HOW
WE LIVE NOW

Contemporary Multicultural Literature

HOW
WE LIVE NOW

Contemporary Multicultural Literature

Edited by

JOHN REPP

Edinboro University of Pennsylvania

Bedford Books *of* St. Martin's Press · Boston

For Bedford Books

Publisher: Charles H. Christensen
Associate Publisher: Joan E. Feinberg
Managing Editor: Elizabeth M. Schaaf
Developmental Editor: Karen S. Henry
Production Editor: Lori Chong
Copyeditor: Daniel Otis
Text Design: Claire Seng-Niemoeller
Cover Design: Hannus Design Associates
Cover Art: Detail of "Reflections" (1982–83), Billy Morrow Jackson. Collection of Busey Bank, Urbana, IL. Through the cooperation of the Jane Haslem Gallery, Washington, D.C.
Cover Photograph: Courtesy of University of Illinois Press, Urbana and Chicago, publishers of *Billy Morrow Jackson, Interpretations of Time and Light,* by Howard E. Wooden, © 1990.

Library of Congress Catalog Card Number: 90–71626

6   5   4   3   2

f   e   d   c   b   a

For information, write: St. Martin's Press, Inc.
175 Fifth Avenue, New York, NY 10010
Editorial Offices: Bedford Books *of* St. Martin's Press
29 Winchester Street, Boston, MA 02116

ISBN: 0–312–05191–3

ACKNOWLEDGMENTS

Alice Adams, "Waiting for Stella." From *Return Trips* by Alice Adams. Copyright © 1984 by Alice Adams. Reprinted by permission of Alfred A. Knopf, Inc.

Maggie Anderson, "Heart Fire." Reprinted from *Cold Comfort* by Maggie Anderson, by permission of the University of Pittsburgh Press. © 1986 by Maggie Anderson.

Antler, "Raising My Hand." From *Last Words* by Antler (Ballantine Books' Available Press). Reprinted by permission of the author.

Jimmy Santiago Baca, "Perfecto Flores." From *Black Mesa Poems*. Copyright © 1989 by Jimmy Santiago Baca. Reprinted by permission of New Directions Publishing Corporation.

John Balaban, "Words for My Daughter." From *Words for My Daughter* by John Balaban. Copyrighted 1991 by John Balaban. Reprinted by permission of Copper Canyon Press.

Charles Baxter, "Gryphon." From *Through the Safety Net* by Charles Baxter. Copyright © 1985 by Charles Baxter. Used by permission of Viking Penguin, a division of Penguin Books USA Inc.

Acknowledgments and copyrights are continued at the back of the book on pages 889–892, which constitute an extension of the copyright page.

 The text of this book is printed on recycled paper.

PREFACE

How We Live Now takes for granted the power of imaginative literature to excite readers, inspire writers, and enliven classrooms. By drawing on a broad range of contemporary American literature, the book's one hundred stories, poems, plays, and essays portray American life in all its variety and complication.

But why *this* literature? First, because it *is* literature, and so gives what we go to that ancient spring to get: the magical satisfaction of living someone else's joy and terror, being thus reminded we're not alone. Second, though American culture has been "multicultural" from the start, it has never before been so eloquently multivoiced, nor have its college campuses ever been so bewilderingly heterogeneous. Since imaginative literature makes the alien not just familiar, but compellingly intimate, students will find reading and writing about work that offers a wide variety of outlooks deeply instructive. Third, because of this variety, and because few of the selections in *How We Live Now* were published before 1980, students will be more likely to see their experience reflected in their reading, and therefore less likely to see literature as beside the point, as a battlement to be scaled, or merely as an opportunity to learn a lesson that will increase their chances for happiness. Finally, students who have used this book will be more easily persuaded that literary traditions aren't corpses exhumed each September and reinterred each June. Someone who's wrestled with Tim O'Brien's "The Things They Carried" or John Balaban's "Words for My Daughter" won't easily find Stephen Crane dry and distant; a student who has read and written about Yusef Komunyakaa's "Facing It" will be hard put to dismiss "The Death of the Ball-Turret Gunner"; the close reader of Bharati Mukherjee's "Fathering" will discover the power of unreliable narration, thereby gaining more ready access to Bartleby's stale corner; and no "Twice-Told Tale" will appear impenetrable to the young writer who has contemplated Charles Johnson's "Exchange Value."

In short, the selections in *How We Live Now* — whether written by such well-known writers as John Updike, Adrienne Rich, and Amy Tan or writers who deserve a wider audience such as Lewis Nordan, Jesse Lee Kercheval, and Judith Ortiz Cofer — demonstrate that good writing resolves nothing for all time, that the questions students have are shared by accomplished writers, that a piece of writing may be, perhaps should be, deeply satisfying and deeply disturbing at the same time. Students and teachers will find in this book an introduction to literature grounded in the instructive pleasure all literature provides.

ORGANIZATION

How We Live Now is meant to be written about. Divided into seven thematic parts, the selections cluster around familiar themes — the individual's relationship to the self, to family, to community, and so on. The theme of each part provides an immediate focus and a context for thinking and writing about the selections. For example, Part One, "With Ourselves," asks students to consider their relationship to themselves — their memories, values, hopes, regrets — by gathering selections that portray individuals declaring who they are or want to be, struggling to forgive themselves for past failure, creating an identity separate from the family, renewing self-confidence, confronting loss. Subsequent parts continue this exploration of contemporary life through the lens of relationship: "In Families," "With Friends," "In and Out of Communities," "On and Off the Job," "In and Out of Love," "With Eternal Questions and Everyday Absurdities." Because students will have thought much about these themes before arriving in the classroom — and because they will write about them continuously as they work through each part — writers and cultures that may at first be unfamiliar or strange will become more readily accessible.

EDITORIAL FEATURES

The design of the book's apparatus is based in part on the assumption that critical thinking, writing, and reading most richly develop inductively, via the complicated pleasures of literature. By eliciting writing drawn from memory and experience, the "Write Before Reading" exercises that follow each part introduction bring students into immediate dialogue with part themes and prepare them for active engagement with the reading and writing they will do

in each part. For instance, the "Write Before Reading" exercise that opens Part
Two, "In Families," reads as follows:

> Take some time to recall memorable family stories, "legends" that may have
> been handed down for generations. Pick the story that best dramatizes your
> family's "personality," its particular way of being in the world, and narrate it
> as fully as you can.

After each selection, students are asked to consider "Investigations," questions for discussion or writing that frequently refer to the part's "Write Before
Reading" exercise or draw connections to other selections. Parts conclude with
"Connections and Elaborations," writing assignments that challenge students
to deepen their reflections on the part's theme and selections, often by referring
back to the "Write Before Reading" exercise.

RESOURCES FOR INSTRUCTORS AND STUDENTS

Resources for Teaching How We Live Now, bound with the text in an instructor's edition, offers part overviews discussing the theme and related issues,
selection overviews commenting on teaching challenges and opportunities, and
a discussion of and possible answer for each of the "Investigations." The
manual also comments on a number of "Connections and Elaborations" questions, and provides suggestions for condensing parts when teaching time is
limited. Finally, biographical information in the manual supplements the text's
biographical footnotes.

Writing About How We Live Now: A Brief Guide for Students, prepared
by Ellen Darion, is a booklet available to instructors who adopt *How We Live
Now.* The booklet discusses the elements of fiction, poetry, and drama and
guides students through the process of writing about literature, from finding a
topic to documenting sources.

ACKNOWLEDGMENTS

Gratitude, like the collaboration that made *How We Live Now* possible, is an
illuminating labor, a naming and passing-on of gifts. Literary tradition is itself
a circle of gifts, and is, as the poet Hayden Carruth once said, "always unexpected, like the taste of the pomegranate, so sweet." How sweet and unexpected, then, that this book owes its title and to some extent its shape to two
other books: Anthony Trollope's 1875 satire of the London literary scene, *The
Way We Live Now,* and L. Rust and Penney Chapin Hills's 1968 anthology,
How We Live: Contemporary Life in Contemporary Fiction.

My work would not have borne fruit, sweet or otherwise, without the
work of many gifted people, to whom my thanks. Alice Adams (University of
Iowa), John Alberti (Northern Kentucky University), Kathleen Shine Cain (Mer-

rimack College), Marilyn Rye (Rutgers University), and Randy Woodland (University of California at Los Angeles) reviewed the book, asking crucial questions, offering alternative selections and assignments, and challenging easy assumptions, all the while bringing to a difficult task their passion for good writing and teaching.

I am also grateful to David Kaufman and Michael Feingold for their expert advice about contemporary drama.

At Bedford Books, Chuck Christensen does what he does better than anyone else, and college writing and literature classes are far the better for it. Joan Feinberg brought to the project her characteristic calm, wit, and an uncanny talent for saying the right thing at the right time. Kim Chabot prepared manuscripts and mailings, did biographical research, made copies, found books, and answered questions, all with uncommon grace and good humor. Lori Chong guided the manuscript through production and was kind to an editor unschooled in the arcana of "pages" and the rest. Christine Peter did research on short notice. With almost no time left, Tara Masih drafted questions that found all net, preventing the book from going into overtime. Karen S. Henry's talents as a development editor are outshone only by her qualities of character, without which this book and its editor would be much the poorer.

And last but never least, Ellen Darion wrote the instructor's manual, demonstrated yet again her love and knowledge of contemporary letters, and laughed at the right times.

CONTENTS

> I never liked Marvin Pruitt. Never liked him, never knew him, even though there
> were only three of us in the class. Three black kids. In our school there were
> fourteen classrooms of thirty-odd white kids (in '66, they considered Chicanos
> provisionally white) and three or four black kids. Primary school in primary colors.
> Neat division. Alphabetized. They didn't stick us in the back, or arrange us by
> degrees of hue, apartheidlike. This was real integration, a ten-to-one ratio as tidy
> as upper-class landscaping.

> Beneath stones engraved in Arabic
> my grandfather, my grandmother.
> Beneath this earth
> grandpa whose sad eyes
> could not endure
> the pain of legs numbed
> forever, grandma
> who smiled although cells
> crushed her brain.

> I am what I am and I am U.S. American   I haven't wanted to say it because if I
> did you'd take away the Puerto Rican but now I say go to hell   I am what I am
> and you can't take it away with all the words and sneers at your command
> I am what I am I'm not hiding under no stoop

Free Student Supplement

Writing About How We Live Now: A Brief Guide for Students, which is shrink-wrapped with this Instructor's Edition, will be bound into the back of the student edition of *How We Live Now* for easy reference. Please disregard the note to the contrary inside the front cover of the Instructor's Edition.

BUSINESS REPLY MAIL

FIRST CLASS   PERMIT NO. 1147   NEW YORK, NY

POSTAGE WILL BE PAID BY

**College Department
ST. MARTIN'S PRESS, INC.**
175 FIFTH AVENUE
NEW YORK, N.Y. 10010

This examination copy of

How We Live Now
by John Repp

is sent to you with the compliments of
your St. Martin's Press representative.

Your comments on our books help us estimate printing requirements, assist us in preparing revisions, and guide us in shaping future books to your needs. Will you please take a moment to fill out and return this postpaid card?

☐ you may quote me for advertising purposes
☐ I have adopted this book for _____ semester, 19 _____ .
☐ I am seriously considering it.

Date _____

Comments

Name _____ Department _____
School _____ Phone Number ( ) _____
City _____ State _____ Zip _____

Course Title _____ Enrollment _____
Present Text _____
Do you plan to change texts this year? Yes ☐ No ☐ When is your decision due? _____
Is your text decision individual ☐ committee ☐ department ☐
If committee or department, please list others involved _____

I remember Ann's eyes and the hat she wore the day we first looked at each other. Our babies had just stepped howling out of the sandbox on their new walking legs. We picked them up. Over their sandy heads we smiled. I think a bond was sealed then, at least as useful as the vow we'd all sworn with husbands to whom we're no longer married.

Lucy Anguiano, Texas girl who smells like corn, like Frito Bandito chips, like tortillas, something like that warm smell of *nixtamal* or bread the way her head smells when she's leaning close to you over a paper cutout doll or on the porch when we are squatting over marbles trading this pretty crystal that leaves a blue star on your hand for that giant cat-eye with a grasshopper-green spiral in the center like the juice of bugs on the windshield when you drive to the border, like the yellow blood of butterflies.

Maybe Claudia knew my parents were away. Maybe she had watched them load their suitcases into the cab from some hiding place in the park. All I knew was that if I saw her, if I looked through the peephole and saw Claudia soaked to the bone, water streaming from the ends of the long blond hair that I had never, in the twelve years I had known her, seen dirty or uncombed, I would not be able to turn her away.

What was I trying to do, you growled
Show you up?
Make the teachers like me, pet me,
Tell me what a credit to my people I was?
I was playing right into their hands, you challenged
And you would have none of it.

I have a friend who still believes in heaven.
Not a stupid person, yet with all she knows, she literally talks to god,
she thinks someone listens in heaven.
On earth, she's unusually competent.
Brave, too, able to face unpleasantness.

Actually, Stella has always been a sort of unifying principle for this group, in that they have generally been united in opposition to whatever she was doing. Not actual opposition to her views, but Stella always, somehow, went too far.

> What about
> "your" friends? We want playmates we can own.
> Could these be yours? Since every friendship
>
> grows from some furtive apotheosis
> of oneself, who were these dim intruders
> presuming they inhabited your pain?

> When near your death a friend
> Asked you what he could do,
> "Remember me," you said.
> We will remember you.

> BONNIE: Because what I wanna know about maybe is you, and why you would put
> a friend of yours like me in that kind of jeopardy. Why you would let me go
> with this creep, if I was begging, let alone instigate it, that's what I'm wondering
> when I get right down to it, though I hadn't even thought about it. But maybe
> it's having a goddamn friendship with you is the source of jeopardy for a person.

> That is where we lost track
> of one another. The silence that followed
> your last letter grew longer,
> becoming a tunnel of snow
> the train you were riding whistled through.

> Wilhelmina was my best friend when we were stationed in France together, in
> Fontainebleau just south of Paris in the golden pre–de Gaulle years. I had already
> been an army wife for ten years by then, but Willy was an outsider. To the wife
> part anyway. She'd been a WAC major — the 41st WAC to go regular army, she
> told me.

> He was quiet again,
> driving east on 113,
> near the slaughterhouse
> on the day after Christmas,
> not mourning,
> but almost bowed,
> like it is after the funeral
> of a distant relative,
> thoughtful,
> sorrow on the border at dusk.

CONNECTIONS AND ELABORATIONS   365

BARRY: You're pathetic. I despise each and every one of you . . . You've got nothing. Nothing. Absolutely nothing. No brains. No power. No future. No hope. No God. The only thing you believe in is me. What are you if you don't have me? I'm not afraid, see. I come up here every night and I make my case, I make my point. . . . I say what I believe in. I have to, I have no choice, you frighten me! I come up here every night and I tear into you, I abuse you, I insult you . . . and you just keep calling.

My childhood was the oral tradition of the Acoma Pueblo people — Aaquumeh hano — which included my immediate family of three older sisters, two younger sisters, two younger brothers, and my mother and father. My world was our world of the Aaquumeh in McCartys, one of the two villages descended from the ageless mother pueblo of Acoma. My world was our Eagle clan-people among other clans.

My father could have passed as European, but we couldn't. My brother and I both have our mother's black hair and olive skin, and so we lived in El Building and visited our great-uncle and his fair children on the next block. It was their private joke that they were the German branch of the family. Not many years later that area too would be mainly Puerto Rican. It was as if the heart of the city map were being gradually colored brown — *café con leche* brown. Our color.

We peeled trees, drilled boulders, dug sumps, took sweat baths
   together.
That house finished we went on
Built a schoolhouse, with a hundred wheelbarrows,
   held seminars on California paleo-indians during lunch.

On and Off the Job

Tasks defined as *work* are not only graded, they are compensated; they have a worth that is unarguable because it translates into hard currency. Wage labor — and in the beginning, this generally means a confining, repetitive chore for which we are quickly overqualified — paradoxically brings a sense of blooming freedom. At the outset, the complaint to a peer that business supersedes fun is oddly liberating — no matter what drudgery requires your attention, it is by its very required nature serious and adult.

I sleep very well after I've pitched a good game, not so well after a bad one, and I sleep very badly the night before I pitch, and the day of the game I force myself to eat. It's one of the things that makes the game exciting, but a lot of times, especially in late season, I long for the time when I'll have a job I can predict, can wake up on the ranch knowing what I'm going to do and that I'm not going to fail.

Some mornings we woke to find him
asleep on the couch, his foreman's tie twisted
into words we couldn't spell.
We ate our cereal as carefully as communion
until our mother shook him ready for another day.

Steel: durable, impregnable, indestructible. I cut through it like butter. At a touch, the flame of my torch turns that sturdy mass of steel into flowing liquid. What power!

All the way across the Bay Bridge I sang
to the cool winds buffeting my Ford,
for I was on my way to a life of buying
untouched drive shafts, universal joints,
perfect bearings so steeped in Cosmoline
they could endure a century and still retain
their purity of functional design.

GARFINKLE: I'm not your best friend — I'm your only friend. I care about you in the only way that matters in business. I don't make anything? I'm making you money. And, lest we forget, that's the only reason any of you became stockholders in the first place. To make money. You don't care if they manufacture wire and cable, fry chicken, or grow tangerines. You want to make money. I'm making you money. I'm the only friend you got.

"I just had a thought!" Benny says. "A big thought! This could become some kind of craze! We could become the Budweiser of this!" He puts his hands in the air and then draws them apart to form the banner he sees in his mind. "The Veritas Grit World Championship Belt-Sander Races!"
    "Think wild, babe!" says Dwight.

When the cart is empty he sells the cart.
When the cart is sold he sells the ox,
harness and yoke, and walks
home, his pockets heavy
with the year's coin for salt and taxes.

I'd be lying if I said that the possibility of covering a Ku Klux Klan rally didn't cause me a few moments' concern about my physical well-being. But when another reporter came over to tell me about the May 28th Klan rally in front of Clearwater City Hall, I reasoned, "It's just another assignment. I am a reporter, and I know my life isn't all budget meetings."

He has nothing that glows his face
so much as stories of his working years,
feats of courage in the mines
when he was called upon to defuse dynamite
that didn't explode.

Only one at a time could get
so close, his nose
to the anthracite, funneling
light from a helmet, chipping,
with his eyes like points of fire.

She didn't want his flowers. She didn't want him on her platform. She didn't want him in her 13' by 13' sanctuary, touching her things, poking around, asking stupid questions, making small talk. "Look," she said finally, talking to the glass but looking through him, beyond him, scanning the infinite as she'd trained herself to do, no matter what the problem, "I've got a job to do up here."

"For beauty is why we live," Uncle Ralph said when he talked of precious things only the Pawnees know. "We die for it, too." He called himself an ancient Pawnee warrior when he was quite young. He told us that warriors must brave all storms and odds and stand their ground. He knew intimate details of every battle the Pawnees ever fought since Pawnee time began, and Sister and I knew even then that Uncle Ralph had a great battlefield of his own.

The window in his office is one-way glass, allowing Lamar to observe his sixteen men while cloaked in smoky invisibility. The situation, Lamar muses, is analogous to that of a god, looking down from a screen of clouds at the unhappy mortals below who believe with touching urgency that their frenetic schemes and counter-schemes are extensions of conscious ideals.

PART SIX   651

In and Out of Love

Now, when he and I meet, after all these years,
I say to the bitch inside me, don't start growling.
He isn't a trespasser anymore.
Just an old acquaintance tipping his hat.

"Are you loving and snuggling? May I join?"
He flops down between us and hugs us and snuggles himself to sleep,
his face gleaming with satisfaction at being this very child.

On what would be his last night to walk about the city we sat in the courtyard of
the Picasso Museum. There under a dusk-deep sapphire sky I turned to him and
said, "I'm so lucky," and it was as if the time alloted to him to teach this lesson,
the time alloted to me to learn it had been consumed, and there was nothing left
but the facts of things to play out.

With Eternal Questions and Everyday Absurdities

Why should we sit by the Adige and destroy
Anything, even our enemies, even the prey
God caused to glitter for us
Defenseless in the sun?
We are not exhausted. We are not angry, or lonely,
Or sick at heart.
We are in love lightly, lightly.

As the sun rises
high enough to
warm the frost
off the pine needles,

I rise to make
four prayers of
thanksgiving

On hot summer days, whenever the two girls walked by them, the villagers would feel as if the icy notes of xylophones were playing gently on the surface of their skin or as if a breeze from the ocean had just whistled through the branches of the trees in the parched plaza square.

Each form is furled into its hollow,
white in the dark curl,
the sea a mausoleum, with countless shelves,
cradling the prone effigies of our unearthly selves

The idea that we live
a second life, or third,
makes for good science fiction
but no one really believes it.
We're born, we die.
In and out. Up and down.
Truth and truth.

Regretful that I had let secret questions drop out of my mouth, I couldn't look into her eyes. My hands began to fan out, grow like a liar's nose until they hung by my side like low weights. Abuelita made a balm out of dried moth wings and Vicks and rubbed my hands, shaped them back to size and it was the strangest feeling. Like bones melting. Like sun shining through the darkness of your eyelids.

I was raised on the Old Testament.
In it God talks to Moses, Noah,
Samuel, and they answer.
People confer with angels. Certain
animals converse with humans.
It's a simple world, full of crossovers.

I stared hard at the shot of the cathedral on the TV. How could I even begin to describe it? But say my life depended on it. Say my life was being threatened by an insane guy who said I had to do it or else.

HOW
WE LIVE NOW

Contemporary Multicultural Literature

PART ONE

WITH

OURSELVES

We begin with questions of identity so basic they've become clichés: Who am I? What do I want? Why did I do that? Difficult as they are by themselves, these questions are further complicated by the fundamental role the idea of individualism plays in American culture. "Be all that you can be" is much more than an advertising gimmick: Think how often you've heard that injunction and others like it on the playground, in the classroom, and on TV. We hear that each of us is unique, each of us has a particular destiny to fulfill and the freedom to pursue it. This can be exhilarating. As we successfully test our abilities and values, we gain the confidence necessary to take the next step, and the next. Yet this self we're busy building often seems a jumble of conflict and confusion, much of it having to do with circumstances over which we have little or no control.

The selections in "With Ourselves" introduce you to people trying to come to grips with who they are. In Reginald McKnight's "The Kind

1

of Light That Shines on Texas," a sixth-grader confronts his betrayal of a classmate; Lawrence Joseph's "Driving Again" asks us to consider how the world of dreams and waking life intersect; in Rosario Morales's "I Am What I Am," a woman speaks in voices that may or may not be her own; in "Customs of the Country," a woman tries to make up for past neglect; in 'night, Mother, by Marsha Norman, a mother and daughter wrestle with the question of suicide and family obligation; in Yusef Komunyakaa's "Facing It" a Vietnam veteran tries to make peace with the war at the Vietnam Veterans Memorial; in Peter Cameron's "Jump or Dive" an adolescent boy feels pressured to make a decision the terms of which are murky, at best; in John Edgar Wideman's "Valaida" a survivor of the Holocaust makes a confession he hopes and fears will ease his loneliness; in Joy Harjo's "Ordinary Spirit" a Native American writer shows how ancestors, animals, the summer air itself can instruct us; in Richard McCann's "My Mother's Clothes: The School of Beauty and Shame" a teenage boy discovers the price of violating the categories of "masculine" and "feminine"; Antler's "Raising My Hand" asks us to rethink one of the basic customs of school; John Haines's "Moments and Journeys" argues for a view of life measured in something other than "clock time"; and in "The Northside at Seven," by Lucia Maria Perillo, a woman struggles to understand how much of who she is depends on who her father is.

WRITE BEFORE READING

Tell the story of the single experience or set of closely related experiences that caused you the most self-doubt. Then, tell the story of the single experience or set of closely related experiences that most confirmed or strengthened your sense of who you are.

REGINALD McKNIGHT

The Kind of Light
That Shines on Texas

I never liked Marvin Pruitt. Never liked him, never knew him, even though there were only three of us in the class. Three black kids. In our school there were fourteen classrooms of thirty-odd white kids (in '66, they considered Chicanos provisionally white) and three or four black kids. Primary school in primary colors. Neat division. Alphabetized. They didn't stick us in the back, or arrange us by degrees of hue, apartheidlike. This was real integration, a ten-to-one ratio as tidy as upper-class landscaping. If it all worked, you could have ten white kids all to yourself. They could talk to you, get the feel of you, scrutinize you bone deep if they wanted to. They seldom wanted to, and that was fine with me for two reasons. The first was that their scrutiny was irritating. How do you comb your hair — why do you comb your hair — may I please touch your hair — were the kinds of questions they asked. This is no way to feel at home. The second reason was Marvin. He embarrassed me. He smelled bad, was at least two grades behind, was hostile, dark-skinned, homely, close-mouthed. I feared him for his size, pitied him for his dress, watched him all the time. Marveled at him, mystified, astonished, uneasy.

He had the habit of spitting on his right arm, juicing it down till it would glisten. He would start in immediately after taking his seat when we'd finished with the Pledge of Allegiance, "The Yellow Rose of Texas," "The Eyes of Texas Are upon You," and "Mistress Shady." Marvin would rub his spit-flecked arm with his left hand, rub and roll as if polishing an ebony pool cue. Then he would rest his head in the crook of his arm, sniffing, huffing deep like black-jacket boys huff bagsful of acrylics. After ten minutes or so, his eyes would close, heavy. He would sleep till recess. Mrs. Wickham would let him.

There was one other black kid in our class, a girl they called Ah-so. I never learned what she did to earn this name. There was nothing Asian about this big-shouldered girl. She was the tallest, heaviest kid in school. She was quiet, but I don't think any one of us was subtle or sophisticated enough to nickname our classmates according to any but physical attributes. Fat kids were called Porky or Butterball; skinny ones were called Stick or Ichabod. Ah-so was big, thick, and African. She would impassively sit, sullen, silent as Marvin. She wore the same dark blue pleated skirt every day, the same ruffled white blouse

REGINALD McKNIGHT, born in Germany in 1956 and raised as an "air force brat" in a number of places, didn't think of himself as a writer until he spent a year in Senegal in the early 1980s. He is the author of *Moustapha's Eclipse* (1988) and *I Get on the Bus* (1991) and teaches writing at Carnegie Mellon University.

3

every day. Her skin always shone as if worked by Marvin's palms and fingers. I never spoke one word to her, nor she to me.

Of the three of us, Mrs. Wickham called only on Ah-so and me. Ah-so never answered one question, correctly or incorrectly, so far as I can recall. She wasn't stupid. When asked to read aloud she read well, seldom stumbling over long words, reading with humor and expression. But when Wickham asked her about Farmer Brown and how many cows, or the capital of Vermont, or the date of this war or that, Ah-so never spoke. Not one word. But you always felt she could have answered those questions if she'd wanted to. I sensed no tension, embarrassment, or anger in Ah-so's reticence. She simply refused to speak. There was something unshakable about her, some core so impenetrably solid, you got the feeling that if you stood too close to her she could eat your thoughts like a black star eats light. I didn't despise Ah-so as I despised Marvin. There was nothing malevolent about her. She sat like a great icon in the back of the classroom, tranquil, guarded, sealed up, watchful. She was close to sixteen, and it was my guess she'd given up on school. Perhaps she was just obliging the wishes of her family, sticking it out till the law could no longer reach her.

There were at least half a dozen older kids in our class. Besides Marvin and Ah-so there was Oakley, who sat behind me, whispering threats into my ear; Varna Willard with the large breasts; Eddie Limon, who played bass for a high school rock band; and Lawrence Ridderbeck, whom everyone said had a kid and a wife. You couldn't expect me to know anything about Texan educational practices of the 1960s, so I never knew why there were so many older kids in my sixth-grade class. After all, I was just a boy and had transferred into the school around midyear. My father, an air force sergeant, had been sent to Vietnam. The air force sent my mother, my sister Claire, and me to Connolly Air Force Base, which during the war housed "unaccompanied wives." I'd been to so many different schools in my short life that I ceased wondering about their differences. All I knew about the Texas schools is that they weren't afraid to flunk you.

Yet though I was only twelve then, I had a good idea why Wickham never once called on Marvin, why she let him snooze in the crook of his polished arm. I knew why she would press her lips together, and narrow her eyes at me whenever I correctly answered a question, rare as that was. I knew why she badgered Ah-so with questions everyone knew Ah-so would never even consider answering. Wickham didn't like us. She wasn't gross about it, but it was clear she didn't want us around. She would prove her dislike day after day with little stories and jokes. "I just want to share with you all," she would say, "a little riddle my daughter told me at the supper table th'other day. Now, where do you go when you injure your knee?" Then one, two, or all three of her pets would say for the rest of us, "We don't know, Miz Wickham," in that skin-chilling way suck-asses speak, "where?" "Why, to Africa," Wickham would say, "where the knee grows."

The thirty-odd white kids would laugh, and I would look across the room at Marvin. He'd be asleep. I would glance back at Ah-so. She'd be sitting still as a projected image, staring down at her desk. I, myself, would smile at Wickham's stupid jokes, sometimes fake a laugh. I tried to show her that at least one of us was alive and alert, even though her jokes hurt. I sucked ass, too, I suppose. But I wanted her to understand more than anything that I was not like her other nigra children, that I was worthy of more than the nonattention and the negative attention she paid Marvin and Ah-so. I hated her, but never showed it. No one could safely contradict that woman. She knew all kinds of tricks to demean, control, and punish you. And she could swing her two-foot paddle as fluidly as a big-league slugger swings a bat. You didn't speak in Wickham's class unless she spoke to you first. You didn't chew gum, or wear "hood" hair. You didn't drag your feet, curse, pass notes, hold hands with the opposite sex. Most especially, you didn't say anything bad about the Aggies, Governor Connolly, LBJ, Sam Houston, or Waco. You did the forbidden and she would get you. It was that simple.

She never got me, though. Never gave her reason to. But she could have invented reasons. She did a lot of that. I can't be sure, but I used to think she pitied me because my father was in Vietnam and my uncle A.J. had recently died there. Whenever she would tell one of her racist jokes, she would always glance at me, preface the joke with, "Now don't you nigra children take offense. This is all in fun, you know. I just want to share with you all something Coach Gilchrest told me th'other day." She would tell her joke, and glance at me again. I'd giggle, feeling a little queasy. "I'm half Irish," she would chuckle, "and you should hear some of those Irish jokes." She never told any, and I never really expected her to. I just did my Tom-thing. I kept my shoes shined, my desk neat, answered her questions as best I could, never brought gum to school, never cursed, never slept in class. I wanted to show her we were not all the same.

I tried to show them all, all thirty-odd, that I was different. It worked to some degree, but not very well. When some article was stolen from someone's locker or desk, Marvin, not I, was the first accused. I'd be second. Neither Marvin nor Ah-so nor I were ever chosen for certain classroom honors — "Pledge leader," "flag holder," "noise monitor," "paper passer-outer," but Mrs. Wickham once let me be "eraser duster." I was proud. I didn't even care about the cracks my fellow students made about my finally having turned the right color. I had done something that Marvin, in the deeps of his never-ending sleep, couldn't even dream of doing. Jack Preston, a kid who sat in front of me, asked me one day at recess whether I was embarrassed about Marvin. "Can you believe that guy?" I said. "He's like a pig or something. Makes me sick."

"Does it make you ashamed to be colored?"   10

"No," I said, but I meant yes. Yes, if you insist on thinking us all the same. Yes, if his faults are mine, his weaknesses inherent in me.

"I'd be," said Jack.

I made no reply. I was ashamed. Ashamed for not defending Marvin and ashamed that Marvin even existed. But if it had occurred to me, I would have asked Jack whether he was ashamed of being white because of Oakley. Oakley, "Oak Tree," Kelvin "Oak Tree" Oakley. He was sixteen and proud of it. He made it clear to everyone, including Wickham, that his life's ambition was to stay in school one more year, till he'd be old enough to enlist in the army. "Them slopes got my brother," he would say. "I'mna sign up and git me a few slopes. Gonna kill them bastards deader'n shit." Oakley, so far as anyone knew, was and always had been the oldest kid in his family. But no one contradicted him. He would, as anyone would tell you, "snap yer neck jest as soon as look at you." Not a boy in class, excepting Marvin and myself, had been able to avoid Oakley's pink bellies, Texas titty twisters, moon pie punches, or worse. He didn't bother Marvin, I suppose, because Marvin was closer to his size and age, and because Marvin spent five-sixths of the school day asleep. Marvin probably never crossed Oakley's mind. And to say that Oakley hadn't bothered me is not to say he had no intention of ever doing so. In fact, this haphazard sketch of hairy fingers, slash of eyebrow, explosion of acne, elbows, and crooked teeth, swore almost daily that he'd like to kill me.

Naturally, I feared him. Though we were about the same height, he out-weighed me by no less than forty pounds. He talked, stood, smoked, and swore like a man. No one, except for Mrs. Wickham, the principal, and the coach, ever laid a finger on him. And even Wickham knew that the hot lines she laid on him merely amused him. He would smile out at the classroom, goofy and bashful, as she laid down the two, five, or maximum ten strokes on him. Often he would wink, or surreptitiously flash us the thumb as Wickham worked on him. When she was finished, Oakley would walk so cool back to his seat you'd think he was on wheels. He'd slide into his chair, sniff the air, and say "Some-thin's burnin. Do y'all smell smoke? I swanee, I smell smoke and fahr back here." If he had made these cracks and never threatened me, I might have grown to admire Oakley, even liked him a little. But he hated me, and took every opportunity during the six-hour school day to make me aware of this. "Some Sambo's gittin his ass broke open one of these days," he'd mumble. "I wanna fight somebody. Need to keep in shape till I git to Nam."

I never said anything to him for the longest time. I pretended not to hear   15
him, pretended not to notice his sour breath on my neck and ear. "Yep," he'd whisper. "Coonies keep ya in good shape for slope killin." Day in, day out that's the kind of thing I'd pretend not to hear. But one day when the rain dropped down like lead balls, and the cold air made your skin look plucked, Oakley whispered to me, "My brother tells me it rains like this in Nam. Maybe I ought a go out at recess and break your ass open today. Nice and cool so you don't sweat. Nice and wet to clean up the blood." I said nothing for at least half a minute, then I turned half right and said, "Thought you said your brother was dead." Oakley, silent himself, for a time, poked me in the back with his pencil and hissed, "*Yer* dead." Wickham cut her eyes our way, and it was over.

It was hardest avoiding him in gym class. Especially when we played murderball. Oakley always aimed his throws at me. He threw with unblinking intensity, his teeth gritting, his neck veining, his face flushing, his black hair sweeping over one eye. He could throw hard, but the balls were squishy and harmless. In fact, I found his misses more intimidating than his hits. The balls would whizz by, thunder against the folded bleachers. They rattled as though a locomotive were passing through them. I would duck, dodge, leap as if he were throwing grenades. But he always hit me, sooner or later. And after a while I noticed that the other boys would avoid throwing at me, as if I belonged to Oakley.

One day, however, I was surprised to see that Oakley was throwing at everyone else but me. He was uncommonly accurate, too; kids were falling like tin cans. Since no one was throwing at me, I spent most of the game watching Oakley cut this one and that one down. Finally, he and I were the only ones left on the court. Try as he would, he couldn't hit me, nor I him. Coach Gilchrest blew his whistle and told Oakley and me to bring the red rubber balls to the equipment locker. I was relieved I'd escaped Oakley's stinging throws for once. I was feeling triumphant, full of myself. As Oakley and I approached Gilchrest, I thought about saying something friendly to Oakley: Good game, Oak Tree, I would say. Before I could speak, though, Gilchrest said, "All right boys, there's five minutes left in the period. Y'all are so good, looks like, you're gonna have to play like men. No boundaries, no catch outs, and you gotta hit your opponent three times in order to win. Got me?"

We nodded.

"And you're gonna use these," said Gilchrest, pointing to three volleyballs at his feet. "And you better believe they're pumped full. Oates, you start at that end of the court. Oak Tree, you're at th'other end. Just like usual, I'll set the balls at mid-court, and when I blow my whistle I want y'all to haul your cheeks to the middle and th'ow for all you're worth. Got me?" Gilchrest nodded at our nods, then added, "Remember, no boundaries, right?"

I at my end, Oakley at his, Gilchrest blew his whistle. I was faster than Oakley and scooped up a ball before he'd covered three-quarters of his side. I aimed, threw, and popped him right on the knee. "One-zip!" I heard Gilchrest shout. The ball bounced off his knee and shot right back into my hands. I hurried my throw and missed. Oakley bent down, clutched the two remaining balls. I remember being amazed that he could palm each ball, run full out, and throw left-handed or right-handed without a shade of awkwardness. I spun, ran, but one of Oakley's throws glanced off the back of my head. "One-one!" hollered Gilchrest. I fell and spun on my ass as the other ball came sailing at me. I caught it. "He's out!" I yelled. Gilchrest's voice boomed, "No catch outs. Three hits. Three hits." I leapt to my feet as Oakley scrambled across the floor for another ball. I chased him down, leapt, and heaved the ball hard as he drew himself erect. The ball hit him dead in the face, and he went down flat. He rolled around, cupping his hands over his nose. Gilchrest sped to his side, helped him to his feet, asked him whether he was OK. Blood flowed from Oakley's nose, dripped in startlingly bright spots on the floor, his shoes, Gilchrest's shirt. The coach removed Oakley's T-shirt and pressed it against the big kid's nose to stanch the bleeding. As they walked past me toward the office I mumbled an apology to Oakley, but couldn't catch his reply. "You watch your filthy mouth, boy," said Gilchrest to Oakley.

The locker room was unnaturally quiet as I stepped into its steamy atmosphere. Eyes clicked in my direction, looked away. After I was out of my shorts, had my towel wrapped around me, my shower kit in hand, Jack Preston and Brian Nailor approached me. Preston's hair was combed slick and plastic looking. Nailor's stood up like frozen flames. Nailor smiled at me with his big teeth and pale eyes. He poked my arm with a finger. "You fucked up," he said.

"I tried to apologize."

"Won't do you no good," said Preston.

"I swanee," said Nailor.

"It's part of the game," I said. "It was an accident. Wasn't my idea to use volleyballs."

"Don't matter," Preston said. "He's jest lookin for an excuse to fight you."

"I never done nothing to him."

"Don't matter," said Nailor. "He don't like you."

"Brian's right, Clint. He'd jest as soon kill you as look at you."

"I never done nothing to him."

"Look," said Preston, "I know him pretty good. And jest between you and me, it's cause you're a city boy — "

"Whadda you mean? I've never — "

"He don't like your clothes — "

"And he don't like the fancy way you talk in class."

"What fancy — "

"I'm tellin him, if you don't mind, Brian."

"Tell him then."

"He don't like the way you say 'tennis shoes' instead of sneakers. He don't like colereds. A whole bunch a things, really."

"I never done nothing to him. He's got no reason — "

"*And,*" said Nailor, grinning, "*and,* he says you're a stuck-up rich kid." Nailor's eyes had crow's-feet, bags beneath them. They were a man's eyes.

"My dad's a sergeant," I said.

"You chicken to fight him?" said Nailor.

"Yeah, Clint, don't be chicken. Jest go on and git it over with. He's whupped pert near ever'body else in the class. It ain't so bad."

"Might as well, Oates."

"Yeah, yer pretty skinny, but yer jest about his height. Jest git im in a headlock and don't let go."

"Goddamn," I said, "He's got no reason to — "

Their eyes shot right and I looked over my shoulder. Oakley stood at his locker, turning its tumblers. From where I stood I could see that a piece of cotton was wedged up one of his nostrils, and he already had the makings of a good shiner. His acne burned red like a fresh abrasion. He snapped the locker open and kicked his shoes off without sitting. Then he pulled off his shorts, revealing two paddle stripes on his ass. They were fresh red bars speckled with white, the white speckles being the reverse impression of the paddle's suction holes. He must not have watched his filthy mouth while in Gilchrest's presence. Behind me, I heard Preston and Nailor pad to their lockers.

Oakley spoke without turning around. "Somebody's gonna git his skinny black ass kicked, right today, right after school." He said it softly. He slipped his jock off, turned around. I looked away. Out of the corner of my eye I saw him stride off, his hairy nakedness a weapon clearing the younger boys from his path. Just before he rounded the corner of the shower stalls, I threw my toilet kit to the floor and stammered, "I — I never did nothing to you, Oakley." He stopped, turned, stepped closer to me, wrapping his towel around himself. Sweat streamed down my rib cage. It felt like ice water. "You wanna go at it right now, boy?"

"I never did nothing to you." I felt tears in my eyes. I couldn't stop them even though I was blinking like mad. "Never."

He laughed. "You busted my nose, asshole."   50

"What about before? What'd I ever do to you?"

"See you after school, Coonie," Then he turned away, flashing his acne-spotted back like a semaphore. "Why?" I shouted. "Why you wanna fight me?" Oakley stopped and turned, folded his arms, leaned against a toilet stall. "Why you wanna fight *me*, Oakley?" I stepped over the bench. "What'd I do? Why me?" And then unconsciously, as if scratching, as if breathing, I walked toward Marvin, who stood a few feet from Oakley, combing his hair at the mirror. "Why not him?" I said. "How come you're after *me* and not *him?*" The room froze. Froze for a moment that was both evanescent and eternal, somewhere between an eye blink and a week in hell. No one moved, nothing happened; there was no sound at all. And then it was as if all of us at the same moment looked at Marvin. He just stood there, combing away, the only body in motion, I think. He combed his hair and combed it, as if seeing only his image, hearing only his comb scraping his scalp. I knew he'd heard me. There's no way he could not have heard me. But all he did was slide the comb into his pocket and walk out the door.

"I got no quarrel with Marvin," I heard Oakley say. I turned toward his voice, but he was already in the shower.

I was able to avoid Oakley at the end of the school day. I made my escape by asking Mrs. Wickham if I could go to the restroom.

" 'Restroom,' " Oakley mumbled. "It's a damn toilet, sissy."   55

"Clinton," said Mrs. Wickham. "Can you *not* wait till the bell rings? It's almost three o'clock."

"No ma'am," I said. "I won't make it."

"Well, I should make you wait just to teach you to be more mindful about . . . hygiene . . . uh things." She sucked in her cheeks, squinted. "But I'm feeling charitable today. You may go." I immediately left the building, and got on the bus. "Ain't you a little early?" said the bus driver, swinging the door shut. "Just left the office," I said. The driver nodded, apparently not giving me a second thought. I had no idea why I'd told her I'd come from the office, or why she found it a satisfactory answer. Two minutes later the bus filled, rolled and shook its way to Connolly Air Base.

When I got home, my mother was sitting in the living room, smoking her Slims, watching her soap opera. She absently asked me how my day had gone and I told her fine. "Hear from Dad?" I said.

"No, but I'm sure he's fine." She always said that when we hadn't heard from him in a while. I suppose she thought I was worried about him, or that I felt vulnerable without him. It was neither. I just wanted to discuss something with my mother that we both cared about. If I spoke with her about things that happened at school, or on my weekends, she'd listen with half an ear, say something like, "Is that so?" or "You don't say?" I couldn't stand that sort of thing. But when I mentioned my father, she treated me a bit more like an adult, or at least someone who was worth listening to. I didn't want to feel like a boy that afternoon. As I turned from my mother and walked down the hall I thought about the day my father left for Vietnam. Sharp in his uniform, sure behind his aviator specs, he slipped a cigar from his pocket and stuck it in mine. "Not till I get back," he said. "We'll have us one when we go fishing. Just you and me, out on the lake all day, smoking and casting and sitting. Don't let Mamma see it. Put it in y'back pocket." He hugged me, shook my hand, and told me I was the man of the house now. He told me he was depending on me to take good care of my mother and sister. "Don't you let me down, now, hear?" And he tapped his thick finger on my chest. "You almost as big as me. Boy, you something else." I believed him when he told me those things. My heart swelled big enough to swallow my father, my mother, Claire. I loved, feared, and respected myself, my manhood. That day I could have put all of Waco, Texas, in my heart. And it wasn't till about three months later that I discovered I really wasn't the man of the house, that my mother and sister, as they always had, were taking care of me.

For a brief moment I considered telling my mother about what had happened at school that day, but for one thing, she was deep down in the halls of "General Hospital," and never paid you much mind till it was over. For another thing, I just wasn't the kind of person — I'm still not, really — to discuss my problems with anyone. Like my father I kept things to myself, talked about my problems only in retrospect. Since my father wasn't around, I consciously wanted to be like him, doubly like him, I could say. I wanted to be the man of the house in some respect, even if it had to be in an inward way. I went to my room, changed my clothes, and laid out my homework. I couldn't focus on it. I thought about Marvin, what I'd said about him or done to him — I couldn't tell which. I'd done something to him, said something about him; said something about and done something to myself. *How come you're after* me *and not* him? I kept trying to tell myself I hadn't meant it that way. *That* way. I thought about approaching Marvin, telling him what I really meant was that he was more Oakley's age and weight than I. I would tell him I meant I was no match for Oakley. *See, Marvin, what I meant was that he wants to fight a*

60

colored guy, but is afraid to fight you cause you could beat him. But try as I did, I couldn't for a moment convince myself that Marvin would believe me. I meant it *that* way and no other. Everybody heard. Everybody knew. That afternoon I forced myself to confront the notion that tomorrow I would prob-ably have to fight both Oakley and Marvin. I'd have to be two men.

I rose from my desk and walked to the window. The light made my skin look orange, and I started thinking about what Wickham had told us once about light. She said that oranges and apples, leaves and flowers, the whole multicolored world, was not what it appeared to be. The colors we see, she said, look like they do only because of the light or ray that shines on them. "The color of the thing isn't what you see, but the light that's reflected off it." Then she shut out the lights and shone a white light lamp on a prism. We watched the pale splay of colors on the projector screen; some people ooohed and aaahed. Suddenly, she switched on a black light and the color of everything changed. The prism colors vanished, Wickham's arms were purple, the buttons of her dress were as orange as hot coals, rather than the blue they had been only seconds before. We were all very quiet. "Nothing," she said after a while, "is really what it appears to be." I didn't really understand then. But as I stood at the window, gazing at my orange skin, I wondered what kind of light I could shine on Marvin, Oakley, and me that would reveal us as the same.

I sat down and stared at my arms. They were dark brown again. I worked up a bit of saliva under my tongue and spat on my left arm. I spat again, then rubbed the spittle into it, polishing, working till my arm grew warm. As I spat, and rubbed, I wondered why Marvin did this weird, nasty thing to himself, day after day. Was he trying to rub away the black, or deepen it, doll it up? And if he did this weird nasty thing for a hundred years, would he spit-shine himself invisible, rolling away the eggplant skin, revealing the scarlet muscle, blue vein, pink and yellow tendon, white bone? Then disappear? See through, all colors, no colors. Spitting and rubbing. Is this the way you do it? I leaned forward, sniffed the arm. It smelled vaguely of mayonnaise. After an hour or so, I fell asleep.

I saw Oakley the second I stepped off the bus the next morning. He stood outside the gym in his usual black penny loafers, white socks, high water jeans, T-shirt, and black jacket. Nailor stood with him, his big teeth spread across his bottom lip like playing cards. If there was anyone I felt like fighting, that day, it was Nailor. But I wanted to put off fighting for as long as I could. I stepped toward the gymnasium, thinking that I shouldn't run, but if I hurried I could beat Oakley to the door and secure myself near Gilchrest's office. But the moment I stepped into the gym, I felt Oakley's broad palm clap down on my shoulder. "Might as well stay out here, Coonie," he said. "I need me a little target practice." I turned to face him and he slapped me, one-two, with the back, then the palm of his hand, as I'd seen Bogart do to Peter Lorre in *The Maltese Falcon.* My heart went wild. I could scarcely breathe. I couldn't swallow.

"Call me a nigger," I said. I have no idea what made me say this. All I   65
know is that it kept me from crying. "Call me a nigger, Oakley."

"Fuck you, ya black ass slope." He slapped me again, scratching my eye.
"I don't do what coonies tell me."

"Call me a nigger."

"Outside, Coonie."

"Call me one. Go ahead."

He lifted his hand to slap me again, but before his arm could swing my   70
way, Marvin Pruitt came from behind me and calmly pushed me aside. "Git
out my way, boy," he said. And he slugged Oakley on the side of his head.
Oakley stumbled back, stiff-legged. His eyes were big. Marvin hit him twice
more, once again to the side of the head, once to the nose. Oakley went down
and stayed down. Though blood was drawn, whistles blowing, fingers pointing,
kids hollering, Marvin just stood there, staring at me with cool eyes. He spat
on the ground, licked his lips, and just stared at me, till Coach Gilchrest and
Mr. Calderon tackled him and violently carried him away. He never struggled,
never took his eyes off me.

Nailor and Mrs. Wickham helped Oakley to his feet. His already fattened
nose bled and swelled so that I had to look away. He looked around, bemused,
walleyed, maybe scared. It was apparent he had no idea how bad he was hurt.
He didn't even touch his nose. He didn't look like he knew much of anything.
He looked at me, looked me dead in the eye in fact, but didn't seem to recognize
me.

That morning, like all other mornings, we said the Pledge of Allegiance,
sang "The Yellow Rose of Texas," "The Eyes of Texas Are upon You," and
"Mistress Shady." The room stood strangely empty without Oakley, and without Marvin, but at the same time you could feel their presence more intensely
somehow. I felt like I did when I'd walk into my mother's room and could
smell my father's cigars, or cologne. He was more palpable, in certain respects,
than when there in actual flesh. For some reason, I turned to look at Ah-so,
and just this once I let my eyes linger on her face. She had a very gentle-looking
face, really. That surprised me. She must have felt my eyes on her because she
glanced up at me for a second and smiled, white teeth, downcast eyes. Such a
pretty smile. That surprised me too. She held it for a few seconds, then let it
fade. She looked down at her desk, and sat still as a photograph.   1989

INVESTIGATIONS

1. Note each instance where the narrator, Clint Oates, does his "Tom-thing."
   What specific skills are involved? How would Clint's feelings for Marvin
   Pruitt change if Marvin did *his* "Tom-thing"?
2. Imagine that you're Marvin Pruitt. Describe, as concretely as possible, Mrs.
   Wickham, Ah-so, "Oak Tree" Oakley, Clint, yourself. Why would Oakley
   have a quarrel with Clint and not you? Why did you fight Oakley?

3. Why is it important for Clint to show Mrs. Wickham "we were not all the same"? How does his "Tom-thing" help him do this? Do you think it hurts him? If so, how?

4. At the end of the story, Clint sees Ah-so in a different light than he had before. How did the events in the story cause him to see her differently? How does he see himself differently?

LAWRENCE JOSEPH

Driving Again

Driving again,
this time Van Dyke Avenue.
Just beyond my window
October wind raises
a leaf from a sewer,   5
a gray-haired man standing in a crowd
before the Mount Zion Temple
tips his hat, "not bad, and you?"
When I was a child
I saw this church through the window   10
of a '51 Chevrolet
huddled beside my grandmother
in the backseat, her small
soft hands holding mine,
her perfume and the smell from squirrel   15
fur around her neck
spinning me to sleep.
Now I pass a woman,
her brown-blond face spotted purple,
who lowers her head   20
to spit, I see
a boy's words, "Dirty Killer Hood,"
in spray paint
on the wall of U.A.W. Local 89.

Born in Detroit in 1948 and currently living in New York City, LAWRENCE JOSEPH is a third-generation Lebanese-American, a professor of law at St. John's University School of Law, and a widely published poet. The University of Pittsburgh Press has published two collections of his poems: *Shouting at No One* (1982) and *Curriculum Vitae* (1988).

Where was it? I stumbled   25
through the darkness to the door
before I realized
I was waking from a dream
of this street, this smoke
from Eldon Axle foundry, these   30
motor blocks stacked against
this dull sky. Too many times
I stood on a loading dock
and watched morning air change
from red to iron.   35
"Gimme coffee, gimme a cigarette,"
a face asked me, "ain't no life,"
another warned.
Here is the cemetery.
Beneath stones engraved in Arabic   40
my grandfather, my grandmother.
Beneath this earth
grandpa whose sad eyes
could not endure
the pain of legs numbed   45
forever, grandma
who smiled although cells
crushed her brain.
Years ago, on a day like this,
I fell to my knees   50
with my father to pull grass
from their stones.
I did not cry.
When I closed my eyes I did not pray.
Now, in a car, on Van Dyke,   55
I cry for them and for me.   1983

INVESTIGATIONS

1. In lines 25–28, the speaker realizes he's "waking from a dream." How much of the poem is part of the dream? How does this realization affect the speaker?
2. What issues in the speaker's past does he confront in the poem? If you faced one or more of these issues, how would you respond?
3. Using as evidence as many details from the poem as possible, write a paragraph or two in which you say why the speaker cries for himself at the end of the poem.

ROSARIO MORALES

I Am What I Am

I am what I am and I am U.S. American   I haven't wanted to say it because
if I did you'd take away the Puerto Rican but now I say go to hell   I am
what I am and you can't take it away with all the words and sneers at your
command   I am what I am   I am Puerto Rican   I am U.S.
American   I am New York Manhattan and the Bronx   I am what I am
I'm not hiding under no stoop   behind no curtain   I am what I am   I
am Boricua as boricuas come from the isle of Manhattan and I croon Carlos
Gardel tangoes in my sleep and Afro-Cuban beats in my blood and Xavier
Cugat's lukewarm latin is so familiar and dear   sneer dear but he's familiar
and dear   but not Carmen Miranda   who's a joke because I never was a
joke   I was a bit of a sensation   See! here's a real true honest-to-god
Puerto Rican girl and she's in college   Hey! Mary   come here and look
she's from right here   a South Bronx girl and she's honest-to-god in college
now   Ain't that something   who would believed it Ain't science wonderful or some such thing a wonder a wonder

And someone who did languages for a living stopped me in the subway
because how I spoke was a linguist's treat   I mean there it was yiddish and
spanish and fine refined college educated english and irish which I mainly keep
in my prayers   It's dusty now   I haven't said my prayers in decades but
try my Hail Marrrry full of grrrace with the nun's burr with the nun's disdain
its all true and its all me   do you know I got an English accent from
the BBC I always say   For years in the mountains of Puerto Rico when I
was 22 and 24 and 26   all those young years   I listened to the BBC and
Radio Moscow's English   english announcers announce and denounce and
then I read Dickens all the way thru three or four times at least and then later
I read Dickens aloud in voices and when I came back to the U.S. I spoke
mockdickens and mockBritish especially when I want to be crisp efficient I
know what I am doing and you can't scare me   tough   that's why I am
what I am and I'm a bit of a snob too   Shit! why am I calling myself
names   I really really dig the funny way the British speak   and it's real
it's true   and I love too the singing of yiddish sentences that go with shrugs
and hands and arms doing melancholy or lively dances   I love the sound
and look of yiddish in the air   in the body   in the streets   in the English
language   nooo   so what's new   so go by the grocer and buy some

---

A native of New York City, ROSARIO MORALES (b. 1920) currently lives in Cambridge, Massachusetts, where she is working on short stories. In 1986, Firebrand Books published a semiautobiographical collection of poems and essays that Morales coauthored with her daughter, Aurora Levins Morales.

fruit   oye vey   gevalt gefilte fish   raisele   oh and those words hundreds of them dotting the english language like raisins in the bread   shnook and schlemiel   suftik   tush schmata   all those soft sweet sounds saying sharp sharp things   I am what I am and I'm naturalized Jewish-American   wasp is foreign and new but Jewish-American is old show familiar   schmata familiar and its me dears its me   bagels blintzes and all   I am what I am   Take it or leave me alone.   1983

INVESTIGATIONS

1. According to Morales's speaker, what does it mean to be "U.S. American"?
2. Compare the speaker's definition of herself with Clint Oates's in "The Kind of Light That Shines on Texas." "What kind of light" would "reveal [them] as the same"? In other words, what point or points of view would you need to adopt to see these two people as essentially the same?
3. In a paragraph or two, write your own "I Am What I Am," imitating the style and tone of Morales's original. To what extent does the result reflect how you tend to see yourself?
4. What would Morales's speaker think of Jessie (*'night, Mother,* p. 28)? What advice could she offer Jessie? Would it make a difference? Why or why not?

MADISON SMARTT BELL

Customs of the Country

I don't remember much about that place anymore. It was nothing but somewhere I came to put in some pretty bad time, though that was not what I had planned on when I went there. I had it in mind to improve things, but I don't think you could fairly claim that's what I did. So that's one reason I might just as soon forget about it. And I didn't stay there all that long, not more than about nine months or so, about the same time, come to think, that the child I was there to try to get back had lived inside my body.

Born in Tennessee in 1957, MADISON SMARTT BELL has published two collections of short stories and five novels, including *The Year of Silence* (1987), *Straight Cut* (1986), and *Dr. Sleep* (1991). He writes, "[I'm] skeptical of any analysis that's based on demographics. I'm much more interested in the accommodations one individual makes to another."

It was a cluster-housing thing a little ways north out of town from Roanoke, on a two-land road that crossed the railroad cut and went about a mile farther up through the woods. The buildings looked something like a motel, a little raw still, though they weren't new. My apartment was no more than a place that would barely look all right and yet cost me little enough so I had something left over to give the lawyer. There was fresh paint on the walls and the trim in the kitchen and bathroom was in fair shape. And it was real quiet mostly, except that the man next door used to beat up his wife a couple of times a week. The place was soundproof enough I couldn't usually hear talk but I could hear yelling plain as day and when he got going good he would slam her bang into our common wall. If she hit in just the right spot it would send my pots and pans flying off the pegboard where I'd hung them above the stove.

Not that it mattered to me that the pots fell down, except for the noise and the time it took to pick them up again. Living alone like I was, I didn't have the heart to do much cooking and if I did fix myself something I mostly used an old iron skillet that hung there on the same wall. All the others I only had out for show. The whole apartment was done about the same way, made into something I kept spotless and didn't much care to use. I wore my hands out scrubbing everything clean and then saw to it that it stayed that way. I sewed slipcovers for that threadbare batch of Goodwill furniture I'd put in the place, and I hung curtains and found some sunshiny posters to tack on the walls, and I never cared a damn about any of it. It was an act, and I wasn't putting it on for me or for Davey, but for all the other people I expected to come to see it and judge it. And however good I could get it looking, it never felt quite right.

I felt even less at home there than I did at my job, which was waitressing three snake-bends of the counter at the Truckstops of America out at the I-81 interchange. The supervisor was a man named Tim that used to know my husband Patrick from before we had the trouble. He was nice about letting me take my phone calls there and giving me time off to see the lawyer, and in most other ways he was a decent man to work for, except that now and then he would have a tantrum over something or other and try to scream the walls down. Still, it never went beyond yelling, and he always acted sorry once he got through. The other waitress on my shift was an older lady named Prissy, and I liked her all right in spite of the name.

We were both on a swing shift that rolled over every ten days, which was the main thing I didn't like about that job. The six-to-two I hated the worst because it would have me getting back to my apartment building around three in the morning, not the time it looked its best. It was the kind of place where at that time of night I could expect to find the deputies out there looking for somebody, or else some other kind of trouble. I never got to know the neighbors any too well, but a lot of them were pretty sorry — small-time criminals, dope dealers and thieves, none of them much good at whatever it was they did.

There was one check forger that I knew of, and a man who would break into the other apartments looking for whiskey. One thing and another, along that line.

The man next door, the one that beat up his wife, didn't do crimes or work either that I ever heard. He just seemed to lay around the place, maybe drawing some kind of welfare. There wasn't a whole lot of him, he was just a stringy little man, hair and mustache a dishwater-brown, cheap green tattoos running up his arms. Maybe he was stronger than he looked, but I did wonder how come his wife would take it from him, since she was about a head taller and must have outweighed him an easy ten pounds. I might have thought she was whipping on him — stranger things have been known to go on — but she was the one that seemed like she might break out crying if you looked at her crooked. She was a big fine-looking girl with a lovely shape, and long brown hair real smooth and straight and shiny. I guess she was too hammered down most of the time to pay much attention to how she dressed, but still she had pretty brown eyes, big and long-lashed and so soft, sort of like a cow's eyes, except I never saw a cow that looked that miserable.

At first I thought maybe I might make a friend of her, she was about the only one around there I felt like I might want to. Our paths crossed pretty frequent, either around the apartment building or in the Kwik Sack back toward town, where I'd find her running the register some days. But she was shy of me, shy of anybody I suppose. She would flinch if you did so much as say hello. So after a while I quit trying. She'd get hers about twice a week, maybe other times I wasn't around to hear it happen. It's a wonder all the things you can learn to ignore, and after a month or so I was that accustomed I barely noticed when they would start in. I would just wait till I thought they were good and through, and then get up and hang those pans back on the wall where they were supposed to go. And all the while I would just be thinking about some other thing, like what might be going on with my Davey.

The place where he had been fostered out was not all that far away, just about ten or twelve miles up the road, out there in the farm country. The people were named Baker. I never got to first names with them, just called them Mr. and Mrs. They were older than me, both just into their forties, and they didn't have any children of their own. The place was only a small farm but Mr. Baker grew tobacco on the most of it and I'm told he made it a paying thing. Mrs. Baker kept a milk cow or two and she grew a garden and canned in the old-time way. Thrifty people. They were real sweet to Davey and he seemed to like being with them pretty well. He had been staying there almost the whole two years, which was lucky too, since most children usually got moved around a whole lot more than that.

And that was the trouble, like the lawyer explained to me, it was just too good. Davey was doing too well out there. He'd made out better in the first grade than anybody would have thought. So nobody really felt like he needed to be moved. The worst of it was the Bakers had got to like him well enough they were saying they wanted to adopt him if they could. Well, it would have been hard enough for me without that coming into it.

Even though he was so close, I didn't go out to see Davey near as much as I would have liked to. The lawyer kept telling me it wasn't a good idea to look like I was pressing too hard. Better take it easy till all the evaluations came in and we had our court date and all. Still, I would call and go on out there maybe a little more than once a month, most usually on the weekends, since that seemed to suit the Bakers better. They never acted like it was any trouble, and they were always pleasant to me, or polite might be a better word yet. The way it sometimes seemed they didn't trust me did bother me a little. I would have liked to take him out to the movies a time or two, but I could see plain enough the Bakers wouldn't have been easy about me having him off their place.

But I can't remember us having a bad time, any of those times I went. He was always happy to see me, though he'd be quiet when we were in the house, with Mrs. Baker hovering. So I would get us outside quick as ever I could and, once we were out, we would just play like both of us were children. There was an open pasture, a creek with a patch of woods, a hay barn where we would play hide-and-go-seek. I don't know what all else we did, silly things mostly. That was how I could get near him the easiest, he didn't get a whole lot of playing in, way out there. The Bakers weren't what you would call playful and there weren't any other children living near. So that was the thing I could give him that was all mine to give. When the weather was good we would stay outside together most all the day and he would just wear me out. But over the winter those visits seemed to get shorter and shorter, like the days.

Davey called me Momma still, but I suppose he had come to think your mother was something more like a big sister or just some kind of a friend. Mrs. Baker was the one doing for him all the time. I don't know just what he remembered from before, or if he remembered any of the bad part. He would always mind me but he never acted scared around me, and if anybody says he did they lie. But I never really did get to know what he had going on in the back of his mind about the past. At first I worried the Bakers might have been talking against me, but after I had seen a little more of them I knew they wouldn't have done anything like that, wouldn't have thought it right. So I expect whatever Davey knew about that other time he remembered on his own. He never mentioned Patrick hardly and I think he really had forgotten about him. Thinking back I guess he never saw that much of Patrick even when we were all living together. But Davey had Patrick's mark all over him, the same eyes and the same red hair.

Patrick had thick wavy hair the shade of an Irish setter's, and a big rolling mustache the same color. Maybe that was his best feature, but he was a good-looking man altogether, still is I suppose, though the prison haircut don't suit him. If he ever had much of a thought in his head I suspect he had knocked it clean out with dope, yet he was always fun to be around. I wasn't but seventeen when I married him and I didn't have any better sense myself. Right to the end I never thought anything much was the matter, all his vices looked so small to me. He was good-tempered almost all the time, and good with Davey when he did notice him. Never once did he raise his hand to either one of us. In little ways he was unreliable, late, not showing up at all, gone out of the house for days sometimes. Hindsight shows me he ran with other women, but I managed not to know anything about that at the time. He had not quite finished high school and the best job he could hold was being an orderly down at the hospital, but he made a good deal of extra money stealing pills out of there and selling them on the street.

That was something else I didn't allow myself to think on much back then. Patrick never told me a lot about it anyhow, always acted real mysterious about whatever he was up to in that line. He would disappear on one of his trips and come back with a whole mess of money, and I would spend up my share and be glad I had it too. I never thought much about where it was coming from, the money or the pills either one. He used to keep all manner of pills around the house, Valium and ludes and a lot of different kinds of speed, and we both took what we felt like whenever we felt in the mood. But what Patrick made the most on was Dilaudid. I used to take it without ever knowing what it really was, but once everything fell in on us I found out it was a bad thing, bad as heroin they said, and not much different, and it was what they gave Patrick most of his time for.

I truly was surprised to find out that it was the strongest dope we had,   15
because I never really even felt like it made you all that high. You would just take one and kick back on a long slow stroke and whatever trouble you might have, it would not be able to find you. It came on like nothing but it was the hardest habit to lose, and I was a long time shaking it. I might be thinking about it yet if I would let myself, and there were times, all through the winter I spent in that apartment, I'd catch myself remembering the feeling.

You couldn't call it a real bad winter, there wasn't much snow or anything, but I was cold just about all the time, except when I was at work. All I had in the apartment was some electric baseboard heaters, and they cost too much for me to leave them running very long at a stretch. I'd keep it just warm enough so I couldn't see my breath, and spend my time in a hot bathtub or under a big pile of blankets on the bed. Or else I would just be cold.

There was some kind of strange quietness about that place all during the cold weather. If the phone rang it would make me jump. Didn't seem like there was any TV or radio ever playing next door. The only sound coming out of there was Susan getting beat up once in a while. That was her name, a sweet name, I think. I found it out from hearing him say it, which he used to do almost every time before he started on her. "Su-*san*," he'd call out, loud enough I could hear him through the wall. He'd do it a time or two, he might have been calling her to him, and I suppose she went. After that would come a bad silence that reminded you of a snake being somewhere around. Then a few minutes' worth of hitting sounds and then the big slam as she hit the wall, and the clatter of my pots falling on the floor. He'd throw her at the wall maybe once or twice, usually when he was about to get through. By the time the pots had quit spinning on the floor it would be real quiet over there again, and the next time I saw Susan she'd be walking in that ginger way people have when they're hiding a hurt, and if I said hello to her she'd give a little jump and look away.

After a while I quit paying it much mind, it didn't feel any different to me than hearing the news on the radio. All their carrying on was not any more to me than a bump in the rut I had worked myself into, going back and forth from the job, cleaning that apartment till it hurt, calling up the lawyer about once a week to find out what was happening, which never was much. He was forever trying to get our case before some particular doctor or social worker or judge who'd be more apt to help us than another, so he said. I would call him up from the TOA, all eager to hear what news he had, and every time it was another delay. In the beginning I used to talk it all over with Tim or Prissy after I hung up, but after a while I got out of the mood to discuss it. I kept ahead making those calls but every one of them just wore out my hope a little more, like a drip of water wearing down a stone. And little by little I got in the habit of thinking that nothing really was going to change.

Somehow or other that winter passed by, with me going from one phone call to the next, going out to wait on that TOA counter, coming home to shiver and hold hands with myself and lie awake all through the night, or the day, depending what shift I was on. It was springtime, well into warm weather, before anything really happened at all. That was when the lawyer called *me*, for a change, and told me he had some people lined up to see me at last.

Well, I was all ready for them to come visit, come see how I'd fixed up   20
my house and all the rest of my business to get set for having Davey back with me again. But as it turned out, nobody seemed to feel like they were called on to make that trip. "I don't think that will be necessary" was what one of them said, I don't recall which. They both talked about the same, in voices that sounded like filling out forms.

So all I had to do was drive downtown a couple of times and see them in their offices. That child psychologist was the first and I doubt he kept me more than half an hour. I couldn't tell the point of most of the questions he asked. My second trip I saw the social worker, who turned out to be a black lady once I got down there, though I never could have told it over the phone. Her voice sounded like it was coming out of the TV. She looked me in the eye while she was asking her questions, but I couldn't tell a thing about what she thought. It wasn't till I was back in the apartment that I understood she must have already had her mind made up.

That came to me in a sort of a flash, while I was standing in the kitchen washing out a cup. Soon as I walked back in the door I saw my coffee mug left over from breakfast, and I kicked myself for letting it sit out. I was giving it a hard scrub with a scouring pad when I realized it didn't matter anymore.

I might just as well have dropped it on the floor and got what kick I could out of watching it smash, because it wasn't going to make any difference to anybody now. But all the same I rinsed it and set it in the drainer, careful as if it was an eggshell. Then I stepped backward out of the kitchen and took a long look around that cold shabby place and thought it might be for the best that nobody was coming. How could I have expected it to fool anybody else when it wasn't even good enough to fool me? A lonesomeness came over me, I felt like I was floating all alone in the middle of cold air, and then I began to remember some things I would just as soon as have not.

No, I never did like to think about this part, but I have had to think about it time and again, with never a break for a long, long time, because I needed to get to understand it at least well enough to believe it never would ever happen anymore. And I had come to believe that, in the end. If I hadn't, I never would have come back at all. I had found a way to trust myself again, though it took me a full two years to do it, and though of course it still didn't mean that anybody else would trust me.

What had happened was that Patrick went off on one of his mystery trips and stayed gone a deal longer than usual. Two nights away, I was used to that, but on the third I did start to wonder. He normally would have called at least, if he was going to be gone that long of a stretch. But I didn't hear a peep until about halfway through the fourth day. And it wasn't Patrick himself that called, but one of those public-assistance lawyers from downtown.

Seemed like the night before Patrick had got himself stopped on the interstate loop down there. The troopers said he was driving like a blind man, and he was so messed up on whiskey and ludes I suppose he must have been pretty near blind at that. Well, maybe he would have just lost his license or something like that, only that the backseat of the car was loaded up with all he had lately stole out of the hospital.

So it was bad. It was so bad my mind just could not contain it, and every hour it seemed to be getting worse. I spent the next couple of days running back and forth between the jail and that lawyer, and I had to haul Davey along with me wherever I went. He was too little for school and I couldn't find anybody to take him right then, though all that running around made him awful cranky. Patrick was just grim, he would barely speak. He already knew pretty well for sure that he'd be going to prison. The lawyer had told him there wasn't no use in getting a bondsman, he might just as well stay on in there and start pulling his time. I don't know how much he really saved himself that way, though, since what they ended up giving him was twenty-five years.

That was when all my troubles found me, quick. Two days after Patrick got arrested, I came down real sick with something. I thought at first it was a bad cold or the flu. My nose kept running and I felt so wore out I couldn't hardly get up off the bed and yet at the same time I felt real restless, like all my nerves had been scraped bare. Well, I didn't really connect it up to the fact that I'd popped the last pill in the house a couple of days before. What was really the matter was me coming off that Dilaudid, but I didn't have any notion of that at the time.

I was laying there in bed not able to get up and about ready to jump right out of my skin at the same time when Davey got the drawer underneath the stove open. Of course he was getting restless himself with all that had been going on, and me not able to pay him much mind. All our pots and pans were down in that drawer then, and he began to take them out one at a time and throw them on the floor. It made a hell of a racket, and the shape I was in, I felt like he must be doing it on purpose to devil me. I called out to him and asked him to quit. Nice at first: "You stop that, now, Davey. Momma don't feel good." But he kept right ahead. All he wanted was to have my attention, I know, but my mind wasn't working right just then. I knew I should get up and just go lead him away from there, but I couldn't seem to get myself to move. I had a picture of myself doing the right thing, but I just wasn't doing it. I was still lying there calling to him to quit and he was still banging those pots around and before long I was screaming at him outright, and starting to cry at the same time. But he never stopped a minute. I guess I had scared him some already and he was just locked into doing it, or maybe he wanted to drown me out. Every time he flung a pot it felt like I was getting shot at. And the next thing I knew I got myself in the kitchen someway and I was snatching him up off the floor.

To this day I don't remember doing it, though I have tried and tried. I thought if I could call it back then maybe I could root it out of myself and be shed of it for good and all. But all I ever knew was one minute I was grabbing a hold of him and the next he was laying on the far side of the room with his right leg folded up funny where it was broke, not even crying, just looking surprised. And I knew that it had to be me that threw him over there because as sure as hell is real there was nobody else around that could have done it.

I drove him to the hospital myself. I laid him straight on the front seat   30 beside me and drove with one hand all the way so I could hold on to him with the other. He was real quiet and real brave the whole time, never cried the least bit, just kept a tight hold on my hand with his. Well, after a while, we got there and they ran him off somewhere to get his leg set and pretty soon the doctor came back out and asked me how it had happened.

It was the same hospital where Patrick had worked and I even knew that doctor a little bit. Not that being connected to Patrick would have done me a whole lot of good around there at that time. Still, I have often thought since then that things might have come out better for me and Davey both if I just could have lied to that man, but I was not up to telling a lie that anybody would be apt to believe. All I could do was start to scream and jabber like a crazy person, and it ended up I stayed in that hospital quite a few days myself. They took me for a junkie and I guess I really was one too, though I hadn't known it till that very day. And I never saw Davey again for a whole two years, not till the first time they let me go out to the Bakers'.

Sometimes you don't get but one mistake, if the one you pick is bad enough. Do as much as step in the road one time without looking, and your life could be over with then and there. But during those two years I taught myself to believe that this mistake of mine could be wiped out, that if I struggled hard enough with myself and the world I could make it like it never had been.

Three weeks went by after I went to see that social worker, and I didn't have any idea what was happening, or if anything was. Didn't call anybody, I expect I was afraid to. Then one day the phone rang for me out there at the TOA. It was the lawyer and I could tell right off from the sound of his voice I wasn't going to care for his news. Well, he told me all the evaluations had come in now, sure enough, and they weren't running in our favor. They weren't against *me*, he made sure to say that, it was more like they were *for* the Bakers. And his judgment was it wouldn't pay me anything if we went on to court. It looked like the Bakers would get Davey for good anyhow, and they were likely to be easier about visitation if there wasn't any big tussle. But if I drug them into court, then we would have to start going back over that whole case history —

That was the word he used, *case history,* and it was around about there that I hung up. I went walking stiff-legged back across to the counter and just let myself sort of drop on a stool. Prissy had been covering my station while I was on the phone and she came right over to me then.

"What is it?" she said. I guess she could tell it was something by the look on my face.

"I lost him," I said.

"Oh, hon, you know I'm so sorry," she said. She reached out for my hand but I snatched it back. I know she meant it well but I just was not in the mood to be touched.

"There's no forgiveness," I said. I felt bitter about it. It had been a hard road for me to come as near forgiving myself as I ever could. And Davey forgave me, I really knew that, I could tell it in the way he acted when we were together. And if us two could do it, I didn't feel like it ought to be anybody else's business but ours. Tim walked up then and Prissy whispered something to him, and then he took a step nearer to me.

"I'm sorry," he told me.

"Not like I am," I said. "You don't know the meaning of the word."

"Go ahead and take off the rest of your shift if you feel like it," he said. "I'll wait on these tables myself, need be."

"I don't know it would make any difference," I said.

"Better take it easy on yourself," he said. "No use in taking it so hard. You're just going to have to get used to it."

"Is that a fact?" I said. And I lit myself a cigarette and turned my face away. We had been pretty busy, it was lunchtime, and the people were getting restless seeing all of us standing around there not doing a whole lot about bringing them their food. Somebody called out something to Tim, I didn't hear just what it was, but it set off one of his temper fits.

"Go on and get out of here if that's how you feel," he said. He was getting red in the face and waving his arms around to include everybody there in what he was saying. "Go on and clear out of here, every last one of you, and we don't care if you never come back. There's not one of you couldn't stand to miss a meal anyhow. Take a look at yourselves, you're all fat as hogs . . . "

It seemed like he might be going to keep it up a good while, and he had already said I could leave, so I hung up my apron and got my purse and I left. It was the first time he ever blew up at the customers that way, it had always been me or Prissy or one of the cooks. I never did find out what came of it all because I never went back to that place again.

I drove home in such a poison mood I barely knew I was driving a car or that there were any others on the road. I was ripe to get killed or kill somebody, and I wouldn't have cared much either way. I kept thinking about what Tim had said about having to get used to it. It came to me that I was used to it already, I really hadn't been all that surprised. That's what I'd been doing all those months, just gradually getting used to losing my child forever.

When I got back to the apartment I just fell in a chair and sat there staring across at the kitchen wall. It was in my mind to pack my traps and leave that place, but I hadn't yet figured out where I could go. I sat there a good while, I guess. The door was ajar from me not paying attention, but it wasn't cold enough out to make any difference. If I turned my head that way I could see a slice of the parking lot. I saw Susan drive up and park and come limping toward the building with an armload of groceries. Because of the angle I couldn't see her go into their apartment but I heard the door open and shut and after that it was quiet as a tomb. I kept on sitting there thinking about how used to everything I had got. There must have been generous numbers of other people too, I thought, who had got themselves accustomed to all kinds of things. Some were used to taking the pain and the rest were used to serving it up. About half of the world was screaming in misery, and it wasn't anything but a habit.

When I started to hear the hitting sounds come toward me through the wall, a smile came on my face like it was cut there with a knife. I'd been expecting it, you see, and the mood I was in I felt satisfied to see what I had expected was going to happen. So I listened a little more carefully than I'd been inclined to do before. It was *hit hit hit* going along together with a groan and a hiss of the wind being knocked out of her. I had to strain pretty hard to hear that breathing part, and I could hear him grunt too, when he got in a good one. There was about three minutes of that with some little breaks, and then a longer pause. When she hit the wall it was the hardest she had yet, I think. It brought down every last one of my pots at one time, including that big iron skillet that was the only one I ever used.

It was the first time they'd managed to knock that skillet down, and I was so impressed that I went over and stood looking down at it like I needed to make sure it was a real thing. I stared at the skillet so long it went out of focus and started looking more like a big black hole in the floor. That's when it dawned on me that this was one thing I didn't really have to keep on being used to.

It took three or four knocks before he came to the door, but that didn't worry me at all. I had faith, I knew he was going to come. I meant to stay right there till he did. When he came, he opened the door wide and stood there with his arms folded and his face all stiff with his secrets. It was fairly dark behind him, they had all the curtains drawn. I had that skillet held out in front of me in both my hands, like maybe I had come over to borrow a little hot grease or something. It was heavy it kept wanting to dip down toward the floor like a water witch's rod. When I saw he wasn't expecting anything, I twisted the skillet back over my shoulder like baseball players do their bats, and I hit him bang across the face as hard as I knew how. He went down and out at the same time and fetched up on his back clear in the middle of the room.

Then I went in after him, with the skillet cocked and ready in case he made to get up. But he didn't look like there was a whole lot of fight left in him right then. He was awake, at least partly awake, but his nose was just spouting blood and it seemed like I'd knocked out a few of his teeth. I wish I could tell you I was sorry or glad, but I didn't feel much of anything really, just that high lonesome whistle in the blood I used to get when I took all that Dilaudid. Susan was sitting on the floor against the wall, leaning down on her knees and sniveling. Her eyes were red but she didn't have any bruises where they showed. He never did hit her on the face, that was the kind he was. There was a big crack coming down the wall behind her and I remember thinking it probably wouldn't be too much longer before it worked through to my side.

"I'm going to pack and drive over to Norfolk," I told her. I hadn't thought of it before but once it came out my mouth I knew it was what I would do. "You can ride along with me if you want to. With your looks you could make enough money serving drinks to the sailors to buy that Kwik Sack and blow it up."

She didn't say anything, just raised her head up and stared at me kind of bug-eyed. And after a minute I turned around and went out. It didn't take me any time at all to get ready. All I had was a suitcase and a couple of boxes of other stuff. The sheets and blankets I just pulled off the bed and stuffed in the trunk all in one big wad. I didn't care a damn about that furniture, I would have lit it on fire on a dare.

When I was done I stuck my head back into the other apartment. The door was still open like I had left it. What was she doing but kneeling down over that son of a bitch and trying to clean off his face with a washrag. I noticed he was making a funny sound when he breathed, and his nose was still bleeding pretty quick, so I thought maybe I had broke it. Well, I can't say that worried me much.

"Come on now if you're coming, girl," I said. She looked up at me, not telling me one word, just giving me a stare out of those big cow eyes of hers like I was the one had been beating on her that whole winter through. And I

55

saw then that they were both of them stuck in their groove and that she would not be the one to step out of it. So I pulled back out of the doorway and went on down the steps to my car.

I was speeding on the road to Norfolk, doing seventy, seventy-five. I'd have liked to gone faster if the car had been up to it. I can't say I felt sorry for busting that guy, though I didn't enjoy the thought of it either. I just didn't know what difference it had made, and chances were it had made none at all. Kind of a funny thing, when you thought about it that way. It was the second time in my life I'd hurt somebody bad, and the other time I hadn't meant to do it at all. This time I'd known what I was doing for sure, but I still didn't know what I'd done.   1988

INVESTIGATIONS

1. What customs are involved in the story? To what extent do you share them?
2. Early in the story, the narrator says, "It's a wonder all the things you can learn to ignore." Locate each instance where she ignores something. To what extent *must* she do so? In what ways has it been necessary for you to "learn to ignore" things going on around you? What have you risked by doing so?
3. The narrators of both "Customs of the Country" and "The Kind of Light That Shines on Texas" do things they don't intend to, things they later regret and try to understand. Do they succeed? Do you think understanding something you regret doing helps you not to repeat it? Why or why not?
4. At the end of the story, the narrator says that her "busting" her neighbor probably hadn't made any difference. Do you agree? Do you think the narrator changes during the course of the story? If so, how?

MARSHA NORMAN

'night, Mother

Characters

JESSIE CATES, in her late thirties or early forties, is pale and vaguely unsteady physically. It is only in the last year that Jessie has gained control of her mind and body, and tonight she is determined to hold on to that control. She wears pants and a long black sweater with deep pockets, which contain scraps of paper, and there may be a pencil behind her ear or a pen clipped to one of the pockets of the sweater.

As a rule, Jessie doesn't feel much like talking. Other people have rarely found her quirky sense of humor amusing. She has a peaceful energy on this night, a sense of purpose, but is clearly aware of the time passing moment by moment. Oddly enough, Jessie has never been as communicative or as enjoyable as she is on this evening, but we must know she has not always been this way. There is a familiarity between these two women that comes from having lived together for a long time. There is a shorthand to the talk and a sense of routine comfort in the way they relate to each other physically. Naturally, there are also routine aggravations.

THELMA CATES, "MAMA," is Jessie's mother, in her late fifties or early sixties. She has begun to feel her age and so takes it easy when she can, or when it serves her purpose to let someone help her. But she speaks quickly and enjoys talking. She believes that things *are* what she says they are. Her sturdiness is more a mental quality than a physical one, finally. She is chatty and nosy, and this is *her* house.

Time and Place

The play takes place in a relatively new house built way out on a country road, with a living room and connecting kitchen, and a center hall that leads off to the bedrooms. A pull cord in the hall ceiling releases a ladder which leads to the attic. One of these bedrooms opens directly onto the hall, and its entry should be visible to everyone in the audience. It should be, in fact, the focal point of the entire set, and the lighting should make it disappear completely at times and draw the entire set into it at others. It is a point of both threat and promise. It is an ordinary door that opens onto absolute nothingness. That

---

Before becoming a playwright, MARSHA NORMAN (b. 1948) was a teacher and a journalist, once writing a children's column for the *Louisville* (Kentucky) *Times*. Her plays, which include *Getting Out* (1978), *Third and Oak* (1978), and *Circus Valentine* (1979), have won a number of awards and been widely produced. *'night, Mother* won the 1983 Pulitzer Prize for Drama.

door is the point of all the action, and the utmost care should be given to its design and construction.

The living room is cluttered with magazines and needlework catalogues, ash-trays, and candy dishes. Examples of Mama's needlework are everywhere — pillows, afghans, and quilts, doilies, and rugs, and they are quite nice examples. The house is more comfortable than messy, but there is quite a lot to keep in place here. It is more personal than charming. It is not quaint. Under no circumstances should the set and its dressing make a judgment about the intelligence or taste of Jessie and Mama. It should simply indicate that they are very specific real people who happen to live in a particular part of the country. Heavy accents, which would further distance the audience from Jessie and Mama, are also wrong.

The time is the present, with the action beginning about 8:15. Clocks onstage in the kitchen and on a table in the living room should run throughout the performance and be visible to the audience.

> *(Mama stretches to reach the cupcakes in a cabinet in the kitchen. She can't see them, but she can feel around for them, and she's eager to have one, so she's working pretty hard at it. This may be the most serious exercise Mama ever gets. She finds a cupcake, the coconut-covered, raspberry-and-marshmallow-filled kind known as a snowball, but sees that there's one missing from the package. She calls to Jessie, who is apparently somewhere else in the house.)*

MAMA (*unwrapping the cupcake*): Jessie, it's the last snowball, sugar. Put it on the list, OK? And we're out of Hershey bars, and where's that peanut brittle? I think maybe Dawson's been in it again. I ought to put a big mirror on the refrigerator door. That'll keep him out of my treats, won't it? You hear me, honey? (*Then more to herself.*) I hate it when the coconut falls off. Why does the coconut fall off?

> *(Jessie enters from her bedroom, carrying a stack of newspapers.)*

JESSIE: We got any old towels?

MAMA: There you are!

JESSIE (*holding a towel that was on the stack of newspapers*): Towels you don't want anymore. (*Picking up Mama's snowball wrapper.*) How about this swimming towel Loretta gave us? Beach towel, that's the name of it. You want it? (*Mama shakes her head no.*)

MAMA: What have you been doing in there?

JESSIE: And a big piece of plastic like a rubber sheet or something. Garbage bags would do if there's enough.

MAMA: Don't go making a big mess, Jessie. It's eight o'clock already.

JESSIE: Maybe an old blanket or towels we got in a soap box sometime?

MAMA: I said don't make a mess. Your hair is black enough, hon.

JESSIE (*continuing to search the kitchen cabinets, finding two or three more towels to add to her stack*): It's not for my hair, Mama. What about some old pillows anywhere, or a foam cushion out of a yard chair would be real good.

MAMA: You haven't forgot what night it is, have you? (*Holding up her finger-nails.*) They're all chipped, see? I've been waiting all week, Jess. It's Saturday night, sugar.

JESSIE: I know. I got it on the schedule.

MAMA (*crossing to the living room*): You want me to wash 'em now or are you making your mess first? (*Looking at the snowball.*) We're out of these. Did I say that already?

JESSIE: There's more coming tomorrow. I ordered you a whole case.

MAMA (*checking the* TV Guide): A whole case will go stale, Jessie.

JESSIE: They can go in the freezer till you're ready for them. Where's Daddy's gun?

MAMA: In the attic.

JESSIE: Where in the attic? I looked your whole nap and couldn't find it anywhere.

MAMA: One of his shoeboxes, I think.

JESSIE: Full of shoes. I looked already.

MAMA: Well, you didn't look good enough, then. There's that box from the ones he wore to the hospital. When he died, they told me I could have them back, but I never did like those shoes.

JESSIE (*pulling them out of her pocket*): I found the bullets. They were in an old milk can.

MAMA (*as Jessie starts for the hall*): Dawson took the shotgun, didn't he? Hand me that basket, hon.

JESSIE (*getting the basket for her*): Dawson better not've taken that pistol.

MAMA (*stopping her again*): Now my glasses, please. (*Jessie returns to get the glasses.*) I told him to take those rubber boots, too, but he said they were for fishing. I told him to take up fishing.

(*Jessie reaches for the cleaning spray, and cleans Mama's glasses for her.*)

JESSIE: He's just too lazy to climb up there, Mama. Or maybe he's just being smart. That floor's not very steady.

MAMA (*getting out a piece of knitting*): It's not a floor at all, hon, it's a board now and then. Measure this for me. I need six inches.

JESSIE (*as she measures*): Dawson could probably use some of those clothes up there. Somebody should have them. You ought to call the Salvation Army before the whole thing falls in on you. Six inches exactly.

MAMA: It's plenty safe! As long as you don't go up there.

JESSIE (*turning to go again*): I'm careful.

MAMA: What do you want the gun for, Jess?

JESSIE (*not returning this time. Opening the ladder in the hall*): Protection. (*She steadies the ladder as Mama talks.*)

MAMA: You take the TV way too serious, hon, I've never seen a criminal in my life. This is way too far to come for what's out here to steal. Never seen a one.

JESSIE (*taking her first step up*): Except for Ricky.

MAMA: Ricky is mixed up. That's not a crime.

JESSIE: Get your hands washed. I'll be right back. And get 'em real dry. You dry your hands till I get back or it's no go, all right?

MAMA: I thought Dawson told you not to go up those stairs.

JESSIE (*going up*): He did.

MAMA: I don't like the idea of a gun, Jess.

JESSIE (*calling down from the attic*): Which shoebox, do you remember?

MAMA: Black.

JESSIE: The box was black?

MAMA: The shoes were black.

JESSIE: That doesn't help much, Mother.

MAMA: I'm not trying to help, sugar. (*No answer.*) We don't have anything anybody'd want, Jessie. I mean, I don't even want what we got, Jessie.

JESSIE: Neither do I. Wash your hands. (*Mama gets up and crosses to stand under the ladder.*)

MAMA: You come down from there before you have a fit. I can't come up and get you, you know.

JESSIE: I know.

MAMA: We'll just hand it over to them when they come, how's that? Whatever they want, the criminals.

JESSIE: That's a good idea, Mama.

MAMA: Ricky will grow out of this and be a real fine boy, Jess. But I have to tell you, I wouldn't want Ricky to know we had a gun in the house.

JESSIE: Here it is. I found it.

MAMA: It's just something Ricky's going through. Maybe he's in with some bad people. He just needs some time, sugar. He'll get back in school or get a job or one day you'll get a call and he'll say he's sorry for all the trouble he's caused and invite you out for supper someplace dress-up.

JESSIE (*coming back down the steps*): Don't worry. It's not for him, it's for me.

MAMA: I didn't think you would shoot your own boy, Jessie. I know you've felt like it, well, we've all felt like shooting somebody, but we don't do it. I just don't think we need . . .

JESSIE (*interrupting*): Your hands aren't washed. Do you want a manicure or not?

MAMA: Yes, I do, but . . .

JESSIE (*crossing to the chair*): Then wash your hands and don't talk to me any more about Ricky. Those two rings he took were the last valuable things *I* had, so now he's started in on other people, door to door. I hope they put him away sometime. I'd turn him in myself if I knew where he was.

MAMA: You don't mean that.

JESSIE: Every word. Wash your hands and that's the last time I'm telling you.

(Jessie sits down with the gun and starts cleaning it, pushing the cylinder out, checking to see that the chambers and barrel are empty, then putting some oil on a small patch of cloth and pushing it through the barrel with the push rod that was in the box. Mama goes to the kitchen and washes her hands, as instructed, trying not to show her concern about the gun.)

MAMA: I shoulda got you to bring down that milk can. Agnes Fletcher sold hers to somebody with a flea market for forty dollars apiece.

JESSIE: I'll go back and get it in a minute. There's a wagon wheel up there, too. There's even a churn. I'll get it all if you want.

MAMA *(coming over, now, taking over now)*: What are you doing?

JESSIE: The barrel has to be clean, Mama. Old powder, dust gets in it . . .

MAMA: What for?

JESSIE: I told you.

MAMA *(reaching for the gun)*: And I told you, we don't get criminals out here.

JESSIE *(quickly pulling it to her)*: And I told you . . . *(Then trying to be calm.)* The gun is for me.

MAMA: Well, you can have it if you want. When I die, you'll get it all, anyway.

JESSIE: I'm going to kill myself, Mama.

MAMA *(returning to the sofa)*: Very funny. Very funny.

JESSIE: I am.

MAMA: You are not! Don't even say such a thing, Jessie.

JESSIE: How would you know if I didn't say it? You want it to be a surprise? You're lying there in your bed or maybe you're just brushing your teeth and you hear this . . . noise down the hall?

MAMA: Kill yourself.

JESSIE: Shoot myself. In a couple of hours.

MAMA: It must be time for your medicine.

JESSIE: Took it already.

MAMA: What's the matter with you?

JESSIE: Not a thing. Feel fine.

MAMA: You feel fine. You're just going to kill yourself.

JESSIE: Waited until I felt good enough, in fact.

MAMA: Don't make jokes, Jessie. I'm too old for jokes.

JESSIE: It's not a joke, Mama.

(Mama watches for a moment in silence.)

MAMA: That gun's no good, you know. He broke it right before he died. He dropped it in the mud one day.

JESSIE: Seems OK. *(She spins the chamber, cocks the pistol, and pulls the trigger. The gun is not yet loaded, so all we hear is the click, but it will definitely work. It's also obvious that Jessie knows her way around a gun. Mama cannot speak.)* I had Cecil's all ready in there, just in case I couldn't find this one, but I'd rather use Daddy's.

MAMA: Those bullets are at least fifteen years old.

JESSIE (*pulling out another box*): These are from last week.

MAMA: Where did you get those?

JESSIE: Feed store Dawson told me about.

MAMA: Dawson!

JESSIE: I told him I was worried about prowlers. He said he thought it was a good idea. He told me what kind to ask for.

MAMA: If he had any idea . . .

JESSIE: He took it as a compliment. He thought I might be taking an interest in things. He got through telling me all about the bullets and then he said we ought to talk like this more often.

MAMA: And where was I while this was going on?

JESSIE: On the phone with Agnes. About the milk can, I guess. Anyway, I asked Dawson if he thought they'd send me some bullets and he said he'd just call for me, because he knew they'd send them if he told them to. And he was absolutely right. Here they are.

MAMA: How could he do that?

JESSIE: Just trying to help, Mama.

MAMA: And then I told you where the gun was.

JESSIE (*smiling, enjoying this joke*): See? Everybody's doing what they can.

MAMA: You told me it was for protection!

JESSIE: It *is*! I'm still doing your nails, though. Want to try that new Chinaberry color?

MAMA: Well, I'm calling Dawson right now. We'll just see what he has to say about this little stunt.

JESSIE: Dawson doesn't have any more to do with this.

MAMA: He's your brother.

JESSIE: And that's all.

MAMA (*stands up, moves toward the phone*): Dawson will put a stop to this. Yes he will. He'll take the gun away.

JESSIE: If you call him, I'll just have to do it before he gets here. Soon as you hang up the phone, I'll just walk in the bedroom and lock the door. Dawson will get here just in time to help you clean up. Go ahead, call him. Then call the police. Then call the funeral home. Then call Loretta and see if *she'll* do your nails.

MAMA: You will not! This is crazy talk, Jessie!

(*Mama goes directly to the telephone and starts to dial, but Jessie is fast, coming up behind her and taking the receiver out of her hand, putting it back down.*)

JESSIE (*firm and quiet*): I said no. This is private. Dawson is not invited.

MAMA: Just me.

JESSIE: I don't want anybody else over here. Just you and me. If Dawson comes over, it'll make me feel stupid for not doing it ten years ago.

MAMA: I think we better call the doctor. Or how about the ambulance. You like that one driver, I know. What's his name, Timmy? Get you somebody to talk to.

JESSIE (*going back to her chair*): I'm through talking, Mama. You're it. No more.

MAMA: We're just going to sit around like every other night in the world and then you're going to kill yourself? (*Jessie doesn't answer.*) You'll miss. (*Again there is no response.*) You'll just wind up a vegetable. How would you like that? Shoot your ear off? You know what the doctor said about getting excited. You'll cock the pistol and have a fit.

JESSIE: I think I can kill myself, Mama.

MAMA: You're not going to kill yourself, Jessie. You're not even upset! (*Jessie smiles, or laughs quietly, and Mama tries a different approach.*) People don't really kill themselves, Jessie. No, mam, doesn't make sense, unless you're retarded or deranged, and you're as normal as they come, Jessie, for the most part. We're all *afraid* to die.

JESSIE: I'm not, Mama. I'm cold all the time, anyway.

MAMA: That's ridiculous.

JESSIE: It's exactly what I want. It's dark and quiet.

MAMA: So is the back yard, Jessie! Close your eyes. Stuff cotton in your ears. Take a nap! It's quiet in your room. I'll leave the TV off all night.

JESSIE: So quiet I don't know it's quiet. So nobody can get me.

MAMA: You don't know what dead is like. It might not be quiet at all. What if it's like an alarm clock and you can't wake up so you can't shut it off. Ever.

JESSIE: Dead is everybody and everything I ever knew, gone. Dead is dead quiet.

MAMA: It's a sin. You'll go to hell.

JESSIE: Uh-huh.

MAMA: You will!

JESSIE: Jesus was a suicide, if you ask me.

MAMA: You'll go to hell just for saying that. Jessie!

JESSIE (*with genuine surprise*): I didn't know I thought that.

MAMA: Jessie!

(*Jessie doesn't answer. She puts the now-loaded gun back in the box and crosses to the kitchen. But Mama is afraid she's headed for the bedroom.*)

MAMA (*in a panic*): You can't use my towels! They're my towels. I've had them for a long time. I like my towels.

JESSIE: I asked you if you wanted that swimming towel and you said you didn't.

MAMA: And you can't use your father's gun, either. It's mine now, too. And you can't do it in my house.

JESSIE: Oh, come on.

MAMA: No. You can't do it. I won't let you. The house is in my name.

JESSIE: I have to go in the bedroom and lock the door behind me so they won't arrest you for killing me. They'll probably test your hands for gunpowder, anyway, but you'll pass.

MAMA: Not in my house!

JESSIE: If I'd known you were going to act like this, I wouldn't have told you.

MAMA: How am I supposed to act? Tell you to go ahead? OK by me, sugar? Might try it myself. What took you so long?

JESSIE: There's just no point in fighting me over it, that's all. Want some coffee?

MAMA: Your birthday's coming up, Jessie. Don't you want to know what we got you?

JESSIE: You got me dusting powder, Loretta got me a new housecoat, pink probably, and Dawson got me new slippers, too small, but they go with the robe, he'll say. (*Mama cannot speak.*) Right? (*Apparently Jessie is right.*) Be back in a minute.

(*Jessie takes the gun box, puts it on top of the stack of towels and garbage bags, and takes them into her bedroom. Mama, alone for a moment, goes to the phone, picks up the receiver, looks toward the bedroom, starts to dial, and then replaces the receiver in its cradle as Jessie walks back into the room. Jessie wonders, silently. They have lived together for so long there is very rarely any reason for one to ask what the other was about to do.*)

MAMA: I started to, but I didn't. I didn't call him.

JESSIE: Good. Thank you.

MAMA (*starting over, a new approach*): What's this all about, Jessie?

JESSIE: About?

(*Jessie now begins the next task she had "on the schedule," which is refilling all the candy jars, taking the empty papers out of the boxes of chocolates, etc. Mama generally snitches when Jessie does this. Not tonight, though. Nevertheless, Jessie offers.*)

MAMA: What did I do?

JESSIE: Nothing. Want a caramel?

MAMA (*ignoring the candy*): You're mad at me.

JESSIE: Not a bit. I am worried about you, but I'm going to do what I can before I go. We're not just going to sit around tonight. I made a list of things.

MAMA: What things?

JESSIE: How the washer works. Things like that.

MAMA: I know how the washer works. You put the clothes in. You put the soap in. You turn it on. You wait.

JESSIE: You do something else. You don't just wait.

MAMA: Whatever else you find to do, you're still mainly waiting. The waiting's the worst part of it. The waiting's what you pay somebody else to do, if you can.

JESSIE (*nodding*): OK. Where do we keep the soap?

MAMA: I could find it.

JESSIE: See?

MAMA: If you're mad about doing the wash, we can get Loretta to do it.

JESSIE: Oh now, that might be worth staying to see.

MAMA: She'd never in her life, would she?

JESSIE: Nope.

MAMA: What's the matter with her?

JESSIE: She thinks she's better than we are. She's not.

MAMA: Maybe if she didn't wear that yellow all the time.

JESSIE: The washer repair number is on a little card taped to the side of the machine.

MAMA: Loretta doesn't ever have to come over here again. Dawson can just leave her at home when he comes. And we don't ever have to see Dawson either if he bothers you. Does he bother you?

JESSIE: Sure he does. Be sure you clean out the lint tray every time you use the dryer. But don't ever put your house shoes in, it'll melt the soles.

MAMA: What does Dawson do, that bothers you?

JESSIE: He just calls me Jess like he knows who he's talking to. He's always wondering what I do all day. I mean, I wonder that myself, but it's my day, so it's mine to wonder about, not his.

MAMA: Family is just accident, Jessie. It's nothing personal, hon. They don't mean to get on your nerves. They don't even mean to be your family, they just are.

JESSIE: They know too much.

MAMA: About what?

JESSIE: They know things about you, and they learned it before you had a chance to say whether you wanted them to know it or not. They were there when it happened and it don't belong to them, it belongs to you, only they got it. Like my mail-order bra got delivered to their house.

MAMA: By accident!

JESSIE: All the same . . . they opened it. They saw the little rosebuds on it. (*Offering her another candy.*) Chewy mint?

MAMA (*shaking her head no*): What do they know about you? I'll tell them never to talk about it again. Is it Ricky or Cecil or your fits or your hair is falling out or you drink too much coffee or you never go out of the house or what?

JESSIE: I just don't like their talk. The account at the grocery is in Dawson's name when you call. The number's on a whole list of numbers on the back cover of the phone book.

MAMA: Well! Now we're getting somewhere. They're none of them ever setting foot in this house again.

JESSIE: It's not them, Mother. I wouldn't kill myself just to get away from them.

MAMA: You leave the room when they come over, anyway.

JESSIE: I stay as long as I can. Besides, it's you they come to see.

MAMA: That's because I stay in the room when they come.

JESSIE: It's not them.

MAMA: Then what is it?

JESSIE (*checking the list on her note pad*): The grocery won't deliver on Saturday anymore. And if you want your order the same day, you have to call before ten. And they won't deliver less than fifteen dollars' worth. What I do is tell them what we need and tell them to add on cigarettes until it gets to fifteen dollars.

MAMA: It's Ricky. You're trying to get through to him.

JESSIE: If I thought I could do that, I would stay.

MAMA: Make him sorry he hurt you, then. That's it, isn't it?

JESSIE: He's hurt me, I've hurt him. We're about even.

MAMA: You'll be telling him killing is OK with you, you know. Want him to start killing next? Nothing wrong with it. Mom did it.

JESSIE: Only a matter of time, anyway, Mama. When the call comes, you let Dawson handle it.

MAMA: Honey, nothing says those calls are always going to be some new trouble he's into. You could get one that he's got a job, that he's getting married, or how about he's joined the army, wouldn't that be nice?

JESSIE: If you call the Sweet Tooth before you call the grocery, that Susie will take your fudge next door to the grocery and it'll all come out together. Be sure you talk to Susie, though. She won't let them put it in the bottom of a sack like that one time, remember?

MAMA: Ricky could come over, you know. What if he calls us?

JESSIE: It's not Ricky, Mama.

MAMA: Or anybody could call us, Jessie.

JESSIE: Not on Saturday night, Mama.

MAMA: Then what is it? Are you sick? If your gums are swelling again, we can get you to the dentist in the morning.

JESSIE: No. Can you order your medicine or do you want Dawson to? I've got a note to him. I'll add that to it if you want.

MAMA: Your eyes don't look right. I thought so yesterday.

JESSIE: That was just the ragweed. I'm not sick.

MAMA: Epilepsy is sick, Jessie.

JESSIE: It won't kill me. (*A pause.*) If it would, I wouldn't have to.

MAMA: You don't *have* to.

JESSIE: No, I don't. That's what I like about it.

MAMA: Well, I won't let you!

JESSIE: It's not up to you.

MAMA: Jessie!

JESSIE: I want to hang a big sign around my neck, like Daddy's on the barn. GONE FISHING.

MAMA: You don't like it here.

JESSIE (*smiling*): Exactly.

MAMA: I meant here in my house.

JESSIE: I know you did.

MAMA: You never should have moved back in here with me. If you'd kept your little house or found another place when Cecil left you, you'd have made some new friends at least. Had a life to lead. Had your own things around you. Give Ricky a place to come see you. You never should've come here.

JESSIE: Maybe.

MAMA: But I didn't force you, did I?

JESSIE: If it was a mistake, we made it together. You took me in. I appreciate that.

MAMA: You didn't have any business being by yourself right then, but I can see how you might want a place of your own. A grown woman should . . .

JESSIE: Mama . . . I'm just not having a very good time and I don't have any reason to think it'll get anything but worse. I'm tired. I'm hurt. I'm sad. I feel used.

MAMA: Tired of what?

JESSIE: It all.

MAMA: What does that mean?

JESSIE: I can't say it any better.

MAMA: Well, you'll have to say it better because I'm not letting you alone till you do. What were those other things? Hurt . . . (*Before Jessie can answer.*) You had this all ready to say to me, didn't you? Did you write this down? How long have you been thinking about this?

JESSIE: Off and on, ten years. On all the time, since Christmas.

MAMA: What happened at Christmas?

JESSIE: Nothing.

MAMA: So why Christmas?

JESSIE: That's it. On the nose.

(*A pause. Mama knows exactly what Jessie means. She was there, too, after all.*)

JESSIE (*putting the candy sacks away*): See where all this is? Red hots up front, sour balls and horehound mixed together in this one sack. New packages of toffee and licorice right in back there.

MAMA: Go back to your list. You're hurt by what?

JESSIE (*Mama knows perfectly well*): Mama . . .

MAMA: OK. Sad about what? There's nothing real sad going on right now. If it was after your divorce or something, that would make sense.

JESSIE (*looking at her list, then opening the drawer*): Now, this drawer has everything in it that there's no better place for. Extension cords, batteries for the radio, extra lighters, sandpaper, masking tape, Elmer's glue, thumbtacks, that kind of stuff. The mousetraps are under the sink, but you call Dawson if you've got one and let him do it.

MAMA: Sad about what?

JESSIE: The way things are.

MAMA: Not good enough. What things?

JESSIE: Oh, everything from you and me to Red China.

MAMA: I think we can leave the Chinese out of this.

JESSIE (*crosses back into the living room*): There's extra light bulbs in a box in the hall closet. And we've got a couple of packages of fuses in the fuse box. There's candles and matches in the top of the broom closet, but if the lights go out, just call Dawson and sit tight. But don't open the refrigerator door. Things will stay cool in there as long as you keep the door shut.

MAMA: I asked you a question.

JESSIE: I read the paper. I don't like how things are. And they're not any better out there than they are in here.

MAMA: If you're doing this because of the newspapers, I can sure fix that!

JESSIE: There's just more of it on TV.

MAMA (*kicking the television set*): Take it out, then!

JESSIE: You wouldn't do that.

MAMA: Watch me.

JESSIE: What would you do all day?

MAMA (*desperately*): Sing. (*Jessie laughs.*) I would, too. You want to watch? I'll sing till morning to keep you alive, Jessie, please!

JESSIE: No. (*Then affectionately.*) It's a funny idea, though. What do you sing?

MAMA (*has no idea how to answer this*): We've got a good life here!

JESSIE (*going back into the kitchen*): I called this morning and canceled the papers, except for Sunday, for your puzzles; you'll still get that one.

MAMA: Let's get another dog, Jessie! You liked a big dog, now, didn't you? That King dog, didn't you?

JESSIE (*washing her hands*): I did like that King dog, yes.

MAMA: I'm so dumb. He's the one run under the tractor.

JESSIE: That makes him dumb, not you.

MAMA: For bringing it up.

JESSIE: It's OK. Handi-Wipes and sponges under the sink.

MAMA: We could get a new dog and keep him in the house. Dogs are cheap!

JESSIE (*getting big pill jars out of the cabinet*): No.

MAMA: Something for you to take care of.

JESSIE: I've had you, Mama.

MAMA (*frantically starting to fill pill bottles*): You do too much for me. I can fill pill bottles all day, Jessie, and change the shelf paper and wash the floor when I get through. You just watch me. You don't have to do another thing in this house if you don't want to. You don't have to take care of me, Jessie.

JESSIE: I know that. You've just been letting me do it so I'll have something to do, haven't you?

MAMA (*realizing this was a mistake*): I don't do it as well as you. I just meant if it tires you out or makes you feel used . . .

JESSIE: Mama, I know you used to ride the bus. Riding the bus and it's hot

and bumpy and crowded and too noisy and more than anything in the
world you want to get off and the only reason in the world you don't get
off is it's still fifty blocks from where you're going? Well, I can get off
right now if I want to, because even if I ride fifty more years and get off
then, it's the same place when I step down to it. Whenever I feel like it, I
can get off. As soon as I've had enough, it's my stop. I've had enough.

MAMA: You're feeling sorry for yourself!

JESSIE: The plumber's helper is under the sink, too.

MAMA: You're not having a good time! Whoever promised you a good time?
Do you think I've had a good time?

JESSIE: I think you're pretty happy, yeah. You have things you like to do.

MAMA: Like what?

JESSIE: Like crochet.

MAMA: I'll teach you to crochet.

JESSIE: I can't do any of that nice work, Mama.

MAMA: Good time don't come looking for you, Jessie. You could work some
puzzles or put in a garden or go to the store. Let's call a taxi and go to
the A&P!

JESSIE: I shopped you up for about two weeks already. You're not going to
need toilet paper till Thanksgiving.

MAMA (*interrupting*): You're acting like some little brat, Jessie. You're mad and
everybody's boring and you don't have anything to do and you don't like
me and you don't like going out and you don't like staying in and you
never talk on the phone and you don't watch TV and you're miserable
and it's your own sweet fault.

JESSIE: And it's time I did something about it.

MAMA: Not something like killing yourself. Something like . . . buying us all
new dishes! I'd like that. Or maybe the doctor would let you get a driver's
license now, or I know what let's do right this minute, let's rearrange the
furniture.

JESSIE: I'll do that. If you want. I always thought if the TV was somewhere
else, you wouldn't get such a glare on it during the day. I'll do whatever
you want before I go.

MAMA (*badly frightened by those words*): You could get a job!

JESSIE: I took that telephone sales job and I didn't even make enough money
to pay the phone bill, and I tried to work at the gift shop at the hospital
and they said I made people real uncomfortable smiling at them the way
I did.

MAMA: You could keep books. You kept your dad's books.

JESSIE: But nobody ever checked them.

MAMA: When he died, they checked them.

JESSIE: And that's when they took the books away from me.

MAMA: That's because without him there wasn't any business, Jessie!

JESSIE (*putting the pill bottles away*): You know I couldn't work. I can't do
anything. I've never been around people my whole life except when I went

to the hospital. I could have a seizure any time. What good would a job do? The kind of job I could get would make me feel worse.

MAMA: Jessie!

JESSIE: It's true!

MAMA: It's what you think is true!

JESSIE (*struck by the clarity of that*): That's right. It's what I think is true.

MAMA (*hysterically*): But I can't do anything about that!

JESSIE (*quietly*): No. You can't. (*Mama slumps, if not physically, at least emotionally.*) And I can't do anything either, about my life, to change it, make it better, make me feel better about it. Like it better, make it work. But I can stop it. Shut it down, turn it off like the radio when there's nothing on I want to listen to. It's all I really have that belongs to me and I'm going to say what happens to it. And it's going to stop. And I'm going to stop it. So. Let's just have a good time.

MAMA: Have a good time.

JESSIE: We can't go on fussing all night. I mean, I could ask you things I always wanted to know and you could make me some hot chocolate. The old way.

MAMA (*in despair*): It takes cocoa, Jessie.

JESSIE (*gets it out of the cabinet*): I bought cocoa, Mama. And I'd like to have a caramel apple and do your nails.

MAMA: You didn't eat a bite of supper.

JESSIE: Does that mean I can't have a caramel apple?

MAMA: Of course not. I mean . . . (*Smiling a little.*) Of course you can have a caramel apple.

JESSIE: I thought I could.

MAMA: I make the best caramel apples in the world.

JESSIE: I know you do.

MAMA: Or used to. And you don't get cocoa like mine anywhere anymore.

JESSIE: It takes time, I know, but . . .

MAMA: The salt is the trick.

JESSIE: Trouble and everything.

MAMA (*backing away toward the stove*): It's no trouble. What trouble? You put it in the pan and stir it up. All right. Fine. Caramel apples. Cocoa. OK.

(*Jessie walks to the counter to retrieve her cigarettes as Mama looks for the right pan. There are brief near-smiles, and maybe Mama clears her throat. We have a truce, for the moment. A genuine but nevertheless uneasy one. Jessie, who has been in constant motion since the beginning, now seems content to sit.*

Mama starts looking for a pan to make the cocoa, getting out all the pans in the cabinets in the process. It looks like she's making a mess on purpose so Jessie will have to put them all away again. Mama is buying time, or trying to, and entertaining.)

JESSIE: You talk to Agnes today?

MAMA: She's calling me from a pay phone this week. God only knows why. she has a perfectly good Trimline at home.

JESSIE (*laughing*): Well, how is she?

MAMA: How is she every day, Jessie? Nuts.

JESSIE: Is she really crazy or just silly?

MAMA: No, she's really crazy. She was probably using the pay phone because she had another little fire problem at home.

JESSIE: Mother . . .

MAMA: I'm serious! Agnes Fletcher's burned down every house she ever lived in. Eight fires, and she's due for a new one any day now.

JESSIE (*laughing*): No!

MAMA: Wouldn't surprise me a bit.

JESSIE (*laughing*): Why didn't you tell me this before? Why isn't she locked up somewhere?

MAMA: 'Cause nobody ever got hurt, I guess. Agnes woke everybody up to watch the fires as soon as she set 'em. One time she set out porch chairs and served lemonade.

JESSIE (*shaking her head*): Real lemonade?

MAMA: The houses they lived in, you knew they were going to fall down anyway, so why wait for it, is all I could ever make out about it. Agnes likes a feeling of accomplishment.

JESSIE: Good for her.

MAMA (*finding the pan she wants*): Why are you asking about Agnes? One cup or two?

JESSIE: One. She's your friend. No marshmallows.

MAMA (*getting the milk, etc.*): You have to have marshmallows. That's the old way, Jess. Two or three? Three is better.

JESSIE: Three, then. Her whole house burns up? Her clothes and pillows and everything? I'm not sure I believe this.

MAMA: When she was a girl, Jess, not now. Long time ago. But she's still got it in her, I'm sure of it.

JESSIE: She wouldn't burn her house down now. Where would she go? She can't get Buster to build her a new one, he's dead. How could she burn it up?

MAMA: Be exciting, though, if she did. You never know.

JESSIE: You do too know, Mama. She wouldn't do it.

MAMA (*forced to admit, but reluctant*): I guess not.

JESSIE: What else? Why does she wear all those whistles around her neck?

MAMA: Why does she have a house full of birds?

JESSIE: I didn't know she had a house full of birds!

MAMA: Well, she does. And she says they just follow her home. Well, I know for a fact she's still paying on the last parrot she bought. You gotta keep your life filled up, she says. She says a lot of stupid things. (*Jessie laughs, Mama continues, convinced she's getting somewhere.*) It's all that okra she eats. You can't just willy-nilly eat okra two meals a day and expect to get away with it. Made her crazy.

JESSIE: She really eats okra twice a day? Where does she get it in the winter?

MAMA: Well, she eats it a lot. Maybe not two meals, but . . .

JESSIE: More than the average person.

MAMA (*beginning to get irritated*): I don't know how much okra the average person eats.

JESSIE: Do you know how much okra Agnes eats?

MAMA: No.

JESSIE: How many birds does she have?

MAMA: Two.

JESSIE: Then what are the whistles for?

MAMA: They're not real whistles. Just little plastic ones on a necklace she won playing Bingo, and I only told you about it because I thought I might get a laugh out of you for once even if it wasn't the truth, Jessie. Things don't have to be true to talk about 'em, you know.

JESSIE: Why won't she come over here?

(*Mama is suddenly quiet, but the cocoa and milk are in the pan now, so she lights the stove and starts stirring.*)

MAMA: Well now, what a good idea. We should've had more cocoa. Cocoa is perfect.

JESSIE: Except you don't like milk.

MAMA (*another attempt, but not as energetic*): I hate milk. Coats your throat as bad as okra. Something just downright disgusting about it.

JESSIE: It's because of me, isn't it?

MAMA: No, Jess.

JESSIE: Yes, Mama.

MAMA: OK. Yes, then, but she's crazy. She's as crazy as they come. She's a lunatic.

JESSIE: What is it exactly? Did I say something, sometime? Or did she see me have a fit and's afraid I might have another one if she came over, or what?

MAMA: I guess.

JESSIE: You guess what? What's she ever said? She must've given you some reason.

MAMA: Your hands are cold.

JESSIE: What difference does that make?

MAMA: "Like a corpse," she says, "and I'm gonna be one soon enough as it is."

JESSIE: That's crazy.

MAMA: That's Agnes. "Jessie's shook the hand of death and I can't take the chance it's catching, Thelma, so I ain't comin' over, and you can understand or not, but I ain't comin'. I'll come up the driveway, but that's as far as I go."

JESSIE (*laughing, relieved*): I thought she didn't like me! She's scared of me! How about that! Scared of me.

MAMA: I could make her come over here, Jessie. I could call her up right now and she could bring the birds and come visit. I didn't know you ever thought about her at all. I'll tell her she just has to come and she'll come, all right. She owes me one.

JESSIE: No, that's all right. I just wondered about it. When I'm in the hospital, does she come over here?

MAMA: Her kitchen is just a tiny thing. When she comes over here, she feels like . . . (*Toning it down a little.*) Well, we all like a change of scene, don't we?

JESSIE (*playing along*): Sure we do. Plus there's no birds diving around.

MAMA: I hate those birds. She says I don't understand them. What's there to understand about birds?

JESSIE: Why Agnes likes them, for one thing. Why they stay with her when they could be outside with the other birds. What their singing means. How they fly. What they think Agnes is.

MAMA: Why do you have to know so much about things, Jessie? There's just not that much *to* things that I could ever see.

JESSIE: That you could ever *tell,* you mean. You didn't have to lie to me about Agnes.

MAMA: I didn't lie. You never asked before!

JESSIE: You lied about setting fire to all those houses and about how many birds she has and how much okra she eats and why she won't come over here. If I have to keep dragging the truth out of you, this is going to take all night.

MAMA: That's fine with me. I'm not a bit sleepy.

JESSIE: Mama . . .

MAMA: All right. Ask me whatever you want. Here.

(*They come to an awkward stop, as the cocoa is ready and Mama pours it into the cups Jessie has set on the table.*)

JESSIE (*as Mama takes her first sip*): Did you love Daddy?

MAMA: No.

JESSIE (*pleased that Mama understands the rules better now*): I didn't think so. Were you really fifteen when you married him?

MAMA: The way he told it? I'm sitting in the mud, he comes along, drags me in the kitchen, "She's been there ever since"?

JESSIE: Yes.

MAMA: No. It was a big fat lie, the whole thing. He just thought it was funnier that way. God, this milk in here.

JESSIE: The cocoa helps.

MAMA (*pleased that they agree on this, at least*): Not enough, though, does it? You can still taste it, can't you?

JESSIE: Yeah, it's pretty bad. I thought it was my memory that was bad, but it's not. It's the milk, all right.

MAMA: It's a real waste of chocolate. You don't have to finish it.

JESSIE (*putting her cup down*): Thanks, though.

MAMA: I should've known not to make it. I knew you wouldn't like it. You never did like it.

JESSIE: You didn't ever love him, or he did something and you stopped loving him, or what?

MAMA: He felt sorry for me. He wanted a plain country woman and that's what he married, and then he held it against me the rest of my life like I was supposed to change and surprise him somehow. Like I remember this one day he was standing on the porch and I told him to get a shirt on and he went in and got one and then he said, real peaceful, but to the point, "You're right, Thelma. If God had meant for people to go around without any clothes on, they'd have been born that way."

JESSIE (*sees Mama's hurt*): He didn't mean anything by that, Mama.

MAMA: He never said a word he didn't have to, Jessie. That was probably all he'd said to me all day, Jessie. So if he said it, there was something to it. but I never did figure that one out. What did that mean?

JESSIE: I don't know. I liked him better than you did, but I didn't know him any better.

MAMA: How could I love him, Jessie. I didn't have a thing he wanted. (*Jessie doesn't answer.*) He got his share, though. You loved him enough for both of us. You followed him around like some . . . Jessie, all the man ever did was farm and sit . . . and try to think of somebody to sell the farm to.

JESSIE: Or make me a boyfriend out of pipe cleaners and sit back and smile like the stick man was about to dance and wasn't I going to get a kick out of that. Or sit up with a sick cow all night and leave me a chain of sleepy stick elephants on my bed in the morning.

MAMA: Or just sit.

JESSIE: I liked him sitting. Big old faded blue man in the chair. Quiet.

MAMA: Agnes gets more talk out of her birds than I got from the two of you. He could've had that GONE FISHING sign around his neck in that chair. I saw him stare off at the water. I saw him look at the weather rolling in. I got where I could practically see the boat myself. But you, you knew what he was thinking about and you're going to tell me.

JESSIE: I don't know, Mama! His life, I guess. His corn. His boots. Us. Things. You know.

MAMA: No, I don't know, Jessie! You had those quiet little conversations after supper every night. What were you whispering about?

JESSIE: We weren't whispering, you were just across the room.

MAMA: What did you talk about?

JESSIE: We talked about why black socks are warmer than blue socks. Is that something to go tell Mother? You were just jealous because I'd rather talk to him than wash the dishes with you.

MAMA: I was jealous because you'd rather talk to him than anything! (*Jessie reaches across the table for the small clock and starts to wind it.*) If I had died instead of him, he wouldn't have taken you in like I did.

JESSIE: I wouldn't have expected him to.

MAMA: Then what would you have done?

JESSIE: Come visit.

MAMA: Oh, I see. He died and left you stuck with me and you're mad about it.

JESSIE (*getting up from the table*): Not anymore. He didn't mean to. I didn't have to come here. We've been through this.

MAMA: He felt sorry for you, too, Jessie, don't kid yourself about that. He said you were a runt and he said it from the day you were born and he said you didn't have a chance.

JESSIE (*getting the canister of sugar and starting to refill the sugar bowl*): I know he loved me.

MAMA: What if he did? It didn't change anything.

JESSIE: It didn't have to. I miss him.

MAMA: He never really went fishing, you know. Never once. His tackle box was full of chewing tobacco and all he ever did was drive out to the lake and sit in his car. Dawson told me. And Bennie at the bait shop, he told Dawson. They all laughed about it. And he'd come back from fishing and all he'd have to show for it was . . . a whole pipe-cleaner *family* — chickens, pigs, a dog with a bad leg — it was creepy strange. It made me sick to look at them and I hid his pipe cleaners a couple of times but he always had more somewhere.

JESSIE: I thought it might be better for you after he died. You'd get interested in things. Breathe better. Change somehow.

MAMA: Into what? The Queen? A clerk in a shoe store? Why should I? Because he said to? Because you said to? (*Jessie shakes her head.*) Well I wasn't here for his entertainment and I'm not here for yours either, Jessie. I don't know what I'm here for, but then I don't think about it. (*Realizing what all this means.*) But I bet you wouldn't be killing yourself if he were still alive. That's a fine thing to figure out, isn't it?

JESSIE (*filling the honey jar now*): That's not true.

MAMA: Oh no? Then what were you asking about him for? Why did you want to know if I loved him?

JESSIE: I didn't think you did, that's all.

MAMA: Fine then. You were right. Do you feel better now?

JESSIE (*cleaning the honey jar carefully*): It feels good to be right about it.

MAMA: It didn't matter whether I loved him. It didn't matter to me and it didn't matter to him. And it didn't mean we didn't get along. It wasn't important. We didn't talk about it. (*Sweeping the pots off the cabinet.*) Take all these pots out to the porch!

JESSIE: What for?

MAMA: Just leave me this one pan. (*She jerks the silverware drawer open.*) Get me one knife, one fork, one big spoon, and the can opener, and put them out where I can get them. (*Starts throwing knives and forks in one of the pans.*)

JESSIE: Don't do that! I just straightened that drawer!

MAMA (*throwing the pan in the sink*): And throw out all the plates and cups. I'll use paper. Loretta can have what she wants and Dawson can sell the rest.

JESSIE (*calmly*): What are you doing?

MAMA: I'm not going to cook. I never liked it, anyway. I like candy. Wrapped in plastic or coming in sacks. And tuna. I like tuna. I'll eat tuna, thank you.

JESSIE (*taking the pan out of the sink*): What if you want to make apple butter? You can't make apple butter in that little pan. What if you leave carrots on cooking and burn up that pan?

MAMA: I don't like carrots.

JESSIE: What if the strawberries are good this year and you want to go picking with Agnes.

MAMA: I'll tell her to bring a pan. You said you would do whatever I wanted! I don't want a bunch of pans cluttering up my cabinets I can't get down to, anyway. Throw them out. Every last one.

JESSIE (*gathering up the pots*): I'm putting them all back in. I'm not taking them to the porch. If you want them, they'll be here. You'll bend down and get them, like you got the one for the cocoa. And if somebody else comes over here to cook, they'll have something to cook in, and that's the end of it!

MAMA: Who's going to come cook here?

JESSIE: Agnes.

MAMA: In my pots. Not on your life.

JESSIE: There's no reason why the two of you couldn't just live here together. Be cheaper for both of you and somebody to talk to. And if the birds bothered you, well, one day when Agnes is out getting her hair done, you could take them all for a walk!

MAMA (*as Jessie straightens the silverware*): So that's why you're pestering me about Agnes. You think you can rest easy if you get me a new babysitter? Well, I don't want to live with Agnes. I barely want to talk with Agnes. She's just around. We go back, that's all. I'm not letting Agnes near this place. You don't get off as easy as that, child.

JESSIE: OK, then. It's just something to think about.

MAMA: I don't like things to think about. I like things to go on.

JESSIE (*closing the silverware drawer*): I want to know what Daddy said to you the night he died. You came storming out of his room and said I could wait it out with him if I wanted to, but you were going to watch "Gunsmoke." What did he say to you?

MAMA: He didn't have *anything* to say to me, Jessie. That's why I left. He didn't say a thing. It was his last chance not to talk to me and he took full advantage of it.

JESSIE (*after a moment*): I'm sorry you didn't love him. Sorry for you, I mean. He seemed like a nice man.

MAMA (*as Jessie walks to the refrigerator*): Ready for your apple now?

JESSIE: Soon as I'm through here, Mama.

MAMA: You won't like the apple, either. It'll be just like the cocoa. You never liked eating at all, did you? Any of it! What have you been living on all these years, toothpaste?

JESSIE (*as she starts to clean out the refrigerator*): Now, you know the milkman comes on Wednesdays and Saturdays, and he leaves the order blank in an egg box, and you give the bills to Dawson once a month.

MAMA: Do they still make that orangeade?

JESSIE: It's not orangeade, it's just orange.

MAMA: I'm going to get some. I thought they stopped making it. You just stopped ordering it.

JESSIE: You should drink milk.

MAMA: Not anymore, I'm not. That hot chocolate was the last. Hooray.

JESSIE (*getting the garbage can from under the sink*): I told them to keep delivering a quart a week no matter what you said. I told them you'd run out of Cokes and you'd have to drink it. I told them I knew you wouldn't pour it on the ground . . .

MAMA (*finishing her sentence*): And you told them you weren't going to be ordering anymore?

JESSIE: I told them I was taking a little holiday and to look after you.

MAMA: And they didn't think something was funny about that? You who doesn't go to the front steps? You, who only sees the driveway looking down from a stretcher passed out cold?

JESSIE (*enjoying this, but not laughing*): They said it was about time, but why didn't I take you with me? And I said I didn't think you'd want to go, and they said, "Yeah, everybody's got their own idea of vacation."

MAMA: I guess you think that's funny.

JESSIE (*pulling jars out of the refrigerator*): You know there never was any reason to call the ambulance for me. All they ever did for me in the emergency room was let me wake up. I could've done that here. Now, I'll just call them out and you say yes or no. I know you like pickles. Ketchup?

MAMA: Keep it.

JESSIE: We've had this since last Fourth of July.

MAMA: Keep the ketchup. Keep it all.

JESSIE: Are you going to drink ketchup from the bottle or what? How can you want your food and not want your pots to cook it in? This stuff will all spoil in here, Mother.

MAMA: Nothing I ever did was good enough for you and I want to know why.

JESSIE: That's not true.

MAMA: And I want to know why you've lived here this long feeling the way you do.

JESSIE: You have no earthly idea how I feel.

MAMA: Well, how could I? You're real far back there, Jessie.

JESSIE: Back where?

MAMA: What's it like over there, where you are? Do people always say the right thing or get whatever they want, or what?

JESSIE: What are you talking about?

MAMA: Why do you read the newspaper? Why don't you wear that sweater I made for you? Do you remember how I used to look, or am I just any old woman now? When you have a fit, do you see stars or what? How did you fall off the horse, really? Why did Cecil leave you? Where did you put my old glasses?

JESSIE (*stunned by Mama's intensity*): They're in the bottom drawer of your dresser in an old Milk of Magnesia box. Cecil left me because he made me choose between him and smoking.

MAMA: Jessie, I know he wasn't that dumb.

JESSIE: I never understood why he hated it so much when it's so good. Smoking is the only thing I know that's always just what you think it's going to be. Just like it was the last time, right there when you want it and real quiet.

MAMA: Your fits made him sick and you know it.

JESSIE: Say seizures, not fits. Seizures.

MAMA: It's the same thing. A seizure in the hospital is a fit at home.

JESSIE: They didn't bother him at all. Except he did feel responsible for it. It *was* his idea to go horseback riding that day. It was his idea I could do *anything* if I just made up my mind to. I fell off the horse because I didn't know how to hold on. Cecil left for pretty much the same reason.

MAMA: He had a girl, Jessie. I walked right in on them in the toolshed.

JESSIE (*after a moment*): OK. That's fair. (*Lighting another cigarette.*) Was she very pretty?

MAMA: She was Agnes's girl, Carlene. Judge for yourself.

JESSIE (*as she walks to the living room*): I guess you and Agnes had a good talk about that, huh?

MAMA: I never thought he was good enough for you. They moved here from Tennessee, you know.

JESSIE: What are you talking about? You liked him better than I did. You flirted him out here to build your porch or I'd never even met him at all. You thought maybe he'd help you out around the place, come in and get some coffee and talk to you. God knows what you thought. All that curly hair.

MAMA: He's the best carpenter I ever saw. That little house of yours will still be standing at the end of the world, Jessie.

JESSIE: You didn't need a porch, Mama.

MAMA: All right! I wanted you to have a husband.

JESSIE: And I couldn't get one on my own, of course.

MAMA: How were you going to get a husband never opening your mouth to a living soul?

JESSIE: So I was quiet about it, so what?

MAMA: So I should have let you just sit here? Sit like your daddy? Sit here?

JESSIE: Maybe.

MAMA: Well, I didn't think so.

JESSIE: Well, what did you know?

MAMA: I never said I knew much. How was I supposed to learn anything living out here? I didn't know enough to do half the things I did in my life. Things happen. You do what you can about them and you see what happens next. I married you off to the wrong man, I admit that. So I took you in when he left. I'm sorry.

JESSIE: He wasn't the wrong man.

MAMA: He didn't love you, Jessie, or he wouldn't have left.

JESSIE: He wasn't the wrong man, Mama. I loved Cecil so much. And I tried to get more exercise and I tried to stay awake. I tried to learn to ride a horse. And I tried to stay outside with him, but he always knew I was trying, so it didn't work.

MAMA: He was a selfish man. He told me once he hated to see people move into his houses after he built them. He knew they'd mess them up.

JESSIE: I loved that bridge he built over the creek in back of the house. It didn't have to be anything special, a couple of boards would have been just fine, but he used that yellow pine and rubbed it so smooth . . .

MAMA: He had responsibilities here. He had a wife and son here and he failed you.

JESSIE: Or that baby bed he built for Ricky. I told him he didn't have to spend so much time on it, but he said it had to last, and the thing ended up weighing two hundred pounds and I couldn't move it. I said, "How long does a baby bed have to last, anyway?" But maybe he thought if it was strong enough, it might keep Ricky a baby.

MAMA: Ricky is too much like Cecil.

JESSIE: He is not. Ricky is as much like me as it's possible for any human to be. We even wear the same size pants. These are his, I think.

MAMA: That's just the same size. That's not you're the same person.

JESSIE: I see it on his face. I hear it when he talks. We look out at the world and we see the same thing: Not Fair. And the only difference between us is Ricky's out there trying to get even. And he knows not to trust anybody and he got it straight from me. And he knows not to try to get work, and guess where he got that. He walks around like there's loose boards in the floor, and you know who laid that floor, I did.

MAMA: Ricky isn't through yet. You don't know how he'll turn out!

JESSIE (*going back to the kitchen*): Yes I do and so did Cecil. Ricky is the two of us together for all time in too small a space. And we're tearing each other apart, like always, inside that boy, and if you don't see it, then you're just blind.

MAMA: Give him time, Jess.

JESSIE: Oh, he'll have plenty of that. Five years for forgery, ten years for armed assault . . .

MAMA (*furious*): Stop that! (*Then pleading.*) Jessie, Cecil might be ready to try it again, honey, that happens sometimes. Go downtown. Find him. Talk to him. He didn't know what he had in you. Maybe he sees things different now, but you're not going to know that till you go see him. Or call him up! Right now! He might be home.

JESSIE: And say what? Nothing's changed, Cecil, I'd just like to look at you, if you don't mind? No. He loved me, Mama. He just didn't know how things fall down around me like they do. I think he did the right thing. He gave himself another chance, that's all. But I did beg him to take me with him. I did tell him I would leave Ricky and you and everything I loved out here if only he would take me with him, but he couldn't and I understood that. (*Pause.*) I wrote that note I showed you. I wrote it. Not Cecil. I said "I'm sorry, Jessie, I can't fix it all for you." I said I'd always love me, not Cecil. But that's how he felt.

MAMA: Then he should've taken you with him!

JESSIE (*picking up the garbage bag she has filled*): Mama, you don't pack your garbage when you move.

MAMA: You will not call yourself garbage, Jessie.

JESSIE (*taking the bag to the big garbage can near the back door*): Just a way of saying it, Mama. Thinking about my list, that's all. (*Opening the can, putting the garbage in, then securing the lid.*) Well, a little more than that. I was trying to say it's all right that Cecil left. It was . . . a relief in a way. I never was what he wanted to see, so it was better when he wasn't looking at me all the time.

MAMA: I'll make your apple now.

JESSIE: No thanks. You get the manicure stuff and I'll be right there.

> (*Jessie ties up the big garbage bag in the can and replaces the small garbage bag under the sink, all the time trying desperately to regain her calm. Mama watches, from a distance, her hand reaching unconsciously for the phone. Then she has a better idea. Or rather she thinks of the only other thing left and is willing to try it. Maybe she is even convinced it will work.*)

MAMA: Jessie, I think your daddy had little . . .

JESSIE (*interrupting her*): Garbage night is Tuesday. Put it out as late as you can. The Davises' dogs get in it if you don't. (*Replacing the garbage bag in the can under the sink.*) And keep ordering the heavy black bags. It doesn't pay to buy the cheap ones. And I've got all the ties here with the hammers and all. Take them out of the box as soon as you open a new one and put them in this drawer. They'll get lost if you don't, and rubber bands or something else won't work.

MAMA: I think your daddy had fits, too. I think he sat in his chair and had little fits. I read this a long time ago in a magazine, how little fits go, just little blackouts where maybe their eyes don't even close and people just call them "thinking spells."

JESSIE (*getting the slipcover out of the laundry basket*): I don't think you want this manicure we've been looking forward to. I washed this cover for the sofa, but it'll take both of us to get it back on.

MAMA: I watched his eyes. I know that's what it was. The magazine said some people don't even know they've had one.

JESSIE: Daddy would've known if he'd had fits, Mama.

MAMA: The lady in this story had kept track of hers and she'd had eighty thousand of them in the last eleven years.

JESSIE: Next time you wash this cover, it'll dry better if you put it on wet.

MAMA: Jessie, listen to what I'm telling you. This lady had anywhere between five and five hundred fits a day and they lasted maybe fifteen seconds apiece, so that out of her life, she'd only lost about two weeks altogether, and she had a full-time secretary job and an IQ of 120.

JESSIE (*amused by Mama's approach*): You want to talk about fits, is that it?

MAMA: Yes. I do. I want to say . . .

JESSIE (*interrupting*): Most of the time I wouldn't even know I'd had one, except I wake up with different clothes on, feeling like I've been run over. Sometimes I feel my head start to turn around or hear myself scream. And sometimes there *is* this dizzy stupid feeling a little before it, but if the TV's on, well, it's easy to miss.

(*As Jessie and Mama replace the slipcover on the sofa and the afghan on the chair, the physical struggle somehow mirrors the emotional one in the conversation.*)

MAMA: I can tell when you're about to have one. Your eyes get this big! But, Jessie, you haven't . . .

JESSIE (*taking charge of this*): What do they look like? The seizures.

MAMA (*reluctant*): Different each time, Jess.

JESSIE: OK. Pick one, then. A good one. I think I want to know now.

MAMA: There's not much to tell. You just . . . crumple, in a heap, like a puppet and somebody cut the strings all at once, or like the firing squad in some Mexican movie, you just slide down the wall, you know. You don't know what happens? How can you not know what happens?

JESSIE: I'm busy.

MAMA: That's not funny.

JESSIE: I'm not laughing. My head turns around and I fall down and then what?

MAMA: Well, your chest squeezes in and out, and you sound like you're gagging, sucking air in and out like you can't breathe.

JESSIE: Do it for me. Make the sound for me.

MAMA: I will not. It's awful-sounding.

JESSIE: Yeah. I felt like it might be. What's next?

MAMA: Your mouth bites down and I have to get your tongue out of the way fast, so you don't bite yourself.

JESSIE: Or you. I bite you, too, don't I?

MAMA: You got me once real good. I had to get a tetanus! But I know what to watch for now. And then you turn blue and the jerks start up. Like I'm standing there poking you with a cattle prod or you're sticking your finger in a light socket as fast as you can . . .

JESSIE: Foaming like a mad dog the whole time.

MAMA: It's bubbling, Jess, not foam like the washer overflowed, for God's sake; it's bubbling like a baby spitting up. I go get a wet washcloth, that's all. And then the jerks slow down and you wet yourself and it's over. Two minutes tops.

JESSIE: How do I get to the bed?

MAMA: How do you think?

JESSIE: I'm too heavy for you now. How do you do it?

MAMA: I call Dawson. But I get you cleaned up before he gets here and I make him leave before you wake up.

JESSIE: You could just leave me on the floor.

MAMA: I want you to wake up someplace nice, OK? (*Then making a real effort.*) But, Jessie, and this is the reason I even brought this up! You haven't had a seizure for a solid year. A whole year, do you realize that?

JESSIE: Yeah, the phenobarb's about right now, I guess.

MAMA: You bet it is. You might never have another one, ever! You might be through with it for all time!

JESSIE: Could be.

MAMA: You are. I know you are!

JESSIE: I sure am feeling good. I really am. The double vision's gone and my gums aren't swelling. No rashes or anything. I'm feeling as good as I ever felt in my life. I'm even feeling like worrying or getting mad and I'm not afraid it will start a fit if I do, I just go ahead.

MAMA: Of course you do! You can even scream at me, if you want to. I can take it. You don't have to act like you're just visiting here, Jessie. This is your house, too.

JESSIE: The best part is, my memory's back.

MAMA: Your memory's always been good. When couldn't you remember things? You're always reminding me what . . .

JESSIE: Because I've made lists for everything. But now I remember what things mean on my lists. I see "dish towels," and I used to wonder whether I was supposed to wash them, buy them, or look for them because I wouldn't remember where I put them after I washed them, but now I know it means wrap them up, they're a present for Loretta's birthday.

MAMA (*finished with the sofa now*): You used to go looking for your lists, too, I've noticed that. You always know where they are now! (*Then suddenly worried.*) Loretta's birthday isn't coming up, is it?

JESSIE: I made a list of all the birthdays for you. I even put yours on it. (*A small smile.*) So you can call Loretta and remind her.

MAMA: Let's take Loretta to Howard Johnson's and have those fried clams. I *know* you love that clam roll.

JESSIE (*slight pause*): I won't be here, Mama.

MAMA: What have we just been talking about? You'll be here. You're well, Jessie. You're starting all over. You said it yourself. You're remembering things and . . .

JESSIE: I won't be here. If I'd ever had a year like this, to think straight and all, before now, I'd be gone already.

MAMA (*not pleading, commanding*): No, Jessie.

JESSIE (*folding the rest of the laundry*): Yes, Mama. Once I started remembering, I could see what it all added up to.

MAMA: The fits are over!

JESSIE: It's not the fits, Mama.

MAMA: Then it's me for giving them to you, but I didn't do it!

JESSIE: It's not the fits! You said it yourself, the medicine takes care of the fits.

MAMA (*interrupting*): Your daddy gave you those fits, Jessie. He passed it down to you like your green eyes and your straight hair. It's not my fault!

JESSIE: So what if he had little fits? It's not inherited. I fell off the horse. It was an accident.

MAMA: The horse wasn't the first time, Jessie. You had a fit when you were five years old.

JESSIE: I did not.

MAMA: You did! You were eating a popsicle and down you went. He gave it to you. It's *his* fault, not mine.

JESSIE: Well, you took your time telling me.

MAMA: How do you tell that to a five-year-old?

JESSIE: What did the doctor say?

MAMA: He said kids have them all the time. He said there wasn't anything to do but wait for another one.

JESSIE: But I didn't have another one.

(*Now there is a real silence.*)

JESSIE: You mean to tell me I had fits all the time as a kid and you just told me I fell down or something and it wasn't till I had the fit when Cecil was looking that anybody bothered to find out what was the matter with me?

MAMA: It wasn't *all the time,* Jessie. And they changed when you started to school. More like your daddy's. Oh, that was some swell time, sitting here with the two of you turning off and on like light bulbs some nights.

JESSIE: How many fits did I have?

MAMA: You never hurt yourself. I never let you out of my sight. I caught you every time.

JESSIE: But you didn't tell anybody.

MAMA: It was none of their business.

JESSIE: You were ashamed.

MAMA: I didn't want anybody to know. Least of all you.

JESSIE: Least of all me. Oh, right. That was mine to know, Mama, not yours. Did Daddy know?

MAMA: He thought you were . . . you fell down a lot. That's what he thought. You were careless. Or maybe he thought I beat you. I don't know what he thought. He didn't think about it.

JESSIE: Because you didn't tell him!

MAMA: If I told him about you, I'd have to tell him about him!

JESSIE: I don't like this. I don't like this one bit.

MAMA: I didn't think you'd like it. That's why I didn't tell you.

JESSIE: If I'd known I was an epileptic, Mama, I wouldn't have ridden any horses.

MAMA: Make you feel like a freak, is that what I should have done?

JESSIE: Just get the manicure tray and sit down!

MAMA (*throwing it to the floor*): I don't want a manicure!

JESSIE: Doesn't look like you do, no.

MAMA: Maybe I did drop you, you don't know.

JESSIE: If you say you didn't, you didn't.

MAMA (*beginning to break down*): Maybe I fed you the wrong thing. Maybe you had a fever sometime and I didn't know it soon enough. Maybe it's a punishment.

JESSIE: For what?

MAMA: I don't know. Because of how I felt about your father. Because I didn't want any more children. Because I smoked too much or didn't eat right when I was carrying you. It has to be something I did.

JESSIE: It does not. It's just a sickness, not a curse. Epilepsy doesn't mean anything. It just is.

MAMA: I'm not talking about the fits here, Jessie! I'm talking about this killing yourself. It has to be me that's the matter here. You wouldn't be doing this if it wasn't. I didn't tell you things or I married you off to the wrong man or I took you in and let your life get away from you or all of it put together. I don't know what I did, but I did it, I know. This is all my fault, Jessie, but I don't know what to do about it now!

JESSIE (*exasperated at having to say this again*): It doesn't have anything to do with you!

MAMA: Everything you do has to do with me, Jessie. You can't do *anything*, wash your face or cut your finger, without doing it to me. That's right! You might as well kill me as you, Jessie, it's the same thing. This has to do with me, Jessie.

JESSIE: Then what if it does! What if it has everything to do with you! What if you are all I have and you're not enough? What if I could take all the rest of it if only I didn't have you here? What if the only way I can get away from you for good is to kill myself? What if it is? I can *still* do it!

MAMA (*in desperate tears*): Don't leave me, Jessie! (*Jessie stands for a moment, then turns for the bedroom.*) No! (*She grabs Jessie's arm.*)

JESSIE (*carefully taking her arm away*): I have a box of things I want people to have. I'm just going to go get it for you. You . . . just rest a minute.

(*Jessie is gone. Mama heads for the telephone, but she can't even pick up the receiver this time and, instead, stoops to clean up the bottles that have spilled out of the manicure tray.*

Jessie returns, carrying a box that groceries were delivered in. It probably says Hershey Kisses or Starkist Tuna. Mama is still down on the floor cleaning up, hoping that maybe if she just makes it look nice enough, Jessie will stay.)

MAMA: Jessie, how can I live here without you? I need you! You're supposed to tell me to stand up straight and say how nice I look in my pink dress, and drink my milk. You're supposed to go around and lock up so I know we're safe for the night, and when I wake up, you're supposed to be out there making the coffee and watching me get older every day, and you're supposed to help me die when the time comes. I can't do that by myself, Jessie. I'm not like you, Jessie. I hate the quiet and I don't want to die and I don't want you to go, Jessie. How can I . . . (*Has to stop a moment.*) How can I get up every day knowing you had to kill yourself to make it stop hurting and I was here all the time and I never even saw it. And then you gave me this chance to make it better, convince you to stay alive, and I couldn't do it. How can I live with myself after this, Jessie?

JESSIE: I only told you so I could explain it, so you wouldn't blame yourself, so you wouldn't feel bad. There wasn't anything you could say to change my mind. I didn't want you to save me. I just wanted you to know.

MAMA: Stay with me just a little longer. Just a few more years. I don't have that many more to go, Jessie. And as soon as I'm dead, you can do whatever you want. Maybe with me gone, you'll have all the quiet you want, right here in the house. And maybe one day you'll put in some begonias up the walk and get just the right rain for them all summer. And Ricky will be married by then and he'll bring your grandbabies over and you can sneak them a piece of candy when their daddy's not looking and then be real glad when they've gone home and left you to your quiet again.

JESSIE: Don't you see, Mama, everything I do winds up like this. How could I think you would understand? How could I think you would want a manicure? We could hold hands for an hour and then I could go shoot myself? I'm sorry about tonight, Mama, but it's exactly why I'm doing it.

MAMA: If you've got the guts to kill yourself, Jessie, you've got the guts to stay alive.

JESSIE: I know that. So it's really just a matter of where I'd rather be.

MAMA: Look, maybe I can't think of what you should do, but that doesn't mean there isn't something that would help. *You* find it. *You* think of it. You can keep trying. You can get brave and try some more. You don't have to give up!

JESSIE: I'm *not* giving up! This *is* the other thing I'm trying. And I'm sure there are some other things that might work, but *might* work isn't good enough anymore. I need something that *will* work. *This* will work. That's why I picked it.

MAMA: But something might happen. Something that could change everything. Who knows what it might be, but it might be worth waiting for! (*Jessie doesn't respond.*) Try it for two more weeks. We could have more talks like tonight.

JESSIE: No, Mama.

MAMA: I'll pay more attention to you. Tell the truth when you ask me. Let you have your say.

JESSIE: No, Mama! We wouldn't have more talks like tonight, because it's this next part that's made this last part so good, Mama. No, Mama. *This* is how I have my say. This is how I say what I thought about it *all* and I say no. To Dawson and Loretta and the Red Chinese and epilepsy and Ricky and Cecil and you. And me. And hope. I say no! (*Then going to Mama on the sofa.*) Just let me go easy, Mama.

MAMA: How can I let you go?

JESSIE: You can because you have to. It's what you've always done.

MAMA: You are my child!

JESSIE: I am what became of your child. (*Mama cannot answer.*) I found an old baby picture of me. And it was somebody else, not me. It was somebody pink and fat who never heard of sick or lonely, somebody who cried and got fed, and reached up and got held and kicked but didn't hurt anybody, and slept whenever she wanted to, just by closing her eyes. Somebody who mainly just laid there and laughed at the colors waving around over her head and chewed on a polka-dot whale and woke up knowing some new trick nearly every day, and rolled over and drooled on the sheet and felt your hand pulling my quilt back up over me. That's who I started out and this is who is left. (*There is no self-pity here.*) That's what this is about. It's somebody I lost, all right, it's my own self. Who I never was. Or who I tried to be and never got there. Somebody I waited for who never came. And never will. So, see it doesn't much matter what else happens in the world or in this house, even. I'm what was worth waiting for and I didn't make it. Me . . . who might have made a difference to me . . . I'm not going to show up, so there's no reason to stay, except to keep you company, and that's . . . not reason enough because I'm not . . . very good company. (*Pause.*) Am I.

MAMA (*knowing she must tell the truth*): No. And neither am I.

JESSIE: I had this strange little thought, well, maybe it's not so strange. Anyway, after Christmas, after I decided to do this, I would wonder, sometimes, what might keep me here, what might be worth staying for, and you know what it was? It was maybe if there was something I really liked, like maybe if I really liked rice pudding or cornflakes for breakfast or something, that might be enough.

MAMA: Rice pudding is good.

JESSIE: Not to me.

MAMA: And you're not afraid?

JESSIE: Afraid of what?

MAMA: I'm afraid of it, for me, I mean. When my time comes. I know it's coming, but . . .

JESSIE: You don't know when. Like in a scary movie.

MAMA: Yeah, sneaking up on me like some killer on the loose, hiding out in the back yard just waiting for me to have my hands full someday and how am I supposed to protect myself anyhow when I don't know what he looks like and I don't know how he sounds coming up behind me like that or if it will hurt or take very long or what I don't get done before it happens.

JESSIE: You've got plenty of time left.

MAMA: I forget what for, right now.

JESSIE: For whatever happens, I don't know. For the rest of your life. For Agnes burning down one more house or Dawson losing his hair or . . .

MAMA (*quickly*): Jessie. I can't just sit here and say OK, kill yourself if you want to.

JESSIE: Sure you can. You just did. Say it again.

MAMA (*really startled*): Jessie! (*Quiet horror.*) How dare you! (*Furious.*) How dare you! You think you can just leave whenever you want, like you're watching television here? No, you can't, Jessie. You make me feel like a fool for being alive, child, and you are so wrong! I like it here, and I will stay here until they make me go, until they drag me screaming and I mean screeching into my grave, and you're real smart to get away before then because, I mean, honey, you've never heard noise like that in your life. (*Jessie turns away.*) Who am I talking to? You're gone already, aren't you? I'm looking right through you! I can't stop you because you're already gone! I guess you think they'll all have to talk about you now! I guess you think this will really confuse them. Oh yes, ever since Christmas you've been laughing to yourself and thinking, "Boy, are they all in for a surprise." Well, nobody's going to be a bit surprised, sweetheart. This is just like you. Do it the hard way, that's my girl, all right. (*Jessie gets up and goes into the kitchen, but Mama follows her.*) You know who they're going to feel sorry for? Me! How about that! Not you, me! They're going to be *ashamed* of you. Yes. *Ashamed!* If somebody asks Dawson about it, he'll change the subject as fast as he can. He'll talk about how much he has to pay to park his car these days.

JESSIE: Leave me alone.

MAMA: It's the truth!

JESSIE: I should've just left you a note!

MAMA (*screaming*): Yes! (*Then suddenly understanding what she has said, nearly paralyzed by the thought of it, she turns slowly to face Jessie, nearly whispering.*) No. No. I . . . might not have thought of all the things you've said.

JESSIE: It's OK, Mama.

(*Mama is nearly unconscious from the emotional devastation of these last few moments. She sits down at the kitchen table, hurt and angry and desperately afraid. But she looks almost numb. She is so far beyond what is known as pain that she is virtually unreachable and Jessie knows this, and talks quietly, watching for signs of recovery.*)

JESSIE (*washes her hands in the sink*): I remember you liked that preacher who did Daddy's, so if you want to ask him to do the service, that's OK with me.

MAMA (*not an answer, just a word*): What.

JESSIE (*putting on hand lotion as she talks*): And pick some songs you like or let Agnes pick, she'll know exactly which ones. Oh, and I had your dress cleaned that you wore to Daddy's. You looked real good in that.

MAMA: I don't remember, hon.

JESSIE: And it won't be so bad once your friends start coming to the funeral home. You'll probably see people you haven't seen for years, but I thought about what you should say to get you over that nervous part when they first come in.

MAMA (*simply repeating*): Come in.

JESSIE: Take them up to see their flowers, they'd like that. And when they say, "I'm so sorry, Thelma," you just say, "I appreciate your coming, Connie." And then ask how their garden was this summer or what they're doing for Thanksgiving or how their children . . .

MAMA: I don't think I should ask about their children. I'll talk about what they have on, that's always good. And I'll have some crochet work with me.

JESSIE: And Agnes will be there, so you might not have to talk at all.

MAMA: Maybe if Connie Richards does come, I can get her to tell me where she gets that Irish yarn, she calls it. I know it doesn't come from Ireland. I think it just comes with a green wrapper.

JESSIE: And be sure to invite enough people home afterward so you get enough food to feed them all and have some left for you. But don't let anybody take anything home, especially Loretta.

MAMA: Loretta will get all the food set up, honey. It's only fair to let her have some macaroni or something.

JESSIE: No, Mama. You have to be more selfish from now on. (*Sitting at the table with Mama.*) Now, somebody's bound to ask you why I did it and you just say you don't know. That you loved me and you know I loved you and we just sat around tonight like every other night of our lives, and then I came over and kissed you and said, " 'Night, Mother," and you heard me close my bedroom door and the next thing you heard was the shot. And whatever reasons I had, well, you guess I just took them with me.

MAMA (*quietly*): It was something personal.

JESSIE: Good. That's good, Mama.

MAMA: That's what I'll say, then.

JESSIE: Personal. Yeah.

MAMA: Is that what I tell Dawson and Loretta, too? We sat around, you kissed me, " 'Night, Mother"? They'll want to know more, Jessie. They won't believe it.

JESSIE: Well, then, tell them what we did. I filled up the candy jars. I cleaned out the refrigerator. We made some hot chocolate and put the cover back on the sofa. You had no idea. All right? I really think it's better that way. If they know we talked about it, they really won't understand how you let me go.

MAMA: I guess not.

JESSIE: It's private. Tonight is private, yours and mine, and I don't want anybody else to have any of it.

MAMA: OK, then.

JESSIE (*standing behind Mama now, holding her shoulders*): Now, when you hear the shot, I don't want you to come in. First of all, you won't be able to get in by yourself, but I don't want you trying. Call Dawson, then call the police, and then call Agnes. And then you'll need something to do till somebody gets here, so wash the hot-chocolate pan. You wash that pan till you hear the doorbell ring and I don't care if it's an hour, you keep washing that pan.

MAMA: I'll make my calls and then I'll just sit. I won't need something to do. What will the police say?

JESSIE: They'll do that gunpowder test, I guess, and ask you what happened, and by that time, the ambulance will be here and they'll come in and get me and you know how that goes. You stay out here with Dawson and Loretta. You keep Dawson out here. I want the police in the room first, not Dawson, OK?

MAMA: What if Dawson and Loretta want me to go home with them?

JESSIE (*returning to the living room*): That's up to you.

MAMA: I think I'll stay here. All they've got is Sanka.

JESSIE: Maybe Agnes could come stay with you for a few days.

MAMA (*standing up, looking into the living room*): I'd rather be by myself, I think. (*Walking toward the box Jessie brought in earlier.*) You want me to give people those things?

JESSIE (*they sit down on the sofa, Jessie holding the box on her lap*): I want Loretta to have my little calculator. Dawson bought it for himself, you know, but then he saw one he liked better and he couldn't bring both of them home with Loretta counting every penny the way she does, so he gave the first one to me. Be funny for her to have it now, don't you think? And all my house slippers are in a sack for her in my closet. Tell her I know they'll fit and I've never worn any of them, and make sure Dawson hears you tell her that. I'm glad he loves Loretta so much, but I wish he knew not everybody has her size feet.

MAMA (*taking the calculator*): OK.

JESSIE (*reaching into the box again*): This letter is for Dawson, but it's mostly about you, so read it if you want. There's a list of presents for you for at least twenty more Christmases and birthdays, so if you want anything special you better add it to this list before you give it to him. Or if you want to be surprised, just don't read that page. This Christmas, you're getting mostly stuff for the house, like a new rug in your bathroom and needlework, but next Christmas, you're really going to cost him next Christmas. I think you'll like it a lot and you'd never think of it.

MAMA: And you think he'll go for it?

JESSIE: I think he'll feel like a real jerk if he doesn't. Me telling him to, like this and all. Now, this number's where you call Cecil. I called it last week and he answered, so I know he still lives there.

MAMA: What do you want me to tell him?

JESSIE: Tell him we talked about him and I only had good things to say about him, but mainly tell him to find Ricky and tell him what I did, and tell Ricky you have something for him, out here, from me, and to come get it. (*Pulls a sack out of the box.*)

MAMA (*the sack feels empty*): What is it?

JESSIE (*taking it off*): My watch. (*Putting it in the sack and taking a ribbon out of the sack to tie around the top of it.*)

MAMA: He'll sell it!

JESSIE: That's the idea. I appreciate him not stealing it already. I'd like to buy him a good meal.

MAMA: He'll buy dope with it!

JESSIE: Well, then, I hope he gets some good dope with it, Mama. And the rest of this is for you. (*Handing Mama the box now. Mama picks up the things and looks at them.*)

MAMA (*surprised and pleased*): When did you do all this? During my naps, I guess.

JESSIE: I guess. I tried to be quiet about it. (*As Mama is puzzled by the presents.*) Those are just little presents. For whenever you need one. They're not bought presents, just things I thought you might like to look at, pictures or things you think you've lost. Things you didn't know you had, even. You'll see.

MAMA: I'm not sure I want them. They'll make me think of you.

JESSIE: No they won't. They're just things, like a free tube of toothpaste I found hanging on the door one day.

MAMA: Oh. All right, then.

JESSIE: Well, maybe there's one nice present in there somewhere. It's Granny's ring she gave me and I thought you might like to have it, but I didn't think you'd wear it if I gave it to you right now.

MAMA (*taking the box to a table nearby*): No. Probably not. (*Turning back to face her.*) I'm ready for my manicure, I guess. Want me to wash my hands again?

JESSIE (*standing up*): It's time for me to go, Mama.

MAMA (*starting for her*): No, Jessie, you've got all night!

JESSIE (*as Mama grabs her*): No, Mama.

MAMA: It's not even ten o'clock.

JESSIE (*very calm*): Let me go, Mama.

MAMA: I can't. You can't go. You can't do this. You didn't say it would be so soon, Jessie. I'm scared. I love you.

JESSIE (*taking her hands away*): Let go of me, Mama. I've said everything I had to say.

MAMA (*standing still a minute*): You said you wanted to do my nails.

JESSIE (*taking a small step backward*): I can't. It's too late.

MAMA: It's not too late!

JESSIE: I don't want you to wake Dawson and Loretta when you call. I want them to still be up and dressed so they can get right over.

MAMA (*as Jessie backs up, Mama moves in on her, but carefully*): They wake up fast, Jessie, if they have to. They don't matter here, Jessie. You do. I do. We're not through yet. We've got a lot of things to take care of here. I don't know where my prescriptions are and you didn't tell me what to tell Dr. Davis when he calls or how much you want me to tell Ricky or who I call to rake the leaves or . . .

JESSIE: Don't try and stop me, Mama, you can't do it.

MAMA (*grabbing her again, this time hard*): I can too! I'll stand in front of this hall and you can't get past me. (*They struggle.*) You'll have to knock me down to get away from me, Jessie. I'm not about to let you . . .

(*Mama struggles with Jessie at the door and in the struggle Jessie gets away from her and —*)

JESSIE (*almost a whisper*): 'Night, Mother. (*She vanishes into her bedroom and we hear the door lock just as Mama gets to it.*)

MAMA (*screams*): Jessie! (*Pounding on the door.*) Jessie, you let me in there. Don't you do this, Jessie. I'm not going to stop screaming until you open this door, Jessie. Jessie! Jessie! What if I don't do any of the things you told me to do! I'll tell Cecil what a miserable man he was to make you feel the way he did and I'll give Ricky's watch to Dawson if I feel like it and the only way you can make sure I do what you want is you come out here and make me, Jessie! (*Pounding again.*) Jessie! Stop this! I didn't know! I was here with you all the time. How could I know you were so alone?

(*And Mama stops for a moment, breathless and frantic, putting her ear to the door, and when she doesn't hear anything, she stands up straight again and screams once more.*)

Jessie! Please!

(*And we hear the shot, and it sounds like an answer, it sounds like No.*

Mama collapses against the door, tears streaming down her face, but not screaming anymore. In shock now.)

Jessie, Jessie, child . . . Forgive me. (*Pause.*) I thought you were mine.

(*And she leaves the door and makes her way through the living room, around the furniture, as though she didn't know where it was, not knowing what to do. Finally, she goes to the stove in the kitchen and picks up the hot-chocolate pan and carries it with her to the telephone, and holds on to it while she dials the number. She looks down at the pan, holding it tight like her life depended on it. She hears Loretta answer.*)

MAMA: Loretta, let me talk to Dawson, honey.   1983

INVESTIGATIONS

1. When did you first figure out what Jessie was up to? When does Mama figure it out? What precipitated your understanding? Mama's?
2. When Mama says "You told me it [the gun] was for protection!" (p. 33), what does she mean? What does Jessie mean when she replies, "It *is*!" (p. 33)?
3. Why does Jessie keep trying to bring Mama's attention back to the list whenever Mama presses her for reasons why she wants to commit suicide?
4. What would Antler ("Raising My Hand," p. 101) say in response to Jessie's speech on page 41:

   > No. You can't. . . . And I can't do anything either, about my life, to change it, make it better, make me feel better about it. Like it better, make it work. But I can stop it. Shut it down, turn it off like the radio when there's nothing on I want to listen to. It's all I really have that belongs to me and I'm going to say what happens to it. And it's going to stop. And I'm going to stop it. So. Let's just have a good time.

5. Of the characters you've met in Part One, which bears the closest resemblance to Jessie? Write a 250–500-word essay that accounts for the differences between Jessie's response to her predicament and the response of the character you've chosen to his or her predicament.

Facing It

My black face fades,
hiding inside the black granite.
I said I wouldn't,
dammit: No tears.
I'm stone. I'm flesh.   5
My clouded reflection eyes me
like a bird of prey, the profile of night
slanted against morning. I turn
this way — the stone lets me go.
I turn that way — I'm inside   10
the Vietnam Veterans Memorial
again, depending on the light
to make a difference.
I go down the 58,022 names,
half-expecting to find   15
my own in letters like smoke.
I touch the name Andrew Johnson;
I see the booby trap's white flash.
Names shimmer on a woman's blouse
but when she walks away   20
the names stay on the wall.
Brushstrokes flash, a red bird's
wings cutting across my stare.
The sky. A plane in the sky.
A white vet's image floats   25
closer to me, then his pale eyes
look through mine. I'm a window.
He's lost his right arm
inside the stone. In the black mirror
a woman's trying to erase names: 30
No, she's brushing a boy's hair.   1988

A Vietnam veteran, YUSEF KOMUNYAKAA (b. 1947) was raised in Bogalusa, Louisiana, and now teaches creative writing and Afro-American studies at Indiana University. His publications include three poetry collections: *I Apologize for the Eyes in My Head* (1986), *Copacetic* (1984), and *Dien Cai Dau* (1988), all from Wesleyan University Press.

INVESTIGATIONS

1. What are the ways the speaker's "black face fades, / hiding inside the black granite"?
2. Does the speaker get caught by the "bird of prey" of his "clouded reflection"? Note each image of transformation in the poem. (An example appears in line 5 when the speaker announces, "I'm stone.") How do these images help characterize the speaker?
3. Why has the speaker come to the Vietnam Veterans Memorial? How has his visit changed him?
4. Do you think the speaker's experience at the Memorial bears any resemblance to the dream in Lawrence Joseph's "Driving Again"? If so, describe the similarities.

PETER CAMERON

Jump or Dive

Jason, my uncle's lover, sat in the dark kitchen eating what sounded like a bowl of cereal. He had some disease that made him hungry every few hours — something about not enough sugar in his blood. Every night, he got up at about three o'clock and fixed himself a snack. Since I was sleeping on the living-room couch, I could hear him.

My parents and I had driven down from Oregon to visit my Uncle Walter, who lived in Arizona. He was my father's younger brother. My sister Jackie got to stay home, on account of having just graduated from high school and having a job at the Lob-Steer Restaurant. But there was no way my parents were letting me stay home: I had just finished ninth grade and I was unemployed.

My parents slept in the guest room. Jason and Uncle Walter slept together in the master bedroom. The first morning, when I went into the bathroom, I saw Jason sitting on the edge of the big unmade bed in his jockey shorts. Jason was very tan, but it was an odd tan: His face and the bottom three-quarters of his arms were much darker than his chest. It looked as if he was wearing a T-shirt.

PETER CAMERON was born in 1959 in Pompton Plains, New Jersey, and graduated from Hamilton College in 1982. His publications include *One Way or Another* (1986), a collection of short stories, and *Leap Year* (1988), a novel.

The living-room couch was made of leather and had little metal nubs stuck all over it. It was almost impossible to sleep on. I lay there listening to Jason crunch. The only other noise was the air conditioner, which turned itself off and on constantly to maintain the same, ideal temperature. When it went off, you could hear the insects outside. A small square of light from the opened refrigerator appeared on the dining-room wall. Jason was putting the milk away. The faucet ran for a second, and then Jason walked through the living room, his white underwear bright against his body. I pretended I was asleep.

After a while, the air conditioner went off, but I didn't hear the insects.   5
At some point in the night — the point that seems closer to morning than to evening — they stopped their drone, as though they were unionized and paid to sing only so long. The house was very quiet. In the master bedroom, I could hear bodies moving, and murmuring, but I couldn't tell if it was people making love or turning over and over, trying to get comfortable. It went on for a few minutes, and then it stopped.

We were staying at Uncle Walter's for a week, and every hour of every day was planned. We always had a morning activity and an afternoon activity. Then we had cocktail hour, then dinner, then some card game. Usually hearts, with the teams switching: some nights Jason and Walter versus my parents, some nights the brothers challenging Jason and my mother. I never played. I watched TV, or rode Jason's moped around the deserted roads of Gretna Green, which was the name of Uncle Walter's condominium village. The houses in Gretna Green were called villas, and they all had different names — some for gems, some for colors, and some for animals. Uncle Walter and Jason lived in Villa Indigo.

We started each morning on the patio, where we'd eat breakfast and "plan the day." The adults took a long time planning the day so there would be less day to spend. All the other villa inhabitants ate breakfast on their patios, too. The patios were separated by lawn and rock gardens and pine trees, but there wasn't much privacy: Everyone could see everyone else sitting under uniformly striped umbrellas, but everyone pretended he couldn't. They were mostly old people, retired people. Children were allowed only as guests. Everyone looked at me as if I was a freak.

Wednesday morning, Uncle Walter was inside making coffee in the new coffee machine my parents had brought him. My mother told me that whenever you're invited to someone's house overnight you should bring something — a hostess gift. Or a host gift, she added. She was helping Uncle Walter make breakfast. Jason was lying on a chaise in the sun, trying to even out his tan. My father was reading the *Wall Street Journal*. He got up early every morning and drove into town and bought it, so he could "stay in touch." My mother made him throw it away right after he read it so it wouldn't interfere with the rest of the day.

Jason had his eyes closed, but he was talking. He was listing the things we could do that day. I was sitting on the edge of a big planter filled with pachysandra and broken statuary that Leonard, my uncle's ex-boyfriend, had dug up somewhere. Leonard was an archeologist. He used to teach paleontology at Northern Arizona University, but he didn't get tenure, so he took a job with an oil company in South America, making sure the engineers didn't drill in sacred spots. The day before, I'd seen a tiny, purple-throated lizard in the vines, and I was trying to find him again. I wanted to catch him and take him back to Oregon.

Jason paused in his list, and my father said, "Uh-huh." That's what he always says when he's reading the newspaper and you talk to him.

"We could go to the dinosaur museum," Jason said.

"What's that?" I said.

Jason sat up and looked at me. That was the first thing I'd said to him, I think. I'd been ignoring him.

"Well, I've never been there," he said. Even though it was early in the morning, his brown forehead was already beaded with sweat. "It has some reconstructed dinosaurs and footprints and stuff."

"Let's go there," I said. "I like dinosaurs."

"Uh-huh," said my father.

My mother came through the sliding glass doors carrying a platter of scrambled eggs. Uncle Walter followed with the coffee.

"We're going to go to the dinosaur museum this morning," Jason said.

"Please, not that pit," Uncle Walter said.

"But Evan wants to go," Jason said. "It's about time we did something he liked."

Everyone looked at me. "It doesn't matter," I said.

"Oh, no," Uncle Walter said. "Actually, it's fascinating. It just brings back bad memories."

As it turned out, Uncle Walter and my father stayed home to discuss their finances. My grandmother had left them her money jointly, and they're always arguing about how to invest it. Jason drove my mother and me out to the dinosaur museum. I think my mother came just because she didn't want to leave me alone with Jason. She doesn't trust Uncle Walter's friends, but she doesn't let on. My father thinks it's very important we all treat Uncle Walter normally. Once he hit Jackie because she called Uncle Walter a fag. That's the only time he's ever hit either of us.

The dinosaur museum looked like an airplane hangar in the middle of the desert. Inside, trenches were dug into the earth and bones stuck out of their walls. They were still exhuming some of the skeletons. The sand felt oddly damp. My mother took off her sandals and carried them; Jason looked around quickly, and then went outside and sat on the hood of the car, smoking, with his shirt off. At the gift stand, I bought a small bag of dinosaur bone chips. My mother bought a 3-D panoramic postcard. When you held it one way, a dinosaur stood with a creature in its toothy mouth. When you tilted it, the creature disappeared. Swallowed.

On the way home, we stopped at a Safeway to do some grocery shopping.

Both Jason and my mother seemed reluctant to push the shopping cart, so I did. In the produce aisle, Jason picked up cantaloupes and shook them next to his ear. A few feet away, my mother folded back the husks to get a good look at the kernels on the corncobs. It seemed as if everyone was pawing at the food. It made me nervous, because once, when I was little, I opened up a box of chocolate Ding Dongs in the grocery store and started eating one, and the manager came over and yelled at me. The only good thing about that was that my mother was forced to buy the Ding Dongs, but every time I ate one I felt sick.

A man in Bermuda shorts and a yellow cardigan sweater started talking to Jason. My mother returned with six apparently decent ears of corn. She dumped them into the cart. "Who's that?" she asked me, meaning the man Jason was talking to.

"I don't know," I said. The man made a practice golf swing, right there in the produce aisle. Jason watched him. Jason was a golf pro at a country club. He used to be part of the golf tour you see on television on weekend afternoons, but he quit. Now he gave lessons at the country club. Uncle Walter had been one of his pupils. That's how they met.

"It's hard to tell," Jason was saying. "I'd try opening up your stance a little more." He put a cantaloupe in our shopping cart.

"Hi," the man said to us.

"Mr. Baird, I'd like you to meet my wife, Ann," Jason said.   30

Mr. Baird shook my mother's hand. "How come we never see you down the club?"

"Oh . . . " my mother said.

"Ann hates golf," Jason said.

"And how 'bout you?" The man looked at me. "Do you like golf?"

"Sure," I said.   35

"Well, we'll have to get you out on the links. Can you beat your dad?"

"Not yet," I said.

"It won't be long," Mr. Baird said. He patted Jason on the shoulder. "Nice to see you, Jason. Nice to meet you, Mrs. Jerome."

He walked down the aisle and disappeared into the bakery section. My mother and I both looked at Jason. Even though it was cold in the produce aisle, he was sweating. No one said anything for a few seconds. Then my mother said, "Evan, why don't you go find some Doritos? And some Gatorade, too, if you want."

Back at Villa Indigo, my father and Uncle Walter were playing cribbage.   40
Jason kissed Uncle Walter on the top of his semibald head. My father watched and then stood up and kissed my mother. I didn't kiss anyone.

Thursday, my mother and I went into Flagstaff to buy new school clothes. Back in Portland, when we go into malls we separate and make plans to meet at a specified time and place, but this was different: It was a strange mall, and since it was school clothes, my mother would pay for them, and therefore she could help pick them out. So we shopped together, which we hadn't done in a while. It was awkward. She pulled things off the rack which I had ignored, and when I started looking at the Right Now for Young Men stuff she entered the Traditional Shoppe. We finally bought some underwear, and some orange and yellow socks, which my mother said were "fun."

Then we went to the shoe store. I hate trying on shoes. I wish the sales-people would just give you the box and let you try them on yourself. There's something about someone else doing it all — especially touching your feet — that embarrasses me. It's as if the person was your servant or something. And in this case the salesperson was a girl about my age, and I could tell she thought I was weird, shopping with my mother. My mother sat in the chair beside me, her pocketbook in her lap. She was wearing sneakers with little bunny-rabbit tails sticking out the back from her socks.

"Stand up," the girl said.

I stood up.

"How do they feel?" my mother asked.   45

"OK," I said.

"Walk around," my mother commanded.

I walked up the aisle, feeling everyone watching me. Then I walked back and sat down. I bent over and unlaced the shoes.

"So what do you think?" my mother asked.

The girl stood there, picking her nails. "They look very nice," she said.   50

I just wanted to get out of there. "I like them," I said. We bought the shoes.

On the way home, we pulled into a gas station–bar in the desert. "I can't face Villa Indigo without a drink," my mother said.

"What do you mean?" I asked.

"Nothing," she said. "Are you having a good time?"

"Now?"   55

"No. On this trip. At Uncle Walter's."

"I guess so," I said.

"Do you like Jason?"

"Better than Leonard."

"Leonard was strange," my mother said. "I never warmed to Leonard."   60

We got out of the car and walked into the bar. It was dark inside, and empty. A fat woman sat behind the bar, making something out of papier-mâché. It looked like one of those statues of the Virgin Mary people have in their front yards. "Hiya," she said. "What can I get you?"

My mother asked for a beer and I asked for some cranberry juice. They didn't have any, so I ordered a Coke. The woman got my mother's beer from a portable cooler like the ones you take to football games. It seemed very unprofessional. Then she sprayed Coke into a glass with one of those shower-head things. My mother and I sat at a table in the sun, but it wasn't hot, it was cold. Above us, the air conditioner dripped.

My mother drank her beer from the long-necked green bottle. "What do you think your sister's doing right now?" she asked.

"What time is it?"

"Four."

"Probably getting ready to go to work. Taking a shower."

My mother nodded. "Maybe we'll call her tonight."

I laughed, because my mother called her every night. She would always make Jackie explain all the noises in the background. "It sounds like a party to me," she kept repeating.

My Coke was flat. It tasted weird, too. I watched the woman at the bar. She was poking at her statue with a swizzlestick — putting in eyes, I thought.

"How would you like to go see the Petrified Forest?" my mother asked.

"We're going to another national park?" On the way to Uncle Walter's, we had stopped at the Grand Canyon and taken a mule ride down to the river. Halfway down, my mother got hysterical, fell off her mule, and wouldn't get back on. A helicopter had to fly into the canyon and rescue her. It was horrible to see her like that.

"This one's perfectly flat," she said. "And no mules."

"When?" I said.

"We'd go down on Saturday and come back to Walter's on Monday. And leave for home Tuesday."

The bar woman brought us a second round of drinks. We had not asked for them. My Coke glass was still full. My mother drained her beer bottle and looked at the new one. "Oh dear," she said. "I guess we look like we need it."

The next night, at six-thirty, as my parents left for their special anniversary dinner in Flagstaff, the automatic lawn sprinklers went on. They were activated every evening. Jason explained that if the lawns were watered during the day the beads of moisture would magnify the sun's rays and burn the grass. My parents walked through the whirling water, got in their car, and drove away.

Jason and Uncle Walter were making dinner for me — steaks, on their new electric barbecue. I think they thought steak was a good, masculine food. Instead of charcoal, their grill had little lava rocks on the bottom. They reminded me of my dinosaur bone chips.

The steaks came in packs of two, so Uncle Walter was cooking up four. The fourth steak worried me. Who was it for? Would we split it? Was someone else coming to dinner?

"You're being awfully quiet," Uncle Walter said. For a minute, I hope he was talking to the steaks — they weren't sizzling — so I didn't answer.

Then Uncle Walter looked over at me. "Cat got your tongue?" he asked.

"What cat?" I said.

"The cat," he said. "The proverbial cat. The big cat in the sky."

"No," I said.

"Then talk to me."

"I don't talk on demand," I said.

Uncle Walter smiled down at his steaks, lightly piercing them with his chef's fork. "Are you a freshman?" he asked.

"Well, a sophomore now," I said.

"How do you like being a sophomore?"

My lizard appeared from beneath a crimson leaf and clicked his eyes in all directions, checking out the evening.

"It's not something you like or dislike," I said. "It's something you are." 90

"Ah," Uncle Walter said. "So you're a fatalist?"

I didn't answer. I slowly reached out my hand toward the lizard, even though I was too far away to touch it. He clicked his eyes toward me but didn't move. I think he recognized me. My arm looked white and disembodied in the evening light.

Jason slid open the terrace doors, and the music from the stereo was suddenly loud. The lizard darted back under the foliage.

"I need a prep chef," Jason said. "Get in here, Evan."

I followed Jason into the kitchen. On the table was a wooden board, and 95 on that was a tomato, an avocado, and an apple. Jason handed me a knife. "Chop those up," he said.

I picked up the avocado. "Should I peel this?" I asked. "Or what?"

Jason took the avocado and sliced it in half. One half held the pit and the other half held nothing. Then he pulled the warty skin off in two curved pieces and handed the naked globes back to me. "Now chop it."

I started chopping the stuff. Jason took three baked potatoes out of the oven. I could tell they were hot by the way he tossed them onto the counter. He made slits in them and forked the white stuffing into a bowl.

"What are you doing?" I asked.

"Making baked potatoes," he said. He sliced butter into the bowl. 100

"But why are you taking the potato out of the skin?"

"Because these are stuffed potatoes. You take the potato out and doctor it up and then put it back in. Do you like cheese?"

"Yes," I said.

"Do you like chives?"

"I don't know, I said. "I've never had them." 105

"You've never had chives?"

"My mother makes normal food," I said. "She leaves the potato in the skin."

"That figures," Jason said.

After dinner, we went to the driving range. Jason bought two large buckets and we followed him upstairs to the second level. I sat on a bench and watched Jason and my uncle hit ball after ball out into the floodlit night. Sometimes the balls arched up into the darkness, then reappeared as they fell.

Uncle Walter wasn't too good. A few times, he topped the ball and it 110 dribbled over the edge and fell on the grass right below us. When that happened, he looked around to see who noticed, and winked at me.

"Do you want to hit some?" he asked me, offering his club.

"Sure," I said. I was on the golf team last fall, but this spring I played baseball. I think golf is an elitist sport. Baseball is more democratic.

I teed up a ball and took a practice swing, because my father, who taught

me to play golf, told me always to take a practice swing. Always. My first shot
was pretty good. It didn't go too far, but it went straight out and bounced a
ways before I lost track of it in the shadows. I hit another.

Jason, who was in the next cubicle, put down his club and watched me.
"You have a great natural swing," he said.

His attention bothered me, and I almost missed my next ball. It rolled off   115
the tee. I picked it up and reteed it.

"Wait," Jason said. He walked over and stood behind me. "You're swinging much too hard." He leaned over me so that he was embracing me from
behind, his large tan hands on top of mine, holding the club. "Now, just relax,"
he said, his voice right beside my cheek.

I tried to relax, but I couldn't. I suddenly felt very hot.

"OK," Jason said, "nice and easy. Keep the left arm straight." He raised
his arms, and with them the club. Then we swung through, and he held the
club still in the air, pointed out into the night. He let go of the club and ran
his hand along my left arm, from my wrist up to my shoulder. "Straight," he
said. "Keep it nice and straight." Then he stepped back and told me to try
another swing by myself.

I did.

"Looking good," Jason said.   120

"Why don't you finish the bucket?" my uncle said. "I'm going down to
get a beer."

Jason returned to his stall and resumed his practice. I teed up another ball,
hit it, then another, and another, till I'd established a rhythm, whacking ball
after ball, and all around me clubs were cutting the night, filling the sky with
tiny white meteorites.

Back at Villa Indigo, the sprinklers had stopped, but the insects were
making their strange noise in the trees. Jason and I went for a swim while my
uncle watched TV. Jason wore a bathing suit like the swimmers in the Olympics:
red-white-and-blue, and shaped like underwear. We walked out the terrace
doors and across the wet lawn toward the pool, which was deserted and glowed
bright blue. Jason dived in and swam some laps. I practiced diving off the
board into the deep end, timing my dives so they wouldn't interfere with him.
After about ten laps, he started treading water in the deep end and looked up
at me. I was bouncing on the diving board.

"Want to play a game?" he said.

"What?"   125

Jason swam to the side and pulled himself out of the pool. "Jump or Dive,"
he said. "We'll play for money."

"How do you play?"

"Don't you know anything?" Jason said. "What do you do in Ohio?"

"It's Oregon," I said. "Not much."

"I can believe it. This is a very simple game. One person jumps off the   130
diving board — jumps high — and when he's at the very highest the other

person yells either 'Jump' or 'Dive,' and the person has to dive if the other person yells 'Dive' and jump if he yells 'Jump.' If you do the wrong thing, you owe the guy a quarter. OK?"

"OK," I said. "You go first."

I stepped off the diving board and Jason climbed on. "The higher you jump, the more time you have to twist," he said.

"Go," I said. "I'm ready."

Jason took three steps and sprang, and I yelled, "Dive." He did.

He got out of the pool, grinning. "OK," he said. "Your turn."   135

I sprang off the board and heard Jason yell, "Jump," but I was already falling forward head first. I tried to twist backward, but it was still a dive.

"You owe me a quarter," Jason said when I surfaced. He was standing on the diving board, bouncing. I swam to the side. "Here I go," he said.

I waited till he was coming straight down toward the water, feet first, before I yelled, "Dive," but somehow Jason somersaulted forward and dived into the pool.

We played for about fifteen minutes, until I owed Jason two dollars and twenty-five cents and my body was covered with red welts from smacking the water at bad angles. Suddenly the lights in the pool went off.

"It must be ten o'clock," Jason said. "Time for the geriatrics to go to bed."   140

The black water looked cold and scary. I got out and sat in a chair. We hadn't brought towels with us, and I shivered. Jason stayed in the pool.

"It's warmer in the water," he said.

I didn't say anything. With the lights off in the pool, the stars appeared brighter in the sky. I leaned my head back and looked up at them.

Something landed with a splat on the concrete beside me. It was Jason's bathing suit. I could hear him in the pool. He was swimming slowly underwater, coming up for a breath and then disappearing again. I knew that at some point he'd get out of the water and be naked, so I walked across the lawn toward Villa Indigo. Inside, I could see Uncle Walter lying on the couch, watching TV.

Later that night, I woke up hearing noises in the kitchen. I assumed it was   145
Jason, but then I heard talking, and realized it was my parents, back from their anniversary dinner.

I got up off the couch and went into the kitchen. My mother was leaning against the counter, drinking a glass of seltzer. My father was sitting on one of the barstools, smoking a cigarette. He put it out when I came in. He's not supposed to smoke anymore. We made a deal in our family last year involving his quitting: My mother would lose fifteen pounds, my sister would take Science Honors (and pass), and I was supposed to brush Princess Leia, our dog, every day without having to be told.

"Our little baby," my mother said. "Did we wake you up?"

"Yes," I said.

"This is the first one I've had in months," my father said. "Honest. I just found it lying here."

"I told him he could smoke it," my mother said. "As a special anniversary treat." 150

"How was dinner?" I asked.

"OK," my mother said. "The restaurant didn't turn around, though. It was broken."

"That's funny," my father said. "I could have sworn it was revolving."

"You were just drunk," my mother said.

"Oh, no," my father said. "It was the stars in my eyes." He leaned forward 155
and kissed my mother.

She finished her seltzer, rinsed the glass, and put it in the sink. "I'm going to bed," she said. "Good night."

My father and I both said good night, and my mother walked down the hall. My father picked up his cigarette. "It wasn't even very good," he said. He looked at it, then held it under his nose and smelled it. "I think it was stale. Just my luck."

I took the cigarette butt out of his hands and threw it away. When I turned around, he was standing by the terrace doors, looking out at the dark trees. It was windy.

"Have you made up your mind?" he asked.

"About what?" 160

"The trip."

"What trip?"

My father turned away from the terrace. "Didn't Mom tell you? Uncle Walter said you could stay here while Mom and I went down to see the Petrified Forest. If you want to. You can come with us otherwise."

"Oh," I said.

"I think Uncle Walter would like it if he had some time alone with you. I 165
don't think he feels very close to you anymore. And he feels bad Jackie didn't come."

"Oh," I said. "I don't know."

"Is it because of Jason?"

"No," I said.

"Because I'd understand if it was."

"No," I said, "it's not that. I like Jason. I just don't know if I want to stay 170
here. . . ."

"Well, it's no big deal. Just two days." My father reached up and turned off the light. It was a dual overhead light and fan, and the fan spun around some in the darkness, each spin slower. My father put his hands on my shoulders and half pushed, half guided me back to the couch. "It's late," he said. "See you tomorrow."

I lay on the couch. I couldn't fall asleep, because I knew that in a while Jason would be up for his snack. That kept me awake, and the decision about what to do. For some reason, it did seem like a big deal: going or staying. I could still picture my mother, backed up against the wall of the Grand Canyon, as far from the cliff as possible, crying, her mule braying, the helicopter whirring in the sky above us. It seemed like a choice between that and Jason swimming in the dark water, slowly and nakedly. I didn't want to be there for either.

The thing was, after I sprang off the diving board I did hear Jason shout, but my brain didn't make any sense of it. I could just feel myself hanging there, above the horrible bright-blue water, but I couldn't make my body turn, even though I was dropping dangerously, and much too fast.   1986

INVESTIGATIONS

1. Look again at the "self-doubt" episode you narrated in response to "Write Before Reading" at the beginning of Part One. Judging from your experience, is Evan experiencing self-doubt? If so, what advice could you offer him about how to get through it?

2. How would the other characters in the story describe Evan? Is he a fatalist, as Uncle Walter claims? Is he a "window" in the sense the speaker in "Facing It" is?

3. Why does it "seem like a big deal" to Evan whether he goes to the Petrified Forest or stays at Uncle Walter's?

4. Are there any places other than the story's end where Evan seems to be "dropping dangerously, and much too fast"? Where is he "dropping" from? What is he "dropping" into?

JOHN EDGAR WIDEMAN

Valaida

Whither shall I go from thy spirit
Or whither shall I flee from thy presence?

Bobby tell the man what he wants to hear. Bobby lights a cigarette. Blows smoke and it rises and rises to where I sit on my cloud overhearing everything. Singing to no one. Golden trumpet from the Queen of Denmark across my knees. In my solitude. Dead thirty years now and meeting people still. Primping

One of the most widely respected and praised writers in America, JOHN EDGAR WIDEMAN (b. 1941) was raised in Homewood, a largely black neighborhood in Pittsburgh, Pennsylvania. His many books include the novels *Reuben* (1987), *A Glance Away* (1967), and *Philadelphia Fire* (1990; winner of the American Book Award in 1991); *Fever* (1989), a short story collection; and *Brothers and Keepers* (1984), a nonfiction account of his relationship with his brother.

loose ends of my hair. Worried how I look. How I sound. Silly. Because things don't change. Bobby with your lashes a woman would kill for, all cheekbones, bushy brows and bushy upper lip, ivory when you smile. As you pretend to contemplate his jive questions behind your screen of smoke and summon me by rolling your big, brown-eyed-handsome-man eyeballs to the ceiling where smoke pauses not one instant, but scoots through and warms me where I am, tell him, Bobby, about "fabled Valaida Snow who traveled in an orchid-colored Mercedes-Benz, dressed in an orchid suit, her pet monkey rigged out in an orchid jacket and cap, with the chauffeur in orchid as well." If you need to, lie like a rug, Bobby. But don't waste the truth, either. They can't take that away from me. Just be cool. As always. Recite those countries and cities we played. Continents we conquered. Roll those faraway places with strange-sounding names around in your sweet mouth. Tell him they loved me at home too, a down-home girl from Chattanooga, Tennessee, who turned out the Apollo, not a mumbling word from wino heaven till they were on their feet hollering and clapping for more with the rest of the audience. Reveries of days gone by, yes, yes, they haunt me, baby, I can taste it. Yesteryears, yesterhours. Bobby, do you also remember what you're not telling him? Blues lick in the middle of a blind flamenco singer's moan. Mother Africa stretching her crusty, dusky hands forth, calling back her far-flung children. Later that same night both of us bad on bad red wine wheeling round and round a dark gypsy cave. Olé. Olé.

Don't try too hard to get it right, he'll never understand. He's watching your cuff links twinkle. Wondering if they're real gold and the studs real diamonds. You called me Minnie Mouse. But you never saw me melted down to sixty-eight pounds soaking wet. They beat me, and fucked me in every hole I had. I was their whore. Their maid. A stool they stood on when they wanted to reach a little higher. But I never sang in their cage, Bobby. Not one note. Cost me a tooth once, but not a note. Tell him that one day I decided I'd had enough and walked away from their hell. Walked across Europe, the Atlantic Ocean, the whole U.S. of A. till I found a quiet spot put peace back in my soul, and then I began performing again. My tunes. In my solitude. And yes. There was a pitiful little stomped-down white boy in the camp I tried to keep the guards from killing, but if he lived or died I never knew. Then or now. Monkey and chauffeur and limo and champagne and cigars and outrageous dresses with rhinestones, fringe and peekaboo slits. That's the foolishness the reporter's after. Stuff him with your MC b.s., and if he's still curious when you're finished, if he seems a halfway decent sort in spite of himself, you might suggest listening to the trumpet solo in My Heart Belongs to Daddy, *hip him to* Hot Snow, *the next to last cut, my voice and Lady Day's figure and ground, ground and figure* Dear Lord above, send back my love.

He heard her in the bathroom, faucets on and off, on and off, spurting into the sink bowl, the tub. Quick burst of shower spray, rain sound spattering plastic curtain. Now in the quiet she'll be polishing. Every fixture will gleam.

Shine's what people see. See something shiny, don't look no further, most people don't. If she's rushed she'll wipe and polish faucets, mirrors, metal collars around drains. Learned that trick when she first came to the city and worked with gangs of girls in big downtown hotels. *Told me, said, Don't be fussing around behind in there or dusting under them things, child. Give that mirror a lick. Rub them faucets. Twenty more rooms like this one here still to do before noon.* He lowers the newspaper just enough so he'll see her when she passes through the living room, so she won't see him looking unless she stops and stares, something she never does. She knows he watches. Let him know just how much was enough once upon a time when she first started coming to clean the apartment. Back when he was still leaving for work some mornings. Before they understood each other, when suspicions were mutual and thick as the dust first time she bolted through his doorway, into his rooms, out of breath and wary-eyed like someone was chasing her and it might be him.

She'd burst in his door and he'd felt crowded. Retreated, let her stake out the space she required. She didn't bully him but demanded in the language of her brisk, efficient movements that he accustom himself to certain accommodations. They developed an etiquette that spelled out precisely how close, how distant the two of them could be once a week while she cleaned his apartment.

Odd that it took him years to realize how small she was. Shorter than him and no one in his family ever stood higher than five foot plus an inch or so of that thick, straight, black hair. America a land of giants and early on he'd learned to ignore height. You couldn't spend your days like a country lout gawking at the skyscraper heads of your new countrymen. No one had asked him so he'd never needed to describe his cleaning woman. Took no notice of her height. Her name was Clara Jackson and when she arrived he was overwhelmed by the busyness of her presence. How much she seemed to be doing all at once. Noises she'd manufacture with the cleaning paraphernalia, her humming and singing, the gum she popped, heavy thump of her heels even though she changed into tennis sneakers as soon as she crossed the threshold of his apartment, her troubled breathing, asthmatic wheezes and snorts of wrecked sinuses getting worse and worse over the years, her creaking knees, layers of dresses, dusters, slips whispering, the sighs and moans and wincing ejaculations, addresses to invisible presences she smuggled with her into his domain. *Yes, Lord. Save me, Jesus. Thank you, Father.* He backed away from the onslaught, the clamorous weight of it, avoided her systematically. Seldom were they both in the same room at the same time more than a few minutes because clearly none was large enough to contain them and the distance they needed.

She was bent over, replacing a scrubbed rack in the oven when he'd discovered the creases in her skull. She wore a net over her hair like serving girls in Horn and Hardart's. Under the webbing were clumps of hair, defined by furrows exposing her bare scalp. A ribbed yarmulke of hair pressed down on top of her head. Hair he'd never imagined. Like balled yarn in his grandmother's lap. Like a nursery rhyme. *Black sheep. Black sheep, have you any wool?* So different from what grew on his head, the heads of his brothers and sisters and mother and father and cousins and everyone in the doomed village where he was born, so different that he could not truly consider it hair, but some ersatz substitute used the evening of creation when hair ran out. Easier to think of her as bald. Bald and wearing a funny cap fashioned from the fur of some swarthy beast. Springy wires of it jutted from the netting. One dark strand left behind, shocking him when he discovered it marooned in the tub's gleaming, white belly, curled like a question mark at the end of the sentence he was always asking himself. He'd pinched it up in a wad of toilet paper, flushed it away.

Her bag of fleece had grayed and emptied over the years. Less of it now. He'd been tempted countless times to touch it. Poke his finger through the netting into one of the mounds. He'd wondered if she freed it from the veil when she went to bed. If it relaxed and spread against her pillow or if she slept all night like a soldier in a helmet.

When he stood beside her or behind her he could spy on the design of creases, observe how the darkness was cultivated into symmetrical plots and that meant he was taller than Clara Jackson, that he was looking down at her. But those facts did not calm the storm of motion and noise, did not undermine her power any more than the accident of growth, the half inch he'd attained over his next tallest brother, the inch eclipsing the height of his father, would have diminished his father's authority over the family, if there had been a family, the summer after he'd shot up past everyone, at thirteen the tallest, the height he remained today.

Mrs. Clara. Did you know a colored woman once saved my life?

Why is she staring at him as if he's said, Did you know I slept with a   10
colored woman once? He didn't say that. Her silence fusses at him as if he did, as if he'd blurted out something unseemly, ungentlemanly, some insult forcing her to tighten her jaw and push her tongue into her cheek, and taste the bitterness of the hard lump inside her mouth. Why is she ready to cry, or call him a liar, throw something at him or demand an apology or look right through him, past him, the way his mother stared at him on endless October afternoons, gray slants of rain falling so everybody's trapped indoors and she's cleaning, cooking, tending a skeletal fire in the hearth and he's misbehaving, teasing his little sister till he gets his mother's attention and then he shrivels in the weariness of those sad eyes catching him in the act, piercing him, ignoring him, the hurt, iron, and distance in them accusing him. Telling him for this moment, and perhaps forever, for this cruel, selfish trespass, you do not exist.

No, Mistah Cohen. That's one thing I definitely did not know.

His fingers fumble with a button, unfastening the cuff of his white shirt. He's rolling up one sleeve. Preparing himself for the work of storytelling. She has laundered the shirt how many times. It's held together by cleanliness and starch. A shirt that ought to be thrown away but she scrubs and sprays and irons it; he knows the routine, the noises. She saves it how many times, patching, mending, snipping errant threads, the frayed edges of cuff and collar hardened again so he is decent, safe within them, the blazing white breast he puffs out like a penguin when it's spring and he descends from the twelfth floor and conquers the park again, shoes shined, the remnants of that glorious head of hair slicked back, freshly shaved cheeks raw as a baby's in the brisk sunshine of those first days welcoming life back and yes he's out there in it again, his splay-foot penguin walk and gentleman's attire, shirt like a pledge, a promise, a declaration framing muted stripes of his dark tie. Numbers stamped inside the collar. Mark of the dry cleaners from a decade ago, before Clara Jackson began coming to clean. Traces still visible inside the neck of some of his shirts she's maintained impossibly long past their prime, a row of faded numerals like those he's pushing up his sleeve to show her on his skin.

The humped hairs on the back of his forearm are pressed down like grass in the woods where a hunted animal has slept. Gray hairs the color of his flesh, except inside his forearm, just above his wrist, the skin is whiter, blue veined. All of it, what's gray, what's pale, what's mottled with dark spots is meat that turns to lard and stinks a sweet sick stink to high heaven if you cook it.

Would you wish to stop now? Sit down a few minutes, please. I will make a coffee for you and my tea. I tell you a story. It is Christmas soon, no?

She is stopped in her tracks. A tiny woman, no doubt about it. Lumpy now. Perhaps she steals and hides things under her dress. Lumpy, not fat. Her shoulders round and padded. Like the derelict women who live in the streets and wear their whole wardrobes winter spring summer fall. She has put on flesh for protection. To soften blows. To ease around corners. Something cushioned to lean against. Something to muffle the sound of bones breaking when she falls. A pillow for all the heads gone and gone to dust who still find ways at night to come to her and seek a resting place. He could find uses for it. Extra flesh on her bones was not excess, was a gift. The female abundance, her thickness, her bulk reassuring as his hams shrink, his fingers become claws, the chicken neck frets away inside those razor-edged collars she scrubs and irons.

Oh you scarecrow. Death's-head stuck on a stick. Another stick lashed crossways for arms. First time you see yourself dead you giggle. You are a survivor, a lucky one. You grin, stick out your tongue at the image in the shard of smoky glass because the others must be laughing, can't help themselves, the ring of them behind your back, peeking over your scrawny shoulders, watching as you discover in the mirror what they've been seeing since they stormed the gates and kicked open the sealed barracks door and rescued you from the piles of live kindling that were to be your funeral pyre. Your fellow men. Allies. Victors. Survivors. Who stare at you when they think you're not looking, whose eyes are full of shame, as if they've been on duty here, in this pit, this stewpot cooking the meat from your bones. They cannot help themselves. You laugh to help them forget what they see. What you see. When they herded your keepers past you, their grand uniforms shorn of buttons, braid, ribbons, medals, the twin bolts of frozen lightning, golden skulls, eagles' wings, their jackboots

15

gone, feet bare or in peasant clogs, heads bowed and hatless, iron faces unshaven, the butchers still outweighed you a hundred pounds a man. You could
not conjure up the spit to mark them. You dropped your eyes in embarrassment,
pretended to nod off because your body was too weak to manufacture a string
of spittle, and if you could have, you'd have saved it, hoarded and tasted it a
hundred times before you swallowed the precious bile.

A parade of shambling, ox-eyed animals. They are marched past you,
marched past open trenches that are sewers brimming with naked, rotting flesh,
past barbed-wire compounds where the living sift slow and insubstantial as fog
among the heaps of dead. No one believes any of it. Ovens and gas chambers.
Gallows and whipping posts. Shoes, shoes, shoes, a mountain of shoes in a
warehouse. Shit. Teeth. Bones. Sacks of hair. The undead who huddle into
themselves like bats and settle down on a patch of filthy earth mourning their
own passing. No one believes the enemy. He is not these harmless farmers filing
past in pillaged uniforms to do the work of cleaning up this mess someone's
made. No one has ever seen a ghost trying to double itself in a mirror so they
laugh behind its back, as if, as if the laughter is a game and the dead one could
muster up the energy to join in and be made whole again. I giggle. I say, Who
in God's name would steal a boy's face and leave this thing?

Nearly a half-century of rich meals with seldom one missed but you cannot
fill the emptiness, cannot quiet the clamor of those lost souls starving, the child
you were, weeping from hunger, those selves, those stomachs you watched
swelling, bloating, unburied for days and you dreamed of opening them, of
taking a spoon of whatever was growing inside because you were so empty
inside and nothing could be worse than that gnawing emptiness. Why should
the dead be ashamed to eat the dead? Who are their brothers, sisters, themselves? You hear the boy talking to himself, hallucinating milk, bread, honey.
Sick when the spoiled meat is finally carted away.

Mistah Cohen, I'm feeling kinda poorly today. If you don mind I'ma work
straight through and gwan home early. Got all my Christmas still to do and
I'm tired.

She wags her head. Mumbles more he can't decipher. As if he'd offered   20
many times before, as if there is nothing strange or special this morning at
10:47, him standing at the china cupboard prepared to open it and bring down
sugar bowl, a silver cream pitcher, cups and saucers for the two of them, ready
to fetch instant coffee, a tea bag, boil water and sit down across the table from
her. As if it happens each day she comes, as if this once is not the first time,
the only time he's invited this woman to sit with him and she can wag her old
head, stare at him moon-eyed as an owl and refuse what's never been offered
before.

The tattoo is faint. From where she's standing, fussing with the vacuum
cleaner, she won't see a thing. Her eyes, in spite of thick spectacles, watery and
weak as his. They have grown old together, avoiding each other in these musty
rooms where soon, soon, no way round it, he will wake up dead one morning
and no one will know till she knocks Thursday, and knocks again, then rings,

pounds, hollers, but no one answers and she thumps away to rouse the super with his burly ring of keys.

He requires less sleep as he ages. Time weighs more on him as time slips away, less and less time as each second passes but also more of it, the past accumulating in vast drifts like snow in the darkness outside his window. In the wolf hours before dawn this strange city sleeps as uneasily as he does, turning, twisting, groaning. He finds himself listening intently for a sign that the night knows he's listening, but what he hears is his absence. The night busy with itself, denying him. And if he is not out there, if he can hear plainly his absence in the night pulse of the city, where is he now, where was he before his eyes opened, where will he be when the flutter of breath and heart stop?

They killed everyone in the camps. The whole world was dying there. Not only Jews. People forget. All kinds locked in the camps. Yes. Even Germans who were not Jews. Even a black woman. Not gypsy. Not African. American like you, Mrs. Clara.

They said she was a dancer and could play any instrument. Said she could line up shoes from many countries and hop from one pair to the next, performing the dances of the world. They said the Queen of Denmark had honored her with a gold trumpet. But she was there, in hell with the rest of us.

A woman like you. Many years ago. A lifetime ago. Young then as you would have been. And beautiful. As I believe you must have been, Mrs. Clara. Yes. Before America entered the war. Already camps had begun devouring people. All kinds of people. Yet she was rare. Only woman like her I ever saw until I came here, to this country, this city. And she saved my life.

Poor thing.

I was just a boy. Thirteen years old. The guards were beating me. I did not know why. Why? They didn't need a why. They just beat. And sometimes the beating ended in death because there was no reason to stop, just as there was no reason to begin. A boy. But I'd seen it many times. In the camp long enough to forget why I was alive, why anyone would want to live for long. They were hurting me, beating the life out of me but I was not surprised, expected no explanation. I remember curling up as I had seen a dog once cowering from the blows of a rolled newspaper. In the old country lifetimes ago. A boy in my village staring at a dog curled and rolling on its back in the dust outside the baker's shop and our baker in his white apron and tall white hat striking this mutt again and again. I didn't know what mischief the dog had done. I didn't understand why the fat man with flour on his apron was whipping it unmercifully. I simply saw it and hated the man, felt sorry for the animal, but already the child in me understood it could be no other way so I rolled and curled myself against the blows as I'd remembered that spotted dog in the dusty village street because that's the way it had to be.

Then a woman's voice in a language I did not comprehend reached me. A woman angry, screeching, I heard her before I saw her. She must have been screaming at them to stop. She must have decided it was better to risk dying than watch the guards pound a boy to death. First I heard her voice, then she rushed in, fell on me, wrapped herself around me. The guards shouted at her. One tried to snatch her away. She wouldn't let go of me and they began to beat her too. I heard the thuds of clubs on her back, felt her shudder each time a blow was struck.

She fought to her feet, dragging me with her. Shielding me as we stumbled and slammed into a wall.

My head was buried in her smock. In the smell of her, the smell of dust, of blood. I was surprised how tiny she was, barely my size, but strong, very strong. Her fingers dug into my shoulders, squeezing, gripping hard enough to hurt me if I hadn't been past the point of feeling pain. Her hands were strong, her legs alive and warm, churning, churning as she pressed me against herself, into her. Somehow she'd pulled me up and back to the barracks wall, propping herself, supporting me, sheltering me. Then she screamed at them in this language I use now but did not know one word of then, cursing them, I'm sure, in her mother tongue, a stream of spit and sputtering sounds as if she could build a wall of words they could not cross.

The kapos hesitated, astounded by what she'd dared. Was this black one a madwoman, a witch? Then they tore me from her grasp, pushed me down and I crumpled there in the stinking mud of the compound. One more kick, a numbing, blinding smash that took my breath away. Blood flooded my eyes. I lost consciousness. Last I saw of her she was still fighting, slim, beautiful legs kicking at them as they dragged and punched her across the yard.

You say she was colored?

Yes. Yes. A dark angel who fell from the sky and saved me.

Always thought it was just you people over there doing those terrible things to each other.

He closes the china cupboard. Her back is turned. She mutters something at the metal vacuum tubes she's unclamping. He realizes he's finished his story anyway. Doesn't know how to say the rest. She's humming, folding rags, stacking them on the bottom pantry shelf. Lost in the cloud of her own noise. Much more to his story, but she's not waiting around to hear it. This is her last day before the holidays. He'd sealed her bonus in an envelope, placed the envelope where he always does on the kitchen counter. The kitchen cabinet doors have magnetic fasteners for a tight fit. After a volley of doors clicking, she'll be gone. When he's alone preparing his evening meal, he depends on those clicks for company. He pushes so they strike not too loud, not too soft. They punctuate the silence, reassure him like the solid slamming of doors in big sedans he used to ferry from customer to customer. How long since he'd been behind the wheel of a car? Years, and now another year almost gone. In every corner of the city they'd be welcoming their Christ, their New Year with extravagant displays of joy. He thinks of Clara Jackson in the midst of her family. She's little but the others are brown and large, with lips like spoons for serving the sugary babble of their speech. He tries to picture them, eating and drinking, huge people crammed in a tiny, shabby room. Unimaginable, really.

The faces of her relatives become his. Everyone's hair is thick and straight and black.   1989

INVESTIGATIONS

1. How does the opening italicized passage connect with the rest of the story? What is its significance?
2. The narrator tells us that "no one had asked," so Mr. Cohen had "never needed to describe his cleaning woman." She's then described quite vividly. Note other instances in the story of this play of distance and intimacy. How does the characters' distance from each other make their intimacy possible or necessary? How does their intimacy confirm their distance from each other?
3. What does Mr. Cohen want from Mrs. Clara? Does he get it? How does telling his story to her change him? How does it change her?
4. How would the story of his rescue be different if Mr. Cohen were telling it to another survivor of the Holocaust rather than to Mrs. Clara? To the speaker of "Facing It"? To the speaker of "Driving Again"?

JOY HARJO

Ordinary Spirit

I was born in Tulsa, Oklahoma, on May 9, 1951, after a long, hard labor that occurred sporadically for over a week. My mother didn't know it was labor because I wasn't due until mid-July. I also surprised her because I was a single birth; she had been told to possibly expect twins. The birth was hard on both of us. I was kept alive on a machine for the first few days of my life until I made a decision to live. When I looked around I saw my mother, only nineteen, of mixed Cherokee and French blood, who had already worked hard for her short life. And my father, a few years older, a tall, good-looking Creek man who was then working as a mechanic for American Airlines. I don't think I

A member of the Creek Tribe, JOY HARJO was born in Tulsa, Oklahoma, in 1951. In addition to being a screenwriter and a musician, she has published three collections of poetry: *The Last Song* (1973), *What Moon Drove Me to This* (1980), and *She Had Some Horses* (1983). She is currently a professor of English at the University of New Mexico.

was ever what they expected, but I am grateful that they made my life possible and honor them for it.

I was the first of four children who were born evenly spaced over the next eight years or so. And much later had my own children, Phil and Rainy Dawn. We are descended from a long line of tribal speakers and leaders from my father's side. Menawa, who led the Red Stick War against Andrew Jackson, is our great-great (and possibly another great) grandfather. I don't know much about the family on my mother's side except there were many rebels and other characters. They are all part of who I am, the root from which I write, even though I may not always name them.

I began writing around the time I was twenty-two years old. I am now thirty-four and feel that after all this time I am just beginning to learn to write. I am only now beginning to comprehend what poetry is, and what it can mean. Each time I write I am in a different and wild place, and travel toward something I do not know the name of. Each poem is a jumping-off edge and I am not safe, but I take more risks and understand better now how to take them. They do not always work, but when they do it is worth it. I could not live without writing and/or thinking about it. In fact, I don't have to think about it; it's there, some word, concept always being born or, just as easily, dying.

I walk in and out of many worlds. I used to see being born of this mixed-blood/mixed-vision a curse, and hated myself for it. It was too confusing and destructive when I saw the world through that focus. The only message I got was not belonging anywhere, not to any side. I have since decided that being familiar with more than one world, more than one vision, is a blessing, and know that I make my own choices. I also know that it is only an illusion that any of the worlds are separate.

It is around midnight. I often write at this time in my workroom near the front of an old Victorian-style house near downtown Denver. Tonight a thick snow has muffled the sounds of traffic. The world is quiet except for the sound of this typewriter humming, the sometimes dash of metallic keys, and the deep breathing of my dog who is asleep nearby. And then, in the middle of working, the world gives way and I see the old, old Creek one who comes in here and watches over me. He tries to make sense of this world in which his granddaughter has come to live. And often teases me about my occupation of putting words on paper.

I tell him that it is writing these words down, and entering the world through the structure they make, that has allowed me to see him more clearly, and to speak. And he answers that maybe his prayers, songs, and his belief in them has allowed him to create me.

We both laugh, and continue our work through many seasons.

This summer, during one of those sultry summer evenings when the air hums with a chorus of insects and there's the sound of children playing in the street, I sat, writing. Not actually writing but staring into that space above the typewriter where vision telescopes. I began remembering the way the world was before speech in childhood. A time when I was totally conscious of sound, and conscious of being in a world in which the webbed connections between us all were translucent yet apparent. I remember what it felt like to live within that space, where every live thing had a voice, and each voice/sound an aurora of color. It was sometime during that reminiscence that I began this poem:

SUMMER NIGHT

The moon is nearly full,
            the humid air sweet like melon.
Flowers that have cupped the sun all day
                 dream of iridescent wings
under the long dark sleep.
              Children's invisible voices call out
in the glimmering moonlight.
               Their parents play wornout records
of the *cumbia*. Behind the screendoor
                their soft laughter swells
into the rhythm of a smooth guitar.
              I watch the world shimmer
inside this globe of a summer night,
              listen to the wobble of her
spin and dive. It happens all the time, waiting for you
                  to come home.
There is an ache that begins
             in the sound of an old blues song.
It becomes a house where all the lights have gone out
                 but one.
And it burns and burns
           until there is only the blue smoke of dawn
and everyone is sleeping in someone's arms
               even the flowers
even the sound of a thousand silences.
             And the arms of night
in the arms of day.
         Everyone except me.
But then the smell of damp honeysuckle twisted on the vine.
And the turn of the shoulder
            of the ordinary spirit who keeps watch
over this ordinary street
          And there you are, the secret
of your own flower of light
            blooming in the miraculous dark.
(from *Furious Light*, Watershed Foundation cassette, 1986)

For years I have wanted to capture that ache of a summer night. This summer in Denver was especially humid, reminded me of Oklahoma. I wanted to feel, in the poem, of a thick, sweet air. And I wanted the voices I remembered, my parents' talking and scratchy, faint music of the radio. In the poem it is my neighbors I hear, and their old records of the *cumbia*. I also wanted to sustain

a blues mood, pay homage to the blues because I love the blues. There was the
sound of a sensuous tenor saxophone beneath the whole poem. I also added
the part of everyone being in someone else's arms, "everyone except me," for
the blues effect.

But I did not want to leave the poem there, in the center of the ache; I   10
wanted to resolve it. I looked out the front door into the night and caught a
glimpse of someone standing near the streetlight, a protecting spirit who was
keeping watch over the street. I could have made that up, but I believe it is
true. And I knew the spirit belonged in the poem and, because the spirit lives
in the poem, too, helps turn the poem around to a place of tender realization.
Hence, "And there you are, the secret / of your own flower of light / blooming
in the miraculous dark."

When I first began writing, poetry was simply a way for me to speak. I
was amazed that I could write anything down and have it come out a little
more than coherently. Over the years the process has grown more complicated,
more intricate, and the world within the poem more immense. In another recent
poem the process is especially important:

TRANSFORMATIONS

This poem is a letter to tell you that I
have smelled the hatred you have tried
to find me with; you would like to destroy me.
Bone splintered in the eye of one you choose
to name your enemy won't make it better for you
to see. It could take a thousand years if you name it
that way, but then, to see after all that time, never
could anything be so clear. Memory has many forms.
When I think of early winter I think of a blackbird
laughing in the frozen air; guards a piece of light. I
saw the whole world caught in that sound. The sun
stopped for a moment because of tough belief. I don't
know what that has to do with what I am trying to tell you
except that I know you can turn a poem into something
else. This poem could be a bear treading the far northern
tundra, smelling the air for sweet alive meat. Or a piece
of seaweed stumbling in the sea. Or a blackbird, laughing.
What I mean is that hatred can be turned into something
else, if you have the right words, the right meanings
buried in that tender place in your heart where
the most precious animals live. Down the street
an ambulance has come to rescue an old man who is slowly
losing his life. Not many can see that he is already
becoming the backyard tree he has tended for years,
before he moves on. He is not sad, but compassionate
for the fears moving around him.
That's what I mean to tell you. On the other side
of the place you live stands a dark woman.
She has been trying to talk to you for years.
You have called the same name in the middle of a nightmare,

from the center of miracles. She is beautiful.
This is your hatred back. She loves you.

When I began writing the poem, I knew I wanted an actual transformation to be enacted within it. I began with someone's hatred, which was a tangible thing, and wanted to turn it into love by the end of the poem. I was also interested in the process of becoming. I tried to include several states of becoming. The "process of the poem" becoming was one. I entered the poem very consciously with lines such as, "I don't know what that has to do with what I am trying to tell you," and "What I mean is . . ." I also consciously switched tenses partly for that reason, and others. I often change tense within a poem and do so knowing what I am doing. It isn't by accident that it happens. Time doesn't realistically work in a linear fashion.

Within the poem is also the process of the "hater" becoming one who is loved, and who ultimately loves. The "I" is also involved in the process.

Earlier in the day an ambulance came into the neighborhood to pick up an elderly neighbor who had suffered a stroke and was near death. It was a major event. All who witnessed it walked carefully through the rest of the day. I was still thinking of him when I wrote the poem and knew that somehow he, too, belonged in the poem, for he was also part of the transformation.

I was not sure how the poem would end when I began writing it, but 15 looking back I realize the ending must have originated in one of two places. One was a story I heard from a woman who during times of deep emotional troubles would be visited by a woman who looked just like her. She herself would never see her, but anyone passing by her room while she was asleep would see this imaginary woman, standing next to her bed. I always considered the "imaginary" woman as her other self, the denied self who wanted back in.

And I was reminded, too, of the woman who had followed me around at an all-night party in Santa Fe a few years before. We had all drifted around the house, talking, dancing, filled with music and whatever else we had tasted. She finally caught up with me around dawn and told me that she was sorry she was white, and then told me that she believed white people had no souls. I was shocked and sad. And I saw her soul, starved but thinly beautiful, knocking hard on the wall of cocaine and self-hatred she was hiding behind.

So the poem becomes a way of speaking to her.

It is now very late and I will let someone else take over this story. Maybe the cricket who likes to come in here and sing and who probably knows a better way to write a poem than me.

It is not the last song, but to name anything that, only means that I would continue to be amazed at the creation of any new music.   1987

INVESTIGATIONS

1. Harjo says that all her forebears are part of who she is, "the root from which" she writes. List the ways in which your forebears are part of who you are, are root of the tree you are. How might this way of looking at

identity help account for who Evan ("Jump or Dive") and Jessie (*'night, Mother*) are?

2. Do you agree with Harjo that "it is only an illusion that any of the worlds" we "walk in and out of . . . are separate"? Why or why not?

3. To what extent would Harjo share John Haines's ("Moments and Journeys," p. 103) outlook? Joyce Carol Oates's ("Against Nature," p. 789)? What accounts for the similarities? The differences?

4. How might Mr. Cohen's ("Valaida") soul look to Harjo? How might yours look to her?

RICHARD McCANN

My Mother's Clothes: The School of Beauty and Shame

Like every corner house in Carroll Knolls, the corner house on our block was turned backward on its lot, a quirk introduced by the developer of the subdivision, who, having run short of money, sought variety without additional expense. The turned-around houses, as we kids called them, were not popular, perhaps because they seemed too public, their casement bedroom windows cranking open onto sunstruck asphalt streets. In actuality, however, it was the rest of the houses that were public, their picture windows offering dioramic glimpses of early-American sofas and Mediterranean-style pole lamps whose mottled globes hung like iridescent melons from wrought-iron chains. In order not to be seen walking across the living room to the kitchen in our pajamas, we had to close the venetian blinds. The corner house on our block was secretive, as though it had turned its back on all of us, whether in superiority or in shame, refusing to acknowledge even its own unkempt yard of yellowing zoysia grass. After its initial occupants moved away, the corner house remained vacant for months.

The spring I was in sixth grade, it was sold. When I came down the block

Author of *Dream of the Traveler* (1976), a collection of poetry, RICHARD McCANN (b. 1949) has published fiction in numerous magazines and anthologies, including *Editors' Choice: Best New Short Fiction for 1987* (1988). He says, "The process of writing has required that I both find my way into and out of the fictions — my mother's endless memories, my culture's myths — within which I was raised."

from school, I saw a moving van parked at its curb. "Careful with that!" a woman was shouting at a mover as he unloaded a tiered end table from the truck. He stared at her in silence. The veneer had already been splintered from the table's edge, as though someone had nervously picked at it while watching TV. Then another mover walked from the truck carrying a child's bicycle, a wire basket bolted over its thick rear tire, brightly colored plastic streamers dangling from its handlebars.

The woman looked at me. "What have you got there? In your hand."

I was holding a scallop shell spray-painted gold, with imitation pearls glued along its edges. Mrs. Eidus, the art teacher who visited our class each Friday, had showed me how to make it.

"A hatpin tray," I said. "It's for my mother."   5

"It's real pretty." She glanced up the street as though trying to guess which house I belonged to. "I'm Mrs. Tyree," she said, "and I've got a boy about your age. His daddy's bringing him tonight in the new Plymouth. I bet you haven't sat in a new Plymouth."

"We have a Ford." I studied her house dress, tiny blue and purple flowers imprinted on thin cotton, a line of white buttons as large as Necco Wafers marching toward its basted hemline. She was the kind of mother my mother laughed at for cutting recipes out of *Woman's Day*. Staring from our picture window, my mother would sometimes watch the neighborhood mothers drag their folding chairs into a circle on someone's lawn. "There they go," she'd say, "a regular meeting of the Daughters of the Eastern Star!" "They're hardly even *women*," she'd whisper to my father, "and their *clothes*." She'd criticize their appearance — their loud nylon scarves tied beneath their chins, their disintegrating figures stuffed into pedal pushers — until my father, worried that my brother, Davis, and I could hear, although laughing himself, would beg her, "Stop it, Maria, please stop; it isn't funny." But she wouldn't stop, not ever. "Not even thirty and they look like they belong to the DAR! They wear their pearls inside their bosoms in case the rope should break!" She was the oldest mother on the block but she was the most glamorous, sitting alone on the front lawn in her sleek kick-pleated skirts and cashmere sweaters, reading her thick paperback novels, whose bindings had split. Her hair was lightly hennaed, so that when I saw her pillowcases piled atop the washer, they seemed dusted with powdery rouge. She had once lived in New York City.

After dinner, when it was dark, I joined the other children congregated beneath the streetlamp across from the turned-around house. Bucky Trueblood, an eighth-grader who had once twisted the stems off my brother's eyeglasses, was crouched in the center, describing his mother's naked body to us elementary school children gathered around him, our faces slightly upturned, as though searching for a distant constellation, or for the bats that Bucky said would fly into our hair. I sat at the edge, one half of my body within the circle of light, the other half lost to darkness. When Bucky described his mother's nipples, which he'd glimpsed when she bent to kiss him goodnight, everyone giggled; but when he described her genitals, which he'd seen by dropping his pencil on the floor and looking up her nightie while her feet were propped on a hassock as she watched TV, everyone huddled nervously together, as though listening to a ghost story that made them fear something dangerous in the nearby dark. "I don't believe you," someone said; "I'm telling you," Bucky said, "*that's what it looks like.*"

I slowly moved outside the circle. Across the street a cream-colored Plymouth was parked at the curb. In a lighted bedroom window Mrs. Tyree was hanging café curtains. Behind the chain link fence, within the low branches of a willow tree, the new child was standing in his yard. I could see his white T-shirt and the pale oval of his face, a face deprived of detail by darkness and distance. Behind him, at the open bedroom window, his mother slowly fiddled with a valance. Behind me the children sat spellbound beneath the light. Then Bucky jumped up and pointed in the new child's direction — "Hey, you, you want to hear something really *good?*" — and even before the others had a chance to spot him, he vanished as suddenly and completely as an imaginary playmate.

The next morning, as we waited at our bus stop, he loitered by the mailbox   10
on the opposite corner, not crossing the street until the yellow school bus pulled up and flung open its door. Then he dashed aboard and sat down beside me. "I'm Denny," he said. Denny: a heavy, unbeautiful child, who, had his parents stayed in their native Kentucky, would have been a farm boy, but who in Carroll Knolls seemed to belong to no particular world at all, walking past the identical ranch houses in his overalls and Keds, his whitish-blond hair close-cropped all around except for the distinguishing, stigmatizing feature of a wave that crested perfectly just above his forehead, a wave that neither rose nor fell, a wave he trained with Hopalong Cassidy hair tonic, a wave he tended fussily, as though it were the only loveliness he allowed himself.

What in Carroll Knolls might have been described by someone not native to those parts — a visiting expert, say — as *beautiful,* capable of arousing terror and joy? The brick ramblers strung with multicolored Christmas lights? The occasional frontyard plaster Virgin entrapped within a chicken-wire grotto entwined with plastic roses? The spring Denny moved to Carroll Knolls, I begged my parents to take me to a nightclub, had begged so hard for months, in fact, that by summer they finally agreed to a Sunday matinee. Waiting in the backseat of our Country Squire, a red bow tie clipped to my collar, I watched our house float like a mirage behind the sprinkler's web of water. The front door opened, and a white dress fluttered within the mirage's ascending waves: Slipping on her sunglasses, my mother emerged onto the concrete stoop, adjusted her shoulder strap, and teetered across the wet grass in new spectator shoes. Then my father stepped out and cut the sprinkler off. We drove — the warm breeze inside the car sweetened by my mother's Shalimar — past ranch houses tethered to yards by chain link fences; past the Silver Spring Volunteer Fire Department and Carroll Knolls Elementary School; past the Polar Bear Soft-Serv stand, its white stucco siding shimmery with mirror shards; past a bulldozed red-clay field where a weathered billboard advertised IF YOU LIVED HERE YOU'D BE HOME BY NOW, until we arrived at the border — a line of cinder-block discount liquor stores, a traffic light — of Washington, D.C. The red light turned red. We stopped. The breeze died and the Shalimar fell from the air. Exhaust fumes mixed with the smell of hot tar. A drunk man stumbled into the crosswalk, followed by an old woman shielding herself from the sun with an orange umbrella, and two teenaged boys dribbling a basketball back and forth between them. My mother put down her sun visor. "Lock your door," she said.

Then the light changed, releasing us into another country. The station wagon sailed down boulevards of Chinese elms and flowering Bradford pears, through hot, dense streets where black families sat on wooden chairs at curbs, along old streetcar tracks that caused the tires to shimmy and the car to swerve, onto Pennsylvania Avenue, past the White House, encircled by its fence of iron spears, and down 14th Street, past the Treasury Building, until at last we reached the Neptune Room, a cocktail lounge in the basement of a shabbily elegant hotel.

Inside, the Neptune Room's walls were painted with garish mermaids reclining seductively on underwater rocks, and human frogmen who stared longingly through their diving helmets' glass masks at a loveliness they could not possess on dry earth. On stage, leaning against the baby grand piano, a *chanteuse* (as my mother called her) was singing of her grief, her wrists weighted with rhinestone bracelets, a single blue spotlight making her seem like one who lived, as did the mermaids, underwater.

I was transfixed. I clutched my Roy Rogers cocktail (the same as a Shirley Temple, but without the cheerful, girlish grenadine) tight in my fist. In the middle of "The Man I Love" I stood and struggled toward the stage.

I strayed into the spotlight's soft-blue underwater world. Close up, from   15
within the light, the singer was a boozy, plump peroxide blonde in a tight black cocktail dress; but these indiscretions made her yet more lovely, for they showed what she had lost, just as her songs seemed to carry her backward into endless regret. When I got close to her, she extended one hand — red nails, a huge glass ring — and seized one of mine.

"Why, what kind of little sailor have we got here?" she asked the audience.

I stared through the border of blue light and into the room, where I saw my parents gesturing, although whether they were telling me to step closer to her microphone or to step farther away, I could not tell. The whole club was staring.

"Maybe he knows a song!" a man shouted from the back.

"Sing with me," she whispered. "What can you sing?"

I wanted to lift her microphone from its stand and bow deeply from the   20
waist, as Judy Garland did on her weekly TV show. But I could not. As she began to sing, I stood voiceless, pressed against the protection of her black dress; or, more accurately, I stood beside her, silently lip-syncing to myself. I do not recall what she sang, although I do recall a quick, farcical ending in

which she falsettoed, like Betty Boop, "Gimme a Little Kiss, Will Ya, Huh?" and brushed my forehead with pursed red lips.

That summer, humidity enveloping the landfill subdivision, Denny, "the new kid," stood on the boundaries, while we neighborhood boys played War, a game in which someone stood on Stanley Allen's front porch and machine-gunned the rest of us, who one by one clutched our bellies, coughed as if choking on blood, and rolled in exquisite death throes down the grassy hill. When Stanley's father came up the walk from work, he ducked imaginary bullets. "Hi, Dad," Stanley would call, rising from the dead to greet him. Then we began the game again: Whoever died best in the last round got to kill in the next. Later, after dusk, we'd smear the wings of balsa planes with glue, ignite them, and send them flaming through the dark on kamikaze missions. Long after the streets were deserted, we children sprawled beneath the corner streetlamp, praying our mothers would not call us — *"Time to come in!"* — back to our ovenlike houses; and then sometimes Bucky, hoping to scare the elementary school kids, would lead his solemn procession of junior high "hoods" down the block, their penises hanging from their unzipped trousers.

Denny and I began to play together, first in secret, then visiting each other's houses almost daily, and by the end of the summer I imagined him to be my best friend. Our friendship was sealed by our shared dread of junior high school. Davis, who had just finished seventh grade, brought back reports of corridors so long that one could get lost in them, of gangs who fought to control the lunchroom and the bathrooms. The only safe place seemed to be the Health Room, where a pretty nurse let you lie down on a cot behind a folding screen. Denny told me about a movie he'd seen in which the children, all girls, did not have to go to school at all but were taught at home by a beautiful governess, who, upon coming to their rooms each morning, threw open their shutters so that sunlight fell like bolts of satin across their beds, whispered their pet names while kissing them, and combed their long hair with a silver brush. "She never got mad," said Denny, beating his fingers up and down through the air as though striking a keyboard, "except once when some old man told the girls they could never play piano again."

With my father at work in the Pentagon and my mother off driving the two-tone Welcome Wagon Chevy to new subdivisions, Denny and I spent whole days in the gloom of my living room, the picture window's venetian blinds closed against an August sun so fierce that it bleached the design from the carpet. Dreaming of fabulous prizes — sets of matching Samsonite luggage, French Provincial bedroom suites, Corvettes, jet flights to Hawaii — we watched Jan Murray's "Treasure Hunt" and Bob Barker's "Truth or Conse-quences" (a name that seemed strangely threatening). We watched "The Loretta Young Show," worshipping yet critiquing her elaborate gowns. When "The Early Show" came on, we watched old Bette Davis, Gene Tierney, and Joan Crawford movies — *Dark Victory, Leave Her to Heaven, A Woman's Face.* Hoping to become their pen pals, we wrote long letters to fading movie stars, who in turn sent us autographed photos we traded between ourselves. We searched the house for secrets, like contraceptives, Kotex, and my mother's hidden supply of Hershey bars. And finally, Denny and I, running to the front window every few minutes to make sure no one was coming unexpectedly up the sidewalk, inspected the secrets of my mother's dresser: her satin nightgowns and padded brassieres, folded atop pink drawer liners and scattered with loose sachet; her black mantilla, pressed inside a shroud of lilac tissue paper; her heart-shaped candy box, a flapper doll strapped to its lid with a ribbon, from which spilled galaxies of cocktail rings and cultured pearls. Small shrines to deeper intentions, private grottoes of yearning: her triangular cloisonné earrings, her brooch of enameled butterfly wings.

Because beauty's source was longing, it was infused with romantic sorrow; because beauty was defined as "feminine," and therefore as "other," it became hopelessly confused with my mother: Mother, who quickly sorted through new batches of photographs, throwing unflattering shots of herself directly into the fire before they could be seen. Mother, who dramatized herself, telling us and our playmates, "My name is Maria Dolores; in Spanish, that means 'Mother of Sorrows,' " Mother, who had once wished to be a writer and who said, looking up briefly from whatever she was reading, "Books are my best friends." Mother, who read aloud from Whitman's *Leaves of Grass* and O'Neill's *Long Day's Journey into Night* with a voice so grave I could not tell the difference between them. Mother, who lifted cut-glass vases and antique clocks from her obsessively dusted curio shelves to ask, "If this could talk, what story would it tell?"

And more, always more, for she was the only woman in our house, a "people-watcher," a "talker," a woman whose mysteries and moods seemed endless: Our Mother of the White Silk Gloves; Our Mother of the Veiled Hats; Our Mother of the Paper Lilacs; Our Mother of the Sighs and Heartaches; Our Mother of the Gorgeous Gypsy Earrings; Our Mother of the Late Movies and the Cigarettes; Our Mother whom I adored and who, in adoring, I ran from, knowing it "wrong" for a son to wish to be like his mother; Our Mother who wished to influence us, passing the best of herself along, yet who held the fear common to that era, the fear that by loving a son too intensely she would render him unfit — "Momma's boy," "tied to apron strings" — and who therefore alternately drew us close and sent us away, believing a son needed "male influence" in large doses, that female influence was pernicious except as a final finishing, like manners; Our Mother of the Mixed Messages; Our Mother of Sudden Attentiveness; Our Mother of Sudden Distances; Our Mother of Anger; Our Mother of Apology. The simplest objects of her life, objects scattered accidentally about the house, became my shrines to beauty, my grottoes of romantic sorrow: her Revlon lipstick tubes, "Cherries in the Snow"; her Art Nouveau atomizers on the blue mirror top of her vanity; her pastel silk scarves knotted to a wire hanger in her closet; her white handkerchiefs blotted with red mouths. Voiceless objects; silences. The world halved with a cleaver: "masculine," "feminine." In these ways was the plainest ordinary love made com-

25

plicated and grotesque. And in these ways was beauty, already confused with the "feminine," also confused with shame, for all these longings were secret, and to control me all my brother had to do was to threaten to expose that Denny and I were dressing ourselves in my mother's clothes.

Denny chose my Mother's drabbest outfits, as though he were ruled by the deepest of modesties, or by his family's austere Methodism: a pink wrap-around skirt from which the color had been laundered, its hem almost to his ankles; a sleeveless white cotton blouse with a Peter Pan collar; a small straw summer clutch. But he seemed to challenge his own primness, as though he dared it with his "effects": an undershirt worn over his head to approximate cascading hair; gummed hole-punch reinforcements pasted to his fingernails so that his hands, palms up, might look like a woman's — flimsy crescent moons waxing above his fingertips.

He dressed slowly, hesitantly, but once dressed, he was a manic Proteus metamorphosing into contradictory, half-realized forms, throwing his "long hair" back and balling it violently into a French twist; tapping his paper nails on the glass-topped vanity as though he were an important woman kept waiting at a cosmetics counter; stabbing his nails into the air as though he were an angry teacher assigning an hour of detention; touching his temple as though he were a shy schoolgirl tucking back a wisp of stray hair; resting his fingertips on the rim of his glass of Kool-Aid as though he were an actress seated over an ornamental cocktail — a Pink Lady, say, or a Silver Slipper. Sometimes, in an orgy of jerky movement, his gestures overtaking him with greater and greater force, a dynamo of theatricality unleashed, he would hurl himself across the room like a mad girl having a fit, or like one possessed; or he would snatch the chenille spread from my parents' bed and drape it over his head to fashion for himself the long train of a bride. "Do you like it?" he'd ask anxiously, making me his mirror. "Does it look *real*?" He wanted, as did I, to become something he'd neither yet seen nor dreamed of, something he'd recognize the moment he saw it: himself. Yet he was constantly confounded, for no matter how much he adorned himself with scarves and jewelry, he could not understand that this was himself, as was also and at the same time the boy in overalls and Keds. He was split in two pieces — as who was not? — the blond wave cresting rigidly above his close-cropped hair.

"He makes me nervous," I heard my father tell my mother one night as I lay in bed. They were speaking about me. That morning I'd stood awkwardly on the front lawn — "Maybe you should go help your father," my mother had said — while he propped an extension ladder against the house, climbed up through power lines he separated with his bare hands, and staggered across the pitched roof he was reshingling. When his hammer slid down the incline, catching on the gutter, I screamed, "You're falling!" Startled, he almost fell.

"He needs to spend more time with you," I heard my mother say.

I couldn't sleep. Out in the distance a mother was calling her child home. A screen door slammed. I heard cicadas, their chorus as steady and loud as the hum of a power line. *He needs to spend more time with you.* Didn't she know? Saturday mornings, when he stood in his rubber hip boots fishing off the shore of Triadelphia Reservoir, I was afraid of the slimy bottom and could not wade after him; for whatever reasons of his own — something as simple as shyness, perhaps — he could not come to get me. I sat in the parking lot drinking Tru-Ade and reading *Betty and Veronica,* wondering if Denny had walked alone to Wheaton Plaza, where the weekend manager of Port-o'-Call allowed us to Windex the illuminated glass shelves that held Lladro figurines, the porcelain ballerina's hands so realistic one could see tiny life and heart lines etched into her palms. *He needs to spend more time with you.* Was she planning to discontinue the long summer afternoons that she and I spent together when there were no new families for her to greet in her Welcome Wagon car? "I don't feel like being alone today," she'd say, inviting me to sit on their chenille bedspread and watch her model new clothes in her mirror. Behind her an oscillating fan fluttered nylons and scarves she'd heaped, discarded, on a chair. "Should I wear the red belt with this dress or the black one?" she'd ask, turning suddenly toward me and cinching her waist with her hands.

Afterward we would sit together at the rattan table on the screened-in porch, holding cocktail napkins around sweaty glasses of iced Russian tea and listening to big-band music on the Zenith.

"You look so pretty," I'd say. Sometimes she wore outfits I'd selected for her from her closet — pastel chiffon dresses, an apricot blouse with real mother-of-pearl buttons.

One afternoon she leaned over suddenly and shut off the radio. "You know you're going to leave me one day," she said. When I put my arms around her, smelling the dry carnation talc she wore in hot weather, she stood up and marched out of the room. When she returned, she was wearing Bermuda shorts and a plain cotton blouse. "Let's wait for your father on the stoop," she said.

Late that summer — the summer before he died — my father took me with him to Fort Benjamin Harrison, near Indianapolis, where, as a colonel in the U.S. Army Reserves, he did his annual tour of duty. On the propjet he drank bourbon and read newspapers while I made a souvenir packet for Denny: an airsickness bag, into which I placed the Chiclets given me by the stewardess to help pop my ears during takeoff, and the laminated white card that showed the location of emergency exits. Fort Benjamin Harrison looked like Carroll Knolls: hundreds of acres of concrete and sun-scorched shrubbery inside a cyclone fence. Daytimes I waited for my father in the dining mess with the sons of other officers, drinking chocolate milk that came from a silver machine, and desultorily setting fires in ashtrays. When he came to collect me, I walked behind him — gold braid hung from his epaulets — while enlisted men saluted us and opened doors. At night, sitting in our BOQ room, he asked me questions about myself: "Are you looking forward to seventh grade?" "What do you think you'll want to be?" When these topics faltered — I stammered what I hoped were right answers — we watched TV, trying to preguess lines of dialogue on reruns of his favorite shows, "The Untouchables" and "Rawhide." "That Della Street," he said as he watched "Perry Mason," "is almost as pretty as your mother." On the last day, eager to make the trip memorable, he brought me a gift: a glassine envelope filled with punched IBM cards that told me my life story as his secretary typed it into the office computer. Card One: *You live at 10406 Lillians Mill Court, Silver Spring, Maryland.* Card Two: *You are entering seventh grade.* Card Three: *Last year your teacher was Mrs. Dillard.* Card Four: *Your favorite color is blue.* Card Five: *You love the Kingston Trio.* Card Six: *You love basketball and football.* Card Seven: *Your favorite sport is swimming.*

Whose son did these cards describe? The address was correct, as was the   35 teacher's name and the favorite color; and he'd remembered that one morning during breakfast I'd put a dime in the jukebox and played the Kingston Trio's song about "the man who never returned." But whose fiction was the rest? Had I, who played no sport other than kickball and Kitty-Kitty-Kick-the-Can, lied to him when he asked me about myself? Had he not heard from my mother the outcome of the previous summer's swim lessons? At the swim club a young man in black trunks had taught us, as we held hands, to dunk ourselves in water, surface, and then go down. When he had told her to let go of me, I had thrashed across the surface, violently afraid I'd sink. But perhaps I had not lied to him; perhaps he merely did not wish to see. It was my job, I felt, to reassure him that I was the son he imagined me to be, perhaps because the role of reassurer gave me power. In any case, I thanked him for the computer cards. I thanked him the way a father thanks a child for a well-intentioned gift he'll never use — a set of handkerchiefs, say, on which the embroidered swirls construct a monogram of no particular initial, and which thus might be used by anyone.

As for me, when I dressed in my mother's clothes, I seldom moved at all: I held myself rigid before the mirror. The kind of beauty I'd seen practiced in movies and in fashion magazines was beauty attained by lacquered stasis, beauty attained by fixed poses — "ladylike stillness," the stillness of mannequins, the stillness of models "caught" in midgesture, the stillness of the passive moon around which active meteors orbited and burst. My costume was of the greatest solemnity: I dressed like the *chanteuse* in the Neptune Room, carefully shimmying my mother's black slip over my head so as not to stain it with Brylcreem, draping her black mantilla over my bare shoulders, clipping her rhinestone dangles to my ears. Had I at that time already seen the movie in which French women who had fraternized with German soldiers were made to shave their heads and walk through the streets, jeered by their fellow villagers? And if so, did I imagine myself to be one of the collaborators, or one of the villagers, taunting her from the curb? I ask because no matter how elaborate my costume, I made no effort to camouflage my crew cut or my male body.

How did I perceive myself in my mother's triple-mirrored vanity, its endless repetitions? I saw myself as doubled — both an image and he who studied it. I saw myself as beautiful, and guilty: The lipstick made my mouth seem the ripest rose, or a wound; the small rose on the black slip opened like my mother's heart disclosed, or like the Sacred Heart of Mary, aflame and pierced by arrows; the mantilla transformed me into a Mexican penitent or a Latin movie star, like Dolores Del Rio. The mirror was a silvery stream: On the far side, in a clearing, stood the woman who was icily immune from the boy's terror and contempt; on the close side, in the bedroom, stood the boy who feared and yet longed after her inviolability. (Perhaps, it occurs to me now, this doubleness is the source of drag queens' vulnerable ferocity.) Sometimes, when I saw that person in the mirror, I felt as though I had at last been lifted from that dull, locked room, with its mahogany bedroom suite and chalky blue walls. But other times, particularly when I saw Denny and me together, so that his reality shattered my fantasies, we seemed merely ludicrous and sadly comic, as though we were dressed in the garments of another species, like dogs in human clothes. I became aware of my spatulate hands, my scarred knees, my large feet; I became aware of the drooping, unfilled bodice of my slip. Like Denny, I could neither dispense with images nor take their flexibility as pleasure, for the idea of self I had learned and was learning still was that one was constructed by one's images — "*When boys cross their legs, they cross one ankle atop the knee*" — so that one finally sought the protection of believing in one's own image and, in believing in it as reality, condemned oneself to its poverty.

(That locked room. My mother's vanity; my father's highboy. If Denny and I, still in our costumes, had left that bedroom, its floor strewn with my mother's shoes and handbags, and gone through the darkened living room, out onto the sunstruck porch, down the sidewalk, and up the street, how would we have carried ourselves? Would we have walked boldly, chattering extravagantly back and forth between ourselves, like drag queens refusing to acknowledge the stares of contempt that are meant to halt them? Would we have walked humbly, with the calculated, impervious piety of the condemned walking barefoot to the public scaffold? Would we have walked simply, as deeply accustomed to the normalcy of our own strangeness as Siamese twins? Or would we have walked gravely, a solemn procession, like Bucky Trueblood's gang, their manhood hanging from their unzipped trousers?

(We were eleven years old. Why now, more than two decades later, do I wonder for the first time how we would have carried ourselves through a publicness we would have neither sought nor dared? I am six feet two inches tall; I weigh 198 pounds. Given my size, the question I am most often asked about my youth is "What football position did you play?" Overseas I am most commonly taken to be a German or a Swede. Right now, as I write this, I am wearing L. L. Bean khaki trousers, a LaCoste shirt, Weejuns: the anonymous American costume, although partaking of certain signs of class and education, and most recently, partaking also of certain signs of sexual orientation, this costume having become the standard garb of the urban American gay man. Why do I tell you these things? Am I trying — not subtly — to inform us of my "maleness," to reassure us that I have "survived" without noticeable "complexes"? Or is this my urge, my constant urge, to complicate my portrait of myself to both of us, so that I might layer my selves like so many multicolored crinoline slips, each rustling as I walk? When the wind blows, lifting my skirt, I do not know which slip will be revealed.)

Sometimes, while Denny and I were dressing up, Davis would come home   40
unexpectedly from the bowling alley, where he'd been hanging out since entering junior high. At the bowling alley he was courting the protection of Bucky's gang.

"Let me in!" he'd demand, banging fiercely on the bedroom door, behind which Denny and I were scurrying to wipe the makeup off our faces with Kleenex.

"We're not doing anything," I'd protest, buying time.

"Let me in this minute or I'll tell!"

Once in the room, Davis would police the wreckage we'd made, the emptied hatboxes, the scattered jewelry, the piled skirts and blouses. "You'd better clean this up right now," he'd warn. "You two make me *sick*."

Yet his scorn seemed modified by awe. When he helped us rehang the   45
clothes in the closet and replace the jewelry in the candy box, a sullen accomplice destroying someone else's evidence, he sometimes handled the garments as though they were infused with something of himself, although at the precise moment when he seemed to find them loveliest, holding them close, he would cast them down.

After our dress-up sessions Denny would leave the house without goodbyes. I was glad to see him go. We would not see other for days, unless we met by accident; we never referred to what we'd done the last time we'd been together. We met like those who have murdered are said to meet, each tentatively and warily examining the other for signs of betrayal. But whom had we murdered? The boys who walked into that room? Or the women who briefly came to life within it? Perhaps this metaphor has outlived its meaning. Perhaps our shame derived not from our having killed but from our having created.

In early September, as Denny and I entered seventh grade, my father became ill. Over Labor Day weekend he was too tired to go fishing. On Monday his skin had vaguely yellowed; by Thursday he was severely jaundiced. On Friday he entered the hospital, his liver rapidly failing; Sunday he was dead. He died from acute hepatitis, possibly acquired while cleaning up after our sick dog, the doctor said. He was buried at Arlington National Cemetery, down the hill from the Tomb of the Unknown Soldier. After the twenty-one-gun salute, our mother pinned his colonel's insignia to our jacket lapels. I carried the flag from his coffin to the car. For two weeks I stayed home with my mother, helping her write thank-you notes on small white cards with black borders; one afternoon, as I was affixing postage to the square, plain envelopes, she looked at me across the dining room table. "You and Davis are all I have left," she said. She went into the kitchen and came back. "Tomorrow," she said, gathering up the note cards, "you'll have to go to school." Mornings I wandered the long corridors alone, separated from Denny by the fate of our last names, which had cast us into different homerooms and daily schedules. Lunchtimes we sat together in silence in the rear of the cafeteria. Afternoons, just before gym class, I went to the Health Room, where, lying on a cot, I'd imagine the Phys. Ed. coach calling my name from the class roll, and imagine my name, unclaimed, unanswered to, floating weightlessly away, like a balloon that one jumps to grab hold of but that is already out of reach. Then I'd hear the nurse dial the telephone. "He's sick again," she'd say. "Can you come pick him up?" At home I helped my mother empty my father's highboy. "No, we want to save that," she said when I folded his uniform into a huge brown bag that read GOODWILL INDUSTRIES; I wrapped it in a plastic dry-cleaner's bag and hung it in the hall closet.

After my father's death my relationship to my mother's things grew yet more complex, for as she retreated into her grief, she left behind only her mute objects as evidence of her life among us: objects that seemed as lonely and vulnerable as she was, objects that I longed to console, objects with which I longed to console myself — a tangled gold chain, thrown in frustration on the mantel; a wineglass, its rim stained with lipstick, left unwashed in the sink. Sometimes at night Davis and I heard her prop her pillow up against her bedroom wall, lean back heavily, and tune her radio to a call-in show: "*Nightcaps, what are you thinking at this late hour?*" Sunday evenings, in order to help her prepare for the next day's job hunt, I stood over her beneath the bare basement bulb, the same bulb that first illuminated my father's jaundice. I set her hair, slicking each wet strand with gel and rolling it, inventing gossip that seemed to draw us together, a beautician and his customer.

"You have such pretty hair," I'd say.

"At my age, don't you think I should cut it?" She was almost fifty.   50

"No, never."

That fall Denny and I were caught. One evening my mother noticed something out of place in her closet. (Perhaps now that she no longer shared it, she knew where every belt and scarf should have been.)

I was in my bedroom doing my French homework, dreaming of one day visiting Au Printemps, the store my teacher spoke of so excitedly as she played us the Edith Piaf records that she had brought back from France. In the mirror above my desk I saw my mother appear at my door.

"Get into the living room," she said. Her anger made her small, reflected body seem taut and dangerous.

In the living room Davis was watching TV with Uncle Joe, our father's   55
brother, who sometimes came to take us fishing. Uncle Joe was lying in our father's La-Z-Boy recliner.

"There aren't going to be any secrets in this house," she said. "You've been in my closet. What were you doing there?"

"No, we weren't," I said. "We were watching TV all afternoon."

"*We?* Was Denny here with you? Don't you think I've heard about that? Were you and Denny going through my clothes? Were you wearing them?"

"No, Mom," I said.

"Don't lie!" She turned to Uncle Joe, who was staring at us. "Make him   60
stop! He's lying to me!"

She slapped me. Although I was already taller than she, she slapped me
over and over, slapped me across the room until I was backed against the TV.
Davis was motionless, afraid. But Uncle Joe jumped up and stood between my
mother and me, holding her until her rage turned to sobs. "I can't, I can't be
both a mother and a father," she said to him. "I can't do it." I could not look
at Uncle Joe, who, although he was protecting me, did not know I was lying.

She looked at me. "We'll discuss this later," she said. "Get out of my
sight."

We never discussed it. Denny was outlawed. I believe, in fact, that it was
I who suggested he never be allowed in our house again. I told my mother I
hated him. I do not think I was lying when I said this. I truly hated him —
hated him, I mean, for being me.

For two or three weeks Denny tried to speak with me at the bus stop, but
whenever he approached, I busied myself with kids I barely knew. After a while
Denny found a new best friend, Lee, a child despised by everyone, for Lee was
"effeminate." His clothes were too fastidious; he often wore his cardigan over
his shoulders, like an old woman feeling a chill. Sometimes, watching the street
from our picture window, I'd see Lee walking toward Denny's house. "What
a queer," I'd say to whoever might be listening. "He walks like a *girl*." Or
sometimes, at the junior high school, I'd see him and Denny walking down the
corridor, their shoulders pressed together as if they were telling each other
secrets, or as if they were joined in mutual defense. Sometimes when I saw
them, I turned quickly away, as though I'd forgotten something important in
my locker. But when I felt brave enough to risk rejection, for I belonged to no
group, I joined Bucky Trueblood's gang, sitting on the radiator in the main
hall, and waited for Lee and Denny to pass us. As Lee and Denny got close,
they stiffened and looked straight ahead.

"Faggots," I muttered.   65

I looked at Bucky, sitting in the middle of the radiator. As Lee and Denny
passed, he leaned forward from the wall, accidentally disarranging the practiced
severity of his clothes, his jeans puckering beneath his tooled belt, the breast
pocket of his T-shirt drooping with the weight of a pack of Pall Malls. He
whistled. Lee and Denny flinched. He whistled again. Then he leaned back, the
hard lines of his body reassuring themselves, his left foot striking a steady beat
on the tile floor with the silver V-tap of his black loafer.   1986

INVESTIGATIONS

1. In paragraph 25 the narrator talks about "the world halved with a cleaver:
   'masculine,' 'feminine.'" He says this division makes "the plainest ordinary
   love . . . complicated and grotesque." Locate places in the story where the

narrator seems "masculine." In what ways is he "complicated and grotesque" at those times?

2. The narrator says his friend, Denny, was "split in two pieces — as who
was not?" To what extent does the narrator transcend this split? How
might bridging the gap between "masculine" and "feminine" worlds bring
us into greater harmony with ourselves?

3. Assume for a moment that the narrator is correct in saying that "one was
constructed by one's images." What images construct you?

ANTLER

Raising My Hand

One of the first things we learn in school is
    if we know the answer to a question
We must raise our hand and be called on
    before we can speak.
How strange it seemed to me then,   5
    raising my hand to be called on,
How at first I just blurted out,
    but that was not permitted.

How often I knew the answer
And the teacher (knowing I knew)   10
Called on others I knew (and she knew)
    had it wrong!
How I'd stretch my arm
    as if it would break free
    and shoot through the roof   15
    like a rocket!
How I'd wave and groan and sigh,
Even hold up my aching arm
    with my other hand
Begging to be called on,   20
Please, *me,* I know the answer!

ANTLER's *Factory* won the 1985 Walt Whitman Award from the Academy of American Poets. Born
in 1946, Antler considers himself a "Great Lakes Bioregion poet."

Almost leaping from my seat
    hoping to hear my name.

Twenty-nine now, alone in the wilds,
Seated on some rocky outcrop   25
    under all the stars,
I find myself raising my hand
    as I did in first grade
Mimicking the excitement
    and expectancy felt then,   30
No one calls on me
    but the wind.   1986

INVESTIGATIONS

1. What purpose is raising one's hand before speaking designed to serve? In what ways is it strange to have to raise one's hand before speaking? What would school be like if this custom didn't exist? How would you be different if you'd never had to raise your hand?

2. How did school help make the speaker who he is? What emotions does he experience in stanza two? Are these the same emotions as he experiences in stanza three?

3. What has the speaker learned since he first went to school?

4. Write a poem about a school custom that had a particularly strong effect on you. Try ending your poem as Antler does his, with an image of that custom as it influences you now.

JOHN HAINES

Moments and Journeys

The movements of things on this earth has always impressed me. There is a reassuring vitality in the annual rise of a river, in the return of the Arctic sun, in the poleward flight of spring migrations, in the seasonal trek of nomadic peoples. A passage from Edwin Muir's autobiography speaks to me of its significance.

> I remember . . . while we were walking one day on the Mönchsberg — a smaller hill on the opposite side of the river — looking down on a green plain that stretched away to the foothills, and watching in the distance people moving along the tiny roads. Why do such things seem enormously important to us? Why, seen from a distance, do the casual journeys of men and women, perhaps going on some trivial errand, take on the appearance of a pilgrimage? I can only explain it by some deep archetypal image in our minds of which we become conscious only at the rare moments when we realize that our own life is a journey. [Edwin Muir, *An Autobiography* (Sommers, Conn.: Seabury, 1968), p. 217].

This seems to me like a good place to begin, not only for its essential truth, but because it awakens in me a whole train of images — images of the journey as I have come to understand it, moments and stages in existence. Many of these go back to the years I lived on my homestead in Alaska. That life itself, part of the soil and weather of the place, seemed to have about it much of the time an aura of deep and lasting significance. I wasn't always aware of this, of course. There were many things to be struggled with from day to day, chores of one sort or another — cabins to be built, crops to be looked after, meat to kill, and wood to cut — all of which took a kind of passionate attention. But often when I was able to pause and look up from what I was doing, I caught brief glimpses of a life much older than mine.

Some of these images stand out with great force from the continual coming and going of which they were part — Fred Campbell, the old hunter and miner I had come to know, that lean, brown man of patches and strange fits. He and I and my first wife, Peg, with seven dogs — five of them carrying packs — all went over Buckeye Dome one day in the late summer of 1954. It was a clear, hot day in mid-August, the whole troop of us strung out on the trail. Campbell and his best dog, a yellow bitch named Granny, were in the lead. We were in

---

JOHN HAINES (b. 1924) served in the U.S. Navy in World War II, homesteaded in Alaska from 1954 until 1969, and has worked as a trapper, fisherman, freelance writer and editor, and hunter. His many collections of poems include *New Poems: 1980–88* (1990), *The Stars, The Snow, The Fire* (1989), and *News from the Glacier: Selected Poems, 1960–80* (1982).

a hurry, or seemed to be, the dogs pulling us on, straining at their leashes for the first two or three miles, and then, turned loose, just panting along, anxious not be left behind. We stopped only briefly that morning, to adjust a dog pack and to catch our wind. Out of the close timber with its hot shadows and swarms of mosquitoes, we came into the open sunlight of the dome. The grass and low shrubs on the treeless slopes moved gently in the warm air that came from somewhere south, out of the Gulf of Alaska.

At midday we halted near the top of the dome to look for water among the rocks and to pick blueberries. The dogs, with their packs removed, lay down in the heat, snapping at flies. Buckeye Dome was the high place nearest to home, though it was nearly seven miles by trail from Richardson. It wasn't very high, either — only 3,000 feet — but it rose clear of the surrounding hills. From its summit you could see in any direction, as far west as Fairbanks when the air was clear enough. We saw other high places, landmarks in the distance, pointed out to us and named by Campbell: Banner Dome, Cockscomb, Bull Dome, and other I've forgotten. In the southeast, a towering dust cloud rose from the Delta River. Campbell talked to us of his trails and camps, of years made of such journeys as ours, an entire history told around the figure of one man. We were new to the North and eager to learn all we could. We listened, sucking blueberries from a tin cup.

And then we were on the move again. I can see Campbell in faded jeans   5
and red felt hat, bending over one of the dogs as he tightened a strap, swearing and saying something about the weather, the distance, and himself getting too old to make such a trip. We went off down the steep north slope of the dome in a great rush, through miles of windfalls, following that twisting, root-grown trail of his. Late in the evening, wading the shallows of a small creek, we came tired and bitten to his small cabin on the shore of a lake he had named for himself.

That range of images is linked with another at a later time. By then I had my own team, and with our four dogs we were bound uphill one afternoon in the cool September sunlight to pick cranberries on the long ridge overlooking Redmond Creek. The tall, yellow grass on the partly cleared ridge bent over in the wind that came easily from the west. I walked behind, and I could see, partly hidden by the grass, the figures of the others as they rounded the shoulder of a little hill and stopped to look back toward me. The single human figure there in the sunlight under moving clouds, the dogs with their fur slightly ruffled, seemed the embodiment of an old story.

And somewhere in the great expanse of time that made life in the wilderness so open and unending, other seasons were stations on the journey. Coming across the Tanana River on the midwinter ice, we had three dogs in harness and one young female running loose beside us. We had been three days visiting a neighbor, a trapper living on the far side of the river, and were returning home. Halfway across the river we stopped to rest; the sled was heavy, the dogs were tired and lay down on the ice.

Standing there, leaning on the back of the sled, I knew a vague sense of remoteness and peril. The river ice always seemed a little dangerous, even when it was thick and solid. There were open stretches of clear, blue water, and sometimes large, deep cracks in the ice where the river could be heard running deep and steady. We were heading down-river into a cloudy December evening. Wind came across the ice, pushing a little dry snow, and no other sound — only the vast presence of snow and ice, scattered islands, and the dark crest of Richardson Hill in the distance.

To live by a large river is to be kept in the heart of things. We become involved in its life, the heavy sound of it in the summer as it wears away silt and gravel from its cut-banks, pushing them into sandbars that will be islands in another far-off year. Trees are forever tilting over the water, to fall and be washed away, to lodge in a drift pile somewhere downstream. The heavy gray water drags at the roots of willows, spruce, and cottonwoods; sometimes it brings up the trunk of a tree buried in sand a thousand years before, or farther back than that, in the age of ice. The log comes loose from the fine sand, heavy and dripping, still bearing the tunnel marks made by the long dead insects. Salmon come in midsummer, then whitefish, and salmon again in the fall; they are caught in our nets and carried away to be smoked and eaten, to be dried for winter feed. Summer wears away into fall; the sound of the river changes. The water clears and slowly drops; pan ice forms in the eddies. One morning in early winter we wake to a great and sudden silence: The river is frozen.

We stood alone there on the ice that day, two people, four dogs, and a 10 loaded sled, and nothing before us but land and water into Asia. It was time to move on again. I spoke to the dogs and gave the sled a push.

Other days. On a hard-packed trail home from Cabin Creek, I halted the dogs part way up a long hill in scattered spruce. It was a clear evening, not far below zero. Ahead of us, over an open ridge, a full moon stood clear of the land, enormous and yellow in the deep blue of the Arctic evening. I recalled how Billy Melvin, an old miner from the early days at Richardson, had once described to me a moonrise he had seen, a full moon coming up ahead of him on the trail, "big as a rain barrel." And it was very much like that — an enormous and rusty rain barrel into which I looked, and the far end of the barrel was open. I stood there, thinking it might be possible to go on forever into that snow and yellow light, with no sound but my own breathing, the padding of the dog's feet, and the occasional squeak of the sled runners. The moon whitened and grew smaller; twilight deepened, and we went on to the top of the hill.

What does it take to make a journey? A place to start from, something to leave behind. A road, a trail, or a river. Companions, and something like a destination: a camp, an inn, or another shore. We might imagine a journey with no destination, nothing but the act of going, and with never an arrival. But I think we would always hope to find *something* or *someone*, however unexpected and unprepared for. Seen from a distance or taken part in, all journeys may be the same, and we arrive exactly where we are.

One late summer afternoon, near the road to Denali Park, I watched the figures of three people slowly climb the slope of a mountain in the northeast. The upper part of the mountain was bare of trees, and the small alpine plants there were already red and gold from the early frost. Sunlight came through the broken rain clouds and lit up the slope and its three moving figures. They were so far away that I could not tell if they were men or women, but the red jacket worn by one of them stood out brightly in the sun. They climbed higher and higher, bound for a ridge where some large rocks broke through the thin soil. A shadow kept pace with them, slowly darkening the slope below them, as the sun sank behind another mountain in the southwest. I wondered where they were going — perhaps to hunt mountain sheep — or they were climbing to a berry patch they knew. It was late in the day; they would not get back by dark. I watched them as if they were figures in a dream, who bore with them the destiny of the race. They stopped to rest for a while near the skyline, but were soon out of sight beyond the ridge. Sunlight stayed briefly on the high rock summit, and then a rain cloud moved in and hid the mountaintop.

When life is simplified, its essence becomes clearer, and we know our lives as part of some ancient human activity in a time measured not by clocks and calendars but by the turning of a great wheel, the positions of which are not wage-hours, nor days and weeks, but immense stations called Spring, Summer, Autumn, and Winter. I suppose it will seem too obvious to say that this sense of things will be far less apparent to people closed off in the routine of a modern city. I think many people must now and then be aware of such moments as I have described, but do not remember them, or attach no special significance to them. They are images that pass quickly from view because there is no place for them in our lives. We are swept along by events we cannot link together in a significant pattern, like a flood of refugees pushed on by the news of a remote disaster. The rush of conflicting impressions keeps away stillness, and it is in stillness that the images arise, as they will, fluently and naturally, when there is nothing to prevent them.

There is the dream journey and the actual life. The two seem to touch now and then, and perhaps when men lived less complicated and distracted lives the two were not separate at all, but continually one thing. I have read somewhere that this was once true for the Yuma Indians who lived along the Colorado River. They dreamed at will, and moved without effort from waking into dreaming life; life and dream were bound together. And in this must be a kind of radiance, a very old and deep assurance that life has continuity and meaning, that things are somehow in place. It is the journey resolved into one endless present.

And the material is all around us. I retain strong images from treks with my stepchildren: of a night seven years ago when we camped on a mountaintop, a night lighted by snow patches and sparks from a windy fire going out. Sleeping on the frozen ground, we heard the sound of an owl from the cold, bare oak trees above us. And there was a summer evening I spent with a small class of schoolchildren near Painted Rock in central California. We had come to learn about Indians. The voices of the children carried over the burned fields under the red glare of that sky, and the rock gave back heat in the dusk like an immense oven. There are ships and trains that pull away, planes that fly into the night; or the single figure of a man crossing an otherwise empty lot. If such moments are not as easily come by, as clear and as resonant as they once were in the wilderness, it may be because they are not so clearly linked to the life that surrounds them and of which they are part. They are present nonetheless, available to imagination, and of the same character.

One December day a few years ago, while on vacation in California, I went with my daughter and a friend to a place called Pool Rock. We drove for a long time over a mountain road, through meadows touched by the first green of the winter rains, and saw few fences or other signs of people. Leaving our car in a small campground at the end of the road, we hiked four miles up a series of canyons and narrow gorges. We lost our way several times but always found it again. A large covey of quail flew up from the chaparral on a slope above us; the tracks of deer and bobcat showed now and then in the sand under our feet. An extraordinary number of coyote droppings scattered along the trail attracted our attention. I poked one of them with a stick, saw that it contained much rabbit fur and bits of bone. There were patches of ice in the streambed, and a few leaves still yellow on the sycamores.

We came to the rock in mid-afternoon, a great sandstone pile rising out of the foothills like a sanctuary or a shrine to which one comes yearly on a pilgrimage. There are places that take on symbolic value to an individual or a tribe, "soul-resting places," a friend of mine has called them. Pool Rock has become that to me, symbolic of that hidden, original life we have done so much to destroy.

We spent an hour or two exploring the rock, a wind- and rain-scoured honeycomb stained yellow and rose by a mineral in the sand. Here groups of Chumash Indians used to come, in that time of year when water could be found in the canyons. They may have come to gather certain foods in season, or to take part in magic rites whose origin and significance are no longer understood. In a small cave at the base of the rock, the stylized figures of headless reptiles, insects, and strange birdmen are painted on the smoke-black-ened walls and ceiling. These and some bear paw impressions gouged in the rock, and a few rock mortars used for grinding seeds, are all that is left of a once-flourishing people.

We climbed to the summit of the rock, using the worn footholds made   20
long ago by the Chumash. We drank water from the pool that gave the rock its name, and ate our lunch, sitting quietly in the cool sunlight. And then the wind came up, whipping our lunchbag over the edge of the rock; a storm was moving in from the coast. We left the rock by the way we had come, and hiked down the gorge in the windy, leaf-blown twilight. In the dark, just before the rain, we came to the campground, laughing, speaking of the things we had seen, and strangely happy.   1978

INVESTIGATIONS

1. In what ways is Haines's memoir an illustration of what the narrator in "My Mother's Clothes: The School of Beauty and Shame" means by "one was constructed by one's images"?
2. Look back at your response to "Write Before Reading." How can the episodes you narrated be thought of as what Haines calls "stations on the journey"?
3. Haines claims that in the Yuma Indians' ability to move

> without effort from waking into dreaming life . . . must be a kind of radiance, a very old and deep assurance that life has continuity and meaning, that things are somehow in place. It is the journey resolved into one endless present. (p. 106)

What might the speaker in Lawrence Joseph's "Driving Again" think of this?
4. In paragraph 12, Haines says that in making journeys "we would always hope to find *something* or *someone,* however unexpected and unprepared for." How do the journeys he describes in this memoir fit this conception of a journey?

LUCIA MARIA PERILLO

The Northside at Seven

Gray-sulphured light, having risen early this morning
in the west, over the stacks of Solvay, has by now
wafted across the lake and landed here on Lodi Street
where it anoints each particular with the general grace
of decay: the staggering rowhouses, the magazines flapping   5
from the gutter like broken skin, the red Dodge sedan
parked across the street from where I'm hunched in the pickup.
The Dodge's driver was ahead of me at the counter

LUCIA MARIA PERILLO (b. 1958) grew up in Irvington, New York, was educated at McGill University (Montreal) and Syracuse University, and worked for five years in the U.S. Fish and Wildlife Service. Of "The Northside at Seven," she says, "Like many second- and third-generation children, I had felt embarrassed by my parents' ethnicity and the poem chronicles the advent of my acceptance of our collective root."

in Ragusa's Bakery, making confession before an old woman
who was filling pastry shells with sweetened ricotta: 10

I put a new roof on her house, he was telling the woman,
but the lady don't pay me. I do a good job; she got no complaint.
But see, a man must hold his head high so I took her car.
The old woman trilled as she stuffed another log of cannoli.
To me, the man said, *She can call the cops if she wanna —*   15
I'll tell 'em I got kids to take care of, I gotta contract.
I shrugged: all the absolution I could bring myself to deliver
before grabbing the white paper sacks the woman slapped down
and walking out the door, leaving the man dropjawed and
unfinished in what he'd needed to tell me. I don't know;   20

there was something about his Sicilian features, his accent,
his whole goddamned hard-luck story that just gnawed on me so,
like those guys who came to unload on my own old man, muttering
Bobby, Bobby, see we got a little problem here Bobby . . .
the cue for women, kids to leave the room. But since then   25
my father has tried to draw me back into that room,
driving me along the tattered Bronx streets of his boyhood,
sometimes lifting his hands from the steering wheel and
spreading them, saying: *Look, these people are paysan,*
you're paysan, nothing you're ever gonna do can change that . . .   30

We'd spend the rest of the day on food, eating spiedini,
the anchovy sauce quenching what has become a chronic thirst
for salt, and shopping for the dense bread made from black
tailings of prosciutto, I forget the name of it now.
I forget so much. I even forget why tears come on the freeway,   35
mornings I drive by these old buildings when bread is cooking —
why? for what? Sometimes I feel history slipping from my body
like a guilty bone, the only way I have to call it back
is to sit here, slumped behind the wheel licking sugar from
my chin, right hand warmed by the semolina loaves riding shotgun,   40

the way my father might have spent his early mornings years ago,
before he claimed the responsibilities of manhood — of marrying
and making himself a daughter who would not be trapped, as he
felt he was, by streets washed over in the slow decay of light.
Making her different than he was. And making her the same.   1989

INVESTIGATIONS

1. Why does the man at the bakery bother the speaker so much? Why does she cry on the freeway?

2. In what sense is the speaker the same as her father? In what sense are you like your father? Your mother?

3. What would John Haines say about the speaker's experience of memory? How do you think the speaker would feel about Haines's claim that "a very old and deep assurance that life has continuity and meaning" comes from crossing and recrossing the boundary between waking and dream?

CONNECTIONS AND ELABORATIONS

1. a. Choose a selection in which someone confronts self-doubt. After carefully noting what caused that person's self-doubt, how the person responded, and how he or she has changed (or not changed) as a result, write an essay in which you compare this person's experience to yours as you told it in response to "Write Before Reading" at the beginning of Part One.

   b. Choose a selection in which someone confirms or strengthens his or her sense of self. After carefully noting what challenged that person, how he or she responded, and what resources he or she called upon to confront the challenge, write an essay in which you compare this person's experience to yours as you told it in response to "Write Before Reading" at the beginning of Part One.

2. Which of the selections most strongly challenged your ideas about how one maintains a healthy sense of self? Write an essay in which you analyze what made that selection so compelling.

3. Write one of the following dramatic scenes:

   a. An argument in which you, the narrator of Bell's "Customs of the Country," and Mr. Cohen (Wideman's "Valaida") try to convince Jessie (Norman's 'night, Mother) not to commit suicide.

   b. A conversation about the necessity of "selling yourself" between you, Rosario Morales ("I Am What I Am"), and Clint Oates (McKnight's "The Kind of Light That Shines on Texas").

   c. An argument in which the narrator of Bell's "Customs of the Country," Jessie (Norman's 'night, Mother), and the narrator of McCann's "My Mother's Clothes: The School of Beauty and Shame" try to convince you that we can never really understand what we do or why.

4. After reexamining the selections, your response to "Write Before Reading," and any other writing or thinking you've done in response to your reading, write an essay in which you analyze the role of misunderstanding in creating a sense of self.

5. Rewrite John Haines's "Moments and Journeys" from Mr. Cohen's (Wideman's "Valaida") point of view. Then, write a 250–500-word essay in which you discuss how Mr. Cohen's personal history influenced what he saw.

6. In McCann's "My Mother's Clothes: The School of Beauty and Shame" the narrator claims that the source of beauty is longing. Write a persuasive essay that establishes the validity of that idea, using evidence from your own life and from at least two of the selections in this book.

PART TWO

IN FAMILIES

It has been said that Americans live in myth, not history, which may be a way of saying that we like stories better than facts, stories that tell us who we ought to be rather than how to be who we are. One of our most powerful myths tells us that the perfect family is a nuclear one: married parents with children, preferably living in suburbia with other nuclear families. Though myths never precisely mirror the "facts," the one about the nuclear family not only gets less true every day but may also obscure other myths that have more compelling, complicated things to say about the pains and pleasures of family life and about what gives that life value.

In this part, you'll read and write about selections that take you inside families as distinct from one another as perhaps they are from your own. You'll travel to a working-class home in the Pacific Northwest in Tess Gallagher's "The Lover of Horses"; see how Rita Dove's "Grape Sherbet" helps a father teach an important lesson; witness the power and cost of forgiveness in Ed Ochester's "Changing the Name to Ochester"; visit a suburbia more menacing than we might like to believe in Bharati Mukherjee's "Fathering"; hear a Vietnam veteran tell his daughter of the pains and joys of life in "Words for My Daughter," by John Balaban; watch a father celebrate his daughter's growing into adolescence in "Circling the Daughter," by Etheridge Knight; see how a Vietnamese woman, her ex-soldier husband, and their daughter make a home in a West Virginia trailer park in Elizabeth Gordon's "On the Other Side of the War: A Story"; watch a young girl wrestle with her and her family's "Devils" in Cynthia Kadohata's short story; witness an unusual ritual in James Masao Mitsui's "Allowance"; attend a wedding at which a Cuban-American family confronts its past and must come to terms with its present in Eduardo Machado's *Broken Eggs*; discover what it takes for a man to "retrain" himself in "After the Deindustrialization of America, My Father Enters Television Repair," by Peter Oresick; share a mother's struggle with her own preconceptions and expectations in order to accept her son's homosexuality in Agnes G. Herman's "A Parent's Journey Out of the Closet"; meet a blind ex–trapeze artist and her daughter in "The Leap," by Louise Erdrich; and fish in a magical chicken yard in Lewis Nordan's "Sugar Among the Chickens."

WRITE BEFORE READING

Take some time to recall memorable family stories, "legends" that may have been handed down for generations. Pick the story that best dramatizes your family's "personality," its particular way of being in the world, and narrate it as fully as you can.

The Lover of Horses

They say my great-grandfather was a gypsy, but the most popular explanation for his behavior was that he was a drunk. How else could the women have kept up the scourge of his memory all these years, had they not had the usual malady of our family to blame? Probably he was both, a gypsy and a drunk.

Still, I have reason to believe the gypsy in him had more to do with the turn his life took than his drinking. I used to argue with my mother about this, even though most of the information I have about my great-grandfather came from my mother, who got it from her mother. A drunk, I kept telling her, would have had no initiative. He would simply have gone down with his failures and had nothing to show for it. But my great-grandfather had eleven children, surely a sign of industry, and he was a lover of horses. He had so many horses he was what people called "horse poor."

I did not learn, until I traveled to where my family originated at Collenamore in the west of Ireland, that my great-grandfather had most likely been a "whisperer," a breed of men among the gypsies who were said to possess the power of talking sense into horses. These men had no fear of even the most malicious and dangerous horses. In fact, they would often take the wild animal into a closed stall in order to perform their skills.

Whether a certain intimacy was needed or whether the whisperers simply wanted to protect their secret conversations with horses is not known. One thing was certain — that such men gained power over horses by whispering. What they whispered no one knew. But the effectiveness of their methods was renowned, and anyone for counties around who had an unruly horse could send for a whisperer and be sure that the horse would take to heart whatever was said and reform his behavior from that day forth.

By all accounts, my great-grandfather was like a huge stallion himself, and when he went into a field where a herd of horses was grazing, the horses would suddenly lift their heads and call to him. Then his bearded mouth would move, and though he was making sounds that could have been words, which no horse would have had reason to understand, the horses would want to hear; and one by one they would move toward him across the open space of the field. He could turn his back and walk down the road, and they would follow him. He was probably drunk my mother said, because he was swaying and mumbling

5

Author of a collection of essays and a book of short stories, TESS GALLAGHER (b. 1943) will publish a sixth collection of poetry, *Moon Crossing Bridge*, in 1992. She traces her beginnings as a writer to fishing trips with her father, during which she'd invent "charm songs and word-hopes to tempt the fish."

all the while. Sometimes he would stop dead-still in the road and the horses would press up against him and raise and lower their heads as he moved his lips. But because these things were only seen from a distance, and because they have eroded in the telling, it is now impossible to know whether my great-grandfather said anything of importance to the horses. Or even if it was his whispering that had brought about their good behavior. Nor was it clear, when he left them in some barnyard as suddenly as he'd come to them, whether they had arrived at some new understanding of the difficult and complex relationship between men and horses.

Only the aberrations of my great-grandfather's relationship with horses have survived — as when he would bathe in the river with his favorite horse or when, as my grandmother told my mother, he insisted on conceiving his ninth child in the stall of a bay mare named Redwing. Not until I was grown and going through the family Bible did I discover that my grandmother had been this ninth child, and so must have known something about the matter.

These oddities in behavior lead me to believe that when my great-grand-father, at the age of fifty-two, abandoned his wife and family to join a circus that was passing through the area, it was not simply drunken bravado, nor even the understandable wish to escape family obligations. I believe the gypsy in him finally got the upper hand, and it led to such a remarkable happening that no one in the family has so far been willing to admit it: not the obvious transgression — that he had run away to join the circus — but that he was in all likelihood a man who had been stolen by a horse.

This is not an easy view to sustain in the society we live in. But I have not come to it frivolously, and have some basis for my belief. For although I have heard the story of my great-grandfather's defection time and again since child-hood, the one image which prevails in all versions is that of a dappled gray stallion that had been trained to dance a variation of the mazurka. So impressive was this animal that he mesmerized crowds with his sliding step-and-hop to the side through the complicated figures of the dance, which he performed, not in the way of Lippizaners — with other horses and their riders — but riderless and with the men of the circus company as his partners.

It is known that my great-grandfather became one of these dancers. After that he was reputed, in my mother's words, to have gone "completely to ruin." The fact that he walked from the house with only the clothes on his back, leaving behind his own beloved horses (twenty-nine of them to be exact), further supports my idea that a powerful force must have held sway over him, some-thing more profound than the miseries of drink or the harsh imaginings of his abandoned wife.

Not even the fact that seven years later he returned and knocked on his   10 wife's door, asking to be taken back, could exonerate him from what he had done, even though his wife did take him in and looked after him until he died some years later. But the detail that no one takes note of in the account is that when my great-grandfather returned, he was carrying a saddle blanket and the black plumes from the headgear of one of the circus horses. This passes by even my mother as simply a sign of the ridiculousness of my great-grandfather's plight — for after all, he was homeless and heading for old age as a "good-for-nothing drunk" and a "fool for horses."

No one has bothered to conjecture what these curious emblems — saddle blanket and plumes — must have meant to my great-grandfather. But he hung them over the foot of his bed — "like a fool," my mother said. And sometimes when he got very drunk he would take up the blanket and, wrapping it like a shawl over his shoulders, he would grasp the plumes. Then he would dance the mazurka. He did not dance in the living room but took himself out into the field, where the horses stood at attention and watched as if suddenly experiencing the smell of the sea or a change of wind in the valley. "Drunks don't care what they do," my mother would say as she finished her story about my great-grandfather. "Talking to a drunk is like talking to a stump."

Ever since my great-grandfather's outbreaks of gypsy-necessity, members of my family have been stolen by things — by mad ambitions, by musical instruments, by otherwise harmless pursuits from mushroom hunting to child-bearing or, as was my father's case, by the more easily recognized and popular obsession with card playing. To some extent, I still think it was failure of imagination in this respect that brought about his diminished prospects in the life of our family.

But even my mother had been powerless against the attraction of a man so convincingly driven. When she met him at a birthday dance held at the country house of one of her young friends, she asked him what he did for a living. My father pointed to a deck of cards in his shirt pocket and said, "I play cards." But love is such as it is, and although my mother was otherwise a deadly practical woman, it seemed she could fall in love with no man but my father.

So it is possible that the propensity to be stolen is somewhat contagious when ordinary people come into contact with people such as my father. Though my mother loved him at the time of the marriage, she soon began to behave as if she had been stolen from a more fruitful and upright life which she was always imagining might have been hers.

My father's card playing was accompanied, to no one's surprise, by bouts of drinking. The only thing that may have saved our family from a life of poverty was the fact that my father seldom gambled with money. Such were his charm and powers of persuasion that he was able to convince other players to accept his notes on everything from the fish he intended to catch next season to the sale of his daughter's hair.

I know about this last wager because I remember the day he came to me with a pair of scissors and said it was time to cut my hair. Two snips and it was done. I cannot forget the way he wept onto the backs of his hands and held the braids together like a broken noose from which a life had suddenly slipped. I was thirteen at the time and my hair had never been cut. It was his pride and joy that I had such hair. But for me it was only a burdensome difference between me and my classmates, so I was glad to be rid of it. What

15

anyone else could have wanted with my long shiny braids is still a mystery to me.

When my father was seventy-three he fell ill and the doctors gave him only a few weeks to live. My father was convinced that his illness had come on him because he'd hit a particularly bad losing streak at cards. He had lost heavily the previous month, and items of value, mostly belonging to my mother, had disappeared from the house. He developed the strange idea that if he could win at cards he could cheat the prediction of the doctors and live at least into his eighties.

By this time I had moved away from home and made a life for myself in an attempt to follow the reasonable dictates of my mother, who had counseled her children severely against all manner of rash ambition and foolhardiness. Her entreaties were leveled especially in my direction since I had shown a suspect enthusiasm for a certain pony at around the age of five. And it is true I felt I had lost a dear friend when my mother saw to it that the neighbors who owned this pony moved it to pasture elsewhere.

But there were other signs that I might wander off into unpredictable pursuits. The most telling of these was that I refused to speak aloud to anyone until the age of eleven. I whispered everything, as if my mind were a repository of secrets which could only be divulged in this intimate manner. If anyone asked me a question, I was always polite about answering, but I had to do it by putting my mouth near the head of my inquisitor and using only my breath and lips to make my reply.

My teachers put my whispering down to shyness and made special accom-   20
modations for me. When it came time for recitations I would accompany the teacher in the cloakroom and there whisper to her the memorized verses or the speech I was to have prepared. God knows, I might have continued on like this into the present if my mother hadn't plotted with some neighborhood boys to put burrs into my long hair. She knew by other signs that I had a terrible temper, and she was counting on that to deliver me into the world where people shouted and railed at one another and talked in an audible fashion about things both common and sacred.

When the boys shut me into a shed, according to plan, there was nothing for me to do but to cry out for help and to curse them in a torrent of words I had only heard used by adults. When my mother heard this she rejoiced, thinking that at last she had broken the treacherous hold of the past over me, of my great-grandfather's gypsy blood and the fear that against all her efforts I might be stolen away, as she had been, as my father had, by some as yet unforeseen predilection. Had I not already experienced the consequences of such a life in our household, I doubt she would have been successful, but the advantages of an ordinary existence among people of a less volatile nature had begun to appeal to me.

It was strange, then, that after all the care my mother had taken for me in this regard, when my father's illness came on him, my mother brought her appeal to me. "Can you do something?" she wrote, in her cramped, left-handed scrawl. "He's been drinking and playing cards for three days and nights. I am at my wit's end. Come home at once."

Somehow I knew this was a message addressed to the very part of me that most baffled and frightened my mother — the part that belonged exclusively to my father and his family's inexplicable manias.

When I arrived home my father was not there.

"He's at the tavern. In the back room," my mother said. "He hasn't eaten   25 for days. And if he's slept, he hasn't done it here."

I made up a strong broth, and as I poured the steaming liquid into a Thermos I heard myself utter syllables and other vestiges of language which I could not reproduce if I wanted to. "What do you mean by that?" my mother demanded, as if a demon had leapt out of me. "What did you say?" I didn't — I couldn't — answer her. But suddenly I felt that an unsuspected network of sympathies and distant connections had begun to reveal itself to me in my father's behalf.

There is a saying that when lovers have need of moonlight, it is there. So it seemed, as I made my way through the deserted town toward the tavern and card room, that all nature had been given notice of my father's predicament, and that the response I was waiting for would not be far off.

But when I arrived at the tavern and had talked my way past the barman and into the card room itself, I saw that my father had an enormous pile of blue chips at his elbow. Several players had fallen out to watch, heavy-lidded and smoking their cigarettes like weary gangsters. Others were slumped on folding chairs near the coffee urn with its empty "Pay Here" styrofoam cup.

My father's cap was pushed to the back of his head so that his forehead shone in the dim light, and he grinned over his cigarette at me with the serious preoccupation of a child who has no intention of obeying anyone. And why should he, I thought as I sat down just behind him and loosened the stopper on the Thermos. The five or six players still at the table casually appraised my presence to see if it had tipped the scales of their luck in an even more unfavorable direction. Then they tossed their cards aside, drew fresh cards, or folded.

In the center of the table were more blue chips, and poking out from my   30 father's coat pocket I recognized the promissory slips he must have redeemed, for he leaned to me and in a low voice, without taking his eyes from his cards, said, "I'm having a hell of a good time. The time of my life."

He was winning. His face seemed ravaged by the effort, but he was clearly playing on a level that had carried the game far beyond the realm of mere card-playing and everyone seemed to know it. The dealer cocked an eyebrow as I poured broth into the plastic Thermos cup and handed it to my father, who slurped from it noisily, then set it down.

"Tell the old kettle she's got to put up with me a few more years," he said, and lit up a fresh cigarette. His eyes as he looked at me, however, seemed over-brilliant, as if doubt, despite all his efforts, had gained a permanent seat at his table. I squeezed his shoulder and kissed him hurriedly on his forehead. The men kept their eyes down, and as I paused at the door, there was a shifting of chairs and a clearing of throats. Just outside the room I nearly collided with the barman, who was carrying in a fresh round of beer. His heavy jowls waggled as he recovered himself and looked hard at me over the icy bottles. Then he disappeared into the card room with his provisions.

I took the long way home, finding pleasure in the fact that at this hour all the stoplights had switched onto a flashing-yellow caution cycle. Even the teenagers who usually cruised the town had gone home or to more secluded spots. *Doubt,* I kept thinking as I drove with my father's face before me, that's the real thief. And I knew my mother had brought me home because of it, because she knew that once again a member of our family was about to be stolen.

Two more days and nights I ministered to my father at the card room. I would never stay long because I had the fear myself that I might spoil his luck. But many unspoken tendernesses passed between us in those brief appearances as he accepted the nourishment I offered, or when he looked up and handed me his beer bottle to take a swig from — a ritual we'd shared since my childhood.

My father continued to win — to the amazement of the local barflies who poked their faces in and out of the card room and gave the dwindling three or four stalwarts who remained at the table a commiserating shake of their heads. There had never been a winning streak like it in the history of the tavern, and indeed, we heard later that the man who owned the card room and tavern had to sell out and open a fruit stand on the edge of town as a result of my father's extraordinary good luck.

Twice during this period my mother urged the doctor to order my father home. She was sure my father would, at some fateful moment, risk the entire winnings in some mad rush toward oblivion. But his doctor spoke of a new "gaming therapy" for the terminally ill, based on my father's surge of energies in the pursuit of his gambling. Little did he know that my father was, by that stage, oblivious to even his winning, he had gone so far into exhaustion.

Luckily for my father, the hour came when, for lack of players, the game folded. Two old friends drove him home and helped him down from the pickup. They paused in the driveway, one on either side of him, letting him steady himself. When the card-playing had ended there had been nothing for my father to do but to get drunk.

My mother and I watched from the window as the men steered my father toward the hydrangea bush at the side of the house, where he relieved himself with perfect precision on one mammoth blossom. Then they hoisted him up the stairs and into the entryway. My mother and I took over from there.

"Give 'em hell, boys," my father shouted after the men, concluding some conversation he was having with himself.

"You betcha," the driver called back, laughing. Then he climbed with his   40
companion into the cab of his truck and roared away.

Tied around my father's waist was a cloth full of bills and coins which
flapped and jingled against his knees as we bore his weight between us up the
next flight of stairs and into the living room. There we deposited him on the
couch, where he took up residence, refusing to sleep in his bed — for fear, my
mother claimed, that death would know where to find him. But I preferred to
think he enjoyed the rhythms of the household; from where he lay at the center
of the house, he could overhear all conversations that took place and add his
opinions when he felt like it.

My mother was so stricken by the signs of his further decline that she did
everything he asked, instead of arguing with him or simply refusing. Instead of
taking his winnings straight to the bank so as not to miss a day's interest, she
washed an old goldfish bowl and dumped all the money into it, most of it in
twenty-dollar bills. Then she placed it on the coffee table near his head so he
could run his hand through it at will, or let his visitors do the same.

"Money feels good on your elbow," he would say to them. "I played them
under the table for that. Yes sir, take a feel of that!" Then he would lean back
on his pillows and tell my mother to bring his guests a shot of whiskey. "Make
sure she fills my glass up," he'd say to me so that my mother was certain to
overhear. And my mother, who'd never allowed a bottle of whiskey to be
brought into her house before now, would look at me as if the two of us were
more than any woman should have to bear.

"If you'd only brought him home from that card room," she said again
and again. "Maybe it wouldn't have come to this."

This included the fact that my father had radically altered his diet. He   45
lived only on greens. If it was green he would eat it. By my mother's reckoning,
the reason for his change of diet was that if he stopped eating what he usually
ate, death would think it wasn't him and go look for somebody else.

Another request my father made was asking my mother to sweep the
doorway after anyone came in or went out.

"To make sure death wasn't on their heels; to make sure death didn't slip
in as they left." This was my mother's reasoning. But my father didn't give any
reasons. Nor did he tell us finally why he wanted all the furniture moved out
of the room except for the couch where he lay. And the money, they could
take that away too.

But soon his strength began to ebb, and more and more family and friends
crowded into the vacant room to pass the time with him, to laugh about stories
remembered from his childhood or from his nights as a young man at the
country dances where he and his older brother would work all day in the
cotton fields, hop a freight train to town, and dance all night. Then they would
have to walk home, getting there just at daybreak in time to go straight to
work again in the cotton fields.

"We were like bulls then," my father would say in a burst of the old vigor,
then close his eyes suddenly as if he hadn't said anything at all.

As long as he spoke to us, the inevitability of his condition seemed easier   50
to bear. But when, at the last, he simply opened his mouth for food or stared
silently toward the far wall, no one knew what to do with themselves.

My own part in that uncertain time came to me accidentally. I found
myself in the yard sitting on a stone bench under a little cedar tree my father
loved because he liked to sit there and stare at the ocean. The tree whispered,
he said. He said it had a way of knowing what your troubles were. Suddenly
a craving came over me. I wanted a cigarette, even though I don't smoke, hate
smoking, in fact. I was sitting where my father had sat, and to smoke seemed
a part of some rightness that had begun to work its way within me. I went
into the house and bummed a pack of cigarettes from my brother. For the rest
of the morning I sat under the cedar tree and smoked. My thoughts drifted
with its shiftings and murmurings, and it struck me what a wonderful thing
nature is because it knows the value of silence, the innuendos of silence and
what they could mean for a word-bound creature such as I was.

I passed the rest of the day in a trance of silences, moving from place to
place, revisiting the sites I knew my father loved — the "dragon tree," a
hemlock which stood at the far end of the orchard, so named for how the wind
tossed its triangular head; the rose arbor where he and my mother had courted;
the little marina where I sat in his fishing boat and dutifully smoked the hated
cigarettes, flinging them one by one into the brackish water.

I was waiting to know what to do for him, he who would soon be a piece
of useless matter of no more consequence than the cigarette butts that floated
and washed against the side of his boat. I could feel some action accumulating
in me through the steadiness of water raising and lowering the boat, through
the sad petal-fall of roses in the arbor and the tossing of the dragon tree.

That night when I walked from the house I was full of purpose. I headed
toward the little cedar tree. Without stopping to question the necessity of what
I was doing, I began to break off the boughs I could reach and to pile them
on the ground.

"What are you doing?" my brother's children wanted to know, crowding   55
around me as if I might be inventing some new game for them.

"What does it look like?" I said.

"Pulling limbs off the tree," the oldest said. Then they dashed away in a
pack under the orchard trees, giggling and shrieking.

As I pulled the boughs from the trunk I felt a painful permission, as when
two silences, tired of holding back, give over to each other some shared regret.
I made my bed on the boughs and resolved to spend the night there in the
yard, under the stars, with the hiss of the ocean in my ear, and the maimed
cedar tree standing over me like a gift torn out of its wrappings.

My brothers, their wives, and my sister had now begun their nightly vigil
near my father, taking turns at staying awake. The windows were open for the
breeze and I heard my mother trying to answer the question of why I was
sleeping outside on the ground — "like a damned fool" I knew they wanted
to add.

"She doesn't want to be here when death comes for him," my mother said, with an air of clairvoyance she had developed from a lifetime with my father. "They're too much alike," she said.

The ritual of night games played by the children went on and on long past their bedtimes. Inside the house, the kerosene lantern, saved from my father's childhood home, had been lit — another of his strange requests during the time before his silence. He liked the shadows it made and the sweet smell of the kerosene. I watched the darkness as the shapes of my brothers and sister passed near it, gigantic and misshapen where they bent or raised themselves or crossed the room.

Out on the water the wind had come up. In the orchard the children were spinning around in a circle, faster and faster until they were giddy and reeling with speed and darkness. Then they would stop, rest a moment, taking quick ecstatic breaths before plunging again into the opposite direction, swirling round and round in the circle until the excitement could rise no higher, their laughter and cries brimming over, then scattering as they flung one another by the arms or chased each other toward the house as if their lives depended on it.

I lay awake for a long while after their footsteps had died away and the car doors had slammed over the good-byes of the children being taken home to bed and the last of the others had been bedded down in the house while the adults went on waiting.

It was important to be out there alone and close to the ground. The pungent smell of the cedar boughs was around me, rising up in the crisp air toward the tree, whose turnings and swayings had altered, as they had to, in order to accompany the changes about to overtake my father and me. I thought of my great-grandfather bathing with his horse in the river, and of my father who had just passed through the longest period in his life without the clean feel of cards falling through his hands as he shuffled or dealt them. He was too weak now even to hold a cigarette; there was a burn mark on the hardwood floor where his last cigarette had fallen. His winnings were safely in the bank and the luck that was to have saved him had gone back to that place luck goes to when it is finished with us.

So this is what it comes to, I thought, and listened to the wind as it mixed gradually with the memory of children's voices which still seemed to rise and fall in the orchard. There was a soft crooning of syllables that was satisfying to my ears, but ultimately useless and absurd. Then it came to me that I was the author of those unwieldy sounds, and that my lips had begun to work of themselves.

In a raw pulsing of language I could not account for, I lay awake through the long night and spoke to my father as one might speak to an ocean or the wind, letting him know by that threadbare accompaniment that the vastness he was about to enter had its rhythms in me also. And that he was not forsaken. And that I was letting him go. That so far I had denied the disreputable world of dancers and drunkards, gamblers and lovers of horses to which I most surely belonged. But from that night forward I vowed to be filled with the first unsavory desire that would have me. To plunge myself into the heart of my life and be ruthlessly lost forever.   1982

INVESTIGATIONS

1. What facts are given about the men in this family? How would their behavior be explained in your family?
2. What stories of odd, irrational, irresponsible, or even supernatural behavior are told in your family? What do these stories say about what makes your family a family, about what it values and doesn't value? In what ways do the oddities described in "The Lover of Horses" make the narrator's family a family? What traits do your family and hers share?
3. The narrator isn't a smoker or a drinker, yet by the end of the story she has taken on many of the "disreputable" characteristics of her forebears. How do you account for this?
4. Near the end of the story, the narrator describes her nieces and nephews playing in the orchard, "spinning around in a circle, faster and faster until they were giddy and reeling with speed and darkness," playing "as if their lives depended on it." In what ways does each of the characters' lives depend on "speed and darkness," on "laughter and cries brimming over"?

RITA DOVE

Grape Sherbet

The day? Memorial.
After the grill
Dad appears with his masterpiece —
swirled snow, gelled light.
We cheer. The recipe's   5
a secret and he fights
a smile, his cap turned up
so the bib resembles a duck.

Currently professor of creative writing at the University of Virginia, RITA DOVE (b. 1952) has published a collection of stories, a novel, and four collections of poetry. One of them, *Thomas and Beulah*, won the 1987 Pulitzer Prize for Poetry, making Dove the second Black poet so honored. (Gwendolyn Brooks was the first.)

That morning we galloped
through the grassed-over mounds   10
and named each stone
for a lost milk tooth. Each dollop
of sherbet, later,
is a miracle,
like salt on a melon that makes it sweeter.   15

Everyone agrees — it's wonderful!
It's just how we imagined lavender
would taste. The diabetic grandmother
stares from the porch,
a torch   20
of pure refusal.

We thought no one was lying
there under our feet,
we thought it
was a joke. I've been trying   25
to remember the taste,
but it doesn't exist.
Now I see why
you bothered,
father.   1983

INVESTIGATIONS

1. Why did the narrator's father "bother" (lines 29–30)? How might the family in Gallagher's "The Lover of Horses" have benefited from this sort of "bothering"?
2. How is the speaker's realization at the end of the poem "a miracle, / like salt on a melon that makes it sweeter" (lines 14–15)? Describe similar "miracles" your parents have performed.
3. How do you reconcile the speaker's claim that she can't "remember the taste" of her father's grape sherbet with her clear memories of this particular day? What does she mean when she says the taste "doesn't exist"?

ED OCHESTER

Changing the Name
to Ochester

When other grandpas came to Ellis Island
the Immigration people asked "Name?"
and they said "Sergius Bronislaus Jgzywglywcz"
and the officer said, "ok, from now on your name's
Sarge Jerko," and Sarge trundled off to the Lower East Side   5
with a lead cross and a sausage wrapped in a hair shirt
and shared a tiny ill-lit room with eight *Landleute*
and next to a pot of boiling diapers began to carve
yo-yos to peddle on the street and forty years later
was Sarge Jerko, Inc., the Yo-Yo King,   10
but my grandfather was born in this country
(no one living knows anything about *his* parents)
and was an engineer for Con Edison
when he married the immigrant girl
Katherina Humrich who everybody said   15
was once very pretty but when I knew her
had a tight bun, thin German lips
and a nose which came to her chin;
her major pleasures were trips to Coney Island
with friends and frightening little children   20
by jumping out from behind curtains, after which
she cackled hilariously. This is all I know for certain
about my grandfather: 1) his name was Olshevski,
and he changed it shortly after his marriage,
when they were living in an Irish neighborhood,   25
2) while working at Con Ed he bought a yacht
my grandmother said, but my mother said, "Mom,
it was just a boat," 3) he left Katherina
after the fourth son was born, and she lived
in a tiny apartment on Chauncy Street   30
which smelled, even when I was eight,
like boiled diapers, 4) he was reported

Born in New York City in 1939, ED OCHESTER directs the Writing Program at the University of Pittsburgh and is the editor of the Pitt Poetry Series. His most recent collection of poetry is *Changing the Name to Ochester* (1988).

to be handsome and have "a roving eye,"
5) my father and his brothers
all of whom are dead now   35
refused to go to his funeral
and never spoke of him.

This is a poem about forgiving Grandpa
for my not knowing him. And father, if you're
reading over my shoulder, I don't forget how   40
you had three cents spending money a week
and gave two cents to the church, or how
Uncle George, the baby who was everybody's
darling, couldn't go to college because he had
to work to support the family like everybody else 45
and how he became a fire chief in the City of New York,
and how Uncle Will, before he died of cancer,
became an advisor to La Guardia and made a bundle
by being appointed trustee of orphans' estates,
or how Uncle Frank, driving his battery truck   50
once was stopped by Will and La Guardia in their big car
and they chatted, and Uncle Frank — my favorite uncle,
neither Olshevski nor Ochester — still talks
about how his partner Paddy kept saying
"Bejasus, it was the Mayor,"   55
or how, because you had to support your brothers,
you couldn't marry till 30
and were engaged for eight years to my mother
who to this day loves you because you did
what you had to do, and how you built your business 60
going door-to-door selling insurance on Chauncy Street
and Myrtle Avenue till late at night, arguing and collecting
quarters and dimes from people who lived
in tiny apartments smelling of boiled diapers.
Nearly twenty years since your death, father,   65
and long ago I've forgiven you, and I think
you did love me really, and who am I, who was born
as you said, "with everything," to condemn
your bitterness toward your father who left you
with nothing?   70

I don't believe in original sin.
I believe if we're strong enough and gather our powers
we could work it out: not petty human misery,
no windrows of the dead slaughtered
in suicide charges, no hearts shrunken   75

and blackened like meat spitted
and held too long to the fire.
But what everybody knows
is enough to make you laugh
and to break your heart.   80
Grandpa, forty years after your death,
by the power vested in me as the oldest
living Ochester in the direct line I hereby
forgive you. And though you died,
my mother says, penniless and alone   85
with no one to talk to
I hope that when you abandoned your family
you lived well. I hope you sailed your 15-foot
yacht out into Long Island Sound
with a pretty woman on board and a bottle   90
of plum brandy. I hope that when the huge yacht
with "Jerko II" on the stern sailed by
you looked up and said "honey,
you'll be sailing one like that some day"
and that she giggled and said, "yeah,   95
hon, gimme a kiss" and afterward tilted
the bottle, and that the sun was shining
on the Sound, and that you enjoyed
the bitter smell of the brine and
the brilliance of the white scud and   100
that when you made love that night
it was good and lasted
a long, long time.   1987

INVESTIGATIONS

1. In lines 38–39, the speaker announces, "This is a poem about forgiving Grandpa for my not knowing him." How do the details listed in lines 11–37 help the speaker forgive his grandfather? Who else does he forgive? How does his father's bitterness enable the speaker to forgive Grandpa?

2. What resources do the speaker's uncles draw upon after having been left "with nothing"? How do you think his grandmother was able to cope with her abandonment?

3. Write a poem about your family and its history that imitates Ochester's technique. How is writing such a poem an act of forgiveness? How is writing this kind of poem about family history different from writing an essay about the same events? What can such a poem do that an essay can't do?

Fathering

Eng stands just inside our bedroom door, her fidgety fist on the doorknob which Sharon, in a sulk, polished to a gleam yesterday afternoon.

"I'm starved," she says.

I know a sick little girl when I see one. I brought the twins up without much help ten years ago. Eng's got a high fever. Brownish stains stiffen the nap of her terry robe. Sour smells fill the bedroom.

"For God's sake leave us alone," Sharon mutters under the quilt. She turns away from me. We bought the quilt at a garage sale in Rock Springs the Sunday two years ago when she moved in. "Talk to her."

Sharon works on this near-marriage of ours. I'll hand it to her, she really   5
does. I knead her shoulders, and I say, "Easy, easy," though I really hate it when she treats Eng like a deaf-mute. "My girl speaks English, remember?"

Eng can outcuss any freckle-faced kid on the block. Someone in the killing fields must have taught her. Maybe her mama, the honeyest-skinned bar girl with the tiniest feet in Saigon. I was an errand boy with the Combined Military Intelligence. I did the whole war on Dexedrine. Vietnam didn't happen, and I'd put it behind me in marriage and fatherhood and teaching high school. Ten years later came the screw-ups with the marriage, the job, women, the works. Until Eng popped up in my life, I really believed it didn't happen.

"Come here, sweetheart," I beg my daughter. I sidle closer to Sharon, so there'll be room under the quilt for Eng.

"I'm starved," she complains from the doorway. She doesn't budge. The robe and hair are smelling something fierce. She doesn't show any desire to cuddle. She must be sick. She must have thrown up all night. Sharon throws the quilt back. "Then go raid the refrigerator like a normal kid," she snaps.

Once upon a time Sharon used to be a cheerful, accommodating woman. It isn't as if Eng was dumped on us out of the blue. She knew I was tracking my kid. Coming to terms with the past was Sharon's idea. I don't know what happened to *that* Sharon. "For all you know, Jason," she'd said, "the baby died of malaria or something." She said, "Go on, find out and deal with it." She said she could handle being a stepmother — better a fresh chance with some orphan off the streets of Saigon than with my twins from Rochester. My

Author of three novels, two books of nonfiction, and two collections of short stories, BHARATI MUKHERJEE was born in 1940 and raised in Calcutta, India. She lived from 1968 to 1980 in Montreal, Quebec, Canada, and now lives in Saratoga Springs, New York. Her collection *The Middleman and Other Stories* won the 1989 National Book Critics Circle Award for fiction.

twins are being raised in some organic-farming lesbo commune. Their mother breeds Nubian goats for a living. "Come get in bed with us, baby. Let Dad feel your forehead. You burning up with fever?"

"She isn't hungry, I think she's sick," I tell Sharon, but she's already tugging her sleeping mask back on. "I think she's just letting us know she hurts."

I hold my arms out wide for Eng to run into. If I could, I'd suck the virus right out of her. In the jungle, VC mamas used to do that. Some nights we'd steal right up to a hootch — just a few of us intense sons of bitches on some special mission — and the women would be at their mumbo jumbo. They'd be sticking coins and amulets in napalm burns.

"I'm hungry, Dad." It comes out as a moan. Okay, she doesn't run into my arms, but at least she's come as far in as the foot of our bed. "Dad, let's go down to the kitchen. Just you and me."

I am about to let that pass though I can feel Sharon's body go into weird little jerks and twitches when my baby adds with emphatic viciousness, "Not her, Dad. We don't want her with us in the kitchen."

"She loves you," I protest. Love — not spite — makes Eng so territorial; that's what I want to explain to Sharon. She's a sick, frightened, foreign kid, for Chrissake. "Don't you, Sharon? Sharon's concerned about you."

But Sharon turns over on her stomach. "You know what's wrong with you, Jase? You can't admit you're being manipulated. You can't cut through the 'frightened-foreign-kid' shit."

Eng moves closer. She comes up to the side of my bed, but doesn't touch the hand I'm holding out. She's a fighter.

"I feel fire-hot, Dad. My bones feel pain."

"Sharon?" I want to deserve this woman. "Sharon, I'm so sorry." It isn't anybody's fault. You need uppers to get through peace times, too.

"Dad. Let's go. Chop-chop."

"You're too sick to keep food down, baby. Curl up in here. Just for a bit?"

"I'd throw up, Dad."

"I'll carry you back to your room. I'll read you a story, okay?"

Eng watches me real close as I pull the quilt off. "You got any scars you haven't shown me yet? My mom had a big scar on one leg. Shrapnel. Boom boom. I got scars. See? I got lots of bruises."

I scoop up my poor girl and rush her, terry robe flapping, to her room which Sharon fixed up with white girlish furniture in less complicated days. Waiting for Eng was good. Sharon herself said it was good for our relationship. "Could you bring us some juice and aspirin?" I shout from the hallway.

"Aspirin isn't going to cure Eng," I hear Sharon yell. "I'm going to call Dr. Kearns."

Downstairs I hear Sharon on the phone. She isn't talking flu viruses. She's talking social workers and shrinks. My girl isn't crazy; she's picked up a bug in school as might anyone else.

"The child's arms are covered with bruises," Sharon is saying. "Nothing major. They look like . . . well, they're sort of tiny circles and welts." There's nothing for a while. Then she says, "Christ! no, Jason can't do enough for her! That's not what I'm saying! What's happening to this country? You think we're perverts? What I'm saying is the girl's doing it to herself."

"Who are you talking to?" I ask from the top of the stairs. "What happened to the aspirin?"

I lean as far forward over the railing as I dare so I can see what Sharon's up to. She's getting into her coat and boots. She's having trouble with buttons and snaps. In the bluish light of the foyer's broken chandelier, she looks old, harrowed, depressed. What have I done to her?

"What's going on?" I plead. "You deserting me?"

"Don't be so fucking melodramatic. I'm going to the mall to buy some aspirin."

"How come we don't have any in the house?"

"Why are you always picking on me?"

"Who was that on the phone?"

"So now you want me to account for every call and every trip?" She ties an angry knot into her scarf. But she tells me. "I was talking to Meg Kearns. She says Dr. Kearns has gone hunting for the day."

"Great!"

"She says he has his beeper on him."

I hear the back door stick and Sharon swear. She's having trouble with the latch. "Jiggle it gently," I shout, taking the stairs two at a time. But before I can come down, her Nissan backs out of the parking apron.

Back upstairs I catch Eng in the middle of a dream or delirium. "They got Grandma!" she screams. She goes very rigid in bed. It's a four-poster with canopy and ruffles and stuff that Sharon put on her MasterCard. The twins slept on bunk beds. With the twins it was different, totally different. Dr. Spock can't be point man for Eng, for us.

"She bring me food," Eng's screaming. "She bring me food from the forest. They shoot Grandma! Bastards!"

"Eng?" I don't dare touch her. I don't know how.

"You shoot my grandmother?" She whacks the air with her bony arms. Now I see the bruises, the small welts all along the insides of her arms. Some have to be weeks old, they're that yellow. The twins' scrapes and cuts never turned that ochre. I can't help wondering if maybe Asian skin bruises differently from ours, even though I want to say skin is skin; especially hers is skin like mine.

"I want to be with Grandma. Grandma loves me. I want to be ghost. I don't want to get better."

I read to her. I read to her because good parents are supposed to read to their kids laid up sick in bed. I want to do it right. I want to be a good father. I read from a sci-fi novel that Sharon must have picked up. She works in a camera store in the mall, right next to a B. Dalton. I read three pages out loud, then I read four chapters to myself because Eng's stopped up her ears. Aliens have taken over small towns all over the country. Idaho, Nebraska: No state is safe from aliens.

Some time after two, the phone rings. Since Sharon doesn't answer it on the second ring, I know she isn't back. She carries a cordless phone everywhere around the house. In the movies, when cops have bad news to deliver, they lean on your doorbell; they don't call. Sharon will come back when she's ready. We'll make things up. Things will get back to normal.

"Jason?"

I know Dr. Kearns's voice. He saw the twins through the usual immunizations.

"I have Sharon here. She'll need a ride home. Can you drive over?"

"God! What's happened?"

"Nothing to panic about. Nothing physical. She came for a consultation."

"Give me a half-hour. I have to wrap Eng real warm so I can drag her out in this miserable weather."

"Take your time. This way I can take a look at Eng, too."

"What's wrong with Sharon?"

"She's a little exercised about a situation. I gave her a sedative. See you in a half-hour."

I ease delirious Eng out of the overdecorated four-poster, prop her against my body while I wrap a blanket around her. She's a tiny thing, but she feels stiff and heavy, a sleepwalking mummy. Her eyes are dry-bright, strange.

It's a sunny winter day, and the evergreens in the front yard are glossy with frost. I press Eng against my chest as I negotiate the front steps. Where the gutter leaks, the steps feel spongy. The shrubs and bushes my ex-wife planted clog the front path. I've put twenty years into this house. The steps, the path, the house all have a right to fall apart.

I'm thirty-eight. I've let a lot of people down already.

The inside of the van is deadly cold. Mid-January ice mottles the windshield. I lay the bundled-up child on the long seat behind me and wait for the engine to warm up. It feels good with the radio going and the heat coming on. I don't want the ice on the windshield to melt. Eng and I are safest in the van.

In the rearview mirror, Eng's wrinkled lips begin to move. "Dad, can I have a quarter?"

"May I, kiddo," I joke.

There's all sorts of junk in the pockets of my parka. Buckshot, dimes and quarters for the vending machine, a Blistex.

"What do you need it for, sweetheart?"

Eng's quick. Like the street kids in Saigon who dove for cigarettes and sticks of gum. She's loosened the blanket folds around her. I watch her tuck the quarter inside her wool mitt. She grins. "Thanks, soldier."

At Dr. Kearns's, Sharon is lying unnaturally slack-bodied on the lone vinyl sofa. Her coat's neatly balled up under her neck, like a bolster. Right now she

45
50
55
60

looks amiable, docile. I don't think she exactly recognizes me, although later she'll say she did. All that stuff about Kearns going hunting must have been a lie. Even the stuff about having to buy aspirins in the mall. She was planning all along to get here.

"What's wrong?"

"It's none of my business, Jason, but you and Sharon might try an honest-to-goodness heart-to-heart." Then he makes a sign to me to lay Eng on the examining table. "We don't look so bad," he says to my daughter. Then he excuses himself and goes into a glass-walled cubicle.

Sharon heaves herself into a sitting position of sorts on the sofa. "Everything was fine until she got here. Send her back, Jase. If you love me, send her back." She's slouched so far forward, her pointed, sweatered breasts nearly touch her corduroy pants. She looks helpless, pathetic. I've brought her to this state. Guilt, not love, is what I feel.

I want to comfort Sharon, but my daughter with the wild, grieving pygmy face won't let go of my hand. "She's bad, Dad. Send *her* back."

Dr. Kearns comes out of the cubicle balancing a sample bottle of pills or caplets on a flattened palm. He has a boxer's tough, squarish hands. "Miraculous stuff, this," he laughs. "But first we'll stick our tongue out and say *ahh*. Come on, open wide."

Eng opens her mouth real wide, then brings her teeth together, hard, on Dr. Kearns's hand. She leaps erect on the examining table, tearing the disposable paper sheet with her toes. Her tiny, funny toes are doing a frantic dance. "Don't let him touch me, Grandma!"

"He's going to make you all better, baby." I can't pull my alien child down, I can't comfort her. The twins had diseases with easy names, diseases we knew what to do with. The thing is, I never felt for them what I feel for her.

"Don't let him touch me, Grandma!" Eng's screaming now. She's hopping on the table and screaming. "Kill him, Grandma! Get me out of here, Grandma!"

"Baby, it's all right."

But she looks through me and the country doctor as though we aren't here, as though we aren't pulling at her to make her lie down.

"Lie back like a good girl," Dr. Kearns commands.

But Eng is listening to other voices. She pulls her mitts off with her teeth, chucks the blanket, the robe, the pajamas to the floor; then, naked, hysterical, she presses the quarter I gave her deep into the soft flesh of her arm. She presses and presses that coin, turning it in nasty half-circles until blood starts to pool under the skin.

"Jason, grab her at the knees. Get her back down on the table."

From the sofa, Sharon moans. "See, I told you the child was crazy. She hates me. She's possessive about Jason."

The doctor comes at us with his syringe. He's sedated Sharon; now he wants to knock out my kid with his cures.

65

70

75

"Get the hell out, you bastard!" Eng yells. "*Vamos!* Bang bang!" She's   80
pointing her arm like a semiautomatic, taking out Sharon, then the doctor. My
Rambo. "Old way is good way. Money cure is good cure. When they shoot
my grandma, you think pills do her any good? You Yankees, please go home."
She looks straight at me. "Scram, Yankee bastard!"

Dr. Kearns has Eng by the wrist now. He has flung the quarter I gave her
on the floor. Something incurable is happening to my women.

Then, as in fairy tales, I know what has to be done. "Coming, pardner!"
I whisper. "I got no end of coins." I jiggle the change in my pocket. I jerk her
away from our enemies. My Saigon kid and me: We're a team. In five minutes
we'll be safely away in the cold chariot of our van.   1988

INVESTIGATIONS

1. Find evidence to support Sharon's claim that Eng is manipulating Jason.
   What would each of the characters gain from such manipulation?

2. Note the places in the story where Jason blames himself for things gone
   wrong. Then note places where he refuses responsibility for shortcomings
   or takes credit for things gone right. How might this internal struggle
   account for how he acts?

3. At one point Jason thinks of Sharon and Eng as "my women." Locate
   other instances of his thinking of either one or both of them this way.
   How might this explain Eng's actions? Sharon's?

4. Why does Jason end up thinking of Dr. Kearns and Sharon as "our enemies"? What does he think he's rescuing Eng from?

Words for My Daughter

About eight of us were nailing up forts
in the mulberry grove behind Reds' house
when his mother started screeching and
all of us froze except Reds — fourteen, huge
as a hippo — who sprang out of the tree so fast   5
the branch nearly bobbed me off. So fast,
he hit the ground running, hammer in hand,
and seconds after he got in the house
we heard thumps like someone beating a tire
off a rim   his dad's howls the screen door   10
banging open   Saw   Reds barreling out
through the tall weeds towards the highway
the father stumbling after his fat son
who never looked back across the thick swale
of teazel and black-eyed Susans until it was safe   15
to yell fuck you at the skinny drunk
stamping around barefoot and holding his ribs.

Another time, the Connelly kid came home to find
his alcoholic mother getting fucked by the milkman.
Bobby broke a milk bottle and jabbed the guy   20
humping on his mom. I think it really happened
because none of us would loosely mention that
wraith of a woman who slippered around her house
and never talked to anyone, not even her kids.

Once a girl ran past my porch   25
with a dart in her back, her open mouth
pumping like a guppy's, her eyes wild.
Later that summer, or maybe the next,
the kids hung her brother from an oak.
Before they hoisted him, yowling and heavy   30

JOHN BALABAN's most recent books include *Blue Mountain* (1982) and *Words for My Daughter* (1991), collections of poetry, and a novel entitled *Coming Down Again* (1985). Currently professor of English at the Pennsylvania State University, Balaban (b. 1943) taught at the University of Can Tho, South Vietnam, during 1967 and 1968. He served as a conscientious objector with the International Voluntary Services during the Vietnam War.

on the clothesline, they made him claw the creekbank
and eat worms. I don't know why his neck didn't snap.

Reds had another nickname you couldn't say
or he'd beat you up: "Honeybun."
His dad called him that when Reds was little.   35

So, these were my playmates. I love them still
for their justice and valor and desperate loves
twisted in shapes of hammer and shard.
I want you to know about their pain
and about the pain they could loose on others.   40
If you're reading this, I hope you will think,
Well, my dad had it rough as a kid, so what?
If you're reading this, you can read the news
and you know that children suffer worse.

Worse for me is a cloud of memories   45
still drifting off the South China Sea,
like the nine-year-old boy, naked and lacerated,
thrashing in his pee on a steel operating table
and yelling "Dau. Dau," while I, trying to translate
in the mayhem of Tet for surgeons who didn't know   50
who this boy was or what happened to him, kept asking
"Where? Where's the pain?" until a surgeon
said "Forget it. His ears are blown."

I remember your first Halloween
when I held you on my chest and rocked you,   55
so small your toes didn't touch my lap
as I smelled your fragrant peony head
and cried because I was so happy and because
I heard, in no metaphorical way, the awful chorus
of Soeur Anicet's orphans writhing in their cribs.   60
Then the doorbell rang and a tiny Green Beret
was saying trick or treat and I thought oh oh
but remembered it was Halloween and where I was.
I smiled at the evil midget, his map light and night
paint, his toy knife for slitting throats, said,   65
"How ya doin', soldier?" and, still holding you asleep
in my arms, gave him a Mars bar. To his father

waiting outside in fatigues I hissed, "You shit,"
and saw us, child, in a pose I know too well.

I want you to know the worst and be free from it.   70
I want you to know the worst and still find good.
Day by day, as you play nearby or laugh
with the ladies at People's Bank as we go around town
and I find myself beaming like a fool,
I suspect I am here less for your protection   75
than you are here for mine, as if you were sent
to call me back into our helpless tribe.   1989

INVESTIGATIONS

1. Think of the worst thing your parents have had to tell you. To what extent
   was your reaction to this bad news influenced by *how* your parents broke
   it to you? If your parents had told you "the worst" in the way the speaker
   in "Words for My Daughter" does, would you have been "free from it"?
   Would you be able to "still find good"? Why or why not?

2. How is the "protection" the speaker suspects he gets from his daughter
   similar to what Jason gets from Eng in Mukherjee's "Fathering"?

3. In what ways is it cruel to "protect" people from knowledge of the pain
   of life?

ELIZABETH GORDON

On the Other Side
of the War: A Story

I. The Way We Came to America

The way we came to America was this: My father, who was in the Army, made an overseas call to his mom and dad in West Virginia.

"Listen," he said, "I've decided to adopt this poor little Vietnamese baby and bring her to America. What do you think?"

Now, both Grandma and Grandpa were true hillbillies in their lineage, habits, and mental faculties — which means they were as broke, as stubborn, and as sharp as folks can be. Not that my father's story required much genius to be seen right through. A twenty-four-year-old enlisted man wanting to bring home some mysterious oriental infant? They hadn't brought him up *that* good.

"It's all right, Skip," they told him. "You can get married, if you love her, and bring 'em both. Bring 'em both on home."

II. No One Had Expected

No one had expected anything like that to happen, least of all the people it happened to.

My father had been quite prepared to meet and marry a sweet girl with a name like Layuna or Ginny Lee. A girl who hailed from one of the good neighboring towns of Beckley or Rainelle. A girl with a daddy, like his, who liked to work on cars, who'd every once in a while hit the booze and start cursing about black lung. There'd been no Nguyen Ngoc Huong from Saigon in *his* crystal ball.

And my mother never dreamed she'd live in an aluminum house on wheels, or see shaved ice swirling down from the sky. Her kitchen window looked out onto a pasture of cows, who stood utterly still with the weather piling up around their legs. It was a difficult thing for her to understand.

So while my father was out climbing telephone poles for Ma Bell, my mother was in the trailer with me, crying and crying for the cows who had not a plank against the cold.

ELIZABETH GORDON was born in 1964 to an American father and a Vietnamese mother in Saigon (now Ho Chi Minh City) and raised in Tennessee. She received a master's degree in creative writing from Brown University, and she currently works as a free-lance writer in Providence, Rhode Island.

III. Things Got Mixed Up

Things got mixed up sometimes between them. Though it was my father's unshakable belief that Common Sense prevailed in all circumstances, he seemed to forget that Common Sense is commonly rendered senseless whenever it crosses a few time zones.

For example, my mother would constantly confuse "hamburger" with "pancake," presumably because both were round, flat, and fried in a pan. So my father, after asking for his favorite breakfast, would soon smell the juicy aroma of sizzling ground beef coming from the kitchen. Other times, he'd find a stack of well-buttered flapjacks, along with a cold bottle of Coca-Cola, waiting for him at the dinner table.

One morning, before my father left for work, he asked my mother to make corn bread and pinto beans for supper. The result of this request was that my mother spent the remainder of the day peeling, one by one, an entire pound of pinto beans. How could she have known any better?

When my father returned home that night, he found her with ten sore fingers and a pot full of mush. He didn't know whether to laugh or cry, but he kissed her because there was nothing he could say.

IV. The Photograph

The photograph, circa 1965, is somewhat unusual. In the background there is a row of neat, nearly identical frame houses. The street in front of the houses is spacious and clean, as wholesome and as decent as sunshine.

Up a little closer, there is a car. It's a two-tone Chevy with curvaceous fenders, gleaming as though it's just been washed and waxed by hand. The weather looks like Sunday.

In the foreground not unexpectedly, a woman with a small child. The woman is a wife because she wears a gold ring. She is also a mother because of the way she holds her child.

The woman has a slim, dainty figure. Her smile is wide and loose, as though she is close to laughter. Maybe her husband, who is taking her picture, is telling a joke or making a silly face. It seems quite natural that the photographer is the husband. Who else would it be?

But something in the photograph seems not quite right. Strangers often tilt their heads when looking at it, as if it is uncomfortable to view straight up and down. Possibly, it's the incomparable blackness of the woman's hair, or the way it seems forced into a wave it can barely hold. Or maybe it has something to do with the baby's eyes which, though blue, are shaped exactly like the woman's: round at the center, narrow at the corners, and heavy-lidded.

What are eyes like that doing among frame houses and a shiny Chevrolet? It seems a reasonable thing to ask.

V. When I Started School

When I started school there were numerous forms to be filled out. Some of the questions were so simple, I could have answered them myself.

The task belonged to my mother, though. She handled most of the questions　20 with ease, and I liked to watch the way she filled all those boxes and blanks with her pretty handwriting.

There was one question, however, that gave my mother a lot of trouble. Even though it was multiple choice, none of the answers seemed to fit. She decided to ask my father what to do.

He didn't have an answer right away, and for some reason that made him angry. The problem was, I was supposed to be in a race, but he couldn't figure out which one.

Finally, he told my mother to put an "H" in that blank. "For *human* race," he said.

I didn't understand what that meant, back then. But it sounded like a good race to me.　　　　　　　　　　　　　　　　　　　　　　　　　　　1989

INVESTIGATIONS

1. To what extent do you think the narrator exhibits the "true hillbilly" qualities of being "as broke, as stubborn, and as sharp as folks can be" (para. 3)? Which of her mother's qualities do you detect in her telling of the story?

2. Consider the question the narrator asks at the end of section IV: "What are eyes like that doing among frame houses and a shiny Chevrolet?" Why does she think this "a reasonable thing to ask"?

3. In what ways does Skip, the narrator's father, add to the problems caused by racial distinctions when he tells Nguyen Ngoc Huong to "put an 'H' . . . for *human* race" (para. 23) on the school questionnaire?

4. Remember one or two times in your life when what you considered common sense was "commonly rendered senseless." Which of your assumptions were called into question? Which of those assumptions can be traced to your upbringing? To your social class? Your education?

ETHERIDGE KNIGHT

Circling the Daughter

For Tandi

You came / to be / in the Month of Malcolm,
And the rain fell with a fierce gentleness,
Like a martyr's tears,
On the streets of Manhattan when your light was lit;
And the City sang you Welcome. Now I sit,   5
Trembling in your presence. Fourteen years
Have brought the moon-blood, the roundness,
The girl-giggles, the grand-leaps.
We are touch-tender in our fears.

You break my eyes with your beauty: 10
Oouu-oo-baby-I-love-you.

Do not listen to the lies of old men
Who fear your power,
Who preach that you were "born in sin."
A flower is moral by its own flowering.   15
Reach always within
For the Music and the Dance and the Circling.

O Tandiwe, my Beloved of this land,
Your spring will come early and
When the earth begins its humming,   20
Begin your dance with men
With a Grin and a Grace of whirling.
Your place is neither ahead nor behind,
Neither right nor left. The world is round.
Make the sound of your breathing   25
A silver bell at midnight
And the chilling wet of the morning dew . . .

ETHERIDGE KNIGHT (1933–1991) received fellowships from the National Endowment for the Arts and the Guggenheim Foundation, and in 1985 was awarded the Shelley Memorial Award by the Poetry Society of America. His most recent collection of poems is *The Essential Etheridge Knight* (1986).

You break my eyes with your beauty:
Oouu-oo-baby-I-love-you.   1986

INVESTIGATIONS

1. What does the speaker mean by "A flower is moral by its own flowering" (line 15)?
2. What are the similarities between how the speakers in "Circling the Daughter" and Balaban's "Words for My Daughter" address their children? What might each of them say to the narrator of Gordon's "On the Other Side of the War: A Story" about the events in that story?
3. Imagine that you're the speaker's daughter. Write either a poem or brief essay called "Circling the Father."

CYNTHIA KADOHATA

Devils

My mother liked to tell me never to close the door of a closet or an empty room at night, because the devil might grow inside it while you were sleeping. I thought the devil was some sort of fungus that grew the way mold used to grow on old tomatoes in the recesses of our refrigerator. I say "used to" because once my mother became a Christian everything changed. I didn't like that. I didn't like how we now had to dust the furniture daily and dress for dinner, and how we could no longer put our feet on the coffee table. What did all this have to do with religion? Still, I always opened my closet door wide at bedtime. I did not want any devil growing in there. I pictured this devil fungus growing on the tops of my patent-leather Sunday-school shoes, or on the collars of my favorite dresses. That was my big mistake: I thought a devil would grow on the outside of things, not the inside.

Of course, none of this new regimen was what my mother learned at church but her own idea, which she somehow extrapolated from the weekly sermons of our flamboyant minister. My mother became a Christian a month

Cynthia Kadohata (b. 1956), author of the novel *The Floating World* (1989), says, "The most helpful thing I ever heard about writing was advice . . . a composition teacher once gave his . . . students: 'Make a mess, then clean it up.'" Kadohata lives in Los Angeles where she works as a full-time writer. In 1991 she received a creative writing fellowship from the National Endowment for the Arts.

after she and my father divorced, and she remained a Christian for about eight months, until we left the town where we were living — Chesterville, Arkansas — and moved to Chicago. We'd lived in Arkansas for a few years, because my father worked sexing chickens at a hatchery, like most of the other Japanese in town. My parents' marriage was already falling apart when we got to Arkansas, so our years there were unhappy ones. After the divorce, my father moved to Georgia, where he'd found another hatchery job. Despite the divorce, he wanted us to move to Georgia, too, but my mother declined.

With my father gone, my mother needed a job. She got crates of newborn chicks from a friend at a hatchery and practiced separating them — male, female, male, male, female, female — until late at night. My sister, my brother, and I would creep into the garage and watch her practicing in her old clothes. She moved her body in jerks back and forth, and every now and then she paused to wipe her beautiful hair out of her eyes. When the chicks got too old to be of use to her, we would take them on. We cut up worms and bugs to feed them and gave the sick ones water with eyedroppers. After a while almost all of them were sick. We spread them out on newspapers — old Chesterville *Stars* — laid out on the dining-room table, and every morning we checked them for stiffness. The stiff ones we threw out. Each chicken was different, you noticed. Some had brown streaks across their foreheads, some white puffs on their backs. We minded when they died, but we didn't mind giving away the survivors to be eaten; I think in rural areas what you learn early to mind is not death but waste. By the time they were all gone, my mother had already found a different kind of job — in an office — and we went on to other projects.

Around the same time my mother also found a new boyfriend. His name was Mr. Mason. Mr. Mason was a member of the church my mother had just joined, but he wasn't a Christian, in my opinion. Sometimes he told my mother she was stupid or ugly, and once we saw him threaten to hit her. But because he was in the church she trusted him. I, too, felt he possessed a certain authority. I hated it when he called my mother names, but I disliked myself for disliking him, because I thought it was wrong of me.

I thought Mr. Mason's features were off somehow, exaggerated — big hands, big feet, and big, big eyes. My sister, who didn't like him either, said he was handsome, and his feet, hands, and eyes were perfectly normal. Everyone agreed he seemed very strong. Whenever our numerous aunts called, they said my mother should get married again, because we needed a father. I didn't understand this at all. We already had a father. I talked to him on the phone all the time.

Whenever my mother went out with Mr. Mason, the Irvings from next door kept an eye on us. We stayed home, and every so often one of them came over to check on us. My sister, Kate, was a year and a half older than I; Sean was four years younger. I was eight.

One night, my mother returned from an outing with Mr. Mason looking for a fight, and she yelled at us to clean up — we'd been painting at the table. As she yelled, she swung her arms, accidentally sending a container of white paint spinning across the table and splattering to the floor. She looked stricken as she saw the paint being absorbed by the rug, and she ran to her room and didn't come out. Of course, we all thought it was because she had spilled the paint. We wanted to pound on her door and tell her it was OK: "Spill all the paint you want!" Kate knocked and said the paint came out with water — it was no big deal at all. My mother murmured, "OK," but she didn't come out of her room until the next day.

After that, she didn't see Mr. Mason for a couple of weeks, and then suddenly she was seeing him all the time, and all she talked about was Mr. Mason and the church. One day, a traveling revival meeting came to town. The tent was set up near our house. After school on the first day of the revival, Kate and I took our bikes — Sean always rode with me — across the highway from the revival tent. We watched from a parking lot, watched that big gray tent billow and sway with the wind. I don't know what we were expecting to happen. Inside the revival tent, you could hear noises like moaning. Every day on the way to school, Kate and I rode the long way, past the tent, to listen to the moaning. We wondered whether our mother moaned like that in church, or whether she might even be going to the revival and moaning there.

The evening before the tent left, my mother came home late from work with her hair all wet. It scared me. Nearly every day brought some odd change in our lives at home. We sat down to supper in our school clothes, the way we always did lately. While our mother said grace, we tilted our heads down, eyes peering up at her wet hair. My brother had an unbreakable habit of seesawing his chair so that he was resting on just two legs. He often lost his balance and fell over, and we would all jump to check on him. You could be talking to him face to face and all of a sudden he wouldn't be there anymore. I remember that after saying grace my mother told us she had been baptized, and right then Sean fell over with an especially big bang. My mother said, "I've been baptized," and my brother disappeared — crash! So her announcement didn't have quite the effect she'd probably expected.

While I didn't like events at home, I admit I liked going to church. I liked singing the hymns, which I got very emotional about, and I liked the way the minister shouted during sermons. Sometimes he walked back and forth with his hands on his heart and pretended he was dying. The minister, who was friendly with Mr. Mason, liked my mother. He was so pleased to have her in the church and she could be so charming that he gave her a set of keys so we could go into the church whenever it wasn't in use. There was a dusty back room with a piano, and we took lessons there. We brought sandwiches for lunch and sat and listened to each other practice — songs about birthday parties, baseball, kangaroos, and rabbits. All my friends from school owned pianos, and now I felt we did, too.

Most of the back rooms smelled of dust. One room I especially liked was full of supplies for the church like notebooks, pencils, erasers, and chalk. Every time I ran out of school supplies, I felt a little sad, so I was happy in the supply room, with its evidence that the world had plenty of all those things I would need again and again every year into the foreseeable future.

Another room I liked was filled with assorted junk — piles of old papers, a few shadeless lamps, an old desk. I liked it because it was so dusty that if you fanned the door back and forth the dust flew into the air, sparkling and smoking and swirling. It was as if you could suddenly see molecules and the room were thick with them.

The last thing I liked about church was Sunday-school storybooks. They were so much more fun than regular schoolbooks. I loved the stories, and I loved the beautiful colored pictures. These books, which we wrote our names in and were allowed to keep, were precious to me. Still, I had questions. For instance, why could all those astounding things happen only a long time ago? Why not now? Where was Samson *now*?

I liked the minister, too, but I didn't entirely trust him, partly because he was friends with Mr. Mason and partly because I thought they were both changing our mother and taking her away from us. I was having dreams lately in which everything I saw was a certain color — all red or all yellow or all blue. Sometimes I woke up and opened my eyes and the whole room would be awash in blue, and I would lie there, scared to move, until everything was normal again. That's the way I saw my mother's newfound religion — as if she had turned all blue overnight.

We were really evil. We used to make voodoo dolls, which consisted of pieces of rolled-up tissue stuffed into flat tissue and secured with a rubber band. We would take out my mother's sewing case and stick pins into these dolls, to which we'd taped the names of Mr. Mason and his children. His children were OK, but we disliked them on principle. Actually, I admired how Mr. Mason and his kids could throw rocks so expertly they could hit cans in our front yard from across the road. His kids threatened to throw rocks at me once, but I threatened to throw a curse on them. Usually, Kate refused to participate when Sean and I made voodoo dolls. She said she didn't like the Masons either but it was wrong to try to curse them.

Sean and I were cohorts in everything. I think life was hardest for Sean. I had school, but he didn't, and there were no other kids around who were his age — at least no Japanese kids. All my parents' friends had been part of the tiny cluster of Japanese who lived across town, and none of them had young children. There were a few other Japanese — all men — living in the Chesterville Arms, one of the few apartment buildings in town. These men, who all worked in hatcheries, were divorced, looking for wives from Japan, or too poor to buy houses. There was at that time something a little risqué about living in an apartment in Chesterville. One associated these men with prostitutes and gambling.

On our tiny street, there was just us, the Irvings, and, on our right, a wild family — the Ryans — whom Mr. Mason wouldn't let us talk to. Before, we'd

15

approached them only shyly, sometimes exchanging unusual stones or branches we'd found. One of the girls had gotten pregnant once, and the boys all used swear words and sometimes started small fires in their driveway just for their amusement. I'd always been scared of them, but I envied those kids, too — now more than ever. I was still afraid of them, yet also dizzier and dizzier with desire to know them. I wanted to swear and to eat supper on the front porch every night, the way they did.

The Irvings, our other neighbors, were a couple whose children had grown up and gotten married. Every Christmas, they let us help decorate their tree with beautiful ornaments filled with bubbling lava of intense colors. Everyone in town liked the Irvings, but no one liked the Ryans. Sometimes people in town discussed ways to get them to leave, and the Irvings often spoke wistfully of selling their home and moving to a better area. If Mr. Mason caught us even looking toward the Ryans' house, he would give us a rap on the head. It was very difficult, because I didn't know who was evil, Mr. Mason, the Ryans, or the people in town — or me, for pondering all this every night. I started opening the closet doors wider before I went to sleep. Previously, I'd made sure to open the hall-closet doors a few inches. Now I opened them several feet. One night I heard a cry and a commotion, and everyone in the house jumped out of bed. But it was only that Sean had walked into a door I'd opened wider than usual. When I saw how perplexed he looked, I thought, Poor Sean — he's too young to be worrying about such things as devils. But when I told him I wouldn't open the doors so wide any longer, he said he wanted them like that.

After about half a year of seeing Mr. Mason, my mother announced that she was going to marry him. All her sisters called us and were very proud and excited that it had taken her such a short time to catch another husband. They couldn't wait to come down to Arkansas for the wedding. Whenever any of them visited, they and our uncles took Kate and me bowling every night, which they said would help make us "well-rounded girls," even though I'd never scored higher than fourteen. They pointed out that Mr. Mason owned a dry cleaner's, and a home in a nicer neighborhood than ours. So I knew my mother's sisters were right and I was wrong, but I still didn't like him. We hardly talked to him at all, and it didn't make sense to me to go so suddenly from "Mr. Mason" to "Father" with nothing in between, just as it hadn't made sense to me to go from never thinking about church to thinking about it all the time, the way my mother had months earlier.

I remember a couple of weeks after she told me they were getting married   20
I wanted to talk to someone about it, but no one was around. I called Weather Information, just to hear an adult voice. Chesterville was too small to have its own weather number, so I called long-distance, to St. Louis or Atlanta or somewhere. I sat there listening for a long time. I had a vague awareness of time passing as I listened, the weather repeating itself over and over. I knew I would get in trouble when the phone bill came, but I couldn't stop listening. I loved it when the report changed, without a break, at the hour, and I loved

the comforting monotony, like the sound of steady rain. I daydreamed, I played with my collection of little plastic dinosaurs, I leafed through a book, all with the phone cradled next to my ear. At some point an operator broke in and asked, "What do you want?" I replied, "The weather!," and she said, "OK," and clicked off.

After that I hung up and sat at a window. My brother was playing out back. One of the younger Ryan boys wandered over, and for a while he and Sean played peacefully. Then they got into a fight about something, so I ran outside. When I had reached the yard, they were ineffectually throwing punches at each other. I was still hurrying over to them when something whizzed in front of me. It landed — *whop* — on little Joe Ryan's back, and he sort of flopped over. I remember he took a small hop before he fell, as if he'd just got an electric shock. There was nothing to pad his fall, because the ground was cracked and grassless from drought. My brother and I stood there for a moment, stunned. Then Mr. Mason, who had come to see my mother, walked forward. I was sure Joe Ryan was dead, so I was very surprised when he jumped up and broke into a hard run toward his house. "Hey!" I shouted, meaning to help him, but he ran even harder. There was a blotch of red on the back of his white shirt, from where the rock had hit.

My mother was appalled when she heard about this incident, but it didn't affect her plans to marry Mr. Mason. Strange weeds had begun to grow in the cracks in the back yard, and I thought devils were sprouting up all over. A few days later, I told my mother a lie. I told her that Mr. Mason had slapped me so hard it had sent me flying across the room. She and Mr. Mason sat me down on the livingroom couch, one of them on either side of me, and tried to get me to change my story. Mr. Mason said to make myself at home. He said I could put my feet on the coffee table. They offered me Heath bars — my favorite candy — and coffee ice cream. I was terrified that if I ate some I would accidentally blurt out the truth and then my mother would certainly go ahead and marry Mr. Mason. I wasn't scared that he would hurt one of us, but that he *could*. My father was just as big, but I never thought of him as someone who might hurt people. So I held my ground. In about fifteen minutes we were all shouting at each other, yet somehow in the middle of all the yelling we heard my sister's soft voice say, "I saw it." We looked to the doorway, where she was standing. My sister was the most well behaved of the three of us — the quietest, the smartest, the sweetest. "I saw him hit her," she said. And that was that.

Our house had been packed up for the impending move to Mr. Mason's. Instead, two days later truckers came to take away our things and my mother took Kate, Sean, and me to the Chesterville Arms. She told us that Mr. Hiro-kane, a man we'd met a number of times when he'd worked with my father, was going to look after us while she talked with Mr. Mason. The apartments were shaped like a small motel — a one-story building of single rooms around a courtyard. The outsides were painted white with forest-green awnings. In the middle of the courtyard sat a wooden swing that was very dirty and looked as if no one ever used it. Across the street was a tire store with a huge tire on top of it that looked just like the huge doughnut over the doughnut shop downtown, except the tire was black and the doughnut was brown. Mr. Hirokane rented a small room with one bed and two bureaus. There was a hot plate on one of the bureaus and a TV in a corner. We watched TV while Mr. Hirokane sat outside talking with some other men. Poring over the *Racing Form*, discussing horses, they became quite animated. Every so often, Mr. Hirokane peered through the screen door and said, "How you kids doing in there?" or, "You kids need anything?" or, "Everything OK in there?" Kate shyly said everything was fine and he went back to talking with the men. For dinner, we ate rice with sliced ham, and then we washed dishes in his bathroom sink. Finally, the other men left and he sat outside alone. He kept peeking in to check, but he never came in, as if he thought he would be bothering us. Before ten he told us to go to sleep, and we changed and lay down in his bed. He still sat outside, waiting for my mother's return, I guess. I was closest to the window, and sometimes I peeked out and saw him, still sitting there alone. He had put a jacket on over his T-shirt, and he was leaning against a wooden post, snoring loudly. A *Racing Form* blew across the porch. At some point, our mother returned to take us to a motel. We said thank you to Mr. Hirokane, whom we never saw again, and my mother shook his hand.

The next day we took the main street — the highway — out of Chesterville. It was almost autumn, so the air was cool and tart that morning, and a few trees were tinged orange. When we moved into town, we'd come on the highway, too. I watched out the window as we passed everything we'd passed when we first came: the church, our school, the doughnut shop. I tried to pretend we were going backward in time, to before we came to Chesterville, but then I noticed how the huge brown doughnut, new when we came, was chipped now and weathered.

My brother was examining a map of the country, but he was holding it   25
upside down. I turned it right side up for him, then leaned my head against the window. We were heading for Chicago. That's where all those aunts of ours lived.

                                                                      1989

INVESTIGATIONS

1. In paragraph 18 the narrator says, "It was very difficult, because I didn't know who was evil, Mr. Mason, the Ryans, or the people in town — or me, for pondering all this every night." Who do you think is evil in this story? Why?
2. Why does the narrator's mother want to marry Mr. Mason? Why does the narrator call the long-distance weather number instead of talking to her mother (or her father, for that matter) about the impending marriage?

3. How would this family's situation be different if they were white? If the narrator's mother were a lawyer? If she had become a Buddhist rather than a Christian? If the narrator's father had vanished like the grandfather in "Changing the Name to Ochester"? If the narrator and her brother and sister had more directly confronted their mother about Mr. Mason?

4. Using material derived from as many selections in Part Two as possible, as well as from your own experience, write a 250–500-word essay describing the process you'd recommend for exorcising the narrator's devils.

JAMES MASAO MITSUI

Allowance

I am ten.
My mother sits in a black
rocking chair in the parlor
and tells stories of a country school
surrounded by ricefields   5
and no roads.

I stand in the kerosene light
behind her,
earning my allowance.
A penny   10
for each white hair I pull.   1978

INVESTIGATIONS

1. What "allowances" are given and received in this poem? How might the ritual the poem describes be seen as a duty? How might it be seen as a way of creating intimacy?

2. This poem withholds the details of the stories the mother tells. How does this reticence increase the poem's effectiveness? How does it limit its effectiveness?

A nisei (second-generation Japanese-American) born in Skykomish, Washington, JAMES MASAO MITSUI (b. 1940) has received a National Endowment for the Arts Creative Writing Fellowship and has published three collections of poetry: *Journal of the Sun* (1974), *Crossing the Phantom River* (1978), and *After the Long Train* (1986). He is a high school teacher.

3. Using "Allowance" as a model, rewrite one of the other poems in Part Two, concentrating on paring that poem down to its most vivid and suggestive details.

4. In as brief a space as possible, write a poem that embodies the essence of your relationship with one of your parents. In what ways might explaining this essence be pointless? In what ways might such an explanation be necessary?

EDUARDO MACHADO

Broken Eggs

Characters

SONIA MARQUEZ HERNANDEZ, a
    Cuban woman
LIZETTE, Sonia's daughter, nineteen
    years old
MIMI, Sonia's daughter
OSCAR, Sonia's son

MANUELA RIPOL, Sonia's mother
OSVALDO MARQUEZ, Sonia's ex-
    husband
MIRIAM MARQUEZ, Osvaldo's sister
ALFREDO MARQUEZ, Osvaldo's and
    Miriam's father

Time and Place

A hot January day, 1979. A country club in Woodland Hills, California, a suburb of Los Angeles.

ACT ONE

(A waiting room off the main ballroom of a country club in Woodland Hills, California, a suburb of Los Angeles. The room is decorated for a wedding. Up center, sliding glass doors leading to the outside; stage right, a hallway leading to the dressing room; stage left, an archway containing the main entrance to the room and a hallway leading to the ballroom. A telephone booth in one corner. Two round tables, one set with coffee service and the other for the cake.).

(In the dark, we hear Mimi whistling the wedding march. As the lights come up, Lizette is practicing walking down the aisle. Mimi is

---

Born in Havana, Cuba, in 1953, EDUARDO MACHADO "was a terrible student" in high school, "except in Shakespeare." Although broke when he moved to New York in the late 1970s, Machado's family wouldn't help, so he stopped believing that "family is family and they care about you more than anybody else."

drinking a Tab and watching Lizette. They are both dressed in casual clothes.)

MIMI: I never thought that any of us would get married, after all —

LIZETTE: Pretend you come from a happy home.

MIMI: We were the audience to one of the worst in the history of the arrangement.

LIZETTE: Well, I'm going to pretend that Mom and Dad are together for today . . .

MIMI: That's going to be hard to do if that mustached bitch, whore, cunt, Argentinian Nazi shows up to your wedding.

LIZETTE: Daddy promised me that his new wife had no wish to be here. She's not going to interfere. *(Mimi starts to gag.)* Mimi, why are you doing this.

MIMI: The whole family is going to be here.

LIZETTE: They're our family. Don't vomit again, Mimi, my wedding.

MANUELA *(offstage)*: Why didn't the bakery deliver it?

MIMI: Oh, no!

LIZETTE: Oh my God.

(Mimi and Lizette run to the offstage dressing room.)

MANUELA *(offstage)*: Who ever heard of getting up at 6 A.M.?

SONIA *(offstage)*: Mama, please —

(Manuela and Sonia enter. Sonia is carrying two large cake boxes. Manuela carries a third cake box.)

MANUELA: Well, why didn't they?

SONIA: Because the Cuban bakery only delivers in downtown L.A. They don't come out this far.

(Manuela and Sonia start to assemble the cake.)

MANUELA: Then Osvaldo should have picked it up.

SONIA: It was my idea.

MANUELA: He should still pick it up, he's the man.

SONIA: He wanted to get a cake from this place, with frosting on it. But I wanted a cake to be covered with meringue, like mine.

MANUELA: You let your husband get away with everything.

SONIA: I didn't let him have a mistress.

MANUELA: Silly girl, she ended up being his wife!

SONIA: That won't last forever.

MANUELA: You were better off with a mistress. Now you're the mistress.

SONIA: Please, help me set up the cake. . . . Osvaldo thought we should serve the cake on paper plates. I said no. There's nothing worse than paper plates. They only charge a dime a plate for the real ones and twenty dollars for the person who cuts it. I never saw a paper plate till I came to the USA.

MANUELA: She used witchcraft to take your husband away, and you did nothing.

SONIA: I will.

MANUELA: Then put powder in his drinks, like the lady told you to do.

SONIA: I won't need magic to get him back, Mama, don't put powders in his drink. It'll give him indigestion.

MANUELA: Don't worry.

SONIA: Swear to me. On my father's grave.

(*The cake is now assembled.*)

MANUELA: I swear by the Virgin Mary, Saint Teresa my patron saint, and all the Saints, that I will not put anything into your husband's food . . . as long as his slut does not show up. Here. (*She hands Sonia a little bottle.*)

SONIA: No.

MANUELA: In case you need it.

SONIA: I won't.

MANUELA: You might want it later. It also gives you diarrhea for at least three months. For love, you kiss the bottle, and thank the Virgin Mary. For diarrhea, you do the sign of the cross twice.

SONIA: All right.

MANUELA: If your father was alive, he'd shoot him for you.

SONIA: That's true.

MANUELA: Help me roll the cake out.

SONIA: No. They'll do it. They're getting the room ready now. They don't want us in there. We wait here — the groom's family across the way.

MANUELA: The Jews.

SONIA: The Rifkins. Then we make our entrance —

MANUELA: I see —

SONIA (*looks at cake*): Perfect. Sugary and white . . . pure.

MANUELA: Beautiful.

SONIA: I'm getting nervous.

MANUELA: It's your daughter's wedding. A very big day in a mother's life, believe me.

SONIA: Yes, a wedding is a big day.

MANUELA: The day you got married your father told me, "We are too far away from our little girl." I said to him, "But, Oscar, we live only a mile away." He said, "You know that empty acre on the street where she lives now?" I said "Yes." He said, "I bought it and we are building another house there, then we can still be near our little girl."

SONIA: He loved me.

MANUELA: Worshipped you.

SONIA: I worshipped him. He'll be proud.

MANUELA: Where's your ex-husband, he's late.

(*Lizette enters and makes herself a cup of coffee. Sonia helps her.*)

SONIA: So how do you feel, Lizette, my big girl?

LIZETTE: I'm shaking.

MANUELA: That's good. You should be scared.

LIZETTE: Why, Grandma?

MANUELA: You look dark, did you sit out in the sun again?

LIZETTE: Yes, I wanted to get a tan.

MANUELA: Men don't like that, Lizette.

LIZETTE: How do you know?

SONIA: Mama, people like tans in America.

MANUELA: Men like women with white skin.

LIZETTE: That's a lie. They don't.

MANUELA: Don't talk back to me like that.

SONIA: No fights today, please, no fights. Lizette, tell her you're sorry. I'm nervous. I don't want to get a migraine, I want to enjoy today.

LIZETTE: Give me a kiss, Grandma. *(They kiss.)* Everything looks so good.

SONIA: It should — eight thousand dollars.

MANUELA: We spent more on your wedding and that was twenty-nine years ago. He should spend money on his daughter.

SONIA: He tries. He's just weak.

MANUELA: Don't defend him.

SONIA: I'm not.

MANUELA: Hate him. Curse him.

SONIA: I love him.

MANUELA: Sonia! Control yourself.

LIZETTE: He's probably scared to see everybody.

MANUELA: Good, the bastard.

(Lizette exits to dressing room.)

SONIA: Did I do a good job? Are you pleased by how it looks? *(She looks at the corsages and boutonnieres on a table.)* Purples, pinks, and white ribbons . . . tulle. Mama, Alfredo, Pedro. . . . No, not Pedro's . . . Oscar's . . . He just looks like Pedro. Pedro! He got lost. He lost himself and then we lost him.

MANUELA: Sonia!

SONIA: I'll pin yours on, Mama.

MANUELA: Later, it'll wilt if you pin it now.

(Miriam enters. She is wearing a beige suit and a string of pearls.)

SONIA: Miriam, you're here on time. Thank you, Miriam.

MIRIAM: Sonia, look. *(Points at pearls.)* They don't match. That means expensive. I bought them for the wedding.

MANUELA: Miriam, how pretty you look!

MIRIAM: Do you think the Jews will approve?

MANUELA: They're very nice, the Rifkins. They don't act Jewish. Lizette told me they put up a Christmas tree but what for I said to her?

MIRIAM: To fit in?

MANUELA: Why? Have you seen your brother?

MIRIAM: He picked us up last night from the airport . . .

MANUELA: Did he say anything to you?

MIRIAM: Yes, how old he's getting. . . . That's all he talks about.

MANUELA: Where's your husband?

MIRIAM: He couldn't come: business.

MANUELA: That's a mistake.

MIRIAM: I'm glad I got away.

MANUELA: But is he glad to be rid of you?

SONIA: Mama, go and see if Lizette needs help, please.

MANUELA: All right. Keep your husband happy, that's the lesson to learn from all this. Keep them happy. Let them have whatever they want. . . . Look at Sonia. *(She exits to dressing room.)*

SONIA: Thank God for a moment of silence. Osvaldo this, Osvaldo that. Powder Curse him. Poisons, shit . . .

MIRIAM: Are you all right? That faggot brother of mine is not worth one more tear: coward, mongoloid, retarded creep.

SONIA: Does he look happy to you?

MIRIAM: No.

SONIA: He looks sad?

MIRIAM: He always looked sad. Now he looks old and sad.

SONIA: Fear?

MIRIAM: Doesn't the Argentinian make him feel brave?

SONIA: He'll be mine again. He'll remember what it was like before the revolution. Alfredo and you being here will remind him of that. He'll remember our wedding — how perfect it was; how everything was right . . . the party, the limo, walking through the rose garden late at night, sleeping in the terrace room. I'm so hot I feel like I have a fever.

MIRIAM: "My darling children, do not go near the water, the sharks will eat you up." That's the lesson we were taught.

SONIA: Today I am going to show Osvaldo who's in control. Be nice to him today.

MIRIAM: He left you three months after your father died. He went because he knew you had no defense. He went off with that twenty-nine-year-old wetback. You know, we *had* to come here, but they *want* to come here. And you still want him back?

SONIA: If he apologizes, yes.

MIRIAM: Don't hold your breath. He lets everyone go. Pedro needed him —

SONIA: Don't accuse him of that, he just forgot —

MIRIAM: What? How could he forget. Pedro was our brother.

SONIA: He got so busy here working, that he forgot, he couldn't help him anyway. He was here, Pedro stayed in Cuba, you were in Miami, and I don't think anyone should blame anyone about that. No one was to blame!

MIRIAM: Oh, I'm having an attack . . . *(She shows Sonia her hands.)* See how I'm shaking? It's like having a seizure. Where's water? *(Sonia gets her a glass of water. She takes two Valium.)* You take one, too.

SONIA: No. Thank you.

(Mimi enters, goes to the pay phone, dials.)

MIRIAM: A Valium makes you feel like you are floating in a warm beach.

SONIA: Varadero?

MIRIAM: Varadero, the Gulf of Mexico, Santa Mariá del Mar. It's because of these little pieces of magic that I escaped from the path. I did not follow the steps of my brothers and end up an alcoholic.

SONIA: Osvaldo never drank a lot.

MIRIAM: You forget.

SONIA: Well, drinking was not the problem.

MANUELA *(entering)*: I made Mimi call the brothel to see why your husband's late.

MIRIAM: Where's Lizette?

MANUELA: Down the hall. It says "Dressing Room."

MIRIAM: I got five hundred dollars, brand-new bills. *(She exits.)*

SONIA: The world I grew up in is out of style; will we see it again, Mama?

MIMI *(comes out of phone booth)*: She answered. She said "Yes?" I said "Where's my father?" She said "Gone." I said "Already!" She said "I'm getting ready for. . . ." I said "For what? Your funeral?" She hung up on me. She sounded stoned . . .

MANUELA: Sonia, someday it will be reality again, I promise.

MIMI: What?

SONIA: Cuba. Cuba will be a reality.

MIMI: It was and is a myth. Your life there is mythical.

MANUELA: That's not true. Her life was perfect. In the mornings, after she was married, Oscar would get up at six-thirty and send one of his bus drivers ten miles to Guanabacoa to buy bread from her favorite bakery, to buy bread for his little married girl.

SONIA: At around nine, I would wake up and walk out the door through the yard to the edge of the rose garden and call, "Papa, my bread."

MANUELA: The maid would run over, cross the street, and hand her two pieces of hot buttered bread . . .

SONIA: I'd stick my hand through the gate and she'd hand me the bread. I'd walk back — into Alfredo's kitchen, and my coffee and milk would be waiting for me.

MIMI: Did you read the paper?

SONIA: The papers? I don't think so.

MIMI: Did you think about the world?

SONIA: No. I'd just watch your father sleep and eat my breakfast.

MANUELA: Every morning, "Papa, my bread." *(She goes to the outside doors and stays there, staring out.)*

MIMI: You will never see it again. Even if you do go back, you will seem out of place; it will never be the same.

SONIA: No? You never saw it.

MIMI: And I will never see it.

SONIA: Never say never —

MIMI: What do you mean "Never say never"?!

SONIA: Never say never. Never is not real. It is a meaningless word. Always is a word that means something. Everything will happen always. The things that you feared and made your hands shake with horror, and you thought "not to me," will happen always.

MIMI: Stop it!

SONIA: I have thoughts, ideas. Just because I don't speak English well doesn't mean that I don't have feelings. A voice — a voice that thinks, a mind that talks.

MIMI: I didn't say that.

SONIA: So never say never, dear. Be ready for anything. Don't die being afraid. Don't, my darling.

MIMI: So simple.

(*Miriam enters.*)

SONIA: Yes, very simple, darling.

MIRIAM: What was simple?

SONIA: Life, when we were young.

MIRIAM: A little embarrassing, a little dishonest, but without real care; that's true. A few weeks ago I read an ad. It said "Liberate Cuba through the power of Voodoo." There was a picture of Fidel's head with three pins stuck through his temples.

MANUELA: They should stick pins in his penis.

SONIA: Mama! (*She laughs.*)

MANUELA: Bastard.

MIRIAM: The idea was that if thousands of people bought the product, there would be a great curse that would surely kill him — all that for only $11.99. Twelve dollars would be all that was needed to overthrow the curse of our past.

(*Lizette enters wearing a robe.*)

MANUELA: We should try everything, anything.

LIZETTE: Today is my wedding, it is really happening in an hour, here, in Woodland Hills, California, Los Angeles. The United States of America, 1979. No Cuba today please, no Cuba today.

SONIA: Sorry.

MIMI: You want all the attention.

SONIA: Your wedding is going to be perfect. We are going to win this time.

LIZETTE: Win what?

MANUELA: The battle.

MIRIAM: "Honest woman" versus the "whore."

MIMI: But who's the "honest woman" and who's the "whore"?

MANUELA: Whores can be easily identified — they steal husbands.

MIRIAM: They're from Argentina.

SONIA: They say "yes" to everything. The good ones say "no."

LIZETTE: And we're the good ones.

SONIA: Yes. I am happy today. You are the bride, the wedding decorations came out perfect and we are having a party. Oo, oo, oo, oo, oo . . . *uh.*

(The women all start doing the conga in a circle. They sing. Osvaldo enters.)

Join the line.

LIZETTE: In back of me, Daddy.

MIRIAM: In front of me, Osvaldo.

(They dance. Miriam gooses Osvaldo.)

OSVALDO: First I kiss my daughter — *(He kisses Lizette.)* then my other little girl — *(He kisses Mimi)* then my sister — *(He and Miriam blow each other a kiss.)* — then my wife. *(He kisses Sonia.)*

SONIA: Your old wife.

OSVALDO: My daughter's mother.

SONIA: That's right.

(Miriam lights a cigarette and goes outside.)

MIMI: We were together once, family: my mom, my dad, my big sister, my big brother. We ate breakfast and dinner together and drove down to Florida on our vacations, looked at pictures of Cuba together.

SONIA: And laughed, right?

MIMI: And then Papa gave us up.

OSVALDO: I never gave you up.

MIMI: To satisfy his urge.

MANUELA: Stop right now.

OSVALDO: Don't ever talk like that again.

SONIA: Isn't it true?

OSVALDO: It's more complex than that.

SONIA: More complex — how? No, stop.

LIZETTE: Please stop.

MANUELA: Don't fight.

MIMI: You see, Daddy, I understand you.

OSVALDO: You don't.

MIMI: I try.

OSVALDO: So do I.

MIMI: You don't.

OSVALDO: I'm going outside.

LIZETTE: Come, sit with me.

SONIA: You have to start getting dressed.

LIZETTE: Thank you for making *me* happy.

ACT ONE   OSVALDO: I try.

(*Lizette and Osvaldo exit to dressing room.*)

SONIA: Mimi, no more today. Please, no more.

MIMI: When you're born the third child, the marriage is already half apart, and being born into a family that's half over, half apart, is a disturbing thing to live with.

SONIA: Where did you read that?

MIMI: I didn't read it. It's my opinion. Based on my experience, of my life.

SONIA: We were never half apart.

MIMI: No, but that's what it felt like.

MANUELA: It's unheard of. It's unbelievable —

MIMI: What is she talking about now?

MANUELA: A Catholic does not get a divorce. They have a mistress and a wife but no divorce, a man does not leave everything.

SONIA (*to Mimi*): As difficult as it might be for you to understand, we were together and a family when you were born. I wanted, we wanted, to have you. We had just gotten to the U.S., Lizette was ten months old. Your father had gotten his job as an accountant. We lived behind a hamburger stand between two furniture stores, away from everything we knew, afraid of everything around us. We were alone, no one spoke Spanish. Half of the people thought we were Communist, the other half traitors to a great cause; three thousand miles away from our real lives. But I wanted you and we believed in each other more than ever before. We were all we had.

MIMI: I wish it would have always stayed like that.

SONIA: So do I.

MANUELA: In Cuba, not in California, we want our Cuba back.

MIMI: It's too late for that, Grandma.

MANUELA: No.

MIMI: They like their government.

MANUELA: Who?

MIMI: The people who live there like socialism.

MANUELA: No, who told you that?

MIMI: He's still in power, isn't he?

MANUELA: Because he oppresses them. He has the guns, Fidel has the bullets. Not the people. He runs the concentration camps. He has Russia behind him. China. We have nothing behind us. My cousins are starving there.

MIMI: At least they know who they are.

MANUELA: You don't? Well, I'll tell you. You're Manuela Sonia Marquez Hernández. A Cuban girl. Don't forget what I just told you.

MIMI: No, Grandma. I'm Manuela Sonia Marquez, better known as Mimi Mar-kwez. I was born in Canoga Park. I'm a first-generation white Hispanic American.

MANUELA: No you're not. You're a Cuban girl. Memorize what I just told you.

(Lizette and Osvaldo enter. Lizette is in her bra and slip.)

LIZETTE: My dress, Mama, help me, time to dress.

SONIA: The bride is finally ready, Mama, help me dress her in her wedding dress. Miriam, Mimi, she's going to put on her wedding dress.

(Miriam enters.)

MANUELA: You're going to look beautiful.

SONIA: And happy, right, dear?

LIZETTE: I'm happy. This is a happy day, like they tell you in church, your baptism, your first communion, and your wedding. Come on, Mimi.

(All the women except Sonia exit to dressing room.)

SONIA: That's how I felt. I felt just like her.

OSVALDO: When, Sonia?

SONIA: Twenty-nine years ago.

(Sonia exits to dressing room. Osvaldo goes to the bar and pours himself a double of J&B. Alfredo enters.)

ALFREDO: You the guard?

OSVALDO: No.

ALFREDO: Drinking so early in the morning.

OSVALDO: My nerves, Daddy.

ALFREDO: Nervous, you made your bed, lie in it.

OSVALDO: I do. I do lie in it.

ALFREDO: So don't complain.

OSVALDO: I'm just nervous, little Lizette is a woman now.

ALFREDO: You're lucky.

OSVALDO: Why?

ALFREDO: She turned out to be decent.

OSVALDO: Why wouldn't she?

ALFREDO: In America it's hard to keep girls decent, especially after what you did.

OSVALDO: I never deserted them.

ALFREDO: But divorce, you're an idiot. Why get married twice, once is enough. You can always have one on the side and keep your wife. But to marry your mistress is stupid, crazy, and foolish. It's not done, son. It's not decent.

OSVALDO: And you know a lot about decency?!

ALFREDO: I stayed married.

OSVALDO: Daddy, she loved me. I loved her. We couldn't be away from each other. She left her husband.

ALFREDO: She wanted your money.

OSVALDO: What money?

ALFREDO: To a little immigrant you're Rockefeller.

OSVALDO: Women only wanted you for your money.

ALFREDO: I know. And I knew how to use my position.

OSVALDO: She loves me.

ALFREDO: Good, she loves you — you should have taken her out dancing. Not married her.

OSVALDO: I did what I wanted to do, that's all.

ALFREDO: You did what your mistress wanted you to do. That is all.

OSVALDO: I wanted to marry her. That's why I did it. I just didn't do what my family thought I was supposed to do.

ALFREDO: You're still a silly boy *(Looking at wedding decorations and cake.)* Well, very nice. Sonia still has taste.

OSVALDO: Yes, she does.

ALFREDO: When she was young I was always impressed by the way she dressed, by the way she looked, how she spoke. The way she treated my servants, my guests.

OSVALDO: She was very well brought up.

ALFREDO: Now your new one is common, right?

OSVALDO: She loves me. Respect her, please.

ALFREDO: So did Sonia. The only thing the new one had to offer is that she groans a little louder and played with your thing a little longer, right?

OSVALDO: That's not true.

ALFREDO: Boring you after five years?

OSVALDO: . . . A little.

ALFREDO: Then why?

(Lizette enters. She is dressed in her bride's dress.)

LIZETTE: I'm ready for my photographs, Bride and Father.

OSVALDO: You look better than Elizabeth Taylor in *Father of the Bride.*

ALFREDO: Sweetheart, you look beautiful.

LIZETTE: Thank you. He took pictures of Mama dressing me, putting on my veil. Now he wants pictures of you and me — then Mama, you, and me — then Grandpa, you and me and Miriam — then Mama and me and Grandma — then with Mimi, et cetera, et cetera, et cetera, et cetera; all the combinations that make up my family.

OSVALDO: Are you excited?

LIZETTE: Yes, I am. And nervous, Daddy, I'm so excited and nervous.

SONIA *(enters)*: Time for the pictures, Mimi will call me when he needs me again.

OSVALDO: Do I look handsome?

ALFREDO: Look at this place, beautiful, Sonia, a beautiful job. *(He gives Sonia a little kiss.)*

SONIA: Thank you.

ALFREDO: She knows how to throw parties. Hmmm, Osvaldo, with taste. With class.

OSVALDO: With class.

SONIA: Osvaldo, come here a moment. Pin my corsage. *(Osvaldo goes over to the table with the corsages on it.)* I bought myself a purple orchid. It goes with the dress. I bought your wife the one with the two white gardenias. I figured she'd be wearing white, trying to compete with the bride. She's so young and pure, hmmm . . . *(She laughs.)*

OSVALDO: She's not coming.

SONIA: It was a joke; I was making a little joke. I can joke about it now. Laugh. Did you dream about me again last night?

OSVALDO: Shh. Not in front of Lizette.

SONIA: I want to.

OSVALDO: We spent too much money on this, don't you think?

SONIA: No, I don't. I could have used more. Mama said they spent twice as much on our wedding.

OSVALDO: Did you tell them the exact number of people that RSVP'd so that we don't have to pay money for extra food?

SONIA: Lizette did, I can't communicate with them, my English —

OSVALDO: Your English is fine. I don't want to spend extra money.

SONIA: How much did you spend on your last wedding?

OSVALDO: She paid for it, she saved her money. She works, you know. She wanted a fancy wedding. I already had one. A sixteen-thousand-dollar one, according to your mother.

SONIA: Didn't *she*? Or was she not married to the guy she left for you?

OSVALDO: She was married. She doesn't live with people.

SONIA: Fool. When you got near fifty you turned into a fool; a silly, stupid, idiotic fool.

LIZETTE: No fights today.

(Osvaldo and Lizette start to exit.)

SONIA: I'm sorry. I swear, no fights . . . Osvaldo . . .

OSVALDO: Yes?

SONIA: You look debonair.

OSVALDO: Thank you, Sonia.

ALFREDO: Don't let it go to your head.

OSVALDO: You look magnifique.

SONIA: Thank you, Osvaldo.

(Lizette and Osvaldo exit to ballroom.)

ALFREDO: Don't let it go to your head.

SONIA: He's insecure, about his looks.

ALFREDO: I tried to talk some sense into my son.

SONIA: Today we'll be dancing every dance together, in front of everybody. And I'll be the wife again. Divorces don't really count for Catholics. We're family, him and me.

ALFREDO: When you married him and moved in with us, I always thought you were like brother and sister.

SONIA: No, lovers. Stop teasing me. He's my only friend.

ALFREDO: Even now?

SONIA: Always, Alfredo, forever.

MIRIAM *(enters from ballroom)*: Sonia, your turn for more snapshots — Father, Mother, and Bride.

SONIA: She's happy, don't you think!

MIRIAM: The bride is in heaven.

SONIA: Excuse me, Alfredo, if you want breakfast, ask the waiter.

(Sonia exits. Miriam sits down. Alfredo looks at the coffee and sits down.)

ALFREDO: Go get me a cup of coffee.

MIRIAM: No. Call the waiter, he'll get it for you.

ALFREDO: You do it for me.

MIRIAM: No.

ALFREDO: When did you stop talking to waiters?

MIRIAM: When I started talking to the gardener.

ALFREDO: What a sense of humor! What wit! What a girl, my daughter.

MIRIAM: Ruthless, like her dad.

ALFREDO: Exactly like me; you need to conquer. Go! Make sure it's hot! *(Miriam pours the coffee.)* If I were your husband I'd punish you every night: no money for you, no vacations, no cars, no credit cards, no pills, no maid. The way you exhibit yourself in your "see-through blouses" with no bras and your skimpy bikinis.

MIRIAM *(teasing Alfredo)*: Ooooh!

ALFREDO: How many horns did you put on his head?

MIRIAM: It excites him.

ALFREDO: That's not true.

MIRIAM: He feels lucky when he gets me, that I did not whither like all the other girls from my class, from our country, with their backward ways. Sugar, Daddy?

ALFREDO: Two lumps. No, three, and plenty of milk.

MIRIAM: There's only cream.

ALFREDO: Yes, cream is fine.

MIRIAM: Here, Daddy.

ALFREDO *(takes one sip and puts coffee down)*: What a vile taste American coffee has.

MIRIAM: I'm used to it, less caffeine.

ALFREDO: You did keep in shape.

(Mimi enters from ballroom in her bridesmaid's gown.)

MIRIAM: So did you. Greed and lust keep us in shape.

MIMI: Grandpa, your turn. Both sets of grandparents, the Cubans and the Jews, the bride and the groom.

ALFREDO: How do I look, sweetheart?

MIMI: Dandy, Grandpa, dandy.

(*Alfredo exits.*)

Who do you lust after?

MIRIAM: Your father.

MIMI: Your own brother?!

MIRIAM: I was joking — your father's too old now. Your brother, maybe.

MIMI: You are wild.

MIRIAM: If I would have been born in this country, to be a young girl in this country, without eyes staring at you all the time. To have freedom. I would never have gotten married. I wanted to be a tightrope walker in the circus . . . that's what I would have wanted.

MIMI: I never feel free.

MIRIAM: Do you get to go to a dance alone?

MIMI: Naturally.

MIRIAM: Then you have more freedom than I ever did.

MIMI: How awful for you.

MIRIAM: It made you choke, you felt strangled.

MIMI: What did you do?

MIRIAM: I found revenge.

MIMI: How?

MIRIAM: I'll tell you about it, one day, when there's more time.

MIMI: Can I ask you a question? Something that I wonder about? Did Uncle Pedro kill himself, was it suicide? Did Grandpa have mistresses?

MIRIAM: How do you know?

MIMI: Information slips out in the middle of a fight.

MIRIAM: He drank himself to death.

MIMI: Oh, I thought he did it violently.

MIRIAM: And your grandpa had a whole whorehouse full of wives.

(*Mimi and Miriam laugh.*)

MIMI: I'm like Grandpa. I'm pregnant . . .

MIRIAM: Don't kid me.

MIMI: Aunt Miriam, I am.

MIRIAM: Oh God.

MIMI: What are you doing?

MIRIAM: I need this. (*She takes a Valium.*) Don't you use a pill?

MIMI: With my mother.

MIRIAM: I don't understand.

MIMI: She'd kill me.

MIRIAM: True. Why did you do it?

MIMI: Freedom.

MIRIAM: Stupidity.

MIMI: Will you help me?

(*Oscar enters.*)

MIRIAM: My God, a movie star.

OSCAR: No, just your nephew, Oscar.

MIRIAM: Your hair is combed. You cut your fingernails?

OSCAR: Better than that, a manicure. You two look sexy today.

MIRIAM: Thank you. She's not a virgin . . .

OSCAR: So?

MIMI: I'm pregnant —

MIRIAM: Don't tell him.

OSCAR: Oh, Mimi.

MIRIAM: What are you going to do?

OSCAR: Pretend she didn't say it. Poor Mimi.

MIMI: You're no saint.

OSCAR: I'm not pregnant.

MIMI: Not because you haven't tried.

OSCAR: Oh, I love *you.*

(*Manuela enters.*)

MIRIAM: You better not talk.

MANUELA: You're here. Good.

MIMI: If you tell her, I'll tell her you're a fruit.

OSCAR: I don't care.

MIMI: Swear.

OSCAR: I swear.

MANUELA: You look beautiful. Here, sit on my lap.

(*Oscar sits on Manuela's lap.*)

MIRIAM: He'll get wrinkled.

MIMI: This is revolting.

MANUELA: I promised your mother that we will be polite.

MIMI: The slut is not coming.

OSCAR: Good. A curse on Argentina.

MANUELA: Oscar, if you ever see her, it is your duty to kick her in the ass. But be good to your father today. It's not his fault. We all know that your father is a decent man. We all know that she got control of him with as they say "powders."

MIMI: I think they call it "blowing."

MANUELA: Blowing? She blowed-up his ego, is that what you think?

MIMI: Right.

MANUELA: No. You are wrong. She did it with drugs. But your mother wants you not to fight with your father. She wants him back.

OSCAR: I'll have to react however I feel.

MANUELA: Your mother is weak and she cannot take another emotional scene. And these Jewish people that Lizette is marrying would never understand about witchcraft, after all they don't even believe in Christ.

OSCAR: I can't promise anything.

MANUELA: Today will be a happy day. Lizette is marrying a nice boy, he's buying her a house. And your mother has a plan.

OSCAR: Right . . .

MANUELA: Right, Miriam?

MIRIAM: You're right. But if I ever see that Argentinian.

MANUELA: You're going to be a good girl, right Mimi?

MIMI: I'll do whatever the team decides.

OSCAR: Spoken like a true American.

SONIA *(enters)*: You made it in time for the pictures, thank God.

OSCAR: Do I have to pose with Dad?

SONIA: No fights.

OSCAR: All right. But I'm standing next to you.

SONIA: Thank you. Miriam, Mama, they want more pictures with you. And in ten minutes "The Family Portrait."

MIMI: That'll be a sight.

MANUELA: Is my hair all right?

SONIA: Yes. Here, put on your corsage.

MANUELA: Thank you.

MIRIAM: And for me?

SONIA: The gardenias.

(Miriam and Manuela exit.)

You look neat, Oscar. Thank God. The photographer suggested a family portrait, the entire family. He said it will be something we will cherish forever.

OSCAR: Why?

(Osvaldo enters.)

SONIA: Well, the family portrait will be a record, proof that we were really a family. That we really existed, Oscar. Oscar, my father's name.

OSCAR: I'm glad you named me after him and not Osvaldo.

SONIA: At first I thought of naming you after your father, but then I thought, "That's so old-fashioned, it's 1951, time for something new."

OSCAR: Good for you.

MIMI: What a sign of liberation.

OSVALDO: Oh?!

OSCAR: So . . . continue, Mama.

SONIA: You like the story?

OSCAR: Yes.

SONIA: You, Mimi?

MIMI: Fascinating.

SONIA: Well, and since your grandpa has no son, I named you after him.

OSCAR: I bet he liked that.

SONIA: It made him very happy. I keep thinking he'll show up today. He'll walk in soon, my father. "Papa do you like it?" And he would say . . .

ACT ONE   MIMI: "We have to get back to Cuba."

OSCAR: "We have to fight!"

MIMI: "Where papayas grow as large as watermelons and guayabas and man-
goes grow on trees. How could anyone starve in a place like that?"

OSVALDO: Then someone took it all away.

OSCAR: He had everything. He had pride, honor —

OSVALDO: True but someone took it away.

OSCAR: That doesn't matter.

OSVALDO: Well it does, he lost.

SONIA: You loved him, I know you did, everyone did.

OSVALDO: Yes, right, I did.

OSCAR: He fought and he knew what he believed in. He knew what his life
was about.

OSVALDO: Maybe that's why he wanted to die.

SONIA: No, just a stroke.

(Pause.)

OSCAR: Daddy, do you like my suit?

OSVALDO: Well, it's really a sports coat and pants.

OSCAR: It's linen.

OSVALDO: It'll wrinkle.

OSCAR: I wanted to look nice.

SONIA: It does.

OSVALDO: It doesn't matter.

OSCAR: No, I don't suppose it really does.

OSVALDO: It means nothing.

OSCAR: What means something, Daddy?

OSVALDO: Columns that add up, neatly. Formulas where the answer is always
guaranteed!

OSCAR: Guarantees mean something?!

OSVALDO: The answer. That's what means something.

OSCAR: Then I have a meaningless life.

OSVALDO: Stop it.

OSCAR: I never found any answers.

OSVALDO: Stop your melodrama.

OSCAR: I'm going to pretend you didn't say that. I'm twenty-eight years old
and I refuse to get involved with you in the emotional ways that you used
to abuse our relationship.

MIMI: Time for a Cuba Libre. (She exits.)

OSVALDO: How much did that piece of dialogue cost me?

OSCAR: Let's stop.

OSVALDO: From which quack did you get that from?

OSCAR: From the one that told me you were in the closet.

OSVALDO: What closet?

(Sonia goes to check if anyone's listening.)

OSCAR: It's an expression they have in America for men who are afraid, no, they question, no, who fears that he wants to suck cock.

(*Osvaldo slaps Oscar.*)

OSVALDO: Control yourself, learn to control your tongue!

OSCAR: Did that one hit home?

OSVALDO: Spoiled brat.

OSCAR: Takes one to know one. God, I despise you.

OSVALDO: I'm ashamed of you, you're such a nervous wreck, all those doctors, all the money I spend.

OSCAR: Thanks, Daddy, I had such a fine example of Manhood from you.

OSVALDO: Bum!

OSCAR: Fool.

SONIA: You're both the same, you're both so selfish, think of Lizette, her fiancé's family, what if they hear this. Quiet!

OSCAR: Leave us alone.

SONIA: No. I belong in this argument too, I'm the mother and the wife.

OSCAR: The ex-wife, Mama.

SONIA: No, in this particular triangle, the wife.

OSCAR (*to Sonia*): Your life is a failure.

OSVALDO: Because of you.

SONIA: Don't say that, Osvaldo. He's our son.

OSVALDO: He's just like you.

SONIA: What do you mean by that?!

OSVALDO: An emotional wreck.

OSCAR: That's better than being emotionally dead.

OSVALDO: I hate him.

SONIA: No. Osvaldo, how dare you! (*She cries.*)

OSCAR: See what you've made, turned her into?!

OSVALDO: It's because of you.

SONIA: I refuse to be the cause of this fight, today we're having a wedding, so both of you smile.

OSVALDO: You're right, Sonia, I'm sorry.

OSCAR: God.

SONIA: I'm going to be with Lizette. You two control yourselves.

OSCAR (*whispers*): Faggot.

(*Sonia exits.*)

Sissy.

OSVALDO: I bet you know all about that?!

OSCAR: Yes, want to hear about it?

(*Alfredo enters.*)

OSVALDO: Not in front of your grandfather.

OSCAR: There's no way to talk to you, you petty bastard. (*He starts to cry.*)

OSVALDO: Exactly like her, crying.

OSCAR *(stops crying)*: Because we were both unfortunate enough to have to know you in an intimate way.

OSVALDO: Other people don't feel that way.

OSCAR: That's because they're made of ice. A lot of Nazis in Argentina.

OSVALDO: Your sister needs me today. I'm going to make sure she's happy. Men don't cry. Now stop it. *(He exits.)*

OSCAR: Right.

ALFREDO: Be careful.

OSCAR: About what?

ALFREDO: You show too much. Be on your guard.

OSCAR: So what?

ALFREDO: You let him see too much of you.

OSCAR: He's my father.

ALFREDO: He's a man first, my son second, your father third.

OSCAR: That's how he feels? He told you that? Did he?!

ALFREDO: Be a little more like me. And a little less like your other grandfather. He's dead. I'm still alive.

OSCAR: He was ill. It wasn't his fault.

ALFREDO: He was a fool.

OSCAR: No. That's not true.

ALFREDO: He was foolish. He trusted mankind. Money made him flabby. He thought if you gave a starving man a plate of food, he thanks you. He didn't know that he also resents you, he also waits. No one wants to beg for food, it's humiliating.

OSCAR: Of course no one wants to.

ALFREDO: So they wait. And when they regain their strength, they stab you in the back.

OSCAR: How can you think that's true?!

ALFREDO: We are the proof of my theory — Cubans. He did it to us — Fidel, our neighbors, everybody. So never feed a hungry man.

OSCAR: You don't really believe that.

MIMI *(enters)*: The picture, Grandpa. Oscar, the family portrait!

ALFREDO: I'm on my way. Comb your hair. Fix your tie. Your suit is already wrinkled.

OSCAR: Real linen does that.

(Alfredo exits with Mimi. Oscar takes out a bottle of cocaine — the kind that premeasures a hit. He goes outside but leaves the entrance door open. He snorts.)

Ah, breakfast.

(Oscar snorts again. Osvaldo enters but does not see Oscar. He goes straight to the bar, comes back with a drink — a J&B double — and gulps it down. He looks at the corsages. We hear Oscar sniffing coke.)

OSVALDO *(to himself)*: White, compete with the bride . . . very funny, Sonia.

SONIA *(enters)*: Osvaldo, we are waiting for you. The family portrait, come.

OSVALDO: No, I can't face them.

SONIA: Don't be silly.

OSVALDO: They love you. They hate me, my sister, my father, my children, they all hate me.

SONIA: They don't. No one hates their own family. It's a sin to hate people in your immediate family.

OSVALDO: They always hated me. Till I was seventeen I thought —

SONIA: That they found you in a trash can, I know, Osvaldo. We need a record, a family portrait. The last one was taken at Oscar's seventh birthday. It's time for a new one.

OSVALDO: You don't need me.

SONIA: It wouldn't be one without you.

OSVALDO: For who?

SONIA: For everybody. Be brave. Take my hand. I won't bite. *(Osvaldo holds her hand.)* After all, I'm the mother and you are the father of the bride.

OSCAR *(sticks his head in)*: The Argentinian just drove up.

OSVALDO: Liar.

OSCAR: She looks drunk.

OSVALDO: Liar.

OSCAR: What do they drink in Argentina?

SONIA: Behave!

(A car starts honking.)

OSCAR: Sounds like your car.

OSVALDO: How dare she. How can she humiliate me. How can she disobey me.

SONIA: Oscar go out and say your father is posing with his past family. Tell her that after the portrait is taken, she can come in.

OSCAR: But she has to sit in the back.

SONIA: No, I'm going to be polite. That's what I was taught.

OSVALDO: Go and tell her.

OSCAR: Remember Mama, I did it for you. *(He exits.)*

OSVALDO: Thank you. Hold my hand.

SONIA: Kiss me.

OSVALDO: Here?

SONIA: Yes, today I'm the mother and the wife.

(Osvaldo and Sonia kiss.)

OSVALDO: You did a good job.

SONIA: You do like it?

OSVALDO: I mean with our daughters. They're good girls . . . like their mother.

SONIA: They have a good father.

OSVALDO: That's true.

(*Osvaldo and Sonia exit, Oscar reenters.*)

OSCAR: The family portrait? This family. . . . My family. The Father, Jesus
Christ his only son, and the Holy Ghost (*Crossing himself.*) . . . why the
fuck did you send me to this family.

(*Blackout.*)

ACT TWO

(*Afternoon. Offstage, the band is playing "Snow," an Argentinian folk
song, and a woman is singing. Miriam is in the phone booth. Mimi is
looking at the bridal bouquet and pulling it apart. Sonia enters eating
cake.*)

WOMAN'S VOICE (*singing offstage*):
Don't sing brother, don't sing,
I hear Moscow is covered with snow.
And the wolves run away out of hunger.
Don't sing 'cause Olga's not coming.

Even if the sun shines again.
Even if the snow falls again.
Even if the sun shines again.
Even if the snow falls again.

Walking to Siberia tomorrow, oh,
Out goes the caravan,
Who knows if the sun
Will light our march of horror.

While in Moscow, my Olga, perhaps,
To another, her love she surrenders.
Don't sing brothers, don't sing.
For God's sake, oh God, no.

United by chains to the steppes
A thousand leagues we'll go walking.
Walking to Siberia, no.
Don't sing, I am filled with pain.
And Moscow is covered with snow.
And the snow has entered my soul.
Moscow now covered with snow.
And the snow has entered my soul.

SONIA: It's insult to injury an Argentinian song about going to Siberia, Russia.
Moscow is covered with snow . . . what do Argentinians know about
Moscow? I wish she'd go to Siberia tomorrow. (*To Mimi.*) They are

walking a thousand leagues to their exile . . . I took a plane ride ninety-nine miles, a forty-five minute excursion to my doom.

MIRIAM *(to phone)*: No, shit no! Liars.

SONIA: Don't sing, Sonia . . . *(She sings.)* 'cause Moscow is covered with snow, right Mimi?

MIMI: Right.

SONIA: When I first got here this place looked to me like a farm town. Are you happy, dear?

MIMI: I don't think so.

SONIA: No, say yes!

MIMI: Yes.

SONIA: That's good.

MIMI: Ciao!

(Mimi runs to the bathroom to puke. Osvaldo enters.)

SONIA: So, you had to play a song for her?

OSVALDO: She told the band she wanted to sing it. But it's the only Argentinian song they know.

SONIA: Good for the band! Remember when we thought Fidel was going to send us to Russia, to Moscow? Siberia, Siberia, this place is like Siberia!

OSVALDO: It's too warm to be Siberia. *(He kisses Sonia passionately.)* It was a beautiful ceremony. *(He kisses her again.)*

SONIA: Dance with me. Tell them to play a danzón.

OSVALDO: Let's dance in here.

SONIA: She'll get angry? It's our daughter's wedding.

OSVALDO: She's my wife.

SONIA: I was first.

OSVALDO: You're both my wife.

(Osvaldo and Sonia dance.)

SONIA: Before my sixteenth birthday your family moved to Cojimar . . . your cousin brought you to the club.

OSVALDO: You were singing a Rita Hayworth song called "Put the Blame on . . . Me"?

SONIA: No, "Mame". . . . I was imitating her . . . did I look ridiculous?

OSVALDO: No!

SONIA *(starts to do Rita's number, substituting "Cuban" for "Frisco")*:
    Put the blame on Mame, boys
    Put the blame on Mame
    One night she started to shim and shake
    That began the Cuban quake
    So-o-o, put the blame on Mame, boys
    Put the blame on Mame . . .

OSVALDO: You look sexy.

SONIA: I let you kiss me, then you became part of the club.

OSVALDO: On your seventeenth birthday I married you.

SONIA: Well, I kissed you.

OSVALDO: Was I the only one?

SONIA: Yes.

OSVALDO: And by your eighteenth birthday we had Oscar. I should go back to
the party. She'll start looking for me.

SONIA: Tell her to relax. Tell the band to stop playing that stupid song. I want
to dance. I want more Cuban music.

OSVALDO: All right! What song?

SONIA: "Guantanamera."

OSVALDO: They might know "Babalú."

SONIA: That's an American song.

(Manuela and Alfredo enter, in the middle of a conversation. Osvaldo
exits to the ballroom. Sonia goes outside.)

MANUELA: The trouble is Americans are weak . . . they don't know how to
make decisions.

ALFREDO: At least they are happy —

MANUELA: Why?

ALFREDO: Money!

MANUELA: You had that in Cuba, Alfredo, but —

ALFREDO: Look at my son — he has an accounting firm —

MANUELA: He's only a partner.

ALFREDO: He has a Lincoln Continental, a classy car, two beautiful houses,
with pools and —

MANUELA: Don't talk about the prostitute's house in front of me, Alfredo,
please.

ALFREDO: Forgive me.

MANUELA: We knew how to make decisions, we —

ALFREDO: Of course.

MANUELA: Fight who you don't agree with, do not doubt that you are right,
and if they use force, you use force, bullets if you have to. Only right and
wrong, no middle, not like Americans always asking questions, always in
the middle, always maybe. Sometimes I think those Democrats are Communists —

ALFREDO: No, Manuela, you see in demo —

MANUELA: Democracy, Communism, the two don't go together, at least the
Russians know that much. They don't let people complain in Russia, but
here, anybody can do anything. (The band is playing "Guantanamera.")
At last some good music, no more of that Argentinian shit. (She hums
some of the song.)

ALFREDO: That's one of my favorite songs.

MANUELA: Yes, beautiful.

ALFREDO: May I have this dance?

MANUELA: Yes . . . but do I remember how?

MIMI (who has reentered): It'll come back to you, Grandma.

> (Manuela, Alfredo, and Mimi exit to the dance floor. Miriam is still
> sitting in the phone booth, smoking. Sonia enters. Miriam opens the
> phone-booth doors.)

MIRIAM: I just made a phone call to Cuba, and you can.

SONIA: They got you through?

MIRIAM: Yes. The overseas operator said, "Sometimes they answer, but only if
they feel like it."

SONIA: Who did you call?

MIRIAM: My . . . our house. . . . I sometimes think that I live at the same time
there as here. That I left a dual spirit there. When I go to a funeral I look
through the windows as I drive and the landscapes I see are the streets
outside the cemetery in Guanabacoa, not Miami. A while ago I looked out
at the dance floor and I thought I was in the ballroom back home. That's
why I had to call. I miss the floor, the windows, the air, the roof.

SONIA: The house is still standing, though, it is still there.

MIRIAM: But we are not.

SONIA: I saw a picture of it. It hasn't been painted in twenty years, we painted
it last.

MIRIAM: Sonia, she said upstairs he's crying again.

SONIA: You're sending chills up my spine.

MIRIAM: Is it Pedro crying?

SONIA: No, she was trying to scare you. We have to hold on to it, the way we
remember it, painted.

MIRIAM: I think I heard Pedro screaming in the garden before she hung up.

SONIA: No, he's dead, he went to heaven.

MIRIAM: No, he's in hell. If there's a heaven he's in hell. Suicides go to hell.
He was the only one that managed to remain, death keeps him there.
Maybe the house filled with strangers is his hell.

SONIA: Why he did it I'll never understand. Maybe he had to die for us?

MIRIAM: No, he didn't do it for *me*.

SONIA: Maybe that's the way things are, maybe one of us had to die. Maybe
there's an order to all these things.

MIRIAM: There's no order to things, don't you know that by now? It's chaos,
only chaos.

> (Mimi enters.)

SONIA: No, there's a more important reason, that's why he did it.

MIMI: What?

SONIA: This conversation is not for your ears.

MIMI: Why not?

(*Lizette enters.*)

SONIA: Because it isn't, that's all.

LIZETTE: Mama! Daddy started dancing with her and Oscar's whistling at
   them, whispering "Puta, putica."

MIRIAM: The Americans won't understand what they are saying.

LIZETTE: Americans know what "puta" means. My husband is embarrassed.
   Other people get divorces and don't act like this. Tell him he must stop.
   No name-calling in Spanish or in English. This is a bilingual state.

MIMI: No, Mama, don't do it.

MIRIAM: Mimi's right, let them do whatever they want.

SONIA: Right, why should I protect her?

LIZETTE: How about me? Who's going to protect me?

SONIA: Your husband.

MIMI: Tell him to tell them to stop, you've got your husband now, your own
   little family unit.

LIZETTE: Fuck off, Mimi. I'm begging you Mama, please. Just take him to the
   side and tell him to leave her alone, to let her have a good time.

SONIA: To let her have a good time?!

MIMI: I'll take care of it. (*She yells out to the ballroom.*) Hey you slut, Miss
   Argentina. Don't use my sister's wedding for your crap. Come in here and
   fight it out with us!

MIRIAM: Mimi, she's flipping the bird at you. She's gesturing fuck you.

MIMI: Fuck yourself!

LIZETTE: Mama! Stop her! Oh God —

MIMI (*yells to ballroom*): You're just a bitch, lady.

LIZETTE (*starts to cry*): Oh, God, oh, God —

SONIA: In a little while everybody will forget about it —

LIZETTE: Oh God, Mama. Everybody's looking at us. They are so embarrassed.
   You let them ruin my wedding. You promised. I hate you. It's a fiasco. I
   hate you, Mimi.

SONIA: Sorry, promises are something nobody keeps, including me.

LIZETTE: You're such assholes.

SONIA: Everybody's got their faults, learn to live with it!

LIZETTE: You failed me.

MIMI: That was great, Aunt Miriam.

SONIA: I'm sorry.

MIRIAM: Thanks Mimi, it was fun.

OSVALDO (*enters*): How could you . . .

MIRIAM: Careful!

OSVALDO: Help me, Sonia.

SONIA: Osvaldo, I've put up with a lot.

OSVALDO: How about me? I want you and your children to apologize to her.

SONIA: No.

MIMI: Never.

MIRIAM: She should leave the party and let the rest of us have a good time. What the hell is she doing here?

OSVALDO: For my sake, Sonia.

SONIA: I'm sorry, I can't.

OSVALDO: What am I going to do?

SONIA: Who do you love, me?

OSVALDO: Yes.

SONIA: Who do you love, her?

OSVALDO: Yes.

SONIA: So full of contradictions, so confused. I'll go tell her that. He loves both of us, Cuba and Argentina!

OSVALDO: This is not the time to kid me, look at Lizette, she's upset.

LIZETTE: I'll never be able to talk to my mother-in-law again.

MIRIAM: It's your fault, Osvaldo. He never moved from the garden.

OSVALDO: Miriam?! Who never moved from the garden?

MIRIAM: Pedro. He never left the garden.

OSVALDO: None of us have.

MIRIAM: He stayed. He took a razor blade but remained locked forever in our family's garden.

OSVALDO: He was a coward.

MIRIAM: Maybe you are the coward, you keep running away.

OSVALDO: From what?

OSCAR (enters, trying not to laugh): I'm sorry. I behaved badly.

OSVALDO: Tell me, Miriam, from what? (He exits.)

OSCAR: Don't cry Lizette, forgive me? Hmm?

LIZETTE: Oscar, now they're starting to fight about Cuba. I just want to cry. They're going to tell my husband, "Your wife is from a crazy family. Are you sure she's not mentally disturbed?"

MIMI: Are you sure you're not mentally disturbed?

(Mimi and Oscar laugh. Osvaldo reenters.)

OSVALDO: What do I run away from that he faced?

MIRIAM: That we lost everything.

SONIA: Everything, no.

OSVALDO: You think I don't know that?

MIRIAM: Pedro knew. He became invisible but remains in silence, as proof.

OSVALDO: As proof of what?

SONIA: That we are not a very nice family? Is that what you are saying?

OSVALDO: He had nothing to do with us, he was an alcoholic.

SONIA: He killed himself because of our sins.

OSVALDO: No, Sonia, that was Christ, Pedro was a drunk, not a Christ figure.

MIRIAM: Because of our lies, Sonia.

OSVALDO: What lies?

MIRIAM: Why did you desert him? You, his brother, you were the only one he spoke to, the only one he needed.

OSVALDO: He made me sick.

MIRIAM: You were always together, you always spent your days together.

OSVALDO: He was an alcoholic.

MIRIAM: We were all alcoholics.

SONIA: I was never an alcoholic.

MIRIAM: He needed you.

OSVALDO: He was perverted.

MIRIAM: We were all perverted. That's why the new society got rid of us.

OSVALDO: Our mother is not perverted!

MIRIAM: No, just insane.

SONIA: No, she's an honest woman, now your father —

OSVALDO: My father was just selfish, he had too many mistresses.

SONIA: Fifteen.

OSCAR: Fifteen?

MIMI: All at once?

LIZETTE: Who gives a fuck? Everybody in this family is a —

MIRIAM: I'm the one that suffered from that, not you, Osvaldo. You take after Daddy so don't complain. Why did you let Pedro kill himself?

OSVALDO: He wanted too much from me.

MIRIAM: He needed you.

OSVALDO: He wanted my mind, he wanted my . . . , my . . . , he wanted everything.

MIRIAM: You're glad he did it?

OSVALDO: I was relieved.

MIRIAM: He knew too much, ha!

SONIA: Too much of what?

MIRIAM: The perversions.

SONIA: What perversions?

MIRIAM: Too much about his perversions, darling Sonia, you married a corrupted family, you really deserved better.

OSCAR: Uh-huh.

LIZETTE: I'm closing the door.

(*Manuela and Alfredo enter.*)

MANUELA: I'll never forget what he said.

ALFREDO: When?

MANUELA: In 1959, after the son-of-a-bitch's first speech, he said, "That boy is going to be trouble . . . he's full of Commie ideals."

ALFREDO: I must say I did not suspect it. I was so bored with Batista's bullshit I thought, a revolution, good. We'll get rid of the bums, the loafers, but instead, they got rid of us.

MANUELA: I hope he rots. Rot, Fidel Castro, die of cancer of the balls.

ALFREDO: Let's hope.

MANUELA: Then they came. And they took our businesses away, one by one. And we had to let them do it. They took over each of them, one after the other. It took the milicianos three days. I looked at Oscar while they did it, for him it was like they . . . for him, that was his life's work, he felt like . . .

OSCAR: Like they were plucking out his heart. Like they were sticking pins into his brain. Like they were having birds peck out his genitals. Like he was going betrayed.

MANUELA: Yes, that's it.

ALFREDO: I hate myself for helping them, bastards.

MANUELA: All he wanted after that was —

SONIA: To fight back.

OSCAR: Right.

MIRIAM: I still do. I still want to fight somebody!

SONIA: But he did fight back. Till the day he died, he never gave up. Right, Mama?

MANUELA: "We are in an emergency," that's how he put it, "an emergency."

MIRIAM: Daddy. Daddy, I am in an emergency now. I have taken six Valiums and it's only noon.

ALFREDO: Why?

MIRIAM: Because I want to strangle you every time I look at you.

LIZETTE: Quiet, they're going to want an annulment.

MANUELA: My God, Miriam!

OSCAR: Who?

ALFREDO: Why?

MIRIAM: Why?!

LIZETTE: The Jews, they're a quiet people.

ALFREDO: Yes, Miriam, why?

MIRIAM: Why did you send your mistresses' daughters to my school?!

MANUELA: Miriam, not in front of the children.

ALFREDO: Because it was a good school.

MIRIAM: People in my class wouldn't talk to me because of you!

ALFREDO: Sorry.

OSVALDO: Sorry? That's all you have to say to her?! That's the only answer you give?!

ALFREDO: I don't know, what else should I say?

OSVALDO: Why did you not once congratulate me for finishing the university?! Why did you let me drink? Why did you let Pedro drink?

ALFREDO: I never noticed that you drank.

MIMI: Why did you leave my mother, and leave me . . . and never came to see me play volleyball?

OSVALDO: Leave me alone, I'm talking to my father.

MIMI: And who are you to me?

MANUELA: Good girl, good question.

OSVALDO: You? Why did you make your daughter think that the only person in the world who deserved her love was your husband?!

MANUELA: He was strong.

OSVALDO: He got drunk. He was a coward when he died.

OSCAR: No. That's not true.

MANUELA: He was a real man. What are you?

LIZETTE: You mean old hag, don't you ever talk to my dad again like . . .

SONIA: Don't you ever call your grandmother that. She's my mother!

LIZETTE: I'm going back to the wedding. *(She exits.)*

OSCAR: Why did they kick us out?

(Silence.)

OSVALDO: We left. We wanted to leave.

OSCAR: No one asked me.

SONIA: We had to protect you from them.

MIRIAM: That's right.

OSVALDO: They wanted to brainwash you, to turn you into a Communist.

OSCAR: No one explained it to me. You told me I was coming here for the weekend.

OSVALDO: It was not up to you.

SONIA: You were just a child, it was up to us.

OSVALDO: That's right.

MIRIAM: And we made the right decision, believe me.

OSCAR: Miriam, why did you let me be locked out? That day in Miami, November, 1962. The day the guy from the Jehovah's Witnesses came to see you. And you took him to your room to discuss the end of the world.

MIRIAM: It was a joke. I was only twenty. I don't believe in God.

OSCAR: Well, you locked me out. And I sat outside and you laughed at me, and I sat there by a tree and I wanted to die. I wanted to kill myself at the age of ten. I wanted to beat my head against the tree, and I thought, "Please stop working, brain, even they locked me out, even my family, not just my country, my family too." Bastards! Fidel was right. If I had a gun, I'd shoot you. I curse you, you shits. Who asked me?

OSVALDO: The revolution had nothing to do with you. You don't *really* remember it, and believe it or not, it did not happen just for you, Oscar.

OSCAR: Yeah, I didn't notice you damaged.

OSVALDO: I had to go to the market at age thirty-two and shop for the first time in my life.

MIMI: So what?

OSCAR: God.

OSVALDO: And I could not tell what fruit was ripe and what fruit was not ripe. I did not know how to figure that out. I cried at the Food King market in Canoga Park. Some people saw me. *(He cries.)*

OSCAR: Big deal.

OSVALDO *(stops crying)*: And Sonia, you refused to come and help me! You made me go do it alone. And shopping is the wife's duty.

SONIA: I couldn't. I felt weak. I was pregnant with Mimi. I'm sorry, Osvaldo. *(To Oscar.)* I wanted you to live a noble life.

OSCAR: How?

SONIA: I don't know. I taught you not to put your elbows on the table. You had perfect eating habits . . .

OSCAR: What does that have to do with nobility?

SONIA: It shows you're not common. That's noble.

OSCAR: No, Mama, nobility —

SONIA: Yes.

OSCAR: No, nobility has to do with caring about the ugly things, seeing trash and loving it. It has to do with compassion, not table manners. It has to do with thought, not what people think about you.

SONIA: Stop picking on me.

OSCAR: I'm not picking on you.

SONIA: Everybody is always picking on me. I failed, I know I failed.

OSCAR: No, you just don't try. Why don't you try?

SONIA: Try what?

OSCAR: To do something.

SONIA: No.

OSCAR: Why?

SONIA: I'm not some whore that can go from guy to guy.

OSVALDO: Are you talking about my wife?

OSCAR: Try it.

SONIA: Don't insult me. Stop insulting me.

OSCAR: You need somebody.

SONIA: Stop it!

OSVALDO: Leave her alone.

(Osvaldo grabs Sonia. They walk toward the ballroom, then stop. We hear the band playing "Que Sera, Sera.")

MANUELA: I think they're going to dance.

MIRIAM: I want to see the Argentinian's expression.

(Sonia and Osvaldo are now dancing. The others watch. Mimi and Oscar go into the phone booth to snort coke.)

ALFREDO: Leave all three of them alone. (He goes outside to smoke a cigar.)

(Miriam and Manuela walk past Sonia and Osvaldo toward the ball-room.)

MIRIAM: Why are you dancing out in the hall . . . afraid of Argentina?

(Miriam and Manuela exit.)

OSVALDO: I'd like to take a big piece of wood and beat some sense into her. . . . No, I want to beat her to death!

SONIA: She went too far . . . she lost control . . . she gets excited.

OSVALDO: They always lose control. Pedro thought there was no limit . . . that you did not have to stop anywhere . . . life was a whim. . . . But I knew that you have to stop yourself . . . that's being civilized, that's what makes us different than dogs . . . you can't have everything you feel you want . . .

SONIA: He was a tortured soul . . . and you loved him . . .

OSVALDO: My big brother. *(He starts to cry.)*

SONIA: And you tried to help him . . .

OSVALDO: How?

SONIA: The only way you knew how, with affection.

OSVALDO: Affection?

SONIA: Yes, and that's decent.

OSVALDO: Maybe it is. Maybe I am.

(Sonia and Osvaldo kiss. He takes her out to the dance floor. She smiles. Oscar and Mimi come out of the phone booth. Oscar continues to snort cocaine.)

OSCAR: He did it. Well, at least he had the balls to take her out and dance. She won. You see if you have a plan and follow it . . . *(Sniff, sniff.)* Ah, hurray for the American dream.

MIMI: It's pathetic. They're still dancing. Oh God help us, she believes anything he tells her.

OSCAR: She had to endure too many things.

MIMI: What, losing her maid?

OSCAR: They never tell her the truth.

MIMI: And you do? You tell her the truth? Well, I'm gonna tell her.

OSCAR: I think you should get an abortion.

MIMI: Why should I?

OSCAR: To protect her?

MIMI: Why should I protect her?

OSCAR: I don't know. Lie to her. Tell Dad.

MIMI: Never mind. Pour me some more champagne.

(Lizette enters.)

I hope one of those horny Cubans just off the boat is ready to rock and roll.

LIZETTE: No more scenes, Mimi. Dad and Mom are enough.

(Mimi toasts Lizette with champagne.)

MIMI: Arrivederci. *(She exits.)*

LIZETTE: They're out there dancing like they were in love or something —

OSCAR: Maybe they are.

LIZETTE: Never, he's being polite and she's showing off. And the Argentinian is complaining to me. And I don't want any part of any of you.

OSCAR: You don't! You think your husband is going to take you away from all this. Does he know about the suicides, how they drink till they explode

. . . the violence we live with, the razor blades, the guns, the hangings, the one woman in our family who set herself on fire while her three kids watched?

ALFREDO (who has reentered): We are just hot-blooded and passionate, that's all.

OSCAR: Grandpa told me a week before . . . "Oscar," he told me . . . "they'll tell you soon I'm in the hospital. That means that I'm on my way out . . . this life here is ridiculous."

ALFREDO: Oscar Hernández was a fool. That's a fool's kind of suicide, that's what I told you.

OSCAR: A lot of drinks when your blood pressure is high is not a fool's kind of suicide, it's just suicide. Despair, that's always the story of people that get kicked out, that have to find refuge, you and me . . . us.

LIZETTE: No, you. Everybody dies on the day that they're supposed to. Forget about it.

OSCAR: How can I?

ALFREDO: You better teach yourself to.

OSCAR: How can I? Have you taught yourself? Tell me, why do you want to live? For what?

ALFREDO: Because of me . . . here or over there, I still need me!

OSCAR: You don't have any honor.

ALFREDO: Honor for what?

OSCAR: For our country.

ALFREDO: That little island? . . . Look, Oscar, when Columbus first found it there were Indians there, imagine, Indians. So we eliminated the Indians, burned all of them, cleaned up the place. . . . We needed somebody to do the Indians' work so we bought ourselves slaves . . . and then the Spaniards, that's us, and the slaves started to . . . well, you know.

OSCAR: I can only imagine.

ALFREDO: Well, then we started calling ourselves natives. Cubans.

LIZETTE: That's right, a name they made up!

ALFREDO: Right! And we became a nation . . .

OSCAR: A race.

ALFREDO: Yes. And then the U.S. came and liked it, and bought and cheated their way into this little place. They told us (He imitates a Texan accent.) "Such a pretty place you have, a valuable piece of real estate. We will help you!" So, they bought us.

OSCAR: We should have eliminated them!

ALFREDO: Maybe. But, what we did . . . was sell it to them and fight against each other for decades, trying to have control of what was left of this pretty place, this valuable piece of real estate. And a bearded guy on a hill talked to us about liberty, and justice, and humanity and humility — and we bought his story. And he took everything away from everybody. And we were forced to end up here. So, we bought their real estate. Do you know how Miami was built?

LIZETTE: With sand that they shipped in from Cojimar! Right?

ALFREDO: That's right. And your other grandfather could not accept the fact that it was just real estate. So he got drunk when he knew he had high blood pressure. What a fool.

LIZETTE: He tells the truth, Oscar.

OSCAR: And Mama thinks it was her country. And someday she'd go back. And I hoped it was my country. What a laugh, huh?

LIZETTE: If you ever tell Mama this, it'll kill her.

OSCAR: Maybe it wouldn't.

LIZETTE: She can't deal with real life, believe me. I'm her daughter. I know what she's really like.

OSCAR: And you can deal with everything?

LIZETTE: Sure. I grew up here, I have a Jewish name now . . . Mrs. Rifkin, that's my name.

OSCAR: Well, Mrs. Rifkin, I'm jealous of you.

ALFREDO: Time for a dance. I haven't danced with the mother of the groom. *(He exits.)*

LIZETTE: Try to get away, Mrs. Rifkin!

OSCAR: And the new Mrs. Rifkin is running away. You got away.

LIZETTE: Don't be jealous, Oscar. It's still all back here. *(She points to her brain.)*

OSVALDO *(enters)*: One o'clock, Lizette.

LIZETTE: One more dance.

OSCAR: Why do you have to leave so soon?

LIZETTE: It's another two thousand for the entire day.

OSCAR: God.

OSVALDO: God what?

OSCAR: You have no class.

SONIA *(enters)*: Osvaldo, I have to talk to you.

OSVALDO: Why?

SONIA: Please, just do me a favor. I have to talk to you.

LIZETTE: Want to dance?

OSCAR: All right.

(*Lizette and Oscar exit.*)

OSVALDO: What do you want, Sonia? Tell me, sweetheart.

SONIA *(hysterical)*: Don't be angry at me, there's no more wedding cake, we've run out of wedding cake. There's no more, nothing, no more wedding cake.

OSVALDO: That's all right, we should start getting them out. Tell them to start passing out the packages of rice.

SONIA: No, some people are asking for wedding cake. What do we do? What?

OSVALDO: They've had plenty to eat, a great lunch, a salad, chicken cacciatore, a pastry, all they could drink, champagne, coffee. Tell them to pass out the rice, get this over with, and let's go home.

SONIA: At a wedding, wedding cake is something people expect. I can't embarrass the groom's family again. What do we do, what are you going to do?!

OSVALDO: Let's go up to people we know . . .

SONIA: Only Cubans!

OSVALDO: All right, let's go up to all the Cubans we know and ask them not to eat the cake. Then serve it to the Jews. The Cubans won't care.

SONIA: You do it, I can't. I can't face them.

OSVALDO: No, do it, with me, come on.

(Oscar enters. He is about to eat a piece of cake. Sonia grabs it away from him.)

OSCAR: What are you doing?

SONIA: You can't eat it, there's not enough.

OSCAR: Why?

OSVALDO: Just do what your mother says. Please, let's go.

SONIA: You do it.

OSVALDO: You're not coming with me?

SONIA: No, I'm sorry. I can't, I'm too embarrassed.

(Osvaldo exits.)

OSCAR: Okay, give it back to me now.

SONIA: No, take it to that man over there.

OSCAR: Why should I?

SONIA: He didn't get any cake. I think the waiters stole one of the layers. You take it to him. I think his name is Mr. Cohen, the man who's looking at us.

OSCAR: All right. Who?

SONIA (points discreetly): The bald man.

OSCAR: Great.

(Manuela and Miriam enter.)

MANUELA: Oh my God, Jesus Sonia. Osvaldo just told me that we are out of cake.

OSCAR: We are. (He exits.)

MANUELA: We were winning.

SONIA: The stupid waiters cut the pieces too big, Mama.

MANUELA: Americans! This is one of the great follies of my life.

SONIA: Of course, Mama, this is worse than the revolution.

(Manuela goes outside.)

MIRIAM: No, in the revolution people died.

SONIA: They really did, didn't they?

MIRIAM: Real blood was shed, real Cuban blood.

SONIA: I forget sometimes.

ACT TWO   MIRIAM: Only when I'm calm, that's when I remember, when I'm waking up
    or when I'm half asleep . . . at those moments.

SONIA: Let's go out to the dance floor and dance like we did at the Tropicana.

LIZETTE *(enters):* I ripped my wedding dress.

SONIA: Oh well, dear, it's only supposed to last one day. Maybe the next
    wedding you go to, Lizette, will be mine.

LIZETTE: Who did you find, Mama?

SONIA: Your father.

LIZETTE: Mama, Daddy can't afford another wife.

SONIA: I'm not another wife, Lizette.

LIZETTE: I hope you are right.

MIRIAM: Wait a minute. *(She gives Lizette five hundred dollars.)* In case you
    decide you need something else when you are on your honeymoon.

LIZETTE: Another five hundred. I think we have three thousand dollars in cash.

*(Lizette exits to dressing room. Miriam lights two cigarettes. She gives
one to Sonia.)*

MIRIAM: Let's go. Remember when we thought Fidel looked sexy.

SONIA: Shh.

*(Miriam and Sonia sashay off to the ballroom. Osvaldo and Alfredo
enter. Osvaldo is eating a big piece of cake.)*

ALFREDO: All women are hysterical.

OSVALDO: I got out there, took the cake from the Cubans, who were outraged.
    A couple of them called me a Jew. I took it to the Jews and they were as
    happy as can be. I offered them the cake but nobody wanted any. She
    made me go through all that for nothing.

ALFREDO: They were being polite, Jews don't like to appear greedy.

OSVALDO *(eats the cake):* Well it's delicious.

ALFREDO: It's Cuban cake.

OSVALDO: The only thing that I like Cuban is the food.

ALFREDO: Then start acting like a man. You have one crying in the back and
    the other demanding in the front!

OSVALDO: I do.

ALFREDO: You don't have the energy to play it both ways.

OSVALDO: What are you talking about?

ALFREDO: Your wife . . . Sonia!

OSVALDO: She'll never change.

ALFREDO: Why should she?!

OSVALDO: To be acceptable.

(Alfredo slaps Osvaldo. Mimi enters.)

MIMI: The rice, we have to hit her with the rice.

(Osvaldo and Alfredo, glaring at each other, exit with Mimi. Lizette

enters in her honeymoon outfit and goes outside. She sees Manuela.
They come back in.)

LIZETTE: Grandma, you've been in the sun!
MANUELA: I was taking a nap. You know when you get old you need rest.
LIZETTE: You were crying, Grandma. Don't.
MANUELA: We didn't have enough cake!
LIZETTE: Nothing turned out right, Grandma, that's the truth.
MANUELA: You're right. Oscar would have made sure that we had a good time.
    My husband would have spent more money. I would have been proud.
    Your mother would have been proud. You would have been proud.
LIZETTE: Grandma, aren't you proud of me?
MANUELA: Yes.
LIZETTE: Did you love each other?
MANUELA: Yes dear, we did.
LIZETTE: And you never doubted it?
MANUELA: No dear.
LIZETTE: I hope I can do it. Wish me luck, Grandma. I don't want to fail. I
    want to be happy.
MANUELA: I hope that you know how to fight. Everything will try to stop and
    corrupt your life. I hope your husband is successful and that you have
    enough children.
LIZETTE: And that I never regret my life.
MANUELA: That will be my prayer.
LIZETTE: That if anyone goes, it's me, that I'm the one that walks. That he'll
    be hooked on me forever.
MANUELA: That's right.
LIZETTE: Thank you.
MANUELA: A beautiful dress. I'll get the rice.
LIZETTE: No, we are sneaking out. I don't want rice all over my clothes. In ten
    minutes tell them we tricked them, that we got away.
MANUELA: Go. Don't be nervous. Tonight everything will be all right. Don't
    worry, have a nice vacation.
LIZETTE: It's eighty degrees in Hawaii, it's an island, like Cuba.
MANUELA: Cuba was more beautiful.

(Lizette exits.)

Then politicians got in the way.

LIZETTE *(offstage)*: Honey, we did it. Give me a kiss.

(Manuela goes outside.)

ENTIRE CAST *(offstage)*: Ah! Uh-Uh! Noooooooooo!
LIZETTE *(offstage)*: My God, rice, run!

(Sonia enters, covered with rice, followed by Osvaldo.)

OSVALDO: It was a beautiful wedding.

SONIA: You're coming home with me?

OSVALDO: I can't.

SONIA: Yes, come with me.

OSVALDO: Not tonight.

SONIA: When?

OSVALDO: Never. *(Pause.)* Nothing is left between you and me.

SONIA: Nothing?

OSVALDO: Nothing.

SONIA: I'm not even your mistress?

OSVALDO: That's right. Revolutions create hell for all people involved.

SONIA: Don't do this. We belong together, we were thrown out. Discarded. We stayed together, Cubans, we are Cubans. Nothing really came between us.

OSVALDO: Something did for me.

　　　(Mimi enters.)

SONIA: What about our family? What we swore to Christ?

OSVALDO: I don't believe in anything, not even Christ.

SONIA: And me?

OSVALDO: I have another wife, she's my wife now. I have another life.

SONIA: If I was my father, I'd kill you!

MIMI *(to Osvaldo)*: Your wife is waiting in the car. *(To Sonia.)* She told me to tell him.

OSVALDO: Sonia, I'm starting fresh. You should too.

SONIA: I should, yes, I should. *(She takes out the bottle that Manuela gave her in Act One and makes the sign of the cross twice.)*

OSVALDO: That's right. *(He starts to exit.)*

SONIA: Wait. One last toast.

OSVALDO: To the bride?

SONIA: No, to us. *(She goes to the fountain to pour them champagne, and puts the potion into Osvaldo's drink.)*

MIMI: Osvaldo?

OSVALDO: How dare you call me that!

MIMI: Okay, Daddy, is that better? This family is the only life I know. It exists for me.

OSVALDO: This is between your mother and me.

MIMI: No, listen Daddy, the family is continuing. I'm going to make sure of that.

OSVALDO: How? Mimi, how?

MIMI: Never mind, Osvaldo.

　　　(Sound of car horn.)

OSVALDO: She's honking the horn, hurry Sonia!

　　　(Sonia hands Osvaldo the drink.)

SONIA: Money, love and the time to enjoy it, for both of us!

OSVALDO: Thanks. *(He gulps down the drink and exits.)*

MIMI: Osvaldo, you jerk. Bastard!

SONIA: Don't worry Mimi, he's going to have diarrhea till sometime in March.

MIMI: Finally.

SONIA: Put the blame on me. I don't speak the right way. I don't know how to ask the right questions.

MIMI: That's not true, Mama.

SONIA: When I first got here . . . I got lost, I tried to ask an old man for directions. I could not find the right words to ask him the directions. He said to me, "What's wrong with you, lady, somebody give you a lobotomy?" I repeated that word over and over to myself, "lobotomy, lobotomy, lo-bo-to-meee!" I looked it up. It said an insertion into the brain, for relief, of tension. I remembered people who had been lobotomized, that their minds could not express anything, they could feel nothing. They looked numb, always resting, then I realized that the old man was right.

MIMI: No. Mama.

SONIA: So I decided never to communicate or deal with this country again. Mimi, I don't know how to go back to my country. He made me realize that to him, I looked like a freak. Then I thought, but I'm still me to Osvaldo, he's trapped too. He must feel the same way too. Put the blame on me.

(Miriam and Oscar enter.)

MIMI: Aunt Miriam, tell me, how did you find revenge?

MIRIAM: Against what?

MIMI: Your father.

MIRIAM: Oh, when my mother and father got to America, I made them live with me. I support them. Now they are old and they are dependent on me for everything.

MIMI: It's not worth it, Aunt Miriam.

MIRIAM: Yes it is.

MIMI: Grandma, I'm in the car.

MIRIAM: It's revenge.

OSCAR *(shows Miriam the coke bottle)*: My revenge!

MIRIAM: Everyone in this family's got a drug.

MANUELA *(enters)*: Mimi is taking me home?

SONIA: Yes, Mama, she's waiting in the car —

MANUELA: You didn't do it right.

SONIA: I'm sorry, Mama . . . I did it the way I was taught.

(Manuela kisses Oscar good-bye and then exits.)

Why can't life be like it was? Like my coming-out party. When my father introduced me to our society in my white dress.

MIRIAM: Sonia, they threw the parties to give us away . . . perfect merchandising; Latin women dressed like American movies, doing Viennese waltzes. "Oh, beautiful stream, so clear and bright, a radiant dream we sing to you, by shores that . . ."

SONIA: I wonder what it would have been like if we would have stayed?

MIRIAM: They would have ridiculed us.

SONIA: We would have had a country.

MIRIAM: We didn't have a choice.

(Oscar exits to ballroom.)

SONIA: Miriam, Pedro took his life because of that.

MIRIAM: No. Pedro did it because of days like today — afternoons like this one: when you are around the people you belong with and you feel like you're choking and don't know why. *(She takes out Valium.)* I'll give you a piece of magic.

SONIA: How many?

MIRIAM: One . . . no, two. A Valium — that's the only certain thing. It reassures you. It lets you look at the truth. That's why psychiatrists prescribe them.

SONIA: You guarantee me Varadero? I'll be floating in Varadero Beach?

MIRIAM: If you take three you get to Varadero, Cuba.

(Miriam and Sonia take the Valium. From the offstage ballroom we hear Oscar speaking over the microphone.)

OSCAR *(sniff . . . sniff):* . . . One, two, three, testing, one, three, three, two, testing. Lenin or some Commie like that said that "you cannot make an omelet without breaking a few eggs." Funny guy. Testing. All right, now from somewhere in the armpit of the world, a little tune my mother taught me.

(He sings "Isla.")

In an island
Far away from here
I left the life I knew
Island of mine
Country of mine
Mine and only mine
Terraces and houses
Country do you remember
Do you remember
Remember me?

MIRIAM *(takes cushions from chair and puts them on the floor):* I want to float down Key Biscayne back to Varadero. Varadero, please, please come.

(Miriam lies on the cushions. Sonia looks at her.)

SONIA: Why is he making so much noise?!

MIRIAM: Shhh. I'm already there . . . miles and miles into the beach and the

water is up to my knees . . . I float. The little fish nibble at my feet. I kick
them. I'm in. I'm inside the place where I'm supposed to be.

OSCAR *(singing offstage)*:
> You were once my island
> I left you all alone
> I live without your houses
> Beautiful houses
> Houses remembered.

SONIA: Sonia is not coming back. Cojimar, Sonia will never be back.

OSCAR *(singing offstage)*:
> Eran mias
> You were only mine
> Never forget me
> Don't forget me
> Mi amor.

MIMI *(enters)*: Mama, what's she doing?

SONIA: Relaxing.

MIMI: Want to dance, Mama?

SONIA: Us?

MIMI: Yes.

SONIA: Yes.

OSCAR *(singing offstage)*:
> En una isla
> Lejos de aqui
> Dejé
> La vida mia
> Madre mia
> Isla mia

MIMI: They're going to kick us out.

SONIA: That's all right, Mimi. I've been kicked out of better places.

OSCAR *(singing offstage)*: Te dejé.

*(Sonia and Mimi begin to dance. Lights fade as we hear the end of
the song.)*   1984

INVESTIGATIONS

1. How would you describe Sonia? How does she change as the play progresses? How could she have more successfully resolved her problems by
   the end of the play?

2. On p. 175 Miriam says that Pedro (her and Osvaldo's dead brother) "never
   left the garden," and Osvaldo replies, "None of us have." What does he
   mean?

3. During a conversation about Pedro's suicide, Sonia says, "Maybe that's
   the way things are, maybe one of us had to die. Maybe there's an order

to all these things," to which Miriam replies, "There's no order to things, don't you know that by now? It's chaos, only chaos" (p. 173). What evidence can you find in *Broken Eggs* in support of each of these attitudes? Which attitude better reflects your personal view of family? Why?

4. In what ways do the conflicts in this family help to bind them, help to give them an identity as a family? How might their lives have been better if they'd stayed in Cuba? Would they "know who they are," as Mimi seems to think (p. 158)? How does being immigrants complicate their efforts to "know who they are"?

PETER ORESICK

After the Deindustrialization of America, My Father Enters Television Repair

My hands hold, my father's solder the wires —
picture rolls once, then steadies . . . an English castle!
The voice-over drones about Edward I,
who, to subdue the Welsh, built castles.
Some sixty years, dozens of engineers, the masses   5
conscripted from the villages.

My father moves on to a Zenith
with a bad tuner. TVs interest him, not the English
with their damp, historical programming.

Here there were Indians, mound builders.   10
Here, an English fort, a few farmers.
And here the industrialist settled his ass,
John Ford on the river dredging sand

PETER ORESICK (b. 1955) grew up in Ford City, Pennsylvania, a mill town north of Pittsburgh where his grandparents, Ukrainian-Ruthenian immigrants, had found jobs as glassworkers around the turn of the century. His collections of poems include *An American Peace* (1985), *Other Lives* (1984), *The Story of Glass* (1977), and *Definitions* (1990).

for making glass. Plate glass.
(Why should America buy from Europe?)   15
Some half dozen years, German engineers, and hundreds of Slavic peasants.

Grandfather sat on his samovar
warming himself and making excuses,
but finally, he set off.
Got a room, became a shoveler.   20
Got a wife, a company house.
Ford City: a valley filling with properties.

No one got along —
not Labor and Capital, not Germans and Slavs,
not husbands and wives, for that matter.   25

Edward's castles were ruins
by the 15th century. Not from Welsh armies,
but the rise of the middle class.
The towns around a castle thrived:
tailors, smithies, cobblers, coopers.   30
Drawing in the Welsh peasants.
And what with intermarriage and the rise of capitalism . . .
a castle grew obsolescent.

I turn off the set. My father hunts
cigarettes at the Kwik-Mart on the corner.   35
Overhead, my mother's footsteps,
the tonk of bottles,
the scraping of plates.

During Eisenhower's reign
my grandfather retired and mowed his lawn   40
until I took over. He primed the filter,
set the choke, then we took turns pulling
till the sputtering engine caught.
("Somanabitch," he'd spit.)
And watch me as I mowed   45
back and forth for two dollars.

Once in the garage he showed me a scythe.
He mowed hay in the old country, and the women
would follow, raking it in windrows.

The factories today are mostly closed down,   50
or full of robots or far off in Asia.
Ford City lives through the mail:
compensation, a thin pension,
and, of course, Social Security.

I always drive along the factory, windows rolled down;   55
I want my kids in the back seat to see.
Seven or eight, probably pensioners, congregate
on the corner, each man dressed quite alike:
Sears jacket, cigarette, salt-and-pepper hair.

"Honk the horn," my oldest begs.   60
He waves and waves zealously
until a man turns — a man
with my face, but full of sweetness now,
silence and clarity.   1990

INVESTIGATIONS

1. Return to your response to "Write Before Reading" (p. 114). How do you account for the similarities and differences between the "legend" of your family and the legends told here by Oresick?
2. Why does the speaker describe the TV show about Edward I? What connects what we hear about Edward I to what we know of the speaker's family? How does knowing about Edward I clarify what we know of the speaker's family?
3. What reasons can you give for this family remaining in Ford City? What reasons are there for them to leave? What would your family do in their place? Why?

AGNES G. HERMAN

A Parent's Journey
Out of the Closet

When we agreed to adopt seven-month-old Jeff, we knew that his life as a member of a Jewish family would begin the moment we brought him to our home. We celebrated that joyous homecoming with appropriate religious ritual, with blessings recited by Jeff's rabbi father as our gurgling, happy baby teethed on his infant kiddush cup and enjoyed his challah. There, in the warmth of our extended family circle of grandparents, an aunt, an uncle, and the Temple Board, our small son passed comfortably through his bris, his initial Jewish milestone. There would be many more.

By the time he was two, Jeff ate an ice cream cone without spilling a drop; his face came out of the sticky encounter clean. At five, he watched other kids play ball in the alley, standing aside because he had been told not to play there. Besides, he seemed more comfortable playing with the little girl next door. There were awkward moments as he began to grow up, such as the times when the baseball bat, which his father insisted upon, was not comfortable in his hands, but the rolling pin, which his father decried, was. His grandmother, whom he adored, remarked, "Jeff is too good."

I knew she was right, and privately I felt a nagging fear I could hardly express to myself. Was Jeff a "sissy"? That archaic term was the only one I dared whisper to myself. "Gay" only meant "lively and fun-loving"; "homosexual" was a label not to be used in polite society and certainly never to be mentioned in the same sentence with a child's name. Such a term would certainly stigmatize a youngster and humiliate a family.

Jeff continued to be an eager volunteer in the kitchen and a reluctant participant on the ballfield. We fought the former and pressed to correct the latter, frustrating our son while we all grew tense. As to our silent fears, we repressed them.

Jeff developed reading problems in school. We worried, but accepted the   5
inappropriate assurance offered by his teacher. "He is such a good boy — don't confuse him with counseling." We bought it, for a while. As the reading problems continued, Jeff did enter therapy and was helped to become less anxious and learn how to read all over again. At our final parental consultation with the psychiatrist, I hesitantly asked, "Doctor, I often worry that Jeff is

Born in New York City in 1922, AGNES G. HERMAN holds a B.A. from the University of Michigan and a master's degree in social work from Columbia University. Retired since 1979, she helped found the Union of American Hebrew Congregations program on the Changing Jewish Family and the Synagogue and currently serves on its Committee on AIDS.

effeminate. What do you think?" I held my breath while he offered his reassurance: "There is nothing wrong with your son. He is a sensitive boy — not aggressive or competitive. So he likes girls! In a few years you will be worrying about that for other reasons."

Jeff looked forward eagerly to religious school. He accompanied his dad, helped around the temple, and received many kudos. He was quick, efficient, and willingly took instructions. In later years, even after his father was no longer in the pulpit, Jeff continued his role as a temple volunteer. He moved chairs and carried books; later, he changed fuses, focused spotlights, and handled sound equipment. Jeff was comfortable; it was "his" temple. Other children there shared his interests and became his friends, later forming the temple youth group.

Bar mitzvah class, however, was a difficult obstacle. When Hebrew became a daily family battle, we withdrew him from Hebrew school to be tutored instead by his father. He spent a substantial amount of time, which otherwise was not available, with his dad. As a result, a potential failure was transformed into another family milestone. Jeff yawned his way through formal bar mitzvah training, but when his big day arrived, he was prepared, and pleased even himself.

During confirmation and youth group years, Jeff seemed to be struggling to be like his peers. Temple became the center of his life. He worked and played there, dated, went steady, and attended meetings and dances. He shared with no one — not his parents, his friends, or his rabbi — his own feelings of being "different."

When Jeff was sixteen, we moved from New Rochelle to Los Angeles. It was a difficult move for him, cutting off relationships and sources of recognition and acceptance. As we settled into our new home, Jeff began to explore the San Fernando Valley, enrolled in high school, and tried to make new friends. At our insistence, he attended one meeting of the local temple youth group, but felt rejected by the youngsters there. That marked the unfortunate beginning of Jeff's disenchantment with synagogues and withdrawal from family religious observances and celebrations.

Jeff gradually acclimated to his new environment. He took Amy, a Jewish girl his own age, to the senior prom; he cruised Van Nuys Boulevard on Wednesdays with Ann. He was always on the move — coming home to eat, shower, change clothes, and zip out again. We blamed it on the fast pace of California and the novelty of having his own "wheels": first a motorcycle, and then a car. There were several accidents — none serious, thank heavens! Again, in retrospect, the furious struggle with his identity must have played a part in his fast-paced behavior. At the time, though, we buried our heads in the sand, believing that Jeff was merely behaving like every other teenager.

After high school, the pace seemed to slow down a bit. So when Jeff was nineteen and we decided to leave him in charge for the six months of our sabbatical world tour, we had no hesitation. Conscientious and cautious, he could handle the cars and the checkbook. He would continue in college and be available to his sister Judi, also attending college. We flew off to Europe and Israel, confident and secure.

When an overseas call came three months later in Jerusalem, my heart beat fast, and my sense of well-being faltered slightly. "Everything is fine, no problem. I have quit college. Now don't get excited . . . I want to go to business school and study interior design. Jobs are plentiful; I know a guy who will hire me the minute I graduate."

Jeff had always shown a creative flair for color and design. He constantly rearranged our furniture, changing one room after another. All this raced through my mind as I held the phone, separated from him by 9000 miles. Erv and I looked at each other, wished Jeff luck, and told him to write the check for his tuition.

When we finally returned home, Jeff was obviously depressed. His answers to our questions were surly, clipped, and evasive. Behaving unlike his usual loving self, he ran in and out of the house silently, furtively, always in a hurry. He seemed uninterested in our trip and was clearly trying to avoid us.

One day during Passover, Erv was searching for a favorite cantorial record   15
that Jeff often appropriated. He checked Jeff's record collection and poked about among the torn jeans. Speechless and ashen, Erv returned to the breakfast room and dropped a book into my lap: *Homosexuality in Modern Society.* "This was hidden in Jeff's room." My heart raced and skipped. Confrontation was finally at hand, not only with Jeff, but with my own fears as well.

Then our son came through the front door on the run: "I'm late . . . can't stop . . . talk to you later."

The tone of our response and expressions on our faces stopped him mid-flight. "Son, stand still! Something is going on, you are not yourself! Are you in trouble? Drugs, maybe? Is one of your girlfriends pregnant? Or, are you, is it possible that you are . . . homosexual?"

I waited, trembling. The faces of my beloveds were creased with anger and worry. I could barely breathe.

"Yes, I am gay." A simple sentence, yet I did not understand. Nothing was "gay"!

We asked in unison, "What does that mean?"   20

"I am homosexual," he explained. After long minutes of uncomfortable conversation, we sent Jeff on his way with "we'll talk later." I ran from the room to what was to become my comfort zone, the cool tile of the bathroom floor, and I cried my eyes out. I guess Erv went to work. All we can recall now is that neither of us could face the reality right then.

That evening and the next, we did an enormous amount of soul-searching. What did I, a social worker, know about homosexuality? What did my husband, the rabbi, know? Our academic credentials were impressive — professionally we were both well-trained to help other people in pain. But in our personal distress, we felt helpless.

Everything I had ever heard about homosexuality destroyed all my dreams about our son's future. He would never marry and have children. His warmth, caring, good looks, and so many other wonderful traits would not be passed along to a son or daughter, a grandchild. We wondered whether we could keep him in our family circle, or would we lose him to "that other world" of homosexuality, a world that was foreign to us.

We wracked ourselves with self-blame — what did we do wrong? I accepted all the myths about homosexuality. First, the myth of the strong mother — I was a strong mother, but what mother doesn't overexert her influence on her children? Second, the myth of the absent father — Erv spent so much time crisscrossing the country, berating himself for not being at home enough. Third was the myth of seduction — had someone lured Jeff into this awful lifestyle? And then, finally, I believed the myth of "the cure" — that the right therapist could change Jeff's sexual orientation.

We did seek help from a therapist. He was patient, caring, and accepting   25
of Jeff and his lifestyle. He helped us begin to sort out myth from reality and guided us through a tangled web of grief, pain, and disappointment. He gently destroyed our unrealistic hope of "changing" Jeff. Our abiding love for our son was, of course, the key to this difficult yet hopeful journey.

I did not like Jeff's lifestyle at that time, but that did not interfere with my love for him. Understanding and acceptance gradually grew, but the path to real comfort continued to be bumpy.

Jeff sought help, too. At nineteen, he admitted that there was much that he wanted to know about himself. During that time, he offered a comment that we gratefully accepted: "Please stop blaming yourselves. It is not your fault that I have grown up gay." With those words, Jeff erased our most devastating, yet unspoken, anxiety.

Time moved along for all of us. We grieved the loss of deeply held expectations for our son's life. We experienced inner turmoil. Jeff struggled to make peace with himself. We learned to support one another.

Over time, we came to understand that a child who is homosexual needs no less understanding, support, and acceptance than one who is heterosexual. Clearly, our gay son has the same human needs that his straight sister has: for empathy and patience, for security and success, for caring and love. Rejection is difficult for both our children, yet perhaps more so for our gay child. Society has taught him that he will experience less validation and more unnecessary pain. He, and all of us who love him, are vulnerable to that pain.

It became clear that Jeff's sexual orientation was only one part of his life.   30
There remained the ordinary concerns and controversies intrinsic to raising any child. Jeff rode the roller coaster of financial and vocational problems. We provided advice, which he sometimes accepted, and loans, which he often repaid. Jeff's married sister behaved in much the same manner.

Jeff became ill and required the usual chicken soup and tender care in his apartment. He preferred receiving that attention from friends, but also expected Mother and Dad to stop by regularly with reassurance and love. His sister behaved the same way when she broke her leg and was living alone.

When a love affair went sour, Jeff became depressed and sad. We worried and tried to be especially sensitive to his pain. The same support was called for when his sister faced divorce with sadness and depression. We were happier when Jeff was living with a friend who cared about him and about whom he cared, and we felt the same way about his sister, now happily remarried.

During all this time, it never occurred to us to turn to the Jewish community for support, though we knew its resources well. We kept our concerns about Jeff's lifestyle to ourselves: We were in the closet. A child's homosexuality was not something one discussed in 1969 and throughout the 1970s. And sharing intimacies with others was not our way — these were matters we had to work out ourselves. We had decided alone, together, to marry each other; we decided alone, together, to have children. And we decided alone, together, to tough out our son's homosexuality, confront it, embrace him, and then face the world together.

I recall sitting with close friends one evening. Naturally, the conversation turned to our kids. At one point, someone said, "I think we have something in common." We all agreed, but even then, none of us could articulate it. In fact, on the way home, Erv asked, "Are you sure their oldest son is gay?"

Finally we came "halfway out," sharing only with family. We found almost unanimous acceptance; affection for Jeff did not falter. But it was seventeen long years before we went public in the Jewish community. Even during the years when my husband was deeply involved in supporting the establishment of a gay outreach synagogue in Los Angeles, when he was busy teaching others that Judaism must not turn its back on any of its children, we did not share our son's homosexuality with the Jewish public.

I "came out" for us, with Jeff's permission, in 1986, with an article in *The Reconstructionist*, a national Jewish magazine. The response was over-whelming. Support from rabbis, lay leaders, and friends poured in from around the country. Even at that late date, comfortable as we had become with Jeff's lifestyle, we found those messages heartwarming and reassuring.

Some of our friends were angry that we had not shared our pain with them. Perhaps we did not trust people to practice compassion and acceptance. Perhaps we did not trust them to understand that we are not failures as parents. We did not want our son to suffer rejection from those we loved. We did not want to be rejected by those we loved!

The pressure was greater on Jeff. Because he is a rabbi's child, he felt, correctly, that the expectations of him were high. Jeff was not alone in fearing the expectations of others; he had learned that sensitivity from us. Every family feels a need to be without flaws: a nonsensical, impossible attitude, but it is real. Among rabbis' families it is often exaggerated.

Should we have trusted our friends and colleagues from the beginning? Could we have dared to test the support of the synagogue leaders with whom Erv worked daily? Should we have risked our own self-image and left the closet earlier? Would any of that have made our son more comfortable at our seder table or at services? I do not have the answers. I believe we came out only when we were ready; getting ready took a long time.

There are Jewish parents who shut out their gay and lesbian children and   40
erect a wall of alienation. There is little solace in that course of action, or in
believing that their child can be "changed" to heterosexuality. Those who reject
the person rather than accept the reality, or who chase fantasies rather than
learning facts, deserve our compassion and understanding. It is difficult to face
the disappointment, grief, and guilt that often precede true acceptance. Parents
need to be helped to mourn broken dreams, to keep communication open, and
to prevent love and parental devotion from being overwhelmed by pain and
confusion.

Some parents actually chant Kaddish[1] for their "wayward" children. For
us, our Jewish dedication to family left no room for such behavior. Disappointment hurts, but is curable. Alienation, on the other hand, can kill relationships,
love, and family. Thank God, our love — and our religious faith — did not
falter.

We Jewish parents love our offspring, sometimes desperately. We can
survive the shock of learning that a son is gay, or a daughter is lesbian.
Eventually we can find that love will crumble the walls of alienation and that
time is an ally. Our children, too, can learn to be patient with us as we grow.

Would we have done anything differently? Yes. We would have paid heed
to the "flashing lights," the warnings of parenthood. We would have helped
our son as early as possible to like himself and to make peace with himself.
And when he did break the news to us in 1969, I wish we would have been
wise enough to hug our beloved son and say, "We love you very much. Let's
talk about it."

When strangers ask me today if our son is married, I do not hesitate to
explain, "He is not. He is gay." We are out of the closet. It has been a long
road, but well worth it.   1985

INVESTIGATIONS

1. Where did Herman's "nagging fear" that Jeff was a "sissy" come from?
   To what extent did she and Erv fear for themselves, and not for Jeff?
2. In paragraph 21 Jeff's parents cannot "face the reality" of his being gay,
   though he's just told them. If they had "faced the reality" sooner, what
   details in the account of Jeff's upbringing on pages 193–195 would have
   been different?
3. What purpose does the extended comparison between Jeff and his sister
   serve?
4. What would the narrator of McCann's "My Mother's Clothes: The School
   of Beauty and Shame" have to say about Herman's "inner turmoil" concerning Jeff's sexual orientation?

---

[1] A prayer for the dead. [Ed.]

LOUISE ERDRICH

The Leap

My mother is the surviving half of a blindfold trapeze act, not a fact I think about much even now that she is sightless, the result of encroaching and stubborn cataracts. She walks slowly through her house here in New Hampshire, lightly touching her way along walls and running her hands over knick-knacks, books, the drift of a grown child's belongings and castoffs. She has never upset an object or as much as brushed a magazine onto the floor. She has never lost her balance or bumped into a closet door left carelessly open.

It has occurred to me that the catlike precision of her movements in old age might be the result of her early training, but she shows so little of the drama or flair one might expect from a performer that I tend to forget the Flying Avalons. She has kept no sequined costume, no photographs, no fliers or posters from that part of her youth. I would, in fact, tend to think that all memory of double somersaults and heart-stopping catches had left her arms and legs were it not for the fact that sometimes, as I sit sewing in the room of the rebuilt house in which I slept as a child, I hear the crackle, catch a whiff of smoke from the stove downstairs, and suddenly the room goes dark, the stitches burn beneath my fingers, and I am sewing with a needle of hot silver, a thread of fire.

I owe her my existence three times. The first was when she saved herself. In the town square a replica tent pole, cracked and splintered, now stands cast in concrete. It commemorates the disaster that put our town smack on the front page of the Boston and New York tabloids. It is from those old news-papers, now historical records, that I get my information. Not from my mother, Anna of the Flying Avalons, nor from any of her in-laws, nor certainly from the other half of her particular act, Harold Avalon, her first husband. In one news account it says, "The day was mildly overcast, but nothing in the air or temperature gave any hint of the sudden force with which the deadly gale would strike."

I have lived in the West, where you can see the weather coming for miles, and it is true that out here we are at something of a disadvantage. When extremes of temperature collide, a hot and cold front, winds generate instan-taneously behind a hill and crash upon you without warning. That, I think, was the likely situation on that day in June. People probably commented on the pleasant air, grateful that no hot sun beat upon the striped tent that stretched

A member of the Turtle Mountain Band of Chippewa, LOUISE ERDRICH (b. 1954) grew up in Wahpeton, North Dakota. Author of three novels and two collections of poetry, she most recently collaborated with her husband, Michael Dorris, on *The Crown of Columbus* (1991), a novel.

over the entire center green. They bought their tickets and surrendered them
in anticipation. They sat. They ate carmelized popcorn and roasted peanuts.
There was time, before the storm, for three acts. The White Arabians of Ali-
Khazar rose on their hind legs and waltzed. The Mysterious Bernie folded
himself into a painted cracker tin, and the Lady of the Mists made herself
appear and disappear in surprising places. As the clouds gathered outside,
unnoticed, the ringmaster cracked his whip, shouted his introduction, and
pointed to the ceiling of the tent, where the Flying Avalons were perched.

   They loved to drop gracefully from nowhere, like two sparkling birds, and   5
blow kisses as they threw off their plumed helmets and high-collared capes.
They laughed and flirted openly as they beat their way up again on the trapeze
bars. In the final vignette of their act, they actually would kiss in midair,
pausing, almost hovering as they swooped past one another. On the ground,
between bows, Harry Avalon would skip quickly to the front rows and point
out the smear of my mother's lipstick, just off the edge of his mouth. They
made a romantic pair all right, especially in the blindfold sequence.

   That afternoon, as the anticipation increased, as Mr. and Mrs. Avalon tied
sparkling strips of cloth onto each other's face and as they puckered their lips
in mock kisses, lips destined "never again to meet," as one long breathless
article put it, the wind rose, miles off, wrapped itself into a cone, and howled.
There came a rumble of electrical energy, drowned out by the sudden roll of
drums. One detail not mentioned by the press, perhaps unknown — Anna was
pregnant at the time, seven months and hardly showing, her stomach muscles
were that strong. It seems incredible that she would work high above the
ground when any fall could be so dangerous, but the explanation — I know
from watching her go blind — is that my mother lives comfortably in extreme
elements. She is one with the constant dark now, just as the air was her home,
familiar to her, safe, before the storm that afternoon.

   From opposite ends of the tent they waved, blind and smiling, to the crowd
below. The ringmaster removed his hat and called for silence, so that the two
above could concentrate. They rubbed their hands in chalky powder, then
Harry launched himself and swung, once, twice, in huge calibrated beats across
space. He hung from his knees and on the third swing stretched wide his arms,
held his hands out to receive his pregnant wife as she dove from her shining
bar.

   It was while the two were in midair, their hands about to meet, that
lightning struck the main pole and sizzled down the guy wires, filling the air
with a blue radiance that Harry Avalon must certainly have seen through the
cloth of his blindfold as the tent buckled and the edifice toppled him forward,
the swing continuing and not returning in its sweep, and Harry going down,
down into the crowd with his last thought, perhaps, just a prickle of surprise
at his empty hands.

   My mother once said that I'd be amazed at how many things a person can
do within the act of falling. Perhaps, at the time, she was teaching me to dive
off a board at the town pool, for I associated the idea with midair somersaults.

But I also think she meant that even in that awful doomed second one could think, for she certainly did. When her hands did not meet her husband's, my mother tore her blindfold away. As he swept past her on the wrong side, she could have grasped his ankle, the toe-end of his tights, and gone down clutching him. Instead, she changed direction. Her body twisted toward a heavy wire and she managed to hang on to the braided metal, still hot from the lightning strike. Her palms were burned so terribly that once healed they bore no lines, only the blank scar tissue of a quieter future. She was lowered, gently, to the sawdust ring just underneath the dome of the canvas roof, which did not entirely settle but was held up on one end and jabbed through, torn, and still on fire in places from the giant spark, though rain and men's jackets soon put that out.

Three people died, but except for her hands my mother was not seriously   10
harmed until an overeager rescuer broke her arm in extricating her and also, in the process, collapsed a portion of the tent bearing a huge buckle that knocked her unconscious. She was taken to the town hospital, and there she must have hemorrhaged, for they kept her, confined to her bed, a month and a half before her baby was born without life.

Harry Avalon had wanted to be buried in the circus cemetery next to the original Avalon, his uncle, so she sent him back with his brothers. The child, however, is buried around the corner, beyond this house and just down the highway. Sometimes I used to walk there just to sit. She was a girl, but I rarely thought of her as a sister or even as a separate person really. I suppose you could call it the egocentrism of a child, of all young children, but I considered her a less finished version of myself.

When the snow falls, throwing shadows among the stones, I can easily pick hers out from the road, for it is bigger than the others and in the shape of a lamb at rest, its legs curled beneath. The carved lamb looms larger as the years pass, though it is probably only my eyes, the vision shifting, as what is close to me blurs and distances sharpen. In odd moments, I think it is the edge drawing near, the edge of everything, the unseen horizon we do not really speak of in the eastern woods. And it also seems to me, although this is probably an idle fantasy, that the statue is growing more sharply etched, as if, instead of weathering itself into a porous mass, it is hardening on the hillside with each snowfall, perfecting itself.

It was during her confinement in the hospital that my mother met my father. He was called in to look at the set of her arm, which was complicated. He stayed, sitting at her bedside, for he was something of an armchair traveler and had spent his war quietly, at an air force training grounds, where he became a specialist in arms and legs broken during parachute training exercises. Anna Avalon had been to many of the places he longed to visit — Venice, Rome, Mexico, all through France and Spain. She had no family of her own and was taken in by the Avalons, trained to perform from a very young age.

They toured Europe before the war, then based themselves in New York. She was illiterate.

It was in the hospital that she finally learned to read and write, as a way of overcoming the boredom and depression of those weeks, and it was my father who insisted on teaching her. In return for stories of her adventures, he graded her first exercises. He bought her her first book, and over her bold letters, which the pale guides of the penmanship pads could not contain, they fell in love.

I wonder if my father calculated the exchange he offered: one form of flight for another. For after that, and for as long as I can remember, my mother has never been without a book. Until now, that is, and it remains the greatest difficulty of her blindness. Since my father's recent death, there is no one to read to her, which is why I returned, in fact, from my failed life where the land is flat. I came home to read to my mother, to read out loud, to read long into the dark if I must, to read all night.

Once my father and mother married, they moved onto the old farm he had inherited but didn't care much for. Though he'd been thinking of moving to a larger city, he settled down and broadened his practice in this valley. It still seems odd to me, when they could have gone anywhere else, that they chose to stay in the town where the disaster had occurred, and which my father in the first place had found so constricting. It was my mother who insisted upon it, after her child did not survive. And then, too, she loved the sagging farmhouse with its scrap of what was left of a vast acreage of woods and hidden hayfields that stretched to the game park.

I owe my existence, the second time then, to the two of them and the hospital that brought them together. That is the debt we take for granted since none of us asks for life. It is only once we have it that we hang on so dearly.

I was seven the year the house caught fire, probably from standing ash. It can rekindle, and my father, forgetful around the house and perpetually exhausted from night hours on call, often emptied what he thought were ashes from cold stoves into wooden or cardboard containers. The fire could have started from a flaming box, or perhaps a buildup of creosote inside the chimney was the culprit. It started right around the stove, and the heart of the house was gutted. The baby-sitter, fallen asleep in my father's den on the first floor, woke to find the stairway to my upstairs room cut off by flames. She used the phone, then ran outside to stand beneath my window.

When my parents arrived, the town volunteers had drawn water from the fire pond and were spraying the outside of the house, preparing to go inside after me, not knowing at the time that there was only one staircase and that it was lost. On the other side of the house, the superannuated extension ladder broke in half. Perhaps the clatter of it falling against the walls woke me, for I'd been asleep up to that point.

As soon as I awakened, in the small room that I now use for sewing, I smelled the smoke. I followed things by the letter then, was good at memorizing instructions, and so I did exactly what was taught in the second-grade home

15

20

fire drill. I got up, I touched the back of my door before opening it. Finding it hot, I left it closed and stuffed my rolled-up rug beneath the crack. I did not hide under my bed or crawl into my closet. I put on my flannel robe, and then I sat down to wait.

Outside, my mother stood below my dark window and saw clearly that there was no rescue. Flames had pierced one side wall, and the glare of the fire lighted the massive limbs and trunk of the vigorous old elm that had probably been planted the year the house was built, a hundred years ago at least. No leaf touched the wall, and just one thin branch scraped the roof. From below, it looked as though even a squirrel would have had trouble jumping from the tree onto the house, for the breadth of that small branch was no bigger than my mother's wrist.

Standing there, beside Father, who was preparing to rush back around to the front of the house, my mother asked him to unzip her dress. When he wouldn't be bothered, she made him understand. He couldn't make his hands work, so she finally tore it off and stood there in her pearls and stockings. She directed one of the men to lean the broken half of the extension ladder up against the trunk of the tree. In surprise, he complied. She ascended. She vanished. Then she could be seen among the leafless branches of late November as she made her way up and, along her stomach, inched the length of a bough that curved above the branch that brushed the roof.

Once there, swaying, she stood and balanced. There were plenty of people in the crowd and many who still remember, or think they do, my mother's leap through the ice-dark air toward that thinnest extension, and how she broke the branch falling so that it cracked in her hands, cracked louder than the flames as she vaulted with it toward the edge of the roof, and how it hurtled down end over end without her, and their eyes went up, again, to see where she had flown.

I didn't see her leap through air, only heard the sudden thump and looked out my window. She was hanging by the backs of her heels from the new gutter we had put in that year, and she was smiling. I was not surprised to see her, she was so matter-of-fact. She tapped on the window. I remember how she did it, too. It was the friendliest tap, a bit tentative, as if she was afraid she had arrived too early at a friend's house. Then she gestured at the latch, and when I opened the window she told me to raise it wider and prop it up with the stick so it wouldn't crush her fingers. She swung down, caught the ledge, and crawled through the opening. Once she was in my room, I realized she had on only underclothing, a bra of the heavy stitched cotton women used to wear and step-in, lace-trimmed drawers. I remember feeling light-headed, of course, terribly relieved, and then embarrassed for her to be seen by the crowd undressed.

I was still embarrassed as we flew out the window, toward earth, me in her lap, her toes pointed as we skimmed toward the painted target of the fire fighter's net.

I know that she's right. I knew it even then. As you fall there is time to think. Curled as I was, against her stomach, I was not startled by the cries of

25

the crowd or the looming faces. The wind roared and beat its hot breath at our back, and flames whistled. I slowly wondered what would happen if we missed the circle or bounced out of it. Then I wrapped my hands around my mother's hands. I felt the brush of her lips and heard the beat of her heart in my ears, loud as thunder, long as the roll of drums.   1990

INVESTIGATIONS

1. In what ways is the narrator's return home "to read to [her] mother, to read out loud, to read long into the dark . . . to read all night" (para. 15) just as breathtaking as the rescue during the house fire?

2. Locate each "leap" in the story. How might an ability to live "comfortably in extreme elements" be considered crucial to making each of these leaps? Where else in this part's selections can you see this ability at work? How might the story you wrote in response to "Write Before Reading" be seen as evidence of an ability to live "comfortably in extreme elements"?

3. In paragraph 15 the narrator wonders if her "father calculated the exchange he offered" when he taught her mother to read and write. What sort of "exchange" is it? What other "exchanges" can you find in the story? Describe them and how they serve to make this family a family.

LEWIS NORDAN

Sugar Among the Chickens

I had been fishing for an hour and still hadn't caught anything. I was fishing for chickens. Mama wouldn't let me walk to the town pond by myself. What else was I going to fish for?

I looked back over my shoulder through the torn-out screened door and tried to see Mama in there. I said, "Mama." I was using the voice that says you're being real good and not fishing for chickens.

Mama said, "You better not be fishing for chickens, Sugar Mecklin, you going to get switched." She's got this ability.

She was out in the kitchen, that was good anyway. I put a fresh kernel on my hook and scattered shelled corn on the slick dirt yard below the porch and

Born in 1939 in Itta Bena, Mississippi, LEWIS NORDAN has published two collections of short stories: *Welcome to the Arrow-Catcher Fair* (1983) and *The All-Girl Football Team* (1986). He regards his inability to tell the unvarnished truth as "a flaw, but it is also a gift for which I am grateful."

dusted off my hands on my white blue jeans. A handful of old hens came bobbing and clucking up to the corn and poked at it with their heads and then raised their heads up and looked around, and then started poking at it again.

I dropped the bait hook in amongst them. I wished I could figure out some way to use a cork. The chickens bobbed and pecked and poked and scratched. I moved my baited hook into the middle of the chickens and eased it down onto the ground and waited. I still didn't get a bite.

My daddy didn't much care whether I fished for chickens or not. My daddy knew I never would catch one, never had, never would. It was my mama who was the problem. She said it would ruin your life if you fished for chickens.

I wasn't studying ruining my life right now. I was thinking about hooking and landing some poultry.

I wasn't using a handline, which is easy to hide if your mama comes up on you. I was using a cane pole and a bream hook, little bitty rascal of a hook. I liked a handline all right, I wasn't complaining. Nothing better for fishing in real tight places, like up under your house on a hot day when the chickens are settled down in the cool dirt and have their neck feathers poked out like a straw hat and a little blue film of an eyelid dropped down over their eyes. A handline is fine for that. A cane pole is better from off your porch, though.

Or I guessed it was. I never had caught a chicken. I had had lots of bites, but I never had landed one, never really even set the hook in one. They're tricky, a chicken.

I really wanted to catch one, too. I wanted the hook to snag in the beak, I wanted to feel the tug on the line. I wanted to haul it in, squawking and heavy and beating its wings and sliding on its back and flopping over its breast and dragging along and the neck stretched out a foot and a half and the stupid old amazed eyes bright as Beau dollars.

I dreamed about it, asleep and awake. Sometimes I let myself believe the chicken I caught was not just any old chicken but maybe some special one, one of the Plymouth Rocks, some fat heavy bird, a Leghorn, or a blue Andalusian. And sometimes, as long as I was making believe, I thought I might catch an even finer specimen, the finest in the whole chicken yard. I thought I caught the red rooster itself.

The red rooster was a chicken as tall as me. It seemed like it, I swear, when I was ten. It was a chicken, I'm telling you, like no chicken you ever saw before. It could fly. There was no half-assed flying about it. It could fly long distance. Daddy said it could migrate if it had anywhere to go. It couldn't do that, but it could fly fifty times farther than any other chicken you ever saw. This was a chicken that one time killed a stray dog.

I dreamed about that rooster. The best dream was when I caught it not on a handline and not on a cane pole. I dreamed I caught it on a limber fine six-and-a-half-foot Zebco rod and spinning reel, like the ones in the Western Auto store in Arrow Catcher. That's the town I used to live right outside of when I was little, in the Delta. The line on that Zebco spool was almost invisible.

I watched the chickens. There was a fine old Plymouth Rock I would just love to catch. She dusted her feathers and took long steps like a kid wearing his daddy's hip boots. I moved the bait closer to her and held my breath. She started poking around at the corn. She hit the bait once but didn't pick up the hook. My line was taut, so I felt the strike vibrate through the line and down the cane pole to my hands, which I noticed were sweating. I thought, If she hit it once, she just might . . . But she didn't. She stopped eating corn altogether and scratched herself with her foot like a dog.

I tried to listen for my mama. Mama couldn't be expected to stay in the   15 kitchen forever. I needed to say something to her in my I-ain't-fishing-for-chickens voice, but I couldn't. The Plymouth Rock pecked the earth a few times, but not the bait. Then, all of a sudden, she shifted position a little and pecked right down on the corn with the hook in it, the bait. For the second time that day I felt a strike vibrate through my hands. But the chicken missed the hook again and I jerked the bait out of her mouth. She didn't know what happened to it. She looked like, What in the world?

I repositioned the bait, and the hen started pecking around it again. I had to say something to Mama. I held real still and tried to talk in a voice that maybe a chicken couldn't hear. In my head I invented a voice that seemed like it was going to be all throaty and hoarse and animallike when it came out, but when it did come out, it didn't make any sound at all, not even a whisper, just a little bit of released breath and a wormy movement of my lips. I said, "Mama, I ain't fishing for chickens." Nobody heard it, not even me. The Plymouth Rock hit the bait a third time.

It wasn't possible to catch a chicken. I knew that. My daddy had convinced me. He said, "A chicken is dumb, but not dumb enough." So I knew it was impossible. But I also knew it had happened. I had the Plymouth Rock.

I jerked my pole skyward and set the hook hard in the chicken's beak.

The sound that rose up out of the chicken's throat was a sound that nobody who has never caught a chicken on a hook has ever heard. It sounded like chicken-all-the-way-back-to-the-beginning-of-chicken.

I was anchored to the porch, with the butt end of the pole dug into my   20 groin for support. The heavy flopping squalling bird was hanging off the end of my line in midair. The sound didn't stop. The sound was like the fire siren in Arrow Catcher. As beautiful and as scary as that. It was like a signal. I thought it signaled danger and adventure and beauty.

I was screaming too, along with the chicken. I didn't even know I was screaming. I heaved on the heavy bird. The pole was bent double. I wanted to land the chicken. I wanted the Plymouth Rock on the porch with me.

I couldn't pick it up high enough. It was too heavy for me. It was up off the ground, all right, but I couldn't get it high enough to sling it onto the porch. The chicken was beating its wings and spinning in a wild circle. I held it there.

I heaved on the pole again. The bird swung up and around, but was still not high enough. It hit the side of the house and then swung back out into midair.

Mama came out on the porch and stood behind me. I knew she was back there, because I heard the door slap shut.

At first I didn't look back. I just stopped hauling on the chicken. I was still holding it up off the ground, though. I couldn't give it up yet, not all of it, even though I had stopped trying to land it. 25

Finally I did look back. The face of my mama, I thought, was the saddest face on this earth. It just had to be. I said, "Hey, Mama," real subdued, trying not to provoke her. I was still holding the chicken off the ground, and it still hadn't stopped making its noise. I said, "I been fishing for chickens." No use lying about it now.

I expected my mama to say, "I swan," like she always said when she meant "I swear." What she really said surprised me. She said she was a big failure in life. She said she was such a big failure in life she didn't see why she didn't just go off and eat some poison.

I eased the chicken down onto the ground. It got loose and scooted off toward the garage with its feathers sticking out.

Mama cut a switch off a crape myrtle and switched me good on my bare legs and went back inside the house. She lay across her bed on the wedding-ring quilt my grandmama Sugar gave her when she got married, with hers and Daddy's names sewed in a corner and a heart stitched around the names, and had herself a long hard cry. And so that part of it was over.

Some time passed. Some days and, I guess, some weeks. I watched my 30 mama around the house. At night, after supper, and after she had wiped the table, she would do what she liked best. She would lay out on the table a new piece of cloth from Kamp's Low Price Store and pin to it a tissue-paper Simplicity pattern. She would weight the pattern down all around with pieces of silverware from the dark chest lined with green felt. The silver came from my mama's grandmama who lost her mind and threw away the family Bible and almost everything else and so left only the silverware, which she forgot to throw away. Mama would get the pattern all weighted down, and she would look around for a minute, in her sewing basket or in a kitchen drawer, and say, "Has anybody seen my good scissors?" She would find the scissors and bring them to the table and cut through the paper and the cloth. She would poke through her sewing basket. I saw the faded pin-cushion and the cloth measuring tape and a metal thimble and about a jillion buttons and the pinking shears.

She would lay down a towel to keep from scratching the dining room table and then heft the heavy old portable Kenmore onto it. She might have to thread the bobbin. She might lift the cloth to her nose and breathe its new-smell before she put it into the machine, under the needle, and on the shiny metal plate. She would touch the pedal with her foot.

Before any of this would happen, before supper even, my daddy would come home from work. I could hear the car pull into the drive and head around back of the house. He would get out of the car, and he would be wearing white overalls and a paper cap with the name of a paint store printed on it. He would smell like paint and turpentine and maybe a little whiskey.

Daddy would shoo the chickens back from the gate in the fence where the chickens would flock when they heard his car. He would open the gate and ease inside, real quick, before anybody could get out. I would watch him.

The chickens were gossipy and busy and fat and fine. Daddy would scatter shelled corn from a white metal dishpan and pour out mash for those that needed it and run well water into the troughs.

I always wished Mama would watch him do this. I thought that if she did she would stop thinking she was a big failure in life.   35

I went down the steps and into the chicken yard with him. He let me reach my hand into the fragrant dusty corn and pelt the old birds with it.

Then there was the part where the rooster attacks you. Every day I forgot it was going to happen, and then it would happen and I would think, Now why didn't I remember that?

It happened today, this particular day, I mean, a Tuesday and just before sunset. The rooster was on top of us. It hadn't been there before, and now it was all I could see, the red furious rooster. Its wings were spread out and its bones were creaking and clacking and its beak was wide open and its tongue was blazing black as blood. And the rooster's eye — it looked like it had only one eye, and the eye was not stupid and comical like the other chickens'. It seemed lidless and magical, like it could see into a person's heart and know all its secrets and read his future. And the feet — they were blue-colored, but blue like you never saw before except in a wound. And the spurs.

And then it was over. Today, like other days, Daddy kicked the chicken in the breast with the toe of his work shoe and it flopped over on its back. It righted itself and stood up and started pecking at the corn on the ground. Daddy walked over to the rooster and petted its neck. The bird made a stretching motion with its head like a cat.

Then there was the next part. We watched the rooster eat. Without warn-   40
ing, as we knew it would, it stopped eating. It stood straight up and cocked its head so far that the comb flopped over. It looked like somebody who has just remembered something real important.

Then the rooster took off. Any other flying chickens you see are all hustle and puffing and heaving and commotion and getting ten feet maybe, not matter how hard they work at it. This chicken could fly like a wild bird, like a peacock, maybe, or a wild turkey. There was nothing graceful about it, nothing pretty. It was just so amazing to watch. When the rooster flew, it looked like some fat bad child who has rung your doorbell and is running down the street away from your house, slow and obvious and ridiculous, but padding on anyway, uncatchable. It flew out and out, over the chicken-yard fence, over a little side yard where Mr. Love kept a goat, over the trailer the midgets lived in, out farther like a kite, over a house, and finally into the branches of a line of hardwood trees across the railroad tracks.

We went inside the house then, and Daddy went into the bathroom and came out after a long time with his new smells of Wildroot and Aqua Velva and his wet combed hair. The whiskey smell was a little stronger, a little sweeter.

After supper, and after the sewing machine was turned off and put away, Mama said, "Now all I have to do is hem it, and it'll be all done." She was on the sofa, so she sat up straight and held the dress up to her front and pretended like she was modeling it. Daddy was moving out of the room. He was weaving a little when he walked, on his way to the kitchen.

I looked at Mama. She had a pleased look on her face that made me think she thought she looked pretty. She did look kind of pretty.

I picked up the package the pattern came in. There was a color picture of   45
two women on it. I said, "Where do these ladies live, Mama?"

She took the package out of my hand and looked at it with the same look on her face. She looked off somewhere away from my eyes and said, "I think maybe these two ladies live in New York City. They live across the hall from one another in a penthouse apartment. I think they just met up downtown by accident." She looked at me and smiled and handed the pattern package back to me.

I said, "What are they talking about?"

Mama said, "Hm." She took the package from me again and looked at it, serious. She said, "I think maybe, well, maybe the lady in the red dress is saying why don't we go somewhere real nice today. She's saying why don't they shop around a little and then maybe go to a picture show. They might even be talking about going to the opera, you don't know."

I tried to think about the opera, men in turbans and women in white-powdered wigs. The men carried sabers at their sides, and the women had derringers in their purses. I said, "I ain't studying no opera."

Mama laid the package down and put the new dress aside too. She started   50
poking through her sewing basket for something, but then stopped without finding it. She had lost the look she had before.

I said, "Are you going to the opera?"

She said, "No."

I said, "When you put on that dress, you know what?"

She didn't answer.

I said, "You ain't going to look like neither one of those ladies." I don't   55
know why I said that.

Mama got up from where she was sitting. She said, "Don't say *ain't*, Sugar. It will ruin your life." She got up off the sofa and went into the bedroom and closed the door.

Daddy came back into the living room. He was wobbly and ripe with whiskey. He said, "What happened to Mama?"

I said, "She's lying down."

He eased back into his chair and started to watch "Gilligan's Island" on the television.

I went to my room. I sat on the bed and let my feet hang off. I had to do   60
something. I felt like I was working a jigsaw puzzle with my family. I saw my
mama and my daddy and the chickens and the midgets and Mr. Love's goat
and I thought I could never get it worked.

I started to fish for the rooster. Sometimes I fished with a handline, sometimes with a cane pole. The rooster never looked at my bait.

I fished every day, and every day I got older and the rooster didn't get
caught. School started up again and I got new shoes. The leaves finally fell off
the trees and I helped Mama rake them up in the afternoons. The rooster hated
my bait. He couldn't stand to look at it.

I changed bait. I used raisins. I used jelly beans. I used a dog turd. You
got to want to catch a chicken to bait a hook with dog turd. Chickens eat
them all the time, no reason it wouldn't work. It didn't though.

I threw the cat in the chicken yard. I had ten hooks dangling off the cat,
feet and tail and flea collar, everywhere you can put a hook on a cat. The
rooster killed the cat, but it didn't take a hook. Too bad about the cat. You're
not going to catch a rooster without making a sacrifice or two.

After a while fishing for the rooster and keeping Mama from knowing   65
about it became like a job, like an old habit you never would think about
breaking. All that mattered was that I fish for him, that I never give up, no
matter how hopeless, no matter how old or unhappy I got.

Something happened then that changed things. It was Saturday. I got on
my bike and pedaled from my house to the picture shown in Arrow Catcher.
There was always a drawing at the matinee.

Mrs. Meyers, the old ticket-taker-upper with the white hair and shaky
hands and snuff-breath — she would do the same thing every time. She would
take your ticket out of your hand and tear it into halves and tell you what a
fine young man you were growing up to be and to hold onto your ticket stub,
you might win the drawing.

I walked down the aisle and found me a seat up close to the front. I looked
at the torn ticket in my hands, and the other seats filled up with people.

Mr. Gibbs owned the picture show, called it the Strand Theater. The lights
were all on bright and Mr. Gibbs climbed up on the stage by a set of wooden
steps around the side. He was huffing and sweating, waving his hands for
everybody to be quiet. Like he said every Saturday, he said, "Be quiet, boys
and gulls, be quite, please." We laughed at him, and the underarms of his white
shirt were soaked with sweat.

I watched Mr. Gibbs crank the handle of a wire basket filled with ping-   70
pong balls. Every ball had a number on it. Mr. Gibbs would draw them out,
one at a time, and put each one on a little cushioned platform with the number
facing out to the audience, until he had four of them. He would draw them
out slow and teasing and smiling. It was something he loved to do, you could
tell. He would call out each number in its turn, real loud and exaggerated. He

would say, "Fo-urrr," or "Nye-unn," and he would hold up the white ball and show everyone he wasn't cheating, and then he would put the ball on the cushioned stand. You had to like Mr. Gibbs.

Then it started happening. The first number he called out was the first number on my ticket stub. And then so was the second. It seemed impossible that the number in my ear was the same number as in my eye. It kept on being the same number, digit by digit, right down to the end. I had won the drawing.

I had never won anything before. One time I won a pink cake in a cakewalk. It tasted terrible and I hated it, but I ate all of it anyway, same night I won it. I had never won anything except that cake, so it was impressive enough to win the drawing.

But winning was nothing compared to the prize I was going to take home. I had won the Zebco rod and spinning reel from the Western Auto.

Mr. Gibbs was standing up on that little stage like a sweaty fat angel. He was giving his heartfelt thanks to the Western Auto store, homeowned and homeoperated by Mr. Sooey Leonard, and to all the other fine local merchants of Arrow Catcher who donated these fine prizes and made these drawings possible.

I went up on the stage. I climbed the same dusty wooden steps that Mr.   75
Gibbs had climbed. I showed Mr. Gibbs my ticket stub. I was trembling. He shook my hand, and my hand was sweaty and slick against his manly palm and fingers. Mr. Gibbs asked me if I didn't think every single person in this fine audience ought to take his patronage to the Western Auto store and all the other fine local merchants of Arrow Catcher.

I said, "Yessir," and everybody laughed and clapped their hands.

Mr. Gibbs said what was I going to do with my fine prize.

I said, "Go fishing," and everybody laughed again.

Mr. Gibbs said why didn't everybody give this fine young fisherman another round of applause, and so everybody did.

I don't know what was on the movie. I sat through it, and I watched it,   80
with the fishing rod between my legs, but I didn't see it. I remember a huffing train and some wreckage, I remember an icy train platform and taxicabs and a baby growing up rich instead of poor. Barbara Stanwyck married John Lund, I remember that. Whatever was on the movie, one thing was all I was thinking about and that was that I was definitely going fishing, no doubt about it. The fish I was going to catch was as tall as me and had red feathers and was big enough and fine enough to ruin the life of every soul in Arrow Catcher, Mississippi.

I look back at the day I caught the rooster. I see the familiar yard, the fence of chicken wire. I smell the sweet fresh fragrance of grain and mash and lime and chickenshit and water from a deep well poured through troughs of corrugated metal. I smell creosote and the green pungent shucks of black walnuts under the tree. I see the trailer the midgets lived in and the goat next door. I see myself, a boy, holding the Zebco rod I won at the Strand Theater. The Zebco moves back, then whips forward.

The line leaps away from the reel, from the rod's tip. It leaps into S's and figure eights. It floats like the strand of a spider's web. At the end of the line I see the white fleck of sunlight that covers the hook: the bait, the kernel of corn. I watch it fly toward the rooster.

I look ahead of the corn, far down the chicken yard, and see the rooster. It seems to be on fire in the sunlight. For one second I lose my mind and believe that the rooster means something more than a rooster. I don't believe it long. I come to my senses and know that the rooster is a chicken, that's all. A very bad chicken. He is the same miserable wretched mean bad son-of-a-bitch that my daddy has called him every day of the rooster's life. I remember that the rooster is smarter than me, and faster and stronger and crazier. I remember that I am in the chicken yard with him and that he doesn't like me and that my daddy ain't home from work to protect me and my ass is in trouble, Jack.

I understand, at last, what the rooster is going to do. He is going to catch the bait in the air, like a dog catching a Frisbee. I can't believe what I am watching. The rooster has positioned itself, flat-footed, with its mouth open, its head cocked to one side. Until this moment I have not believed I would catch the rooster. I have meant to catch it, but the habit of fishing for it is all I have thought about for a long time. And now, in the presence of an emotion something like awe, I understand that the rooster is about to catch me.

It happens. The rooster, at the last moment, has to lurch a step forward, 85
it has to duck its head, but it does so with perfect accuracy. The bird might as well have been a large red-feathered frog plucking a fly from the air. He catches the baited hook in his mouth.

I do not move to set the hook. There is no point. The rooster has been fishing for me for three years, and now it has caught me. I have become old enough to believe that doom will always surprise you, that doom is domestic and purrs like a cat.

The bird stands quiet with the bait in its mouth. The line droops to the ground from his chicken lips. I stand attached to him by the line. It is no help to remember that the rooster is a beast and without humor.

Then it does move. At first I thought the creature was growing taller. Nothing could have surprised me. I might have been growing smaller. Neither was true. I was watching what I had watched many times. I was watching the rooster take flight.

It left the ground. The hook was still in its mouth, attached to nothing. The rooster was holding the hook in its mouth like a peanut.

More than ever the bird seemed on fire. It flew out and out, away from 90
me. The nylon line trailed it in flight. The sun shone on the rooster and on the line and told me that I was in big trouble and had not yet figured out how.

It flew over the chicken-yard fence, over the goat, over the midgets. It gained altitude. I watched the line be stripped in coils from my open-face reel.

The bird flew and flew, high as the housetops, and then the treetops, out toward the railroad tracks. I was a child flying a living kite.

It took me a minute to see what the rooster was up to. I had never seen him do this before. Just when he was almost out of sight, out over the railroad tracks and ready, I thought, to light in the hardwood trees, the bird seemed to hang suspended. It seemed to have hung itself in midair and to have begun to swell out like a balloon. I was holding the fishing rod limp in my hand and studying the rooster's strange inflation. The rooster, above the treetops, ballooned larger and larger. It grew large enough that I could distinguish its particular features again, the stretched neck and popped-out eyes, the sturdy wings and red belly feathers. Nothing about the appearance of the rooster made sense.

And then everything did. I was not looking at the bird's tail-feathers, as I should have been. I was looking him in the face. He was not growing larger, he was coming closer. I looked at my reel and saw that the line was still. The rooster had turned around in flight and was coming back after me.

I looked at him. The rooster had cleared the goat and the midgets. It was big as a goose, big as a collie. Its feet were blue and as big as yard rakes. I dropped the fishing rod into the dirt. I turned to the gate and tried to open the latch. I could hear the rooster's bones creaking and clacking. I could hear the feathers thudding against the air. My hands were clubs, the gate would not come unlatched. I pounded at the gate.

I heard the rooster set its wings like a hawk about to land on a fence post.   95
The rooster landed on my head. It didn't fall off. I thought it might, but it did not. It clung to my scalp by its fierce toenails. I clubbed at the gate with my useless hands. The bird stood on my head, and its wings kept up their motion and clatter. I could not appreciate the mauling I was receiving by the wings for the fire the feet had lit in my brain. I tried to climb the gate, but my feet had turned to stumps.

The chicken yard was in hysterics, the Plymouth Rocks and Leghorns and blue Andalusians. I clung to the gate with the rooster on my head. I imagined flames the shape of an angry chicken rising from my head.

I screamed, and still the rooster held on. It drubbed me with its wings. My eyes were blackened and swollen, my nose ran with blood. I didn't care, so long as someone put out the fire in my scalp.

I got the idea that it could be put out with water. I gave up at the gate and ran stumbling across the chicken yard. Layers and pullets and bantams, all the curious and hysterical, fanned away from me in droves. The rooster hung on.

I reached the hydrant hopeless. There was no hope of putting my head under the spigot while wearing the chicken. There was a garden hose in the old garage, but it was of no use. If I could not open the simple latch of the gate, there was no chance I could retrieve the garden hose from its wall hook and screw it to the spigot.

My mama was standing on the back porch watching. I longed for the days 100
when I was young enough to be switched with crape myrtle. I saw her start to
move toward me. She was moving toward me but I knew she would never
reach me in time. Blood and chickenshit ran down the sides of my face and
into my ears. The wings kept up the pounding, and the rooster's bones and
ligaments kept up the creaking and clacking and clicking.

I had not noticed my daddy drive up, but now I saw his car in the driveway.
He left the car and was headed toward me. He also moved in slow motion.

I left the spigot. My motion and my parents' motion had become the same.
They stood at the gate and pounded at it. Their hands were clubs too and the
gate would not open for them.

I motioned for them to stay where they were. They saw that I knew what
I was doing. Something had changed in me. I was not running now. The rooster
was still riding my head. I walked, purposeful, like a heavy bear through the
chicken yard.

And yet my steps were not heavy. My life was not ruined. I could wear
this chicken on my head forever. I could bear this pain forever. In a year no
one would notice the chicken but myself. Then even I would not notice. My
mama had believed that spending your life in the place of your birth, absorbing
its small particulars into your blood, was ruination. I looked at my parents
beside the gate. My daddy held my mama in his arms as they looked at me.
My daddy had gotten the gate open now but again I held up my hand and
stopped him. I knew now what I could give them. It was a picture of myself
that I would live the rest of my life to prove true: They watched their son wear
this living crowing rooster like a crown.

They were proud of me. I knew they were. They were frightened also but 105
pride was mainly what I saw in their faces as I kept them from helping me.
They believed that my life would not be ruined. They believed that a man
who has worn a chicken on his head — worn it proudly, as I was beginning
to do — would never be a fool to geography or marriage or alcohol.

I stood tall in the chicken yard. My parents looked at me from the gate
and I felt their love and pride touch me. They believed that a man and his wife
with such a son could not be ruined either, not yet, not forever.

The rooster had stopped flapping its wings. It was heavy on me, but I
straightened my back and did not slump. Now it balanced itself with more
ease, it carried more of its own weight and was easier to hold. It stood on my
head like an eagle on a mountain crag. I strode toward my parents and they
toward me. The three of us, and the rooster, moved through the chicken yard
in glory.

1986

INVESTIGATIONS

1. Why is Sugar's mother so sad after she catches him fishing for chickens?
   What does this habit signify for her?

2. If the rooster doesn't "mean more than a rooster," why does Sugar try so hard to catch him?

3. Describe the pieces in the "jigsaw puzzle" of Sugar's family and make an attempt to "get it worked." Describe the picture you get when you "work" the "jigsaw puzzle" of your family. How much of the picture can be seen in the writing you did in "Write Before Reading"?

4. Write a 250–500-word essay in which you support this assertion: "In Lewis Nordan's 'Sugar Among the Chickens,' each of Sugar Mecklin's actions demonstrates that instinct heals what reason might harm."

PART TWO
CONNECTIONS AND ELABORATIONS

1. After reexamining the selections in Part Two, your response to "Write Before Reading" on page 114, and any other writing and thinking you've done in response to the selections, write an essay that defines what makes a family a family.

2. Using the writing you did in response to "Write Before Reading" and any appropriate evidence from the selections, write an essay analyzing the ways a family's "legends" act as obstacles to change within the family.

3. After deciding which instance of family discord in Part Two you find most compelling, write a scene (in the case of a story), some dialogue (in the case of the play), or a stanza (in the case of a poem) that transforms the discord into harmony. Then write a short essay in which you say what in the characters or situation prevents the reconciliation you've imagined.

4. After choosing an appropriate selection, write an essay supporting or refuting this assertion: "The members of this family should stop rationalizing destructive behavior and take responsibility for their actions."

5. Using as evidence material from Balaban's "Words for My Daughter," Gallagher's "The Lover of Horses," Mitsui's "Allowance," and Erdrich's "The Leap," write an essay that argues that family obligation can be liberating, not burdensome.

6. Using as evidence material from Machado's *Broken Eggs*, Nordan's "Sugar Among the Chickens," Mukherjee's "Fathering," Gallagher's "The Lover of Horses," and Herman's "A Parent's Journey Out of the Closet," write an essay

   a. in which you argue that we have much less control than we think we do over how and why we act, *or*

   b. in which you analyze how accepting our lack of control over our actions changes how we think about what we do.

7. You've witnessed a number of instances of family love in Part Two. After reexamining Erdrich's "The Leap," write an essay in which you show how these instances can be seen as "forms of flight."

216

PART THREE

WITH FRIENDS

Most of us consider friendship to be as important as any other relationship in our lives. Sometimes, in fact, we feel closer to our friends
than to anyone else: Friends share secrets, explore one another's unique
outlooks on life, confess innermost doubts and pleasures, share adventures, try to help each other through times of trouble, and swear to
remain friends no matter what. Despite all this it often seems easier to
say what friendship isn't than to say what it is.

In Part Three you'll read and write about friends of various ages
and cultures. In Grace Paley's "Friends," a group of women visit a sick
friend, trying to comfort her and one another; "My Lucy Friend Who
Smells Like Corn," by Sandra Cisneros, recalls the delight of a childhood friendship; a sixteen-year-old girl has to choose between loyalty
and responsibility in Ellen Darion's "Claudia"; in "Para Teresa," by
Inés Hernandez, two schoolchildren develop mutual respect despite their
differences; Louise Glück's "Celestial Music" shows how friends sometimes teach one another; in Alice Adams's "Waiting for Stella," aging
friends reflect on their own past and future as they remember the lively
Stella, "the first of them to die"; in David Rabe's *Hurlyburly* four men

rage at one another, the women in their lives, and the circumstances in which they find themselves; and in Richard Howard's "The Victor Vanquished," Thom Gunn's "Memory Unsettled," Cathy Song's "Losing Track," Jesse Lee Kercheval's "Willy," and Martín Espada's "Manuel Is Quiet Sometimes," friendship is tested by loss.

WRITE BEFORE READING

We often hear how crucial it is to "be there" when our friends need us. After calling to mind your most significant friendships, tell the story of a time when you or a friend of yours *failed* to "be there," yet the friendship continued. Then write a paragraph or two analyzing the changes caused by the failure, and the reasons you and your friend were able to go on being friends.

Friends

To put us at our ease, to quiet our hearts as she lay dying, our dear friend Selena said, Life, after all, has not been an unrelieved horror — you know, I *did* have many wonderful years with her.

She pointed to a child who leaned out of a portrait on the wall — long brown hair, white pinafore, head and shoulders forward.

Eagerness, said Susan. Ann closed her eyes.

On the same wall three little girls were photographed in a school yard. They were in furious discussion; they were holding hands. Right in the middle of the coffee table, framed, in autumn colors, a handsome young woman of eighteen sat on an enormous horse — aloof, disinterested, a rider. One night this young woman, Selena's child, was found in a rooming house in a distant city, dead. The police called. They said, Do you have a daughter named Abby?

And with *him*, too, our friend Selena said. We had good times, Max and I. You know that. 5

There were no photographs of *him*. He was married to another woman and had a new, stalwart girl of about six, to whom no harm would ever come, her mother believed.

Our dear Selena had gotten out of bed. Heavily but with a comic dance, she soft-shoed to the bathroom, singing, "Those were the days, my friend . . ."

Later that evening, Ann, Susan, and I were enduring our five-hour train ride to home. After one hour of silence and one hour of coffee and the sandwiches Selena had given us (she actually stood, leaned her big soft excavated body against the kitchen table to make those sandwiches), Ann said, Well, we'll never see *her* again.

Who says? Anyway, listen, said Susan. Think of it. Abby isn't the only kid who died. What about that great guy, remember Bill Dalrymple — he was a noncooperator or a deserter? And Bob Simon. They were killed in automobile accidents. Matthew, Jeannie, Mike. Remember Al Lurie — he was murdered on Sixth Street — and that little kid Brenda, who O.D.'d on your roof, Ann? The tendency, I suppose, is to forget. You people don't remember them.

What do you mean, "you people"? Ann asked. You're talking to *us*. 10

I began to apologize for not knowing them all. Most of them were older than my kids, I said.

Grace Paley (b. 1922) grew up in the Bronx, New York. A political activist since the 1950s, she sees "this whole masculine enterprise of war" as humanity's fundamental problem. Besides *Leaning Forward* (1985), a collection of poems, she has published three collections of stories, most recently *Later the Same Day* (1985).

Of course, the child Abby was exactly in my time of knowing and in all my places of paying attention — the park, the school, our street. But oh! It's true! Selena's Abby was not the only one of that beloved generation of our children murdered by cars, lost to war, to drugs, to madness.

Selena's main problem, Ann said — you know, she didn't tell the truth. What?

A few hot human truthful words are powerful enough, Ann thinks, to steam all God's chemical mistakes and society's slimy lies out of her life. We all believe in that power, my friends and I, but sometimes . . . the heat.

Anyway, I always thought Selena had told us a lot. For instance, we knew she was an orphan. There were six, seven other children. She was the youngest. She was forty-two years old before someone informed her that her mother had *not* died in childbirthing her. It was some terrible sickness. And she had lived close to her mother's body — at her breast, in fact — until she was eight months old. Whew! said Selena. What a relief! I'd always felt I was the one who'd killed her.

Your family stinks, we told her. They really held you up for grief.

Oh, people, she said. Forget it. They did a lot of nice things for me too. Me and Abby. Forget it. Who has the time?

That's what I mean, said Ann. Selena should have gone after them with an ax.

More information: Selena's two sisters brought her to a Home. They were ashamed that at sixteen and nineteen they could not take care of her. They kept hugging her. They were sure she'd cry. They took her to her room — not a room, a dormitory with about eight beds. This is your bed, Lena. This is your table for your things. This little drawer is for your toothbrush. All for me? she asked. No one else can use it? Only me. That's all? Artie can't come? Franky can't come? Right?

Believe me, Selena said, those were happy days at Home.

Facts, said Ann, just facts. Not necessarily the *truth*.

I don't think it's right to complain about the character of the dying or start hustling all their motives into the spotlight like that. Isn't it amazing enough, the bravery of that private inclusive intentional community?

It wouldn't help not to be brave, said Selena. You'll see.

She wanted to get back to bed. Susan moved to help her.

Thanks, our Selena said, leaning on another person for the first time in her entire life. The trouble is, when I stand, it hurts me here all down my back. Nothing they can do about it. All the chemotherapy. No more chemistry left in me to therapeut. Ha! Did you know before I came to New York and met you I used to work in that hospital? I was supervisor in gynecology. Nursing. They were my friends, the doctors. They weren't so snotty then. David Clark, big surgeon. He couldn't look at me last week. He kept saying, Lena . . . Lena . . . Like that. We were in North Africa the same year — '44, I think. I told him, Davy, I've been around a long enough time. I haven't missed too much.

He knows it. But I didn't want to make him look at me. Ugh, my damn feet are a pain in the neck.

Recent research, said Susan, tells us that it's the neck that's a pain in the feet.

Always something new, said Selena, our dear friend.

On the way back to the bed, she stopped at her desk. There were about twenty snapshots scattered across it — the baby, the child, the young woman. Here, she said to me, take this one. It's a shot of Abby and your Richard in front of the school — third grade? What a day! The show those kids put on! What a bunch of kids! What's Richard doing now?

Oh, who knows? Horsing around someplace. Spain. These days, it's Spain. Who knows where he is? They're all the same.

Why did I say that? I knew exactly where he was. He writes. In fact, he found a broken phone and was able to call every day for a week — mostly to give orders to his brother but also to say, Are you OK, Ma? How's your new boyfriend, did he smile yet?

The kids, they're all the same, I said.

It was only politeness, I think, not to pour my boy's light, noisy face into that dark afternoon. Richard used to say in his early mean teens, You'd sell us down the river to keep Selena happy and innocent. It's true. Whenever Selena would say, I don't know, Abby has some peculiar friends, I'd answer for stupid comfort, You should see Richard's.

Still, he's in Spain, Selena said. At least you know that. It's probably interesting. He'll learn a lot. Richard is a wonderful boy, Faith. He acts like a wise guy but he's not. You know the night Abby died, when the police called me and told me? That was my first night's sleep in two years. I *knew* where she was.

Selena said this very matter-of-factly — just offering a few informative sentences.

But Ann, listening, said, Oh! — she called out to us all, Oh! — and began to sob. Her straightforwardness had become an arrow and gone right into her own heart.

Then a deep tear-drying breath: I want a picture too, she said.

Yes. Yes, wait, I have one here someplace. Abby and Judy and that Spanish kid Victor. Where is it? Ah. Here!

Three nine-year-old children sat high on that long-armed sycamore in the park, dangling their legs on someone's patient head — smooth dark hair, parted in the middle. Was that head Kitty's?

Our dear friend laughed. Another great day, she said. Wasn't it? I remember you two sizing up the men. I *had* one at the time — I thought. Some joke. Here, take it. I have two copies. But you ought to get it enlarged. When this you see, remember me. Ha-ha. Well, girls — excuse me, I mean ladies — it's time for me to rest.

She took Susan's arm and continued that awful walk to her bed.

30

35

40

We didn't move. We had a long journey ahead of us and had expected a little more comforting before we set off.

No, she said. You'll only miss the express. I'm not in much pain. I've got lots of painkiller. See?

The tabletop was full of little bottles.

I just want to lie down and think of Abby.   45

It was true, the local could cost us an extra two hours at least. I looked at Ann. It had been hard for her to come at all. Still, we couldn't move. We stood there before Selena in a row. Three old friends. Selena pressed her lips together, ordered her eyes into cold distance.

I know that face. Once, years ago, when the children were children, it had been placed modestly in front of J. Hoffner, the principal of the elementary school.

He'd said, No! Without training you cannot tutor these kids. There are real problems. You have to know *how to teach.*

Our P.T.A. had decided to offer some one-to-one tutorial help for the Spanish kids, who were stuck in crowded classrooms with exhausted teachers among little middle-class achievers. He had said, in a written communication to show seriousness and then in personal confrontation to *prove* seriousness, that he could not allow it. And the board of ed itself had said no. (All this no-ness was to lead to some terrible events in the schools and neighborhoods of our poor yes-requiring city.) But most of the women in our P.T.A. were independent — by necessity and disposition. We were, in fact, the soft-speaking tough souls of anarchy.

I had Fridays off that year. At about 11 A.M. I'd bypass the principal's   50
office and run up to the fourth floor. I'd take Robert Figueroa to the end of the hall, and we'd work away at storytelling for about twenty minutes. Then we would write the beautiful letters of the alphabet invented by smart foreigners long ago to fool time and distance.

That day, Selena and her stubborn face remained in the office for at least two hours. Finally, Mr. Hoffner, besieged, said that because she was a nurse, she would be allowed to help out by taking the littlest children to the modern, difficult toilet. Some of them, he said, had just come from the barbarous hills beyond Maricao. Selena said OK, she'd do that. In the toilet she taught the little girls which way to wipe, as she had taught her own little girl a couple of years earlier. At three o'clock she brought them home for cookies and milk. The children of that year ate cookies in her kitchen until the end of the sixth grade.

Now, what did we learn in that year of my Friday afternoons off? The following: Though the world cannot be changed by talking to one child at a time, it may at least be known.

Anyway, Selena placed into our eyes for long remembrance that useful stubborn face. She said, No. Listen to me, you people. Please. I don't have lots of time. What I want . . . I want to lie down and think about Abby. Nothing special. Just think about her, you know.

In the train Susan fell asleep immediately. She woke up from time to time, because the speed of the new wheels and the resistance of the old track gave us some terrible jolts. Once, she opened her eyes wide and said, You know, Ann's right. You don't get sick like that for nothing. I mean, she didn't even mention him.

Why should she? She hasn't even seen him, I said. Susan, you still have   55
him-itis, the dread disease of females.

Yeah? And you don't? Anyway, he *was* around quite a bit. He was there every day, nearly, when the kid died.

Abby. I didn't like to hear "the kid." I wanted to say "Abby" the way I've said "Selena" — so those names can take thickness and strength and fall back into the world with their weight.

Abby, you know, was a wonderful child. She was in Richard's classes every class till high school. Good-hearted little girl from the beginning, noticeably kind — for a kid, I mean. Smart.

That's true, said Ann, very kind. She'd give away Selena's last shirt. Oh yes, they were all wonderful little girls and wonderful little boys.

Chrissy *is* wonderful, Susan said.   60

She *is,* I said.

Middle kids aren't supposed to be, but she is. She put herself through college — I didn't have a cent — and now she has this fellowship. And, you know, she never did take any crap from boys. She's something.

Ann went swaying up the aisle to the bathroom. First she said, Oh, all of them — just wohunderful.

I loved Selena, Susan said, but she never talked to me enough. Maybe she talked to you women more, about things. Men.

Then Susan fell asleep.   65

Ann sat down opposite me. She looked straight into my eyes with a narrow squint. It often connotes accusation.

Be careful — you're wrecking your laugh lines, I said.

Screw you, she said. You're kidding around. Do you realize, I don't know where Mickey is? You know, you've been lucky. You always have been. Since you were a little kid. Papa and Mama's darling.

As is usual in conversations, I said a couple of things out loud and kept a few structured remarks for interior mulling and righteousness. I thought: She's never even met my folks. I thought: What a rotten thing to say. Luck — isn't it something like an insult?

I said, Annie, I'm only forty-eight. There's lots of time for me to be totally   70
wrecked — if I live, I mean.

Then I tried to knock on wood, but we were sitting in plush and leaning on plastic. Wood! I shouted. Please, some wood! Anybody here have a matchstick?

Oh, shut up, she said. Anyway, death doesn't count.

I tried to think of a couple of sorrows as irreversible as death. But truthfully nothing in my life can compare to hers: a son, a boy of fifteen, who disappears before your very eyes into a darkness or a light behind his own, from which neither hugging nor hitting can bring him. If you shout, Come back, come back, he won't come. Mickey, Mickey, Mickey, we once screamed, as though he were twenty miles away instead of right in front of us in a kitchen chair; but he refused to return. And when he did, twelve hours later, he left immediately for California.

Well, some bad things had happened in my life, I said.

What? You were born a woman? Is that it?   75

She was, of course, mocking me this time, referring to an old discussion about feminism and Judaism. Actually, on the prism of isms, both of those do have to be looked at together once in a while.

Well, I said, my mother died a couple of years ago and I still feel it. I think *Ma* sometimes and I lose my breath. I miss her. You understand that. Your mother's seventy-six. You have to admit it's nice still having her.

She's very sick, Ann said. Half the time she's out of it.

I decided not to describe my mother's death. I could have done so and made Ann even more miserable. But I thought I'd save that for her next attack on me. These constrictions of her spirit were coming closer and closer together. Probably a great enmity was about to be born.

Susan's eyes opened. The death or dying of someone near or dear often   80
makes people irritable, she stated. (She's been taking a course in relationships *and* interrelationships.) The real name of my seminar is Skills: Personal Friendship and Community. It's a very good course despite your snide remarks.

While we talked, a number of cities passed us, going in the opposite direction. I had tried to look at New London through the dusk of the windows. Now I was missing New Haven. The conductor explained, smiling: Lady, if the windows were clean, half of you'd be dead. The tracks are lined with sharpshooters.

Do you believe that? I hate people to talk that way.

He may be exaggerating, Susan said, but don't wash the window.

A man leaned across the aisle. Ladies, he said, I do believe it. According to what I hear of this part of the country, it don't seem unplausible.

Susan turned to see if he was worth engaging in political dialogue.   85

You've forgotten Selena already, Ann said. All of us have. Then you'll make this nice memorial service for her and everyone will stand up and say a few words and then we'll forget her again — for good. What'll you say at the memorial, Faith?

It's not right to talk like that. She's not dead yet, Annie.

Yes, she is, said Ann.

We discovered the next day that give or take an hour or two, Ann had been correct. It was a combination — David Clark, surgeon, said — of being sick unto real death and having a tabletop full of little bottles.

Now, why are you taking all those hormones? Susan had asked Selena a   90
couple of years earlier. They were visiting New Orleans. It was Mardi Gras.

Oh, they're mostly vitamins, Selena said. Besides, I want to be young and beautiful. She made a joking pirouette.

Susan said, That's absolutely ridiculous.

But Susan's seven or eight years younger than Selena. What did she know? Because: People *do* want to be young and beautiful. When they meet in the street, male or female, if they're getting older they look at each other's face a little ashamed. It's clear they want to say, Excuse me, I didn't mean to draw attention to mortality and gravity all at once. I didn't want to remind you, my dear friend, of our coming eviction, first from liveliness, then from life. To which, most of the time, the friend's eyes will courteously reply, My dear, it's nothing at all. I hardly noticed.

Luckily, I learned recently how to get out of that deep well of melancholy. Anyone can do it. You grab at roots of the littlest future, sometimes just stubs of conversation. Though some believe you miss a great deal of depth by not sinking down down down.

Susan, I asked, you still seeing Ed Flores?   95

Went back to his wife.

Lucky she didn't kill you, said Ann. I'd never fool around with a Spanish guy. They all have tough ladies back in the barrio.

No, said Susan, she's unusual. I met her at a meeting. We had an amazing talk. Luisa is a very fine woman. She's one of the office-worker organizers I told you about. She only needs him two more years, she says. Because the kids — they're girls — need to be watched a little in their neighborhood. The neighborhood is definitely not good. He's a good father but not such a great husband.

I'd call that a word to the wise.

Well, you know me — I don't want a husband. I like a male person around.   100 I hate to do without. Anyway, listen to this. She, Luisa, whispers in my ear the other day, she whispers, Suzie, in two years you still want him, I promise you, you got him. Really, I may still want him then. He's only about forty-five now. Still got a lot of spunk. I'll have my degree in two years. Chrissy will be out of the house.

Two years! In two years we'll all be dead, said Ann.

I know she didn't mean all of us. She meant Mickey. That boy of hers would surely be killed in one of the drugstores or whorehouses of Chicago, New Orleans, San Francisco. I'm in a big beautiful city, he said when he called last month. Makes New York look like a garbage tank.

Mickey! Where?

Ha-ha, he said, and hung up.

Soon he'd be picked up for vagrancy, dealing, small thievery, or simply   105 screaming dirty words at night under a citizen's window. Then Ann would fly to the town or not fly to the town to disentangle him, depending on a confluence of financial reality and psychiatric advice.

How *is* Mickey? Selena had said. In fact, that was her first sentence when

we came, solemn and embarrassed, into her sunny front room that was full of
the light and shadow of windy courtyard trees. We said, each in her own way,
How are you feeling, Selena? She said, OK, first things first. Let's talk about
important things. How's Richard? How's Tonto? How's John? How's Chrissy?
How's Judy? How's Mickey?

I don't want to talk about Mickey, said Ann.

Oh, let's talk about him, talk about him, Selena said, taking Ann's hand.
Let's all think before it's too late. How did it start? Oh, for godsake talk about
him.

Susan and I were smart enough to keep our mouths shut.

Nobody knows, nobody knows anything. Why? Where? Everybody has an   110
idea, theories, and writes articles. Nobody knows.

Ann said this sternly. She didn't whine. She wouldn't lean too far into
Selena's softness, but listening to Selena speak Mickey's name, she could sit in
her chair more easily. I watched. It was interesting. Ann breathed deeply in
and out the way we've learned in our Thursday-night yoga class. She was able
to rest her body a little bit.

We were riding the rails of the trough called Park-Avenue-in-the-Bronx.
Susan had turned from us to talk to the man across the aisle. She was explaining
that the war in Vietnam was not yet over and would not be, as far as she was
concerned, until we repaired the dikes we'd bombed and paid for some of the
hopeless ecological damage. He didn't see it that way. Fifty thousand American
lives, our own boys — we'd paid, he said. He asked us if we agreed with Susan.
Every word, we said.

You don't look like hippies. He laughed. Then his face changed. As the
resident face-reader, I decided he was thinking: Adventure. He may have hit a
mother lode of late counterculture in three opinionated left-wing ladies. That
was the nice part of his face. The other part was the sly out-of-town-husband-
in-New-York look.

I'd like to see you again, he said to Susan.

Oh? Well, come to dinner day after tomorrow. Only two of my kids will   115
be home. You ought to have at least one decent meal in New York.

Kids? His face thought it over. Thanks. Sure, he said. I'll come.

Ann muttered, She's impossible. She did it again.

Oh, Susan's OK, I said. She's just right in there. Isn't that good?

This is a long ride, said Ann.

Then we were in the darkness that precedes Grand Central.   120

We're irritable, Susan explained to her new pal. We're angry with our
friend Selena for dying. The reason is, we want her to be present when we're
dying. We all require a mother or mother-surrogate to fix our pillows on that
final occasion, and we were counting on her to be that person.

I know just what you mean, he said. You'd like to have someone around.
A little fuss, maybe.

Something like that. Right, Faith?

It always takes me a minute to slide under the style of her public-address system. I agreed. Yes.

The train stopped hard, in a grinding agony of opposing technologies. 125

Right. Wrong. Who cares? Ann said. She didn't have to die. She really wrecked everything.

Oh, Annie, I said.

Shut up, will you? Both of you, said Ann, nearly breaking our knees as she jammed past us and out of the train.

Then Susan, like a New York hostess, began to tell that man all our private troubles — the mistake of the World Trade Center, Westway, the decay of the South Bronx, the rage in Williamsburg. She rose with him on the escalator, gabbing into evening friendship and, hopefully, a happy night.

At home Anthony, my youngest son, said, Hello, you just missed Richard. 130 He's in Paris now. He had to call collect.

Collect? From Paris?

He saw my sad face and made one of the herb teas used by his peer group to calm their overwrought natures. He does want to improve my pretty good health and spirits. His friends have a book that says a person should, if properly nutritioned, live forever. He wants me to give it a try. He also believes that the human race, its brains and good looks, will end in his time.

At about 11:30 he went out to live the pleasures of his eighteen-year-old nighttime life.

At 3 A.M. he found me washing the floors and making little apartment repairs.

More tea, Mom? he asked. He sat down to keep me company. OK, Faith. 135 I know you feel terrible. But how come Selena never realized about Abby?

Anthony, what the hell do I realize about you?

Come on, you had to be blind. I was just a little kid, and *I* saw. Honest to God, Ma.

Listen, Tonto. Basically Abby was OK. She was. You don't know yet what their times can do to a person.

Here she goes with her goody-goodies — everything is so groovy wonderful far-out terrific. Next thing, you'll say people are darling and the world is *so* nice and round that Union Carbide will never blow it up.

I have never said anything as hopeful as that. And why to all our knowledge 140 of that sad day did Tonto at 3 A.M. have to add the fact of the world?

The next night Max called from North Carolina. How's Selena? I'm flying up, he said. I have one early-morning appointment. Then I'm canceling everything.

At 7 A.M. Annie called. I had barely brushed my morning teeth. It was hard, she said. The whole damn thing. I don't mean Selena. All of us. In the train. None of you seemed real to me.

Real? Reality, huh? Listen, how about coming over for breakfast — I don't have to get going until after nine. I have this neat sourdough rye?

No she said. Oh Christ, no. No!

I remember Ann's eyes and the hat she wore the day we first looked at each other. Our babies had just stepped howling out of the sandbox on their new walking legs. We picked them up. Over their sandy heads we smiled. I think a bond was sealed then, at least as useful as the vow we'd all sworn with husbands to whom we're no longer married. Hindsight, usually looked down upon, is probably as valuable as foresight, since it does include a few facts. 145

Meanwhile, Anthony's world — poor, dense, defenseless thing — rolls round and round. Living and dying are fastened to its surface and stuffed into its softer parts.

He was right to call my attention to its suffering and danger. He was right to harass my responsible nature. But I was right to invent for my friends and our children a report on these private deaths and the condition of our lifelong attachments.   1985

INVESTIGATIONS

1. In paragraph 53 the narrator, Faith, says, "Selena placed into our eyes for long remembrance that useful stubborn face." Go through the story and find evidence of the usefulness of that "stubborn face," both for Selena and for her three friends. How much of the friendship among these four women comes from the use each friend has been to the others?

2. Several times in the story Faith doesn't say entirely what she thinks: She says "a couple of things out loud" and keeps "a few structured remarks for interior mulling and righteousness" (para. 69). After locating each of these instances and reflecting on your own experience with friendship, analyze the extent to which friendship depends on not telling the whole truth.

3. Compare the friendship described in "Claudia" (p. 231) to the friendships described in this story. To what extent are the differences a product of the difference in the characters' ages? What accounts for the similarities, despite the difference in the characters' ages?

4. At the end of the story, Faith says, "I was right to invent for my friends and our children a report on these private deaths and the condition of our lifelong attachments." What does she mean? In what sense is friendship itself an invention?

SANDRA CISNEROS

My Lucy Friend
Who Smells Like Corn

Lucy Anguiano, Texas girl who smells like corn, like Frito Bandito chips, like tortillas, something like that warm smell of *nixtamal* or bread the way her head smells when she's leaning close to you over a paper cutout doll or on the porch when we are squatting over marbles trading this pretty crystal that leaves a blue star on your hand for that giant cat-eye with a grasshopper-green spiral in the center like the juice of bugs on the windshield when you drive to the border, like the yellow blood of butterflies.

Have you ever eated dog food? I have. After crunching like ice, she opens her big mouth to prove it, only a pink tongue rolling around in there like a blind worm, and Janey looking in because she said, Show me. But me, I like that Lucy, corn-smell hair and aqua flip-flops just like mine that we bought at the K-Mart for only seventy-nine cents same time.

I'm going to sit in the sun, don't care if it's a million trillion degrees outside, so my skin can get so dark it's blue where it bends like Lucy's. Her whole family like that. Eyes like knife slits. Lucy and her sisters. Norma, Margarita, Ofelia, Herminia, Nancy, Olivia, Cheli, y la Amber Sue.

Screen door with no screen. BANG! Little black dog biting his fur. Fat couch on the porch. Some of the windows painted blue, some pink because her daddy got tired that day or forgot. Mama in the kitchen feeding clothes into the wringer washer and clothes rolling out all stiff and twisted and flat like paper. Lucy got her arm stuck once and had to yell, Maaa! and her mama had to put the machine in reverse and then her hand rolled back, the finger black and later, her nail fell off. *But did your arm get flat like the clothes? What happened to your arm? Did they have to pump it with air?* No, only the finger, and she didn't cry neither.

Lean across the porch rail and pin the pink sock of the baby Amber Sue 5
on top of Cheli's flowered T-shirt, and the blue jeans of la Ofelia over the inside seam of Olivia's blouse, over the flannel nightgown of Margarita so it don't stretch out, and then you take the work shirts of their daddy and hang them upside down like this, and this way all the clothes don't get so wrinkled and take up less space and you don't waste pins. The girls all wear each other's clothes, except Olivia who is stingy, because there ain't no boys here. Only

A second-generation Mexican-American, SANDRA CISNEROS (b. 1954) is "trying to write the stories that haven't been written." She says, "I'm determined to fill a literary void." She has most recently published *Woman Hollering Creek* (1991), a story collection, and *My Wicked Wicked Ways* (1987), a book of poetry.

girls and one father who is never home hardly and one mother who says, *Ay! I'm real tired,* and so many sisters there's no time to count them.

I'm sitting in the sun even though it's the hottest part of the day, the part that makes the streets dizzy, when the heat makes a little hat on the top of your head and bakes the dust and weed grass and sweat up good, all steamy and smelling like sweet corn.

I want to rub heads and sleep in a bed with little sisters, some at the top and some at the feets. I think it would be fun to sleep with sisters you could yell at one at a time or all together, instead of alone on the fold-out chair in the living room.

When I get home Abuelita will say, *Didn't I tell you?* and I'll get it because I was supposed to wear this dress again tomorrow. But first I'm going to jump off an old pissy mattress in the Anguiano yard. I'm going to scratch your mosquito bites, Lucy, so they'll itch you, then put Mercurochrome smiley faces on them. We're going to trade shoes and wear them on our hands. We're going to walk over to Janey Ortiz's house and say, *We're never ever going to be your friend again forever!* We're going to run home backwards and we're going to run home frontwards, look twice under the house where the rats hide and I'll stick one foot in there because you dared me, sky so blue and heaven inside those white clouds. I'm going to peel a scab from my knee and eat it, sneeze on the cat, give you three M&Ms I've been saving for you since yesterday, comb your hair with my fingers and braid it into teeny-tiny braids real pretty. We're going to wave to a lady we don't know on the bus. Hello! I'm going to somersault on the rail of the front porch even though my *chones* show. And cut paper dolls we draw ourselves, and color in their clothes with crayons, my arm around your neck.

And when we look at each other, our arms gummy from an orange Popsicle we split, we could be sisters, right? We could be, you and me waiting for our teeths to fall and money. You laughing something into my ear that tickles, and me going, Ha Ha Ha Ha. Her and me, my Lucy friend who smells like corn.   1991

INVESTIGATIONS

1. Why are these girls friends? What draws them to each other?
2. Write a paragraph or two in Cisneros's style about one of your childhood friendships. What qualities of friendship does this style evoke particularly well? Rewrite a paragraph or two of Grace Paley's "Friends" using this style. How does the change improve upon the original? What is thereby "lost in translation"?
3. In the final paragraph, the narrator says, "And when we look at each other, our arms gummy from an orange Popsicle we split, we could be sisters, right?" In what ways are the friends sisters? What besides the fact that

they come from different families shows they're not sisters? In your experience, to what extent are friends defined as "not quite family"?

ELLEN DARION

Claudia

The trees at the end of my block were trying to wrench themselves out of the
ground. From the top of the hill I watched, smelling the Hudson in the hot
wind, the faint odor of sewage under the stronger smell of salt. I smelled earth,
too, damp from the earlier rain — damp as the back of my neck and my chest
and the T-shirt that flattened against my sweating stomach. Beyond the park
and the highway the river rushed south, whitecaps riding the current. I started
downhill and my hair shot out behind me like some crazy kite tail, bobbing
and ducking in the wind.

When I reached the alley next to my building, I checked for the landlord's
car. It sat where it always sat, five floors beneath our kitchen window, even
more directly below my best friend's kitchen window, two stories down. We
used to lean out and spit on the roof of the car when we were younger, or
bombard it with the dinners we didn't eat — corned beef hash, for instance,
which fell slowly, settling into continent-shaped clumps on the gleaming black
metal. Tiny islands splattered off their coastlines and across the roof of the car,
and we'd invent names for them. Sometimes we dropped burning matchbooks,
too, but they always went out before they hit their target. I looked up at
Claudia's window now, but it was dark.

There were lights on in our windows, but I had left them on. My parents
were away, visiting friends in California. Upstairs I let myself into the apartment, fighting the wind tunnel I created when I opened the front door. The
living room curtains flapped wildly out the window and the hanging plants
twisted in the wind. The ends of the curtains were filthy and wet, the newspapers from the coffee table were all over the floor, and there were leaves from
the plants everywhere. I didn't care. I was sixteen, working as a counselor at
a day camp from which I now had a fifteen-hour reprieve, and I had two weeks

---

Born and raised in Manhattan, ELLEN DARION (b. 1958) is a graduate of Oberlin College and the
University of Pittsburgh Writing Program. She has published stories in a number of journals, including
The Gettysburg Review, Epoch, and *Special Report: Fiction.*

to clean up. It was all mine — this apartment, the crazy wind, the bucking trees, the river, even the Palisades beyond.

"If there's a forecast for rain," my mother had said, "close the windows before you leave." I left them open. The place turned into a sauna with all the windows closed in August. "Turn everything off before you leave." Everything meant the coffee-maker, fans, and stove. The lights stayed on, different ones every day, so people would think we were home. "Be careful," my mother continued. "Be good." This last was about my friend Mark, though my mother wouldn't say so. My parents liked Mark, but to mention his name would be to admit they knew he'd be staying over in their absence — knew and approved, or at least knew and were leaving town anyway. My mother went on. "Don't open the door for anyone you don't know." And then, casually, "Claudia's back. She's been showing up in the middle of the night again." This was news. "Don't let her in."

Claudia had been gone for over a year. She left because her mother wouldn't allow Claude's boyfriend into the apartment. No one would. Ray had filthy hair and rotting teeth and his mottled skin had a yellowish tone. I could never stand to look at him long enough to get more details. Claudia met him in the park. She had disappeared with him when her mother kicked her out. Those were Claudia's words — *kicked her out* — though I knew that was not what her mother had intended. She just wanted Claudia to stop seeing Ray. But Claudia was wild. I wasn't — at least, I never tried anything when there was a chance I'd get caught. I despised myself for this lack of spine.

The sound of the doorbell pulled me away from the window. Mark leered at me through the peephole and I let him in. His face was flushed from the heat, and his wiry hair had sprung into curls around his forehead. Tiny beads of sweat decorated his cheeks and nose, sat poised waiting to creep into his beard. He kissed me and pressed the shopping bag he was holding into my hand at the same time. I stepped back and peered into it.

"Dinner," he said. "It's going to storm any minute. This way we won't have to go out and buy anything."

"Thanks," I said. He'd brought a box of vermicelli and a jar of gourmet tomato sauce, which was all the cooking I was interested in when it was still ninety-seven degrees out. "Maybe the rain will cool things off." I started for the kitchen with the bag.

"Now why would we want to do that?" Mark said, moving into my path, snaking one leg behind me, clasping his hands in the small of my back. He kissed me again, pulling me tight against him, one hand sliding lower, seeking the hem of my T-shirt, slipping under it, palm finding bare skin. I closed my eyes. His fingertips were silk, brushing my waist, playing over my ribs. I dropped the bag. Mark smelled like heat, like steam and sweat but clean, like baby powder. He must have taken a shower right before he left. I pressed my face into his neck and walked him backward down the hall.

5

We lay sweating on my parents' bed. This was where we slept, in my
parents' absence, because of the air conditioner and the double bed. At first
I wouldn't do it. It was too strange. But after one night wedged together in
my narrow bed, where I was unable to tell Mark's breathing from my own,
where three times I woke startled from dreams about falling, I agreed to
move.

"I'm starved," Mark said. I didn't answer. I was listening to the staccato
ping the rain made against the window. A clap of thunder rolled in the distance.
The wind was still fierce: I could hear trash cans rolling in the alley, lids
skittering up the street. Claudia and Ray were sleeping in the park, my mother
had told me. "They must be on something," she had said.

"Hello?" Mark said. "I'm talking to you."

"Sorry," I said, reaching for him. But he was up already, standing near the
door. "Food," he said. "I need food."

"Okay," I said. "Don't you want to take a shower?"

"Nope," he said "Too hungry. You go ahead, though. I'll start dinner."

"At least put your pants on," I said. Mark liked to walk around nude as
often as possible, but in his parents' apartment the blinds were usually closed.
Which made it dark and depressing, I thought, so we spent most of our time
here. Besides, my parents came home from work later, so we had more time
alone together here.

We were eating in front of the TV when the doorbell rang. I didn't move.
I wasn't expecting anyone, and I didn't need some well-intentioned neighbor
checking in and discovering me and Mark in our underwear. Also, we were
watching a rerun of "The Avengers," an episode I'd never seen. Diana Rigg
was on her way to rescue Mr. Steed, who was outnumbered. The doorbell rang
again.

"Maybe it's important," Mark said.

"If it's so important," I said, "let them use the telephone." Diana Rigg
was doing her thing now, karate-chopping one guy in the neck, kicking the
other one in the chin, laying out the first guy when he tried to get up. I wanted
to move like that. I wanted the doorbell to stop ringing, but whoever was there
wasn't going away.

"At least go see who it is," Mark said. "You don't have to let anyone in."

Actually I had a pretty good idea who it was. The rain had been splashing
down in sheets for hours. The park would be a swamp by now. Maybe Claudia
knew my parents were away. Maybe she had watched them load their suitcases
into the cab from some hiding place in the park. All I knew was that if I saw
her, if I looked through the peephole and saw Claudia soaked to the bone,
water streaming from the ends of the long blond hair that I had never, in the
twelve years I had known her, seen dirty or uncombed, I would not be able to
turn her away.

"If I answer it," I said, "we're going to have company."

"What are you talking about?"

"It's Claudia," I said. "Remember, my friend from downstairs?"

I had not told Mark that Claudia was back, for a lot of reasons. I hadn't
seen her yet myself, wouldn't really believe it until I did. And Mark had never
known her in the first place. The truth was that I hadn't seen much of Claudia
in the two or three years before her disappearance. Before that, though, we
were inseparable. When we weren't trying to cause permanent damage to the
landlord's car, we devised new and crueler ways of driving off Claudia's mother's boyfriends. We put salt in their drinks and honey in their shaving kits. If
they had cars we put honey on the upholstered seats. One guy discovered a
dead mole we had found in the park in his coat pocket. When there was no
one to torment, we played a game called Jimmy and Susie, in which we were
orphans on the run. Jimmy and Susie were constantly getting stuck on an island
in the middle of the ocean with the tide rapidly rising. I always played Jimmy,
and Jimmy always saved Susie — though in real life I had been the one afraid
to put my face in the water. Claudia had made the rules. Now someone was
leaning on the doorbell so it made one long, harsh, continuous buzz.

"Do you want *me* to answer it?" Mark asked. "That noise is making me
crazy."

"No," I said. I stood and carried our plates up the hall. The truth was, I
didn't believe Claudia was dangerous. I didn't believe anyone else thought so,
either. I thought our parents' refusal to let her in was intended as punishment,
as censure for being with a boy no one approved of. I didn't approve of him
either, but Claudia and I went back too far. She needed help, and I could help
her. Here was another chance to save her from drowning.

Her turned out to be *them*. I hadn't thought she'd bring Ray with her,
somehow. I hadn't seen him through the peephole. My first instinct was to
close the door, but they were both inside before I could act on it. Ray looked
exactly as I remembered him: like Ratso Rizzo, only taller — sniffling, unshaven, hunched over, his movement forward more a shuffle than a walk. But
it was Claudia who really frightened me. In fact she looked much better than
Ray did, cleaner and less beaten down. The difference was in how far she had
fallen. Claudia's blue eyes shone coldly from her hollow face, as if they were
lit by tiny bulbs from behind, but they shone more gray than blue, a gray that
matched the grayness of her skin. She was so thin her T-shirt hung in waves
from her bony shoulders. Instinctively I reached for her hand, and almost
dropped it just as quickly. It felt like balsa wood. I had always envied her long
slender fingers, especially in piano class, where Claudia's effortless reach
spanned two octaves while mine could barely cover one. But the fingers I held
now weren't strong enough to hold down a piano key. These fingers were
empty, bones filled with air.

Claudia pulled her hand back and jerked her head in Mark's direction.
"This your boyfriend?" she asked.

Mark said, "Hi." He was sitting up uncharacteristically straight. He had   30
abandoned completely the manner he usually cultivated around my friends he
didn't know — the half-closed lids, the surly slouch, the whole attempt to look
unimpressed. He was alert, the tips of his fingers drumming lightly on the edge

of the dining-room table, where he had settled himself when he came up the hall. Besides his fingers there wasn't a sound in the room but Ray's wheezing.

"Is he okay?" I asked Claudia. She shrugged. She was looking at our plates on the table, still half-full of food. "Sit down," I said. "I'll get you something to eat." Ray looked like he was about to fall down. Claudia guided him into a chair. I turned the flame on under the tomato sauce I hadn't put away yet and put on more water for spaghetti.

Claudia appeared in the kitchen doorway. "Can I take a shower?"

"Of course," I said. "You know where everything is." She looked at me blankly, then turned to Ray.

"Come on," she said. When he didn't move she took his hand and pulled him out of his chair. I followed them down the hall through my bedroom to the back bathroom and showed them where the towels were. I lent Claudia some clean clothes, but I didn't have anything to fit Ray.

"Maybe you could wash his clothes while he's in the shower," I suggested. I wasn't just thinking of him. I really didn't want him sitting on our chairs in what he was wearing.

"Sure," Claudia said "Where's your machine?"

We didn't have a machine. "I meant downstairs. In the laundry room," I said slowly. "In the basement." The laundry had been a weekly job for us both since we were old enough to reach the coin slots in the machines. We used to do it at the same time because it was so boring, and because there were waterbugs in the basement as big as our feet. I looked closely at Claudia, but all she said was "Oh. Well, maybe later." She went into my bedroom, where I could see Ray sprawled face down on the bed.

"Take your time," I said when she started to close the door. I turned to discover Mark, who had been watching all this from the front hall.

"Well?" he said.

"Well what?"

"Would you like to tell me what the hell is going on?"

So I told him about Claudia. I told him that when we were small, Claudia brought me along on weekend visits to her father, because they didn't know what to say to each other. She barely knew him. She was a baby when her parents got divorced. Her mother worked two jobs, so Claudia came with us everywhere: the park, the library, the beach in the summer. Our family photo albums were filled with pictures of Claude's birthday parties next to the pictures of mine. There were other pictures, too: me and Claudia hanging upside down from the monkey bars in the playground, Claudia waving with both hands, always one step more daring than me. Claudia and me at a bay beach somewhere, me treading water while she arced into another one of her perfect dives off the dock, chin tucked, legs together and unbent, arms and fingers extended, her flying braids the only part of her not perfectly aligned with her arrow-straight body.

Then there were pictures that weren't in the albums: Claudia and me convincing Arnold Fenton that he was on the verge of a nervous breakdown

and it was only his mile-thick glasses and the fierce stutter that kept his eyeballs
and tongue from falling out; Claudia and me following home a high-school
boy she liked to see where he lived, then sitting on a stoop across the street
from his building smoking cigarettes so he could be impressed if he came out.
Claudia smoked. I just held a lit cigarette and moved it up to my mouth every
so often.

"That's very interesting," Mark said when I was done. "Now how do you
plan to get them out of here?"

I hadn't thought of that. I shrugged.   45

"Great," Mark said. "Wonderful. You realize they're going to steal everything your parents own."

"I doubt it," I said. Claudia had left the door to my bedroom slightly ajar,
and I could see Ray on the bed. He hadn't moved. "Look," I said, pointing.

"That's good," Mark said. "If he's dead, he can't steal anything."

"Shut up."

"I can't believe you let these people in."   50

"She's my best friend."

"Sure," Mark said. "Ask her about something that happened when you
were eight years old."

"Shut up," I said again. But I knew he was right. She didn't know there
was a laundry room in the basement, much less where my mother kept her
towels. She probably didn't remember what had happened yesterday. But this
wasn't about memory. It was about common decency. It was about friendship
and loyalty and betrayal. It was about my inability to leave Claudia standing
in the hall with no place to go but Riverside Park in the pouring rain.

"Let's take this from the top," Mark said. He was using his okay-I'll-be-
reasonable-for-both-of-us tone of voice. "We have a situation here. You let
them take showers; we feed them; we send them on their way."

"Where are they supposed to sleep?"   55

"That's not your problem."

But it was. I couldn't refuse Claudia. I couldn't kick her out. It would be
like going over to the other side. "Look, Mark," I said, "if you're so disturbed
by all this, why don't you just go home?"

"Right," Mark said. "And leave you alone with a couple of starving
junkies — "

"Claudia is not a junkie."

"You couldn't prove it by me." Mark stalked down the hall toward the   60
bedroom. In a couple of minutes I heard the shower go on. In the other
bathroom, Claudia's had gone off awhile ago, but she hadn't emerged from
the back bedroom. Maybe they were too tired to eat. I cleared off the table
and washed our dishes, then turned off the stove. Most of the water had boiled
away anyway, and the sauce was beginning to burn on the bottom of the pan.
I couldn't wait for them all night. I had to get up early for work. If they came
out and were hungry, they could take care of themselves. Provided they didn't
set the place on fire by accident.

Mark wanted me to get rid of them, and I knew I should try. But it was too late. I could ask them to leave but I knew they wouldn't go, not into the flooded park and thunder and lightning, not when they had already waited this long outside my clean, dry apartment for sanctuary and had finally been admitted inside. The only way I could get rid of them was to call the police, and I wasn't about to do that. Claudia was a runaway, a juvenile offender. She had no doubt been stealing food to stay alive, and I didn't want to think about what else she might have done. I wished there was some way I could turn Ray over without Claudia, but we already knew she wouldn't be separated from him. I couldn't call the cops. I had to let them stay.

I moved around the apartment, turning out lights. In the kitchen my gaze focused on the knife rack. Maybe Mark was right. Maybe they were planning to rob us blind, and then they would slit our throats when they discovered there wasn't enough cash in the house for their next fix. You heard stories on the news about it all the time, people getting killed for drug money. I didn't like Ray having access to all those knives. I picked up the butcher block and brought the whole thing down the hall to the bedroom. I was half serious about wanting to keep the knives away from Ray. Also, I knew Mark would think it was funny, and I wanted to make him laugh. He was always making fun of me for being paranoid.

But when I opened the bedroom door, Mark was asleep in front of the TV. He was so sure we were going to be ax-murdered he had fallen asleep in the middle of the evening news.

"You really are an asshole," I said, closing the door. How could he fall asleep if he really believed Claudia and Ray were going to ransack the apartment? And if he didn't believe it, what was he being such a pain in the ass for?

I stepped out of my shorts and looked at Mark, who was on his side, facing the wall. Careful not to touch him, I eased myself on to the bed. It bothered me that he couldn't understand why I had to let Claudia in. It bothered me that he didn't *want* to understand enough to stay awake until I came to bed. I heard a noise in the hall and froze. The back bedroom door was opening. I listened to footsteps — two sets — going up the hall. The kitchen was too far away for me to hear what they were doing. They were probably just hungry. That, or they were calling their friends to bring the van so they could clean this place out. It occurred to me then that anyone who slept in the park probably had a knife of his own. I pictured Ray charging into the bedroom, breaking the flimsy hook-and-eye lock with no effort, pulling his knife from his pocket as he entered. Mark wasn't going to be any help. He'd sleep through his own murder.

There *was* another way out of this room: the fire-escape window. It was a nice idea, but the gate over that window would have kept the Goths out of ancient Rome. I would never have time to unlock it if I really had to get out of here fast. Floorboards creaked in the hall. Someone was coming back. I held my breath until the footsteps continued past my door. The door to the

65

back bedroom opened and closed, but I wasn't sure I'd heard them both walk by. I gave up. I was too tired to play detective anymore.

A blaring car alarm startled me awake in the morning. The car could have been parked under the bed, it was so loud. Mark groaned and covered his head with his pillow. He could actually go to sleep like that. I was up for good. Up and remembering Claudia and Ray. So. We had gotten through the night alive. We had not even been threatened, but somehow I was not comforted by this knowledge. I felt invaded. What if they were gone, had taken things? What if they were still asleep? I'd have to wake them. What if they wouldn't leave? Suppose they wanted to stay another night, or longer, or refused to leave before my parents came home? I pulled on my clothes and walked up the hall.

The door to my bedroom was open. The bed was made. I didn't know how to read these signs. But when I got to the dining room I was relieved and happy and ashamed all at the same time. Here were Claudia and Ray looking clean for what had to be the first time in weeks. And rested. They had gotten their first good night's sleep in ages, in a real bed, where they didn't have to worry about anyone bothering them, or being hit by lightning, or getting bitten by a rat if they did manage to fall asleep in some puddle near a tree.

"Good morning," I said.

Claudia smiled. "Good morning." The hunted look she wore last night   70 had softened some. "We did the wash." She pointed to the laundry basket full of neatly folded sheets and towels. Which meant they weren't asking to stay another night. I had done the right thing. All they had wanted was a little kindness, and I gave it to them. I had made the right choice, done something not so much generous as simply humane. I had counted on Claudia, had counted on trust and loyalty and love, and here was proof that my instincts were good. Claudia and Ray were decent people, and I was decent for giving them the chance to prove it. I had done the right thing.

But at work that day, during morning swim, the icy pool water jolted me awake to something I hadn't thought about: the tool drawer in the kitchen where my father kept the spare keys and some extra cash, tucked under the level. Claudia and Ray could easily have discovered these last night, could have stumbled across them looking for napkins or silverware. If they had, they would be back to steal everything. They would have access to my parents' bedroom now, too: my mother's jewelry, my parents' checkbook, the key to their safety deposit box. Their signatures on dozens of documents, waiting to be forged.

I shivered, though the sun was moving higher in a cloudless sky. Even if nothing was missing when I got home, I had no way of knowing whether Claudia and Ray had found those keys. By now they had had plenty of time to copy them and return the originals, so no one would know. One night a month, a year, five years from now my father would awake, hearing noises. He would get up to see about them and be shot or stabbed or bludgeoned by

Ray or some other doped-up member of his gang, who would be in the midst of burglarizing the apartment. Claudia would be standing watch outside. Or maybe she'd be driving the getaway car. I would have to change the locks. And I would have to tell my parents, who would ask why the locks had been changed.

At home that night I checked the apartment for signs of anything wrong. The keys in the kitchen drawer did not look like they had been moved, and the twenty-dollar bills were still there. Claudia and Ray wouldn't have taken the keys and not the cash. Living hand-to-mouth the way they did I doubted they were capable of such a ruse. I counted the twenties and began to feel better. Maybe I didn't have to change the locks. My mother's jewelry was untouched too, at least everything I could remember to check for: the diamond earrings, the pearls, the amethyst necklace and pin. She had been wearing her lapis beads when they left. I checked everything else I could think of — the bankbooks, the key to the safety deposit box, the key to the fire-escape gate. Everything was in its place. Everything except Claudia, who was out on the street somewhere, planning her next meal.

I had spent the day feeling stupid and angry — angry that Claudia had showed up with Ray, angry at her for endangering me this way, angry at myself for letting her in. I would never know if those dry, weightless fingers had lifted the spare keys out of that kitchen drawer. But now the anger was gone — or not gone entirely, but floating, suspended, as if the person who had been angry were someone other than me. What I felt now was empty, just empty and sad. I knew I had not done the right thing last night. I knew that I had just been lucky. But I also knew that I'd do it again if I had to, that I would do anything to pull Claudia back into the world of perfect dives, where she did not need saving, so I could save her again and again and again.   1991

INVESTIGATIONS

1. Why is Mark so unimpressed by the narrator's explanation for letting Claudia and Ray into the apartment (para. 44)? If an estranged friend, a friend you had some reason to fear, needed your help, what would you do? Why?

2. What insight into this friendship does the "Jimmy and Susie game" (para. 25) provide?

3. In paragraph 27 the narrator says, "She needed help, and I could help her." To what extent does she succeed? Suppose the narrator hadn't allowed Claudia and Ray into the apartment. In what sense would that have been more help to them? In what sense might "helping" Claudia be failing to "be there" for her?

4. Reread the story's final paragraph. Why does the narrator feel "empty, just empty and sad"? What does she mean when she says, "I knew I had not

done the right thing last night. I knew that I had just been lucky." What
connection does paragraph 70 have to these realizations?

INÉS HERNANDEZ

Para Teresa[1]

A tí-Teresa Compean
Te dedico las palabras estás
que explotan de mi corazón[2]

That day during lunch hour
at Alamo which-had-to-be-its-name   5
Elementary
my dear raza[3]
That day in the bathroom
Door guarded
Myself cornered   10
I was accused by you, Teresa
Tú y las demas de tus amigas
Pachucas todas
Eran Uds. cinco.[4]

Me gritaban que porque me creía tan grande[5]   15
What was I trying to do, you growled
Show you up?
Make the teachers like me, pet me,
Tell me what a credit to my people I was?
I was playing right into their hands, you challenged   20

---

[1] For Teresa. [Au.]
[2] To you, Teresa Compean, I dedicate these words that explode from my heart. [Au.]
[3] Literally, "race," used to mean "the people." [Ed.]
[4] You and the rest of your friends, all Pachucas, there were five of you. [Au.]
[5] You were screaming at me, asking me why I thought I was so hot. [Au.]

Author of Con Razon, Corazon: Poetry (1977), INÉS HERNANDEZ considers "the Chicano-Chicana voice" part of "a collective voice . . . which is seeking a more humanistic society." Born in Texas in 1947, she currently teaches in the Native American Studies Department at the University of California at Davis.

And you would have none of it.
I was to stop.

I was to be like you
I was to play your game of deadly defiance
Arrogance, refusal to submit.   25
The game in which the winner takes nothing
Asks for nothing
Never lets his weaknesses show.

But I didn't understand.
My fear salted with confusion   30
Charged me to explain to you
I did nothing *for the teachers.*
I studied for my parents and for my grandparents
Who cut out honor roll lists
Whenever their nietos'[6] names appeared   35
For my shy mother who mastered her terror
to demand her place in mothers' clubs
For my carpenter-father who helped me patiently with my math.
For my abuelos que me regalaron lápices en la Navidad[7]
And for myself.   40

Porque reconocí en aquel entonces
una verdad tremenda
que mi hizo a mi un rebelde
Aunque tú no te habías dadocuenta.[8]
We were not inferior   45
You and I, y las demás de tus amigas
Y los demás de nuestra gente[9]
I knew it the way I know I was alive
We were good, honorable, brave
Genuine, loyal, strong   50

And smart.
Mine was a deadly game of defiance, also.
My contest was to prove
beyond any doubt
that we were not only equal but superior to them. 55

---

[6] Grandchildren's. [Au.]
[7] Grandparents who gave me gifts of pencils at Christmas. [Au.]
[8] Because I recognized a great truth then that made me a rebel, even though you didn't realize it. [Au.]
[9] And the rest of your friends / And the rest of our people. [Au.]

That was why I studied.
If I could do it, we all could.

You let me go then,
Your friends unblocked the way
I who-did-not-know-how-to-fight   60
was not made to engage with you-who-grew-up-fighting
Tu y yo, Teresa[10]
We went in different directions
Pero fuimos juntas.[11]

In sixth grade we did not understand   65
Uds. with the teased, dyed-black-but-reddening hair,
Full petticoats, red lipsticks
and sweaters with the sleeves
pushed up
Y yo conformándome con lo que deseaba mi mamá[12]   70
Certainly never allowed to dye, to tease, to paint myself
I did not accept your way of anger,
Your judgments
You did not accept mine.

But now in 1975, when I am twenty-eight   75
Teresa Compean
I remember you.
Y sabes —
Te comprendo,
Es más, te respeto.   80
Y, si me permites,
Te nombro — "hermana."[13]   1977

INVESTIGATIONS

1. Why does the speaker respect Teresa? How much does "fear salted with confusion" (line 30) have to do with it? Why doesn't their mutual lack of acceptance (lines 72–74) fail to prevent mutual respect?

2. In what ways does the "deadly game of defiance" bind the two girls? What's deadly about the game? How can they each play this game yet be "good, honorable," and "genuine" (lines 49–50)?

[10] You and I. [Au.]
[11] But we were together. [Au.]
[12] And I conforming to my mother's wishes. [Au.]
[13] And do you know what, I understand you. Even more, I respect you. And, if you permit me, I name you my sister. [Au.]

3. How is the sisterhood claimed by the narrator of Cisneros's "My Lucy Friend Who Smells Like Corn" similar to the sisterhood claimed in this poem's final stanza?
4. If Teresa were to read this poem, how do you think she'd react?

LOUISE GLÜCK

Celestial Music

I have a friend who still believes in heaven.
Not a stupid person, yet with all she knows, she literally talks to god,
she thinks someone listens in heaven.
On earth, she's unusually competent.
Brave, too, able to face unpleasantness.   5

We found a caterpillar dying in the dirt, greedy ants crawling over it.
I'm always moved by weakness, by disaster, always eager to oppose vitality.
But timid, also, quick to shut my eyes.
Whereas my friend was able to watch, to let events play out
according to nature. For my sake, she intervened,   10
brushing a few ants off the torn thing, and set it down across the road.

My friend says I shut my eyes to god, that nothing else explains
my aversion to reality. She says I'm like the child who buries her head
                                                              in the pillow

so as not to see, the child who tells herself   15
that light causes sadness —
My friend is like the mother. Patient, urging me
to wake up an adult like herself, a courageous person —

In my dreams, my friend reproaches me. We're walking
on the same road, except it's winter now;   20
she's telling me that when you love the world you hear celestial music;
look up, she says. When I look up, nothing.
Only clouds, snow, a white business in the trees

LOUISE GLÜCK's most recent collections of poetry are *Ararat* (1990) and *The Triumph of Achilles* (1985), winner of the National Book Critics Circle Award. Born in New York City in 1943, Glück now lives in Plainfield, Vermont, and teaches at Williams College.

like brides leaping to a great height —
Then I'm afraid for her; I see her   25
caught in a net deliberately cast over the earth —

In reality, we sit by the side of the road, watching the sun set,
from time to time the silence pierced by a birdcall.
It's this moment we're both trying to explain, the fact
that we're at ease with death, with solitude.   30
My friend draws a circle in the dirt; inside, the caterpillar doesn't move.
She's always trying to make something whole, something beautiful, an image
capable of life apart from her.
We're very quiet. It's peaceful sitting here, not speaking, the composition
fixed, the road turning suddenly dark, the air   35
going cool, here and there the rocks shining and glittering —
it's this stillness that we both love.
The love of form is a love of endings.   1989

INVESTIGATIONS

1. In line 17 the speaker says, "My friend is like the mother." Compare the relationship this poem dramatizes to any of the mother-child relationships about which you've read. What characteristics distinguish this friendship from the mother-child relationships?

2. What significant effect does the dream described in lines 19–26 have on how the speaker thinks about her friend?

3. How does being "at ease with death, with solitude" help these friends stay friends?

4. Write a paragraph or two in which you argue for "a love of endings" as an essential ingredient of friendship.

ALICE ADAMS

Waiting for Stella

Actually it is Jimmy, Stella's fourth and final husband (Stella died a month ago), for whom everyone is waiting, all these old people, in this large sunny clearing in a grove of ancient redwoods. It is high noon, on a bright October day, and time for lunch, but Rachel, the hostess, has delayed serving the food, because of Jimmy's lateness. This will be everyone's first sight of him since Stella's death; he took off for Santa Barbara just afterward to visit a sister there, and presumably to recuperate, traveling in Stella's old car. Perhaps the car is making him late this morning? The guests, old friends, sip nervously at tomato juice or club soda, while a few of the hardier ones have white wine; they are all in their seventies or eighties, except for a young dark, vividly pretty girl, Day, a visiting friend of Rachel's, who will help with lunch.

Everyone, including Rachel and her husband, Baxter, and Day, the visiting girl, is seated at a long bandanna-cloth-covered table, on benches. Not far from the table is a small oval concrete swimming pool, its unused murky water now flat and still. Here and there in the grove are clumps of huge thick-fronded ferns, a dusty gray green, quite motionless, in the moted sunlight.

They are all waiting for Jimmy, of course, but it is Stella whose lively absence dominates the mood, so that several people, especially Rachel and Baxter, have to remind themselves that they are waiting for Jimmy, not for Stella.

Rachel and Baxter's house is up on a knoll, invisible from the pool, among tall thick eucalyptus trees, gray thickets of manzanita. It is a big house, though cheaply and somewhat flimsily constructed of clapboard, now nicely weathered to silver. It was a great bargain forty years ago when Rachel and her first husband had it built. Now it is probably worth a lot of money, as she and Baxter wryly say to each other from time to time, and they add, "but only if we sell it." (Baxter is Rachel's third husband, and surely her last, she thinks.) Near the house, a little way down toward the pool, is the guest cabin, slatted, green.

All the houses in this small enclave, in the Santa Cruz Mountains, are somewhat similar, as, not quite accidentally, are their owners; friends, they all were professional people, "liberals," mildly intellectual. Rachel was a doctor, a professor of medicine, rather distinguished; Baxter, although he inherited money, was an art critic. Stella was a painter.

ALICE ADAMS (b. 1926), winner of the 1982 O. Henry Special Award for Continuing Achievement and a 1978 Guggenheim Fellowship, has written four short story collections, including *After You've Gone* (1989), and six novels, most recently *Caroline's Daughter* (1991). Adams lives and writes in San Francisco.

What once were vacation homes now house their retirements.

In those younger, summer days, feelings sometimes ran high: Dissensions occurred over love affairs, real or imagined; opposing political views split their ranks. But now old feuds are quieted, if not forgotten — especially today, as in an almost unified way they think about Stella, the first of them to die, and they think about Jimmy, who is *very* late.

Now, conferring with Day, Rachel decides to go ahead and serve the first course, a gazpacho, which has already been brought down and is sitting there on the table, in its huge green-glazed tureen. And so Rachel ladles out the soup, and Day takes the bowls around to everyone.

Actually, Stella has always been a sort of unifying principle for this group, in that they have generally been united in opposition to whatever she was doing. Not actual opposition to her views, but Stella always, somehow, went too far. Wonderful of her to march in Selma at already sixty-odd, but did she have to get arrested, so purposefully, and spend a week in that jail? Or, more recently, was it necessary, really, that she scale the fence at Diablo Canyon, protesting nuclear power? Not to mention the fact that she often drank too much, and almost always talked too much, with her proud white tooth-flashing grin; she had too many husbands and lovers (though fortunately, it was sometimes remarked, no children).

Her final marriage to Jimmy Scott, a former alcoholic, former film director   10
(not important), was hard to understand, the other husbands having been, in their ways, almost predictable: Jack, a Communist, and Jewish (this was daring, in 1922, for a New England girl of "good" — Republican, Unitarian — family); Horace, a black longshoreman; and Yosh, a Japanese painter, whom she married just after Pearl Harbor (of course). But — Jimmy?

During the illness preceding Stella's death, however, the mercifully short three months, Jimmy's behavior toward her was observed to be exemplary. It was hardly a time when anyone would have behaved badly, but still his patience was remarkable. He searched for out-of-print books that Stella mentioned wanting to reread, for out-of-season flowers for her bedroom (they were not rich people, not at all), for special delicate foods, rare fruits to tempt her waning appetite.

In the last awful month of her life, although she stayed at home, in the house up the road from Rachel and Baxter's, Stella refused (through Jimmy, of course) to let anyone visit her; not even Rachel, a doctor, was allowed to see her then, which no one quite understood, except, just possibly, Rachel.

Of the dozen people there — thirteen, counting Day — only Day is not thinking in a concentrated way about Stella. Day is thinking painfully, obsessively of Allen, the lover whom she came to California to see, but with whom things did not work out; they just broke up in San Francisco, where Allen lives. Scenes and quarrels, all terrible to recall. Passing breadsticks, Day considers the phrase "to break up." It is odd, she thinks, that people always say "break up *with*," since the whole point of breaking up is that you are no longer *with* but alone.

In order not to think about Allen, and then, too, because it seems appropriate, Day makes a conscious effort to think about Stella, whom she met fairly often, over the years, at Rachel's. (Day's mother, also a doctor, a friend of Rachel's, named Day for her heroine, Dorothy Day, who was also much admired by Rachel.) Stella was perfectly all right, Day thinks, but she talked so much. And that hair. Bright red hair, for a woman in her seventies or (probably) eighties? More generously, Day then admits to herself that you can't tell what you'll do that far ahead. She herself at eighty might dye her hair purple, or green, a one-person revival of punk, in the year two thousand and whatever, out of sheer boredom with living that long.

Stella never seemed bored with her old age — you had to give her that. And even if Jimmy bored her she never let it be known. ("Jimmy was actually more interesting as an alcoholic," Baxter has remarked. "Poor Stella! No luck at all with men.")

Day, who in her grief is not even aware of how pretty she is, now sits down with her own cold bowl of soup, next to Baxter, who must have been extremely handsome, a long time ago, Day imagines.

Baxter, who dislikes gazpacho (the peppers seem to disagree with him, or perhaps the cucumbers), looks for diversion at Day's long thin brown legs, now exposed beneath her loose flowered skirt, in high rope clogs. Day's legs, which Baxter much admires, lead him back to a sensual dream of Stella. He sees a room in the Sherry Netherland, in New York (he has just married Rachel; she is waiting for him, up in Connecticut — she is giving a seminar at Yale). Gold coverlets drawn back on sumptuous beds, in the half-light of an August afternoon. Champagne in a silver bucket, two chilled glasses. And Stella: all that pink-gold flesh (she was fairly plump in those days), all that flesh, half revealed, half concealed. Silk, rows of lace. That flesh, breasts, and that brilliant hair, spread on her pillow, his pillow.

But even in his dream he, Baxter, is actually sitting there alone, and fully dressed. And he never saw any flesh of Stella's beyond that revealed in a modest bathing suit. For Stella, if the truth were known, and he trusts that it is not — Stella had stood him up. There he was, expecting her, in that room, with champagne, and the next day she had the consummate gall to say, "But Baxter, darling, I can't believe you were serious." And that awful laugh. What a bitch, when you came right down to it — really surprising that more people didn't see through her. He wonders if Rachel did; he has never been sure just how Rachel felt about Stella. Well, there's no possibility of understanding women, as he has always said.

More crossly than he meant to, Baxter whispers to Day, "Why do you think Rachel serves this damned soup so often?"

Startled, Day answers him literally. "She thinks it's good in hot weather, I guess." And then she says the next thing that enters her grief-dulled mind: "And it seems a more leftist sort of soup than vichyssoise."

Baxter emits a loud cackling laugh. "Oh, very good," he tells Day, who has not meant to be funny, especially. "A leftist soup. That's *very good.*"

Baxter's laugh and some words of this small exchange have caught everyone's attention, so that it all has to be repeated several times, and explained, many of those old ears not being quite what they once were. No one seems to think "leftist soup" is quite as funny as Baxter did. (Rachel especially, in the way of wives, did not find it awfully funny. Why did she marry Baxter, she wonders. But even if she knew, it is much too late to reconsider.) However, at least a diversion was created, from so many sad thoughts of Stella, and such anxiety as how to deal with Jimmy: How will he be?

This October day is unseasonably hot; everyone has agreed on that, and commented at length. Even in this shaded glen, where usually it is cool, often cold, almost always too cold for swimming in the dark greenish pool, today it is very warm, so that swimming is at least discussed. Warm shafts of light fall dustily between the redwoods, on the thick, still, tessellated fronds of ferns.

Stella, of course, would have been in hours ago, flopping around like a porpoise and exhorting everyone else to come in, too. No one has remarked on this probability, but what Stella would have been doing has occurred to everyone there. They will continue to think, in other contexts, of what Stella would have done.

However, the heat is actually a relief to so many old bones; they bask and relax in it. And the warm weather seems a reprieve of sorts, to these old people. The fact is that their location, in these mountains south of San Francisco, is not an ideal spot for the retired, for the very old. They are vulnerable to such extremes of cold, and to floods, from mountain streams, as well as to spectres of isolation, loneliness, helplessness. Danger. They have all thought and talked from time to time of moving somewhere else, but where? And for them to move would seem a sort of giving up, giving in, a yielding to old age and infirmity.

This day, though, is reassuring; they are still all right, exactly where they are.

And, as no one says, and perhaps no one is really aware, it is rather a relief not to have Stella around, loudly splashing in the pool, and always urging them all to exceed themselves, somehow.

Although they were very close friends, as far as anyone knew, and were almost exactly the same age, Rachel's and Stella's personal styles were very different. Rachel's low-key, toned-down quiet mode could almost have been developed in opposition to Stella's flamboyance. All three of Rachel's husbands, including Baxter, have affectionately compared her to a wren, a coincidence that tactful Rachel has mentioned to no one, surely not to Baxter, who despite his money and good looks is quite insecure.

Rachel is small, with neat gray-brown hair and finely lined lightly tanned skin. When Baxter came home to her that time in Connecticut, just mentioning that he had "caught a glimpse" of Stella in New York, Rachel quite accurately surmised what had happened: Baxter had made a pass, of some sort, and Stella in some way had turned him down. Curiously, at first she was a little annoyed at Stella: Poor Baxter, aging is hard on such a handsome man. But it soon came to her, causing a wry, inward smile, that after all if Stella had said yes, she, Rachel, would have been considerably more annoyed.

Standing just off from the group, near the end of the table, Day and Rachel now consult with each other, Rachel saying, "Well, I just don't know. Jimmy's usually so punctual," and she frowns.   30

"He might feel worse if we waited," Day offers. "Worse about everything, I mean."

Rachel gives Day an attentive, interested look. (Rachel listens to what other people say.) "Well, of course you're absolutely right," she says. "Besides, it's making everyone nervous. We'll just go ahead with the salmon."

"He might always call and say that he isn't coming after all," Day further contributes. She is thinking: Allen might call.

"Oh, right," says Rachel.

It is true that the prolonged absence of Jimmy is nervously felt, all around.   35
People speculate about what could have happened. Flat tires are mentioned, as well as being out of gas, or lost. What no one voices is the fear, felt by almost all of them, that he could have started drinking again. Stella was believed to have helped get him off the bottle.

Someone, more mean-spirited than the rest, has just said, "I hope our dear Jimmy hasn't stopped off at some bar," when fortunately Rachel and Day arrive with their platters of cold salmon, the glistening silvery pink surrounded by various shades of green — parsley and several sauces — so that everyone can exclaim over the beauty of the food.

One moment after everyone is served, there comes the sound and then a quick flashed glimpse in the driveway above of a hastily braked and parked red sports car.

What an odd car for a man whose wife has just died is what everyone instantly, simultaneously thinks — everyone but Day, who has recognized the car. It is not Jimmy's car but Allen's, and she begins to run back up the path that she has just come down with her platter, now going several times as fast as before: She is almost flying.

Behind her, a guest who has not yet understood that it is not Jimmy's car after all, and who has apparently not forgotten some ancient political feud, is heard to mutter, "Perfect car for a red-haired Communist!"

Half an hour later (still no sign of Jimmy), a few people are on their second helpings of salmon. Rachel keeps an experienced-hostess eye on all the plates; she is hoping for not much left over, Baxter not being overly fond of salmon (hard to think what he does like, really), and she cannot bear waste. It is sad, she thinks, the loss of appetite suffered by the old, and she remembers her own gnawing hungers as a scrawny Brooklyn girl. It is far worse than the diminution of sexual appetite, one's lessening interest in food. After all, most people eat three times a day, most not truly poor Americans.

She is allowing her mind to wander foolishly. Rachel looks across the table at Day and Allen, who appear to be absolutely, heedlessly absorbed in each other. She looks at her watch, unobtrusively, she hopes, and frowns.

It is so strange, Day is thinking, her feelings on being with Allen. Now. He is so near that she can smell him, his known scents of clean skin and recent soap, clean cotton work shirt just slightly perspired on. He is so near, so known and loved (she supposes) and still so strange, unreal to her. Their quarrels, too, are unreal, all suddenly dissolved. "Whatever was that all about?" Allen asked her, after their long greeting kiss, as hand in hand they walked down to the shaded dell together, and Day said, "Oh, I don't *know.*"

Now, though, it is as if she had known all along that Allen would come to her here; she has been waiting for Allen, as everyone else waited for Jimmy, and thought about Stella.

But, most curiously, she is aware in some depth of herself of the faintest disappointment that he has come, after all. She feels the lack of her recent misery; weirdly, she misses its bite; the very sharpness of that anguish seems a loss.

Then quite suddenly everything that is happening is interrupted, all the eating and serving and clearing, all the intense thoughts of everyone there, all rudely broken into by the sharp repeated blast of a horn, the country sound of a very old Ford. Stella's car: It is Jimmy at last, of course.

Straining to look up through the immense, thick trees, enormous trunks of the venerable redwoods, the smaller eucalyptus, manzanitas, they can just see the old rattletrap that Stella always drove, as shabby and dusty as though she drove it still. The door slams three, then four times (it is remembered that Stella never could get that door shut), and from way up there comes the jaunty sound of Jimmy calling, "Hallooo, hallooo!"

"Oh dear, he must be drunk," someone says.

"Oh, I hope not," says Baxter eagerly, clearly hoping that he is.

"He is not drunk," Rachel fiercely tells them both.

What Day first sees of Jimmy, and maybe the others, too, are the bright stripes of the sweater he is wearing, a brilliant orangy red, on a darker background. What Day thinks is: How amazing, his sweater is striped with the color of Stella's hair.

In a curious way, Jimmy looks both smaller and livelier than usual. He fairly runs down the path toward them all.

Watching him, as everyone is, several people seem to decide that perhaps so much attention paid to his arrival will be awkward, and small attempts are made at conversation, here and there. However, none succeed, and by the time Jimmy, quite out of breath, arrives at the end of the table, Rachel's end, they are all staring, and smiling welcomes in his direction.

"Well," Jimmy at last gets out, "you all look like you'd been waiting for somebody more important. Or bigger, anyway," and with an odd quirky smile he actually turns to look behind him, as though the larger, more important person had followed him down the path.

"Jimmy dear, don't be silly," Rachel chides him. "But what ever happened? You're so late."

"Well, it's that damned old car of Stell's, of course. Damned old thing wouldn't start, and then I had to wait for the tow truck."

"Well, fortunately everything's cold, and there's lots left. Here's a plate, just sit right here by me." A small catch can be heard in Rachel's voice, as she speaks to Jimmy, and tears are seen in her eyes. But since all these people are so old, and given to emotional moments, no one wonders why at this particular moment of first seeing Jimmy Rachel should be so moved.

Across the table from Rachel and Jimmy, Baxter has been struck by a new thought, one that makes him very happy. Alcoholics are almost always impotent, he thinks; that fellow Jimmy very likely never had her, either, the poor dumb sod.

Vastly cheered (and quite wrong: Stella and Jimmy enjoyed a spirited sexual rapport), Baxter thinks again of Stella, her often imagined, forever inaccessible flesh — ah, no one now! And he smiles in a warm, comradely way in Jimmy's direction.

Jimmy is talking about his labors with Stella's papers. "So much!" he tells everyone, with a pixieish widening of his old bright blue eyes. "So many papers! She wrote to everyone, you know, and they always wrote her back, and she kept everything. Even foolish letters from me. I was proud to come upon them." With a look of surprise he beams at his audience, then stops for a bite of salmon.

They are all regarding Jimmy as though he were a brand-new person, some visitor of charm and distinction. (It is Baxter who makes this observation to himself, and quite without pleasure.)

"It's going to take me a good ten years to get through it all," announces Jimmy (as though he could count on living ten more years). Everyone smiles at him with happy approval (as though they, too, could live that long).

Almost from one moment to the next, the day that seemed so unseasonably warm has turned cool — a sudden chill in the air, and a breeze, reminding everyone that the season is actually autumn, that summery warmth at noon was delusional. And they are none of them as young as they once were.

"I could go up and get some sweaters," Rachel offers. "Day and I — "

But they all decline. They have all been there long enough, they almost say.

It is somehow assumed that when everyone leaves Rachel will have some   65
time alone with Jimmy, which they no doubt need — they will want to talk about Stella — and that Day will go off with that fellow, that young Allen (well, off to bed). And that Baxter will take a nap, by himself.

All these things do take place, but not quite as anyone would have expected.

In bed, after a brief interval of love, Day and Allen take up their argument again.

Allen believes that they should marry. In a fast-disintegrating world, a personal commitment is almost all that is left, he thinks. Let us love one another or die, he says. Ah, love, let us be true. Besides, he is making a lot of money in San Francisco, in real estate.

Well, Day does not see marriage as an ultimate commitment. She does love Allen, and she is true. But still. And she has hopes of being accepted at law school, in New Haven.

Well, if she must, then why not Stanford, or Berkeley, or Davis?   70

In the waning late-afternoon light, the cool fall end of that golden October day, their words rise in the air, in circles and patterns that then, like smoke, dissolve, and Day and Allen fall asleep, in the high narrow guest bed, in the flimsily slatted green-stained cabin.

In the kitchen, clearing up, Rachel and Jimmy do not fall into a conversation having to do with Stella; they do not even mention Stella. Instead, they discuss Santa Barbara, and Jimmy's plans to go there, to live with his sister.

"It's a most charming place," he tells Rachel, as he polishes glasses (remembering that Stella thought they came out brighter with paper than with linen. "Such an affectation, linen towels," she used to say). "And the flowers," Jimmy now tells Rachel, quickly. Well, the flowers. And it's interesting, he continues, how some people seem to mellow with age: His sister, who for years was such a terror, now is very nice, a kind and pleasant person.

"I suppose that must be true," murmurs Rachel, who is wondering if either of those adjectives, kind and pleasant, would ever apply to Baxter, and if so, when.

"When I'm settled there, you've got to come and visit," Jimmy says.   75

Baxter goes off to bed, alone, of course, but despite the huge new down quilt and the lowered blinds and all the soothing books (his favorites, Ruskin

and Swinburne, odd tastes, perhaps somewhat misleading, having to do with
his mother), despite all the available comforts of the bedroom, poor Baxter is
quite unable to sleep, even to doze for a minute or two.

He is thinking of Day and Allen, rancorously, uncontrollably. His are not
exactly personal thoughts; he is simply thinking of youth, of obviously taken-
for-granted health and sensuality. The condition of youth now seems to Baxter
a club from which he has abruptly and most unfairly been excluded.

A couple of hours later Jimmy has gone. Outside, the night has turned
black and cold, and a wind has come up, rattling leaves, shaking windowpanes,
but Rachel remains in the small bright kitchen. Everything is clean and put
away, and she is tired. She has made herself a small pot of tea, and she sits
sipping, at the kitchen table. She thinks, How wonderful not to be talking to
anyone, not even thinking of people.

However, this is not to last, as she might have known that it would not:
Light footsteps in the passageway hurry toward her, someone else with something to say, or ask.

And of course it is Day.   80

"Well," Day begins, with a smile of pure pleasure at the sight of Rachel
which almost dissolves Rachel's wish that she not be there. "Oh, I hoped I'd
find you," says Day. "I slept for a while, and I had such an odd dream, about
Stella. So vivid." She smiles again, disarmingly. "In the dream, I asked her
point-blank how come she married Jimmy, and she told me, but what's terrible
is that I can't remember what she said!"

"Would you like some tea? The cups are right there behind you."

Day sits down with her tea. In her old loose blue cotton robe, with her
just-washed face, she looks even younger than she is. She says, "Well, it was
really a nice lunch party?"

What was intended as a statement has come out as a question, at which
Rachel smiles. "I guess," she says. "I wanted Jimmy to have a good time, and
to feel that everyone liked him, after all. I wish that damned old car hadn't
made him so late. On the other hand . . ."

She has left her thought dangling, but Day takes it up. "On the other hand,   85
maybe just as well? Time enough?" she asks, in her clear young voice.

"Could be. Enough of all of us. We don't really make up for Stella." She
adds, after the smallest pause, "And I thought Baxter was especially cross. Men
are so much less forgiving than women are, don't you think?" She sighs, at
this quite unintended afterthought.

"Oh really, how do you mean?"

Day is so eager that Rachel regrets her observation. "Well, maybe it's not
even true."

But Day is relentless. "What does Baxter have against Jimmy, do you
think?" she pursues.

"Well, basically just his marrying Stella. It was Stella that Baxter had it in   90
for, so to speak."

Day asks, "Because of her politics, you mean?"

"Well, that among other things. Actually, a lot of men didn't like her, not at all. It was odd, I always thought. Men are supposed to like beautiful women." Rachel's voice is reedy, low and rather tired, an old thrush.

"You mean, men fell in love with her but really didn't like her much?" Day's tone is that of someone zeroing in — perhaps a lawyer's tone.

Rachel smiles. With exhausted emphasis she says, "Exactly. That's just what Stella said, in fact. I think it made her lonely, a lot of the time."

"Especially since no one would see what was going on. Oh, I can see that,"   95
Day improvises.

"And Jimmy liked her very much, it's that simple," Rachel concludes. "She said she could hardly believe it." And she adds, as though it were irrelevant, "I think everyone is a little mad at Stella now for having died."

Ignoring that last (could she not have heard it? did Rachel not actually say it, only think it?), Day smiles; she is in love with this conversation. She now asks, "Did you notice Jimmy's sweater? Those stripes?"

"Exactly the color of Stella's hair. I saw that too."

"Do you think he thought of it?" Day is very serious.

"When he bought the sweater?" Rachel pauses before she answers. "No,   100
I'm sure the choice was quite unconscious. But still."

"Yes, still. He did buy it." And Day smiles again, as though they had, together, understood and settled everything.

And Rachel, who feels that almost nothing has been understood, or settled, who herself does not see how she can get through the coming winter, much less the rest of her life — Rachel smiles back at her.   1985

INVESTIGATIONS

1. The narrator says that Stella would have been in the pool "hours ago, flopping around like a porpoise and exhorting everyone else to come in, too" (para. 24). A few paragraphs later, the narrator says that it is a relief for her friends "not to have Stella around, loudly splashing in the pool, and always urging them all to exceed themselves, somehow" (para. 27). Consider other images of the way Stella behaved with her friends. How do you account for her friends' conflicting impressions of Stella? How do these impressions help you see her as a believable character?

2. Often there is a single person at the heart of a social group. Think of a group to which you belong — a group of school friends, friends in the neighborhood, or friends who play sports together. If there is a single person at the center of the group, characterize this person. What qualities does he or she share with Stella?

3. Rachel's friend Day attends the party to help with lunch. What larger role does this "young dark, vividly pretty girl" (para. 1) play in the story? How does her lover Allen affect this role?

4. Read Grace Paley's "Friends" and make notes about Selena's characteristics. Then make a list of Stella's traits. Compare the two women (noting similarities and differences) and the effect they had on their friends. Would you say they were good friends to their friends? Why or why not?
5. In the last month of her life, Stella refused to let anyone visit her. Why do you think she did this? Apparently, none of her friends "except, just possibly, Rachel," a doctor, understood her wish (para. 12). What do you think Rachel understood?
6. Rachel tells Day that a lot of men didn't like Stella. What about Stella might have irritated men? Why do you think Jimmy liked her so much?

RICHARD HOWARD

The Victor Vanquished

for Tom, 1989

At the going rate, your body gave you
— made you — too much pain for you to call it
yours. Oh not the pain, the pain was all yours

and all you had; by the end you hugged it
closer than their anodine substitutes: 5
pain was your one religion, pain was bliss.

But this body, where almost everything hurt
and what didn't hurt didn't work — *yours*? Never!
Like anybody's, it gave nothing up

that soap and water couldn't wash away.   10
Whose was it then, this desecrated pond
where all fish die, where only scum persists?

RICHARD HOWARD (b. 1929) is considered the translator most responsible for introducing modern French fiction to American readers. His many honors include a Pulitzer Prize in Poetry for *Untitled Subjects* (1969) and an American Book Award in 1984 for his translation of Charles Baudelaire's *Les Fleurs du Mal.*

Anybody's. Nobody's. Like a king
who keeps recognizing as "my people"
the rebels who have pulled him off the throne . . .   15

Your body not your body. What about
"your" friends? We want playmates we can own.
Could these be yours? Since every friendship

grows from some furtive apotheosis
of oneself, who were these dim intruders   20
presuming they inhabited your pain,

as if there could be room for them as well?
You would not have it — let them all go hang!
For two years, the body alone with its pain

suspended friendship like the rope that holds   25
a hanged man. All you wanted was to drop
this burden, even if it meant that you

would be the burden dropped. And "your" lovers?
What about love — was it like "your" disease,
an abnormal state of recognition   30

occurring in a normal man? Love is
not love until it is vulnerable —
then you were in it: up to here in love!

The verdict of their small-claims court: it takes
all kinds to make a sex. Had you made yours?   35
Everything is possible but not

everything is permitted: in love
you were a shadow pursuing shadows,
yet the habit of the chase enthralled you,

and you could not desist. You would make love   40
by listening, as women do. And by lying
still, alone, waiting. You did not wait long.

Life in general is, or ought to be,
as Crusoe said, one universal Act
of Solitude. You made it death as well.   45   1990

INVESTIGATIONS

1. In what ways can this poem be considered an example of how friendship involves "a love of endings" ("Celestial Music," line 38)?
2. What does the speaker risk by "being there" for his friend? How close would you have to feel to one of your friends to "be there" in the ways described in this poem? What risks would such closeness involve?
3. What sacrifices does the speaker's friendship with his dying friend require of him? What sacrifices does his friend make? How are these sacrifices similar to those you read about in Grace Paley's "Friends" and Ellen Darion's "Claudia"? How might the *lack* of such sacrifices help explain the quality of the male friendships portrayed in *Hurlyburly* (p. 258)?

THOM GUNN

Memory Unsettled

Your pain still hangs in air,
Sharp motes of it suspended;
The voice of your despair —
That also is not ended:

When near your death a friend   5
Asked you what he could do,
"Remember me," you said.
We will remember you.

Once when you went to see
Another with a fever   10
In a like hospital bed,
With terrible hothouse cough
And terrible hothouse shiver
That soaked him and then dried him,
And you perceived that he   15
Had to be comforted,

Born in 1929 in Gravesend, England, THOM GUNN has lived in California since 1954. His most recent books include a collection of essays entitled *The Occasions of Poetry* (1982) and *The Passages of Joy* (1982), a book of poems.

You climbed in there beside him
And hugged him plain in view,
Though you were sick enough,
And had your own fears too.　　　20　　　　1990

INVESTIGATIONS

1. According to this poem, what are some of the factors that can limit our ability to help and comfort one another? What do you think the limits are?
2. How is the poet's adherence to a rhyme scheme appropriate to what the poem says?
3. Look again at Cisneros's "My Lucy Friend Who Smells Like Corn." How might that story and "Memory Unsettled" be considered examples of the joy friendship has to offer?

DAVID RABE

Hurlyburly

Characters

EDDIE	DARLENE
PHIL	BONNIE
MICKEY	DONNA
ARTIE	

ACT ONE

Scene 1

(*Time: A little while ago.*)

(*Place: A two-story house crowded into one of the canyons between Sunset Boulevard and Mulholland Drive in the Hollywood Hills.*)

A Vietnam veteran, DAVID RABE (b. 1940) was born in Dubuque, Iowa, and educated at Loras College and Villanova University. His plays have won numerous awards, including the Tony award for *Sticks and Bones* (1971) and the New York Drama Critics Circle Award for *Streamers* (1976).

(*A spacious living room leading into an open kitchen make up the entire first floor of the house. Steps lead upstairs to an exposed balcony which overlooks the living room. A rail runs along the balcony and stairway. Three doors feed onto the balcony — Eddie's bedroom and Mickey's bedroom, which are separated by a bathroom. Stage right there is a couch and a low coffee table with a portable television on top of it and piles of newspapers and magazines on the couch and the floor around it. Directly upstage and yet slightly off center is the door to the outside. Along this wall there is perhaps a closet door with a mirror inside of it. Slightly right of center stage is an armchair angled toward the couch. A hassock sits beside it. Upstage of the couch is a window seat, the outdoor foliage visible beyond it; books, photos, résumés are scattered on the window seat. At the far stage left is a pile of throw pillows; and if the closet door and mirror are inappropriate along the back wall, perhaps they are in this wall. The kitchen area is a nook, with a counter running out downstage and swivel chairs on either side. Upstage are the stove, refrigerator, cabinets. The nook itself has shelves in which there are liquor bottles, magazines, scripts.*

The house is completely surrounded by wild vegetation, which is visible through greenhouselike windows in the living room and kitchen. At the far right is an old rocking chair. It is worth noting that in the characters' speeches phrases such as "whatchamacallit," "thing-amajig," "blah-blah-blah," and "rapateta" abound. These are phrases used by the characters to keep themselves talking and should be said unhesitatingly with the authority and conviction with which one would have in fact said the missing word.)

(*As the curtain rises, Eddie is asleep on the couch. The TV on the coffee table in front of the couch is droning out the early morning news. Eddie is a mess, his shirt out, wrinkled, unbuttoned, his trousers remaining on him only because one leg is yet tangled around one ankle. He lies with his head downstage, and as the door opens and Phil, a muscular, anxious man in a hurry comes rushing in, Eddie instantly sits straight up and appears to be looking right at Phil.*)

PHIL: Eddie.
EDDIE: What? (*Eddie flops back onto the couch as if he has just been hit on the head.*)
PHIL: Eddie, you awake or not?
EDDIE: I don't know. How about you?
PHIL: Eddie, I'm standin' here. How you doin'?
EDDIE: I don't know. Did I leave the door open?
PHIL: It was open.
EDDIE (*sitting up, a man in command, and talking, almost bragging, as he*

turns off the TV): I come home last night, I was feelin' depressed. I sat around, I watched some TV. Somebody called and hung up when I answered. I smoked some dope, took a couple of ludes. The TV got to look very good. It was a bunch of shit, but it looked very good due to the dope and due to the ludes. So I musta fell asleep at some point. *(As nodding a little it appears he might sleep again.)*

PHIL *(heading for the kitchen)*: Maybe I'll make us some coffee. Where is everything? By the stove and stuff?

EDDIE: What time is it?

PHIL *(holding up his left wrist and watch, he yells)*: I can't tell you what time it is: My watch was broken by the blow.

EDDIE: There's a clock on the stove.

PHIL: It's over.

EDDIE: What?

PHIL: Everything.

EDDIE *(rising, staggering toward the kitchen, his trousers dragging along by the ankle)*: What EVERYTHING?

PHIL: Me and Susie.

EDDIE: Whata you mean, "everything"?

PHIL: Everything. The whole thing. You know. Our relationship. I really fucked up this time. I really did. *(Sitting on a swivel chair, Eddie reaches around the counter to soak a towel in the sink. Phil is filling the coffee pot.)*

EDDIE: You had a fight. So what? Give her a little time and call her up, you know that. Don't be so goddamn negative.

PHIL: This was a big one.

EDDIE: Bigger than the last one?

PHIL: Yeah.

EDDIE: So what'd you do, shoot her? *(He covers his face with the wet towel. Silence, as Phil is putting the coffee into the filter for the coffee machine. Eddie peeks out from behind the towel.)* You didn't shoot her, Phil. You got a gun?

PHIL: On me?

EDDIE: You didn't shoot her, Phil.

PHIL: No.

EDDIE *(he puts the towel back over his face, pressing it against his eyes)*: So, she'll take you back. She always takes you back.

PHIL: Not this time.

EDDIE *(bursting out from behind the towel, he begins rummaging around the counter for aspirin, which he finds)*: What happened?

PHIL: I went too far. She ain't going to take me back.

EDDIE: You want me to call her?

PHIL: She'll give you the fucking business. She hates you.

EDDIE: Whata you mean, she hates me?

PHIL: She hates you.

EDDIE: What are you talking about, she hates me? Susie don't hate me. She
    likes me.

PHIL: She hates you; she told me.

EDDIE: She hates me? How can she hate me?

PHIL: She hates you. She tol' me. In the middle of the fight.

EDDIE (*his head killing him, takes some aspirin*): What are you talking about:
    You two are in the middle of this bloodbath — the goddamn climactic go-
    round of your seven-year career in, you know what I mean, marital carnage
    and somewhere in the peak of this motherfucker she takes time out to tell
    you she hates good ol' Eddie. Am I supposed to believe that?

PHIL: I was surprised too. I thought she liked you.

EDDIE: You're serious.

PHIL: Yeah.

EDDIE: So fuck her. What a whore. She hates me. Are you serious? This is
    unacceptable goddamn behavior.

PHIL: She's unbelievable.

EDDIE (*rising, he is kicking at his slacks, stepping on them to get them off, and
    starting toward the stairs and the bathroom*): This is unbelievable. I mean,
    what is she, a goddamn schizophrenic here? Is this a goddamn psychotic
    we've been dealing with here? I mean, isn't she always friendly with me?
    You have seen this, right? I mean, I'm not a goddamn imbecile to have
    thought she liked me. She acted like she liked me.

PHIL (*following after Eddie*): I thought she liked me.

EDDIE (*as they climb the stairs together*): I thought she liked you too. I mean,
    she don't like anybody, is that the situation, the pathetic bitch?

PHIL: I knew she hated Artie.

EDDIE: I knew she hated Artie, too. (*He goes into the bathroom.*) But Artie's
    an obnoxious, anal-obsessive pain in the ass who could make his best
    friend hire crazed, unhappy people with criminal tendencies to cut off his
    legs, which we have both personally threatened to do. So she hates a guy
    who, though we both love him, we both personally know it is somewhat
    in spite of him that we love him. So that proves nothing. (*There is the
    sound of the toilet flushing and then Eddie, carrying a pair of jogging
    shorts, steps back into the hallway.*) I mean, what the hell does she think
    gives her justification to hate me?

PHIL: She didn't say.

EDDIE: She didn't say?

PHIL: No. (*He goes into the bathroom.*)

EDDIE (*pulling on the jogging shorts*): She gave no rhyme or reason? She
    just — you gotta help me picture this — she what? In the middle of
    some goddamn retort, or was it out of the blue?

PHIL: Whata you mean?

EDDIE: I mean, did she have a point of reference, some sort of reference from
    within your blowup out of which she made some goddamn association

which was for her justification that she come veering off to dump all this unbelievable vituperative horseshit over me — whatever it was. I wanna get it straight. *(Toilet is flushed, and Phil comes out of the bathroom.)*

PHIL: You got some weed? I need some weed. *(Followed by Phil, Eddie heads down the stairs to the kitchen counter where he pulls from a shelf his drug box and, opening it, takes out a rolled joint.)*

EDDIE: I got great weed. You wanna toke up?

PHIL: I need somethin'.

EDDIE *(handing a joint to Phil)*: You just help me out, all right; I got to get this straight.

PHIL: I'm tryin', Eddie. You know that.

EDDIE *(as Phil inhales, trying to remember, Eddie sits Phil down on the swivel chair outside the counter)*: So what'd she say about me? You know, think back. So the two of you are hurling insults and she's a bitch, blah, blah, blah, you're a bastard, rapateta. *(Moving to serve coffee to Phil.)* So in the midst of this TUMULT where do I come in?

PHIL *(remembering suddenly)*: You're just like me, she says.

EDDIE: What? *(At the coffee, he freezes midgesture.)* We're alike? She said that?

PHIL: Yeah — we were both whatever it was she was calling me at the time.

EDDIE: I mean, that's sad. She's sad. They're all sad. They're all fucking crazy. What is she thinking about?

PHIL: I don't know.

EDDIE: What do you think she's thinking about?

PHIL: We're friends. You know. So she thinks we got somethin' in common. It's logical.

EDDIE: But we're friends on the basis of what, Phil? On the basis of opposites, right? We're totally dissimilar is the basis of our friendship, right?

PHIL: Of course.

EDDIE: I mean, I been her friend longer than I been yours. What does she think, that I've been — what? More sympathetic to you than her in those god-damn disputes you two have? If that's what she thought she should have had the guts to tell me, confront me!

PHIL: I don't think that's what she thought.

EDDIE: SO WHAT WAS IT?

PHIL: I don't know. I don't think she thinks.

EDDIE *(settling into the swivel chair opposite Phil)*: None of them think. I don't know what they do.

PHIL: They don't think.

EDDIE: They calculate. They manipulate. So what's she up to? They express their feelings. I mean, my feelings are hurt, too.

PHIL *(growing frenzied)*: Mine, too.

EDDIE: They're all nuts.

PHIL *(and more frenzied)*: I pity them, I fuckin' pity them. She makes me crazy. I ain't gonna see her any more.

EDDIE: This is terrible on a certain level. I mean, I liked you two together.

PHIL *(agitated, starting to pace away from Eddie)*: I know. Me, too. A lot of people did. I'm very upset. Let me have some more weed. *(Reaching back he grabs the joint from Eddie, then immediately paces on, roaming the living room.)* It was terrible. It was somethin'. Blah-blah-blah!

EDDIE: Rapateta. Hey, absolutely.

PHIL: Blah-blah-blah! You know, I come home in the middle 'a the night — she was out initially with her girlfriends, so naturally I was alone and went out too. So I come home, I'm ripped, I was on a tear, but I'm harmless, except I'm on a talking jag, you know, who cares? She could have some sympathy for the fact that I'm ripped, she could take that into consideration, let me run my mouth a little, I'll fall asleep, where's the problem? That's what you would do for me, right?

EDDIE: Yeah.

PHIL *(rushing to Eddie to hand him the joint)*: She can't do that.

EDDIE: What's she do? What the hell's the matter with her, she can't do that?

PHIL: I'm on a tear, see, I got a theory how to take Las Vegas and turn it upside down like it's a little rich kid and shake all the money out of its pockets, right?

EDDIE: Yeah. So what was it?

PHIL: It was bullshit, Eddie. *(Sitting back down opposite Eddie.)* I was demented and totally ranting, so to that extent she was right to pay me no attention, seriously, but she should of faked it. But she not only sleeps, she snores. So I gotta wake her up, because, you know, the most important thing to me is that, in addition to this Las Vegas scam, I have this theory on the Far East, you know; it's a kind of vision of Global Politics, how to effect a real actual balance of power. She keeps interrupting me. You know, I'm losing my train of thought everytime she interrupts me. It's a complex fucking idea, so I'm asking her to just have some consideration until I get the whole thing expressed, then she wants to have a counterattack, I couldn't be more ready.

EDDIE: She won't do that?

PHIL: No.

EDDIE: That's totally uncalled for, Phil. All you're asking for is civilization, right? You talk and she talks. That's civilization, right? You take turns!

PHIL: I don't think I'm asking for anything unusual, but I don't get it.

EDDIE: Perverse.

PHIL: Perverse is what she wrote the book on it. I am finally going totally crazy. *(Jumping back up on his feet.)* I've totally lost track of my ideas. I'm like lookin' into this hole in which was my ideas. I arrive thinkin' I can take Vegas and save the world. Forty-five seconds with her and I don't know what I'm talking about. So I tell her — "LISTEN! — lemme think a second, I gotta pick up the threads." She says some totally irrelevant but degrading shit about my idea and starts some nitpicking with which she obviously intends to undermine my whole fucking Far Eastern theory on the balance

of powers, and I'm sayin', "Wait a minute," but she won't. So WHACK!
I whack her one in the face. Down she goes.

EDDIE: You whacked her.

PHIL: I whacked her good. You see my hand. *(Moving to Eddie, Phil holds out his hand.)*

EDDIE *(rising to look at Phil's hand)*: You did that to your hand?

PHIL: Her fuckin' tooth, see.

EDDIE *(teasing Phil a little)*: You were having this political discussion with which she disagreed, so you whacked her out, is that right?

PHIL: It wasn't the politics. I didn't say it was the politics.

EDDIE: What was it? You were ripped?

PHIL: Yeah. But it wasn't that. I don't know what it was. *(Phil sits down on the couch, starts to play with a toy, a magic cube sitting on the table.)*

EDDIE: What was it? *(Moving to sit beside Phil.)*

PHIL: I don't know. I had this idea and then it was gone.

EDDIE *(eager)* Yeah.

PHIL: It was just this disgusting cloud like fucking with me and I went crazy.

EDDIE *(delighted)*: Right. Whata you mean?

PHIL: You know this fog, and I was in it and it was talking to me with her face on it. Right in front of me was like this cloud with her face on it, but it wasn't just her, but this cloud saying all these mean things about my ideas and everything about me, so I was like shit and this cloud knew it. There was no way out. I couldn't get my thoughts together. They were all over the place. And once they were all over the place they weren't anything any more. That was when it happened.

EDDIE: You whacked her.

PHIL: Yeah.

EDDIE: Was she all right?

PHIL: She was scared, and I was scared. I don't know if I was yelling I would kill her or she was yelling she was going to kill me.

EDDIE: Somebody was threatening somebody, though.

PHIL: Definitely.

EDDIE *(rising, he paces in a meditative, investigative manner across the room for more coffee)*: So try and remember how was it before you whacked her or after you whacked her that she made her reference to me?

PHIL: You mean that she hated you?

EDDIE: Yeah.

PHIL: Before. It was in the vicinity of Vegas, I think, but it gets blurry.

EDDIE: So what musta happened is she decided I had some connection to your Vegas scam and this was for her justification to dump all this back-stabbing hostility all over me.

PHIL: She didn't say that. She just says we're both assholes.

EDDIE: But it would be logical that if this petty, cheap-shot animosity was in the vicinity of Vegas, it would have to do with Vegas. THAT WOULD ONLY BE LOGICAL.

PHIL: EXCEPT SHE AIN'T LOGICAL.

EDDIE: True.

PHIL: SHE'S JUST A NASTY BITCH AND I MARRIED HER.

EDDIE: You know what I think?

PHIL: What?

EDDIE: She hates men.

PHIL (*crossing toward Eddie, very interested*): Whata you mean?

EDDIE: She hates you, she hates me. She hates men. I don't know what else to think. It's a goddamn syllogism. Susie hates Phil, Susie hates Eddie. She hates men.

PHIL: And Artie, too.

EDDIE: Artie, Eddie, Phil are men, she hates men. The fucker's irrefutable, except that's not how it works, GODDAMNIT.

PHIL: What?

EDDIE: You go from the general to the particular. I'm talking about a syllogism, here.

PHIL: Yeah.

EDDIE (*irritated, storming off, he slumps into the big armchair, the better to think*): Damnit! What the hell goes the other way?

PHIL: Which way?

EDDIE: Something goes the other goddamn way!

PHIL: What?

EDDIE: You start from the particular in something. Susie hates Eddie, Susie hates Phil. Phil and Eddie are men, therefore, blah, blah, blah. . . . Oh, my god, do you know what it is?

PHIL: What?

EDDIE: Science! What goes the other way is science, in which you see all the shit like data and go from it to the law. This is even better. We have just verified, and I mean scientifically, the bitch has been proven to basically hate all men. She doesn't need a reason to hate me in particular — she already hates me in the fucking abstract.

PHIL: You gonna call her?

EDDIE: You want me to?

PHIL: You said you were gonna!

EDDIE: That was before I understood the situation. Now that I understand the situation, the hell with her. The bitch wants to go around hating me in the fucking abstract! Are you nuts? Call her? I wouldn't piss on her if the flames were about to engulf her goddamn, you know, central nervous system! (*As Mickey staggers out of his bedroom onto the balcony, Phil grabs up a bottle of bourbon from the counter.*)

PHIL: I am going to hole up here and ossify myself.

EDDIE: I MEAN, WHERE THE HELL DOES SHE GET OFF? (*It is important to note that there is an element of play in this whole scene between Phil and Eddie: On some level it is a game, a riff and that Eddie tends to adopt Phil's mannerisms when alone with him.*)

MICKEY: Didn't I beg you to let me have some goddamn quiet this morning? Eddie, I begged you!

EDDIE *(runs to the base of the stairs, yelling up)*: Phil has left Susie again, only this time it's final!

MICKEY: So what are YOU screaming about?

PHIL *(following after Eddie)*: The deceitful bitch has been bad-mouthing Eddie. That's been part of the problem from the beginning.

EDDIE: Her attitude has been deceitful and degrading!

MICKEY: So when did this happen?

PHIL: It's been goin' on.

MICKEY: It'll blow over. *(Mickey goes reeling into the bathroom.)*

EDDIE: No!

PHIL: I don't think so.

EDDIE *(having a fit at the base of the stairs, yet there is a note of sheer delight in it)*: I mean, she thinks she can do this shit and get away with it? He goes back, he's nuts. He deserves her. You go back this time, Phil, I'm never gonna speak to you again.

PHIL: I know that. I agree with you.

MICKEY *(coming out of the bathroom)*: He's not serious, Phil.

EDDIE: Whata you know about it?

MICKEY: You're serious, if Phil goes back to his wife, you don't ever want to speak to him again? *(Descending the stairs, Mickey is all but attacked by Eddie.)*

EDDIE: I'm serious. *(As Mickey moves to the kitchen, Eddie and Phil follow him, both yelling at Mickey and one another, an element of fun between them that they are tormenting Mickey with their noise and craziness when he has just awoken.)*

MICKEY: That's not serious.

EDDIE: Says you! I know when I'm serious and I'm serious, and Phil knows it even if you don't.

PHIL: I hate her anyway!

EDDIE: See! And you'd know it, too, if you were my goddamn friend like you think you are.

PHIL: I'm done with her!

EDDIE *(grabbing his box of cocaine and other drugs from its shelf under the breakfast nook counter)*: See!

MICKEY: You guys are in a fucking frenzy here. Have some breakfast, why don't you? Eat an orange, why don't you? Calm you down. We need some fruit in this house. Where's the fruit? *(As Mickey looks in the refrigerator, Eddie has handed a vial of coke to Phil and has spread a line for himself on the countertop. Phil hovers beside Eddie.)* Where's the food? We need some food in this house. Eddie, where's all the food? *(Seeing Eddie preparing to snort some cocaine.)* What are you doing?

EDDIE: What's it look like I'm doin?

MICKEY: It looks like — What does it look like? It looks like you are doin' a line of coke on the kitchen counter here at eight forty-five in the morning.

EDDIE: Very good. (*Eddie and Phil snort coke and exchange glances and pokes throughout this, clearly a conspiracy against Mickey; almost like two bad little boys with a baby-sitter they don't much respect.*)

MICKEY: What are you becoming, a coke fiend, Eddie?

EDDIE: How'm I gonna wake up? I gotta wake up!

MICKEY: Some people have coffee.

EDDIE: The caffeine is fucking poison, don't you know that?

MICKEY: Right. So what is this, Bolivian health food? Some people risk it with coffee to wake up in the morning, rather than this shit which can make you totally chemically insane. Don't you watch the six o'clock news?

EDDIE: I watch all the news.

MICKEY (*looking under the counter, he finds a package of English muffins containing two muffins which he waves with a flourish*): Bread. I found some fucking bread. All right, we can have some muffins for breakfast. We can have some moldy muffins along with our Bolivian Blow for break-fast. How long have I slept? Last time I saw you, you were a relatively standard everyday alcoholic Yahoo, Eddie. Now the bread's moldy and you're sniffin' around the goddamn breakfast nook like a wart hog.

EDDIE: I had a rough night. Whata you want from me?

MICKEY: You should go to bed. (*Mickey is cutting a muffin, putting butter and jelly on it.*)

EDDIE: How'm I going to get to bed?

MICKEY: I don't know. Most people manage it. I don't know. Is this an out-rageous suggestion, that he should get to bed? He's down here half the night, Phil, crashing around and talking to the TV like a goddamn maniac. Want half a dead English muffin, Phil? (*Offering jellied muffins on a plate to Phil, who looks at Eddie, and Mickey shifts the plate toward Eddie.*) Eddie?

EDDIE (*clearly snubbing Mickey, Eddie turns to Phil, who is spooning coke from the vial*): I gotta wake up. (*As Phil puts the coke to one of Eddie's nostrils.*) I got a lot of work today. (*Phil puts coke to Eddie's other nostril and Eddie snorts, then grabs Phil's face between his hands.*) The shit that went down here last night was conspiratorial. It was unbelievable. (*Eddie walks toward the front door, Phil following along.*) I mean, first of all the eleven o'clock news has just devastated me with this shitload of horror in which it sounds like not only are we headed for nuclear devastation if not by the Russians then by some goddamn primitive bunch of middle-eastern motherfuckers — (*Opening the front door, he reaches out and picks up several newspapers, glancing at them as he talks to Phil. Mickey, aban-doned in the kitchen nook, eats the muffins.*) — and I don't mean that racially but just culturally, because they are so far back in the forest in some part of their goddamn mental sophistication, they are likely to drop the bomb just to see the light and hear the big noise. I mean, I am talking not innate ability, but sophistication here. They have got to get off the camels and wake up! *(Handing the newspapers to Phil, Eddie starts up the stairs.)* So on top of this, there's this accidental electrical fire in which an entire family is incinerated, the father trying to save everybody by hurling them out the window, but he's on the sixth floor, so he's, you know — they're like eggs on the sidewalk. So much for heroics. *(Having paused partway up the stairs, he now pivots to hasten up the remainder.)* So then my wife calls! You wanna have some absurdity?

PHIL: I thought you was divorced.

EDDIE: I am.

PHIL: You said, "wife."

EDDIE *(pausing on the balcony to look down)*: Why would I do that? I hate my ex-wife. I might have said "mother" instead of "ex-wife," but not "wife."

PHIL: Why would you do THAT?

EDDIE *(playfully exasperated)*: Because I could have made a Freudian slip!

PHIL: You don't believe in that shit, do you?

EDDIE: Whata you know about it?

PHIL: Somethin'. I know somethin'. I was in prison.

EDDIE *(going into his room)*: Mickey, what'd I say?

MICKEY: I wasn't listening.

PHIL *(with all the newspapers, he sits on the arm of the couch and yells up at Eddie's door)*: I mean, how would that shit work? You'd have WHAT? — all that stuff from your neighborhood like chasing you?

MICKEY: You mean like from your background.

PHIL: You believe in that Freudian shit, Mickey?

MICKEY: What Freudian shit?

PHIL: You know. All those books!

MICKEY: No.

PHIL: Me neither. *(Crossing to join Mickey.)* I mean, how would that work? What? Ghosts?

MICKEY: It wouldn't.

PHIL: So assholes pay all this money, right. *(As Eddie, having come out of his room, buttoning a clean shirt but still wearing the jogging shorts, is descending the stairs.)* It's unbelievable; and it don't work.

MICKEY: Eddie's done it.

PHIL: You done it, Eddie?

EDDIE *(taking a newspaper from Phil)*: What?

PHIL: What we're talkin' about here. You were just talkin' about it, too!

MICKEY: Freud.

EDDIE *(as he settles in the armchair to read)*: Right. One of the real prestige guys of blow. A pioneer. *(And opening the paper, he closes the conversation.)*

MICKEY: So, Phil, you left your wife. I liked your wife.

PHIL: You can have her. *(Rising, he moves off to the couch carrying what's left of the newspapers.)*

MICKEY: Don't kid yourself. You find anybody whatsoever with her when you go back, let alone me, of whom your affection is borderline to say the least, you'll kill them.

PHIL: I ain't going back.

MICKEY: So your personal life's a shambles, how's your career?

PHIL: I'm up for some very interesting parts at the moment, and on several of them — my agent says on this new copy show for NBC, my agent says I'm a lock, that's how close I am. I been back six times; the director and I have hit it off. It's very exciting.

MICKEY: Who's the director?

PHIL: He's this terrific Thomas Leighton.

EDDIE *(quite exasperated)*: This is the Thomas Leighton thing? *(It is clearly a topic he put time and energy in trying to make clear for Phil.)* He's a scumbag, I tol' you, Phil. He's a scumbag faggot who likes to jerk tough guys like you around. He'll bring you back a hundred times, you'll get nothing.

PHIL *(a little distressed that Eddie is saying these things in front of Mickey)*: My agent says he likes me, and it's between me and this other guy who is taller, and that the only problem is when they cast the lead, if he's a different physical type than me, then I'll have a very good shot.

EDDIE: The leads are always a different physical type than you, Phil. This is America. This is TV.

PHIL *(leaping to his feet, he bolts for the door)*: What are you tryin' to discourage me for?

EDDIE *(rushing to stop Phil from leaving)*: I'm not trying to discourage you.

MICKEY *(easing toward the stairs)*: This is Eddie's particular talent — to effortlessly discourage people.

EDDIE *(his hand on Phil, he almost follows Mickey up the stairs so urgent is his point)*: If Phil wants to obliquely pick my brain about our area of expertise here, Mickey, am I supposed to pretend that you and I are not casting directors or I haven't noticed the whys and wherefores of how the thing happens in this town? I mean, right, Phil?

PHIL *(a little like a kid on a street corner, he hangs around one of the balcony support beams)*: I mean, Eddie, I trust that you are not deliberately trying to discourage me, but in all honesty, I gotta tell you, I'm feelin' very discouraged.

EDDIE *(genuinely wanting to impart sincere and friendly wisdom to Phil)*: No, no. Look, you have to exploit your marketable human qualities, that's all. You have certain qualities and you have to exploit them. I mean, basically we all know the M.O. out here is they take an interesting story, right? They distort it, right? Cut whatever little truth there might be in it out on

the basis of it's unappealing, but leave the surface so it looks familiar —
cars, hats, trucks, trees. So, they got their scam, but to push it they have
to flesh it out, so this is where you come in because then they need a lot
of authentic-sounding and -looking people — high-quality people such as
yourself, who need a buck. So like every other whore in this town, myself
included, you have to learn to lend your little dab of whatever truth you
can scrounge up in yourself to this total, this systematic sham — so that
the fucking viewer will be exonerated from ever having to confront directly
the fact that he is spending his life face to face with total shit. So that's all
I'm sayin'. "Check with me," is all I'm sayin'. Forget about this Leighton
thing. *(Together, they have ended up back by the couch and TV.)*

PHIL: Forget about it? I got nothin' else to do. What about the things you're
currently working on? Anything for me?

MICKEY *(descending the steps, dressed for work, and carrying a handful of
résumés and photographs)*: Nothing.

PHIL: Who asked you? *(Mickey settles down on the window seat to sort the
résumés.)*

EDDIE: There's a thing down the road a month or so, it might be a good thing
for you. *(He crosses to the breakfast nook counter where scripts are piled
on shelves.)*

PHIL: What is it?

EDDIE: It's a special or a pilot, they haven't decided. *(Picking a joint from an
ashtray on the counter, he prepares to light up.)*

PHIL: But there might be somethin' in it for me. You got a script? *(He strides
over and takes the script that Eddie is pulling from the pile.)*

EDDIE: This is shit, though. I don't wanna hear about the quality, because this
is total shit. *(He inhales the joint.)*

MICKEY: Don't get fucked up, Eddie. We got that meeting with the guy.

EDDIE: So maybe you could handle things this morning? Whataya think?

MICKEY: I think they're expecting both of us, that's what I think.

PHIL *(leaning against the wall, he has been leafing through the script)*: This is
shit, huh?

EDDIE: Total.

PHIL: But there might be somethin' in it for me?

EDDIE: Yeah. *(Phil, grabbing his coat, starts off. Eddie jumps after him, fearful
Phil's feelings have been hurt again.)* Where you goin'?

PHIL *(indicating the stairs)*: I'm going to read it. And also, I'm beat. I'm really
beat. It's been one exhausting thing I went through. I'm gonna pass out in
your room, Eddie, okay?

EDDIE *(as Phil is going up the stairs)*: We'll do something later. *(Eddie takes a
huge toke on the joint.)*

MICKEY: Do you realize, Eddie, that you are now toking up at eight fifty-eight
in the morning on top of the shit you already put up your nose? You're
going to show up at work looking like you got a radish for a nose. You're
going to show up talking like a fish.

EDDIE: Don't worry about it, okay?

MICKEY: Is that supposed to fuck me up? *(Mickey moves from the window seat to the couch where he sits.)*

EDDIE: You don't have to worry about me, Mickey.

MICKEY: What kind of tone is that?

EDDIE: What do you mean, what kind of tone is that? That's my tone.

MICKEY: So what does it mean?

EDDIE: My tone? What does my tone mean? I don't have to interpret my fucking tone to you, Mickey. I don't know what it means. What do you think it means?

MICKEY: Just don't get clandestine on me, Eddie; that's all I'm saying.

EDDIE: But there are not a lot of dynamite ladies around anywhere you look, Mickey, as we both know, and I am the one who met Darlene first. I am the one who brought her by, and it was obvious right from the get-go that Darlene was a dynamite lady, this was a very special lady.

MICKEY: We hit it off, Eddie, you know. I asked you.

EDDIE *(all ease and smiles, he seems to be only after clarity)*: Absolutely. Look, I'm not claiming any reprehensible behavior on anybody's part, but don't ask me not to have my feelings hurt, okay. I'm not saying anything went on behind my back or I was deceived or anything. Nevertheless, the situation has had an effect on me. I mean, we are all sophisticated people, and Darlene and I most certainly had no exclusive commitment of any kind whatsoever to each other, blah-blah-blah.

MICKEY *(moving to the kitchen to get some coffee, he is relieved at their agreement)*: That's exactly what I'm saying, Rapateta.

EDDIE: There's no confusion here, Mickey, but have a little empathy for crissake. *(Mickey nods, for "empathy" is certainly something he can afford to give.)* I bring this very special lady to my house to meet my roommate, my best friend, and I haven't been interested in a woman for years, seriously, I have this horror show of a marriage in my background, and everybody knows it, so blah-blah-blah, they have THIS ATTRACTION to each other. *(Seeing now that Eddie is after more than "empathy," Mickey pretends exasperation and bows his head to the counter in mock self-abasement.)* My roommate and my new girl — I'm just trying to tell the story here, Mickey; nobody's to blame. *(Patting Mickey on the back.)* Certainly not you. I mean, you came to me, you had experienced these vibes between yourself and Darlene — isn't that what you said — I mean, you correct me if I'm wrong — but would I mind, you wondered, if you and Darlene had dinner in order to, you know, determine the nature of these vibes, or would that bother me? That's a fair — I mean, reasonable representation of what you asked.

MICKEY *(moving out with his coffee toward the armchair, he addresses invisible masses — his voice, of course, slightly self-mocking, not totally, by any means, serious)*: I just — I mean, from my point of view, the point is — the main point is, I asked.

EDDIE: I know this.

MICKEY: That — in my opinion — is the paramount issue, the crucial issue. And I don't want it forgotten.

EDDIE (*though charming, he is not without an ominous note in his tone and smile*): Nothing from yesterday is forgotten, Mickey. You don't have to worry about that.

MICKEY: Why do we have to go through this? I just wanna have some breakfast. I mean, couldn't you have said, "no"? Couldn't you have categorically, definitively said "no" when I asked? But you said — "Everybody's free, Mickey." That's what you said.

EDDIE: Everybody is free.

MICKEY: So what's this then?

EDDIE: This? You mean this? This conversation?

MICKEY: Yeah.

EDDIE: This is JUST ME trying to maintain a, you know, viable relationship with reality. I'm just trying to make certain I haven't drifted off into some, you know, solitary paranoid fantasy system of my own, totally unfounded and idiosyncratic invention. I'm just trying to stay in reality, Mickey, that's all. Don't you want me to be in reality? I personally want us both to be in reality.

MICKEY: Absolutely. That's what I want. (*And Mickey almost rushes to the chair opposite Eddie at the counter, as if with this move he will end the conversation on this note.*) I mean, I want us both to be in reality. Absolutely.

EDDIE (*very reassuring*): So that's what's going on here, you know, blah-blah-blah. Don't take it personally.

MICKEY (*very affirmative*): Blah-blah-blah!

EDDIE: So I was just wondering. You came in this morning at something like six-oh-two, so your dinner must have been quite successful. These vibes must have been serious. I mean, sustaining, right?

MICKEY: Right. Yeah. You know.

EDDIE: Or does it mean — and I'm just trying to get the facts straight here, Mickey — does it mean you fucked her?

MICKEY: Darlene?

EDDIE: Right.

MICKEY: Darlene? Did I fuck Darlene? Last night? Eddie, hey, I asked you. I thought we were clear on this thing.

EDDIE: We're almost clear.

MICKEY (*with a take-charge manner, as if he has at last figured out what it is that Eddie wants*): What I mean, Eddie is, THINGS HAPPEN, but if this bothers you, I mean, if this bothers you, I don't have to see her again. This is not worth our friendship, Eddie; you know that.

EDDIE (*recoiling in a mockery of shock, yet not without a real threat*): Wait a minute. You're not saying that you took my new girl, my very special dynamite girl out and fucked her on a whim, I mean, a fling and it meant nothing!? You're not saying that?

MICKEY: No, no, no.

EDDIE: I mean, these vibes were serious, right? These vibes were the beginnings of something very serious, right? They were the first, faint, you know, things of a serious relationship, right?

MICKEY: Hey, whatever.

EDDIE *(munching the remnants of one of the muffins, he is quite happy)*: I mean, I don't want to interfere with any possibilities for happiness in your life, Mickey.

MICKEY: Believe me, this is not a possibility for happiness in my life.

EDDIE: Well, it was in mine. It was such a possibility in mine.

MICKEY: I think you just have it maybe all out of proportion here, Eddie.

EDDIE: Yeah? So do me a breakdown.

MICKEY: I just think maybe she's not as dynamite as you might think. *(Mickey's remark nearly catapults Eddie across the room.)*

EDDIE: Fuck you!

MICKEY: You always go a little crazy about women, Eddie.

EDDIE: You wanna let it alone, Mickey.

MICKEY: It's not a totally, you know, eccentric thing to happen to a guy, so don't get fucking defensive.

EDDIE: I mean, there's nothing here that necessitates any sort of underground smear campaign against Darlene.

MICKEY: No, no, no. I just want you to think about the possibility that things have gotten a little distorted, that's all.

EDDIE: No.

MICKEY: You won't think about it?

EDDIE: I mean, bad-mouthing her just to get yourself off the hook — don't think you can do that.

MICKEY: Never.

EDDIE: It's not that I DON'T understand — it's that I DO understand. It's just that I'm not so fucking sophisticated as to be totally beyond this entire thing, you see what I'm saying, Mickey. Blah-blah-blah — my heart is broken — blah-blah-blah. *(He flops down on the couch, as if he might go back to sleep.)*

MICKEY: Blah — blah — blah. Absolutely. So you want me to toast you what's left of the muffin? We can put some raisins on it — be a sort of Danish. Somebody's got to go shopping.

EDDIE: You think we couldn't handle a dog around here?

MICKEY: I wouldn't want to be a fucking dog around here. Dogs need stability.

EDDIE: I like dogs.

MICKEY *(as he goes into the kitchen to start cleaning up the mess there)*: You could borrow Artie's dog.

EDDIE: I hate Artie's dog. It looks like a rat; it doesn't look like a dog. I like big dogs.

MICKEY: So did you get any sleep at all?

EDDIE: Fucking Agnes had to call. Why does she have to call?

MICKEY: Why do you talk to her is the real question?

EDDIE: I have to talk to her. We have a kid.

MICKEY: That's a thought to turn the mind to pure jello — you or any man daring to get that close to Agnes. Are you sure you did it?

EDDIE: Only with a borrowed cock.

MICKEY: I mean, you might as well put your balls in her teeth as pick up the phone.

EDDIE: Because she thinks she's smarter than me; she thinks I'm afraid of her and that I agree with her assessment of what went wrong between us.

MICKEY (*quite superior*): But every time you talk to her, you end up in this total, this absolute nonproductive shit-fit over what she said, or meant, or might have been implying, and in the process deliver her conclusive proof of what for her is already irrefutable — namely that you're a mess. (*As Artie and Donna come in the front door.*) And then you go crazy for days!

EDDIE: What do you want me to do, abandon my kid in her hands and with no other hope? Forget about it! (*He is turning over as if to hide his head or go to sleep, so he doesn't see Artie or Donna.*)

(*Artie is about ten years older than Eddie and Mickey. He is slick in appearance, dressed very California; a mix of toughness and arrogance, a cunning desperation; he carries a shoulder satchel or briefcase. With him is Donna; blonde, about fifteen. Carrying a Walkman tape player, she has earphones on. Under her arm she has a record album which she will carry everywhere. She wears tattered shorts, a T-shirt, a buckskin jacket, and beat-up cowboy boots. Seeing Artie, Mickey addresses him as if he's been standing there for years.*)

MICKEY: Artie, so what's the haps, here?

ARTIE: You guys in the middle of something, or what?

MICKEY: You didn't tell us you got married.

ARTIE: Her? I found her on the elevator.

DONNA: Where's the bathroom?

EDDIE: What kind of accent is that? What kind of accent you got?

DONNA: I'm from the Midwest, so that's it.

ARTIE (*to Mickey*): You want her?

MICKEY: Whata you mean?

ARTIE: It's too crowded, see?

DONNA: Artie, they got a bathroom?

ARTIE: Sure they got a bathroom.

EDDIE (*from the couch*): What's she want with our bathroom, Artie? Is this a goddamn coke fiend you brought with you here?

DONNA: I gotta go.

EDDIE: Where?

DONNA: I gotta go to the bathroom.

ARTIE: This is Eddie.

DONNA: Hi, you got a bathroom?

EDDIE: It's upstairs.

DONNA: Great.

MICKEY *(as Donna hurries up the stairs)*: I'm Mickey. It's the first door.

DONNA: Great, Mickey. I'm Donna. *(She goes into the bathroom, shutting the door.)*

MICKEY: Cute, Artie, very cute.

ARTIE *(to Mickey)*: You want her?

EDDIE: You keep sayin' that, Artie.

ARTIE *(as if irritated at her)*: She was on the goddamn elevator. In the hotel. I'm going out for coffee in the morning, I take the elevator, there she is.

MICKEY *(moving to get Artie some coffee)*: You want coffee. We got coffee, muffins, coke, and raisins.

ARTIE *(glancing at his watch, he settles into the swivel chair in front of the counter)*: It's too early for breakfast, but I'll have some coffee. This was yesterday. So I come back from coffee, she's in the elevator. It's an hour. So that's a coincidence. Then I'm going out for dinner. Right? This is seven — eight hours later. She's in the elevator.

MICKEY: She's livin' in the elevator.

ARTIE: Yeah, so after dinner, there she is. So I ask her: Is she livin' in the elevator? She says her boyfriend tried to kill her, so she's stayin' off the street.

MICKEY *(handing Artie the coffee, Mickey stands behind the counter, leaning on it toward Artie)*: Why'd he want to kill her?

ARTIE: She says he was moody. So, I took her in. But I figured, I don't need her, you know, like you guys need her. You guys are a bunch of desperate guys. You're very desperate guys, right? You can use her. So I figured on my way to the studio, I'd drop her by, you can keep her. Like a CARE package, you know. So you can't say I never gave you nothing.

EDDIE *(from the couch)*: You're giving her to us?

ARTIE: Yeah.

EDDIE: What are we going to do with her?

ARTIE: What do you want to do with her?

EDDIE: Where's she from?

MICKEY *(as if Eddie is an imbecile)*: What has that got to do with anything?

EDDIE: I wanna know.

MICKEY: Somewhere in the Middle West. I heard her.

EDDIE: That could be anywhere.

MICKEY: So what?

EDDIE *(crossing toward them to get coffee)*: I'm just trying to figure out what we're going to do with her. You wanna pay attention.

ARTIE *(intervening on Mickey's behalf)*: What do you want, Eddie, an instruction manual? This is a perfectly viable piece of ass I have brought you, and you're acting totally like WHAT? What's going on here? Are we in sync or not?

EDDIE: Like she'll be a pet, is that what you're saying, Artie?

ARTIE: Right.

MICKEY (*patting Artie, his arm ending up around Artie*): Right.

ARTIE: You can keep her around. (*Artie and Mickey exchange a look with which to patronize Eddie.*)

EDDIE: She'll be like this pet we can keep and fuck her if we want to?

ARTIE: Sure. Just to stay in practice. In case you run into a woman.

EDDIE: I guess he hasn't heard about Darlene. (*It is as if the name, "Darlene," is a punch from which Mickey reels.*) I guess you haven't heard about Darlene, Artie.

ARTIE: No. Is this important?

EDDIE: Mickey has gotten involved with this truly dynamite bitch in a very serious relationship.

MICKEY: Bullshit. (*Rising, Mickey escapes across the room to the window seat where he sits down, picking up a* Variety.)

ARTIE: Is this true, Mickey? Is this the same Darlene, Eddie? You had a Darlene.

EDDIE (*leaning across the counter to Artie*): What I'm inferring here, Artie, is that Mickey is unlikely to be interested in this bimbo you have brought by for fear of, you know, contaminating his feelings and catching some vile disease in addition.

ARTIE: So when did this happen, Mickey? You guys switched, or what? I miss everything. So you're in a serious relationship, Mickey. That's terrific.

MICKEY: Except I ain't serious about anything, Artie, you know that. (*As Donna comes out of the bathroom and down the stairs, her shoes clumping loudly.*)

EDDIE: You wanna live with us for a while, Donna?

DONNA (*pausing at the base of the stairs to look at Eddie*): Hmmmmmmmmmmmmm?

ARTIE (*he crosses toward her, as Mickey comes up behind her*): Okay, I gotta go. All she has to do for me is go down to the hotel twice a day and walk my dog.

MICKEY (*arm around her*): Right. (*As he blows the word in her ear, Donna yelps and scurries several steps away.*)

EDDIE: What if she runs away?

ARTIE: What do you want from me, Eddie, a guarantee? (*Draping an arm over her shoulder, Artie slides a hand under her shirt and fiddles with her breast.*) I can't guarantee her. She worked last time I used her. You want a guarantee, talk to the manufacturer. I'm not the manufacturer.

EDDIE (*settling down on the swivel chair and picking up the phone*): You're the retailer.

ARTIE: Frankly, from the look of you, what I am is a goddamn charity organization having some compassion on some pathetic fuck who is you, that's what I am. (*After all, Eddie sits there still in his jogging shorts, and his partially buttoned shirt.*) I'm having some generosity toward the heartbreaking desperation I encounter here every time I come by and have to look at you. You don't mind if I have a little mercy.

EDDIE: So where you goin? You goin' to the studio?

ARTIE: I said that.

EDDIE: You didn't say what for.

ARTIE: You didn't ask what for. I got a meeting.

EDDIE: You know what happens to you doesn't happen to normal people.

ARTIE: I did good deeds in an earlier lifetime. How do I know?

EDDIE: Yeah, but being a highly developed bullshit artist does not normally translate into this kind of situation.

ARTIE: He's a blocked writer, and my stories about my life unblock him. You know, it was his idea, and secretly, I always dreamed of it.

EDDIE: Dreamed of what?

ARTIE *(advancing on Eddie, he leaves Donna)*: Having an interesting life and a capacity to relate some of it does not constitute a criminal offense against you personally, Eddie.

EDDIE: Hey, you're misinterpreting my whole slant here; forget about it.

ARTIE: I intend to forget about it.

EDDIE: You're an ungrateful prick, Artie.

ARTIE *(in a state of total delight, he pats Eddie's cheek)*: I'm desperate. *(And he starts for the door.)*

EDDIE: Just keep me informed. I want to be of help. You got a deal, right?

ARTIE *(the door open, his hand on the knob, he stops, and, looking back, he is very happy, very confident, almost grand: He will, it seems, soon own the entire town of Hollywood)*: Things look VERY good. They look VERY good. You know, who can tell in this town?

EDDIE: Did they write the check? If they wrote the check, you got a deal.

ARTIE: So they didn't.

EDDIE: Then you don't.

ARTIE: YET. They didn't YET.

EDDIE: Then you don't YET. If they didn't YET, you don't YET.

ARTIE: But we're close. We're very close.

EDDIE: The game in this town is not horseshoes, Artie.

ARTIE *(rushing back to Eddie to make his point)*: How come you're being such a prick to me?

EDDIE: Envy!

ARTIE: I didn't think you knew.

EDDIE: Of course I know. What do you think, I don't know what I'm feeling?

ARTIE: It happens.

EDDIE: Everything happens. *(Standing up, the phone still in his hand.)* But what I'm after here, I mean ultimately, is for your own good, for your clarity. You lose your clarity in this town next thing you know you're waking up in the middle of the night on the beach with dogs pissing on you, you think you're on vacation. You panic in this town, Artie, they can smell it in your sweat.

ARTIE: Who's gonna panic? I been learning these incredible, fantastic relaxation techniques.

EDDIE *(sitting back down, he begins dialing the phone)*: Who's the producer you're most often in the room with?

ARTIE: Simon! He's got a distribution deal now with Universal.

MICKEY: What relaxation techniques?

ARTIE: They are these ones that are fantastic, Mickey, in as much as you can do them under the table, you're in some goddamn meeting, you just tense your feet and —

EDDIE: HERB Simon? HERB Simon? Is this who we're talking about? (*He slams down the phone.*)

ARTIE: What about him?

EDDIE (*standing, Eddie leans toward Artie like a fighter in his corner*): This is the guy you're dealing with? This guy's a known snake. I got the right guy, Artie. Herb Simon.

ARTIE: Yeh. Universal.

EDDIE: THIS GUY'S AN ANACONDA. HE'S A KNOWN ANACONDA.

ARTIE (*shrugging, he's heard everything*): I heard that.

EDDIE: I mean, you gotta make this guy pay you if you say "Hello" to him right? You're not crossing the street free for this guy, are you?

ARTIE: We gotta do a treatment.

EDDIE: No!

ARTIE: It's nothin'. He's a major guy. I don't want to piss him off.

EDDIE: These fucking snakes are sharks out here, Artie, you know that.

MICKEY: He's right, Artie.

ARTIE: We have hit it off, Mickey. He likes me.

MICKEY: Good.

EDDIE: If it's true, it's good.

ARTIE: Fuck you. The guy is at this juncture where he's sick of himself; he's looking for some kind of fucking turnaround into decency.

EDDIE: You base this opinion on what, Artie, your desperate desire to succeed?

ARTIE: Something happened and I saw it, goddamnit.

MICKEY: So what happened?

ARTIE: It was the other day after lunch.

EDDIE: Who paid?

ARTIE (*snapping at Eddie, snarling*): He did. He paid. (*And then back to Mickey, developing a manner of high confidence, his story that of an amazing and rare intimacy with a creature of almost royal importance.*) So we're crossing the street. You know, he gets this terrible pain in his stomach. I mean, his stomach made a noise and he doubles over like this. It's a noise like a gorilla could have made it. And he's over like this and he's paralyzed. We're all paralyzed in the middle of the street. So we get across the street. I'm asking him, is he okay. Maybe the food was bad. "No," he says. "Maybe," I says. "No. It's all the lies I tell," he says. He looks me in the eye and says, "It's this town and all the lies it makes me tell," See? He tol' me that.

MICKEY: Herb Simon said that?

ARTIE: Yeah!

EDDIE: So?

ARTIE *(moving in righteous anger at Eddie)*: So, he was straight with me, you cynical prick.

EDDIE: So, what's the point? This fucking snake tells you he lies a lot, so you figure you can trust him? That's not clear, Artie. Wake up! This guy is legendary among snakes. He is permanently enshrined in the reptilian hall of Hollywood fucking fame, this guy. You don't wake up, they are going to eat you alive. As an appetizer! You won't even be the main course. They're just going to whet their appetites on what is to you your entire motherfucking existence.

ARTIE *(caught, his words are light little chunks of fury)*: You're making me nervous.

EDDIE: I'm trying to make you nervous. Don't you know a ploy when you see one?

ARTIE: I considered whether it was a ploy, and I come down on the side of I would trust him a little.

EDDIE: Why trust him at all?

ARTIE: I gotta work with him.

EDDIE: You're not telling me you can't work with somebody you don't trust.

ARTIE: No.

EDDIE: I'm not saying, "Don't work with him!" I'm saying, "Don't trust him!"

ARTIE: I'll talk to him! *(Looking at his watch, Artie panics and starts scurrying around, gathering his things.)*

EDDIE: Get some money! Get some bucks!

ARTIE: For crissake, I'm gonna be late with this bullshit you put me through, Eddie. What do you do this to me for? He's gonna be pissed at me, goddamnit! *(He rushes out the door.)*

DONNA: Bye, Artie.

EDDIE: You think I was too hard on him?

MICKEY: No.

EDDIE: You gotta be hard on him, right? — he's a hard-head himself.

MICKEY *(on the move toward Donna)*: So how is Goldilocks doing here? You had any breakfast? *(His fingers are in her hair.)*

EDDIE *(heading for the refrigerator)*: You want a beer?

DONNA *(rising, she moves toward the counter)*: Sure.

EDDIE *(at the refrigerator)*: Where'd you say you were from?

MICKEY *(lighting a joint, he follows along after her)*: She said Midwest. I remember. Isn't that what you said?

DONNA: Yeah.

MICKEY: See.

EDDIE *(handing her a beer)*: So you came out here to get into the movies?

DONNA: We were hitchhiking.

MICKEY: Where to?

DONNA: The Grand Canyon.

EDDIE: It's not in L.A.

DONNA: I just kept going.

MICKEY: So you were in Artie's elevator? *(Having drawn the smoke in, he puts his mouth on Donna's and blows the smoke into her.)*

DONNA: It wasn't his. Can I turn on the TV?

EDDIE *(imitating her accent)*: Sure. *(Donna goes scurrying to the TV, which she turns on and sits in front of.)* So if Artie hadn't invited you off the elevator, would you still be on it?!

DONNA: I saw some interesting things I was on it!

MICKEY *(yelling over the loud volume of the TV)*: Like what?! *(He crosses to sit beside her on the couch.)*

DONNA *(yelling)*: Different people!

EDDIE *(yelling)*: This was interesting! *(Eddie crosses to stand leaning against the side of the armchair facing the couch.)*

DONNA *(yelling)*: You could hear their conversation! Some were about their rooms and the hotel carpeting, or the pictures in the hall! There was sometimes desperation you couldn't get a handle on it! They talked about their clothes! *(Mickey, reaching forward, turns off the volume of the TV.)*

MICKEY: So you evidently would have starved to death mesmerized by the spellbinding panorama on this elevator, it wasn't for Artie.

DONNA: I'da got off to eat. That's crazy. It was nice of Artie nevertheless to take a chance on me and everything. He's been just, you know, fantastic. *(Again Mickey puts his mouth to Donna's and blows the smoke into her, and then he pulls back.)* Except it is boring how he sits sometimes at the table, he's got these pencils, and he doesn't say anything to you. *(Moving to the floor, Mickey pulls her boot off, and her sock. She quickly grabs up her boot, clutching it.)* And he's got this paper, and I couldn't watch any TV except with the sound off because the noises would bother his train of thought. It was interesting for a while to watch TV in silence like old-time movies, except you didn't have a clue. *(When Mickey goes to work on her second boot, pulling it off, she grabs it from him, trying to interest him in her points about TV.)* You know, how they would put those words up every now and then in old-time movies so you could sort of hang on to the direction things were taking. And they acted like deaf people talking. Well, on TV there was none of these advantages, so I had to work up my own story a lot. *(As Mickey is reaching up to unbuckle the waist of her shorts, she leaps to her feet.)* Did he say what time I should walk his dog? *(Mickey grabs her arm to tug her back onto the couch while Eddie moves to take from her the record she carries.)*

EDDIE: What's this?

DONNA: It's just my favorite record for very particular reasons.

EDDIE: Willie Nelson sings "Stardust," "Unchained Melody," "All of Me?"

DONNA: Nobody ever agrees with me, people just scream at me.

MICKEY: What?

DONNA *(as she talks, Mickey, his arm around her, nuzzles her)*: My friends, when I argue with them, they just scream at me, but it's these really terrific old songs sung by this new guy, right, Willie Nelson, only he's an old guy, and they're all like these big-city songs like Chicago or New York, right, Sinatra kind of songs, only Willie, who they are sung by, is this cowboy, so it's like this cowboy on the plains singing to his cows, and the mountains are there but it's still the deep, dark city streets, so it's like the mountains and the big sky are this nightclub in the night and this old cowboy, this old, old cowboy under a street light in the middle of the mountains is singing something old and modern, and it's everything, see. You wanna hear it?

EDDIE: No.

MICKEY: Sure. *(He kisses Donna, his hand moving to unbuckle her shorts as Eddie's bedroom door opens and Phil steps out, hair tousled, shirt off.)*

PHIL: Anybody got any Valium around here, Eddie?

EDDIE: Look at this. Artie brought her by.

PHIL: Where's Artie?

MICKEY: He's gone.

PHIL: Artie was here?

EDDIE: Yeah.

PHIL: Who's this?

EDDIE: He brought her by for us. Like a CARE package. *(Reaching, Eddie takes Donna by the arm and lifts her from Mickey.)*

PHIL: Yeah? Whata you mean?

EDDIE: Not for Mickey, though.

MICKEY *(certain it's a joke)*: Get off my back, you —

EDDIE *(arms around Donna)*: This is for Phil and me because we don't have any serious relationships. This is a CARE package. Didn't you hear him? This is a CARE package for people without serious relationships.

MICKEY: You prick.

DONNA: What're you guys talking about?

EDDIE: Fucking you.

DONNA: Oh.

EDDIE: Phil and me, but not Mickey because he has a serious relationship. He has to preserve it.

DONNA: You gotta work at it, Mickey.

PHIL: You're sayin' seriously this is includin' me?

EDDIE: So we'll go upstairs, okay, Donna?

DONNA *(a little stoned and scared)*: Okay. *(She carries her boots and record as she and Eddie head for the stairs.)*

PHIL: He can't, but I can?

EDDIE: Yeah.

MICKEY: You sonofabitch. *(Mickey is about to follow Eddie and Donna up the stairs.)*

EDDIE *(whirling at the base of the stairs to face Mickey)*: Don't you even think about it. Right, Phil?

MICKEY: I'll — *(Looking up, Mickey meets Phil's eyes.)* You jerk-off, Eddie! You jerk-off! I'll get her sometime you're not around.

EDDIE *(bounding up the stairs)*: I can only do so much for you, Mickey. That'll be on your conscience.

MICKEY: Give me a break.

EDDIE *(looking down on Mickey)*: This is for your own good.

PHIL *(joining Eddie)*: I got here just in time.

EDDIE *(to Mickey)*: You'll thank me later! *(And whirling, Eddie follows Donna into his room.)*

MICKEY: You're nuts, Eddie; you're fucking nuts!

PHIL: So this is the bachelor life!

(Phil goes into the bedroom, slamming the door, and the music starts: Willie Nelson singing "All of Me" as Mickey stands, looking up for a beat, and the music plays.)

(Blackout.)

(The music continues.)

Scene 2

(Time: Evening of the same day.)

(The music, Willie Nelson singing "All of Me," continues. Darlene, beautiful and fashionable, is seated on one of the swivel chairs at the breakfast nook counter. Photography equipment is on the floor beside the chair. She is examining a contact sheet of photographs as the lights come up, and then the door opens and Eddie comes in dressed for work, carrying several scripts and a New York Times, which he is reading as he walks, so he doesn't see Darlene. The music goes out.)

DARLENE: Hi.

EDDIE *(though he is startled, we would never know it)*: Hi, Darlene. Mickey around?

DARLENE: I'm supposed to meet him. Is it okay?

EDDIE: Sure. What?

DARLENE: I was going to wait outside.

EDDIE *(heading for the refrigerator for a beer, he is all smiles)*: What? Are you crazy? No, no, no. Sit down. How you doing? You look good.

DARLENE: It's a facade.

EDDIE: What isn't? That's what I meant, you know. I wasn't saying anything more. That's what I was saying. It's a terrifically successful facade. *(He sits in the swivel chair opposite her.)* So, how's life in the world of photojournalism, Darlene?

DARLENE: Can I have a beer, too? I just feel . . . wow . . . you know?

EDDIE: What?

DARLENE: Weird, weird, weird.

EDDIE: I mean, you're not giving this whole situation a second thought, are you?

DARLENE: I certainly am. I . . .

EDDIE: No, no, no.

DARLENE: What situation? What do you mean? Do you —

EDDIE: Us. Mickey, you, me. Us.

DARLENE: Of course I am. That's what I thought you meant.

EDDIE: Don't be crazy.

DARLENE: Well, I have my mad side, you know. I have my feelings.

EDDIE: I don't mean "mad" by "crazy." I mean, "mad" has a kind of grandeur about it. I mean more like "silly." Is that what I mean?

DARLENE: Well, if you don't know, maybe you should stop talking till you figure it out and not go around just spewing out all this incomprehensible whatever it is you're saying and you know, hurting a person's feelings. That might have some value.

EDDIE: I opted for spontaneity, you know.

DARLENE: Well, sure. I'm just saying, "strike a balance."

EDDIE: Is that what you were saying?

DARLENE: Yes. That's right. What did you think I was saying?

EDDIE: I mean, we've all had our feelings hurt. That's the one thing this situation has given us all in common, I would say. I would hope you're not trying to construct some unique, you know, strictly personal interpretation of things on that basis.

DARLENE: What are you getting at?

EDDIE: I'm not exactly certain.

DARLENE: Well . . . are you exactly uncertain?

EDDIE: Possibly.

DARLENE: Where's Mickey?

EDDIE: I haven't checked. Is he late?

DARLENE: This is a perfect example of what could drive a person right off the wall about you. I mean, you are totally off the wall sometimes.

EDDIE: In what way? Everybody has their flaws, Darlene.

DARLENE *(rising, she roots around in her camera case)*: This total way you exaggerate this enchantment you have with uncertainty — the way you just prolong it and expect us all to think we ought to try and live in it and it's meaningful. It's shit.

EDDIE: This bothers you.

DARLENE: It bothers everyone.

EDDIE: No, it bothers you. And don't think this is a surprise. I am well aware of how what might to another person appear as honesty, but to you, it's —

DARLENE: Some other person such as who?

EDDIE: You want a list?

DARLENE: I want an answer. And a beer.

EDDIE: The beer is in the refrigerator. *(She storms past Eddie, who lifts his knees up to his chest to make room for her as she rushes to the refrigerator.)* And the answer, if you want it from me, is coming along the lines I am speaking it, which is the only way it can come, since it's my answer, and if it is to come at all, it —

DARLENE *(charging past him with her beer)*: I don't have time. I mean, your thoughts are a goddamn caravan trekking the desert, and then they finally arrive and they are these senseless, you know, beasts, you know, of burden. Okay? So just forget about it.

EDDIE: You asked me a question.

DARLENE *(pacing away from him)*: I also asked you to forget about it.

EDDIE: But I don't want to forget about it.

DARLENE: I made a mistake.

EDDIE *(rising)*: But you don't deny you asked it.

DARLENE: Eddie, you look like a man with a hammer in his hand.

EDDIE: So what? And I don't. Or are you a liar on top of everything else? You asked me a question!

DARLENE: All right!

EDDIE: Some sensitivity is the quality a person might have. Sure, I can come up with all the bullshit anytime — some clearcut diagnosis totally without a solid, actual leg to stand on but presented with all the necessary postures and tones of voice full of conviction and all the necessary accessories and back-up systems of control and sincerity to lend total credibility to what is total bullshit; but I chose instead, and choose quite frequently, to admit it if I don't know what I'm talking about; or if I'm confused about what I'm feeling, I admit it. But this is too much of SOMETHING for you — I don't know what — so at least we found out in time. That's some good luck.

DARLENE: Liar on top of WHAT ELSE?

EDDIE: Whata you mean?

DARLENE: You said, "liar on top of everything else."

EDDIE: I did?

DARLENE: Just a minute ago.

EDDIE: What was I talking about?

DARLENE: Me.

EDDIE: I did? No. What'd I say? *(The front door opens, and Mickey, carrying a bag of groceries, comes in directly behind Darlene.)*

DARLENE: "LIAR ON TOP OF EVERYTHING ELSE!"

MICKEY: Hi.

DARLENE: Hi.

MICKEY: How you doing?

EDDIE *(heading for the armchair, where he sits, picking up the newspaper)*: Great. You?

MICKEY *(moving to the kitchen, he sets the bag down on the counter, taking out beers)*: Terrific. Anybody need a beer?

EDDIE: No.

DARLENE: Sure. *(Mickey pops open a beer for her and then moves to start up the stairs where he abruptly halts.)*

MICKEY: You know what I'm going to do? I'm going to venture a thought that I might regret down the road. And anticipating that regret makes me, you know, hesitate. In the second of hesitation, I get a good look at the real feeling that it is, this regret — a kind of inner blackmail that shows me even further down the road where I would end up having to live with myself as a smaller person, a man less generous to his friends than I would care to be. *(Slowly, carefully, he descends the stairs.)* So, you know, we'll have to put this through a multiprocessing here, but I was outside, I mean, for a while; and what I heard in here was — I mean, it really was passion. Sure, it was a squabble, and anybody could have heard that, but what I heard was more. We all know — everybody knows I'm basically on a goof right now. I'm going back to my wife and kids sooner or later — I don't hide that fact from anybody. And what I really think is that fact was crucial to the development of this whole thing because it made me WHAT? Safe. A viable diversion from what might have actually been a genuine, meaningful, and to that same extent and maybe even more so — threatening — connection between you two. I'm not going to pretend I wasn't up for it, too — but I was never anything but above board. You know — a couple jokes, nice dinner, that's my style. Good wine, we gotta spend the night — and I don't mean to be crass — because the point is maybe we have been made fools of here by our own sophistication, and what am I protecting by not saying something about it, my vanity? Ego? Who needs it? So, I'm out in the yard and I'm thinking, "Here is this terrific guy, this dynamite lady, and they are obviously, definitely hooked up on some powerful, idiosyncratic channel, so what am I doing in the middle?" Am I totally off base here, Eddie, or what? *(He ends huddling with Eddie, who is in the armchair, while Darlene is seated on the swivel chair behind Mickey.)*

EDDIE: You're — I mean, obviously you're not TOTALLY. You know that.

MICKEY: That's exactly what I'm saying.

EDDIE: I mean, from my end of it.

MICKEY: For my own well-being, I don't want to serve as the instrument of some neurotic, triangular bullshit being created here between you two. That's the main issue for me. I mean, from my point of view.

EDDIE: Right.

DARLENE *(leaning forward, trying to insert herself into their attention)*: I mean, I certainly haven't felt right — I mean, good about it, that's —

MICKEY *(whirling toward her)*: Everything went so fast.

DARLENE: Everything just happened.

MICKEY: You met him, you met me.

DARLENE: I met Eddie, and then Eddie, you know, introduces me to you.

EDDIE: It's too fast.

DARLENE: It was fast.

MICKEY (*he strides about between them*): Just — What is this, the electronic age? Sure. But we're people, not computers; the whole program cannot be just reprogrammed without some resolution of the initial, you know, thing that started everything. So I'm going to — I don't know what — but go. Somewhere. Out. And you two can just see where it takes you. Go with the flow. I mean, you guys should see yourselves.

DARLENE: I'm just — I mean, I don't — weird, weird, weird.

MICKEY (*patting Darlene's hand*): In all honesty, Darlene, you told me this is what you wanted in more ways than I cared to pay attention to. (*Backing for the door, he looks at Eddie.*) And you, you prick, you were obviously madly in love. (*To Darlene.*) Go easy on him. I'll catch you later.

EDDIE: Down the road.

DARLENE: Bye.

MICKEY: Just remember, Darlene, you made the wrong choice. (*Mickey goes.*)

EDDIE (*pacing toward the door as if in awe of Mickey*): Where the hell did he come up with the . . . I mean, clarity to do that?

DARLENE: That wasn't clarity.

EDDIE (*turning toward Darlene, he perches on the couch arm*): No, no, I mean, it wasn't clarity. But he had to HAVE clarity.

DARLENE: I don't know what it was. Generosity?

EDDIE: Whatever it was, you don't see it very often. I don't expect that from Mickey, I mean, that kind of thing.

DARLENE: Who expects that from anybody? We're all so all over the place.

EDDIE: Self-absorbed.

DARLENE: And distracted. I'm distracted by everything. I mean, I'm almost always distracted, aren't you?

EDDIE: Absolutely.

DARLENE: Everything is always distracting me from everything else.

EDDIE: Everything is very distracting, but what I've really noticed is that mainly, the thing I'm most distracted by is myself. I mean, I'm my own major distraction, trying to get it together, to get my head together, my act together.

DARLENE: Our little minds just buzzzzzzzz! What do they think they're doing?

EDDIE: However Mickey managed to get through it, though, I know one thing — I'm glad he did.

DARLENE: Are you really?

EDDIE: I really missed you. It was amazing. That was probably it — he got his clue from the fact that I never shut up about you. I think I was driving him crazy. How do you feel?

DARLENE: Great. I think I was, you know, into some form of obsession about you, too, some form of mental loop. I feel scared is what I feel. Good, too. I feel good, but mainly scared.

EDDIE: I'm scared.

DARLENE: I mean, a year ago, I was a basket case. If we had met a year ago, I wouldn't have had a prayer.

EDDIE: Me, too. A year ago, I was nuts. And I still have all kinds of things to think through. Stuff coming up, I have to think it through.

DARLENE: Me, too.

EDDIE: And by thinking, I don't mean just some ethereal mental thing either, but being with people is part of it, being with you is part of the thinking, that's how I'm doing the thinking, but I just have to go slow, there's a lot of scar tissue.

DARLENE: There's no rush, Eddie.

EDDIE: I don't want to rush.

DARLENE: I don't want to rush.

EDDIE: I can't rush. I'll panic. If I rush, I'll panic.

DARLENE: We'll just have to keep our hearts open, as best we can.

EDDIE: No pressure.

DARLENE: And no guilt, okay?

EDDIE: No guilt.

DARLENE: We don't want any guilt. I mean, I'm going to be out of town a lot. We both have our lives.

EDDIE: We just have to keep our options open.

DARLENE: And our hearts, okay?

EDDIE: I mean, the right attitude. . . .

DARLENE: Exactly. If we have the right attitude. . . .

EDDIE: Attitude is so important. And by attitude I don't mean just attitude either, but I mean real emotional space.

DARLENE: We both need space.

EDDIE: And time. We have to have time.

DARLENE: Right. So we can just take the time to allow the emotional space for things to grow and work themselves out.

EDDIE: So you wanna go fuck?

(*They kiss and the music starts: Willie Nelson singing "Someone to Watch Over Me."*)

(*Blackout.*)

(*Note: It might be that as the scene progresses, they end up on the couch, undressing each other as they conduct their negotiations; or perhaps it is more strictly a negotiation with distance between them. Or perhaps it is a combination so that each time there is a sense of the negotiations being completed so that physical contact can begin — an embrace, a kiss — some bit of outstanding business is then remembered, and one or the other moves away.*)

Scene 3

(*Time: Late afternoon of the next day.*)

(*The music, Willie Nelson singing "Someone to Watch Over Me," continues. Donna, moving to the music, crosses, carrying a beer, and*

*turns on the TV, the volume loud. She flops down on the couch,
picking up a magazine, while the music and TV are both playing. The
door opens and Phil comes in looking disheveled, in a hurry. He starts
talking almost immediately, clearly thinking Eddie is around. He carries two six-packs of beer and a grocery bag containing meat and
bread for sandwiches and two huge bags of popcorn. In his pocket is
a pint of bourbon in a paper bag from which he sips every now and
then.)*

PHIL: So this broad is always here, you know what I mean? What is she, a
    chair? What are you, a goddamn chair? You sit around here and you
    would let anybody do anything to you, wouldn't you? Whatsamatter with
    you? Don't you have any self-respect? You're all alike. She is!

DONNA: Who you talkin' to?

PHIL (*yelling up the stairs toward Eddie's room*): She's got the goddamn TV
    on and the record player on! Who you workin' for, the electric company?
    (*He turns off the record player.*)

DONNA: Who you talkin' to, Phil?

PHIL: Don't call me Phil, okay. Just don't. I'm talkin' to you. Who asked you
    anyway?

DONNA: You ain't talkin' to me, I could tell by your tone. Who you talkin' to?

PHIL: You're very observant. You're very smart. Who was I talkin' to?

DONNA: I don't know. I'm the only one here.

PHIL: I was talkin' to Eddie.

DONNA: Eddie ain't here.

PHIL: He's up in his room.

DONNA: He ain't.

PHIL (*running up the stairs to look into the bathroom and then Eddie's room*):
    EDDIE! EDDIE! Where the hell are you? (*Stepping out of Eddie's room.*)
    I was just talkin' to him.

DONNA: That's what I been trying to explain to you.

PHIL (*leaning over the railing to yell down to her*): Get off my back, will you?
    You dumb bitch. Get off it. You're on me all the time.

DONNA: I ain't.

PHIL (*heading toward Mickey's room, he opens the door and looks in*): The
    fuck you ain't.

DONNA: I'm sorry. I'm just sittin' here.

PHIL: Like hell you are.

DONNA: I'm sorry.

PHIL (*coming down the stairs*): You oughta be sorry. You're a sorry goddamn
    piece of just whatever the hell you are.

DONNA: Am I botherin' you? I am just sitting here.

PHIL: With your head up your ass.

DONNA: I was readin' a magazine.

PHIL: With your head up your ass.

DONNA: Boy, you are really an insulting form of person. Honest to god. Let a person have some rest. *(On his way to the kitchen, Phil freezes and then whirls to face her.)*

PHIL: Meaning me?

DONNA: Whata you mean?

PHIL: I mean, "meanin' me?" Who's SOMETHIN'?

DONNA: I didn't mean nothin'. I never mean nothin'.

PHIL: You said it though, didn't you?

DONNA: What?

PHIL: What you said? You fuckin' said it.

DONNA: I don't know what you're talkin' about. Exactly.

PHIL *(heading into the kitchen where he starts to pour the popcorn in a bowl and tries to make sandwiches)*: What I'm talkin' about is how you are and what you said. You see a guy has undergone certain difficulties so his whole appearance thing is a mood thing of how he is obviously in a discouraged state, he's full of turmoil, does it occur to you to say a kindly thing or to cut his fuckin' heart out? You got your tongue out to sharpen your knife is what you're up to, or do you want to give me some other explanation?

DONNA: Sure, because —

PHIL: So what is it?

DONNA: What?

PHIL: Your so-called explanation! Let's hear it.

DONNA: I'm just —

PHIL: Bullshit. Bull Shit!

DONNA: No.

PHIL *(as Eddie comes in the front door with a bag of pretzels and clothes from the cleaners)*: Would you listen to this air head?

EDDIE: How's everything?

PHIL: Terrific. It's all totally fucked up, which I wouldn't have it any other way. I thought you was here.

EDDIE: I hadda go out.

PHIL *(moving toward Eddie)*: Your car was here. What the fuck is going on?

EDDIE: It wasn't far, so I walked. Donna, hey, I thought you were on your way to —

PHIL: Listen, Eddie! I saw the car, I thought you were here, you know, I was talkin' to you, you wasn't here, so I sounded like this asshole, so the ditz here has got to get on me about it.

EDDIE: Don't fuck with Phil, Donna.

DONNA: I wasn't, Eddie.

EDDIE: I mean, did you bring her, Phil?

PHIL: Who?

DONNA: No, no, no.

EDDIE: She's here ain't she!

DONNA: I was hitchhiking, Eddie, and it was like he come outa nowhere and it was, wow, Mickey. Whata hot car. So I set out for San Francisco like we talked about but I ended up here.

PHIL: I mean, what is it with this goddamn broad that makes her tick? I wanna know what makes her fuckin' tick. You answer me that goddamn question, will you?

DONNA: What?

PHIL: What makes you tick? I come here to see Eddie, you gotta be here. I wanna watch the football game and talk over some very important issues which pertain to my life, you gotta be here. What the fuck makes you tick?

DONNA: What's he talkin' about?

EDDIE: I don't know.

PHIL: What I'm talkin' about is —

EDDIE: Listen, Phil, if Darlene comes by, you just introduce Donna as your ditz, okay? *(He starts up the stairs for his room.)*

PHIL: What?

EDDIE: You found her, you know. Darlene's gonna be by at any second, we're goin' to the desert for the weekend. Can you do that? *(As he goes running into his room.)*

DONNA: Who's Darlene, Phil?

PHIL *(crossing to get some of his food)*: I'm beggin' you. I'm beggin' you. I don't wanna see you, okay? I don't wanna see you.

DONNA: Okay.

PHIL: I mean, I come in here and you gotta be here; I'm thinkin' about football, and you gotta be here with your tits and your ass and this tight shrunken clothes and these shriveled jeans, so that's all I'm thinking about from the minute I see you is tits and ass. Football doesn't have a chance against it. It's like this invasion of tits and ass overwhelming my own measly individuality so I don't have a prayer to have my own thoughts about my own things except you and tits and ass and sucking and fucking and that's all I can think about. My privacy has been demolished. You think a person wants to have that kind of thing happen to their heads — they are trying to give their own problems some serious thought, the next thing they know there's nothing in their brains as far as they can see but your tits and ass? You think a person likes that?

DONNA: Who's playin'?

PHIL: You think a person likes that?

DONNA: No.

PHIL: Who's playin' what?

DONNA: Football.

PHIL: None of your fuckin' business.

DONNA: I like it.

PHIL: What are you talkin' about? I don't know what you're talkin' about.

DONNA: Football.

PHIL: You're nuts.

DONNA: I wanna watch it with you.

PHIL: You're nuts! You wanna watch the game? You're talkin' about you wanna watch the football game? Are you nuts? Are you crazy?

DONNA: What?

PHIL: How you gonna watch it? You don't know about it. You don't know nothing about it.

DONNA: I do. I know the points, and the insignias, and the —

PHIL: That's not the game.

DONNA: And when they go through the air and they catch it.

PHIL: Get outta here. I don't want you here.

DONNA: I know about the mascots.

PHIL: You wanna know about the game? You wanna know about it? *(He has moved to grab her head between his two hands.)* You don't know about the fucking game. Hut, hut, hut —

DONNA: What are you doin'? What are you — *(He butts his head into hers.)*

PHIL: That's the game. That's the game.

DONNA: Ohh, ouch, ouch, awwwww owwwwww. *(Eddie comes out of his bedroom, a bunch of clothes in his hands.)*

EDDIE: What's this now?

PHIL: She's cryin'. What the fuck is the matter with her?

DONNA: He hit me, he hit me.

PHIL: She says she wants to know about the game.

EDDIE: What game?

DONNA: Football —

PHIL: — football!

DONNA: That's all.

PHIL: She's nuts.

DONNA: He hurt me. Am I bleedin'? Eddie, Eddie, Eddie.

EDDIE: No.

DONNA *(running to the record player, grabbing the record)*: This is shit, this is shit. This is shit.

EDDIE: What happened?

PHIL: I don't know. It was over too fast.

EDDIE: What? *(Donna is running up the stairs now.)*

PHIL: This thing here, whatever it was that happened here. She wanted to know about football, you know, the crazy bitch. She can't know about football. It's impossible. It's totally one hundred percent impossible. So this is what happens. *(Going into the bathroom, Donna slams the door.)* So how you doin?

EDDIE: Great. Me and Darlene are goin' to the desert.

PHIL: So guess what?

EDDIE *(he disappears back into his room)*: What?

PHIL *(heading up the stairs)*: It's almost decided. I'm almost decided about going back to Susie.

EDDIE *(from off)*: What?

PHIL *(hovering outside Eddie's room)*: I can't stand it. The loneliness. And some form of totally unusual and unpredictable insanity is creeping up on me about to do I don't know WHAT — God forbid I find out. So I been thinkin' maybe if we had the kid, everything, or at least the main things, might be okay.

EDDIE (*coming out of his bedroom*): What kid?

PHIL: We were tryin' to have a kid. That's what we been doin'.

EDDIE: You and Susie?

PHIL: Eddie, wake up here! Who you think? Yeah, me and Susie. She wants a kid. All her friends have been havin' 'em.

EDDIE (*as he backs along the balcony toward the bathroom door*): It's that goddamn age where it hits 'em like a truck, this maternal urge; they gotta have a kid — they don't know what hit 'em. (*Eddie knocks on the bathroom door.*)

PHIL: So it hit Susie; but maybe it's what I need, you know.

EDDIE: Were you doin' that insanity with the thermometer and, you know, you gotta fuck on schedule?

PHIL: Unbelievable!

EDDIE: Because that stuff is insanity. (*And again Eddie knocks on the bathroom door, which opens, and Donna comes out, walking straight to Mickey's room.*)

PHIL: The trouble is though, what if it doesn't work out the way I planned it?

EDDIE: Nothin' does, Phil. (*He steps into the bathroom, and Phil comes around to stand looking in at Eddie.*)

PHIL: I mean, I wanna have a kid sometimes, and sometimes I'm scared to death, and mostly though, I mean, for the last month or so it was like in my thoughts in my mind sometimes this little baby had this big gun to my head and she would shoot me sooner or later.

EDDIE (*as Eddie comes out of the bathroom, zipping up a shaving kit, and heading for his room*): So you don't want a kid.

PHIL: I do and I don't. I do and I don't.

EDDIE (*pausing on the balcony, he faces Phil*): I think this might be the thing here, you know, about which you two have been fighting so much lately. You shouldn't probably have one now. Just go back and get some, you know, clarity, so you both know what the issues are. This is the relationship I'm talkin' about. Straighten that out.

PHIL: Right. And then see. That makes sense.

EDDIE: Sure. (*Eddie steps into his room.*)

PHIL: Except she has to have one.

EDDIE (*coming out of his room, carrying a small suitcase, the shaving kit, and a garment bag*): She don't have to have one.

PHIL (*following Eddie as they descend the stairs*): I tried tellin' her that, because you know I got three kids, two little boys and a girl who are now, you know, I don't know how old, in Toledo, I haven't seen 'em since I went to prison. I don't want any more kids out there, you know, rollin' around their beds at night with this sick fucking hatred of me. I can't stand it.

EDDIE: Who could stand it?

PHIL: Right.

EDDIE: So don't have the kid now.

PHIL: Right. *(As Eddie, at the kitchen counter grabs his dope box in order to pack it.)* Except she's desperate. I can't stand it when she cries.

EDDIE: You can't stand it when she cries is no reason to have a kid, Phil. I mean, a kid is a big fuckin' gamble.

PHIL: Hey, as we both well know, Eddie, what isn't a gamble? You're alive, you gamble!

EDDIE: Yeh, but the collateral here is, you know, this other person you can't even ask what they think of the odds. There is involved here an innocent helpless person totally dependent on your good will.

PHIL: It's fuckin' depressing. How about some weed? I want some weed.

EDDIE: What I'm sayin', Phil, is first things first.

PHIL: Like what?

EDDIE: The marriage; the marriage. *(Giving a joint to Phil, Eddie lights it for him and gives Phil complete attention now at the kitchen counter.)* I mean, no kid and a divorce is who-gives-a-fuck, but you have a kid and it's seismic. A big ten on the Richter scale. Carnage, man, that's what I'm sayin', gore on the highway. Add in the kid and it's a major disaster.

PHIL *(passing the lit joint to Eddie, Phil sits on the swivel chair outside the counter)*: Right. Sure. Except, see, the trouble is, Susie has wanted to be a mother since she was twelve, you know. She had dolls and teddy bears and she dressed them up in diapers — you know — she still does it, sometimes. It was all she ever dreamed about.

EDDIE: Still does what?

PHIL: I wanna make her happy, Eddie. I mean, if she's happy, maybe I'll be happy. So she's got teddy bears, so what.

EDDIE *(sitting opposite Phil)*: I mean, you're not thinkin' of going back and just, you know, hoping for the best; I mean, just trusting it to luck that she won't get pregnant. You're not thinkin' that.

PHIL: No, fuck, no.

EDDIE: Because you won't have a chance if you're sayin' that, and you go back.

PHIL: I got it covered, Eddie.

EDDIE: She'll eat you alive.

PHIL: I got it covered, Eddie, is what I'm sayin'. I got the situation totally covered. There's nothin' to worry about on that score. I been takin' this stuff and messing the whole thing up, which is why we ain't pregnant at this very minute.

EDDIE: Whata you mean?

PHIL: You know, my sperm count is monstrous on its own.

EDDIE: Whata you mean?

PHIL: I have a very high sperm count. It's record setting.

EDDIE: What stuff?

PHIL: Stuff. You know, it's harmful to the sperm and I'm messing myself up.

EDDIE: You're taking some kind of — Wait a minute! You're telling me you're taking some kind of poison?

PHIL: That's why I hadda talk to you, Eddie.

EDDIE: Do you know what the hell you're saying to me?

PHIL: What?

EDDIE *(leaping to his feet, Eddie marches to the clothes from the cleaners)*: This is insane! You're taking some kind of goddamn poison because — This is crazy, Phil! This is nuts! It's fucking nuts!

PHIL: It's not poison.

EDDIE *(ripping open the paper wrapped around the box containing the shirts)*: Listen to me. Do me a favor. Tell her what's been going on. You can tell her, can't you?

PHIL: Sure.

EDDIE *(putting shirts into the suitcase)*: So do it. If you're going back, you gotta do it. She's your wife, for god's sake, you can talk to her.

PHIL: Sure.

EDDIE: So explain the situation to here. *(Grabbing the dope box, he starts to go with it to put it in the suitcase.)* I mean, don't you think maybe this is why the hell you two been fighting?

PHIL: Are you mad at me?

EDDIE: No.

PHIL: You're sure.

EDDIE: I'm just excited. Sometimes I get like I'm angry when I get excited. *(He is putting the sport jacket and trousers from the cleaners in the clothing bag.)*

PHIL: Right. Because you are absolutely without a doubt one hundred percent right in everything you're saying, but if I don't do it, what's gonna happen?

EDDIE: You gotta do it.

PHIL: She gets so sad. Eddie, she gets so goddamn sad, I can't stand it.

EDDIE: But it'll be worse if you have the kid — it'll just all be a million zillion times worse. You know that. That's what we've been talking about here.

PHIL: Without a doubt. And I'm going to do it, I just want to know what kind of latitude I have regarding our friendship if my mind gets changed.

EDDIE: Listen to me — are you a deaf man? Am I only under the delusion that I'm speaking? What you're telling me is a horror story — one part of you is begging another part to stop, but you don't hear you. But I do, I hear — you have got to stop, Phil.

PHIL: I know this, Eddie. But what if I can't? Give me some sort of hint regarding your reaction, so I know.

EDDIE: What's she do, hypnotize you? Is this voodoo? You're a grown man. You have asked me to tell you. I'm telling you: "Tell her!"

PHIL: You're not answering my question. I'm talking about our friendship here!

EDDIE: You're switching the goddamn subject is what you're doing.

PHIL: What the hell are you talking about? Why are you avoiding my question?

EDDIE: Our friendship doesn't matter here. Our friendship is totally, categorically, one hundred percent irrelevant here.

PHIL: Eddie, listen to yourself! This is our friendship — this conversation — these very exchanges. We are in our friendship. What could be more important?

EDDIE: I mean, I don't feel . . . What?

PHIL: Scorn. You feel scorn for me.

EDDIE: No.

PHIL: It's in your eyes.

EDDIE: No. What? *(He unzips the shaving kit to get out a container of Alka Seltzer.)*

PHIL: These dark thoughts, Eddie, I see them reflected in your eyes, they pertain to something other than me, or what?

EDDIE: I'm not having dark thoughts.

PHIL: Beyond the thoughts you're thinking, Eddie.

EDDIE *(crossing to the sink for water)*: No!

PHIL: Then what the hell are you thinking about? I come for advice and you're off on some other totally unrelated tangent, is that the thing here, the goddamn bottom line? I need your attention, and you're off in some fucking daydream? I'm desperate and you are, for crissake, distracted? Is this friendship, Eddie? Tell me!

EDDIE: Wait a minute.

PHIL: You want a fucking minute?

EDDIE: I don't know what you're talking about. *(He drops the tablets in a glass of water.)*

PHIL *(trying to be helpful, to explain)*: Dark thoughts. Your dark thoughts, Eddie. This is not uncommon for people to have them. You were provoked; think nothing of it. But please — this, now — dark thoughts and everything included, this is our friendship. Pay attention to it, it's slipping by.

EDDIE: Right! Yeh! I wanna!

PHIL *(patiently explaining)*: I mean, if I do something you consider foolhardy, you won't just dismiss my feelings and my effort and the fact that I came to you.

EDDIE: I feel like you're drillin' little fuckin' chunks of cottage cheese into my brain. I'm gettin' confused here, Phil, I tol' you, I don't feel good. *(He is moving, almost staggering toward the couch.)*

PHIL *(following along, puffing a joint)*: It's chaotic is why you're confused Eddie. That's why you're confused. Think nothin' of it. I'm confused. The goddamn situation is like this masked fucking robber come to steal the goods, but we don't even know is he, or isn't he. I mean, we got these dark thoughts, I see 'em in you, you don't think you're thinkin' 'em, so we can't even nail that down, how we going to get beyond it? They are the results of your unnoticed inner goings-on or my gigantic paranoia, both of which exist, so the goddamn thing in its entirety is on the basis of what has got to be called a coin toss.

EDDIE: I can figure it, I can — It's not a goddamn coin toss!

PHIL: You think I'm being cynical when I say that? Nothing is necessary, Eddie. Not a fucking thing! We're in the hands of something, it could kill us now or later, it don't care. Who is this guy that makes us just — you know — WHAT? THERE'S A NAME FOR THIS — IT HAPPENS — THERE'S A WORD FOR IT — EVERYBODY KNOWS IT, I CAN'T THINK OF IT. IT'S LIKE A LAW. IT IS A LAW. WHAT'S A LAW? WHAT THE FUCK IS A LAW? Cynicism has nothing to do with it, Eddie, I've done my best. The fucking thing is without a clue, except the mess it leaves behind it, the guts and gore. What I'm sayin' is, if my conclusion is contrary to your wishes, at least give me the fucking consideration and respect that you know that at least from my point of view it is based on solid thought and rock hard evidence that has led me to I have no other choice, so you got no right to fuck with me about it. I want your respect, Eddie. *(He ends leaning intently toward Eddie on the couch.)*

EDDIE: You got that, Phil.

PHIL: I do?

EDDIE: Don't you know that? I'm just sayin — all I'm sayin' is, "Don't have the baby thoughtlessly."

PHIL: Eddie, for god sake, don't terrify me that you have paid no attention! If I was thoughtless would I be here? I feel like I have pushed thought to the brink where it is just noise and of no more use than a headful of car horns, because the bottom line here that I'm getting at is just this — I got to go back to her. I got to go back to Susie, and if it means havin' a kid, I got to do it. I mean, I have hit a point where I am going round the bend several times a day now, and so far I been on the other side to meet me, but one a these days it might be one time too many, and who knows who might be there waitin'? If not me, who? I'm a person, Eddie, and I have realized it, who needs like a big-dot-thing, you know — this big-dot-thing around which I can just hang and blab my thoughts and more or less formulate everything as I go, myself included. I mean, I used to spend my days in my car; I didn't know what the fuck I was doin' but it kept me out of trouble until nothin' but blind luck led me to I-am-married, and I could go home. She was my big-dot-thing. Now I'm startin' in my car again, I'm spendin' days on the freeways and rain or no rain I like the wipers clickin' and all around me the other cars got people in 'em the way I see them when they are in cars. These heads, these faces. These boxes of steel with glass and faces inside. I been the last three days without seeing another form of human being in his entirety except gas station attendants. The family men in the day with their regular food and regular hours in their eyes. And then in the night, these moonlighters; they could be anything. In the wee hours of the morning, it's derelicts, and these weird spooky kids like they have recently arrived from outer space, but not to stay. The cloverleafs, they got a thing in them, it spins me off. There's little back roads and little towns sometimes I never heard of them. I start to expect the gas station attendants to know me when I arrive. I get excited that I've been there before. I want them to welcome me. I'm disappointed when they don't. Something that I don't want to be true starts lookin' like it's all that's true only I don't know what it is. No. No. I need my marriage. I come here to tell you. I got to stay married. I'm lost without her.

(The door to Mickey's room slams loudly as out comes Donna. She is dressed in shorts far too snug for her, and a tight T-shirt shortened above her belly button, and she carries her record and other belongings.)

DONNA *(at the top of the stairs)*: You guys have cooked your goose. You can just walk your own dog, and fuck yourselves. These particular tits and ass are taking a hike. *(She stomps down the stairs and struts to the door, opens it, turns, looks at Eddie who is staring at her, quite ill.)* So this is good-bye. *(She goes out, slamming the door.)*

ACT TWO

Scene 1

(Time: Night. A year later.)

(Place: The same.)

(Eddie lies on the floor, nestled on pillows, while Mickey is seated, legs dangling through the spokes of the second floor railing. Each has a drink. Phil and Artie are a twosome, a kind of team, standing and drinking, both involved with one another and their memory of the event in which they recently participated and which they are trying to communicate to Mickey and Eddie. Phil has ice wrapped in a towel around his right hand. Artie is so proud of Phil you would think he had himself performed the deed they are excitedly relating. At the breakfast nook, he pours drinks for himself and Phil.)

PHIL: This guy, what a fuckin' guy.

ARTIE: You shoulda seen him. He was unbelievable.

EDDIE: So what happened?

PHIL: I decked him; he deserved it.

EDDIE: So what happened?

PHIL: He made me mad.

ARTIE: He was a jerk.

EDDIE: So you decked this guy.

ARTIE *(rushing near to Phil, hugging him, patting him)*: You shoulda seen it. The guy went across the room. He looked like he was on wheels.

EDDIE: So what'd he do?

PHIL: He got up.

ARTIE: The dumb fuck.

EDDIE: I mean, why'd you hit him?

PHIL: He got up!

EDDIE (*sitting up, trying to make his point*): I mean, before he got knocked down — the first time you hit him, why'd you hit him?

ARTIE: You wouldn't believe this guy. He was genuinely irritating.

PHIL: This is the pitiful part. I don't think he could help himself.

ARTIE: I mean, this is the way this pathetic jerk-off must go through his life. IRRITATING!

PHIL: It's a curse to be this guy! I shoulda had some consideration.

EDDIE (*going to the kitchen*): BUT WHAT HAPPENED?

ARTIE: He was sayin' this unbelievable dumb stuff to this broad.

EDDIE (*in the kitchen Eddie pours another drink*): Some broad you knew?

ARTIE: Noooo! (*As if this is the dumbest question anybody ever could have asked.*) Just this genuinely repulsive broad.

PHIL: And he's talkin' to her like she's somethin' gorgeous. THIS DOG! It was offensive. Who'd he think he was with, you know? This was nobody of any even remotely dynamite qualities, you know what I mean? You don't talk to some dog in the manner he's talking. It's disgusting!

ARTIE: Very irritating guy.

EDDIE: I can see that.

PHIL: You shoulda been there. I ask him to shut up, and he says he isn't botherin' anybody. I says he is botherin' me; he looks at me like I'm an asshole; I can see he's askin' for it, so I warn him one more time.

EDDIE: What'd you say?

PHIL: I don't SAY nothing. I look at him very seriously, you know, bullets and razors and bloodshed in my eyes, but all under control, so he can have the option of knowing nothing need happen if he don't push me. But he's gotta push me.

MICKEY: So what happened?

PHIL: It all went very quickly —

ARTIE: — the guy goes right off the stool!

EDDIE (*with his drink, Eddie leans intently in toward Phil, exasperated, yet playing at the exasperation, enjoying the fact that they cannot seem to make any sense to one another*): But what happened?

ARTIE: He got up.

EDDIE: He got up?

MICKEY: He got up? This is unbelievable. You knock him down, he gets up?

ARTIE: Phil don't just knock him down. He knocks him across the room. (*And now Artie in order to demonstrate, runs crashing backwards into a wall.*) It's like this goddamn vortex just snarfs him up and fucking magnetizes him to the wall for a full second before he slides to the floor. SO THEN HE GETS UP! Do you believe this guy?

PHIL: Personally, this is where the guy gets a raw deal, though, 'cause the second time I was wired into some other frequency, and the whack I put on him was beyond the realm of normal human punches. That he didn't disintegrate was both his and my good fortune.

MICKEY: This is some tough guy, huh?

ARTIE AND PHIL: NOOOOO! NOOOO! (*As if this is an insanely stupid question.*)

PHIL: Absolutely not. This is a weak link on the chain of humanity other than in his particular capacities of irritating; and this is where the real irony comes in. Because I don't think, looking back, that when he got up on his feet again he any longer had a clue to where he was or what he was doin'.

ARTIE: He was totally fuckin' unconscious.

PHIL: Exactly. Looking back, I can see he was no longer from his point of view in the bar even. From his point of view he was on his way to catch a bus or something.

ARTIE: It was his reflexes.

PHIL: Exactly, but I don't see he's harmless in time to take charge of my own reflexes, which see nothing at all except that he's comin' toward me. So I gotta let him have it. It's him or me.

ARTIE: But as far as attacking Phil, it's the farthest thing from his mind.

PHIL: No, he's like going shopping or something. He don't know what he's doing. It's just his reflexes.

ARTIE: His reflexes got the best of him.

PHIL: So we are both victims of our reflexes.

MICKEY (*pronouncing from where he sits on high*): So, this is a tragedy here.

PHIL: I don't know about that, but it was a mess, and I coulda got into real trouble, because the force with which I hit him is even in my memory of it nerve-wracking.

ARTIE: Don't get morose, Phil, huh? (*Patting Phil, trying to cheer him up.*) Pay attention to the upside.

PHIL: You pay attention to the upside — you're the big deal — I'm the fuck-up. (*Pulling away from Artie, Phil moves over to the TV where he has spied a vial of coke.*)

EDDIE (*following after Phil*): You let off some steam, Phil. This is the purpose of this kind of, you know, out-and-out bullshit.

PHIL (*picking up the coke*): You wanna tell me how come I have all the necessary realizations that any normal human being might have — only I have them too late, so that I understand he's a pathetic, unconscious jerk-off who can't help irritating people and is oblivious to the fact that he is on his feet — only by the time I understand it, he's unconscious and nothing but luck has kept me from doing a lifetime in the can; so the realizations can serve no possible useful purpose on earth but to torment me with the thought that I am a merciless, totally out of control prick. Whata you wanna call that? I call it horseshit.

ARTIE: Phil has got violent karma, that's all; it's in the cards. (*Behind the breakfast nook counter he has a notebook in which he starts to scribble.*)

PHIL: Yeh, well, I am running out of patience with being good for nothing but whacking people in the face they do some irrelevant thing that drives me nuts. If this is my karma, to be an asshole and have such a thing as this, fuck it.

MICKEY (*rising languidly to his feet*): Absolutely, right; fuck destiny, fate, and all metaphysical stuff.

PHIL (*bolting to the base of the stairway where he glares up at Mickey*): You, you cynical bastard, watch the fine line you are walking between my self-awareness and my habitual trend to violence. 'Cause on the one hand I might appear worried, but on the other I could give a fuck, you know, and my urge to annihilate anyone might just fixate on you.

MICKEY (*descending the stairs toward a bottle of scotch by the TV*): And the vortex get me — fling me, you might say, wallward, magnetically.

PHIL: Exactly. So you can help us both out by watching your goddamn, you know — right? Am I making myself clear?

MICKEY (*slipping by Phil*): Step.

PHIL: Yeah. P's and Q's. (*Moving after Mickey, but yelling to Artie who is busy scribbling at the breakfast nook.*) So, Artie, you got any inside dope on this karma thing, or you just ranting?

ARTIE: Everybody knows something, it's a popular topic.

PHIL (*turning to Artie*): But what I'm asking you is, "You said it, do you know it?"

EDDIE (*moving near Phil*): I mean, Phil, isn't the fact of the matter here that you signed your divorce papers today?

PHIL: Who said anything about that? One thing does not lead to another.

EDDIE: I mean, I think that's what you're wired up about.

PHIL: Eddie, you're jumpin' around on me, here, what's your point?

EDDIE: The baby, the baby. The divorce. This is the ambush you been worried about. They got you. They blew you the fuck right out of orbit, and if you see maybe that's what's cooking under the whole thing, you might just get a hold of yourself.

MICKEY: And pull yourself back into orbit.

PHIL: But what orbit? I'm in an orbit.

MICKEY: It's just it's a useless fucking orbit.

PHIL (*crossing slowly to Mickey*): Do you know, Mickey, I could kick your eyes out and never think about it a second time, that's the depths to which my animosity runs?!

MICKEY: I know that.

PHIL: So why do you take these chances and risk ruining both our lives?

MICKEY: This is the very point Artie was, I think, making.

PHIL: Artie, is this your point? (*Turning, looking for Artie.*)

ARTIE: What? (*Unnoticed by the others, Artie has settled down in the corner on a pile of pillows and he does not even look up from his scribbling, as Phil comes rushing toward him.*)

PHIL: Is this your point?

ARTIE: What?

EDDIE (*moving in on Mickey*): Mickey! Will you just cut the goofy shit for a second? This is a serious point I'm trying to make here.

MICKEY: He knows his life is a mess.

EDDIE: He doesn't know it enough.

MICKEY: He knows it so goddamn well he's trying to avoid it.

EDDIE: That's my point! I mean, Phil, if you see the goddamn issue here. PHIL!

PHIL (*looking up from Artie's endeavor*): YEAH. What's Artie doin'?

ARTIE: I had a thought.

PHIL: So you wrote it down? Everybody has a thought, Artie, this is no justification they go around writing them down.

EDDIE (*approaching Phil, trying to force his attention*): You're just on a goddamn wild roll here because of the state of your life being a shambles! The baby's born and you sign the divorce papers all in the same month, so you're under stress.

PHIL: I'm aware of that.

EDDIE: So that's what I'm sayin'. See the connection.

PHIL: But why are you trying to torment me, Eddie? I thought I could count on you.

EDDIE: But lighten up is what I'm saying. Give yourself a break. I mean, the real issues are not you hitting people or not hitting people, but are these other issues of your divorce and baby. You enjoy hitting people and you know it.

PHIL: My point is not that I don't enjoy it but that it is dangerous, and mostly dangerous that I do enjoy it, so what's the point in that? And my point is that I am wired beyond my reasons. I know my reasons, but I am wired beyond them.

MICKEY (*moving near, his manner a seeming friendliness*): You're right on schedule, Phil, that's all. You're a perfectly, rapateta, blah-blah-blah, modern statistic; you have the baby, you get the divorce. You're very "now" is all, but not up to it. You're the definitive representative of the modern male in this year, but you're not willing to accept it.

PHIL (*undergoing an impulse to throw Mickey through a wall*): This is what I gotta talk to Artie about. (*He turns and finds Artie at the breakfast nook, picking up the phone.*) Artie, what the fuck are you doing?

ARTIE: I'm checking my messages.

PHIL (*hurrying to Artie*): You got a minute, this is a disaster here. I'm on the brink and you're checking your fucking messages. Have some compassion. (*He is trying to get Artie to hang up.*)

ARTIE: Just a second. (*He beeps his beeper into the phone.*)

EDDIE: So who'd you hear from, huh? You got studio executives lined up on your goddamn machine beep after beep. (*Mimicking different voices.*) "Great project, Arthur." "Terrific treatment." "Must have lunch."

ARTIE: I have a career. I am not ashamed, I have a career. You want me to be ashamed?

EDDIE: What I want you to understand, Artie, is the absurdity of this business, and the fact that you're a success in it is a measure of the goddamn absurdity of this business to which we are all desperate to belong as a bunch of dogs.

ARTIE: You're a small-minded prick, Eddie; I hope you know that.

MICKEY *(having settled down on the window seat)*: He does.

EDDIE: I am familiar with the opinion. However, I do not myself hold it.

PHIL *(unable to wait any longer, he grabs at the phone, but Artie eludes him, determined to get his messages)*: But what I need, Artie, is a little more, you know what I mean, Artie. What I'm wondering here is, you got any particularly useful, I mean, hard data on this karma stuff, you know, the procedures by which this cosmic shit comes down. That's what I'm asking: Do you know what you're talking about?

MICKEY: He's a Jew.

PHIL: I know he's a Jew. I'm talking to him, ain't I? Destiny is a thing you have to be somewhat educated to have a hint about it, so he might know somebody, right, Artie? You know anybody?

EDDIE: But it's another tradition, Phil.

PHIL: Who gives a fuck!? Of course I know that. But I'm not talking about tradition here — I'm asking him about the cosmos and has he come upon anything in all the fucking books he reads that might tell me more than I pick up off the TV which is, strictly speaking, dip-shit.

ARTIE *(behind Phil, hanging up the phone)*: Sure.

PHIL: See. So what is it?

ARTIE: Hey, you know, past lives, you have past lives and the karmic stuff accrues to it. You have debts and credits and you have to work your way out from under the whole thing, so you —

MICKEY: Artie! This is not your investment counselor we're talking about here.

EDDIE: This is not cosmic Visa, Artie.

(Mickey and Eddie are both laughing now — Mickey, wanting fun and to keep Phil from being taken seriously by anyone, and Eddie because he is irritated that Phil seems more interested in Artie's opinions than in the advice Eddie himself has tried to give.)

ARTIE: We could be in the process of working out the debits and credits of our past lives with the very way we relate to each other at this very instant. It could be that Phil owes some affection to me, I owe him some guidance, and —

EDDIE *(laughing even more now. Mickey and Eddie both breaking up)*: Guidance?

MICKEY: The fact that you're talking, Artie, does not necessarily make it destiny speaking, I hope you know this.

ARTIE: And you two pricks owe some negative shit to everybody.

PHIL: Artie, he's right. You make it sound like the cosmos is in your opinion this loan shark. This is disappointing.

ARTIE: You asked me.

PHIL: Because I thought you might know.

MICKEY: That's the TV fucking version, and don't you pretend you learned that anywhere but on the evening news.

EDDIE: Some goddamn Special Project.

PHIL: I was hoping, you know, he's a Jew. He's got this insane religious history running out behind him, he might have picked up something, you know. That's what I was hoping. There might be some crazed Hasidic mother-fucker in his family; you know, he came to dinner, he had his pigtail, nobody could shut him up about karma, destiny, the way of the stars; it might have rubbed off on Artie.

MICKEY: You disappointed him, Artie. You built him up, you disappointed him.

ARTIE: It happens.

MICKEY: He's at a critical juncture in his life, here.

ARTIE: Who isn't?

EDDIE: You guys need to get laid.

MICKEY: You, however, don't, huh?

EDDIE: I am, in fact, sustaining a meaningful relationship.

ARTIE (*irritated that Eddie and Mickey have teased him, he thinks he will tease back, snapping out his real feelings*): The only thing sustaining that relationship is the fact that she's out of town two out of every three weeks.

EDDIE (*glaring at Artie*): Well, she's in town tomorrow.

MICKEY (*after an uneasy second*): I wouldn't mind getting laid. What are we thinking about?

EDDIE: We could call somebody.

PHIL: Do it.

ARTIE: Do it now!

EDDIE: I was thinking primarily of setting Phil up, that's what I meant, primarily.

ARTIE: What about me?

EDDIE: Give me a break, Artie. Phil is in a totally unique situation, here, back out in the single life.

PHIL: I'm in a totally fucked-up state of mind, too.

ARTIE: I mean, that little blonde might still be around, you hadn't decided to beat the shit out of her.

PHIL: Is everything my fault, Artie? I mean, relent, I beg you, I am feeling suicidal. Haven't I explained myself?

ARTIE: She liked us. She would have stayed a long time.

PHIL: I was teaching her football. It was an accident. I went too far.

EDDIE: So I could call Bonnie.

ARTIE: You're not going to get Bonnie for Phil?

PHIL: I don't believe this treachery. Artie, have some mercy.

(*Phil and Artie spin off into their own little squabble, Phil pushing at Artie, trying to shut him up, while Eddie goes to the phone to start dialing and Mickey watches them all.*)

ARTIE: This is sex we're talking about now, Phil. Competitive sex.

PHIL: That's what I'm saying. I need help.

ARTIE: You're such a jerk-off, you're such a goof-off. I don't believe for a second you were seriously desperate about trying to pick that bitch up.

PHIL: That's exactly how out of touch I am, Artie — I have methods so outdated they appear to you a goof.

ARTIE (*Artie runs toward Mickey, Phil chasing playfully after him*): Fuck you. He's got this thing.

PHIL: Styles have changed. Did you see the look of disgust on that bimbo's excuse for a face? It was humiliating.

ARTIE (*trying to tell Mickey*): He's got this thing!

PHIL: It used to work. (*Pulling Artie away from Mickey, Phil throws him toward the couch, where the two of them collapse, giggling.*)

MICKEY: What thing? (*Eddie is at the phone, dialing.*)

PHIL: It's a vibrator that I carry around, see.

MICKEY: You carry around a vibrator with you?

PHIL: As a form of come-on, so they see I'm up for anything right from the get-go. It's very logical if you think about it. But tonight there were extenuating circumstances.

ARTIE: It's a logic apparent to you alone, Phil.

EDDIE (*slamming down the phone*): Bonnie, get off the fucking phone!

MICKEY: He had a vibrator.

PHIL: I had a vibrator. So what?

EDDIE: It's logical.

PHIL: Right. Eddie understands me, thank god for it. So when I'm coming on to the broad, see, I sort of pull it out, and have it there. It's like some other guy might have a nail file or something only I got a vibrator — so this Bonnie's a terrific broad, huh?

EDDIE: Terrific.

ARTIE: So you got your thing.

PHIL: So I'm delivering my pitch, you know, and we can have a good time if we get an opportunity to be alone, and as a kind of mood-setter, I turn it on, you know. Except I forgot about the goddamn weights.

EDDIE: What?

MICKEY: THE WEIGHTS? YOU FORGOT ABOUT THE WEIGHTS?

PHIL: I forgot about 'em. Unbelievable!

MICKEY: UNBELIEVABLE! YOU FORGOT ABOUT THE WEIGHTS! (*To Eddie across the room.*) HE FORGOT ABOUT THE GODDAMN WEIGHTS!

ARTIE: Do you know what he's talking about?

MICKEY: No, I don't know what he's talking about!

PHIL: You prick. You disgust me. I'm talking about the weights.

ARTIE: See, he has been transporting his barbells and weights in the back of the car, with all his inability to know where he lived.

PHIL: So the weights were in the back of the car.

MICKEY: Right.

PHIL: The train of events in this thing is perfectly logical to anybody with half a heart to see them, unless that person is a nasty prick. So what had to happen, happened, and I threw the weights into the trunk of the car carelessly and hit the vibrator without thinking about it.

EDDIE: So you pulled out a broken vibrator on this broad.

PHIL: Exactly.

EDDIE: This is an emergency. I think this is an emergency situation here. *(Whirling back to the phone he begins furiously dialing.)*

PHIL: This is what I'm trying to tell you.

EDDIE: You're a desperate human being, Phil.

PHIL: I'm begging. Get Bonnie! I got this broken vibrator, and so when I turn it on, it goes round sort of all weird like, you know, and the motor's demented sounding, it's going around all crooked and weird, changing speeds. She's looking at me.

EDDIE *(dialing again and again)*: This really happened to you?

PHIL: What can I do, Eddie? Help me.

EDDIE: I'm trying.

PHIL: So this broad is looking at me. She's givin' me this look. This thing's in my hand, arrrgghhh, like I'm offering to put this goddamn model airplane inside her. It's liable to come apart and throw her across the room.

EDDIE: Bonnie, please. *(He slams down the phone.)*

ARTIE: This thing's goin', arrrggghhh, arrrghhh. Phil's sayin', "Want to come home with me?"

PHIL: Arrghhhhh, arghhh, want to come home with me? *(Eddie, on the stool by the phone, stares at Phil.)*

EDDIE: You really did this, Phil?

PHIL: Yeah.

EDDIE: Listen to me. You're a rare human being.

PHIL *(very pleased)*: So how come everything turns to shit?

EDDIE: I don't know, but we're going to find out. You're a rare, precious human being.

PHIL: I suspected as much.

EDDIE: Underneath all this bullshit, you have a real instinctive thing, you know what I mean. It's like this wide open intuition.

PHIL *(rising now, he glides across the room to stand beside Eddie)*: This is what I think sometimes about myself.

EDDIE: I mean, it's unique; this goddamn imagination — you could channel it.

PHIL: I have thoughts sometimes they could break my head open.

EDDIE: Whata you mean?

PHIL: I mean, these big thoughts. These big goddamn thoughts. I don't know what to do with them.

EDDIE: This is what I'm saying: if you could channel them into your talent. I mean, under all this crazed bullshit you've been forced to develop —

PHIL: I get desperate. I feel like my thoughts are all just going to burst out of my head and leave me; they're going to pick me up and throw me around the room. I fight with them. It's a bloodbath this monster I have with my thoughts. Maybe if I channeled them.

EDDIE: I never took you so seriously before. I mean, quite so seriously.

PHIL: Me neither.

EDDIE: I'm calling Bonnie, Phil. I'm calling her for you.

PHIL: So call her.

MICKEY (*leaning from his window seat toward Artie on the couch*): Could this be it, Artie?

ARTIE: What? (*Though busy with the phone, Eddie and Phil are clearly eavesdropping on Mickey and Artie.*)

MICKEY: Could this be destiny in fact at work, Artie, and we are witnessing it? — the pattern in the randomness, so that we see it: man without a home, careless weights; broken vibrator, disappointed broad. And from this apparent mess, two guys fall in love.

EDDIE: He's jealous, Phil. Don't worry about his petty jealousy.

PHIL: He could choke on his own spit, I would feel nothing. No. I would feel glee. I would be a kid at an amusement park. (*As Eddie disgustedly hangs up the phone.*) She's still busy?

EDDIE: I'm gonna get her for you, Phil, don't worry.

PHIL: So who is this bitch she's on the phone forever, some goddamn agent?

EDDIE: No, no, she's terrific, you're gonna love her. This is a bitch who dances naked artistically in this club. That's her trip.

MICKEY: With a balloon.

EDDIE: That's what makes it artistic. Without the balloon, what is she?

ARTIE: A naked bitch.

EDDIE: You would wanna fuck her, though.

ARTIE: Anybody would.

EDDIE: She's a good bitch, though, you know what I mean? She's got a heart of gold.

MICKEY: What's artistic about her is her blow jobs.

PHIL (*grabbing Eddie, turning him back to the phone*): Get her, Eddie; get her.

MICKEY: She's critically acclaimed.

EDDIE: And the best part about her is that she's up for anything.

MICKEY: Like the airport.

EDDIE: What airport? (*Then he screams into the phone.*) Bonnie, please!

MICKEY: So we ask her to go to the airport.

EDDIE (*remembering, he puts down the phone*): Oh Jesus, the airport!

(*Eddie moves to Mickey as the story, the claims of old times, the competitiveness of memory, and telling the story draw Mickey and Eddie into a teamlike intimacy, leaving Phil to flop down in the big armchair.*)

MICKEY: This was amazing. Robbie Rattigan was coming in.

EDDIE: He was coming in, see, he was up for this major part in this pilot for an ABC series. Right? He's flying in, we wanna make him feel welcome.

MICKEY: He's gonna be all screwed up from the flight, he's got this big meeting.

EDDIE: Bonnie jumps at the chance. She's seen him as a featured killer on several cop shows which he was on almost every one of them as a killer. "Meet him at the airport," we tell her.

MICKEY: "He's a friend of ours," we tell her. We want you to relax him on the drive back to town.

EDDIE: She says to us that she has been very impressed by his work when she saw it.

MICKEY: She's a fuckin' critic.

EDDIE: So we meet the plane. Robbie gets off, you know; we meet him, we get in the car. Hey, hey, blah-blah, blah-blah-blah. We're on the freeway, she's in the back seat with Robbie.

MICKEY: She's just there.

EDDIE: We made a point of just introducing her like she's somebody's girlfriend, you know, or just some bitch we know, she happens to be in the back seat when we pick him up.

MICKEY: An accident.

EDDIE: No big deal.

MICKEY: So Robbie's talkin' about the part he's up for, and getting very serious, "rapateta." So Bonnie reaches over and unzips his fly. He looks at her like she just fell out of a tree. "Don't mind me," she says. (*Having drifted together to the kitchen, Eddie is again on the chair by the phone; Mickey, behind the counter.*)

EDDIE: I'm tellin' him to keep on talkin'.

MICKEY: We're acting like we don't know what's goin' on.

EDDIE: She just had this impulse. He's irresistible.

MICKEY: That's the impression.

EDDIE: That he's this irresistible guy. That's the impression we want to make.

MICKEY: So she's gone down on him.

EDDIE: You can tell by his face.

MICKEY: She's very energetic.

EDDIE (*dialing one more time*): So he starts to curse us out. You would not believe the cursing he does.

MICKEY: "Robbie," I tell him, "Welcome to L.A.!"

EDDIE (*into the phone*): Bonnie! Hello! (*Everybody freezes.*) Hello. Hey. Bonnie. Eddie. Yeah. C'mon over. Yeah. C'mon over. (*He hangs up.*) She's comin' over.

PHIL: She's comin' over? She's really comin'?

EDDIE: Yeah. Oh, the look on Robbie's face, and the look on the kid's face. Remember that?

MICKEY: No. What?

EDDIE: The kid. Oh, yeah. Christ, the kid. She's got a six-year-old daughter, and she was there.

MICKEY: She was with us?

EDDIE: In the front seat. I forgot about the kid. Wasn't she there?

MICKEY: Yeah. Remember?

EDDIE: Yeah.

MICKEY: So Robbie's wong comes out, and he's got one. I mean, this guy is epic.

EDDIE: Monstrous. The kid is petrified.

MICKEY: I mean, there's her mother goin' into combat with this horse.

EDDIE: It's a goddamn snake.

MICKEY: This is sick, isn't it? I'm gettin' a little sick.

EDDIE: We were ripped though, weren't we? We were ripped.

MICKEY: Maybe we were blotto.

EDDIE: Then we woulda forgot the whole thing. Which we didn't.

MICKEY: We nearly did. I mean, about the kid, right?

EDDIE: I don't think the mitigating circumstances are sufficient! I ended up takin' care of her. She started to cry, remember?

MICKEY: No.

EDDIE: Sure. I mean, she didn't start to cry, but she looked like somebody whacked her in the back of the head with a rock. So I hadda take care of her. You remember, Mickey!

MICKEY: Almost. I was drivin'. So then what happened? I was personally blotto.

EDDIE: Bullshit! We ended up, I'm holdin' her, we're tellin' her these goddamn stories, remember? She was there. We were makin' up this story about elves and shit, and this kingdom full of wild rabbits, and the elves were getting stomped to death by gangs of wild rabbits.

MICKEY: Jungle Bunnies, I think, is what we called them.

EDDIE: Fuck. Everywhere I turn I gotta face my own depravity. Jungle Bunnies are stomping elves to death so the elves start to hang them. Is that the story?

MICKEY: Yeah. And we were doin' the voices. (*Now they are moaning and pounding their heads on the counter in a mix of mock and real remorse.*)

EDDIE: I don't wanna think about it. High-pitched, right?

MICKEY: Yeah, high-pitched . . .

MICKEY AND EDDIE: And rural!

EDDIE: The kid was catatonic. I think maybe that was it, Mickey; we turned the corner in this venture.

MICKEY: Right. What venture?

EDDIE: Life. That was the nose dive. I mean, where it began. We veered at that moment into utter irredeemable depravity. (*As they collapse upon the counter.*)

MICKEY: I feel sick to my stomach about myself. A little. That I could do that. How could I do that?

PHIL (*leaping to his feet*): Hey! You guys! Don't get crazy! You had a WHIM. This is what happens to people. THEY HAVE WHIMS. So you're sittin' around, Robbie's comin'. You want him to like you, you want him to think well of you. So you have this whim. Did she have to do it? Did anybody twist her arm? (*Mickey and Eddie have straightened slowly.*)

MICKEY: Phil's right, Eddie. What'd we do? I mean, objectively. Did anybody say, "Bring your kid."

EDDIE: It's the airwaves.

MICKEY: Exactly. (*Mickey heads up the stairs.*)

EDDIE: TV. TV. Once it was a guy from TV, what chance did she have? (*Phil lounges in the armchair while Artie is flopped on the couch. Mickey goes upstairs and emerges from the bathroom with a huge hashish pipe and a* Variety *with which he flops down on the floor of the balcony.)* She couldn't help herself. And I think subconsciously we knew this. Didn't we know it? I mean, what does she watch? About a million hours of TV a week, so the airwaves are all mixed with the TV waves and then the whole thing is scrambled in her brain waves so, you know, her head is just full of this static, this fog of TV thoughts, to which she refers for everything. I mean, this is an opportunity to mix with the gods we're offering her in the back seat of our car.

(As Eddie finishes, he is reclining on top of the kitchen counter, his back against the wall. Mickey has given up reading and is flat on the floor, his arm dangling through the rails. The door opens and in comes Bonnie.)

BONNIE: Hi!

EDDIE: Bonnie.

ARTIE: Hi!

BONNIE: Hi, Artie, hi, Mickey. Your call was a miracle, Eddie.

MICKEY: Hi.

EDDIE: This is Phil.

BONNIE: Hi.

PHIL: Hi.

EDDIE: He's recently divorced.

BONNIE: Everybody I know is either recently married or recently divorced, some of them the same people. It's a social epidemic.

PHIL: I'm recently divorced.

BONNIE: I've got to have some blow, Eddie, can you spare it?

EDDIE: Sure, hey.

BONNIE: Doom and gloom have come to sit in my household like some permanent kind of domestic appliance. My brain has been invaded with glop. If you could spare some blow to vacuum the lobes, I would be eternally grateful.

PHIL: We could go buy some.

EDDIE: I got plenty. *(Bonnie has moved to Eddie, who is digging out some coke for her as Phil drifts toward them.)*

PHIL: She and me could go. I know where to buy it like it grows on trees.

BONNIE: I was in mortal longing for someone to call me. I was totally without hope of ever having worthwhile companionship tonight, a decent fucking conversation. *(Phil, sidling up to Bonnie, puts his arm around her as Eddie spoons her some coke.)*

PHIL: Eddie's got some stuff here to really round off your — you know, rough spots.

BONNIE: I couldn't be happier.

PHIL: We been having a good time, too.

BONNIE: Is this particular guy just being ceremonial here with me, Eddie, or does he want to dick me?

EDDIE: I thought we'd get around to that later.

BONNIE *(to Phil)*: Eddie thought we'd get around to that later.

PHIL *(hands off, backing away)*: Hey, if I have overstepped some invisible boundary here, you notify me fast because I respond quickly to clear-cut information while, you know, murk and innuendo make me totally demented.

ARTIE: We couldn't have less of any idea what we're doing here, Bonnie.

BONNIE: I'm sure he has his saving graces.

MICKEY: Why don't you list them? I bet he'd like you to list them! *(With this Mickey breaks himself up; Artie erupts in a fit of giggles as Phil tries awkwardly to join in.)*

PHIL: You could make a list of what you think might be my saving graces based on some past savings account in the sky.

BONNIE: Is everybody ripped here?

MICKEY: We're involved in a wide variety of pharmaceutical experiments. *(This, of course, keeps them laughing.)*

EDDIE: Testing the perimeters of the American Dream of oblivion.

BONNIE *(giving Eddie a little kiss on the forehead)*: Well, I can't express my gratitude for your generosity that led you to including me.

PHIL: You want people to call, you might spend less time on the phone.

BONNIE *(turning to look for Phil, who is sitting on the arm of the couch with a bottle)*: This is exactly my point. This bozo would not get off the phone.

MICKEY: You could hang up.

BONNIE *(moving toward Mickey)*: His reaction was to call me back so quickly I considered whether he had magical powers or not.

PHIL: You could leave the phone off the hook.

BONNIE: Which I did. *(As she moves to Phil for the bottle.)*

PHIL: This explains the infinite length of your busy signal.

BONNIE *(to Phil)*: See! This is what I was afraid of: Friends might call. You see the dilemma I was in.

PHIL *(almost scolding her)*: Eddie called and called.

EDDIE: We called as if it was a religious duty.

BONNIE: Thank god you persisted. *(She crosses to Eddie.)* This guy was pushing me beyond my own rational limits so I was into hallucinatory kinds of, you know, considerations, like would I invite him over and then hack him to death with a cleaver.

PHIL: Who is this guy? *(Moving after her, he drops into the armchair, kneeling in the seat looking over the back toward her and Eddie.)* I know ways to make guys stop anything. They might think they couldn't live without it until I talk to them. They might think they have the courage of cowboys, but I can change their minds. Who is this guy?

BONNIE: This is what I'm getting at, Eddie, a person like this guy can only be found in your household. What's your name again?

PHIL: Phil.

ARTIE: He's dangerous, Bonnie.

BONNIE: Who isn't?

ARTIE: I mean, in ways you can't imagine.

BONNIE: That's very unlikely, Artie. (*Eddie hands her a lighted joint.*) Drugs. I mean, I'm telling this guy on the phone that drugs are and just have been as far as I can remember, an everpresent component of my personality. I am a drug-person. And I would not, if I were him, consider that anything unusual, unless he is compelled to reveal to the entire world his ignorance of the current situation in which most people find themselves — so that's what I'm telling this guy.

PHIL: Who is this guy? He's drivin' me nuts, this guy.

BONNIE: Some guy. Don't worry about it. (*Crossing to Phil to give him a joint and almost to console him with her explanation, as she sits on the hassock beside the armchair.*) I mean, my life in certain of its segments has just moved into some form of automation on which it runs as if my input is no longer required. So my girlfriend Sarah gets involved with this guy who is totally freaked out on EST, so she gets proportionally freaked out on EST, this is what love can do to you, so then they are both attempting to freak me out on EST, as if my certainty that they are utterly full of shit is some nonnegotiable threat to them rather than just my opinion and so they must — out of their insecurity, assault me with this goddamn EST ATTACK so that everywhere I turn I am confronted with their booklets and god knows what else, these pictures of this Werner Shmerner and the key to them that I must get rid of is my drug-desires, which is the subject of their unending, unvaried, you know, whatchamacallit.

EDDIE: Proselytizing.

BONNIE (*looking to Eddie*): They will not shut up about it. So I am trying to make to this guy what is for me an obvious point, which is that unlike those who have lost their minds to EST, I am a normal person: I need my drugs! (*Phil has coke which he gives her. They have booze to share, grass.*) Has he been in the hospital lately? I am asking him. Because you go in the hospital, where I have recently had reason to go, and along with everything else you can get there, the anesthesiologist, the minute I am strong enough, he is offering to sell me coke of which he says he is himself deeply fond along with twenty or thirty percent of the nurses and a sprinkling of the interns, as he reported it. I am scoffed at for this remark, so, being civilized, I attempt to support my point with what Sarah and I both know from our mutual girlfriend Denise. "Does Denise not work as a legal secretary in this building full of lawyers?" I tell him. Well, she says these lawyers are totally blow oriented, and you go in there in the after-hours where some of them are still working, it sounds like a goddamn hog farm, she says. Well, Sarah and this guy react to this with two absolutely unaltered onslaughts, and while they're yelling at me, I'm yelling at them, that since I am a drug-person, I must give them a drug-person's answer: (*Sliding off the hassock to the pillows on the floor.*) "Thbgggggggggghhhhhhhgggggghhhhh!" I go, and slam down the phone and hang it up. (*Ending up lying on her back on the floor at Phil's feet.*)

PHIL: So that's when we called.

BONNIE: When I picked it up, you were there. Eddie was there.

PHIL: And now you're here.

MICKEY (*gazing down on Phil and Bonnie*): Is this the hand of destiny again, Eddie, look at it.

EDDIE (*still lying on the counter*): I'm looking.

MICKEY: The hand of destiny again emerging just enough from, you know, all the normal muck and shit, so that, you know, we get a glimpse of it.

BONNIE: Whata you mean, Mickey? What's he mean?

EDDIE: It's a blind date.

BONNIE: Ohh, you invited me over for this guy, Eddie?

EDDIE: Yeah. Why?

BONNIE: Oh, you know, I thought. . . .

PHIL: She don't have to, Eddie. (*Phil storms away toward the kitchen.*)

BONNIE: No, no. I just didn't know it was a setup.

PHIL (*behind the counter getting a beer*): I mean, she should know it could be the final straw for me to justify some sort of butchery, but that's just a fact of life and not in any way meant to influence the thing here.

EDDIE (*dropping off the counter, Eddie moves to join Bonnie on the floor*): You disappointed in Phil?

BONNIE: I wasn't thinking about it.

EDDIE: What were you thinking about?

BONNIE: Eddie, look, it doesn't matter.

EDDIE: He's nervous.

PHIL (*at the counter with his drink*): I'm very nervous.

BONNIE (*standing up*): Right. So what's the agenda?

EDDIE (*giving her some coke*): Hey, I figured I'd just sort of rough in the outline, you'd have the rest at your fingertips; you know, operating at an instinctual level.

BONNIE (*walking to Phil, she spoons coke to his nose, and he snorts*): So you wanna go upstairs? (*Phil shakes his head no.*) No?

PHIL: Out. Eddie, can I borrow your car? I don't have a car.

BONNIE: So we'll go over to my place. (*Picking up a joint.*) Can I take this, Eddie?

EDDIE: What happened to your car?

PHIL: My wife got all the keys. She put one a those locks on it so it fuckin' screams at you.

BONNIE: I got a car.

PHIL: You got a car? (*Bonnie is running around, collecting supplies, picking up her shoes.*)

BONNIE: So we'll be back in a little, you guys'll be here?

EDDIE: Where else?

BONNIE: Bye.

MICKEY (*as Bonnie and Phil go out the door*): Have a nice time, kids.

EDDIE: Bye.

MICKEY: She's some bitch.

EDDIE (*settling back on the pillows on the floor*): Balloons. Balloons.

ARTIE (*lounging, staring at the ceiling*): Eddie, can I ask you something? I wanna ask you something.

EDDIE: Sure.

ARTIE: You don't mind?

EDDIE: What?

ARTIE: I'm just very curious about the nature of certain patterns of bullshit by which people pull the wool over their own eyes.

EDDIE: Yeah?

ARTIE: So could you give me a hint as to the precise nature of the delusion with which you hype yourself about this guy, that you treat him the way you do?

EDDIE: Artie, hey, you know, I have a kind of intuitive thing with Phil. Don't get in a fuckin' snit about it.

ARTIE: Because you desert me for this fucking guy all the time. What is it about you, you gotta desert me?

EDDIE: I don't desert you.

ARTIE (*rising now, he moves toward Eddie*): But what is it you really think about me, so that in your estimation you can dump on me, and treat Phil like he's some — I don't know what — but you lost a paternity suit and he was the result.

EDDIE: Artie, you're the only one old enough around here to be everybody's father, so what are you talking about?

ARTIE: Age don't mean shit in a situation like this.

EDDIE: First of all, I don't consider your statement that I dump on you accurate, so why should I defend against it? (*Slowly now, Eddie is getting to his feet, his back to Artie.*)

ARTIE: It's subtle. Hey, you think that means I'm gonna miss it? It's an ongoing, totally pervasive attitude with which you dump on me subtly so that it colors almost every remark, every gesture. And I'm sick of it.

EDDIE (*turning, he faces Artie*): I'm sorry your deal fell through. (*And walks away, looking for something, heading toward Mickey, who lies on the balcony as he has been, arm dangling, watching everything.*)

ARTIE: You lie to yourself, Eddie.

EDDIE: Yeah?

ARTIE (*pursuing Eddie*): That's right. You lie to yourself.

EDDIE (*as Mickey hands Eddie the big hashish pipe*): Just because you're Jewish doesn't make you Freud, you prick.

ARTIE: And just because you're whatever the fuck you are doesn't make you whatever the hell you think you are. The goddamn embodiment of apple pie here is full of shit.

EDDIE (*sitting down on the stairs to light the pipe*): So I lie, huh? Who better? I'm a very good liar, and I'm very gullible. This makes for an accomplishment in the field never before imagined.

ARTIE: And my deal didn't fall through, anyway. That's just stunningly diversionary on your part even if it did. Which it didn't. You're a deceptive sonofabitch, Eddie. Is everything a ploy to you?

EDDIE: What are you talking about?

ARTIE: You know what I mean.

EDDIE: I don't.

ARTIE: The hell you don't. Doesn't he Mickey? He knows.

EDDIE: I don't. I swear it.

ARTIE: You're just avoiding the goddamn confrontation here.

EDDIE: What confrontation?

ARTIE: We're having a confrontation here.

EDDIE: We are?

ARTIE: Yeah! I am! I'm gettin' out of here. Mickey, you wanna get out of here?

MICKEY: Sure. (*Artie starts up the stairs, but Eddie blocks the way.*)

EDDIE: Where you goin'?

ARTIE: I'm goin' to the can, and then I'm getting out of here. (*He squeezes past Eddie.*) And you, you sonofabitch, I'm going to tell you the goddamn bottom line because if you don't know it, you are — I mean, a thousand-fold — just utterly — and you fucking know it!

EDDIE: What?

ARTIE (*retreating toward the door of the bathroom*): Hey, you don't have to deal any further with my attempts at breathing life into this corpse of our friendship. Forget about it. (*He bolts into the bathroom, slamming the door.*)

EDDIE: You're a schmuck, Artie! You're a schmendrick! Go check your messages! (*Flopping down on the stairs, he turns to Mickey, lying on the balcony floor just above Eddie's head.*) What was that?

MICKEY (*unmoving*): I think what he was trying to get at is that he, you know, considers your investment in Phil, which is in his mind sort of disproportionate and maybe even — and mind you, this is Artie's thought, not mine — but maybe even fraudulent and secretly self-serving on your part. So you know, blah-blah-blah, rapateta — that this investment is based on the fact that Phil is very safe because no matter how far you manage to fall, Phil will be lower. You end up crawling along the sidewalk, Phil's gonna be on his belly in the gutter looking up in wide-eyed admiration. (*Bolting upright, Eddie heads for the couch, where he grabs up a bottle.*)

EDDIE: This is what Artie thinks.

MICKEY (*getting slowly to his feet now, Mickey starts dressing to go out with Artie: putting on a belt, tucking in a shirt, putting on his shoes*): Yeah. And it hurts his feelings, because, you know, he'd like to think he might be capable of an eyeball-to-eyeball relationship with you based not necessarily on equality, but on, nevertheless, some real affinity — and if not the actuality, at least the possibility of respect. So your, you know, decision, or whatever — compulsion — to shortchange yourself, in his estimation, and hang out with Phil is for him a genuine disappointment, which you just saw the manifestation of.

EDDIE *(has been drinking quite a bit throughout the evening and is now taking in great quantities, throwing his head back to drink from the bottle)*: That was his hurt feelings.

MICKEY: Yeah.

EDDIE: What's everybody on my case for all of a sudden?

MICKEY: Nobody's on your case.

EDDIE: What do you think you're doing, then, huh? What is this, What was Artie doing?

MICKEY *(having descended the stairs, Mickey is now sitting down in the armchair, putting on his shoes)*: You have maybe some misconceptions is all, first of all about how smart you are. And then maybe even if you are as smart as you think you are, you have some misconception about what that entitles you to regarding your behavior to other human beings. Such facts being pointed out is what's going on here, that's all. Don't take it personally.

EDDIE: What would make you mad, Mickey?

MICKEY: Hey, I'm sure it's possible. *(Mickey moves now into the kitchen, looking for something to eat in the refrigerator.)*

EDDIE: What would it be? I'm trying to imagine.

MICKEY: The truth is, Artie isn't really that pissed at you anyway.

EDDIE: He got close enough.

MICKEY: You know, his feelings got hurt.

EDDIE: That's what I'm talking about. Don't I have feelings, too?

MICKEY *(standing at the breakfast nook, eating ice cream)*: Except it makes him feel good to have his feelings hurt, that's why he likes you. You're a practicing prick. You berate him with the concoction of moral superiority which no doubt reassures him everything is as it should be, sort of reminding him in a cozy way of his family in whose eyes he basked most of his life as a glowing disappointment.

EDDIE: You're just too laid back for human tolerance sometimes, Mickey. A person wonders if you really care.

MICKEY: I get excited.

EDDIE: You have it figured somehow. What's it according to — some schematic arrangement — grids of sophistication — what's the arrangement by which you assess what's what so you are left utterly off the hook?

MICKEY: It's a totally unconscious process.

EDDIE: Fuck you, Mickey.

MICKEY: Ask Darlene if she won't let you go back to coke, why don't you? Booze seems to bring out some foul-spirited streak in you.

EDDIE: That's the fucking bottom line, though, huh, nobody's going to take substantial losses in order to align and endure with what are totally peripheral — I mean, transient elements in their life. I mean, we all know we don't mean shit in one another's eyes, finally.

MICKEY: Do you realize you're turning nasty right before my eyes?

EDDIE: I'm feeling a little grim, if you don't mind. *(He takes a drink.)*

MICKEY: Just so you're aware of it.

EDDIE: Hey, if I wasn't, there's plenty of judgmental jerks around here to remind me. *(He takes another drink.)*

MICKEY: You gonna remember any of this tomorrow, or is this one of your, you know, biodegradable moments?

EDDIE: Lemme in on your point of view, Mickey, we can have a dialectic.

MICKEY: Hey. Just in case you notice me walk out of the room, you can reflect back on this, all right?

EDDIE: All right. On what?

MICKEY *(now backing toward the door)*: That, you know, this foul mood of yours might have been sufficient provocation to motivate my departure, see. You know, lock that in so you can minimize the paranoia.

EDDIE: You sound like my goddamn mother.

ARTIE *(as coming out of the bathroom, he starts down the stairs)*: Father.

EDDIE: Mother.

ARTIE: So you coming with us, Eddie, or not?

EDDIE *(slumped on the couch, drinking)*: Where you going?

ARTIE: I don't know. Where we going, Mickey?

MICKEY: It was your idea.

EDDIE: No.

MICKEY *(to Eddie)*: We'll go somewhere. We'll think of somewhere; change the mood.

EDDIE: No. Fuck no. I'm gonna get ripped and rant at the tube.

MICKEY: What's a matter with you?

EDDIE: Nothing.

ARTIE: You don't wanna.

EDDIE: No. *(As Mickey, shrugging, goes strolling out the door.)*

ARTIE: You gonna be all right?

EDDIE: Who cares?

ARTIE: This is not caring I'm expressing here. This is curiosity. Don't misconstrue the behavior here and confuse yourself that anybody cares!

MICKEY *(from off)*: Artie, let's go.

EDDIE: Artie, relax. You're starting to sound like an imitation of yourself, and you're hardly tolerable the first time.

ARTIE: Eddie, don't worry about a thing. This is just some sort of irreversible chemical pollution of your soul. Your body has just gone into shock from all the shit you've taken in, so you're suffering some form of virulent terminal toxic nastiness. Nothing to worry about.

(Artie, with his last word, is out the door, and the phone is ringing. Eddie looks at the phone and starts toward it.)

EDDIE: Who's worried? The only thing worrying me, Artie, was that you might decide to stay. *(Grabbing up the phone.)* Yeah. Agnes. Whata you want? *(As he talks, he arranges a nest of pillows onto which he flops with the phone and his bottle of vodka.)* I said, were you worried I might be having a pleasant evening, you didn't want to take any chances that I might not be miserable enough without hearing from you? No, I did not make an obscene call to you. What'd he say? It can't be too dirty to say, Agnes, HE said it. Every call you make to me is obscene. Everything you say to me is obscene. Of course I'm drunk. If you don't want to talk to me when I'm drunk, call me in the daytime. I'm sober in the daytime, but of course we both know you do want to talk to me when I'm drunk. You get off on it, don't you. Reminds you of the good old days. If you hurt my little girl, I'll kill you . . . I said, "If you hurt my little girl, I'll kill you!"

(Bonnie enters through the front door, her clothing ripped and dirty, her knee scraped. Limping, she carries one of her shoes in her hand. Seeing her, Eddie gets to his feet.)

BONNIE: Eddie . . . !

EDDIE *(into the phone)*: I have to go. I'll call you tomorrow. Good-bye. *(He hurries toward Bonnie who, leaning against one of the balcony support beams, starts hobbling toward him.)* Where's Phil?

BONNIE: You know, Eddie, how come you gotta put me at the mercy of such a creep for? Can I ask you that?

EDDIE: Where is he? *(He is helping her toward the armchair.)*

BONNIE: He threw me out of my own car, Eddie.

EDDIE: What'd you do?

BONNIE *(pulling away from him, slapping at his arms in a little fit)*: Whata you mean, what'd I do? He's a fucking guy, he should be in a ward somewhere! You could have at least warned me!

EDDIE *(struggling to help her)*: Nobody listens to me.

BONNIE *(still pushing or hitting at him)*: I listen to you and you damn well know it.

EDDIE: You're all right. *(Patting her, as she sits in the armchair, he heads for the bar to make her a drink and wet a washcloth in the sink with which to wash off her knee.)*

BONNIE: I'm alive, if that's what you mean, but I am haunted by the suspicion that it is strictly a matter of luck. Nor is it enough that I have my various limbs, you know, operational. I wouldn't mind having a little, you know — LIKE A GODDAMN, YOU KNOW, A SLEEPING CAT HAS IT!

EDDIE: Contentment.

BONNIE: I'm a nervous wreck! This guy is a debilitating experience. I mean, you should reconsider your entire evaluation of this guy, Eddie. *(Hobbling toward him, as if with urgent news.)* This is a guy, he is totally without redeeming social value!

EDDIE *(handing her the drink, he guides her back to the chair)*: Where is he?

BONNIE: I mean, I came down here in good faith, Eddie, I hope you are not going to miss that point.

EDDIE (*as he kneels down to tend her knee with the washcloth*): Will you get off your high horse about Phil, all right? So he took your car, so what. He'll bring it back.

BONNIE: He didn't just take my car, Eddie; HE THREW ME OUT OF IT.

EDDIE (*trying to shrug the whole thing off*): So what?

BONNIE (*ripping the washcloth from his hands*): Whata you mean, "so what?"

EDDIE: So what? (*Reaching to get the washcloth back.*)

BONNIE: Eddie, it was moving!

EDDIE: He slowed it down. (*Still he tries to get the washcloth, but she will not let him have it.*)

BONNIE: Right. He slowed it down. But he didn't slow it down enough. I mean, he didn't stop the fucking car. He slowed it down. Whata you mean, "he slowed it down?" As if that was enough to make a person feel, you know, appropriately handled. He threw me out of my own slowly moving car and nearly killed me.

EDDIE (*indicating her knee, which is right in front of him*): You scraped your knee!

BONNIE: I just missed cracking open my head on a boulder that was beside the road.

EDDIE: What boulder?

BONNIE: Whata you mean, what boulder? This boulder beside the road. THAT boulder.

EDDIE: Will you please get to the fucking point?

BONNIE: No.

EDDIE: Then shut up! (*Whirling, he flops furiously back on his pillows. Grabbing up his bottle, he drinks.*)

BONNIE: No! (*Rising now, she starts to angrily pull off her skirt and then her pantyhose in order to tend to her knee and other wounds.*) Because what I wanna know about maybe is you, and why you would put a friend of yours like me in that kind of jeopardy. Why you would let me go with this creep, if I was begging, let alone instigate it, that's what I'm wondering when I get right down to it, though I hadn't even thought about it. But maybe it's having a goddamn friendship with you is the source of jeopardy for a person. (*Swinging her skirt at him, she storms over to the bar for more to drink, for water and ice for her wounds.*)

EDDIE (*his feelings have been hurt: As far as he's concerned, he's been trying to help*): You want to take that position.

BONNIE: It could be.

EDDIE: You wanna — you take it if you want to.

BONNIE: I'm not sayin' I want to. I'm saying maybe I should want to, and if I think about it, maybe that's what I'll do and you ought to know I am going to think about it.

(*Due to his drinking, Eddie, from the instant Bonnie first hurled the shoe or hit at him, has been reacting increasingly as a little boy. Scolded*) *by Artie and scolded by Mickey, he tries to hold his ground against Bonnie, yet to placate her. When she yells at him, he winces, as if her words are physical. Behind her back he sometimes mimics her as she talks. When she, out of her own frustration, swings at him with a shoe, a blouse, her pantyhose, he recoils as a child might. Though he is attempting to contend with Bonnie, he is far away and with someone from long ago.)*

EDDIE: Don't, you know, strain yourself.

BONNIE: I hurt my foot, too, and my hip and my elbow along with my knee.

EDDIE: I'm sorry about that.

BONNIE: Maybe you might show something more along the lines of your feelings and how you might explain yourself so that I might have them to think about when I'm thinking about it all, so I give you a fair shot. I mean, this guy, Eddie, is not just, you know, semiweird; he is working on genuine berserk. Haven't you noticed some clue to this?

EDDIE: You must have done SOMETHING.

BONNIE: I SAT THERE. *(Behind the bar, she drinks, puts ice on her wounds.)* He drove; I listened to the music on the tape deck like he wanted, and I tol' him the sky was pretty, just trying, you know, to put some sort of fucking humanity into the night, some sort of spirit so we might, you know, appear to one another as having had at one time or another a thought in our heads and were not just these totally fuck-oriented, you know, things with clothes on.

EDDIE: What are you getting at?

BONNIE: What I'm getting at is I did nothing, and in addition, I am normally a person who allots a certain degree of my energy to being on the alert for creeps, Eddie. I am not so dumb as to be ignorant of the vast hordes of creeps running loose in California as if every creep with half his screws loose has slid here like the continent is tilted. But because this guy was on your recommendation, I am caught unawares and nearly maimed. That's what I'm getting at. I mean, this guy is driving, so I tell him we can go to my house. He says he's hungry, so I say, "Great, how about a Jack-In-The-Box?" He asks me if that's code for something. So I tell him, "No, it's California-talk, we have a million of 'em, is he new in town?" His answer is, do I have a water bed? "No," I tell him, but we could go to a sex motel, they got water beds. They got porn on the in-house video. Be great! So then I detect he's lookin' at me, so I smile, and he says, "Whata you smilin' about?" I say, "Whata you mean?" He says, like he's talkin' to the steering wheel, "Whata you thinkin'?" or some shit. I mean, but it's like to the steering wheel; he's all bent out of shape.

EDDIE: See. You did something.

BONNIE: What?

EDDIE: I don't know.

BONNIE: I smiled.

EDDIE: Then what?

BONNIE *(hitting at him with her pantyhose)*: I smiled, Eddie, for chrissake, I smiled is what I did. It's a friendly thing in most instances, but for him it promotes all this paranoid shit he claims he can read in it my secret opinions of him, which he is now saying. The worst things anybody could think about anybody, but I ain't saying nothing. He's sayin' it. Then he screams he knew this venture was a one-man operation and the next thing I know he's trying to push me out of the car. He's trying to drive it, and slow it down, and push me out all at once, so we're swervin' all over the road. So that's what happened. You get it now?

EDDIE: He's been having a rough time.

BONNIE: Eddie, it's a rough century all the way around — you say so yourself, Eddie. Who does anybody know who is doing okay? So this is some sort of justification for us all to start pushing each other out of cars? — things aren't working out personally the way we planned?

EDDIE: Aren't you paying any fucking attention to my point here? I'm talking about a form of desperation you are maybe not familiar with it.

BONNIE: Oh.

EDDIE: I'm talking about a man here, a guy he's had his entire thing collapse. Phil has been driven to the brink.

BONNIE: Oh. Okay. *(Now, angrily, Bonnie begins to dress.)* You consider desperation you and your friend's own, private, so-called — thingamajig. Who would have thought other? I mean, I can even understand that due to the attitude I know you hold me in, which is of course mainly down. Because deep down, a person does not live in an aura of — you know, which we all have them, auras — and they spray right out of us and they are just as depressing and pushy on the people in our company as anything we might, you know, knowingly and overtly badmouth them with. But at the same time, you certainly should be told that in my opinion you are totally, one hundred percent, you know, with your head up your ass about me.

EDDIE: Yeah.

BONNIE: That's what I'm saying. "Wrong," is what I'm saying. See, because I am a form of human being just like any other, get it! And you wanna try holding onto things on the basis of your fingernails, give me a call. So desperation, believe it or not, is within my areas of expertise, you understand? I am a person whose entire life with a child to support depends on her tits and this balloon and the capabilities of her physical grace and imaginary inventiveness with which I can appear to express something of interest in the air by my movement and places in the air I put the balloon along with my body, which some other dumb bitch would be unable to imagine or would fall down in the process of attempting to perform in front of crowds of totally incomprehensible and terrifying bunch of audience members. And without my work what am I but an unemployed scrunt on the meat market of these streets? Because this town is nothin' but mean in spite of the palm trees. So that's my point about desperation, and I can give you references, just in case you never thought of it, you know; and just thought I was over here — some mindless twat over here with blonde hair and big eyes.

EDDIE: I hadn't noticed your hair or eyes.

BONNIE: I'm gonna level with you, Eddie, I came here for a ride home and an apology. *(Finished dressing, she pivots furiously and starts for the door.)*

EDDIE *(rising up on his knees)*: Don't you fuck everybody you meet?

BONNIE: Whata you mean? WHAT?

EDDIE: You know what I'm talking about.

BONNIE *(coming back at him)*: I fuck who I want. What does one thing have to do with — I mean, what's the correlation, huh?

EDDIE *(he is headed toward her on his knees)*: You fuck everybody.

BONNIE: I fuck a lot of different guys: That's just what I do. It's interesting. You know that. You learn a lot about 'em. That's no reason to assume I can be thrown out of a car as random recreation, however. If I want to jump, I'll jump. Not that that's the point, I hope.

EDDIE: It's not far from it.

BONNIE: I mean, I fuck different guys so I know the difference. That's what I'm saying. There's a lot of little subtleties go right by you don't have nothing to compare them to.

EDDIE: But you're getting these airs is what I'm getting at. I mean you're assuming some sort of posture, like some attitude of I pushed you into some terrible, unfamiliar circumstances and normally you're very discreet about who you ball and who you don't, when normally you —

BONNIE: He coulda hurt me, Eddie.

EDDIE *(trying to stand up)*: I don't care!

BONNIE: Don't tell me that.

EDDIE *(Eddie careens backward against the stairway and bounces forward onto the floor on his hands and knees)*: You're just some bitch who thinks it matters that you run around with balloons and your tits out. Nobody's going to take substantial losses over what are totally peripheral, totally transient elements. You know, we're all just background in one another's life. Cardboard cutouts bumping around in this vague, you know, hurly-burly, this spin-off of what was once prime-time life; so don't hassle me about this interpersonal fuck-up on the highway, okay? *(Having struggled to the sink, he is putting water on his face.)*

BONNIE: You oughta have some pity.

EDDIE: I'm savin' it.

BONNIE: For your buddies.

EDDIE: For myself. *(The front door opens and Phil bursts in, sweating, looking worried, clutching a handkerchief.)*

BONNIE: Oh, no. *(Bonnie flees away from Phil toward Eddie behind the counter.)*

PHIL: I'm perfectly, you know, back to earth now. I can understand if you don't believe me, but there's nothing to be concerned about.

BONNIE: I oughta call the cops, you prick.

PHIL: Your car's outside; it's okay.

BONNIE: I'm talking about murder almost.

PHIL *(grabbing the phone as if he will present it to her)*: You want me to dial it for you, Bonnie; you have every right.

EDDIE: Shut up. Can you do that? Can you just SHUT UP? *(Grabbing the phone from Phil, he storms away from both of them.)*

PHIL: I'm sorry, Eddie.

EDDIE: I mean, I'm disgusted with the both of you.

PHIL: I don't blame you, Eddie.

EDDIE *(trying to get away, to be alone, he goes to the far corner, the couch. Done with them, he grabs up a newspaper, yet he is too angry)*: I did my best for the both of you. I did everything I could to set you up nicely, but you gotta fuck it up. Why is that?

PHIL: I'm some kind of very, very unusual jerk, is what I figure.

BONNIE: You had no rhyme nor reason for what you did to me.

PHIL *(following after Eddie, perhaps sitting down next to Eddie, as in an odd way he's giving an explanation for Eddie's sake)*: It's broads, Eddie. I got all this hubbub for a personality with which I try to make do, but they see right through it to where I am invisible. I see 'em see through; it makes me crazy, but it ain't their fault.

EDDIE: I go out of my way for you, Phil; I don't know what more I can do. Now I have Artie pissed at me, I have Bonnie pissed.

PHIL: She has every right; you have every right. Artie's pissed, too?

EDDIE: You know that.

PHIL: I didn't know it.

EDDIE: In your heart I'm talkin' about, Phil; that's what I'm talking about.

PHIL: It's — you know, my imaginary side, Eddie — like we were sayin', I get lost in it. I gotta channel it into my work more.

EDDIE: Fuck your work. What work? *(Getting up, backing away, yet towering over Phil.)* You don't have any work, Phil, you're background, don't you know that? They just take you on for background. They got all these bullshit stories they want to fill the air with, they want to give them some sense of reality, some fucking air of authenticity, don't they? So they take some guy like you and stick him around the set to make the whole load of shit look real. Don't you know that? You're a prop. The more guys like you they got looking like the truth, the more bullshit they can spread all around you. You're like a tree, Phil. *(Phil is standing.)* You're like the location! They just use you to make the bullshit look legitimate! *(Grabbing up a vodka bottle from the coffee table.)*

PHIL: What about my, you know, talent; you said I ought to . . . you know. . . . Remember?

EDDIE *(moving to slump down in the rocking chair)*: That was hype. I don't know what I was doin'.

PHIL: Oh.

EDDIE: Hype. You know.

PHIL: You were what — puttin' me on?

EDDIE: This is the real goods.

PHIL: You mean, all that you said about how I oughta, you know, have some faith in myself, it wasn't true.

EDDIE: Whata you think? Did you ever really believe it?

PHIL: Yeah. Sorta.

EDDIE: Not really. No.

PHIL: Well, you know. No.

EDDIE: So who we been kiddin'?

PHIL: Me. We been kiddin' me. *(Moving nearer to Eddie now.)* But this is the real goods . . . now, right? I mean, we're gettin' down to the real goods now.

EDDIE: Yeah.

PHIL: So you musta decided it would be best for me to hear the truth.

EDDIE: Naw.

PHIL: So I could try and straighten myself out. *(By this eerie, unrelenting positiveness, Phil seems to be almost demanding an escalation from Eddie.)*

EDDIE: I'm just sick of you, Phil.

PHIL: Oh. How long you been sick of me? It's probably recent.

EDDIE: No.

PHIL: So it's been a long time. . . . So what caused it?

EDDIE: I'm gonna let you off the hook now, Phil. I'm not gonna say any more. *(Clutching his newspaper and bottle, Eddie bolts away, heading for the stairs.)*

PHIL: You gotta.

EDDIE: I'm gonna lighten up. I'm gonna give you a break.

PHIL *(grabbing Eddie partway up the stairs)*: Eddie, you gotta give me the entire thing now. I don't need a break. I want it all. I can take it. It's for my own good, right? I can take it. I gotta have it. I got a tendency to kid myself everything is okay. So, you know, you tell me what are the things about me that are for you, you know, disgusting. I want to know. Tell me what they are.

EDDIE: Everything. Everything about you.

PHIL: Everything? Everything? You really had me fooled, Eddie.

EDDIE: That was the point. *(Nodding, he slumps head bowed, on the stairs.)*

BONNIE: You guys are crazy.

EDDIE: Whata you mean? *(Looking drunkenly up at Phil.)* What does she mean? You . . . look terrible, Phil. *(As trying to stand, he slips and bumps down several steps.)*

BONNIE: You ain't lookin' so good yourself, Eddie.

EDDIE: I feel awful.

BONNIE: Whatsamatter?

EDDIE: I dunno. I'm depressed.

PHIL: What about?

EDDIE: Everything. *(Gesturing, the newspaper still in his hand, he notices it.)* You read this shit. Look at this shit.

PHIL: You depressed about the news, Eddie?

EDDIE: Yeh.

PHIL: You depressed about the newspaper?

EDDIE: It's depressing. You read about this fucking neutron bomb? Look at this. *(Hands a part of the paper to Phil, as Bonnie is inching nearer. Phil sits on the arm of the couch, looking at the paper. Eddie, clutching a part of the paper, is trying to stand.)*

PHIL: It's depressing. You depressed about the neutron bomb, Eddie?

EDDIE: Yeah.

(There is an element here of hope in both Bonnie and Phil that Eddie may tell them something to explain, in fact, what's been going on.)

BONNIE: It's depressing. *(Kneeling on the armchair, she looks over the back at Eddie and Phil with their newspapers.)* The newspaper is very depressing. I get depressed every time I read it.

EDDIE: I mean, not that I would suggest that, you know, the anxiety of this age is an unprecedented anxiety, but I'm fucking worried about it, you know. *(Taking a big drink, which empties the bottle he has.)*

PHIL: So it's the newspaper and all the news got you down, huh, Eddie?

EDDIE *(crossing with his tattered newspaper to the coffee table for another bottle sitting there)*: I mean, the aborigine had a lot of problems — nobody is going to say he didn't — tigers in the trees, dogs after his food; and in the Middle Ages, there was goblins and witches in the woods. But this neutron bomb has come along and this sonofabitch has got this ATTI-TUDE. I mean, inherent in the conception of it is this fucking ATTITUDE about what is worthwhile in the world and what is worth preserving. And do you know what this fastidious prick has at the top of its hierarchy — what sits at the pinnacle? THINGS! *(He takes a huge drink of vodka.)* Put one down in the vicinity of this room and we're out. The three of us — out, out, out! "Well, I think I'll go downtown tomorrow and buy some new shoe — " WHACK! You're out! *(He goes reeling toward the kitchen.)* "Well, I thought I'd apologize for my reprehensible — " You're out! No shoes, no apologize. But guess what? The glasses don't even crack. *(He has a glass.)* The magazine's fine. The chairs, the table — *(He knocks a chair over.)* The phone'll ring if there's anybody to call. The things are unfucking-disturbed. It annihilates people and saves THINGS. It loves things. It is a thing that loves things. Technology has found a way to save its own ass! And whether we know it or not, we KNOW it — that's eating at us. *(Lurching now, he grabs up a wastebasket, appears about to vomit in it, clutches it.)* And where other, older, earlier people — the Ancients might have had some consolation from a view of the heavens as inhabited by this thoughtful, you know, meditative, maybe a trifle unpredictable and wrathful, but nevertheless UP THERE — this divine onlooker — *(Staggering about with his bottle and basket.)* — we have bureaucrats devoted to the accumulation of incomprehensible data — we have connoisseurs of graft and the filibuster — virtuosos of the three-martini lunch for whom we vote on the basis of their personal appearance. The air's bad, the water's got poison in it, and into whose eyes do we find ourselves staring when we look for providence? We have emptied out the heavens and put oblivion in the hands of a bunch of aging insurance salesmen whose jobs are insecure. *(He ends up leaning against the counter, the basket under his arm, the bottle in his hand.)*

BONNIE: Yeah, well, Eddie, it's no reason to be mean to your friends.

EDDIE: Says you.

BONNIE: Exactly.

EDDIE: You want me to have reasons? I got to have fucking reasons? *(Suddenly woozy, Eddie is trying to move away, collapsing onto his hands and knees and crawling.)* And you probably want me to say them, don't you. And you probably want them to be the right reasons, and I say them. They're whores, don't you know that? Logic is a slut. Be consoled that inasmuch as you are indiscreet you are logical.

PHIL *(jumping to his feet, heading for the door)*: I gotta get something from the car.

EDDIE: What?

PHIL: I'll be right back. *(He goes out the door.)*

EDDIE: No. I say no. You want me "nice." You want me "polite." "Good." *(Crawling as he talks, dragging along his bottle and basket.)* "Kinder." "More considerate." But I say no. I will be a thing. I will be a thing and loved; a thing and live. *(At his nest of pillows, he drops.)* Be harder, colder, a rock or polyurethane, that's my advice. Be a thing and live . . . that's my advice. . . . *(He is on his back now, clutching his garbage can and his bottle. He turns onto his side as if to sleep. Bonnie walks to him and stands looking down.)*

BONNIE: Boy, Eddie, you are just transforming right before my eyes, and I used to have an entirely optimistic opinion of you. What is going on with you? *(She pokes him with her foot.)*

EDDIE *(he tries to look up)*: Pardon me?

BONNIE: You know what I'm saying. I mean, you were once upon a time a totally admirable person, but it's reached the point I feel like a goddamn magnifying glass couldn't find what's left of your good points.

EDDIE: Suck my dick.

BONNIE: I'm being serious here, Eddie, I thought you had this girlfriend and it was a significant, you know, mutually fulfilling relationship, but you're hardly a viable social entity at the moment, that's what I think.

EDDIE: Things have taken a turn for the worse, that's all. Suck my dick, Bonnie.

BONNIE: Like what?

EDDIE: Everything has gotten relatively unconventional within me, but who'm I going to complain to? *(Turning away as if to hide or sleep.)* Who's listenin'? And even if they are, what can they do about it?

BONNIE: I'm listenin'.

EDDIE: She doesn't love me.

BONNIE: Who?

EDDIE: My girlfriend.

BONNIE: Whata you mean?

EDDIE: Whata you mean, whata I mean? She doesn't love me. *(Trying to get away, crawling, and dragging with him his bottle, his garbage can, his pillow. He doesn't get far, but has a new nest of sorts.)* Is that some sort of arcane, totally off-the-wall, otherworldly sentiment that I am some oddity to find distressing so that nobody to whom I mention it has any personal reference by which they can understand me? What is going on here? My girlfriend doesn't love me.

BONNIE: Sure she does.

EDDIE: No.

BONNIE: Why?

EDDIE: I don't know, but she doesn't.

BONNIE: Are you sure?

EDDIE *(angry, pounding on the pillow in petulance, having a little fit)*: She's out of town all the time. She's always out of town. She takes every job that comes across her desk, you know, as long as it takes her out of town.

BONNIE: So you miss her.

EDDIE: She's a photographer, you know. Fuck her. There's pictures here. It's Hollywood.

BONNIE: Sure. You should tell her.

EDDIE: Talking about love makes you feel like you're watching TV, Bonnie, that why you're so interested? *(Suddenly sitting up, startled, focusing on her.)* I'm real, Bonnie. I'm real. I'm not a goddamn TV image in front of you, here; this is real. I'm a real person, Bonnie, you know that, right? Suck my dick.

BONNIE: You know, if your manner of speech is in any way a reflection of what goes on in your head, Eddie, it's a wonder you can tie your shoes.

EDDIE: You're right. You ever have that experience where your thoughts are like these totally separate, totally self-sustaining phone booths in this vast uninhabited shopping mall in your head? You ever have that experience? My inner monologue has taken on certain disquieting characteristics, I mean, I don't feel loved. Even if she loves me, I don't feel it. I don't feel loved, and I'm sick of it, you know what I mean?

BONNIE: I'm gonna go.

EDDIE: What for?

BONNIE: Home. I'm going home. Maybe you been doin' too much shit, Eddie. Even outlaws have to take precautionary measures.

EDDIE: Says who?

(Artie and Mickey come in the door. Mickey heads up to his room, while Artie goes to the kitchen for a drink.)

MICKEY: Hi.
ARTIE: Hey.

BONNIE: I'm going home. (*Eddie is scrambling to his feet, trying to appear okay.*)

MICKEY: How was your date?

ARTIE: We saw your date out in the bushes there like a madman. What's the haps, here, huh?

BONNIE: The hell with the bunch of you.

EDDIE: He threw her out of her car. (*Staggering to the couch where he flops down.*)

BONNIE: Can't you just keep your mouth shut, Eddie? Does everybody have to know?

EDDIE: Suck my dick.

BONNIE (*heading for the door*): Good-bye.

ARTIE: Whata you doin' tomorrow, Bonnie?

BONNIE: Why?

ARTIE: I wanna know.

BONNIE: I don't wanna tell you, it's none of your business, I'm taking my kid to Disneyland. We're goin' for the day, so I won't be home.

EDDIE: You haven't been to Disneyland yet?

BONNIE: Of course we been. We been a hundred times. We like it.

ARTIE: I'll go with you.

BONNIE: You wanna?

ARTIE: Sure.

BONNIE: Great. Come by about eleven.

ARTIE: Okay.

BONNIE: Bye. (*As she goes out the door, Mickey comes down the stairs and crosses into the kitchen to join Artie.*)

MICKEY: Bye.

ARTIE: Bye.

EDDIE: You guys see Phil outside?

ARTIE: So she likes to be thrown out of cars. I threw a bitch out of bed once.

EDDIE: It ain't the same thing.

ARTIE: Did I say it was?

MICKEY: What happened?

EDDIE: You implied it.

ARTIE: She was harassing me. We were ballin' away, she's tellin' me, "Faster, faster, slower, higher, do this, do that. Faster. Higher." So I says to her, "Hey, listen, am I in your way here, or what?" (*The front door opens, and Phil comes in carrying a baby wrapped in a blanket.*)

PHIL: I got my baby.

ARTIE: What?

MICKEY: Phil.

PHIL: I got my baby.

MICKEY: Whata you mean?

PHIL: I went and took her.

ARTIE: He got his kid. You got your kid, Phil.

MICKEY: Where's your wife?

PHIL: Sleepin'.

MICKEY: She doesn't know? *(Tentatively, Artie and Mickey move to gather around Phil and peek at the baby.)*

PHIL: I snuck. I coulda been anybody. I coulda done anything. You like her?

ARTIE: You kidnaped her.

PHIL: You want me to kill you, Artie? This is my baby here. She's mine.

MICKEY: She looks like you, Phil.

ARTIE: Around the eyes.

MICKEY: And the mouth. Look at the mouth. That's Phil's mouth.

PHIL: I don't see it.

ARTIE: It's unmistakable.

MICKEY: You don't see it in the eyes?

PHIL: No, I look real hard, and I try like to think I'm looking into my own eyes, but I don't see anything of my own at all. I wish I did. Nothing familiar. Just this baby. Cute. But like I found her.

ARTIE: Look how she's looking at you.

PHIL: They can't see. It's the sound vibrations and this big blur far away like a cloud, that's all. Wanna hold her, Eddie?

EDDIE: My hands are dirty.

PHIL: 'At's okay. You want her, Mickey?

MICKEY: Sure.

PHIL *(carefully he passes the baby to Mickey)*: She's light as a little feather, huh? You can hold her in one hand.

ARTIE: Does she cry?

PHIL: She's very good-natured.

MICKEY: What if she cries? *(Mickey, eager to get rid of the baby, passes her to Eddie.)*

ARTIE: Tell her a joke.

EDDIE *(taking the baby)*: Ohh, she's real cute. What's happenin', little baby? Makes me miss my kid, huh?

ARTIE: Makes me miss my kid.

MICKEY: I got two of 'em.

EDDIE: This really makes me hate my ex-wife. *(Eddie laughs a little, and looks at Mickey, who laughs.)* I mean, I really hate my ex-wife. *(Now they start to make jokes, trying to break each other up, and top each other, all except, of course, Phil.)*

ARTIE: And this little innocent thing here, this sweet little innocent thing is a broad of the future.

MICKEY: Hard to believe, huh?

EDDIE: Awesome.

ARTIE: Depressing.

EDDIE: Maybe if we kept her and raised her, she could grow up and be a decent human being.

MICKEY: Unless it's just biologically and genetically inevitable that at a certain age they go nasty.

PHIL: Except for the great ones.

MICKEY: The great ones come along once in a lifetime.

ARTIE: Not in my lifetime.

PHIL: Like the terrific athletes of any given generation, there's only a few.

MICKEY: You think it might be wise or unwise to pay attention to the implications of what we're saying here?

EDDIE: Who has time?

MICKEY: Right. Who has time?

EDDIE: It's hard enough to say what you're sayin', let alone to consider the goddamn implications.

ARTIE: Lemme see her, okay? *(As the baby is briefly in Phil's hands while on her way from Eddie to Artie, Phil stares at the child.)*

PHIL: We was all that little: each one of us. I'm gonna ask Susie to give me one more try. Just one more. I'm gonna beg her.

MICKEY: You oughta call her, Phil; tell her you got the kid, anyway.

PHIL: I'll take the kid back. I'll beg her. I can beg.

EDDIE: Phil, listen to me; you're a rare fuckin' human being. Underneath it all, you got this goddamn potential, this unbelievable potential. You really do; you could channel it.

PHIL *(unable to look at Eddie, he pulls away)*: I mean, I'm startin' in my car again, Eddie. I was three days on the highway last week. Three whole days with nothing but gas station attendants. You know what I'm sayin', Eddie? I'll beg her. I'll follow her around on my hands and knees throughout the house. I won't let her out of my sight. *(Artie yelps and stares down at the baby.)* What happened?

ARTIE *(hurrying to pass the baby back to her father)*: She shit herself.

MICKEY: Look at that smile. Ohhh, she shit herself, and look at that big smile.

PHIL *(cradling the baby)*: They're very honest.

ARTIE: Yeah, well, she's a broad already, Phil. Just like every other broad I ever met, she hadda dump on me.

ACT THREE

Scene I

(Time: Several days later, early evening.)

(Place: The same.)

(Mickey and Darlene are laughing. They are at the breakfast nook counter, Mickey behind it, pouring wine, while Darlene is seated in front of it.)

MICKEY: All I said was "Has anybody seen him levitate?" So she says to me, "Well, he's an honest person and he has been working at it for years, so if he says he levitates, I see no reason for you to doubt it."

DARLENE: Yeah, Mickey, what are you, a cynic?

MICKEY: I mean, not only is she miffed at me, but the entire room is in sympathy. This is the group consensus: The guy has worked at it, so for asking a question such as, "Has anybody seen him levitate?" I'm crude. Or I don't know what.

DARLENE (tapping his nose with her forefinger): Bad, bad, bad. Bad, bad.

(As Mickey imitates the moans of a guilty dog, Eddie comes in through the front door and stands for a beat, looking at them.)

EDDIE: Bad what?

MICKEY: Dog.

DARLENE: Hi, honey.

(Everyone, a little embarrassed, is avoiding one another's eyes.)

MICKEY: We were talking about that levitation guy, right?

DARLENE: Which led to bad dog. Somehow.

EDDIE: It would have to.

MICKEY: I think it was a logical but almost untraceable sequence of associations.

EDDIE: Been waiting long?

(Mickey and Darlene speak almost simultaneously.)

DARLENE: No.

MICKEY: Yeah. (Pause.) I have, she hasn't. I gotta go.

EDDIE: Phil call?

MICKEY (rushing about now, preparing to leave): Not that I know of. How's he doin'?

EDDIE: I got a lot of frantic messages at work, and when I tried his house, Susie called me an "asshole" and hung up, and from then on the phone was off the hook. So much for reconciliation.

MICKEY: It would appear they've found a pattern to their liking.

DARLENE: I mean, Phil's a lot of fun, but on a day-to-day basis, I would have to have a lot of sympathy for Susie.

EDDIE (heading to the kitchen and the refrigerator): She's a very sympathetic bitch. That's her staple attribute.

MICKEY (near the door): You want me to try and hook up with you later, or you up for privacy?

EDDIE: Depends on do I locate Phil or not.

DARLENE: You could call, or we could leave a message.

MICKEY: I'll check my service. See you. (Mickey goes out the door.)

EDDIE: Let's just hang around a little in case he calls.

DARLENE: I'm tired anyway.

EDDIE: It's the kid thing, you know, that's the thing. He could walk in a second it wasn't for the kid.

DARLENE: He should have then.

EDDIE: Exactly. But he couldn't. *(Heading for the stairs, beginning to take off his jacket.)* So what am I talking about? It's just a guy like Phil, for all his appearances, this is what can make him nuts. You don't ever forget about 'em if you're a guy like Phil. I mean, my little girl is a factor in every calculation I make — big or small — she's a constant. You can imagine, right?

DARLENE: Sure. I had a, you know — and that was — well, rough, so I have some sense of it, really, in a very funny way.

EDDIE *(as he goes into his bedroom)*: What?

DARLENE: My abortion. I got pregnant. I wasn't sure exactly which guy — I wasn't going crazy or anything with a different guy every night or anything, and I knew them both very well, but I was just not emotionally involved with either one of them, seriously. *(Emerging from the bedroom, he freezes, staring down at her, his shirt half off.)* Though I liked them both. A lot. Which in a way made the whole thing even more confusing on a personal level, and you know, in terms of trying to figure out the morality of the whole thing, so I finally had this abortion completely on my own without telling anybody, not even my girlfriends. I kept thinking in my mind that it wasn't a complete baby, which it wasn't, not a fully developed person, but a fetus which it was, and that I would have what I would term a real child later, but nevertheless, I had these nightmares and totally unexpected feelings in which in my dreams I imagined the baby as this teenager, a handsome boy of real spiritual consequences, which now the world would have to do without, and he was always like a refugee, full of regret, like this treasure that had been lost in some uncalled-for way, like when a person of great potential is hit by a car. I felt I had no one to blame but myself, and I went sort of out of my mind for a while, so my parents sent me to Puerto Rico for a vacation, and I got myself back together there enough to come home with my head on my shoulders at least semistraight. I was functional, anyway. Semifunctional, anyway. But then I told everybody what had happened. I went from telling nobody to everybody.

EDDIE: This was . . .

DARLENE: What?

EDDIE: When?

DARLENE: Seven-and-a-half years ago.

EDDIE: That's what I mean, though; those feelings.

DARLENE: I know. I understood, see, that was what you meant, which was my reason for trying to make the effort to bring it up, because I don't talk about it all that much at all anymore, but I wanted you to know that when you said that about your daughter, I, in fact, in a visceral sense, knew what you were talking about.

EDDIE (*moving down the stairs toward her, as it seems they agree on every-thing*): I mean, everybody has this baggage, and you can't ignore it or what are you doing?

DARLENE: You're just ignoring it.

EDDIE: You're just ignoring the person then, that's all. But at the same time your own feelings are — it's overwhelming or at least it can be. You can't take it all on.

DARLENE: No.

EDDIE (*holding her hand, he pats her in consolation*): There's nothing I can do about all that, you know, that happened to you.

DARLENE: No.

EDDIE: It really messed you up, though.

DARLENE: For a while. But I learned certain things from it, too, you know.

EDDIE (*still holding her hand*): Sure.

DARLENE: It was painful, but I learned these things that have been a help ever since, so something came out of it good.

EDDIE: So . . . these two guys. . . . Where are they?

DARLENE: Oh, I have no idea. This was in Cincinnati.

EDDIE: Right. (*Now he rises and begins mixing drinks for them both.*)

DARLENE: I don't know what happened to them. I think one got married and I have this vague sense that — I don't know what EXACTLY — but . . . No. I can't remember. But I have this sense that SOMETHING happened to him. I don't know what. Anyway, I rarely think about it anymore. I'm a very different person.

EDDIE: Did . . . they know each other?

DARLENE: The two guys?

EDDIE: Yeah.

DARLENE: No. I mean, not that I know of. Why?

EDDIE: Just wondering.

DARLENE: What?

EDDIE: Nothing. Just . . . you know.

DARLENE: You must have been wondering something. People don't just wonder nothing.

EDDIE: No, no. I was just wondering, you know, was it a pattern? That's all.

DARLENE: No.

EDDIE: I mean, don't get irritated. You asked me.

DARLENE: You asked me. I mean, I was trying to tell you something else entirely.

EDDIE: I know that.

DARLENE: So what's the point?

EDDIE: I'm aware absolutely of what you were trying to tell me. And I heard it. But am I just supposed to totally narrow down my whole set of perceptions, just filter out everything, just censor everything that doesn't support your intention? I made an association. And it was not an unreasonable association.

DARLENE: It was totally off the wall, and hostile.

EDDIE: Hostile?

DARLENE: And you know it.

EDDIE: Give me a break! What? I'm supposed to sit still for the most arcane association I ever heard in my life, that levitation leads to dogs? But should I come up with an equally — I mean, equally, shit — when I come up with a hundred percent more logical association, I'm supposed to accept your opinion that it isn't?

DARLENE: No, no, no.

EDDIE: Well, that's all it was. An association. That's all it was.

DARLENE: Okay.

EDDIE: I mean, for everybody's good, it appeared to me a thought worth some exploration, and if I was wrong, and I misjudged, then I'm sorry.

DARLENE: It's just something I'm very, sometimes, sensitive about.

EDDIE: Sure. What? The abortion.

DARLENE: Yeah.

EDDIE *(handing her the drink, he pats her hand)*: Sure. Okay, though? You okay now? You feel okay?

DARLENE: I'm hungry. You hungry?

EDDIE: I mean, if we don't talk these things out, we'll just end up with all this, you know, unspoken shit, following us around. You wanna go out and eat? Let's go out. What are you hungry for? How about Chinese?

DARLENE: Sure.

EDDIE *(grabbing up the phone and starting to dial)*: We could go to Mr. Chou's. Treat ourselves right.

DARLENE: That's great. I love the seaweed.

EDDIE: I mean, you want Chinese?

DARLENE: I love Mr. Chou's.

EDDIE: We could go some other place. How about Ma Maison?

DARLENE: Sure.

EDDIE *(hanging up the phone)*: You like that better than Mr. Chou's?

DARLENE: I don't like it better, but it's great. Which one is your preference?

EDDIE: Well, I want — you know — this should be — I'd like this to be your choice.

DARLENE: It doesn't matter to me.

EDDIE: Which one should I call?

DARLENE: Surprise me.

EDDIE: I don't want to surprise you. I want to, you know, do whatever you say.

DARLENE: Then just pick one. Call one. Either.

EDDIE: I mean, why should I have to guess? I don't want to guess. Just tell me. I mean, what if I pick the wrong one?

DARLENE: You can't pick the wrong one. Honestly, Eddie, I like them both the same. I like them both exactly the same.

EDDIE: Exactly?

DARLENE: Yes. I like them both.

EDDIE: I mean, how can you possibly think you like them both the same? One is French and one is Chinese. They're different. They're as different as — I mean, what is the world, one big blur to you out there in which everything that bears some resemblance to something else is just automatically put at the same level in your hierarchy, for chrissake, Darlene, the only thing they have in common is that they're both restaurants!

DARLENE: Are you aware that you're yelling?

EDDIE: My voice is raised for emphasis, which is a perfectly legitimate use of volume. Particularly when, in addition, I evidently have to break through this goddamn cloud in which you are obviously enveloped in which everything is just this blur totally void of the most rudimentary sort of distinction.

DARLENE: Just call the restaurant, why don't you?

EDDIE: Why are you doing this?

DARLENE: I'm hungry. I'm just trying to get something to eat before I faint.

EDDIE: The fuck you are. You're up to something.

DARLENE: What do you mean, what am I up to? You're telling me I don't know if I'm hungry or not? I'm hungry!

EDDIE: Bullshit!

DARLENE *(leaping up from her chair, she strides across the room)*: "Up to?" Paranoia, Eddie. Para-fucking-noia. Be alert. Your tendencies are coming out all over the place.

EDDIE: I'm fine.

DARLENE *(pacing near the base of the stairs)*: I mean, to stand there screeching at me about what-am-I-up-to is paranoid.

EDDIE: Not if you're up to something, it's not.

DARLENE: I'm not. Take my word for it, you're acting a little nuts.

EDDIE: I'm supposed to trust your judgment of my mental stability? I'm supposed to trust your evaluation of the nuances of my sanity? You can't even tell the difference between a French and a Chinese restaurant!

DARLENE: I like them both.

EDDIE: But they're different. One is French, and the other is Chinese. They are totally fucking different.

DARLENE: Not in my inner, subjective, emotional experience of them.

EDDIE: The tastes, the decors, the waiters, the accents. The fucking accents. The little phrases the waiters say. And they yell at each other in these whole totally different languages, does none of this make an impression on you?

DARLENE: It impresses me that I like them both.

EDDIE: Your total inner emotional subjective experience must be THIS EPIC FUCKING FOG! I mean, what are you on, some sort of dualistic trip and everything is in twos and you just can't tell which is which so you're just pulled taut between them on this goddamn high wire between people who might like to have some kind of definitive reaction from you in order to know!

DARLENE: Fuck you!

EDDIE: What's wrong with that?

DARLENE: Is that what this is all about? Those two guys. I happened to mention two guys!

EDDIE: I just want to know if this is a pattern. Chinese restaurants and you can't tell the difference between people. *(They stand, staring at each other.)*

DARLENE: Oh, Eddie. Oh, Eddie, Eddie.

EDDIE: What?

DARLENE: Oh, Eddie, Eddie. *(Moving to the couch, she slumps down, sits there.)*

EDDIE: What?

DARLENE: I just really feel awful. This is really depressing. I really like you. I really do.

EDDIE: I mean . . .

DARLENE: What?

EDDIE: Well, don't feel too bad, okay?

DARLENE: I do, I feel bad. I feel bad.

EDDIE *(moving now, he sits down on the edge of the armchair, and leans toward her)*: But, I mean, just — we have to talk about these things, right? That's all. This is okay.

DARLENE: No, no.

EDDIE: Just don't — you know, on the basis of this, make any sort of grand, kind of overwhelming, comprehensive, kind of, you know, totally conclusive assessment here. That would be absurd, you know. I mean, this is an isolated, individual thing here, and —

DARLENE: No.

EDDIE *(moving to the couch, he tries to get close to her, settles on his knees on the floor beside the couch)*: Sure. I mean, sometimes what is it? It's stuff, other stuff; stuff under stuff, you're doing one thing you think it's something else. I mean, it's always there, the family thing, the childhood thing, it's — sometimes it comes up. I go off. I'm not even where I seem anymore. I'm not there.

DARLENE: Eddie, I think I should go.

EDDIE: I'm trying to explain.

DARLENE *(sliding away from him)*: I know all about it.

EDDIE: Whata you know all about?

DARLENE: Your fucking childhood, Eddie. You tol' me.

EDDIE: Whata you know?

DARLENE: I know all I — what is this, a test? I mean, I know: Your parents were these religious lunatics, these pious frauds, who periodically beat the shit out of you.

EDDIE: They weren't just religious, and they didn't just —

DARLENE: Your father was a minister, I know.

EDDIE: What denomination?

DARLENE: Fuck you. *(She bolts away, starts gathering up her things: She's going to leave.)*

EDDIE: You said you knew.

DARLENE: I don't think there's a lot more we ought to, with any, you know, honesty, allow ourselves in the way of bullshit about our backgrounds to exonerate what is our just plain mean behavior to one another.

EDDIE: That's not what I'm doing.

DARLENE: So, what are you doing?

EDDIE (*following her*): They took me in the woods; they prayed and then they beat the shit out of me; they prayed and beat me with sticks. He talked in tongues.

DARLENE: She broke your nose and blacked your eyes, I know.

EDDIE: Because I wanted to watch "Range Rider" on TV, and she considered it a violent program. (*Phone rings.*) So she broke my nose. That's insane.

DARLENE: But I don't care, Eddie. I don't care. (*She's really ready to go now.*)

EDDIE: Whata you mean?

DARLENE: I mean, it doesn't matter. (*She steps for the door.*)

EDDIE: It doesn't matter? What are you talking about? (*Grabbing her by the arm to detain her.*)

DARLENE: It doesn't.

EDDIE: No, no, no. (*As he grabs up the phone and yells into it.*) Hold on. (*Clutching Darlene in one hand and the phone in the other, he turns to her.*) No, no; it matters, and you care. What you mean is, it doesn't make any difference. (*Releasing her, he speaks into the phone.*) Hello.

DARLENE: I can't stand this goddamn semantic insanity anymore, Eddie — I can't be that specific about my feelings — I can't. Will you get off the phone!

EDDIE (*into the phone*): What? Oh, no. No, no. Oh, no.

DARLENE: What?

EDDIE: (*into phone*): Wait there. There. I'll come over. (*He hangs up and stands.*)

DARLENE: Eddie, what? You look terrible. What? (*He starts toward the front door.*) Eddie, who was that? What happened? Eddie!

EDDIE: Phil's dead.

DARLENE: What?

EDDIE: Car. Car.

DARLENE: Oh, Eddie, Eddie.

EDDIE: What?

DARLENE: I'm so sorry.

(*Eddie gives her a look and goes, and as he leaves her alone in the room, "Someone to Watch Over Me" sung by Willie Nelson starts to play.*)

(*Blackout.*)

(*The music continues.*)

Scene 2

(*Time: Several days later. Evening.*)

(*Place: The same.*)

(*In the dark "Someone to Watch Over Me" continues. Mickey, Artie, and Eddie come in through the front door. They wear dark suits. Eddie is carrying a stack of mail. As Mickey turns on the lights, the music goes out.*)

ARTIE: So now what? (*Eddie walks to the kitchen, where he stands sorting the mail, while Mickey, oddly buoyant, straightens up the room a little.*)

MICKEY: I'm beat. What's his name, his agent, wasn't there. You see him?

ARTIE: He's an asshole. (*Settling into the swivel stool at the counter.*) He probably would have gone berserk to be at Phil's funeral. I was almost berserk.

MICKEY: So it was just as well he didn't come.

ARTIE: Fuck him. There's no excuse.

MICKEY: Funerals aren't for everybody, Artie. You know. Life . . . isn't for everybody. As Phil demonstrated. Life wasn't for him. (*Moving behind the counter, he empties an ashtray in the waste can.*)

ARTIE: You think he meant it?

MICKEY: As much as he meant anything. How you doin'?

ARTIE: I'm okay. Except I feel, though, somewhat like at any moment I could turn into a hysterical like, you know, rabbit.

MICKEY: Yeah. What would that be like?

ARTIE: I think I'm gonna go home. I think I'm gonna go home, Eddie. What time is it? I'm whipped.

MICKEY: Ten twenty . . . two.

ARTIE: Ten? Ten? It feels like goddamn four in the morning. I feel like I been awake for years.

MICKEY: It's ten twenty-two.

ARTIE: It is, isn't it. My watch is stopped. What happened to my watch? I'm whipped. It takes it out of you, huh, Eddie, a day like this.

MICKEY: Death . . . takes it out of you?

ARTIE: Yeah.

EDDIE: What you gonna do tomorrow?

ARTIE: I got a bunch of meetings. We got a development deal.

EDDIE: Yeah?

ARTIE: Set, too. On paper. Good terms; very good terms. Terms I'm totally overjoyed about. (*There is an echo in this of their first-act scene: Artie is aggressive and positive here; he is not going to let Eddie get at him again.*)

EDDIE (*smiling*): Come by, okay?

ARTIE: Sure. Late. (*Starting for the door.*)

EDDIE: Whatever.

ARTIE: Take care, you guys.

MICKEY: You, too, Artie. Fuck him, huh? *(At the door, Artie hesitates, glances back.)*

ARTIE: The jerk-off. *(He goes.)*

(Mickey, crossing behind Eddie, pats him lightly on the back.)

MICKEY: How you doin', Edward?

EDDIE: I don't know. You?

MICKEY: Okay. *(Starting for the stairs.)*

EDDIE: Oh, I'm okay. I mean, I'm okay. Is that what you're askin'?

MICKEY: Yeah.

EDDIE: Yeah, shit. I'm okay.

MICKEY: Good.

(As Mickey climbs the stairs, Eddie freezes and stands staring at a letter.)

EDDIE: Holy Jesus holy Christ, I got a letter. Phil. Phil.

MICKEY: What?

EDDIE *(tearing open the letter)*: Yeah.

MICKEY: What's it say? *(Coming to the stairway rail to stare down at Eddie.)*

EDDIE: What? WHAT? *(Reads.)* "The guy who dies in an accident understands the nature of destiny. Phil."

MICKEY: What?

EDDIE: That's what it says. *(Handing the letter up through the rails to Mickey, Eddie is examining the envelope.)* It's postmarked — the — this is the day. He mailed it on the day.

MICKEY *(staring at the letter)*: "The guy who dies in an accident understands the nature of destiny."

EDDIE: To die in — what the fuck? I mean, Mickey, what, what, what?

MICKEY *(with a shrug)*: It's a fucking fortune cookie. *(He hands the letter back down to Eddie, who takes it.)*

EDDIE: I mean, if he killed himself, this is the note.

MICKEY: Whata you mean "if"?

EDDIE: I'm giving him the benefit of the doubt. *(Sitting back against the swivel chair to intently study the letter.)*

MICKEY: Eddie, c'mon, you wanna look this thing in the eye. You don't do a hundred down that narrow crease in the high ground because you're anxious to get home. A hundred MPH down Mulholland on a star-filled night is not the way to longevity. The guy behaved often, and finally, like some, you know, soulful jerk-off. Fuck him and forget him. What more can I say. *(He starts for his room.)*

EDDIE: I'm gonna look up the words. *(Standing up, he heads for the stairway.)*

MICKEY: What?

EDDIE: On the thing here, I'm gonna see if the dictionary might help.

MICKEY (*as Eddie comes running up the stairs*): Look up the words? Are you out of your mind? Don't get involved in this thing. Don't waste your time.

EDDIE: But this is it — this is what he wanted to tell us. (*Eddie goes into his bedroom.*)

MICKEY: He had somethin' to say he could a give us a phone call; he could have stopped by; our door was open. He wants to get some information to me now, he's going to have to bridge the gap directly; he's going to have to make an appearance, difficult as it might be. (*Eddie, carrying a dictionary, comes out of the bedroom.*) Listen to me: Stay away from this shit. He's dead: He didn't want to discuss it before, I don't want to discuss it after. (*He grabs the dictionary from Eddie's hands.*) He had enough to keep him goin', Eddie — the wife, the kid, the career was decent — blah, blah, blah — but he had some secrets and he kept 'em, they ate a hole in his brain where his self-restraint might have been, his sense of proportion might have lingered, and without that —

EDDIE (*grabbing the dictionary back*): But that's exactly what I'm talking about — this is the clue. To something. Maybe why. I want to know why. (*And Eddie heads down the stairs with Mickey rushing after him.*)

MICKEY: What why? There's no why in a disaster like this. You know, the earth moved. He was in the wrong place; this big hole opens up, what's he gonna do?

EDDIE: Your attitude, Mickey — will you please examine your fucking attitude?

MICKEY: This is a dead end is all I'm saying. There's no traffic with this thing. You go in, you don't come out. The guy made a decision beyond communication.

EDDIE (*waving the note at Mickey, who grabs it*): He left a note.

MICKEY: The note is tangential. It's part of his goof, you know, that he was a rational human being, when he wasn't. (*Balling up the note, he throws it on the floor.*) I want no part of this fucking, beyond-the-grave extension of his jerk-off sensibility.

EDDIE (*grabbing the note up protectively, he smooths it out on the kitchen counter in preparation to study it*): The note is what he wanted us to think.

MICKEY: Bullshit.

EDDIE: He left it.

MICKEY: To drive us nuts from long distance. Lemme see that — what is this?

(*Mickey grabs the note and paces around while Eddie, sitting on the swivel chair on the living room side of the counter, focuses on the dictionary.*)

EDDIE: I'm gonna look up the words.

MICKEY: It's a fucking fortune cookie. What's to look up? "A guy who." That's him. "Dies." In case we didn't know, he gave us a demonstration. "Accident" is to propel yourself into a brief but unsustainable orbit, and then attempt to land in a tree on the side of a clifflike incline. "Understand" is what he had no part of. "Nature" is the tree, and "destiny" is, if you're him, you're an asshole.

EDDIE *(he is busily turning pages in the dictionary)*: Look. Count the letters.

MICKEY: What?

EDDIE: Count the words and the letters, I want to know how many letters.

MICKEY: Eddie, this is dementia, here. You've flipped a circuit. Grief has put you out of order.

EDDIE: You never heard of an anagram?

MICKEY: Sure.

EDDIE: So maybe it's an anagram.

MICKEY: You think this is an anagram?

EDDIE: I'd like to find out.

MICKEY: You think this is an anagram?

EDDIE *(leaping up, Eddie grabs Mickey by the arm and marches him to the armchair where he sits Mickey down, handing him a pencil)*: You don't have to have any faith in the fucking thought, but just as a favor, you know, participate, okay. Help me move it along. That's all I'm asking. And keep your sarcasm to yourself.

MICKEY: What sarcasm?

EDDIE *(getting back to the counter, the dictionary)*: Can you do that?

MICKEY: What sarcasm? I'm — you know — this is — What sarcasm? This is insulting.

EDDIE: You're getting sidetracked.

MICKEY: I'll do this goddamn lunacy. I'll count the letters here, but get one thing straight, all right? There's no sarcasm here. *(He is so irritated, he cannot stay seated. He's up, he's down, dropping the pencil, picking it up, he steps toward Eddie, then back to the armchair.)* I've indulged in nothing even remotely sarcastic here, and I want that understood because you have obviously not understood it. So I'll make allowances, but if I've been flip, it's to put some humor into what could be totally and utterly morbid — and there have been times in the goddamn history of mankind where a little humor won a person some affection for the effort, you know, not to go under; anybody can go under. I mean, we're all goin' fuckin' under, so how about a little laugh along the way? So I'm flip. So what!

EDDIE: I don't feel like being flip.

MICKEY: Right. But you wanna do a goddamn anagram, right? On his death note. Whata you expect to uncover, the buried treasure of his midlife crisis, and how it might hope to be viewed retrospectively? Fine. I'll give you a hand, but if you think there's blood in this stone, man, just forget about it.

EDDIE: "Flip" IS "sarcastic," Mickey.

MICKEY *(rising, starting to cross toward Eddie)*: It is not. It's — "flip." On a whole other level, a whole other lower level and just lighter.

EDDIE: To me, it's "sarcastic." *(Eddie is bowed over the dictionary, his fingers marking pages as Mickey, carrying the note comes up behind him.)*

MICKEY: But that's crazy! Sarcastic is "heavy." It's mean. Funny, sure, but mean. I do both, but this was flip.

EDDIE: You shoulda heard yourself.

MICKEY: I did.

EDDIE: You shoulda listened closer.

MICKEY: You wanna get on with this. *(He crosses around to the kitchen side of the counter and flops into the other swivel chair, starting to pour himself a drink.)* So whata you got there?

EDDIE *(reading from the dictionary)*: So I have "accident" here, and "destiny." "Accident: a happening that is not expected, foreseen, or intended. Two, an unfortunate occurrence or mishap, sudden fall, collision, usually resulting in physical injury." Blah-blah, just repeats basically. And "destiny," we have, "The inevitable or necessary succession of events. What will necessarily happen to any person or thing." So, if you die in a happening that is not expected, foreseen, or intended, you understand the inevitable or necessary succession of events.

MICKEY: Fuck him. *(He tosses the note into the trash can.)*

EDDIE: It makes sense.

MICKEY *(moving off toward the couch and TV)*: It makes no sense.

EDDIE *(following Mickey)*: I mean, we owe him to understand as best we can what he wanted. Nobody has to believe it.

MICKEY: Anyway, he did it on purpose, so it was no goddamn accident. *(Sitting down on the couch, Mickey grabs the* TV Guide.*)* And if it was no accident, then his note is categorically, definitively irrelevant.

EDDIE *(sinking onto the edge of the armchair, squeezing the dictionary, looking at Mickey)*: But how did he get there? Exactly how did he get to that point where in his own mind he could do it on purpose? That's what —

MICKEY: It's not that big a deal — that's the fucking truth, you know, you make an adjustment, that's all — you shift your point a view a little and what was horrible looks okay. All the necessary information that might deter you gets locked away. Little gremlins divert the good thoughts so you don't hear them. You just hear the bad thoughts, which at this point are convincing you they're a good idea. *(Rising, loosening his tie, taking off his jacket, Mickey moves toward the kitchen.)* You get an idea, that's all. You don't understand the scope of it; you just lose the scope of it. So there you are, foot's on the gas, you're flying. So far so good. No big deal. Road, trees, radio. What's a little flick of the steering wheel? Maybe an inch's rotation. Nothing to it. An inch, what's that? So you do it. *(From the cabinets he grabs a bowl and a box of Cheerios.)* But with that, what? You've gone beyond what you can come back from. You've handed control over now, it's gravity and this big machine, which is a car, who are in charge now. Only it's not a car anymore. It's this hunk of metal rearranging itself according to the laws of physics, force and reaction, stress and resistance; heat, friction, collapse, and then you're gone, who knows where. *(With a shrug, he heads triumphantly for the refrigerator to get some milk.)*

EDDIE: So how many letters?

MICKEY: Right. The fucking anagram. This is exciting, Eddie; I've never been involved with a being from another planet before. *(Picking the crumpled note from the trash can, he tosses it toward Eddie.)* Twelve and fifty-four. *(The note lands on the floor, and Mickey pours milk on his cereal.)*

EDDIE: Twelve words and fifty-four letters. That's interesting. *(Picking up the note.)*

MICKEY: It's interesting, huh?

EDDIE *(with the note and dictionary, he settles on the floor, making a little desk of the coffee table)*: Don't you see?

MICKEY *(standing behind the counter, he eats)*: You're in charge here, Eddie.

EDDIE: But don't you see?

MICKEY: Yes. I almost see.

EDDIE: I mean, they're both even. For one thing. There's lots of relationships.

MICKEY: Can I ask you something?

EDDIE: Sure. No!

MICKEY: I can't?

EDDIE: No.

MICKEY: How ripped are you?

EDDIE: I don't have time for your question. *(Furious, Eddie rises up on his knees.)* You can make a worthwhile contribution to this project here, or you can forget about it, but your animosity, or whatever it is — resistance — it's nothing but static. I need some goddamn support and you're delivering all this — whatever it is. I mean, give me a break.

MICKEY: Common sense.

EDDIE *(advancing on Mickey, carrying the dictionary and note)*: Is that what you think you're going to talk me into? Like what, for example, based on your vast experience with common sense is the take on this?

MICKEY: It happens.

EDDIE *(something wild is entering into Eddie as he faces Mickey across the counter)*: "It happens?" On a friend's death, you absolutely ransack the archives of your whole thing and come up with "It happens." *(As it appears Eddie is now going to work on the counter, Mickey grabs a* Daily Variety *and starts away.)* You need some help, Mickey. Common sense needs some help.

MICKEY *(moving with his* Daily Variety *to the couch, he flops down to read)*: You need some sleep.

EDDIE *(working at the counter)*: I mean, I think if he did it this way, if it is an anagram, it wouldn't be cryptic. The cryptic element would have been, you know, more than handled by the fact that it was in a fucking anagram to begin with, right?

MICKEY *(reading)*: Sure.

EDDIE: I mean, that makes sense, right?

MICKEY *(turning a page)*: Absolutely.

EDDIE: Mickey, for crissake, have all the goddamn private disdain you want in reserve, but follow the logic of what I'm saying. It's logical.

MICKEY *(glancing up)*: I'm in total fucking agreement. Anagram would more than handle cryptic.

EDDIE: I tried to warn him, you know. She was a snake. And I tried to tell him, you know, she was out to absolutely undermine the little faith he had in himself. I saw it coming; she hadda see it coming. I mean, for all his toughness, he was made out of thin air, he was a pane of glass, and if you went near him, you knew it. I'm gonna call her. *(Whirling, Eddie reaches for the phone.)*

MICKEY: Who? Susie? *(Rushing to the phone to stop Eddie.)* Eddie, you don't know what you're doing. You can't call her up in the middle of the night; she's a widow. She just put her husband in the ground.

EDDIE: I want her to have some fucking cognizance of this event.

MICKEY: She knows.

EDDIE: She killed him? You ain't sayin' she's looking at it from the context she killed him?

MICKEY: What?

EDDIE: You bet you're not because what she knows is he's dead and that's how much better than him she is. No more teddy bears — she's takin' care of business, so she's a together bitch, and he's weak, he punked out. A person cannot keep up their self-respect they know they look like some goddamn crazed insensitive prick who goes around dropping kids out of his life like they're trash to him. I saw it in him. She should have. What the hell was she thinking about?

MICKEY: Herself. I don't know. What do people think about?

EDDIE: Fuck her. What's she got to think about?

MICKEY: She wanted things. I don't know. So she thought about the things she wanted. You want to kill her for what she was doing — to get things she wanted. You can't kill people for that.

EDDIE *(grabbing his box of dope and coke from its shelf under the counter)*: She killed him.

MICKEY: You're gonna die a this shit, Eddie. Does it not cross your mind?

EDDIE: Hey, don't get serious here, Mickey. You know, don't get morbid here and ruin a nice evening. *(Spreading his vials out on the counter.)* Die of it is a little extreme. You have to admit that. And even if it isn't, take care of myself for what? For some state-of-the-art bitch to get her hooks into me. They're fucking ghouls, Mickey. They eat our hearts.

MICKEY: You don't know what you're saying. You don't. *(Pouring a large glass of vodka.)*

EDDIE: I do.

MICKEY (*moving restlessly with his vodka and* Variety, *not quite knowing where to go, he ends up perched then on the edge of the big armchair*): I know what you think you're saying, but you're not saying it.

EDDIE: I do. I do. I know what I'm saying. I don't know what I mean, but I know what I'm saying. Is that what you mean?

MICKEY: Yeah.

EDDIE (*snorting a line of coke off the kitchen counter*): Right. But who knows what anything means, though, huh? It's not like anybody knows that, so at least I know I don't know, which is more than most people. They probably think they know what they mean, not just what they think they mean. You feel that, Mickey, huh? (*He starts to move around behind Mickey, coming up on his right side.*) About death, that when it comes, you're just going along in this goddamn ongoing inner rapateta, rapateta, blah-blah-blah, in which you understand this or that, and tell yourself about it, and then you ricochet on, and then it just cuts out — midsomething. Midrealization. "Oh, now I under — " Blam! You're gone. Wham! Comatose. Dead. You think that's how it is? (*Ending up close to Mickey's head, stretched around the armchair, whispering into Mickey's right ear.*)

MICKEY: I'm going to bed. (*He stands and takes a gulp of vodka.*) And you should, too. Go to bed. You're a mess. Phil would want you to get your rest.

EDDIE: Fuck you about him, Mickey. (*Getting to his feet.*) I mean, where do you get the goddamn cynicism, the goddamn scorn to speak his name, let alone —

MICKEY: Eddie, Eddie, is everything my fault?

EDDIE: What'd you ever do but mock him and put him down?

MICKEY: Relent, I beg you.

EDDIE (*advancing on Mickey*): You ain't saying you ever did one good thing for him, are you, not one helpful thing!?

MICKEY: No, Eddie, what I'm saying is that unlike you, I never lied to him.

EDDIE (*trapping Mickey against the counter*): And you never loved him either.

MICKEY: Right, Eddie. Good taste has no doubt deprived me of a great many things. (*Slipping free now, Mickey glides behind the counter to get a drink.*)

EDDIE: You lie to yourself, Mickey.

MICKEY: Who better?

EDDIE: No guts. No originality; no guts. (*He moves toward the couch, as Mickey, behind the counter is furiously pouring himself some vodka in a water glass.*)

MICKEY: You want this goddamn ultramodern, post-hip, comprehensive, totally fucking cost-efficient explanation of everything by which you uncover the preceding events which determined the following events, but you're not gonna find it. (*And Mickey takes a drink.*)

EDDIE: Says you.

MICKEY: You wanna believe that if you do or don't do certain things now, certain other things will or won't happen down the road, accordingly. You think you're gonna parlay this finely tuned circuitry you have for a brain into some form of major participation in the divine conglomerate, man, but all you're gonna really do is make yourself and everyone around you, nuts. *(And Mickey drinks again.)*

EDDIE: Hey, I'm just tryin' to level out here, Mick — the lobes are humming, you know — I got sonar bouncing off the moon; I got —

MICKEY: I mean, to whatever extent THIS FUCKING TORMENT OF YOURS is over whatshername, Darlene, believe me, she isn't worth it.

EDDIE: Ohhh, that move you made when you gave her up for her own good, that was genius. Whatever prayer I might have had was gone. She had you down as some form of totally unique, altruistic phenomenon, instead of the fact that you had a low opinion of her and what you really wanted was to fuck the bubble-brain Artie had brought us.

MICKEY: So what?

EDDIE: You're not better off than me.

MICKEY: Just slightly.

EDDIE: You don't have any feelings at all.

MICKEY: I don't have your feelings, Eddie; that's all. I have my own. They get me by.

EDDIE: So what kind of friendship is this?

MICKEY: Adequate. Good night. *(Turning, he starts for the stairs.)*

EDDIE: Somethin' terrible is goin' on, Mickey. It's a dark time.

MICKEY: People been sayin' that since the beginning of time, Eddie. Don't feel particularly put upon, okay. Forget about it.

EDDIE: That doesn't mean forget about it. That just means it's been going on a long time.

MICKEY *(at the top of the stairs, he turns to look down)*: I mean, Eddie, it's not the time that's dark, it's just you. You know? It's just you.

EDDIE *(a mix of fury and scorn)*: C'mon, scumbag, where you goin'? We'll rant at the tube.

MICKEY: No.

EDDIE: The tube, the tube — it's the asshole of our times. You'll love it.

MICKEY: Wait up for Phil, why don't you? Wouldn't that be great if Phil came by? To keep you company. I'm sure he will. He always did.

EDDIE *(turning on the TV and getting, instantly "The Tonight Show," the intro music loud)*: I can't hear you, Mickey. I got the tube. The tube and twenty-seven cable channels. I'm set for life.

MICKEY: Good night. *(Mickey goes toward his bedroom door.)*

EDDIE: The tube. The tube. The best and brightest predigested. The dream devoured and turned to incandescent shit. *(Mickey's door slams.)* Fuck you, Mickey. All right. All right. I'm on my own. *(He starts talking to Johnny Carson on the TV.)* How you doin', huh, John? *(Rushes to the counter, his coke vial in his hand. Behind the counter, he pulls out booze bottles, several joints, and then a bunch of vials of pills.)* Hey, Carson! Hey, you motherfucker, huh? It's you and me, that's right. Head to head.

Eyeball to eyeball, John. And I am fortified. *(Holding up his various drugs and vials.)* Here's for my left lobe. Here's for my right lobe. And here's to keep the spark plugs blasting. *(From the TV, the audience is shouting "Yo" to Johnny.)* Yo! Yo! *(Johnny announces that this is "The Tonight Show"'s nineteenth anniversary.)* Your anniversary! Oh, my god. Your anniversary! No, you didn't get my card because I didn't send you a fucking card, John! *(Johnny says that Ed looks like a "large penguin," as Eddie at the counter begins sorting pills from vials; he drops pills into a large water glass.)* Penguins? You think that's funny? Bullshit! Funny is your friends disappearing down roads and hallways. Out of cars and behind closed doors. We got a skull in our skin, John, and we got ghosts. That's funny. *(John talks about "foreplay.")* Foreplay? Foreplay? Grow up! They're talking about quarks. They want us to think about quarks. They're going to teach our children about quarks. And Black Holes. Imagine that. Black holes, John. The heavens. Astronauts, Men in — OH! *(Suddenly remembering.)* This morning, John, there was this guy — *(Running to the TV, carrying his glass of pills and a bottle of booze, which he sets down)* — Oh, you want funny? This one'll put you away, John — *(Grabbing the newspaper.)* We got this guy on the obit page — he WAS an astronaut, who went round the moon and ended up in Congress and had surgery for a malignancy in his nose, then passed away six months later. *(Having rummaged in the paper, he now finds the page.)* I know, I know, it's touchy material, John, but it's rich, it's ripe, you'll love it. His campaign slogan was, "I was privileged to be one of the few who viewed our earth from the moon, and that vision taught me that technology and commitment can overcome any challenge." Here's a guy who went into orbit; he rendezvoused with the moon, and from that vantage what most impressed him was HIS OWN ABILITY TO GET THERE! Hovering in the heavens, what he saw was the MAGNIFICENCE OF MEN AND MACHINES! HE MIGHT AS WELL HAVE BEEN IN DETROIT. Right? And if technology and commitment are the instruments to overcome any challenge, I want to ask him, what about his nose?! *(Laughter from the TV. The front door is slowly opened, as Donna comes in, fearfully, quite slowly. She stares at Eddie, ranting at the TV. She looks around and sneaks closer, moving along behind the couch to see what he's looking at. She is heavily made up, her clothing in disarray, and tattered, her makeup old and smeared in some places.)* I know, I know, I could have crossed the boundary here of discretion. It's possible: My own sense of discrimination has taken quite a blast. I've been humbled, John. I been blasted. And I mean, I'm not tryin' to make a finished thing here, just rough in a couple of ideas. You could refine 'em, put your stable on 'em. Right? *(He takes a huge drink of vodka.)* Right, John?? You're not listening to me. You never listen to me. *(He is hitting the TV with a newspaper. Donna has been reaching to touch him, to get his attention.)* You never listen to me! *(And now her hand hits his shoulder. He jumps. She jumps back, moving backwards so she ends up in front of him.)*

DONNA: Hey, Eddie! I ain't mad anymore. You mad? See my, ah, you know, outfit? I got a little bit from everywhere I been so I'm like my own, you know, whatchamacallit. Right? Bits and pieces. So you can look at me and get the whole picture. See — here's Florida. *(She points to a patch on her clothes.)* And here's Vermont. *(Another patch.)* Which is a New England state. So if you put it together with a little thought, you can see I hitchhiked up and down the entire East Coast.

EDDIE: Unless you took a plane.

DONNA: Oh, no. I didn't. Airplane? Where would I get the money? How you been?

EDDIE: I'm a wreck.

DONNA *(hobbling a little, she leans against the armchair to pull off one shoe. She is weary; her sock is torn, her foot sore)*: You look a wreck, actually, but I didn't want to be impolite and mention it.

EDDIE: I don't know what I'm doing, you know what I mean?

DONNA: You're watchin' TV.

EDDIE: Right.

DONNA *(tentatively, she is looking about for something to eat and drink; she is edging for the kitchen)*: I'm gonna eat something, okay?

EDDIE: I don't know when I thought of you last, and in you walk. I don't get it.

DONNA: I'm a surprise is all.

EDDIE *(rising, Eddie moves after her)*: But I mean, I don't know what pertains to me and what doesn't.

DONNA *(a little startled by his sudden movement, she falters)*: Whata you mean?

EDDIE: I mean, everything. Right? I don't know what of everything going on pertains to me and what is of no account at all.

DONNA: Everything pertains to you, Eddie.

EDDIE: Yeah?

DONNA: Sure. *(Finding a plate with leftover bread on it.)* It's all part of the flow of which we are a part, too, and everything pertains to everything one way or another, see what I mean?

EDDIE: But I don't know, see, I don't KNOW.

DONNA: It doesn't matter.

EDDIE: So I'm just in this flow, right, like you in your elevator.

DONNA *(finding an open bottle of water)*: It wasn't mine.

EDDIE: So how'm I supposed to feel about it? See that's what I don't know.

DONNA *(moving to the armchair to eat)*: You have total, utter, complete freedom on that score, Eddie, because it doesn't make a bit of difference.

EDDIE *(following her)*: What I feel, it doesn't matter? This flow don't care!

DONNA: I don't think so.

EDDIE: So fuck it then! What good is it?

DONNA: I don't know.

EDDIE: Wait a minute, wait a minute — I don't think you know what I'm talking about. And I'm trying to grasp and, you know, incorporate as good advice what is your basic and total misunderstanding. I mean, is it pertinent, for example, that you came by?

DONNA: It doesn't matter.

EDDIE: I know that's what you think, but that's only because you have totally missed my point.

DONNA: Oh, no. So what is it?

EDDIE: I'm trying to say.

DONNA: Great!

EDDIE: I HAVE SO MUCH TO FIGURE OUT. (*Pacing near the TV, Eddie grabs up the newspaper.*) I mean, there's you there, and then there's other items like this and this, and does it pertain to me, FOR EXAMPLE, that I read that-my-government-is-selling-baby-milk-formula-to-foreign-countries-in-order-that-the-mother's-milk-will-dry-up-from-lack-of-use-and-the-formula-supply — you following me so far? — the-formula-supply-is-cut-off-and-the-babies-starve. I mean, how am I supposed to feel about that? First of all, I can't even be certain that it's even true. All I can be sure of is that it's printed in this goddamn newspaper. And I can't find out. How'm I supposed to find out? Write my congressman? Hire a goddamn private detective? Bring my private life to a screeching halt and look into it? I couldn't even if I wanted to. And should I ever figure it out, how the hell do I influence the course of these things? I mean, what am I supposed to do about all these things?

DONNA: I don't know.

EDDIE: That's my point, that's what I'm saying.

DONNA: So I do know your point.

EDDIE: But do they pertain to me?

DONNA: You're certainly worried about them.

EDDIE: I'm aware that I'm worried about them.

DONNA: I mean, I was saying to you that they all pertain to you as much as they're part of everything, right? That's what I was saying.

EDDIE: But as real things or as rumors?

DONNA: Whichever they are.

EDDIE: Which we don't know.

DONNA: Right. So this would qualify as a mystery, Eddie, right?

EDDIE: Yeah.

DONNA: So you can't straighten out a mystery, right? That's all I'm saying.

EDDIE: Did you know Phil is dead?

DONNA: Wow. What happened?

EDDIE: He drove his car off Mulholland.

DONNA: What happened?

EDDIE: The car crashed.

DONNA: No shit. I read about that. I read about that in the paper, but I didn't recognize his name, even though it was the same name.

EDDIE: Funeral was today.

DONNA: Wow. So that's why you're such a wreck, Eddie. No wonder. You were at the funeral.

EDDIE: Yeah.

DONNA: That'd wreck anybody.

EDDIE: Yeah.

DONNA: Was it sad?

EDDIE *(with a shrug, Eddie gets through it quickly, not seeming to care at all)*: You know, everybody wears the suits, you do the things. Everybody's there; you hang around, you know. The cars. Everybody gets to the church. So the priest is there, he blah-blah, blah-blah-blah, some guy is singing, mmmmmmmmmmmmmnnnnnnnnn, mmmmm, you drive to the cemetery, right. Everybody's in a line, cars all in a line. Brrrmmmm, brrrrrrmmmm. Everybody's in the cars; blah-blah, blah-blah-blah. So we get to the cemetery, the priest's got some more to say, rapateta, rapateta. So there's the hole, put him in. Blah-blah, blah-blah-blah.

DONNA: Was it sad?

EDDIE *(somewhere, here it hits him, a grief that, though there are tears, is beyond them: It is in his body, which heaves, and wracks him)*: There was in the church we were all like a bunch of dogs. This guy would sing with his beautiful voice. He had this beautiful high voice. All alone. No organ or anything. Just his voice. And we would all start to cry. The priest could say anything, a lot a nice things; sad things. Nothin'. But then this guy from way in the back of the church would sing, and you couldn't hear the words even, just this high, beautiful, sad sound, this human sound, and we would all start to cry along with him. *(He gasps, tries to breathe.)*

DONNA: You know somethin', Eddie. I didn't really go to all these actual places on my clothes.

EDDIE: No.

DONNA: No. *(Moving closer to him.)* I thought about them all though, and bought the souvenirs at a local souvenir place, and I dreamed these big elaborate dreams about these places. First, I would buy this book all about these places like Lauderdale, and Miami and Boston, and then I knew what I was dreaming about, and I could dream with accurate and convincing details, but actually I went out of here north toward San Francisco, but I got no further than Oxnard.

EDDIE *(sitting up, trying to get himself under control)*: I know where Oxnard is.

DONNA *(with immense enthusiasm)*: Great!

EDDIE *(laughing a little)*: What's so great about me knowing where Oxnard is?

DONNA: It's great when people know what each other are talking about, right, isn't that what we been talking about? I fell in love with a Mexican there. But after a while it wasn't love.

EDDIE: What was it?

DONNA: A mess. So I'm gonna sleep here if you don't mind. You got room?

EDDIE: I'm gonna be up for a while.

DONNA (*standing up, looking around*): Oh, I don't care. I'm just happy to get off the streets at the moment. The desperation out there is paranormal.

EDDIE: I don't know if I'm going to sleep ever again. I might stay awake forever.

DONNA: That's okay; should I lay down on the floor?

EDDIE: No, there's room here.

(*Eddie slides to one end of the couch, while Donna, carrying her coat, settles in against him, covering herself with her coat, then she looks up at him.*)

DONNA: You wanna fuck me or anything, Eddie, before I go to sleep?

EDDIE: No.

DONNA: Great. Not that I don't want to. I'm just sleepy.

EDDIE: You want a lude, or anything?

DONNA: No. (*Turning back to go to sleep.*)

EDDIE: Valium?

DONNA: No. 'Night.

EDDIE: Good night.

DONNA: Pleasant dreams.

(*He holds her.*)

(*Blackout.*)   1984

INVESTIGATIONS

1. On page 262 Eddie says, "But we're friends on the basis of what, Phil? On the basis of opposites, right? We're totally dissimilar is the basis of our friendship, right?" What are the ways in which Eddie and Phil *aren't* "totally dissimilar"? How do their similarities help bind them together? If you agree with Eddie that he and Phil are "opposites," explain how this forms the basis of their friendship.

2. Locate all the references the characters make to friendship and compare the male characters' ideas of friendship with those of the female characters. To what extent does your experience reflect similar distinctions between how men and women see friendship?

3. After reviewing your response to "Write Before Reading" on page 218 write a letter to Eddie in which you offer him advice for getting through his troubles with Mickey and Phil.

4. How do you account for each of the characters' relationship to Phil? After locating the situation in which Phil most disturbed or intrigued you, write

two or three paragraphs describing how you would have acted toward him and what you would have said to him.

5. Locate instances throughout the play of what Eddie calls "a form of desperation" (p. 320). What are the ways in which each of the characters is desperate? How does their desperation help account for how Eddie, Artie, Phil, and Mickey talk about and act toward women? To what extent does it account for their self-pity? Their paranoia? To what extent does this desperation explain Eddie's remarking about Phil's daughter, "Maybe if we kept her and raised her, she could grow up and be a decent human being" (p. 328)?

CATHY SONG

Losing Track

Last night I saw a documentary
on China. The camera crew
had traveled to the far western
province of Xinjiang. In the brief
green meadows of summer in the hills   5
I thought I recognized you,
but she was younger,
a girl who could have been your sister.
She was leaping in a game,
trying to catch the tail's end, a small boy,   10
in a snake of children
weaving through the tall grass.
Her long braids were flying like the tassels
tying her cotton quilted vest.
The camera almost touched her face: sturdy and earnest, 15
she seemed to smile against her will.

If you remained in China,
you would be pedaling an ancient
bicycle in Beijing. I received two letters.

A Chinese-American raised in Honolulu, Hawaii, CATHY SONG (b. 1955) earned a B.A. from Wellesley College and an M.A. from Boston University and now teaches at the University of Hawaii at Manoa. Her poetry collections include *Picture Bride* (1983), which won the Yale Series of Younger Poets Award, and *Frameless Windows, Squares of Light* (1988).

The students were so polite   20
they made you feel venerable
Beyond your years, waiting after class
to hand you rice cakes and panfried doughnuts.
I can hear them reciting
your stilted English sentences: at school,   25
I had once mistaken you for a foreigner,
your speech halting and deliberate.
You described your room, writing
how cold it was to face
the northern slant of the sun.   30
The light made you think of Michigan,
driving home through the woods with your father.
You made tentative plans to return
to the family house,
to finish a book of stories   35
you began writing in an upstairs room.
And then you wrote that you had fallen
in love with one of your students
but as if thinking it over,
you were riding an inland train   40
with someone else, a safe companion,
a woman with unfeminine features.

That is where we lost track
of one another. The silence that followed
your last letter grew longer,   45
becoming a tunnel of snow
the train you were riding whistled through.
Our words had been what had kept
us alive to one another and when they stopped,
a jade fish, an old coin,   50
was dropped into the blue China Sea.
Last night I found myself alone
when your face was brought back to life.
I dreamt I went to find you
in the drafty halls of the school   55
where in the mausoleum silence
of the library we would study, side by side,
our identical hair covering
the English language we both loved.

The story you began writing in Michigan   60
was a notebook you carried
across the snow quiet fields of the campus.

Walking in the shadow of the lights
along College Road, our tracks
had already begun to diverge   65
with our good night and a stack of books
at the frozen lily pond.
I watched you trudge up the hill
toward the observatory.
I see you as you were then,   70
so serious you did not mean to scowl,
your black ponytail, an ink brush,
dipping into the night air,
dotting the points to a constellation
you had yet to name.   75   1988

INVESTIGATIONS

1. What about the girl in the documentary (lines 1–16) reminds the speaker of her friend? What do these similarities say about why the speaker misses her friend?
2. In lines 52–53, the speaker says, "Last night I found myself alone / when your face was brought back to life." What does she mean? In what sense was she *not* alone before seeing the documentary?
3. Imagine you're the speaker's friend. Write a poem or a letter to the speaker (addressing her as "you") in which you respond to what she says in "Losing Track."

Willy

When Walt called at 6:30, I was drunk. He knew I would be, of course. Ever since he moved out, he times his communications with me for thirty minutes into the bourbon and after my 6:00 Valium. That way he doesn't have to worry about me asking any questions. Not that I questioned him when he said he had to have an apartment in the shadow of the Pentagon to be closer to his work — Walt is busy selling back to Defense all the knowledge they paid him to accumulate in his thirty years in the army. I knew the truth was that he couldn't face me the way I was, come home to a wife with problems after a day of solving ones with world consequences. But I didn't have the energy to try to make him say out loud that he was really leaving me, abandoning me — even if it was in a house whose bills he paid promptly and with a sense of duty.

" 'lo, Helen," he'd say and then launch into the list of the expenses. That day, when I heard him get as far as "forty gallons of heating oil," I put the phone down on the desk and let him talk to the philodendron while I went into the kitchen for some goldfish crackers. I got back in the middle of something different.

"Ted, after all these years — damn surprise. And him in consulting too." I started to put the phone back down, but I caught, " . . . kids fine, but Wilhelmina's in Walter Reed." Then I realized which Ted he was talking about. Wilhelmina's Ted. My Wilhelmina.

"In the hospital?" I said, startling Walt. "What's wrong? Is it serious? Is it cancer?"

"I didn't ask," he said.   5

How could you not ask, Walt?

Wilhelmina was my best friend when we were stationed in France together, in Fontainebleau just south of Paris in the golden pre–de Gaulle years. I had already been an army wife for ten years by then, but Willy was an outsider. To the wife part anyway. She'd been a WAC major — the 41st WAC to go regular army, she told me. A WAC until she got pregnant and her Ted proposed

---

The daughter of career army officers, JESSE LEE KERCHEVAL was born in 1956 in Fontainebleau, France, and now lives in Madison, Wisconsin, where she teaches at the University of Wisconsin. Her collection of stories, *The Dogeater* (1987), won the 1986 Associated Writing Programs Award in Short Fiction.

with a gallant, "The C.O. says to make an honest woman out of you." One cold day when we were watching my Anna and her Johnny chase dead leaves in the Forest of Fontainebleau, Willy told me the army had offered her an abortion when she was pregnant. Willy shook her head, "I couldn't believe they'd break the law." That was Willy — her years in the army had given her great faith in rules. But THE RULES then said NO PREGNANT WACs, so Willy made her late entrance into my social world. Or I tried to convince her to. I took to Willy right away. Here was someone who could explain to me the military side of the army — all the things Walt was too busy to talk about. But Willy didn't try to mix with the other wives, play bridge, go to Hospital Circle meetings, join Refreshment Committees. I was hard on her for it at the time — I was like a high school girl, wanting all my friends to be popular. The army life stressed doing things in groups, was as strict as the nuns back in grammar school in its aversion for "particular friends." Group friendships were a protection against constant loss through transfer, retirement. Willy always thought such friendships were shallow — how could friends be as interchangeable in the support they gave as bras? And it was true that no one really talked to anyone else, not like Willy and I did, but someone in the chain was always there — if you had to have a babysitter or got too drunk at the Officers' Club and needed to be taken to the ladies' room to lie down. But in all my army years, Wilhelmina was my one best friend. Maybe I shouldn't have allowed myself even one.

The Officers' Club Autumn Ball came along, and that was too big a social event for even Willy to ignore. To get her excited about going, I had a dress-maker in Fontainebleau copy us gowns out of *Vogue*. I was too short for the season's square padded shoulders — my dress swallowed me up. But Willy looked smashing. Tall, blond, like Kate Hepburn mixed with Betty Grable. Then, the night of the ball, Walt told me Ted had gotten orders for Texas, and the fun went out of my plan.

Around ten — the invitations read eight, but only Walt believed it — the ballroom got crowded and hot. Willy grabbed my elbow and said she felt sick. We went into the garden. She sat down and put her head between her legs. "Oh, God," she said, "I think I'm pregnant again." We cried, Willy and I, out there in that damp French garden, hugging each other, crushing our new gowns. "Listen," Willy said at last, holding me at arm's length, "I don't want any Christmas cards with mimeographed newsletters in them. I don't want to send you a fruitcake and get it back 'Moved — No Forwarding Address.' We say good-bye first-rate friends, and when we meet up again, we start right where we left off. OK?" I must have said something back — OK, I guess — but all I remember is Willy's voice, tight, demanding, "No fade-out friendship — you hear me?" We sat on the stone bench, our arms around each other's padded shoulders, staring into the darkness as if our future was out there, waiting to run us down like a tank. When Willy left France, I was sure I would never see her again.

Then Walt, twenty years later, mentions her between the heating oil and   10
the "Bye, Helen, gotta run" — with no idea what the news meant to me at all.

I called Walter Reed as soon as he hung up, but they wouldn't let me talk
to Willy. "She's been medicated," a cool young voice said.

I went to see her the next morning, after my 10:00 A.M. Valium. I got the
car carefully out of the garage at the time when, in the old days, I would have
been at the commissary finding Walt something wonderful for dinner. It was a
joke with us — how I'd found my way to his heart through his stomach. Every
night, after I told him what was for dessert, he'd say, "Strawberry short-
cake — you can read me like a book," and kiss me on my temple, right where
the blood leaves the head for the heart. But over the years dinner got quicker
and quicker. He brought work home, then there were meetings to go to. You
could see the nervousness in his eyes as he hurried even through dessert —
afraid decisions were being made without him, maybe afraid they didn't really
need him. Like a gambler who can't stand to be in the clubroom when the
horses are running. So instead of grocery shopping, I drove carefully through
D.C. where all the streets seemed to run one way the wrong direction. I finally
asked a cop I'd circled three times how to get on Georgia Avenue, but after he
told me, I missed the turn and went by him again. He raised his hands to
heaven, "Jesus H. Christ!" his lips said.

Willy was down a very quiet hall. I thought this was a bad sign, being on
a floor where no one was well enough to have "The Price Is Right" on loud. I
was right to be worried. She looked God-awful. I'd already double-checked the
number on the door before I recognized Willy's eyes in the swollen lumpy face
on the pillow. Willy's eyes, though, knew who I was at once. "Helen," she
said, and didn't sound surprised. "God, don't look at me — I sure wouldn't
want to. Turn on the TV, and we'll both look at that."

I stayed all day. Right through the game shows and into the soaps. She
was still Willy. She complained about the way the WACs had been swallowed
up by the army, women never training together, *esprit de corps* down the toilet.
She mocked her civilian doctors — the army doesn't have enough doctors even
to staff Walter Reed, its showcase, these days. How they weren't sure what she
had in her, cancer, benign growth, just old rubbish. But fluid wasn't draining
down through all the clever little valves and faucets in her liver. "Call Roto-
Rooter, that's the name," she sang, "and away go troubles down the drain."
Just like Willy, but she got serious for a minute when "General Hospital" came
on and the pale green room on the TV looked the same as hers.

She turned her eyes on me. "You don't look so good yourself, kiddo.   15
You're not sick are you?"

"No, not really sick," I said. "I just don't feel well sometimes."

"Be well," she said, leaning out of her bed to put a swollen hand on my
arm. "Once you give in to being sick, what happens isn't up to you anymore."
She took her hand back and closed her eyes. "You get well and stay well. You
hear me, Helen?"

"I will," I said. "Willy, I promise."

The nurse finally shooed me out when Willy's bowl of dinner came. When I got home, in spite of my promise, I felt so not well that I took two Valiums and got into the bourbon before the sun was over the yardarm, and still I shook as I lay on the couch watching Dan Rather. The phone rang promptly at 6:30, but I didn't answer it.

Why did you buy this house, Walt, if you weren't going to stay put?   20

Three years ago he bought this house, put me in it, and then ran back to his classified paper wars — where, as in any war, thoughts of family were put away for the duration, and men gave their all for the national defense. What was I supposed to do out here, in this suburb grown out of a cornfield, when he didn't even stay home to be fed breakfast and lunch? I had imagined the two of us flying around the world military space available, staying at Officers' Clubs in Calcutta and Nome. Or buying a Winnebago and having cactus fruit for dessert on the south rim of the Grand Canyon. I wanted us to be together. Instead I unpacked our green footlockers. Sent one of them off with Anna, packed with her *Playgirls* and her teddy bear, when she left to go to the University of Paris, to go back to France where she too had been happy. I put pictures on the walls for the first time in thirty years.

Walt had his consulting business to get going, and on the vast plain of civilian life, there was nowhere to go and no one to go there with. There were no Wives' Bus Tours, no Officers' Club Bazaars. No one to come and sit with me and calm me down with endless hands of gin rummy and tiny tuna sandwiches. I couldn't relax. I paced from basement to attic and down again. I hung wallpaper. It wasn't straight. I took it down again. I cooked dinner for Walt and either burnt the food or burnt my fingers. I forgot to make dessert. I couldn't sleep and kept Walt awake when he had important meetings in the morning. He sent me to a doctor, a civilian specialist in internal medicine, whose waiting room was filled by women with vague interior complaints.

"Valium," a woman in his waiting room told me, "is what doctors give to women who cry in their offices, who take to their beds but can't sleep, who are in pain but aren't sick." The doctor prescribed 15 mg. ones for me.

Even then I couldn't relax. One day I walked out of the housing development — heeding the warning on the Valium label about handling heavy machinery — to the ABC Liquor a mile down the road. And walked home again along the busy road with no sidewalk, ignoring the honking horns and startled looks, with a fifth of bourbon under my arm. At 5:00 I took a drink. At 5:15 I took another. Then I felt something give, something hard. Then I relaxed. For two years.

I got to Walter Reed a little earlier the next morning. I'd only missed   25
Georgia Avenue once this time, so I stopped in the gift shop and bought Art Buchwald's latest paperback. That would cheer Willy up. Buchwald had gotten his start writing on the *International Herald-Tribune* when we were in France,

and Willy was a big fan. We'd even met him once, at a USO luncheon, although he was very shy and not at all funny in person.

I took the book upstairs with me, but Willy's room was empty. I thought I'd gotten the wrong floor and went all the way down in the elevator and retraced my steps. She still wasn't there. I sat down on the army-tight sheets of her vacant bed. I think I knew by then, but still, I decided I would wait. Surely they'd wheel her in any minute from one of the endless tests she'd joked about yesterday. I was thinking about turning on the TV when the nurse came in. She was pissed, of course, to find me wrinkling her sterile sheets, but I'm sure she thought she was being polite enough — they teach them that in nursing school. "You'll have to talk to her husband," she said. "He's already picked up her effects."

Oh, Willy.

Another nurse came in, a big black woman, who had taken her politeness course more to heart. "She died in her sleep, honey," she said, "not a bit of pain." Died medicated, she was really saying. With enough pills you don't even feel your own death.

Driving home everything seemed sharp enough to cut. Cracks in the road, starlings on phone lines — it was like Willy's death was an electric shock, jump-starting nerves that hadn't worked in years. It was weird, and painful, but also as sweet and sour as a key lime pie. Suddenly I wanted to be alive even if it hurt like hell.

I pulled into the driveway and noticed for the first time that the house was the same puckery green as a cooking apple. I could taste it. I went straight upstairs to the kitchen, got down my refillable bottle of Valium, and dropped it down the garbage disposal. God, what a sound it made. The plastic screamed against the metal teeth. "There, Willy," I said, "well and getting weller." Then I got a lemon out of the refrigerator and stuffed it down after the pills. Nothing in this world smells lovelier than lemon rind down the garbage disposal. It made me cry to smell it. It made my head light. I left the kitchen to go down to the living room whistling, feeling buoyant as a party balloon. Then I fell down the stairs. I landed on my right shoulder, like a linebacker making a good tackle. Something went crack-snap, and there was such a stab of Valium-less pain I couldn't breathe. When I tried to stand, something went gently pop in my left hip, and I couldn't get up at all. "I'm not sick, Willy," I said lying there on the floor. "Just give me a minute."

At 6:30 the phone rang, and I thought, "Please Walt, no answer two days in a row. Get worried. Come looking."

Instead a neighbor found me, Mrs. Pinter, a Korean war bride who was collecting for the Heart Fund but took me to the hospital instead. I had only dislocated my hip, but I had broken my collar bone, and that seemed to require that my entire upper body, including my right arm, be bound tight as a mummy. Mrs. Pinter waited for me, drove me home, tucked me into bed with the new

30

pain pills that the doctor prescribed for me within easy reach on the night stand. She bowed politely before she left, refusing to consider my suggestion that she take whatever money was in my purse to help the hearts of America. I couldn't make it into the kitchen, so I flushed the pills down the toilet, then I lay back down on the bed and thought about dying. About lying there all wrapped up until I starved and dried up in my wrappings and turned into a real mummy. "Here I come, Willy," I said.

But I didn't. Quiet as cats the women of the neighborhood crept in. *Abandoned. Too sick to cook. Shouldn't be alone.* There, but for the grace of God, *go I, go I, go I.* They brought casseroles, congealed salads. The first couple of days I was too sick to eat what they brought. I threw up, and it seemed I could smell Valium in my urine, my sweat. Finally I managed to eat some congealed salad, holding it on my tongue until it dissolved. The women sat with me and told me where they'd come from and who they'd left behind, and I told them about Walt and about Willy.

A week after my accident, I was up, eating blintze and playing gin with Emma Rosen, a tiny Jewish woman who had lost every single member of her family in the concentration camps. She cried, and I held her hand as she showed me the official lists that traced her dead down through second cousins, then the phone rang, and it was Walt. He had just read the *Post,* he said, and first he called Ted, then me. Wilhelmina's funeral was today, 4:00 at Arlington. She had passed away last Wednesday, but there had been an autopsy, and Arlington wouldn't schedule until the body was released. "I'm sorry, Helen," he said. "Should I come and get you?"

It would take Walt an hour from the Pentagon then maybe more going back as rush hour started. Mrs. Rosen held out her watch — it was almost 2:30. "No," I said, "I can get to Arlington. Will you be there?"

"I'll try," Walt said.

I ransacked the closets for something black to wear to the funeral and found a wool skirt that was probably Anna's, but with my arm lashed down none of my blouses would fit.

Mrs. Rosen took me across the street to Mrs. Gjerde's house — she of the congealed salad — and I borrowed a black tent top from the very back of her closet. "My size 16 wardrobe," she explained, "for right after Christmas."

"Can you drive?" I asked Mrs. Gjerde. She shook her head. I told Walt I'd get there. I looked at Mrs. Rosen. Her face flushed.

"They took my license away," she said.

"Well," I said, "you can work the turn signal."

I couldn't turn around to back the car out, but luckily I'd left it in the middle of the double-car garage. And luckily, to Walt a car wasn't a car without an automatic transmission and power steering. Still, every pothole brought unmuffled pain. Tears came out of my eyes and dried where I could taste them. But my mind was as clear as the pain, and I pulled into Arlington at 3:30 without having gotten lost once.

Walt was waiting on the steps of the reception building. A girl in a blue

35

40

blazer with an American flag on the pocket tried to take my arm, but I waved her away. She took Mrs. Rosen's instead and led her inside.

I walked up to Walt.

"You're hurt," he said. He didn't seem surprised — maybe the neighborhood women had been talking to him too.

"A war wound," I said. Walt considered me and nodded, almost with respect. I considered him and thought he looked as bad as I did.

"You're all right, then?" he asked.

"Almost," I said, "and you?"

"I've never been so tired."

"We're not young."

"No."

I started up the stairs, wanting to go in together on this note of agreement, but Walt stopped me.

"I can't stay — a meeting," he said, but with no excitement in his voice. Sounding as tired as he looked.

"That's all right."

"No," Walt said, "it's not."

"No," I said, and we stood, in agreement for a second time. I waved him down the stairs. "Come by the house," I said. "We'll talk."

Ted was in the waiting room talking to Mrs. Rosen. I almost didn't recognize him in civilian clothes.

"I had to pull strings," he was explaining, "to get my wife into Arlington. These days it's for field-ranking officers only, full colonel and up." Mrs. Rosen nodded. "Hell, I'm a lieutenant colonel, and *I* don't even qualify." He made a face. "But Wil's being the 41st WAC cut the mustard with this woman general I got hold of. That's the army," he shrugged, "an exception for every rule."

And since he'd gotten Willy in, I knew that Ted would also be an exception to the rule. A man has a right to be buried with his wife, and Willy's body was holding Ted's place.

Ted saw me in the door and stood up. He didn't recognize me, so I reminded him, and he looked nervous. Afraid, I think, that I might do something awkward like cry.

A woman wearing a corsage of mums with petals like white cockatoo feathers came in and introduced herself as the Defense Department Representative. Then the girl in the blue blazer shooed us out into waiting limousines. Ted got in one with the woman from Defense, and Mrs. Rosen and I got in the other.

It was a splendid funeral, Willy.

Full Military Honors. A company of Old Guards from Fort Myers, all six feet tall, formed the honor guard, and there was a marching band, complete with tuba. Four gray horses pulled the caisson with Willy's flag-draped coffin, and behind it was a tall black horse with an empty saddle. A mount for the fallen rider, for Wilhelmina.

The woman soldier who was our driver said the horse was Black Jack Pershing, and this was his last funeral before being retired to Virginia. "Black Jack followed President John Kennedy to his grave," she said.

We rolled slowly through Arlington, to a measured drumbeat from the band. On the reviewing stand in front of the Veterans' Day Memorial, a hundred or so tourists watched us, the last full honors funeral of the day. They were wearing shorts, sneakers, Instamatics, but they stood as Black Jack passed, quiet and respectful.

65

Willy's grave was on the flat land near the Potomac, not up on one of the green hills, but it was a nice site, close to a small tulip tree. The four of us sat in folding chairs facing a patch of Astroturf that covered the open grave, and Mrs. Rosen began to cry softly. The chaplain gave a short eulogy based on Willy's military record. "Honorably discharged," he concluded, "Wilhelmina went on to send two sons into military service. John is serving on the USS *Lexington,* and his brother, Victor, is stationed in Turkey." Until then I hadn't known Willy's French pregnancy had given her another son. Then the honor guard folded the flag from Willy's coffin, snapping it crisply, and the chaplain presented it to Ted. "For your wife's service to her country," he said. The band started playing something low and sad, like a hymn but with a touch of military march; the honor guard fired the twenty-one-gun salute, aiming toward the Pentagon. A soldier lifted the Astroturf, and four Old Guards lowered Willy slowly into the grave. The soldier laid the green carpet back over her. Mrs. Rosen cried harder.

Then the woman from Defense stood up. The band started playing something snappy. Ted stood. The honor guard formed in ranks on the road. Mrs. Rosen stood. The band marched off, the horses starting after them. Mrs. Rosen raised her hands toward Willy, then to the sky, and began to moan. Her voice starting low, hoarse, then rising. The woman from Defense turned toward her, even her cockatoo corsage looking startled. Mrs. Rosen went down on her knees on the Astroturf. Ted turned away. Mrs. Rosen moaned louder, shaking her head from side to side. And then I moaned too, feeling something moving deep under my bandages. Not even the army can make partings painless. To feel loss, to grieve — this is a promise we make when we love. I would feel this for Walt, or he for me. It was inevitable. And it made him precious, Willy precious.

"Willy, Willy, my friend," I was crying, "I'll miss you, I'll miss you." Black Jack screamed, his bridle rattling as he shook his head, but Mrs. Rosen's voice rose higher even than that. Our sorrow rising into the air above Arlington, above the Potomac, up to meet the jets taking off from Bowling Green, from Andrews, up to the very boundaries of the national defense.   1987

INVESTIGATIONS

1. For Helen's circle of army wives, "group friendships were a protection against constant loss through transfer, retirement" (para. 7). In what ways

are the neighborhood women who help Helen after her fall a "group friendship"? If you have experienced similar group friendships, discuss the pleasures they offer that particular friendships don't. What sort of "protection" do they offer? If you have avoided group friendships, talk about why. Do you regret missing the pleasures and protection they offer? Explain your answer.

2. Why does Willy's death make Helen want "to be alive even if it hurt like hell"? Compare Helen's grief to Eddie's at the end of David Rabe's *Hurlyburly*. To what extent does Phil's death cause Eddie "to be alive even if it hurt like hell"?

3. How do you explain Mrs. Rosen's grief (paras. 67–68)?

4. How can this story be seen as an example of Richard Howard's claim that "every friendship / grows from some furtive apotheosis / of oneself" ("The Victor Vanquished," lines 18–20)?

MARTÍN ESPADA

Manuel Is Quiet Sometimes

He was quiet again,
driving east on 113,
near the slaughterhouse
on the day after Christmas,
not mourning,   5
but almost bowed,
like it is after the funeral
of a distant relative,
thoughtful,
sorrow on the border at dusk.   10

Vietnam was a secret.
Some men there collected ears,
some gold teeth.
Manuel collected the moist silences
between bursts of mortar.   15

A lawyer as well as a poet, MARTÍN ESPADA (b. 1958) says, "What I'm doing is using the power of the word to fight against what I consider to be wrong." Raised in a Brooklyn housing project, he now lives in Boston. His most recent collection of poetry, *Rebellion Is the Circle of a Lover's Hands* (1990), was awarded the 1991 Paterson Poetry Prize.

He would not tell
what creatures laughed in his sleep,
or what blood was still drying
from bright to dark
in moments of boredom   20
and waiting.
A few people knew
about the wound,
a jabbing in his leg
(though he refused   25
to limp);
I knew about the time
he went AWOL.

Driving east on 113,
he talked   30
about how he keeps
the car running
in winter. It's
a good car,
he said.   35
There was the brief illumination
of passing headlights,
and slaughterhouse smoke
halted in the sky.

Another night,   40
the night of the Chicano dance,
Manuel's head swung low and lazy
with drinking.
He smiled repeatedly,
a polite amnesiac,   45
and drank other people's beer,
waiting for the dancers
to leave their tables
so he could steal the residue
in plastic cups.   50

It was almost 2 AM
when he toppled,
aimless as something beheaded,
collapsing so he huddled
a prisoner on the floor.   55

The shell of his body
swung elbows
when we pulled him up.
He saw me first,
seeing a stranger.   60
His eyes were the color
of etherized dreams,
eyes that could
castrate the enemy,
easy murder watching me   65
with no reflection.

This is what he said:
"I never lied
to you, man."   1987

INVESTIGATIONS

1. For Manuel, "Vietnam was a secret" (line 11). What kind of secret? In what ways is this poem secretive? In your experience, what part do secrets play in friendship?

2. After Manuel falls down, "aimless as something beheaded" (line 53), "he huddled / a prisoner on the floor." Who is his jailer? What crime has been committed?

3. "Seeing a stranger" (line 60), Manuel tells the speaker, "I never lied / to you, man." Who is he talking to? What effect does this have on the speaker? What does not lying have to do with keeping secrets?

4. Compare the Vietnam experience as it is represented in "Manuel Is Quiet Sometimes," "Facing It" (p. 64), "Words for My Daughter" (p. 135), and "The Things They Carried" (p. 437). What common portrait of the war emerges?

PART THREE
CONNECTIONS AND ELABORATIONS

1. After reviewing the part of Rabe's *HurlyBurly* (p. 258) you found most troubling, do one of the following:

   a. Keeping the circumstances as close as possible to those in the passage, do a 250–500-word rewrite in which all the characters are women.

   b. Keeping the circumstances as close as possible to those in the passage, do a 250–500-word rewrite in which the male characters speak and act in ways consistent with your experience.

   Then write a 250–500-word analysis in which you account for the differences between your rewrite and the original.

2. Using as evidence images, lines, and scenes from the selections, your response to "Write Before Reading" on page 218, and any other writing and thinking you've done in response to the selections, write an essay that defines friendship.

3. Using the writing you did in response to "Write Before Reading" and any appropriate evidence from the chapter selections, write an essay that identifies qualities essential to friendship and analyzes their relative importance.

4. Using as evidence material from your response to "Write Before Reading" and from Paley's "Friends," Darion's "Claudia," Howard's "The Victor Vanquished," Rabe's *Hurlyburly,* Kercheval's "Willy," and Espada's "Manuel Is Quiet Sometimes," write an essay that

   a. demonstrates how our ability to help our friends is limited *and/or*

   b. demonstrates how our inability to help our friends has little to do with the essential qualities of friendship.

5. Using as evidence material from Paley's "Friends," Cisneros's "My Lucy Friend Who Smells Like Corn," Darion's "Claudia," Kercheval's "Willy," and Glück's "Celestial Music," write an essay that compares friendships formed in childhood to those formed in adulthood.

6. Using as evidence material from Paley's "Friends," Adams's "Waiting for Stella," Gunn's "Memory Unsettled," Rabe's *HurlyBurly,* Song's "Losing Track," and Kercheval's "Willy," write an essay in which you identify those individuals you'd most want as friends and those you'd least want, and why. (You may limit your choice to three selections.)

7. From your own experience and from your reading of the selections in Part Three, write an essay that explores the extent to which friendship is similar to a family relationship.

8. From your own experience and from your reading of the selections in this book, write an essay that analyzes the ways in which friendship is distinct from other kinds of relationships.

PART FOUR

IN AND OUT OF
COMMUNITIES

Where do we belong? How do we come to feel "at home" in a particular place? How do we transform ourselves from "outsiders" to "insiders," from strangers to part of the team, the neighborhood, the city, the country? How does a collective heritage influence the individual? What does it cost to violate the unwritten rules? What does it cost to *follow* those rules? These are some of the questions addressed by the selections in Part Four, selections that ask you to consider "community" not as a narrowly political phenomenon, but as a condition having to do with "common possession or participation," one of the dictionary's definitions of the word.

In Part Four you'll meet individuals and groups coming to terms with various kinds of community life, and in some cases with community illness or death. In Shay Youngblood's "Snuff Dippers," a worldly sort of faith binds a group of maids; in "Twice an Outsider: On Being Jewish and a Woman," Vivian Gornick compares her experience of being Jewish to that of Woody Allen, Mel Brooks, and Saul Bellow; "The Body Politic," by Theodore Weesner, takes us inside a Midwestern junior-high basketball team; Patricia Hampl recalls what it meant to belong to a Catholic parish in "Parish Streets"; the Mormon missionary tradition yields unintended results in "The New Timothy," by Walter Kirn; Lucille Clifton writes about reading her poetry "in white amer-ica"; Wendy Rose speaks against "a temporary tourism / of our souls" in "For the White Poets Who Would Be Indian"; in "Aria: A Bilingual Childhood," Richard Rodriguez reflects on the conflicting demands of home and school; in Amy Tan's "Two Kinds," a Chinese-American girl discovers what it means to be the "wrong" kind of daughter; Lorna Dee Cervantes's "Refugee Ship" dramatizes the "captivity" implicit in losing one's heritage; a platoon of "grunts" in Vietnam struggle to bear the weight of "The Things They Carried" in Tim O'Brien's short story; Kitty Tsui's "Don't Let Them Chip Away at Our Language" dramatizes the threat to community life posed by loss of language; the host of a talk radio program acts as the focus of a fluid, virtually faceless com-munity in Eric Bogosian's *Talk Radio*; in "The Language We Know," Simon J. Ortiz celebrates "the oral tradition of the Acoma Pueblo people"; in Judith Ortiz Cofer's "Silent Dancing," a home movie trig-gers memories of a Puerto Rican family's life in a Paterson, New Jersey, apartment building; and Gary Snyder reflects on the relationship be-tween building community and building homes in his poem "Building."

WRITE BEFORE READING

After listing the various communities of which you consider yourself a part, recall a particularly memorable time when you felt like an outsider and write two or three paragraphs detailing that experience. Then tell the story of how you became an *insider,* paying special attention to the process by which you figured out what joining that community required of you. Was the effort worthwhile? Why or why not?

Snuff Dippers

I have always had a deep and undying respect for the wisdom of snuff dippers. Big Mama raised me in the company of wise old Black women like herself who had managed to survive some dangerous and terrible times and live to tell bout them. These were hard-working, honest women whose only admitted vice, aside from exchanging a lil bit of no-harm-done gossip now and then, was dipping snuff.

Big Mama and her friends was always sending me to Joe's grocery store on the corner to buy silver tins of the fine brown powder wrapped in labels with names like Bruton's Sweet Snuff, Georgia Peach, and Three Brown Monkeys. The summer I was six my mean older cousin, DeeDee, told me that snuff was really ground up monkey dust, a delicacy in the royal palaces of Africa. She told me to mix three heaping tablespoons of snuff with a glass of milk and to drink it through a straw fast like a chocolate milkshake.

"If you drink it all," she said, shaking her nine-year-old hips, "you'll wake up and be real pretty like them African dancing girls we saw on TV. They drink it every day. It'll make your teeth white too."

"How come you know so much?" I asked suspiciously.

"Cause when I went to New York to see Aunt Louise she lived next door   5
to a African dancing girl. She told me herself that's how come she was so pretty."

DeeDee was so convincing, especially when she made me promise on the Bible not to tell nobody.

I took one of Big Mama's good glasses with flowers painted on it down from the top shelf of the china cabinet. Then I mixed the milk and monkey dust, stirring it in the pretty glass till it made me sneeze. Holding my nose, I stuck a plastic straw into the foaming brown stuff and began to drink my way to beauty. Big Mama heard me coughing and crying and come in the kitchen. When she found out what I was doing she shook her head and tried not to laugh at me. She gave me some baking soda to rinse my mouth out and a lecture on not believing everything I heard. Said I was already pretty, and all the monkey dust in the world couldn't give me a good, kind, honest heart. I never forgave DeeDee for that trick. I was dizzy for hours, and the taste of the nasty, bittersweet snuff lingered on my tongue long after the humiliation had gone.

SHAY YOUNGBLOOD's *Shakin' the Mess Outta Misery,* a play based on *The Big Mama Stories* (1989), has recently been produced in a number of cities. Born in 1959 in Columbus, Georgia, Youngblood now lives in Providence, Rhode Island, where she is enrolled in the graduate writing program at Brown University.

When I was a few years wiser and had the nerve to question Big Mama, I asked her why she dipped snuff. Big Mama leaned back, deep into her rocking chair. She slowly drew a fresh tin of snuff from her apron pocket. After opening the can, she took a big pinch of the brown stuff between her index and forefinger like I'd seen her do a million times. With her other hand she stretched out her bottom lip to take in the dip of snuff. She slapped her hands together and wiped them on her apron before she answered me. By the way she took her time I knew she was gonna tell me a story. Big Mama started out by defending herself.

"Snuff ain't no worse than them cancer sticks that be killing folks left and right. I ain't never heard tell of snuff harming nobody. But as I recollect, back in '57 when the only place colored folks could sit on a bus was in the back, Emma Lou came close to getting us killed on the #99."

Big Mama told me that over twenty years ago the #99 bus was known as the "maids' bus." It arrived downtown at the corner of Broadway and 12th streets every weekday morning at 6:00 A.M. to pick up the Black domestic workers bound for the rich white suburb of Northend, ninety minutes away. The sun would just be creeping up behind the glass-and-steel office buildings to light the women's way. From a distance, the #99 bus stop looked like any other corner where buses stopped. Bout forty Black women stood there dressed as if on their way to a church social. They all carried shopping bags made of plastic, paper, or straw, advertising the names of places they would never see or stores where they weren't welcome. In the bags were maids' uniforms that pride prevented them from wearing outside the places where they worked in them.

Everybody had a regular seat on the #99 so that friends and neighbors could sit together recreating communities. Miss Emma Lou sat in the seventh row, right-hand side next to the window, and Miss Mary sat next to her. Seats weren't assigned, but all hell cut loose when the pattern was broken by a newcomer. Newcomers sat up front — period.

Big Mama said that conversations on the #99 went something like this.

Miss Emma Lou: "My lady asked me to come in on a Sunday afternoon, would you believe, to pour tea for some English foreigners visiting her mama. I told her that her mama was gonna have to pour that tea herself cause I had to go to church on Sunday. The Lord wouldn't preciate my missing a prayer service to pour tea for the Queen of England."

Miss Mary: "My white lady, bless her heart, is as simple as a chile. When the boss was near bout fifty years old he turn round and left the other missus and two grown children to marry this girl right out of college. This chile, believe me when I tell you, sends her drawers to the dry cleaners. Ain't that nothin? A woman that cain't wash her own drawers."

Miss Mary and Miss Emma Lou lived in one-bedroom apartments on either side of me and Big Mama in the housing projects by the river. Miss Mary was a tall, straight-backed, thin Black woman, somewhere in her sixties, who looked like a gypsy. She wore big gold earrings and bright-colored head ties that matched her dresses. Sometimes in the middle of a conversation with her Miss Mary would see into your future and start to tell it if you didn't stop her. Folks said she come from a line of West Indian root women, seers and healers, and couldn't help it. Miss Emma Lou tried to convince her to charge for the privilege of knowing people's future, but Miss Mary said that would be highway robbery, charging money for a gift give to her by God.

Miss Emma Lou was Miss Mary's best friend. She was a short, heavyset brown-skin woman who was as bowlegged as Miss Mary was straight in the back. Unlike the other maids, Miss Emma Lou wore her white uniform most of the time — said it was the mark of a professional. She made her white folks refer to her as a domestic engineer and got paid a lil bit extra for it. Miss Emma Lou wasn't nobody's fool. And she was a snuff-dipping woman who said what was on her mind and emphasized her point by spitting snuff juice in a can she carried with her everywhere.

Then there was Ralph, a big, red-faced Irishman with laughing green eyes and curly, blond hair, who had been the driver for the #99 since the service began in 1952. Dr. J. R. Whittenhauser, the millionaire doctor, had stopped Ralph's gypsy cab on Peachtree Street and offered him an easier job with a steadier income. All he had to do was pick up the domestic help for Northend by 6:00 A.M. Monday through Friday and pick them up again at 3:30 P.M. in a bus Northend residents bought for that purpose. Even if the city buses went on strike or riots broke out, white ladies in Northend would have their meals cooked, children looked after, and laundry done.

Ralph was one of the nicest white men she ever met, according to Big Mama. If one of the regular riders was late, Ralph would wait a few more minutes knowing that on Fridays Miss Lamama had to walk her grandchildren to school and on Mondays Miss Mary did a sunrise ritual. If it was raining real hard or the temperature was real cold, Ralph would drive some of the older women with arthritis, bursitis, and bad knees across town right up to their door. In return the women baked him cakes, brought him lunch, and treated him like one of them.

Big Mama said Ralph was like one of them cause white folks treated him the same as if he was colored cause he was a foreigner. She said he even stood up to a white man for them.

Big Mama's face got real serious when she started telling me one of her stories bout the not-so-long-ago days. 20

"As I seem to recall, it was a scorching hot day in the middle of July when Emma Lou liketa got in a whole heap of trouble over some snuff and Ralph stood up for us like a soldier," Big Mama said.

"Not only was the weather hot, but colored folks was stirred up over the lynchings and killings of colored mens all over the South by evil white men. The whites was getting meaner as the summer got hotter. A colored woman had just been found dead. She was raped and sawed open by six white men who made her brother watch em ravish her. Some awful bloody things happened that summer." Big Mama closed her eyes and drew herself up like a chill had passed over her.

"What happened, Big Mama?" I asked impatiently, as children do.

"Hold on, chile, I'm getting to it. A story ain't something you just read off like ingredients on a soap box. A story's like a map — you follow the lines and they'll take you somewhere. There's a way to do anything, and with a story you take your time." She shook a finger in my direction.

"I'm sorry, Big Mama." I was afraid I'd messed up and she wouldn't finish   25
the story. I promised to hush and not interrupt her again.

Big Mama shifted herself into a more comfortable position for storytelling and cocked her head back for better memory.

"As I was bout to say, the #99 was rolling toward town. Most of the women on the bus was talking bout how hot it was. Breakfast milk spoiling on the table, clothes drying stiff on the line quick as lightning strike, and lil babies crying all day long they was so miserable. We was all real hot, sweaty, and wore out. Emma Lou was sitting in her regular seat by the window. Mary was next to her, and I was sitting behind them at my window seat.

"I was sitting there listening to Emma Lou go on bout how her white folks was going on a vacation in Europe, or somewhere like that, and just looking out the window. We was still in Northend, where most of the rich white folks live, and I took notice of this brand new white convertible Cadillac cruising long side of the bus. It was a white man and woman in the car. She had on a pretty white dress and looked just as brown as your Cousin DeeDee, but she had long yellow hair that was blowing all round her face. The white man was driving. He had yellow hair too, but he was real red; his skin was peeling off him like a boiled tomato. Look like he'd been to Florida and stayed in the sun too long. He had on a pair of them mirror sunglasses so you couldn't see his eyes like them small-town redneck sheriffs useta wear to scare coloreds. You can tell a whole heap bout a person by looking in they eyes. You can just bout see what's going on in they mind, and some people have some terrible things on they mind."

Big Mama stopped talking again, but I didn't say nothing, and in a minute or two she kept on.

"Well, you know Emma Lou got to have her a dip of snuff. Don't care   30
where she is or who she with, she gonna have her a taste. That day wasn't no different, but that day Emma Lou didn't have her spit cup with her. She probably left it at her white lady's house. She asked Lamama if she could use her fancy Ethiopian handkerchief, but Lamama was offended. Told her to use her bag, but Emma Lou had her white folks' lace tablecloths in there. Wouldn't you know it, just as them white folks in they brand new Cadillac was passing the bus, Emma Lou stuck her head out the window and let out a long stream of thick, brown snuff spit right in that white woman's face and on her pretty white dress.

"When the other womens on the bus saw what had happened, they started falling off they seats they was laughing so hard. Ralph hear what happen and he laugh too, but pretty soon we all realize they wasn't nothing to laugh at. Them white folks drove up side the bus cussing and carrying on like I never heard and hope not to hear no more. All that white man could see was blood. Ralph got hold of the situation and threw the bus in high gear. That Cadillac speeded up too. Folks on the bus got quiet. All we could hear was the bus tires hitting the road and that raging white man calling us every kind of nigger he could think of. Ralph say, 'I'm trying to get rid of this fool. Hang on, ladies.'

"For a few minutes we thought Ralph had lost them, but before we got out of Northend a police car with flashing blue lights and a crying siren signaled for the bus to pull over. Ralph started cussing like a sailor, but he had to pull over for the law. Out of the corner of my eye I saw the colored Catholic woman from up North cross herself. I started praying myself cause I saw the white Cadillac pull up and park behind the police car.

"The white woman jumped outta that car looking ugly like somebody called her mama nigger. She had wiped most of the spit off her face, but she still had brown snuff stains on the front of her dress. The white man had evil and ugly wrote all over him. He was hollering at the policeman and waving his fist round. The police officer, a blond-headed boy with cold blue eyes, had to hold him back from getting on the bus. The policeman got on though and look us over like we stole something. He say out loud, 'Which one of you aunties spit on Mr. Roger's friend?' As if we was children and any one of us could've been his mama, grandma, or help raise him.

"Nobody made a sound. Then he put his hand on his hip by his gun and say real nasty, 'I'm gonna have to lock every one of y'all up if don't nobody speak up right now.' We didn't hardly breathe. When he ask Ralph who spit on the white lady, Ralph say, 'Might be a pigeon thought he was flying over the ocean and took a notion to shit in the sea. Why you want to bother these nice ladies?' That made the police mad. He say, 'They a bunch of niggers and one of em spit on a white lady. I don't know where you from, but we don't tolerate disrespect from our niggers here in Georgia, or from nigger-loving foreigners.'

"When Ralph stood up in front of that policeman you could see the blood rush to his face. He was mad as all git out. The policeman back off the bus with his hand on his gun. He say loud, looking hard at Ralph, 'I want all you niggers to get off the bus. That mean everybody.' Ralph was the first one to get off the bus. Then we all got off and the policeman made us line up by the road in that hot sun like he was gonna let that crazy white man shoot us. Cars was passing long the highway with folks looking at us like we was from the moon. Then the policeman just left us standing there and went over to his patrol car and started talking on his radio.

"Before we knowed anything, that crazy white man was hollering at us, 'Somebody's gonna pay for this.' The white woman was leaning on the Cadillac looking hateful and mean as a snake. Then that fool white man started picking up rocks and dirt and throwing em at us. Mary still got a scar where one of them rocks split her knee. Ralph rush over to stop him, but the white man throwed dirt in his eyes. We all run screaming and hollering behind us into a patch of weeds and up against a fence a lil piece from the road till we couldn't go no further. I thought for sure we was gonna be killed. Finally the policeman see what was happening and pull the white man to the side. They look over at us standing in them knee-high weeds and briars and laughed at something that was said between em. Do you know that no-good policeman watch that crazy white man come over to where we was backed up against the fence like dogs and hark spit on each one of us. Lamama wiped our faces with her fancy handkerchief, weeping like a widow. Then the white man laughed and got in his Cadillac with his woman.

"Mary was behind me calling on her West Indian spirits and making signs. That white man pulled onto the highway, his tires kicking up dust every which way, right in the path of a tractor-trailer truck. I'll never forget it as long as I live. The sight of that big, brand new white Cadillac being knocked in the side and the surprise on them white folks' faces. It was a mess of twisted steel and burning white flesh. Mary was smiling. She crossed herself and said, 'Thank you, Jesus. Thank you, Ogun.'

"Emma Lou turned to me and said, 'Ain't it a shame that folks can be so mean with the Lord watching they every move.' She clicked her tongue like she do and spit in the direction of the wreck.

"I said to her, 'Emma Lou, it be the truth. Folks act like God don't be on the case recording everything in his Book of Life.' "

Big Mama shook her head in wonder and spit in the big tin can with the   40
yellow peach label on it, the one she kept under her chair, to let me know she was through. I went over and hugged her tight round the middle, glad she took the time to remember with me the way things used to be.   1989

INVESTIGATIONS

1. In paragraph 8, the narrator asks Big Mama why she "dipped snuff," and Big Mama responds by telling the story of the #99 bus. How does this story answer the narrator's question? How does it bear out Big Mama's conviction that "a story's like a map — you follow the lines and they'll take you somewhere"?

2. What besides their shared occupation and their race defines the women of the #99 bus as a community? How does Ralph fit in? Describe how each of the characters helps bind the group together.

3. After looking up the definition of the word *mores*, write a 250–500-word essay comparing the mores of the "#99 bus group" to those of the white police officer and the couple in the Cadillac.

4. In what ways are the sentiments expressed in paragraphs 37–39 thoroughly praiseworthy? How would you compare the religious beliefs dramatized here to those described in "Parish Streets" (p. 397)?

VIVIAN GORNICK

Twice an Outsider:
On Being Jewish
and a Woman

When I was growing up, the whole world was Jewish. The heroes were Jewish and the villains were Jewish. The landlord, the doctor, the grocer, your best friend, the village idiot, the neighborhood bully: all Jewish. We were working-class and immigrant as well, but that just came with the territory. Essentially, we were Jews on the streets of New York. We learned to be kind, cruel, smart, and feeling in a mixture of language and gesture that was part street slang, part grade-school English, part kitchen Yiddish. We learned about politics and society in much the same way: Down the block were a few Orthodox Jews, up the block a few Zionists, in between a sprinkling of socialists. For the most part, people had no politics at all, only a cautious appetite for the goods of life. It was a small, tight, hyphenated world that we occupied, but I didn't know that; I thought it *was* the world.

One Sunday evening when I was eight years old my parents and I were riding in the back seat of my rich uncle's Buick. We had been out for a drive and now we were back in the Bronx, headed for home. Suddenly, another car sideswiped us. My mother and my aunt shrieked. My uncles swore softly. My father, in whose lap I was sitting, said out the window at the speeding car, "That's all right. Nothing but a bunch of kikes in here." In an instant I knew everything. I knew there was a world beyond our streets, and in that world my father was a humiliated man, without power or standing. By extension, we were all vulnerable out there; but *we* didn't matter so much. It was my father, my handsome, gentle father, who mattered. My heart burned for him. I burrowed closer in his lap, pressed myself against his chest. I wanted to warm the place in him that I was sure had grown cold when he called himself a kike.

That was in the middle of the Second World War — *the* watershed event for the men and women of my generation. No matter what your social condition, if you were a child growing up in the early 1940s you entered the decade destined for one kind of life and came out of it headed for another. For those of us who had gone into the war the children of intimidated inner-city Jews, 1945 signified an astonishing change in the atmosphere. The end of the

Formerly a college teacher and a staff writer for *The Village Voice*, VIVIAN GORNICK (b. 1935) now works full-time as a free-lance writer, focusing on women's issues. Her books include *Women in Science* (1983) and *Fierce Attachments* (1987).

war brought frozen food and nuclear fission, laundromats and anticommunists, Levittown and the breakup of the college quota system. The trolley tracks were torn up, and the streets paved over. Buses took you not only to other parts of the Bronx but into Manhattan as well. When my brother graduated from the Bronx High School of Science in 1947 my father said, "Now you can become a salesman." But my cousin Joey had been a bombardier in the Pacific and was now one of the elite: a returned GI at City College. My brother sat down with my father and explained that even though he was not a genius he had to go to college. It was his right and his obligation. My father stared at his son. Now we were in the new world.

When I was sixteen a girl in the next building had her nose straightened; we all trooped in to see Selma Shapiro lying in state, swathed in bandages from which would emerge a person fit for life beyond the block. Three buildings away a boy went downtown for a job, and on his application he wrote "Arnold Brown" instead of "Arnold Braunowitz." The news swept through the neighborhood like wildfire. A nose job? A name change? What was happening here? It was awful; it was wonderful. It was frightening; it was delicious. Whatever it was, it wasn't stasis. Things felt lively and active. Chutzpah was on the rise, passivity on the wane. We were going to run the gauntlet. That's what it meant to be in the new world. For the first time we could *imagine* ourselves out there.

But who exactly do I mean when I say we? I mean Arnie, not Selma. I mean my brother, not me. I mean the boys, not the girls. My mother stood behind me, pushing me forward. "The girl goes to college, too," she said. And I did. But my going to college would not mean the same thing as my brother's going to college, and we all knew it. For my brother, college meant getting from the Bronx to Manhattan. But for me? From the time I was fourteen I yearned to get out of the Bronx, but get out into *what?* I did not actually imagine myself a working person alone in Manhattan, and nobody else did either. What I did imagine was that I would marry, and that the man I married would get me downtown. He would brave the perils of class and race, and somehow I'd be there alongside him.

The greater chain of social being obtained. Selma straightened her nose so that she could marry upward into the Jewish middle class. Arnie changed his name so that he could wedge himself into the Christian world. It was the boys who would be out there facing down the terrors of the word "kike," not the girls. The boys would run the gauntlet, for themselves and for us. We would be standing not beside them but behind them, egging them on. And because we knew we'd be behind them we — the girls — never experienced ourselves directly as Jews. I never shivered inside with the fear of being called a kike. I remember that. Somehow I knew that if I were insulted in that way I might feel stunned, but the fear and shame would be once removed. I knew I'd run home to Arnie, and I'd say, "Arnie, they called me a kike," and he'd look miserable, and I'd say, "Do something!" and the whole matter would be out of my hands the minute I said "Do something." It was Arnie who'd have to

5

stand up to the world, search his soul, test his feelings, discover his capacity for courage or action. Not me. And that is why Arnie grew up to become William Paley, and the other boys on the block — the ones who sneered and raged and trembled, who knew they'd have to run that gauntlet, get into that new world like it or not, and were smart and sensitive, and hated and feared and longed for it all — they grew up to become Philip Roth and Woody Allen. Me and Selma? We grew up to become women.

The confusion is historic; the distinction is crucial.

Woody Allen is exactly my age. I remember as though it were yesterday listening to Allen's first stand-up comic monologues in the late fifties at the Bitter End Cafe. We were all in our twenties, my friends and I and Allen. It was as though someone on the block had suddenly found it in himself to say to a world beyond the street, "Listen. You wanna know how it is? This is how it is," and with more courage than anxiety he had shaped our experience. This wasn't Milton Berle or Henny Youngman up there, a Borscht Belt comic speaking half Yiddish, half English, all outsiderness. No, this was one of us, describing how it felt to be our age and in our place: on the street, at a party, in the subway, at home in the Bronx or Brooklyn; and then out there, down-town, in the city. Half in, half out.

Philip Roth, of course, cut closer to the bone. His sentence structure deepened the experience, drove home better than Allen could the pain and the excitement, the intelligence and the anguish, the hilarity and the madness of getting so close you could touch it and *still* you weren't inside.

Behind both Allen and Roth stood Saul Bellow, who made the words   10
"manic" and "Jewish" synonymous, whose work glittered with a wild flood of feeling that poured from a river of language, all pent-up brilliance, the intelligence driven to an edge of hysteria that resembled Mel Brooks as much as it did Philip Roth. Although Bellow had been writing since the forties, it was only now in the fifties and sixties that his work and its meaning traveled down from a small community of intellectual readers to the reading populace at large. Here was a street-smart writing Jew who was actually extending the American language, using us — our lives, our idiom — to say something about American life that had not been said before. In the process, he gave us — me and my contemporaries — the equipment to define ourselves, and therefore become ourselves.

These men are on a continuum. From Milton Berle and Mel Brooks to Saul Bellow, Philip Roth, and Woody Allen — the subtle alterations of tone and voice among them constitute a piece of social history, chart a progress of the way Jews felt about themselves in America, embody a fine calibration of rage, resentment, and hunger.

My mother hated Milton Berle, and I understood why — he was hard to take. But I laughed against my will, and I knew he was the real thing. To see the idiom of your life coming back at you, shaped and enlarged by a line of humorous intelligence as compelling as a poem in the sustained nature of its thesis and context, was to experience one of life's deepest satisfactions. When that famous chord of recognition strikes, it is healing — illuminating and healing.

Milton Berle was my first experience of an artist's work applied to the grosser materials of my own environment. Berle, operating at a lower level of genius, was just as sinister as the Marx brothers. It was the wildness of his humor and the no-holds-barred atmosphere that it generated. Berle was coarse and vulgar, fast and furious, frightening in the speed of his cunning and his rage. My mother was repelled. She knew this was Jewish self-hatred at its most vicious.

Mel Brooks was more of the same, only ten years younger, and the ten years made a difference. A few years ago Brooks reminisced about how, when he began writing for Sid Caesar, his mother asked him how much money he was making, and he told her sixty dollars a week. He knew if he told her what he was really making she'd have a heart attack. "The heart," he said. "It would attack her." That story was for us: Woody Allen built on it. Brooks — also marked by a Borscht Belt coarseness that spoke to an uneducated sense of America, a lack of conversance with the larger culture — was still the shrewd, wild Jew talking, but his tone was a bit sadder, a bit quieter than Milton Berle's, less defended against the fears that dominated our lives. The lessened defense was the sign of change.

With Woody Allen, we passed through into a crucial stage of development.   15 Allen built a persona, an identity, a body of work out of the idea of the mousy Jew who makes a fool of the gentile rather than of another Jew. This had not happened before. Its meaning was unmistakable.

The Woody Allen character is obsessed with getting laid. Everyone else does it; he alone can't do it. Everywhere he goes — in the street, on the subway, at a party — he gazes mournfully at the golden shiksas all around him, always beyond reach. It's not a Jewish girl he's trying to get into bed; it's Diane Keaton. The Jewish girl is Brooklyn; Annie Hall is Manhattan.

And what does sexual success mean? It means everything. It means the defeat of all that life bitterly withholds, already characterized by the fact that one has been born a Jew instead of Humphrey Bogart. If Allen can just get that blue-eyed beauty into bed. He wants it so bad he's going to die of it. He's going to expire from this hunger right there before your eyes.

The humor turns on Allen's extraordinary ability to mock himself. He's as brilliant as Charlie Chaplin at making wonderful his own smallness. And he's as successful as Chaplin at making a hero of the little man, and a fool of the withholding world in the person of the pretty girl. When Diane Keaton wrings her hands and moans, "I can't," and Allen blinks like a rabbit and says, "Why? Because I'm Jewish?" — he accomplishes a minor miracle on the screen. The beautiful woman is made ridiculous. The golden shiksa has become absurd, inept, incapable: the insincere and the foolish cut down to size so that Allen can come up to size.

When was the first time I saw it? Which movie was it? I can't remember.

I remember only that at one of them, in the early seventies, I suddenly found myself listening to the audience laugh hysterically while Allen made a dreadful fool of the girl on the screen, and I realized that he had to make a fool of her, that he would always have to make a fool of her, because she was the foil: the instrument of his unholy deprivation, the exasperating source of life's mean indifference. I said to myself, "This is dis-*gust*-ting," and as I said it I knew I'd been feeling this way all my life: from Milton Berle to Saul Bellow to Woody Allen. I had always laughed, but deep inside I'd frozen up, and now I saw why. Milton Berle with his mother-in-law jokes, Saul Bellow with the mistresses who hold out and the wives who do him in, Mel Brooks and Woody Allen with the girl always and only the carrot at the end of the stick. Every last one of them was trashing women. Using women to savage the withholding world. Using us. Their mothers, their sisters, their wives. To them, we weren't friends or comrades. We weren't even Jews or gentiles. We were just girls.

At that moment I knew that I would never again feel myself more of a Jew than a woman. I had never suffered as men did for being a Jew in a Christian world because, as a Jew, I had not known that I wanted the world. Now, as a woman, I knew I wanted the world and I suffered.

Hannah Arendt, watching the Nazis rise to power in Germany, had denied the meaning of her own Jewishness for a long time. When she acknowledged it, she did so by saying, "When one is attacked as a Jew, one must defend oneself *as a Jew*. Not as a German, not as a world-citizen, not as an upholder of the Rights of Man [emphasis in original]." I read that and I was ready to change the sentences to read, "When one is attacked as a woman, one must defend oneself *as a woman*. Not as Jew, not as a member of the working class, not as a child of immigrants."

My father had to be Jewish; he had no choice. When he went downtown he heard "kike." I live downtown, and I do not hear "kike." Maybe it's there to be heard and I'm not tuned in, but it can't be there all that much if I don't hear it. I'm out in the world, and this is what I *do* hear:

I walk down the street. A working-class man puts his lips together and makes a sucking noise at me.

I enter a hardware store to purchase a lock. I choose one, and the man behind the counter shakes his head at me. "Women don't know how to use that lock," he says.

I go to a party in a university town. A man asks me what I do. I tell him I'm a journalist. He asks if I run a cooking page. Two minutes later someone asks me not if I have a husband but what my husband does.

I go to another party, a dinner party on New York's Upper West Side. I'm the only woman at the table who is not there as a wife. I speak a few sentences on the subject under discussion. I am not responded to. A minute later my thought is rephrased by one of the men. Two other men immediately address it.

Outsiderness is the daily infliction of social invisibility. From low-grade humiliation to life-threatening aggression, its power lies in the way one is seen, and how that in turn affects the way one sees oneself. When my father heard the word "kike" the life-force within him shriveled. When a man on the street makes animal-like noises at me, or when a man at a dinner table does not hear what I say, the same thing happens to me. This is what makes the heart pound and the head fill with blood. This is how the separation between world and self occurs. This is outsiderness alive in the daily way. It is here, on the issue of being a woman, not a Jew, that I must make my stand and hold my ground.

A few years ago I taught at a state university in a small Western town. One night at a faculty party a member of the department I was working in, a man of modest intelligence, said of another teacher who had aroused strong feeling in the department, "He's a smart Jew crashing about in all directions." I stared at this man, thinking, "How interesting. You *look* civilized." Then I said, quite calmly, "What a quaint phrase. In New York we don't hear ourselves described as smart Jews any more. Is that still current out here?" The man turned dull red, and the exchange was at an end.

A few weeks later at another party I saw this same man engaged in conversation with another member of the department, a woman. I knew this woman, and in my view her gifts of mind and spirit were comparable to the man's. She was not a scholar and he was not a scholar. She was not intellectual and neither was he. They were both hard-working university teachers. I watched the two standing together, talking. The woman gestured widely as she spoke, smiled inordinately, fingered her hair. Her eyes were bright; her tone was eager. She exclaimed; she enthused; she performed. The man stood there, pulling at a pipe, silent, motionless, his body slack, his face immobile, his entire being unreadable except for his eyes and his mouth: in them an expression of mockery and patronage as the woman grew ever more frantic in her need to gain a response. It was clear that the harder she tried, the more secure he felt. At a certain point it became obvious that he was deliberately withholding what he knew she needed. I was watching a ritual exchange of petition and denial predicated on a power structure that in this instance turned wholly on his maleness and her femaleness.

I watched these two for a long time, and as I watched I felt my throat tighten, my arms and legs begin to tingle, a kind of sick feeling spread through my chest and belly. I wanted to put her up against the wall, but I wanted to put him through the wall. I realized I'd been absorbing this kind of thing twenty times a day in this department, in this university, in this town; and it was making me ill.

This daily feeling, this awareness of the subtle ways in institutional life that the most ordinary men accord each other the simplest of recognitions and withhold these recognitions from the equally ordinary women with whom they work, is palpable, and it burns inside every woman who experiences it — whether she is aware of what is happening or has numbed herself to what is happening.

When I hear an anti-Semitic remark I am hurt, I am angered, but I am not frightened. I do not fear for my life or my livelihood or my right to pursue the open expression of my convictions. When I hear a sexist remark I feel all of the above. I feel that stomach-churning rage and pain that tells me that I am in trouble, that I am up against threat and wipeout. I am in the presence of something virulent in the social scheme directed against me not because of what I actually am but because of an immutable condition of birth. Something I might once have experienced as a Jew but today can feel only as a woman.

Bellow, Roth, Allen: These are writers who have had only the taste of their own lives as the stimulus for creative work — and a rich, lively taste it has been: tart and smart, full of bite and wisdom. But these writers were allowed to become so fabulously successful precisely because the stigma of Jewishness was fading even as they were recording it. When Bellow wrote *Herzog,* being Jewish was no longer the open wound it had been when he wrote *The Victim;* and by the time Allen and Roth were coming into their own they were far more integrated into the larger world than their work suggested. Therefore, for Allen or Roth to go on making the golden shiksa the foil, or for Bellow to keep portraying the Jewish intellectual who can't arrive as his foil, is tiresome and unpersuasive. It does not speak to the lives that any of us are now living. Such work strikes no chord of recognition; it strikes only chords of memory and sentiment. The thing about outsiderness is that one feels it in the flesh every day; one feels oneself invisible in the ordinary social way. These are requirements of the condition.

This invisibility once made Jews manic and Blacks murderous. It works on women in a variety of ways:

I leaned across the counter in the hardware store and said to the man who had told me women didn't know how to use the lock I'd chosen, "Would you say that to me if I were Black?" He stared lightly at me for a long moment. Then he nodded. "Gotcha," he said. 35

To the man at the university party I explained my work in great and careful detail. The man, a sixty-year-old Ivy Leaguer, was frankly puzzled at why I spoke of something fairly simple at such excessive length. I knew this was the first time he had heard what I was *really* saying, and I didn't expect it to sink in. What I did expect was that the next time he heard a woman speak these words, they would begin to take hold.

At the dinner party in New York I made a scene. I brought harmless sociability to an end. I insisted that everyone see that the little social murders committed between men and women were the real subtext of the evening, and that civilized converse was no longer possible unless this underlying truth was addressed. I did this because these were liberal intellectuals. They had heard it all before, many times, and *still* they did not get it. It was as terrible for me to go home that evening with the taste of ashes in my mouth as it was for everyone else — we had all come expecting the warm pleasures of good food and good conversation — but I couldn't have lived with myself that night if I hadn't spoken up. Just as I would have had to speak up if the conversation had suddenly turned politely anti-Semitic. Which it would not have in this company.

The Jewishness inside me is an education. I see more clearly, can think more inventively, because I can think analogously about "them" and "us." That particular knowledge of being one among the many is mine twice over. I have watched masters respond to "them" and "us," and I have learned. I wouldn't have missed being Jewish for the world. It lives in me as a vital subculture, enriching my life as a writer, as an American, and certainly as a woman.   1986

INVESTIGATIONS

1. Look again at the writing you did in response to "Write Before Reading" (p. 368). To what extent does it verify Gornick's assertion that "outsiderness is the daily infliction of social invisibility" (para. 27)? How does Gornick think one stops being invisible?
2. Gornick makes a distinction between who she actually is and how she's seen "because of an immutable condition of birth" (para. 32). How does she use this distinction to define herself? What aspects of her personality originate in her "immutable condition of birth"?
3. What would the speaker of "in white america" (p. 413) think of Gornick's statement that hearing a sexist remark makes her "feel that stomach-churning rage and pain" (para. 32) that means she's "up against threat and wipeout"? What would Big Mama ("Snuff Dippers") think?
4. Write a 250–500-word account of one of "the little social murders committed between men and women" (para. 37) that you've witnessed. What harm came to each party to the crime? What did each party gain? To what extent are these "little social murders" self-inflicted?

THEODORE WEESNER

The Body Politic

Five-five and one-twelve, thirteen years old, out of an obscure elementary school, a complete unknown, Glen Whalen walks into the boys' locker room to spin the dial of his combination lock. Emerson Junior High. It's a school with a double gym with a whiskey-colored floor upon which street shoes are never allowed.

The occasion: seventh-grade basketball tryouts.

Glen removes items from his gym bag and places them on the bench. Two pairs of white wool socks, white hi-top sneakers, gym shorts, T-shirt, jock. All but the T-shirt are new. He has to remove staple and paper label from a pair of socks, the jock from the box. The new sneakers, a once-a-year event, promise speed, new squeak-grips on the polished wooden floor, sudden turns, spring. This pair, he has told himself, he'll keep strictly for indoor use, a promise he made to himself in sixth grade too, only to break it during a sunny February thaw to the more immediate promise of running outdoors with seeming lightning speed.

The gym bag is new too, his first, navy blue with brown leather handles, a spontaneous gift from his father as they shopped on Saturday. Except for the sneakers, P. F. Flyers, and the jock, a Bike — a slight necessity, but his first and thus no slight event after all — the items are free of racing stripes and product names, as apparently uncomplicated as other forces at work in the era in which this otherwise unnoticed chapter in sports history is quietly unfolding.

Glen and his father, Red Whalen — the two live alone together in an apartment on Buick Street, in the obscure elementary school district, just up the hill from Buick Plant Three where Red works the second shift — picked out the items at Hubbard's Hardware & Sporting Goods Store downtown. Glen's list from school did not include a gym bag, and he imagined carrying everything in a paper bag, much as his father always had a bottle in a paper bag nearby, in glove box, trunk, under the driver's seat. But his father had already tipped one of those bags a few times by midday Saturday, the last a sizable snort as they parked in the alley behind Hubbard's, and there were the gym bags on a shelf before them.

"How you going to carry all that gear?"

Glen, looking in the same direction, did not say.

A native of Flint, Michigan, and a graduate of the Iowa Writers Workshop, THEODORE WEESNER (b. 1935) spent three years in the army after leaving school at sixteen. The author of four novels, most recently *The True Detective* (1988) and *Winning the City* (1990), he currently teaches at Emerson College and lives in Portsmouth, New Hampshire.

"Let's do it right," his father said. "Fight them to the end. On land, in the air, on the sea." There was that reddish glow in his cheeks, the film over his eyes, his Mona Lisa grin.

Blue is the wrong color, though, Glen realizes when a string of five boys — tall, renowned Ray Peaks among them — enters the locker room, each carrying a kelly green gym bag. The school colors are green and white, Glen knows, alas, in this moment, even as he knew it all along. Green and white, fight fight! "Shoot!" he says aloud.

"Belly high . . . without a rubber," one of the five boys sings out as they   10
turn into a nearby aisle.

Glen's plain white T-shirt also identifies him as an outsider. It's true that other white T-shirts are present in the gathering of twenty-five or thirty, but each is worn by a boy who handles a basketball with his elbows out, or one who cannot get his feet, in concert with his hands, to comprehend the concept of *steps*. Then two more boys wearing white T-shirts walk in, but the two — they have to be twins — are blubbery with jelly rolls around their middles, with near-breasts, and each wears knee guards, elbow guards, and wire cages over glasses. Otherwise most of the boys wear kelly green basketball jerseys, although no such item was included on the mimeographed list. One boy wears a flowered bathing suit that he had outgrown perhaps a year earlier.

Coach Bass walks into the gym carrying a new ball, blowing his whistle, shouting at them to return the balls to the ball bin, to *never* take a ball from that bin unless he says to! Appearing then, making a jogging entrance from the tunnel onto the glossy floor, are the boys of the green gym bags. The five, Glen notices, wear uniform gray sweatshirts — over green sleeveless jerseys, it will turn out — above white gym shorts and, laced in a military staircase braid into their white sneakers, matching green shoe laces. They are the ones, everything about them seems to say, who know the score, who already have it made at Emerson Junior High.

Coach Bass, ball under his arm, tweets his whistle, tells them to sit down. He paces to and fro before them, shifts the new ball hand-to-hand as he talks. He introduces the locker-room man, "Slim" who stands at the tunnel entrance watching. The best players and hardest workers will make the traveling squad of ten, he tells them. That's the way it is. This isn't elementary school anymore and that is the black-and-blue reality of competitive sports. A list will be posted on the bulletin board outside his office after practice on Friday. BUT, he adds, raising a finger. That's not all. Any boy — any one of them who has the desire. Who is willing to do the work. Can continue to attend practices. AND — from among THOSE boys — TWO alternates will be selected to dress for each home game.

Glen sits watching and wondering. Two alternates for each home game. It means everyone has a chance. Sort of. But does the Coach mean the *same two*, or two *new* ones each time? There are so many students here in junior high — hundreds more than in the small brick elementary school he attended last year.

Building and grounds cover acres. And any number of ninth-grade boys actually have mustaches, are over six feet tall. And some of the girls — wow!

The Coach blows his whistle again. He snaps, "On your feet!" and they   15
jump, almost as one, as if the process of selection is related to how quickly one can get upright. All but Ray Peaks, Glen notices. Ray Peaks — his arms appear to reach his knees — pushes up from one hand and is the last to stand. Still he is the first to receive a pass, as the Coach snaps the new ball to him and tells him to lead a line along the wall of folding doors.

Glen follows into the line and performs as instructed. He joins rows of five, back-pedals, sidesteps side-to-side, starts and stops. However anxious he feels, he does not have the problems of any number of boys who move left when they should move right, cross their feet when they should sidestep, stop when they should start. He dribbles in and around strategically placed folding chairs. He exchanges passes along a line of others and takes his place at the other end. He follows through one line to shoot a lay-up, and another to rebound and pass off. He begins to perspire, to breathe more deeply, to relax a little, and begins to observe the others in their turns as he waits in lines. And, like others, he glances to the Coach now and then, to see if he can see whatever it is the man is taking in.

Junior-high basketball. For home games the panels will be folded away, bleachers will unfold from either side, and the space and glossy floor — the surface is no less than beautiful, precious, an expanse of fixed lacquer upon which to perform — will offer a dimension that is possibly magical. Ray Peaks, Glen hears in one of the moving lines, could play with the senior team if he wanted.

Glen tries harder, tries to concentrate. However new he is to organized drills and dashes, shouts and whistles, it is becoming increasingly apparent that he is far from the worst. For while the gang of five seems to know all of the moves, any number of others, here and there, now and again, continue to reveal various shortcomings. And — that most promising sign — going in on a bounce pass down the middle, to go UP! and lay the ball over the front edge of the rim without crashing into the Coach where he is positioned just under the backboard, Glen hears at his back that phrase which shoots him through with sudden hope. "Nice shot there."

Friday waits before them as the week moves along, but Glen goes about life and school in his usual ways. He has never *made* anything like a team before, and even as he entertains his degree of hope, he hardly takes on any of the anxieties of expectation. Good things come home when you don't stand at the door waiting, his father has told him, and Glen gives little thought to what it will mean if he does or does not make the team. He will probably keep trying, he thinks, on the chance of dressing as an alternate.

He begins to eat lunch with Norman Van Slyke, who sits in front of him   20
in homeroom. Glen's father leaves him a dollar on the kitchen table every morning for lunch and on his own Glen has fallen into a habit of walking three

blocks from school to a small corner grocery he spotted sometime previously. Cold weather has yet to arrive and at the store — Sam Jobe's Market — he stands inside near a red pop case to eat, or he sits outside in the sun. Lunch is a packaged pie, usually pineapple but sometimes cherry, a Clark bar or two, and from a glass-bowl machine, five or six pennies' worth of Spanish peanuts to feed into his bottle of Hire's Root Beer, which salty beetles, as he thinks of them — perhaps Japanese, which are popular at the time, although he has never seen one — he pops to oblivion between his teeth as he drinks his root beer.

Norman Van Slyke's looks made Glen smile the first time he saw him in homeroom. Sparse hairs sprout already from the short, thin boy's upper lip, just under his adhesive-tape-hinged glasses, and his extensive nose projects in the midst of this confusion like an animal reaching its head from a hole in the ground. Norman's features twitch; the periscope that is his nose seems to look around at times, to glance up and down and to the side.

Glen calls him Rat Nose at once, and the name brings immediate snickers of pleasure from the other boy. In turn, Rat Nose identifies Glen as Weasel, and they take on the names and wear them along the street as easily as old sweatshirts.

After-school practices continue. Each morning, coming out of Civics and turning right, headed for Geometry, Glen discovers that he passes Ray Peaks going the other way. On Thursday morning, the lanky boy utters, "Say," in passing, and on Friday, when Glen speaks first, says, "Hi," to the school's already-famous athlete, Ray Peaks winks in a natural and friendly way that reminds Glen of his father's winks.

Glen also hears or learns in the days passing that the boys of the kelly green gym bags all attended the elementary school attached to the very end of Emerson Junior High. So it is that they had used the glossy hardwood double gymnasium all those years, stopped by after school to see home games and, as it also comes out, played together for two years as teammates in a Saturday-morning league. In practices, when teams are identified, and when they scrimmage, the five boys, Ray Peaks ever the nucleus, move as one.

Glen's basketball experience was different. His elementary school, near   25
Buick Plants Two and Three along a branch of the city river, had neither gymnasium nor coach. A basement classroom served as a gym, under the guidance of the gym teacher, Mrs. Roland. Painted blackish brown, its high windows and ceiling light fixtures caged, the room offered a single netless rim fixed flush to the wall, eight or nine feet from the floor and perhaps eighteen inches from the ceiling. The clearance was enough for either lay-ups or line drives.

No matter, Glen always thought, for in gym class they only played little kid games in circles anyway and only once was basketball ever given a try. Mrs. Roland, whistle around her neck, glasses on a separate lanyard, demonstrated — to introduce that one game — by hoisting the cumbersome ball from her side with both hands, kicking up one ankle as she tossed it at the basket, hitting the *bottom* of the rim. Then she selected teams — which selections for any real sport, indoors or out, were always maddening to Glen, as she chose captains and teams by height rather than ability. And she officiated the year's single basketball game by calling one jump ball after another, the contest lasting three minutes or less, concluding on a score of 2–0.

Tall boys will always be given the breaks, Mrs. Roland seemed to say. And if your last name starts with W, your place will always be at the end of the line.

Glen did play outdoors. At least a year earlier, as an eleven-year-old, he paused on a sidewalk beside a cement driveway at the side of a church along Buick Avenue and discovered not Jesus but basketball. The church was First Nazarene and the boys playing under the outdoor hoop were high-school age. Glen stood and watched, and when a loose ball came his way, he shagged it and walked it back several steps to throw it to the boy walking toward him.

"Wanna play, come on," the boy said.

Glen was too thrilled to be able to say. He did walk toward the action, though, nodding, although he had just a moment ago touched a basketball for the first time in his life. "You're on my side," the boy said. "Gives us three on a side."

Anxious, Glen moved into the area as instructed. The boy who had invited him — who was pointing out the sides, treating him as some actual person he had never known himself to be — turned out to be the seventeen-year-old son of the church's minister. Glen had never encountered a generous teenager before, and his wonder was such that he might have been a possible convert to nearly anything, but no such strings were attached. The seventeen-year-old boy was merely that rarest of individuals in Glen's life, a teenager who wasn't mean.

The game — Twenty-one — progressed, and passes were sent Glen's way as if he knew what to do. He did not. He passed the ball back each time, another time bounced it once and passed it back, and no one said anything critical, nor cast any critical glances, and the minister's son, who was already a memorable figure to Glen, said at last, when Glen single-dribbled again and return-passed the ball, "That's the way."

It would seem that Glen was being indulged, but something in the way the game was managed made it no less real as a contest. The minister's son had Glen put the ball in play each time it was his team's turn to do so, and in time he said to him, "Don't be afraid to take a shot," and when Glen passed off instead, he said, "Go ahead, take a shot or you'll never learn." A chance came again, and even as it may not have been the best opportunity, Glen pushed the ball two-handed toward the basket, only to see it fall short by two or three feet.

His teammates recovered the ball, passed and circled, and the boy said to him, "That's okay, good try, try it again." In time there came another opportunity, closer in, and this time the ball hit on the rim, hesitated, and, alas, dropped through, and the boy said only, "There you go, that's the way," as if

30

it were just another basket among all that might pass through such a metal ring and not Glen Whalen's very first. Glen continued with the game, too, as if nothing out of the ordinary had happened. But by the time evening air was descending he had grown so happy a glow was in his eyes, and for the first time in his life he was falling in love with something.

He had to be told to go home. When the sky was so dark the ball could   35
be spotted only directly overhead, a black moon against the night sky, and three of the other boys had drifted away, the minister's son finally said to him that he had better head on home, it was getting late. As Glen started off, though, the boy called after him, said they played every night at that time, to stop by again, and if he wanted to shoot by himself, the ball would be just inside that side door and he was welcome to use it just so he put it back when he was done.

Glen shot baskets, hours on end, entering into any number of imaginary schemes and games, and that summer and fall alone, until snow and ice covered the driveway, he played away a hundred or more evenings with the older boys, game after game, unto darkness. The games were three-on-three, although there were evenings when enough boys showed up to make three or four teams and to continue to play a threesome had to win or go to the end of the line. Glen loved it; he learned most of the moves and absorbed them into his system as one does. And so it is, on Friday after school, when practice ends and he follows along with the others to the bulletin board between gym and locker room and reads the typed list there between shoulders, reads it from the top — *Raymond Peaks* — down, the tenth name on the list is *Glen Whalen*.

He is invited to lunch. In school on Monday, outside his homeroom, one of the boys of the green gym bags — Keith Klett, also a guard — appears at Glen's side and doesn't ask him but tells him to meet them out front at lunch time. His house is only two blocks away, the boy adds; it's where they go to eat.

Seeing Rat Nose later, Glen mentions that he is going to eat lunch with the basketball team, and he experiences but the slightest twinge of betrayal. When he gathers with the others by the mailbox, though, there are only six of them who cross the street to walk along the residential sidestreet and Glen realizes, for whatever reason, that he is being selected by the five as a sixth man. He is being taken in. And he is not so naive that he doesn't know the reason; basketball is at the heart of it and some one person or another, or the Coach, has to have noted, as the line goes, that he is good.

Four of the five — all but Keith Klett — carry home-packed lunches in paper bags, and Glen is asked about the whereabouts of his own. "You can make a sandwich at my house," Keith Klett says. "No charge."

So Glen does — nutty peanut butter on fluffy Wonder Bread — in a large   40
kitchen and large house which if not elegant are far more middle-class than any house he has ever visited in a similar way. He is impressed by the space; there seem to be so many rooms, rooms of such size, a two-car garage outside,

a sun porch, a den; then, up a carpeted turning stairway to a second floor, Keith Klett's bedroom is larger than the living room in the four-room walk-up apartment he and his father have called home for the last couple years.

No less noticeable to Glen's eyes are the possessions, the furnishings and appliances, a boy's bedroom seemingly as filled with sports equipment as Hubbard's Hardware, and, on a counter, a globe that lights and an aquarium with bubbles but no fish — "the dumb jerk peed in the tank and they all croaked," Ray Peaks says — and model planes, ships, tanks, a desk with a lampshade shaped like a basketball, and, in its own bookcase, an *Encyclopaedia Britannica* set just like the set in the junior-high Reference Room. And — the reason they can troop through the house at will, the reason to troop here for lunch in the first place — Keith Klett's parents are both at work.

Making a sandwich in the kitchen, following each of Keith Klett's steps, including the pouring of a glass of milk, Glen follows into the den where the others sit around eating. Hardly anything has been said about basketball, and some joke seems to be in the air, but Glen has yet to figure out what it is. Sandwich packed away in two or three bites, two-thirds of his glass of milk poured in after, Keith Klett, smiling, is soon on his feet, saying to Glen, "There's something you have to see," slipping away to run upstairs as Ray Peaks calls after him, "Keith, leave that crap alone, it makes me sick."

There is no response.

"What's he doing?" Glen asks.

"You'll see — it'll make you toss your cookies."

Reappearing, a grin on his face, holding something behind his back, Keith Klett moves close before Glen where he sits chewing a mouthful of peanut-butter sandwich. The others titter, giggle, offer expressions of sickness, as Keith Klett hangs near Glen's face and sandwich a white rectangle of gauze blotched at its center with a blackish red stain. Even as Glen doesn't know exactly what it is, he has an idea and pulls his neck back enough, turtle-fashion, not to be touched by the daintily held object.

"Get out of here, Keith!" Gene Elliott says, adding to Glen, to them all, "Anybody who gets a charge out of that has to be a pervert."

Not entirely certain of the function of the pad of gauze, Glen decides not to ask. As Keith returns upstairs, white object in a pinch of fingertips, Glen finishes his sandwich, drinks away his milk, and carries the glass to the kitchen sink where he rinses it out, as he does at home. Perhaps it has to do with his father working second shift, leaving him to spend his evenings generally alone, or maybe it has to do with his not having brothers or sisters with whom to trade jokes and stories, but Glen has a sense, realized for probably the first time, as he and the others are walking back to school, that maybe he is shy or maybe he doesn't have much that he wishes to say. It's a disappointing realization in its way, and he is disappointed too, in some attic area of thoughts, with the group of five that has decided to take him in. He had imagined something else. And a twinge continues in him over Rat Nose going off on his own. One thing Glen does seem to see; he is a person. Each of them is a person, and each of them is different, and so is he, which is something he had never thought about before.

The season's first game is away, Friday after school. Lowell Junior High.

Thursday, at the end of practice, they are issued green satin trunks and 50
white jerseys with green satin letters and numbers. Glen will always remember that first digital identity, Number 5, will feel a kinship with all who wear it. Cheerleaders and a busload of students are scheduled to leave at 3 P.M. the next day, the Coach, clipboard in hand, tells them as they check the uniforms for size. Team members are to gather at the rear door at exactly 2:30.

"You have a parent who can drive?" the Coach all at once asks Glen.

"No," Glen says, feeling that old rush of being from the wrong side of something.

"You don't — your mother can't drive?"

"I just live with my father," Glen says.

"He can't drive?" 55

"Works second shift."

The Coach makes a mark on his clipboard, goes on to question others. In a moment, in the midst of assigning rides, he says, "Keep those uniforms clean now, and be sure to bring clean socks and a towel."

Four cars, including the Coach's own, will be making the drive, he announces at last. "Two-thirty on the button," he adds. "If you're late, you miss the game. And no one will change cars. Everybody will come back in the same car they go in."

The next afternoon, entering the strange school building across town, filing into a strange locker room, they select lockers to use and the Coach comes along, giving each of them a new pair of green shoelaces. Glen — he rode over in the Coach's car with two other silent second-stringers — continued more or less silent now, sitting on the bench, removing his still-clean white laces, placing them in his gym bag, replacing them with the green laces. He also unstaples his second new pair of wool socks, thinking that later he will remove the new green laces and save them and the second pair of socks for games only.

At last, dressed in the school uniform — Number 5; he loves the number 60
already and tries, unsuccessfully, to glimpse it over his shoulder — and new socks and bright shoelaces, he stands up from the bench to shake things out, to see how he feels. Nervous, he realizes. Frightened, although of what exactly, he isn't sure. Goose-bumped in locations — along thighs, under biceps — where he has not known the chilled sensation to visit him before, he notices that one, and then another and another, all of them, have laced in the green laces in the stairway military pattern, while his make their way in X's. He feels himself a fool. Was there time to change? Should he say something?

The Coach holds up both hands. "Now I know you all want to play," he says. "Chances are you won't. Depends on how things go. One thing — I want each and every one of you to understand before we go out that door. You will

listen to what I say and you will do as I tell you. There will be no debates.
There will be no complaints during or after this game. Anyone who complains,
about the game, or about teammates, or about anything, will find himself an
ex-member of this team. Nor will there be any arguing with officials. No calls
will be disputed. Remember: Losers complain and argue — men get the job
done. They stand up to adversity. They win.

"Now, we're going to go out there and have a good warm-up. The starting
five will be the starting five from practice and Ray Peaks will be our captain
for this game. Now: Let it be said of you that you tried your hardest, that you
did your best. Now: Everyone pause, take a deep breath.

"Let's go! Green and white!"

Throughout the warm-up, throughout the entire first half, in a continuing
state of awe and shock, Glen's goose bumps maintain their topography in
unusual places. It is the first time he has ever performed or even moved before
a group of people purposely assembled to watch and judge and count, and
even as this occasions excitement in him, a roller-coaster thrill, his greater
sense, sitting on the bench in the middle of the second-stringers, is one of high-
wire anxiety. His eyes feel froglike, his neck has unforeseen difficulty turning
in its socket, chills chase over his arms and legs like agitated sled dogs.

From folded-down bleachers on this side of the gym only — opposite is a
wall with high, wire-covered windows — Lowell Junior High students, teachers,
and parents clap, cheer, and shout as the game moves along. Glen sits there.
He looks around. His neck continues to feel stiff and sluggish. It occurs to him
as he glances to the lighted score board at the left end of the gym, that he does
not know how long the halves are. Six minutes and departing seconds remain
in the first half, then, all at once, five minutes and a new supply of seconds
begin to disappear into some tunnel of time gone by.

To Glen's right, before the narrow width of bleachers next to the door
that leads to their locker room, the cheerleaders from his school, half a dozen
seventh-grade girls in green and white, work, against all odds, it seems, to do
their job:

Peaks, Peaks — he's our man!
If he can't do it — nobody can! Yayyy!

Glen does not quite look at the cheerleaders; so carefully dressed, he feels
he has gone to a dance of some kind when he has never danced a step in his
life and would have declined the invitation if he had known it would lead to
this. The seconds on the clock chase each other away; then, again, another
fresh supply. Glen looks to the action out on the floor without knowing quite
what is happening. Nor can he entirely grasp what it was he is doing sitting
there on the bench. Even as he went through the warm-up drills, he did not
look at any of the spectators; rather he looked ahead, or at the floor, or kept
his eye on the ball as it moved here and there. How has it come to this? Where

is he? His team, he realizes, is behind 17–11, and he could not tell anyone how this had come to pass.

No substitutions. As the first half ends and the Coach stands up, Glen moves with the other second-stringers to follow along with the starting five to the locker room. Glen feels no disappointment that he has spent this time sitting and watching, nor any urge to be put into the game. Sitting on the bench in that costume, getting his neck to swivel; it seemed contribution enough. As they pass before the group from their school, however, and names and remarks of encouragement are called out, he hears distinctly, "Go get 'em, Weasel," and looks over to see Rat Nose's face looking at him, smiling, pleased, and a pleasure of friendship leaps up in Glen's chest.

The Coach paces and talks and points. They are behind 19–11. He slaps a fist into an opened palm. Glen continues to feel overwhelmed by all that surrounds him, but on the thought of Rat Nose sitting out there, calling him Weasel, he has to stop himself from tittering and giggling out loud. For one moment, then another, it seems to be the funniest thing that has ever happened to him.

"Now we don't have much time," the Coach is saying. "We have to get   70
the ball in to Ray Peaks. If we're going to pull this out, we have to get the ball in to Ray under the basket! Now let's get out there and do it. Green and white, fight — okay?" he inquires with some uncertainty.

On the floor, going through a confused warm-up, Glen glances back at the group from his school, looks to see Rat Nose there in particular, but the group is too far away and at such an angle that he cannot be sure. Then they're being herded back to their bench; maybe they aren't supposed to warm up for the second half — no one seems to know.

Glen sits in the middle of those on the bench and stares at the game as before. Five-on-five, two officials in black-and-white striped shirts. Whistles. The scrambled movement of basketball at ground level. Hands raised. Shouts from the bleachers. Yet again he has forgotten to check the beginning time. Nine minutes thirty seconds remain as he looks for the first time. The score? His next realization is that he has not been keeping score. He is too nervous for math, he thinks. Home 25/Visitors 16. The next time he looks, the clock shows eight minutes forty-four seconds. His team, he realizes, has scored but five points so far in the half. The other team's lead is increasing. It looks like his team is going to lose. That's what it looks like. There is Keith Klett snapping a pass to the side to Gene Elliott as they move before the scrambled concentration of players at the far end and Glen experiences a vague sense that they are somehow progressing in the wrong direction, and he experiences a vague sense, too, of hearing his name called out: "Whalen — Whalen!"

It is his name in fact, and there is the Coach's face as he looks, his fingers indicating sharply that he is to move to his side. The next thing Glen seems to know, as if he had received a blast of frozen air, is that he is crouched, one hand on the floor, next to the Coach's knee. In this location the volume of the game, the cheers, and spectators, seems to have increased three times over. "Check in at the table, next whistle, for Klett, get that ball to Ray Peaks!" Glen hears, sees the Coach spit the words at him from the side of his mouth all the time continuing to watch the action at the far end.

Stealing along in the same crouch, Glen reports in over the table top, says, "Whalen for Klett — I mean Number 5 for Number 7."

Taking a duck-step or two to the center line, Glen looks up to the score   75
board. Home 27/Visitors 16. Seven minutes thirty-one seconds.

A whistle blows out on the floor and at once a horn honks behind him, giving him so sudden a scare, he seems to lose some drops in his pants. "Substitution Emerson," the man calls.

Glen moves onto the floor, into the view of all, seeking Keith Klett; spotting him, he says, "In for you," and believing he is the object of all eyes, moves past him toward the end of the court where the other team is putting the ball in play, not knowing, in the blur of things, if it is the consequence of a basket or not.

Nor does he see Gene Elliott for the moment as, before him, an official hands the ball to a Lowell player. The boy passes it at once to a player who turns to start dribbling downcourt and Glen dashes toward him and the ball, slaps the ball away, chases it, grabs it in both hands, pivots, looks to find his fellow guard, to get rid of the ball, as he is poked in wrist and forearm by someone's fingers and whistle blows sharply, close-by.

"Foul! Lowell! Number 13!" the official snaps. "One shot! Number 5!"

The players return, taking their positions. "That's the way! Way to go!"   80
comes from Glen's teammates.

He stands waiting at the free-throw line. The others settle in, lean, wait. He has done this a thousand times, and never. The ball is handed over. "One shot," the official says. Glen looks to the distant hoop; he finds presence of mind enough to call up something of the endless shots in the church driveway, although the message remains elusive. He shoots, from the chest, as he had in the driveway, although they were taught in practice to shoot from between their legs. Hitting the rim with a thud, the ball holds, rolls, tries to get away to the side, cannot escape, falls through.

"Way to go, Whalen," a teammate remarks, passing him on the way down the floor. "That's the way," comes from another.

Glen moves toward the out-of-bounds line again, toward the other guard, as the ball is about to be put in play. He looks over for Gene Elliott again, but doesn't spot him, as the ball is passed in, and the guard receiving the ball, more alert this time, starts to dribble up court as Glen rushes him, explodes over him, somehow hits the ball as the boy swings it in both hands, knocks it loose, chases it, dribbles it once in the chase, looks again for his teammate as the Lowell player is on him, jumps, shoots — sees the ball hit the backboard, hit the rim, go through — and hears an explosion of applause from the other end of the gym.

At once he moves back in, pursuing the ball, as a teammate slaps his back, says, "Great shot!" and hears his coach call out, "Go ahead with that press, that's the way!" and hears the other team's coach, close-by, snarl to his guards, "Keep it away from that guy will you?" and hears Gene Elliott, inches away, say, "Coach says to go ahead with the press."

There he is, poised, ready, so thrilled already that his eyes seem aflame, as the Lowell players are all back down-court and are taking more time. He glances to the clock: seven minutes twenty seconds. In about ten seconds, he realizes, he has scored three points, which message keeps coming to him, that he has, in about ten seconds scored three points, that it is true, he has, and it is something, it is all things, and everything he has ever known in his life is different now.   85

The ball is moved along this time. At the other end, in their zone defense, the other team loses possession near the basket, and players run and lope past Glen as he circles back, and the ball is passed to him, and he dribbles along, eluding a Lowell player, passes off to Gene Elliott, sees Ray Peaks ranging to the right of the basket, and when the ball comes back to him — it will be his most satisfying play, one which is no way accidental, no way lucky — he immediately fires a long one-handed pass, more football than basketball, hard and high, and to his amazement Ray Peaks leaps high, arms extended, whips the ball out of the air with both hands, dribbles at once on a pivot-turn and lays it in neatly off the board, and there comes another explosion from behind them. And there is Ray Peaks seeking him out, grabbing his arm, hissing in a wild, feverish whisper, "That's the way to pass! Keep it up! Keep it up! We're going to beat these guys!"

The game progresses. Glen intercepts a pass and goes two-thirds of the court to put in a lay-up just over the front edge of the rim, as they were instructed, and he scores two or more free throws, to go three for three, bringing his point total to seven, but his most satisfying play is the first long, high pass, and the most exciting experience of the game is the fever which infects them all, especially Ray Peaks, who scores any number of added baskets on his high, hard passes, and Gene Elliott, too, who passes harder, as they all become caught up in the fever, including the Coach, who is on his feet shouting, clapping, waving, and the group from their school, whose explosions of applause keep becoming louder and wilder, until, suddenly to Glen, both horn and whistle sound, and there comes another explosion of applause, and the Coach and players from the bench are on the floor, grabbing, slapping, shouting, for the game is over and they have won, and they know things they had not known before, and none can quite get enough, it seems, of what it is they have not known until this very moment.

As they move and are being moved toward the locker room, Ray Peaks is slapped and congratulated, and so is Glen. There is the Coach, arm around Glen's shoulders, voice close, calling to him, "That full-court press was the thing to do! You ignited that comeback! You turned it around!"

The celebration continues in the locker room. The final score: Home 29/ Visitors 33. Locker doors are slammed, towels are thrown around, there is the Coach congratulating Glen again, slapping his shoulder, calling to them all, "That full-court press turned it around!" Glen learns, too, in the melee, that only two players on his team have scored, he and Ray Peaks, seven points and twenty-six, and everything, all of it, keeps occurring over again for him as a surprise, and as a surprise all over again, and he lets it go on as it will, a dozen Christmases and birthdays combined, accepts the compliments, knows in some part of himself already that he is changed by what has happened, has been granted something, knows these things, and does not volunteer in any way that at the time he simply chased the ball because he was so confused by all that was happening around him that he did not know, otherwise, what it was that he was supposed to do.

Monday it is back to school and lunch hour as usual. After school, though, as practice moves along, as they run through drills with the dozen or so alternates, there comes a time for the Coach to name squads of five, and the name, Glen Whalen, is called to run out and join the first team, in place of Keith Klett, who is left to stand with the others. It is not something Glen anticipated — is a small surprise — but as it happens the logic is not unreasonable to him. Nor is anything unreasonable to the other four, who congratulate him in small ways as he takes his place on the floor. 90

Keith Klett stands among the others, retreats, Glen notices, to the back row. His eyes appear not to focus on anything in particular as he stands looking ahead, glancing around.

They come face-to-face after practice in the locker room. Glen, sitting on the bench to untie his shoes, looks to the end of his aisle and sees Keith Klett staring at him. "You suck-ass," the boy says.

Keith Klett walks on. Glen doesn't say anything. He sits looking that way for a moment and doesn't know what to say or do.

Nor does he see the other boy when, undressed, towel around his waist, he walks along the main aisle to the shower. He wonders if they will fight, there in the locker room or out behind the school, and although the prospect of everyone streaming along uttering "Fight, fight," excites and terrifies him at once — he'll do it, he thinks — nothing of the kind happens. The remark stays within him like a speck; it stays and stays.

At home that night he thinks of resurrecting his friendship with Rat Nose and the thought appeals to him, as if to return home after having been away. Then he wonders if Rat Nose might turn his back on him — who would blame him? — and he worries about it until the next day when he encounters Rat Nose near his locker in the hall. 95

"Still go to Jobe's Market?" Glen asks.

"Sometimes," Rat Nose says.

"Wanna go?"

"Sure — I don't care — wanna go?"

They walk along the hall toward the door. There is no mention of a change 100
of any kind and they move along as if nothing has happened, as if it is merely
another day.   1989

INVESTIGATIONS

1. According to Vivian Gornick ("Twice an Outsider: On Being Jewish and
   a Woman"), imagination can play an important role in an outsider's
   attempts to move away from the margins. How does Glen use his imagination in this way? What other powers does he use to gain acceptance?

2. When Glen first discovers "not Jesus but basketball" (para. 28), he is
   treated "as some actual person he had never known himself to be" (para.
   31). What about basketball makes him an "actual person"? How is he not
   "actual" otherwise?

3. When Glen goes to lunch at Keith Klett's house, "he experiences but the
   slightest twinge of betrayal" (para. 38) because he's not eating lunch with
   his friend Rat Nose. Think of a time when you've been on either side of a
   similar situation. How did you reconcile the demands of friendship and
   those of community? In what ways does becoming a member of a group
   guarantee such "twinges of betrayal"?

4. When Glen's team wins the game, "they know things they had not known
   before, and none can quite get enough, it seems, of what it is they have
   not known until this very moment" (para. 87). What are these "things
   they had not known before"? What things do we discover in community
   that we don't discover anywhere else?

PATRICIA HAMPL

Parish Streets

Lexington, Oxford, Chatsworth, continuing down Grand Avenue to Milton and Avon, as far as St. Albans — the streets of our neighborhood had an English, even an Anglican, ring to them. But we were Catholic, and the parishes of the diocese, unmarked and ghostly as they were, posted borders more decisive than the street signs we passed on our way to St. Luke's grade school or, later, walking in the other direction to Visitation Convent for high school.

We were like people with dual citizenship. I *lived* on Linwood Avenue, but I *belonged* to St. Luke's. That was the lingo. Mothers spoke of daughters who were going to the junior-senior prom with boys "from Nativity" or "from St. Mark's," as if from fiefdoms across the sea.

"Where you from?" a boy livid with acne asked when we startled each other lurking behind a pillar in the St. Thomas Academy gym at a Friday night freshman mixer.

"Ladies' choice!" one of the mothers cried from a dim corner where a portable hi-fi was set up. She rasped the needle over the vinyl, and Fats Domino came on, insinuating a heavier pleasure than I yet knew: *I found my thrill . . . on Blueberry Hill.*

"I'm from Holy Spirit," the boy said, as if he'd been beamed in to stand   5
by the tepid Cokes and tuna sandwiches and the bowls of sweating potato chips on the refreshments table.

Parish members did not blush to describe themselves as being "from Immaculate Conception." Somewhere north, near the city line, there was even a parish frankly named Maternity of Mary. But then, in those years, the 1950s and early 1960s, breeding was low-grade fever pulsing amongst us unmentioned, like a buzz or hum you get used to and cease to hear. The white noise of matrimonial sex.

On Sundays the gray stone nave of St. Luke's church, big as a warehouse, was packed with families of eight or ten sitting in the honey-colored pews. The fathers wore brown suits. In memory they appear spectrally thin, wraithlike and spent, like trees hollowed of their pulp. The wives were petite and cheerful with helmetlike haircuts. Perkiness was their main trait. But what did they say, these small women, how did they talk? Mrs. Healy, mother of fourteen ("They can afford them," my mother said, as if to excuse her paltry two. "He's a

---

Patricia Hampl (b. 1946) once said, "I write about all the things I intended to leave behind, to grow out of, or deny: being a Midwesterner, a Catholic, a woman." Now professor of English at the University of Minnesota, Hampl's books include *Resort and Other Poems* (1983) and a memoir entitled *A Romantic Education* (1981).

doctor."), never uttered a word, as far as I remember. Even pregnant, she was somehow wiry, as if poised for a tennis match. Maybe these women only wore a *look* of perkiness, and like their lean husbands, they were sapped of personal strength. Maybe they were simply tense.

Not everyone around us was Catholic. Mr. Kirby, a widower who was our next door neighbor, was Methodist — whatever that was. The Nugents across the street behind their cement retaining wall and double row of giant salvia, were Lutheran, more or less. The Williams family, who subscribed to the *New Yorker* and had a living room outfitted with spare Danish furniture, were Episcopalian. They referred to their minister as a priest — a plagiarism that embarrassed me for them because I liked them and their light, airy ways.

As for the Bertrams, our nearest neighbors to the west, it could only be said that Mrs. Bertram, dressed in a narrow suit with a peplum jacket and a hat made of the same heathery wool, went *somewhere* via taxi on Sunday mornings. Mr. Bertram went nowhere — on Sunday or on any other day. He was understood, during my entire girlhood, to be indoors, resting.

Weekdays, Mrs. Bertram took the bus to her job downtown. Mr. Bertram   10
stayed home behind their birchwood Venetian blinds in an aquarium half-light, not an invalid (we never thought of him that way), but a man whose occupation it was to rest. Sometimes in the summer he ventured forth with a large wrench-like gadget to root out the masses of dandelions that gave the Bertram lawn a temporary brilliance in June.

I associated him with the Wizard of Oz. He was small and mild-looking, going bald. He gave the impression of extreme pallor except for small, very dark eyes.

It was a firm neighborhood rumor that Mr. Bertram had been a screen-writer in Hollywood. Yes, that pallor was a writer's pallor; those small dark eyes were a writer's eyes. They saw, they noted.

He allowed me to assist him in the rooting-out of his dandelions. I wanted to ask him about Hollywood — had he met Audrey Hepburn? I couldn't bring myself to maneuver for information on such an important subject, But I did feel something serious was called for here. I introduced religion while he plunged the dandelion gadget deep into the lawn.

No, he said, he did not go to church. "But you do believe in God?" I asked, hardly daring to hope he did not. I longed for novelty.

He paused for a moment and looked up at the sky where big, spreading   15
clouds streamed by. "God isn't the problem," he said.

Some ancient fissure split open, a fine crack in reality: So there *was* a problem. Just as I'd always felt. Beneath the family solidity, the claustrophobia of mother-father-brother-me, past the emphatic certainties of St. Luke's catechism class, there was a problem that would never go away. Mr. Bertram stood amid his dandelions, resigned as a Buddha, looking up at the sky which gave back nothing but drifting white shapes on the blue.

What alarmed me was my feeling of recognition. Of course there was a problem. It wasn't God. Life itself was a problem. Something was not right, would never be right. I'd sensed it all along, some kind of fishy vestigial quiver in the spine. It was bred in the bone, way past thought. Life, deep down, lacked the substantiality that it *seemed* to display. The physical world, full of detail and interest, was a parched topsoil that could be blown away.

This lack, this blankness akin to chronic disappointment, was everywhere, under the perkiness, lurking even within my own happiness. "What are you going to do today?" my father said when he saw me digging in the backyard on his way to work at the greenhouse.

"I'm digging to China," I said.

"Well, I'll see you at lunch," he said, "if you're still here."   20

I wouldn't bite. I frowned and went back to work with the bent tablespoon my mother had given me. It wasn't a game. I wanted out. I was on a desperate journey that only looked like play. I couldn't explain.

The blank disappointment, masked as weariness, played on the faces of people on the St. Clair bus. They looked out the windows, coming home from downtown, unseeing: Clearly nothing interested them. What were they thinking of? The passing scene was not beautiful enough — was that it? — to catch their eye. Like the empty clouds Mr. Bertram turned to, their blank looks gave back nothing. There was an unshivered shiver in each of us, a shudder we managed to hold back.

We got off the bus at Oxford where, one spring, in the lime green house behind the catalpa tree on the corner, Mr. Lenart (whom we didn't know well) had slung a pair of tire chains over a rafter in the basement and hanged himself. Such things happened. Only the tight clutch of family life ("The family that prays together stays together.") could keep things rolling along. Step out of the tight, bright circle, and you might find yourself dragging your chains down to the basement.

The perverse insubstantiality of the material world was the problem: Reality refused to be real enough. Nothing could keep you steadfastly happy. That was clear. Some people blamed God. But I sensed that Mr. Bertram was right not to take that tack. *God is not the problem.* The clouds passing in the big sky kept dissipating, changing form. That was the problem — but so what? Such worries resolved nothing and were best left unworried — the unshivered shiver.

There was no one to blame. You could only retire, like Mr. Bertram, stay   25
indoors behind your birchwood blinds, and contemplate the impossibility of things, allowing the Hollywood glitter of reality to fade away and become a vague local rumor.

There were other ways of coping. Mrs. Krueger, several houses down with a big garden rolling with hydrangea bushes, held as her faith a passionate belief in knowledge. She sold *World Book* encyclopedias. After trying Christian Science and a stint with the Unitarians, she had settled down as an agnostic. There seemed to be a lot of reading involved with being an agnostic, pamphlets and books, long citations on cultural anthropology in the *World Book*. It was an abstruse religion, and Mrs. Krueger seemed to belong to some ladies' auxiliary of disbelief.

But it didn't really matter what Mrs. Krueger decided about "the deity-idea," as she called God. No matter what they believed, our neighbors lived not just on Linwood Avenue; they were in St. Luke's parish too, whether they knew it or not. We claimed the territory. And we claimed them — even as we dismissed them. They were all non-Catholics, the term that disposed nicely of all spiritual otherness.

Let the Protestants go their schismatic ways; the Lutherans could splice themselves into synods any which way. Believers, nonbelievers, even Jews (the Kroners on the corner) or a breed as rare as the Greek Orthodox whose church was across the street from St. Luke's — they were all non-Catholics, just so much extraneous spiritual matter orbiting the nethersphere.

Or maybe it was more intimate than that, and we dismissed the rest of the world as we would our own serfs. We saw the Lutherans and Presbyterians, even those snobbish Episcopalians, as rude colonials, non-Catholics all, doing the best they could out there in the bush to imitate the ways of the homeland. *We* were the homeland.

Jimmy Guiliani was a bully. he pulled my hair when he ran by me on   30
Oxford as we all walked home from St. Luke's, the girls like a midget army in navy jumpers and white blouses, the boys with the greater authority of free civilians without uniforms. They all wore pretty much the same thing anyway: corduroy pants worn smooth at the knees and flannel shirts, usually plaid.

I wasn't the only one Jimmy picked on. He pulled Moira Murphy's hair, he punched Tommy Hague. He struck without reason, indiscriminately, so full of violence it may have been pent-up enthusiasm released at random after the long day leashed in school. Catholic kids were alleged, by public school kids, to be mean fighters, dirty fighters.

Jimmy Guiliani was the worst, a terror, hated and feared by Sister Julia's entire third-grade class.

So, it came as a surprise when, after many weeks of his tyranny, I managed to land a sure kick to his groin and he collapsed in a heap and cried real tears. "You shouldn't *do* that to a boy," he said, whimpering. He was almost primly admonishing. "Do you know how that feels?"

It's not correct to say that it was a sure kick. I just kicked. I took no aim and had no idea I'd hit paydirt — or why. Even when the tears started to his eyes and he doubled over clutching himself, I didn't understand.

But I liked it when he asked if I knew how it felt. For a brief, hopeful   35
moment I thought he would tell me, that he would explain. Yes, tell me: How *does* it feel? And what's *there*, anyway? It was the first time the male body imposed itself.

I felt an odd satisfaction. I'd made contact. I wasn't glad I had hurt him, I wasn't even pleased to have taken the group's revenge on the class bully. I hadn't planned to kick him. It all just *happened* — as most physical encounters do. I was more astonished than he that I had succeeded in wounding him, I think. In a simple way, I wanted to say I was sorry. But I liked being taken seriously and could not forfeit that rare pleasure by making an apology.

For a few weeks after I kicked him, I had a crush on Jimmy Guiliani. Not because I'd hurt him. But because he had paused, looked right at me, and implored me to see things from his point of view. *Do you know how it feels?*

I didn't know — and yet I did. As soon as he asked, I realized obscurely that I did know how it felt. I knew what was there between his legs where he hurt. I ceased to be ignorant at that moment. And sex began — with a blow.

The surprise of knowing what I hadn't realized I knew seemed beautifully private, but also illicit. That was a problem. I had no desire to be an outlaw. The way I saw it, you were supposed to know what you had been *taught*. This involved being given segments of knowledge by someone (usually a nun) designated to dole out information in measured drams, like strong medicine.

Children were clean slates others were meant to write on. 40

But here was evidence I was not a blank slate at all. I was scribbled all over with intuitions, premonitions, vague resonances clamoring to give their signals. I had caught Mr. Bertram's skyward look and its implicit promise: Life will be tough. There was no point in blaming God — the Catholic habit. Or even more Catholic, blaming the nuns, which allowed you to blame Mother and God all in one package.

And here was Jimmy Guiliani drawing out of me this other knowledge, bred of empathy and a swift kick to his privates. *Yes, I know how it feels.*

The hierarchy we lived in, a great linked chain of religious being, seemed set to control every entrance and exit to and from the mind and heart. The buff-colored *Baltimore Catechism*, small and square, read like an owner's manual for a very complicated vehicle. There was something pleasant, lulling and rhythmic, like heavily rhymed poetry, about the singsong Q-and-A format. Who would not give over heart, if not mind, to the brisk nannyish assurance of the Baltimore prose:

Who made you?
God made me.

Why did God make you?
God made me to know, love and serve Him in this world, in order to be happy with Him forever in the next.

What pleasant lines to commit to memory. And how harmless our Jesuitical discussions about what, exactly, constituted a meatless spaghetti sauce on Friday. Strict constructionists said no meat of any kind should ever, at any time, have made its way into the tomato sauce; easy liberals held with the notion that meatballs could be lurking around in the sauce, as long as you didn't eat them. My brother lobbied valiantly for the meatball *intactus* but present. My mother said nothing doing. They raged for years.

Father Flannery, who owned his own airplane and drove a sports car, had   45
given Peter some ammunition when he'd been asked to rule on the meatball
question in the confessional. My mother would hear none of it. "I don't want
to know what goes on between you and your confessor," she said, taking the
high road.

"A priest, Ma, a *priest,*" my brother cried, "This is an ordained priest
saying right there in the sanctity of the confessional that meatballs are OK."

But we were going to heaven my mother's way.

Life was like that — crazy. Full of hair-splitting, and odd rituals. We got
our throats blessed on St. Blaise day in February, with the priest holding
oversized beeswax candles in an X around our necks, to ward off death by
choking on fishbones. There were smudged foreheads on Ash Wednesday and
home May altars with plaster statuettes of the Virgin festooned with lilacs.
Advent wreaths and nightly family rosary vigils during October (Rosary
Month), the entire family on their knees in the living room.

There were snatches of stories about nuns who beat kids with rulers in the
coat room; the priest who had a twenty-year affair with a member of the Altar
and Rosary Society; the other priest in love with an altar boy — they'd had to
send him away. Not St. Luke's stories — oh no, certainly not — but stories,
floating, as stories do, from inner ear to inner ear, respecting no parish boundaries. Part of the ether.

And with it all, a relentless xenophobia about other religions. "It's going   50
to be a mixed marriage, I understand," one of my aunts murmured about a
friend's daughter who was marrying an Episcopalian. So what if he called
himself High Church? What did that change? He was a non-Catholic.

And now, educated out of it all, well climbed into the professions, the
Catholics find each other at cocktail parties and get going. The nun stories, the
first confession traumas — and a tone of rage and dismay that seems to bewilder
even the tellers of these tales.

Nobody says, when asked, "I'm Catholic." It's always, "Yes, I was brought
up Catholic." Anything to put it at a distance, to diminish the presence of that
grabby heritage that is not racial but acts as if it were. "You never get over it,
you know," a fortyish lawyer told me a while ago at a party where we found
ourselves huddled by the chips and dip, as if we were at a St. Thomas mixer
once again.

He seemed to feel he was speaking to someone with the same hopeless
congenital condition. "It's different now, of course," he said, "But when we
were growing up back there. . . ." Ah yes, the past isn't a time. It's a place.
And it's always there.

He had a very Jimmy Guiliani look to him. A chastened rascal. "I'm
divorced," he said. We both smiled: There's no going to hell anymore. "Do
they still have mortal sin?" he asked wistfully.

The love-hate lurch of a Catholic upbringing, like having an extra set of   55
parents to contend with. Or an added national allegiance — not to the Vatican,
as we were warned that the Baptists thought during John Kennedy's campaign

for president. The allegiance was to a different realm. It was the implacable loyalty of faith, that flawless relation between self and existence which we were born into. A strange country where people prayed and believed impossible things.

The nuns who taught us, rigged up in their bold black habits with the big round wimples stiff as frisbees, walked our parish streets; they moved from convent to church in twos or threes, dipping in the side door of the huge church "for a little adoration," as they would say. The roly-poly Irish-born monsignor told us to stand straight and proud when he met us slouching along Summit toward class. And fashionable Father Flannery who, every night, took a gentle, companionable walk with the old Irish pastor, the two of them taking out white handkerchiefs, waving them for safety, as they crossed the busy avenue on the way home in the dark, swallowed in their black suits and cassocks, invisible in the gloom.

But the one I would like to summon up most and to have pass me on Oxford as I head off to St. Luke's in the early morning mist, one of those mid-May weekdays, the lilacs just starting to spill, that one I want most to materialize from "back there" — I don't know her name, where, exactly, she lived, or who she was. We never spoke, in fact. We just passed each other, she coming home from six o'clock daily Mass, I going early to school to practice the piano for an hour before class began.

She was a "parish lady," part of the anonymous population that thickened our world, people who were always there, who were solidly part of us, part of what we were, but who never emerged beyond the bounds of being parishioners to become persons.

We met every morning, just past the Healys' low brick wall. She wore a librarian's cardigan sweater. She must have been about forty-five, and I sensed she was not married. Unlike Dr. and Mrs. Harrigan who walked smartly along Summit holding hands, their bright Irish setter accompanying them as far as the church door where he waited till Mass was over, the lady in the cardigan was always alone.

I saw her coming all the way from Grand where she had to pause for the traffic. She never rushed across the street, zipping past a truck, but waited until the coast was completely clear, and passed across keeping her slow, almost floating pace. A lovely, peaceful gait, no rush to it.

When finally we were close enough to make eye contact, she looked up, straight into my face, and smiled. It was such a *complete* smile, so entire, that it startled me every time, as if I'd heard my name called out on the street of a foreign city.

She was a homely woman, plain and pale, unnoticeable. But I felt — how to put it — that she shed light. The mornings were often frail with mist, the light uncertain and tender. The smile was a brief flood of light. She loved me, I felt.

I knew what it was about. She was praying. Her hand, stuck in her cardigan pocket, held one of the crystal beads of her rosary. I knew this. I'd once seen

60

her take it out of the left pocket and quickly replace it after she had found the handkerchief she needed.

If I had seen a nun mumbling the rosary along Summit (and that did happen), it would not have meant much to me. But here on Oxford, the side street we used as a sleepy corridor to St. Luke's, it was a different thing. The parish lady was not a nun. She was a person who prayed, who prayed alone, for no reason that I understood. But there was no question that she prayed without ceasing, as the strange scriptural line instructed.

She didn't look up to the blank clouds for a response, as Mr. Bertram did   65
in his stoic way. Her head was bowed, quite unconsciously. And when she raised it, keeping her hand in her pocket where the clear beads were, she looked straight into the eyes of the person passing by. It was not an invasive look, but one brimming with a secret which, if only she had words, it was clear she would like to tell.   1986

INVESTIGATIONS

1. Why is it that in Hampl's memory the fathers in their brown Sunday suits "appear spectrally thin, wraithlike and spent, like trees hollowed of their pulp" (para. 7)? How might their belonging to St. Luke's parish have this effect?

2. Compare the "blankness akin to chronic disappointment" (para. 18) Hampl describes to the disappointment Glen Whalen ("The Body Politic") feels after he eats lunch with the good basketball players who accept him as one of them. What does this feeling have to do with being inside a community? To what extent did you feel this "unshivered shiver" (para. 22) in the situation you described in your response to "Write Before Reading" (p. 368)?

3. How might Vivian Gornick ("Twice an Outsider: On Being Jewish and a Woman") explain the lack of "contact" (para. 36) Hampl describes? How does the "contact" Hampl creates by kicking Jimmy Guiliani threaten her belonging to St. Luke's? How does it threaten *her*?

4. Why does the man Hampl meets at a party sound wistful when he asks, "Do they still have mortal sin?" (para. 54)?

WALTER KIRN

The New Timothy

When the older boys in our ward came home from their two-year missions to Panama or Guam or wherever the men in Salt Lake had sent them, the first things they usually wanted to do were not the things you'd think, such as date girls and grow out their buzz cuts. Not for the first few weeks, at least. The boys had grown into statesmen while abroad, diplomats of the Gospel, and what they wanted to do when they got back, after their big reception in the airport with everyone waving bouquets and crying and pushing in to shake the hands that had blessed and baptized new foreign Mormons, was teach us younger guys about the world, its peoples, and their many customs, so we would know what was waiting for us when we went off on our own missions someday.

"A significant fact about Koreans," Timothy Breeden told us one night, "is that they see Americans as spoiled. They admire our institutions, sure — democracy and that — but basically they think we're pretty soft."

We were sitting around in Timothy's bedroom, four of us boys who had come there straight from church, sipping hot cider his mother had made and handing around a stack of snapshots showing crowded streets and blurry statues. When one of us would linger with a picture or hold it up to the light to see it better, Timothy would sway out forward from where he sat cross-legged on his bed and give us an expert description.

"That's a Buddha you have in your hand," Timothy told me. "Buddhas are their gods." He took back the picture and waved it around. "Who can guess how old this figure is?"

Someone dumb said, "A hundred years," like someone dumb always says.   5

Timothy looked at me. "Guess, Karl. Can you guess?"

I shook my head and tried not to yawn. I had run out of comments for Timothy. I had been in his room for over two hours, curious at first, then bored, waiting along with the other boys for Timothy to tire himself out. He had been back in Phoenix only three days and I could see he needed rest — there were shadows under his eyes and in his cheeks — but when I had asked him a moment ago if we should leave so he could go to bed, he'd told me he didn't need to sleep now that he knew how to meditate. "I don't have to eat as much, either," he said. "You can go a whole day on one slice of bread — you just have to burn it slowly."

WALTER KIRN (b. 1962) lived on a farm in Minnesota before earning a bachelor's degree at Princeton University and a master's degree at Oxford University. *My Hard Bargain,* his first collection of stories, appeared in 1990.

"But don't you need liquids, too?" asked Kevin Smith. Kevin's cousin Donna was the girl who'd been picked by Bishop Geertz to write Timothy letters in Korea. At church that day, when Donna heard that Timothy was inviting us over, she had asked me to call her afterwards and give her a report.

"In point of fact," said Timothy, turning over his hands in his lap and staring at his palms, "liquids are *all* you need."

I looked at Kevin, whose eyes had gone wide, and wondered what I was going to tell Donna.   10

Probably that she would just have to wait.

Donna Smith was seventeen, six months older than me, and a popular girl in our school because of her nonstop activities schedule. She captained the volleyball "A" squad, she starred in the aqua-ballet, and whenever there was a charity drive to help the school buy new computers or combat muscular dystrophy worldwide, Donna would chair the planning committee and be the person who painted fresh red lines on the funds barometer next to the flagpole. The reason she had time for all these things was that she never studied. Beautiful Mormon girls don't have to. Chances are they'll be married by eighteen, or, if they want to go to college, BYU or Ricks will accept them no matter how low they graduate.

To keep the non-Mormon boys from bothering Donna while she was writing to Timothy, I had pretended to be her boyfriend. We even went out on dates together. Her rule was that I could touch her in public but not when we were alone. I obeyed. I liked Donna plenty — any boy would have who'd seen her perform, exploding out of water, *ta-da!* — but what was I supposed to do? Donna had made it clear to me that keeping her faithful to Timothy was a duty I had to take seriously, or lose.

"You watch, he's going to appreciate this," Donna would often tell me, usually at the end of a date when we were sitting around in my Nova, digging the popcorn hulls out of our molars and trying to say good-bye without kissing. "You'll want to feel secure too," she'd tell me, "when you go away."

"I guess so," I'd say. "I suppose."   15

"Don't fool yourself," Donna would say. "You will. Out there all alone like that, having to cook your own meals. Not only that, they have riots there. Timothy says he got caught in one. Riots and murders all day long."

"You're right," I'd say. "It must be awful. I'll see you tomorrow. It's late."

"Well, don't just *agree* with me," Donna would say, giving my knee a backhanded slap that made her charm bracelet jingle. "Tell me what you *think*."

Sometimes, these talks would go on for so long and would get so incredibly pointless and dumb that I would have to climb out of the car and walk around the front and open Donna's door for her.

With Timothy home from Korea, though, Donna should have been through   20
with me. According to the deal we'd made, I was supposed to watch from the sidelines as Donna and Timothy got engaged, went off to BYU together, and

eventually set up house in one of the married dormitories there. That was Donna's plan, the plan that had worked so well for other couples, including her parents and my older sister. But Timothy had been home for three months and he still hadn't asked her out.

"Karl, can we talk?" Donna asked me at school one day. I took this as kind of a joke. I laughed. We were sitting in the library, where talking was all we ever did.

You had to have a book open though, so I balled up my sheet of doodles and opened one of Donna's books: *Crime and Punishment*.

"What are you reading this for?" I said. It made me sad that a girl with her looks suddenly felt she had something to gain by reading classic foreign literature.

Donna said, "Timothy's so confused now. Did you hear that he got an apartment downtown? His parents tried to stop him, so he borrowed a hundred dollars off Kevin to make the security payment."

All I said was, "Huh." Except for the downtown part, this sounded to me 25 like good news. Timothy was twenty-one years old, he spoke a foreign language now — a tough one. He couldn't very well stay in that bedroom with Disneyland curtains and Noah's Ark wallpaper.

"I heard that he doesn't have furniture," she said. "No sofa, no table, no lamp." Donna looked at me, pausing, as if she thought I needed time to picture an empty room. "I want you to visit him, Karl. There's something I want you to give him for me."

"All we can give him," I said, "is love and patience." It was a thing I could say without thinking that sounded like something I'd thought about.

Donna didn't seem to hear me. She lifted her knapsack off the chair back and took out a fat brown envelope crisscrossed with black electrical tape.

"Can't you just mail this?" I said.

"No," said Donna. "They open things." 30

I reached across and touched the envelope. I knew I would probably open it myself, so I thought it was only right to give her a second chance: "Have Kevin take it."

Donna shook her head. "Kevin's a Buddhist now too, Karl. Someone stable has to do this, someone who's on *my* side."

Then Donna leaned over and kissed me on the cheek.

We were in public, so it was allowed.

There had been cases worse than Timothy's — of boys who came home 35 from the mission field actually physically wounded, or on drugs, or in love with a girl from wherever they'd taught, or even in love with the boy they'd taught with, since Mormons go off on their missions in pairs. The same way I knew what went on in the Temple without ever having been inside the Temple — mostly from overhearing my parents or talking with friends who had overheard theirs — I knew about boys who lost weight in the field and never gained it back, a worm in their stomachs that just dug in for life, and of one boy who went away to New Guinea and witnessed a levitation in the jungle, and could not forget it, and lived in his car now, thirty-four years old.

I was thinking all this as I drove down Central, a straight shot south between palm trees and malls to Timothy's new apartment. I had Donna's envelope up on the dashboard, with all the tape stuck back in place, and I was driving slowly, buying time, because of what I was delivering.

The pictures must have been taken with a timer — Donna propping the camera on a shelf, then scurrying backwards into position, with only seconds to fluff up her bangs and settle her hands on the hips of her swimsuit. Some of Donna's poses I recognized from spectacular moments in the aqua-ballet. Other poses she must have seen in fashion magazines. One shot showed her suit strap slipping off, accidentally on purpose, it looked like. No matter what the pose was, though — whether Donna's arms were up or down, doing an arching backwards dive or softly paddling out toward the camera — her mouth was always stern, a line, as if she did not plan to do this again and wanted that fact known.

Not by me, of course, but by Timothy. He was the one she was trying to save, and I had no choice but to help her.

The low adobe apartment building was set around a gravel courtyard junked up with lawn chairs and tipped-over trikes and ruled by a pack of runty Mexicans playing whatever game those kids play instead of Cowboys and Indians. The kids carried pistols and droopy plastic swords. The moment I closed the gate behind me, two little girls with lopsided crew cuts charged at my knees and held on tight as three screaming boys closed in with machetes. Stripping the girls' small hands off my legs, I remembered something my dad had told me: that if the Apostles sent me to Mexico, I should try to get out of it by pretending I couldn't learn Spanish, because there is just no helping those people.

Some of the doors I passed had number stickers, but most of them just had number-shaped stains where the stickers had rotted away in the sun. I slipped the envelope under my waistband, thinking it would be safer there, and flopped out my shirt to hide it.   40

When I finally found the right-numbered door, Kevin, not Timothy, answered my knock. He was barefoot, with only gym shorts on, and over his shoulder I could see furniture — not a whole lot, but enough.

"Karl, my man," said Kevin, waving me in with two splinted fingers wrapped in dirty tape.

I sat on the couch. "Where's Timothy?" I said.

Kevin said, "Supply run. He'll be back."

"What happened to your hand?" I said.   45

"See that cinder-block wall?" said Kevin. I looked. "Someday I'm going to master it," he said "Someday I'll be stronger than that wall."

I wasn't really listening. I was searching the room for signs of Buddhism and not finding any. I did see a Book of Mormon, though: It was on the

floor by my feet, weighted by a filthy clamshell ashtray. I leaned down
to take the ashtray away and I felt Donna's envelope bending, all those
pictures.

"Leave that ashtray be," said Kevin. "Everything has a place in this apartment."

I straightened back up, embarrassed. "Is Timothy teaching you something?" I said.

Kevin shrugged. "Stuff about Korea, that's all."

"Stuff like what?" I said.

"Tae-Kwon-Do karate, different techniques to focus my mind. Mostly, we
just smoke here, though. That's why Timothy took this place, to have a place
to smoke."

"Just to smoke?" I said.

Kevin nodded. "Timothy picked it up in Korea. He says he can't quit —
he's a smoker now. He's breaking the Word of Wisdom and he doesn't know
what to do. He'll probably leave the church about it."

"Smoking?" I said. "That's all that's going on here?"

"Pretty much," said Kevin. "What's sad is that Timothy knows he'd be
perfect if this one thing wasn't ruining him."

I thought about this for a while. Then I said, "That's crazy. He should just
ask the bishop for help. Bishop Geertz was a smoker once himself."

"You don't understand," said Kevin. "Timothy's not at that stage anymore.
He doesn't ask for help. He stands alone."

"Does that go for Donna, too?" I said. "I hope he knows she's crying
every night."

Just for a moment, Kevin looked angry — I watched his jaw muscles bunch
together — but then, and it was amazing how he did this, he looked to the
side and shut his eyes and when he turned back to look at me again his face
was like a baby's, all washed-out and bright.

"That's none of my business," said Kevin. "Not yours, either."

Nothing else was said until I asked if I could use the bathroom. I wanted
to adjust the envelope, and maybe have one last look at the pictures, especially
that falling-strap one.

"Sorry, the toilet's dry," said Kevin. "We hardly ever use it." He picked
at his splint and eyed the wall. "We're at this stage where we hardly ever have
to."

I told him that sounded very unhealthy.

"Only to Westerners," Kevin said.

A loaf of bread, a jug of grape juice, a carton of filterless Camels — that's
what came out of Timothy's bag when he finally got back from the store. He
set out his items neatly on the shelf, lining them up so they didn't touch, as if
he planned to do a painting of them. I noticed then that his furniture was also
spaced for a painting.

"You here for a karate lesson?" Timothy asked me. "Or just as a spy for the brotherhood?" A cigarette was burning in his fingers, but I hadn't seen him puff on it yet.

"I wanted to see how you're doing," I said. I felt the envelope poking my rib cage. "I wasn't in church last week."

"Nor, alas, was I," said Timothy, using a word I'd read in books but had never actually heard in life. He tapped off his ash on the leg of his jeans and rubbed it in with the heel of his hand. "I presume you have scoped why that is," he said.

It struck me then that Timothy had forgotten how to speak English in   70
Korea and was building a whole new language for himself.

Kevin, starting to pace and chop the air, said, "Come on, let's go outside. We'll get all the kids and hold a class for Karl."

Timothy dragged on his cigarette. "You go ahead, Number Two. I'll be out in a triple jiff."

When Kevin had gone outside, Timothy stubbed out his cigarette, then lit a second one and frowned at me. At the edge of his still short haircut, just above and in back of his ear, I noticed a white shaved circle divided in half by a line of fuzz. It looked like something someone had stamped there without his necessarily knowing it.

"More propaganda from Bishop Geertz," said Timothy. He pointed at my bulging shirt.

"It's from Donna," I said, bringing out the envelope. "It's personal, though,   75
so you might want to — "

Timothy took the envelope from me and started peeling the tape off. His expression and all the smoke around his body made him look like a man in his own private vampire movie.

"She told me it's very personal," I said.

Timothy frowned and went on peeling. "Don't worry, I've seen these before," he said. "Or others of similar character."

Timothy held up the envelope and shook out the pictures onto the couch. Some of the worst ones landed faceup and Timothy lined them up on the cushion, making their corners even. He gazed at them for a moment, then picked out a butt from the ashtray on his knee, put it in his lips, and relit it. He squinted at the pictures through the smoke. "Which are your favorites?" he asked me.

I reached around to adjust my collar.   80

Timothy said, "The bending-over ones?"

I kept my mouth shut.

"Those are the saddest of all," he said. "She's pushing it in those. The essence of beauty is stillness and simplicity."

Kevin poked his head in the door then. "Any time," he said. "They're ready."

I glanced out into the courtyard. About a dozen barefoot Mexicans were   85
standing in a perfect line, not moving.

"Warm them up," said Timothy. He looked at me, grinning. "My troops," he said. "Assuming the meek shall inherit the earth — and there is every evidence they will — what you want to be, Karl, if you're smart, you want to be a general of the meek."

That's when I pushed myself up off the cushion. "Donna told me to tell you to call her. I see that you don't have a phone, though, so forget it."

"Hey, amigo. Chill," said Timothy. He shuffled the pictures into a pile and slid them back into the envelope. "For the pornography file," he said.

"Do whatever you want," I said.

Timothy shook his head. "At least she's learned some modesty," he said. 90
"In Korea, she sent me the wide-open spaces. You know what I mean by the 'wide-open spaces'? Photograph-wise? Anatomy-wise? Ever seen a Korean girl open a bottle of Coke? No hands?"

I didn't know what to say to this. I didn't know how to breathe and still be here. Out in the courtyard, the kids were screaming now, shooting out their little fists and screaming.

What I said next was a line from TV, but I knew it was the only line there is. "She's not going to wait any longer," I said. "I'll make sure of that."

Timothy said, "You do that," and stood up off the couch. He held out the envelope stuffed with secret pictures. "I guess these are yours then," he said. "Sorry you can't have the others — I burned them."

I let him hand me the envelope.

"I want you to promise me something," said Timothy, standing in the   95
doorway and kicking off his shoes. "Promise you'll go on a mission, Karl. I recommend it oh so highly. It helps you get your priorities straight when you see how outnumbered we are."

I remember those next few days as a dangerous time when I couldn't stop laughing. Everything was a joke, except for jokes. Jokes seemed very serious to me. Other things, though — the sacrament service, the way it was only torn-up Wonder Bread, yet everyone kept it for ages on their tongue — the president's hair on the morning news being whipped down flat by helicopter wind — even the thought of my sister's husband supposed to be some all-star saint because he'd converted a whole Brasilian village — all that kind of stuff just cracked me up no end.

If my parents had been at home I probably wouldn't have gone so crazy, but they were over in Mesa that week, staying with my sister and doing Temple work. They were baptizing the dead. They were standing knee-deep in a golden font and watching a TV screen flash the names of people who had died in ignorance, before Joseph Smith restored the Church and after Jesus started it. The Church had collected these names from books and graveyards all over the world and had put them onto microfilm and stored them in a bomb-proof vault inside a Utah mountain. Every time another corpse's name flashed, Mom or Dad got dunked in its behalf.

Baptizing the dead — another laugh.

I did not go to school, my mood was that tricky. I was afraid I'd see Donna and bite her — I didn't know what I might do. I stapled her pictures onto a string the way you show off Christmas cards and hung them over the tub in my bathroom. I liked to slide down under the water, watching the pictures blur away. I did this every night. Then, on my third day home, a friend stopped over and told me that Donna was home from school herself, exhausted after a marathon car wash held to raise money for vanishing sea turtles.

"Is Donna there?" I asked her father. I was standing in the living room, 100 the phone cord spooled around my chest because I was slowly spinning in place, trying to calm myself down. The turning and turning living room walls with all their framed verses and family portraits felt like the cyclorama I'd seen once of Brigham Young crossing the plains, that same dizziness.

"Timothy's sent a note," said Donna before I could get a word in. "Listen, everyone's bawling here. Come get me."

Heading out of town that evening, before we realized where we were driving, I tried to ask about Timothy's note, but Donna did not want to talk about that. "More sad confusion" was all she would tell me, and something about him moving to the mountains. She wanted to talk about science instead. It was high time she knew more about it, she told me, draping her arm around my neck, and as I drained my gas tank making what felt like pointless right turns, she asked me all kinds of heartbreaking questions she could have had answered in seventh grade, if only she'd paid attention then. Why do planets rotate? How can ships built of steel float in water? Why does a car need four different gears?

When I told her my answers would take some time, she said that she knew that but had to start somewhere, which made me wonder where Donna had been or where she would have ended up, not even knowing the sun was a star.

And then we saw the sign and knew we had been driving somewhere after all.

Check-in was easy. The key fit the lock. The curtains were already drawn. 105 The hardest part of our first time together there in the Day Rates Motel was pretending we didn't know what we were doing. It was having to fake we were virgins, though we were.   1990

INVESTIGATIONS

1. What are the similarities and differences between life in St. Luke's parish ("Parish Streets") and the Mormon ward in which Karl lives? How are ward attitudes toward the outside world similar to parish attitudes? How do they differ?

2. In paragraph 24 Donna says, "Timothy's so confused now." Why does she think so? Why might Timothy think Donna is the confused one? What do you think caused the change in Timothy?

3. After his meeting with Timothy, Karl thinks "everything was a joke, except

for jokes. Jokes seemed very serious to me" (para. 96). What does he mean?

4. In what ways do Karl and Donna remain "inside" the Mormon church, even in the final paragraph?

LUCILLE CLIFTON

in white america

1   i come to read them poems

i come to read them poems,
a fancy trick i do
like juggling with balls of light.
i stand, a dark spinner,
in the grange hall,   5
in the library, in the
smaller conference room,
and toss and catch as if by magic,
my eyes bright, my mouth smiling,
my singed hands burning.   10

2   the history

1800's in this town
fourteen longhouses were destroyed
by not these people here.
not these people
burned the crops and chopped down   15
all the peach trees.
not these people. these people
preserve peaches, even now.

A native of Depew, New York, LUCILLE CLIFTON (b. 1936) is the author of many children's books, a memoir (*Generations: A Memoir*, 1986), and seven books of poetry, most recently *Quilting: Poems 1987–1990* (1991). She once said, "I am a Black woman poet, and I sound like one."

3   *the tour*

"this was a female school.
my mother's mother graduated   20
second in her class.
they were taught embroidery,
and chenille and filigree,
ladies' learning. yes,
we have a liberal history here."   25
smiling she pats my darky hand.

4   *the hall*

in this hall
dark women
scrubbed the aisles
between the pews   30
on their knees.
they could not rise
to worship.
in this hall
dark women   35
my sisters and mothers

though i speak with the tongues
of men and of angels and
have not charity . . .

in this hall   40
dark women,
my sisters and mothers,
i stand
and let the church say
let the church say   45
let the church say
AMEN.

5   *the reading*

i look into none of my faces
and do the best i can.
the human hair between us   50

stretches but does not break.
i slide myself along it and
love them, love them all.

6   *it is late*

it is late
in white america.   55
i stand
in the light of the
7-11
looking out toward
the church   60
and for a moment only
i feel the reverberation
of myself
in white america
a black cat   65
in the belfry
hanging
and
ringing.   1987

INVESTIGATIONS

1. In section 1, why does the speaker feel her "singed hands burning" (line 10)? In what ways does she speak as an outsider? As an insider?

2. Describe how her sense of history influences the speaker of this poem. What does her sense of history have to do with what she says in section 6 (lines 54–69)?

3. How might the women spoken of in section 4 (lines 27–47) be seen as what Patricia Hampl ("Parish Streets") calls "people who were always there, who were solidly part of us, part of what we were, but who never emerged beyond the bounds of being parishioners to become persons"?

4. What does the speaker mean in section 5 (line 48) when she says, "i look into none of my faces"? How do you reconcile this section's final two lines (52–53) with the final line (26) of section 3?

WENDY ROSE

For the White Poets
Who Would Be Indian

just once. Just long enough
to snap up the words, fish-hooked
to your tongues: you think of us now
when you kneel on the earth, when
you turn holy in a temporary tourism   5
of our souls;
                with words you paint your faces,
                chew your doeskin, touch beast
                and tree as if sharing a mother
                were all it takes, could bring   10
instant and primal knowledge.
You think of us only when
your voice wants for roots,
when you have sat back on your heels
and   become   primitive.   15

You finish your poems
and go back.   1977

INVESTIGATIONS

1. Reread lines 7–11. What besides "sharing a mother" does the speaker
   think it "takes" to "be Indian"? Why isn't "sharing a mother" enough to
   "bring / instant and primal knowledge"?
2. Imagine that you're the speaker of this poem. In two or three paragraphs,
   explain why white poets will always be outsiders to your experience, why
   even imagination isn't enough for them to glimpse it "from the inside."
3. Where do the "white poets" "go back" to (line 17)? In what sense did
   they get what they came for?

Anthropologist, editor, visual artist, and poet, WENDY ROSE was born in California in 1948, educated
at the University of California at Berkeley, and now teaches American Indian Studies at Fresno City
College. Her books include the poetry collections *Lost Copper* (1981) and *Halfbreed Chronicles*
(1984).

RICHARD RODRIGUEZ

Aria: A Bilingual Childhood

I

I remember to start with that day in Sacramento — a California now nearly thirty years past — when I first entered a classroom, able to understand some fifty stray English words.

The third of four children, I had been preceded to a neighborhood Roman Catholic school by an older brother and sister. But neither of them had revealed very much about their classroom experiences. Each afternoon they returned, as they left in the morning, always together, speaking in Spanish as they climbed the five steps of the porch. And their mysterious books, wrapped in shopping-bag paper, remained on the table next to the door, closed firmly behind them.

An accident of geography sent me to a school where all my classmates were white, many the children of doctors and lawyers and business executives. All my classmates certainly must have been uneasy on that first day of school — as most children are uneasy — to find themselves apart from their families in the first institution of their lives. But I was astonished.

The nun said, in a friendly but oddly impersonal voice, "Boys and girls, this is Richard Rodriguez." (I heard her sound out: *Rich-heard Road-ree-guess.*) It was the first time I had heard anyone name me in English. "Richard," the nun repeated more slowly, writing my name down in her black leather book. Quickly I turned to see my mother's face dissolve in a watery blur behind the pebbled glass door.

Many years later there is something called bilingual education — a scheme 5 proposed in the late 1960s by Hispanic-American social activists, later endorsed by a congressional vote. It is a program that seeks to permit non-English-speaking children, many from lower-class homes, to use their family language as the language of school. (Such is the goal its supporters announce.) I hear them and am forced to say no: It is not possible for a child — any child — ever to use his family's language in school. Not to understand this is to misunderstand the public uses of schooling and to trivialize the nature of intimate life — a family's "language."

Memory teaches me what I know of these matters; the boy reminds the

The son of working-class Mexican immigrants, RICHARD RODRIGUEZ (b. 1944) grew up in Sacramento, California. Now a writer, lecturer, and educational consultant, Rodriguez holds a Ph.D. in English literature from the University of California at Berkeley and is the author of *Hunger of Memory* (1982) and *Mexico's Children* (1991).

adult. I was a bilingual child, a certain kind — socially disadvantaged — the son of working-class parents, both Mexican immigrants.

In the early years of my boyhood, my parents coped very well in America. My father had steady work. My mother managed at home. They were nobody's victims. Optimism and ambition led them to a house (our home) many blocks from the Mexican south side of town. We lived among *gringos* and only a block from the biggest, whitest houses. It never occurred to my parents that they couldn't live wherever they chose. Nor was the Sacramento of the fifties bent on teaching them a contrary lesson. My mother and father were more annoyed than intimidated by those two or three neighbors who tried initially to make us unwelcome. ("Keep your brats away from my sidewalk!") But despite all they achieved, perhaps because they had so much to achieve, any deep feeling of ease, the confidence of "belonging" in public was withheld from them both. They regarded the people at work, the faces in crowds, as very distant from us. They were the others, *los gringos*. That term was interchangeable in their speech with another, even more telling, *los americanos*.

I grew up in a house where the only regular guests were my relations. For one day, enormous families of relatives would visit and there would be so many people that the noise and the bodies would spill out to the backyard and front porch. Then, for weeks, no one came by. (It was usually a salesman who rang the doorbell.) Our house stood apart. A gaudy yellow in a row of white bungalows. We were the people with the noisy dog. The people who raised pigeons and chickens. We were the foreigners on the block. A few neighbors smiled and waved. We waved back. But no one in the family knew the names of the old couple who lived next door; until I was seven years old, I did not know the names of the kids who lived across the street.

In public, my father and mother spoke a hesitant, accented, not always grammatical English. And they would have to strain — their bodies tense — to catch the sense of what was rapidly said by *los gringos*. At home they spoke Spanish. The language of their Mexican past sounded in counterpoint to the English of public society. The words would come quickly, with ease. Conveyed through those sounds was the pleasing, soothing, consoling reminder of being at home.

During those years when I was first conscious of hearing, my mother and father addressed me only in Spanish; in Spanish I learned to reply. By contrast, English (*inglés*), rarely heard in the house, was the language I came to associate with *gringos*. I learned my first words of English overhearing my parents speak to strangers. At five years of age, I knew just enough English for my mother to trust me on errands to stores one block away. No more.

I was a listening child, careful to hear the very different sounds of Spanish and English. Wide-eyed with hearing, I'd listen to sounds more than words. First, there were English (*gringo*) sounds. So many words were still unknown that when the butcher or the lady at the drugstore said something to me, exotic polysyllabic sounds would bloom in the midst of their sentences. Often, the speech of people in public seemed to me very loud, booming with confidence. The man behind the counter would literally ask, "What can I do for you?" But by being so firm and so clear, the sound of his voice said that he was a *gringo;* he belonged in public society.

I would also hear then the high nasal notes of middle-class American speech. The air stirred with sound. Sometimes, even now, when I have been traveling abroad for several weeks, I will hear what I heard as a boy. In hotel lobbies or airports, in Turkey or Brazil, some Americans will pass, and suddenly I will hear it again — the high sound of American voices. For a few seconds I will hear it with pleasure, for it is now the sound of *my* society — a reminder of home. But inevitably — already on the flight headed for home — the sound fades with repetition. I will be unable to hear it anymore.

When I was a boy, things were different. The accent of *los gringos* was never pleasing nor was it hard to hear. Crowds at Safeway or at bus stops would be noisy with sound. And I would be forced to edge away from the chirping chatter above me.

I was unable to hear my own sounds, but I knew very well that I spoke English poorly. My words could not stretch far enough to form complete thoughts. And the words I did speak I didn't know well enough to make into distinct sounds. (Listeners would usually lower their heads, better to hear what I was trying to say.) But it was one thing for *me* to speak English with difficulty. It was more troubling for me to hear my parents speak in public: their high-whining vowels and guttural consonants; their sentences that got stuck with "eh" and "ah" sounds; the confused syntax; the hesitant rhythm of sounds so different from the way *gringos* spoke. I'd notice, moreover, that my parents' voices were softer than those of *gringos* we'd meet.

I am tempted now to say that none of this mattered. In adulthood I am   15
embarrassed by childhood fears. And, in a way, it didn't matter very much that my parents could not speak English with ease. Their linguistic difficulties had no serious consequences. My mother and father made themselves understood at the county hospital clinic and at government offices. And yet, in another way, it mattered very much — it was unsettling to hear my parents struggle with English. Hearing them, I'd grow nervous, my clutching trust in their protection and power weakened.

There were many times like the night at a brightly lit gasoline station (a blaring white memory) when I stood uneasily, hearing my father. He was talking to a teenaged attendant. I do not recall what they were saying, but I cannot forget the sounds my father made as he spoke. At one point his words slid together to form one word — sounds as confused as the threads of blue and green oil in the puddle next to my shoes. His voice rushed through what he had left to say. And, toward the end, reached falsetto notes, appealing to his listener's understanding. I looked away to the lights of passing automobiles. I tried not to hear anymore. But I heard only too well the calm, easy tones in the attendant's reply. Shortly afterward, walking toward home with my father, I shivered when he put his hand on my shoulder. The very first chance that I got, I evaded his grasp and ran on ahead into the dark, skipping with feigned boyish exuberance.

But then there was Spanish. *Español*: my family's language. *Español*: the language that seemed to me a private language. I'd hear strangers on the radio and in the Mexican Catholic church across town speaking in Spanish, but I couldn't really believe that Spanish was a public language, like English. Spanish speakers, rather, seemed related to me, for I sensed that we shared — through our language — the experience of feeling apart from *los gringos*. It was thus a ghetto Spanish that I heard and I spoke. Like those whose lives are bound by a barrio, I was reminded by Spanish of my separateness from *los otros, los gringos* in power. But more intensely than for most barrio children — because I did not live in a barrio — Spanish seemed to me the language of home. (Most days it was only at home that I'd hear it.) It became the language of joyful return.

A family member would say something to me and I would feel myself specially recognized. My parents would say something to me and I would feel embraced by the sounds of their words. Those sounds said: *I am speaking with ease in Spanish. I am addressing you in words I never use with* los gringos. *I recognize you as someone special, close, like no one outside. You belong with us. In the family.*

(*Ricardo.*)

At the age of five, six, well past the time when most other children no longer easily notice the difference between sounds uttered at home and words spoken in public, I had a different experience. I lived in a world magically compounded of sounds. I remained a child longer than most; I lingered too long, poised at the edge of language — often frightened by the sounds of *los gringos*, delighted by the sounds of Spanish at home. I shared with my family a language that was startlingly different from that used in the great city around us.

For me there were none of the gradations between public and private society so normal to a maturing child. Outside the house was public society; inside the house was private. Just opening or closing the screen door behind me was an important experience. I'd rarely leave home all alone or without reluctance. Walking down the sidewalk, under the canopy of tall trees, I'd warily notice the — suddenly — silent neighborhood kids who stood warily watching me. Nervously, I'd arrive at the grocery store to hear there the sounds of the *gringo* — foreign to me — reminding me that in this world so big, I was a foreigner. But then I'd return. Walking back toward our house, climbing the steps from the sidewalk, when the front door was open in the summer, I'd hear voices beyond the screen door talking in Spanish. For a second or two, I'd stay, linger there, listening. Smiling, I'd hear my mother call out, saying in Spanish (words): "Is that you, Richard?" All the while her sounds would assure me: *You are home now; come closer; inside. With us.*

"*Sí,*" I'd reply.

Once more inside the house I would resume (assume) my place in the family. The sounds would dim, grow harder to hear. Once more at home, I would grow less aware of that fact. It required, however, no more than the blurt of the doorbell to alert me to listen to sounds all over again. The house would turn instantly still while my mother went to the door. I'd hear her hard

20

English sounds. I'd wait to hear her voice return to soft-sounding Spanish, which assured me, as surely as did the clicking tongue of the lock on the door, that the stranger was gone.

Plainly, it is not healthy to hear such sounds so often. It is not healthy to distinguish public words from private sounds so easily. I remained cloistered by sounds, timid and shy in public, too dependent on voices at home. And yet it needs to be emphasized: I was an extremely happy child at home. I remember many nights when my father would come back from work, and I'd hear him call out to my mother in Spanish, sounding relieved. In Spanish, he'd sound light and free notes he never could manage in English. Some nights I'd jump up just at hearing his voice. With *mis hermanos* I would come running into the room where he was with my mother. Our laughing (so deep was the pleasure!) became screaming. Like others who know the pain of public alienation, we transformed the knowledge of our public separateness and made it consoling — the reminder of intimacy. Excited, we joined our voices in a celebration of sounds. *We are speaking now the way we never speak out in public. We are alone — together*, voices sounded, surrounded to tell me. Some nights, no one seemed willing to loosen the hold sounds had on us. At dinner, we invented new words. (Ours sounded Spanish, but made sense only to us.) We pieced together new words by taking, say, an English verb and giving it Spanish endings. My mother's instructions at bedtime would be lacquered with mock-urgent tones. Or a word like *sí* would become, in several notes, able to convey added measures of feeling. Tongues explored the edges of words, especially the fat vowels. And we happily sounded that military drum roll, the twirling roar of the Spanish *r*. Family language: my family's sounds. The voices of my parents and sisters and brother. Their voices insisting: *You belong here. We are family members. Related. Special to one another. Listen!* Voices singing and sighing, rising, straining, then surging, teeming with pleasure that burst syllables into fragments of laughter. At times it seemed there was steady quiet only when, from another room, the rustling whispers of my parents faded and I moved closer to sleep.

2

Supporters of bilingual education today imply that students like me miss a   25
great deal by not being taught in their family's language. What they seem not to recognize is that, as a socially disadvantaged child, I considered Spanish to be a private language. What I needed to learn in school was that I had the right — and the obligation — to speak the public language of *los gringos*. The odd truth is that my first-grade classmates could have become bilingual, in the conventional sense of that word, more easily than I. Had they been taught (as upper-middle-class children are often taught early) a second language like Spanish or French, they could have regarded it simply as that; another public language. In my case such bilingualism could not have been so quickly achieved. What I did not believe was that I could speak a single public language.

Without question, it would have pleased me to hear my teachers address me in Spanish when I entered the classroom. I would have felt much less afraid. I would have trusted them and responded with ease. But I would have delayed — for how long postponed? — having to learn the language of public society. I would have evaded — and for how long could I have afforded to delay? — learning the great lesson of school, that I had a public identity.

Fortunately, my teachers were unsentimental about their responsibility. What they understood was that I needed to speak a public language. So their voices would search me out, asking me questions. Each time I'd hear them, I'd look up in surprise to see a nun's face frowning at me. I'd mumble, not really meaning to answer. The nun would persist, "Richard, stand up. Don't look at the floor. Speak up. Speak to the entire class, not just to me!" But I couldn't believe that the English language was mine to use. (In part, I did not want to believe it.) I continued to mumble. I resisted the teacher's demands. (Did I somehow suspect that once I learned public language my pleasing family life would be changed?) Silent, waiting for the bell to sound, I remained dazed, diffident, afraid.

Because I wrongly imagined that English was intrinsically a public language and Spanish an intrinsically private one, I easily noted the difference between classroom language and the language of home. At school, words were directed to a general audience of listeners. ("Boys and girls.") Words were meaningfully ordered. And the point was not self-expression alone but to make oneself understood by many others. The teacher quizzed: "Boys and girls, why do we use that word in this sentence? Could we think of a better word to use there? Would the sentence change its meaning if the words were differently arranged? And wasn't there a better way of saying much the same thing?" (I couldn't say. I wouldn't try to say.)

Three months. Five. Half a year passed. Unsmiling, ever watchful, my teachers noted my silence. They began to connect my behavior with the difficult progress my older sister and brother were making. Until one Saturday morning three nuns arrived at the house to talk to our parents. Stiffly, they sat on the blue living room sofa. From the doorway of another room, spying the visitors, I noted the incongruity — the clash of two worlds, the faces and voices of school intruding upon the familiar setting of home. I overheard one voice gently wondering, "Do your children speak only Spanish at home, Mrs. Rodriguez?" While another voice added, "That Richard especially seems so timid and shy."

That Rich-heard!   30

With great tact the visitors continued, "Is it possible for you and your husband to encourage your children to practice their English when they are home?" Of course, my parents complied. What would they not do for their children's well-being? And how could they have questioned the Church's authority which those women represented? In an instant, they agreed to give up the language (the sounds) that had revealed and accentuated our family's closeness. The moment after the visitors left, the change was observed. "*Ahora,* speak to us *en inglés,*" my father and mother united to tell us.

At first, it seemed a kind of game. After dinner each night, the family gathered to practice "our" English. (It was still then *inglés,* a language foreign to us, so we felt drawn as strangers to it.) Laughing, we would try to define words we could not pronounce. We played with strange English sounds, often overanglicizing our pronunciations. And we filled the smiling gaps of our sentences with familiar Spanish sounds. But that was cheating, somebody shouted. Everyone laughed. In school, meanwhile, like my brother and sister, I was required to attend a daily tutoring session. I needed a full year of special attention. I also needed my teachers to keep my attention from straying in class by calling out, *Rich-heard* — their English voices slowly prying loose my ties to my other name, its three notes, *Ri-car-do*. Most of all I needed to hear my mother and father speak to me in a moment of seriousness in broken — suddenly heartbreaking — English. The scene was inevitable: One Saturday morning I entered the kitchen where my parents were talking in Spanish. I did not realize that they were talking in Spanish however until, at the moment they saw me, I heard their voices change to speak English. Those *gringo* sounds they uttered startled me. Pushed me away. In that moment of trivial misunderstanding and profound insight, I felt my throat twisted by unsounded grief. I turned quickly and left the room. But I had no place to escape to with Spanish. (The spell was broken.) My brother and sisters were speaking English in another part of the house.

Again and again in the days following, increasingly angry, I was obliged to hear my mother and father: "Speak to us *en inglés.*" (*Speak.*) Only then did I determine to learn classroom English. Weeks after, it happened: One day in school I raised my hand to volunteer an answer. I spoke out in a loud voice. And I did not think it remarkable when the entire class understood. That day, I moved very far from the disadvantaged child I had been only days earlier. The belief, the calming assurance that I belonged in public, had at last taken hold.

Shortly after, I stopped hearing the high and loud sounds of *los gringos.* A more and more confident speaker of English, I didn't trouble to listen to *how* strangers sounded, speaking to me. And there simply were too many English-speaking people in my day for me to hear American accents anymore. Conversations quickened. Listening to persons who sounded eccentrically pitched voices, I usually noted their sounds for an initial few seconds before I concentrated on *what* they were saying. Conversations became content-full. Transparent. Hearing someone's *tone* of voice — angry or questioning or sarcastic or happy or sad — I didn't distinguish it from the words it expressed. Sound and word were thus tightly wedded. At the end of a day, I was often bemused, always relieved, to realize how "silent," though crowded with words, my day in public had been. (This public silence measured and quickened the change in my life.)

At last, seven years old, I came to believe what had been technically true since my birth: I was an American citizen.

But the special feeling of closeness at home was diminished by then. Gone was the desperate, urgent, intense feeling of being at home; rare was the experience of feeling myself individualized by family intimates. We remained a loving family, but one greatly changed. No longer so close; no longer bound tight by the pleasing and troubling knowledge of our public separateness. Neither my older brother nor sister rushed home after school anymore. Nor did I. When I arrived home there would often be neighborhood kids in the house. Or the house would be empty of sounds.

Following the dramatic Americanization of their children, even my parents grew more publicly confident. Especially my mother. She learned the names of all the people on our block. And she decided we needed to have a telephone installed in the house. My father continued to use the word *gringo*. But it was no longer charged with the old bitterness or distrust. (Stripped of any emotional content, the word simply became a name for those Americans not of Hispanic descent.) Hearing him, sometimes, I wasn't sure if he was pronouncing the Spanish word *gringo* or saying gringo in English.

Matching the silence I started hearing in public was a new quiet at home. The family's quiet was partly due to the fact that, as we children learned more and more English, we shared fewer and fewer words with our parents. Sentences needed to be spoken slowly when a child addressed his mother or father. (Often the parent wouldn't understand.) The child would need to repeat himself. (Still the parent misunderstood.) The young voice, frustrated, would end up saying, "Never mind" — the subject was closed. Dinners would be noisy with the clinking of knives and forks against dishes. My mother would smile softly between her remarks; my father at the other end of the table would chew and chew at his food, while he stared over the heads of his children.

My *mother!* My *father!* After English became my primary language, I no longer knew what words to use in addressing my parents. The old Spanish words (those tender accents of sound) I had used earlier — *mamá* and *papá* — I couldn't use anymore. They would have been too painful reminders of how much had changed in my life. On the other hand, the words I heard neighborhood kids call *their* parents seemed equally unsatisfactory. *Mother* and *Father*; *Ma, Papa, Pa, Dad, Pop* (how I hated the all-American sound of that last word especially) — all these terms I felt were unsuitable, not really terms of address for *my* parents. As a result, I never used them at home. Whenever I'd speak to my parents, I would try to get their attention with eye contact alone. In public conversations, I'd refer to "my parents" or "my mother and father."

My mother and father, for their part, responded differently, as their children spoke to them less. She grew restless, seemed troubled and anxious at the scarcity of words exchanged in the house. It was she who would question me about my day when I came home from school. She smiled at small talk. She pried at the edges of my sentences to get me to say something more. (What?) She'd join conversations she overheard, but her intrusions often stopped her children's talking. By contrast, my father seemed reconciled to the new quiet. Though his English improved somewhat, he retired into silence. At dinner he spoke very little. One night his children and even his wife helplessly giggled at his garbled English pronunciation of the Catholic Grace before Meals. Thereafter he made his wife recite the prayer at the start of each meal, even on formal occasions, when there were guests in the house. Hers became the public

40

voice of the family. On official business, it was she, not my father, one would usually hear on the phone or in stores, talking to strangers. His children grew so accustomed to his silence that, years later, they would speak routinely of his shyness. (My mother would often try to explain: Both his parents died when he was eight. He was raised by an uncle who treated him like little more than a menial servant. He was never encouraged to speak. He grew up alone. A man of few words.) But my father was not shy, I realized, when I'd watch him speaking Spanish with relatives. Using Spanish, he was quickly effusive. Especially when talking with other men, his voice would spark, flicker, flare alive with sounds. In Spanish, he expressed ideas and feelings he rarely revealed in English. With firm Spanish sounds, he conveyed confidence and authority English would never allow him.

The silence at home, however, was finally more than a literal silence. Fewer words passed between parent and child, but more profound was the silence that resulted from my inattention to sounds. At about the time I no longer bothered to listen with care to the sounds of English in public, I grew careless about listening to the sounds family members made when they spoke. Most of the time I heard someone speaking at home and didn't distinguish his sounds from the words people uttered in public. I didn't even pay much attention to my parents' accented and ungrammatical speech. At least not at home. Only when I was with them in public would I grow alert to their accents. Though, even then, their sounds caused me less and less concern. For I was increasingly confident of my own public identity.

I would have been happier about my public success had I not sometimes recalled what it had been like earlier, when my family had conveyed its intimacy through a set of conveniently private sounds. Sometimes in public, hearing a stranger, I'd hark back to my past. A Mexican farmworker approached me downtown to ask directions to somewhere. "*¿Hijito . . . ?*" he said. And his voice summoned deep longing. Another time, standing beside my mother in the visiting room of a Carmelite convent; before the dense screen which rendered the nuns shadowy figures, I heard several Spanish-speaking nuns — their busy, singsong overlapping voices — assure us that yes, yes, we were remembered, all our family was remembered in their prayers. (Their voices echoed faraway family sounds.) Another day, a dark-faced old woman — her hand light on my shoulder — steadied herself against me as she boarded a bus. She murmured something I couldn't quite comprehend. Her Spanish voice came near, like the face of a never-before-seen relative in the instant before I was kissed. Her voice, like so many of the Spanish voices I'd hear in public, recalled the golden age of my youth. Hearing Spanish then, I continued to be a careful, if sad, listener to sounds. Hearing a Spanish-speaking family walking behind me, I turned to look. I smiled for an instant, before my glance found the Hispanic-looking faces of strangers in the crowd going by.

Today I hear bilingual educators say that children lose a degree of "individuality" by becoming assimilated into public society. (Bilingual schooling was popularized in the seventies, that decade when middle-class ethnics began to resist the process of assimilation — the American melting pot.) But the bilingualists simplistically scorn the value and necessity of assimilation. They do not seem to realize that there are *two* ways a person is individualized. So they do not realize that while one suffers a diminished sense of *private* individuality by becoming assimilated into public society, such assimilation makes possible the achievement of *public* individuality.

The bilingualists insist that a student should be reminded of his difference from others in mass society, his heritage. But they equate more separateness with individuality. The fact is that only in private — with intimates — is separateness from the crowd a prerequisite for individuality. (An intimate draws me apart, tells me that I am unique, unlike all others.) In public, by contrast, full individuality is achieved, paradoxically, by those who are able to consider themselves members of the crowd. Thus it happened for me: Only when I was able to think of myself as an American, no longer an alien in *gringo* society, could I seek the rights and opportunities necessary for full public individuality. The social and political advantages I enjoy as a man result from the day that I came to believe that my name, indeed, is *Rich-heard Road-ree-guess*. It is true that my public society today is often impersonal. (My public society is usually mass society.) Yet despite the anonymity of the crowd and despite the fact that the individuality I achieve in public is often tenuous — because it depends on my being one in a crowd — I celebrate the day I acquired my new name. Those middle-class ethnics who scorn assimilation seem to me filled with decadent self-pity, obsessed by the burden of public life. Dangerously, they romanticize public separateness and they trivialize the dilemma of the socially disadvantaged.

My awkward childhood does not prove the necessity of bilingual education. My story discloses instead an essential myth of childhood — inevitable pain. If I rehearse here the changes in my private life after my Americanization, it is finally to emphasize the public gain. The loss implies the gain: The house I returned to each afternoon was quiet. Intimate sounds no longer rushed to the door to greet me. There were other noises inside. The telephone rang. Neighborhood kids ran past the door of the bedroom where I was reading my schoolbooks — covered with shopping-bag paper. Once I learned public language, it would never again be easy for me to hear intimate family voices. More and more of my day was spent hearing words. But that may only be a way of saying that the day I raised my hand in class and spoke loudly to an entire roomful of faces, my childhood started to end.   1982

45

INVESTIGATIONS

1. In paragraph 5 Rodriguez says, "It is not possible for a child — any child — ever to use his family's language in school." To what extent is this true of your own experience? Is it easier for members of one particular social class rather than another to make the transition from "the nature of intimate life — a family's 'language' " to the language of the school?

2. If Rodriguez had grown up in the barrio, how would his experience of home and school have been different?

3. Look back at the writing you did in response to "Write Before Reading" (p. 368). In what ways did your transition from outsider to insider involve learning what Rodriguez calls a "public language"? Describe the structure, the *grammar*, of that language. Who was in charge of teaching it? How was it taught?

4. To what extent does moving from one community to another always involve forsaking a private language for a public one?

5. Review Vivian Gornick's distinction ("Twice an Outsider: On Being Jewish and a Woman") between her actual self and how she's perceived by others because of her gender, because of what she calls "an immutable condition of birth." In what sense can you make a similar distinction in Rodriguez's case? How "immutable" is his "condition of birth"? To what extent does he change who he "actually" is?

AMY TAN

Two Kinds

My mother believed you could be anything you wanted to be in America. You could open a restaurant. You could work for the government and get good retirement. You could buy a house with almost no money down. You could become rich. You could become instantly famous.

"Of course you can be prodigy, too," my mother told me when I was nine. "You can be best anything. What does Auntie Lindo know? Her daughter, she is only best tricky."

America was where all my mother's hopes lay. She had come here in 1949 after losing everything in China: her mother and father, her family home, her first husband, and two daughters, twin baby girls. But she never looked back with regret. There were so many ways for things to get better.

We didn't immediately pick the right kind of prodigy. At first my mother thought I could be a Chinese Shirley Temple. We'd watch Shirley's old movies

---

It wasn't until AMY TAN (b. 1952) visited China in 1987 that she could say, "I'm both Chinese and American. . . . Suddenly some piece fit in the right place and something became whole." A native of Oakland, California, Tan is the author of *The Joy Luck Club* (1989) and *The Kitchen God's Wife* (1991).

on TV as though they were training films. My mother would poke my arm and say, "*Ni kan*" — You watch. And I would see Shirley tapping her feet, or singing a sailor song, or pursing her lips into a very round O while saying, "Oh my goodness."

"*Ni kan*," said my mother as Shirley's eyes flooded with tears. "You already know how. Don't need talent for crying!"   5

Soon after my mother got this idea about Shirley Temple, she took me to a beauty training school in the Mission district and put me in the hands of a student who could barely hold the scissors without shaking. Instead of getting big fat curls, I emerged with an uneven mass of crinkly black fuzz. My mother dragged me off to the bathroom and tried to wet down my hair.

"You look like Negro Chinese," she lamented, as if I had done this on purpose.

The instructor of the beauty training school had to lop off these soggy clumps to make my hair even again. "Peter Pan is very popular these days," the instructor assured my mother. I now had hair the length of a boy's, with straight-across bangs that hung at a slant two inches above my eyebrows. I liked the haircut and it made me actually look forward to my future fame.

In fact, in the beginning, I was just as excited as my mother, maybe even more so. I pictured this prodigy part of me as many different images, trying each one on for size. I was a dainty ballerina girl standing by the curtains, waiting to hear the right music that would send me floating on my tiptoes. I was like the Christ child lifted out of the straw manger, crying with holy indignity. I was Cinderella stepping from her pumpkin carriage with sparkly cartoon music filling the air.

In all of my imaginings, I was filled with a sense that I would soon become   10
perfect. My mother and father would adore me. I would be beyond reproach. I would never feel the need to sulk for anything.

But sometimes the prodigy in me became impatient. "If you don't hurry up and get me out of here, I'm disappearing for good," it warned. "And then you'll always be nothing."

Every night after dinner, my mother and I would sit at the Formica kitchen table. She would present new tests, taking her examples from stories of amazing children she had read in *Ripley's Believe It or Not*, or *Good Housekeeping*, *Reader's Digest*, and a dozen other magazines she kept in a pile in our bathroom. My mother got these magazines from people whose houses she cleaned. And since she cleaned many houses each week, we had a great assortment. She would look through them all, searching for stories about remarkable children.

The first night she brought out a story about a three-year-old boy who knew the capitals of all the states and even most of the European countries. A teacher was quoted as saying the little boy could also pronounce the names of the foreign cities correctly.

"What's the capital of Finland?" my mother asked me, looking at the magazine story.

All I knew was the capital of California, because Sacramento was the name   15
of the street we lived on in Chinatown. "Nairobi!" I guessed, saying the most
foreign word I could think of. She checked to see if that was possibly one way
to pronounce "Helsinki" before showing me the answer.

The tests got harder — multiplying numbers in my head, finding the queen
of hearts in a deck of cards, trying to stand on my head without using my
hands, predicting the daily temperatures in Los Angeles, New York, and London.

One night I had to look at a page from the Bible for three minutes and
then report everything I could remember. "Now Jehoshaphat had riches and
honor in abundance and. . . . that's all I remember, Ma," I said.

And after seeing my mother's disappointed face once again, something
inside of me began to die. I hated the tests, the raised hopes and failed expectations. Before going to bed that night, I looked in the mirror above the
bathroom sink and when I saw only my face staring back — and that it would
always be this ordinary face — I began to cry. Such a sad, ugly girl! I made
high-pitched noises like a crazed animal, trying to scratch out the face in the
mirror.

And then I saw what seemed to be the prodigy side of me — because I
had never seen that face before. I looked at my reflection, blinking so I could
see more clearly. The girl staring back at me was angry, powerful. This girl
and I were the same. I had new thoughts, willful thoughts, or rather thoughts
filled with lots of won'ts. I won't let her change me, I promised myself. I won't
be what I'm not.

So now on nights when my mother presented her tests, I performed list-   20
lessly, my head propped on one arm. I pretended to be bored. And I was. I got
so bored I started counting the bellows of the foghorns out on the bay while
my mother drilled me in other areas. The sound was comforting and reminded
me of the cow jumping over the moon. And the next day, I played a game with
myself, seeing if my mother would give up on me before eight bellows. After
a while I usually counted only one, maybe two bellows at most. At last she
was beginning to give up hope.

Two or three months had gone by without any mention of my being a
prodigy again. And then one day my mother was watching "The Ed Sullivan
Show" on TV. The TV was old and the sound kept shorting out. Every time
my mother got halfway up from the sofa to adjust the set, the sound would go
back on and Ed would be talking. As soon as she sat down, Ed would go silent
again. She got up, the TV broke into loud piano music. She sat down. Silence.
Up and down, back and forth, quiet and loud. It was like a stiff embraceless
dance between her and the TV set. Finally she stood by the set with her hand
on the sound dial.

She seemed entranced by the music, a little frenzied piano piece with this
mesmerizing quality, sort of quick passages and then teasing lilting ones before
it returned to the quick playful parts.

"*Ni kan,*" my mother said, calling me over with hurried hand gestures. "Look here."

I could see why my mother was fascinated by the music. It was being pounded out by a little Chinese girl, about nine years old, with a Peter Pan haircut. The girl had the sauciness of a Shirley Temple. She was proudly modest like a proper Chinese child. And she also did this fancy sweep of a curtsy, so that the fluffy skirt of her white dress cascaded slowly to the floor like the petals of a large carnation.

In spite of these warning signs, I wasn't worried. Our family had no piano and we couldn't afford to buy one, let alone reams of sheet music and piano lessons. So I could be generous in my comments when my mother bad-mouthed the little girl on TV.   25

"Play note right, but doesn't sound good! No singing sound," complained my mother.

"What are you picking on her for?" I said carelessly. "She's pretty good. Maybe she's not the best, but she's trying hard." I knew almost immediately I would be sorry I said that.

"Just like you," she said. "Not the best. Because you not trying." She gave a little huff as she let go of the sound dial and sat down on the sofa.

The little Chinese girl sat down also to play an encore of "Anitra's Dance" by Grieg. I remember the song, because later on I had to learn how to play it.

Three days after watching "The Ed Sullivan Show," my mother told me what my schedule would be for piano lessons and piano practice. She had talked to Mr. Chong, who lived on the first floor of our apartment building. Mr. Chong was a retired piano teacher and my mother had traded housecleaning services for weekly lessons and a piano for me to practice on every day, two hours a day, from four until six.   30

When my mother told me this, I felt as though I had been sent to hell. I whined and then kicked my foot a little when I couldn't stand it anymore.

"Why don't you like me the way I am? I'm *not* a genius! I can't play the piano. And even if I could, I wouldn't go on TV if you paid me a million dollars!" I cried.

My mother slapped me. "Who ask you be genius?" she shouted. "Only ask you be your best. For you sake. You think I want you to be genius? Hnnh! What for! Who ask you!"

"So ungrateful," I heard her mutter in Chinese. "If she had as much talent as she has temper, she would be famous now."

Mr. Chong, whom I secretly nicknamed Old Chong, was very strange, always tapping his fingers to the silent music of an invisible orchestra. He looked ancient in my eyes. He had lost most of the hair on top of his head and he wore thick glasses and had eyes that always looked tired and sleepy. But he must have been younger than I thought, since he lived with his mother and was not yet married.   35

I met Old Lady Chong once and that was enough. She had this peculiar smell like a baby that had done something in its pants. And her fingers felt like a dead person's, like an old peach I once found in the back of the refrigerator; the skin just slid off the meat when I picked it up.

I soon found out why Old Chong had retired from teaching piano. He was deaf. "Like Beethoven!" he shouted to me. "We're both listening only in our head!" And he would start to conduct his frantic silent sonatas.

Our lessons went like this. He would open the book and point to different things, explaining their purpose: "Key! Treble! Bass! No sharps or flats! So this is C major! Listen now and play after me!"

And then he would play the C scale a few times, a simple chord, and then, as if inspired by an old, unreachable itch, he gradually added more notes and running trills and a pounding bass until the music was really something quite grand.

I would play after him, the simple scale, the simple chord, and then I just 40 played some nonsense that sounded like a cat running up and down on top of garbage cans. Old Chong smiled and applauded and then said, "Very good! But now you must learn to keep time!"

So that's how I discovered that Old Chong's eyes were too slow to keep up with the wrong notes I was playing. He went through the motions in half-time. To help me keep rhythm, he stood behind me, pushing down on my right shoulder for every beat. He balanced pennies on top of my wrists so I would keep them still as I slowly played scales and arpeggios. He had me curve my hand around an apple and keep that shape when playing chords. He marched stiffly to show me how to make each finger dance up and down, staccato like an obedient little soldier.

He taught me all these things, and that was how I also learned I could be lazy and get away with mistakes, lots of mistakes. If I hit the wrong notes because I hadn't practiced enough, I never corrected myself. I just kept playing in rhythm. And Old Chong kept conducting his own private reverie.

So maybe I never really gave myself a fair chance. I did pick up the basics pretty quickly, and I might have become a good pianist at that young age. But I was so determined not to try, not to be anybody different that I learned to play only the most ear-splitting preludes, the most discordant hymns.

Over the next year, I practiced like this, dutifully in my own way. And then one day I heard my mother and her friend Lindo Jong both talking in a loud bragging tone of voice so others could hear. It was after church, and I was leaning against the brick wall wearing a dress with stiff white petticoats. Auntie Lindo's daughter, Waverly, who was about my age, was standing farther down the wall about five feet away. We had grown up together and shared all the closeness of two sisters squabbling over crayons and dolls. In other words, for the most part, we hated each other. I thought she was snotty. Waverly Jong had gained a certain amount of fame as "Chinatown's Littlest Chinese Chess Champion."

"She bring home too many trophy," lamented Auntie Lindo that Sunday. 45 "All day she play chess. All day I have no time do nothing but dust off her winnings." She threw a scolding look at Waverly, who pretended not to see her.

"You lucky you don't have this problem," said Auntie Lindo with a sigh to my mother.

And my mother squared her shoulders and bragged: "Our problem worser than yours. If we ask Jing-mei wash dish, she hear nothing but music. It's like you can't stop this natural talent."

And right then, I was determined to put a stop to her foolish pride.

A few weeks later, Old Chong and my mother conspired to have me play in a talent show which would be held in the church hall. By then, my parents had saved up enough to buy me a secondhand piano, a black Wurlitzer spinet with a scarred bench. It was the showpiece of our living room.

For the talent show, I was to play a piece called "Pleading Child" from Schumann's *Scenes from Childhood*. It was a simple, moody piece that sounded more difficult than it was. I was supposed to memorize the whole thing, playing the repeat parts twice to make the piece sound longer. But I dawdled over it, playing a few bars and then cheating, looking up to see what notes followed. I never really listened to what I was playing. I daydreamed about being somewhere else, about being someone else.

The part I liked to practice best was the fancy curtsy: right foot out, touch the rose on the carpet with a pointed foot, sweep to the side, left leg bends, look up and smile.

My parents invited all the couples from the Joy Luck Club to witness my debut. Auntie Lindo and Uncle Tin were there. Waverly and her two older brothers had also come. The first two rows were filled with children both younger and older than I was. The littlest ones got to go first. They recited simple nursery rhymes, squawked out tunes on miniature violins, twirled Hula Hoops, pranced in pink ballet tutus, and when they bowed or curtsied, the audience would sigh in unison, "Awww," and then clap enthusiastically.

When my turn came, I was very confident. I remember my childish excitement. It was as if I knew, without a doubt, that the prodigy side of me really did exist. I had no fear whatsoever, no nervousness. I remember thinking to myself, This is it! This is it! I looked out over the audience at my mother's blank face, my father's yawn, Auntie Lindo's stiff-lipped smile. Waverly's sulky expression. I had on a white dress layered with sheets of lace, and a pink bow in my Peter Pan haircut. As I sat down I envisioned people jumping to their feet and Ed Sullivan rushing up to introduce me to everyone on TV.

And I started to play. It was so beautiful. I was so caught up in how lovely I looked that at first I didn't worry how I would sound. So it was a surprise to me when I hit the first wrong note and I realized something didn't sound quite right. And then I hit another and another followed that. A chill started at the top of my head and began to trickle down. Yet I couldn't stop playing, as though my hands were bewitched. I kept thinking my fingers would adjust themselves back, like a train switching to the right track. I played this strange jumble through two repeats, the sour notes staying with me all the way to the end.

When I stood up, I discovered my legs were shaking. Maybe I had just been nervous and the audience, like Old Chong, had seen me go through the right motions and had not heard anything wrong at all. I swept my right foot out, went down on my knee, looked up and smiled. The room was quiet, except for Old Chong, who was beaming and shouting, "Bravo! Bravo! Well done!" But then I saw my mother's face, her stricken face. The audience clapped weakly, and as I walked back to my chair, with my whole face quivering as I tried not to cry, I heard a little boy whisper loudly to his mother, "That was awful," and the mother whispered back, "Well, she certainly tried."

And now I realized how many people were in the audience, the whole world it seemed. I was aware of eyes burning into my back. I felt the shame of my mother and father as they sat stiffly throughout the rest of the show.

We could have escaped during intermission. Pride and some strange sense of honor must have anchored my parents to their chairs. And so we watched it all: the eighteen-year-old boy with a fake mustache who did a magic show and juggled flaming hoops while riding a unicycle. The breasted girl with white makeup who sang from *Madama Butterfly* and got honorable mention. And the eleven-year-old boy who won first prize playing a tricky violin song that sounded like a busy bee.

After the show, the Hsus, the Jongs, and the St. Clairs from the Joy Luck Club came up to my mother and father.

"Lots of talented kids," Auntie Lindo said vaguely, smiling broadly.

"That was somethin' else," said my father, and I wondered if he was referring to me in a humorous way, or whether he even remembered what I had done.

Waverly looked at me and shrugged her shoulders. "You aren't a genius like me," she said matter-of-factly. And if I hadn't felt so bad, I would have pulled her braids and punched her stomach.

But my mother's expression was what devastated me: a quiet, blank look that said she had lost everything. I felt the same way, and it seemed as if everybody were now coming up, like gawkers at the scene of an accident, to see what parts were actually missing. When we got on the bus to go home, my father was humming the busy-bee tune and my mother was silent. I kept thinking she wanted to wait until we got home before shouting at me. But when my father unlocked the door to our apartment, my mother walked in and then went to the back, into the bedroom. No accusations. No blame. And in a way, I felt disappointed. I had been waiting for her to start shouting, so I could shout back and cry and blame her for all my misery.

I assumed my talent-show fiasco meant I never had to play the piano again. But two days later, after school, my mother came out of the kitchen and saw me watching TV.

"Four clock," she reminded me as if it were any other day. I was stunned, as though she were asking me to go through the talent-show torture again. I wedged myself more tightly in the front of the TV.

"Turn off TV," she called from the kitchen five minutes later. 65

I didn't budge. And then I decided. I didn't have to do what my mother said anymore. I wasn't her slave. This wasn't China. I had listened to her before and look what happened. She was the stupid one.

She came out from the kitchen and stood in the arched entryway of the living room. "Four clock," she said once again, louder.

"I'm not going to play anymore," I said nonchalantly. "Why should I? I'm not a genius."

She walked over and stood in front of the TV. I saw her chest was heaving up and down in an angry way.

"No!" I said, and I now felt stronger, as if my true self had finally emerged. 70 So this was what had been inside me all along.

"No! I won't!" I screamed.

She yanked me by the arm, pulled me off the floor, snapped off the TV. She was frighteningly strong, half pulling, half carrying me toward the piano as I kicked the throw rugs under my feet. She lifted me up and onto the hard bench. I was sobbing by now, looking at her bitterly. Her chest was heaving even more and her mouth was open, smiling crazily as if she were pleased I was crying.

"You want me to be someone that I'm not!" I sobbed. "I'll never be the kind of daughter you want me to be!"

"Only two kinds of daughters," she shouted in Chinese. "Those who are obedient and those who follow their own mind! Only one kind of daughter can live in this house. Obedient daughter!"

"Then I wish I wasn't your daughter. I wish you weren't my mother," I 75 shouted. As I said these things I got scared. I felt like worms and toads and slimy things were crawling out of my chest, but it also felt good, as if this awful side of me had surfaced, at last.

"Too late change this," said my mother shrilly.

And I could sense her anger rising to its breaking point. I wanted to see it spill over. And that's when I remembered the babies she had lost in China, the ones we never talked about. "Then I wish I'd never been born!" I shouted. "I wish I were dead! Like them."

It was as if I had said the magic words. Alakazam! — and her face went blank, her mouth closed, her arms went slack, and she backed out of the room, stunned, as if she were blowing away like a small brown leaf, thin, brittle, lifeless.

It was not the only disappointment my mother felt in me. In the years that followed, I failed her so many times, each time asserting my own will, my right to fall short of expectations. I didn't get straight As. I didn't become class president. I didn't get into Stanford. I dropped out of college.

For unlike my mother, I did not believe I could be anything I wanted to   80
be. I could only be me.

And for all those years, we never talked about the disaster at the recital
or my terrible accusations afterward at the piano bench. All that remained
unchecked, like a betrayal that was now unspeakable. So I never found a way
to ask her why she had hoped for something so large that failure was inevitable.

And even worse, I never asked her what frightened me the most: Why had
she given up hope?

For after our struggle at the piano, she never mentioned my playing again.
The lessons stopped. The lid to the piano was closed, shutting out the dust,
my misery, and her dreams.

So she surprised me. A few years ago, she offered to give me the piano,
for my thirtieth birthday. I had not played in all those years. I saw the offer as
a sign of forgiveness, a tremendous burden removed.

"Are you sure?" I asked shyly. "I mean, won't you and Dad miss it?"   85

"No, this your piano," she said firmly. "Always your piano. You only one
can play."

"Well, I probably can't play anymore," I said "It's been years."

"You pick up fast," said my mother, as if she knew this was certain. "You
have natural talent. You could been genius if you want to."

"No I couldn't."

"You just not trying," said my mother. And she was neither angry nor   90
sad. She said it as if to announce a fact that could never be disproved. "Take
it," she said.

But I didn't at first. It was enough that she had offered it to me. And after
that, every time I saw it in my parents' living room, standing in front of the
bay windows, it made me feel proud, as if it were a shiny trophy I had won
back.

Last week I sent a tuner over to my parents' apartment and had the piano
reconditioned, for purely sentimental reasons. My mother had died a few
months before and I had been getting things in order for my father, a little bit
at a time. I put the jewelry in special silk pouches. The sweaters she had knitted
in yellow, pink, bright orange — all the colors I hated — I put those in moth-
proof boxes. I found some old Chinese silk dresses, the kind with little slits up
the sides. I rubbed the old silk against my skin, then wrapped them in tissue
and decided to take them home with me.

After I had the piano tuned, I opened the lid and touched the keys. It
sounded even richer than I remembered. Really, it was a very good piano.
Inside the bench were the same exercise notes with handwritten scales, the
same second-hand music books with their covers held together with yellow
tape.

I opened up the Schumann book to the dark little piece I had played at
the recital. It was on the left-hand side of the page, "Pleading Child." It looked

more difficult than I remembered. I played a few bars, surprised at how easily the notes came back to me.

And for the first time, or so it seemed, I noticed the piece on the right-hand side. It was called "Perfectly Contented." I tried to play this one as well. It had a lighter melody but the same flowing rhythm and turned out to be quite easy. "Pleading Child" was shorter but slower; "Perfectly Contented" was longer but faster. And after I played them both a few times, I realized they were two halves of the same song.   95

1989

INVESTIGATIONS

1. Why is Jing-mei "so determined not to try, not to be anybody different" (para. 43)? Why is her mother so bent on Jing-mei's achieving some kind of public success?

2. Why doesn't Jing-mei realize "how many people were in the audience, the whole world it seemed" (para. 56) till after her performance at the talent show? How do she and her family fit into this "whole world"?

3. In paragraph 80 Jing-mei says, "For unlike my mother, I did not believe I could be anything I wanted to be. I could only be me." To what extent does your experience bear this out? To what extent are both Jing-mei and her mother mistaken?

4. Compare this story to Richard Rodriguez's account of private and public life in "Aria: A Bilingual Childhood." What would Rodriguez think of Jing-mei's realization that "Perfectly Contented" and "Pleading Child" "were two halves of the same song" (para. 95)?

LORNA DEE CERVANTES

Refugee Ship

like wet cornstarch
I slide past *mi abuelita's*[1] eyes
bible placed by her side
she removes her glasses
the pudding thickens   5

[1] My grandmother's.

Born in 1954 in San Francisco, California, LORNA DEE CERVANTES founded Mango Publications, a press mainly devoted to Chicano literature. She received a National Endowment for the Arts fellowship in 1978 and is the author of *Emplumada* (1981), a collection of poems.

mamá raised me with no language
I am an orphan to my spanish name
the words are foreign, stumbling on my tongue
I stare at my reflection in the mirror
brown skin, black hair   10

I feel I am a captive
aboard the refugee ship
a ship that will never dock
a ship that will never dock   1975

INVESTIGATIONS

1. What is the significance of the speaker's initial comparison? How is "wet cornstarch" connected to the last line of the poem's first stanza?
2. The speaker claims her mother raised her "with no language / I am an orphan to my spanish name," yet calls her mother "*mamá*" and her grandmother "*mi abuelita.*" How do you explain this?
3. What would Richard Rodriguez ("Aria: A Bilingual Childhood") think about the speaker's feeling that she is "a captive / aboard the refugee ship / a ship that will never dock"?
4. What might free the speaker from her feelings that she's trapped on "a ship that will never dock"?

TIM O'BRIEN

The Things They Carried

First Lieutenant Jimmy Cross carried letters from a girl named Martha, a junior at Mount Sebastian College in New Jersey. They were not love letters, but Lieutenant Cross was hoping, so he kept them folded in plastic at the bottom of his rucksack. In the late afternoon, after a day's march, he would dig his foxhole, wash his hands under a canteen, unwrap the letters, hold them with the tips of his fingers, and spend the last hour of light pretending. He would imagine romantic camping trips into the White Mountains in New Hampshire.

Born in Worthington, Minnesota, in 1946 and a graduate of Macalester College, TIM O'BRIEN was an infantryman in Vietnam from 1969 to 1970. His books include *The Things They Carried* (1990) and *Going After Cacciato* (1978), winner of the 1979 National Book Award for fiction.

He would sometimes taste the envelope flaps, knowing her tongue had been there. More than anything, he wanted Martha to love him as he loved her, but the letters were mostly chatty, elusive on the matter of love. She was a virgin, he was almost sure. She was an English major at Mount Sebastian, and she wrote beautifully about her professors and roommates and midterm exams, about her respect for Chaucer and her great affection for Virginia Woolf. She often quoted lines of poetry; she never mentioned the war, except to say, Jimmy, take care of yourself. The letters weighed ten ounces. They were signed "Love, Martha," but Lieutenant Cross understood that "Love" was only a way of signing and did not mean what he sometimes pretended it meant. At dusk, he would carefully return the letters to his rucksack. Slowly, a bit distracted, he would get up and move among his men, checking the perimeter, then at full dark he would return to his hole and watch the night and wonder if Martha was a virgin.

The things they carried were largely determined by necessity. Among the necessities or near necessities were P-38 can openers, pocketknives, heat tabs, wristwatches, dog tags, mosquito repellent, chewing gum, candy, cigarettes, salt tablets, packets of Kool-Aid, lighters, matches, sewing kits, Military Payment Certificates, C rations, and two or three canteens of water. Together, these items weighed between fifteen and twenty pounds, depending upon a man's habits or rate of metabolism. Henry Dobbins, who was a big man, carried extra rations; he was especially fond of canned peaches in heavy syrup over pound cake. Dave Jensen, who practiced field hygiene, carried a toothbrush, dental floss, and several hotel-size bars of soap he'd stolen on R&R in Sydney, Australia. Ted Lavender, who was scared, carried tranquilizers until he was shot in the head outside the village of Than Khe in mid-April. By necessity, and because it was SOP,[1] they all carried steel helmets that weighed five pounds including the liner and camouflage cover. They carried the standard fatigue jackets and trousers. Very few carried underwear. On their feet they carried jungle boots — 2.1 pounds — and Dave Jensen carried three pairs of socks and a can of Dr. Scholl's foot powder as a precaution against trench foot. Until he was shot, Ted Lavender carried six or seven ounces of premium dope, which for him was a necessity. Mitchell Sanders, the RTO,[2] carried condoms. Norman Bowker carried a diary. Rat Kiley carried comic books. Kiowa, a devout Baptist, carried an illustrated New Testament that had been presented to him by his father, who taught Sunday school in Oklahoma City, Oklahoma. As a hedge against bad times, however, Kiowa also carried his grandmother's distrust of the white man, his grandfather's old hunting hatchet. Necessity dictated. Because the land was mined and booby-trapped, it was SOP for each man to carry a steel-centered, nylon-covered flak jacket, which weighed 6.7 pounds, but which on hot days seemed much heavier. Because you could die so quickly, each man carried at least one large compress bandage, usually in the helmet band for easy access. Because the nights were cold, and because

---

[1] Standard Operating Procedure. [Ed.]
[2] Radio Telephone Operator. [Ed.]

the monsoons were wet, each carried a green plastic poncho that could be used as a raincoat or ground sheet or makeshift tent. With its quilted liner, the poncho weighed almost two pounds, but it was worth every ounce. In April, for instance, when Ted Lavender was shot, they used his poncho to wrap him up, then to carry him across the paddy, then to lift him into the chopper that took him away.

They were called legs or grunts.

To carry something was to "hump" it, as when Lieutenant Jimmy Cross humped his love for Martha up the hills and through the swamps. In its intransitive form, "to hump" meant "to walk," or "to march," but it implied burdens far beyond the intransitive.

Almost everyone humped photographs. In his wallet, Lieutenant Cross carried two photographs of Martha. The first was a Kodachrome snapshot signed "Love," though he knew better. She stood against a brick wall. Her eyes were gray and neutral, her lips slightly open as she stared straight-on at the camera. At night, sometimes, Lieutenant Cross wondered who had taken the picture, because he knew she had boyfriends, because he loved her so much, and because he could see the shadow of the picture taker spreading out against the brick wall. The second photograph had been clipped from the 1968 Mount Sebastian yearbook. It was an action shot — women's volleyball — and Martha was bent horizontal to the floor, reaching, the palms of her hands in sharp focus, the tongue taut, the expression frank and competitive. There was no visible sweat. She wore white gym shorts. Her legs, he thought, were almost certainly the legs of a virgin, dry and without hair, the left knee cocked and carrying her entire weight, which was just over one hundred pounds. Lieutenant Cross remembered touching that left knee. A dark theater, he remembered, and the movie was *Bonnie and Clyde,* and Martha wore a tweed skirt, and during the final scene, when he touched her knee, she turned and looked at him in a sad, sober way that made him pull his hand back, but he would always remember the feel of the tweed skirt and the knee beneath it and the sound of the gunfire that killed Bonnie and Clyde, how embarrassing it was, how slow and oppressive. He remembered kissing her good night at the dorm door. Right then, he thought, he should've done something brave. He should've carried her up the stairs to her room and tied her to the bed and touched that left knee all night long. He should've risked it. Whenever he looked at the photographs, he thought of new things he should've done.

What they carried was partly a function of rank, partly of field speciality.

As a first lieutenant and platoon leader, Jimmy Cross carried a compass, maps, code books, binoculars, and a .45-caliber pistol that weighed 2.9 pounds fully loaded. He carried a strobe light and the responsibility for the lives of his men.

As an RTO, Mitchell Sanders carried the PRC-25 radio, a killer, twenty-six pounds with its battery.

As a medic, Rat Kiley carried a canvas satchel filled with morphine and plasma and malaria tablets and surgical tape and comic books and all the things a medic must carry, including M&Ms for especially bad wounds, for a total weight of nearly twenty pounds.

As a big man, therefore a machine gunner, Henry Dobbins carried the M-60, which weighed twenty-three pounds unloaded, but which was almost always loaded. In addition, Dobbins carried between ten and fifteen pounds of ammunition draped in belts across his chest and shoulders.

As PFCs or Spec 4s, most of them were common grunts and carried the standard M-16 gas-operated assault rifle. The weapon weighed 7.5 pounds unloaded, 8.2 pounds with its full twenty-round magazine. Depending on numerous factors, such as topography and psychology, the riflemen carried anywhere from twelve to twenty magazines, usually in cloth bandoliers, adding on another 8.4 pounds at minimum, fourteen pounds at maximum. When it was available, they also carried M-16 maintenance gear — rods and steel brushes and swabs and tubes of LSA oil — all of which weighed about a pound. Among the grunts, some carried the M-79 grenade launcher, 5.9 pounds unloaded, a reasonably light weapon except for the ammunition, which was heavy. A single round weighed ten ounces. The typical load was twenty-five rounds. But Ted Lavender, who was scared, carried thirty-four rounds when he was shot and killed outside Than Khe, and he went down under an exceptional burden, more than twenty pounds of ammunition, plus the flak jacket and helmet and rations and water and toilet paper and tranquilizers and all the rest, plus the unweighed fear. He was dead weight. There was no twitching or flopping. Kiowa, who saw it happen, said it was like watching a rock fall, or a big sandbag or something — just boom, then down — not like the movies where the dead guy rolls around and does fancy spins and goes ass-over-teakettle — not like that, Kiowa said, the poor bastard just flat-fuck fell. Boom. Down. Nothing else. It was a bright morning in mid-April. Lieutenant Cross felt the pain. He blamed himself. They stripped off Lavender's canteens and ammo, all the heavy things, and Rat Kiley said the obvious, the guy's dead, and Mitchell Sanders used his radio to report one U.S. KIA and to request a chopper. Then they wrapped Lavender in his poncho. They carried him out to a dry paddy, established security, and sat smoking the dead man's dope until the chopper came. Lieutenant Cross kept to himself. He pictured Martha's smooth young face, thinking he loved her more than anything, more than his men, and now Ted Lavender was dead because he loved her so much and could not stop thinking about her. When the dust-off arrived, they carried Lavender aboard. Afterward they burned Than Khe. They marched until dusk, then dug their holes, and that night Kiowa kept explaining how you had to be there, how fast it was, how the poor guy just dropped like so much concrete. Boom-down, he said. Like cement.

In addition to the three standard weapons — the M-60, M-16, and M-79 — they carried whatever presented itself, or whatever seemed appropriate as a means of killing or staying alive. They carried catch-as-catch-can. At various times, in various situations, they carried M-14s and CAR-15s and Swedish Ks and grease guns and captured AK-47s and Chi-Coms and RPGs and Simonov carbines and black-market Uzis and .38-caliber Smith & Wesson handguns and 66-mm LAWs and shotguns and silencers and blackjacks and bayonets and C-4 plastic explosives. Lee Strunk carried a slingshot; a weapon of last resort, he called it. Mitchell Sanders carried brass knuckles. Kiowa carried his grandfather's feathered hatchet. Every third or fourth man carried a Claymore antipersonnel mine — 3.5 pounds with its firing device. They all carried fragmentation grenades — fourteen ounces each. They all carried at least one M-18 colored smoke grenade — twenty-four ounces. Some carried CS or teargas grenades. Some carried white-phosphorus grenades. They carried all they could bear, and then some, including a silent awe for the terrible power of the things they carried.

In the first week of April, before Lavender died, Lieutenant Jimmy Cross received a good-luck charm from Martha. It was a simple pebble, an ounce at most. Smooth to the touch, it was a milky-white color with flecks of orange and violet, oval-shaped, like a miniature egg. In the accompanying letter, Martha wrote that she had found the pebble on the Jersey shoreline, precisely where the land touched water at high tide, where things came together but also separated. It was this separate-but-together quality, she wrote, that had inspired her to pick up the pebble and to carry it in her breast pocket for several days; where it seemed weightless, and then to send it through the mail, by air, as a token of her truest feelings for him. Lieutenant Cross found this romantic. But he wondered what her truest feelings were, exactly, and what she meant by separate-but-together. He wondered how the tides and waves had come into play on that afternoon along the Jersey shoreline when Martha saw the pebble and bent down to rescue it from geology. He imagined bare feet. Martha was a poet, with the poet's sensibilities, and her feet would be brown and bare, the toenails unpainted, the eyes chilly and somber like the ocean in March, and though it was painful, he wondered who had been with her that afternoon. He imagined a pair of shadows moving along the strip of sand where things came together but also separated. It was phantom jealousy, he knew, but he couldn't help himself. He loved her so much. On the march, through the hot days of early April, he carried the pebble in his mouth, turning it with his tongue, tasting sea salts and moisture. His mind wandered. He had difficulty keeping his attention on the war. On occasion he would yell at his men to spread out the column, to keep their eyes open, but then he would slip away into daydreams, just pretending, walking barefoot along the Jersey shore, with Martha, carrying nothing. He would feel himself rising. Sun and waves and gentle winds, all love and lightness.

What they carried varied by mission.

When a mission took them to the mountains, they carried mosquito netting, machetes, canvas tarps, and extra bug juice.

If a mission seemed especially hazardous, or if it involved a place they knew to be bad, they carried everything they could. In certain heavily mined AOs,[3] where the land was dense with Toe Poppers and Bouncing Betties, they took turns humping a twenty-eight-pound mine detector. With its headphones and big sensing plate, the equipment was a stress on the lower back and shoulders, awkward to handle, often useless because of the shrapnel in the earth, but they carried it anyway, partly for safety, partly for the illusion of safety.

On ambush, or other night missions, they carried peculiar little odds and ends. Kiowa always took along his New Testament and a pair of moccasins for silence. Dave Jensen carried night-sight vitamins high in carotin. Lee Strunk carried his slingshot; ammo, he claimed, would never be a problem. Rat Kiley carried brandy and M&Ms. Until he was shot, Ted Lavender carried the starlight scope, which weighed 6.3 pounds with its aluminum carrying case. Henry Dobbins carried his girlfriend's pantyhose wrapped around his neck as a comforter. They all carried ghosts. When dark came, they would move out single file across the meadows and paddies to their ambush coordinates, where they would quietly set up the Claymores and lie down and spend the night waiting.

Other missions were more complicated and required special equipment. In mid-April, it was their mission to search out and destroy the elaborate tunnel complexes in the Than Khe area south of Chu Lai. To blow the tunnels, they carried one-pound blocks of pentrite high explosives, four blocks to a man, sixty-eight pounds in all. They carried wiring, detonators, and battery-powered clackers. Dave Jensen carried earplugs. Most often, before blowing the tunnels, they were ordered by higher command to search them, which was considered bad news, but by and large they just shrugged and carried out orders. Because he was a big man, Henry Dobbins was excused from tunnel duty. The others would draw numbers. Before Lavender died there were seventeen men in the platoon, and whoever drew the number seventeen would strip off his gear and crawl in head first with a flashlight and Lieutenant Cross's .45-caliber pistol. The rest of them would fan out as security. They would sit down or kneel, not facing the hole, listening to the ground beneath them, imagining cobwebs and ghosts, whatever was down there — the tunnel walls squeezing in — how the flashlight seemed impossibly heavy in the hand and how it was tunnel vision in the very strictest sense, compression in all ways, even time, and how you had to wiggle in — ass and elbows — a swallowed-up feeling — and how you found yourself worrying about odd things — will your flashlight go dead? Do rats carry rabies? If you screamed, how far would the sound carry? Would your buddies hear it? Would they have the courage to drag you out? In some respects, though not many, the waiting was worse than the tunnel itself. Imagination was a killer.

On April 16, when Lee Strunk drew the number seventeen, he laughed and muttered something and went down quickly. The morning was hot and very still. Not good, Kiowa said. He looked at the tunnel opening, then out across

[3] Area(s) of Operation. [Ed.]

a dry paddy toward the village of Than Khe. Nothing moved. No clouds or birds or people. As they waited, the men smoked and drank Kool-Aid, not talking much, feeling sympathy for Lee Strunk but also feeling the luck of the draw. You win some, you lose some, said Mitchell Sanders, and sometimes you settle for a rain check. It was a tired line and no one laughed.

Henry Dobbins ate a tropical chocolate bar. Ted Lavender popped a tran-   20
quilizer and went off to pee.

After five minutes, Lieutenant Jimmy Cross moved to the tunnel, leaned down, and examined the darkness. Trouble, he thought — a cave-in maybe. And then suddenly, without willing it, he was thinking about Martha. The stresses and fractures, the quick collapse, the two of them buried alive under all that weight. Dense, crushing love. Kneeling, watching the hole, he tried to concentrate on Lee Strunk and the war, all the dangers, but his love was too much for him, he felt paralyzed, he wanted to sleep inside her lungs and breathe her blood and be smothered. He wanted her to be a virgin and not a virgin, all at once. He wanted to know her. Intimate secrets — why poetry? Why so sad? Why that grayness in her eyes? Why so alone? Not lonely, just alone — riding her bike across campus or sitting off by herself in the cafeteria. Even dancing, she danced alone — and it was the aloneness that filled him with love. He remembered telling her that one evening. How she nodded and looked away. And how, later, when he kissed her, she received the kiss without returning it, her eyes wide open, not afraid, not a virgin's eyes, just flat and uninvolved.

Lieutenant Cross gazed at the tunnel. But he was not there. He was buried with Martha under the white sand at the Jersey shore. They were pressed together, and the pebble in his mouth was her tongue. He was smiling. Vaguely, he was aware of how quiet the day was, the sullen paddies, yet he could not bring himself to worry about matters of security. He was beyond that. He was just a kid at war, in love. He was twenty-two years old. He couldn't help it.

A few moments later Lee Strunk crawled out of the tunnel. He came up grinning, filthy but alive. Lieutenant Cross nodded and closed his eyes while the others clapped Strunk on the back and made jokes about rising from the dead.

Worms, Rat Kiley said. Right out of the grave. Fuckin' zombie.

The men laughed. They all felt great relief.   25

Spook City, said Mitchell Sanders.

Lee Strunk made a funny ghost sound, a kind of moaning, yet very happy, and right then, when Strunk made that high happy moaning sound, when he went *Ahhooooo*, right then Ted Lavender was shot in the head on his way back from peeing. He lay with his mouth open. The teeth were broken. There was a swollen black bruise under his left eye. The cheekbone was gone. Oh shit, Rat Kiley said, the guy's dead. The guy's dead, he kept saying, which seemed profound — the guy's dead. I mean really.

The things they carried were determined to some extent by superstition. Lieutenant Cross carried his good-luck pebble. Dave Jensen carried a rabbit's foot. Norman Bowker, otherwise a very gentle person, carried a thumb that had been presented to him as a gift by Mitchell Sanders. The thumb was dark brown, rubbery to the touch, and weighed four ounces at most. It had been cut from a VC corpse, a boy of fifteen or sixteen. They'd found him at the bottom of an irrigation ditch, badly burned, flies in his mouth and eyes. The boy wore black shorts and sandals. At the time of his death he had been carrying a pouch of rice, a rifle, and three magazines of ammunition.

You want my opinion, Mitchell Sanders said, there's a definite moral here.

He put his hand on the dead boy's wrist. He was quiet for a time, as if counting a pulse, then he patted the stomach, almost affectionately, and used Kiowa's hunting hatchet to remove the thumb.   30

Henry Dobbins asked what the moral was.

Moral?

You know. *Moral.*

Sanders wrapped the thumb in toilet paper and handed it across to Norman Bowker. There was no blood. Smiling, he kicked the boy's head, watched the flies scatter, and said, It's like with that old TV show — Paladin. Have gun, will travel.

Henry Dobbins thought about it.   35

Yeah, well, he finally said. I don't see no moral.

There it *is,* man.

Fuck off.

They carried USO stationery and pencils and pens. They carried Sterno, safety pins, trip flares, signal flares, spools of wire, razor blades, chewing tobacco, liberated joss sticks and statuettes of the smiling Buddha, candles, grease pencils, *The Stars and Stripes,* fingernail clippers, Psy Ops[4] leaflets, bush hats, bolos, and much more. Twice a week, when the resupply choppers came in, they carried hot chow in green Mermite cans and large canvas bags filled with iced beer and soda pop. They carried plastic water containers, each with a two-gallon capacity. Mitchell Sanders carried a set of starched tiger fatigues for special occasions. Henry Dobbins carried Black Flag insecticide. Dave Jensen carried empty sandbags that could be filled at night for added protection. Lee Strunk carried tanning lotion. Some things they carried in common. Taking turns, they carried the big PRC-77 scrambler radio, which weighed thirty pounds with its battery. They shared the weight of memory. They took up what others could no longer bear. Often, they carried each other, the wounded or weak. They carried infections. They carried chess sets, basketballs, Vietnamese-English dictionaries, insignia of rank, Bronze Stars and Purple Hearts, plastic cards imprinted with the Code of Conduct. They carried diseases, among them malaria and dysentery. They carried lice and ringworm and leeches and paddy algae and various rots and molds. They carried the land itself — Vietnam, the place, the soil — a powdery orange-red dust that covered their boots and

---

[4] Psychological Operations. [Ed.]

fatigues and faces. They carried the sky. The whole atmosphere, they carried it, the humidity, the monsoons, the stink of fungus and decay, all of it, they carried gravity. They moved like mules. By daylight they took sniper fire, at night they were mortared, but it was not battle, it was just the endless march, village to village, without purpose, nothing won or lost. They marched for the sake of the march. They plodded along slowly, dumbly, leaning forward against the heat, unthinking, all blood and bone, simple grunts, soldiering with their legs, toiling up the hills and down into the paddies and across the rivers and up again and down, just humping, one step and then the next and then another, but no volition, no will, because it was automatic, it was anatomy, and the war was entirely a matter of posture and carriage, the hump was everything, a kind of inertia, a kind of emptiness, a dullness of desire and intellect and conscience and hope and human sensibility. Their principles were in their feet. Their calculations were biological. They had no sense of strategy or mission. They searched the villages without knowing what to look for, not caring, kicking over jars of rice, frisking children and old men, blowing tunnels, sometimes setting fires and sometimes not, then forming up and moving on to the next village, then other villages, where it would always be the same. They carried their own lives. The pressures were enormous. In the heat of early afternoon, they would remove their helmets and flak jackets, walking bare, which was dangerous but which helped ease the strain. They would often discard things along the route of march. Purely for comfort, they would throw away rations, blow their Claymores and grenades, no matter, because by night-fall the resupply choppers would arrive with more of the same, then a day or two later still more, fresh watermelons and crates of ammunition and sunglasses and woolen sweaters — the resources were stunning — sparklers for the Fourth of July, colored eggs for Easter. It was the great American war chest — the fruits of science, the smokestacks, the canneries, the arsenals at Hartford, the Minnesota forests, the machine shops, the vast fields of corn and wheat — they carried like freight trains; they carried it on their backs and shoulders — and for all the ambiguities of Vietnam, all the mysteries and unknowns, there was at least the single abiding certainty that they would never be at a loss for things to carry.

After the chopper took Lavender away, Lieutenant Jimmy Cross led his 40 men into the village of Than Khe. They burned everything. They shot chickens and dogs, they trashed the village well, they called in artillery and watched the wreckage, then they marched for several hours through the hot afternoon, and then at dusk, while Kiowa explained how Lavender died, Lieutenant Cross found himself trembling.

He tried not to cry. With his entrenching tool, which weighed five pounds, he began digging a hole in the earth.

He felt shame. He hated himself. He had loved Martha more than his men, and as a consequence Lavender was now dead, and this was something he would have to carry like a stone in his stomach for the rest of the war.

All he could do was dig. He used his entrenching tool like an ax, slashing, feeling both love and hate, and then later, when it was full dark, he sat at the bottom of his foxhole and wept. It went on for a long while. In part, he was grieving for Ted Lavender, but mostly it was for Martha, and for himself, because she belonged to another world, which was not quite real, and because she was a junior at Mount Sebastian College in New Jersey, a poet and a virgin and uninvolved, and because he realized she did not love him and never would.

Like cement, Kiowa whispered in the dark. I swear to God — boom-down. Not a word.

I've heard this, said Norman Bowker.   45

A pisser, you know? Still zipping himself up. Zapped while zipping.

All right, fine. That's enough.

Yeah, but you had to see it, the guy just —

I *heard,* man. Cement. So why not shut the fuck *up?*

Kiowa shook his head sadly and glanced over at the hole where Lieutenant   50
Jimmy Cross sat watching the night. The air was thick and wet. A warm, dense fog had settled over the paddies and there was the stillness that precedes rain.

After a time Kiowa sighed.

One thing for sure, he said. The Lieutenant's in some deep hurt. I mean that crying jag — the way he was carrying on — it wasn't fake or anything, it was real heavy-duty hurt. The man cares.

Sure, Norman Bowker said.

Say what you want, the man does care.

We all got problems.   55

Not Lavender.

No, I guess not. Bowker said. Do me a favor, though.

Shut up?

That's a smart Indian. Shut up.

Shrugging, Kiowa pulled off his boots. He wanted to say more, just to   60
lighten up his sleep, but instead he opened his New Testament and arranged it beneath his head as a pillow. The fog made things seem hollow and unattached. He tried not to think about Ted Lavender, but then he was thinking how fast it was, no drama, down and dead, and how it was hard to feel anything except surprise. It seemed un-Christian. He wished he could find some great sadness, or even anger, but the emotion wasn't there and he couldn't make it happen. Mostly he felt pleased to be alive. He liked the smell of the New Testament under his cheek, the leather and ink and paper and glue, whatever the chemicals were. He liked hearing the sounds of night. Even his fatigue, it felt fine, the stiff muscles and the prickly awareness of his own body, a floating feeling. He enjoyed not being dead. Lying there, Kiowa admired Lieutenant Jimmy Cross's capacity for grief. He wanted to share the man's pain, he wanted to care as Jimmy Cross cared. And yet when he closed his eyes, all he could think was Boom-down, and all he could feel was the pleasure of having his boots off and

the fog curling in around him and the damp soil and the Bible smells and the plush comfort of night.

After a moment Norman Bowker sat up in the dark.

What the hell, he said. You want to talk, *talk*. Tell it to me.

Forget it.

No, man, go on. One thing I hate, it's a silent Indian.

For the most part they carried themselves with poise, a kind of dignity. Now and then, however, there were times of panic, when they squealed or wanted to squeal but couldn't, when they twitched and made moaning sounds and covered their heads and said Dear Jesus and flopped around on the earth and fired their weapons blindly and cringed and sobbed and begged for the noise to stop and went wild and made stupid promises to themselves and to God and to their mothers and fathers, hoping not to die. In different ways, it happened to all of them. Afterward, when the firing ended, they would blink and peek up. They would touch their bodies, feeling shame, then quickly hiding it. They would force themselves to stand. As if in slow motion, frame by frame, the world would take on the old logic — absolute silence, then the wind, then sunlight, then voices. It was the burden of being alive. Awkwardly, the men would reassemble themselves, first in private, then in groups, becoming soldiers again. They would repair the leaks in their eyes. They would check for casualties, call in dust-offs, light cigarettes, try to smile, clear their throats and spit, and begin cleaning their weapons. After a time someone would shake his head and say, No lie, I almost shit my pants, and someone else would laugh, which meant it was bad, yes, but the guy had obviously not shit his pants, it wasn't that bad, and in any case nobody would ever do such a thing and then go ahead and talk about it. They would squint into the dense, oppressive sunlight. For a few moments, perhaps, they would fall silent, lighting a joint and tracking its passage from man to man, inhaling, holding in the humiliation. Scary stuff, one of them might say. But then someone else would grin or flick his eyebrows and say, Rodger-dodger, almost cut me a new asshole, *almost*.

There were numerous such poses. Some carried themselves with a sort of wistful resignation, others with pride or stiff soldierly discipline or good humor or macho zeal. They were afraid of dying but they were even more afraid to show it.

They found jokes to tell.

They used a hard vocabulary to contain the terrible softness. *Greased,* they'd say. *Offed, lit up, zapped while zipping.* It wasn't cruelty, just stage presence. They were actors and the war came at them in 3-D. When someone died, it wasn't quite dying, because in a curious way it seemed scripted, and because they had their lines mostly memorized, irony mixed with tragedy, and because they called it by other names, as if to encyst and destroy the reality of death itself. They kicked corpses. They cut off thumbs. They talked grunt lingo. They told stories about Ted Lavender's supply of tranquilizers, how the poor guy didn't feel a thing, how incredibly tranquil he was.

There's a moral here, said Mitchell Sanders.

They were waiting for Lavender's chopper, smoking the dead man's dope.   70

The moral's pretty obvious, Sanders said, and winked. Stay away from drugs. No joke, they'll ruin your day every time.

Cute, said Henry Dobbins.

Mind-blower, get it? Talk about wiggy — nothing left, just blood and brains.

They made themselves laugh.

There it is, they'd say, over and over, as if the repetition itself were an act   75
of poise, a balance between crazy and almost crazy, knowing without going. There it is, which meant be cool, let it ride, because oh yeah, man, you can't change what can't be changed, there it is, there it absolutely and positively and fucking well *is*.

They were tough.

They carried all the emotional baggage of men who might die. Grief, terror, love, longing — these were intangibles, but the intangibles had their own mass and specific gravity, they had tangible weight. They carried shameful memories. They carried the common secret of cowardice barely restrained, the instinct to run or freeze or hide, and in many respects this was the heaviest burden of all, for it could never be put down, it required perfect balance and perfect posture. They carried their reputations. They carried the soldier's greatest fear, which was the fear of blushing. Men killed, and died, because they were embarrassed not to. It was what had brought them to the war in the first place, nothing positive, no dreams of glory or honor, just to avoid the blush of dishonor. They died so as not to die of embarrassment. They crawled into tunnels and walked point and advanced under fire. Each morning, despite the unknowns, they made their legs move. They endured. They kept humping. They did not submit to the obvious alternative, which was simply to close the eyes and fall. So easy, really. Go limp and tumble to the ground and let the muscles unwind and not speak and not budge until your buddies picked you up and lifted you into the chopper that would roar and dip its nose and carry you off to the world. A mere matter of falling, yet no one ever fell. It was not courage, exactly; the object was not valor. Rather, they were too frightened to be cowards.

By and large they carried these things inside, maintaining the masks of composure. They sneered at sick call. They spoke bitterly about guys who had found release by shooting off their own toes or fingers. Pussies, they'd say. Candy-asses. It was fierce, mocking talk, with only a trace of envy or awe, but even so, the image played itself out behind their eyes.

They imagined the muzzle against flesh. They imagined the quick, sweet pain, then the evacuation to Japan, then a hospital with warm beds and cute geisha nurses.

They dreamed of freedom birds.   80

At night, on guard, staring into the dark, they were carried away by jumbo jets. They felt the rush of takeoff. *Gone!* they yelled. And then velocity, wings and engines, a smiling stewardess — but it was more than a plane, it was a real bird, a big sleek silver bird with feathers and talons and high screeching. They were flying. The weights fell off, there was nothing to bear. They laughed and held on tight, feeling the cold slap of wind and altitude, soaring, thinking *It's over, I'm gone!* — they were naked, they were light and free — it was all lightness, bright and fast and buoyant, light as light, a helium buzz in the brain, a giddy bubbling in the lungs as they were taken up over the clouds and the war, beyond duty, beyond gravity and mortification and global entanglements — *Sin loi!*[5] they yelled, *I'm sorry, motherfuckers, but I'm out of it, I'm goofed, I'm on a space cruise, I'm gone!* — and it was a restful, disencumbered sensation, just riding the light waves, sailing that big silver freedom bird over the mountains and oceans, over America, over the farms and great sleeping cities and cemeteries and highways and the golden arches of McDonald's. It was flight, a kind of fleeing, a kind of falling, falling higher and higher, spinning off the edge of the earth and beyond the sun and through the vast, silent vacuum where there were no burdens and where everything weighed exactly nothing. *Gone!* they screamed, *I'm sorry but I'm gone!* And so at night, not quite dreaming, they gave themselves over to lightness, they were carried, they were purely borne.

On the morning after Ted Lavender died, First Lieutenant Jimmy Cross crouched at the bottom of his foxhole and burned Martha's letters. Then he burned the two photographs. There was a steady rain falling, which made it difficult, but he used heat tabs and Sterno to build a small fire, screening it with his body, holding the photographs over the tight blue flame with the tips of his fingers.

He realized it was only a gesture. Stupid, he thought. Sentimental, too, but mostly just stupid.

Lavender was dead. You couldn't burn the blame.

Besides, the letters were in his head. And even now, without photographs, Lieutenant Cross could see Martha playing volleyball in her white gym shorts and yellow T-shirt. He could see her moving in the rain.

When the fire died out, Lieutenant Cross pulled his poncho over his shoulders and ate breakfast from a can.

There was no great mystery, he decided.

In those burned letters Martha had never mentioned the war, except to say, Jimmy, take care of yourself. She wasn't involved. She signed the letters "Love," but it wasn't love, and all the fine lines and technicalities did not matter.

The morning came up wet and blurry. Everything seemed part of everything else, the fog and Martha and the deepening rain.

It was a war, after all.

Half smiling, Lieutenant Jimmy Cross took out his maps. He shook his head hard, as if to clear it, then bent forward and began planning the day's

---

[5] Sorry about that. [Ed.]

march. In ten minutes, or maybe twenty, he would rouse the men and they would pack up and head west, where the maps showed the country to be green and inviting. They would do what they had always done. The rain might add some weight, but otherwise it would be one more day layered upon all the other days.

He was realistic about it. There was that new hardness in his stomach.

No more fantasies, he told himself.

Henceforth, when he thought about Martha, it would be only to think that she belonged elsewhere. He would shut down the daydreams. This was not Mount Sebastian, it was another world, where there were no pretty poems or midterm exams, a place where men died because of carelessness and gross stupidity. Kiowa was right. Boom-down, and you were dead, never partly dead.

Briefly, in the rain, Lieutenant Cross saw Martha's gray eyes gazing back   95
at him.

He understood.

It was very sad, he thought. The things men carried inside. The things men did or felt they had to do.

He almost nodded at her, but didn't.

Instead he went back to his maps. He was now determined to perform his duties firmly and without negligence. It wouldn't help Lavender, he knew that, but from this point on he would comport himself as a soldier. He would dispose of his good-luck pebble. Swallow it, maybe, or use Lee Strunk's slingshot, or just drop it along the trail. On the march he would impose strict field discipline. He would be careful to send out flank security, to prevent straggling or bunching up, to keep his troops moving at the proper pace and at the proper interval. He would insist on clean weapons. He would confiscate the remainder of Lavender's dope. Later in the day, perhaps, he would call the men together and speak to them plainly. He would accept the blame for what had happened to Ted Lavender. He would be a man about it. He would look them in the eyes, keeping his chin level, and he would issue the new SOPs in a calm, impersonal tone of voice, an officer's voice, leaving no room for argument or discussion. Commencing immediately, he'd tell them, they would no longer abandon equipment along the route of march. They would police up their acts. They would get their shit together, and keep it together, and maintain it neatly and in good working order.

He would not tolerate laxity. He would show strength, distancing himself.   100

Among the men there would be grumbling, of course, and maybe worse, because their days would seem longer and their loads heavier, but Lieutenant Cross reminded himself that his obligation was not to be loved but to lead. He would dispense with love; it was not now a factor. And if anyone quarreled or complained, he would simply tighten his lips and arrange his shoulders in the correct command posture. He might give a curt little nod. Or he might not. He might just shrug and say Carry on, then they would saddle up and form into a column and move out toward the villages of Than Khe.   1986

INVESTIGATIONS

1. What do the names the soldiers have for one another and "the things they carry" reveal about their attitudes toward themselves and what they do? How might the soldiers' language be considered a "private" one, in the sense Richard Rodriguez ("Aria: A Bilingual Childhood") uses the term?

2. The soldiers carry things necessary for physical survival or comfort, but they also carry hopes, dreams, love, and other "weightless" things. Locate places where the story mentions these things and write a 500–750-word essay that shows how they "weigh" at least as much as the equipment the soldiers carry.

3. How is the soldiers' relationship to one another a closer one than friendship? In what other kinds of community is such intimacy possible?

4. In paragraph 29 Mitchell Sanders says, "There's a definite moral here" and Henry Dobbins asks what it is. In what ways is Sanders's response a satisfactory one? What would you tell Dobbins the "moral" is? How is Kiowa's pleasure in being alive (para. 60) moral?

KITTY TSUI

Don't Let Them Chip Away at Our Language

haa-low, okay,
dank que, gut bye.

the only words
my grandmother knew.
the only words of english   5
she spoke
on a regular basis
in her rhythm of

Born "in the City of Nine Dragons [Kowloon, Hong Kong] in the Year of the Dragon [1952–53]," KITTY TSUI grew up "in England and Hong Kong, and immigrated to Gold Mountain in 1969." An artist, actor, and competitive bodybuilder, Tsui is the author of *The Words of a Woman Who Breathes Fire* (1983), a poetry collection.

city cantonese
mixed with   10
chinatown slang:
du pont guy,
low-see beef,
and, you good gel,
sic gee mah go,   15
sic apple pie
yum coca co-la.

a few proper nouns
were also part of
her vocabulary.   20
ny name, kit-ee
san fan-see,
pete gid-ding
her favorite
weatherman on tv,   25
say-fu-way
where she would
stock up on
rolls of toilet paper,
sponges and ajax.   30
on sale, of course.

in the spring of 1985
a republican assemblyman
proposed a bill
to make english   35
the official language
of the state.
his rationale:
we're no longer
going to let them   40
chip away at our language.
if they can't
understand english
they shouldn't be here
at all.   45

we first came
in 1785, three seamen
stranded in baltimore.
later we were
merchants and traders,   50

cooks and tailors,
contract laborers hired
to work in the mines,
in construction,
in the canneries,   55
hired to do what no man would:
hang from cliffs in a basket,
endure harsh winters
and blast through rock
to build the iron horse.   60

we became sharecroppers
growing peanuts,
strawberries,
cabbage and
chrysanthemums.   65
opened restaurants
and laundries,
worked in rich homes,
on ranches and farms
tending stock,   70
cleaning house,
cooking and ironing,
chopping firewood,
composing letters home
dreaming of a wife, a son.   75

we are tong yan,
american born
and immigrants
living in l.a., arizona,
brooklyn and the bronx,   80
san mateo and the sunset.
we eat burgers and baw,
custard tart and bubblegum.
we are doctors, actors,
artists, carpenters,   85
maids and teachers,
gay and straight.
we speak in many tongues:
sam yup, say yup, street talk,
the queen's english.   90

please don't let them
chip away at our language.   1989

INVESTIGATIONS

1. Compare what the speaker means by "please don't let them chip away at our language" to what the "republican assemblyman" means in line 41. Describe what each of them sees as a threat to "our language."
2. Compare this poem to Lucille Clifton's "in white america." Why do both poems make historical references? In what ways do the two poems describe similar divisions in American culture?
3. What does this poem demonstrate about how the language we speak binds us to others? About how it can alienate us?

ERIC BOGOSIAN

Talk Radio

Characters

SID GREENBERG, financial talk show host

BERNIE, Sid's operator

SPIKE, engineer

DAN WOODRUFF, executive producer, WTLK

STU NOONAN, Barry's operator

LINDA MAC ARTHUR, assistant producer of "Nighttalk"

BARRY CHAMPLAIN, "Nighttalk" host

KENT, guest

DR. SUSAN FLEMING, talk show host

OPERATOR FOR DR. FLEMING

CALLERS

(*The set is a stripped-down version of a radio studio — WTLK, a "talk radio" station operating out of Cleveland, Ohio. Two console tables occupy the main space. One, stage left, faces the audience and is equipped with a small computer screen, a phone unit with buttons for several lines, and a studio mike on a "Luxo" armature. Two office chairs are on either side of the table facing the audience. This is the talk radio host's console. The second table, stage right, faces away from the audience and is equipped with a computer screen and key-*

Raised in Woburn, Massachusetts, and a graduate of Oberlin College, ERIC BOGOSIAN (b. 1953), like other performance artists, turns social commentary into theater. His plays include *Drinking in America* (1986), *Talk Radio* (1987), and *Sex, Drugs and Rock 'n' Roll* (1989).

board, a larger phone unit, and a headset. This is the operator's console. Behind and above the operator's desk is a little balcony with three steps leading up to it. The balcony leads to a door, which in turn leads to the sound engineer's booth. The booth is separated from the main space by a large plate-glass window. Thus the engineer can look out over the space and see both the operator and the host. In extreme downstage right is a coffee machine on a small table along with cups, sugar, and spoon and another office chair, where the assistant producer sits. Behind this chair is a coat rack.)

(As the audience enters the theater the set is bathed in dim light. Soft "easy listening" music is played over the sound system. The set is empty. The music grows louder as house lights and stage lights fade to black. The music begins changing rapidly as if someone were switching channels, then finally "finding" WTLK. In black an announcer's voice booms out.)

ANNOUNCER'S VOICE: Coming up in just a few minutes, "Nighttalk" with Barry Champlain right after the news and weather . . . and now, back to Sidney Greenberg and "Your Taxes and You."

(Sid is heard in the dark, a nasal, clipped voice.)

SID: . . . All righty, now, Richard, are you still with me?

(Stage light snaps on to reveal Sid Greenberg at the host's desk. He is hunched over the microphone, smoking a cigar. The desk is a mess of take-out containers and coffee cups. At the operator's desk sits Sid's assistant, Bernie, and in the engineer's booth sits Spike, the engineer.)

(Sid speaks with a flowing energy that gives little room for the caller.)

SID: OK, now with the cash that you have in hand from the second mortgage on the first property, the property on the lake . . . you've either taken a second mortgage or completely refinanced that property. Now you have cash in hand. What are you gonna do with that cash?

RICHARD *(caller)*: That's why I —

SID: Figuring the property is probably worth in the neighborhood of two hundred thousand, you pay off the existing mortgage of ten thousand bucks with a hundred-and-seventy-five-thousand-dollar refinancing loan. Simple arithmetic leaves you with a hundred and sixty-five thousand dollars. . . . Now you could *pocket* this money, but that isn't going to get you *anywhere*. 'Cause you're not using the money! And the last thing you want to do is *sell*, 'cause that means *capital gains tax* and that means you gotta send a check to . . . yeah, you guessed it, our Fat Uncle in Washington. . . . Don't wanna do that, so hold on to that property! Now, . . . Richard, you still with me?

RICHARD: Uh-huh.

SID: Richard, do you have a paper and pencil? . . . Good, 'cause now we're gonna make some money! What you need is a tax break and some income, so you take that hundred and sixty-five thousand and you fly to Florida and you look for an office building going for somewhere in the neighborhood of one or two million bucks. You use that hundred and sixty-five thousand *and* the fifty grand your uncle left you *and* the hundred thou you're gonna make off the second mortgage on your house and you put that all together and you use that three hundred and fifteen thousand dollars as a *down payment* on the office building in, let's say, Cocoa Beach.

RICHARD: Florida?

SID: You take the income you make on the rentals in that building and put the excess income beyond your monthly finance payments on the two notes into either a zero-coupon bond or a T-bill —

RICHARD: What about a Ginnie Mae?

SID: Ginnie Maes, Fannie Maes, Willie Mays, you'll never lose with bonds. . . . Establish an annuity trust and your kids will have plenty when college days roll around *and* you'll be sitting pretty with a tax break in Florida, two places to go on vacation, and, *get this, Richard,* over two million dollars' worth of property. . . . Unbelievable, but guess what, Richard, using my method, you've just become a millionaire! How about that!

(While Sid gives the last speech, Stu Noonan, Barry Champlain's operator, has entered and perched himself on the railing of the balcony, waiting for Bernie to vacate his seat.)

RICHARD: But what about — ?

SID *(cutting him off)*: All righty, the big clock on the wall tells me that it's time to wrap this episode of "Your Taxes and You" up for this evening. Stay tuned for the news and weather, followed by some stimulating conversation from the master, Mister Barry Champlain. . . . I'm Sidney Greenberg, reminding you that "it's not how much you make, it's how much you take home." *(Stands, sticks his cigar in his mouth.)* All right, we're off. . . . So . . . are we going from here?

(Bernie has grabbed coats and hats from the coatrack and gives Sid his. Stu enters and pours himself a coffee, goes to his desk as Linda MacArthur, the assistant producer, enters. Passing Sid and Bernie, she cleans off the desk and preps it for Barry.)

BERNIE: Sure, why not?

SID: Good, good, good . . .

BERNIE: You know, Sid, it's gonna be a wet track.

SID: 'Course it's gonna be a wet track. Been raining all day, how they gonna keep it dry? Wipe it off with a towel? . . . Can't be done!

BERNIE: So who do you like in the third race?

SID: We keep talkin' we're not gonna make it till the fifth. Did you see my car when you came in?

BERNIE: No.

SID: I was coming out of the Pick-N-Pay and there's this kid sitting on the hood of my car. And he's got circles, you know, around all the rust spots.

BERNIE: What, a whacko?

(Bernie and Sid exit.)

SID *(offstage)*: No, a black kid. So he tells me for ninety-five dollars he can take out every ding and rust spot. I couldn't believe it . . .

(The news and weather can be heard over the sound system as Linda and Stu get ready for their show. They work efficiently, hardly speaking. Linda cleans Barry's desk off, checks his mike and headset, puts out pencils and paper, and pours him a fresh cup of coffee. Linda's job during the show is to make sure Barry has everything he needs, to keep track of when commercials are aired, and generally to make sure the show is running smoothly. It is no coincidence that Linda is a very sexy blonde. Stu likewise cleans off Bernie's mess from his operator's desk, whipping the garbage into a small trash basket next to Barry's desk. Stu's job is to field the phone calls that come in to Barry, screen them, and pass them on to Barry's desk. He also helps to cue Barry when a commercial is coming up. His job is something like an air traffic controller's. Stu looks over at Barry's desk, the empty chair. Lights a cigarette. Stu looks at his watch, takes a deep breath.)

STU: Two minutes . . .

LINDA *(as she refreshes Stu's coffee)*: I called my mother in New Jersey this morning. I told her the show was going national. . . . She wanted to know if that meant we were gonna be on TV! Isn't that a riot?

(Barry Champlain enters. He's a wiry man who's moving a little too fast. He acts very sure of himself, but there's an edge.)

BARRY *(coming in the door past Spike)*: Spike, how ya doin' tonight? Stu! *(Slaps hands with Stu, then launches into a story.)* Hey, listen to this. Last night I call this Chinese restaurant. I'm ordering take out. I'm celebrating, figure it's the last time in my life I ever have to eat take-out Chinese food. I dial the phone wrong. I get this Chinese betting parlor. I'm talking on the phone to this Chinaman bookie. . . . Guy doesn't take bets on sports or horses, he takes bets on animals that *fight* each other . . . Dog fights, pit bull fights, Chihuahua fights, poodle fights! Cockfights! Monkey fights! Frog fights! *Frog* fights, Stu! I put down some money, won a hundred bucks on a frog named Hung Far Low! *(Turns to Linda.)* Linda, come on, let's go. We're wasting time!

(Linda has been waiting with clippings in her hand.)

LINDA: You wanna hear these?

BARRY: I'm here, am I here?

STU: Sixty seconds to air, Bar.

(*Stu looks at his watch. Barry has seated himself at his desk during the interchange, starts pushing buttons, sipping coffee, getting ready. Linda puts the clippings down in front of him and reads the headlines from her clipboard. Barry half-listens, makes little grunts after each item ["yeah," "uh-huh," etc.], flips through the clippings.*)

LINDA: North American Boy-Love Association has a chapter in Shaker Heights. . . . They found a woman with sixty-seven cats in her house; she was raising them for their pelts! . . . A guy was arrested this morning; he had three women chained to the wall in his basement, said they were his "harem" —

STU: Thirty seconds.

LINDA: — Three out of four people say that they prefer watching —

BARRY (*testing his mike*): Spike, beam me up, baby, beam me up!

LINDA: Are you listening to this?

BARRY (*patronizing*): I'm listening. I'm listening. Yeah?

(*Barry scrutinizes the clippings on his desk.*)

LINDA: Three out of four people say that they prefer watching television over having sex with their spouse. . . . A guy in San Jose, California, wants to be a surrogate mother, says he can do it. . . . Report on AIDS —

BARRY: I don't wanna talk about AIDS —

STU: Fifteen.

LINDA: OK . . . uh . . . Homeless people are living in an abandoned meat-packing plant in Willard. Some of them used to work there before it shut down —

BARRY: Where's Willard?

LINDA: Stu, you know where Willard is?

STU: Here we go in five!

LINDA: Dan called, said he'd drop by.

(*This interests Barry.*)

BARRY: Why?

LINDA: Guess he's nervous.

(*Linda exits.*)

BARRY: I'll make him nervous . . .

(*As he says the words, the room fills with the chords of George Thorogood's "Bad to the Bone." A pretaped announcer's voice follows.*)

ANNOUNCER'S VOICE-OVER: "And now from the heart of the Great Lakes, it's time for Cleveland's most popular and controversial talk show: 'Nighttalk' with Barry Champlain! And now, ladies and gentlemen, here's Barry . . ."

(Barry has taken a last sip of coffee, leans into the microphone. Stu points at him, and Barry picks up the beat perfectly.)

BARRY: Last night an eighty-year-old grandmother was knifed to death on Euclid Avenue, twenty people were watching, not one lifted a finger. Some kids need money for crack, so they stuck a knife in her throat. In Shaker Heights our good citizens . . . your doctors, your lawyers, your dentists . . . have formed a little club, they're having sex with children. . . . And on the West Side, fifteen churches were busted last week, for, get this, illegal gambling activities . . . and that's just in Cleveland!

This country, where culture means pornography and slasher films, where ethics means payoffs, graft, and insider schemes, where integrity means lying, whoring, and intoxication . . . this country is in deep trouble, this country is rotten to the core. . . . And somebody better do something about it!

Tomorrow night, this show, "Nighttalk," begins national broadcasting. That is to say some smart guys at the Metroscan network have decided to pick us up for the benefit of people all over America. Two hundred and fifty-seven stations in the United States and Canada. How about that? How about that?

Some people have asked me if I'm gonna soften my touch on the national show. That's impossible. It can't be done. If I had to do that I might as well quit. This decadent country needs a loud voice, needs somebody to shake it up . . . and that somebody is me!

I have a job to do and I'm gonna do it . . . and I need your help. . . . Now this is what I want you to do. . . . Are you listening? I want you to do something very simple. There's a thing in your house called a telephone. I want you to pick it up. . . . Go ahead, put your hand out and grab it, hold it up to your face, and dial 555-T-A-L-K. . . . Open your mouth and tell me what we're going to do about the mess this country's in!

This show goes national tomorrow night and that means the nation is listening. You better have something to say. . . . I know I do. *(Picks up his headset and puts it on as he speaks.)* This is Barry Champlain, hold on to your radios. . . . Let's go to the first caller. Francine.

FRANCINE: Yes, Barry.

BARRY: How's your life tonight?

FRANCINE: I have a little problem I'd like to discuss . . .

BARRY: Shoot.

FRANCINE: I'm a transvestite.

BARRY: Uh-huh.

FRANCINE: And I'm trying to save money for an operation —

BARRY: Francine . . .

FRANCINE: What?

BARRY: This isn't interesting —

FRANCINE: Let me finish what I was saying!

BARRY: Francine . . . in your wildest imagination . . . what possible interest do you think your personal adventures in surgery would hold for my listeners?

FRANCINE: I don't care about your listeners, it's something I *have* to talk about!

BARRY: I don't. *(Cuts Francine off.)* "Nighttalk. . . ." Yeah, Josh?

JOSH: Thanks a lot, Barry. Uh, Barry, don't you think that the policies the World Bank is following only hurts the economies of Third World countries to the benefit of American banks?

BARRY: Hold on! "Third World countries!" "Third World countries!" Where'd you learn that phrase, in college? Something you saw on "Sixty Minutes"?

JOSH: It's a commonly used term —

BARRY: Uh-huh. I hear it used all the time. It intrigues me. . . . You know what it means?

JOSH: Of course I do.

BARRY: Please tell us.

JOSH: Well, it means developing countries . . . small poor countries.

BARRY: Small countries . . . so India's not Third World?

JOSH: Well, India is . . .

BARRY: What about communist countries. . . . Red China, for instance?

JOSH: No, not communist countries. . . . We're getting off the track. . . . What I was trying —

BARRY: We're not getting off the track, Josh, we're getting *on* the track. The track is that you don't know what the hell you're talking about! You call me up and start spouting a bunch of left-wing mumbo jumbo about a subject you know nothing about! Yugoslavia is communist, it's a Third World country, so's Nicaragua, so's Cuba. Josh, go back to college and when you graduate gimme a call. *(Cuts him off.)* "Nighttalk," you're on.

JUNIOR: *Barry!* Yeah, hey man, what do you think about the Indians this year?

BARRY: In a word I'd say they suck.

JUNIOR: Hey, I disagree with you on that one, Bar! They're gonna take the pennant. Niekro's gonna win twenty!

BARRY: Are you *nuts?* Niekro's fifty years old!

JUNIOR: Well, listen, you Mister Fuckin' Big Shot, Niekro has played better ball than any other —

BARRY: Yeah. Yeah. Yeah. *(Cuts him off.)* The Indians are gonna be watching the Series on the boob tube. Toronto will take the pennant, and the Astros will take the Series. On that deep note, let's break for a commercial. . . . This is "Nighttalk."

(Barry pulls his headset off as Stu signals to Spike to begin running an ad.)

STU: This is a sixty, Barry.

BARRY: Stu, let's cool it with the baseball calls tonight, all right? How's the board?

STU: Board's good. Warming up. I got five hanging already . . . two look good . . .

(Linda enters holding a bottle of Jack Daniel's and an empty glass. She is followed closely by Dan Woodruff, executive producer of "Nighttalk." He's a young businessman, nattily dressed.)

DAN: Barry! *(Barry watches Linda pour him a stiff double.)* Just wanted to come by, say hello. *(Nodding to Stu.)* Stu. We did it, Barry!

BARRY: What do you mean, "we," Dan? You. You did it!

DAN: You know what it is, Barry? They can't say no to ratings. That's the key. Do what you want but get the ratings . . . then they can't say no. . . . You become an irresistible force.

BARRY: Yup. Dan, we're in the middle of a show right now, gotta move it along —

STU: Thirty seconds, Barry.

DAN: I'm out. I'm out. "Genius at work." I know. . . . I'll leave you guys alone. *(Leaving.)* Make it a hot show tonight!

BARRY: It's always a hot show, Dan.

DAN: Yeah, but tonight . . . *extra* hot. Don't wanna fuck this up. . . . We got a contract for six months, we want it for six years!

BARRY *(friendly)*: Sixty years! Six hundred years! Six thousand years!

(Barry gives Dan a Nazi salute.)

STU: Six seconds.

DAN *(laughing)*: Sounds good. Sounds good. Oh, Barry, if you need anything, I'll be upstairs.

(As Dan leaves, Barry settles in at his desk, waiting for the ad to wind down. Dan gives Linda a conspiratorial wink on his way out. Barry lights a cigarette, glances at his screen. Stu gives him a "go.")

BARRY: Ruth, you're on.

RUTH: You're such a good man.

BARRY: Hello.

RUTH: You're so good, you care so much.

BARRY: Hello, is this Ruth?

RUTH: Yes, Ruth, this is Ruth. I was just listening to what you were saying, Barry, and you're so right! There is no more love, Barry. There is no more hope!

BARRY: Well, I wasn't saying that exactly. I was saying that I can't help but wonder why —

RUTH: No. No. You're right, Barry. . . . Look at the world today. Hundreds of thousands of people starving in Africa. . . . And no one cares . . . that's all. . . . They'll die. . . . And it can't be stopped, Barry. *(Barry, resigned to letting this one run a bit, finds his cigarette pack empty. He signals to Linda for a fresh pack. She comes over, disposes of the old pack, and leaves to get another.)* Who can stop the toxic wastes, the terrorism, the

nuclear buildup, the starvation, . . . the assassinations? They tried to kill
the Pope, Barry, what about that? You know, they killed Jack Kennedy!

BARRY: Yeah, I think I remember reading about that somewhere. . . . Listen,
Ruth, you can't take the world's problems personally —

RUTH: No, Barry, don't deny it. Don't act naive for our sake! You know the
truth because you are an educated and wise man. And you're a courageous
man to tell it. I'm so glad that your show will be finally heard all over this
country because it's time that people started to listen to someone with a
level head —

BARRY: Especially people like you, huh, Ruth?

RUTH: — the pollution is killing the trees, animals are becoming extinct. No
more elephants, no more eagles, no more whales. Not to mention the
rhinos, the condors, the grizzlies, the panda bears. No more panda bears!
. . . What's the point, will someone tell me that?

(*Linda has entered with fresh cigarettes. She presses them into his
hand.*)

BARRY: Ruth, cheer up! Somehow the world will struggle on without the panda
bears. . . ."Every cloud has a silver lining."

RUTH: That's nice of you to say, Barry. But I know you don't believe it. You're
just saying it to make all of us feel better. Because you are so good and
kind. But, Barry, we don't deserve it . . . we don't deserve your love. It's
our own fault . . . it's all our own fault . . .

BARRY: Look, Ruth, the point is that I feel —

RUTH: Thank you, Barry, for being such a good man. You are a prick in the
conscience of the country. . . . If it weren't for you I don't know what I'd
do. Take care of yourself. And good luck with your new show, we need it
now more than ever.

BARRY: Ruth, I was saying the point is that — (*A loud click is heard on the
line; she's hung up.*) I guess we've lost Ruth. . . . No more panda bears
. . . no more Ruth! Gonna miss 'em. Hey, Stu, did she just call me a prick?

STU: She called you a prick, Bar!

BARRY: I think she called me a prick! . . . Makes you think . . . What do you
think? What do you say? Call me, I want to know. . . ."Nighttalk," Glenn,
hello, you're on.

GLENN: Hello, Barry?

BARRY: You got 'im.

GLENN: Oh. Phew. I never called before, I'm a little nervous . . .

BARRY: That's all right. Relax. . . . Take your time . . .

GLENN: Your show is great. You're great. I've been listening to you for a long
time. . . . I used to listen to you when you were in Akron —

BARRY: Goin' back to my hippie days.

GLENN: Yeah. Heh. Heh. . . . You were great then too. Uh . . .

BARRY: Yeah, OK. Thanks a lot, Glenn, what's on your mind tonight?

GLENN: Well, something that woman was saying before about whales?

BARRY: What about them?

GLENN: Well, going extinct and, you know, the baby seals and everything . . .

BARRY: Uh-huh. Ecology. Yeah?

GLENN: Yeah . . . well, yeah, but what I was gonna say was more about animals in general, we should pay more attention to animals. . . . We should give them more respect. I have a cat, Muffin, . . . and sometimes, uh, I live alone, and, uh, sometimes, I will come home from work and we, well, I make dinner, we have, uh, dinner together, you know?

BARRY: You have dinner with your cat? At the table, you have dinner? What, with a tablecloth, candles, that kind of thing?

GLENN: Well, no, heh-heh, of course not . . .

BARRY: Oh.

GLENN: She has her own plate. On the floor . . .

BARRY: Oh, good!

GLENN: But we'll eat the same things. Like if I have pork chops, she has pork chops . . . if I have a veal, she has a veal. . . . And anyway, we spend time together. . . . And sometimes I just think, that well, there are so many crazy, loud people in the world and then there's Muffin. Quiet. Not hurting anybody. Clean. Why can't people be more like that?

BARRY: Lemme ask you something, Glenn. You and Muffin sound pretty intimate. You're not into anything funny, are you? She's fixed, isn't she?

GLENN: Huh? Yeah, she's . . . hey, I don't like what you're saying about my cat!

BARRY: There's a name for people who prefer animals over human beings, Glenn. . . . I mean, Glenn, Muffin's fixed, maybe the way to get people to act like Muffin is to get them fixed? What do you think about that idea? Sound good? Snip off the old cojones?

GLENN: No . . . that's not what I said at all! I don't think —

BARRY: You don't think? You don't think? Maybe we should all get fixed. Then we'd be quiet like little kittens! Isn't that what you want, Glenn, huh?

GLENN: *No!*

BARRY: *What are we alive for, Glenn? We are not house cats!* Glenn, you got a choice, either start living, or go get fixed. . . . Take my advice, stop hanging around with the pussy and go find some! . . . "Nighttalk," Betty.

BETTY: You think you're so smart!

BARRY: Hello?

BETTY: You're so smart, aren't ya? Cutting everyone off all the time. You know everything, don't ya?

BARRY: Not everything, Betty. No one can know everything. Even I can't know about everything!

BETTY: Why are you always making fun of this country? Why are you always talking about drugs and niggers and Jews? Isn't there anything else to talk about?

BARRY: You know what I hate, Betty? I hate people who call me up and tell

me what they *don't* want to talk about. . . . If you don't want to talk
about AIDS and *blacks* why do you bring them up in the first place? Huh?
Sounds to me like you *like* talking about them. . . . If you don't want to
talk about 'em then tell me what you wanna talk about or get off the
phone!

BETTY: Why don't you start telling the truth?

BARRY: About what, Betty?

BETTY: You know what I'm talkin' about. . . . The people behind your show.
. . . The people who pay the bills!

BARRY: Lemme guess. You're talking about the sponsors now?

BETTY: Don't act dumb with me. What kind of name is Champlain anyway?
That's not a real name. You changed it, didn't you? Why? Maybe because
it sounded a little too Jewish? Change the name, get a nose job . . . same
old story. You think people are so stupid! No one's as smart as you are.
. . . You think people never gonna find out about this propaganda that
you and your bosses and the State of Israel are perpetrating on the American —

BARRY: Wait a sec. . . . Hold on! State of Israel? *State of Israel!* Come on!

BETTY: You know, there are two kinds of Jews —

BARRY: Oh yeah?

BETTY: — the quiet types and the big-mouthed types and you're one of the big-
mouthed types . . . cut me off, I know you're gonna do it, go ahead!

BARRY: I'm not going to cut you off, Betty. You're too interesting to cut off.
. . . What you are saying reminds me of a little story . . . *(Pause. He looks
at his drink, swirling it in his glass.)* Two years ago, I visited Germany,
never had been there and wanted to take a look at Hitler's homeland. Are
you familiar with Adolf Hitler, Betty?

BETTY: I'm familiar with Hitler.

BARRY: Good. . . . Now, although in fact, I'm not Jewish, I decided to visit
what is left of a concentration camp on the outskirts of Munich. Dachau.
You join a little tour group, go out by bus, everyone gets out at the gates.
. . . It's rather chilling. A sign over the gate says: "Arbeit Macht Frei." It
means "Work will make you free," something the Nazis told their prisoners. . . . Of course most of them never left. . . . Are you still listening,
Betty?

BETTY: I hear all your lies . . .

BARRY: Good. I want to make sure you're not missing any of this. . . . Now,
as I walked along the gravel path between what remained of the barracks,
where the prisoners slept, and the gas chambers, where they died, I saw
something glitter in among the stones of the gravel. I bent over to see what
it was. What I had found was a tiny Star of David. Very old. Who knows,
it might have belonged to one of the prisoners of the camp, perhaps a
small boy torn from his parents as they were dragged off to the slaughterhouse. . . . I kept that Star of David. . . . I know I shouldn't have, but I

did. I keep it right here on my desk. I like to hold it sometimes. *(Swirling his glass of booze and studying it.)* In fact . . . well, I am holding it right now. . . .

    I hold it in my hand to give me courage . . . maybe a little of the courage that that small boy had as he faced unspeakable evil can enter me as I face the trials in my own life . . . when I face the cowardly and the narrow-minded . . . the bitter, bigoted people who hide behind anonymous phone calls full of hatred and poisonous bile. . . . People who have no guts, no spine, so they lash out at the helpless. . . . The grotesquely ignorant people, like you, Betty, who make me puke. . . . People who have nothing better to do than desecrate history, perhaps . . . only to repeat it. . . . Are you still with me, Betty? *(Pause.) Betty!*

BETTY: Keep talkin', Jew boy. Life is short . . . *(Click.)*

BARRY: Uh-huh, Stu, let's send a microwave oven out to Betty. . . . "Nighttalk," Debbie, you're on.

DEBBIE: Hello, Barry? Oh, I can't believe I'm actually on!

BARRY: You're actually on. What's on your mind tonight, Debbie?

DEBBIE: My boyfriend.

BARRY: How old are you, Debbie?

DEBBIE: I'm almost sixteen, Barry, and —

BARRY: Goin' to school?

DEBBIE: Yes, ummmm . . .

BARRY: And your boyfriend, what's he, a senior or something?

DEBBIE: He, uh, doesn't go to school, Barry . . .

BARRY: Doesn't go to school, where's he work?

DEBBIE: I don't see him all the time, so I don't really know . . .

BARRY: You don't know whether your boyfriend works or not? That's interesting.

DEBBIE: Well, see, the reason I don't know is that he leaves town sometimes and he kind of lives in his pickup truck. It's one of those that's all customized with tons of chrome on it. . . . He even has license plates that say "STAN-3" and everything and, ummmm, he tells me that he loves me, Barry, and I love him . . .

BARRY: Uh-huh. Love is a hard thing to define. Fifteen, huh? Tell me something, Debbie, is he a nice guy?

DEBBIE: Yes.

BARRY: Well, you're a lucky girl to have a nice guy with a pickup truck in love with you. So what's the problem?

DEBBIE: Well, see, I, um . . . *(Quiet.)*

BARRY: Debbie, hello? You still with us?

DEBBIE: Yes . . . *(Sniffing.)*

BARRY: Debbie?

DEBBIE *(outburst)*: I'm going to have a baby, Barry . . . and now Stan isn't around. I'm going to have to tell my parents pretty soon . . . *(Whimpering.)*

BARRY: Now, now, hold on there, Deb. Nothing's that bad. You're pregnant. We used to call it "being in trouble." It's bad, but it's not the worst thing that could happen.

DEBBIE: But my parents are gonna kill me, you don't understand!

BARRY: Look at it this way, people have babies all the time. It's not the end of the world, it's the beginning! A little baby is coming! A little pink baby! Things could be worse, a lot worse. You could be sick, or dying. Stan could be driving around in his pickup truck and have a head-on collision, go through the windshield and die!

DEBBIE: Barry, I want to die.

BARRY: No you don't, young lady.

DEBBIE: Yes I do!

BARRY: No you don't, young lady! Now let's not start taking ourselves too seriously here. . . . You got yourself in a little trouble. You let your animal passions get out of hand and now the fiddler has to be paid, Debbie, right?

DEBBIE: But, Barry, . . . he told me that —

BARRY: Right? Am I right or am I wrong? Sounds to me like you want to blame the world for what *you* did. Well, don't expect a shoulder to cry on here, little girl, because you didn't think of these things in the wet heat of passion. You liked the feel of sex, you like the feel of being in love, you better like the feel of being pregnant.

DEBBIE *(crying)*

BARRY: Hey, now, no crying. Crying isn't going to fix anything. You're just gonna get the baby all upset. Debbie. Debbie. Now listen to me . . . is the baby kicking?

DEBBIE: No of course not, I just found out! *(Crying.)*

BARRY: What?

DEBBIE: I just barely found out!

BARRY *(laughing)*: Well, gee, the way you're going on there you sound like you're in labor! Come on! Snap out of it. . . . Debbie, can I ask you a serious question?

DEBBIE: What?

BARRY: Do you understand what has happened?

DEBBIE: I wish I wasn't pregnant and I could go to school!

BARRY: Yes, but, Debbie, are you sorry for what you've done? Debbie?

DEBBIE: Huh?

BARRY: Are you genuinely sorry for what you did to Stan?

DEBBIE: Stan? But Stan did it to me!

BARRY: But, Debbie. . . . You're not listening to me. . . . Now listen to me, Debbie!

DEBBIE: What?

BARRY: It takes two to tango! You seduced poor old Stan with your cute little fifteen-year-old body and now you want everybody to feel sorry for you! You did it so you could trap Stan into sticking around. Right? No wonder the guy can't find a job! Right?

DEBBIE: Uh . . .

BARRY: That's what I think happened. You think maybe that's what happened?

DEBBIE: I don't know. . . . I guess so . . .

BARRY: Well then you have to deal with the consequences.

DEBBIE *(pause)*: So uh, then what should I do?

BARRY: Do you know where Stan is?

DEBBIE: No! *(Crying again.)* I don't know where he is!

BARRY: All right, all right, don't start crying again, spare me the crying. . . . OK, Debbie, listen. This is what we're gonna do. We're gonna find Stan. Someone out there knows where he is, and I want them to call me here at the station. . . . You leave your number with Stu and we're gonna call you as soon as we come up with something. And we will, don't worry. And let me say to anybody listening right now who knows where Stan is, you know, the guy who lives in the pickup truck, the one with all the chrome and the vanity plates that say "STAN-3." . . . Don't call the police. . . . Give me a call at 216-555-T-A-L-K because we got a little girl here who's lookin' for her daddy. . . . OK, Debbie?

DEBBIE: Uh . . . yeah . . . I guess . . .

BARRY: You're not gonna do anything crazy?

DEBBIE: No.

BARRY: Good. Stay warm, drink lots of milk, and away from the stuff under the sink and we'll talk in a little while. . . . A young lady with a problem. But here on "Nighttalk" every problem has a solution and that's why we're here. Let's go to a commercial. We'll be back with more . . . "Nighttalk . . ."

(During the commercial, Barry pushes his chair back from his desk, rubs his face. Linda gets up and goes over to him.)

LINDA: You hungry?

(Barry just points at his shoulders, and Linda comes up behind him and starts rubbing.)

STU *(has spun his chair to face Barry)*: Hey, Barry, that guy talking about the old days in Akron. . . . It reminds me of that night that truck driver called who was stuck in his bathtub?

BARRY: Oh, yeah! *(Laughing.)*

(Barry puts his feet up on his desk as Stu gets up to get a cookie from the coffee bar. Stu plays out the story to Barry's amusement.)

STU: Linda, this guy must have weighed four hundred and fifty pounds . . . stuck in the tub. What does Barry do? The guy doesn't want a rescue squad, so Barry calls up this massage parlor. Has 'em send over three hookers and a locksmith. And while these three bimbos baste this guy with joy jell, the locksmith's trying to pry him out with a crowbar! *(Barry's*

laughing now.) Great sound effects. . . . Guy popped when he came
out —

BARRY: Like a cork! Linda, you shoulda been there . . .

LINDA: I'll get you a sandwich.

BARRY: Four hundred pounds? No one weighs that much!

STU: This guy did. . . . Ten seconds.

(Linda is gone. Barry and Stu are getting back in the saddle.)

BARRY: That was in Akron?

STU: Spring 'eighty-one . . .

BARRY: Akron's ancient history . . . this is Cleveland.

STU: You're on.

BARRY: We're back. I'm Barry Champlain and you're listening to "Nighttalk."
We got a pretty freewheeling show for you tonight. You call it, we'll talk
about it. Your state of mind, the state of the union, whatever statements
you wanna make, we're listenin'. Hello, Cathleen . . . you're on "Nighttalk."
CATHLEEN: Yes, am I on?

BARRY: You're on!

CATHLEEN: Boy oh boy . . . lots of good stuff to talk about tonight!

BARRY: What's up, Cathleen?

CATHLEEN: I loved what you were saying about your show going national and
everything. It's important to say all that stuff —

BARRY: Someone has to say it, Cathleen.

CATHLEEN: I know, I know. I don't miss one of your shows because you tell it
like it is, Barry. God bless ya! God bless ya. My best friend, Judy, she hates
the show, she doesn't understand why I listen. . . . But to each his own,
that's what I say. You tell it like it is and you've got guts —

BARRY: I'm glad you feel that way —

CATHLEEN: I have strong feelings and I don't hide them. Judy thinks your show
is for nut jobs and psychos, but I don't agree. You say a lot of good
stuff —

BARRY: Yeah, Cathleen, I think you have to be more careful how you choose
your friends.

CATHLEEN: Yeah, I don't like her that much anyway —

BARRY: She doesn't sound very likable —

CATHLEEN: Only problem is, she's my only real friend.

BARRY: Oh, yeah? I don't think someone who calls your beliefs "nutty and
psycho" is a friend. . . . You got a real friend here, Cathleen —

CATHLEEN: You're kidding me —

BARRY: I don't kid when I'm talking about something serious like friendship.
As your friend, I'm giving you good advice when I tell you to stay away
from Judy . . . she's a bitter, cynical, pessimistic person . . .

CATHLEEN: Maybe you're right.

BARRY: Of course I'm right. Thanks for the call . . . *(Cut off.)* . . . and we have
Kent on the line. . . . Hello, Kent.

KENT: Uh, I need help.

BARRY: Shoot.

KENT: What?

BARRY: Shoot. Shoot. Tell me what the problem is.

KENT: Well . . . uh, I party a lot . . . you know, with my girlfriend —

BARRY: How old are you, Kent?

KENT: Eighteen.

BARRY: How old is your girlfriend?

KENT: She's sixteen.

BARRY: All right, go ahead.

KENT: So, we, uh . . . like to, uh, party, you know?

BARRY: Kent. When you do all this partying, where are your parents?

KENT: They go away a lot. Vacations.

BARRY: Where are they right now?

KENT: I don't know.

BARRY: You don't know!

KENT: They're on a vacation. . . . Wait a minute, I remember . . . uh . . . Fiji. Is that right? Is there a place called Fiji?

BARRY: Your parents are on vacation in a place called Fiji. So what are you up to? Partying?

KENT: Yeah . . . except . . . well, that's what I wanted to ask you about . . . uh . . . we been partying for a couple a days . . .

BARRY: A couple of days? What do you mean exactly when you say "partying"?

KENT: You know, having sex . . . hanging around, eating, watching cable, getting high, listening to tapes . . .

BARRY: Hold on. Back up a sec. Gettin' high? Smokin' pot?

KENT: Well, yeah, we always smoke.

BARRY: If you always smoke, what do you mean by "gettin' high"?

KENT: Free-base. Smokin' coke. Crack.

BARRY: Sounds pretty sordid. . . . You've been smokin' crack for a couple of days . . . with your girlfriend. . . . What else . . . you been doing?

KENT: And drinkin'. And I dunno. I drank some Wild Turkey yesterday 'cause I was gettin' paranoid. . . . Jill was doin' acid, I think. I'm not sure. Some Valiums.

BARRY: You don't need to call me, Kent, you need to call a doctor and have your stomach pumped! Lemme give you a number to call —

KENT: Yeah, but . . . see that's why I'm callin' you, Barry!

BARRY: Why?

KENT: Jill . . . she . . . uh, she's been sleepin' and uh . . .

BARRY (*evenly*): No. No. No.

KENT: She's been sleepin' and she won't, uh, . . . wake up, you know?

BARRY: Don't waste my time with this baloney —

KENT: Hey, she won't wake up! She's turning blue!

BARRY: Oh, she's turning blue. . . . You just tell Stu your address and we'll send —

KENT: Hey, no, you gotta help my girlfriend!

BARRY: Tell Stu where —

KENT: No . . . that . . . I can't . . . I can't . . . . *(Click.)*

BARRY: Hello! *(Shoots a look at Stu. Stu makes a throat-cutting gesture indicating that he hung up.)* Confusion reigns in Cleveland tonight. . . . Let's break for a little commercial and we'll be back with . . ."Nighttalk." *(Stu signals to Spike, and sound cuts to upbeat station identification.)* What's the problem tonight, *Stu?* You're throwing me some real curveballs, man.

(Stu turns to face him.)

STU: What's wrong with curveballs, Bar?

BARRY: Control, Stu, control! I don't need shit like that kid tonight! . . . Something on your mind? Something wrong at home?

STU: No, Bar, there's nothing wrong at home —

BARRY: Well then stay on the ball, all right? Gimme the meat, not the poison.

STU *(ignores Barry's mounting fury and turns back to his console)*: You got it.

BARRY *(jumps up and stalks over to Stu)*: Stu, lemme see your board. Come on, run it! Who's this Henry guy, this nukes guy, you didn't gimme that! What about this Denise here, I didn't get that either. . . . What about the professor —

STU: Barry, the professor is a stiff. All those people are stiffs. You want stiffs, I'll send you stiffs —

BARRY *(interrupting him)*: Stu . . . Stu . . . Stu . . . Stu . . . Stu, I don't want stiffs. *(Shouting now.)* Am I speaking English? Read my lips. . . . Keep the show moving, gimme stuff I can work with! *(Practically screaming at Stu.)* You having trouble understanding me tonight?

(Barry goes back to his desk.)

STU: No, Barry, I'm not having trouble understanding you. In fact, I hear you loud and clear —

BARRY: *Good!*

(Barry slumps in his chair, turns away from the audience. Stu addresses the audience, turning in his chair, then standing and walking upstage center.)

STU: I met Barry Champlain in nineteen seventy-two. I was a DJ for a "progressive rock" station down in Akron and one day this guy shows up from Cambridge, Mass. . . . At least that's where he said he came from. . . . We were both hard-ass hippies . . . which meant of course that we were into subversive radio. . . . We thought we were changing the whole goddamn world right there in the studio 'cause we were playin' Lou Reed. . . . and Frank Zappa or David Bowie. . . . Barry Champlain would . . . go beyond the tolerable. He'd play "Let It Bleed" twenty-five times in a row just for the effect . . . or find a record with a particularly good skip on it and just let it go. And I'd come by and we'd be hanging out, throwing down tequila and sucking limes, watching this record going round and round while the station manager is pounding on the studio door. . . . One time they had to knock the door down just to get Barry to take the record off. He didn't get fired, he got a raise. *(Laughs.)* And the more I watched Barry the more I wondered why I was a DJ at all. I'd say things like "Here's the latest from Cream, it's called 'Wheels of Fire' and it's . . . really heavy. . . ." Very embarrassing. Then Barry would get in the saddle to do his show and one second he's talking about his secret crush on Jane Fonda's breasts, next minute he's giving out the home phone number of every FBI agent in the state. . . . Then he started having people call in to the show. No one had done this in Akron before and I'm hanging out pretty much every day watching all this energy coming out of Barry. . . . And more and more people are calling in to the show 'cause Barry would say stuff like "Call me and tell me about your most intense orgasm . . ." and people would do it. He'd say: "Call me and tell me about your worst experience with a cop . . ." and they would be off to the races for the rest of the show. . . . He'd say, "Call me and tell me the one thing you've never told anybody else before in your entire life." One guy . . . one guy called up Barry and tells him that he fragged his lieutenant in Khesanh. He confessed it right on the radio. And he was cryin'. The guy wouldn't stop crying. Around that time Barry got his talk show here in Cleveland. I figured, to hell with being a DJ, I jumped ship and went with him. I listen to Barry Champlain take off for outer space every night, then the show's over and we go home. I mean, I go home to Cheryl and our kid. . . . Barry . . . I don't know what Barry Champlain does anymore. . . . It's not like the old days when we'd pick up a couple of girls and fifth of scotch and head for a room at the Holiday Inn. . . . Now he just splits, says he has to work on the show. And I can see him sitting at home making cups of coffee, chain-smoking cigarettes, and reading the fucking encyclopedia. Or worse. Maybe he just sits and waits to come back to the studio. He lost his voice once in nineteen eighty-three. Freaked him the fuck out. At first he was climbing the walls . . . then he started getting depressed. . . . Real depressed. I know what it was. He missed the sound of his own voice. You see, for Barry Champlain talking is like thinking out loud. That's why he loves radio. It's his life. He simply talks and all those people out there become part of him, part of his mind. I do too, I guess . . .

(Lights back up on Barry at his desk, as Stu walks back to the console.)

BARRY: John, calling from Lorain.

JOHN: Barry, hello, I'd like to comment if I may on what that lady was saying a few minutes before . . . the one who called you a Jew.

BARRY: Yeah.

JOHN: Well, I'm black —

BARRY: Good for you. You wanna medal?

JOHN: Heh-heh. No . . . I don't. No, don't play with me like them other people.

I want you to know that I enjoy listening to your show and I have many friends who are Jewish —

BARRY: How many?

JOHN: Oh . . . three or four —

BARRY: I wouldn't call that many —

JOHN: They're very nice people, very educated —

BARRY: Yeah, John, what's the point?

JOHN: I like Jews and I think —

BARRY: I don't know how to break this to you, John, but they're never gonna let you in the B'nai B'rith.

JOHN: Heh-heh . . . that's not what I —

BARRY: Hey, John . . . you're black . . . don't you know how Jews feel about blacks? They hate you. You know those slums over on the East Side where the rats eat little babies for breakfast? Jews own those slums. . . . What do you mean "I like Jews." What are you, some kind of Uncle Tom?

JOHN: What the hell you know about Uncle Tom? I think you got your facts confused and I —

BARRY: *I don't care what you think! No one does!* . . . You know why? 'Cause you're trying to kiss the master's butt, that's why! You call me up and try to get deep with me about how much you love Jews and you're lying. You hate them —

JOHN: I don't kiss nobody's butt —

BARRY: Sure you do! You kiss my butt. You're kissing it right now. If you weren't, you'd hang up on me!

JOHN: That's what I'm trying to say, I don't want to hang up on you!

BARRY: Then I'll do you the favor. *(Cut off.)* "Nighttalk," Henry . . . you're on.

HENRY: Yeah, hello, Barry —

BARRY: Yessir.

HENRY: Calling from Wheeling.

BARRY: Long distance! How's the weather?

HENRY: Good. Good. Um . . . I wanna talk about that nuclear power plant over on the river —

BARRY: The Liberty Power Facility.

HENRY: Yes.

BARRY: I think it's a great idea. It's gonna cut our electric bills in half. You got a problem with that?

HENRY *(clears throat, then monotone, as if reading)*: "The Liberty Nuclear Power Facility is an infringement on the health and well-being of all the people living within a five-hundred-mile radius of its reactor core. We, the members of the Life and Liberty Alliance, protest the building, sale, or manufacture of — "

BARRY: Wait a minute, wait a minute, hold on there one second, Henry —

HENRY: " — nuclear and nuclear-related materials for any purpose, whether for armaments or so-called peaceful — "

BARRY: Hey! Now shut up for a minute! Are you reading that? Stu, is he reading that?

HENRY: " — utilization that endangers the life of millions of people in the Ohio River Valley."

BARRY: Hey, shut up for a second. *Are . . . you . . . reading . . . that?*

HENRY: That is our manifesto —

BARRY: I don't care if it's the Magna Charta, you don't read anything over the air on this show. . . . Now, you got something to say, say it or you're off.

HENRY: The use of nuclear energy is as irresponsible as nuclear war. We feel —

BARRY: Oh, now it's nuclear war! Two minutes ago it was a power plant. How about toxic waste, that bothers you too, I bet. What about baby seals? Panda bears?

HENRY: That has nothing to do with our protest —

BARRY: Uh-huh.

HENRY: We're talking about poison. We're all condemning ourselves with this nuclear doomsday machine. Our children . . .

(They're talking over each other. Barry wins out.)

BARRY: Cut it, Henry, all right? What are you telling us? That we're all gonna die? I got news for you pal, we all die sooner or later. A nuclear war would probably be the best thing to ever happen to this country. Wake some people up.

HENRY: I don't know how you can joke about nuclear war . . . this is —

BARRY: Who says I'm joking, pal? Hey, I did my protest march bit back in the sixties. I been there, man. It was a lot of fun! I bet it's still a lot of fun. . . . *You don't care about anybody else, you just wanna go out there and have a good time!* Why don't you stop all this whining and start doing something more constructive with your time —

HENRY: That's exactly what I am doing! I'm doing something constructive! Which is more —

BARRY: Hold on, I'm not finished. You had your say, now lemme have mine. . . . You're just a spoiled, spineless little baby. You want to go crying to Mommy about what a nasty world this is, and then she'll fix it and make it all better. Put out that marijuana joint you're smoking, pal, and face the facts: Yes, a nuclear war is a very great possibility. And yes, Henry, it's scary. And, yes, we don't like it. But all the weepy pseudointellectuals in the world aren't going to change things one bit. . . . *(Pause.)*

HENRY: Your attitude is immoral.

BARRY: Did I hurt your feelings, pal? Go tell it to your shrink —

HENRY: *When that plant explodes and kills a few thousand people it will be on your head!*

(Barry taunts him while he screams, finally cutting him off.)

BARRY: Too bad you can't keep up an intelligent conversation in a normal tone of voice. *(Cut off.)* Bob . . . how's tricks?

BOB: Barry, my friend.

BARRY: Bob, what a relief. How you doing tonight?

BOB: Terrific. Very well. Thank you. How are you?

BARRY: Pretty well. Pretty well.

BOB: Congratulations.

BARRY: Thank you.

BOB: I hope you're not gonna get too busy to take my calls.

BARRY: Bob, no show is complete without your call.

BOB: Hee-hee!

BARRY: How are the legs?

BOB: Oh they're fine. An ache or two, but not bad. You know what I say, "When they give you the lemons, make lemonade — "

BARRY: You can't cry over spilt milk —

BOB: Cry and you cry alone.

BARRY: Because you can't lose what you never had.

BOB: Because you don't know what you've got till you've lost it.

BARRY: So don't lose hope, this too shall pass.

BOB: Because today is the first day of the rest of your life.

BARRY: Yeah, and it's always darkest before dawn. Bob, can I just — ?

BOB: Because tomorrow never comes —

BARRY: Yeah, and if you play with fire you will get burnt. . . . Bob, can I say something, please?

BOB: Of course, Barry.

BARRY: Thank you. We are all inspired by your courage. You are a brave man and an example to all of us. As they say, Bob, the hero and coward both feel fear. The difference is that the coward runs away. You didn't run away. And we thank you for that.

BOB: Well, thank you, Barry. But you know, people think that life in a wheel-chair must be the worst thing in the world. That's not the way I look at it. I imagine the worst thing in the world would be being unthankful for all the good things that come our way every day: the smiles of little children, flowers blooming, little birds chirping, sitting on the budding branches on a bright spring day . . . hell! Just the sun coming up every day is a miracle!

BARRY: I couldn't agree with you more, Bob, especially the part about the sun. . . . You know, I think we get too bogged down in our daily trouble, we forget about the simple things.

BOB: Oh, I left out one more thing to be thankful for.

BARRY: What's that?

BOB: The Barry Champlain show.

BARRY *(pause)*: Thank you, Bob, . . . us both being vets, it means a lot to me that you would say that.

BOB: I mean it.

BARRY: I know you do. . . . Look we gotta move along, be well.

BOB: Oh, no!

BARRY: Sorry, gotta run. . . . I know you can't but we can.

BOB: OK then. . . . And good luck with that kid . . .

BARRY: Who?

BOB: The one on drugs there? I hope he calls back.

BARRY: Me too. . . . Look, Bob: Don't put all your eggs in one basket!

BOB: And a bird in hand —

BARRY: G'night Bob. *(Cuts him off.)* And we have Denise on the line, hello, Denise —

DENISE: I'm scared, Barry.

BARRY: What are you scared of, babe?

DENISE: Nothing specifically, but on the other hand . . . you know, it's like everywhere I go . . .

BARRY: Yeah?

DENISE: Well, like, Barry, you know, like we've got a garbage disposal in our sink in the kitchen, I mean my mother's kitchen . . .

BARRY: Um-hmmm.

DENISE: And sometimes a teaspoon will fall into the garbage disposal . . . *(As Denise continues to talk, Barry turns to Stu with a "what the hell is this?" gesture. Stu begs a cigarette. Barry, looking very sour, nudges the pack of cigarettes toward Stu, and he rolls over in his chair. Barry puts his hand over the mike and [inaudibly] asks Stu if he heard what he was saying five minutes ago. Stu says he asked for the call. Barry continues to listen to the call but gets more restless, finally cutting in on Denise.)* . . . ya, so like, you know how you feel when you have to reach down into that garbage disposal and you have to feel around down there for that teaspoon. You don't want to do it. Who knows what's down there? Could be garbage, a piece of something, so much stuff goes down there . . . or germs, which you can't see. You can't see germs, but if they're gonna be anywhere, they're gonna be down that disposal. They grow there, see? They come back up the pipes. Salmonella, yeast, cancer, even the common cold, who knows? But, Barry, even without all that, what if, and I'm just saying "what if," 'cause it would probably never happen, but what if the garbage disposal came on while your hand is down there?

BARRY *(joking)*: Boy, that would be a handful, wouldn't it?

DENISE: I get so scared of thinking about it that I usually leave the teaspoon there. I don't even try to get it out. But then I'm afraid that my mother will get mad if she finds it down there, so I turn the disposal on, trying to make it go down the drain. But all it does is make a huge racket. And I stand in the middle of the kitchen and the spoon goes around and around and I get sort of paralyzed, you know? It makes a lot of noise, incredible noise. But Barry, I kind of like that noise, because I know the teaspoon is getting destroyed and annihilated and that's good 'cause I hate the teaspoon for scaring me like that —

BARRY: Denise, Denise, Denise, Denise! . . . Lemme get this straight, you're afraid of the garbage disposal in your mother's kitchen?

DENISE: Well it's not just the disposal, it's everything. What about insects? Termites. Hornets. Spiders. Ants. Centipedes. Mites. You can't even see the mites, they're like the germs. Tiny, impossible to see! I like things to be clean, you know. Dirty ashtrays bother me . . . *(Barry is fed up, shoots Stu a look [still sitting next to him], noticing for the first time that Dan is standing next to Spike in the control booth, watching Barry. When they meet eyes, Dan indicates that he wants to speak to Barry. Barry turns back to his microphone as Stu scurries back to his desk.)* . . . just one more unknown. Just like the houses on our street. Used to be we knew who lived on our street. But that was years ago. Now all kinds of people live on our street. Even foreigners, people with accents. What are they doing on our street? What are their habits? Are they clean? Are they sanitary?

BARRY: Why don't you ask them?

DENISE: Oh, sure, that would be a great idea just to go to somebody's house and just knock on the door. What if a serial murderer lived there? Ted Bundy? What if Ted Bundy or the Boston Strangler was just sitting inside watching television eating potato chips and I came to the door? Great! Come on in!

BARRY: Wait a minute. Ted Bundy lives in your neighborhood, is that what you're saying?

DENISE: I don't go to strange people's houses. I keep the doors locked at all times. I stopped driving, but that isn't going to solve anything. . . . You're not going to stop a plane from crashing into your house, now are you?

BARRY: No.

(Dan has entered onto the balcony, holds up one finger as if to say: "Just one minute, please.")

DENISE: The mailman brings me unsolicited mail and the postage stamp was licked by someone with AIDS. Right? My mother is a threat to my life just by persisting in going out there —

BARRY: Out where? Where does your mother go?

DENISE: Do you know that there's this dust storm in California that has these little fungus spores in it? And these spores get in people's lungs and it goes into their bloodstreams and grows inside them and kills them? Strange air . . . strange air . . . you have to . . . Oh! There's my mother. I hear her key in the door. She'll kill me if she finds out I used the phone.

(Denise hangs up. Click.)

BARRY: Strange air . . . that's what we've got for you tonight. I think I see my producer, Dan Woodruff, lurking in the corner warning me that if I don't wedge in a word here for our sponsors he's gonna do something outrageous, like remove his toupee. Don't wanna have that happen. . . . So lemme tell you where to eat . . .

(Barry signals to Stu, and an ad gets thrown on. It runs under the following scene, audible as Dan exits.)

DAN: Barry —

BARRY: Linda! Coffee please?

DAN: Barry, I need your opinion on something —

BARRY *(ignoring Dan)*: Stu, check the level on line three, I'm getting a buzz there —

DAN: Barry, I need ten seconds of your time —

BARRY: What, Dan, what? I'm in the middle of a show here. I don't have time to chew the fat with you!

STU: Thirty seconds . . .

DAN *(has come down to stand next to Barry)*: Barry, that kid who called, the one on drugs, with the girlfriend —

BARRY: Kent, yeah?

DAN: Kent . . . is a problem. We've got sponsors listening tonight, national sponsors. They just called and they're concerned about Kent. They think you should do something, say something.

BARRY: What do they want me to say, Dan? It's a hoax. There's no girlfriend. I get calls like this all the time —

DAN: They don't know that.

BARRY: *Who* doesn't?

DAN *(gently)*: The sponsors, Barry. The people who are going to put you on the air coast to coast tomorrow night —

BARRY *(jumping up)*: Dan, all right! All right! *(Walks over to Stu.)* Stu, chances are this kid Kent is gonna call again. When he does, shoot him to me and I'll talk him out. . . . Make you happy, Dan?

(Barry stalks back to his desk, pissed.)

DAN: Thank you, Barry. I know you know what to do. . . . Oh . . . what if it isn't a hoax? What if the girl *is* dead?

BARRY: We'll send her a wreath.

(Dan exits.)

STU: Harry's Restaurant . . . runs long . . .

(Barry is sitting at his desk, boiling. Harry's Restaurant ad is droning on. [Done as a "live spot," with Barry's voice prerecorded to sound live, very folksy.] "And with that you get your choice of french fries, baked or delmonico potatoes. Choice of two vegetables. Cup of coffee or tea or soft drink with your meal. And . . . dessert from the dessert bar. . . . Lots of good things to choose from. Can you beat it for five ninety-five? I don't think so. . . . Harry's Restaurant for good solid food. You'll be happy to leave a tip . . . for your waitress . . . at Harry's Restaurant, I know I always do. I go there as often as I can. . . . Really excellent. . . . Tell 'em Barry sent you.")

BARRY: Wait a minute, before I take any more callers I have to say something. . . . Isn't that the most sickening ad copy you've ever heard? Harry's Restaurant? Home cooking? You ever go back into the kitchen of that place and you'd think you were in a taco stand in Tijuana! That was a pretaped commercial you just heard, everybody, something the *sponsors* force me to do. They like to make Barry sound homey and candid. Makes me wanna throw up. Which I usually do whenever I eat at Harry's. . . . "Nighttalk," Joe.

JOE: Barry!

BARRY: Yessir.

JOE: I been drivin' cab for eleven years. . . . Last week I picked up a lady at the airport, rich bitch, you know what I'm saying? Wanted to know if I could take a check. . . . I said, "Lady, I'm a working man . . . gimme cash. . . ." She said she don't got it. I said, "Well, gimme that fancy watch a yours there and when you come up with the dough, I'll give it t'ya back. . . ." She ran outta the cab.

BARRY: She stiffed you.

JOE: You're damned right, she did. 'Cause she's got rocks in her head. Like the jerks who call your show. What the hell's wrong with that kid who just called? The one with the girlfriend who OD'd? . . . He got a problem? What he needs is a good bust in the chops.

BARRY: You're referring to Kent, the guy who likes to "party"?

JOE: Yeah. Yeah. Kid like that needs some discipline.

BARRY: You think that would do it, huh, Joe?

JOE: Lemme tell you something, Barry. I got two kids and they gimme any trouble and I just take off my belt. They see the belt and that's it.

BARRY: How old are your children, Joe?

JOE: My little girl's five and my boy's three and a half.

BARRY: You hit them with a belt?

JOE: A brush, a belt, a newspaper. Whatever. The wife thinks I'm too hard on 'em. Hey . . . they're either gonna get it from me, or they're gonna get it out there. . . . *(Barry is getting seriously angry. He glowers at Stu for letting this call through.)* The world's a crazy place, Barry, filled with crazy people. . . . You make a small mistake, you pay for it the rest of your life.

BARRY: Tell me something, Joe. What was your mistake?

JOE: Being at the wrong place at the wrong time.

BARRY: You were set up?

JOE: You could say that.

BARRY: And let me guess, you went to jail.

JOE: Did a dime.

BARRY: Ten years. Must've been quite the wrong place.

JOE: Armed robbery.

BARRY: Tell me something, Joe, what's jail like?

JOE: Waste of my time.

BARRY: And you've got better things to do with your time.

JOE: You better believe it.

BARRY: Like beat your kids with brushes and belts.

JOE: Huh?

BARRY: You're the jerk. You're a child-molesting lunatic.

JOE: Yeah. . . . And what are you? A faggot?

BARRY: What are you, a prick?

JOE: How about this? . . . I come down to the station right now, pal, and bust your faggot face in?

BARRY *(starts laughing)*: Who ya gonna get to help ya? Ya brother?

JOE: Don't say nothin' about my brother!

BARRY: Your brother's a creep and a pinhead just like you are. Your wife still sleepin' with him?

JOE: The wife don't screw around. Don't get me angry.

BARRY: What do you beat your wife with, Joe, a baseball bat?

JOE: I'm coming down there . . .

BARRY: Please . . . we're all waiting. . . . You want me to call you a cab? Oh, I forgot, you drive one!

JOE: I know what you look like. I know where you live. You're dead. *(Click.)*

(Deadly pause. Barry is steaming.)

BARRY: "Nighttalk," June.

JUNE: Hello?

BARRY: Hello.

JUNE: Hello? Am I on?

BARRY: You're on.

JUNE: Oh, Barry, I wanted to say something about the people who don't pick up after their doggies when they are walking them. . . . My Buttons is just a small poodle so all I have to take along is a little garden spade. I think some people would need a snow shovel.

BARRY: Yeah, that's pretty disgusting, June.

JUNE: It is disgusting . . . it really is . . . but, Barry . . . that young man who was having a drug overdose . . . is he going to die? Eh?

BARRY: We all die someday, June.

JUNE: I . . . hah . . . I never thought about it that way before. . . . Do you have a doggie, Barry?

BARRY: I own no pets.

JUNE: What's that?

BARRY: I don't have a dog, a cat, a mouse, a goldfish, or a gerbil. I own no pets.

JUNE: Oh, but you have to have a pet! How can you live without a pet, Barry, eh?

BARRY: Well, I'll tell you, June, when I was a kid my father gave me a golden Lab for my tenth birthday. Beautiful dog . . . very friendly. All the kids loved her —

JUNE: Oh, yes, they're lovely doggies . . . lovely . . .

BARRY: We used to go on long walks through the woods. . . . Goldie, that was her name, Goldie —

JUNE: Like Goldie Hawn . . . what a nice name!

BARRY: Yeah, well, one day we were out walking in the woods. Beautiful autumn day. The leaves were just changing on the trees. We came out to this highway. Goldie saw a male German shepherd on the other side, didn't look where she was going . . . got hit dead on by a Greyhound tour bus doing around ninety —

JUNE: Did she die?

BARRY: Of course she died, June. She was dragged for around a quarter mile.

JUNE: Awwwww!

BARRY: I never could bring myself to get another dog after that. . . . You never know what might happen . . . to your dog. Especially the small ones, little poodles like yours. . . . Always getting their heads caught in slamming car doors . . . or falling down garbage disposals . . . or sometimes, when you're talking on the phone, they get all wrapped up in that plastic that comes with the dry cleaning. And they're barking and strangling to death and you can't hear them. . . . You know what I'm saying, June? *(Silence.)* June? June? *June?* Guess she had to go walk her doggie. . . . *(Furious.)* Listen to this . . .

(Barry gives Stu the signal and whirls around in his chair, leaving his back to the audience. The lights dim to begin Linda's monologue. The audience can hear a snatch of the station ID Spike has just flipped on, a sweet woman's voice: "555-T-A-L-K . . . you'll be picked up when it's your turn to talk to Barry." The station sound dims, and Linda turns to face the audience.)

LINDA: One night, after the show, I stopped by the lunchroom. I was thirsty, I was gonna get a Coke out of the machine. Barry was there. Sitting at the crummy table under the crummy fluorescent light. I didn't know him. I had been working here two months and he had said three words to me the whole time. He was sitting there staring at this ashtray full of butts. Just sitting. I asked him if anything was wrong. . . . He looked up at me like he'd never seen me before. Like he didn't even know where he was. He said, "I'm outta cigarettes." I said, "There's a machine down the hall. I'll get you some. . . ." I mean, he coulda gotten the cigarettes himself, I know, but he seemed like he couldn't at that moment. . . . He looked at me again and said, "Linda. Can I go home with you tonight? Can I sleep with you?" Now, I've had a lot of guys come on to me in a lot of ways. I expected this Barry guy to have a smooth approach but this was unexpectedly unique. I didn't say yes. I didn't say no. We went to this diner he likes and I watched him eat a cheeseburger. He was talking about something, what was it? Euthanasia. I remember, because I thought, This guy really knows how to sweet-talk a girl. And the whole time smoking cigarettes, looking around, tapping his fingers. . . . Of course, we ended up at my place. As I was getting us drinks, I said to myself, "Linda, you know you're gonna go to bed with this guy, so let's get the ball rolling." He was nervous, like he was gonna jump out of his skin, so I started giving him a shoulder massage. The next thing, we're on the floor and he's kissing me like he was in the middle of the ocean, trying to get on a life raft! I got us into the bedroom . . . and I go to the bathroom for two seconds to get myself together and anyway, when I get back to the bed, he's asleep, curled up in a ball. All that night, while he slept, he's throwing himself around, tossing and turning, grinding his teeth, clenching his fists. It was scary. Next morning, he's up before me. Comes out of the shower, he's a different guy. Says he never slept so well. Then he comes over to the bed and . . . we made love. . . . Since then, we've spent maybe a dozen nights together. . . . Lemme put it this way, Barry Champlain is a nice place to visit, but I wouldn't want to live there.

(*Lights back up on Barry on the phone.*)

BARRY: And now a caller we've all been waiting to hear from. . . . Where are you calling from, sir?

STAN: Calling from Fort Wayne —

BARRY: Been doing a little driving in the pickup?

STAN: Yeah, I guess you could say that —

BARRY: I just did. So tell us something, Stan, what are you going to do about your girlfriend here in Cleveland? She tells us you're gonna be a daddy.

STAN: I just heard. . . . I didn't know. How could I know? I just stopped by here at Al's, I was getting gas and a couple of beers . . . and, uh, he asked me if I had a girlfriend in Cleveland.

BARRY: Yeah, well the question is, Are you gonna have a wife in Cleveland?

STAN: Yeah, I guess that's the question.

BARRY: Well, you know what I think?

STAN: What?

BARRY: I think you better get your ass up to Cleveland.

STAN: Hey, I just got here. I been drivin' all night! You think you can get me to turn around?

BARRY: Yes, I do. I have your make, model, and tags —

STAN: No, hey —

BARRY: Don't "hey" me, buddy. You know what you did. We're talking about a fifteen-year-old girl!

STAN: I didn't know she was fifteen! Anyway, it's none of your damn business, bud!

BARRY: Well, that's just too bad, isn't it, Stan? You know why? Because they don't let you keep your pickup truck when you go to prison. I hear they love rapists there. You better bring along a large jar of Vaseline —

STAN (*nervous*): I ain't goin' to no jail. . . . That's crazy.

BARRY: Stu, we still have the number of the Indiana State Troopers?

STAN: *No!* Hey! What the hell you think you're trying to do?

BARRY: This is what you're gonna do, Stan. You're gonna call Debbie, get in your truck, fill the tank, and start driving. I'll give you five hours.

STAN: Shit! *(Click.)*

BARRY: And we have Rose on the line. Hello, Rose.

ROSE: I'm so excited, this is my first time!

BARRY: I'll be gentle!

ROSE *(laughing)*: I'm so happy for you, Barry, and I just wanted to call you and congratulate you on doing a very good job!

BARRY: Well, thank you, dear. And how's your life?

ROSE: Well, I don't know what I'd do without your show. I listen every night. . . . I am the mother of five children: Mike Junior, Cindy, Charlie, Robert, and Nancy. She's the baby, she'll be four next month. And of course, Skippy, our beagle.

BARRY: That's good news, Rose. Tell me something, are they good kids?

ROSE: They're wonderful kids, Barry. Mike just finished college, . . . Robert was elected president of his class, and Cindy wants to be a brain surgeon and/or marry Jon Bon Jovi as of last week.

BARRY: Heh-heh. I'm impressed.

ROSE: Barry, can I just say something?

BARRY: Sure, Rose. Make it quick.

ROSE: My husband, Mike Senior, died four years ago, he had an accident with the lawn mower and —

BARRY: I'm sorry to hear that.

ROSE: Well, yes, so things have been a little tough for all of us. . . . But the kids have been terrific.

BARRY: They sound terrific. You sound terrific.

(Barry is obviously bored by this call. He gets ready to cut Rose off.)

ROSE: They are terrific and I'm getting better all the time. . . . I get tired. . . . My job gets me tired at the end of the day, but then I come home and I turn on your show and presto, I'm a new woman —

BARRY: Well, thank you, dear. It means a lot to me. Thanks for the call —

ROSE: *Barry?*

BARRY: Yup?

ROSE: Sometimes you remind me of my late husband, who was very gentle and loving and a good man —

BARRY: I'm sure he was.

ROSE: Barry, Mike died around the time of his birthday . . . so his presents were never unwrapped. . . . I know this sounds . . . I feel almost silly saying this, but what's your shirt size, Barry?

BARRY: Oh, well . . . heh-heh.

ROSE: Everyone can use shirts. They're brand-new. They're just too nice to send to the Salvation Army! Silk shirts —

BARRY: The station doesn't allow gifts. . . . I wish they would, but they don't. I can't accept any gifts —

ROSE: I could deliver them personally. Gold cuff links —

BARRY: Yeah, . . . uh, Rose, can I ask you a question?

ROSE: You can ask me anything you want.

BARRY: Well, you know I sit here every night alone in the studio happily chatting with people and I have no idea . . . I mean I can tell from your voice that you are a very, very attractive woman . . . and I was wondering, you know . . . *(Leans back in his chair, puts his feet up, and keeps talking.)* I can see you at home right now, sitting in your kitchen . . . you've got the radio on there next to you and maybe a cup of coffee. Here we are talking on the phone, I've got my coffee and you've got yours. Two kindred souls sitting with our cups of coffee in the middle of the night. Alone together. . . . And I just, uh, was wondering what you were wearing . . .

ROSE: Wearing?

BARRY: You're wearing something?

ROSE: Well, yes. . . . I'm wearing my bathrobe right now.

BARRY: Uh-huh, sure. . . . You just got home from work. You put on your bathrobe. What sort of bathrobe is it, Rose?

ROSE: Well, it's cotton and it has a sort of a blue print all over it . . .

BARRY *(has become sultry and whispery)*: Uh-huh. . . . Uh-huh. . . . Are you wearing slippers?

ROSE: Yes.

BARRY: Furry ones?

ROSE: Yes.

BARRY: Stockings?

ROSE: No.

BARRY: Panty hose?

ROSE *(pause)*: No.

BARRY: Are you alone right now, Rose?

(Rose's voice becomes halting. Barry eggs her on with soothing "Uh-huhs" and "yeahs.")

ROSE: I am alone right now, Barry. I haven't been, uh, dating for a while, well, uh, not since Mike died and so it's a nice feeling to hear your voice . . . on the phone . . . right now. . . . It's nice to have someone special to talk to — *(Behind Rose we can hear children: "Mommy! Mommy!")* Shhhhh! Please! I'm on the phone right now!

BARRY: Gee, Rose, you told me you were alone. You just said you were alone, Rose!

ROSE: I'm sorry, Barry, . . . uh, . . . should I send the shirts?

BARRY: Well, when would you have the time, you sound so busy there. Listen, Rose, this is what you do. . . . Don't give those shirts to anyone else, save 'em for me, will you, please?

ROSE: Of course!

BARRY: And call me back in a month . . . make it two months, will you call me back in a couple of months, Rose?

ROSE: Of course . . .

BARRY: You promise you'll call me back?

(*Stu has hastily scribbled a note and passed it over to Barry during this exchange. Barry reads the note as he continues to talk to Rose.*)

ROSE: I'll call you back in two months!

BARRY: Good. Look, I got a very important commercial coming up, so I gotta move it along here, Rose, but I want to thank you very much for calling.

ROSE: Thank you, Barry. I think —

(*Barry cuts her off.*)

BARRY: What a lovely, lovely woman you are, Rose . . . and me? I'm Barry Champlain . . . and you, you're listening to Cleveland's most popular talk show, "Nighttalk." Gotta break for a little station ID here, but we'll be back . . . with more . . . "Nighttalk"! (*Turns to Stu. Theme music comes up.*) What do you think?

STU: I think he's lyin'.

BARRY: Lemme have 'im.

STU: Here we go.

BARRY (*back to his mike*): And we have Kent with us once again. . . . Kent . . .

KENT: I didn't mean to hang up on you.

BARRY: But you did.

KENT: Yeah . . . I . . .

BARRY: Listen, Kent, . . . you're a fake. You're a hoax. You call me with some fake-o story about how you and your girlfriend are taking drugs and she's OD'd and your parents are in Acapulco —

KENT: Fiji.

BARRY: What? . . . Fiji . . . an important detail. . . . And you're just this mixed-up kid who doesn't know what to do —

KENT: It's true —

BARRY: I don't believe you.

KENT: Well, there's no way to prove it to you —

BARRY: Sure there is, give Stu your address and we'll send somebody over there —

KENT: No. Uh-uh. No way!

BARRY: Kent. . . . What are you trying to tell me, that your girlfriend . . . what's her name?

KENT: Uh, Jill.

BARRY: OK, Jill. Jill has what . . . OD'd?

KENT: I don't know. . . . I can't get her to wake up —

BARRY: Yeah. Yeah. OK, we heard that already, you were smokin' crack and she won't wake up. . . . What you think, I was born yesterday? OK, OK, I'll go along with you . . . just for fun. . . . Just for fun, is she breathing?

KENT: I'll check . . .

BARRY: Oh, I can't believe this. . . . Stu, can you believe this? Why am I talking to this guy? I must have some kind of morbid curiosity. Some dark force compels me to listen to this garbage.

(*Dan Woodruff has entered the studio.*)

KENT: Yeah, she's breathin'. I think. It's hard to tell. . . . There's some, like, foam coming out of her mouth —

BARRY: *What?*

KENT: There's foam coming out of her mouth!

BARRY: All right, all right. . . . I've had enough of this baloney. You and I both know you're lying. I'm cutting you off . . . get off my show!

KENT: No, wait!

BARRY: That's it.

KENT: *Listen!* My parents *are* in Fiji . . . but, uh, . . . the stuff about my girlfriend —

BARRY: What?

KENT: She . . .

BARRY: Come on, Kent, spit it out!

KENT: You'll cut me off!

BARRY: I won't cut you off.

KENT: You promise?

BARRY: I promise I won't cut you off, Kent.

KENT (*starts laughing*): I made the whole thing up!

BARRY (*glances slightly over toward Dan*): Kent?

KENT: What?

BARRY: I lied, I'm cutting you off, you've wasted too much time for one night —

KENT: *No! No! Please!*

BARRY: You think you've been jerking me around and I knew from the minute I heard your voice you were lying. . . . Sayonara. Good-bye.

KENT: Please! Please! I'm not lying now! I gotta talk to you . . . please!

BARRY: Oh, yeah, and what are you gonna tell me now? That your mother just slit her wrists and she's bleeding to death? How about your father? What's he got, a shotgun in his mouth? Gonna blow his brains out? Who else is dead, Kent?

KENT: No one's dead.

BARRY: Come on, who's dead? Who's dead, Kent? Who's dead?

KENT: No one's dead. You're making me nervous! I just wanna talk!

BARRY: We're talkin'. You got two seconds, talk!

KENT: I listen all the time. I think about what you say. You say such cool stuff and I, . . . uh, . . . wanted to meet you.

BARRY: Now you are goofing on me. Cut it out. . . . You wanted to meet me? You can meet me anytime you want. I'm right here at the station.

KENT: At the station?

BARRY: I'm not the president, for God's sake. I'm right here. Downtown. In the Terminal Tower in the studio.

KENT: I could just come down?

BARRY: You could just come down —

KENT: Now?

BARRY: Now?

KENT: Right now?

BARRY: What do you mean, right now?

KENT: Right now. Could I come down . . . and meet you?

BARRY: I'm on the air, Kent.

KENT: *Please!*

> (*Barry looks over to Dan. Dan shakes his head no and emphasizes this with a gesture. Barry pauses, then:*)

BARRY: Uh, sure, Kent, why not? Come on down. I'd love to meet you.

KENT: Really? Really? Great!

BARRY: Just hurry it up, we're already halfway through the show.

KENT: Wait. Wait. Oh. I'll be right down. (*Click.*)

> (*Theme music comes over the sound system.*)

BARRY: We're at the end of the first hour of exciting and intellectual conversation. Don't go away. . . . We have the news and the weather coming up and then we'll be back with more . . . "Nighttalk"!

> (*His words are followed by a blast of theme music and station IDs. Ads and five minutes of the news, all of which runs under the following:*)

DAN: Barry . . .

> (*Barry gets up, walks past Dan to go to the coffee table. Stu checks his levels; once the news is on he leaves to go to the coffee room. Linda comes in.*)

BARRY: Dan? Oh, you're still hanging around! Linda, go down and tell security this kid is coming. . . . Dan, you want anything? Coffee, tea, insulin, crack? We have it all right here.

> (*Linda starts to exit; Dan motions for her to stay. Barry pours himself some water, then turns to face Dan.*)

DAN: Barry, you should ask me if you want to have guests on the show.

BARRY: Why?

DAN: Because I'm the producer, Barry, that's why.

BARRY: Dan, you asked me to talk to him and I did.

DAN: Well, he's not coming on the show. That's it. There's too much riding on what's happening tonight.

BARRY: What's happening tonight, Dan?

DAN: I told you, the sponsors are listening tonight. Ralston-Purina, the dog food people!

BARRY: Dan, this is *my* show. The sponsors bought *my* show. If I want to have this kid on my show, I'll have him on the show. I put who I want on my show. . . . If I want to have Charlie Manson on my show, I'll have him on. Or Ted Bundy, or John Wayne Gacy . . . or Sirhan Sirhan. . . . *(He's on a tear.)* Or how about this, Dan? I get David Berkowitz, Bernhard Goetz, and John Hinckley on, and we do a special on *gun control*! Or wait . . . even better, we can get a few of those guys who go into shopping centers with automatic weapons, M-16s. . . . *(Turning to Linda.)* What was the name of that guy in San Diego, McDonald's?

LINDA: Huberty?

BARRY: That's it! Huberty, James Huberty! We get James Huberty and we get the Texas tower guy, Charles Whitman . . . make a great show, Dan. Dan, you gotta think about these things, 'cause you're the producer. . . . *(Turning to Linda.)* What ever happened to Richard Speck? And the nurses? Let's bring them on the show! *Wayne Williams* . . . bring him up from Atlanta! Look, Dan, I gotta take a piss, gotta get going. . . . *(Starts to exit, from the balcony.)* Wait! I got it! What ever happened to that postman from Oklahoma? He killed fourteen people, Dan. He *killed his boss*! We bring him on the show. . . . Bring *you* on as a special guest! *(As he exits.)* That's it, that's what we gotta do.

(Linda has found this amusing. She looks at Dan, who just glares. She exits.)

DAN *(addresses the audience)*: Mantovani . . . Bacharach . . . Mancini . . . the Living Strings . . . the Jackie Gleason Orchestra. . . . The name for it is "easy listening," . . . "beautiful music," . . . gentle, . . . serene, . . . melodic, . . . reassuring. The kind of shit you hear on elevators. The kind of shit this station played between nineteen sixty and nineteen eighty. Mindless. Insipid. Disturbing. They hired me in 'eighty-one because their easy-listening format was losing the battle against the Rolling Stones and Grand Funk Railroad. I told them I wanted to put together something new: an all-talk station. I wanted to grab all the top talk talent in the Midwest and create a team that would be unbeatable. That was *my* idea, an all-talk station. I told them take it or leave it. They took it and I got myself the best sports commentator, a financial whiz, a psychologist, a home handy-man specialist, and a sweet old guy that old ladies just loved to chat with. I had myself a full deck . . . but I was missing the joker. . . . Then I heard Barry Champlain. He was down in Akron. A crazy DJ who liked to take callers. Liked to get people wound up. . . . I also heard he was a pretty self-involved guy. Figured. "Champlain." His real name was Paleologus! I went down to see him. Had lunch. Told him my plan. I looked over his résumé, saw that he had been stationed at Fort Dix for six months in 1969, got discharged for a hernia or something like that. So I turned him into a Vietnam vet. I asked him if he ever smoked pot. He said he did maybe once or twice, so I turned him into a hippie too. Barry Champlain marched in all the antiwar marches . . . after he saw the horrors of war in Southeast Asia, of course. He also knew how to fly a plane, lived in a tent in the Yukon for a year, and pitched minor-league baseball for the Toledo Mudhens. . . . Oh, yeah, I'm particularly proud of this one: He got a Ph.D. in history at the University of Chicago after writing a book on Martin Luther and the Reformation. A Renaissance man. . . . Barry just sat there chewing his tuna fish sandwich, staring at me. . . . The gears were turning in his head. Then I hit him with the zinger . . . the name of the show: "Nighttalk with Barry Champlain." His name would be *part* of the name of the show. . . . He stopped chewing. . . . I had my joker. *(Stu and Spike resume their places in the studio.)* Talent comes and goes. Like trains in and out of the train station. Trains wear out, they get derailed, they crash. Sooner or later, they're out of commission. The faster they go, the harder they crash. . . . Barry's my train. *(Barry enters, rushed, puffing on a cigarette. He goes directly to his place, not seeing Dan.)* I put him on the track. I keep him on the track. I keep him oiled and on the track. I let him go as fast as he can. The faster the better. *(As he leaves.)* This is a great job. It's fun, I enjoy myself every day. And it's a challenge. . . . And you make a pretty good buck. . . . I'd say it's just about perfect. . . . You get into trouble when you forget it's a job. When you start to think you're doing something more. . . . It'll fuck you up every time. Every time. That's Barry's problem, not mine.

(Dan exits.)

BARRY *(resumes taking calls)*: "Nighttalk," Vincent.

VINCENT: I been listening to you for five years —

BARRY: Yeah?

VINCENT: Yeah, the guys here at the store put you on every night. We sit around and laugh at you cause you're a jerkoff and a loser —

BARRY *(cuts him off)*: "Nighttalk," Agnes?

AGNES: Barry, can I ask you a question?

BARRY: Hit me, babe . . .

AGNES: Oh, I wouldn't hit you for the world! "I Love Lucy" . . . Why don't they make more of 'em?

BARRY: What?

AGNES: The "I Love Lucy" show. It's so good, why don't they make more of them? I feel like I've seen each one at least ten times! It's time to make some new ones —

BARRY: Those shows are ancient, Agnes! Lucille Ball is an old woman and the rest of the cast is dead!

AGNES: No, she's not that old. I saw her on the show the other night, she looked to be around thirty-five! And that Ricky Ricardo, boy can he play the bongos —

BARRY: *No one can be this stupid!* Are you serious, Agnes? Do you know what year this is? *(Cuts her off.)* "Nighttalk," Chris!

CHRIS: Good evening, Barry.

BARRY: Yeah?

CHRIS: Some people think God is dead. Do you think God is dead, Barry?

BARRY: I happen to know that God is alive and well and living in Gary, Indiana. He's a black steelworker with seven kids who works the night shift pouring off slag.

CHRIS: I see. But, Barry, do you believe in God?

BARRY: What?

CHRIS: Do you believe in God?

BARRY: Are we being serious here, Chris?

CHRIS: I'm serious. I think it's very important.

BARRY: Why is it very important what I believe? Can't you think for yourself?

CHRIS: Don't you think that without some kind of belief in God our actions in this world are meaningless? It would just be physics and chemicals without God . . . just shapes and colors . . .

BARRY: Shapes and colors? Come on! Chris! We been reading William Blake?

CHRIS: I think you do believe in God.

BARRY: Oh, you do?

CHRIS: Yes, you believe in God.

BARRY: Really? What makes you so sure?

CHRIS: It's simple. You think you *are* God. And aren't you ashamed?

(Kent is being led by Linda and is visible through the studio glass. As soon as Linda sees Barry's off-air she brings Kent in through the door.)

BARRY *(pause, sideways glance at Stu)*: On that note, let's hear from our sponsors. Hope you stick around for the Second Coming. *(Turns on Stu, furious.)* What are you doing to me, Stu? You're killing me, you're killing me right on the air. . . . *(Sees Kent. Kent is standing there, shag haircut, torn jeans, tie-dye T-shirt — suburban deadhead — soaking up the ambience of the studio. He's amazed and proud that he's actually here.)* Wait, don't tell me, I can guess . . .

LINDA: He seems harmless . . .

(Linda brings Kent to Barry's desk.)

BARRY *(glares at Stu)*: Harmless as a baboon.

LINDA: You'll sit over here, Kent. This is your microphone. Speak directly into it, keeping your mouth about six inches away. . . . Remember the ground rules: no phone numbers, no brand names, no last names over the air. . . . Otherwise, act and speak normally. . . . This is Mr. Champlain . . .

KENT: This is great! You're Barry?

BARRY: You got 'im.

KENT: Wow . . .

(Kent just stares at Barry.)

BARRY: What's wrong with him?

LINDA: I think he's star struck.

(*Linda returns to her seat.*)

STU: We're going in five . . . four . . . three . . .

BARRY: Come on, pal, . . . we're on.

STU: You're on with the kid.

BARRY (*swings back into the show*): We're back. With me right now is a very special guest. . . . Kent. . . . Say hi to everyone, Kent.

KENT: Wow . . .

BARRY: My sentiments exactly. We've brought Kent on board to give us an inside look at the future of America. Kent is the classic American youth: energetic and resourceful . . . spoiled, perverse, and disturbed. . . . Would you say that's an accurate description, Kent?

KENT: Yeah, sure . . .

BARRY: What do you call that haircut?

KENT: Uh . . . I dunno . . . rock and roll . . .

BARRY: Are you high right now, Kent?

KENT: High?

BARRY: Are you on drugs? Or is this just your naturally moronic self? Wipe the drool off your mouth, you're getting the desk all wet.

KENT: I can't believe I'm . . . Does this work?

(*Kent speaks into the mike.*)

BARRY: This is a radio station, Kent. You're sitting in front of a live mike. . . . When you speak, thousands of people hear your voice. It penetrates their minds.

KENT (*screams a rock howl*): Wanna send that one out to Diamond Dave and Billy the bass player and all the babes at the mall —

BARRY: Kent, we're discussing America here tonight. You have any thoughts on that subject?

KENT: America . . . is a country . . .

BARRY: That's a good start.

KENT: It's where the revolution was. . . . It's the home of democracy, like you were saying before . . .

BARRY: Yeah, go on . . . uh-huh.

KENT: That's how come we can have, you know, talk shows and TV and stuff. There's freedom in America. I wouldn't wanna live in Russia. You know, because they don't have freedom. And their TV shows suck. I think all they have is news. . . . I mean, the news sucks here too. All they ever talk about is Nicaragua and Iran. All these boring places filled with boring people. Who cares, you know? How come they never talk about cool places like London or Lauderdale or Antarctica . . .

BARRY: Or Fiji? How about Fiji? You forgot Fiji, Kent.

KENT: Yeah . . . yeah . . .

(Kent spaces out.)

BARRY: Oh, I'm sorry, I broke your train of thought. Keep going, this is exhilarating.

KENT: Well . . . Nobody talks about what the kids are doing. I mean, it's not like I'm not into political stuff. The Live Aid concert was pretty good, you know. Hands Across America. I dunno. I like Bruce. And he's political.

BARRY: Bruce? Bruce Springsteen. I hear he's a communist.

KENT: Naw, he's from New Jersey. His babe's supposed to be pretty nice —

BARRY: Whose babe?

KENT: Bruce's!

BARRY: Oh, Bruce Springsteen's wife. Yes, what about her?

KENT: Julianne. She was a model. All the rock stars go with models. Keith and Patti. Mick and Jerry. Prince. I guess that's the way it works out. . . . The models hang around with the guys they think are the coolest and they want to make it with them. The stars.

BARRY: Oh, really?

KENT: You know what I'm talking about, Barry. Look at you, big star, famous guy . . . you've got that fine fox right over there that works for you. *(Flips his tongue at Linda.)* Models. *So,* if you've got some cash, and you're cool, you get to have a model . . .

BARRY: So you're not into women's liberation?

KENT: Yeah, I am. I'm into everybody being liberated. Women, South Africans, all those kind of people. I saw a show about all that stuff. . . . Revolution is pretty important, you know? There's gonna be a lot more revolutions. When the people get together, solidarity, you know? Like that song by MegaDeath *(Singing and pounding on the desk.)* "Peace sells, but who's buying?" Plus . . . plus I saw a show about how people will have two-way televisions so they can see each other and then they won't be able to stop the revolution —

BARRY: Who won't be able to stop it?

KENT: Big Brother . . . the government . . . They're all a bunch of fascists, they wanna control everybody's mind. But freedom's an important thing. Like you always say. You say the best things, Barry. I listen to you all the time. You're great.

BARRY: Swell, Kent, and I mean that from my heart. So you just felt like calling tonight and making my life miserable? You got thousands of people worried about your girlfriend, Jill . . .

KENT: Yeah, I guess I shouldna done that . . .

BARRY: Is Jill dead, Kent?

KENT: Nah. She's listening to the show right now. She's taping it.

BARRY: For posterity I'm sure. *(Pause.)* Kent, you're an idiot. . . . I sincerely hope that you don't represent the future of this country, 'cause if you do, we are in sad shape.

KENT: Barry, . . . you're so funny! That's why I love to listen to ya show. . . .
   All the kids listen. . . . You're the best thing on the radio —
BARRY: Kent, America is waiting for you and your friends . . . indeed the world
   is. . . . The future looks difficult in this country and in the world at large.
   . . . What are you planning to do about the armaments race, toxic wastes,
   organized crime, the breakdown of the political system? How are you
   going to prepare for the future?
KENT: By listening to your show, Barry!
BARRY: That's pretty funny. You're a funny guy, like to party, have fun. . . .
   Am I part of your good time?
KENT: Sure.
BARRY: Kent, we discuss a lot of disturbing subjects on this show. Tragic things.
   Frightening things. Doesn't any of that bother you?
KENT: No.
BARRY: Why not?
KENT: It's just a show!
BARRY: It's just one big rock video, huh?
KENT: Yeah, Barry, you know . . . it's your show!
BARRY: Yeah . . . that it is . . . that it is . . . my show. Let's get back to the
   callers on *my* show.
KENT: Sure thing, Barry!
BARRY: Julia.
JULIA: Barry, hello, yes . . . I think . . . these people who have been calling you
   tonight are a bunch of I-don't-know-whats! It's crazy. And that crazy kid
   you got on there. . . . that's terrible. I've been listening to you for five
   years straight, Barry, and I love you and your show. I think it's terrific that
   more people are gonna be listening. I just hope you have time for your
   longtime friends —
BARRY: I always have time for my friends, Julia.
JULIA: Your show's terrific. You're terrific and I don't know what else to
   say . . .
BARRY: Well, tell me something, Julia, since you listen all the time, what is it
   that you like about the show?
JULIA: Well . . . I don't know . . . a lot of things . . .
BARRY: Well, what? For instance . . .
JULIA: Well, I love you, Barry . . .
BARRY: Yeah. That's a given. . . . OK, what about me do you love?
JULIA: Well, you're very funny . . .
BARRY: Uh-huh . . .
JULIA: And I love to hear you talk about all the things you have to say!
BARRY: OK, OK, well, let's get back to the show . . . the show must serve some
   kind of purpose for you . . .
JULIA: Now, I wouldn't say that . . .
BARRY: What would you say?
JULIA: Well, I don't know? I . . .

BARRY: What do you mean, you don't know? You've said that at least five
times now! What don't you know? You been listening to this show for
five years and you don't know why you listen to it?

JULIA: I just said —

BARRY: I heard what you said, you said you don't know why you listen! Why
don't I tell you why? You listen to this show so that you can feel superior
to the other losers who call in!

JULIA: Barry!

BARRY: Don't "Barry" me! You've got sawdust between your ears instead of
brains. Just listen to you. If I sounded as stupid as you did, I'd be too
embarrassed to open my mouth!

JULIA: I'm hanging up!

BARRY: Good. And don't call back.

(*She hangs up. Barry is silent. Pause.*)

KENT: Wow.

BARRY: "Nighttalk." You're on.

CALLER: I just have one thing to ask you, Barry . . .

BARRY: Hit me.

CALLER: Are you as ugly looking as you sound?

BARRY: Uglier.

CALLER: Yeah, I thought you'd say something like that. But as usual you avoid
the question . . .

BARRY (*pause*): What's the question?

CALLER: I think you know the question.

BARRY: Is it animal, vegetable, or mineral?

CALLER: The question is obvious, why does an intelligent fellow like yourself
spend so much energy hurting other people? Do you not love yourself?

BARRY: People who love themselves are in love with a fool.

CALLER: Well put. Good night, Barry. (*Click.*)

BARRY (*stares at his microphone. He's feeling trapped.*): "Nighttalk." Allan.

ALLAN: You love to cut people off, Champlain. You wanna push folks around,
you know why? 'Cause you're a lonely, sorry mother . . . you're a failure.
That jerk kid is making a jackass out of you —

BARRY (*cut off*): "Nighttalk," Ralph.

RALPH: They asked me, why did you do it? Why are you so angry? . . . They
don't understand, Barry, me and you, Barry, we're the kind of people we
feel too much —

BARRY: Hey, Ralph, you playing with a full deck or what?

RALPH: I'm not saying I have the answers, who does? I used to think I knew,
but now, who knows? Take for instance, take cancer. What is it? A virus?
A bacteria? What difference does it make? It kills you just the same . . .
just as fast. I never saw an atom bomb explode, never did. . . . The guys
who did, they're dead. . . . All we got is movies and the guys who made
the movies, where are they? They tell me the little babies in Africa are

starving. . . . OK, I'll buy that . . . but where? Exactly where? And what am I supposed to do about it? See, all I know is me . . . and me, I'm gettin' screwed. . . . Barry, they say that they're gonna come here and take my TV set and take my refrigerator. . . . What are they gonna do with my TV set?

BARRY: Probably watch it. That's what people do with TV sets.

RALPH: But when they do, what do they see? They see people killing people, babies starving. Floods. And for what? For nothing. Beer commercials. Tampax ads. MTV. A yacht in the ocean. A diamond earring. A racehorse. I guess so. All I know is what I read in the papers. And that's a lot of talk-talk-talk-talk-talk —

BARRY: Ralph, Ralph, Ralph, Ralph, Ralph . . . tell me something, I'm curious, how do you dial the phone with a straitjacket on?

RALPH: Sure, I'll listen, I'll listen to common sense. But who's got it anymore? Barry, even if you got it, you're the only one . . . just you and me. Nobody else. Everybody knows God is dead. You know why?

BARRY *(subdued)*: Why?

RALPH: 'Cause God said he would destroy Sodom and he did 'cause you know why?

BARRY: Why?

RALPH: 'Cause Lot couldn't keep the Sodomites away from the angels. . . . They were trying to do it with the angels. . . . Lot tried to tell 'em, don't do it . . . but they wouldn't listen. And now the guy's dead. See what I'm sayin'? *(Barry has had enough, he's fed up. Pulls himself together to make a final assault on Ralph.)* I don't know much about God, I never was very religious, but you can't help feeling like something's wrong, like no one's drivin' the train . . . the system. Too many people gettin' sick and the traffic is always jammin' up and even the weather's not been very good lately. I don't get it, Barry, I don't —

(Barry whirls toward the microphone, mouth open. But another voice is talking; it's Kent, shouting into his mike.)

KENT: You don't get it, wimp? Here's what you get: You get a dollar fifty-nine, go down to the drugstore, buy a pack of razor blades, and slash your fucking wrists, pinhead!

(Kent is proud of his Barryism, while Barry's mouth is agape; he's unable to believe what is happening on his show.)

BARRY *(pause)*: Let's hear from our sponsors. *(Whirls at Linda, unaware that Dan has entered during Kent's interview.)* Linda! Get Kent a drink of water or something.

(Linda gets up and starts moving toward Kent.)

BARRY *(under his breath)*: Get him out of here, now.

LINDA: Come on, Kent.

(*Linda starts leading Kent out.*)

KENT: Hey! Barry!

(*Kent whirls around. He has something in his hand. He points it at Barry. A gun? No, a small flash camera. He flashes Barry, a few feet from his face. Barry is standing, temporarily blinded. Kent bounds out of the studio, past Stu with Linda in pursuit. As Kent passes Dan, he flashes him as well. Barry steadies himself at his desk.*)

STU: Thirty seconds, Bar.

(*Dan is standing on the balcony, smiling at the floor with patient embarrassment.*)

DAN: Barry, I gotta say it. . . . You dispelled any doubts I had. . . . I loved it! Great choice, great work. Unorthodox show, but . . . interesting. . . . See you tomorrow, champ. . . . Stu.

(*Dan turns to leave.*)

BARRY: Dan! Where are you going?

DAN: You don't need me here anymore tonight. See you tomorrow.

BARRY: Dan! (*Sitting down in his chair.*) What would happen if I don't come in tomorrow night?

DAN: Huh? . . . Oh, well, I think they're holding your slot back in Akron, Barry . . . if you want it!

(*Dan winks and leaves. Barry stares at his microphone, a crooked smile on his face.*)

STU: Ten seconds, Barry.

BARRY: Fuckit.

STU: Spike, pop me an ID, we need time here.

(*Stu is looking at Barry for a cue.*)

BARRY (*snaps out of it, looks at Stu*): What are you staring at?

STU: Tell the truth, Barry, I was thinking maybe we should send Linda out to pick up a bottle for after the show. Whaddyou say?

BARRY: Show's a washout, Stu!

STU: So we'll hash it out over at the Red Coach. . . . (*Pause.*) C'mon, Barry, it's not that important, it's just one show.

BARRY: If it's not that important, Stu, why am I doing it?

STU: You don't like the heights, Barry, don't climb the mountains.

BARRY: Fuck you.

STU: No, not fuck me, fuck you. It's like the kid said, it's your show . . .

BARRY (*can't argue*): Hold the calls. (*Stu points the "go" finger. Barry with bemusement turning to shouting anger into the mike.)* I'm here, I'm here every night, I come up here every night. This is my job, this is what I do for a living. I come up here and I do the best I can. I give you the best I can. I can't do better than this. I can't. I'm only a human being up here. I'm not God, . . . uh, . . . a lot of you out there are not. . . . I may not be the most popular guy in the world. That's not the point. I really don't care what you think about me. I mean, Who the hell are you anyways? You . . . "audience." . . . You call me up and you try to tell me things about myself. . . . You don't know me. You don't know anything about me. You've never seen me. . . . You don't know what I look like. You don't know who I am, what I want, what I like, what I don't like in this world. I'm just a voice. A voice in the wilderness. . . . And you . . . like a pack of baying wolves descend on me, 'cause you can't stand facing what it is you are and what you've made. . . . Yes, the world is a terrible place! Yes, cancer and garbage disposals will get you! Yes, a war is coming. Yes, the world is shot to hell and you're all goners. . . . Everything's screwed up and you like it that way, don't you? You're fascinated by the gory details. . . . You're mesmerized by your own fear! You revel in floods and car accidents and unstoppable diseases. . . . You're happiest when others are in pain! And that's where I come in, isn't it? . . . I'm here to lead you by the hand through the dark forest of your own hatred and anger and humiliation. . . . I'm providing a public service! You're so scared! You're like the little child under the covers. You're afraid of the boogeyman, but you can't live without him. Your fear, your own lives have become your entertainment! Tomorrow night, millions of people are going to be listening to this show, *and you have nothing to talk about*! Marvelous technology is at our disposal and instead of reaching up for new heights, we try to see how far down we can go . . . how deep into the muck we can immerse ourselves! What do you wanna talk about? Baseball scores? Your pet? Orgasms? You're pathetic. I despise each and every one of you. . . . You've got nothing. Nothing. Absolutely nothing. No brains. No power. No future. No hope. No God. The only thing you believe in is me. What are you if you don't have me? I'm not afraid, see. I come up here every night and I make my case, I make my point. . . . I say what I believe in. I have to, I have no choice, you frighten me! I come up here every night and I tear into you, I abuse you, I insult you . . . and you just keep calling. Why do you keep coming back, what's wrong with you? I don't want to hear any more, I've had enough. Stop talking. Don't call anymore! Go away! Bunch of yellow-bellied, spineless, bigoted, quivering, drunken, insomniatic, paranoid, disgusting, perverted, voyeuristic little obscene phone callers. That's what you are. Well, to hell with ya. . . . I don't need your fear and your stupidity. You don't get it. . . . It's wasted on you. Pearls before swine. . . . *(Catches his breath.)* If one person out there had any idea what I'm talking about . . . *(Suddenly starts taking callers again.)* Fred, you're on!

FRED: Oh . . . hello . . . yes . . . well . . . you see, . . . Barry, . . . I know it's depressing that so many people don't understand that you're just joking —

BARRY *(cut off)*: Jackie, you're on!

JACKIE: I've been listening for many years, and I find you a warm and intelligent voice in the —

BARRY *(cut off)*: Debbie, you're on!

DEBBIE: Stan called. . . . He told me that he never wants to see me again!

BARRY *(cut off)*: Arnold . . .

ARNOLD: What you were saying before about loneliness, I'm an electrical engineer —

BARRY: Lucy!

LUCY: Barry, my mother is from Akron and she wants to know if you went to high school with —

BARRY: Larry!

LARRY: Why do people insist on calling homosexuals normal? I —

BARRY: Ralph!

RALPH: I'm in my house. . . . I'm at home, which is where you should be. I'm not far away. Come over if you want. . . . I have some cold cuts . . . beer. . . . Come over and we can talk some more . . . 'cause you and me, we're the same kind of people. I know you know what I'm talking about. . . . I have beer. Soup. I'm here. Come by later. I'll wait . . .

(Barry stares at the mike. He starts to speak, but doesn't know what to say.)

STU: Barry, forty-five seconds left in the show! *(Barry is confused, still silent.)* This is dead air, Barry, dead air . . .

(Barry realizes that he wants "dead air." He stares at the mike, smiles to himself, closes his eyes, waits. Long pause.)

BARRY: I guess we're stuck with each other. This is Barry Champlain. *(Signals to Stu. Theme music comes up. Barry gets up from his desk. Starts to leave, unsure of what he's just done. As he passes Stu's desk, he slaps his hand as he did when he arrived at the top of the show. In the doorway.)* Tomorrow, Stu . . .

STU: Tomorrow, Bar . . .

(Barry exits.)

(A quick news and weather report comes on. Stu packs it in. Susan Fleming's operator takes Stu's place and sets up. Dr. Susan Fleming enters, goes straight to the desk. Her show begins.)

SUSAN: This is Dr. Susan Fleming. . . . Before I take the first caller, I'd like to comment on something I saw on the way over to the station this evening.

There was a man standing on a street corner, obviously mentally disturbed. . . . It made me think about something we don't often talk about . . .

(*Blackout.*)   1987

INVESTIGATIONS

1. Toward the end of Barry's introduction to his show, he says, "I have a job to do and I'm gonna do it . . . and I need your help" (p. 459). What are the ways in which Barry's listeners help him do his job? In what sense do Barry and his listeners "speak the same language"? How might Barry's insults be considered essential to binding this community together?

2. How do you explain Barry's anger? To what extent can it be traced to the "blankness akin to chronic disappointment" Patricia Hampl ("Parish Streets") finds in belonging to a particular community? To what extent can this "blankness" make each of us, as Linda says of Barry, "a nice place to visit, but I wouldn't want to live there" (p. 481)?

3. After reviewing your response to "Write Before Reading" on page 368, write a 250–500-word essay comparing how you became an insider to how Kent becomes an insider.

4. On page 488, Dan claims Barry's "problem" is that he thinks he's "doing something more" than a job. Do you agree? Why or why not? How would Barry's realizing he's *not* "doing something more" than a job change his relationship with his listeners? With his coworkers? How might a conviction that he's "doing something more" be necessary to his listeners? To himself?

5. After rereading Rodriguez's "Aria: A Bilingual Childhood," compare Barry's "public language" when he's on the air to his "private language" when he's talking to his coworkers. What are the ways in which his speech on pages 496–497 illustrates how public language tends to make one a stranger in one's home?

SIMON J. ORTIZ

The Language We Know

I don't remember a world without language. From the time of my earliest childhood, there was language. Always language, and imagination, speculation, utters of sound. Words, beginnings of words. What would I be without language? My existence has been determined by language, not only the spoken but the unspoken, the language of speech and the language of motion. I can't remember a world without memory. Memory, immediate and far away in the past, something in the sinew, blood, ageless cell. Although I don't recall the exact moment I spoke or tried to speak, I know the feeling of something tugging at the core of the mind, something unutterable uttered into existence. It is language that brings us into existence. It is language that brings us into being in order to know life.

My childhood was the oral tradition of the Acoma Pueblo people — Aaquumeh hano — which included my immediate family of three older sisters, two younger sisters, two younger brothers, and my mother and father. My world was our world of the Aaquumeh in McCartys, one of the two villages descended from the ageless mother pueblo of Acoma. My world was our Eagle clan-people among other clans. I grew up in Deetziyamah, which is the Aaquumeh name for McCartys, which is posted at the exit off the present interstate highway in western New Mexico. I grew up within a people who farmed small garden plots and fields, who were mostly poor and not well schooled in the American system's education. The language I spoke was that of a struggling people who held ferociously to a heritage, culture, language, and land despite the odds posed them by the forces surrounding them since A.D. 1540, the advent of Euro-American colonization. When I began school in 1948 at the BIA (Bureau of Indian Affairs) day school in our village, I was armed with the basic ABC's and the phrases "Good morning, Miss Oleman" and "May I please be excused to go to the bathroom," but it was an older language that was my fundamental strength.

In my childhood, the language we all spoke was Acoma, and it was a struggle to maintain it against the outright threats of corporal punishment, ostracism, and the invocation that it would impede our progress towards Americanization. Children in school were punished and looked upon with disdain if they did not speak and learn English quickly and smoothly, and so I

Born and raised in Acoma Pueblo, New Mexico, SIMON J. ORTIZ (1941) has taught creative writing and Native American literature at a number of colleges. His many books include *Fightin': New and Collected Stories* (1983) and *From Sand Creek* (1981), a collection of poems.

learned it. It has occurred to me that I learned English simply because I was forced to, as so many other Indian children were. But I know, also, there was another reason, and this was that I loved language, the sound, meaning, and magic of language. Language opened up vistas of the world around me, and it allowed me to discover knowledge that would not be possible for me to know without the use of language. Later, when I began to experiment with and explore language in poetry and fiction, I allowed that a portion of that impetus was because I had come to know English through forceful accultur-ation. Nevertheless, the underlying force was the beauty and poetic power of language in its many forms that instilled in me the desire to become a user of language as a writer, singer, and storyteller. Significantly, it was the Acoma language, which I don't use enough of today, that inspired me to become a writer. The concepts, values, and philosophy contained in my original language and the struggle it has faced have determined my life and vision as a writer.

In Deetziyamah, I discovered the world of the Acoma land and people firsthand through my parents, sisters, and brothers, and my own perceptions, voiced through all that encompasses the oral tradition, which is ageless for any culture. It is a small village, even smaller years ago, and like other Indian communities it is wealthy with its knowledge of daily event, history, and social system, all that make up a people who have a many-dimensioned heritage. Our family lived in a two-room home (built by my grandfather some years after he and my grandmother moved with their daughters from Old Acoma), which my father added rooms to later. I remember my father's work at enlarging our home for our growing family. He was a skilled stoneworker, like many other men of an older Pueblo generation who worked with sandstone and mud mortar to build their homes and pueblos. It takes time, persistence, patience, and the belief that the walls that come to stand will do so for a long, long time, perhaps even forever. I like to think that by helping to mix mud and carry stone for my father and other elders I managed to bring that influence into my con-sciousness as a writer.

Both my mother and my father were good storytellers and singers (as my mother is to this day — my father died in 1978), and for their generation, which was born soon after the turn of the century, they were relatively educated in the American system. Catholic missionaries had taken both of them as children to a parochial boarding school far from Acoma, and they imparted their discipline for study and quest for education to us children when we started school. But it was their indigenous sense of gaining knowledge that was most meaningful to me. Acquiring knowledge about life was above all the most important item; it was a value that one had to have in order to be fulfilled personally and on behalf of his community. And this they insisted upon im-parting through the oral tradition as they told their children about our native history and our community and culture and our "stories." These stories were common knowledge of act, event, and behavior in a close-knit pueblo. It was

5

knowledge about how one was to make a living through work that benefited his family and everyone else.

Because we were a subsistence farming people, or at least tried to be, I learned to plant, hoe weeds, irrigate and cultivate corn, chili, pumpkins, beans. Through counsel and advice I came to know that the rain which provided water was a blessing, gift, and symbol and that it was the land which provided for our lives. It was the stories and songs which provided the knowledge that I was woven into the intricate web that was my Acoma life. In our garden and our cornfields I learned about the seasons, growth cycles of cultivated plants, what one had to think and feel about the land; and at home I became aware of how we must care for each other: All of this was encompassed in an intricate relationship which had to be maintained in order that life continue. After supper on many occasions my father would bring out his drum and sing as we, the children, danced to themes about the rain, hunting, land, and people. It was all that is contained within the language of oral tradition that made me explicitly aware of a yet unarticulated urge to write, to tell what I had learned and was learning and what it all meant to me.

My grandfather was old already when I came to know him. I was only one of his many grandchildren, but I would go with him to get wood for our households, to the garden to chop weeds, and to his sheep camp to help care for his sheep. I don't remember his exact words, but I know they were about how we must sacredly concern ourselves with the people and the holy earth. I know his words were about how we must regard ourselves and others with compassion and love; I know that his knowledge was vast, as a medicine man and an elder of his kiva, and I listened as a boy should. My grandfather represented for me a link to the past that is important for me to hold in my memory because it is not only memory but knowledge that substantiates my present existence. He and the grandmothers and grandfathers before him thought about us as they lived, confirmed in their belief of a continuing life, and they brought our present beings into existence by the beliefs they held. The consciousness of that belief is what informs my present concerns with language, poetry, and fiction.

My first poem was for Mother's Day when I was in the fifth grade, and it was the first poem that was ever published, too, in the Skull Valley School newsletter. Of course I don't remember how the juvenile poem went, but it must have been certain in its expression of love and reverence for the woman who was the most important person in my young life. The poem didn't signal any prophecy of my future as a poet, but it must have come from the forming idea that there were things one could do with language and writing. My mother, years later, remembers how I was a child who always told stories — that is, tall tales — who always had explanations for things probably better left unspoken, and she says that I also liked to perform in school plays. In remembering, I do know that I was coming to that age when the emotions and thoughts in me began to moil to the surface. There was much to experience and express in that age when youth has a precociousness that is broken easily or made to flourish. We were a poor family, always on the verge of financial disaster, though our parents always managed to feed us and keep us in clothing. We had the problems, unfortunately ordinary, of many Indian families who face poverty on a daily basis, never enough of anything, the feeling of a denigrating self-consciousness, alcoholism in the family and community, the feeling that something was falling apart though we tried desperately to hold it all together.

My father worked for the railroad for many years as a laborer and later as a welder. We moved to Skull Valley, Arizona, for one year in the early 1950s, and it was then that I first came in touch with a non-Indian, non-Acoma world. Skull Valley was a farming and ranching community, and my younger brothers and sisters and I went to a one-room school. I had never really had much contact with white people except from a careful and suspicious distance, but now here I was, totally surrounded by them, and there was nothing to do but bear the experience and learn from it. Although I perceived there was not much difference between *them* and *us* in certain respects, there was a distinct feeling that we were not the same either. This thought had been inculcated in me, especially by an Acoma expression — *Gaimuu Mericano* — that spoke of the "fortune" of being an American. In later years as a social activist and committed writer, I would try to offer a strong positive view of our collective Indianness through my writing. Nevertheless, my father was an inadequately paid laborer, and we were far from our home land for economic-social reasons, and my feelings and thoughts about that experience during that time would become a part of how I became a writer.

Soon after, I went away from my home and family to go to boarding   10
school, first in Santa Fe and then in Albuquerque. This was in the 1950s, and this had been the case for the past half-century for Indians: We had to leave home in order to become truly American by joining the mainstream, which was deemed to be the proper course of our lives. On top of this was termination, a U.S. government policy which dictated that Indians sever their relationship to the federal government and remove themselves from their lands and go to American cities for jobs and education. It was an era which bespoke the intent of U.S. public policy that Indians were no longer to be Indians. Naturally, I did not perceive this in any analytical or purposeful sense; rather, I felt an unspoken anxiety and resentment against unseen forces that determined our destiny to be un-Indian, embarrassed and uncomfortable with our grandparents' customs and strictly held values. We were to set our goals as American working men and women, singlemindedly industrious, patriotic, and unquestioning, building for a future which ensured that the United States was the greatest nation in the world. I felt fearfully uneasy with this, for by then I felt the loneliness, alienation, and isolation imposed upon me by the separation from my family, home, and community.

Something was happening; I could see that in my years at Catholic school and the U.S. Indian school. I remembered my grandparents' and parents' words:

Educate yourself in order to help your people. In that era and the generation who had the same experience I had, there was an unspoken vow: We were caught in a system inexorably, and we had to learn that system well in order to fight back. Without the motive of a fight-back we would not be able to survive as the people our heritage had lovingly bequeathed us. My diaries and notebooks began then, and though none have survived to the present, I know they contained the varied moods of a youth filled with loneliness, anger, and discomfort that seemed to have unknown causes. Yet at the same time, I realize now, I was coming to know myself clearly in a way that I would later articulate in writing. My love of language, which allowed me to deal with the world, to delve into it, to experiment and discover, held for me a vision of awe and wonder, and by then grammar teachers had noticed I was a good speller, used verbs and tenses correctly, and wrote complete sentences. Although I imagine that they might have surmised this as unusual for an Indian student whose original language was not English, I am grateful for their perception and attention.

During the latter part of that era in the 1950s of Indian termination and the Cold War, a portion of which still exists today, there were the beginnings of a bolder and more vocalized resistance against the current U.S. public policies of repression, racism, and cultural ethnocide. It seemed to be inspired by the civil rights movement led by black people in the United States and by decolonization and liberation struggles worldwide. Indian people were being relocated from their rural homelands at an astonishingly devastating rate, yet at the same time they resisted the U.S. effort by maintaining determined ties with their heritage, returning often to their native communities, and establishing Indian centers in the cities they were removed to. Indian rural communities, such as Acoma Pueblo, insisted on their land claims and began to initiate legal battles in the areas of natural and social, political and economic human rights. By the retention and the inspiration of our native heritage, values, philosophies, and language, we would know ourselves as a strong and enduring people. Having a modest and latent consciousness of this as a teenager, I began to write about the experience of being Indian in America. Although I had only a romanticized image of what a writer was, which came from the pulp rendered by American popular literature, and I really didn't know anything about writing, I sincerely felt a need to say things, to speak, to release the energy of the impulse to help my people.

My writing in my late teens and early adulthood was fashioned after the American short stories and poetry taught in the high schools of the 1940s and 1950s, but by the 1960s, after I had gone to college and dropped out and served in the military, I began to develop topics and themes from my Indian background. The experience in my village of Deetziyamah and Acoma Pueblo was readily accessible. I had grown up within the oral tradition of speech, social and religious ritual, elders' counsel and advice, countless and endless stories, everyday event, and the visual art that was symbolically representative of life all around. My mother was a potter of the well-known Acoma clayware, a traditional art form that had been passed to her from her mother and the generations of mothers before. My father carved figures from wood and did beadwork. This was not unusual, as Indian people know; there was always some kind of artistic endeavor that people set themselves to, although they did not necessarily articulate it as "Art" in the sense of Western civilization. One lived and expressed an artful life, whether it was in ceremonial singing and dancing, architecture, painting, speaking, or in the way one's social-cultural life was structured. When I turned my attention to my own heritage, I did so because this was my identity, the substance of who I was, and I wanted to write about what that meant. My desire was to write about the integrity and dignity of an Indian identity, and at the same time I wanted to look at what this was within the context of an America that had too often denied its Indian heritage.

To a great extent my writing has a natural political-cultural bent simply because I was nurtured intellectually and emotionally within an atmosphere of Indian resistance. Aacquu did not die in 1598 when it was burned and razed by European conquerors, nor did the people become hopeless when their children were taken away to U.S. schools far from home and new ways were imposed upon them. The *Aaquumeh hano*, despite losing much of their land and surrounded by a foreign civilization, have not lost sight of their native heritage. This is the factual case with most other Indian peoples, and the clear explanation for this has been the fight-back we have found it necessary to wage. At times, in the past, it was outright armed struggle, like that of present-day Indians in Central and South America with whom we must identify; currently, it is often in the legal arena, and it is in the field of literature. In 1981, when I was invited to the White House for an event celebrating American poets and poetry, I did not immediately accept the invitation. I questioned myself about the possibility that I was merely being exploited as an Indian, and I hedged against accepting. But then I recalled the elders going among our people in the poor days of the 1950s, asking for donations — a dollar here and there, a sheep, perhaps a piece of pottery — in order to finance a trip to the nation's capital. They were to make another countless appeal on behalf of our people, to demand justice, to reclaim lost land even though there was only spare hope they would be successful. I went to the White House realizing that I was to do no less than they and those who had fought in the Pueblo Revolt of 1680, and I read my poems and sang songs that were later described as "guttural" by a Washington, D.C., newspaper. I suppose it is more or less understandable why such a view of Indian literature is held by many, and it is also clear why there should be a political stand taken in my writing and those of my sister and brother Indian writers.

The 1960s and afterward have been an invigorating and liberating period   15
for Indian people. It has been only a little more than twenty years since Indian writers began to write and publish extensively, but we are writing and publish-

ing more and more; we can only go forward. We come from an ageless, continuing oral tradition that informs us of our values, concepts, and notions as native people, and it is amazing how much of this tradition is ingrained so deeply in our contemporary writing, considering the brutal efforts of cultural repression that was not long ago outright U.S. policy. We were not to speak our languages, practice our spiritual beliefs, or accept the values of our past generations; and we were discouraged from pressing for our natural rights as Indian human beings. In spite of the fact that there is to some extent the same repression today, we persist and insist in living, believing, hoping, loving, speaking, and writing as Indians. This is embodied in the language we know and share in our writing. We have always had this language, and it is the language, spoken and unspoken, that determines our existence, that brought our grandmothers and grandfathers and ourselves into being in order that there be a continuing life.					1987

INVESTIGATIONS

1. Look again at "Parish Streets." Describe the similarities between Hampl's awareness of the world outside St. Luke's to Ortiz's awareness of the world outside Acoma Pueblo. How do they differ in their descriptions of life outside their communities?

2. Write a 500–750-word essay in which you show how you received an "indigenous sense of gaining knowledge" (para. 5), how community "knowledge of act, event, and behavior" was taught to you.

3. In paragraph 10, Ortiz tells about how going away to school "had been the case for the past half-century for Indians: We had to leave home in order to become truly American by joining the mainstream." In what ways is staying home un-American? How would it be dangerous if each of us belonged in and to a particular place?

4. In paragraph 13, Ortiz calls his heritage "my identity, the substance of who I was." Define your heritage. In what ways is this heritage the substance of who you are?

JUDITH ORTIZ COFER

Silent Dancing

We have a home movie of this party. Several times my mother and I have watched it together, and I have asked questions about the silent revelers coming in and out of focus. It is grainy and of short duration, but it's a great visual aid to my memory of life at that time. And it is in color — the only complete scene in color I can recall from those years.

We lived in Puerto Rico until my brother was born in 1954. Soon after, because of economic pressures on our growing family, my father joined the United States Navy. He was assigned to duty on a ship in Brooklyn Yard — a place of cement and steel that was to be his home base in the States until his retirement more than twenty years later. He left the Island first, alone, going to New York City and tracking down his uncle who lived with his family across the Hudson River in Paterson, New Jersey. There my father found a tiny apartment in a huge tenement that had once housed Jewish families but was just being taken over and transformed by Puerto Ricans, overflowing from New York City. In 1955 he sent for us. My mother was only twenty years old, I was not quite three, and my brother was a toddler when we arrived at *El Building,* as the place had been christened by its newest residents.

My memories of life in Paterson during those first few years are all in shades of gray. Maybe I was too young to absorb vivid colors and details, or to discriminate between the slate blue of the winter sky and the darker hues of the snow-bearing clouds, but that single color washes over the whole period. The building we lived in was gray, as were the streets, filled with slush the first few months of my life there. The coat my father had bought for me was similar in color and too big; it sat heavily on my thin frame.

I do remember the way the heater pipes banged and rattled, startling all of us out of sleep until we got so used to the sound that we automatically shut it out or raised our voices above the racket. The hiss from the valve punctuated my sleep (which has always been fitful) like a nonhuman presence in the room — a dragon sleeping at the entrance of my childhood. But the pipes were also a connection to all the other lives being lived around us. Having come from a house designed for a single family back in Puerto Rico — my mother's extended-family home — it was curious to know that strangers lived

Born in 1952 in Hormigueros, Puerto Rico, JUDITH ORTIZ COFER feels that "the place of birth itself becomes a metaphor for the things we all must leave behind." Her books include *Silent Dancing: A Partial Remembrance of a Puerto Rican Childhood* (1990) and *Terms of Survival* (1987), a book of poetry.

under our floor and above our heads, and that the heater pipe went through everyone's apartments. (My first spanking in Paterson came as a result of playing tunes on the pipes in my room to see if there would be an answer.) My mother was as new to this concept of beehive life as I was, but she had been given strict orders by my father to keep the doors locked, the noise down, ourselves to ourselves.

It seems that Father had learned some painful lessons about prejudice while searching for an apartment in Paterson. Not until years later did I hear how much resistance he had encountered with landlords who were panicking at the influx of Latinos into a neighborhood that had been Jewish for a couple of generations. It made no difference that it was the American phenomenon of ethnic turnover which was changing the urban core of Paterson, and that the human flood could not be held back with an accusing finger. 5

"You Cuban?" one man had asked my father, pointing at his name tag on the Navy uniform — even though my father had the fair skin and light-brown hair of his northern Spanish background, and the name Ortiz is as common in Puerto Rico as Johnson is in the United States.

"No," my father had answered, looking past the finger into his adversary's angry eyes. "I'm Puerto Rican."

"Same shit." And the door closed.

My father could have passed as European, but we couldn't. My brother and I both have our mother's black hair and olive skin, and so we lived in El Building and visited our great-uncle and his fair children on the next block. It was their private joke that they were the German branch of the family. Not many years later that area too would be mainly Puerto Rican. It was as if the heart of the city map were being gradually colored brown — *café con leche* brown. Our color.

The movie opens with a sweep of the living room. It is "typical" immigrant 10 *Puerto Rican decor for the time: The sofa and chairs are square and hard-looking, upholstered in bright colors (blue and yellow in this instance), and covered with the transparent plastic that furniture salesmen then were so adept at convincing women to buy. The linoleum on the floor is light blue; if it had been subjected to spike heels (as it was in most places), there were dime-sized indentations all over it that cannot be seen in this movie. The room is full of people dressed up: dark suits for the men, red dresses for the women. When I have asked my mother why most of the women are in red that night, she has shrugged, "I don't remember. Just a coincidence." She doesn't have my obsession for assigning symbolism to everything.*

The three women in red sitting on the couch are my mother, my eighteen-year-old cousin, and her brother's girlfriend. The novia *is just up from the Island, which is apparent in her body language. She sits up formally, her dress pulled over her knees. She is a pretty girl, but her posture makes her look insecure, lost in her full-skirted dress, which she has carefully tucked around her to make room for my gorgeous cousin, her future sister-in-law. My cousin*

*has grown up in Paterson and is in her last year of high school. She doesn't
have a trace of what Puerto Ricans call* la mancha *(literally, the stain: the mark
of the new immigrant — something about the posture, the voice, or the humble
demeanor that makes it obvious to everyone the person has just arrived on the
mainland). My cousin is wearing a tight, sequined, cocktail dress. Her brown
hair has been lightened with peroxide around the bangs, and she is holding a
cigarette expertly between her fingers, bringing it up to her mouth in a sensuous
arc of her arm as she talks animatedly. My mother, who has come up to sit
between the two women, both only a few years younger than herself, is somewhere between the poles they represent in our culture.*

It became my father's obsession to get out of the barrio, and thus we were
never permitted to form bonds with the place or with the people who lived
there. Yet El Building was a comfort to my mother, who never got over yearning
for *la isla*. She felt surrounded by her language: The walls were thin, and voices
speaking and arguing in Spanish could be heard all day. *Salsas* blasted out of
radios, turned on early in the morning and left on for company. Women seemed
to cook rice and beans perpetually — the strong aroma of boiling red kidney
beans permeated the hallways.

Though Father preferred that we do our grocery shopping at the supermarket when he came home on weekend leaves, my mother insisted that she
could cook only with products whose labels she could read. Consequently,
during the week I accompanied her and my little brother to *La Bodega* — a
hole-in-the-wall grocery store across the street from El Building. There we
squeezed down three narrow aisles jammed with various products. Goya's and
Libby's — those were the trademarks that were trusted by *her mamá,* so my
mother bought many cans of Goya beans, soups, and condiments, as well as
little cans of Libby's fruit juices for us. And she also bought Colgate toothpaste
and Palmolive soap. (The final *e* is pronounced in both these products in
Spanish, so for many years I believed that they were manufactured on the
Island. I remember my surprise at first hearing a commercial on television in
which Colgate rhymed with "ate.") We always lingered at La Bodega, for it
was there that Mother breathed best, taking in the familiar aromas of the foods
she knew from Mamá's kitchen. It was also there that she got to speak to the
other women of El Building without violating outright Father's dictates against
fraternizing with our neighbors.

Yet Father did his best to make our "assimilation" painless. I can still see
him carrying a real Christmas tree up several flights of stairs to our apartment,
leaving a trail of aromatic pine. He carried it formally, as if it were a flag in a
parade. We were the only ones in El Building that I knew of who got presents
on both Christmas day AND *día de Reyes,* the day when the Three Kings
brought gifts to Christ and to Hispanic children.

Our supreme luxury in El Building was having our own television set. It   15
must have been a result of Father's guilt feelings over the isolation he had
imposed on us, but we were among the first in the barrio to have one. My

brother quickly became an avid watcher of Captain Kangaroo and Jungle Jim, while I loved all the series showing families. By the time I started first grade, I could have drawn a map of Middle America as exemplified by the lives of characters in "Father Knows Best," "The Donna Reed Show," "Leave It to Beaver," "My Three Sons," and (my favorite) "Bachelor Father," where John Forsythe treated his adopted teenage daughter like a princess because he was rich and had a Chinese houseboy to do everything for him. In truth, compared to our neighbors in El Building, *we* were rich. My father's Navy check provided us with financial security and a standard of life that the factory workers envied. The only thing his money could not buy us was a place to live away from the barrio — his greatest wish, Mother's greatest fear.

In the home movie the men are shown next, sitting around a card table set up in one corner of the living room, playing dominoes. The clack of the ivory pieces was a familiar sound. I heard it in many houses on the Island and in many apartments in Paterson. In "Leave It to Beaver," the Cleavers played bridge in every other episode; in my childhood, the men started every social occasion with a hotly debated round of dominoes. The women would sit around and watch, but they never participated in the games.

Here and there you can see a small child. Children were always brought to parties and, whenever they got sleepy, were put to bed in the host's bedroom. Babysitting was a concept unrecognized by the Puerto Rican women I knew: A responsible mother did not leave her children with any stranger. And in a culture where children are not considered intrusive, there was no need to leave the children at home. We went where our mother went.

Of my preschool years I have only impressions: the sharp bite of the wind in December as we walked with our parents towards the brightly lit stores downtown; how I felt like a stuffed doll in my heavy coat, boots, and mittens; how good it was to walk into the five-and-dime and sit at the counter drinking hot chocolate. On Saturdays our whole family would walk downtown to shop at the big department stores on Broadway. Mother bought all our clothes at Penney's and Sears, and she liked to buy her dresses at the women's specialty shops like Lerner's and Diana's. At some point we'd go into Woolworth's and sit at the soda fountain to eat.

We never ran into other Latinos at these stores or when eating out, and it became clear to me only years later that the women from El Building shopped mainly in other places — stores owned by other Puerto Ricans or by Jewish merchants who had philosophically accepted our presence in the city and decided to make us their good customers, if not real neighbors and friends. These establishments were located not downtown but in the blocks around our street, and they were referred to generically as *La Tienda, El Bazar, La Bodega, La Botánica.* Everyone knew what was meant. These were the stores where your face did not turn a clerk to stone, where your money was as green as anyone else's.

One New Year's Eve we were dressed up like child models in the Sears catalogue: my brother in a miniature man's suit and bow tie, and I in black patent-leather shoes and a frilly dress with several layers of crinoline underneath. My mother wore a bright red dress that night, I remember, and spike heels; her long black hair hung to her waist. Father, who usually wore his Navy uniform during his short visits home, had put on a dark civilian suit for the occasion: We had been invited to his uncle's house for a big celebration. Everyone was excited because my mother's brother Hernan — a bachelor who could indulge himself with luxuries — had bought a home movie camera, which he would be trying out that night.

Even the home movie cannot fill in the sensory details such a gathering left imprinted in a child's brain. The thick sweetness of women's perfumes mixing with the ever-present smells of food cooking in the kitchen: meat and plantain *pasteles,* as well as the ubiquitous rice dish made special with pigeon peas — *gandules* — and seasoned with precious *sofrito* sent up from the Island by somebody's mother or smuggled in by a recent traveler. *Sofrito* was one of the items that women hoarded, since it was hardly ever in stock at La Bodega. It was the flavor of Puerto Rico.

The men drank Palo Viejo rum, and some of the younger ones got weepy. The first time I saw a grown man cry was at a New Year's Eve party: He had been reminded of his mother by the smells in the kitchen. But what I remember most were the boiled *pasteles* — plantain or yucca rectangles stuffed with corned beef or other meats, olives, and many other savory ingredients, all wrapped in banana leaves. Everybody had to fish one out with a fork. There was always a "trick" pastel — one without stuffing — and whoever got that one was the "New Year's Fool."

There was also the music. Long-playing albums were treated like precious china in these homes. Mexican recordings were popular, but the songs that brought tears to my mother's eyes were sung by the melancholy Daniel Santos, whose life as a drug addict was the stuff of legend. Felipe Rodríguez was a particular favorite of couples, since he sang about faithless women and brokenhearted men. There is a snatch of one lyric that has stuck in my mind like a needle on a worn groove: *De piedra ha de ser mi cama, de piedra la cabezera . . . la mujer que a mi me quiera . . . ha de quererme de veras. Ay, Ay, Ay, corazón, porque no amas.*[1] . . . I must have heard it a thousand times since the idea of a bed made of stone, and its connection to love, first troubled me with its disturbing images.

The five-minute home movie ends with people dancing in a circle — the creative filmmaker must have set it up, so that all of them could file past him. It is both comical and sad to watch silent dancing. Since there is no justification for the absurd movements that music provides for some of us, people appear

---

[1] My bed must be stone, my pillow, stone . . . the woman who loves me must truly love me. Ay, ay, ay, heart, why don't you love. [Ed.]

frantic, their faces embarrassingly intense. It's as if you were watching sex. Yet for years I've had dreams in the form of this home movie. In a recurring scene, familiar faces push themselves forward into my mind's eye, plastering their features into distorted close-ups. And I'm asking them: "Who is *she*? Who is the old woman I don't recognize? Is she an aunt? Somebody's wife? Tell me who she is."

"See the beauty mark on her cheek as big as a hill on the lunar landscape of her face — well, that runs in the family. The women on your father's side of the family wrinkle early; it's the price they pay for that fair skin. The young girl with the green stain on her wedding dress is *La Novia* — just up from the Island. See, she lowers her eyes when she approaches the camera, as she's supposed to. Decent girls never look at you directly in the face. *Humilde*, humble, a girl should express humility in all her actions. She will make a good wife for your cousin. He should consider himself lucky to have met her only weeks after she arrived here. If he marries her quickly, she will make him a good Puerto Rican–style wife; but if he waits too long, she will be corrupted by the city — just like your cousin there."

"She means me. I do what I want. This is not some primitive island I live on. Do they expect me to wear a black mantilla on my head and go to mass every day? Not me. I'm an American woman, and I will do as I please. I can type faster than anyone in my senior class at Central High, and I'm going to be a secretary to a lawyer when I graduate. I can pass for an American girl anywhere — I've tried it. At least for Italian, anyway — I never speak Spanish in public. I hate these parties, but I wanted the dress. I look better than any of these *humildes* here. *My* life is going to be different. I have an American boyfriend. He is older and has a car. My parents don't know it, but I sneak out of the house late at night sometimes to be with him. If I marry him, even my name will be American. I hate rice and beans — that's what makes these women fat."

"Your *prima* is pregnant by that man she's been sneaking around with. Would I lie to you? I'm your *Tiá Política*, your great-uncle's common-law wife — the one he abandoned on the Island to go marry your cousin's mother. *I* was not invited to this party, of course, but I came anyway. I came to tell you that story about your cousin that you've always wanted to hear. Do you remember the comment your mother made to a neighbor that has always haunted you? The only thing you heard was your cousin's name, and then you saw your mother pick up your doll from the couch and say: 'It was as big as this doll when they flushed it down the toilet.' This image has bothered you for years, hasn't it? You had nightmares about babies being flushed down the toilet, and you wondered why anyone would do such a horrible thing. You didn't dare ask your mother about it. She would only tell you that you had not heard her right, and yell at you for listening to adult conversations. But later, when you were old enough to know about abortions, you suspected.

"I am here to tell you that you were right. Your cousin was growing an *Americanito* in her belly when this movie was made. Soon after she put something long and pointy into her pretty self, thinking maybe she could get rid of the problem before breakfast and still make it to her first class at the high school. Well, *Niña,* her screams could be heard downtown. Your aunt, her mamá, who had been a midwife on the Island, managed to pull the little thing out. Yes, they probably flushed it down the toilet. What else could they do with it — give it a Christian burial in a little white casket with blue bows and ribbons? Nobody wanted that baby — least of all the father, a teacher at her school with a house in West Paterson that he was filling with real children, and a wife who was a natural blonde.

"Girl, the scandal sent your uncle back to the bottle. And guess where your cousin ended up? Irony of ironies. She was sent to a village in Puerto Rico to live with a relative on her mother's side: a place so far away from civilization that you have to ride a mule to reach it. A real change in scenery. She found a man there — women like that cannot live without male company — but believe me, the men in Puerto Rico know how to put a saddle on a woman like her. *La Gringa,* they call her. Ha, ha, ha. *La Gringa* is what she always wanted to be. . . . "

The old woman's mouth becomes a cavernous black hole I fall into. And as I fall, I can feel the reverberations of her laughter. I hear the echoes of her last mocking words: *La Gringa, La Gringa!* And the conga line keeps moving silently past me. There is no music in my dream for the dancers.

When Odysseus visits Hades to see the spirit of his mother, he makes an   25
offering of sacrificial blood, but since all the souls crave an audience with the living, he has to listen to many of them before he can ask questions. I, too, have to hear the dead and the forgotten speak in my dream. Those who are still part of my life remain silent, going around and around in their dance. The others keep pressing their faces forward to say things about the past.

My father's uncle is last in line. He is dying of alcoholism, shrunken and shriveled like a monkey, his face a mass of wrinkles and broken arteries. As he comes closer I realize that in his features I can see my whole family. If you were to stretch that rubbery flesh, you could find my father's face, and deep within *that* face — my own. I don't want to look into those eyes ringed in purple. In a few years he will retreat into silence, and take a long, long time to die. *Move back, Tío,* I tell him. *I don't want to hear what you have to say. Give the dancers room to move. Soon it will be midnight. Who is the New Year's Fool this time?*   1990

INVESTIGATIONS

1. In paragraph 2 Cofer talks about her family's move to the Paterson "tenement that had once housed Jewish families but was just being taken over and transformed by Puerto Ricans, overflowing from New York City." Carefully examine Cofer's memoir for evidence of how living this "beehive life" transformed her, her family, and her community.

2. Reread paragraph 11. What do you think Puerto Rican immigrants lose when they lose "la mancha"?

3. Compare Cofer's father's "obsession to get out of the barrio" (para. 12)

with Jing-mei's mother's aspirations for her daughter ("Two Kinds"). What accounts for the similarities between their attitudes despite their distinct heritages?

4. Look back at the writing you did for "Write Before Reading" (p. 368). In what ways could you consider yourself an immigrant in the situation you discussed? How well did you assimilate? How possible do you think it is to keep "the best of both worlds," to retain old values while assimilating new ones?

GARY SNYDER

Building

We started our house midway through the Cultural Revolution,[1]
The Vietnam war, Cambodia, in our ears,
   tear gas in Berkeley,
Boys in overalls with frightened eyes, long matted hair, ran
   from the police.   5
We peeled trees, drilled boulders, dug sumps, took sweat baths
   together.
That house finished we went on
Built a schoolhouse, with a hundred wheelbarrows,
   held seminars on California paleo-indians during lunch.   10
We brazed the Chou dynasty form of the character "Mu"[2]
   on the blacksmithed brackets of the ceiling of the lodge,
Buried a five-prong vajra[3] between the schoolbuildings
   while praying and offering tobacco.
Those buildings were destroyed by a fire, a pale copy rebuilt   15
   by insurance.

[1] A violent wave of repression against "enemies of the revolution" launched by Mao Zedung and his followers in China from the mid-sixties to the mid-seventies. [Ed.]
[2] Japanese character after the Chinese character *Wu. Mu* suggests "nothingness." [Ed.]
[3] Sanskrit name for a sacred object that often appears in Buddhist ritual and art, usually depicted as a thunderbolt or a diamond. The *vajra* is capable of breaking another substance but is itself unbreakable. [Ed.]

GARY SNYDER (b. 1930) once said that "intelligence, insight, sensitivity, and brilliance are not limited to educated people." Author of fourteen volumes of poetry, he has worked as a seaman, logger, and college professor and studied Zen Buddhism for a number of years in a Japanese monastery. Snyder's book of poetry, *Turtle Island*, won the 1975 Pulitzer Prize.

Ten years later we gathered at the edge of a meadow.
The cultural revolution is over, hair is short,
    the industry calls the shots in the Peoples Forests.
Single mothers go back to college to become lawyers.   20

Blowing the conch, shaking the staff-rings
    we opened work on a Hall,
Forty people, women carpenters, child labor, pounding nails,
Screw down the corten roofing and shape the beams
    with a planer,   25
The building is done in three weeks.
We fill it with flowers and friends and open it up to our hearts.

Now in the year of the Persian Gulf,
Of Falsehoods and Crimes in the Government held up as Virtues,
    this dance with Matter   30
Goes on: our buildings are solid, to live, to teach, to sit,
To sit, to know for sure the sound of a bell —

This is history. This is outside of history.
Buildings are built in the moment,
    they are constantly wet from the pool   35
        that renews all things
      naked and gleaming.

The moon moves
Through her twenty-eight nights.
Wet years and dry years pass;   40
Sharp tools, good design.   1988

INVESTIGATIONS

1. The speaker refers to "we" throughout the poem. Who makes up "we," and why is identifying this group necessary for understanding the poem? Does the speaker include or exclude the reader in "we"?
2. Snyder describes the literal buildings in his poem and he also uses the metaphor of building to structure the poem. How do these two levels of meaning reinforce each other? How is "building" a metaphor like constructing a building?

3. First, examine the speaker's home, schoolhouse, and hall: (1) How is each built? (2) Who works on them? (3) Where is each located? Then consider each structure within the historical period during which it was built. What can you learn about the periods' politics by studying these structures?

4. Reread lines 28–32. What does the speaker mean by: "To sit, to know for sure the sound of a bell — "? What does this knowledge have to do with contemporary life? In a few paragraphs, describe a building you think fits today's politics.

5. Describe in your own words what Snyder means by the following (lines 33–37):

> This is history. This is outside history.
> Buildings are built in the moment,
>   they are constantly wet from the pool
>   that renews all things
>   naked and gleaming.

PART FOUR
CONNECTIONS AND ELABORATIONS

1. After reexamining the selections in Part Four, your response to "Write Before Reading" (p. 368), and any other writing and thinking you've done in response to the selections, write an essay in which you imagine how community is both a burden and a blessing.

2. After reviewing Gornick's "Twice an Outsider: On Being Jewish and a Woman," write your own version, beginning with "When I was growing up, the whole world was . . ."

3. Write a critique of Rodriguez's "Aria: A Bilingual Childhood" from Simon Ortiz's ("The Language We Know") point of view.

4. Write a critique of Ortiz's "The Language We Know" from Richard Rodriguez's ("Aria: A Bilingual Childhood") point of view.

5. Using as evidence material from Tsui's "Don't Let Them Chip Away at Our Language," Bogosian's *Talk Radio,* Rodriguez's "Aria: A Bilingual Childhood," Cervantes's "Refugee Ship," O'Brien's "The Things They Carried," and Ortiz's "The Language We Know," write an essay analyzing the role of language in forming and maintaining a community's sense of itself.

6. Using as evidence material from your response to "Write Before Reading," Gornick's "Twice an Outsider: On Being Jewish and a Woman," Weesner's "The Body Politic," Hampl's "Parish Streets," Rose's "For the White Poets Who Would Be Indian," Rodriguez's "Aria: A Bilingual Childhood," and Snyder's "Building," write an essay in which you examine how an individual's membership in a community contributes to the construction of an authentic sense of self.

7. Using as evidence material from your response to "Write Before Reading," Youngblood's "Snuff Dippers," Gornick's "Twice an Outsider: On Being Jewish and a Woman," Hampl's "Parish Streets," Kirn's "The New Timothy," Clifton's "in white america," Cofer's "Silent Dancing," and Snyder's "Building," write an essay in which you examine the extent to which we're free to choose the communities to which we belong.

8. Using as evidence material from appropriate selections in this book and from your own experience, write an essay in which you analyze why the demands of friendship and those of community frequently conflict.

PART FIVE

ON AND
OFF THE JOB

Most of us spend a great deal of our lives not only working but looking for work, thinking about what kind of work we want, talking about the work we do, and, not least, living where and how our jobs, or our parents' jobs, determine we'll live. In fact, work so permeates our lives that we gain a vantage point from which to survey what it means — or has meant, or could mean — only after an arduous mental climb.

In Part Five, you'll read about the way desire and chance influence a young man's job search in Michael Dorris's "Life Stories"; see the terrible pressure a "game" can put on one of its players in Andre Dubus's "After the Game"; visit the Detroit home of a factory foreman in Jim Daniels's "My Father Worked Late"; hear Trudy Pax Farr talk about the power and fear of her job in "Steelworker"; read how "Buying and Selling," by Philip Levine, involves several kinds of exchange; watch a New York "takeover artist" make his move on a New England industrial firm in Jerry Sterner's *Other People's Money*; enjoy the bi-

517

zarre exploits of advertising wizards in Ralph Lombreglia's "Late Early Man"; observe the deceptively simple rhythms of the year in Donald Hall's "Ox Cart Man"; witness an African-American reporter struggling to resolve personal and professional pressures in Rachel L. Jones's "The Price of Hate: Thoughts on Covering a Ku Klux Klan Rally"; feel the effects of work and friendship in Jimmy Santiago Baca's "Perfecto Flores"; go down in a coal mine in Jay Parini's "Working the Face"; see the simple, solitary job of a Forestry Service fire-watcher turn into a nightmare in T. Coraghessan Boyle's "Sitting on Top of the World"; read how a Pawnee man answers his traditional calling in "The Warriors," by Anna Lee Walters; experience the politics, the deceptions, and the desperation in the defense industry in "The Flowers of Boredom," by Rick DeMarinis; and watch the harrowing work roofers do in "Tar," by C. K. Williams.

WRITE BEFORE READING

First, take a few minutes to jot down all the jobs you've held (including any jobs for which you weren't paid). Next, after considering the effects each has had on you, describe as fully as possible the one job that's most fundamentally changed you. Finally, tell the story of the single episode from your time at this job that most vividly dramatizes how it changed you.

MICHAEL DORRIS

Life Stories

In most cultures, adulthood is equated with self-reliance and responsibility, yet often Americans do not achieve this status until we are in our late twenties or early thirties — virtually the entire average lifespan of a person in a traditional non-Western society. We tend to treat prolonged adolescence as a warm-up for real life, as a wobbly suspension bridge between childhood and legal maturity. Whereas a nineteenth-century Cheyenne or Lakota teenager was expected to alter self-conception in a split-second vision, we often meander through an analogous rite of passage for more than a decade — through high school, college, graduate school.

Though he had never before traveled alone outside his village, the Plains Indian male was expected at puberty to venture solo into the wilderness. There he had to fend for and sustain himself while avoiding the menace of unknown dangers, and there he had absolutely to remain until something happened that would transform him. Every human being, these tribes believed, was entitled to at least one moment of personal, enabling insight.

Anthropology proposes feasible psychological explanations for why this flash was eventually triggered: Fear, fatigue, reliance on strange foods, the anguish of loneliness, stress, and the expectation of ultimate success all contributed to a state of receptivity. Every sense was quickened, alerted to perceive deep meaning, until at last the interpretation of an unusual event — a dream, a chance encounter, or an unexpected vista — reverberated with metaphor. Through this unique prism, abstractly preserved in a vivid memory or song, a boy caught foresight of both his adult persona and of his vocation, the two inextricably entwined.

Today the best approximations that many of us get to such a heady sense of eventuality come in the performance of our school vacation jobs. Summers are intermissions, and once we hit our teens it is during these breaks in our structured regimen that we initially taste the satisfaction of remuneration that is earned, not merely doled. Tasks defined as *work* are not only graded, they are compensated; they have a worth that is unarguable because it translates into hard currency. Wage labor — and in the beginning, this generally means a confining, repetitive chore for which we are quickly overqualified — para-

Born in Dayton, Washington, in 1945, MICHAEL DORRIS, a member of the Modoc tribe, taught for many years in the Department of Native American Studies at Dartmouth College. He is the author of *The Broken Cord* (1987) and *A Yellow Raft in Blue Water* (1987), and coauthored *The Crown of Columbus* (1991) with his wife, Louise Erdrich.

doxically brings a sense of blooming freedom. At the outset, the complaint to
a peer that business supersedes fun is oddly liberating — no matter what
drudgery requires your attention, it is by its very required nature serious and
adult.

At least that's how it seemed to me. I come from a line of people hard hit   5
by the Great Depression. My mother and her sisters went to work early in their
teens — my mother operated a kind of calculator known as a comptometer
while her sisters spent their days, respectively, at a peanut factory and at
Western Union. My grandmother did piecework sewing. Their efforts, and the
Democratic Party, saw them through, and to this day they never look back
without appreciation for their later solvency. They take nothing for granted.
Accomplishments are celebrated, possessions are valuable, in direct proportion
to the labor entailed to acquire them; anything easily won or bought on credit
is suspect. When I was growing up we were far from wealthy, but what money
we had was correlated to the hours some one of us had logged. My eagerness
to contribute to, or at least not diminish, the coffer was countered by the
arguments of those whose salaries kept me in school: My higher education was
a sound group investment. The whole family was adamant that I have the
opportunities they had missed and, no matter how much I objected, they stinted
themselves to provide for me.

Summer jobs were therefore a relief, an opportunity to pull a share of the
load. As soon as the days turned warm I began to peruse the classifieds, and
when the spring semester was done, I was ready to punch a clock. It even felt
right. Work in June, July, and August had an almost Biblical aspect: In the hot,
canicular weather your brow sweated, just as God had ordained. Moreover,
summer jobs had the luxury of being temporary. No matter how bizarre, how
onerous, how off my supposed track, employment terminated with the falling
leaves and I was back on neutral ground. So, during each annual three-month
leave from secondary school and later from the university, I compiled an eclectic
résumé: lawn cutter, hair sweeper in a barber shop, lifeguard, delivery boy,
temporary mail carrier, file clerk, youth program coordinator on my Montana
reservation, ballroom dance instructor, theater party promoter, night-shift hospital records keeper, human adding machine in a Paris bank, encyclopedia
salesman, newspaper stringer, recreation bus manager, salmon fisherman.

The reasonable titles disguise the madness of some of these occupations.
For instance, I seemed inevitably to be hired to trim the yards of the unconventional. One woman followed beside me, step by step, as I traversed her yard
in ever tighter squares, and called my attention to each missed blade of grass.
Another client never had the "change" to pay me, and so reimbursed my
weekly pruning with an offering culled from his library. I could have done
without the *Guide to Artificial Respiration* (1942) or the many well-worn copies
of Reader's Digest Condensed Books, but sometimes the selection merited the
wait. Like a rat lured repeatedly back to the danger of mild electric shock by
the mystique of intermittent reenforcement, I kept mowing by day in hopes of
turning pages all night.

The summer I was eighteen a possibility arose for a rotation at the post office, and I grabbed it. There was something casually sophisticated about work that required a uniform, about having a federal ranking, even if it was GS-1 (Temp/Sub), and it was flattering to be entrusted with a leather bag containing who knew what important correspondence. Every day I was assigned a new beat, usually in a rough neighborhood avoided whenever possible by regular carriers, and I proved quite capable of complicating what would normally be fairly routine missions. The low point came on the first of August when I diligently delivered four blocks' worth of welfare checks to the right numbers on the wrong streets. It is no fun to snatch unexpected wealth from the hands of those who have but moments previously opened their mailboxes and received a bonus.

After my first year of college, I lived with relatives on an Indian reservation in eastern Montana and filled the only post available: Coordinator of Tribal Youth Programs. I was seduced by the language of the announcement into assuming that there existed Youth Programs to be coordinated. In fact, the Youth consisted of a dozen bored, disgruntled kids — most of them my cousins — who had nothing better to do each day than to show up at what was euphemistically called "the gym" and hate whatever Program I had planned for them. The Youth ranged in age from fifteen to five and seemed to have as their sole common ambition the determination to smoke cigarettes. This put them at immediate and ongoing odds with the Coordinator, who on his first day naively encouraged them to sing the "Doe, a deer, a female deer" song from *The Sound of Music*. They looked at me, that bleak morning, and I looked at them, each boy and girl equipped with a Pall Mall behind an ear, and we all knew it would be a long, struggle-charged battle. It was to be a contest of wills, the hearty and wholesome vs. prohibited vice. I stood for dodge ball, for collecting bugs in glass jars, for arts and crafts; they had pledged a preternatural allegiance to sloth. The odds were not in my favor and each waking dawn I experienced the lightheadedness of anticipated exhaustion, that thrill of giddy dissociation in which nothing seems real or of great significance. I went with the flow and learned to inhale.

The next summer, I decided to find work in an urban setting for a change,   10 and was hired as a general office assistant in the Elsa Hoppenfeld Theatre Party Agency, located above Sardi's restaurant in New York City. The Agency consisted of Elsa Hoppenfeld herself, Rita Frank, her regular deputy, and me. Elsa was a gregarious Viennese woman who established contacts through personal charm, and she spent much of the time courting trade away from the building. Rita was therefore both my immediate supervisor and constant companion; she had the most incredible fingernails I had ever seen — long, carefully shaped pegs lacquered in cruel primary colors and hard as stone — and an attitude about her that could only be described as zeal.

The goal of a theater party agent is to sell blocks of tickets to imminent Broadway productions, and the likely buyers are charities, B'nai Briths, Hadassahs, and assorted other fund-raising organizations. We received commissions on volume, and so it was necessary to convince a prospect that a play — preferably an expensive musical — for which we had reserved the rights to seats would be a boffo smash hit.

The object of our greatest expectation that season was an extravaganza called *Chu Chem,* a saga that aspired to ride the coattails of *Fiddler on the Roof* into entertainment history. It starred the estimable Molly Picon and told the story of a family who had centuries ago gone from Israel to China during the diaspora, yet had, despite isolation in an alien environment, retained orthodox culture and habits. The crux of the plot revolved around a man with several marriageable daughters and nary a kosher suitor within 5,000 miles. For three months Rita and I waxed eloquent in singing the show's praises. We sat in our little office, behind facing desks, and every noon while she redid her nails I ordered out from a deli that offered such exotic (to me) delicacies as fried egg sandwiches, lox and cream cheese, pastrami, *tongue.* I developed of necessity and habit a telephone voice laced with a distinctly Yiddish accent. It could have been a great career. However, come November, *Chu Chem* bombed. Its closing was such a financial catastrophe for all concerned that when the following January one Monsieur Dupont advertised on the Placement Board at my college, I decided to put an ocean between me and my former trusting clientele.

M. Dupont came to campus with the stated purpose of interviewing candidates for teller positions in a French bank. Successful applicants, required to be fluent in *français,* would be rewarded with three well-paid months and a rent-free apartment in Paris. I headed for the language lab and registered for an appointment.

The only French in the interview was *Bonjour, ça va?,* after which M. Dupont switched into English and described the wonderful deal on charter air flights that would be available to those who got the nod. Round-trip to Amsterdam, via Reykjavik, leaving the day after exams and returning in mid-September, no changes or substitutions. I signed up on the spot. I was to be a *banquier,* with *pied-à-terre* in Montparnasse!

Unfortunately, when I arrived with only $50 in travelers checks in my pocket — the flight had cleaned me out, but who needed money since my paycheck started right away — no one in Paris had ever heard of M. Dupont. *Alors.*

I stood in the Gare du Nord and considered my options. There weren't any. I scanned a listing of Paris hotels and headed for the cheapest one: the Hotel Villedo, $10 a night. The place had an ambiance that I persuaded myself was antique, despite the red light above the sign. The only accommodation available was "the bridal suite," a steal at $20. The glass door to my room didn't lock and there was a rather continual floor show, but at some point I must have dozed off. When I awoke the church bells were ringing, the sky was pink, and I felt renewed. No little setback was going to spoil my adventure. I stood and stretched, then walked to a mirror that hung above the sink next to

15

the bed. I leaned forward to punctuate my resolve with a confident look in the eye.

The sink disengaged and fell to the floor. Water gushed. In panic I rummaged through my open suitcase, stuffed two pair of underwear into the pipe to quell the flow, and before the dam broke, I was out the door. I barreled through the lobby of the first bank I passed, asked to see the director, and told the startled man my sad story. For some reason, whether from shock or pity, he hired me at $1.27 an hour to be a crosschecker of foreign currency transactions, and with two phone calls found me lodgings at a commercial school's dormitory.

From eight to five each weekday my duty was to sit in a windowless room with six impeccably dressed people, all of whom were totaling identical additions and subtractions. We were highly dignified with each other, very professional, no *tutoyer*ing. Monsieur Saint presided, but the formidable Mademoiselle was the true power; she oversaw each of our columns and shook her head sadly at my American-shaped numbers.

My legacy from that summer, however, was more than an enduring penchant for crossed sevens. After I had worked for six weeks, M. Saint asked me during a coffee break why I didn't follow the example of other foreign students he had known and depart the office at noon in order to spend the afternoon touring the sights of Paris with the Alliance Française.[1]

"Because," I replied in my halting French, "that costs money. I depend upon my full salary the same as any of you." M. Saint nodded gravely and said no more, but then on the next Friday he presented me with a white envelope along with my check.

"Do not open this until you have left the Société Générale," he said ominously. I thought I was fired for the time I had mixed up krøners and guilders, and, once on the sidewalk, I steeled myself to read the worst. I felt the quiet panic of blankness.

"Dear Sir," I translated the perfectly formed script. "You are a person of value. It is not correct that you should be in our beautiful city and not see it. Therefore we have amassed a modest sum to pay the tuition for a two-week afternoon program for you at the Alliance Française. Your wages will not suffer, for it is your assignment to appear each morning in this bureau and reacquaint us with the places you have visited. We shall see them afresh through your eyes." The letter had thirty signatures, from the director to the janitor, and stuffed inside the envelope was a sheaf of franc notes in various denominations.

I rushed back to the tiny office. M. Saint and Mademoiselle had waited, and accepted my gratitude with their usual controlled smiles and precise handshakes. But they had blown their Gallic cover, and for the next ten days and

[1] A non-profit institution devoted to promoting the French language through cultural and educational programs. [Ed.]

then through all the days until I went home in September, our branch was awash with sightseeing paraphernalia. Everyone had advice, favorite haunts, criticisms of the Alliance's choices or explanations. Paris passed through the bank's granite walls as sweetly as a June breeze through a window screen, and ever afterward the lilt of overheard French, a photograph of Sacré Coeur or the Louvre, even a monthly bank statement, recalls to me that best of all summers.

I didn't wind up in an occupation with any obvious connection to the careers I sampled during my school breaks, but I never altogether abandoned those brief professions either. They were jobs not so much to be held as to be weighed, absorbed, and incorporated, and, collectively, they carried me forward into adult life like overlapping stairs, unfolding a particular pattern at once haphazard and inevitable.   1989

INVESTIGATIONS

1. Recall your first experiences with paid work. What moment or moments most closely correspond to what Dorris calls "one moment of personal, enabling insight" (para. 2)? To what extent did your early work experience provide "foresight of both [an] adult persona and . . . vocation" (para. 3)?

2. Dorris calls school "neutral ground" (para. 6). What does he mean? How is work not "neutral ground"?

3. Note the ways in which Dorris's jobs changed him, how he had to adapt to the demands of the kinds of work he did and to the people with whom he worked. How does the experience you recounted in your response to "Write Before Reading" (p. 518) compare to Dorris's experience? How have the jobs you've held changed you? What has having to adapt to different work situations taught you?

4. What "particular pattern at once haphazard and inevitable" (para. 25) can you discern in the jobs you've held? To what extent have you "weighed, absorbed, and incorporated" (para. 25) those jobs?

ANDRE DUBUS

After the Game

I wasn't in the clubhouse when Joaquin Quintana went crazy. At least I wasn't there for the start of it, because I pitched that night and went nine innings and won, and the color man interviewed me after the game. He is Duke Simpson, and last year he was our first baseman. He came down from the broadcasting booth, and while the guys were going into the clubhouse, and cops and ushers were standing like soldiers in a V from first to third, facing the crowd leaving the park, I stood in front of the dugout with my jacket on, and Duke and I looked at the camera, and he said: "I'm here with Billy Wells."

This was August and we were still in it, four games back, one and a half out of second. It was the time of year when everybody is tired and a lot are hurt and playing anyway. I wanted a shower and a beer, and to go to my apartment for one more beer and then sleep. I sleep very well after I've pitched a good game, not so well after a bad one, and I sleep very badly the night before I pitch, and the day of the game I force myself to eat. It's one of the things that makes the game exciting, but a lot of times, especially in late season, I long for the time when I'll have a job I can predict, can wake up on the ranch knowing what I'm going to do and that I'm not going to fail. I know must jobs are like that, and the people who have them don't look like they've had a rush of adrenaline since the time somebody ran a stop sign and just missed colliding broadside with them, but there's always a trade-off and, on some days in late season, their lives seem worth it. Duke and I talked about pitching, and our catcher Jesse Wade and what a good game he called behind the plate, so later that night I thought it was strange, that Joaquin was going crazy while Duke and I were talking about Jesse, because during the winter the club had traded Manuel Fernandez, a good relief pitcher, to the Yankees for Jesse. Manuel had been Joaquin's roommate, and they always sat together on the plane and the bus, and ate together. Neither one could speak much English. From shortstop, Joaquin used to call to Manuel out on the mound: *Baja y rápido.*[1]

We ended the interview shaking hands and patting each other on the back, then I went between the cops and ushers but there were some fans waiting for autographs at one end of the dugout, so I went over there and signed three

---

[1] Low and fast. [Ed.]

ANDRE DUBUS was born in Lake Charles, Louisiana, in 1936 and has lived for many years in Haverhill, Massachusetts. A Marine Corps veteran and a graduate of the Iowa Writers' Workshop, Dubus is the author of many collections of short fiction, including *Last Worthless Evening* (1986), *Selected Stories* (1988), and *The Cagekeeper and Other Stories* (1990).

baseballs and a dozen scorecards and said thank you twenty or thirty times, and shook it seemed more hands than there were people, then went into the dugout and down the tunnel to the clubhouse. I knew something was wrong, but I wasn't alert to it, wanting a beer, and I was thinking maybe I'd put my arm in ice for a while, so I saw as if out of the corner of my eye, though I was looking right at it, that nobody was at the food table. There was pizza. Then I heard them and looked that way, down between two rows of lockers. They were bunched down there, the ones on the outside standing on benches or on tiptoes on the floor, stretching and looking, and the ones on the inside talking, not to each other but to whoever was in the middle, and I could hear the manager Bobby Drew, and Terry Morgan the trainer. The guys' voices were low, so I couldn't make out the words, and urgent, so I wondered who had been fighting and why now, with things going well for us, and we hadn't had trouble on the club since Duke retired; he was a good ballplayer, but often a pain in the ass. I went to the back of the crowd but couldn't see, so took off my spikes and stepped behind Bruce Green on a bench. Bruce is the only black on the club, and plays right field. I held his waist for balance as I brought my other foot from the floor. I stay in good running shape all year round, and I am overly careful about accidents, like falling off a bench onto my pitching elbow.

I kept my hands on Bruce's waist and looked over his shoulder and there was Joaquin Quintana, our shortstop, standing in front of his locker, naked except for his sweat socks and jockstrap and his gold Catholic medal, breathing through his mouth like he was in the middle of a sentence he didn't finish. He was as black as Bruce, so people who didn't know him took him for a black man, but Manuel told us he was from the Dominican Republic and did not think of himself as a black, and was pissed off when people did; though it seemed to me he was a black from down there, as Bruce was a black from Newark. His left arm was at his side, and his right forearm was out in front of him like he was reaching for something, or to shake hands, and in that hand he held his spikes. It was the right shoe.

Bruce looked at me over his shoulder.

"They can't move him," he said. Bruce was wearing his uniform pants and no shirt. I came to Boston in 1955, as a minor-league player to be named later in a trade with Detroit, when I was in that organization, and I have played all my seven years of major-league ball with the Red Sox; I grew up in San Antonio, so Bruce is the only black I've ever really known. People were talking to Joaquin. Or the people in front were trying to, and others farther back called to him to have some pizza, a beer, a shower, telling him it was all right, everything was all right, telling him settle down, be cool, take it easy, the girls are waiting at the parking lot. Nobody was wet or wrapped in a towel. Some still wore the uniform and some, like Bruce, wore parts of it, and a few had taken off as much as Joaquin. Most of the lockers were open. So was Joaquin's, and he stood staring at Bobby Drew and Terry Morgan, both of them talking, and Bobby doing most of it, being the manager. He was talking softly and

telling Joaquin to give him the shoe and come in his office and lie down on
the couch in there. He kept talking about the shoe, as if it was a weapon,
though Joaquin held it with his hand under it, and not gripped for swinging,
but like he was holding it out to give to someone. But I knew why Bobby
wanted him to put it down. I felt the same: If he would just drop that shoe,
things would get better. Looking at the scuffed toe and the soft dusty leather
and the laces untied and pulled wider across the tongue folded up and over,
and the spikes, silver down at their edges, resting on his palm, I wanted to talk
that shoe out of his hand too, and I started talking with the others below me,
and on the bench across the aisle from me and Bruce, and the benches on the
other side of the group around Joaquin.

That is when I saw what he was staring at, when I told him to come on
and put down that shoe and let's go get some dinner, it was on me, and all the
drinks too, for turning that double play in the seventh; and Bruce said And the
bunt, and Jesse said Perfect fucking bunt, and I saw that Joaquin was not
staring at Bobby or Terry, but at nothing at all, as if he saw something we
couldn't, but it was as clear to him as a picture hanging in the air right in front
of his face.

I lowered myself off the bench and worked my way through the guys, most
of them growing quiet while some still tried to break Joaquin out of it. A few
were saying their favorite curse, to themselves, shaking their heads or looking
at the floor. Everyone I touched was standing tense and solid, but they were
easy to part from each other, like pushing aside branches that smelled of sweat.
I stepped between Bobby and Terry. They were still dressed, Bobby in his
uniform and cap, Terry in his red slacks and white tee shirt.

"Quintana," I said. "Joaquin: It's me, old buddy. It's Billy."

I stared into his eyes but they were not looking back at me; they were   10
looking at something, and they chilled the backs of my knees. I had to stop
my hands from going up and feeling the air between us, grabbing for it, pushing
it away.

There is something about being naked. Duke Simpson and Tommy Lutring
got in a fight last year, in front of Duke's locker, when they had just got out
of the shower, and it was not like seeing a fight on the field when the guys are
dressed and rolling in the dirt. It seemed worse. Once in a hotel in Chicago a
girl and I started fighting in bed and quick enough we were out of bed and
putting on our underpants; the madder we got the more clothes we put on,
and when she ended the fight by walking out, I was wearing everything but
my socks and shoes. I wished Joaquin was dressed.

"Joaquin," I said. "Joaquin, I'm going to take the shoe."

Some of the guys told him to give Billy the shoe. I put my hand on it and
he didn't move; then I tried to lift it, and his arm swung a few degrees, but
that was all. His bicep was swollen and showing veins.

"Come on, Joaquin. Let it go now. That's a boy."

I put my other hand on it and jerked, and his arm swung and his body   15
swayed and my hands slipped off the shoe. He was staring. I looked at Bobby

and Terry, then at the guys on both sides; my eyes met Bruce's, so I said to
him: "He doesn't even know I'm here."

"Poor bastard," Bobby said.

Somebody said we ought to carry him to Bobby's couch, and Terry said
we couldn't because he was stiff as iron, and lightly, with his fingertips, he
jabbed Joaquin's thighs and belly and arms and shoulders, and put his palms
on Joaquin's cheeks. Terry said we had to wait for Doc Segura, and Bobby
told old Will Hammersley, the clubhouse man, to go tell the press he was sorry
but they couldn't come in tonight.

Then we stood waiting. I smelled Joaquin's sweat and listened to his
breathing, and looked up and down his good body, and at the medal hanging
from his neck, and past his eyes, into his locker: the shaving kit and underwear
and socks on the top shelf, with his wallet and gold-banded wristwatch and
box of cigars. A couple of his silk shirts hung in the locker, one aqua and one
maroon, and a sport coat that was pale yellow, near the color of cream; under
it some black pants were folded over the hanger. I wondered what it was like
being him all the time. I don't know where the Dominican Republic is. I know
it's in the Caribbean, but not where. Over the voices around me, Tommy
Lutring said: "Why the *fuck* did we trade Manuel?" Then he said: "Sorry,
Jesse."

"I wish he was here," Jesse said.

The guys near Jesse patted him on the shoulders and back. Lutring is the   20
second baseman and he loves working with Joaquin. They are something to
see, and I like watching them take infield practice. In a game it happens very
fast, and you feel the excitement in the moments it takes Joaquin and Tommy
to turn a double play, and before you can absorb it, the pitcher's ready to
throw again. In practice you get to anticipate, and watch them poised for the
ground ball, then they're moving, one to the bag, one to the ball, and they
always know where the other guy is and where his glove is too, because
whoever's taking the throw knows it's coming at his chest, leading him across
the bag. It's like the movies I used to watch in San Antonio, with one of those
dances that start with a chorus of pretty girls, then they move back for the
man and woman: He is in a tuxedo and she wears a long white dress that rises
from her legs when she whirls. The lights go down on the chorus, and one
light moves with the man and woman dancing together and apart but always
together. Light sparkles on her dress, and their shadows dance on the polished
floor. I was a kid sitting in the dark, and I wanted to dance like that, and felt
if I could just step into the music like into a river, the drums and horns would
take me, and I would know how to move.

That is why Tommy said what he did. And Jesse said he wished Manuel
was here too, which he probably did but not really, not at the price of him
being back with the Yankees where he was the back-up catcher, while here he
is the regular and also has our short left field wall to pull for. Because we
couldn't do anything and we started to feel like Spanish was the answer, or the
problem, and if just somebody could speak it to Joaquin he'd be all right and

he'd put down that shoe and use his eyes again, and take off his jockstrap and socks, and head for the showers, so if only Manuel was with us or one of us had learned Spanish in school.

But the truth is the president or dictator of the Dominican Republic couldn't have talked Joaquin into the showers. Doc Segura gave him three shots before his muscles went limp and he dropped the shoe and collapsed like pants you step out of. We caught him before he hit the floor. The two guys with the ambulance got there after the first shot, and stood on either side of him, behind him so they were out of Doc's way; around the end, before the last shot, they held Joaquin's arms, and when he fell Bobby and I grabbed him too. His eyes were closed. We put him on the stretcher and they covered him up and carried him out and we haven't seen him since, though we get reports on how he's doing in the hospital. He sleeps and they feed him. That was three weeks ago.

Doc Segura had to wait thirty minutes between shots, so the smokers had their cigarettes and cigars going, and guys were passing beers and pizza up from the back, where I had stood with Bruce. He was still on the bench, drinking a beer, with smoke rising past him to the ceiling. I didn't feel right, drinking a beer in front of Joaquin, and I don't think Bobby did either. Terry is an alcoholic who doesn't drink anymore and goes to meetings, so he didn't count. Finally when someone held a can toward Bobby he didn't shake his head, but got it to his mouth fast while he watched Doc getting the second needle ready, so I reached for one too. Doc swabbed the vein inside Joaquin's left elbow. This time I looked at Joaquin's eyes instead of the needle: He didn't feel it. All my sweat was long since dried, and I had my jacket off except the right sleeve on my arm.

I know Manuel couldn't have helped Joaquin. The guys keep saying it was because he was lonesome. But I think they say that because Joaquin was black and spoke Spanish. And maybe for the same reason an alcoholic who doesn't drink anymore may blame other people's troubles on booze: He's got scary memories of blackouts and sick hangovers and D.T.'s, and he always knows he's just a barstool away from it. I lost a wife in my first year in professional ball, when I was eighteen years old and as dumb about women as I am now. Her name was Leslie. She left me for a married dentist, a guy with kids, in Lafayette, Louisiana, where I was playing my rookie year in the Evangeline League, an old class C league that isn't there anymore. She is back in San Antonio, married to the manager of a department store; she has four kids, and I hardly ever see her, but when I do there are no hard feelings. Leslie said she felt like she was chasing the team bus all season long, down there in Louisiana. I have had girlfriends since, but not the kind you marry.

By the time Joaquin fell I'd had a few beers and some pizza gone cold, and I was very tired. It was after one in the morning and I did not feel like I had pitched a game, and won it too. I felt like I had been working all day on the beef-cattle ranch my daddy is building up for us with the money I send him every payday. That's where I'm going when my arm gives out. He has

25

built a house on it, and I'll live there with him and my mom. In the showers people were quiet. They talked, but you know what I mean. I dressed then told Hammersley I wanted to go into the park for a minute. He said Sure, Billy, and opened the door.

I went up the tunnel to the dugout and stepped onto the grass. It was already damp. I had never seen the park empty at night, and with no lights, and all those empty seats and shadows under the roof over the grandstand, and under the sky the dark seats out in the bleachers in right and center field. Boston lit the sky over the screen in left and beyond the bleachers, but it was a dull light, and above the playing field there was no light at all, so I could see stars. For a long time, until I figured everybody was dressed and gone or leaving and Hammersley was waiting to lock up, I stood on the grass by the batting circle and looked up at the stars, thinking of drums and cymbals and horns, and a man and woman dancing.   1988

INVESTIGATIONS

1. Write a dialogue between you and Billy Wells in which you begin by saying, "Look, Billy, you're whistling in the dark. There's no such thing as 'a job I can predict,' a time when I 'can wake up on the ranch knowing what I'm going to do and that I'm not going to fail' " (para. 2).
2. Why do the players feel that if Joaquin Quintana "would just drop that shoe, things would get better" (para. 6)?
3. Describe the part of any of the jobs you've done that most resembles Billy's description in paragraph 20 of Joaquin and Tommy Lutring turning the double play. How much of the pleasure of doing what you did came from "knowing where the other guy" was and what he'd do? What is the price of such dancelike precision?
4. How does their work continue to affect the players after the game? How do these effects compare to those you've experienced after your day's work is done?

My Father Worked Late

Some nights we were still awake
my brother and I, our faces smearing the window
watching the headlights bounce up the driveway
like wild pitches of light
thrown by a tired moon.   5
We breathed in the huge silence
after the engine died
then ran to the door, grabbing his legs
as if we could hold him there
through night, morning, forever.   10

Some nights when he wasn't too tired
he took off his shirt
and sat in the middle of the floor.
We wrestled, trying to pin
back his arms, sitting on his chest   15
digging our heads into the yellow stains
under the arms of his T-shirt.
Each time we thought we had him
Do you give, huh, do you give?
he sat up, cradling us both in headlocks   20
in the closest thing to an embrace
that I remember, and carried us to bed.

Other nights he looked right through us
mechanically eating his late dinner
yelling at anything that moved.   25
Some mornings we woke to find him
asleep on the couch, his foreman's tie twisted
into words we couldn't spell.
We ate our cereal as carefully as communion
until our mother shook him ready for another day.   30
My father carries no wallet full of lost years
carries no stubs, no guarantees, no promises.

JIM DANIELS (b. 1956) tries "to give a voice to those who are often shut out of poetry, to explore
their lives both in and out of the workplace." Author of *Places/Everyone* (1985) and *Punching Out*
(1990), Daniels teaches at Carnegie Mellon University.

We could drive toward each other all night
and never cross the distance of those missing years.

Today, home for a visit,   35
I pull in front of the house.
My father walks down the steps
limping from his stroke
he is coming toward me
both of us pinned to the wind   40
he is looking at me as if to say
give, give, I give,
as if either of us
had anything left to give.   1985

INVESTIGATIONS

1. Compare the weariness of the speaker's father to that of Billy Wells ("After the Game"). How similar are the effects of their work on their loved ones? On themselves?
2. Reread paragraph 25 of Michael Dorris's "Life Stories." To what extent has the speaker in "My Father Worked Late" "weighed, absorbed, and incorporated" the lessons of his father's work?
3. In line 19, the speaker and his brother ask their father, "*Do you give, huh, do you give?*" Describe the meanings that this question accumulates by poem's end.
4. Reflect on the work your parents have done. In what ways can you "never cross the distance" of the "missing years" (line 34) their work has taken?

TRUDY PAX FARR

Steelworker

My first day. The BOP (Basic Oxygen Process) Shop towers some six or seven stories. Everywhere there is equipment of gigantic proportions. Ladles, cranes, transfer cars. We workers are dwarfed beside them. Forklift trucks and bulldozers run around like beetles.

I stand mesmerized when the huge furnace tips and slowly pours out its liquid fire — what other name can I give that brilliant soup? "Don't look at it," another worker says, "you need these," and he gives me some small blue-lensed glasses that I can clip on my safety glasses and flip up or down as I need. As the steel flows from the tap hole of the furnace into the waiting ladle, a sunset glow sweeps over everything and, for a brief moment, there is color in this drab, relentlessly gray building.

Many feet above — I can barely make out the operator in the cab — runs the crane, its runway spanning the width of the building. It comes now, and with much creaking and straining, laboriously lifts the filled ladle. When it does, some steel sloshes over and a glowing puddle sits on the ground after the crane glides away.

I become a burner. I don a stiff metallic-like coat and leggings, strap leather gaiters over shoes. A welder-type shield over my face, leather one-fingered mitts for my hands. All to protect me from the "sparks" (in fact, small droplets of hot steel) that shower down when oxygen, flame, and air meet molten steel. Still, those sparks find their way down my shirt front, into my gloves. At first, I stop to inspect each small burn, but before long I do as the seasoned burners do: simply shake the spark out of my glove the best I can, hold my shirt away from my body and let it tumble down, and continue at the job. Under all that fireproof clothing, my T-shirt and bra are filled with small burn holes. My hands are pock-marked.

Steel: durable, impregnable, indestructible. I cut through it like butter. At a touch, the flame of my torch turns that sturdy mass of steel into flowing liquid. What power!

Sometimes I cut scrap — old rods from the stoppers that close the opening on the ladles. Sometimes I help prepare molds for the next batch of steel — I cut off the steel that has spilled over the edges and has hardened there. Sometimes I'm called to the ladle liners — steel has worked its way in between the

5

TRUDY PAX FARR grew up on a farm in Celina, Ohio, and lived in Chicago for many years before moving recently to rural Minnesota. Besides working in a steel mill, Farr has worked as an English as a Second Language teacher and as a writer. Her essays have appeared in *Tradeswomen*, *Hard-Hatted Women* (1988), and elsewhere.

bricks of the ladle lining and now they need to get those "frozen bricks" out. (This is tricky: Cut the spilled steel, but not the ladle that it's attached to.) Sometimes I work the mixers (large heated drums that hold the molten iron until the furnaces are ready for it) — then it's iron, not steel, that we cut away. It has sloshed around the opening, building up layer after layer until we need to clean away big chunks. Sometimes there are spills on the railroad tracks — a mold full of molten steel has toppled and the hardened metal has to be cleared. All these jobs are small and are done with a hand-held torch.

But more often than not, I work in the "strawberry patch." What a colorful name for yet another ugly spot: an area just outside the BOP Shop where they dump the leftovers from ladles — big bowl-shaped chunks of steel and sediment that must be cut in half before a crane can lift them. Then I work with an unwieldy fifteen-foot rod that can reach far into the crevice I create as I burn. Out of that crevice comes a waterfall of fantastic colors. Through my blue-tinted glasses (now I use those glasses my fellow worker gave me on that first day), I watch it flow like candle wax: red, bright orange, magenta — snaking out, layer upon layer, each quickly fading to a paler shade. A thing of beauty. The only beauty in this gray and dusty place.

One day I meet a photographer — he's come to make an ad for Ford. It will show a spanking-new car springing effortlessly and ready-made from the molten steel. He is surprised to find women working in the mill and asks about burning. I proudly explain the process. Then, "Tell me," he says, "how do you breathe in here?" How indeed? I develop a chronic cough.

Little by little, I begin to feel like a real part of the mill crew. I know I have made it when I begin breaking in new workers. Occasionally the new worker is a woman. On those days, the mill seems different: less austere, more hospitable. We relax, work smoothly; we have to answer to no one, have nothing to prove.

I try to befriend some of the old-time women — those left from the days   10 of World War II when women did so many of the mill jobs: welders, track gang, crane operators, observers. I am fascinated with their life stories: how they came to the mill during the war; how they managed to stay on after everyone told them that their patriotic duty of taking a job in the mill was over, that their patriotic duty *now* was to go home and be a full-time wife. But, for the most part, they seem to resent us newcomers. They complain because we have it easier than they did, because we don't work hard enough, because we demand too much. And sometimes because too many of us are black.

We — all of us in the mill — work around the clock. There are no weekends, no holidays. Steelmaking, they tell us, can take no rest. We come and go — at eight, at four, at midnight. We meet briefly, passing the baton, so to speak, of our particular job. If no relief shows up, we stay for an extra turn (shift).

For single mothers with small children, the schedule is pure hell. Some might call it irony; I call it injustice: Single mothers who so desperately need these relatively well-paying jobs have to face impossible conditions. And no exceptions can be made. (Although I've seen a man get a "special schedule" to accommodate his working wife.)

Each week, people cluster around the bulletin board to decipher their schedule for the coming week. Some read it and are silent: pleased or perhaps resigned. Others object. "Sunday, first turn! No way! Let me talk to that scheduler!" And off they stomp to Nurven's office — a small shanty next to the general foreman's. More often than not they soon come back, sit glumly and silently in the shanty. Nurven is not easily persuaded.

Accidents happen everywhere in the mill. But none so gruesome as those in the BOP Shop. I am on the midnight turn when the first fatality happens. I am working in another area, but hear the voice on the intercom. I don't suspect death — the voice is urgent, but not panicky: "Get a foreman down here. We have a problem." In the morning, I learn it was amiable, deliberate, soft-spoken Slow Joe, his forklift truck tipped over by a railroad transfer car. Not long after, there is the remote-control train operator, squashed by the very cars he is manipulating. Then the millwright caught in the huge cables of the crane he was working on. Another millwright crushed when the equipment he is repairing collapses on him. A man burned to death by steel that spills over the edge of the ladle. Each death wrenches me, twists my heart for days. But despite it all, I feel immune. Confident no such thing will happen to me.

Confident, until it happens to a burner. 15

They tell me about it when I come into the mill for my afternoon turn. A freak accident, they say. He was working on a strawberry, cutting it in half as usual, when the molten steel that had gathered in the crevice "backfired" and spewed out on him. He has third degree burns on most of his body. He is still alive, they say, but barely. Better to die, they say.

I go to the spot where it happened. I stand looking at the half-finished strawberry — a strawberry like any of the dozens I had worked on. I nudge a piece of something on the ground with my metal-tipped shoe. It is a portion of the burner's safety glasses, melted and contorted. And I think: The only reason I'm standing here and not lying in a burn unit somewhere in the city is a question of schedule. I decide I no longer want to be a burner.

I put aside the tools of the burner: torch and striker, rods and hoses. I put aside my fireproof clothing. I take up a trowel and hammer; I become a ladle liner.

The ladle liners' job: Build a floor and wall of firebrick inside the ladle, to keep the molten steel from burning right through the ladle. I heft the eighty-pound bags of cement, mixing it in big drums to make the "soup" that will seal the bricks together. I climb down into the huge container, big enough to hold two hundred tons of molten steel. I slap the bricks in place — clack, clack, clack — one layer, two layers. A wall to hold in all that heat and fire. Like a mason, I tap the brick with my hammer to make it break just so, the exact place, the exact size I need to fit this space, to snug this row.

Some of the ladles come to us direct from the teeming aisle, still hot from 20 the recently poured steel. A pleasant thing on a cold night; not so in the summer.

Steelmaking — that's the heart of it. But the process, despite all our technological know-how, is still a surprisingly seat-of-the-pants operation. The final product is always iffy, and the furnace men are always nervous, often frantic. We try to have as little as possible to do with them, but all our work revolves around them. The ladles we line will carry the steel they create, poured fresh and boiling hot from the furnaces.

A good day — things are perking along. One after another, the torpedo-shaped railroad cars come rolling in, bringing iron from the blast furnace. Iron, scrap, a few bags of this and that dumped into the furnaces. Then what wild rushing sounds: flame and fire, roar and grumble. Steel is being made. Frenzy everywhere. Prepare the molds. Are there enough? On what track shall they be put? Send for the crane: Take this ladle here, bring one from there. Workers pull on their metallic-like coats, ready to approach the heat and fire. On the platform, the steel pourers crook their arms over their faces, a futile attempt to shield themselves from the heat, the glare. They move in quickly, manipulate the flow, take a sample, and move away. Mold after mold is filled with the molten steel.

But not always — things do not always perk. Some fuck-up somewhere: no iron from the blast furnace; a torpedo car "frozen," the iron crusted and unpourable; a furnace down. No steel is made for hours.

Then there is time to sit. We gather in the shanty. (A name that reveals historical origins. Now it is no more than a room to the side of the foreman's office.) We talk about many things. (How Americans never live to be a hundred. "Speak for yourself!" says Love, indignant.) About the general foreman. (How he gives you days off, at the drop of a hat. "He don't know no number smaller than three," says Medicine Man.) Stories of the mill, perhaps already told too often, but part of our culture. There's always one newcomer who has not yet heard them. (How Beefco's dentures fell down through the opening in the ladle he was working on, landed in a bucket of mud and slush in front of Casper, who went running to the office, pale as the ghost for whom he is named. How Beefco went to retrieve them, wiped them on his pants, put them back in his mouth . . . How they tied Potato's shoes together while he slept . . . How Richie the foreman got fired for stealing . . . How. . . .)

On those slow days, there's time for a leisurely lunch. We put packets of tacos, jars of soup, and foil-wrapped ears of corn on the salamanders, and stand around those drums of burning coke while the food heats. Once there was even a whole fish, wrapped and cooked, then spread open for everyone to feast on.

In summer, the heat is unbearable: In addition to nature's heat, we have the steelmaking heat and our heavy protective clothing. Everyone has their theory on how to combat it. Ice cubes in drinks, under hard hats, down shirts. The ice machine they installed in the shanty works overtime. But College Joe make pot after pot of strong coffee on his little hot plate. "The hotter it gets," he insists, "the more coffee you hafta drink."

Seasons come and go in the mill. As far as I know, they will go on forever.

But one day, when the new schedule appears on the board, my name is on

25

a separate list — the one entitled "furlough." I don't mind. This has happened before, and it is a welcome break. A chance to forget about shift work, a chance to live a normal life for a week or two. There are rumors that this layoff is bigger, farther-reaching, but I dismiss those rumors. I have just invested in a pair of new metatarsal shoes — I am sure I will be using them for a long time. I walk to the locker room in my new shoes, put them and the rest of my work clothes in my locker, walk out the gate, and never set foot there again. The big layoff has hit.

Reporters begin trekking to this far southeast corner of Chicago — an area foreign to most of them. Nothing of consequence happens here. But now! Thousands laid off in one fell swoop. Mills closing with hardly a day's notice.

But what have they come to investigate? They nod listlessly, pencils sus- 30 pended over their notebooks when we talk of women's hopes dashed, or returning to humdrum low-paying jobs. A Santa-less Christmas — that is what they want to hear. A starving child, foreclosures, suicides — these are the stories they drool over. And there *are* those stories. When one surfaces, they perk up, smile. They begin scribbling in their notebooks.

Despite all the attention, we feel invisible to the nonsteelworker world. For some time, among ourselves, we keep our identity: We continue to meet at the union hall; government cheese, milk, and honey are distributed; a job training program is started. But there is not much hope. Other mills — and other industries, too — are closing. Even workers with training — machinists, plumbers, welders, electricians — find it hard to get a job. Workers are being shepherded through a funnel into the shrinking job pool. A few make it through. Most are left to flounder. There is a feeling of life having come to a halt; a feeling of depression: What will become of us, our community? A feeling of betrayal: So many loyal years given to the mill; now the company turns its back.

Little by little, our ties weaken, and we scatter.

What has happened to that small group of women who once called them-selves steelworkers? I have lost track of all but a handful.

Some sought jobs similar to the mill — construction, apprenticeships. A few succeeded; most didn't. Some went back to previous jobs. Jobs that, when you came right down to it, they preferred all along. Jobs that pay less, but are less dirty, less dangerous, and, most importantly, have a decent work schedule — a schedule more compatible with raising kids. Some (like me) went back to school, seeking security and stability in nursing, computing, word pro-cessing, teaching. A few fled the Rust Belt, along with the industries, looking for the much-touted jobs in the Sunbelt. I don't know what happened to them.

Sometimes, when I go past that deserted parking lot, now overgrown with 35 weeds, the fences battered and falling, and I see the BOP Shop looming there just beyond, I recall the days at the mill. Then a part of me sighs with relief — the part of me that hated the midnight turns, the dirt, the danger, the harassment, the chaotic life. But another part of me is rather nostalgic — the part that felt the satisfaction of overcoming trepidation, that liked being a part of something BIG. The part of me that enjoyed so much the banter, the camaraderie, the oneness of the mill life. And if today, I were offered a chance to do it all over again, I'm not at all sure what my answer would be.   1988

INVESTIGATIONS

1. Write three or four paragraphs about the job you currently hold (or the one you held most recently) in the "language" of that job. In other words, imitate Farr's descriptive explanations of the tools of the steelworker's trade. What sort of power do (or did) the tools of your trade provide? What sort of power does the "language" of the job provide? To what extent does that language give a "colorful name" to each "ugly spot" of the job (para. 7)?

2. Why does Farr "feel immune" to the danger posed by her work (para. 14)? Why does she lose that immunity when another burner has a serious accident? What about the accidents Farr recounts isn't accidental?

3. What stories do you and your coworkers tell one another? In what ways are these stories similar to those Farr recounts in paragraph 24? What purpose does telling such stories serve for those who work together?

4. In the final paragraph, Farr describes feeling both hatred and nostalgia when she remembers working in the mill. In what ways might this particular mix of feelings be common to any job of this kind? To what extent has it been true in your experience?

PHILIP LEVINE

Buying and Selling

All the way across the Bay Bridge I sang
to the cool winds buffeting my Ford,
for I was on my way to a life of buying
untouched drive shafts, universal joints,
perfect bearings so steeped in Cosmoline   5
they could endure a century and still retain

Born in Detroit in 1928, PHILIP LEVINE tries "to pay homage to the people who taught me my life was a holy thing." Winner of National Endowment for the Arts and Guggenheim fellowships, Levine has published many books of poetry including *A Walk with Tom Jefferson* (1988) and *What Work Is* (1991).

their purity of functional design, they
could outlast everything until like us
their usefulness became legend and they
were transformed into sculpture. At Benicia   10
or the Oakland Naval Yard or Alameda
I left the brilliant Western sun behind
to enter the wilderness of warehouses
with one sullen enlisted man as guide.
There under the blinking artificial light   15
I was allowed to unwrap a single sample,
to hack or saw my way with delicacy
through layer after layer of cardboard,
metallic paper, cloth webbing, wax
as hard as wood until the dulled steel   20
was revealed beneath. I read, if I could,
the maker's name, letters, numbers,
all of which translated into functions
and values known only to the old moguls
of the great international junk companies   25
of Chicago, Philadelphia, Brooklyn,
whose young emissary I was. I, who at
twenty had wept publicly in the Dexter-
Davison branch of the public library
over the death of Keats in the Colvin   30
biography and had prayed like him
to be among the immortals, now lived
at thirty by a code of figures so arcane
they passed from one side of the brain
to the other only in darkness. I, who   35
at twenty-six had abandoned several careers
in salesmanship — copper kitchenware,
Fuller brushes, American encyclopedias —
from door to unanswered door in the down
and out neighborhoods of Detroit, turning   40
in my sample cases like a general handing
over his side arms and swagger stick, I
now relayed the new gospels across mountains
and the Great Plains states to my waiting masters.
The news came back: Bid! And we did   45
and did so in secret. The bids were
awarded, so trucks were dispatched,
Mohawks, Tam O'Shanters, Iroquois.
In new Wellingtons, I stood to one side
while the fork lifts did their work,   50
entering only at the final moment to pay

both loaders and drivers their pittances
not to steal, to buy at last what could
not be bought. The day was closing down.
Even in California the afternoon skies   55
must turn from blue to a darker blue
and finally take the color of coal, and stars
— the same or similar ones — hidden so long
above the Chicago River or the IRT
to Brooklyn, emerge stubbornly not in ones   60
but in pairs, for there is safety in numbers.
Silent, alone, I would stand in the truck's
gray wake feeling something had passed,
was over, complete. The great metal doors
of the loading dock crashed down, and in   65
the sudden aftermath I inhaled a sadness
stronger than my Lucky Strike, stronger
than the sadness of these hills and valleys
with their secret ponds and streams unknown
even to children, or the sadness of children   70
themselves, who having been abandoned believe
their parents will return before dark.   1980

INVESTIGATIONS

1. What similarities do you find between the speaker's description of the tools of his trade and Trudy Pax Farr's description of hers in "Steelworker"? How about Garfinkle's description of his tools in *Other People's Money* (p. 541)? How might a lawyer describe the tools of her trade? How about a doctor, a teacher, a writer? What do you see as the essential distinctions between how individuals with these jobs see their work and how a salesman or a steelworker sees his or her work?

2. In line 43, the speaker calls the information he sends his superiors "the new gospels." What does he mean? How are the "gospels" the speaker sends connected to the "pittances" he gives "both loaders and drivers . . . / not to steal, to buy at last what could / not be bought" (lines 52–54)? What other details in the poem might be considered biblical?

3. Why does the speaker feel such sadness at the end of the poem?

JERRY STERNER

Other People's Money

Characters

WILLIAM COLES, mid-forties. Attractive, polished, president of New England Wire and Cable.

ANDREW JORGENSON, chairman of New England Wire and Cable, sixty-eight years of age.

BEA SULLIVAN, longtime assistant and friend of Jorgenson. An attractive woman in her early sixties.

LAWRENCE GARFINKLE, an obese, elegant, cunning New York "takeover artist." About forty. Hails from the Bronx and speaks in a "New York" accent.

KATE SULLIVAN, Bea's daughter. An attractive, sexy, Wall Street attorney, about thirty-five.

Time and Place
The present. New York and Rhode Island.

ACT ONE

(*We hear two long bursts of a factory whistle followed by some fifteen seconds or so of music with a driving tempo incorporating sounds of an industrial plant during the working day. Music stops suddenly. Bill Coles is center stage with a spotlight on him. All else is dark.*)

COLES: It's been said that you have to be a storyteller to tell a story. It's also been said that businessmen aren't good storytellers . . . not that we don't have a story to tell . . . we do. We tell it in numbers: you know, sales, earnings, dividends. We also express it in ratios: net worth to long-term debt, long-term debt to working capital. And we tell it every year. Have you ever read an annual report? . . . We're not good storytellers. Which is too bad. For there's an important story that needs to be told. It goes way beyond numbers. It's about loyalty, tradition, friendship, and of course, money. Lots of money. It's one heck of a story. And if it hasn't already affected your life, it will. It affected mine. It only started a few years back.

Formerly president of a large real estate company, JERRY STERNER once said, "I think money is the single most revealing thing about a person. When somebody looks at a dollar bill, you can see their reflection." Sterner lives in Brooklyn, New York, where he works as a full-time playwright.

We were all naive then. But, you know something? I knew. I knew as soon as the old man told me about our expected visitor.

(Lights up on Andrew Jorgenson's office upstage right. He is seated behind his modest desk. Two steps down is the New England Wire and Cable conference room, which extends all the way stage right. It is dominated by a large table. Unseen at this time is Garfinkle's office downstage right. It has a desk and chair, a chair for a visitor, and a separate table with a stock-quote machine. Along the perimeter of the stage, U-shaped, is the area Garfinkle roams. Jorgenson is a "hand's on" type, more comfortable with his sleeves rolled up tinkering with a machine than sitting in a boardroom.)

JORGENSON: Why are you so nervous? Stop acting like an expectant father.

COLES *(entering from center stage)*: I heard that name before.

JORGENSON: So what?

COLES: Why would he come all the way from New York? We've never had anyone from New York before.

JORGENSON: Sure we have. Had someone directly from Wall Street a couple of years back.

COLES: I've been here twelve years. I've never seen anyone south of Connecticut.

JORGENSON: . . . Twelve years? Has it been that long? . . . The guy was sitting right there — all stiff and proper taking notes on a clipboard. Some kind of analyst. Wouldn't get close to any of the walls. Scared of a little dust. Three-piece suit, pointy shoes, tie up to here. He starts asking me all kinds of questions and I noticed he wasn't looking at me, looking at the wall back there. I turn around and wouldn't you know — meanest-looking spider was halfway up the ceiling. You know what he says? Bill, you listening? He says, "Could you please get someone to dispose of it?" Not kill it, mind you — dispose of it. I told him since he was the one with the pointy shoes the job was his. *(Laughs at the memory.)* Didn't ask another question. Got up and left. Didn't even say good-bye.

COLES: Be careful what you say to him.

JORGENSON: Don't worry about me. Better check for spiders. *(Rises, puts arm around Coles's shoulder.)* C'mon. C'mon. I was joking. I've never seen you this way.

COLES: Let me do the talking.

JORGENSON: You do the talking. I'll do the listening. "Nu Yawkas" are fun to listen to . . . Where the hell was that guy from? . . . Aha — Barney Smith.

COLES: Smith, Barney.

JORGENSON: Smith, Barney. Figures. Wall Street generally does things ass backwards.

COLES: Have you looked at our stock lately?

JORGENSON: I already got a call from Ozzie at the bank. Happier than a pig in shit. Told me it's up a couple of points. He owns fifteen thousand shares, you know. Has for years. I remember the day he bought. Same day I was

made president. I was really scared. He called. Told me he was buying the
stock to show his confidence in me. Told me he wouldn't sell till I retired.
The man kept his word for . . . thirty-eight years now.

COLES: More shares traded in the last month than did all last year.

JORGENSON: Bill, what's wrong with you? The stock is going up. Worry when
the stock goes down.

(*Bea enters hurriedly. She's excited. Bea is an attractive woman in her
early sixties.*)

BEA: Come. Look. Look! (*She ushers them quickly to an imaginary window
downstage.*) Is that something, Jorgy?

JORGENSON: That's a goddamned big car.

COLES: It's a stretch limo.

BEA (*to Jorgenson*): You see — manners. The chauffeur gets out first, walks all
the way around . . . opens the door. You could learn from that, Jorgy.

JORGENSON: Goddamned big car.

(*Lights up on Garfinkle, cross stage. He is an immense man of forty,
though he looks older. He is always elegantly dressed, surprisingly
graceful for his bulk. He is in some way, larger than life. His deep,
rich voice fills the stage. He speaks in a New York rhythm. He looks
about.*)

GARFINKLE: Haven't seen a place this shitty since I left the Bronx.

BEA (*moving to Garfinkle, her hand extended*): Welcome. You must be Lawrence Garfinkle. I'm Bea Sullivan, Mr. Jorgenson's assistant. He's expecting
you. (*She shakes his hand. They begin walking to Jorgenson's office.*)
Would you like to invite your chauffeur in? We have a small reception
area where he could wait — keep warm.

GARFINKLE: He's a "yard" chauffeur. Bring him inside and you'll spoil him.

BEA: . . . Right this way please. (*They enter office.*) This is Mr. Jorgenson, our
chairman. Mr. Coles, our president. Mr. Garfinkle.

JORGENSON: Call me Jorgy. Everyone else does. (*Moves from his desk. They
shake.*) Welcome to New England Wire and Cable.

COLES: How do you do, Mr. Garfinkle?

GARFINKLE: I do good. Mind if I have a seat? I do even better when I sit.

JORGENSON (*laughs*): I know what you mean. (*Garfinkle dusts off chair in
conference room with a handkerchief.*) Uh-oh, Bill . . . Better check for
spiders. (*Moving to Garfinkle.*) Wire and Cable is man's work. Gotta
expect a little grime.

BEA: May I get you some coffee?

GARFINKLE: Is there a Dunkin' Donuts in this town?

BEA: Dunkin' Donuts? . . .

JORGENSON: Never saw one.

GARFINKLE: Krispy Kremes? . . . Something?

JORGENSON: There's Sam's on Beaver. Doesn't he make donuts?

BEA: I believe he does. He'd be your best bet. Just make a left when you leave the plant. Beaver is your second —

GARFINKLE (*taking a large roll of cash from his pocket and handing Bea several bills*): Why don't you be a sweetheart and take a ride with Arthur and pick up a couple of dozen. Bring one here and leave one in the car for the trip back.

BEA: . . . They might not have much of a selection. Which kind do you like?

GARFINKLE: I like them all. (*Smiling for the first time.*) Can't you tell? (*Bea exits.*)

JORGENSON: Have a nice ride, Bea. You watch, she's going to take him the long way to Beaver. What'd you say your first name was?

GARFINKLE: Lawrence.

JORGENSON: Larry, you made her day. Last limo we saw up here was in '48 when Harry Truman was running for president. Came right here to the plant. Come, I'll show you. (*Takes him to imaginary window downstage.*) Stood right out there. Right there. Gave a speech. Just after the war. It was the golden age, rebuilding America and all. Had thirty-five hundred men working right here. Right at this plant. Going twenty-four hours a day, seven days a week. Truman gave a fine talk. Very impressive. Only Democrat I ever voted for.

COLES: What can we do for you, Mr. Garfinkle? What brings a busy man like you up this way?

GARFINKLE: Harry Truman stories don't grab you, huh?

COLES: We're all busy.

GARFINKLE: You're right. Let's do business. I got a computer back in New York. Call her Carmen. Every morning when I wake up — before I even brush my teeth, I punch out "Carmen computer on the wall, who's the fairest of them all?" You'll forgive me — my programmer isn't Shakespeare.

COLES: Go on.

GARFINKLE: Most mornings she spits out "You are, Garfinkle, you're the fairest of them all." But once in a while, maybe two, three times a year she says something else. Six weeks ago she said: "Garfinkle, Garfinkle, scratch your balls, New England Wire and Cable is the fairest of them all." (*Jorgenson laughs.*) I thought it was funny too. "Wire and Cable — gross me out." I yell back to Carmen. And I do it again. "Carmen computer on the wall, who's the fairest of them all?" She responds, "Don't be a schmuck, Garfinkle — do the numbers!"

COLES: I'm interested. Do the numbers.

GARFINKLE: Get a paper and pencil. Carmen will educate you. (*Coles takes a pad and pencil from Jorgenson's desk.*) The Wire and Cable business is a little soft. Has been for the last ten years. What's it worth?

JORGENSON: This would not be a good time to —

GARFINKLE: I know. I'm not blaming you. You've done a hell of a job. You've kept it alive. That's an accomplishment. Carmen agrees. I'll bet she thinks it's worth more than you do. She says you got equipment up here that cost one hundred twenty million. Worth, even at salvage, thirty to thirty-five million. Write down thirty million. How many acres you got here?

COLES: One hundred ten.

GARFINKLE: What's that worth?

JORGENSON: It would depend on what it's used for.

GARFINKLE: Worst-case basis. Grazing land. Ten million fair? (*Coles nods.*) Good. Write down ten. Put it underneath the thirty.

JORGENSON: We have other businesses, you know. Bill here has diversified us a good deal. He's done a hell of a job, despite my kicking and screaming.

COLES: What does Carmen think the rest of the company is worth, Mr. Garfinkle?

GARFINKLE: Let's see . . . What do you got? Plumbing supplies, electrical distribution, adhesives . . . boring. Nothing my friends on the street would get excited about. But dependable. Decent cash flow.

JORGENSON: With our cumulative losses at Wire and Cable we keep all the earnings from our other businesses. We haven't paid federal taxes in years.

GARFINKLE: You haven't made money in years.

JORGENSON: It'll turn. We got a good crew up here. Best in the business. When it does we're gonna knock their socks off.

GARFINKLE: Everything is possible. Maybe a Dunkin' Donuts will open up next door.

COLES: What does your computer tell you the rest of our businesses are worth, Mr. Garfinkle?

GARFINKLE: Conservative . . . six times cash flow.

COLES: We had ten million in flow last year. This year we're projecting a fifteen percent increase.

GARFINKLE: Carmen only knows what happened. She can't predict. Write down sixty . . . underneath the ten.

COLES: What else, Mr. Garfinkle?

GARFINKLE: Working capital. You got twenty-five million — ten million of it in cash — write down twenty-five.

COLES: Anything else?

GARFINKLE: Add it up. What do you got?

COLES: One hundred and twenty-five million.

GARFINKLE: Good. Now let's say Carmen was suffering from premenstrual syndrome. (*Jorgenson looks at him quizzically.*) A little crazed. Too optimistic. Forget twenty-five million. Take it off. What do you got?

COLES: One hundred million.

GARFINKLE: Nice round number. I like nice round numbers. Now make a line. Right down the middle of the page. Start a new column. Call it liabilities. Let's see what you got. Any debt?

JORGENSON: Not a penny. Don't believe in it.

GARFINKLE: Any lawsuits? Any environmental bullshit?

JORGENSON: None. We've complied with every law. That's a good part of our losses right there.

GARFINKLE: Pension liabilities?

COLES: Fully funded.

GARFINKLE: OK. Add it up. What do you got?

JORGENSON: Didn't write anything.

GARFINKLE: That's exactly what I said to Carmen. Now here comes the fun part. How many shares you got outstanding?

COLES: Four million.

GARFINKLE: Divide four million into the hundred million. what do you got?

COLES: Twenty-five.

GARFINKLE: Good. Now that was all foreplay. Let's go for the real thing. What's your stock selling at?

COLES: You know very well what it's selling at, Mr. Garfinkle.

GARFINKLE: Aw, don't do that. I came all the way from New York. Don't break my rhythm. Let me do my thing. What's the stock at?

COLES: Ten — before you started buying.

GARFINKLE: That's a ten for a twenty-five dollar number. Forty cents on the dollar. Carmen almost came. I had to change my underwear.

JORGENSON: This is a fine company, Larry. We've worked hard. We have a nice story to tell but unless you make those little microchips or fry chicken it's hard to interest you money guys on Wall Street.

COLES: How many shares have you bought?

GARFINKLE: One hundred and ninety-six thousand. I recognize a good job when I see it. I'm happy to put my money here.

JORGENSON (*laughing*): I'll have to tell Ozzie at the bank. He'll be mighty grateful to you. If you have time we'll have lunch together. Get him to spring for it. Tell him you're selling if he don't spring for it. Ozzie's tighter than a duck's ass. How'd you figure out to buy such an odd amount? Why not two hundred thousand — nice even number. Thought you liked nice even numbers.

COLES: Two hundred thousand is five percent of our shares. At five percent he has to file a 13-D with the Securities and Exchange Commission. It becomes public knowledge. (*To Garfinkle.*) Plan on buying more?

GARFINKLE: Never can tell. Got to talk to Carmen.

JORGENSON: That's his business, Bill. He'll let us know when he wants to . . . or when he has to. It's nice to know you have that confidence in us. Nice to have you as a stockholder.

GARFINKLE: Don't let me down. Get us to twenty-five. That's what we're worth.

JORGENSON: You know I can't control that. We do the best we can running the company. I can promise you one thing — we spend the stockholder's money with care. We don't squander it.

GARFINKLE: Not on paint at any rate.

JORGENSON: Not on anything. You watch the nickels and dimes and the dollars take care of themselves. My dad always said that. He founded this company. I guess I do too. As true today as when he said it.

(*Bea enters with a bag of donuts.*)

JORGENSON: Bea, Larry here is our newest stockholder. Give the man a donut.

BEA: All they had were honey and whole wheat. I left six of each in the car. (*She holds out bag. Garfinkle takes one out, grimaces, and puts it back.*)

JORGENSON: How was the ride?

BEA: Everyone stared. It's got a television, a bar, telephone, stock-quote machine —

JORGENSON: And now donuts. If you have no objection, Larry, we're going to call you the "donut man."

GARFINKLE: Where's my change?

BEA (*handing him the change*): Oh — I'm sorry. Just a little flustered, I guess . . . sorry.

GARFINKLE: I like to watch the nickels and dimes too.

(*Garfinkle takes the bag and exits the playing area. They stare after him for a beat.*)

JORGENSON: So, you really like being chauffeured around? I thought you'd be embarrassed.

BEA: Jorgy, riding in a limousine is not an acquired taste. One takes to it all at once.

(*Lights out in Jorgenson's office. Lights up downstage left. Garfinkle is alone checking out the donuts.*)

GARFINKLE: Whole wheat and honey. What — do I look sick? You eat this when you're sick — with tea. Step on it, Arthur. This whole goddamned place stinks. Make sure you get the car washed when we get home. (*Garfinkle moves toward his office.*)

(*Coles moves to center stage. Lights up on Garfinkle's office as Coles enters.*)

COLES: That's an impressive office you have out there.

GARFINKLE: No big deal. Only lawyers. What can I do for you?

COLES: Thanks for seeing me on such short notice. I'm not really here on business. My wife and I came down to spend the evening with Bill, Jr. He's attending Columbia. Got two more after him. Both girls. Claire's out shopping now. It's always a treat to come to this city.

GARFINKLE: Great.

COLES: We're from small towns in Florida. Met at Florida State.

GARFINKLE: What'd you come here for — to give me your biography?

COLES: I didn't know I was boring you.

GARFINKLE: Now you know.

COLES (*trying to control himself*): . . . I'll get to the point. I see by the latest 13-D you hold just over four hundred thousand shares. That's ten percent.

GARFINKLE: Four hundred and twenty-five thousand. Bought some this morning.

COLES: The filing says they were purchased for "investment purposes only."

GARFINKLE: I never read filings.

COLES: What does "investment purposes only" mean?

GARFINKLE: Means I bought them to make money.

COLES: How much more do you intend on buying?

GARFINKLE: That's none of your business.

COLES: Can we speak frankly?

GARFINKLE: No. Lie to me. Tell me how thrilled you are to know me. Tell me how gorgeous I am.

COLES: You don't want to speak frankly?

GARFINKLE: I always speak frankly. I don't like people who say "Can we speak frankly?" Means they're bullshitting me the rest of the time.

COLES: I'm sorry. I won't use that phrase anymore.

GARFINKLE: What do you want?

COLES: Two years. I want two years.

GARFINKLE: For what?

COLES: Jorgenson is sixty-eight. In two years he'll be seventy. He steps down at seventy.

GARFINKLE: Says who?

COLES: It's an agreement he has with the board. His employment contract expires at seventy.

GARFINKLE: The board are his cronies. He is the board. What he wants done gets done.

COLES: He gave me his word. He's a man of his word.

GARFINKLE: Stop playing with yourself.

COLES: Twelve years ago he told me if I did the job it'd be my company to run when he steps down. That's why I came to that godforsaken place. It's the same reason I'm here. I don't want the rug pulled out from under me so close to the finish line.

GARFINKLE: You're wasting your time. I don't have two years.

COLES: Listen, Mr. Garfinkle. I said we could grow our other businesses by fifteen percent. I was being conservative. We'll grow them in excess of twenty. I can manage. I can manage the hell out of a company. In two years we'll be worth considerably more.

GARFINKLE: Billy boy, look at me. I weigh a ton. I smoke three packs a day. I walk from here to there I'm out of breath. I can't even steal life insurance. Two years for me is forever. Do what you have to do now. I'm not a long-term player.

COLES: I can't do it now. I can't do it till he leaves. If I try I'm out on my ear.

GARFINKLE (*handing Coles his briefcase*): That's the problem with working for a living.

COLES: Two years is not a long time. I have waited a lifetime for the opportunity.

GARFINKLE: Hey — you got stock, don't you?

COLES: Yes.

GARFINKLE: Fifty, seventy-five thousand, right?

COLES: Sixty.

GARFINKLE: Well, shit, look — want to feel better? (*Garfinkle taps out stock on his quote machine.*) Before you heard my name your stock was ten. Now it's fourteen and a half. In two months I made you a quarter of a million dollars. Billy boy, the least you can do is smile. Ozzie at the bank, he's sending me flowers. All I'm asking from you is a smile.

COLES (*rises, takes his briefcase, and silently moves center stage to conference room. He is alone. All else is black.*): Several years ago my doctor told me my right arm is three-fourths of an inch longer than the left. "How do I correct that?" I asked. "Carry the briefcase with your left arm for the next twenty-five years," he said. (*Switches the briefcase to the left arm.*) Charged me a hundred fifty dollars and wished me a good day.

GARFINKLE (*in the darkness*): Smile, Billy boy, I just made you a quarter of a million dollars.

COLES: How come I like that doctor more than that pig? (*He turns and faces Jorgenson's darkened office.*) Jorgy, it's important.

(*Lights up in office as Jorgenson rises to greet him.*)

JORGENSON: Come on in. My door is always open. You know that.

(*Coles enters.*)

JORGENSON: Welcome home. How was your trip to New York? How's Bill Jr.?

COLES: Fine.

JORGENSON: You must be exhausted. A day in New York is like a month anywhere else. Goddamned crazy city. Claire do any shopping?

COLES: Some.

JORGENSON: Only some? You got away lucky. Fay used to love to shop there — God rest her soul. Went to this Bergdorf's department store, Lord and Taylor's department store, but she only bought at this Alexander's department store. She was a tight little so and so. Should've married Ozzie.

COLES: She died the year before I got here. Jorgy —

JORGENSON: Last time we were in New York was maybe . . . ten, fifteen years ago. We were in a taxicab on that highway coming in from the airport. Traffic? Nobody moved for maybe half an hour. Cars standing still as far as the eye can see. Suddenly some guy behind us went "beep!" Next guy went "beep beep" a little louder. Before you knew it there were these thousands of cars just parked, blaring away, like an orchestra gone mad. Just one giant "beeeeeep." Including my driver. You'd think he'd been thrilled just sitting there on his ass with his foot on the brake listening to that meter go tick tick tick.

COLES: I stopped by at Garfinkle's office.

JORGENSON: Let me just finish. You could hardly hear yourself think. I shout to the driver, "If you ever reach the next exit, turn around and take us back to the airport." And that's exactly what he did. Fay didn't say a word. Didn't have the nerve. That was the last time we were in New York City . . . And you know what was the most amazing thing? It wasn't even rush hour.

COLES: He intends to take over the company.

JORGENSON: Say that again?

COLES: He intends to take over the company.

JORGENSON: He said that?

COLES: He didn't have to. A man with a gun in his hand doesn't have to announce when he pulls the trigger. When you find out you're dead.

JORGENSON: What are you talking about? What gun?

COLES: He now owns eleven percent of the stock.

JORGENSON: I have a million shares. That's twenty-five percent. If he has a gun — I have a cannon.

COLES: And he's still buying.

JORGENSON: So would you. This is an undervalued company. Give him the credit for recognizing that and putting his money where his mouth is. As it is it's turned out to be a pretty good investment for him. The stock's a lot higher now than when he started buying in.

COLES: Because his buying is moving it up.

JORGENSON: Don't be ridiculous. I'm not saying that's not a factor but it's not the only one. Ozzie told me he bought five thousand shares himself last week. And there are others.

COLES: You don't understand. He's well known. What he does is not a secret. He's called "Larry the Liquidator" on Wall Street. He finds companies worth more dead than alive, gains control, and kills them. Then he pockets the proceeds and goes on to the next one. He spelled it out for us right here in this office. It couldn't be any more clear.

JORGENSON: Suppose you're right. What would you like me to do? Last time I looked it was a free country.

COLES: We could do things to protect ourselves.

JORGENSON: Like what?

COLES: We could change our by-laws to call for a two-thirds majority to effect control rather than fifty-one percent.

JORGENSON: Would that make you feel better?

COLES: Of course it would. At least we'd be fighting back. We wouldn't be rolling over and playing dead.

JORGENSON: Nobody's playing dead. What you propose . . . what would it entail?

COLES: Not much. We'd have to change our state of incorporation from Rhode Island to Delaware.

JORGENSON: Delaware? I've never even been to Delaware.

COLES: Neither have I. We needn't be there. We needn't even visit there. All we'd have to do is hire a local lawyer and get a post office box.

JORGENSON: What would it cost?

COLES: One hundred and seventy-five thousand dollars the first year. Fifty thousand dollars a year thereafter, for local counsel.

JORGENSON: Reclaiming the old stock and issuing the new?

COLES: About two hundred fifty thousand. But that would be a one-shot deal.

JORGENSON: For lawyers?

COLES: Primarily.

JORGENSON: Why can't we keep it a Rhode Island company?

COLES: It's easier to get those changes done in Delaware. They're — geared to corporate needs. And we'll show Garfinkle we're not a sitting duck. We intend to fight.

JORGENSON: By running away?

COLES: Running away?

JORGENSON: From Rhode Island to Delaware.

COLES: Nobody's running anywhere. It's a paper transaction.

JORGENSON: I call it running away. This company was founded in Rhode Island. It thrived in Rhode Island. It will remain in Rhode Island.

COLES: It will remain in Rhode Island. All that's moving is the paper.

JORGENSON: And the paper will remain in Rhode Island. Don't talk to me about playing dead. You know me better than that. Our industry is littered with dead bodies. This country is infested with dead bodies. But we're still here. And the lights go on and the telephone rings and orders come in and product goes out and we have money in the bank. And we didn't get there by playing dead.

COLES: At least talk to a lawyer.

JORGENSON: I am not talking to a lawyer. Lawyers are like cab drivers stuck in traffic. They don't do anything — but their meter is always ticking.

COLES: Please . . . just think about it.

JORGENSON: I have thought about it. Maybe you ought to think about something. I own twenty-five percent of this company. The board owns another ten percent. The employee's stock ownership plan five percent. That's forty percent. How is he going to get control?

COLES: From the sixty left.

JORGENSON: Please. They're long-term holders. If they were looking to sell they would've sold when the stock was sixty. I'm sorry, I take your advice most of the time but in this instance you don't know what you're talking about.

COLES: I do know what —

JORGENSON: You are paid to manage this company. Manage it. It's my company. I'll see to it it stays that way, thank you. (*Coles pauses a beat, turns, and moves center stage.*)

(*Lights out on Jorgenson.*)

COLES: "It's my company." Lord of the Manor with the House on the Hill . . . How long do you work for something till it's finally yours?

(*Lights up on Garfinkle in his office.*)

GARFINKLE: How long do you deliver the mail before they give you the post office? Billy boy, they don't give pots of gold to errand boys. They give pensions.

COLES (*whirling to Garfinkle*): What?

GARFINKLE: Talk to me. What's happening? How come I don't hear from you? What am I — a creditor?

COLES: I'm busy running a company, Mr. Garfinkle. What can I do for you?

GARFINKLE: Talk to me. Have they broken ground on the Dunkin' Donuts next door?

COLES: I'm afraid not.

GARFINKLE: That's disappointing. Got any more disappointing news? (*Long silence.*) . . . Hellooooo.

COLES: How many shares do you own now, Mr. Garfinkle?

GARFINKLE: You got a one-track mind. That's all you're ever interested in. Aren't you interested in me — my wife — my kids?

COLES: How are you, your wife, your kids?

GARFINKLE: I'm not married. Never was. Don't have any kids. Who would marry me? . . . Come to think of it, you might. Shit, with my five hundred thousand shares we're engaged already. Bought the last this morning at fifteen and one-eighth . . . Hellooooo . . . Ozzie at the bank stopped sending me flowers. Now it's plants. Looks like a fucking greenhouse in here. Have you talked to him?

COLES: I don't talk to Ozzie.

GARFINKLE: Not Ozzie. Yorgy.

COLES: About what?

GARFINKLE: Don't act stupid with me, Billy boy. It doesn't become you — not to your fiancée. About restructuring.

COLES: Not yet.

GARFINKLE: You intend to?

COLES: Yes.

GARFINKLE: What are you waiting for?

COLES: The right opportunity.

GARFINKLE: You figure that could occur in my lifetime?

COLES: I don't know, Mr. Garfinkle. I'm not your doctor.

GARFINKLE: You got two weeks.

COLES: Two weeks?

GARFINKLE: Talk to him. Get back to me. Otherwise I'll have to take a ride up there again. Believe me, you don't want to see that happen. I'm less charming the second time.

COLES: Two weeks is unrealistic. I need —

GARFINKLE: Two weeks. Say good-bye.

COLES: Mr. Garfinkle, two weeks —

GARFINKLE: Say good-bye! (*Lights out on Coles. Garfinkle, breathing hard, turns and yells offstage.*) Arthur — get the car ready. We're going back to the shitpit of the world. Bring donuts — and oxygen. (*Lights out on Garfinkle.*)

(Lights up on Jorgenson's office. Coles and Bea are seated. Jorgenson rises from behind his desk cheerfully.)

JORGENSON: Welcome, Larry, nice to see you again.

(Garfinkle enters.)

GARFINKLE: Yumpin' yimminy, Yorgy, was that the sun I almost saw?

JORGENSON: It sure was. Come — look at it again. *(Leads him to window. They stare out.)*

GARFINKLE: Living up here is like living in a limo. You're always looking out from tinted windows.

JORGENSON: Larry, spring is here.

GARFINKLE: Why not? It's been everywhere else.

JORGENSON: Come on. If a beautiful spring day doesn't bring out the sunshine in your soul we'll have to — Bea, c'mon. Let's do it.

BEA: Now?

JORGENSON: Now. *(Bea exits, excited.)* Wait till you see this, Larry. I haven't even told Bill about it. *(Impatient, yells offstage.)* C'mon, Bea. We're all waiting.

BEA *(offstage)*: Hold your horses, Jorgy. I'll be right there.

JORGENSON: Been with me for thirty-seven years. Yelled at me the same way back then.

BEA *(offstage)*: Ready?

JORGENSON: Ready. Ready. *(Bea enters pushing a standup rack of donuts.)* C'mere — I'll show you how it works. *(He turns handle on top and donuts move up and down like a ferris wheel — different flavored donuts in each rack. Ingenious, actually.)*

BEA: Jorgy designed and built it this morning.

JORGENSON: Willard helped. He's our line foreman. And Kyle at the machine shop lent a hand. Larry, you're looking at a New England Wire and Cable product. Designed and built right here.

BEA: Keep turning.

JORGENSON *(continuing to turn handle)*: This lady drove all the way down to Providence this morning, almost thirty miles — sixty round trip — to get them.

BEA: Closest Dunkin' Donuts I could find. Will you keep turning, Jorgy.

GARFINKLE: With all the pricks in the world I got to do business with a nice guy.

BEA: Look. Raspberry . . . toasted coconut.

JORGENSON: It comes apart. You could take it back to New York with you. Keep it in your office. A donut wheel for the donut man.

BEA: Chocolate sprinkles . . . chocolate icing . . . chocolate fudge . . . chocolate cream . . .

GARFINKLE *(looking wistfully at the donuts)*: How unlucky can you get.

JORGENSON: Know the best part? Know who paid for the donuts? Ozzie at the bank.

GARFINKLE: . . . Well, Ozzie . . . it's you and me, Babe . . . let's get to work.

(*Music comes up as stage goes black. Pause a beat. Lights go back up in conference room. Everyone is there. Time has passed.*)

JORGENSON: Larry, do me a favor. I'm a simple man. Restructuring, redeploying, maximizing — don't talk to me in Wall Street. Talk to me in English.

COLES: He wants you to sell the company.

JORGENSON: Is that what it's all about, Larry?

GARFINKLE (*singing*): "What's it all about, Larry?"

COLES: Tell him. He won't believe me. Tell him.

GARFINKLE: Not the company. Not the company. It's worth bupkus. You're lucky if you get the sixteen dollars a share it's selling at now.

JORGENSON: Then what, Larry? What do you want?

GARFINKLE: I want what every other stockholder wants. I want to make money.

JORGENSON: You are making money.

GARFINKLE: That's right. For all of us. I'm doing my part. Now you do yours.

JORGENSON: Do what? I don't have a printing press out there. I can't simply crank it out.

GARFINKLE: Get rid of the Wire and Cable division. It's a financial cancer. And it's starving out all the other boring things Billy boy runs. Nobody sees them. All they see is the cancer.

JORGENSON: So you want me to sell Wire and Cable.

GARFINKLE: Surgically remove it.

JORGENSON: To who, Mr. Garfinkle? Know anyone interested in buying a surgically removed cancer?

GARFINKLE: I'll find you a buyer.

JORGENSON: Who?

GARFINKLE: What's the difference?

JORGENSON: Who?

GARFINKLE: Some paper-shuffling Wall Street types. They'll give you a buck for every four you give them in equipment. I told you that.

COLES: And they'll close this down, and deduct it from their taxes.

GARFINKLE: Easy. Just a paper transaction. Your hands won't even get dirty.

JORGENSON: And what happens to the plant?

GARFINKLE: Gets sold for scrap.

JORGENSON: And the men? And the town?

GARFINKLE: Not your problem. You're not the mayor. You're not a missionary.

JORGENSON: So that's what they mean when they talk about restructuring — maximizing shareholder values?

GARFINKLE: That's what they mean.

JORGENSON: Nice turn of phrase. We used to call it "going out of business."

GARFINKLE: Welcome to the wonderful world of Wall Street.

JORGENSON: Shouldn't surprise me. Those boys down there can't charge millions by going out of business. First they become lawyers and investment bankers — then they restructure.

GARFINKLE: On Wall Street, "Restructuring means never having to say you're sorry." Got it?

JORGENSON: I got it. Now you get it. I understand what you want. Thank you for coming.

GARFINKLE: Yorgy, are you dismissing me?

JORGENSON: I have no time for this. I have a company to run.

GARFINKLE (*to Bea*): Sweetheart, pass me a donut. (*She looks at him, uncertain.*) Come on, the chocolate cream.

BEA: Get it yourself.

COLES: Please leave before it becomes unpleasant.

GARFINKLE: Unpleasant? How quaint — how antiseptic — how "New England."

JORGENSON: Get out before I physically throw you out.

GARFINKLE: All right, forget the donut.

JORGENSON (*rising*): Out!

GARFINKLE: Don't get your bowels in an uproar. We're just doing business.

JORGENSON: Do it somewhere else. You're not welcome here.

GARFINKLE: Now I'm going to tell you something. I don't like the way my company is being run. There is a goddamned fire raging here and this whole industry is up in flames. And you call the Fire Department and who shows up? Nobody. Because they're all in Japan and Singapore and Malaysia and Taiwan and every other shithole place where they're crazy about pollution. And they build factories over there and they stuff them full of little dedicated people who work for twelve cents an hour, ten hours a day, six days a week and then they go home at night and pray for their health so they can come back and do it again tomorrow. And while that goddamned inferno is raging you're out front tidying up, mowing the lawn, playing with your putz on my money.

JORGENSON: Now you listen to me. This plant was here before you were born and — I promise you — will be here long after you're gone. Its products helped build the roads, bridges, and buildings throughout the face of New England. And I will not — do you understand me — will not have it commit suicide and kill these people and this town so you and your cronies can pocket the insurance money.

GARFINKLE: Don't think of it as suicide. Think of it as euthanasia.

JORGENSON: Go back to those other parasites on Wall Street. Tell them to restructure somewhere else. (*Garfinkle moves out of the office toward center stage. Bea takes a donut from bin, and hurls it in his direction.*)

BEA: Here's your lousy donut!

JORGENSON (*kicks over the bin. The donuts litter the floor.*): Here's all your lousy donuts! (*They laugh. She comes over and they hug.*) God damn it, Bea. It feels good to fight something other than imports for a change. (*Lights out in Jorgenson's office. Garfinkle is alone center stage.*)

ACT ONE   GARFINKLE: Geez . . . You'd think I was asking them for a loan.

> (*Lights out. Music plays for several beats as donuts are retrieved from floor.*)

KATE (*in darkness, laughing*): Takeover!

> (*Lights up on Kate alone onstage as she talks to her unseen mother. Kate is an attractive, sexy woman, about thirty-five.*)

KATE: What's so funny? Taking over New England Wire and Cable is like taking over the psychiatric ward at Bellevue. It could be done but who wants to . . . Mother, I'm sorry if it was in poor taste. That's who I am . . . well, why not take the money and run? You should have retired a long time ago. Now's your chance . . . Because I'm busy . . . Busy in like having no time.

> (*Lights up on Bea — in Jorgenson's office.*)

BEA: You can take one day off from Stanley Morgan and fly up here —

KATE: Morgan, Stanley.

BEA: Morgan, Stanley and fly up here and talk to us. Jorgy was always crazy about you.

KATE: I was never crazy about him.

BEA: I did not ask your opinion. I am stating that he would be more at ease speaking to you than some stranger. I expect you to give us a day.

KATE: . . . All right. I'm booked solid through the month. One day early next month.

BEA: I'll expect you here tomorrow.

KATE: Tomorrow?

BEA: Tomorrow. Catch the early flight. Come to the plant. We'll all be here.

KATE (*sighs, resigned*): . . . Coming, Mother. (*Lights out on Bea.*) Why is it that a grown woman, a lawyer, an executive with a staff of thirty and a budget of eight million plus, responsible for making hundreds of decisions every day, can revert to a spineless infant every time she talks to her mother. (*Kate picks up briefcase and moves to conference room.*)

> (*Lights go up there. Bea, Coles, and Jorgenson await.*)

KATE: I understand what you said, but I don't understand what you want. Do you want me to help you negotiate a deal with him?

JORGENSON: There is no deal to be made with him.

KATE: Have you tried?

BEA: We want him to go away.

KATE: He's got a half-million shares. No one walks away from half a million shares.

COLES: What do you suggest?

KATE: I'm a lawyer. Lawyers don't like to go to court. You never know what can happen there. I suggest you settle.

JORGENSON: Meaning?

KATE: The man is motivated by dollars. Make it worth his while to leave.

COLES: Greenmail. Done all the time. Let's explore it.

JORGENSON (*rising*): Excuse me. If this discussion continues on this tack I am leaving. We are wasting our time. There is no deal to be made with predators. You kill it or it kills you.

KATE: I was asked what I suggested. It is not my company and it is not my decision. (*She begins to rise as well.*)

BEA (*to Kate*): Please Kate, we want to explore our options. Help us defend ourselves.

KATE (*reluctantly*): All right. Let's say, I'm not at this point recommending anything. Just going over what others in your position have done. "Exploring options," Mother.

(*Lights up on Garfinkle as he views, unseen by them, their meeting.*)

GARFINKLE (*to audience*): Wait till you hear this.

KATE: Traditionally, first thing, you hire some private investigators, to see what dirt there is. We know some good ones. Hopefully, they'll find something that will make him go away.

GARFINKLE: Aw Kate, you can do better than that.

BEA: Do you think there's a chance? Hasn't he been investigated before?

GARFINKLE (*to audience*): Investigated? I get sued or subpoenaed every week. I've become a professional witness.

KATE: It's unlikely we'll find anything. He's reasonably well known. I think the S.E.C. got him on a few technical violations.

GARFINKLE (*to audience*): That's right, girly. You mug somebody — you're walking the streets the same day. You don't file just one of fourteen hundred bullshit forms they want to put you away for ten years.

COLES: We should do it. We have nothing to lose.

GARFINKLE (*to audience*): It's not his money. Us "stuckholders" will pay for it.

JORGENSON: Doesn't sound promising. We have better things to do with our money.

GARFINKLE: The man's got class . . . or he's cheaper than shit.

KATE: Get the board to authorize a search for a white knight.

BEA: White knight?

KATE: A protector. A larger company that will buy you out and allow you to do business the way you want. You know, someone to rescue the damsel in distress . . . a white knight.

JORGENSON: I don't know anyone like that.

BEA (*to Kate*): Do you?

GARFINKLE (*to audience*): Of course she doesn't. (*Smiles, pats his middle.*) You got to have the stomach for it.

JORGENSON: Next.

KATE: We can formulate a "shark repellent."

BEA: Come again?

KATE: The purpose of a "shark repellent" is to make yourself undesirable to an unwanted suitor, i.e., shark.

BEA: How would that work?

GARFINKLE (to audience): Listen close. It's an education.

KATE: Take the most attractive part of the company — in this case I assume it's the non-wire and cable divisions — give someone, anyone — the option to buy that part of the business for a song. The option only gets triggered if and when anyone not presently on the board acquires thirty percent or more of the company's stock. Garfinkle buys more shares, the option gets triggered. He now owns a lot of shares that are worth considerably less than he paid for them.

JORGENSON: So do we. So do all stockholders.

KATE: That's the risk. The hope is the shark will go elsewhere to feed.

GARFINKLE (to audience): Ingenious, isn't it? Next.

JORGENSON: Next.

GARFINKLE: Mah man!

KATE: We could create a poison pill. It's a form of shark repellent, but one you might find more acceptable. Get the board to authorize three million shares of preferred stock, one share for each share held by all but Garfinkle. If he gains control of thirty percent or more, issue them for, say — a dollar a share.

JORGENSON: A dollar a share!

COLES: What a great idea. We'd make Garfinkle's shares worth less. We'd dilute them.

JORGENSON: We would be diluting ours as well. Book value and earnings per share would be halved.

KATE: Exactly. Once you swallow the poison pill you're no longer desirable. But you can still keep your businesses. To most everyone nothing has changed.

GARFINKLE (to audience): Except the stuckholder. People get paid big money — honored people — pillars of the community — to sit and dream this shit up. You know what I said when I first heard it?

JORGENSON: That's legal?

GARFINKLE (to audience): That's what I said.

KATE: So far.

GARFINKLE (to audience): Would you believe it?

KATE: It's not new. I can give you a list of companies — household names — that have it in their corporate by-laws.

GARFINKLE (to audience): If you or me tried it they'd have us committed.

JORGENSON: How much would your firm charge for taking us on?

KATE: I don't know. That's not my department.

JORGENSON: Rough guess?

KATE: It would depend on how involved it got. If we were able to work it out peacefully and quickly — a million. Maybe two. If it turned out to be war it could go to ten, twenty times that.

JORGENSON: Kate, your mother is the only assistant I ever had. She is also the best friend I ever had. I remember clearly the day you were born. The whole plant shut down a full afternoon while we had birthday cake and celebrated. This whole plant . . .

BEA: Jorgy, please.

JORGENSON: And it is out of respect for that lady that I don't have you bodily thrown out of this office.

GARFINKLE: Bravo, Yorgy!

KATE: I'm sorry you feel that way. I'm only telling you how corporations under attack defend themselves. Don't blame the messenger for the message.

JORGENSON: The messenger, as I hear it, is saying pay him off or self-destruct. Either way, pay me my fee.

KATE: It is not my fee. Unfortunately, I'm only an employee. (*Picking up her briefcase to leave.*) I'm sorry we wasted each other's time.

JORGENSON: Have your firm send me a bill. That way only our time will have been wasted. I trust it'll be for something less than a million dollars.

KATE: It will. This one is on the house. And as long as it's my nickel I want to tell you something. You, as they say on the street, are "in play." Garfinkle put you there. And now, right this second, all over the country there sit all kinds of boring, dull little men, hunched over their IBM PCs buried under mountains of 13-D filings, looking for an edge to make a buck. And some of their little minicomputers have already noticed an obscure over-the-counter stock with a sixty percent move in the last two months. "What's this? How come? What's going on?" they mutter. And then they notice Garfinkle's 13-D and his half-million shares, and they don't have to know diddly-doo about wire and cable. They know Garfinkle and they ride the coattails. Congratulations. You're now "in play" in the big leagues where the game is called hardball and winner takes all. So if you want to play Mr. High and Mighty, Mr. Principled, Mr. Roberts Rule of Order, better go to work for the Peace Corps where you'll be appreciated because you won't have any company left here to run. (*Begins to exit, turns.*) And the shame of it is I would be perfect for this deal. Garfinkle is a blatant sexist. I love blatant sexists. They're my meat. But I wouldn't work for you if you begged me. I like being associated with winners.

(*Lights out in conference room.*)

GARFINKLE (*fanning himself*): Phew . . . some piece of work.

(*Lights out on Garfinkle.*)

BEA: How dare you talk to him that way.

KATE: Will you stop defending him. He is making the wrong decision. He will lose this company.

BEA: He is making the right decision. We will not lose this company.

KATE: We!? Since when is it "we"? He loses this company he walks away with millions. You walk away with memories.

BEA: Don't you worry about me. I'm well provided for.

KATE: "Well provided for." You have running water you think you're well provided for.

BEA: Why are we talking about my finances? What is this all about?

KATE: Anger. About thirty-five years' worth.

BEA: At whom?

KATE: At him. At you. And this god-awful company. It's your life. It always was. When he was happy you were ecstatic. When he was depressed you were distraught. When she died you almost moved in. It was the talk of the town. With Dad keeping the dinner warm.

BEA: I loved him.

KATE: You were married, Mother.

BEA: Listen to me, Kate. In a life filled with rumors and gossip and sideways glances — I apologized to no one. Don't expect it of me now. You won't get it. You were asked here as our attorney, not our judge. If you can't handle the position — leave.

KATE: Why in God's name did you ever marry Dad?

BEA: I was nineteen. He asked. I thought I loved him. Until one day, thank God, I walked through that door. And there stood the most beautiful, scared young man I had ever seen. Had on blue jeans and a red flannel shirt with the sleeves rolled up. Said he just became president. I remember thinking, "How peculiar for a president. This company'll never last." And then the magic words: "How about it, Miss? I'm ready to take a chance with you. Ready to take one with me?" (*Turns to Kate.*) Sometimes life presents us with very limited choices.

KATE: I know.

BEA: Like now.

KATE: I don't believe you.

BEA: He trusts you. Don't make us deal with strangers in three-piece suits. Maybe we can't play the game the way you want us to — help us play our game the best we can.

KATE: Oh Mother, don't you think I want to? Going up against Garfinkle, he's the best. And I'm as good as he is. It's the career opportunity of a lifetime.

BEA: So?

KATE: So I said I wouldn't. Even if he begged me.

BEA: He's not. I am. (*Kate pauses a beat, picks up her briefcase, and crosses to her mother on the way to Jorgenson's office. Looks back.*)

KATE: Well c'mon. (*Bea moves to her and they begin their exit.*)

BEA: And you'll do something about those fees. They're horrendous.

KATE (*laughing*): Don't push it. (*They exit.*)

(*Lights up on Garfinkle.*)

GARFINKLE (*to audience*): You know what kills me? I've done maybe seven — eight deals like this. Know who I negotiate with? Skinny little joggers with contact lenses all stinking from the same after-shave. Don't believe me?

Ever seen an arbitrageur? Ugliest people on the face of the earth. They won't use her. You'll see. I never luck out with a broad like that. Excuse me, woman like that. I've been accused of being a "womanizer." That's someone who likes broads. I remember when that used to be a good thing . . . Although when you cut through the "Woman's Lib" bullshit all it really means is you can't call them "sweetheart" and "darling" unless you're schtuping them . . . then you can't call them anything else. (*Sits behind his desk, smiles.*) I can live with that.

(*Kate enters his office. Hands him her business card.*)

KATE: That's me. We're the investment banker for New England Wire and Cable.

GARFINKLE (*looking at card*): What are you — a fucking lawyer?

KATE (*smiling*): Depends on who I'm with.

GARFINKLE (*rises — opens arms — beams*): Welcome to my life!

KATE: All those cubbyholes have lawyers in them?

GARFINKLE: Mostly. (*She gives him a sad look.*) It's not as bad as you think. I don't have to talk to them. I just have to pay them.

KATE: You don't talk to them?

GARFINKLE: Talk to them? I'd rather talk to my mother. I write to them. (*Takes top sheet from pile on desk. Writes.*) "Fuck . . . them." (*Looks up at Kate.*) Sue. (*Picks up the next sheet. Writes.*) "Trouble." (*Looks up at Kate.*) Settle. (*Picks up the next sheet. Writes.*) "They're . . . morons." (*Looks up at Kate.*) Let them sue. Don't give them a quarter. (*Kate laughs.*) See? Nothing to it. Sue. Settle. Defend. Which one are you?

KATE: I came to talk.

GARFINKLE: Now that's trouble. Lawyers want to talk, it's nothing but trouble. Who are you? How come I never heard of you?

KATE: They generally keep me locked away at bond closings, due diligence meetings, good stuff like that.

GARFINKLE: Life in the fast lane.

KATE: I'm not complaining. They pay well. I meet a lot of people. (*Garfinkle yawns.*) Well . . . it's true. They don't have your . . . something.

GARFINKLE (*opening desk drawer*): Want a donut?

KATE: No thanks.

GARFINKLE: Why not — you a health food freak?

KATE: No. Just not hungry.

GARFINKLE (*incredulous*): You have to be hungry to have a donut?

KATE: . . . you don't?

GARFINKLE: Are you shitting me? In all my life I never heard of such a thing. Have to be hungry? Why? It don't taste better that way.

KATE: How would you know?

GARFINKLE: My luck. A broad with a mouth.

KATE: Show me a broad worth knowing who doesn't have one.

GARFINKLE: I like you. Can you tell?

KATE: Not yet.

GARFINKLE: Hang in. You will.

KATE: That's what I came to see you about. I need a month to hang in.

GARFINKLE: Get lost.

KATE: I just got involved. I need time to get everybody's act together.

GARFINKLE: My act is together.

KATE: If you give me some time I think we can work something out.

GARFINKLE: Settle?

KATE: Work something out.

GARFINKLE: I only settle when I'm in trouble.

KATE: Or when it makes sense.

GARFINKLE: It only makes sense when I'm in trouble.

KATE: If you'd prefer we'll go to court, get an injunction, have a fight, all kinds of allegations, cost them, cost you, and for what?

GARFINKLE: I live in court. You got to do better than that.

KATE: . . . I won't love you anymore.

GARFINKLE: . . . You got two weeks.

KATE: Standstill agreement.

GARFINKLE: Both sides.

KATE: No more buying.

GARFINKLE: Two weeks.

KATE: Thank you. (*She begins to exit.*)

GARFINKLE: Now let's talk about what I want to talk about.

KATE: What's that?

GARFINKLE: Your legs . . . your ass . . . your tits —

KATE: Garfinkle, sit. (*Beat.*) Sit!! (*He sits.*) Listen close. I don't want to repeat this. You listening? Now take your right hand out of that donut drawer and put it between your legs. (*He looks at her, uncertain.*) Come on. They visit each other all the time. (*He laughs . . . a little nervously.*)

GARFINKLE: . . . Can't.

KATE: Why?

GARFINKLE: I'm a lefty. (*Switches hands. Fumbles a bit, but does it.*)

KATE: Good. Now look directly down at the little guy and say — "You must behave yourself when you're in the presence of a lady." (*Garfinkle laughs.*) Garfinkle, if you don't say exactly that, right now, I'm resigning from this case. You'll deal with the Morgan Stanley "B" team. They think arbitrageurs are fun. (*He remains motionless. She rises, begins to exit.*)

GARFINKLE: All right. All right.

KATE: "You must behave yourself when you're in the presence of a lady."

GARFINKLE: . . . You must — (*Kate motions him to put his chin on chest. He does.*) "You must behave yourself when you're in the presence of a lady."

KATE: See, not so hard. (*He does a double take to his crotch as she rises to exit.*) Hey, Garfinkle, what kind of donuts you got in that drawer?

GARFINKLE: The good kind.

KATE: Toss one over. (*He reaches into drawer.*) With the right hand. (*He switches hands and tosses one over. She catches it.*) See you in two weeks. (*She exits. He rises, takes a step or two downstage, his voice filled with wonder.*)

GARFINKLE: . . . I think I'm falling in love . . . (*Lights out on Garfinkle — up on Kate as she munches donut.*)

KATE: The man does have . . . a certain undeniable . . . charm.

(*Lights up in conference room. Jorgenson, Coles, and Bea await.*)

BEA: Charm? He has as much charm as a beached whale.

(*Kate enters office.*)

KATE: Don't knock it. It bought us two weeks.

JORGENSON: For what?

KATE: For getting our act together.

JORGENSON: What did it cost?

KATE: A donut.

COLES: Where do we go from here?

KATE (*to Jorgenson*): Have you reconsidered the defenses we spoke about?

JORGENSON: We won't do that.

KATE: Can I threaten it?

JORGENSON: I don't make threats I won't fulfill.

KATE: It's probably too late in the game for that anyway. Here's what you can do. Get the board together. Authorize the purchase of as many shares as you can afford. Do it right away.

JORGENSON: The dollars we have are our safety net. Most of it is earmarked for future expansion.

KATE: Then borrow the money.

COLES: We have excellent credit. There's a dozen banks happy to lend us the money. It would be no problem.

JORGENSON: It's never a problem borrowing money. It's only a problem paying it back. (*To Kate.*) What would that do?

KATE: Three things. One: For every share you acquire it's one less Garfinkle can get. Two, and more important, you'll drive the price of the stock up. Eighteen sounds terrific when the stock is ten. Twenty is not so terrific when the stock is eighteen. The more it costs the more negotiable he becomes. Get the stock up.

JORGENSON: I understand what you're saying. I'm not sure I want to do that. We've been debt-free since the Depression. It's what's permitted us to survive.

KATE: And it's that gorgeous balance sheet that also makes you so attractive — which is the third reason to buy the shares.

JORGENSON: What a strange new world. A strong, liquid balance sheet is no longer an asset. It's a liability.

KATE: Next, get a letter out to shareholders. Tell them how great business is and how wonderful the future looks. Tell them how pleased you are that the investment community is finally beginning to recognize, in some small way, the real worth of the company. Thank them for their loyalty and support. Talk to as many of the larger shareholders as you can, personally. Under no circumstances mention any potential takeover.

BEA: I'll compile a list of everyone with more than five thousand shares.

JORGENSON: I don't need a list. I know who they are.

KATE: You have any political clout?

BEA: We're friendly with the mayor and city council.

KATE: Forget them. Too small. Do you have a relationship with the governor?

BEA: Are you kidding? He's a Democrat.

KATE: That's OK. I'll set it up from New York. We'll get some of our legislative people up here to talk to him. Prepare a statistical analysis of your dollar contribution to the local economy: jobs, payroll, taxes, etc. Make it as complete as possible.

COLES: You'll have it Monday.

KATE: Maybe we can get some antitakeover legislation passed — quickly.

COLES: I don't mean to be crass . . . but . . . shouldn't we deal with something commonly called . . . "golden parachutes"?

BEA: Golden parachutes?

KATE: You're premature. Don't muddy the water. We'll have time for that later.

JORGENSON: I think you've given us enough to tackle for the moment. We still have a business to run.

KATE: I agree. The important thing for now is to get the stock up. I'll coordinate everything else. (*Begins to exit.*)

JORGENSON: Before you go, will you answer the question I asked you earlier?

KATE: What's that?

JORGENSON: Why did he give us two weeks? What did it cost?

KATE (*smiling*): . . . I told you — A donut. Chocolate fudge with sprinkles. (*Kate exits. Jorgenson moves center stage. Lights go out in his office.*)

JORGENSON: Donut my ass. Garfinkle would never give two weeks. He'd sell them.

BEA: Jorgy, what the hell is a "golden parachute"? (*Lights go out on Jorgenson and Bea as they exit.*)

(*Kate screams in the darkness.*)

KATE: You son of a bitch! You goddamned son of a bitch!

(*Lights up in Garfinkle's office. Kate enters. Flings papers at him.*)

KATE: Goddamned hypocrite liar!

GARFINKLE: But, sweetie pie, but, honey lamb —

KATE: We had an agreement. You gave me your word.

GARFINKLE: But, baby poo —

KATE: Stop that. You lied to me.

GARFINKLE: Me?

KATE: We had a standstill. No more buying.

GARFINKLE: So?

KATE: So? What's this tender to buy New England Wire and Cable at twenty dollars a share all about?

GARFINKLE: Not me.

KATE: I bet. (*Picks up papers.*) OPM holdings — you know nothing about it?

GARFINKLE: OPM? Not a lot to know.

KATE: I'm sure . . . Where's the money coming from — junk bonds?

GARFINKLE: Through Drexel. Give them fifteen percent plus a fee and they'll get you the bucks to buy a slag heap in Mound City, Missouri.

KATE: Why did you have to lie to me? You embarrassed me with my firm. You embarrassed me with my clients.

GARFINKLE (*slams his hand on desk. The ferocity of the blow startles Kate.*): Enough! Who am I dealing with here — Mother Teresa? Don't come on so goddamned holy with me, girly. You think I'm a fool — I sit here and twiddle my thumbs while you drive the price of the stock up?

KATE: I did no such thing.

GARFINKLE: You're full of shit. All the buying was coming from some cock-a-mamie little brokerage firm in Rhode Island.

KATE: I know nothing about it.

GARFINKLE: Give me a break, will you? That cheapskate is so tight he won't put paint on the walls. The only way he'd be paying seventeen for his stock is if someone stood behind him with a cattle prod. I got as good an imagination as most but I tell you it's tough picturing Mother Teresa with a cross in one hand and a cattle prod in the other. (*Kate begins to leave.*) Don't go, Katie. I'm not through. You want to play the game — let's play. Only I don't watch while you do "holier than thou." That's not the way this game is gonna get played.

KATE: Is that what it is for you, a game?

GARFINKLE: Goddamned right. The best game in the world.

KATE: You're playing Monopoly with people's lives here.

GARFINKLE: I'm doing them a favor. I'm making them money. I thought that's what they were in the business for.

KATE: I know this might be difficult for you to believe — for some people business means more than making money. They don't know how to play your game.

GARFINKLE: I'll teach them. It's easy. You make as much as you can for as long as you can.

KATE: And then what?

GARFINKLE: And then what? Whoever has the most when he dies — wins.

KATE: Good-bye, Garfinkle.

GARFINKLE: Aw Katie, don't leave so soon. We haven't spoken about your thighs, your nipples, your —

KATE: See you in court.

GARFINKLE: At least have a donut.

KATE: Stuff it.

ACT ONE   GARFINKLE (*downstage right*): You didn't have to leave. I'm not mad at you. Lying to protect your client is just doing your job good.

KATE: Round One to the fat man. It ain't over till it's over, fat man.

GARFINKLE: And you didn't even ask me what OPM stands for. (*A short burst of music. Smiling.*) "Other People's Money."

(*Blackout.*)

ACT TWO

(*Music plays — ending with a champagne "Pop." Lights come up on Kate with champagne bottle in hand in conference room. Jorgenson, Coles, and Bea are standing expectantly.*)

KATE: To Judge Pollard.

BEA: Judge Jim Pollard? For what?

KATE: For granting us an injunction preventing Garfinkle from buying more shares. (*They cheer, delighted.*)

COLES: A permanent injunction?

KATE: No. Pending the results of a suit we filed in Washington with the S.E.C. But since our annual meeting is in five weeks, for the purposes of taking control at that time, you could consider it permanent.

COLES: No more buying?

KATE: No more buying. He'll look to overturn it but he doesn't have time.

JORGENSON: Not with Jim Pollard presiding. Used to play football together in high school. Slowest son of a bitch on the team.

KATE: Didn't move slowly here. Granted us the injunction in two hours.

GARFINKLE (*sings*): "Territory folks should stick together."

KATE: Our legislative people met yesterday with the governor and his secretary of commerce to discuss immediate antitakeover legislation. They seem, I am told, very sympathetic.

GARFINKLE (*sings*): "Territory folks should all be pals."

KATE: I want to organize bus trips to the state capitol. Get the workers, management, local politicians, everyone in town up there to see the legislators. And demonstrate, demonstrate, demonstrate.

GARFINKLE (*sings*): "Cowboys dance with the farmer's daughters."

KATE: I want to see babies. I want to see balloons. I want to see "Save Our Town, Save Our Future" posters hung from every school, church, bank, and whorehouse in this city. I want visibility. I want prayer meetings. I want pressure!

GARFINKLE (*sings*): "Farmers dance with the rancher's gals!" (*Lights fade in conference room. Kate moves center stage.*)

KATE: God save me . . . I love this!

(Lights up in Garfinkle's office as he berates his unseen staff. Kate looks on in amusement.)

GARFINKLE: Seventeen lawyers on my payroll. Three goddamned law firms on retainer. And all of you together ain't worth some broad wet behind the ears. Some crew — you managed to work it out so in a free market in a free country I can't buy some shit-ass stock that every other asshole can buy. Congratulations. You know what? You — all of you — are destroying the capitalist system. And you know what happens when capitalism is destroyed, don't you? The Communists take over. And you know the one good thing that happens when the Commies take over? The first thing they do, they kill all the lawyers. And if they miss any of you — I'll do it myself. *(Kate, moving into his office, applauds.)* You liked it?

KATE: Loved it.

GARFINKLE: The Wall Street version of "Let's win one for the Gipper."

KATE: It was wonderful. It's a shame Judge Pollard couldn't hear you.

GARFINKLE: Stop gloating. It doesn't become you. What do you want?

KATE: A donut.

GARFINKLE *(mimicking her)*: It's too early to be hungry.

KATE *(mimicking him)*: You have to be hungry to have a donut?

GARFINKLE *(tossing her a donut)*: I see gloating is good for the appetite.

KATE: Who would know better than you.

GARFINKLE: My luck. I meet a broad . . . sweet, nice, Irish. In two weeks she turns into Don Rickles. *(Kate laughs.)* I like it when you laugh. You laugh nice.

KATE: You have the most incredible sense of humor. You make me laugh.

GARFINKLE: Uh-oh. Here it comes. I'm in trouble.

KATE: Let's be friends. Let's work it out. Let's settle.

GARFINKLE: You've been eating too many donuts.

KATE: You only settle when you're in trouble. I thought I heard, "I'm in trouble."

GARFINKLE: Only with you. You're wet behind the ears. I want you wet between your legs. *(Kate chokes on her donut.)* Aha — gotcha. *(She nods, still choking.)* Nice to see a girl blush nowadays. *(He moves behind her, gently and awkwardly patting her back as one would a child.)*

KATE: . . . Not blushing . . . choking.

GARFINKLE: . . . Are you all right? *(She nods.)* Good. I don't want you to sue Dunkin' Donuts. The only thing better than their donuts is their stock.

KATE: Now that you almost killed me, can we talk?

GARFINKLE: Talk. I'm listening. Just don't die on me.

KATE: What do you want to go away?

GARFINKLE: . . . What do you mean?

KATE: What number do we buy you out at? *(Garfinkle, feigning horror, pretends to draw drapes, check for bugs, etc.)* What are you doing?

GARFINKLE: Greenmail! Are you offering me greenmail?

ACT TWO

KATE: Will you stop it!

GARFINKLE: Are you?

KATE: Stop acting like it's new to you. You've done it three times in the past.

GARFINKLE: I've done shit in the past. I don't play that way. It was never my idea. (*Talking into her briefcase.*) And I want the record to show it's not in this case either.

KATE: Why are you so uptight about it? It's not illegal.

GARFINKLE: No, it's not. It's immoral. That distinction has no relevance for you lawyers — but it matters to me.

KATE: For someone who has nothing nice to say about lawyers you certainly have enough of them around.

GARFINKLE: You have to. They're like nuclear warheads. They have theirs so you need yours — but once you use them they fuck everything up. They're only good in their silos.

KATE (*laughs*): I'll have to remember that.

GARFINKLE: Let me ask you something? You have authorization to offer me greenmail? . . . Bet your ass you don't. The others didn't either. It only comes from the lawyers. It's a lawyer's scheme. Everybody walks out happy. I get paid off. You get paid off. Yorgy keeps his company. Billy boy keeps his inheritance. The employees keep their jobs. Everyone comes out.

KATE: Sounds pretty good to me.

GARFINKLE: Except the stuckholders. Their stock falls out of bed. They won't know what hit them.

KATE: I don't believe this. We better stop hanging out together. I turn into Don Rickles and you turn into Albert Schweitzer.

GARFINKLE: Not Albert Schweitzer — Robin Hood. I'm a modern-day Robin Hood. I take from the rich and give to the middle class. (*Kate laughs derisively.*) Well . . . upper middle class.

KATE: Can we be serious now?

GARFINKLE: I am serious. I really believe that . . . So what's your number?

KATE: The stock is eighteen. We'll buy it back at eighteen.

GARFINKLE: First you laugh at me and then you insult me.

KATE: Why? Who else you know would buy a million shares of New England Wire and Cable at eighteen?

GARFINKLE: Me. I'll pay twenty for them.

KATE: You can't. You got trouble.

GARFINKLE: No trouble. Just delay.

KATE: I could maybe . . . get them to stretch to twenty.

GARFINKLE: Now why would I sell you something at the same price I was willing to pay for it?

KATE: Your average cost was thirteen. Thirteen from twenty, times a million, isn't a bad day's pay on one little deal.

GARFINKLE: I'm not interested in seven million. I'm interested in value. The value here is no secret. I spelled it out for them. I was being conservative.

KATE: Spell it out for me. What's the number?

GARFINKLE: Twenty-five.

KATE: Impossible.

GARFINKLE: What's impossible — it's worth it or they'll pay it?

KATE: Both. That stock hasn't seen twenty-five in ten years.

GARFINKLE: You want history? That stock was once sixty. I was once skinny . . . well, skinnier.

KATE: Take twenty.

GARFINKLE: Take a walk. Twenty-five is my number. And that's a favor.

KATE: I can't deliver that.

GARFINKLE: I know. Let's talk about something nice. Let's talk about your eyes.

KATE (*getting up to leave*): I really thought we could work something out.

GARFINKLE: We can't. You're too far away.

KATE: You could lose it all.

GARFINKLE: I could. That's why so few of us have the balls to play the game.

KATE: Thanks for the donut.

GARFINKLE: Don't be depressed. You're in a tough place. Go fight your fight. It's not personal — it's principle. Hey, no matter what — it's better than working at the post office.

KATE (*softly*): Oh yeah . . . It's better than the post office. (*She smiles sadly and exits. He is alone.*)

GARFINKLE: A lot better than working at the post office. It's the best there is. Like in the old westerns, didn't everyone want to be a gunslinger? Didn't everyone want to be Butch Cassidy and the James Boys? There's just a few of us — us modern-day gunslingers. There's T. Boone and the Bass Brothers out of Texas. Irwin Jacobs out of Minneapolis. Would you believe a gunslinger named Irwin Jacobs? The Belzberg Boys up north in Canada. And here in New York we got Saul Steinberg and Ronald Perlman and Carl Icahn. (*Places his hand on his heart.*) Out of respect for the stupid a moment of silence for our gunned-down colleague Ivan Boesky. (*With a big smile.*) It's assholes like him that give assholes like us a bad name. And last, but not least, Garfinkle from the wilds of the Bronx. But instead of galloping in with a six-gun a-blazing in each hand, we're driven in, escorted by a herd of lawyers and investment bankers, waving our limited partnerships in one hand and our 13-D filings in the other. But they quake just as hard. And they wind up just as dead. And it's legal. And it's exciting. And it's fun. (*Moves to desk.*) And the money ain't bad either. (*Sits at desk.*) And every so often, every once in a while, we even wind up with the girl. (*Begins looking at papers on desk. Looks up.*) It's a nice business.

(*As he works quietly for a beat, we hear Kate shouting offstage.*)

KATE (*offstage*): What? What are you so hysterical about — interrupting my meeting.

(*She enters his office.*)

ACT TWO

KATE: What the hell is so important? You having a stroke — a nervous break-down?

GARFINKLE: Just taking care of business.

KATE: You're worse than my mother.

GARFINKLE: Please. I know we're on different sides here —

KATE: I'm busy. What's so important? What do you want?

GARFINKLE: I feel bad about our last meeting. You left, you looked so depressed. I want us to be friends. I want us to end our dispute. I have two propositions. I'll give them to you in my order of preference. (*She sits.*) Sure. If I was having a stroke you'd tell me to dial 911. — Now you're ready to spend the afternoon. How about the evening?

KATE: Proposition number one?

GARFINKLE: We leave here, right now, and go to my place where we make wild, passionate love for the rest of the afternoon.

KATE: Number two?

GARFINKLE: I'm not finished. The first one who comes, loses.

KATE: Loses what?

GARFINKLE: The deal. I come first I sell you back my shares at cost. I slink away never to be seen or heard from again. You come first, you tender all your shares to me at twenty.

KATE: You're serious?

GARFINKLE: Well. — I don't slink. Big men don't slink. I . . . saunter away.

KATE: How do you suggest we write this up for the proxy statement?

GARFINKLE: Delicately. Under the heading, "easy come, easy go."

KATE: The garment center is too classy for you.

GARFINKLE: Come on, what do you got to lose — your virginity? I could lose millions.

KATE: You've thought of everything!

GARFINKLE: Not everything. What happens if we come together?

KATE: We call and make sure your life insurance premiums are paid. (*Kate moves out of office to center stage.*)

GARFINKLE: Hey, premiums are paid. (*Lights out on Garfinkle. Kate is alone.*)

KATE: You think he was serious? So help me, I don't know. On the one hand if he was serious . . . (*She laughs.*) We would have made Wall Street history . . . maybe. (*Moving to conference room.*) On the other hand, proposition number two is something to talk about.

(*Lights up in conference room. Bea, Coles, and Jorgenson excitedly greet Kate as she enters.*)

KATE: Don't get excited. Don't break out the champagne. He gave me two propositions. Here's the one worth talking about. Inasmuch as Judge Pollard will not lift his injunction and inasmuch as his money is tied up, and, if I may say so, inasmuch as your lawyer can be very persuasive, he's agreeable to swap you his shares for the Wire and Cable division.

BEA: . . . What?

KATE: He owns a million shares. He gives them to us. We give him the Wire and Cable division.

COLES: Makes sense. It costs him thirteen million for something he'll sell for thirty — thirty-five million.

JORGENSON (*trying to control himself*): What are the alternatives?

KATE: Don't dismiss it so quickly. On Wall Street this is known as "restructuring." Look what happens. The losses at Wire and Cable disappear. The earnings of the other divisions surface. Your stock skyrockets.

JORGENSON: What are the alternatives?

KATE: Better yet, you get back his million shares you absolutely control this company. It's yours. No one can take it away.

JORGENSON: I'm asking you for the last —

KATE: I can't play with him in the courts forever. Ultimately he gets the injunction withdrawn, buys more shares . . . don't you understand?

BEA: We're not stupid — we understand. What are the alternatives!

KATE: Greenmail. Poison pills. Restructuring. I wouldn't even dare mention a leveraged buyout. You choose. I have given you the alternatives.

JORGENSON: You've given me nothing but different ways to kill myself.

COLES: Jorgy, this idea works. We're rid of the losses. We're in total control. Our stock doubles.

JORGENSON: To hell with the price of our stock. I will not do Garfinkle's dirty work for him.

KATE: I'm pleading with you. I'm imploring you.

JORGENSON: I will not do it. I will not kill these people and this town to enrich the man who is trying to destroy me.

KATE: You're a fool. You're a Neanderthal. You deserve to lose this company!

BEA: Stop that. This is not a chess game. It's not simply a matter of tactics. What's the matter with you? This used to be your home. This is family.

KATE: Family!?

BEA: Yes. The kids you went to school with dream their dreams at this plant. Family.

KATE: Oh good God. OK, let's talk about family. Let's start with Dad. Let's start with his dreams and his family.

BEA: Your father is dead, Kate. But we're not dead. And this plant is not dead. And our dreams aren't over. And they'll never end with greenmail and poison pills.

KATE: Stop talking dreams. Look at the reality.

BEA: I am looking at the reality and I don't like what I see. It scares me. Who are you, Kate? Whatever happened to that brave young girl who set out to do battle to heal all the world's ills? (*Distraught.*) Whatever happened to my baby? (*Jorgenson moves to Bea. With his arm around her shoulder, he begins ushering her off.*)

JORGENSON: Please.

BEA: What are you doing? She is my daughter. This is my fight.

JORGENSON: This is our company. This is my fight, too. I won't embarrass you.

Promise. (*Bea reluctantly exits. Kate begins to leave.*) Hold on a minute
. . . What do you want of me, Kate? Want me to say "I'm sorry"? For
what? For loving your mother? I'm not. Look, we are fighting for our
lives — here and now . . . Why are we even talking about this?

KATE: Because it still hurts.

JORGENSON: Well, what do we do now Kate? Go over it — resolve thirty-some-
odd years of hurt in the next fifteen minutes? Is that what you expect?

KATE: No I don't. But I'll tell you what I do expect. I expect not to be lectured
to about "family" by my mother and not be abused by you.

JORGENSON: Abused?

KATE: I turned my life upside down to come up here to help you out. I don't
even get to take off my jacket and you're ready to have me "bodily thrown
out of your office." Well I'll make it easy for you. I'll leave. (*She turns to
exit.*)

JORGENSON: Well go ahead then and leave. You're a lousy lawyer anyway.

KATE (*returning*): Lousy lawyer!? I want to tell you something. I'm a goddamned
good lawyer. You are a lousy client. You say "No" to everything. You say
"No" to what ninety-nine percent of other corporations say "Yes" to. If
this was any other outfit they'd put a statue out there in the yard of the
woman that saved this company.

JORGENSON: Saved this company? You're not looking to save this company.
You're looking to save your own ass.

KATE: . . . What?

JORGENSON: Being beaten by Garfinkle wouldn't look so good on your résumé,
would it? Damn it Kate — you want to win so badly, you don't even know
what this fight is all about!

KATE: Oh yes I do. It's about your incredible — pigheadedness.

JORGENSON: OK. Sure it is. But it's more than that. It's also about the twelve
hundred men who work here and their families — and their future. Let's
ask them if you're trying to "save this company."

KATE: Why ask them? They're not stockholders.

JORGENSON: Does that mean they don't matter?

KATE: . . . OK . . . Look. They matter. Nothing gets resolved but everything
matters.

JORGENSON: What matters most is this is now my nickel. So let's stop fighting
about what I won't do and let's start fighting about what I will do.

KATE: OK. Here's my problem. I'm a good lawyer. I'm a lousy mindreader.
What will you do?

JORGENSON: I'll leave it up to the stockholders. (*Kate laughs in exasperation.*)

KATE: You will leave it up to the stockholders?

JORGENSON: They haven't let me down yet.

KATE: They haven't met Garfinkle yet.

JORGENSON: I don't have a choice. I do — not — have a choice I can live with.

KATE: Oh, why couldn't you be an asshole like everybody else?

JORGENSON: I'm sorry. I thought I was doing my best.

KATE: OK — look. This forty percent . . . This faithful forty percent . . . Can you absolutely count on them?

JORGENSON: Absolutely. Come on, let's kick his ass all the way back to Wall Street.

KATE: Jorgy, if I play Garfinkle right. If I massage that ego just right, this could work. (*Kate and Jorgenson cross into his office.*)

(*Coles enters alone, addresses audience.*)

COLES: It didn't seem the appropriate time to ask: "And what happens to me if we lose?" It never seemed the appropriate time to ask that. When you spend your life managing a business you're trained to think in contingencies. What happens if sales don't meet expectations? What happens if costs go up — the economy down? What happens if . . .

So . . . later that afternoon, with a lump in my throat, I asked, "What happens to me if we lose? I deserve," I said, "a golden parachute. Managements with far worse records than mine routinely give themselves at least five years' pay. It's done all the time. And it wouldn't cost you a thing. . . ." Know what he said?

JORGENSON (*in his darkened office*): Up here we don't plan the funeral until someone dies.

COLES: Isn't that something? (*Coles exits.*)

(*Lights up in Jorgenson's office. Kate is preparing to leave.*)

JORGENSON: So . . . You think he'll go for it?

KATE: . . . I don't know.

JORGENSON: You can do it. Use some of that home-grown New England charm. Talk nice. Smile sweet. You'll get him.

KATE: Don't go away. (*She turns to Garfinkle's darkened office.*) Hey Garfinkle! Rumor has it you got balls.

(*Lights go up on Garfinkle in his office.*)

GARFINKLE: I've been trying to show you for weeks.

KATE (*moving into conference room area*): Show me now. Let's leave it up to the stockholders. We'll let you run your own slate of directors at the annual meeting. You get fifty-one percent of the votes, it's your company. You buy everybody out at twenty. You don't get the votes, you sell us back your shares at thirteen. You slink away, never to be seen or heard from again . . . What do you say, Garfinkle? Hardball. Winner takes all.

GARFINKLE: Is that what you want?

KATE: A lot.

GARFINKLE: I don't know. It's a tough proposition. You control forty percent of the votes going in.

KATE: What do you got to lose? On a worst-case basis you come out even. It only cost you thirteen.

GARFINKLE: I don't know. It's gonna be close.

ACT TWO

KATE: Robin Hood makes the deal.

GARFINKLE: . . . Yeah. Do it. (*Lights out on Garfinkle's office.*)

(*Kate turns to Jorgenson's office. Lights come up. Bea and Jorgenson are present.*)

KATE: Done. (*She moves to exit.*)

JORGENSON: Hold on. Where are you going?

KATE: The airport.

JORGENSON: I'll give you a lift.

KATE: Don't bother.

JORGENSON: At least let me tell you how great you did.

KATE: We'll see at the annual meeting.

BEA: I know this wasn't your preference. Thanks for sticking your neck out. How does it feel?

KATE: Scary. It's going to be close.

JORGENSON: Close? We have forty percent. He has twenty-five. We would only need ten of the remaining thirty-five. That's less than one in three. If we can't get that — Christ, Richard Nixon could get that.

BEA (*to Kate*): Always wanted to be a politician.

JORGENSON: I did. Always wanted to be Harry Truman. Goddamned son of a bitch just went out and told the truth. (*To Bea.*) And that's what we're going to do. We're going out there and tell the truth. Send a letter to the stockholders? We'll visit them. Hell, we'll even have them over for dinner.

KATE: Harry and Bess hit the campaign trail. (*Begins to leave.*)

JORGENSON: Before you go. You said he gave you two propositions. What was the other?

KATE: Oh, just Garfinkle's idea of a tender offer. Come on. Drive me to the airport.

(*Blackout. Lights up on Garfinkle alone in his office. Coles enters, briefcase in hand.*)

GARFINKLE: Aw Christ, what do *you* want?

COLES: Good morning, Mr. Garfinkle.

GARFINKLE: Are you about to regale me with the latest saga of Bill Jr., at Columbia?

COLES: Strictly business. As you know I had sixty thousand shares of New England stock when we first met.

GARFINKLE: Excuse me — it'll be a history lesson instead.

COLES: Since becoming aware of your investment I have purchased an additional forty thousand shares. I now have a hundred thousand shares.

GARFINKLE: Congratulations.

COLES: I'm prepared to sell you the right to vote those shares at the annual meeting. Are you interested?

GARFINKLE: Sit down. I'm interested. (*Coles sits.*) How much?

COLES: A million.

GARFINKLE: Too much.

COLES: You need a million shares above what you already own. I can get you ten percent of the way there in one transaction. Better yet, it's votes they're counting on for themselves. I think what I'm asking is fair.

GARFINKLE: If your shares make a difference — if I win by less than a hundred thousand you got your million. Otherwise I don't need them. I won't vote them.

COLES: I'm not selling you an option. I'm selling you the right to vote the shares. How you vote them, if you vote them, is your business. It's of no concern to me.

GARFINKLE: . . . If they make the difference, you got a million. If they don't half a million.

COLES: Agreed. (*Reaching into his briefcase.*) I've prepared the papers. I just left the numbers blank. Have your lawyers review it. I'm staying over. I'll pick it up in the morning — along with a check. (*Places papers neatly on Garfinkle's desk.*) Good day, Mr. Garfinkle. (*Exits Garfinkle's office. Moves center stage. Garfinkle shouts after him, a beat after his exit.*)

GARFINKLE: And how is Bill Jr. doing with his studies? (*Lights out on Garfinkle. Coles is alone.*)

COLES: Don't look at me like that. Everybody looks out after their own self-interest. "What's in it for me?" Isn't that, ultimately, what it's all about? Jorgenson looks out for his monument. Garfinkle for his money. Bea for her man. Kate for her career. The employees for their paycheck. I kept this company alive. I helped make it all possible. Who looks out for me? (*A burst of music as lights slowly fade on Coles.*)

(*Lights up on Bea as she tries to get her bearings.*)

BEA: This way? . . . Through there . . .

(*Lights up on Garfinkle in his office. She enters.*)

BEA: Good afternoon, Mr. Garfinkle.

GARFINKLE: Oh no — the donut thrower. Wait — I got to get my catcher's mask.

BEA: I'm sorry. I didn't bring any.

GARFINKLE: Aw . . . And I was looking forward to some of your nutritious health donuts — you know — yogurt sprinkles — penicillin-filled.

BEA: . . . These offices are every bit as impressive as my daughter said they were.

GARFINKLE: . . . What do you know . . . I like your daughter. She's hot shit.

BEA: . . . I think so too . . . assuming I know what you mean.

GARFINKLE: You know what I mean. She's terrific. And she didn't get that way working for those clowns at Morgan, Stanley. She must've got it from you.

BEA: That's kind of you.

GARFINKLE: Did she send you? I wouldn't put it past her.

BEA: She didn't send me. She would be upset with me if she knew. I expect this meeting will be held in confidence.

GARFINKLE: Have a seat. (*She sits.*) What can I do for you?

ACT TWO

BEA: You can take the million dollars I'm about to offer you.

GARFINKLE (*sitting*): . . . This is gonna be some day.

BEA: I thought that might interest you. There is a trust fund, in my name, with a million dollars, primarily in treasury notes, in it. I will turn it over to you if you call off your fight with us. We will buy back your shares at thirteen, which Kate informs me gets you even, plus you'll have a million dollars profit.

GARFINKLE: How come I never had a mother like you?

BEA: Is that acceptable?

GARFINKLE: My mother — I gotta send a check once a month. Would you like to meet her?

BEA: Is that acceptable?

GARFINKLE: How much money you make a year?

BEA: I don't see —

GARFINKLE: How much?

BEA: Forty thousand. Plus health insurance.

GARFINKLE: Why would you give up a million to save forty?

BEA: That's my affair. Is it agreeable to you?

GARFINKLE: Who are you doing it for?

BEA: Myself. I don't need the money.

GARFINKLE: I don't either.

BEA: Then why are you doing it?

GARFINKLE: That's what I do for a living. I make money.

BEA: You will have made money. If you accept my offer you will have made a million dollars. For a few weeks' effort you will have made more than most working a lifetime.

GARFINKLE: Go home. I don't want your money.

BEA: Why? Isn't it good enough for you?

GARFINKLE: It's good. It's just not enough.

BEA: I know a million dollars is not a great deal of money to you. It's all I have. If I had more I'd give you more. I had really hoped to appeal to whatever decent instincts you have left. I'm here to plead for my company.

GARFINKLE: Go home.

BEA: Please, Mr. Garfinkle.

GARFINKLE: I don't take money from widows and orphans. I make them money.

BEA: Before or after you put them out of business?

GARFINKLE: You're getting on my nerves. Go home.

BEA: I intend to. Before I go I'd like to know — I'd like you to tell me — how you can live with yourself?

GARFINKLE: I have no choice. No one else will.

BEA: How? How can you destroy a company . . . its people . . . for the sake of dollars you don't even need?

GARFINKLE: Because it's there.

BEA: . . . Because it's there?

GARFINKLE: What? People climb mountains — swim oceans — walk through fire — 'cause it's there. This way is better. You don't get all sweated up.

BEA: There are people there. There are dreams there —

GARFINKLE: Do you want to give a speech or do you want an answer? 'Cause the answer is not complicated. It's simple. I do it for the money. I don't need the money. I want the money. Shouldn't surprise you. Since when do needs and wants have anything to do with one another? If they did I'd be back in the Bronx and you'd be getting Yorgy his coffee up in Grimetown. You don't need the job. You need the million dollars. But you're prepared to give up what you need — a million dollars — for what you want — a stinking job. You're fucked up, lady. You're sick. Go see a psychiatrist.

BEA: You are the sick one. Don't you know that?

GARFINKLE: Why? 'Cause I know what I want and I know how to get it? Lady, I *looooove* money. I love money more than I love the things it can buy. And I love the things it can buy. You know why? Money is unconditional acceptance. It don't care whether I'm good or not, whether I snore or don't, which God I pray to — it still gets me as much interest in the bank as yours does. There's only three things in this world that give that kind of unconditional acceptance — dogs, donuts, and money. Only money is better. It don't make you fat and it don't shit all over the living room floor.

BEA: I hope you choke on your money and die! (*She exits. Garfinkle smiles sadly.*)

GARFINKLE: How come I always bring out the best in people?

KATE (*in conference room*): You bring out the best in me.

GARFINKLE: I know I do that, Katie, me girl.

KATE: The Irish in me.

GARFINKLE: . . . Same thing.

KATE: What's the matter? Are you becoming melancholy on me?

GARFINKLE: Melancholy? Why would you say that? Just 'cause the governor calls every hour . . . the unions are picketing my house . . . prayer meetings daily chant for my demise —

KATE (*moving to his office*): You're in the wrong profession. You should head the U.N. Nobody can bring people together like you . . . not even a chuckle? You must really be in bad shape. Feeling unloved?

GARFINKLE: Unappreciated. I'm doing the right thing. I'm taking unproductive assets and making them productive. Just following the law of free enterprise economics.

KATE: What law is that?

GARFINKLE: Survival of the fittest.

KATE: The Charles Darwin of Wall Street!

GARFINKLE (*laughing*): . . . I like that. The Charles Darwin of Wall Street.

KATE: Maybe they don't see it that way. Maybe they don't see it as survival of the fittest. Maybe they see it as survival of the fattest.

GARFINKLE: Aw, Katie, why are you so hard on me?

ACT TWO

KATE: 'Cause you're not nice.

GARFINKLE: Since when do you have to be nice to be right?

KATE: You're not right. You're "What's happening." One day we'll smarten up and pass some laws and put you out of business. Ten years from now they'll be studying you at the Wharton School. They'll call it the "Garfinkle Era" and rinse out their mouths when they leave the room.

GARFINKLE: That's how you talk about family?

KATE: Family?

GARFINKLE: Immediate family. For every deal I find, you guys bring me ten. We happen to be in bed together, lady. Calling it family that's being nice. Look at me, Kate.

KATE: I'm going to put you away, Garfinkle.

GARFINKLE: I'm not going away. They can pass all the laws they want — All they can do is change the rules — they can't stop the game. I don't go way. I adapt. Look at me, Kate. Look at you. God damn it! We're the same!

KATE: We are not the same. We are not the same! We sit on opposite sides here. I like where I sit. You sit in shit.

GARFINKLE: You sit with me.

KATE: You sit alone.

GARFINKLE: Alone? Get off it, will you? We've come from "Ask not what your country can do for you" to "What's in it for me?" to "What's in it for me — today!" all in one short generation. That's why those stockholders all love me and that's why you guys all work for me. Nobody's putting a gun to anyone's head. Everybody's got their hand out.

KATE: Not everybody. Not me. Not them.

GARFINKLE: Forget them. It's about you and me now, Kate. I'm the last thought you have when you fall asleep at night and the first when you wake in the morning. I make your juices flow and you know it.

KATE: Garfinkle, if you knew what you do to me you wouldn't brag about it.

GARFINKLE: And you know what makes the two of us so special? What sets us apart? We care more about the game than we do the players. That's not bad. That's smart.

KATE: That's grotesque, Garfinkle. You don't know me. You're not capable of knowing me. You can't see beyond your appetite.

GARFINKLE: Then what the fuck are you doing here!? You can't keep away. You don't want to keep away. Come . . . *play* with me. Be a *player* — not a technician. Feel the power. This is where you belong, Kate. With me. I know you. I know who you are. I like who you are. I want you, Kate.

KATE (*moving away*): I'm going to nail you, Garfinkle. I'm going to send you back to Wall Street with donuts up your ass and everyone's going to know how some broad wet behind the ears did you. And whatever happens from this day forward, whatever success I achieve, none — none will be sweeter than this one! (*She exits. Garfinkle, a beat after the exit yells to her.*)

GARFINKLE: You're so perfect for me! (*Turns, begins to exit.*) To be continued. In Grimetown. (*He exits.*)

(*Lights up on Jorgenson alone in his office. Bea enters, gently singing "Hey, Good Lookin'." Jorgenson smiles weakly.*)

BEA: You OK?

JORGENSON: Just going over in my head what I want to say.

BEA: They're putting speakers out in the hallways. The auditorium won't fit everyone. I feel like we're Harry and Bess on election night.

JORGENSON: Harry was a better man than me. Went to sleep election night. I haven't slept good for days.

BEA: Talk to me.

JORGENSON: I'm scared, Bea. I'm scared time has passed us by. I'm scared I don't know this new environment. I'm scared what I do know doesn't count for anything anymore.

BEA (*moves behind him. Rubs his neck.*): I'm not scared. I'm proud. I'm proud of the business we built. Most of all I'm proud of you. And if what we are counts for nothing anymore, that won't be our failing — it'll be theirs. (*He smiles. Squeezes her hand.*) It'll be all right. Just go out and tell the truth. Go out and give them hell, Harry. (*They remain frozen.*)

(*Garfinkle enters. Looks at them.*)

GARFINKLE: The truth? Why don't you tell the truth, lady? The truth is Harry Truman is dead.

(*A burst of music. Lights dim on Bea and Jorgenson though they continue visible. Garfinkle moves to his darkened office. Bea moves downstage center. We're at the annual meeting. Scene is played as if audience were the stockholders. Kate, Coles, and Jorgenson sit at conference room table.*)

BEA: That concludes the formal aspect of our annual meeting. The one remaining item of business is the election of directors. Is there anyone entitled to vote who does not have a ballot? Please raise your hand. (*She looks about at the audience.*) Will the inspector of elections distribute the ballots. Please keep your hand raised so you can receive your ballot. Thank you. (*Jorgenson rises from table and moves to downstage center.*)

JORGENSON (*addressing audience as if they were the stockholders*): It's nice to see so many familiar faces . . . so many old friends . . . many of you I haven't seen for years. Thank you for coming and welcome to the seventy-third annual meeting of New England Wire and Cable — the thirty-eighth of which I am addressing you as your chief executive.

   Bill Coles, our able president, has told you about our year; what we accomplished — where we need to make further improvements — what our business goals are for next year and the years beyond.

I'd like to talk to you about something else. On this, our seventy-third year, I'd like to share with you some of my thoughts concerning the vote you are about to make in the company you own.

We've had some very good years. We've had some difficult ones as well. Though the last decade has been troubling for us it's been devastating for our industry. Ten short years ago we were the twelfth largest manufacturer of wire and cable in the country, the fourth largest in New England. We're now the third largest in the country and the largest in New England.

We might not have flourished — but we survived. And we're stronger for it. I'm proud of what we accomplished.

So, we're at that point, where this proud company, which has survived the death of its founder, numerous recessions, a major depression, and two world wars, is in imminent danger of self-destructing this day in the town of its birth.

And there is the instrument of our destruction. I want you to see him in all his glory. Larry the Liquidator — the entrepreneur in post-industrial America — playing God with other people's money.

(*Garfinkle nods to the audience.*)

At least the robber barons of old left something tangible in their wake. A coal mine. A railroad. Banks. This man leaves nothing. He creates nothing. He builds nothing. He runs nothing. In his wake lies nothing but a blizzard of paper to cover the pain.

If he said, "I could run this business better." Well, that's something worth talking about. He's not saying that. He's saying, "I am going to kill you because at this particular moment in time you're worth more dead than alive."

Well maybe that's true. But it is also true that one day this industry will turn. One day when the dollar is weaker or the yen stronger or when we finally begin to rebuild the roads, the bridges, the infrastructure of our country, demand will skyrocket. And when those things happen we will be here — and we will be stronger for our ordeal — stronger for having survived. And the price of our stock will make his offer pale by comparison.

God save us if you vote to take his paltry few dollars and run. God save this country if (*pointing to Garfinkle*) "that" is truly the wave of the future. We will then have become a nation that makes nothing but hamburgers, creates nothing but lawyers, and sells nothing but tax shelters.

And if we have come to the point in this country where we kill something because at the moment it's worth more dead than alive, then turn around and take a good look at your neighbor. You won't kill him because it's called "murder" and it's illegal. This too is murder, on a mass scale, only on Wall Street they call it "maximizing shareholder values" and they call it legal and they substitute dollar bills where a conscience should be.

Damn it. A business is more than the price of its stock. It is the place where we make our living, meet our friends, and dream our dreams. It is, in every sense, the very fabric that binds our society together. So let us, right now, at this meeting, say to every Garfinkle in this land, that here we build things, we don't destroy them. Here, we care for more than the price of our stock. Here . . . we care about people. (*Jorgenson moves from lectern back to table. Bea, Coles, and Kate stand and applaud. Garfinkle follows Jorgenson back and as the applause dies, says to Bea, Coles, and Jorgenson respectively.*)

GARFINKLE: Amen . . . And Amen . . . And Amen. Say "Amen," someone, please! (*To audience.*) You'll excuse me. I'm not familiar with the local custom . . . The way I was brought up you always said "Amen" after you heard a prayer. You hear someone praying, after he finishes, you say "Amen" and drink a little wine.

'Cause that's what you just heard — a prayer. The way I was brought up we called the particular prayer — the prayer for the dead. You just heard the prayer for the dead, and fellow stuckholders, you didn't say "Amen" and you didn't even get to sip the wine.

What — You don't think this company is dead? Steel — you remember steel, don't you? Steel used to be an industry. Now heavy metal is a rock group.

This company is dead. Don't blame me. I didn't kill it. It was dead when I got here. It is too late for prayers, for even if the prayers were answered and a miracle occurred and the yen did this and the dollar did that and the infrastructure did the other thing we would still be dead. Know why? Fiberoptics. New technologies. Obsolescence.

We're dead all right. We're just not broke. And you know the surest way to go broke? Keep getting an increasing share of a shrinking market. Down the tubes. Slow but sure. You know, at one time there must have been dozens of companies making buggy whips. And I'll bet you anything the last one around was the one that made the best goddamned buggy whip you ever saw. How would you have liked to have been a stuckholder of that company?

You invested in a business. And that business is dead. Let's have the intelligence, let's have the decency, to sign the death certificate, collect the insurance, and invest the money in something with a future.

Aha — But we can't, goes the prayer — we can't because we have a responsibility — a responsibility to our employees, our community. What will happen to them? I got two words for that — "Who cares?" Care about them? They didn't care about you. They sucked you dry. You have no responsibility to them.

For the last ten years this company has bled your money. Did this community care? Did they ever say, "I know things are tough. We'll lower your taxes, reduce water and sewer"? Check it out. We're paying twice what we paid ten years ago. And the mayor is making twice what he made ten years ago. And our devoted employees, after taking no increases for three years, are still making twice what they made ten years ago. And our stock is one-sixth what it was ten years ago. Who cares? I'll tell you — me!

I'm not your best friend — I'm your only friend. I care about you in the only way that matters in business. I don't make anything? I'm making you money. And, lest we forget, that's the only reason any of you became stockholders in the first place. To make money. You don't care if they manufacture wire and cable, fry chicken, or grow tangerines. You want to make money. I'm making you money. I'm the only friend you got.

Take that money. Invest it somewhere else. Maybe — maybe you'll get lucky and it will be used productively — and if it is — you'll create more jobs and provide a service for the economy and God forbid — even make a few bucks for yourself. Let the government and the mayor and the unions worry about what you paid them to worry about. And if anyone asks, tell them you gave at the plant.

And it pleases me that I'm called "Larry the Liquidator." You know why, fellow stuckholders? Because at my funeral you'll leave with a smile on your face . . . and a few bucks in your pocket. Now that's a funeral worth having. (*Breathing heavily, Garfinkle pauses a beat and sits.*)

BEA: . . . Will the inspector of elections please collect the ballots.

(*The lights dim. Players are now in shadows. Coles rises, moves slowly center stage, addresses audience.*)

COLES: That's what happened. That's it. All of it.

BEA: Is there anyone entitled to vote who has not turned in a ballot?

COLES: It's happening everywhere. No one is immune.

BEA: To retain the present board: 1,741,416.

COLES: I think the old man gave the speech of his life. I can't think how he could have said it better.

BEA: For the opposition slate: 2,219,901.

COLES: What do we do? Pass another law. There's already a law against murder. All he did was supply the weapon.

BEA: Not voting: 176,111.

COLES: Garfinkle won in a landslide. Didn't even need my votes. Cost me the second half million but I feel good about that. I feel better about getting the first half million. I feel best it cost him money he didn't have to spend. That's the only kind of lasting satisfaction you get when you deal with people like him.

BEA: Mr. Garfinkle, your slate is elected.

COLES: He had the nerve to ask me to stay on while he dismembered the company. Even offered me a raise. I said no, of course. There's a point at which we all draw the line.

JORGENSON (*in his office*): We can't leave now. I have to tell the men.

BEA: They know.

JORGENSON: . . . Already?

BEA: Let's go home. There'll be time tomorrow.

JORGENSON: Even . . . Ozzie voted for him. (*He exits. She remains.*)

COLES: He didn't take it well. From me . . . I think he expected it. Ozzie . . . kind of threw him. With all his money you'd think he would have left. Gone somewhere nice . . . somewhere warm. He didn't. Stayed right here. Died almost two years later. Left more than thirty million.

BEA: Jorgy, you only made one mistake in your life. You lived two years too long.

COLES: Bea became executor of his estate. Bought the land the plant used to sit on. Put up a kind of . . . Employee Retraining Center — Actually placed a few people . . . about a hundred of the twelve hundred or so that worked there when the plant closed. It wasn't easy retraining middle-aged men who are used to working with their hands. Some went to work for McDonald's . . . or as night watchmen.

Me? I didn't do too badly. I moved back to Florida. Run a midsized division for a nationally known food processor. I won't ever run the company . . . but I'm financially secure. And you can't beat the weather.

(*Lights up on Garfinkle. He speaks to Kate who is seated at conference table.*)

GARFINKLE: I'm sorry, Kate. I'm surprised myself. See, you do bring out the best in me. Come, ride back to New York with me . . . You worried it wouldn't look right? Don't. It's the perfect ending . . . Come . . . Come. (*She doesn't move.*) I got donuts in the car.

COLES: Kate and Garfinkle? Well, three months later, which was as soon as she could work things out at Morgan, Stanley, she went to work for him. (*Kate rises from table and moves to Garfinkle's office.*) She was very good. Three months after that she became his partner. (*Kate takes a folder from Garfinkle and sits at his desk.*) . . . then his wife. (*Garfinkle beams. Bea exits.*) They have two kids. Set of twins. Call them their "little bull and little bear." Friend of mine saw them the other day . . . Said he never saw them happier. (*Kate and Garfinkle smile at one another. A short burst of music.*)

(*Blackout.*)

1987

INVESTIGATIONS

1. On page 565, the following exchange takes place:

> KATE: Is that what this is for you, a game?
> GARFINKLE: Goddamned right. The best game in the world.

To what extent does Kate consider her job a game? What conditions influence the extent to which a person considers his or her work a game? To what extent might the individuals you've read about so far in Part Five think of their jobs as games? What characteristics of game-playing can make work rewarding?

2. On page 575, William Coles says to the audience, "Don't look at me like that. Everybody looks out after their own self-interest. 'What's in it for me?' Isn't that, ultimately, what it's all about?" Write a 500–750-word essay in which you answer him.

3. On page 577, Garfinkle says his reason for doing what he does "is not complicated. It's simple." He tells Bea, "I do it for the money. I don't need the money. I want the money. Shouldn't surprise you. Since when do needs and wants have anything to do with one another?" Do you agree with him that needs and wants don't have anything to do with one another? Why or why not? What is the connection between needs and wants for the speakers of Levine's "Buying and Selling" and Daniels's "My Father Worked Late"? For Rachel L. Jones ("The Price of Hate: Thoughts on Covering a Ku Klux Klan Rally," p. 606)?

RALPH LOMBREGLIA

Late Early Man

"I was talking to your girlfriend this morning," announces Anita, speaking from the carpeted floor of our editing suite, where she's sprawled like a stranded whale, her head cushioned by a coil of video cables, her silky blue harem pants pulled up above her knees. She's buffing her face with an ice cube as though taking a gravestone rubbing. After lunch she lost the ability to sit up in a chair, and I had to take over at the controls. Our suite contains the only air conditioner in all of Paradise Productions, and it broke down last night, and this is the two-week stretch of hell we go through every summer in Boston, when you can't buy an air conditioner no matter how much money you're willing to spend. The hardware commando, Marco Tempesto, was supposed to come over and fix the one we have, but apparently he's too busy building one of his lasers, or simulating reality on a computer somewhere. "She was telling me she wants you to do this to her," Anita says.

RALPH LOMBREGLIA has spoken of his desire "to make fiction" as a "golden yearning . . . to wander [his] garden bestowing names on the creatures, things still good between [him] and God." Recipient of a Wallace Stegner Fellowship from Stanford University and a National Endowment for the Arts grant, Lombreglia has published short stories in *The Atlantic*, *The Iowa Review*, *The Agni Review*, and *Best American Short Stories* (1987, 1988). His first novel, *Men Under Water*, appeared in 1990.

I twiddle a knob on the console to stop the videotape. "Wants me to do what?"

"You know. Knock her up. Make her pregnant. I'm supposed to plant that suggestion in your mind."

Anita has been with child now for as long as anyone can remember. The baby was due a week ago, and there's still no sign it plans to throw in the towel and come out. Everybody in the office lost the birth-date lottery; we had to make new guesses and put them in the hat all over again.

"Rebecca told you that?" I say. "When?"

"This morning. She was leaving for work when I came in. You were in the shower."

"And she said she wanted me to knock her up."

"Yup."

I have to say, this amazes me. Rebecca and I had a terrible fight this morning before I got in the shower. She was gone when I got out. We fight all the time, and later I can never remember what the fights were about. Rebecca makes documentary films for a station in town, and she stays with me here half the time. I sublet the apartment downstairs — that's how I came to work at Paradise Productions. It's how I met Rebecca, too. She and Anita go back a long way. Anita fixed us up.

"Can I give you some advice?" Anita says. "Do it so she has the kid in the spring. Everybody told me, 'Anita, whatever you do, don't be pregnant in the summertime.' That was the one thing I was supposed to remember. So what do I go and do?" She raises herself up on one elbow. "In fact, right now would be the perfect time."

"Anita? Didn't you kind of get pregnant by accident?"

"Walter!" she cries. "We always thought we might have a baby someday. Maybe, anyway. It crossed our minds. Don't call my baby an accident!"

"I just meant you're not really the family-planning type, you and Dwight."

"No, you're right. We're more the walk-off-the-edge-of-a-cliff type." She selects a new ice cube from the bucket and burnishes her face some more. Then she stops, lapsing into reflection. "Do you think that's a problem?"

"Me? No. I have a lot of respect for people who walk off cliffs."

"You're nice, Walter," she says, continuing with the ice. "I'm glad we found you. Now what's going on up there? You're not telling me anything."

"Benny's molecules are attacking the other molecules. Benny's are winning."

"Oh, good. We're up to the molecules. What's after that?"

"The scientist comes on and starts talking."

"Right. Stop it there," she says. "Let's think this through. We have the nice molecules. Why do we need a scientist talking about them?"

"Because Benny said we have to?"

"Yeah, but that can't be the reason. Scientists are boring. People turn off when they see scientists. No offense."

"What do you mean 'no offense'? I'm not a scientist."

5

10

15

20

"But maybe you played a scientist once. Like the guy in that commercial who says, 'I'm not a doctor, but I play one on TV.' "

"I've never played a scientist."

25

"Well, forget it then," she says. "What am I apologizing to you for?"

"I think we should crowbar the scientist in. Benny wants him."

"I know, I know," she sighs, rearranging herself on the floor and resting her arms on top of the medicine ball her belly has become. "Don't you sometimes wish Benny never found his niche in life?" Then she starts to giggle, but that jostles the baby too much. "Ow. It always kicks me when I laugh. It hates it when I'm happy."

Benny is Benjamin Silk, our client. Anita and Dwight are actually fond of Benny, partly because he's one of their best accounts, but also because he sees reality the way they do, as a collection of bites — verbal ones in Benny's case, the maxims and mottoes by which he orders the world. "Niche in life" is one of his favorites. He found his, and now everybody else had better find theirs. Me in particular. Benny sees me up here, an out-of-work actor writing video scripts, and he pegs me for a guy wandering through life in his boxer shorts, trying to remember what he did with his niche. He would like to save me from this fate. But that's the problem: I think niches are fate. Consider the unlikely people who manage to rendezvous with their niche. I've known a carpenter named Tilt and a tree surgeon named Wilde. Rebecca goes to a dentist named Payne. Once I was stopped by a State Trooper named Officer Crook.

And then there's Benny Silk himself. The first time I encountered him I   30
thought he was the most abrasive person I'd ever met. Then I found out his line of work: abrasives. Benny's the marketing director for an abrasives manufacturer. If it can scrape the surface off an object, if it can grind something down to a nub, if it can scour, sand, buff, or polish to a deep luster, Benny's company makes it. But he wasn't always in abrasives. He's done laminates and films, adhesives and coatings. Did a long stretch in lubrication. They all had their rewards, but they weren't his niche. Then Benny entered the realm of grit and found himself. He became an abrasives evangelist. "You gotta be rough to be smooth, son," he barked at me the moment we met, apropos of nothing except perhaps my scratchy, chapped hand crushed in his lotion-soft one.

Anita and I have been editing Benny's latest project — an infomercial about a fabulous new line of synthetic sandpaper — for two weeks now, twice the editing time prescribed in the budget, and it's still lying there dead. We can't figure out how to jolt it into life. The sandpaper in question is called Veritas Grit — christened by one of Benny's young marketeers from the Harvard Business School. Benny couldn't be more proud of his new stuff if it came from inside his own body, but he knows he's got a hard sell on his hands. Our tape claims that Veritas Grit works as well on metal as on wood, works even better on plastic, works wet or dry, and lasts longer than the competition's best stuff. The problem is it costs about twice as much. People will see the price in the store and go for the other brand. We have to convince them. To this end we've cut in testimonials from users in the field, official company demos, Tempesto's computer-animated molecules. Today, we spent the morning playing with the idea that Veritas Grit is "the premium sandpaper" before we finally dropped that out of shame. Still, Benny wants some compelling something, and whenever clients want something and don't know what it is, they go with an authority figure. Benny has forbidden us to remove this scientist.

Dwight lurches in, a skinny six-foot-six-inch man in a red T-shirt with a yellow peace symbol on the front, sharkskin slacks, low-slung tasselled loafers, translucent green nylon socks. "How's that old rough cut?" he says. "Getting it smoothed out?"

"It's beginning to grate on us," I say.

"Rubbing you wrong?" says Dwight, smiling brightly and joining Anita on the floor. "Going against your grain? Taking the edge off?"

"Dwight," I say, "do you notice anything about this room?"   35

He tumbles one of Anita's ice cubes in his mouth for a minute as though polishing a jewel. "Hot in here," he says around the ice.

"We can't work under these conditions, Dwight. Look at poor Anita."

"I told Anita she should be home, where it's cool," Dwight says, patting her head. "But she's a big girl. She wants to work."

Alongside Dwight's bony frame, Anita seems to have doubled in size in the heat, like bread dough. "I just want to wrap this tape," she says to the ceiling. "I just want to finish this project and go have my baby. And I can. I can. I just have to do it lying down, without moving."

"Dwight, you have to get Tempesto over here to fix this air conditioner,"   40
I say.

"Not possible, Walter. Tempesto's working on something else for me right now. Very important."

"More important than finishing this wretched tape?"

"As a matter of fact, that's what he is working on. I've enlisted his help."

"I thought we were doing that for laughs," Anita says. "You can't put that in this tape, Dwight."

"I think it's just what this tape needs," Dwight says. "We need to show   45
Benny's sandpaper in action. Show people the power of Veritas Grit!"

"Benny'll never go for it," Anita says.

"Anita, don't say that. We haven't even pitched it to him yet."

"Pitched what?" I say.

"What are you doing tonight, Walter?"

"Busy. Tied up."   50

"With Rebecca? She's invited."

"To what?"

"I already told her about it," Anita says. "She thinks it's stupid."

The intercom beeps, and Susie's transistorized voice issues forth from the speaker. Susie is our new Korean receptionist, discovered by Dwight in the corner store just days after her family arrived in the States. "Dwight, Tempasta on two," Susie says. "Tempasta for Dwight."

"Speak of the devil," Dwight says.   55

I dive for the phone and punch Line 2. "Tempesto, we're being roasted alive! You're torturing a pregnant woman! Get over here right now!"

Then Dwight and I wrestle for the phone. He wins, because my hands are too sweaty to hold on. "What's up?" he asks Tempesto.

"Fix our air conditioner, you bum!" Anita calls out.

"What happened?" Dwight says. "Again? For God's sake, Tempesto. Do they have our stuff? Great. OK, I'll grab Walter and we'll be right over."

"No! You can't take Walter!" Anita cries, waving her arms like an over-   60
turned crab.

Dwight hits the intercom button. "Susie to Editing Suite B," he says. "Suite B calling Miss Susie."

"Where is Tempesto, anyway?" I ask.

"Encountering some difficulties," Dwight says, fanning Anita with a folded Boston *Globe*. "Anita, you're my pregnant wife. I don't want you to be un-happy."

"Then go work on your own project and leave us alone!"

"I finished my project. I came in around three and wrapped that one up."   65

"How can you work with no sleep like that?" I say.

"That's when I'm at my best, Walter. If I'm well rested I think too much. You can really screw yourself up, thinking."

Susie appears in our doorway in a state of excited wonder, her arms and eyelids fluttering like hovering birds. I can never decide if Susie grasps the strangeness of her fate or if she thinks crazy video people await every girl who comes to America.

"Susie," Dwight says. "Anita's very uncomfortable."

"Too hot for mothership!" Susie says, waving at her own perspiring throat.   70

Dwight takes a clump of bills from his pants and extracts a couple of twenties. "Take the rest of the afternoon off, Susie. Take Anita to a nice air-conditioned movie. Eat ice cream."

"Tank you, Dwight!" Susie says.

"It's air-conditioned at home," Anita says. "We could rent *Rosemary's Baby*. Or maybe *The Exorcist*.

"I like romantic," says Susie, following us to the door. "Tempasta have many kidnaping!" she adds.

"Kidnaped?" I say. "Again?"   75

The radio in Dwight's air-conditioned 1964 Bonneville says that joggers shouldn't be jogging today — it's ninety-eight degrees with an air inversion trapping car exhaust like a humidor — but as we cross Storrow Drive they're out in normal numbers, running in place as they wait for the light, poised to inject themselves into Boston's jugular vein. They look like tropical fish school-ing outside our windows in their colorful shorts and shoes, gasping for air. Dwight is talking to Benny Silk on his car phone, taking the sports-fishing approach to client management — paying out some line, letting Benny run a little. "You're absolutely right, Benny," he's saying into the phone. "Yup, yup, I couldn't agree more." We cross the river and take Memorial Drive, past the Harvard sunbathers on the banks of the Charles, and by the time we're turning onto River Street toward Central Square Dwight is reeling Benny in: He will meet us after work at an industrial building in Somerville, next to Route 93, where Dwight will unveil his secret weapon of sandpaper salesmanship. Then Dwight hangs up.

"Can I make a call on that?" I say. "I've never talked to anybody on a car phone."

"What are you, early man? I'm riding in a car with early man?"

I call Rebecca at work. "Guess where I am," I say.

"I called Paradise before," she says. "They wouldn't put me through."   80

"Anita made Susie hold our calls. Because of the crunch we're in."

"Then I left a message on your machine downstairs."

"We didn't have time to stop there. We're going to rescue Tempesto."

"Where are you?"

"Driving down River Street."   85

"I hate that. Why do people have to talk on the phone in their cars?"

"Would you like to ask Dwight? It's his phone."

"I'm mad at Dwight. That's what I was calling about. I ran into Anita this morning. Everybody knows she's a nut, but what's his excuse?"

"For what?"

"For letting her work in her condition, and then taking her to this hippy   90 dippy thing tonight."

"Hippy dippy?"

"You don't think an electric belt-sander race is hippy dippy? Maybe the Merry Pranksters'll be there. Maybe we'll all drink some electric Kool-Aid."

"I've been wanting to get a new outlook on things."

"I'd like a man with all his chromosomes. And when I'm a week overdue you better not pull stuff like this on me."

"We're having a baby?"   95

"I meant if we ever did."

"This is the first I've heard about it."

"I've tried to bring it up plenty of times."

"Not that I can remember."

"I've alluded to it. I've made suggestions. A man who was somewhere   100 besides on Mars would have taken the hint."

"She's mad at both of us," I tell Dwight, holding out the phone. He does resemble Timothy Leary, now that I look at him behind the wheel, the worn-down buildings of Cambridge going by in the background. "Belt-sander races, hugh, Dwight? Fascinating."

"I was planning to tell you," he says to me, and then, into the phone, he says, "I can see being mad at *him,* but what did I do?" Then he gets a good long tongue-lashing. "She insists on working, Rebecca," he finally gets in. "I want her to stay home. I am not a slave driver. It's her tape. She's the producer.

I'm the executive producer. You went to college with her, you know how she is. I need Walter there tonight. Our client has taken a liking to him. You're coming, right? I was counting on you to bring Anita. You'll love it. Tempesto? He's being held for ransom. Yup, again. Don't ask me. OK. Bye."

He hangs up and says, "Are you and Rebecca getting along all right, Walter?"

"I don't know, Dwight. I'm drama. She's documentary. It's a constant struggle."

"I figured you were the real problem. She said I was a negligent husband, a rotten father, and an example of the Peter Pan syndrome. That just doesn't fit."

"Well, you have to admit, Dwight. Belt-sander races. It looks pretty bad."

"Walter. Not you, too. You don't trust me."

"You don't tell me anything."

"You know Veritas Grit is a big deal for Benny's company."

"Right, I know that."

"I'm sure it's great sandpaper and everything, but sandpaper's sandpaper, don't you think? You know the real reason it's such a big deal?"

"This must be the part you didn't tell me."

"Because the guy who named it Veritas Grit is the son of one of the company wigs. Fresh out of B-school, doesn't know a thing, but before long he'll be Benny's boss. He's hot to make his mark. He wants a video people won't forget when they see it at trade shows. He wants a spot for cable that'll be like MTV for the abrasives world. He's talking about taking this account to an ad agency."

"The ambitious little snot!"

"Right. I tell Benny we can do all this for a fraction of the price, but it's not gonna be Benny's call. The wig's son is gonna call it. Veritas Grit's his baby. I'm giving birth to a human being, this guy's giving birth to a piece of sandpaper. And the question is: Whose kid's getting that money?"

"Ours!"

"You bet. So I'm telling all this to Tempesto a few days ago, and he mentions these belt-sander races he goes to sometimes. And, bingo, it hits me."

"What?"

"What do you mean, what? Winners use Veritas Grit."

We've arrived at a used-computer store outside Inman Square. Dwight parks, and we step out into the broiler of the world. "I love this place," he says. "They have everything. All the M.I.T. guys get their iron here."

This is the third time Tempesto has been kidnaped this summer. The first time probably shouldn't count, since he abducted himself — as a publicity stunt for a holographic light show he was projecting on the Hancock building at night without a license to do so. The second time was by a convention of cyberpunk misfits in upstate New York who fed Tempesto magic mushrooms and made him stir-fry hundreds of pounds of chicken in an old satellite dish over a bonfire. But this time it looks for real. The counter clerk takes us to a back room, where Tempesto is playing poker with three other guys. He seems positively jolly about the whole deal, but that's the way he always seems. "This is one for *The Journal of Irreproducible Results*!" he calls out as we come in, a chubby man with a bushy black beard and sunspot-flares of shiny black hair firing out around his head. He's wearing a white jumpsuit despite the heat.

"What do you mean 'irreproducible'?" I say. "You're in captivity again."

"I meant my cards," he says, laying them down. "My fourth full house today!"

One of the men has the bearing of the boss, and a beard like the grandfather of Tempesto's beard. He hands Dwight a computer printout and says, "He stays till we settle that."

The printout appears to be the tab Tempesto has been running at the store. "Good God!" says Dwight, regarding the bottom line. "What have you been doing?"

"Various things," Tempesto says. "Art. Life."

"Give me your Visa card."

"You wouldn't take a man's Visa card."

"Yes, I would. Give." Tempesto surrenders the card. "Try to imagine yourself as early man," Dwight says. "Early man when he had to shoot his horse."

"Early man didn't have guns," says Tempesto.

"All right, then, early man when he had to hit his horse on the head with a rock."

"Early man didn't have horses," I say.

"What sticklers for detail you two are," says Dwight, bending the card back and forth till it breaks in half. Then he hands the clerk his own Visa card. He points to the table. "Are you ahead at least?"

"Yeah, but we're playing for these obsolete memory chips. They wouldn't let me play for my bill."

Out front, Dwight signs the slip and the clerk heaves three identical computer printers onto the counter — big old ones from the dinosaur days of the daisy wheel. Each of us grabs one of the brutish, heavy things and staggers into the parking lot. "Why are we buying these crummy printers?" I ask, on the way to Tempesto's van.

"Because Tempesto has made an amazing discovery," Dwight says. "This particular old crummy printer happens to contain exactly the right gears — "

"With exactly the right spindles and teeth and ratios," adds Tempesto.

"For gearing up a Makita electric belt sander. The kind of belt sander we're racing tonight. No other machine known to man contains those gears."

The most astonishing variety of junk — part electronic, part lumber, part dirty clothes — is tumbled in Tempesto's van. He heaves his printer in with a crash. Dwight and I heave ours in, too.

"I'm starved," Dwight says. "Anything in the fridge?"

"I've got leftovers you wouldn't believe," Tempesto says. "Did a big dinner last night. Had a lot of people over. There's a feast waiting for you guys."

"Tempesto's a great cook, Walter," Dwight says. "Wait'll you see."

"You are, Tempesto? Really? What's your cuisine? Tuscan Transistor?"

For a minute, his incredulity grapples with my incredulity. Then I see that his feelings are hurt. "You never came to my house?" he says. "You never ate my food?"

Tempesto's apartment is basically Tempesto's van on a grander scale,   145
without wheels and with electricity. A lot of electricity. Things are plugged in at Tempesto's place in a way the early electrifiers of America never intended. Power strips are scattered across the floors in every room, not a single empty socket left for one more computer, or television, or synthesizer, or CD player, or oscilloscope, or neon sculpture to take suck, from this address, at Boston Edison's breast.

Copies of *The Journal of Irreproducible Results* are lying on the counter in the kitchen. "I thought you made this up," I say, leafing through an issue.

"Why should I make things up?" Tempesto asks. "There's too much that's real already." He's pulling plastic-wrapped dishes out of the fridge and sliding them onto the counter. He calls out their contents as though announcing the guests at a ball. "Roasted eggplant with herbs and garlic. Veal Marsala, sautéed broccoli rabe. Chicken breasts with red peppers. My famous onion tart. Marinated mushrooms, mozzarella in brine, sun-dried tomatoes in virgin olive oil. Green beans in tomato sauce." He pulls a big flat bread out of a drawer — "Focaccia," he says lovingly — flips open the microwave, cranks up the conventional oven, gets a double boiler going on the stove. The heat drives us from the kitchen into the dining room, where the table is covered with circuit boards and schematic diagrams. Tempesto pushes it all aside, and we sit down with plates of food and goblets of Corvo table white. He is a great cook. These are the best leftovers I've ever had in my life. They're better than most things I've eaten the first time around.

"Drama factoid for you, Walter," Tempesto says, raising his glass. "This serviceable *vino* is exactly what Ben Kingsley and Jeremy Irons drink in the lunch scene of the film version of *Betrayal*."

"Isn't that just the kind of thing Tempesto would know?" Dwight says. "What happens in the lunch scene?"

"That's the scene where Ben Kingsley has just found out that Jeremy Irons   150 has been sleeping with his wife for, like, years," I say. "But Jeremy Irons, who's his best friend, doesn't *know* he knows."

"They drink a load of this wine in that scene," says Tempesto.

"Whatever happened to free love?" Dwight asks. "I kind of miss it."

"It was just an introductory offer," says Tempesto.

"Speaking of cheating," I say. "Are you guys fixing this race?"

"Cheating?" Dwight says. "Progress is cheating? Early man ties a rock to   155 a stick and he's cheating 'cause he has a hammer?"

"Did you consider the seminary?" Tempesto asks me. "You did, didn't you? You know how I know? I did, too. It's the truth. I was gonna be a priest.

I never really escaped it — the red lights, the magic. They may get me yet. I can always spot a brother."

"I never knew that about you, Walter," Dwight says. "Maybe you shouldn't be doing corporate video after all."

"I probably shouldn't. It's probably a place I'm passing through."

"On your way to the priesthood," says Tempesto.

Dwight has one rule for eating — stop before it hurts. Failing to observe it, we finish our supper and waddle to Tempesto's workroom. In the middle of his bench is a plastic gallon jug lying on its side, a power cord coming out its spout, machinery dimly visible through its translucence like a ship in a bottle. The words "Veritas Grit" are written along each side in red Magic Marker. Tempesto holds it up for my admiration. Its bottom side has been sliced off, and a belt of sandpaper occupies the rectangular opening. 160

"That's a belt sander? What happened to it?"

"We modified it, Walter," Dwight says. "This is no longer a street machine."

It doesn't look anything like a belt sander. The plastic hood hangs around it like a lady's hoopskirt. "Didn't that use to be a jug of milk?"

"It was springwater, actually," Tempesto says merrily. He puts a screwdriver bit in his drill and reverse-engineers one of the printers until the precious gears are out. Then he removes the sander's milky housing and puts them in there. "Makes it like lightning," he says. "Except that after a few minutes the teeth start to shear off the gears, which is why we need a steady stream of these printers." When he's finished, he hooks the sander up to some kind of tachometer on his bench. I don't know what's normal for a belt sander, but when he revs this one the needle flies right off the scale.

"Yow!" says Tempesto.   165

"Yow!" says Dwight.

"You're gonna cream those poor guys," I say. "You're gonna sand their faces off."

"Yes!" they both say together.

The sun is going down on the beautiful city. We're heading east on Memorial Drive — me in the passenger seat, Tempesto in back with the sander and video gear and two of his famous lasers. Red-gold light suffuses the Bonneville through its rear window. This is Dwight's favorite stretch of road in Boston, especially at this time of day; the sunset has turned the buildings of Back Bay and Government Center into fiery pillars blazing in the air — geometrical solids made of light, as pure as Tempesto's holograms or computer graphics. Their painterly twins shimmer in the silver-blue river below. The traffic is thick and fast at M.I.T., then thick and slow down around Lotus and Lechmere and the optimistic new structures of East Cambridge. It's a scorching Friday in August, and the prosperous people are making their break for the Cape. We escape the throngs by swinging left at the Museum of Science, wherein some of Tempesto's creations are displayed, and on into the tattered margins of Somerville.

Our destination is a block-square brick building five stories tall, its entrance shadowed by an elevated piece of Route 93. Dwight carries the video camera and a garbage bag with the Makita inside. Tempesto has the two lasers. I have the tripods and the cables and the little color TV. We take the freight elevator to the top, where Tempesto's friends are hosting the belt-sander races in their custom-cabinetry shop. The shop is the whole fifth floor of the building, pulsing with loud Chicago blues from the stereo. There must be a hundred people here, but the shop has floor-standing fans and cross-draft from every direction, and it's not that bad. Sheets of plywood on sawhorses are covered with bottles of hooch and bowls of punch, dishes of hummus and baba ghanouj, salsa, chips, and wheels of cheese. The worktables have been pushed away, and people are dancing beneath springy cords for power tools, which hang like bright-blue pigs' tails from the ceiling. The racetrack runs all the way down one side of this huge warehouse space — a three-foot-wide channel of upright two-by-fours nailed to the floor to keep the sanders inside.

You wouldn't think a two-hundred-pound man in a white jumpsuit with the words "CYBER SWINE" stitched across the back in large red letters could disappear into a crowd, but this is what Tempesto now manages to do. Most of the men here have ponytails and beards, mesh caps advertising lumber-supply houses, big hanks of keys snapped to the belt loops of their jeans. I see several guys wearing T-shirts silk-screened with the legend "HIPPIE TRASH," and more women in attendance than I would have predicted. Unlike the men, they seem to have ventured outside this building since Woodstock days. They have actual haircuts, stylish ones, and color on their faces, glittery earrings and hair clips and slinky legwear, and they all look nice, but the most interesting women in the room are the two over by the stereo, holding drinks and nodding their heads at a large middle-aged man in a gray tropical suit two or three shades lighter than his blow-dried hair.

"Benjamin Silk!" Dwight cries out, and then makes his hand into a gun and shoots Benny with it a few times. Benny scoops us toward him with his outstretched arm. I detect that he doesn't know who Rebecca is — and that he'd like to find out, the weasel.

She casts me a piercing look. "We're learning some secrets of corporate life," she says.

" 'For every back there is a knife'?"

"That's what I always say," says Benny.

"Of course it is, Benny. Where else would I have heard it? Who else has been through the wars the way you have?"

"Have you been introduced?" asks Dwight. "This is Walter's sweetheart, Rebecca."

"No!" Benny says. "I didn't realize that! You and Walter! Well, isn't that wonderful. What's a nice girl like you doing with a bum like this?"

"I've always had a thing about bums," Rebecca says.

"You think you can save 'em, right? Lots of women think that. Can I give   180
you some advice? Forget it."

Anita puts her fingertips on her belly like someone testing a melon at the
market.

"Is it dancing?" Dwight asks.

"It's at the Whisky a Go Go in there," Anita says. She's had all the
ultrasounds and the amniocentesis, but she and Dwight want the baby's gender
to be a surprise.

"It dances?" I say.

"The baby likes music," Dwight says. "I think it's the bass."   185

"Feel the baby, Walter," Rebecca says, pushing me forward.

"My treat," says Anita, raising her blouse.

"I want Walter to learn about babies," Rebecca says.

"Watch yourself there, Walter!" Benny says.

I don't know how you feel a pregnant woman. "I've never done this   190
before," I say. I put my palms on Anita's belly. The first shock is how taut it
is. I didn't think it would feel exactly like a drum. The second shock is that
somebody's in there, drumming. "This is unbelievable," I say. There's an up-
tempo blues playing on the sound system out here, and inside Anita the baby
is carrying on like Philly Joe Jones.

"You could have one of your very own," Rebecca says.

"I don't know. It seems like an awfully big decision."

"Or none at all," Anita says.

Diagonally across the room, beneath one of the big industrial windows
overlooking Route 93, Tempesto has set up his lasers on the camera tripods.
"Streetlamp shooting gallery!" he calls out now over the music. "Three shots
for a buck!" he adds, and we join the crowd in front of the window to see his
demonstration. It's that sublime moment in a cloudless day when the smoggy
yellow horizon dissolves slowly upward through values of blue into an indigo
chamber containing Venus and a few airplanes. Most cars aren't using their
headlights yet, but the mercury-vapor lamps have come halfway on like luminous insects flying in formation over the lanes of 93. The traffic north is moving,
but south to the Cape it seems to be backed up for miles. Tempesto trains one
of his lasers on the highway and presses the button to shoot. He misses a few
times, then hits the photoelectric cell controlling a streetlamp on the north-
bound side. It goes black, to the amazement and cheers of the flock around
him. Dwight pays Tempesto a dollar and aims the other beam. He's done this
before; on his third shot he gets a lamp.

"I'm next!" the carpenters shout, waving their dollar bills. "Let me try!"   195
they cry, pushing one another out of the way.

After a minute a knocked-out lamp wakes up again, and so the underlying
game is to see how many you can zap before they come back on. Little by
little, patches of Route 93 go dark.

"Do men ever grow up?" Rebecca asks Anita.

"No," Anita says.

Meanwhile, Dwight has led Benny across the room to the racetrack behind us, where he stands looking down at the long enclosure on the floor and shaking his head. Dwight moves him toward the drinks. I drift over there around the dancers, and when I arrive Benny is sipping a gin-and-tonic and Dwight is at the plywood bar, drizzling hoisin sauce into a plastic cup. "This is the flakiest thing I've ever seen," Benny says as Dwight pours tomato juice and vodka in on top of the hoisin.

"They don't have any Worcestershire," he explains, and then he takes a sip. "Delicious. Walter, help me out. Benny thinks belt-sander races are a stupid idea."

"No," I say. "Really? Ever seen one?"

"I didn't even know there was any such thing."

"Well, don't judge a book by its cover, Benny. Try to imagine yourself as early man. All around early man are sticks and stones. One day it hits him: Tie a stone to a stick. What's he got?"

"A hammer!" Benny says.

"Right. And then?"

"Civilization!"

"Now you're getting it," says Dwight. He fetches his plastic garbage bag from beneath the bar, and extracts the modified Makita.

"Well, get a load of this!" Benny says, turning it over in his hands, looking at the name of his new product emblazoned on its sides, the fresh belt of Veritas Grit installed on the machine. "We've got a nag running in this race?"

"Tell Benny our idea, Walter," says Dwight.

"It's simple," I say. "Winners use Veritas Grit."

Benny's smile opens up like a streetlamp coming on in the darkness. "You can't argue with that, hey?" He sips his gin-and-tonic, and thinks. "They just might go for this back at the ranch! They just might! But you gotta show us. We're from Missouri."

"I'm from the Bronx," says Dwight. "Follow me."

At the far end of the room, the men have gathered with their precious horses in their hands — Makitas and Milwaukees, Black & Deckers, Skils. The races are held in heats, two sanders at a time until two finalists remain to race the best three out of five. Yellow extension cords emerge from two knife switches at the beginning of the long enclosed track. A racer hooks his sander to a cord, waits for the signal, and throws the switch. Anita starts taping the first racers getting ready to run.

"Can you do that?" Rebecca says. "Are you OK?"

"It's just a tiny little camera," Anita says. "I'm fine. I love shooting."

Her camera goes through a cable to the small monitor propped on a chair. I watch the proceedings on the screen, through Anita's eye. The racers get into position; the official gives the signal; they throw the switches. The whole thing takes about three seconds — the sanders hurtling down the track so fast I'm surprised Anita can pan to get it. Somehow it's not quite the mythic deed I imagined. But Benny's enjoying it thoroughly. "Way to go, boy!" he calls out to the winner.

Most of the thirty or so contenders have shown up with the sanders they use every day, rugged machines that put bread on the table but don't know the taste of glory. After a half hour of heats, all but ten have been eliminated. Tempesto, known to be fast, has skipped the preliminaries. Now he's up. The guys with the "HIPPIE TRASH" T-shirts have the hot sander, an expensive-looking Milwaukee, but Tempesto doesn't go against them at first. He has to grind his way up through the ranks. He approaches the track holding Dwight's garbage bag, and with a grand flourish he unveils Veritas Grit.

"What the hell is that!" the other racers cry, laughing at the ugly home-brew thing. "What's Verified Grit?"

"Veritas," Tempesto corrects them. "It's Latin for Harvard."

He plugs the machine in and places it on the track next to a spanking   220
Black & Decker, lots of heavy chrome. The official counts down to the start. When the Makita gets the juice it makes a cracking sound they haven't heard around here since Yastrzemski retired, bucks into the air, hits the floor and zigzags out of control, pinballs against the wooden boundaries, knocks its opponent over, and finally flips right out of the track and across the floor before Tempesto shuts it down.

"What the hell was that!" the carpenters shout.

Dwight and Benny huddle around Tempesto for a conference. Tempesto seems to know what's wrong. He sticks a screwdriver into the machine to adjust some things, installs a new sandpaper belt, and they run again. Whatever he's done is what it needed, because now Veritas Grit just makes the Black & Decker look silly, smoking past the finish line before the poor Decker is halfway there.

The carpenters are mad. They demand to see the Makita. They want to hold it. "It don't weigh nothin'!" one of them exclaims. "Disqualify this thing!"

"No, boys," says Dwight. "No, no. Nobody said this was a stock-sander race. You don't change the rules in the middle of a game."

The carpenters run their knowing thumbs along the belt of Veritas Grit.   225
"Where did you get this?" one of them asks. "I've never seen this in any store."

"A little bird gave it to me," says Tempesto, winking at Benny, who is glowing on the sidelines, gin-and-tonic coming through the armpits of his suit.

The carpenters call a time-out to tweak their machines. Rebecca puts Anita in a chair by the window and rubs her with ice while Dwight rewinds the tape to look at it.

"I'm liking this!" Benny says, watching the little screen. "I think I can sell the kid on this! This is the kind of thing he just might like!"

"That's the spirit, Benny!" Dwight says.

"I just had a thought!" Benny says. "A big thought! This could become   230
some kind of craze! We could become the Budweiser of this!" He puts his hands in the air and then draws them apart to form the banner he sees in his mind. "The Veritas Grit World Championship Belt-Sander Races!"

"Think wild, babe!" says Dwight. "Dream, Benny!"

"Hold on!" Benny says, putting his arm around my shoulders. "Wait a minute! We could put Walter here in it! Walter here could talk about being a world-class belt-sander racer, and how he would never race without Veritas Grit."

"Great idea, Benny!"

"Except I'm not a world-class belt-sander racer," I say.

Benny gives me a quizzical look. "Of course you're not," he says. "Nobody is. It's just a fantasy we're having." Then the significance of that hits him — he's seriously considering staking his career on a fantasy — and I watch his face go through a couple of surreal changes while he wrestles with that. "We'd be manufacturing a craze, Walter. We'd be sponsoring a sporting event, the way Budweiser does. Nobody in the abrasives industry has ever done that before. They never had a sport to sponsor!"

"Benjamin meant you'd be in the video as an actor," Dwight says. "You remember — acting? Your niche in life? You'd be acting as though you were a world-class belt-sander racer."

"Oh, acting," I say.

"He gets it now," Dwight says to Benny. Then he lowers his voice and points to his head. "A lot of actors are not really all that — you know."

"We wouldn't need Einstein," Benny says. Then he slaps Dwight in the belly. "I'm liking this!"

When the races resume, a few men have removed parts of their sanders' housings to lighten them up, but these half-naked creatures run very wrong, sucking sawdusty wind and finally choking out altogether. Heat after heat, the rogue Makita narrows the field, Anita memorializing its conquest on videotape. I watch her pan for cutaways of an ecstatic Benny cheering from the sidelines. "Go, Veritas Grit!" he cries, urging his sander on with thrusts of his arms, and even here in the pandemonium I can see how nicely those shots will work when the tape is cut together, what a pro Anita really is.

In the end it's Hippie Trash versus Veritas Grit, as Dwight and Tempesto always knew it would be. The men put new belts on their sanders for the finals. I go to trackside to catch the action live. Veritas Grit's gears must be wearing down, because the first runoff looks like a tie to me. I glance back at Anita to see if she got the photo finish, but she's standing there holding her belly, looking like a person who just ate the entire lump of wasabi from her sushi dinner, thinking it was something else.

Rebecca has seen her, too, and beats me there. "The baby!" she says.

Tempesto calls a time-out and sneaks off to put new gears into Veritas Grit. Dwight hustles over and hugs his wife. "Now, look," he says. "Everybody stay cool. There's ten minutes left in this, and I don't see why we can't take care of business and have a baby, too."

"Dwight, you swine," Rebecca says.

"Rebecca, I'm closing an important business deal. We need this business to buy Pampers and strollers and everything, OK? Is your car air-conditioned? No? Here, trade keys with me. You and Walter take Anita to the hospital in the Bonneville, and I'll be over in a half hour in your car. You won't even be in labor yet, honey," he tells Anita.

"She's in labor right now!" Rebecca says.

"She's just starting, Rebecca. You realize this will probably go on for about twenty-four hours? We went to the Lamaze classes, didn't we, babe?"

"You went to the first one," Anita says, not bitterly, just sticking up for the facts.

"We know what to expect," Dwight tells Rebecca. "You're overreacting."

"I'm overreacting?"   250

"You're being considerate. But you're a little worked up."

"I'm worked up?"

"Anita's going to the hospital to have a baby. People do it every day. You'll be fine sweetheart," he says to Anita, though she seems to be going into a trance.

"Walter, you know where Brigham and Women's is, right?"

"It's where all the hospitals are, isn't it? I think so. Do I?" I ask Rebecca.   255

"I know where it is," she says.

The whole concept of a freight elevator takes on new meaning as we transport Anita to ground level in the dark, creaking box. Rushing from the building to open the car for the women, I'm convinced that Hippie Trash did indeed put LSD in the beverages upstairs. I'm picking up the world like a satellite dish. I'm hearing everything. I hear the blades of crabgrass rubbing each other in the crummy sand-soil of the concrete planters along the parking lot. I hear the mechanical noises of the belt-sander race. If I had to be up there right now, the sandpaper would shred my brain. As it is, I can distinguish the scrape of every different shoe on the asphalt out here.

"Does anybody else happen to feel like they're on drugs?" I say.

"I do," Anita says.

"Drugs?" says Rebecca. "You're supposed to be driving the car."   260

"I can drive fine," I say, the way people always say these things.

We get Anita in the back seat of the Bonneville, Rebecca in there with her. Once I get behind the wheel, I understand what's happening to me: I have a friend who has become for the moment a creature, a mammalian creature engaged in the live birth mammals are famous for, and I'm sympathizing with that, resonating with it. I'm an animal now myself.

"Music might help," Anita says. "Could you turn on the radio?"

It's only an AM, and at first all I can find are talk shows — people claiming to have been inside UFOs, telling about having fat vacuumed from their buttocks and bellies. Finally I hit music on an oldies station — Little Eva singing "The Loco-Motion."

"That's good," Anita says. "I like that song."   265

"Remind me what I do now?" I call to Rebecca in back.

"Go down this access road and make a right at the fork. I'll tell you from there. Don't go up the ramp on to 93."

"What's that?"

"Right up there."

It's dark down here below the highway, and I don't see what she means. 270
My skin is screaming thousands of messages at me, and I'm giving birth to a
baby in my brain, and the next thing I know we're rising into the air.

"Walter!" Rebecca cries out. "I just got finished saying don't do this!"

"I got mixed up. I'm sorry. Let's not fight, OK? Dwight and Anita never
fight. We always fight. Plus, I'm having some kind of psychedelic experience."

"Well, go back! Back the car down the ramp and get off!"

But it's too late. We're up there now. The space behind me was the only
free slot on this whole merciless highway, and it's been filled by a car, which
in turn left a space that has been filled by another car, like one of those puzzles
of linked plastic numbers sliding around in a frame. One little mistake and
we're hopelessly locked in a grid.

Beneath the spectral mercury-vapor light, the traffic is moving in geological 275
time. We need a helicopter right now. I open my door and stand on the frame
to look out over the cars. It's just more of the same, forever and ever. The
atmosphere is a kiln where thousands of clay cars are baking. Anita can't stand
it, and I have to get back in. Now that we're not moving at all, the air-
conditioning is dragging Dwight's old behemoth to the tar pits. The temperature
gauge edges into the red as I watch.

"I have this unbelievable urge to push," says Anita.

"Well, don't do it!" I say.

"She must have been in transition at the races," Rebecca tells me.

"Really? Jesus, Anita, didn't you know the baby was coming? I thought
women just sort of, you know, knew things like that."

"I felt a little crampy," she says. "I thought it was the baba ghanouj." 280

On the theory that action is better than inaction, I pull off the road and
make a run for it down the shoulder. This works for about a hundred yards,
until the shoulder suddenly stops. I try to pull back into my lane, but the
people alongside us are getting revenge by not letting me. I'm looking around
the car for something to threaten them with when I see Dwight's car phone.
I'm not used to the idea of phones in cars; I forgot it was there. "I have to
make a call," I say, getting out and closing the door gently on the telephone's
cord. A woman answers when I dial 911. "We've got somebody having a baby
here," I say.

"I'm showing you on a cellular phone," she says. "She's having the baby
in a car?"

"Right. We're stuck in traffic on 93 South."

"Where on 93? Between what exits?"

"No idea. We're at the place where the shoulder of the road disappears." 285

"Where were you coming from?"

"About a quarter mile from here. It was Somerville then."

"What can you see right now?"

"The Schrafft's building."

"In front of you?" 290

"Right. Affirmative."

"You're in Somerville. Describe the car. Year, model, color, plates."

"1964 Bonneville. White. Four-door. I can't see the plates, the phone won't reach that far. It's the father's car. He's not here. Could you send a helicopter?"

"No, sir. We can't land a helicopter on that part of 93. We'll send an ambulance."

"What if it happens before they get here?"   295

"Make sure the baby can breathe. Put it on its mother's breast. Don't cut the cord."

"What about germs? The car is filthy."

"An unread newspaper is relatively germ-free. You can deliver the baby on that if you have to. We'll have somebody there as fast as we can." Then she hangs up.

The traffic has moved a little bit. A Lincoln Town Car is alongside us now, the people in it watching me talk on the phone. They remind me of my mom and dad. I knock on their passenger window. The lady lowers it with the electric button. "Hi. Would you folks happen to have a recent newspaper?" I see a crisp copy of today's *Wall Street Journal* right there on their back seat.

"Need the show times for the movies?" the man calls out sarcastically.   300
"Why don't you just call on your phone there, big fella?"

Maybe he is my father, after all. I crouch down to check. No, he isn't. "We're not going to the movies. A woman in our car is having a baby, and in a pinch you can deliver babies on newspapers. That *Wall Street Journal* right there would be fine."

He makes his wife put up the window, and I see them arguing about it without sound, gesturing wildly. I'm about to knock on the next car when the radiator goes on the Bonneville, sheets of white steam spewing from the grille and hood with a horrid hissing sound. The man gets out of the Lincoln with the newspaper and looks in our car. I look in with him. It's like a wolf den in there, one female hunkering on the floor, another one, heavy with young, lying on the seat. They're breathing rapidly through their mouths and staring out with eyes dilated to black disks. The man pushes the newspaper at me and backs away, but his wife is already out of the Lincoln. "Oh, my God!" she cries when she looks in the car.

I get back in with the phone and open the *Journal* to its deep middle sections. "The lady on 911 told me this," I tell Rebecca. "We're supposed to spread these out over the seat. Anita, an ambulance is on the way. Hang in there, OK?"

"The women in my family have pretty easy births," she says between gasps of air and pain, as though her job were to comfort us. "My doctor says I have a pelvis like the Holland Tunnel." She thinks about this for a second and laughs. "Too bad we can't take it to the hospital."

"Anita, I think you're starting to rave a little bit. Try to be calm."   305

She snorts fiercely like a riled-up horse. I get the number of the cabinetry shop from Information, and ask for Dwight. He's still there. They bring him to the phone.

"I was just leaving," he says. "What's going on?"

I tell him.

"This wasn't the plan, Walter," he says.

"I know it wasn't, Dwight. What can I say? We're stuck in traffic."   310

"What are you doing on 93 in the first place?"

"I made a mistake and got on it. Here, I'm putting you on with Anita."

"You were supposed to be here to tell me to push," she says into the phone.

"No, Dwight, don't tell her that!" I call out. I look outside. The woman from the Lincoln has spread the word, and now about thirty people from other cars are staring in through our steamed-up windows like a gathering of spirits.

"Walter thinks you're mad at him," Anita says. "Tell him you're not."   315

She passes the phone back to me. "Is that you there, where all the people are?" Dwight says. "I think I can see you from here."

"Yeah, we've got a crowd here."

"The Bonneville's overheating, isn't it?"

"Yup."

"It does that when you run the air-conditioning without driving."   320

"I know."

"I'm not mad, Walter," Dwight says. "You're doing your best."

"Thanks, Dwight. I called for an ambulance."

"I see it coming on the shoulder right now. Should be there in a couple of minutes."

"Oh, yeah. I hear the sirens."   325

"You're fine now. I'll meet you at the hospital. Oh, hey! Guess who won the race."

"Who?"

"We did. Veritas Grit. Benny's going wild. He wants to see a proposal for a big promotion. And, Walter? He says he's found your niche for you. You're gonna be the Veritas Grit spokesperson. You could be looking at national TV with this."

"Gee, that's great, Dwight. Thanks."

The radio starts playing "I Second That Emotion," and then all at once   330
the crowd around the car breaks into cheers and applause. When I look in the back seat I see that the baby has left the mother ship and is now half in Rebecca's hands, half space-walking in its birth fluids across the tiny print of the New York Stock Exchange.

"Dwight! You're a father! It's a boy!"

"A boy? The baby's born! I have a son?"

"Look at the size of this kid!"

"Where's Anita?" Dwight cries.

"What do you mean, where is she?"   335

"I mean how is she!"

"She seems fine. She's smiling. She's holding the baby."

"It's a boy!" I hear Dwight shout to the cabinetry shop. "He's big!"

Tempesto grabs the phone over there. "We're firing a twenty-one-gun salute! Look in the steam!"

Sure enough, red filaments flash like pick-up-sticks tumbling through the white cloud around the car. The streetlamps around us start to go out.   340

"Walter," says Dwight. "Hold the phone up to the baby." I do that. "Dwight Junior!" he says, his tiny voice coming out of the phone. "Son! This is your father speaking!"

"Walter, let's have a baby!" Rebecca says as we gaze upon the strapping boy on his mother's breast, born in a '64 Bonneville broken down on the side of the road while Smokey Robinson sang on the radio and his father spoke to him on a car phone. I think: This will be no ordinary child.

"Sure, sweetheart," I say. "Why not?"

And then, just as I kiss Rebecca, our fogged-up car becomes a huge heart attack, throbbing with red light and screaming sounds. Out in the distance, beyond the gaping ghost faces against the steamy glass, the ambulance has pulled to a stop behind the eight or ten cars lined up behind us on the shoulder. I fight through the crowd to meet the men coming toward me with a stretcher and a box of first-aid gear.

"What the hell happened to the lights?" the one is saying to the other.   345

"It's the laser beams!" I shout, gesturing back to the vapors billowing above the Bonneville. "Men in that building over there are shooting them out with laser beams!"

"Is that right?" the first man says, stopping to look where I'm pointing. "Laser beams, Louie," he says to the other guy, but the red ambulance light cancels out the red lasers so you can't see their flicking tongues in the steam anymore. "Been out here a while, huh, pal?"

"I'll never rent on the Cape again," the other man says.

"No, we go to Maine now," the first one replies. "I couldn't take this. We'd like to help you, bud, but we're here for a lady having a baby."

"It already happened!" I cry. "He's born."   350

"The baby we're looking for, or the baby Jesus? We're looking for a Bonneville with a pregnant lady inside."

"Under those people!" I tell them, so drained by birth I should be on that stretcher myself. "But she's not pregnant anymore. It's a boy named Dwight Junior. Go ahead. You'll see him. A big wrinkly red guy on the phone with his dad."   1991

INVESTIGATIONS

1. After reading the story, define "early man." Why is the narrator "*late* early man"?

2. How do you think the story would differ if Tempesto, the "hardware commando," told it? What would be lost? What would be gained?

3. Choose three characters in the story and analyze what is attractive about

them. What do you dislike about them? Which traits seem particularly contemporary? Which traits seem especially suited to the work these characters do? Be sure to refer to particular images and scenes in your discussion of the characters.

4. Compare Lawrence Garfinkle in Sterner's *Other People's Money* with Tempesto. What are the similarities? What are the differences?

5. While watching the "streetlamp shooting gallery," Rebecca asks Anita, "Do men ever grow up?" (para. 197). Discuss the relationships between men and women in the story. How does work affect these relationships?

6. Discuss Anita's pregnancy and delivery. How is Anita's labor related to the other kinds of labor in the story?

DONALD HALL

Ox Cart Man

In October of the year,
he counts potatoes dug from the brown field,
counting the seed, counting
the cellar's portion out,
and bags the rest on the cart's floor.   5

He packs wool sheared in April, honey
in combs, linen, leather
tanned from deerhide,
and vinegar in a barrel
hooped by hand at the forge's fire.   10

He walks by his ox's head, ten days
to Portsmouth Market, and sells potatoes,
and the bag that carried potatoes,
flaxseed, birch brooms, maple sugar, goose
feathers, yarn.   15

DONALD HALL is a poet, essayist, children's author, fiction writer, critic, and editor whose many honors include the National Book Critics Circle Award for *The One Day: A Poem in Three Parts* (1988), two Guggenheim fellowships, and an appointment as poet laureate of New Hampshire. Born in 1928 in New Haven, Connecticut, Hall taught at the University of Michigan for many years before moving to a New Hampshire farm once owned by his grandparents.

When the cart is empty he sells the cart.
When the cart is sold he sells the ox,
harness and yoke, and walks
home, his pockets heavy
with the year's coin for salt and taxes, 20

and at home by fire's light in November cold
stitches new harness
for next year's ox in the barn,
and carves the yoke, and saws planks
building the cart again. 25 1977

INVESTIGATIONS

1. The speaker makes specific references to the months of October, April, and November. Why do you think this is important? What images in the first and last stanzas reflect the cyclical nature of the seasons? Do any other images in the poem reinforce our sense of the cycle?

2. What about the ox cart man do you find praiseworthy? What negative impressions do you receive? Find examples of repetition throughout the poem, and consider how this poetic device helps create your impression of the ox cart man.

3. Study the items packed into the cart and then sold at the market (lines 6–15). Then read lines 19–20. Has the ox cart man made a fair trade? Why or why not? How is the walk to the market different from the walk home?

RACHEL L. JONES

The Price of Hate: Thoughts on Covering a Ku Klux Klan Rally

I was sitting at my computer terminal when I overheard someone in the office mention his concern because he thought a black couple was moving into a house on his street.

He was standing only four feet away from me, yet lacked a mechanism that would prevent him from making racist statements in front of a black person. I stopped typing and stared at his back. He froze momentarily, and the woman he was taking to glanced at me.

I didn't confront him. I had to transmit copy to St. Petersburg and then leave to cover a graduation. Besides, my stomach was churning. Just seven days earlier, at a Ku Klux Klan rally in Clearwater, I had stood only four feet away from a Tarpon Springs man who told me he was tired of "the n-----s getting everything."

I'd be lying if I said that the possibility of covering a Ku Klux Klan rally didn't cause me a few moments' concern about my physical well-being. But when another reporter came over to tell me about the May 28th Klan rally in front of Clearwater City Hall, I reasoned, "It's just another assignment. I am a reporter, and I know my life isn't all budget meetings."

I must also admit to a curiosity about the Klan, and it seemed a good   5
opportunity to take a look at that sideshow of human nature. Now, I *could* have asked to be excused from that particular assignment. As a police reporter, my Saturdays are sometimes very busy. Had I approached my editor to delicately decline, we could have both made ourselves believe it was only natural to send a burly young man into the fray. Anything could have happened that day — traffic accidents, drownings, first-degree murders at the jail.

I couldn't be two places at once, could I?

But two days before the event, I turned to my editor and asked, "I AM covering the rally on Saturday, aren't I?"

She didn't miss a beat. Yes, of course. Just a short story, unless the streets were running with blood or something.

Born in 1961 in Cairo, Illinois, RACHEL L. JONES was educated at Northwestern University and Southern Illinois University. She has worked as a general assignment reporter with the *Miami Herald* and likens reporters to "walking lightning rods, collecting the information, putting [themselves] into someone else's shoes, and then writing about it."

I jokingly told her about the only slightly feigned horror of my older sister, who shrieked into the phone, "They're letting a black reporter cover the KLAN?"

At the Klan rally, the man from Tarpon Springs saw my press badge and figured I was a part of something he called the "Black Associated Press," which he swore was denying white journalism graduates jobs. Mr. Tarpon told me that n-----s weren't qualified to get the jobs they were getting through affirmative action, and that America is for white people.

I paused momentarily and asked what he thought should be done about black people. He didn't know or care.

"Send 'em all to hell," he said, while I took notes.

It's funny — it was all so clinical. My voice held an even tone, and while he talked I searched his contorted face for some glimmer of recognition on his part that *I* was a human being and the words that he spat just might hurt me.

Just as I later waited for Mr. Welcome Wagon to turn around and apologize for his blunder, I waited for the Tarpon Springs man to show some spark of humanity, but he finished his conversation and walked away.

My stomach was still churning hours later as I relived that rally. The whole experience was like being scalded, like having something sharp raked over my flesh until it was raw.

After it was over I went home and drank a shot from the bottle of brandy I'd bought last Christmas. In Harlequin romances, handsome princes always proffered hard liquor to soothe the jangled nerves of a distraught heroine.

But I was alone, and I was no heroine. That night, every noise from the apartment upstairs made me jump, and the pattern of trees against the curtains frightened me as I tossed and turned. I called three of my siblings, but other than offering sympathy, they felt helpless to ease my trauma.

I had been so naive about the whole assignment. The thing is, I never thought it would change me. I figured it would be difficult, but I didn't want it to *change* me.

What you must understand about the Klan is that its members and supporters have been stripped of their humanity. I gained that insight and feel stronger for it. It was easy enough on one level to say, "These people are stupid, so I shouldn't be bothered by what they say."

But that was cold comfort as I walked across the City Hall parking lot, feeling a numbness creep through my arms and legs. I thought I must have been walking like the Scarecrow in *The Wizard of Oz,* but figured if I could just make it to the church across the street, I'd be fine.

At the church, I asked to use the phone and was sent down a hall and to the left. My fingers felt like sausages as I tried to use the rotary dial, muttering curses as I fouled up several times. Finally managing to reach an editor, I was coherent enough to give her information for a brief summary of the rally.

But when the next editor picked up the phone, I dissolved in tears after three words. He was puzzled, and I think unaware of what was wrong at first. I whimpered that I was sorry and didn't know what was wrong, either. I gasped and caught a few breaths before describing in a wavering voice what had happened.

He tried calming me down to discuss the facts. How many people attended? Had there been any clashes? What did police have to say? I planned to write a full story.

The editor said maybe we should just ignore the event. He asked if any of the Klan members had been abusive to me. I mumbled, "Uh hum," and the tears flowed fresh. He told me to get as much police information as I could and to call him back later.

I placed the phone on the hook and buried my face in my hands, letting   25
the sobs come freely. The man who had let me use the church phone brought me a box of tissues and a Coke.

After I splashed my face with cold water and controlled the sobs, I headed back to the rally, just as the Klansmen were loading up to leave. Shouts of "white supremacy" rang through the air as they rolled out, and my photographer walked over to give me the Klansmen's names. I turned away, telling her that I probably wouldn't use them anyway.

"I didn't think it would affect me," I whispered.

"Don't cry. They aren't worth it, Rachel," she said.

But even then, it had started to change me . . .

When you have stared into the twisted face of hate, you *must* change. I   30
remember watching the documentary *Eyes on the Prize,* in particular the segment on the desegregation of Little Rock High School in 1957, and being disturbed by the outpouring of rage against those nine students.

The whites who snarled into the camera back then had no explanation for their vitriol and violence other than that the students were black, and they didn't care who knew it. They weren't going to let those n-----s into the school, no matter what.

I've struggled all my life against a visceral reaction to that kind of racism. I have been mistreated because of my color, but nothing ever came near to what those students went through on a daily basis.

That and countless other examples let me know what I'd been spared, and I decided to choose the path of understanding, realizing that some people are always going to fear or even hate me because of my color alone.

It's a burden blacks must carry no matter how high a level of achievement they reach, and I sought to incorporate that into my own striving. Watching films of what hate turned those people into made me choose to reject it, to deal with people individually and not tarnish all whites with the same obscene images. *I would not hate.*

But as one Klan supporter muttered, "N----- b----," at me as I weaved my   35
way through the crowd, that resolve crumbled. It stung as much as if he *had* slapped me or thrown something.

The leader shouted taunts and epithets at a black woman who was infuriated by the proceedings, and who had even lunged at several people in the small group of supporters.

As the black woman walked away, the leader shouted, "Why don't you go back to Nee-gor Africa where you came from!" I laughed because he sounded foolish, but he saw me and sent a fresh stream of obscenity my way.

A Jewish woman who came to protest was heaped with stinging abuse, and the rabble was ingenious in its varied use of sexual and racial obscenities directed toward her.

Other reporters and photographers eyed me warily throughout the rally, watching for my reaction to the abuse. When the leader started passing out leaflets and avoided my outstretched hand, a photographer asked for two and brought me one.

I said thank you. He said quietly, "You're very, very welcome," and was   40
embarrassed when I caught his eye.

When it was all over, several police officials called me brave. But I felt cold, sick, and empty. I felt like such a naive fool. I felt bitter. So this is what it feels like, I thought. Why *shouldn't* I just hate them right back, why couldn't I diffuse this punch in the gut?

What is noble about not flinching in the face of hate? Slavery, lynchings, rape, inequality, was that not enough? If they want to send me to hell, shouldn't I want to take them along for the ride?

But I still couldn't hate. I was glad I had cried, though. It defied their demented logic. It meant I was human.   1988

INVESTIGATIONS

1. Jones risked her "physical well-being" to cover the Ku Klux Klan rally (para. 4). What would she have risked had she "approached [her] editor to delicately decline" (para. 5)?
2. How is Jones able to be "so clinical" (para. 13) despite feeling like she's had "something sharp raked over [her] flesh until it was raw" (para. 15)?
3. Jones says covering the Klan rally has changed her. How will she think about her job after this episode? How will she think of herself?
4. Compare Jones's memoir to the account you wrote in response to "Write Before Reading" (p. 518). To what extent were the changes you noted caused by what your job required you to do? To what extent were the changes caused by the people with whom your job brought you into contact?

JIMMY SANTIAGO BACA

Perfecto Flores

We banter
back and forth
the price
for laying brick.
"You people only pay   5
the rich, those who
already have money.
I have a whole yard of bricks
collected over thirty years
working as a mason.   10
I offer you a good price,
load them on the truck,
bring sand and gravel,
do the work almost for nothing,
and you won't pay me   15
half what Hunter charges."
He was right, I relented,
paid him seventy cents a block.
The next day
he brought them,   20
towing cement mixer
behind his old truck.
He rounded the weeping willow
trunk with blocks
left over from apartments   25
he worked on
six years ago,
then poured cement
and troweled it smooth.
After he was done, he asked,   30
"Can I have that roll of wire back there?"
He lives my scraps, built three houses
for his daughters with construction site

A *mestizo* (half Chicano, half "detribalized Apache"), JIMMY SANTIAGO BACA (b. 1952) taught himself to read and write while incarcerated in an Arizona prison. Winner of the Wallace Stevens Yale Poetry Fellowship, Baca has published seven books of poetry, including *Black Mesa Poems* (1989) and *Immigrants in Our Own Land & Selected Early Poems* (1990).

scraps.
In English   35
his name is Perfect Flower.
Brawny man with bull shoulders,
who forty years ago came from Mexico,
tired of the mines, the somnolent
spirit of Mexicans. " . . . I was the first one   40
to say I wouldn't ride the old bus.
It was falling apart. I refused, and
the rest followed, and soon a new bus
was brought up the mountain."
I gave him our old Falcon   45
for pouring cement floor
in the guest cottage,
jar of blessed black-purple
Acoma corn kernels
for helping me uproot a tree,   50
gave him seven rabbits
and a box of chickens
for helping me cut adobe arches.
We curse and laugh as we work.
He proudly hefts a wheelbarrow   55
brimmed with cement. "Ah! Sixty-two, *cabrón!*
And you, naa! You would break your back!"
He ribs me, proud of his strength.
He has nothing that glows his face
so much as stories of his working years,   60
feats of courage in the mines
when he was called upon to defuse dynamite
that didn't explode. Short, stocky
gray-haired man, always in his yard
scattering chicken seed, nailing, sawing,   65
always in jean overalls.
Chews a ground weed,
carries a stub pencil and grimy wad of paper
for figuring, and
always turns to me when I drive   70
or walk into his yard
with a roguish grin,
his love of telling stories
competing with mine.
He growls with laughter   75
at the blisters on my hands,
takes his gloves off,
spreads his palms up —

a gallery owner who strips black cloth
off his prized Van Gogh painting,   80
"Look! You could sharpen a file
on these hands," he grins proudly.   1986

INVESTIGATIONS

1. In line 32, the speaker says Perfecto "lives my scraps." What does he mean? How would the speaker's relationship with Perfecto be different if he paid him exclusively with money rather than sometimes with the things he mentions in lines 45–53?
2. Why is competition such an integral part of the relationship between the speaker and Perfecto? In what ways does this competition involve more than winning and losing?
3. In lines 79–80, the speaker compares Perfecto's removing his gloves to "a gallery owner who strips black cloth / off his prized Van Gogh painting." After looking up the word "art" in the dictionary, locate all the details in the poem that could lead you to see Perfecto's work as art. How might Perfecto himself be seen as a work of art? To what extent could Garfinkle's (*Other People's Money*) work be considered art? What in your work experience would you consider art?

JAY PARINI

Working the Face

On his belly with a coal pick
mining underground:
the pay was better for one man
working the face.
Only one at a time could get   5
so close, his nose
to the anthracite, funneling
light from a helmet, chipping,

JAY PARINI (b. 1948) loves "to make things up, believing that truth arises out of it." Professor of English at Middlebury College, Parini is the author of a book of poetry entitled *Anthracite Country* (1982), a critical study entitled *Theodore Roethke: An American Romantic* (1979), and a novel called *The Last Station* (1990).

with his eyes like points of fire.
He worked, a taproot   10
tunneling inward, layer
by layer, digging
in a world of shadows,
thick as a slug against the floor,
dark all day long.   15
Wherever he turned, the facets
showered a million stars.
He was prince of darkness,
stalking the village at 6 P.M.,
having been to the end of it,   20
core and pith
of the world's rock belly.   1976

INVESTIGATIONS

1. After looking up *taproot* in the dictionary, indicate the ways in which the miner fits the definition. What other things is the miner compared to? How do these comparisons influence your attitude toward him?

2. Compare the miner's work to the work of the roofers in Williams's "Tar" (p. 645). What similarities do you find in the speakers' attitudes toward the work being described? How would our impressions of these jobs be different if the workers had written the poems?

3. Look again at the last few paragraphs of "Steelworker." If the miner in "Working the Face" were laid off, to what extent might he feel the mixture of hatred and nostalgia Trudy Pax Farr describes?

4. Reread Baca's "Perfecto Flores." In what ways is the miner in "Working the Face" an artist? What do you ignore when you see him as an artist?

T. CORAGHESSAN BOYLE

Sitting on Top of the World

People would ask her what it was like. She'd watch them from her tower as they weaved along the trail in their baseball caps and day packs, their shorts, hiking boots, and sneakers. The brave ones would mount the 150 wooden steps hammered into the face of the mountain to stand at the highflown railing of the little glass-walled shack she called home for seven months a year. Sweating, sucking at canteens and bota bags, heaving for breath in the undernourished air, they would ask her what it was like. "Beautiful," she would say. "Peaceful."

But that didn't begin to express it. It was like floating untethered, drifting with the clouds, like being cupped in the hands of God. Nine thousand feet up, she could see the distant hazy rim of the world, she could see Mt. Whitney rising up above the crenellations of the Sierra, she could see stars that haven't been discovered yet. In the morning, she was the first to watch the sun emerge from the hills to the east, and in the evening, when it was dark beneath her, the valleys and ridges gripped by the insinuating fingers of the night, she was the last to see it set. There was the wind in the trees, the murmur of the infinite needles soughing in the uncountable branches of the pines, sequoias, and cedars that stretched out below her like a carpet. There was daybreak. There was the stillness of three A.M. She couldn't explain it. She was sitting on top of the world.

Don't you get lonely up here? they'd ask. Don't you get a little stir-crazy?

And how to explain that? Yes, she did, of course she did, but it didn't matter. Todd was up here with her in the summer, one week on, one week off, and then the question was meaningless. But in September he went back to the valley, to his father, to school, and the world began to drag round its tired old axis. The hikers stopped coming then too. In the height of summer, on a weekend, she'd see as many as thirty or forty in the course of a day, but now, with the fall coming on, they left her to herself — sometimes she'd go for days without seeing a soul.

But that was the point, wasn't it?

5

She was making breakfast — a real breakfast for a change, ham and eggs from the propane refrigerator, fresh-dipped coffee and toast — when she spot-

---

Born in 1948 in Peekskill, New York, to Irish immigrant parents, T. CORAGHESSAN BOYLE says, "I don't think I ever read a book until I was eighteen." Now a professor of creative writing at the University of Southern California, Boyle has written four novels, including *World's End* (1987) and *East Is East* (1990), and three books of short stories, most recently *If the River Was Whiskey* (1989).

ted him working his way along one of the switchbacks below. She was immediately annoyed. It wasn't even seven yet and the sign at the trailhead quite plainly stated that visitors were welcome at the lookout between the hours of ten and five *only*. What was wrong with this guy — did he think he was exempt or something? She calmed herself: Maybe he was only crossing the trail. Deer season had opened — she'd been hearing the distant muted pop of gunfire all week — and maybe he was only a hunter tracking a deer.

No such luck. When she glanced down again, flipping her eggs, peering across the face of the granite peak and the steep snaking trail that clung to it, she saw that he was coming up to the tower. Damn, she thought, and then the kettle began to hoot and her stomach clenched. Breakfast was ruined. Now there'd be some stranger gawking over her shoulder and making the usual banal comments as she ate. To them it might have been like Disneyland or something up here, but this was her home, she lived here. How would they like it if she showed up on their doorstep at seven o'clock in the morning?

She was eating, her back to the glass door, hoping he'd go away, slip over the lip of the precipice and disappear, vanish in a puff of smoke, when she felt his footfall on the trembling catwalk that ran round the outside of the tower. Still, she didn't turn or look up. She was reading — she went through a truckload of books in the course of a season — and she never lifted her eyes from the page. He could gawk round the catwalk, peer through the telescope, and hustle himself back on down the steps for all she cared. She wasn't a tour guide. Her job was to watch for smoke, twenty-four hours a day, and to be cordial — if she was in the mood and had the time — to the hikers who made the sweaty panting trek in from the trailhead to join her for a brief moment atop the world. There was no law that said she had to let them in the shack or show them the radio and her plotting equipment and deliver the standard lecture on how it all worked. Especially at seven in the morning. To hell with him, she thought, and she forked up egg and tried to concentrate on her book.

The problem was, she'd trained herself to look up from what she was doing and scan the horizon every thirty seconds or so, day or night, except when she was asleep, and it had become a reflex. She glanced up, and there he was. It gave her a shock. He'd gone round the catwalk to the far side and he was standing right in front of her, grinning and holding something up to the window. Flowers, wildflowers, she registered that, but then his face came into focus and she felt something go slack in her: She knew him. He'd been here before.

"Lainie," he said, tapping the glass and brandishing the flowers, "I brought you something."   10

Her name. He knew her name.

She tried a smile and her face froze around it. The book on the table before her upset the salt shaker and flipped itself shut with a tiny expiring hiss. Should she thank him? Should she get up and latch the door? Should she put out an emergency call on the radio and snatch up the kitchen knife?

"Sorry to disturb you over breakfast — I didn't know the time," he said, and something happened to his grin, though his eyes — a hard metallic blue — held on to hers like pincers. He raised his voice to penetrate the glass: "I've been camping down on Long Meadow Creek and when I crossed the trail this morning I just thought you might be lonely and I'd surprise you" — he hesitated — "I mean, with some flowers."

Her whole body was frozen now. She'd had crazies up here before — it was an occupational hazard — but there was something unnerving about this one, this one she remembered. "It's too early," she said finally, miming it with her hands, as if the glass were impervious to sound, and then she got up from her untouched ham and half-eaten eggs and deliberately went to the radio. The radio was just under the window where he was standing and when she picked up the mike and depressed the talk button she was two feet from him, the thin wall of glass all that separated them.

"Needles Lookout," she said, "this is Elaine. Zack, you there? Over."   15

Zack's voice came right back at her. He was a college student working on a degree in forestry, and he was her relief two days a week when she hiked out and went down the mountain to spend a day with her son, do her shopping, and maybe hit a bar or movie with her best friend and soulmate, Cynthia Furman. "Elaine," he said, above the crackle of static, "what's up? See anything funny out there? Over."

She forced herself to look up then and locate the stranger's eyes — he was still grinning, but the grin was slack and unsteady and there was no joy in the deeps of those hard blue eyes — and she held the black plastic mike to her lips a moment longer than she had to before answering. "Nothing, Zack," she said, "just checking in."

His voice was tinny. "OK," he said. "Talk to you. Over and out."

"Over and out," she said.

And now what? The guy wore a hunting knife strapped to his thigh. His   20
cheeks were caved in as if he were sucking candy and an old-fashioned mustache, thick and reddish, hid his upper lip. Instead of a baseball cap he wore a wide-brimmed felt hat. Wyatt Earp, she thought, and she was about to turn away from the window, prepared to ignore him till he took the hint, till he counted off the 150 wooden steps and vanished down the path and out of her life, when he rapped again on the glass and said, "You got something to put these in — the flowers, I mean?"

She didn't want his flowers. She didn't want him on her platform. She didn't want him in her 13' by 13' sanctuary, touching her things, poking around, asking stupid questions, making small talk. "Look," she said finally, talking to the glass but looking through him, beyond him, scanning the infinite as she'd trained herself to do, no matter what the problem, "I've got a job to do up here and the fact is no one's allowed on the platform between the hours of five in the afternoon and ten in the morning" — now she came back to him and saw that his smile had collapsed — "you ought to know that. It says so in plain English right down there at the trailhead." She looked away, it was over, she was done with him.

She went back to her breakfast, forcing herself to stare at the page before her, though her heart was going and the words meant nothing. Todd had been with her the first time the man had come. Todd was fourteen, tall like his father, blond-headed, and rangy. He was a good kid, her last and final hope, and he seemed to relish the time he spent with her up here. It was a Saturday, the middle of the afternoon, and they'd had a steady stream of visitors since the morning. Todd was in the storage room below, reading comics (in its wisdom, the Forestry Service had provided this second room, twenty-five steps down, not simply for storage but for respite too — it was a box, a womb, with only a single dull high-placed window to light it, antithesis and antidote to the naked glass box above). Elaine was at her post, chopping vegetables for soup and scanning the horizon.

She hadn't noticed him coming — there'd been so many visitors she wasn't attuned to them in the way she was in the quiet times. She was feeling hospitable, lighthearted, the hostess of an ongoing party. There'd been a professor up earlier, an ornithologist, and they'd had a long talk about the golden eagle and the red-tailed hawk. And then there was the young girl from Merced — she couldn't have been more than seventeen — with her baby strapped to her back, and two heavyset women in their sixties who'd proudly made the two-and-a-half mile trek in from the trailhead and were giddy with the thin air and the thrill of their own accomplishment. Elaine had offered them each a cup of tea, not wanting to spoil their fun and point out that it was still two and a half miles back out.

She'd felt his weight on the platform and turned to give him a smile. He was tall and powerful across the chest and shoulders and he'd tipped his hat to her and poked his head in the open door. "Enjoying the view?" he said.

There was something in his eyes that should have warned her off, but she was feeling sociable and buoyant and she saw the generosity in his shoulders and hands. "It's nothing compared to the Ventura Freeway," she deadpanned. 25

He laughed out loud at that, and he was leaning in the door now, both hands on the frame. "I see the monastic life hasn't hurt your sense of humor any — " and then he paused, as if he'd gone too far. "Or that's not the word I want, 'monastic' — is there a feminine version of that?"

Pretty presumptuous. Flirtatious too. But she was in the mood, she didn't know what it was — maybe having Todd with her, maybe just the sheer bubbling joy of living on the crest of the sky — and at least he wasn't dragging her through the same old tired conversation about loneliness and beauty and smoke on the horizon she had to endure about a hundred times a week. "Come in," she said. "Take a load off your feet."

He sat on the edge of the bed and removed his hat. He wore his hair in a modified punk style — hard irregular spikes — and that surprised her: Somehow it just didn't go with the cowboy hat. His jeans were stiff and new and his tooled boots looked as if they'd just been polished. He was studying her — she was wearing khaki shorts and a T-shirt, she'd washed her hair that morning in anticipation of the crowd, and her legs were good — she knew it — tanned and shaped by her treks up and down the trail. She felt something she hadn't felt in a long time, an ice age, and she knew her cheeks were flushed. "You probably had a whole slew of visitors today, huh?" he said, and there was something incongruous in the enforced folksiness of the phrase, something that didn't go with his accent, just as the haircut didn't go with the hat.

"I've counted twenty-six since this morning." She diced a carrot, tossed it into the pan to simmer with the onions and zucchini she'd chopped a moment earlier.

He was gazing out the window, working his hands on the brim of his hat.   30
"Hope you don't mind my saying this, but you're the best thing about this view as far as I can see. You're pretty. Really pretty."

This one she'd heard before. About a thousand times. Probably seventy percent of the day-trippers who made the hike out to the lookout were male, and, if they were alone or with other males, about ninety percent of those tried to hit on her in some way. She resented it, but she couldn't blame them really. There was probably something irresistible in the formula: young woman with blonde hair and good legs in a glass tower in the middle of nowhere — and all alone. Rapunzel, let down your hair. Usually she deflected the compliment — or the moves — by turning officious, standing on her authority as Forestry Service employee, government servant, and the chief, queen, and despot of the Needles Lookout. This time she said nothing. Just lifted her head for a quick scan of the horizon and then looked back down at the knife and the cutting board and began chopping green onion and cilantro.

He was still watching her. The bed was big, a double, one of the few creature comforts the Forestry Service provided up here. There was no headboard, of course — just a big flat hard slab of mattress attached to the wall at window level, so you could be lying in bed and still do your job. Presumably, it was designed for couples. When he spoke again, she knew what he was going to say before the words were out of his mouth. "Nice bed," he said.

What did she expect? He was no different from the rest — why would he be? All of a sudden he'd begun to get on her nerves, and when she turned her face to him her voice was cold. "Have you seen the telescope?" she said, indicating the Bushnell Televar mounted on the rail of the catwalk — beyond the window and out the door.

He ignored her. He rose to his feet. Thirteen by thirteen: Two's a crowd. "You must get awfully lonely up here," he said, and his voice was different now too, no attempt at folksiness or jocularity, "a pretty woman like you. A beautiful woman. You've got sexy legs, you know that?"

She flushed — he could see that, she was sure of it — and the flush made   35
her angry. She was about to tell him off, to tell him to get the hell out of her house and stay out, when Todd came rumbling up the steps, wild-eyed and excited. "Mom!" he shouted, and he was out of breath, his voice high-pitched and hoarse, "there's water leaking all over the place out there!"

Water. It took a moment to register. The water was precious up here, irreplaceable. Once a month two bearded men with Forestry Service patches on their sleeves brought her six twenty-gallon containers of it — in the old way, on the backs of mules. She husbanded that water as if she were in the middle of the Negev, every drop of it, rarely allowing herself the luxury of a quick shampoo and rinse, as she had that morning. In the next instant she was out the door and jolting down the steps behind her son. Down below, outside the storage room where the cartons were lined up in a straight standing row, she saw that the rock face was slick with a finely spread sheen of water. She bent to the near carton. It was leaking from a thin milky stress fracture in the plastic, an inch from the bottom. "Take hold of it, Todd," she said, "we've got to turn it over so the leak's on top."

Full, the carton weighed better than 160 pounds, and this one was nearly full. She put her weight behind it, the power of her honed and muscular legs, but the best she could do, even with Todd's help, was to push the thing over on its side. She was breathing hard, sweating, she'd scraped her knee and there was a stipple of blood on the skin over the kneecap. It was then that she became aware of the stranger standing there behind her. She looked up at him framed against the vastness of the sky, the sun in his face, his big hands on his hips. "Need a hand there?" he asked.

Looking back on it, she didn't know why she'd refused — maybe it was the way Todd gaped at him in awe, maybe it was the old pretty woman/lonely up here routine or the helpless female syndrome — but before she could think she was saying, "I don't need your help: I can do it myself."

And then his hands fell from his hips and he backed away a step, and suddenly he was apologetic, he was smooth and funny and winning and he was sorry for bothering her and he just wanted to help and he knew she was capable, he wasn't implying anything — and just as suddenly he caught himself, dropped his shoulders, and slunk off down the steps without another word.

For a long moment she watched him receding down the trail, and then she turned back to the water container. By the time she and Todd got it upended it was half empty.

Yes. And now he was here when he had no right to be, now he was intruding and he knew it, now he was a crazy defining new levels of the affliction. She'd call in an emergency in a second — she wouldn't hesitate — and they'd have a helicopter here in less than five minutes, that's how quick these firefighters were, she'd seen them in action. Five minutes. She wouldn't hesitate. She kept her head down. She cut and chewed each piece of meat with slow deliberation and she read and reread the same paragraph until it lost all sense. When she looked up, he was gone.

After that, the day dragged on as if it would never end. He couldn't have been there more than ten minutes, slouching around with his mercenary grin and his pathetic flowers, but he'd managed to ruin her day. He'd upset her equilibrium and she found that she couldn't read, couldn't sketch or work on the sweater she was knitting for Todd. She caught herself staring at a fixed point on the horizon, drifting, her mind a blank. She ate too much. Lunch was a ceremony, dinner a ritual. There were no visitors, though for once she longed for them. Dusk lingered in the western sky and when night fell she didn't bother with her propane lantern but merely sat there on the corner of the bed, caught up in the wheeling immensity of the constellations and the dream of the Milky Way.

And then she couldn't sleep. She kept thinking of him, the stranger with the big hands and secretive eyes, kept scanning the catwalk for the sudden black shadow of him. If he came at seven in the morning, why not at three? What was to prevent him? There was no sound, nothing — the wind had died down and the night was clear and moonless. For the first time since she'd been here, for the first time in three long seasons, she felt naked and vulnerable, exposed in her glass house like a fish in a tank. The night was everything and it held her in its grip.

She thought about Mike then, about the house they'd had when Mike had finished his degree and started as an assistant professor at a little state school out in the lost lush hills of Oregon. The house was an A-frame, a cabin with a loft, set down amidst the trees like a cottage in a fairy tale. It was all windows and everywhere you looked the trees bowed down and stepped into the house. The previous owner, an old widower with watery eyes and yellow hair climbing out of his ears, hadn't bothered with blinds or curtains, and Mike didn't like that — he was always after her to measure the windows and order blinds or buy the material for drapes. She'd balked. The openness, the light, the sense of connection and belonging: These were the things that had attracted her in the first place. They made love in the dark — Mike insisted on it — as if it were something to be ashamed of. After a while, it was.

Then she was thinking of a time before that, a time before Todd and graduate school, when Mike sat with her in the dormitory lounge, books spread out on the coffee table before them, the heat and murmur of a dozen other couples locking their mouths and bodies together. A study date. For hours she clung to him, the sofa like a boat pitching in a heavy sea, the tease of it, the fumbling innocence, the interminable foreplay that left her wet and itching while the wind screamed beyond the iced-over windows. That was something. The R.A. would flash the lights and it was quarter to two and they would fling themselves at each other, each step to the door drenched in hormones, sticky with them, desperate, until finally he was gone and she felt the loss like a war bride. Until the next night.

Finally, and it must have been two, three in the morning, the Big Dipper tugged down below the horizon, Orion looming overhead, she thought of the stranger who'd spoiled her breakfast. He'd sat there on the corner of the bed, he'd stood beyond the window with his sad bundle of flowers, devouring the sky. As she thought of him, in that very moment, there was a dull light thump on the steps, a faint rustle, movement, and she couldn't breathe, couldn't move. The seconds pounded in her head and the rustling — it was like the sweep of a broom — was gone, something in the night, a pack rat, the fleeting touch of an owl's wing. She thought of those hands, the eyes, the square of those shoulders, and she felt herself being drawn down into the night in relief, and finally, in gratitude.

She woke late; the sun slanting across the floor to touch her lips and mask her eyes. Zachary was on the radio with the news that Oakland had clinched the pennant and a hurricane was tearing up the East Coast. "You sound awful," he said. "I didn't wake you, did I?"

"I couldn't sleep."

"Star-gazing again, huh?"

She tried out a laugh for him. "I guess," she said. There was a silence. "Jesus, you just relieved me. I've got four more days to put in before I come back down to the ground."

"Just don't get mystical on me. And leave me some granola this time, will you? And if you run out, call me. That's my breakfast we're talking about. And lunch. And sometimes, if I don't feel like cooking — "

She cut him off: "Dinner. I know. I will." She yawned. "Talk to you."

"Yeah. Over and out."

"Over and out."

When she set the kettle on the grill there was gas, but when she turned her back to dig the butter out of the refrigerator, the flame was gone. She tried another match, but there was nothing. That meant she had to switch propane tanks, a minor nuisance. The tanks, which were flown in once a year by helicopter, were located at the base of the stairway, 150 steps down. There was a flat spot there, a gap cut into the teeth of the outcrop and overhung on one side by a sloping twenty-foot-high wall of rock. On the other side, the first step was a thousand feet down.

She shrugged into her shorts, and because it was cold despite the sun — she'd seen snow as early as the fifth of September and the month was almost gone now — she pulled on an oversized sweater that had once belonged to Mike. After she moved out she found it in a pillowcase she'd stuffed full of clothes. He hadn't wanted it back. It was windy and a blast knifed into her when she threw open the door and started down the steps. Big pristine tufts of cumulus hurried across the sky, swelling and attenuating and changing shape, but she didn't see anything dark enough — or big enough — to portend a storm. Still, you could never tell. The breeze was from the north and the radio had reported a storm front moving in off the Pacific — it really wouldn't surprise her to see snow on the ground by this time tomorrow. A good snowfall and the fire season would be over and she could go home. Early.

She thought about that, about the four walls of the little efficiency she rented on a dead street in a dead town to be near Todd during the winter, and hoped it wouldn't snow. Not now. Not yet. In a dry year — and this had been the third dry year in a row — she could stay through mid-November. She reached the bottom of the steps and crouched over the propane tanks, two 300-gallon jobs painted Forestry Service green, feeling depressed over the thought of those four dull walls and the cold in the air and the storm that

50

55

might or might not develop. There was gooseflesh on her legs and her breath
crowded the air round her. She watched a ground squirrel, its shoulders bulky
with patches of bright gray fur, dart up over the face of the overhang, and then
she unfastened the coupling on the empty tank and switched the hose to the
full one.

"Gas problems?"

The voice came from above and behind her and she jumped as if she'd
been stung. Even before she whirled round she knew whose voice it was.

"Hey, hey: didn't mean to startle you. Whoa. Sorry." There he was, the   60
happy camper, knife lashed to his thigh, standing right behind her, two steps
up. This time his eyes were hidden behind a pair of reflecting sunglasses. The
brim of the Stetson was pulled down low and he wore a sheepskin coat, the
fleecy collar turned up in back.

She couldn't answer. Couldn't smile. Couldn't humor him. He'd caught
her out of her sanctuary, caught her out in the open, 150 steep and unforgiving
steps from the radio, the kitchen knife, the hard flat soaring bed. She was
crouching. He towered above her, his shoulders cut out of the sky. Todd was
in school. Mike — she didn't want to think about Mike. She was all alone.

He stood there, the mustache the only thing alive in his face. It lifted from
his teeth in a grin. "Those things can be a pain," he said, the folksy tone
creeping into his voice, "those tanks, I mean. Dangerous. I use electricity
myself."

She lifted herself cautiously from her crouch, the hard muscles swelling in
her legs. She would have risked a dash up the stairs, all 150 of them, would
have put her confidence in her legs, but he was blocking the stairway — almost
as if he'd anticipated her. She hadn't said a word yet. She looked scared, she
knew it. "Still camping?" she said, fighting to open up her face and give him
his smile back, insisting on banality, normalcy, the meaningless drift of meaningless conversation.

He looked away from her, light flashing from the slick convexity of the
sunglasses, and kicked at the edge of the step with the silver-tipped toe of his
boot. After a moment he turned back to her and removed the sunglasses.
"Yeah," he said, shrugging, "I guess."

It wasn't an answer she expected. He guessed? What was that supposed   65
to mean? He hadn't moved a muscle and he was watching her with that look
in his eyes — she knew that look, knew that stance, that mustache and hat,
but she didn't know his name. He knew hers but she didn't know his, not even
his first name. "I'm sorry," she said, and when she put a hand up to her eyes
to shade them from the sun, it was trembling, "but what was your name again?
I mean, I remember you, of course, not just from yesterday but from that time
a month or so ago, but . . ." she trailed off.

He didn't seem to have heard her. The wind sang in the trees. She just
stood there, squinting into the sun — there was nothing else she could do. "I
wasn't camping, not really," he said. "Not that I don't love the wilderness —
and I do camp, backpack and all that — but I just — I thought that's what
you'd want to hear."

What she'd want to hear? What was he talking about? She stole a glance at the tower, sun flashing the windows, clouds pricked on the peak of the roof, and it seemed as distant as the stars at night. If she were only up there she'd put out an emergency, she would, she'd have them here in five minutes . . .

"Actually," and he looked away now, his shoulders slumping in that same hangdog way they had when she'd refused his help with the water carton, "actually I've got a cabin up on Cedar Slope. I just, I just thought you'd want to hear I was camping." He'd been staring down at the toe of his boots, but suddenly he looked up at her and grinned till his back fillings glinted in the light. "I think Elaine's a pretty name, did I tell you that?"

"Thank you," she said, almost against her will, and softly, so softly she could barely hear it herself. He could rape her here, he could kill her, anything. Was that what he wanted? Was that it? "Listen," she said, pushing it, she couldn't help herself, "listen, I've got to get back to work — "

"I know, I know," he said, holding up the big slab of his hand, "back to the nest, huh? I know I must be a pain in the — in the butt for you, and I'll bet I'm not the first one to say it, but you're just too good-looking a woman to be wasted out here on the squirrels and coyotes." He stepped down, stepped toward her, and she thought in that instant of trying to dart past him, a wild thought, instinctual and desperate, a thought that clawed its way into her brain and froze there before she could move. "Jesus," he said, and his voice was harsh with conviction, "don't you get lonely?"

And then she saw it, below and to the right, movement, two bobbing pink hunter's caps, coming up the trail. It was over. Just like that. She could walk away from him, mount the stairs, lock herself in the tower. But why was her heart still going, why did she feel as if it hadn't even begun? "Damn," she said, directing her gaze, "more visitors. Now I really have to get back."

He followed her eyes and looked down to where the hunters sank out of view and then bobbed back up again, working their way up the path. She could see their faces now — two men, middle-aged, wispy hair sticking out from beneath the fluorescent caps. No guns. Cameras. He studied them a moment and then looked into her eyes, looked deep, as if he'd lost something. Then he shrugged, turned his back, and started down the path toward them.

She was in good shape, the best shape of her life. She'd been up the steps a thousand times, two thousand, but she'd never climbed them quicker than she did now. She flew up the stairs like something blown by the wind and she felt a kind of panic beating against her ribs and she smelled the storm coming and felt the cold to the marrow of her bones. And then she reached the door and slammed it shut behind her, fumbling for the latch. It was then, only then, that she noticed the flowers. They were in the center of the table, in a cut-glass vase, lupin, groundsel, forget-me-not.

It snowed in the night, monstrous swirling oversized flakes that clawed at the windows and filled her with despair. The lights would only have made her feel vulnerable and exposed and for the second night running she did

70

without them, sitting there in the dark, cradling the kitchen knife, and listening for his footfall on the steps while the sky fell to pieces around her. But he wouldn't come, not in this weather, not at night — she was being foolish, childish, there was nothing to worry about. Except the snow. It meant that her season was over. And if her season was over, she had to go back down the mountain and into the real world, real time, into the smog and roar and clutter.

She thought of the four walls that awaited her, the hopeless job — wait-ressing or fast food or some such slow crucifixion of the spirit — and she thought of Mike before she left him, saw him there in the black glass of the window, sexless, pale, the little butterfly-wing bifocals perched on the tip of his nose, pecking at the typewriter, pecking, pecking, in love with Dryden, Swift, Pope, in love with dead poets, in love with death itself. She'd met a man at a party a month after she'd left him and he was just like Mike, only he was in love with arthropods. Arthropods. And then she came up to the tower.

She woke late again and the first thing she felt was relief. The sun was out and the snow — it was only a dusting, nothing really — had already begun to recede from the naked high crown of the rock. She put on the kettle and went to the radio. "Zack," she called, "Needle Rock. Do you copy?"

He was there, right at her fingertips. "Copy. Over."

"We had some snow up here — nothing much, just a dusting really. It's clear now."

"You're a little late — Lewis already checked in from Mule Peak with that information. Oversleep again?"

"Yeah, I guess so." She was watching the distant treetops shake off the patina of snow. A hawk sailed across the window. She held the microphone so close to her lips it could have been a part of her. "Zack — " she wanted to tell him about the crazy, about the man in the Stetson, about his hands, wanted to alert him just in case, but she hesitated. Her voice was tiny, detached, lost in the electronic crackle of time and space.

"Lainie?"

"Yes. Yes, I'm here."

"There's a cold front coming through, another storm behind it. They're saying it could drop some snow. The season's still on — Reichert says it will be until we get appreciable precipitation — but this one could be it. It's up to you. You want to come out or wait and see?"

Reichert was the boss, fifty, bald, soft as a clam. The mountains were parched — six inches of powdery duff covered the forest floor and half the creeks had run dry. The season could last till November. "Wait and see," she said.

"OK, it's your choice. Lewis is staying too, if it makes you feel better. I'll keep in touch if anything develops on this end."

"Yeah. Thanks."

"Over and out."

"Over and out."

75

80

85

It clouded over late in the afternoon and the sky closed in on her again. The temperature began to drop. It looked bad. It was early for snow yet, but they could get snow any time of the year at this altitude. The average was twenty-five feet annually, and she'd seen storms drop four and five feet at a time. She talked to Zack at four and he told her it looked pretty grim — they were calling for a seventy percent chance of snow, with the snow level dropping to three thousand feet. "I'll take my chances," she told him. There was a pair of snowshoes in the storage room if it came to that.

The snow started an hour later. She was cooking dinner — brown rice and vegetables — and she'd opened the bottle of wine she'd brought up to commemorate the last day of the season. The flakes were tiny, pellets that shifted down with a hiss, the sort of configuration that meant serious snow. The season was over. She could drink her wine and then think about packing up and cleaning the stove and refrigerator. She put another log on the woodstove and buttoned up her jacket.

The wine was half gone and she'd sat down to eat when she noticed the smoke. At first she thought it must be a trick of the wind, the smoke from her own stove twisting back on her. But no. Below her, no more than five hundred feet, just about where the trail would be, she could see the flames. The wind blew a screen of snow across the window. There hadn't been any lightning — but there was a fire down there, she was sure of it. She got up from the table, snatched her binoculars from the hook by the door, and went out on the catwalk to investigate.

The wind took her breath away. All the universe had gone pale, white above and white beneath: She was perched on the clouds, living in them, diaphanous and ghostly. She could smell the smoke on the wind now. She lifted the binoculars to her eyes and the snow screened them; she tried again and her hair beat at the lenses. It took her a moment, but there, there it was: a fire leaping up out of the swirling grip of the snow. A campfire. But no, this was bigger, fallen trees stacked up in a pyramid — this was a bonfire, deliberate, this was a sign. The snow took it away from her. Her fingers were numb. When the fire came into focus again she saw movement there, a shadow leaping round the flames, feeding them, revelling in them, and she caught her breath. And then she saw the black, jabbing peak of the Stetson and she understood.

He was camping.

Camping. He could die out there — he *was* crazy, he *was* — this thing could turn into a blizzard, it could snow for days. But he was camping. And then the thought came to her: He was camping for her.

Later, when the tower floated out over the storm and the coals glowed in the stove and the darkness settled in around her like a blanket, she disconnected the radio and put the knife away in the drawer where it belonged. Then she propped herself in the corner of the bed, way out over the edge of the abyss, and watched his fire raging in the cold heart of the night. He would be back, she knew that now, and she would be ready for him.   1991

90

95

INVESTIGATIONS

1. When Elaine first realizes that she has seen the unnerving visitor before, she thinks of putting out an emergency call on the radio (para. 12), but she doesn't. Do you think her response is appropriate? Why do you think she stops short of making an emergency call? Why do you think she never tells Zack about the stranger?

2. Choose one of the meeting scenes between Elaine and the disturbing stranger. Keep the given lines of dialogue — for example, Elaine: "Still camping?" Stranger: "Yeah, . . . I guess" (paras. 63, 64) — but retell the scene from the stranger's point of view.

3. Discuss the ways Elaine both fulfills and breaks away from stereotypical images of women.

4. Elaine thinks of her jobs back in the city as a "slow crucifixion of the spirit" (para. 75). If you've had such jobs, analyze what it is about them that crucifies the spirit.

5. What do you make of the last few images: the stranger "leaping around the flames, feeding them, revelling in them" (para. 92), and Elaine propped in the corner of the bed, "way out over the edge of the abyss . . . ready for him" (para. 95)?

ANNA LEE WALTERS

The Warriors

In our youth, we saw hobos come and go, sliding by our faded white house like wary cats who did not want us too close. Sister and I waved at the strange procession of passing men and women hobos. Just between ourselves, Sister and I talked of that hobo parade. We guessed at and imagined the places and towns we thought the hobos might have come from or had been. Mostly they were white or black people. But there were Indian hobos, too. It never occurred to Sister and me that this would be Uncle Ralph's end.

Sister and I were little, and Uncle Ralph came to visit us. He lifted us over his head and shook us around him like gourd rattles. He was Momma's younger

---

A Pawnee/Otoe Indian, ANNA LEE WALTERS (b. 1946) is a painter, writer, and editor at Navajo Community College Press. Her books include a short story collection entitled *The Sun Is Not Merciful* (1985) and *The Spirit of Native America: Beauty and Mysticism in American Indian Art* (1989).

brother, and he could have disciplined us if he so desired. That was part of our custom. But he never did. Instead, he taught us Pawnee words. "*Pari* is Pawnee and *pita* is man," he said. Between the words, he tapped out drumbeats with his fingers on the table top, ghost dance and round dance songs that he suddenly remembered and sang. His melodic voice lilted over us and hung around the corners of the house for days. His stories of life and death were fierce and gentle. Warriors dangled in delicate balance.

He told us his version of the story of Pahukatawa, a Skidi Pawnee warrior. He was killed by the Sioux, but the animals, feeling compassion for him, brought Pahukatawa to life again. "The Evening Star and the Morning Star bore children and some people say that these offspring are who we are," he often said. At times he pointed to those stars and greeted them by their Pawnee names. He liked to pray for Sister and me, for everyone and every tiny thing in the world, but we never heard him ask for anything for himself from *Atius,* the Father.

"For beauty is why we live," Uncle Ralph said when he talked of precious things only the Pawnees know. "We die for it, too." He called himself an ancient Pawnee warrior when he was quite young. He told us that warriors must brave all storms and odds and stand their ground. He knew intimate details of every battle the Pawnees ever fought since Pawnee time began, and Sister and I knew even then that Uncle Ralph had a great battlefield of his own.

As a child I thought that Uncle Ralph had been born into the wrong time. The Pawnees had been ravaged so often by then. The tribe of several thousand when it was at its peak over a century before were then a few hundred people who had been closely confined for more than a hundred years. The warrior life was gone. Uncle Ralph was trapped in a transparent bubble of a new time. The bubble bound him tight as it blew around us.

Uncle Ralph talked obsessively of warriors, painted proud warriors who shrieked poignant battle cries at the top of their lungs and died with honor. Sister and I were little then, lost from him in the world of children who saw everything with children's eyes. And though we saw with wide eyes the painted warriors that he fantasized and heard their fierce and haunting battle cries, we did not hear his. Now that we are old and Uncle Ralph has been gone for a long time, Sister and I know that when he died, he was tired and alone. But he was a warrior.

The hobos were always around in our youth. Sister and I were curious about them, and this curiosity claimed much of our time. They crept by the house at all hours of the day and night, dressed in rags and odd clothing. They wandered to us from the railroad tracks where they had leaped from slow-moving boxcars onto the flatland. They hid in high clumps of weeds and brush that ran along the fence near the tracks. The hobos usually traveled alone, but Sister and I saw them come together, like poor families, to share a can of beans or a tin of sardines that they ate with sticks or twigs. Uncle Ralph also watched them from a distance.

One early morning, Sister and I crossed the tracks on our way to school and collided with a tall, haggard white man. He wore a very old-fashioned pin-striped black jacket covered with lint and soot. There was fright in his eyes when they met ours. He scurried around us, quickening his pace. The pole over his shoulder where his possessions hung in a bundle at the end bounced as he nearly ran from us.

"Looks just like a scared jackrabbit," Sister said, watching him dart away.

That evening we told Momma about the scared man. She warned us about the dangers of hobos as our father threw us a stern look. Uncle Ralph was visiting but he didn't say anything. He stayed the night and Sister asked him, "Hey, Uncle Ralph, why do you suppose they's hobos?" ⟨10⟩

Uncle Ralph was a large man. He took Sister and put her on one knee. "You see, Sister," he said, "hobos are a different kind. They see things in a different way. Them hobos are kind of like us. We're not like other people in some ways and yet we are. It has to do with what you see and feel when you look at this old world."

His answer satisfied Sister for a while. He taught us some more Pawnee words that night.

Not long after Uncle Ralph's explanation, Sister and I surprised a black man with white whiskers and fuzzy hair. He was climbing through the barbed-wire fence that marked our property line. He wore faded blue overalls with pockets stuffed full of handkerchiefs. He wiped sweat from his face. When it dried, he looked up and saw us. I remembered what Uncle Ralph had said and wondered what the black man saw when he looked at us standing there.

"We might scare him," Sister said softly to me, remembering the white man who had scampered away.

Sister whispered, "Hi," to the black man. Her voice was barely audible. ⟨15⟩

"Boy, it's sure hot," he said. His voice was big and he smiled.

"Where are you going?" Sister asked.

"Me? Nowheres, I guess," he muttered.

"Then what you doing here?" Sister went on. She was bold for a seven-year-old kid. I was older but I was also quieter. "This here place is ours," she said.

He looked around and saw our house with its flowering mimosa trees and rich green mowed lawn stretching out before him. Other houses sat around ours. ⟨20⟩

"I reckon I'm lost," he said.

Sister pointed to the weeds and brush further up the road. "That's where you want to go. That's where they all go, the hobos."

I tried to quiet Sister but she didn't hush. "The hobos stay up there," she said. "You a hobo?"

He ignored her question and asked his own. "Say, what is you all? You not black, you not white. What is you all?"

Sister looked at me. She put one hand on her chest and the other hand on me. "We Indians!" Sister said. ⟨25⟩

He stared at us and smiled again. "Is that a fact?" he said.

"Know what kind of Indians we are?" Sister asked him.

He shook his fuzzy head. "Indians is Indians, I guess," he said.

Sister wrinkled her forehead and retorted, "Not us! We not like others. We see things different. We're Pawnees. We're warriors!"

I pushed my elbow into Sister's side. She quieted.

The man was looking down the road and he shuffled his feet. "I'd best go," he said.

Sister pointed to the brush and weeds one more time. "That way," she said.

He climbed back through the fence and brush as Sister yelled, "Bye now!" He waved a damp handkerchief.

Sister and I didn't tell Momma and Dad about the black man. But much later Sister told Uncle Ralph every word that had been exchanged with the black man. Uncle Ralph listened and smiled.

Months later when the warm weather had cooled and Uncle Ralph came to stay with us for a couple of weeks, Sister and I went to the hobo place. We had planned it for a long time. That afternoon when we pushed away the weeds, not a hobo was in sight.

The ground was packed down tight in the clearing among the high weeds. We walked around the encircling brush and found folded cardboards stacked together. Burned cans in assorted sizes were stashed under the cardboards, and there were remains of old fires. Rags were tied to the brush, snapping in the hard wind.

Sister said, "Maybe they're all in the boxcars now. It's starting to get cold."

She was right. The November wind had a bite to it and the cold stung our hands and froze our breaths as we spoke.

"You want to go over to them boxcars?" she asked. We looked at the Railroad Crossing sign where the boxcars stood.

I was prepared to answer when a voice roared from somewhere behind us.

"Now, you young ones, you git on home! Go on! Git!"

A man crawled out of the weeds and looked angrily at us. His eyes were red and his face was unshaven. He wore a red plaid shirt with striped gray and black pants too large for him. His face was swollen and bruised. An old woolen pink scarf hid some of the bruise marks around his neck, and his topcoat was splattered with mud.

Sister looked at him. She stood close to me and told him defiantly, "You can't tell us what to do! You don't know us!"

He didn't answer Sister but tried to stand. He couldn't. Sister ran to him and took his arm and pulled on it. "You need help?" she questioned.

He frowned at her but let us help him. He was tall. He seemed to be embarrassed by our help.

"You Indian, ain't you?" I dared to ask him.

He didn't answer me but looked at his feet as if they could talk so he wouldn't have to. His feet were in big brown overshoes.

"Who's your people?" Sister asked. He looked to be about Uncle Ralph's age when he finally lifted his face and met mine. He didn't respond for a minute. Then he sighed. "I ain't got no people," he told us as he tenderly stroked his swollen jaw.

"Sure you got people. Our folks says a man's always got people," I said softly. The wind blew our clothes and covered the words.

But he heard. He exploded like a firecracker. "Well, I don't! I ain't got no people! I ain't got nobody!" 50

"What you doing out here anyway?" Sister asked. "You hurt? You want to come over to our house?"

"Naw," he said. "Now you little ones, go on home. Don't be walking round out here. Didn't nobody tell you little girls ain't supposed to be going round by themselves? You might git hurt."

"We just wanted to talk to hobos," Sister said.

"Naw, you don't. Just go on home. Your folks is probably looking for you and worrying 'bout you."

I took Sister's arm and told her we were going home. Then we said bye to 55 the man. But Sister couldn't resist a few last words, "You Indian, ain't you?"

He nodded his head like it was a painful thing to do. "Yeah, I'm Indian."

"You ought to go on home yourself," Sister said. "Your folks probably looking for you and worrying 'bout you."

His voice rose again as Sister and I walked away from him. "I told you kids, I don't have no people!" There was exasperation in his voice.

Sister would not be outdone. She turned and yelled, "Oh yeah? You Indian ain't you? Ain't you?" she screamed. "We your people!"

His topcoat and pink scarf flapped in the wind as we turned away from 60 him.

We went home to Momma and Dad and Uncle Ralph then. Uncle Ralph met us at the front door. "Where you all been?" he asked looking toward the railroad tracks. Momma and Dad were talking in the kitchen.

"Just playing, Uncle," Sister and I said simultaneously.

Uncle Ralph grabbed both Sister and me by our hands and yanked us out the door. *"Awkuh!"* he said, using the Pawnee expression to show his dissatisfaction.

Outside, we sat on the cement porch. Uncle Ralph was quiet for a long time, and neither Sister nor I knew what to expect.

"I want to tell you all a story," he finally said. "Once, there were these 65 two rats who ran around everywhere and got into everything all the time. Everything they were told not to do, well they went right out and did. They'd get into one mess and then another. It seems that they never could learn."

At that point Uncle Ralph cleared his throat. He looked at me and said, "Sister, do you understand this story? Is it too hard for you? You're older."

I nodded my head up and down and said, "I understand."

Then Uncle Ralph looked at Sister. He said to her, "Sister, do I need to go on with this story?"

Sister shook her head from side to side. "Naw, Uncle Ralph," she said.

"So you both know how this story ends?" he said gruffly. Sister and I   70
bobbed our heads up and down again.

We followed at his heels the rest of the day. When he tightened the loose
hide on top of his drum, we watched him and held it in place as he laced the
wet hide down. He got his drumsticks down from the top shelf of the closet
and began to pound the drum slowly.

"Where you going, Uncle Ralph?" I asked. Sister and I knew that when
he took his drum out, he was always gone shortly after.

"I have to be a drummer at some doings tomorrow," he said.

"You a good singer, Uncle Ralph," Sister said. "You know all them old
songs."

"The young people nowadays, it seems they don't care 'bout nothing that's   75
old. They just want to go to the Moon." He was drumming low as he spoke.

"We care, Uncle Ralph," Sister said.

"Why?" Uncle Ralph asked in a hard, challenging tone that he seldom
used on us.

Sister thought for a moment and then said, "I guess because you care so
much, Uncle Ralph."

His eyes softened as he said, "I'll sing you an *Eruska* song, a song for the
warriors."

The song he sang was a war dance song. At first Sister and I listened   80
attentively, but then Sister began to dance the men's dance. She had never
danced before and tried to imitate what she had seen. Her chubby body whirled
and jumped the way she'd seen the men dance. Her head tilted from side to
side the way the men moved theirs. I laughed aloud at her clumsy effort, and
Uncle Ralph laughed heartily, too.

Uncle Ralph when in and out of our lives after that. We heard that he
sang at one place and then another, and people came to Momma to find him.
They said that he was only one of a few who knew the old ways and the songs.

When he came to visit us, he always brought something to eat. The Pawnee
custom was that the man, the warrior, should bring food, preferably meat.
Then, whatever food was brought to the host was prepared and served to the
man, the warrior, along with the host's family. Many times Momma and I, or
Sister and I, came home to an empty house to find a sack of food on the table.
Momma or I cooked it for the next meal, and Uncle Ralph showed up to eat.

As sister and I grew older, our fascination with the hobos decreased. Other
things took our time, and Uncle Ralph did not appear as frequently as he did
before.

Once while I was home alone, I picked up Momma's old photo album.
Inside was a gray photo of Uncle Ralph in an army uniform. Behind him were
tents on a flat terrain. Other photos showed other poses but only in one picture
did he smile. All the photos were written over in black ink in Momma's
handwriting. "Ralphie in Korea," the writing said.

Other photos in the album showed our Pawnee relatives. Dad was from   85
another tribe. Momma's momma was in the album, a tiny gray-haired woman

who no longer lived. And Momma's momma's dad was in the album; he wore old Pawnee leggings and the long feathers of a dark bird sat upon his head. I closed the album when Momma, Dad, and Sister came home.

Momma went into the kitchen to cook. She called me and Sister to help. As she put on a bibbed apron, she said, "We just came from town, and we saw someone from home there." She meant someone from her tribal community.

"This man told me that Ralphie's been drinking hard," she said sadly. "He used to do that quite a bit a long time ago, but we thought it had stopped. He seemed to be all right for a few years." We cooked and then ate in silence.

Washing the dishes, I asked Momma, "How come Uncle Ralph never did marry?"

Momma looked up at me but was not surprised by my question. She answered, "I don't know, Sister. It would have been better if he had. There was one woman who I thought he really loved. I think he still does. I think it had something to do with Mom. She wanted him to wait."

"Wait for what?" I asked.   90

"I don't know," Momma said, and sank into a chair.

After that we heard unsettling rumors of Uncle Ralph drinking here and there.

He finally came to the house once when only I happened to be home. He was haggard and tired. His appearance was much like that of the white man that Sister and I met on the railroad tracks years before.

I opened the door when he tapped on it. Uncle Ralph looked years older than his age. He brought food in his arms. "*Nowa,* Sister," he said in greeting. "Where's the other one?" He meant my sister.

"She's gone now, Uncle Ralph. School in Kansas," I answered. "Where   95
you been, Uncle Ralph? We been worrying about you."

He ignored my question and said, "I bring food. The warrior brings home food. To his family, to his people." His face was lined and had not been cleaned for days. He smelled of cheap wine.

I asked again, "Where have you been, Uncle Ralph?"

He forced himself to smile. "Pumpkin Flower," he said, using the Pawnee name, "I've been out with my warriors all this time."

He put one arm around me as we went to the kitchen table with the food. "That's what your Pawnee name is. Now don't forget it."

"Did somebody bring you here, Uncle Ralph, or are you on foot?" I asked   100
him.

"I'm on foot," he answered. "Where's your Momma?"

I told him that she and Dad would be back soon. I started to prepare the food he brought.

Then I heard Uncle Ralph say, "Life is sure hard sometimes. Sometimes it seems I just can't go on."

"What's wrong, Uncle Ralph?" I asked.

Uncle Ralph let out a bitter little laugh. "What's wrong?" he repeated.   105
"What's wrong? All my life, I've tried to live what I've been taught, but
Pumpkin Flower, some things are all wrong!"

He took a folded pack of Camel cigarettes from his coat pocket. His hand
shook as he pulled one from the pack and lit the end. "Too much drink," he
said sadly. "That stuff is bad for us."

"What are you trying to do, Uncle Ralph?" I asked him.

"Live," he said.

He puffed on the shaking cigarette a while and said, "The old people said
to live beautifully with prayers and song. Some died for beauty, too."

"How do we do that, Uncle Ralph, live for beauty?" I asked.   110

"It's simple, Pumpkin Flower," he said. "Believe!"

"Believe what?" I asked.

He looked at me hard. *Awkuh!* he said. "That's one of the things that
is wrong. Everyone questions. Everyone doubts. No one believes in the old
ways anymore. They want to believe when it's convenient, when it doesn't cost
them anything and they get something in return. There are no more believers.
There are no more warriors. They are all gone. Those who are left only want
to go to the Moon."

A car drove up outside. It was Momma and Dad. Uncle Ralph heard it
too. He slumped in the chair, resigned to whatever Momma would say to him.

Momma came in first. Dad then greeted Uncle Ralph and disappeared into   115
the back of the house. Custom and etiquette required that Dad, who was not
a member of Momma's tribe, allow Momma to handle her brother's problems.

She hugged Uncle Ralph. Her eyes filled with tears when she saw how thin
he was and how his hands shook.

"Ralphie," she said, "you look awful, but I am glad to see you."

She then spoke to him of everyday things, how the car failed to start and
the latest gossip. He was silent, tolerant of the passing of time in this way. His
eyes sent me a pleading look while his hands shook and he tried to hold them
still.

When supper was ready, Uncle Ralph went to wash himself for the meal.
When he returned to the table, he was calm. His hands didn't shake so much.

At first he ate without many words, but in the course of the meal he left   120
the table twice. Each time he came back, he was more talkative than before,
answering Momma's questions in Pawnee. He left the table a third time and
Dad rose.

Dad said to Momma, "He's drinking again. Can't you tell?" Dad left the
table and went outside.

Momma frowned. A determined look grew on her face.

When Uncle Ralph sat down to the table once more, Momma told him,
"Ralphie, you're my brother but I want you to leave now. Come back when
you're sober."

He held a tarnished spoon in midair and put it down slowly. He hadn't finished eating, but he didn't seem to mind leaving. He stood, looked at me with his red eyes, and went to the door. Momma followed him. In a low voice she said, "Ralphie, you've got to stop drinking and wandering — or don't come to see us again."

He pulled himself to his full height then. His frame filled the doorway. He leaned over Momma and yelled, "Who are you? Are you God that you will say what will be or will not be?" 125

Momma met his angry eyes. She stood firm and did not back down.

His eyes finally dropped from her face to the linoleum floor. A cough came from deep in his throat.

"I'll leave here," he said. "But I'll get all my warriors and come back! I have thousands of warriors and they'll ride with me. We'll get our bows and arrows. Then we'll come back!" He staggered out the door.

In the years that followed, Uncle Ralph saw us only when he was sober. He visited less and less. When he did show up, he did a tapping ritual on our front door. We welcomed the rare visits. Occasionally he stayed at our house for a few days at a time when he was not drinking. He slept on the floor.

He did odd jobs for minimum pay but never complained about the work or money. He'd acquired a vacant look in his eyes. It was the same look that Sister and I had seen in the hobos when we were children. He wore a similar careless array of clothing and carried no property with him at all. 130

The last time he came to the house, he called me by my English name and asked if I remembered anything of all that he'd taught me. His hair had turned pure white. He looked older than anyone I knew. I marveled at his appearance and said, "I remember everything." That night I pointed out his stars for him and told him how Pahukatawa lived and died and lived again through another's dreams. I'd grown, and Uncle Ralph could not hold me on his knee anymore. His arm circled my waist while we sat on the grass.

He was moved by my recitation and clutched my hand tightly. He said, "It's more than this. It's more than just repeating words. You know that, don't you?"

I nodded my head. "Yes, I know. The recitation is the easiest part but it's more than this, Uncle Ralph."

He was quiet, but after a few minutes his hand touched my shoulder. He said, "I couldn't make it work. I tried to fit the pieces."

"I know," I said. 135

"Now before I go," he said, "do you know who you are?"

The question took me by surprise. I thought very hard. I cleared my throat and told him, "I know that I am fourteen. I know that it's too young."

"Do you know that you are a Pawnee?" he asked in a choked whisper.

"Yes, Uncle," I said.

"Good," he said with a long sigh that was swallowed by the night. 140

Then he stood and said, "Well, Sister, I have to go. Have to move on."

"Where are you going?" I asked. "Where all the warriors go?" I teased.

He managed a smile and a soft laugh. "Yeah, wherever the warriors are, I'll find them."

I said to him, "Before you go, I want to ask you . . . Uncle Ralph, can women be warriors too?"

He laughed again and hugged me merrily. "Don't tell me you want to be one of the warriors too?"

"No, Uncle," I said. "Just one of yours." I hated to let him go because I knew I would not see him again.

He pulled away. His last words were, "Don't forget what I've told you all these years. It's the only chance not to become what everyone else is. Do you understand?"

I nodded and he left.

I never saw him again.

The years passed quickly. I moved away from Momma and Dad and married. Sister left before I did.

Years later in another town, hundreds of miles away, I awoke in a terrible gloom, a sense that something was gone from the world the Pawnees knew. The despair filled days, though the reason for the sense of loss went unexplained. Finally, the telephone rang. Momma was on the line. She said, "Sister came home for a few days not too long ago. While she was here and alone, someone tapped on the door, like Ralphie always does. Sister yelled, 'Is that you, Uncle Ralphie? Come on in.' But no one entered."

Then I understood that Uncle Ralph was dead. Momma probably knew too. She wept softly into the phone.

Later Momma received an official call confirming Uncle Ralph's death. He had died from exposure in a hobo shanty, near the railroad tracks outside a tiny Oklahoma town. He'd been dead for several days and nobody knew but Momma, Sister, and me.

Momma reported to me that the funeral was well attended by the Pawnee people. Uncle Ralph and I had said our farewells years earlier. Momma told me that someone there had spoken well of Uncle Ralph before they put him in the ground. It was said that "Ralphie came from a fine family, an old line of warriors."

Ten years later, Sister and I visited briefly at Momma's and Dad's home. We had been separated by hundreds of miles for all that time. As we sat under Momma's flowering mimosa trees, I made a confession to Sister. I said, "Sometimes I wish that Uncle Ralph were here. I'm a grown woman but I still miss him after all these years."

Sister nodded her head in agreement. I continued. "He knew so many things. He knew why the sun pours its liquid all over us and why it must do just that. He knew why babes and insects crawl. He knew that we must live beautifully or not live at all."

Sister's eyes were thoughtful, but she waited to speak while I went on. "To live beautifully from day to day is a battle all the way. The things that he knew are so beautiful. And to feel and know that kind of beauty is the reason that we should live at all. Uncle Ralph said so. But now, there is no one who knows what that beauty is or any of the other things that he knew."

Sister pushed back smoky gray wisps of her dark hair. "You do," she pronounced. "And I do, too."

"Why do you suppose he left us like that?" I asked.

"It couldn't be helped," Sister said. "There was a battle on."　　160

"I wanted to be one of his warriors," I said with an embarrassed half-smile.

She leaned over and patted my hand. "You are," she said. Then she stood and placed one hand on her bosom and one hand on my arm. "We'll carry on," she said.

I touched her hand resting on my arm. I said, "Sister, tell me again. What is the battle for?"

She looked down toward the fence where a hobo was coming through. We waved at him.

"Beauty," she said to me. "Our battle is for beauty. It's what Uncle Ralph　　165 fought for, too. He often said that everyone else just wanted to go to the Moon. But remember, Sister, you and I done been there. Don't forget, after all, we're children of the stars."　　　　　　　　　　　　　　　　1985

INVESTIGATIONS

1. How are the stories Uncle Ralph tells similar to those told by the steelworkers in "Steelworker"? By Jorgenson in *Other People's Money*? What qualities make Uncle Ralph's stories nothing like what we might call "work stories"?

2. After listing the details of what Pumpkin Flower calls "the warrior life" (para. 5), write a 500–750-word essay in which you discuss the ways in which other selections in this part demonstrate the effects of the loss of "the warrior life."

3. After Pumpkin Flower "pointed out his stars for him and told him how Pahukatawa lived and died and lived again through another's dreams" (para. 131), Uncle Ralph says, "It's more than this. It's more than just repeating words" (para. 132). Describe the "more than just repeating words" part of Uncle Ralph's labor as a warrior. What evidence do you find that Pumpkin Flower has learned well?

4. What makes it difficult for Uncle Ralph to "battle" in order to "live beautifully from day to day" (para. 157)? What would it mean for you to fight such a battle? Who is the enemy?

RICK DeMARINIS

The Flowers of Boredom

He would gladly make the earth a shambles and swallow the world in a yawn.
— Baudelaire, "Au Lecteur"

Lamar sits in his office near the end of the day, looking out at the bent heads of the sixteen men who work for him. The men appear to be engrossed in a new manual that reviews company policy concerning the cost-effectiveness of redundant systems intended to upgrade product reliability. The product is a vital part for a proposed new Mach 3.0 bomber that carries the informal in-house designation Big Buck. Big Buck will probably never be produced, or, if it is, it will most likely be awarded to a company headquartered in Texas, one-time home of the vice president. Favors, like hard currency, are always paid back in Washington. The deck is stacked, as usual, and Lamar's company, Locust Airframes, Inc., is close to the bottom of this one. Still, this going-through-the-motions is necessary, and profitable in itself, since the buyer — in this case the Air Force — picks up the tabs for these ritual dances the defense industry puts on. Lamar's sixteen men are part of the dance, recently hired to fatten the payroll roster of Advanced Proposals Engineering (APE), the section of Locust Airframes whose mission is to bid for contracts. Lamar himself is a new man insofar as he has been promoted from the rank of reliability engineer step III to full-fledged manager. This has involved a change of ID badge color from tepid aqua to radiant orange, an upgraded wardrobe, modifications in demeanor, and a tidy jump in salary and benefits. Job security, of course, is still tied to the shifting sands of Department of Defense wants and desires, which are always creatures of the latest Red Threat scenario and not necessarily a realistic response to the international situation. Lamar has been around long enough to know better — thirteen years now — but he's impressed by his good fortune anyway. He now has his own secretary instead of having to share a pool typist. She is a new employee also, and has eyes for him already. Eyes, that is, for management. Power, Lamar knows, is one of the more dependable aphrodisiacs. Lamar encourages a protective cynicism in himself, but he's only human and knows he would be stupid to look this splendid gift horse in the mouth.

The window in his office is one-way glass, allowing Lamar to observe his sixteen men while cloaked in smoky invisibility. The situation, Lamar muses, is analogous to that of a god, looking down from a screen of clouds at the

---

RICK DeMARINIS was formerly an aerospace worker and is now a teacher of creative writing at the University of Texas at El Paso. Born in New York City in 1934, he has published eight books of fiction including *The Voice of America: Stories* (1991) and *The Year of the Zinc Penny* (1989), a novel.

unhappy mortals below who believe with touching urgency that their frenetic schemes and counterschemes are extensions of conscious ideals. The god maintains this illusion in order to hold the level of human unhappiness constant. He ensures that the noblest projects of those he rules become the *means* of their unhappiness. *Lamar, Lamar,* Lamar thinks, chiding himself for such bloated fantasies, *where do you get such ideas?* He has a partial memory of where such ideas come from — a walk in the dark with a fallen angel — but no, that's literature, something he read years ago in college. In any case, the fantasy is benign, since Lamar has genuine sympathy for his men. He knows, for instance, that he is also being monitored by middle management — carefully jealous men who are halfway up the corporate ladder and do not intend to be bumped by an ambitious underling who doesn't know the rules of climbing. *We are all in the same boat, friends,* Lamar thinks as he looks out at the round-shouldered men. *It's just that I'm on a higher deck than you.*

Lamar sees that one of his new men is hiding his near baldness with wings of yellowish-white hair stretched over his dome from the thriving area above his right ear. The man is in his fifties and is lucky to have been hired at all. This is likely to be the last job he will ever have in the defense industry. After the contract has been let to the Texas company the ax will fall and the sixteen men, along with Lamar himself, will be sent scrambling for other positions within the company. The bald man in his fifties will be cut loose. Age isn't his only albatross. His relatively high salary makes his tenure an impossibility during the austere period following a lost contract. And his chances outside the defense industry are nil. Companies that are connected to legitimate free-enterprise adventures, such as IBM, AT&T, or the small but highly efficient consulting firms, want no part of men who have spent their adult lives in the defense industry. Men such as Lamar's bald man are not what the want ads refer to as "self-starters." Their ponderous, insouciant demeanor makes the personnel interviewers shake their heads in smiling dismay.

The bald man, Lamar knows, has been in the defense industry since the 1950s. B.S. in electrical engineering from Fresno or San Jose State, but has by now forgotten most of his elementary calculus and differential equations. He is what is known in the business as a "Warm Body." The Air Force, before letting a contract, likes to see a company have enough self-confidence to maintain a large, well-paid work force. This results in extreme overhiring in the months before a big contract is about to come down. Lamar has been raised to management to preside over sixteen Warm Bodies. He doesn't mind — it's the system. But only the middle-aged bald man *knows* he is a Warm Body. The others are naive kids, a few years out of college, though the more intelligent ones are becoming restless. They glance, blindly, from time to time at the smoked glass of Lamar's office as if to ask, "Isn't there anything for me to *do?*" Sometimes the blind glance is sharply suspicious — premature inklings of what the bald man knows.

The bald man cannot do real work, anyway. No one expects him to. He, and the others like him, have made their homes through the decades of cold

5

war in such places as Boeing, Lockheed, North American, or McDonnell Douglas, where they grew dim and paunchy reading turgid manuals while dreaming of overseas travel, golf, or a resurrected sexual urge. If such a man is approaching old age and has given up on the vigorous pastimes, it's possible that the simplest pleasures, such as good strong bowel movements or freedom from stiff joints, occupy his reverie. He is terrorized now and again by the streaky pains in his pectorals and arm, sudden sieges of caffeine-instigated vertigo, or shortness of breath. He is probably well past caring about his wife's slow evolution toward complete and self-sufficient indifference. Lamar is not without compassion for the bald man, who was born without ambition, though he once had all the appetites ambition serves. Now he just wants to stay comfortably alive.

Lamar is sympathetic because he knows that he is not substantially different from the bald man. They are brothers in the same tribe. Lamar's single advantage, he believes, is that he knew — and *liked* — the rules of the game when he first hired in, thirteen years ago. He seems to have been born with an instinctive grasp of what the system liked to see in a new man. Early in his career he learned how to appear innovative and energetic while at the same time assuring his superiors that these alarming qualities were empty of substance. And though he was ambitious, he understood the politics of ambition: Never frighten the man immediately above you on the ladder; he is in an excellent position to stomp on your head.

It's a Byzantine institution, the defense industry, with its own rules, rituals, and arcana that confuse and frustrate the uninitiated. And yet it manages to produce weapons of ever-increasing sophistication. That some of these weapons do not work is beside the point, a quibble rooted in a fundamental misunderstanding of the mission of the defense industry, which is, simply, to keep itself well nourished with cost-plus money, to increase steadily in manpower and physical plant, and to reveal itself to the gullible citizenry as an economic savior as well as a vital necessity in a dangerous world. In any case, most of the weapons *do* work, eventually, if not after the first production run of operational units. As long as the fabulous deep pocket of cost-plus money is reachable, the missiles will find their targets, the bombers will get off the ground, and the submarines will float. Lamar's Reliability Section is the arm of Locust Airframes that devotes itself to the creation of documents that further this notion. Reliability achieved through redundant components is costly, but as the number of additional back-up systems increases on a given piece of equipment, the theoretical failure rate dwindles steadily toward the infinitesimal. It's as if men were equipped with one or two extra hearts, or had fresh, supple arteries ready to back up their old, cholesterol-choked ones should they fail. Reliability is the dream of immortality transferred to electronics, hydraulics, and structural mechanics.

With nothing much to do himself, Lamar now studies the stiffening necks of the younger men in his section. They are primed for significant action. They are bright, hard-working, and very well trained. The system will blunt their

keen appetites for real work and discourage their desire to understand their
jobs better by gaining an overview of the entire operation of Locust Airframes,
from design to production. Only a chosen few have such indispensable omnis-
cience. And these few are never seen by men such as Lamar's. Soon, the better
of these young engineers will become deeply frustrated and resign. Though
Lamar is not old — not quite forty — the sight of the young engineers makes
him feel a fatigue rightfully belonging to a man twenty years older. It's their
clear-eyed visionary look, the look that tells you they believe in what they are
doing and that it makes a real difference to the geopolitical future of the planet.
They haven't understood yet that boredom is the soil in which they must grow,
if they are to stay on. The soil of boredom is gray, which is the color of the
walls, the desks, and the carpeting. Lamar has thrived in this gray soil, a hardy
survivor, like mesquite or wild rose. These moments of spiritual fatigue are
few. And though he prefers to wear gray suits, his neckties are always bold.
The effect is: Ambition Under Control.

Across the street from Advanced Proposals Engineering is a topless bar
called The Web. Lamar comes here every day after work for a pick-me-up. The
Web owes its existence to APE, its clientele consisting of engineers, secretaries,
and the occasional manager. And spies. Lamar remembers a time here when
two thick-set men in three-piece suits handcuffed and searched a man wearing
an engineer's badge. "Spy," the bartender told him. "The Feds have had their
eyes on him for months. The guy drank nothing but lime rickeys like it was
summer in Havana. You can spot the type a mile off."

Lamar was required to watch a film, when he first was hired by Locust,   10
that warned about spies. "The pleasant chap occupying the desk next to yours
might be an agent of the Communist conspiracy." The narrator was Ronald
Reagan — a young, pre-office-holding Ronald Reagan — and the tone of the
film was McCarthy-era serious. The statistics given were certified by the FBI.
"There may be as many as four hundred spies in your plant. Think about it."
Lamar thought about it but never saw much in the way of suspicious activity.
He never saw much in the way of *any* kind of activity, except in the factory
areas themselves. But in the vast office buildings all he saw was the interminable
browsing through documents by men fighting a grassroots existential conviction
that a cancer of meaninglessness had taken root in their lives.

Once a pleasant man from Hungary, a refugee, was hauled away from the
desk next to Lamar's by armed guards. It turned out the man had not been
totally candid about his political affiliations when he hired into Locust. He'd
been a member of the Communist party in Hungary, before the 1956 revolt,
though he'd renounced it shortly afterward. But he left this chapter of his life
off his personnel data sheet. The man had a name the other engineers joked
about — Dumbalink Banjo Wits, something like that. Dumbalink was a fierce
and outspoken anti-Communist and an American patriot, but was taken away
in handcuffs and never heard from again. Lamar had liked Dumbalink Banjo
Wits and had called Security with the intention of telling them that the Hun-

garian made most of the engineers in his section look like fellow travelers by comparison, but Security wasn't interested. "He fibbed," the bored Security man had told Lamar.

Lamar, lost in bourbon daydreams, hasn't noticed that someone has slipped into the booth and is sitting opposite him. It's his secretary, a tall, olive-skinned girl with hair so blond it hurts his eyes. Her name is Theresa Keyser but she has told him to please call her Terry. Lamar has fixed her age at twenty-nine, though her job application said twenty-five.

"So, this is where you disappear to," Terry says, smiling. Her blue eyes are intense and, it seems to Lamar, too confident.

"My second home," Lamar says, lifting his bourbon and winking.

"Meanwhile, dinner is in the oven in your *first* home." 15

Lamar is annoyed, but her smile is splendidly straightforward. It makes him believe that she is being aggressive out of nervousness. "Hell," he says, "*APE* is my first home," and she laughs the tension out of her voice and touches his hand.

"I'll have a gimlet," she says to him, though the barmaid, a topless girl with spiders tattooed on her breasts, has been waiting to take her order.

They have two drinks apiece, their conversation gradually changing from office talk to the more revealing narratives alcohol inspires. Lamar learns that Terry has been married and divorced twice and is now unattached. He doesn't try to characterize his own decade-long marriage beyond suggesting that his wife's interests and his own have diverged somewhat over the years. He tells her this in a joking, cavalier manner: His views of marriage are a mixture of fatalism and the always optimistic belief in renewable relationships. This is California, after all, the land of expected transformations. Terry laughs easily at his bittersweet jokes — maybe too easily — but Lamar appreciates it anyway. He likes her, sees that she is intelligent and that her expectations are sober and under control. He reaches across the table and touches her hand. She takes his wrist and applies brief but significant pressure. Her eyes, which had been bold, are now disturbingly vulnerable. *Jesus,* Lamar thinks, knowing that three bourbons and water have inflamed some old romantic notions, *here we go.*

The barmaid brings them two more drinks. "Compliments of the sport in the rubber sandals," she says, gesturing toward a man in a black suit seated at the bar. The man is watching TV — a game show — and is wearing white socks and lipstick-red sandals. He is a Howard Hughes look-alike, trying to create the impression of "renegade genius gone seedy." Even his stringy hair is long and unwashed. The man, sensing Lamar's peevish gaze, looks at him and waves his swizzle stick. His smile is a yellow leer. Lamar knows something about that leer, has seen it before, and is about to tell the barmaid to take the drinks away when Terry returns the man's swizzle-stick salute and says, "Thanks!" just like that, loud enough to make several heads turn toward their booth.

And then it hits Lamar that he knows the man in the rubber sandals. He 20 was a high-level procurement manager for Locust a few years ago. Lamar, in fact, had worked for him when he first hired into Locust. Then there was a big cutback and the man was caught in the middle of an in-company war of attrition. He lost out to men who were more adroit in making the company classify them as indispensable. "Voss," Lamar says, under his breath. When Terry looks at him with raised eyebrows, he says, "Randy Voss. Used to be a wheel. He was supposed to be in line for company president. Crazy genius, they used to say. He must have jumped when he should have ducked."

Lamar is a little rocky when they finally leave The Web. On their way out the door they have to pass by Randy Voss. "Departing so soon?" Voss says to them. Up close his yellow leer is a toxic stain. "The evening is still young, kids. Tell you what, let's make a killer night of it. I'm still fat." He takes out his wallet and taps the bar with it.

Terry starts to answer but Lamar takes her arm and pulls her along. What she doesn't know is that the old ex-manager is a degenerate who thinks it would be nice if the three of them could get together in a downtown motel, in the wino district, and play out some rank fantasy starring himself. Lamar has heard all the Randy Voss stories. When the man had power the stories had the glitter of outré high times. Now he's just flea meat, another unremarkable scumbag.

It's almost dark outside. Terry takes Lamar's arm as they cross the street to the Locust parking lot. "Are you going to come over?" she asks, leaning toward him.

Lamar looks at his watch. "It's late," he says.

"Do you care?"   25

She lives in a fourplex, upstairs, the view of the ocean blocked by a new high-rise condo that has been painted the slate-gray color of the ocean under a winter overcast. "They know how to break your heart, don't they?" Lamar says, mostly to himself.

Terry makes Lamar a bourbon and water and a gimlet for herself. Lamar carries his drink in the palm of his hand as he tours the small apartment. "You do this?" he asks, nodding at a murky painting of a western scene.

"I'm afraid so," she says modestly. "I take art in night school."

"Nice."

"Do you like the condor?"   30

Lamar leans toward the painting which is hanging over the sofa. A bird — it looks like a crow to him — is suspended in midair above a lumpish roadkill on a desert highway.

"It's about to feast on that overripe deer," she explains.

Crow or condor, the bird seems incapable of flight. A stone bird with cast-iron wings. The deer is generic meat, a formless wedge of brown paint streaked with crimson.

"I call it The Angel of Death," Terry says. "But maybe that's too trite. I think I'll change it to Feast of Life. I don't know. I'm torn. What do you think?"

She is standing close to him. He can see her lungs move as she breathes, 35
the rise and fall of her sweater. He begins to see her details: the small, nearly
black mole just above her collarbone, the finely scented neck hair, the lovely
cut of her lips and nostrils. He slips his arm around her and she looks up at
him, lips parting for the kiss. He kisses her chilly lips, and then they both put
down their drinks and kiss again, with heat.

"I vote for Feast," he says. "Feast of Life."

Lamar wakes from a dream frightened, unable to tell himself where he is.
He is reasonably sure he is not home. The rumble of traffic outside is not
familiar. His heart is beating light and fast, like an engine in too high a gear
to have any power. His fear begins to escalate into panic. It's happened to him
before. He has a method for calming himself down. He begins with his name,
the color of his hair and eyes, the ghost-white scar on his left forearm. He
makes a list of keystone events: the year he was born, the years he graduated
high school and college, the year he got married, and the name of the town he
and his wife had eloped to. In this way he gradually finds himself. He reaches
over and touches the woman next to him. She makes a sound he does not
recognize as she turns over to face him.

"Theresa Keyser," he says, not *addressing* but naming her.

"Are you still here?" she says, picking up her clock radio to study its dial.
"Shouldn't you get home?"

His memory, set in motion by the emergency Lamar has declared, continues 40
to fill him in: An image of the man he had forgotten about, the degenerate ex-
manager, Randy Voss, comes to him unbidden. Voss is saying something to
him. They are walking, ten or more years ago, near an assembly-and-checkout
area of the plant. Missiles on huge transport vehicles are slipping slowly out
of a black building. It is a rainy night. Voss is laughing — *crazily,* Lamar
thinks. "Nobody knows jack-shit," Voss is saying to Lamar. "If you are going
to stay in this business, you've got to remember that. Something else, something
besides men and machines gets all this fancy work done."

Lamar, watching the glistening missiles slide through the rain, thinks he
understands what Voss is telling him. A missile, a bomber, a sub, they are all
jigsaw puzzles, the pieces made all over the country. The men who make the
individual pieces don't know — or need to know — the purpose of their work.
The pieces are assembled by other bored functionaries who are also ignorant
of the big picture.

"I see what you mean," Lamar says.

"No you don't. You really don't," Voss says. "What I am telling you is
that there is a great dark . . . *consensus* . . . that sweeps things along to their
inevitable conclusion. There is an intelligence behind it, but, believe me, it is
not human. It is the intelligence of *soil,* the thing that lifts trees and flowers
out of the ground. I am too astonished and thrilled to be frightened by it."

Lamar saw, even then, that Randy Voss was crazy, but what he had said
made a lasting impression. And over the years he has come to adopt Voss's

idea as his own. But it was something he was unable to talk about to anyone else, even his wife. How could you convince anyone that in this industry no single individual, or group of individuals, suspects the existence of a vital sub rosa mechanism that produces and deploys our beautifully elegant weapons? How could you *say* to someone that the process is holistic, that a headstrong organic magic is at work, or that a god presides?   1988

INVESTIGATIONS

1. What would Uncle Ralph ("The Warriors") say about Lamar and his job? In what ways does Lamar battle "to live beautifully from day to day" without fully realizing it?

2. Review the selections in this part. How have "the noblest projects" of the people you've read about "become the *means* of their unhappiness" (para. 2)? What episodes in your working life bear this out?

3. Why would Lamar's "superiors" have found an "innovative and energetic" employee "alarming" (para. 6)? What methods would Lamar propose to "get ahead" in his field? To what extent would these methods work in other fields?

4. Compare Uncle Ralph's ("The Warriors") beliefs about the warrior's function in the scheme of things to Randy Voss's beliefs (paras. 40–43) about the defense industry workers' relationship to the "something else" that "gets all this fancy work done." In what ways are they both crazy? How might they each be seen as completely sane?

C. K. WILLIAMS

Tar

The first morning of Three Mile Island: those first disquieting, uncertain,
    mystifying hours.
All morning a crew of workmen have been tearing the old decrepit roof off
    our building,
and all morning, trying to distract myself, I've been wandering out to watch
    them
as they hack away the leaden layers of asbestos paper and disassemble the
    disintegrating drains.
After half a night of listening to the news, wondering how to know a hundred
    miles downwind   5
if and when to make a run for it and where, then coming bolt awake at seven
when the roofers we've been waiting for since winter sent their ladders shrieking
    up our wall,
we still know less than nothing: The utility company continues making little
    of the accident,
the slick federal spokesmen still have their evasions in some semblance of order.
Surely we suspect now we're being lied to, but in the meantime, there are the
    roofers,   10
setting winch-frames, sledging rounds of tar apart, and there I am, on the curb
    across, gawking.

I never realized what brutal work it is, how matter-of-factly and harrowingly
    dangerous.
The ladders flex and quiver, things skid from the edge, the materials are bulky
    and recalcitrant.
When the rusty, antique nails are levered out, their heads pull off; the under-
    roofing crumbles.
Even the battered little furnace, roaring along as patient as a donkey, chokes
    and clogs,   15
a dense, malignant smoke shoots up, and someone has to fiddle with a cock,
    then hammer it,
before the gush and stench will deintensify, the dark, Dantean broth wearily
    subside.

A native of Newark, New Jersey, C. K. WILLIAMS (b. 1936) has worked as a therapist, editor, ghostwriter, and teacher of creative writing. Winner of the National Book Critics' Circle Award for poetry and a Guggenheim Fellowship, Williams's poetry collections include *Flesh and Blood* (1988) and *Poems 1963–1983* (1988).

In its crucible, the stuff looks bland, like licorice, spill it, though, on your boots
or coveralls,

it sears, and everything is permeated with it, the furnace gunked with burst
and half-burst bubbles,

the men themselves so completely slashed and mucked they seem almost from
another realm, like trolls.   20

When they take their break, they leave their brooms standing at attention in
the asphalt pails,

work gloves clinging like Brer Rabbit to the bitten shafts, and they slouch
along the precipitous lip,

the enormous sky behind them, the heavy noontime air alive with shimmers
and mirages.

Sometime in the afternoon I had to go inside: The advent of our vigil was upon
us.

However much we didn't want to, however little we would do about it, we'd
understood: 25

We were going to perish of all this, if not now, then soon, if not soon, then
someday.

Someday, some final generation, hysterically aswarm beneath an atmosphere
as unrelenting as rock,

would rue us all, anathematize our earthly comforts, curse our surfeits and
submissions.

I think I know, though I might rather not, why my roofers stay so clear to me
and why the rest,

the terror of that time, the reflexive disbelief and distancing, all we should hold
on to, dims so.   30

I remember the president in his absurd protective booties, looking absolutely
unafraid, the fool.

I remember a woman on the front page glaring across the misty Susquehanna
at those looming stacks.

But, more vividly, the men, slivered with glitter from the shingles, clinging like
starlings beneath the eaves.

Even the leftover carats of tar in the gutter, so black they seemed to suck the
light out of the air.

By nightfall kids had come across them: every sidewalk on the block was
scribbled with obscenities and hearts.   1980   35

INVESTIGATIONS

1. Reread lines 8–11. Compare the speaker's attitude toward the "slick federal
   spokesmen" with his attitude toward the roofers. In what sense could lying
   be a "built-in" requirement for working as a federal spokesman? In what
   sense could roofers never be liars?

2. Write three or four paragraphs in which you give examples of how "brutal" a writer's work is, "how matter-of-factly and harrowingly dangerous." Describe what "things skid from the edge" when one writes, how "bulky and recalcitrant" the "materials" are (lines 12–13).

3. Why do the roofers "stay so clear" to the speaker while "the terror of that time" doesn't (lines 29–30)?

PART FIVE
CONNECTIONS AND ELABORATIONS

1. Using as evidence material from the selections in Part Five, your response to "Write Before Reading" (p. 518), and any other writing and thinking you've done in response to the selections,

   a. write an essay that defines what work is and illustrates that definition, *or*

   b. write an essay that classifies the kinds of work you've learned about and that demonstrates the effects of each kind of work on the person doing it, *or*

   c. write an essay that illustrates the essential distinctions between what we might call a "life's work" and a job.

2. Using the writing you did in response to "Write Before Reading" and any appropriate evidence from the selections in Part Five, write a persuasive essay in which you argue one or more of the following points:

   a. We should do the best we can at every job we hold because the qualities thus developed will help us find the job we want.

   b. We shouldn't take work so seriously because jobs are necessary mainly to give us the means to enjoy our leisure time.

   c. Work not done essentially for pleasure is not worth doing at all.

3. After rereading Dubus's "After the Game," Walters's "The Warriors," and Boyle's "Sitting on Top of the World,"

   a. select a scene from "After the Game" and rewrite it from Joaquin's point of view, *and/or*

   b. select a scene from "The Warriors" and rewrite it from Uncle Ralph's point of view, *and/or*

   c. select a scene from "Sitting on Top of the World" and rewrite it from the hiker's point of view.

4. On pages 580–581, Andrew Jorgenson says,

   > Damn it. A business is more than the price of its stock. It is the place where we make our living, meet our friends, and dream our dreams. It is, in every sense, the very fabric that binds our society together.

   Using as evidence appropriate material from your experience and from the selections in Part Five, write a persuasive essay beginning with one of the following sentences:

   a. "Jorgenson's claim in *Other People's Money* that a business 'is the very fabric that binds our society together' helps explain why people so often feel alienated by their work and unfulfilled in their lives."

648

b. "Jorgenson's claim in *Other People's Money* that a business 'is the very fabric that binds our society together' overestimates the power of work to create community."

c. "Jorgenson's claim in *Other People's Money* that a business 'is the very fabric that binds our society together' betrays a complete lack of understanding of contemporary affairs."

d. "Jorgenson's claim in *Other People's Money* that a business 'is the very fabric that binds our society together' is right on the mark."

5. Using as evidence material from Farr's "Steelworker," Sterner's *Other People's Money*, DeMarinis's "The Flowers of Boredom," and Williams's "Tar," write an essay that examines the relationship between lying and work.

6. Using as evidence material from your response to "Write Before Reading," Dubus's "After the Game," Levine's "Buying and Selling," Lombreglia's "Late Early Man," Hall's "Ox Cart Man," Baca's "Perfecto Flores," Parini's "Working the Face," and Walters's "The Warriors," write an essay that examines the relationship between art and work.

7. Using as evidence material from appropriate selections in this book and from your own experience, write an essay in which you analyze the function of the stories coworkers tell one another.

PART SIX

IN AND
OUT OF LOVE

A random sample of television shows, novels, films, poetry, and popular music will convince us of the obvious: No subject so captivates us as love — what it is, how we find it, how we keep it, how we lose it. Yet for all the time we spend thinking about it, we often have enormous difficulty thinking systematically about it, seeing how assumptions and expectations condition our romance with romance. Though the ultimate source of "true love" may remain forever mysterious, an examination of what's "true" about it can bring unexpected rewards.

The selections in Part Six will enable you to study the face of love from angles that may be unfamiliar. In Gish Jen's "What Means Switch" a teacher's well-intentioned unawareness of difference leads to first love between a Chinese-American girl and a Japanese boy; in "Judgment," by Cliff Thompson, a young Black man's relationship with a white woman challenges his naive attitude toward race; in Wendell Berry's "Except," love and the desire for solitude intertwine; a new husband

651

reflects on his sometimes desperate search for identity and love in "Nantucket Honeymoon," by David Mura; a choreographer finds and has trouble accepting the passion she's only half-aware she needs in *Burn This*, by Lanford Wilson; Adrienne Rich's "Love Poem" dramatizes how a couple's love prepares them to accept death's inevitability; in Patricia Dobler's "Hospital Call" a woman declares her willingness to fight the ultimate battle for her husband and herself; in "Long Distance," by Jane Smiley, a man is both relieved and pained when his Japanese lover chooses family duty instead of him; a couple visit a silent battlefield as their marriage ebbs away in "Shiloh," by Bobbie Ann Mason; Thomas Lynch's "The Widow" illustrates how grief sometimes ends; a Navajo woman loses everything but an ancient song in "Lullaby," by Leslie Marmon Silko; in John Updike's "Gesturing," a man's unfaithfulness threatens everything else in his life; in Carolyn Kizer's "Bitch," a woman speaks in two voices about a past love; in "After Making Love We Hear Footsteps," by Galway Kinnell, a married couple's love completes itself in their son; and the loss of his lover to AIDS opens Fenton Johnson to the power of "The Limitless Heart."

WRITE BEFORE READING

First, based on your experience, including any reading, thinking, and observing you've done, identify the stages through which love relationships move, briefly indicating the essential characteristics of each stage. Next, narrate as fully as possible an experience that caused you to move from one stage to another. Finally, identify the kinds of outside influences that can affect the course of an intimate relationship.

GISH JEN

What Means Switch

Here we are, nice Chinese family — father, mother, two born-here girls. Where should we live next? My parents slide the question back and forth like a cup of ginseng neither one wants to drink. Until finally it comes to them, what they really want is a milkshake (chocolate) and to go with it a house in Scarsdale. What else? The broker tries to hint: the neighborhood, she says. Moneyed. Many delis. Meaning rich and Jewish. But someone has sent my parents a list of the top ten schools nationwide (based on the opinion of selected educators "and others"), and so, many-deli or not, we nestle into a Dutch colonial on the Bronx River Parkway. The road is winding where we are, very charming; drivers miss their turns, plow up our flower beds, then want to use our telephone. "Of course," my mom tells them, like it's no big deal, we can replant. We're the type to adjust. You know — the lady drivers weep, my mom gets out the Kleenex for them. We're a bit down the hill from the private-plane set, in other words. Only in our dreams do our parka zippers jam, what with all the lift tickets we have stapled to them, Killington on top of Sugarbush on top of Stowe, and we don't even know where the Virgin Islands are — although certain of us know that virgins are like priests and nuns, which there were a lot more of in Yonkers, where we just moved from, than there are here.

This is my first understanding of class. In our old neighborhood everybody knew everything about virgins and nonvirgins, not to say the technicalities of staying in between. Or almost everybody, I should say; in Yonkers I was the laugh-along type. Here I'm an expert.

"You mean the man. . . . ?" Pigtailed Barbara Gugelstein spits a mouthful of Coke back into her can. "That is *so* gross!"

Pretty soon I'm getting popular for a new girl. The only problem is Danielle Meyers, who wears blue mascara and has gone steady with two boys. "How do *you* know," she starts to ask, and proceeds to edify us all with how she French-kissed one boyfriend and just regular-kissed another. ("Because, you know, he had braces.") We hear about his rubber bands, how once one popped right into her mouth. I realize I need to find somebody to kiss too. But how? I can't do mascara — my eyelashes stick together. Plus, as Danielle the Great Educator points out, I'm *Chinese*.

Luckily, I just about then happen to tell Barbara Gugelstein I know karate.   5

Chinese-American writer GISH JEN (b. 1956) was raised in Scarsdale, New York, and educated at Harvard University, Stanford University, and the Iowa Writers Workshop. Recipient of writing fellowships from the Bunting Institute, the National Endowment for the Arts, and the Copernicus Society, Jen is the author of *Typical American* (1991), a novel.

I don't know why I tell her this. My sister, Callie, is the liar in the family; ask anybody. I'm the one who doesn't see why we should have to hold our heads up. But for some reason I tell Barbara Gugelstein I can make my hands like steel by thinking hard. "I'm not supposed to tell anyone," I say.

She backs away, blinking. I could be the burning bush.

"I can't do bricks," I say — a bit of expectation management. "But I can do your arm if you want." I set my hand in chop position.

"Uhh, it's okay," she says. "I know you can. I saw it on TV last night." That's when I recall that I, too, saw it on TV last night — in fact, at her house. I rush on to tell her I know how to get pregnant with tea.

"With *tea?*"

"That's how they do it in China."

10

She agrees that China is an ancient and great civilization that ought to be known for more than spaghetti and gunpowder. I tell her I know Chinese. "*Be-yeh fa-foon,*" I say. "*Shee-veh. Ji nu.*" Meaning, "Stop acting crazy. Rice gruel. Soy sauce." She's impressed. At lunch the next day Danielle Meyers and Amy Weinstein and Barbara's crush, Andy Kaplan, are all impressed too. Scarsdale is a liberal town, not like Yonkers, where the Whitman Road gang used to throw crab-apple mash at Callie and me and tell us it would make our eyes stick shut. Here we're like permanent exchange students. In another ten years there'll be so many Orientals we'll turn into Asians; but for now, the mid-sixties, what with civil rights on TV, we're not so much accepted as embraced. Especially by the Jewish part of town — which, it turns out, is not all of town at all. That's just an idea people have, Callie says, and lots of them could take us or leave us same as the Christians, who are nice too; I shouldn't generalize. So let me not generalize except to say that pretty soon I've been to so many bar and bas mitzvahs that I can almost say myself whether the kid chants like an angel or like a train conductor, maybe they could use him on the commuter line. At seder I know to get a good pile of that mortar. Also, I know what is schmaltz. I know that I am a goy. This is not why people like me, though. People like me because I do not need to use deodorant, as I demonstrate in the locker room before and after gym. Also, I can explain to them, for example, what is tofu (*der-voo,* we say at home). Their mothers invite me to taste-test their Chinese cooking.

"Very authentic." I try to be reassuring. After all, they're nice people. "Delish." I have seconds. On the question of what we eat, though, I have to admit, "Well, no, it's different from that." I have thirds. "What my mom makes is home style, it's not in the cookbooks."

Not in the cookbooks! Everyone's jealous. Meanwhile, the big deal at home is when we have turkey pot pie. Callie's the one who introduced them — Mrs. Wilder's, they come in this green-and-brown box — and when we have them, we both suddenly get interested in helping out in the kitchen. You know, we stand in front of the oven and help them bake. Twenty-five minutes. She and I have a deal, though, to keep it secret from school, since everybody else thinks they're gross. *We* think they're a big improvement over authentic Chinese home cooking. Oxtail soup — now, that's gross. Stir-fried beef with tomatoes. One day I say, "You know, Ma, I have never seen a stir-fried tomato in any Chinese restaurant we have ever been in, ever."

"In China," she says, pontifical, "we consider tomatoes a delicacy."

"Ma," I say. "Tomatoes are *Italian*."

"No respect for elders." She wags her finger at me, but I can tell it's just to try and shame me into believing her. "I'm tell you, tomatoes *invented* in China."

"*Ma*."

"Is true. Like noodles. Invented in China."

"That's not what they said in *school*."

"*In China*," my mother counters, "we also eat tomatoes uncooked, like apple. And in summertime we slice them, and put some sugar on top."

"Are you sure?"

My mom says of course she's sure, and in the end I give in, even though she once told me that China was such a long time ago, a lot of things she can hardly remember. She said sometimes she has trouble remembering her characters, that sometimes she'll be writing a letter, just writing along, and all of a sudden she won't be sure if she should put four dots or three.

"So what do you do then?"

"Oh, I just make a little sloppy."

"You mean you *fudge?*"

She laughed then, but another time, when she was showing me how to write my name, and I said, just kidding, "Are you sure that's the right number of dots, now?" she was hurt.

"I mean, of course you know," I said. "I mean, *oy*."

Meanwhile, what *I* know is that in the eighth grade what people want to hear does not include the revelation that Chinese people eat sliced tomatoes with sugar on top. For a gross fact, it just isn't gross enough. On the other hand, the fact that somewhere in China somebody eats or has eaten or once ate living monkey brains — now that's conversation.

"They have these special tables," I say, "kind of like a giant collar. With a hole in the middle, for the monkey's neck. They put the monkey in the collar, and then they cut off the top of its head."

"Whadda they use for cutting?"

I think. "Scalpels."

"*Scalpels?*" Andy Kaplan says.

"Kaplan, don't be dense," Barbara Gugelstein says. "The Chinese *invented* scalpels."

Once a friend said to me, You know, everybody is valued for something. She explained how some people resented being valued for their looks; others resented being valued for their money. Wasn't it still better to be beautiful and rich than ugly and poor, though? You should just be glad, she said, that you have something people value. It's like having a special talent, like being good at ice-skating, or opera singing. She said. You could probably make a career out of it.

Here's the irony: I am.   35

Anyway, I am ad-libbing my way through eighth grade, as I've described. Until one bloomy spring day I come in late to homeroom, and to my chagrin discover there's a new kid in class.

Chinese.

So what should I do, pretend to have to go to the girls' room, like Barbara Gugelstein the day Andy Kaplan took his ID back? I sit down; I am so cool I remind myself of Paul Newman. First thing I realize, though, is that no one looking at me is thinking of Paul Newman. The notes fly:

"*I* think he's cute."

"Who?" I write back. (I am still at an age, understand, when I believe a   40
person can be saved by aplomb.)

"I don't think he talks English too good. Writes it either."

"Who?"

"They might have to put him behind a grade, so don't worry."

"He has a crush on you already, you could tell as soon as you walked in, he turned kind of orangish."

I hope I'm not turning orangish as I deal with my mail. I could use a   45
secretary. The second round starts:

"What do you mean who? Don't be weird. Didn't you *see* him??? Straight back over your right shoulder!!!!"

I have to look; what else can I do? I think of certain tips I learned in Girl Scouts about poise. I cross my ankles. I hold a pen in my hand. I sit up as though I have a crown on my head. I swivel my head slowly, repeating to myself, *I could be Miss America.*

"Miss Mona Chang."

Horror raises its hoary head.

"Notes, please."   50

Mrs. Mandeville's policy is to read all notes aloud.

I try to consider what Miss America would do and see myself: back straight, knees together, crying. Some inspiration. Cool Hand Luke, on the other hand, would, quick, eat the evidence. And why not? I should yawn as I stand up, and boom, the notes are gone. All that's left is to explain that it's an old Chinese reflex.

I shuffle up to the front of the room.

"One minute, please," Mrs. Mandeville says.

I wait, noticing how large and plastic her mouth is.   55

She unfolds a piece of paper.

And I, Miss Mona Chang, who got almost straight A's her whole life except in math and conduct, am about to start crying in front of everyone.

I am delivered out of hot Egypt by the bell. General pandemonium. Mrs.

Mandeville still has her hand clamped on my shoulder, though; and the next thing I know, I'm holding the new boy's schedule. He's standing next to me like a big blank piece of paper. "This is Sherman," Mrs. Mandeville says.

"Hello," I say.

"*Non how a,*" I say.   60

I'm glad Barbara Gugelstein isn't there to see my Chinese in action.

"*Ji nu,*" I say. "*Shee veh.*"

Later I find out that his mother asked if there were any other Orientals in our grade. She had him put in my class on purpose. For now, though, he looks at me as if I'm much stranger than anything else he's seen so far. Is this because he understands that I'm saying "soy sauce rice gruel" to him or because he doesn't?

"Sher-man," he says finally.

I look at his schedule card. Sherman Matsumoto. What kind of name is   65
that for a nice Chinese boy?

(Later on, people ask me how I can tell Chinese from Japanese. I shrug. It's the kind of thing you just kind of know, I say. *Oy!*)

Sherman's got the sort of looks I think of as pretty-boy. Monsignor-black hair (not monk-brown, like mine), kind of bouncy. Crayola eyebrows, one with a round bald spot in the middle of it, like a golf hole. I don't know how anybody can think of him as orangish; his skin looks white to me, with pink triangles hanging down the front of his cheeks like flags. Kind of delicate-looking, but the only truly uncool thing about him is that his spiral notebook has a picture of a kitty cat on it. A big white fluffy one, with a blue ribbon above each perky little ear. I get much opportunity to view this, because all the poor kid understands about life in junior high school is that he should follow me everywhere. It's embarrassing. But he's obviously even more miserable than I am, so I try not to say anything. I decide to give him a chance to adjust. We communicate by sign language, and by drawing pictures, which he's better at than I am; he puts in every last detail, even if it takes forever. I try to be patient.

A week of this. Finally I enlighten him. "You should get a new notebook."

His cheeks turn a shade of pink you see mostly only in hyacinths.

"Notebook." I point to his. I show him mine, which is psychedelic, with   70
purple and yellow stick-on flowers. I try to explain that he should have one like this, only without the flowers. He nods enigmatically, and the next day brings me a notebook just like his, except that this cat sports pink bows instead of blue.

"Pret-ty," he says. "You."

He speaks English! I'm dumbfounded. Has he spoken it all this time? I consider: Pretty. You. What does that mean? Plus actually he's said "plit-ty," much as my parents would; I'm assuming he means pretty, but maybe he means pity. Pity. You.

"Jeez," I say finally.

"You are wel-come," he says.

I decorate the back of the notebook with stick-on flowers, and hold it so　　75
that they show when I walk through the halls. In class I keep my book open.
After all, the kid's so new; I think I ought to have a heart. And for a livelong
day nobody notices.

Then Barbara Gugelstein sidles up. "Matching notebooks, huh?"

I'm speechless.

"First comes love, then comes marriage, and then come chappies in a baby
carriage."

"Barbara!"

"Get it?" she says. "Chinese Japs."　　80

"Bar-*bra*," I say to get even.

"Just make sure he doesn't give you any *tea*," she says.

Are Sherman and I in love? Three days later I hazard that we are. My
thinking proceeds this way: I think he's cute, and I think he thinks I'm cute.
On the other hand, we don't kiss and we don't exactly have fantastic conversations. Our talks *are* getting better, though. We started out, "This is a book."

"Book."

"This is a chair."　　85

"Chair."

Advancing to, "What is this?"

"This is a book."

Now, for fun, he tests me. "What is this?" he says.

"This is a book," I say, as if I'm the one who has to learn how to talk.　　90
He claps. "Good!"

Meanwhile, people ask me all about him. I could be his press agent.

"No, he doesn't eat raw fish."

"No, his father wasn't a kamikaze pilot."

"No, he can't do karate."　　95

"Are you sure?" somebody asks.

Indeed he doesn't know karate, but judo he does. I am hurt that I'm not
the one to find this out; the guys know from gym class. They line up to be
flipped, he flips them all onto the floor, and after that he doesn't eat lunch at
the girls' table with me anymore. I'm more or less glad. Meaning, when he was
there, I never knew what to say. Now that he's gone, though, I seem to be
stuck at the "This is a chair" level of conversation. Ancient Chinese eating
habits have lost their cachet; all I get are more and more inquiries about me
and Sherman. "I dunno," I'm saying all the time. *Are* we going out? We do
stuff, it's true. For example, I take him to the department stores, explain to
him who shops in Alexander's, who shops in Saks. I tell him my family's the
type that shops in Alexander's. He says he's sorry. In Saks he gets lost, though
maybe I'm the lost one. (It's true I find him calmly waiting at the front door,
hands behind his back, like a guard.) I take him to the candy store. I take him
to the bagel store. Sherman is crazy about bagels. I explain to him that Lender's
is gross, he should get his bagels from the bagel store. He says thank you.

"Are you going steady?" people want to know.

How can we go steady when he doesn't have an ID bracelet? On the other hand, he brings me more presents than I think any girl's ever gotten before. Oranges. Flowers. A little bag of bagels. But what do they mean? Do they mean thank you, I enjoyed our trip; do they mean I like you; do they mean I decided I liked the Lender's better even if they are gross, and you can have these? Sometimes I think he's acting on his mother's instructions. Also I know that at least a couple of items were supposed to go to our teachers. He told me that and turned red. I figured it still might mean something that he didn't throw them out.

More and more now, we joke. Like, instead of *I'm thinking,* he always   100
says, "I'm sinking," which we both think is so funny that all either one of us has to do is pretend to be drowning and the other one cracks up. And he tells me things — for example, that electric lights are everywhere in Tokyo now.

"You mean you didn't have them before?"

"Everywhere now!" He's amazed too. "Since Olympics!"

"Olympics?"

He hums for me the Olympic theme song. "You know?"

"Sure," I say, and hum with him happily. We could be a picture on a   105
UNICEF poster. The only problem is that I don't really understand what the Olympics have to do with the modernization of Japan, any more than I get this other story he tells me, about that hole in his left eyebrow, which is from some time his father accidentally hit him with a lit cigarette. When Sherman was a baby. His father was drunk, having been out carousing; his mother was very mad but didn't say anything, just cleaned the whole house. Then his father was so ashamed he bowed to ask her forgiveness.

"Your mother cleaned the house?"

Sherman nods solemnly.

"And your father *bowed?*" I find this more astounding than anything I ever thought to make up. "That is so weird," I tell him.

"Weird," he agrees. "This I no forget, forever. *Father* bow to *mother!*"

We shake our heads.   110

As for the things he asks me, they're not topics I ever discussed before. Do I like it here? Of course I like it here, I was born here, I say. Am I Jewish? Jewish! I laugh. *Oy!* Am I American? "Sure I'm American," I say. "Everybody who's born here is American, and also some people who convert from what they were before. You could become American." But he says no, he could never. "Sure you could," I say. "You only have to learn some rules and speeches."

"But I Japanese," he says.

"You could become American anyway," I say. "Like I *could* become Jewish, if I wanted to. I'd just have to switch, that's all."

"But you Catholic," he says.

I think maybe he doesn't get what means switch.   115

I introduce him to Mrs. Wilder's turkey pot pies. "Gross?" he asks. I say they are, but we like them anyway. "Don't tell anybody." He promises. We bake them, eat them. While we're eating, he's drawing me pictures.

"This American," he says, and he draws something that looks like John Wayne. "This Jewish," he says, and draws something that looks like the Wicked Witch of the West, only male.

"I don't think so," I say.

He's undeterred. "This Japanese," he says, and draws a fair rendition of himself. "This Chinese," he says, and draws what looks to be another fair rendition of himself.

"How can you tell them apart?"   120

"This way," he says, and he puts the picture of the Chinese so that it faces the pictures of the American and the Jew. The Japanese faces the wall. Then he draws another picture, of a Japanese flag, so that the Japanese is looking at his flag. "Chinese lost in department store," he says. "Japanese know how go." For fun he draws another Japanese flag, a bigger one, which he attaches to the refrigerator with magnets. "In school, in ceremony, we this way," he explains, and bows to the picture.

When my mother comes in, her face is so red that with the white wall behind her she looks a bit like the Japanese flag herself. Yet I get the feeling I better not say so. First she doesn't move. Then she snatches the flag off the refrigerator, so fast the magnets go flying. Two of them land on the stove. She crumples the paper. She hisses at Sherman, "*This is the U. S. of A., do you hear me!*"

Sherman hears her.

"You call your mother right now, tell her come pick you up."

He understands perfectly. I, on the other hand, am buffaloed. How can   125 two people who don't really speak English understand each other better than I can understand them? "But, Ma," I say.

"Don't *Ma* me," she says.

Later on she explains that the Second World War was in China, too. "Hitler," I say. "Nazis. Volkswagens." I know the Japanese were on the wrong side, because they bombed Pearl Harbor. My mother explains about before that. The Napkin Massacre. "*Nan*-king," she corrects me.

"Are you sure?" I say. "In school they said the war was about putting the Jews in ovens."

"Also about ovens."

"About both?"   130

"Both."

"That's not what they said in school."

"*Just forget about school.*"

Forget about school? "I thought we moved here for the schools."

"We moved here," she says, "for your education."   135

Sometimes I have no idea what she's talking about.

"I like Sherman," I say after a while.

"He's nice boy," she agrees.

Meaning what? I would ask, except that my dad's just come home, which means it's time to start talking about whether they should build a brick wall across the front of the lawn. Recently a car made it almost into our living room, which was so scary that the driver fainted and an ambulance had to come. "We should have discussion," my dad said after that. It's what he says every time. And so for about a week, every night we have them.

"Are you just friends or more than just friends?" Barbara Gugelstein is   140
giving me the cross-ex.

"Maybe," I say.

"Come on," she says. "I told you *everything* about me and Andy."

I actually *am* trying to tell Barbara everything about Sherman, but everything turns out to be nothing. Meaning I can't locate the conversation in what I have to say: Sherman and I go places, we talk, my mother once threw him out of the house because of the Second World War.

"I think we're just friends," I say.

"You think or you're sure?"   145

Now that I do less of the talking at lunch, I notice more what other people talk about — cheerleading, who likes who, this place in White Plains to get earrings. On none of these topics am I an expert. Of course, I'm still friends with Barbara Gugelstein, but I notice that Danielle Meyers has spun away to other groups.

Barbara's analysis goes this way: To be popular you have to have big boobs, a note from your mother that lets you use her Lord & Taylor credit card, and a boyfriend. On the other hand, what's so wrong with being unpopular? "We'll get them in the end," she says. It's what her dad tells her. "Like they'll turn out too dumb to do their own investing," she says, "and then they'll get killed in broker's fees and then they'll have to move to towns where the schools stink. And my dad should know," she winds up. "He's a broker."

"I guess," I say.

But the next thing I know, I have a true crush on Sherman Matsumoto. *Mister* Judo, the guys call him now, with real respect; and the more they call him that, the more I don't care that he carries a notebook with a cat on it.

I sigh. "Sherman."   150

"I thought you were just friends," Barbara Gugelstein says.

"We were," I say mysteriously. This, I've noticed, is how Danielle Meyers talks; everything's secret, she only lets out so much, it's apparent she didn't grow up with everybody telling her she had to share.

And here's the funny thing: The more I intimate that Sherman and I are hot and heavy, the more it seems we actually are. It's the old imagination giving reality a nudge. When I start to blush, he starts to blush; we reach a point where we can hardly talk at all.

"Well, there's first base with tongue, and first base without," I tell Barbara Gugelstein.

In fact, Sherman and I have brushed shoulders, and what actually happened   155
was at least equivalent to first base, I was sure, maybe even second. I felt as though I'd turned into one huge shoulder; that's all I was, one huge shoulder. We not only didn't talk, we didn't breathe. But how can I tell Barbara Gugelstein that? So instead I say, "Well, there's second base and second base."

Danielle Meyers is my friend again. She says, "I know exactly what you mean," just to make Barbara Gugelstein feel bad.

"Like *what* do I mean?" I say.

Danielle Meyers can't answer.

"You know what I think?" I tell Barbara the next day. "I think Danielle's giving us a line."

Barbara pulls thoughtfully on one of her pigtails.   160

If Sherman Matsumoto is never going to give me an ID to wear, he should at least get up the nerve to hold my hand. I don't think he sees this. I think of the story he told me about his parents, and in a synaptic firestorm realize we don't see the same things at all.

So one day, when we happen to brush shoulders again, I don't move away. He doesn't move away either. There we are. Like a pair of bleachers, pushed together but not quite matched up. After a while I have to breathe, I can't help it. I breathe in such a way that our elbows start to touch too. We are in a crowd, waiting for a bus. I crane my neck to look at the sign that says where the bus is going; now our wrists are touching. Then it happens: He links his pinky around mine.

Is that holding hands? Later, in bed, I wonder all night. One finger, and not even the biggest one.

Sherman is leaving in a month. Already! I think, well, I suppose he will leave and we'll never even kiss. I guess that's all right. Just when I've resigned myself to it, though, we hold hands all five fingers. Once when we are at the bagel shop, then again in my parents' kitchen. Then, when we are on the playground, he kisses the back of my hand.

He does it again not too long after that, in White Plains.   165

I invest in a bottle of mouthwash.

Instead of moving on, though, he kisses the back of my hand again. And again. I try raising my hand, hoping he'll make the jump from my hand to my cheek. It's like trying to wheedle an inchworm out the window. You know, *This way, this way.*

All over the world people have their own cultures. That's what we learned in social studies.

If we never kiss, I'm not going to take it personally.

It is the end of the school year. We've had parties. We've turned in our   170
textbooks. Hooray! Outside, the asphalt already steams if you spit on it.
Sherman isn't leaving for another couple of days, though, and he comes to visit
every morning, staying until the afternoon, when Callie comes home from her
big-deal job as a bank teller. We drink Kool-Aid in the back yard and hold
hands until they are sweaty and make smacking noises coming apart. He tells
me how busy his parents are, getting ready for the move. His mother, particularly, is very tired. Mostly we are mournful.

The very last day we hold hands and do not let go. Our palms fill up with
water like a blister. We do not care. We talk more than usual. How much it
will cost to send an airmail letter to Japan, that kind of thing. Then suddenly
he asks, will I marry him?

I'm only thirteen.

But when old? Sixteen?

If you come back to get me.

I come. Or you can come to Japan, be Japanese.   175

How can I be Japanese?

Like you become American. Switch.

He kisses me on the cheek, again and again and again.

His mother calls to say that she's coming to get him. I cry. I tell him how
I've saved every present he's ever given me — the ruler, the pencils, the bags
from the bagels, all the flower petals. I even have the orange peels from the
oranges.

All?   180

I put them in a jar.

I'd show him, except that we're not allowed to go upstairs to my room.
Anyway, something about the orange peels seems to choke him up too. *Mister
Judo,* but I've gotten him in a soft spot. We are going together to the bathroom
to get some toilet paper to wipe our eyes when poor tired Mrs. Matsumoto,
driving her family's car, skids up onto our lawn.

"Very sorry!"

We race outside.

"Very sorry!"   185

Mrs. Matsumoto is so short that all we can see of her is a green cotton
sun hat, with a big brim. It's tied on. The brim is trembling.

I hope my mom's not going to start yelling about the Second World War.

"Is all right, no trouble," she says, materializing on the steps, behind me
and Sherman. She's propped the screen door wide open; when I turn, I see
she's waving. "No trouble, no trouble!"

"No trouble, no trouble!" I echo, twirling a few times with relief.

Mrs. Matsumoto keeps apologizing; my mom keeps insisting she shouldn't   190
feel bad, it was only some grass and a small tree. Crossing the lawn, she insists
that Mrs. Matsumoto get out of the car, even though it means trampling some
lilies of the valley. She insists that Mrs. Matsumoto come in for a cup of tea.
Then she will not talk about anything unless Mrs. Matsumoto sits down, and

unless she lets my mom prepare her a small snack. The coming in and the tea and the sitting down are settled pretty quickly, but they negotiate ferociously over the small snack, which Mrs. Matsumoto will not eat unless she can call Mr. Matsumoto. She makes the mistake of linking Mr. Matsumoto with a reparation of some sort, which my mom will not hear of.

"Please!"

"No no no no."

Back and forth it goes.

"No no no no." "No no no no." "No no no no."

What kind of conversation is that? I look at Sherman, who shrugs. Finally Mr. Matsumoto calls on his own, wondering where his wife is. He comes over in a taxi. He's a heavy-browed businessman, friendly but brisk — not at all a type you could imagine bowing to a lady with a taste for tie-on sun hats. My mom invites him in as if it's an idea she just this moment thought of. And would he maybe have some tea and a small snack?

Sherman and I sneak back outside for another farewell by the side of the house, behind the forsythia bushes. We hold hands. He kisses me on the cheek again, and then — just when I think he's finally going to kiss me on the lips — he kisses me on the neck.

Is this first base?

He does it more. Up and down, up and down. First it tickles, and then it doesn't. He has his eyes closed. I close my eyes too. He's hugging me. Up and down. Then down.

He's at my collarbone.

Still at my collarbone. Now his hand's on my ribs. So much for first base. More ribs. The idea of second base would probably make me nervous if he weren't on his way back to Japan and if I really thought we were going to get there. As it is, though, I'm not in much danger of wrecking my life on the shoals of passion; his unmoving hand feels more like a growth than a boyfriend. He has his whole face pressed to my neck skin so I can't tell his mouth from his nose. I think he may be licking me.

From indoors, a burst of adult laughter. My eyelids flutter. I start to try and wiggle such that his hand will maybe budge upward.

Do I mean for my top blouse button to come accidentally undone?

He clenches his jaw, and when he opens his eyes, they're fixed on that button like it's a gnat that's been bothering him for far too long. He mutters in Japanese. If later in life he were to describe this as a pivotal moment in his youth, I would not be surprised. Holding the material as far from my body as possible, he buttons the button. Somehow we've landed up too close to the bushes.

What to tell Barbara Gugelstein? She says, "Tell me what were his last words. He must have said something last."

"I don't want to talk about it."

"Maybe he said, 'Good-bye?'" she suggests. "'Sayonara?'" She means well.

"I don't want to talk about it."

"Aw, come on, I told you everything about. . . ."

I say, "Because it's private, excuse me."

She stops, squints at me as though I were a far-off face she's trying to   210
make out. Then she nods and very lightly places her hand on my forearm.

The forsythia seemed to be stabbing us in the eyes. Sherman said, more or
less, *You will need to study how to switch.*

And I said, *I think you should switch. The way you do everything is weird.*

And he said, *You just want to tell everything to your friends. You just
want to have boyfriend to become popular.*

Then he flipped me. Two swift moves, and I went sprawling through the
air, a flailing confusion of soft human parts such as had no idea where the
ground was, much less how hard it could be.

It is the fall, and I am in high school, and still he hasn't written, so finally   215
I write him.

I still have all your gifts, I write. *I don't talk so much as I used to. Although
I am not exactly a mouse either. I don't care about being popular anymore. I
swear. Are you happy to be back in Japan? I know I ruined everything. I was
just trying to be entertaining. I miss you with all my heart, and hope I didn't
ruin everything.*

He writes back, *You will never be Japanese.*

I throw all the orange peels out that day. Some of them, it turns out, were
moldy anyway. I tell my mother I want to move to Chinatown.

"Chinatown!" she says.

I don't know why I suggested it.   220

"What's the matter?" she says. "Still boy-crazy? That Sherman?"

"No."

"Too much homework?"

I don't answer.

"Forget about school."   225

Later she tells me that if I don't like school, I don't have to go every day.
Some days I can stay home.

"Stay home?" In Yonkers, Callie and I used to stay home all the time, but
that was because the schools there were *waste of time.*

"No good for a girl be too smart anyway."

For a long time I think about Sherman. But after a while I don't think
about him so much as I just keep seeing myself flipped onto the ground, lying
there shocked as the Matsumotos get ready to leave. My head has hit a rock;
my brain aches as though it's been shoved to some new place in my skull.
Otherwise I am okay. I see the forsythia, all those whippy branches, and can't
believe how many leaves there are on a bush — every one green and perky and
durably itself. And past them real sky. I try to remember why the sky's blue,

even though this one's gone the kind of indescribable gray you associate with the insides of old shoes. I smell grass. Probably I have grass stains all over my back. I hear my mother calling through the back door, "Mona! Everyone leaving now," and "Not coming to say good-bye?" I hear Mr. and Mrs. Matsumoto bowing as they leave — or at least I hear the embarrassment in my mother's voice as they bow. I hear their car start. I hear Mrs. Matsumoto directing Mr. Matsumoto how to back off the lawn so as not to rip any more of it up. I feel the back of my head for blood — just a little. I hear their chug-chug grow fainter and fainter, until it has faded into the whuzz-whuzz of all the other cars. I hear my mom singing, "*Mon*-a! *Mon*-a!" until my dad comes home. Doors open and shut. I see myself standing up, brushing myself off so I'll have less explaining to do if she comes out to look for me. Grass stains — just like I thought.

I see myself walking around the house, going over to have a look at our   230
churned-up yard. It looks pretty sad, two big brown tracks, right through the irises and the lilies of the valley, and that was a new dogwood we'd just planted. Lying there like that. I find myself thinking about my father, having to go dig it up all over again. Adjusting. I think how we probably ought to put up that brick wall. And sure enough, when I go inside, no one's worrying about me, or that little bit of blood at the back of my head, or the grass stains — that's what they're talking about: that wall. Again. My mom doesn't think it'll do any good, but my dad thinks we should give it a try. Should we or shouldn't we? How high? How thick? What will the neighbors say? I plop myself down on a hard chair. And all I can think is, we are the complete only family that has to worry about this. If I could, I'd switch everything to be different. But since I can't, I might as well sit here at the table for a while, discussing what I know how to discuss. I nod and listen to the rest.   1990

INVESTIGATIONS

1. Reread the story, noting where and in what circumstances Mona bends the truth. To what extent does she thereby fulfill her friends' expectations? How does her equivocation contribute to the development of her relationship with Sherman?

2. Compare the "public" Mona-and-Sherman to the "private" Mona-and-Sherman. To what extent can the differences be attributed to their youth? To what extent are fundamental differences between a couple's "public" and "private" personae inevitable? How closely must "public" love and "private" love correspond for love to be genuine?

3. What role does uncertainty play in the development of Mona's affection for Sherman? What role does it continue to play after she realizes she's fallen for him?

4. Compare your experience of first love to Mona's. Through which of the

stages you identified in "Write Before Reading" (p. 652) did each of you move? What accounts for the differences in how you each responded to others' expectations?

5. To what extent can Mona's experience with Sherman be attributed to wish fulfillment? To what extent can it be explained by a new regard for separateness, the kind of "synaptic firestorm" in which Mona realizes that she and Sherman "don't see the same things at all" (para. 161)?

CLIFF THOMPSON

Judgment

"Not too many of *us* here," I said. The two of us stood in the middle of the Bowl, the huge lawn in front of Field College's library.

"You and me, that's about it," she said. This was my first time talking to her, but I'd noticed her before; she was one black student at this tiny school in the middle of Nowhere, Pennsylvania, and I was the other. She was beautiful — her long hair was pulled back, showing off her high, curved forehead and blemishless skin. "Are you a freshman, too?"

"Yeah. My name's Wayne," I said, and we shook hands.

"I'm Roxie. Nice to meet you. Where are you from?"

"D.C."   5

"*Really?* Me too! I'm from Silver Spring."

I gave her a look of mock disgust, and said, "*That's* not D.C."

"All right, then, Maryland," she said, laughing. "Close enough."

We stood there talking for about twenty minutes. I was surprised by her. Before we met I had mentally assigned her a way of speaking and a set of mannerisms which, it turned out, were all wrong. But I liked the real ones — her easy laughter, and the way she tilted her head when she asked a question. Before we parted we made plans to get together for coffee that evening.

Around eight o'clock I left my dorm and headed for Pete's, a diner on the   10
edge of campus. The shortest distance between these two points took me across the Bowl and past the library and the main lecture hall. It was September of 1980, which made these buildings 155 years old; they didn't seem to have been

---

CLIFF THOMPSON was educated at Oberlin College and lived for a time in New York City. "Judgment" is Thompson's first published story. It appeared in *Breaking Ice: An Anthology of Contemporary African-American Fiction,* edited by Terry McMillan.

built so much as just carved out of rock and set among all the trees and grass. In the daytime they looked like a painting of a college campus. Now, silhouetted against the night sky, they looked like medieval castles. They were a little scary, and I thought that a year ago I would've picked up my pace. But I'm in college, I thought; I'm a man now.

"My father's a lawyer," Roxie said. We were in Pete's, hunched over a table in the tiny booth. "I think that's where I get my argumentativeness from. It used to drive the boys in high school crazy."

"If two people agree on everything all the time, one of them is unnecessary," I said. "I can't remember where I heard that, but I like it." She laughed.

"Well, my father's a cabdriver," I said. "Was before he retired, anyway. He's argumentative enough, though. Well, no, that's not really right . . . he doesn't argue with you so much as he just — does what he thinks the situation calls for, and if you're with him on it, fine, and if you're not, then it's just too bad."

"Are you like him?"

"Well . . ." I laughed. "Nobody's really *like* my father. I think I take after   15
him in some ways, though."

"I think I'd like him then," she said and smiled. We looked at each other, longer than people usually do without speaking.

Soon after that night Roxie and I were a couple. I started to think I might just like this college thing.

I liked my roommates, too. Remi and Dave. Coming from D.C., I hadn't spent much time around white people before, and it took some getting used to. They talked differently from the guys I'd grown up with, and about different things — Elvis Costello instead of Chuck Brown and the Soul Searchers, *My Dinner with Andre* instead of *Cooley High*. But the same things made them happy, the same things annoyed them, they had the same little moods. Dave had a good, solid relationship that year with a girl named Nancy, and sometimes Remi longed to be Dave. Remi was always going out with somebody new, and once in a while, when Dave commented on it, I could hear the envy in his lazy Southern voice. After a while I stopped thinking of the two of them as my white roommates and thought of them as just my roommates, and then, gradually, as my friends.

The three of us used to triple-date sometimes. I'd bring Roxie, Dave would bring Nancy, and Remi would drag along whoever he was going out with that week. One night we all went to Lorenzo's, a little pizza place; it sort of marked the border between the campus and the town and was one of the few places where both crowds hung out. The night we went it was full of high school kids, so the six of us squeezed around a square table meant for four and ate greasy pepperoni and mushroom pizza.

"It doesn't get any better than this," Remi said, quoting a TV commercial.   20
We all laughed.

Remi's date that night was an extremely thin, red-haired girl named Michele. She said, "I hate to think what all this grease is gonna do inside my stomach."

I smiled and said, "I figure it'll do like that jar of bacon grease my mother keeps beside the stove. Form a nice, thick, white layer on top, and . . ."

Michele looked shocked. I figured she was going to say, "Stop, you're grossing me out," but she said, "Your mother keeps a jar of bacon grease beside the stove?"

"Yeah," I said.

"Mine does, too," Roxie said.   25

Michele said, "Why?"

"To cook with," I said.

"You're *kidding*."

"Nope."

Michele sort of shuddered. Roxie and I glanced at each other knowingly.   30

Remi said, "This some kind of racial thing?" Remi, Dave, and I looked at each other and smiled, because we were used to this kind of talk. Roxie, Nancy, and Michele looked down at their food; they weren't.

After enough time had passed, Nancy asked me, "How's the econ going?" I made a face. It was a class I was struggling with.

Michele said, "You're taking economics?"

"I'm taking it up the butt," I said. Dave almost spit out his pizza. Everybody laughed.

"You're braver than I am," Michele told me.   35

We stayed a pretty long time, talking and laughing and listening to music on Lorenzo's jukebox. We finished off two pizzas and two pitchers of beer, and the bill, when we finally asked for it, came to around thirty dollars.

"Comes out to six bucks a head, with the tip," Dave said. He, Remi, Michele, and Nancy threw money to the middle of the table. I turned to Roxie and said, "All I have is ten bucks. Do you have anything?"

Roxie reached into her jacket pocket. I noticed Michele looking at Roxie, then at me.

Freshman year seemed to go by very fast. I was on a scholarship then, but I didn't have any other money coming in; sometime around March my savings from the previous summer's job dried up.

"You mind if we go Dutch again tonight?" I asked Roxie. I was in her   40
room, sitting on her bed.

She sat down and sighed. "This is the third Dutch treat this week," she said. "I think you're taking me for granted."

"Look, I'm sorry. My last name's not Rockefeller, okay? It's not that I don't want to take you out, I just can't afford to now."

"Or ever. Why don't you get a campus job, or something?"

"Come on. I'm having a rough enough time with my classes now," I said.

"Anyway . . . what's wrong with going Dutch? Remi and Dave do it all the time. *Everybody* does."

"So you're taking your cues from the white boys now?"   45

I didn't know what to say to that, so I didn't say anything. "Listen," I finally said. "If I have to pay for both of us tonight, we can't go. It's that simple. To tell you the truth, I don't feel much like it now, anyway."

"Fine," she said.

And that was that.

When I left her room I walked around campus for a while because I was too mad to do much else. Soon my anger gave way to hunger. I had missed dinner at the dining hall, so I walked to Lorenzo's, grabbed a small pizza, and took it back to my room.

Remi and Dave were stretched out on their beds listening to The Police   50
when I walked in. I said, "Hello, gentlemen," and fell sideways onto my bed. Remi and Dave sat up and looked at each other, then at me.

Remi said, "That was one fast date."

"Sure nuff," I said, opening my box of pizza.

"What happened?"

"I only had fifteen bucks. I asked if we could go Dutch. She got mad. I got mad. Here I am." I took a bite of pizza.

"You're kidding," Dave said.   55

"Do you see me sittin' here eating this pepperoni and grease pizza? No, I'm not kidding."

Dave said, "What century was *she* born in?"

"You want *my* advice," Remi said, "I'd let her alone for a while."

"Whatever," I said. "If you don't mind, I'd rather not talk about it right now."

"No prob," Remi said, and he and Dave stood up. "We were leaving   60
anyway. We've declared this 'I'm Sick to Death of Being a Student' night. We're going to the game room now, and then later a bunch of us are gonna meet at the disco. You oughtta come." He smiled. "Only costs seventy-five *cents* to get in the *disco*. Seriously, come. Around ten."

"Yeah, maybe," I said. Remi slapped me on the shoulder, and he and Dave left.

I finished my pizza, then just lay back on my bed with my hands clasped behind my head. I stayed like that for the longest time, thinking about things and looking around the room. I stared at the Rolling Stones poster above Remi's bed; at the maps over Dave's bed, those maps of Spain and France and Australia and Russia he loved so much; at the globe on my desk, the one my father had given me just before I left for school ("Take this with you so you don't forget where D.C. is," he'd told me). When I first arrived on campus and got set up in my room, I could spend a lot of time doing exactly what I was doing now, just sitting and looking around the walls. I would think about how I was on my own, and the feeling that gave me was enough to entertain me for the evening. I would wish some of my high school classmates could see me.

But with the passing of the months, my room had lost its power to charm me. All I felt now, lying on my bed and staring at the walls, was boredom.

"What the hell, I'll go to the disco," I said, to no one in particular.

The disco was in a big room in the basement of the student union building. I walked down the hall, toward the pounding, wall-shaking music, and gave my ID to the guy at the door. He stamped my hand, and I went in. It was a good twenty degrees hotter in there. The place was pretty full; I looked out at all the white people — some of them dancing to the rhythm, some of them hopelessly and happily off. I made my way to the edge of the dance floor to look for Remi and Dave. Just about then the strobe light started flashing, and I had to squint and look down to keep my balance.

I felt a hand hit my shoulder. I looked up, and it was Dave. "Hey, guy!"   65
he shouted. "Glad you made it!"

He grabbed my arm and pulled me onto the floor, where Remi and a few other guys and girls were dancing sort of in a circle. I joined in. After a while, I started to really enjoy myself. The D.J. played The Police, The Cars, and The Knack, and also Rick James, songs from Michael Jackson's "Off the Wall" album, and some old Motown. We made periodic trips to the bar, soaked with sweat, and bought cups of beer, which we drank like water. Then we'd head back out to the dance floor.

At one point I felt someone tap me on the back. I turned around, and Dave and Remi were waving good-bye. "I think we've had it," Dave shouted. "You gonna stay a while?"

"I think so," I shouted back.

There was no such thing as partners here; it was a kind of musical free-for-all. I'd dance half a song in front of one person, then she'd wander off, or I'd wander off, and I'd finish the song with someone else — or no one. It didn't seem to matter. That evening, almost nothing did.

I stumbled out of there at about two o'clock. I found myself walking across   70
the Bowl with a blond girl named Joanne, whose dorm was in the same general direction as mine.

"*God*, I needed that," I told Joanne. "I might just make it through the rest of the week now."

"This place getting you down?" she said.

"Ah, this place and a few other things," I said. "My girlfriend's driving me bonkers. She lives to drive me bonkers, I think." All those beers were talking now.

"How does she drive you bonkers?" Joanne asked. We were passing by the library, and under its floodlights, which stayed on all night. I got my first good look at her — at her high, sculpted cheekbones, her nearly pointed nose, the tuft of blond hair that hung down in front and met her eyebrows.

"Oh, man," I said, "it'd take me an hour to tell you. The latest thing is, I   75
can't afford to take her out anywhere 'cuz I'm broke, and she's mad about it. I have to pay for everything, even though I don't have a dime to my name."

She said, "Sounds like you need to either win the lottery or get a new girlfriend."

"I think I have equal shots at both."

"I wouldn't say *that*. You've got about a one-in-a-million shot at the lottery. There are six hundred women on campus. If I were you, I'd save my dollar," she said, smiling.

I remember, then, my lips pressing together to form the word "But," and I remember my mouth expelling the necessary amount of air. No word came out, though.

We reached the walkway that led up to her dorm. We stopped and faced each other. She said, "Well, thanks for walking me." 80

"No problem," I said.

I can describe, but not explain, the moment that followed. It was full of knowledge of what was going to happen, like that half-second between seeing the other car coming and smashing into it. And it was almost that frightening: I was afraid of seeing Roxie after tonight, and afraid, although I wasn't sure why, of crossing this kind of racial line. Afraid — but not ashamed. The certainty that I would go through with it seemed to take it out of my hands, somehow. I stepped toward Joanne feeling scared, excited, and, through it all, blameless.

. . . and after minutes — ten? twenty? — of standing there and exploring each other's mouths with our tongues, after her saying, "I have to get up in the morning," and smiling at me over her shoulder as she went inside, I walked away.

I walked past my own dorm, because I knew I wouldn't be able to sleep, and went several more blocks until I came to the duck pond. I stood at the edge, tossing in pebbles and listening to the ducks quietly talking to each other. Now it started. With Joanne safely back in her room, my cloud of innocence was dissipating; the words *what did I just do?* kept repeating in my mind.

I tossed in a pebble and watched the ripples widen. I watched as they 85 jostled the ducks, and felt bad about disturbing their peace. I wanted to make it up to them, but I didn't have the slightest idea how.

The next morning I woke up and decided that nothing had happened, or at least I would act as if nothing had. As I stood in the shower, hot water cascading over me, it seemed perfectly clear. Nothing had happened. It was that simple.

And it seemed that simple through most of the day. I went to breakfast, and the line servers wore their usual groggy expressions under their white caps. Nothing was different. My classes went as they always did; none of my professors stared at me accusingly. Business as usual.

I got to the dining hall for dinner at six. I got a plate of spinach-something-or-other, then squeezed my way through the mob toward the soda fountain. I was standing in front of it, trying to decide between Coke and Dr. Pepper, when someone to my right said, "Hi there." It was Joanne. She looked a little different from the night before; her hair was tied back, and she looked a lot more put-together than you do after thrashing around on a dance floor.

"Uh. Hi," I said.

She smiled and said, "Are you eating with anyone?" 90

I said, "Um . . ." I looked away, scanning all the faces for Remi or Dave. They weren't anywhere. Joanne didn't know that, though. I turned back to her — looking not in her face, exactly, but toward it — and said, "Yeah."

Before she could respond I was gone, off to find as remote a table as I could, and feeling for all the world like somebody else.

The next day I was walking across the Bowl when I saw her coming toward me. When we were about ten feet apart, our eyes met for the briefest of moments, and then we each looked away. We walked by each other without a word or a glance — which set the tone of our relationship for the rest of freshman year.

Meanwhile, I kept things hobbling along with Roxie. Gradually, without any spoken agreement, things between the two of us became kind of . . . formal. When we saw each other, it was because we had made plans beforehand; we didn't just drop by each other's rooms anymore. I would call her Thursday night about going out on Friday, and when we'd agreed on a time and place, we'd hang up. And it wouldn't cross my mind — or hers either, I don't think — to talk in between making the date and the date itself.

I remember, for some reason, a conversation we had one Friday night. We 95 had just been to see *To Have and Have Not* (in the theater that doubled as the chemistry lab), and I was walking her back to her dorm.

"I'm starting to see one theme over and over again in Bogie's movies," I said. "He's always the guy who swears he's just going to look out for himself, and then he ends up fighting for truth, justice, the American way, and all that other stuff. It was the same thing in *Casablanca, Key Largo, The African* — "

"He wouldn't make it as a leading man today, I'll tell you that," Roxie said.

"Huh?"

"You see how skinny he was? I heard he wasn't but five foot seven, too. He couldn't stand up against some of these muscle-bound men we've got in the movies today."

I was quiet for a second. Then I said, "No. Guess not." 100

We were passing the rear of the library. Across the street were faculty houses. My English professor, Mr. Graham, lived in one of them. The one with the flag on the outside, I thought. It was a clear night; I could see the moon just over one of the houses. It was full and huge and yellow as mustard.

"You ever see any of those movies?" I said. "*Key Largo*, or *The African Queen?*"

"Which one is *The African Queen?*"

"The one with Katharine Hepburn — "

"I love Katharine Hepburn. I saw her in *The Philadelphia Story*. Her and 105
Cary Grant. I *love* Cary Grant."

"I like him, too," I said, and I went back to looking at the moon.

The last day of freshman year around three in the afternoon I was in my room, alone. That morning Remi and I had hugged Dave good-bye and watched him and his family drive off for North Carolina. Around two o'clock I said good-bye to Remi, who was heading back to Brooklyn for the summer. I was packing the last of my junk into a cardboard box on my bed; my father would be there to pick me up in a couple of hours or so. As I tossed in various things — my globe, my desk lamp, a football — I looked around the room. Remi's posters and Dave's maps were gone; the only traces of them were the marks from the tape that had held them up. I couldn't turn on Dave's stereo because it was in the trunk of his father's car, on its way to North Carolina. I had never, I thought, seen a room look as empty as this.

Right about then there was a tap on the door, and Roxie walked in. I remember what she was wearing: white shorts and sneakers and a sky-blue terry-cloth shirt. She looked like summer itself, I thought. "Hi," I said.

"Hi there," she said. "How's it coming?"

"I've about got it under control," I said. "This is the last of it, really.   110
Everything else can go in the car like it is." I looked around the walls again, and said, "Have you ever seen a room look more deserted than this?"

"Looks pretty bare," she said. She sat down on the edge of the mattress; the box I was loading dipped to one side.

I said, "What time are your folks coming?"

"In about three hours."

"You all packed?"

"Just about. I've got a little more to do. I wanted to come over and see   115
you, though."

I said, "Well . . ." and couldn't think what else to say. I put something else in the box, letting it fall more noisily than it had to so it could fill up some of the silence. I finally said, "Did I give you my number at home?"

"Yeah. You have mine, right?"

"Yeah."

She looked around at all my junk, packed in boxes and bags, sitting in heaps on the floor. "Had some good times this year," she said, nodding, still looking at the junk.

"Yeah," I said. I stepped from behind my box and walked over to where   120
she was sitting. I stood in front of her, looking down, my thumbs hooked into the pockets of my jeans. "Had some good times," I said.

She stood up then and put her arms around me, and we hugged for a while. Then we looked at each other and kissed. It was a little more than friendly, but not really passionate; we seemed almost to be saying something to each other through that kiss, something like, "No hard feelings." When it was over she rubbed my chest, then patted it, then started moving away, toward the door. She whispered "'Bye," moved her fingers up and down in a kind of wave, and was gone.

I had wondered how Roxie and I were going to see out the year, and now I guessed I knew. There had been no hideous breakup; we'd made no attempt to smooth out the rough areas. In the end the relationship, all by itself, just dwindled down to nothing.

It felt like a week and a half before I was back on campus again. I roomed with Remi again; we had planned on it being the three of us, but sometime in July Dave's father had gotten pretty sick, and he couldn't come back this semester.

The day before classes started, I was walking across the Bowl when I saw Joanne coming toward me. As a reflex, I started to go into my "ignore" mode — and just think hard about something else until we had passed each other. But then something occurred to me. I looked back at what had happened between us, and now, somehow, I seemed to be looking at it from a great distance. We had necked outside her dorm, once, six months ago. So what? Surely, there must have been some sort of statute of limitations regarding these things, and if there was, it must have been in effect by now. As we got closer, I studied her. She was looking elsewhere, and seemed to be thinking about something I couldn't even guess at (she was in *her* ignore mode now). When we were about four feet apart, I stepped directly in her path. I said, very loudly, "Hi."

She looked startled. But then she saw my expression — my lips were pressed together tightly, in a kind of suppressed smile — and she developed a similar one. With a mock seriousness in my voice, I said, "And where . . . are you going?"

"To . . . the . . . bookstore," she said, imitating me.

"May . . . I . . . accompany you?"

"Why . . . yes . . . you may."

We walked back across the Bowl, around the lecture hall, and through Central Square to the campus bookstore. We talked on the way about our summers. She had spent most of hers in Boston, helping her father add a new room to the house. I had worked delivering packages for an office supply store — which, I told Joanne, was about as exciting as it sounded.

"At least you got to be outside," she said.

"Good point."

In the bookstore she had to get all the books she needed for her classes. The store had carts, miniature versions of grocery store carts, for this purpose. I pulled one out and pushed it behind Joanne while she pulled books from the shelves. "Aagh," I said, after she had pulled out a book on macroeconomics and put it in the cart.

She smiled. "You don't like econ? I think it's fun."

"Fun," I said. "One day when I was six years old, I was running down the street, and I slipped and fell. Landed on my face, and knocked out both my front teeth. *That* was more fun than taking economics."

Joanne made a face and said, "You're weird."   135

When she paid for the books the cashier put them in a brown grocery store bag, and we left. I tried to carry the bag for her, but she insisted on doing it herself. We crossed the street and walked back through Central Square, past the trees and squirrels and stone benches, without talking much. I was working out in my mind how to apologize for last year. The problem now was that it seemed so long ago and trivial, and by bringing it up I would seem to be making a big deal over nothing, yet it didn't seem quite right to pretend that *nothing* had happened. Finally I compromised with myself.

"You ever — um — ever get off on the wrong foot with somebody and not quite know how to get on the right one again?"

She looked at me and smiled, with her lips together. "Yeah," she said. "I think I know what you're talking about."

Later that day I was sitting on my bed, absentmindedly leafing through *The Norton Anthology of English Literature,* when somebody knocked on the door. "It's open," I said, and a second later Roxie walked in.

"Roxie!" I jumped up off the bed.   140

"Hel*lo*," she said. "How *are* you?"

We met in the middle of the floor and hugged, then sat down on the bed. She said, "How was your summer?" At first I thought she meant this as an accusation. Our parents' houses were forty-five minutes apart, and we hadn't seen each other once all summer. But she was smiling; I decided it was an innocent question.

"It wasn't bad," I said.

"What did you do?"

"I was — uh — I delivered packages for an office supply store."   145

"Pret-ty exciting," she said sarcastically.

She had spent June, July, and August, she said, working in a movie theater, which we agreed was about half a notch above my job. Then we talked about what classes we were taking. She said she was looking at an even heavier workload than last year, and I said I was, too.

"So," she said. "What are you doing tonight?"

"Well, I'm kind of busy tonight." Truth was, I was going to the movies with Joanne.

"How about tomorrow night? You want to go have some coffee, or   150
something?"

"Um, yeah," I said, nodding. "Let's do that."

"Okay."

To my surprise, she leaned over and kissed me, and to my disbelief, she stuck her tongue approximately halfway down my throat. Then she stood up, giving me a last peck on the lips, and said, "Talk to you tomorrow." And she left.

For a couple of minutes I just walked around the room — from my bed to my desk to Remi's bed to Remi's desk — with my hand on the back of my head. Then I sat down again. And I decided that if I lived a good long time, if I outlived my children and my children's children, there would still be some things I wouldn't understand.

I picked up Joanne at her room at about seven-thirty. When she opened the door, she looked really great. She wasn't made up or particularly dressed up — she wore beige slacks and a light green plaid top. But she was really . . . pretty. "Hi," she said. "Ready?" 155

The Strand, Field's second-run movie house, was about a block from the campus bookstore. They were showing *The World According to Garp* that night, which neither of us had seen (although we'd both read it). "The writing in that book is so witty," Joanne said, as we walked diagonally through Central Square. "That's most of what I liked about it. I don't know how they're going to capture that on screen."

"Well," I said, "if I know Robin Williams, he can bring it off. As much as it can be brought off, anyway."

"I hope so."

When we were half a block away, I saw someone standing under the marquee. I realized then that the thing I'd been afraid of all day, the thing I'd protected myself against last year, was about to happen.

I don't know why Roxie was standing under the marquee — she was waiting for one of her friends, I guess. "Hi," I said to her, as Joanne and I walked up to the theater; it wasn't quite what I thought I should say, but then I didn't know quite what I thought I should say. 160

"Hi," she said, looking from one of us to the other.

While Joanne paid for her ticket, Roxie and I just looked at each other. Her expression was flat and almost unreadable, except for a slight narrowing of her eyes, which made all the difference; it seemed to be saying, "Uh-huh. I've got your number now."

I bought my ticket, and Joanne and I walked in.

Roxie and I didn't get together for coffee the next night. I didn't hear from her, and I didn't call. To tell the truth, we hardly ever spoke to each other again. Sometimes she looked at me, other times she didn't; but each time, whether we made eye contact or not, her presence made me feel I was being accused of something.

Joanne and I sat on a half-full bus, heading away from the college and into the town of Field itself. We weren't talking, not for the moment, because we'd just reached the point where we were comfortable enough not to talk if we didn't feel like it. We held hands, and she looked out the window, and I looked around the bus. My eyes met the eyes of a white boy, maybe fifteen; he stared at me until he realized I wasn't going to look away, and then *he* looked away. At the front of the bus, two black girls in seats that faced sideways 165 were talking to each other and looking at me. I couldn't hear what they were saying, I could only see their smiles, which weren't really smiles at all.

This wasn't my first trip into town, or Joanne's (we were sophomores now). But it was our first trip together, and our first this school year. We needed a break from campus; we wanted to visit "the real world" for a while, or at least get as close to it as we could. So we rode quietly as the trees and small houses rolled past, and soon there we were in — "Don't blink, or you'll miss it," went the stale joke — downtown Field.

"Where do you want to go first?" Joanne asked me, just as we'd gotten off the bus.

I looked up and down the block. There was a Woolworth's, and beside that a card shop, and beside that a record store, and beside that a pizza joint. Across the street were a post office and a bank.

"Let's go to Woolworth's."

We reached for each other's hand and went down the sidewalk. Now I   170
played a different game from the one on the bus. There I had wanted to see how much direct confrontation I could get away with; here, walking down Main Street, I wanted to see how much I could ignore people. I felt the eyes of the white people, and the few black people, on us; from the corner of my eye I saw their heads turn. But I didn't look at them, and I didn't look at them in a way that must've been obvious.

Looking straight ahead, Joanne said, "I know what *these* people are gonna talk about at dinner tonight." She meant it to sound flip, I could tell. And it did, but only around the edges. Something else was at its center — a kind of little girl's confusion. I squeezed her hand, and she leaned her head toward my shoulder.

We went into Woolworth's. We walked up and down the junk-filled aisles and made fun of everything. I picked up a fake-wood desk lamp; the glue holding the base to the rest of it was showing, and we giggled at that. We giggled at the orange and pea-colored 85 percent polyester clothes that were on sale; at the crushed-velvet paintings of cats and cowboys and Elvis Presley; at everything. The fat white security guard sitting in the corner kept his eyes on us. We giggled at him, too.

When we got tired of that, we went to the pizza joint for lunch. The only person in there, besides us, was the stocky, sweating Italian man behind the counter. He smiled at us when we came in. We smiled back. For a moment I wanted to hug him.

We ate at a table by the window so we could look at the "Pennsylvanians," as Joanne liked to call them. She said, "I talked to my mom last night."

"Oh, yeah?"   175

"Yeah. I told her I started seeing this great new guy. . . ."

"Well, now. Did you tell her what this great new guy looks like?"

"I sure did."

"What did she say?"

"Well, she seemed a little surprised. She said it didn't matter to her, though.   180
She asked me if you were nice, and I said you were. Then she asked me what
you were majoring in, and I told her you were undecided, but leaning toward
English. She liked that. She was an English major."

"You're quite lucky," I said.

"I know. They're great. So have you told your parents about me yet?"

"Not yet. I think I'm gonna wait until I go home for break."

"Is it gonna be that big a deal?"

"To tell you the truth, I don't know. In nineteen years the topic never   185
came up once."

"So . . . if it matters to them, will it matter to you?"

I made a show out of thinking about this. I looked at the ceiling, my brows
knitted; I looked at the floor and scratched my head. Finally I looked her in
the eye and said, "Nope."

This delighted her, and she laughed.

After we left the pizza place, Joanne and I messed around in a record store
for a while, then went to catch the bus back to campus. We stood under one
of those sheltered, Plexiglas bus stops, across the street from the Field Savings
Bank. Two white people were waiting with us — a middle-aged man in a green
polyester leisure suit with white stitches, and a girl who didn't look older than
fifteen.

I looked at Joanne. "Quite a town," I said quietly.   190

"Quite a town," she said.

I felt the urge to kiss her then, but held back. Then I thought about it, and
I went ahead and did it.

A group of white boys, five or six of them, about high school age, came
down the street. They were talking among themselves, and as they passed the
bus stop I heard the words "wrong color." Joanne's eyes met mine for one
brief, alarmed moment. Then I just watched, in silence, as the boys continued
down the street. Finally I shouted, "What?!"

One of the boys looked back; the group kept walking.

"What? What!" I yelled, until Joanne took hold of my arm.   195

During the bus ride back to campus, it rained. First there was a drop here
and there on the windows, and then the sky opened up completely, suddenly,
the way it does on bad TV sitcoms. Soon the black road was shiny, and the
tires of the cars and trucks were reflected in its surface like the edges of some
adjacent, upside-down universe. I felt like going to that universe. Maybe there,
I thought, Joanne and I could walk around together without being stared at or
even noticed by anybody. But I knew it wouldn't work. I knew if I tried to
go there, tried to dive below the surface, I'd never get past the hard, hard
street.   1990

INVESTIGATIONS

1. In paragraph 10, Wayne acknowledges that the campus buildings that "looked like medieval castles . . . were a little scary" but doesn't display fear because he's "a man now." In what ways can Wayne's relationship with Roxie be seen as necessary to his sense of having grown up? How about his relationship with Joanne? How does each relationship reinforce the way he connects reticence with manhood?

2. Why does Wayne feel he "was being accused of something" whenever he runs into Roxie after she sees him with Joanne (para. 164)? What might that "something" be?

3. In paragraph 18, Wayne describes how "after a while" he "stopped thinking" of Remi and Dave as his "white roommates and thought of them as just [his] roommates, and then, gradually, as [his] friends." Compare the ease with which this friendship develops with Wayne's "crossing this . . . racial line" with Joanne (para. 82). Why is interracial love so much more problematic than interracial friendship? How would Wayne's thinking have been different if Joanne were Asian? If she were Hispanic? How much of the "line" do he and Joanne erase during their relationship?

WENDELL BERRY

Except

Now that you have gone
and I am alone and quiet,
my contentment would be
complete, if I did not wish
you were here so I could say,   5
"How good it is, Tanya,
to be alone and quiet."   1980

Raised in Henry County, Kentucky, where he has worked a small farm for many years, WENDELL BERRY (b. 1934) has published more than forty books, including *Collected Poems* (1985), the essay collections *What Are People For?* (1990) and *Standing by Words* (1983), and a novel entitled *The Memory of Old Jack* (1975).

INVESTIGATIONS

1. How is the love embodied in this poem similar to the love expressed in Rich's "Love Poem" (p. 730). Dobler's "Hospital Call" (p. 732), and Silko's "Lullaby" (p. 759)? How would Wayne ("Judgment") feel about the sentiment expressed in the poem?
2. Where along the continuum you constructed in your response to "Write Before Reading" (p. 652) would you place Berry's speaker? Why?
3. What part do you think solitude plays or ought to play in love relationships? In what ways is your thinking on the role of solitude in relationships similar to that implied by the speaker? In what ways different?

DAVID MURA

Nantucket Honeymoon

It's easy for bees to build their combs of honey,
or apples to drop, their light absorbed, but once
only the dazzle and delirium of bodies beneath me,

could sing the tirade taking my life — I was white, yes,
like the bodies I claimed — And when I wanted to say   5
it wasn't my nature, my will, not color, failed. . . .

Since then, I've become someone I never expected.
At times I'd like to think it some great act of character
or even a miracle God was preparing, long before

I finally said: I give. *No mas.* Can't take it anymore.   10
But no, it wasn't like that. You were entering med school,
I felt threatened, I'd been reading Menninger's *Man*

A third-generation Japanese-American, DAVID MURA (b. 1952) grew up near Chicago and now lives in St. Paul, Minnesota. In addition to a poetry collection called *After We Lost Our Way* (1989), Mura has published two books of nonfiction: *A Male Grief: Notes on Pornography and Addiction* (1987) and *Turning Japanese: Memoirs of a Sansei* (1991).

Against Himself,[1] saw myself too often in its pages.
And looking at friends, recent marriages, soon-to-be babies,
I think it was probably just as much the times, just growing up.   15

I learned — how else can I say it? — to love my own sweet skin.

And now on this island of wild mustard, mist
and heather, herring gulls careening in the salty,
rackety Madaket wind, we walk the beach, party

to the triumph of the palpable and small — A conch   20
in your palm, my palm on your shoulder, a fork
you hold up, its lemony halibut, mousse or pate . . .

Later, from our bed, I can see the steeple and its lights,
the full moon; your head a familiar book, bobbing
on my chest. (How far I feel from that Asian island.)   25

Years away our grandchildren will come here saying,
This room is where I began. And returning to Boston,
Paris or Portland, they won't know how bewildered I was,

how alone. They'll think I felt American. I was always at home.   1985

INVESTIGATIONS

1. Why does the speaker "at times . . . like to think" that becoming someone he "never expected . . . [is] some great act of character / or even a miracle / God was preparing, long before I finally said: I give. *No mas*" (lines 7–10)? What compels him to be dissatisfied with that line of thinking?

2. What does line 1 have to do with the rest of the poem? How does the last line help the poem make sense?

3. After reviewing your response to "Write Before Reading" (p. 652) write two or three paragraphs in which you analyze the change that occurs in the speaker between lines 2 and 10. What community influences affect him? How? How do these influences compare with those you mentioned in your response to "Write Before Reading"?

4. Why is it important to the speaker that his grandchildren "won't know how bewildered" he was, "how alone" (lines 28–29)? Compare this solitude to that experienced by the speaker of Berry's "Except."

---

[1] *Man Against Himself,* by Karl A. Menninger, contains psychological case studies of self-destructive behavior. [Ed.]

LANFORD WILSON

Burn This

Characters

ANNA	LARRY
BURTON	PALE

ACT ONE

(*The setting is a huge loft in a converted cast-iron building in lower Manhattan, New York City. Factory windows, a very large sloping skylight, a kitchen area, a sleeping loft, a hall to the bathroom and Larry's bedroom, and another door to Anna's bedroom. The place is sparsely furnished. There is an exercise barre on one mirrored wall and a dining area. There are pipes on the ceiling, and an old sprinkler system is still intact. There is new oak flooring; the walls are white; the only picture is a large framed dance poster. A fire escape runs across the entire upstage.*

It is the sort of place that you would kill for or wouldn't be caught dead in.)

(*The time is the present. It is six o'clock in the evening, mid-October. The sky has the least color left, one lamp has been turned on.*)

(*Anna is huddled on a sofa, smoking. She has a drink. She is thirty-two, very beautiful, tall, and strong. A dancer. A buzzer sounds. A moment later it sounds again. She hears it this time and jumps. She looks at the buzzer. It sounds again. She gets up and goes to it.*)

ANNA: Hello?

BURTON'S VOICE: Hi, it's me. I just heard.

ANNA: Uh, Burton, could we make it another . . . (*Sighs, buzzes him in, opens the apartment door and leaves, going toward the bathroom. After a moment Burton comes in. He is tall, athletic, and rather good-looking. He has big feet and big hands that he admires, cracking his knuckles, stretching*

LANFORD WILSON says, "It's very easy . . . to be pessimistic. To be solidly optimistic and find moments of hope is more difficult." Born in 1937 in Lebanon, Missouri, Wilson has written many plays, including *Hot l Baltimore* (1973), *5th of July* (1977), and *Talley's Folly* (1979), which was awarded the Pulitzer Prize for Drama.

his neck and shoulders. He is a writer and very interested in his process. He is in a sweat suit.)

BURTON: Oh, God, darlin', I heard twenty minutes ago.

ANNA: Yeah, it's not been fun. I didn't know if I wanted to let you in. I think if I have someone to cry on, I'll fall apart completely.

BURTON: Oh, God, how'd it happen?

ANNA: Oh, he and Dom rented a boat — you know, a little motorboat, and some yacht or something ran them down.

BURTON: Goddamn.

ANNA: They were in the middle of the bay — it was just getting dark. Freak accident. They were taking their things off the island. They could have ferried the damn car over, but I guess they thought a boat would be more of an adventure, I don't know. The assholes. I've just been so angry with him. I mean, if you don't swim, damnit! There was a huge picture of Robbie in the *Post*. I threw it out. BRILLIANT YOUNG DANCER DROWNS. That bit. They shipped Dom's body back to California.

BURTON: That's where his folks are? Oh, man. I was gonna run, I saw Kelly in the park, I just hopped in a cab. You went to the funeral?

ANNA: Go? God. Larry and I spent the best years of our lives at that funeral yesterday. And then I got shanghaied into spending the night with the family.

BURTON: Oh, God.

ANNA: Really. I've been smoking one of Robbie's cigarettes that he squirreled away. First cigarette I've had since college. I've forgot how to smoke. And drinking vodka. I feel like a piece of shit, I'm not very good company.

BURTON: No, come on. I just wish I'd been here for you.

ANNA: Who knew where to reach you?

BURTON: I called from the lodge Wednesday, that's the only phone we saw in a week.

ANNA: Yeah, I got the message. Thanks. The kid who took it is a major fan of yours.

BURTON: Of mine?

ANNA: He was impressed all to hell.

BURTON: Nobody knows who writes movies.

ANNA: Sure they do. He's a sci-fi freak. He thinks you and . . . somebody are the two best writers in the business.

BURTON: Exactly.

(*Larry enters holding groceries. He is twenty-seven, medium everything, very bright, gay.*)

LARRY: When the hell did you get home? I've been calling all day.

ANNA: I'm sorry, love, I turned the phone off.

LARRY (*to Burton*): Now you show up.

BURTON: Great timing, huh?

LARRY: Where were you?

ANNA: You don't want to know, really.

BURTON: She got waylaid into spending the night with the family.

LARRY: Oh, God.

ANNA: Really. (*She refills her drink.*)

LARRY: Vodka? Is that two?

ANNA: I think three.

LARRY: You're going to get sloppy. Not that it matters. What do you want? You want bright and cheery, nothing happened? You want quiet, leave me alone? Or maybe talk about it and cry? You know me. I'm always willing to drape the joint in crepe.

ANNA: How are you?

LARRY: Oh, who knows? Hi, beautiful. How was Canada?

BURTON: Great. Cold. Snowy. Exhausting. How's the advertising business?

LARRY: It sucks the big one.

ANNA: Poor baby, everything got dumped on Larry. You were in Canada, I was in Houston. He had to go out there and identify Dom and Robbie, notify their families, get Robbie's suit down for the funeral. Had to buy a dress shirt and tie; Robbie didn't own one.

LARRY: Yeah, it was a lot of laughs. She told you about the funeral?

BURTON: I just walked in.

LARRY: The single most depressing experience of my life.

ANNA: Really. There was this great baroque maroon-and-gold casket with these ormolu geegaws all over it — angels and swags. Robbie would have hated it.

LARRY: It looked like a giant Spode soup tureen.

ANNA: Everything was wrong. The whole company's in Sacramento, so only about six of his friends were there. The eulogy was — the priest hadn't seen him in six years. His folks hadn't seen him in five, did you know that?

LARRY: Jesus.

ANNA: Well, have you ever heard him talk about his family?

LARRY: One brother, I think.

ANNA: Now we know why. (*To Burton.*) There's brothers and sisters, aunts and uncles for days. And none of them had seen him dance!

BURTON: You gotta be kidding.

ANNA: Never. Can you believe it? We couldn't believe it. Oh, God, it was a total nightmare.

LARRY: They had no idea who he was at all.

ANNA: I was the *girlfriend*, can you stand it?

BURTON: Oh, good Lord.

ANNA: It hadn't even crossed my mind. Of course, living with a woman, what else is it going to be?

BURTON: Yeah, but he was hardly living in a closet. I mean, interviews in *The Advocate.*

ANNA: Well, they obviously don't subscribe. Oh, God. Okay. Larry and I take the bus out there.

LARRY: The whole town is a combat zone.

ANNA: I don't know what industry it was built on, but it's not there anymore.

LARRY: In its heyday it couldn't have been much more than a place to leave.

ANNA: At the station we're met by a rented black Cadillac and either the sister or sister-in-law. Did you hear?

LARRY: Not a word.

ANNA: She spoke so softly; we asked three times and finally just pretended to hear. We get to the church —

LARRY: Everyone descended on Anna like a plague of grasshoppers.

ANNA: No joke, they just thrashed me. I'm chaff.

LARRY: She's rushed off to the first five rows, with the family.

ANNA: I said, I'm the grieving —

BURTON: You're the bereaved widow, of course.

ANNA: Some aunt patting my arm, everyone sobbing and beating their breasts. Most of them had never seen him in their lives, you understand. We get to the cemetery. I got the distinct feeling I was expected to throw myself across that hideous casket.

LARRY: Absolutely.

ANNA: I'd have given fifty dollars for a veil. (*Pause.*) I just kept thinking the three of us grew up in such different circumstances. I mean, what could I know about the world living in Highland Park? But, Lord, Robbie grew up in such — I looked for his teacher, I couldn't remember her name; I asked them, they'd never even heard of her.

BURTON: He probably had to sneak off to class.

ANNA: No, he did, literally, I knew that. I tried to tell them about the dance Robbie and I were working on and how important he was to me. With all that drive. Having a friend who was that good pushing you. They wouldn't let me talk about his dancing at all. I thought I could be truthful about something.

BURTON: I wanted to see it.

ANNA: Our dance?

LARRY: It was good.

ANNA: Yeah, even Larry liked it. No, it had no volume, it was too much like Charley's work, anyway. But even my mother keeps a scrapbook, and all she wants is grandchildren.

BURTON: Someone to take over the business.

ANNA: Listen, that's probably all I'm good for, anyway. And quick. Oh, Lord, tell us about Canada. Maybe it'll take my mind off myself.

LARRY: No joke, we've been like this for three days.

BURTON: Feel my thigh. Just her.

ANNA: Good Lord. It must have been beautiful, huh?

BURTON: Yeah, but more strange. Very strange things happen to you up there. Very disconcerting. Two days it's seventy something, we're skiing across this hilltop; we're stark naked, carrying our backpacks.

LARRY: That must have been scenic. (*He goes to his room.*)

BURTON: Oh sure. Next day it was ten degrees and snowing. But amazing country. Incredible skies. Some of the land looks like the moon, all gouged out. Very heavy glacier activity. Very barren, very lonely. I missed you up there. I think I came up with an idea, though.

LARRY: God knows we need it.

ANNA: That's great.

BURTON: Whole new thing, not a space flick. Whole different venue. Takes place in maybe Jasper, way up in northern Alberta in . . . with the aurora and . . . I don't know, about ten different things. This one's weird. Amazing things happen to your mind, you feel like you're all alone, or you're one with the . . . something, or . . . well . . . we don't have to talk about it now.

ANNA: No, what? Something should come from this week.

BURTON (*getting juice from the fridge*): It was like a vision I had while we were going along this ridge, like the top of the world — all this snow, this bright sun, you get into a kind of trance. And I saw this whole story, kind of a weird-ass love story —

ANNA: Burton, a love story?

BURTON: — or really more like a — what? The wives of the whalers or sailors, out to sea . . .

ANNA: The wives out to sea?

BURTON: No, you know. Oh, great. The men, for years on end and the wives waiting on their widow's walk, waiting, walking back and forth, watching the water, the waves coming in, the sun going down, and the men never coming home. Sort of their *heart,* or the men out there on the sea, their *heart.* Where's that love, or what is it, that power that allows those people to sustain that feeling? Through loss, through death. Is it less than the feelings we have? So they can humanly *cope?* Or is it more? I think they felt things in a much more profound way. There's some humongous mega-passion, something felt much deeper than we know. I don't know.

ANNA: I love it when you get an idea. You're so confused and enthusiastic.

BURTON: Am I?

ANNA: It's a good sign.

BURTON: It's there, it's just all fragmented. I had this book of Nordic tales, totally foreign from our stupid urban microcosm, all that crap.

ANNA: You never write urban microcosms, anyway.

BURTON: Well, I know, thank God. But out there . . . or the prairies, hell, the seas of grass, those huge distances, sodbusters, no one within three thousand miles. What *sustains* those people? Out to sea, two or three years at a time, some of those whaling voyages; the fortitude of that kind of love. God . . . But light. Subtle. Don't bang 'em over the head. I don't know. (*Pause.*) I don't think I can use it.

ANNA: Why not? It sounds terrific.

BURTON: No, it's all been done. It's not right. I'd write it, in shooting it'd all be degenerated into some goddamned gothic horror. The handsome sailor away at sea, the evil brother usurps the estate. Seen it a thousand times. Write a sod-buster, they'd turn out *Little House on the Prairie*.

(*Larry reenters.*)

ANNA: No, do it. I want to see it.

BURTON: No, that's just a phantom that haunts you up there. Everything is so good it makes you want to do something good, too. Or I just haven't got that thing yet . . . how that environment impinges on the personalities, what that does to the women, the men . . . the . . . what?

LARRY: Robots.

BURTON: No robots. I love the space stuff, but on this one I'm looking for passions, faith, myths, love, derring-do, for godsake. Heroes and heroines.

LARRY: Senta throwing herself into the sea.

BURTON: Who's Senta?

LARRY: After the Dutchman sails away.

BURTON: I don't know it.

LARRY: *The Flying Dutchman*.

BURTON: I don't know *The Flying* fuckin' *Dutchman*.

ANNA: It's probably in your book of Nordic myths.

LARRY: Really. The Dutchman's this sailor who is like condemned to perdition unless he finds a girl who'll really love him. But he can come ashore only about once every seven years to look for her.

BURTON: Why?

LARRY: You don't ask why in Wagner. So he goes to Norway and Senta falls in love with him, but she has this boyfriend hanging around and the Dutchman gets uptight and sails off again. And Senta throws herself into the . . . fjord.

BURTON: To prove she loved him.

LARRY: To save him from perdition, to break the spell. The sea starts boiling, the Dutchman's ship sinks, all hell breaks loose.

ANNA: Big finish.

BURTON: I like the sea boiling, but I'm not that much of an opera queen.

LARRY: I'm not an opera queen, Burton. I've seen opera queens, and believe me, I rank no higher than Lady-in-Waiting.

BURTON (*looks at his watch*): Oh, Christ, I have to call Signer. I was supposed to have dinner with him tonight.

ANNA: No, don't call it off, tell him the new idea.

BURTON: What do you want to do?

ANNA: I'm going to soak in a tub. Really. I've been in these clothes for two days. You go. Tell him about —

BURTON: No, I'm not ready for him. I shouldn't even be talking about it at this stage. It's the same song every time I see him. God knows what I'd say. Met him once after he'd read a first draft; he's got this crushed look, he hands me the script, says, "What happened to the tiny Australian Bushman?" I still don't know what the fuck he was talking about.

LARRY: Doesn't it just rip you to pieces what they do to your scripts? Did you see *Far Voyager*? After they got through with it?

BURTON: I saw my bank account when they bought it.

LARRY: You don't need money.

BURTON: Tell me what I need.

LARRY: You're rich as Croesus; you were born rich as Croesus.

BURTON: Even Croesus needed money.

LARRY: There was some beautiful writing in —

BURTON: Beautiful writing? It's anathema to a movie. No, you can't get involved with it. You'd kill yourself. You can't worry what they're going to do to it. Start something else; take your two hundred thou and split.

LARRY: It could have been a good movie if you'd —

BURTON: It couldn't have been a good movie; there is no such thing as a good movie.

LARRY: *Far Voyager* was wonderful before —

BURTON: There are no good movies. Did you coach him? It can't happen. There cannot be a good movie. When a good movie happens, which it might, on a roll of the dice, once in five years, it's like this total aberration, a freak of nature like the Grand Canyon, they're ashamed of it. They can't wait to remake it in another ten years and fuck it up the way it's supposed to be. Movies are some banker's speculation about how the American adolescents want to see themselves that week. Period. They're produced by whores, written by whores, directed by —

LARRY: Burton, you don't have to tell me about whores, you're talking to someone who works in advertising. Besides, I don't want to hear it. I think movies are gorgeous: "Who are you? Where did you come from? What do you want? It's me, isn't it? You've always wanted me. You want to have your filthy way with me in the hot desert sun. Ravage me like I've never been ravaged before." *Lust in the Dust.*

BURTON: He memorized that?

LARRY: Burton, you don't memorize. There are some things so true that they enter your soul as you hear them. You should be producing your own stuff, anyway; at least you wouldn't have done that Pit and the Pendulum scene in *Far Voyager*. Saved by forty midgets.

BURTON: *Midgets?*

LARRY: I thought you saw it.

BURTON: No, I just wrote it; I couldn't sit through it. I heard what they did. The cave with the Vampire Queen — hanging upside down. No point in putting yourself through that kind of . . . Midgets?

LARRY: Munchkins. They did everything but sing "Ding Dong the Witch Is Dead."

BURTON: Oh, Jesus. Well, Signer's short, he gets off on little people. I'm not as intrepid as Anna: quitting dance, trying to break into choreography . . .

ANNA: Huh? Oh yeah, at this late date. By myself.

LARRY: What, doll?

ANNA: Nothing. What?

BURTON: We're being insensitive and stupid.

ANNA: No, I'm just out of it.

BURTON: Would it be better if I left?

ANNA: Actually, maybe so.

BURTON: Okay.

ANNA: Really. You should talk about Canada and I want to hear, but all I want to do right now is soak in a hot tub. What time's your dinner?

BURTON: I'll have to get some of this in the computer if I'm going to see him. I came over, I didn't know you'd still be here. You finished with Houston?

ANNA: You kidding? I've got to go back at noon for the reception tomorrow night. I didn't even pack, I just got on a plane. I don't suppose you have any desire to see Houston?

BURTON: Why not?

ANNA: No, I'm okay. I'm glad you're back.

BURTON: When we're not feeling so bad about this, we've got to get away. Go up to the Vineyard. Take a week off.

ANNA: Maybe it's time for us to just move up there permanently.

BURTON: I'd love it.

LARRY: Bye, beautiful.

BURTON: Yeah, sure. Take care of her. I gotta get gone. Call tomorrow.

ANNA: Bye-bye.

   (*Burton exits.*)

LARRY: I don't know why you don't just marry him and buy things.

ANNA: I'm glad he's come up with something. I think he was beginning to panic.

LARRY: I didn't visibly blanch when he said he gets two hundred thousand dollars for a first draft, did I?

ANNA: Well, he's got a name. You know. He's good. God, I'm as stiff as a board. I haven't exercised in two days. I'm completely out of touch with my body.

LARRY: When's your plane tomorrow?

ANNA: Noon. But I'm back the day after. Here for a week, then go to Seattle for no more than six days, and then that's it. No more teaching other companies Charley's dance.

LARRY: Concentrate on your own work.

ANNA: Whatever that is. I've already signed up for a class just to get Charley's damn movements out of my muscles. No lie; I could walk down the street, it's Charley walking down the street, it isn't me.

LARRY: Should we have waited for you? After the funeral. Kelly had to work.

ANNA: No, I should have come with you. God. Just as I think I'm out of there, some relatives drive me back to the house. The place is mobbed. I'm dragged through everybody eating and drinking and talking, to some little back bedroom, with all the aunts and cousins, with the women, right?

Squashed into this room. His mother's on the bed with a washcloth on her forehead. I'm trying to tell them how I've got to get a bus back to civilization.

LARRY: This is very moving, but I'm double-parked.

ANNA: Exactly.

LARRY: This is a *wake*?

ANNA: I couldn't tell you *what* it was, Larry, I guess. In about eight seconds I know they have no idea that Robbie's gay.

LARRY: I could have told you that.

ANNA: They've never heard of Dom. God, I'm making up stories, I'm racking my brain for every interesting thing anyone I know has done to tell them Robbie did it. Wonderful workaholic Robbie, and I couldn't tell them a thing about him. It was all just so massively sad.

LARRY: Oh, Lord.

ANNA: It gets worse, it gets much worse. And they *never saw him dance*! I couldn't believe it. All the men are gorgeous, of course. They all look exactly like Robbie except in that kind of blue-collar, working-at-the-steel-mill kind of way, and *drink*? God, could they knock it back. So then it's midnight and the last bus has left at ten, which they knew, I'm sure, damn them, and I hadn't checked, like an idiot. So I have to spend the night in Robbie's little nephew's room in the attic. The little redhead, did you see him?

LARRY: I didn't see him.

ANNA: He's been collecting butterflies all day, and they're pinned around the room to the walls — a pin in each wing, right?

LARRY: I'm not liking this little redheaded nephew.

ANNA: Darling, wait. So. I get to sleep by about two, I've got them to promise to get me up at six-thirty for the seven-something bus. I wake up, it's not quite light, really; you can't see in the room much — but there's something *in* there.

LARRY: Oh, God.

ANNA: There's this intermittent soft flutter sound. I think what the hell is — Larry, the — oh, Lord, the walls are just pulsating. All those butterflies are alive. They're all beating their bodies against the walls — all around me. The kid's put them in alcohol; he thought he'd killed them, they'd only passed out.

LARRY: Oh, God.

ANNA: I started screaming hysterically. I got the bedsheet around me, ran down to the kitchen; I've never felt so naked in my life. Of course I was naked — a sheet wrapped around me. This glowering older brother had to go get my clothes, unpinned the butterflies, who knows if they lived. I got the whispering sister —

LARRY: What a family!

ANNA: — to drop me off at the bus station; they were glad to get rid of me. I was an hour and a half early, I didn't care. I drank about twenty cups of that vending-machine coffee. Black; the cream and sugar buttons didn't work. The bus-station attendant is ogling me. I'm so wired from the caffeine, if he'd said anything I'd have kneecapped him. There's these two bag ladies yelling at each other, apparently they're rivals. I fit right in.

LARRY: Oh, God. To wake up to those — I can just see them.

ANNA: Oh, Lord, I shrieked like a madwoman. They were glad to get rid of me.

LARRY: I was going to ask if you wanted coffee.

ANNA: No, I don't think that's going to do it.

LARRY: Not one of your better nights.

ANNA: Not one of my better nights. Not one of my better mornings.

LARRY: Jesus. What are we going to do about Robbie's mail?

ANNA: I guess save it. We have to bring Robbie's things down from the loft. Someone's coming over for them.

LARRY: He only had about two pairs of jeans and three sweatshirts. A lot of shoes.

ANNA: Clothes didn't mean much to him.

LARRY: What did, except work and you and Dominic? In the room there's his futon, a candle, and a paperback of *Ancient Evenings*.

ANNA (*Pause. She looks around.*): I left this place, went down to Houston . . . I thought everything important to the future of dance was going to happen in this room. Oh, God. It's too early to go to bed.

LARRY: Go to bed now, you'd be wide awake at 2 A.M.

ANNA: Actually, you want to know the callous truth: If I were still dancing, I'd probably be brilliant tonight. (*Pause.*) How was work? Did they buy the idea?

LARRY: You have no notion of the stupidity involved in designing a Christmas card for a national company. Especially if it's Chrysler. Just for starters, there are a hundred seventy religions in America and only one of them believes in Santa Claus. Nothing religious; that would offend the non-believers. Reindeer are out — Santa Claus again. No snow; that would offend California and Florida. No evergreens, holly, pines — out of the question — mistletoe, no bells. They said the only thing everyone believes in is the family and children. I said that was only going to offend homosexuals.

ANNA: Which didn't matter to them at all.

LARRY: No, I said it as a joke; they bought it.

ANNA: So what?

LARRY: They're still batting it around, but they're leaning toward a car. Which is tantamount to saying the only thing everyone believes in is the auto-mobile.

ANNA: They're probably on to something there.

LARRY: Oh, I have no quarrel with that. A little plastic Chrysler that you can or not hang on your Christmas tree or Hanukkah bush that says *Season's Greetings from Chrysler Corp.* Made in Taiwan, appropriately. It's too complicated, production will get fucked completely, it's going to be late, and the cost is astronomical, but we won't have offended anyone. Except anyone with a modicum of taste. (*He looks at her, she stares off.*) What are you going to do about food? (*A very long pause.*) You wanta order in? Mexican? Pizza? Chinese? (*Pause.*) I haven't stopped thinking about it since it happened.

ANNA: I'm just so annoyed with myself, because all I can feel is anger. I was angry with Robbie and Dom for doing something that stupid; now I'm angry with his family. They just had no goddamned right. He was my friend, damnit. I danced with him for three years. They didn't even know him.

LARRY: They didn't do anything; there's no reason to be angry with them.

ANNA: Well, I am. And there is. And they did. I mean, it's half sentimental horseshit, but damnit, they wouldn't leave me alone. I didn't even have a damn minute to say good-bye. I'll never forgive those bastards for that.

(*Music up, the lights fade. After a moment of darkness there is a pounding on the apartment door.*)

PALE'S VOICE (*offstage*): Annie, hey, Annie — Just go fuck yourself, fella. Get laid, do you good. Annie. Hey. Come on.

(*Anna turns on a light; she has quickly thrown on a Hapi coat. She looks through the peephole.*)

PALE (*offstage*): Come on. Come on. Jesus.

(*She opens the door. Pale comes in. He is thirty-six, shorter than Burton, well built, and can be good-looking, but is certainly sexy. He wears a very good suit.*)

PALE: Goddamn this fuckin' place, how can anybody live this shit city? I'm not doin' it, I'm not drivin' my car this goddamn sewer, every fuckin' time. Who are these assholes? Some bug-eyed, fat-lipped half nigger, all right; some of my best friends, thinks he owns this fuckin' *space.* The city's got this *space* specially reserved for his private use. Twenty-five fuckin' minutes I'm driving around this garbage street; I pull up this space, I look back, this fuckin' baby-shit green Trans Am's on my ass going *beep-beep.* I get out, this fucker says that's my *space.* I showed him the fuckin' tire iron; I told the fucker, You want this space, you're gonna wake up tomorrow, find you slept in your fuckin' car. This ain't your space, you treasure your pop-up headlights, Ho-Jo. Am I right? That shit? There's no talkin' to shit like that.

ANNA: I'm sorry, do I know you?

PALE: How's that?

ANNA: I mean, you're obviously some relation of Robbie's — you could be his double — but —

PALE: Double, shit, with that fuckin' nose of his? Sure you know me — "Do I know you" — we met. I'm the one who saved you from the ferocious butterflies.

ANNA: You have such a large family, I didn't really catch any *names*.

PALE: Jimmy. I was listening to all that molasses you was pouring over Mom and all the cousins and neighbor bitches, I had to go take a shot of insulin.

ANNA: I remember now, you're the older brother.

PALE: Twelve years, so what? What's older? Older than what?

ANNA: Older than Robbie.

PALE: I said, didn't I? Twelve years. You hear me say that? He lived in this joint? I mean no personal disparagement of the neighborhood in which you have your domicile, honey, but this street's dying of crotch rot. The only thing save this part of the city, they burn it down. They call that a street out there? You could lose a Toyota some of those potholes. The people run your fuckin' city's got no respect for the property of the people livin' here. This is why people act the way they do, this shit. (*Beat.*) This has made me not as, you know — whatever — as I usually am. But I'm trying to parallel-park in the only fuckin' space a twenty-block radius, you don't crawl up my butthole in your shit-green Trans Am and go *beep-beep*, you know? (*Looking around.*) So'd you get the stuff together?

ANNA: The what?

PALE: The things, the things, the stuff, Robbie's shit.

ANNA: Wait a minute, you've come for Robbie's things?

PALE: Didn't I say?

ANNA: It's been over a month. I called your mother. She gave me some numbers where I could reach you, but . . .

PALE: Ya, sure. Listen, I don't want you bothering my family, okay? I don't like messages. The first one, you think, okay, fuck, I messed up. I'll take care of it, my fault, something came up, no problem. Then you get, you know, a couple of days, here's another fuckin' message. And it's like I heard you the first time, okay? Don't leave messages for me. I don't need the pool hall and the bar where I go and the auto-repair man on my back saying some bitch called and giving me a little piece of paper.

ANNA: Saying what? Some bitch called? You were the one who was —

PALE: That's the way he talks, what are we talkin'? A fuckin' bartender, what does he know? He's working some dark hole, listening to the dregs of the race vomit their life all over the bar six nights; he's got a low opinion of humanity, okay? I don't like little pieces of paper. You put them in your pocket, you got six or eight little pieces of paper stuffed all over you, it ruins your clothes, you know? I don't read 'em. They're nothin' you don't already know. Somebody *wants* me, big fuckin' deal, take a number. I said I'd come, I'm here. A man would like to think people are gonna believe him. There's a certain satisfaction in being thought of as a man of your — ? There's something wrong with these shoes, my feet are in boiling water. (*He takes off one of his shoes.*) Look at that, oh man, I never had that.

ANNA: Are they new?

PALE: Yeah, first time I put them on. Don't worry about stinkin', I'm clean. They should invent a machine break in shoes — fuckin' killing the top of my foot. That's genuine lizard, two hundred forty-five bucks, fuckin' pinchin' everywhere. Jesus. (*He takes off the second shoe.*) You'd think a lizard's got to be supple, right? They got to move quick. Feel that. Steel plating. (*Walking.*) Oh man. (*Beat.*) What a fuckin' neighborhood. What a place to live.

ANNA: Actually, we like it.

PALE: Yeah, yeah, yeah, yeah, it's supposed to be arty, I know. It's quaint. Look at it — you should make automobile parts here; it's a fuckin' factory. (*Larry stands in the doorway in T-shirt and shorts.*) So who are you?

LARRY: . . . "Where did you come from? What do you want? It's me, isn't it? You've always wanted me. You want to have your filthy way with me in the hot desert sun. Ravage me like I've never been ravaged before." (*To Anna.*) Are you all right?

ANNA: I'm fine. Larry, this is Jimmy, Robbie's brother.

LARRY: I could tell.

PALE: Your girlfriend is in very capable hands.

ANNA: Larry's my other roommate.

PALE: You're the replacement; that didn't take long — in one door, out the other.

LARRY: The three of us got the place together.

PALE: Didn't see you at the wake.

LARRY: I wasn't invited. I'm going to bed, then. (*He exits.*)

ANNA: Good night.

PALE: "Good night," shit. Sleep tight. What am I gonna rip off the TV? He another dancer?

ANNA: No. Listen, Jimmy, Robbie's things are in the basement. No way could you get them tonight without waking up the building. I've already called the Salvation Army, I hadn't been able to reach you.

PALE: So what? What's this huge rush? They're on fire or something? Spontaneous combustion, something? (*There's a noise from the radiator.*) What's that?

ANNA: The heat.

PALE: Heat, yet. The fuckin' room's a oven, bake pizza here, they turn on some heat. (*He takes his jacket and tie off, pulls his shirttail out.*)

ANNA: It's cold. It's the middle of winter.

PALE: I got like a toaster oven I carry around with me in my belly someplace. I don't use heat. I sleep the windows open, no covers, I fuckin' hate things over me. Ray'll tell you: Here comes the dumb fuck Pale with the radiator up his ass. What time they turn it off?

ANNA: Midnight. It comes back on at five.

PALE: Five's ass, shit. It can't be no five. What'd I do with my watch?

ANNA: Actually, I've got to get back to —

PALE: Actually, would you just hold it a second, okay? (*Looking for his watch.*) What'd I do with my — no, it's cool, I got it. (*He opens a window.*) Jesus, it's a fuckin' — you could pass out. How long did he live here?

ANNA: About three years. He was a lot of fun.

PALE: Yeah . . . he was very light, a lotta guys are dark . . . he was very light.

ANNA: Yes he was. (*Pause.*) You want some coffee?

PALE: Sure, whatta you got to drink?

ANNA: Coffee.

PALE: Sure. I'm not difficult.

ANNA: You're Pale.

PALE: V.S.O. Pale, that's me.

ANNA: Robbie mentioned you.

PALE: Yeah? He *mentioned* me? Well, I'm very mentionable.

ANNA: He didn't talk about his family much. You were the one he liked.

PALE (*looking out the window*): That's the bay, huh, the river? Jesus. What a thing to look at. Oh, look, darling, they got tugboats pushin', like, these flatcars; like, five flatcars piled about a mile high with all this city garbage and shit. Who the fuck wants to look at that? You pay for a view of that? Maybe there's people find that fascinating, that's not what I call a view.

ANNA: Are you high?

PALE: How's that?

ANNA: Are you high? I mean, I know you've been drinking; I wondered if you were high, too.

PALE: Yeah, I did maybe a couple lines with Ray, it don't affect me.

ANNA: No, it doesn't affect you. (*She carries the coffee to the living area.*)

PALE: It don't affect me. This is the way I am, what you see, little girl. Straight or high. (*Larry stands in the doorway, only in his shorts.*) What is this, a slow strip act? (*Larry leaves.*) Jesus. Little girls your age don't have roommates, you know? This is not just me, this is prevailing opinion, here. (*He's looking out the window.*)

ANNA: I have a problem with prevailing opinions.

PALE: I could tell.

ANNA: They're putting up that building; it's going to block about half our view.

PALE: No, I'm trying to see where I parked my car. That jerk-off. People aren't human, you ever notice that? This bar tonight, Ray, you know?

ANNA: No.

PALE: Ray, Ray, Ray.

ANNA: No, I don't know him.

PALE: You may not know him. That didn't stop you asking him to write out your number on a piece of paper, give it to me; it didn't stop —

ANNA: Fine; Ray, fine, what about him?

PALE: Boy. So what? You dance here?

ANNA: Robbie and I used it as a studio, yes.

PALE: That's why you got no furniture, no curtains; you'll fall down over 'em, somethin'.

ANNA: Actually, we've tried to keep it as spare as possible.

PALE: This ain't spare. This is a empty fuckin' warehouse. (*He has found a bottle of brandy and pours himself a drink.*)

ANNA: That's not V.S.O.P.

PALE: I can tell. I got one area of expertise: food and drink.

ANNA: Very — Something — Old — Pale.

PALE: "Special." Most people don't even know what that means. Very Special Old Pale. This ain't bad, though, this ain't rotgut.

ANNA: Thank you.

PALE: What? You think it's hot shit? It's okay. It's no better than Rémy. I'd come in, I'd say Very Special Old Pale up, about the third time Ray says, Hey, Pale, on me.

ANNA: This was when?

PALE: When; shit, who knows? Ten, fifteen years. So you dance, too.

ANNA: I did, I've taken off for a while.

PALE: Couldn't stick it.

ANNA: I decided it might be interesting to have a personal life.

PALE: So. You got too good.

ANNA: No, Robbie thought he saw a choreographer in me.

PALE: So what do they do?

ANNA: Choreographers? They make the dance. You have bodies, space, sculptural mass, distance relationships; if they're lucky, they might even discover they have something to say —

PALE: So, you like it?

ANNA: It's an interesting challenge. Well, it's becoming kind of an obsession.

PALE: So you like it.

ANNA: Uh, possibly. Look, if you wanted to come back seven, seven-thirty, we could go down to the basement and get —

PALE: Seven-thirty I'm long outta here. No good. I'm a worker. Part of this country's great working force.

ANNA: What do you do?

PALE: Who me? Whatta I do?

ANNA: It doesn't matter.

PALE: I do anything. On call. Twenty-four hours a day and night. We never close. I deliver. Water. I'm a water deliverer. For fires. I put out fires. I'm a relief pitcher. Like Sparky Lyle.

ANNA: For whom?

PALE: Anybody needs relieving. I'm a roving fireman. Very healthy occupation. I'm puttin' out somebody else's fire, I'm puttin' out my own. *Quid pro —* something; symbiosis. Or sometimes you just let it burn. (*Pause.*)

ANNA: What did you do to your hand?

PALE: No, this bar tonight, Ray, you know?

ANNA: Good ol' Ray, sure. I mean, we've only talked on the phone.

PALE: There was this character runnin' off at the mouth; I told him I'm gonna push his face in, he don't shut up. Now, this should be a fairly obvious statement, right? But this dipshit starts trying to explain to me what he's been saying *ad nauseam* all night, like there was some subtle gradation of thought that was gonna make it all right that he was mouthing this horseshit. So when I'm forced to bust the son of a bitch, he's down on the floor, he's dripping blood from a split lip, he's testing a loose tooth, and that fucker is *still talking.* Now, some people might think that this was the problem of this guy, he's got this motor going, he's not privy to where the shutoff valve is. But I gotta come to the conclusion that I'm weird. Cause I try to communicate with these jerk-offs in what is *essentially* the mother tongue, but no one is picking me up; they're not reading me. There's some mystery here. Okay, sometimes they're just on a rap. I respect rap. You're not supposed to be listening. You can read the paper, watch TV, eat pistachios, I'm not talking that. I'm talking these jerk-offs think you're listening. You said the choreographer organizes what? Sculptured space? What is that?

ANNA: Oh, God. I'm sorry — What did you say? I'm sorry.

PALE: Now, see, that I can't take. I can't stand that.

ANNA: I'm sorry, really, but —

PALE: Well, see, fine, you got these little social phrases and politenesses — all they show me is this — like — giganticness of unconcern with your "I'm sorrys," man. The fuckin' world is going down the fuckin' toilet on "I'm sorrys." I'm sorry is this roll of toilet paper — they're growing whole forests, for people to wipe their asses on with their "I'm sorrys." Be a tree. For one day. And know that that tree over there is gonna be maybe music paper, the Boss is gonna make forty million writin' some poor-slob-can't-get-work song on. This tree is gonna be ten-dollar bills, get passed around, buy things, *mean something,* hear stories; we got sketch pads and fuckin' "I don't love you anymore" letters pinned to some creep's pillow — something of *import.* Headlines, box scores, some great book or movie script — Jack Nicholson's gonna mark you all up, say whatever he wishes to, anyway, out in some fuckin' desert, you're supposed to be his *text,* he's gonna lay out this line of coke on you — Tree over there is gonna be in some four-star restaurant, they're gonna call him parchment, bake pompano in him. And you're stuck in the ground, you can't go nowhere, all you know is some fuckin' junkie's gonna wipe his ass and flush you down the East River. Go floating out past the Statue of Liberty all limp and covered with shit, get tangled up in some Saudi Arabian oil tanker's fuckin' propellers — you got maybe three hundred years before you drift down to Brazil somewhere and get a chance to be maybe a coffee bush. "I'm sorrys" are fuck, man. (*Pause.*) How long did he live here?

ANNA: Three years. Did you know he was studying, Pale?

PALE: Robbie? Didn't do much better than me. I was popular, you know. I don't think he wasn't so popular.

ANNA: Dance, I mean. Did you know he wanted to be a dancer?

PALE: Shit. I don't know. Whatta I know? He was seven, I was outta there. Who knew him? I didn't know him.

ANNA: Actually, I was thinking that.

PALE: Oh, beautiful, I love that. You're gonna be a cunt like everybody else? "You didn't really know him, Pale." *Deeply,* you gotta say. Did you know him deeply, honey? He know you deeply? You guys get deep together? 'Cause neither of you strikes me as the type.

ANNA: Fine.

PALE: What the fuck does that mean, "fine"?

ANNA: It means I'm tired, it's five-thirty in the morning; if you don't want to talk about him, I certainly don't. You're completely closed; you knew him, I didn't. You don't want to hear what I have to say, fine. It means fine.

PALE: What? I don't have feelings? I'm not capable of having a talk here?

ANNA: There's no doubt in my mind that you have completely mastered half the art of conversation. (*Pale whistles.*) I'm tired. I'm sorry. I miss him. You remind me of him.

PALE: Shit.

ANNA: Completely aside from any familial resemblance, just having his brother here reminds me. At the — whatever that wake was after the funeral — it was obvious none of your family knew anything about him. Had you seen him dance? (*Pale shakes his head.*) Well, see, that's impossible for me to understand.

PALE: Anybody good as he was, you said. He was good?

ANNA: Yes.

PALE: Well, see, that shows what the experts know. You saw him and say he was good. I didn't even see him, I know he was shit.

ANNA: Pale, I can't stay up till the people in the building wake up, I have a class at nine, I have to get some rest.

PALE: You teach?

ANNA: What? No, a class I'm taking. I teach too, but this is a class. Then I come back here and work till six, so I've got a long day . . . (*Pause.*) What?

PALE: Awww, shit. (*Pause. He stifles a sob.*) Fuckin' . . . drinkin' and thinkin', man, worse than drinkin' and drivin'. Drinkin' and thinkin'. Aw shit. He wasn't dark, you know, like . . .

ANNA (*pause*): He worked really hard.

PALE: Aww, Jesus . . . feed the fish, man . . . Jesus. (*He sobs enormously and long, she goes to him, he moves away. She touches his shoulder.*)

ANNA: I know.

PALE: Come on, don't mess with me. I don't like being messed with. My heart hurts, I think I'm dying. I think I'm havin' — like — a heart attack. I messed up my stomach, I think I ate somethin'. (*Sobs again.*) I don't do this, this ain't me. (*He gets up, walks around.*) Aww shit. I'm trying to imagine him here.

ANNA: His room was up in the loft.

PALE: Yeah? What'd you do, you guys eat here; you have — like — parties, that shit?

ANNA: Sometimes. When we were all home, which wasn't often enough, we'd trade around. We're all pretty good cooks. Robbie was really the best.

PALE: Robbie cook?

ANNA: He was working his way through *The Cuisine of Southern Italy*. Cookbook . . . Dom . . . someone gave him for Christmas.

PALE: Shit. Fuckin' Christmas parties. Presents and that shit. Look out! Ribbons! I fuckin' hate that crap.

ANNA: What do you like, Pale?

PALE: I like a lot of things. You want bullshit, you want to know what turns me on?

ANNA: Nothing. That's fine. I can imagine.

PALE: Yeah, well, I don't like being imagined. I like the ocean. That hurricane. I stayed on the pier — hanging on to this fuckin' pipe railing, wind blowin' so hard you couldn't breathe. Couldn't open my hands the next day. Try to get excited over some fuckin' roller coaster, some loop-the-loop after that. I like those gigantic, citywide fires — like Passaic, wherever; fuckin' Jersey's burnin' down three times a week. Good riddance. Avalanches! Whole villages wiped out. Somethin' that can — like — amaze you. People don't want to hear that shit, they want — like you should get turned on by some crap — you know, Häagen-Dazs ice cream, "I like everyone to be nice." That shit. Chicks or somethin'. Gettin' laid's okay. A really hot shower's good. Clean underwear, smells like Downy softener. (*Beat.*) So you guys all cook for each other. Sittin' here, makin' polite conversation about the state of the world and shit.

ANNA: Dancers mainly talk about dance.

PALE: Man, I'm fuckin' up my pants all fucked up.

ANNA: That's a nice suit.

PALE: Yeah, I'm a dresser. I keep myself neat. I'm fuckin' up the back of my pants, gettin' all fucked up. Fuckin' linen. Half linen, half wool — fuckin' useless. I could've been the dancer. Who needs it? Our old man, when we was kids, music all over the place. You couldn't hear yourself think. Vivaldi, Puccini, we all knew all that crap, Shostakovich. I've done — like — whole symphonies, amazed people, natural talent, totally original shit, like in the shower. I don't sing Hall & Oates, I compose — like — these tone poems, concertos and shit — huge big orchestrations, use like two orchestras.

ANNA: Do you read music?

PALE: What for? Nobody does that shit. I get going some symphony, these like giant themes come to me, these like world-shaking changes in tempo and these great huge melodies, these incredible variations, man. Get like the whole fuckin' war in it. (*He stops, bends over.*) My heart's killing me. My throat's hurtin', burnin', man. What a fuckin' night. Bust up my hand on that fucker's tooth. (*He looks out the window. Pause.*) Half my fuckin' adult life, I swear to Christ, has been spent looking for a place to park. (*Beat. He looks at her.*) What are you wearin' that thing?

ANNA: I keep hoping I'll have a chance to go back to bed and get my rest.

PALE: Sure. Don't worry about rest, we'll all get our rest. Whatta you call that thing?

ANNA: It's called a Hapi coat.

PALE: That's somethin' to wear, you do your Hapi? The Indians wear that, the Hopis?

ANNA: I got it in Japan.

PALE: Those Orientals are short, it might give them better cover.

ANNA: I just grabbed something.

(*Pause. He looks at her, looks around the room. Back to her.*)

PALE: So the three of you lived here. You and the two faggots.

ANNA: (*A long stunned pause.*) We were all very good friends.

PALE: Tellin' Mom and Aunt Ida and all the neighborhood bitches how you and Robbie did things, horseback, and the races and shit. Said everything except your little boy was a real hot fuck.

ANNA (*pause*): It was very humiliating. They didn't know; it wasn't my place to tell them.

PALE: They know, they just don't know.

ANNA: Well, whatever. I didn't feel it was my place.

PALE (*banging on the sofa*): Fuckin' fruit. Fuck! Fuck! Fuck! Fuck! Fuck! Bastard! Taking his fuckin' little Greek boyfriend out to the island, talking about him in the paper, on that TV thing. "You dance real good." "Well, I get a lot of help from my friend Dominic." Suckin' my dick for me, whatever the fuck they do.

ANNA: Don't you know? I thought you'd know. They have anal intercourse, take turns having oral —

PALE: HEY! HEY! People don't *see* those programs! On TV, Channel Q, whatever, don't matter. People see that. People say, I saw your queer brother on the TV with his boyfriend. People the family works for. That crap. He live here, too? Dominic?

ANNA: He spent about half the time here. We'd been trying to get him to move in, there's plenty of room. Dom was great, you'd have liked him. It's very different here without them.

PALE: I'm just trying to get a picture —

ANNA: Well, don't bother if you didn't give a damn for him; it's a little late to cry now.

PALE: — Robbie cookin', Dominic serving wine, you lighting candles. The fruit in there running around without his clothes on. *What do you know what I feel?* I got my hand bleeding again. Fuckin' myself into little pieces here. I got to wear this look like a fuckin' bum. (*He bends over, starts to cry, stifles it.*) Shit, man; shit, man. Awww shit. (*Taking off his pants.*) I can't get fucked up; you go get your rest, you're worried about rest. I can't fuckin' stand up; I sit down, I'm gonna cry. Come undone. I got to wear these tomorrow — (*Presses them on table.*) I can't fuck myself.

ANNA (*overlapping*): Jimmy, for godsake. Jimmy. If you're worried, I can press them in the morning. Seven o'clock we can go down in the basement. Listen, if you're very quiet, we can sneak down now. We'll take the stairs, 'cause the elevator — Jimmy. Jimmy. (*He has crawled onto the sofa and completely covered himself with an afghan, head and all. His body is racked with crying. Anna looks at him for a moment. She finishes the last of her coffee. What the hell — finishes his brandy as well.*) I know. I miss him like hell. I go to the studio, I think I see him ten times a day. Someone dressed like him, or walking like him. Then I remember he's gone, and it's all that loss all over again. I know.

PALE (*he has poked his head from the afghan*): He was always . . . very . . . (*Gestures light.*)

ANNA: I know. He worked harder than anyone I've ever known.

PALE (*looks around*): Where's my . . .

ANNA: I drank it.

PALE: I'm gonna have to have another. (*She gets up.*) I'll get it.

ANNA: That's okay, you got the last one.

PALE: I'll send you a fuckin' case.

ANNA: It's fine, Jimmy. Just — what? Cool it, okay?

PALE: Jimmy you're callin' me. I like that. Nobody calls me that. Fuckin' place, man. Fuckin' haunted.

ANNA: Yes, it is. So's the studio. So's the streets around the neighborhood. (*Sitting on the sofa.*) So's the whole island of Manhattan.

PALE: So's Jersey. (*Pause.*) I'm gonna be sick here.

ANNA: The brandy doesn't help.

PALE: No, it's good for it. You don't do nothing to your hair? It's just like that?

ANNA: It costs a fortune. (*Pause.*) Oh, God.

PALE: You're done in, huh?

ANNA: No, I'm up. I'm an early riser, anyway. Not usually this early, but . . . No, I'm just . . . blue. Remember that? When people used to feel blue? I'm feeling blue.

PALE: Me too. (*Not looking at her breasts or touching them.*) You almost got no tits at all, you know?

ANNA: I know. Thanks.

PALE: No, that's beautiful. That's very provocative. Guy wants to look, see just how much there is. Tits are very deceptive things. (*Pause. Rubs his chin on the top of her head. Sings very softly, very slowly.*) "I'd . . . rather . . . be . . . blue . . . thinking of you . . ."

ANNA: You're burning up.

PALE (*sings, same*): "Oh . . . oh . . . oh . . . I'm on fire . . ." That's just the toaster oven. Always like that.

ANNA: You're not sick, you don't have a fever?

PALE: Normal temperature about a hundred and ten. Aww, man, I'm so fucked. My gut aches, my balls are hurtin', they're gonna take stitches on my heart; I'm fuckin' *grievin'* here and you're givin' me a hard-on. Come on, don't go away from me — everybody's fuckin' flyin' South, man . . . like I was the . . . aw shit, man. I'm gonna cry all over your hair. (*He does cry in her hair.*)

ANNA: What, Jimmy?

PALE: Come on, don't look at me.

ANNA: Jimmy, stop. Enough already, don't; you're gonna hurt yourself or something.

PALE: Good. Good. Don't look.

ANNA: I was very angry at the funeral. I thought I hadn't had a chance to have a moment, but Larry and I went back to the cemetery a couple of days after and we cried the whole day; but don't break your heart. You know? (*Kisses him lightly.*) Jimmy?

PALE: You went back?

ANNA: Larry and I.

PALE: Come on. You make me upset.

ANNA: You're making yourself upset.

PALE: No, the other way. I'm getting all riled here. I got no place for it. I got like a traffic jam here. (*Kisses her lightly.*) You okay?

ANNA: I'm fine.

PALE: I'm like fallin' outta the airplane here. (*Pause.*) You always smell like that?

ANNA: Shampoo.

PALE: My shampoo don't make me smell like that. Let's just start up the engines real slow here . . . maybe go halfway to the city and stop for somethin' to eat . . . You talk to me, okay? . . . You're gonna find out there's times . . . I'm a real good listener.

(*Music up, fade to black. After a few moments the lights come back up. Very early morning. Sunny. Larry enters from outside.*)

LARRY (*entering yelling*): He might have told me I was going to have to load his car by myself. I adore manual labor at 6:50 A.M. God, I thought he was going to help.

ANNA (*coming in from the bedroom*): He's been on the phone.

LARRY: Where the hell is he?

ANNA: Taking a shower.

LARRY: Any great tone poems come out of there yet?

ANNA: Not a peep.

LARRY: He's probably going to be another big bruiser with a bad back.

ANNA: No, I don't think so.

LARRY: One is not allowed to be smug just because one got laid. (*At Pale's jacket and pants, holds up a pistol.*) Please note.

ANNA: Don't touch it. I saw.

ACT ONE   LARRY: Robbie's address book just happened to fall out of one of the boxes and into my pocket. "Pale: 17 Oak Street, Montclair, New Jersey." Phone number at home, phone number at work.

ANNA: What would you say to an omelette?

LARRY: Uh . . . *Bonjour, omelette.* I'm exhausted, of course; my eyes did not close. I had one hand on the phone and the other with a finger poised to dial 911. Actually, that's not true. With all the music coming out of this room, I abused myself terribly. (*Pale enters, fresh shirt and tie, puts on pants, steps into shoes while dialing.*) You always carry a spare shirt in the car?

PALE: What? Yeah. (*On phone.*) Joe. Pale. Fifteen minutes. You just be damn sure you hold them. Just don't fuck me. Fifteen minutes. You got what? No, no, I can't use it. No. I'm leavin' now. (*Hangs up.*) More fuckin' trouble than my old lady.

LARRY: Than your old what?

PALE: What, you think I'm weird or something? Sure I got an old lady. Two kids, perfect family. (*Hands Anna his opened wallet.*) Boy and girl.

ANNA: Won't she be curious where you spent the night?

PALE: Naw, she trusts me; they're down in Coral Gables. She knows I'm cool. I never cheated on her once.

ANNA (*handing him the wallet*): They're beautiful.

PALE: You get that crap in the car?

LARRY: All loaded.

ANNA: You want coffee? Maybe an omelette?

PALE: Got no time. Don't use food in the morning. I can't drink coffee, burn your guts out. You got my keys? Cigarette lighter?

LARRY: On the counter. That's a great-looking car.

PALE: Fuckin' pain in the ass, too. Okay, people, I'm out of here. (*He exits.*)

LARRY: He's one of those people you know right away isn't going to say, "Have a nice day." So, is he utterly fantastic in the sack?

ANNA: Uh . . . quite interesting.

LARRY (*sings*): "I'd rather be blue, thinking of you — "

ANNA (*glaring at him*): How much did you hear?

LARRY: I'm trying to remember . . . No, I don't think I missed anything.

ANNA: Sorry. Very bad form. It was all very — oh, what the hell. The bird-with-the-broken-wing syndrome.

LARRY: You bring the poor little bird home, doll. You make a splint for its poor little wing. You feed the little bugger chicken soup if you must. You don't, however, fuck it. (*He has been dialing the phone.*) Hello. Is Pale there?

ANNA: You're not.

LARRY: Eleven? What exactly is his position there? Manager. And this is the . . . Da Signate Ristorante.

ANNA: Oh no. Hang up.

LARRY: Thank you. No, no message, he hates them. *Grazie.* (*Hangs up.*) Manages a restaurant. I love it.

ANNA: Oh, God. He's a relief pitcher. Yeah, of sangría.

LARRY: I've been there; it's celebrity city, two stars or something.

ANNA: Well, he said he worked hard.

LARRY: They do, too. Tom managed a restaurant in the Village for two years. He had to be down at the Fulton Fish Market at six in the morning or it was gone.

ANNA: That's probably who he was calling.

LARRY: "This is Pale, hold my fish." I love it. With a gun, though?

ANNA: If he makes the deposits at night.

LARRY: I think you're very wise. One of those people it'd be impossible to get rid of any other way. (*Phone rings.*) That's Burton to tell you how many laps he made around the reservoir.

ANNA: Seven o'clock on the nose.

LARRY (*on the phone*): Hello, beautiful. I get up early sometimes. Part of my charming unpredictability. Actually, I was up with Anna all night. No, nothing serious. Said she felt like she had a terrible weight on her stomach . . . (*Looking at her.*) I just hope she doesn't come down with something. I'm sure she'd love to, only nothing too physical, she looks exhausted.

ANNA (*taking the phone*): Hi, Burt. No, I'm fine, never better.

LARRY: Rub it in.

ANNA: What's to see? Yeah, that'd be fun. Or the other one. No, I don't think so. I've just got no interest in it. The what? (*Covers the phone.*) Would you shut up? That's good, then. Okay, sevenish. (*Hangs up the phone.*)

LARRY: (*sings*): "I'd rather be blue, thinking of you, I'd rather be blue over you. Than be happy with somebody called Burton."

LARRY: Slut.

ANNA: Oh, God. He wants to go out tonight.

LARRY: And of course, out of abject guilt, you said sure. You could always have said, I couldn't possibly, I was fucked blind last night.

ANNA: Go to hell.

LARRY: Please note how contact with your restaurateur has eroded our speech. We're just at the age where we pick that sort of thing up.

ANNA: I'm going back to bed.

LARRY: You'll miss class and you've got work to do.

ANNA: I'll take a shower and think about it.

LARRY: What would you say to a waffle?

ANNA: Get lost, waffle. Get thee behind me. Which is exactly where it would go. (*She starts for the bathroom. Sings.*) "I'd rather be blue, thinking of you, I'd rather be blue over you . . . than be . . ." (*She stops with a shock, turns to look at Larry. Pause. Larry stands looking at her. He sings softly.*)

LARRY: "Oh . . . oh . . . oh . . . I'm on fire . . ."

(*Music up, the lights fade.*)

ACT TWO

(*Late New Year's Eve, 2 A.M. Anna is in a gown, Burton in a tux. Anna has a script in her hands. She finishes reading it.*)

BURTON: That's as far as I've got.

ANNA: Oh, I like it. It's so sad. God.

BURTON: Sad? I thought they were having fun.

ANNA: Oh no, sure. But underneath all that, God, they're so lonely.

BURTON: Yeah, I know, but I don't want to think about that part or I won't be able to do it. Aw, to hell with it, anyway. I want something larger than life. Those people are smaller than life.

ANNA: They're very real, and I think it's exciting. And you have your space. Only it's distance between people rather than distance between places.

BURTON: No, give me kinky or quirky or sadistic — Where's the pain? Where's the joy? Where's the ebullience?

ANNA: It's there. Everything doesn't have to be epic.

BURTON: Yes! Yes! Not in treatment, but at least in feeling. Reach! Reach for something! God! Reach for the sun! Go for it! . . .

ANNA: I don't think I've been sober on New Year's Eve before in my life.

BURTON: Not necessarily recommended.

ANNA: You were doing all that coke.

BURTON: Not the same thing.

ANNA: I've missed you. How was your family?

BURTON: Rich, self-satisfied, alcoholically comatose, boring. (*Pause.*) Before we get off the subject, you really did like it?

ANNA: I really do. That other character is Larry, isn't he?

BURTON: Larry? No. Well, you know. Some him, some — no more than ninety percent. How's it been going here?

ANNA: I'm working like a dog. I almost feel as if I've finally burst my chrysalis after thirty years of incubation. That's the wrong word.

BURTON: Metamorphosis.

ANNA: The day after you left, Fred asked me to do a piece with a company he's putting together.

BURTON: All right!

ANNA: It's kinda exciting, really. Guaranteed coverage, maybe a little more — what? — political than I'd like — three new woman choreographers. Twelve minutes or so each. The first half of a new program he's working on. God. He pays the rent, the advertising. Overall theme, very loosely, is love. Mother love, which God knows I know nothing about — yet. And then something else, and he wants me to do the *pas de deux*. Two couples, not one.

BURTON: *Pas de quatre.*

ANNA: He's got four great kids for me to work with. I try things out here and work with them at Fred's studio. I think it'd be fair to say it's not going well. I'm beginning to think that as an artist I have absolutely no life experience to draw from. Or else I'm just too chicken to let anyone see what I really am.

BURTON: What you need is to do a little research on this love stuff. Tonight.

ANNA: Well, if I'm going to pretend to know anything about it . . .

BURTON: It might get a little X-rated.

ANNA: A *pas de quatre* for Fred, that's absolutely *de rigueur.*

BURTON: What's your schedule tomorrow?

ANNA: Totally clean slate.

BURTON: Me too.

ANNA: Actually, I planned ahead. You've been ambushed. (*She takes a bottle of champagne from the fridge.*) I even bought a new flute. Have you ever seen anything that beautiful in your life? Listen. (*She rings the glass lightly.*) Do you believe that?

BURTON: What's the difference between a flute and a glass?

ANNA: About fifty bucks. Would it be unbearably provocative if I slipped into something less formal?

BURTON: Unbearably, without doubt. Do it.

ANNA: Undo.

BURTON: Whatever happened to zippers? There's nothing so beautiful as the sound of a long zipper down a woman's back.

ANNA: I'll remember.

BURTON: Also, I need the practice. It's been a while, you know.

ANNA: You have to give the story another week — I want to see where it goes. (*Exits into the bedroom.*)

BURTON (*raising his voice slightly*): No, you were saying you were chicken; I think that's what's happening. I don't want to know. I need to get out of the city or something — do something — shake things up. You sure you don't want to give up this loft and move in my place?

ANNA (*offstage*): Never. You want to live with me, you move in here.

BURTON: Maybe I should. Have kids or something.

ANNA (*offstage*): At least then I could do the piece on mother love. That's something I haven't thought about much. Or every time I did, I pushed it out of my mind. But now — I don't know. I think my body chemistry is changing, or maybe I just have time to think of things like that now. I can feel a kind of anxiety or panic creeping up on me. The sound of the biological clock or something. Which is probably only another way of avoiding work. Any excuse.

BURTON: I know the feeling. Every time I start to work on the love story I swiftly segue into droid-busting on Barsoom. I've been working on a kind of extension of the *Far Voyager* story —

ANNA: Do the other one.

BURTON: The space stuff's more fun. The other one isn't fun. I'm talking about myself again! I don't believe it. It's unconscious. (*Anna comes back into the room in full dressing gown.*) That's gorgeous. (*He holds her a moment. They sit and start to toast. There is a noise at the door.*) What the hell?

ANNA: What time is it? It's Harrison across the hall, or maybe Larry coming home.

BURTON: Oh, God, let it be Harrison across the hall. I thought Larry wasn't due back till tomorrow.

ANNA: I think tonight.

BURTON: Well, fuck.

ANNA: Well, later at least.

LARRY (*enters carrying three huge suitcases. He drops them and staggers across the room, collapsing on the sofa.*): I'm dying. Oh, God. Ask me where I was when we rang in the New Year. My arms are dead, they're falling off.

ANNA: Where were you when we rang in the New Year?

LARRY: Circling about ten thousand feet over Queens. And we had been for forty-five minutes. And we continued to for another hour. I was praying we would crash and burn. There was not a happy person on the plane. Everyone was going to a party. Nobody made it. Midnight came and went, nobody said a word. We just glared at each other. The last hour there wasn't a stewardess in sight, they were all up in the cabin with the pilot; we landed, one of them was visibly drunk.

BURTON: I thought you like to travel; you liked meeting people.

LARRY: The man next to me, I strongly suspect, was either Jerry Falwell himself or a member of the Supreme Court. Total Nazi. After half an hour of theories on the Sanctity of the Home and the American Family as the Last Bastion of Christian Liberty (whatever the hell that is) I said, "Well, being a cocksucker, of course, I disagree with everything you've said." I was so angry I didn't even get off on it. That's what going home does to me — I lose my protective sense of humor. My arms are falling off.

ANNA: Happy New Year.

LARRY: Fuck you both. What are you doing here? Why aren't you out partying?

ANNA: It's two-thirty, we're back.

LARRY: From where?

ANNA: We went to a party. I liked it, didn't you?

BURTON: Yeah, it was fun. Up in SoHo.

ANNA: A bunch of the new young geniuses and starlets. I didn't know many of them. Burt can tell you.

BURTON: Nice group. So how's beautiful Detroit?

LARRY: Burton, "beautiful Detroit" is an oxymoron. Detroit is the South's revenge. You don't want to start your New Year with the story of the faggot's Christmas in Wales, believe me. (*He lights a cigarette.*)

ANNA: When did you start smoking?

LARRY: How long have I been gone?

ANNA: You've got a dozen invitations to parties; hop in a cab, have some fun. They'll go all night.

LARRY: Have you ever been to a gay New Year's Eve party? The suicide rate is higher than all of Scandinavia combined. My arms are falling off, my head hurts, I'm exhausted. For the first time in my life I have sympathy for Olga in *Three Sisters*.

ANNA: Go out. Meet someone.

LARRY: Anna, an Olympic gym team performing naked would not turn me on. The defensive front line of the Pittsburgh Steelers could rape me on the floor of the locker room, I'd bring them up on charges. If you're trying to ditch me, forget it. Go to Burton's. Oh, God. I have six nephews I'd never met before. And hope not to see again until they're sixteen. And two nieces. Both of my sisters *and* my brother's wife have turned into baby machines. What is happening to women? Ten years ago they were exciting entities; they're all turning into cows.

BURTON: We were just talking about that.

ANNA: I get more of an image of a brood sow. Flat out in the mud, with about ten piglets squealing around you, trying to nurse. Have you ever seen that? Their eyes rolled back in their heads? Lying back in the sun, in some other world.

LARRY: I hope you don't think you're making it attractive. They all wrote down their kids' birthdays so I'd be sure to send something. There's a doomsday factor in our genes somewhere. Through the entire history of the species it's been the same story — the wrong people reproduce. (*Goes to Anna.*) Happy New Year. (*Kisses her lightly on the lips.*)

ANNA: Happy New Year.

LARRY (*goes to Burton, kisses him lightly on the lips*): Happy New Year.

BURTON: Happy New Year, Uncle Larry.

LARRY: Burton — you're a black belt in karate —

BURTON: Brown.

LARRY: You teach judo at the "Y" —

BURTON: Aikido.

LARRY: I don't care. One more crack and I'll rip your eyes out. Oh, God, when did you last see a grown man cry?

ANNA: Un . . . actually — when was it? The day after you left. I ran into an old friend of yours.

LARRY: I have no old friends. If I do have, I won't after this trip, because I'm going to be unbearable for a month.

ANNA: I think he was actually closer to Robbie than to you.

LARRY: Oh, please. I loved him dearly, but all Robbie's friends talked about dance with that fanatical glazed look across their eyes that always — Closer, how? You don't mean he was crying in his V.S.O. cognac . . . ?

ANNA: I think that's the only thing he drinks.

ACT TWO

LARRY: And this was where . . . ?

ANNA: Midtown. Midmorning. One drink. And I fled.

LARRY: Drinking in the midmorning. You *have* gone downhill without me.

ANNA: I had coffee.

BURTON: Who was this?

LARRY: Just a Pale page from my checkered past. I don't think he came here more than once. Or I should say, I don't think he's *been* here more than once. Please note, my last cigarette. (*He stubs out the cigarette and puts the pack away.*) Did Anna tell you she's working on a dance for Fred?

BURTON: Yeah, that's great.

ANNA: Oh sure — scares the hell out of me.

LARRY: I love it. I come home, she's dancing up a storm.

ANNA: I was flying around here the other day. I flop down, I think that's great; then I thought, I wonder if I could get arrested for that?

LARRY: In some states . . .

ANNA: I think it's all getting a little too personal.

BURTON: Good, it's supposed to be — Make it as personal as you can. Believe me, you can't imagine a feeling everyone hasn't had. Make it personal, tell the truth, and then write "Burn this" on it.

ANNA: Burton, at least, has made a giant leap into the unknown.

BURTON: Yeah, I've taken up skydiving.

ANNA: He's started working on something real.

BURTON: Naw, that's nothing, goes nowhere.

ANNA: It takes place in the city, and is some kind of love story with real people, so, of course, he doesn't trust it.

BURTON: I don't even know why I wrote it down. I was bored.

ANNA: I think it's very hot.

LARRY: So am I gonna hear it?

ANNA: Let him read it — it's only twenty pages.

BURTON: No, it's nothing. Come on.

LARRY: This is the Northern thing?

BURTON: The what? Oh no . . . I tried to do something on the Northern thing; it turned into this city thing.

ANNA: We were about to toast the New Year.

LARRY: Where did those come from? They're gorgeous.

ANNA: Baccarat. They were in the window.

LARRY: How many?

ANNA: Four. It did in my life savings.

LARRY: I'm in love. I'm going to sleep with them.

ANNA: Happy New Year. (*They all toast, say "Happy New Year," and drink.*) Oh, Lord. That makes you understand what they mean by champagne.

LARRY: Home again, home again . . .

ANNA: Jiggity-jig.

(*A distant bell sounds.*)

BURTON: Where the hell is there a bell at this hour?

LARRY: I didn't imagine there was such a thing as a real bell anymore. I thought they were all recordings blasted over loudspeakers.

BURTON: The first year I was in New York I had a job as a messenger. I took a package to this poet's loft —

ANNA: Messenger?

BURTON: I must have been eighteen.

ANNA: God knows you didn't need the money.

BURTON: I know, but I decided I should experience work — I forget why. Anyway, this poet was over on Fourth Avenue, across from the church there. And we got to talking. He asked me what I did and I said I was a writer; turned out he was a poet and I'd read some of his stuff, and he was impressed and I was impressed, and we had a drink and a joint and sat around — this is not a job that I kept for very long.

LARRY: I can see that. Actually, I imagine he was trying to think of a way to get in your pants.

BURTON: Oh, for godsake — why is it always that? Why does it always have to be that with you?

LARRY: Burton, you're talking about a poet. Why does it always have to be that? Ask your priest; I didn't invent people. It's just always that. Anyway.

BURTON: So anyway — the church bells started ringing. We were sitting in the open window, on a big window seat, right across the street from the bell tower, and he said, Poe, Edgar Allan Poe used to live in that apartment. And those bells were the bells, bells, bells, bells, bells, bells, bells.

ANNA: Oh, God. The tintinnabulation. Where?

BURTON: Fourth Avenue and about East Tenth. He got the apartment because of them.

ANNA: Of course he did.

BURTON: Actually, Larry — this'll give you a thrill — he *was* gay and I knew it, and it never crossed my mind he was anything but sincere. I really don't think he was trying to make me.

LARRY: It's possible, Burton. In a different world. But who knows what world poets live in, so —

BURTON: You want to know something? One time — you should know this — when I was twenty — two years later — I'd been here two years and a half. I was up around Columbia. I decided to walk down to the Village. I had to piss so bad — about Fifteenth Street and Eighth or Ninth Avenue — middle of the — say 1 A.M. — and I mean, it's cold. It'd started to snow, so everything was white. I pissed up alongside a doorway, I was feeling very high — on the night, nothing chemical — and this guy sidles up to me from nowhere — there wasn't another person on the street — and he says, "You live around here?" Or some dumb thing.

LARRY: Have you got a match? Yeah.

BURTON: And I think, This is something I should know about. I'm a writer, I'm supposed to know about these things.

LARRY: Always a dangerous supposition.

BURTON: I just shook it off and turned around and leaned against the wall and watched it snow while he went down on me. I came, and he put it away and said thank you, if you believe it, and I said, Have a good life, and went on walking down to the Village. And I never thought about it again. So I'm not completely unversed in your world.

LARRY: That is gorgeous. With the snow falling. God. I mean it's not *Wuthering Heights,* but . . . God.

BURTON: It was very nice, and I never thought about it. And it didn't mean anything, but I've never been sorry it happened or any of that crap.

LARRY: Lord, the innocence and freedom of yesterday.

ANNA: I was just thinking that.

LARRY: Actually, I don't like those ships-that-pass-in-the-night scenes. That doesn't mean that the image of you getting blown in the snow won't haunt me till I die. I think I'll probably be a happier — Did you have your shirt up?

BURTON: I had on a jacket, a scarf, a hat, gloves, galoshes. I had my fly unzipped.

LARRY: You don't care if, in my mind, I sort of push your shirt up to above your navel, and let your pants fall to about midthigh, do you?

BURTON: Be my guest. Larry, we're getting ready to go to bed here — I'm just trying to burn a little clock.

(*There is a noise outside the door.*)

LARRY: What the hell's that?

ANNA: That's got to be Harrison.

LARRY: Happy New Year, Harrison. You old queen.

ANNA: Oh, he is not.

LARRY: He just doesn't know it. He's going to wake up on his fortieth birthday in a dress.

BURTON: Did he knock?

LARRY: No way, shy as a nun. Has anyone ever really seen a shy nun? (*He opens the door, Pale falls in.*) Oh shit. Scare me to death. Are you hurt?

BURTON: What the hell's happening?

LARRY: It's Pale. Not in the best shape. Are you okay?

(*Pale staggers, half on his hands and knees, to the bathroom.*)

ANNA: Absolutely not, Jimmy. No way. I'm sorry. Jimmy! Damnit all! Who the hell does he think he is?

BURTON: Who the hell *is* he?

ANNA: Oh, God. He's a maître d' or . . .

LARRY: Manager.

ANNA: Manager.

LARRY: Of a restaurant.

ANNA: The Il Santalino or something.

LARRY: Da Signate.

ANNA: Over in Short Hills.

LARRY: Montclair.

ANNA (*beat*): New Jersey.

LARRY: If after five attempts, you think you get any points for New Jersey . . .

BURTON: He just walks in? What the fuck's he doing here? He live in the building?

LARRY: He's Robbie's brother.

BURTON: Oh shit.

LARRY: Yeah, he's pretty crushed.

ANNA: Well, he can be crushed somewhere else. Really. He can't just bulldoze his way in here every time he hangs one on. Is he being sick?

LARRY: I would say affirmative, except I try not to talk like that.

ANNA: Oh, God.

BURTON: It's a little late, gang, for a neighborly visit, you know?

LARRY (*at the bathroom door*): Jimmy — are you — yes, he's being sick. Jesus. Doll, are you all right?

PALE (*offstage*): What the fuck do you know, fruit?

LARRY: I beg your pardon?

PALE: What the fuck do you know?

LARRY: What do I know?

PALE: What the fuck do you fuckin' know? Fruit?

LARRY: Jimmy, that's one of those questions one never knows whether to answer with hubris or humility. Are you okay?

PALE: Get the fuck out! (*Slams the door in Larry's face.*)

LARRY: In layout design I could whip his ass. I think this would be a good time to relax and finish the champagne.

BURTON: You want him out of here?

ANNA: Oh, for God's sake. (*Goes to bathroom door.*) Jimmy. Jimmy. Are you — well, obviously he's not all right. Jimmy, what's up? (*Pale opens the door, his face wet, mopping it with a towel, hangs on to her, kisses her.*) Come on. What the hell do you think this is?

BURTON: Hey, fella. What the hell do you think you're doing?

PALE (*drops the towel, drops to one knee, holding the wall to steady himself*): Who the fuck are you?

ANNA: Hey, Burt, come on. Burton, this is Jimmy, Robbie's brother — Jimmy, this is my friend Burton. I feel like an idiot. Larry, shut up. Jimmy, we're not entertaining tonight, so I don't think you can stay.

LARRY: Where the fuck did you come from? What the fuck do you want? It's me, isn't it? You've always wanted to fuck me. You want to have your filthy fuckin' way with me in the hot desert sun . . . Ravage me like I've never been ravaged before.

PALE: You another dancer?

ANNA: Burton's a writer.

PALE: Same thing.

BURTON: Do you need something? Or is this just a friendly visit? Jimmy?

PALE: "Jimmy," shit. Nobody calls me Jimmy. They call me Pale.

BURTON: What?

ANNA: Pale.

BURTON: As in bucket?

ANNA: As in a bucket of brandy. Pale, it's 3 A.M. I know you don't get off work till late, but we're about to call it a . . . year here, you know?

BURTON: You need help getting down to the street or something?

(*Pale gets up, manages to stumble to a chair, almost turning over a table. Sits.*)

ANNA: Oh, you are in great shape. You look like a bum.

BURTON: What do you mean? He is a bum.

ANNA: He's not a bum.

BURTON: Who the hell is he?

ANNA: I told you, Burton, damnit. He's the maître d' —

LARRY: God! Manager! Of the Da Signate Ristorante in Montclair, New Jersey. Jesus.

ANNA: He has a very demanding job.

BURTON: Don't we all. You need help, buddy? 'Cause you're not staying.

PALE: What the fuck do you know?

ANNA: Very little, I'm sure. About anything.

BURTON: I know you're leaving. You call tomorrow. Late, okay?

PALE: About Robbie? Huh? Fuckin' zip.

ANNA: Pale, it's been two months. More. I'm sorry, but you can't grieve forever. Not even you. *I* can't. He gets drunk, he thinks about him. Guilt and that number.

BURTON: He's gonna pass out. Unless you intend to put him up here, I'm gonna help him out into the street. I seem to remember we were having a party.

PALE: You're not "right," are you. You're a little funny.

BURTON: We'll see if you laugh.

PALE (*to Anna*): Tell your friend good night. Let's go.

BURTON: You're the one who's leaving, buddy.

(*Pale lunges at Burton. Burton, with a deft move, drives Pale straight into a wall headfirst. Pale sits on the floor, his back against the wall, staring at them.*)

ANNA: Burt. Pale. Oh, for godsake.

BURTON: What the hell does he think he's doing?

ANNA (*to a blinking Pale*): I should have mentioned, Burt teaches aikido at the "Y."

BURTON: Six years, that's the first time I ever used it.

LARRY (*lighting a cigarette*): Please note, I'm smoking again. Also, that's not the smartest thing to do. He carries a gun.

BURTON: A what? And you let him in here?

LARRY: He fell in.

ANNA: He takes the deposits to the bank at night. I asked; we were right. I don't believe it.

PALE: What fuckin' accident? No fuckin' accident.

LARRY: What's that?

PALE: Robbie and Dominic out in the fuckin' bay — I said there wasn't any fuckin' accident.

ANNA: Not again, Jimmy — I think we've done that number.

PALE: What are you wearin' that thing?

LARRY: What about the accident, Pale?

PALE (*to Anna*): You ain't cold, that thing?

ANNA: No. (*To Larry.*) It's nothing, believe me.

BURTON: Then I'm sorry, fella, we can't serve you here . . . after hours, buddy.

PALE (*looks at Burton*): Who's Bruce Lee? You're cute. You think I can't break a candy-ass like him?

ANNA: When I saw him before, he was saying the mob did it. They have some interest in the restaurant.

LARRY: Oh, please.

BURTON: When was this you saw him?

LARRY: There were definitely no mobster types when I went to the restaurant.

PALE: What assholes. I thought you people was supposed to be *with* it, you're supposed to "swing," you "know what's coming down." Show me a restaurant ain't connected, I'll show you an establishment don't serve food and drink, okay? I can't stay here (*Getting up.*) with you assholes. I got me a reputation to uphold here. You're too stupid for me to stay with.

BURTON: If you know something —

LARRY: Or think you do, you should —

(*As Burton approaches Pale, Pale decks him; tripping him, kicking him in the groin and again in the back as soon as he hits the floor.*)

ANNA: Pale — damnit. Burton, are you all right?

PALE: Nobody does that shit, nobody pulls that shit.

(*Burton is up, winded and shocked; they square off, circle.*)

BURTON: All right, fella, I was being nice; I'm gonna take you apart. I'm gonna enjoy this.

ANNA: Burton, stop it, goddamnit. Both of you. Come on.

PALE: Come on, come on — (*He makes a lunge and Burton sends him flying.*)

ANNA: Burton! Goddamnit, for Christ's sake, this is my apartment! What the fuck do you two think you're doing? (*She steps between them. Burton shoves her aside very roughly; she falls. He clips Pale — Pale sprawls.*) Burton. Goddamnit.

BURTON: No way, buddy, nobody blind-sides me, no way.

ANNA: Okay, leave, then, go on. Burton, damnit, I said leave. (*Pushes him away — Pale stands off.*)

BURTON: I'm not leaving you here with him.

ANNA: Yes, you are, and now.

BURTON: No way am I leaving you alone with this fucker. (*Pale has sat down.*) Go on, buddy, out.

ANNA: You first, just go — Really, I'm not going to have it. That's not the way I live.

BURTON: We were going to have a party — that son of a bitch comes over; no way.

ANNA: Leave, go on. I'll see you tomorrow. I can't have it.

BURTON: Anna, what kind of a man is going to leave you alone with him? Huh? What's he going to do?

ANNA: Nothing.

BURTON: You don't know him.

ANNA: I know him, he's fine. I can't kick him out, so I'm asking you to leave.

BURTON: I'll kick him out, no problem.

ANNA: Go. Damnit. You're the one I don't know right now.

PALE: You fuckin' him, too?

(*A stunned pause.*)

BURTON: What'd you say?

ANNA: Would you please not do this crap?

PALE: Good night.

ANNA: Burton, really, good night.

BURTON: What's he talking about? You're . . .

ANNA: It's utterly beside the point. Good night. Tomorrow.

BURTON: I'm gonna have to rethink everything here. I mean our whole relationship here. This isn't it. This is nothing I want any part of.

ANNA: Good night.

(*Burton gets his coat, goes to the door without looking back, and leaves.*)

PALE: Good night, Bruce.

LARRY: Did you hurt your arm?

ANNA: Oh — no more than I've been hurt every week since I was eight. Pale, you're going to have to — (*Pale puts his arms around her, his hands under her robe.*) Stop it, damnit. I'm not your whore, for you to come and have every time you get drunk. Stop it. (*Pulls away.*) Goddamnit, both of you with that macho bullshit. Okay, now you. Get it together and get it out of here. Up. Go on.

LARRY: Pale? It's not as butch as Burton, but if you don't leave, I'll hit you over the head with a skillet. I'm not joking.

ANNA: I should have had you and Burton carry him out. I didn't want them breaking each other's faces out on the street. *Gunfight at the O.K. Corral.*

PALE: I ain't got it.

LARRY: You ain't got — don't have what?

PALE: The gun. I lost the fucker.

ANNA: When?

PALE: Last week. It's gone. I ain't got it.

ANNA: Where? Well, that's a stupid . . . Pale, don't stretch out and — Pale? Oh, God . . .

LARRY: You don't mean it.

ANNA: Sleeping like a baby.

LARRY: Oh, great. He could have broken Burton's back or something — Oh, Lordy. (*He pours them each a glass of champagne.*) Is it too cold to drag him out?

ANNA: With the antifreeze he's got in him, he should be good for a month. If he'd had the grace to pass out a minute sooner, Burton'd still be here. I had almost decided if he proposed again I was going to accept him.

LARRY: That's why you dressed like Lucia di Lammermoor. (*He hands her her glass.*)

ANNA: Thank you. Happy New Year.

LARRY: A real auspicious beginning.

ANNA: I loathe violence. What is that? I could live my life very well, thank you, without ever seeing another straight man.

LARRY: Me too. Don't hold me to that. What was that about the accident?

ANNA: Oh, when I saw him last week, he was saying he and his dad and their cronies got to drinking, someone says I saw your fruit brother on the TV with his boyfriend. All the usual fag-baiting braggadocio. Someone ought to off the fucker, embarrassment to the family, that crap. And a couple of nights later, Robbie's dead, so he had no way of knowing if —

LARRY: Oh, give me a break.

ANNA: That's what I said. Massive guilt trip.

LARRY: Good. Serves you right, Pale. I have to carry those fuckin' bags down to my room.

ANNA: Get them tomorrow.

LARRY: Never put off till tomorrow what might kill you today. Also, my toothbrush is in there somewhere. God, how it's missed its own glass. Are you going to bed? (*He gets his bags.*)

ANNA: Yes. Pale? Oh damn.

LARRY: Get a blanket down from Robbie's room, I guess.

ANNA: He doesn't like to be covered.

LARRY: That's right. He'll be sorry.

(*Anna turns off the lights. The living room is dark.*)

(*They are both in their rooms.*)

LARRY: My own bed, my own sheets, my own pillow . . .

ANNA: Should I set an alarm or something for him, so he doesn't miss work again?

LARRY: They're probably closed tomorrow.

ANNA: Then to hell with it. (*She goes into the bathroom, turns on the light.*) Good night, love.

ACT TWO LARRY (*offstage*): 'Night, doll. (*Sings.*)
"At night I wake up with the sheets soaking wet
There's a freight train runnin'
Through the middle of my head . . .
And you, you cool my desire.
Oh . . . oh . . . oh . . . I'm on fire . . . "

(*Pale sits up on the sofa. He gets up, looks around, moves to the window, opens it, and steps out into the fire escape. He walks the distance of the windows, lights a cigarette. Anna comes from the bathroom to her room. After a moment Pale flicks his cigarette out into the night. He comes back into the apartment and walks to her room. The lights fade, music up.*)

(*Larry is in the kitchen. Coffee has been made. Pale, dressed in one of Anna's robes, comes from her room.*)

LARRY: It does nothing for you. I couldn't wait to sleep the clock around in my own bed. I woke up at eight.
PALE (*sleepy*): What time is it?
LARRY: About nine. You off today?
PALE: Yeah.
LARRY: Sleep late, for godsake; once, anyway.
PALE: Can't do it.
LARRY: I made coffee, you don't use it. What about tea?
PALE: Whatta you got?
LARRY (*looking through cabinet*): We got: English Breakfast, Irish Breakfast, something that tastes exactly like I imagine burned rubber tires would taste . . .
PALE: Lapsang Souchong.
LARRY: You want it, you'd be doing us a favor.
PALE: You got no plain orange pekoe tea?
LARRY: — Jasmine, Sleepytime, Red Zinger, Chamomile. And plain Red Rose orange pekoe tea. (*Puts the bag in a mug.*) The water's still hot. I thought your familiarity with the finer foods of life —
PALE: Stop. Whattaya doin'? You gonna make a pot a tea, you gonna make one cup? It's not even economical.
LARRY: We actually have a teapot, but I've never seen it used for anything except to put flowers in. (*Takes it out of cabinet.*)
PALE: Get out, go on, you're useless. I thought you clowns were supposed to be worthwhile in the kitchen at least.
LARRY: I never really claimed any expertise in the area. You cook?
PALE (*turns up heat under water until it boils*): I'd better cook. Cook ain't in, I'm it. What? Six — eight times cook don't show, snowstorm, somethin', I gotta cook. I'm okay. (*Pours water in pot, empties it.*)

LARRY: There? Professionally? I've been to your place; twice, actually. It's very good.

PALE: Yeah, I told the cook people couldn't tell the difference. He didn't like it. Next time it snowed he slept inna kitchen. *Gourmet* magazine, they print recipes from like these famous restaurants; I take in the magazine, twice now. I say, So how come you left out the paprika in one; in the other, how come there ain't no lemon juice and no nutmeg? And the butter ain't clarified? He says, Okay, they'll make it at home, then they'll come here and think, Son of a bitch, that man's just a better cook than I am. (*He puts the water and three tea bags in the pot, looks for a tea towel, covers the pot with it.*)

LARRY: Whatever you're doing, I'm impressed.

PALE: What? Twenty years the restaurant business, I can't make a pot of tea, I'm in trouble.

LARRY: You know, it's very unlikely anyone did your family the favor of arranging Robbie's accident.

PALE: I don't wanta talk about it, okay?

LARRY: This would be the situation where the little boy says, "I hate Daddy and I want him to die," and two days later Daddy goes off to the hospital and doesn't come home again. And the little boy thinks it's his fault.

PALE: Yeah? That mighta been the night the angels decided to listen to the little boy.

LARRY: I don't think so.

PALE: That's the way Catholics think; we're fucked.

LARRY: It all sounds very unlikely.

PALE: Yeah, one side of my brain knows that — the other side drinks.

LARRY: Anna said she might be wrong, but she doesn't remember your wife at Robbie's funeral.

PALE: She wasn't there.

LARRY: So she's still in Coral Gables?

PALE: You remember everything everybody says, huh?

LARRY: It's a gift.

PALE: She couldn't take the heat, so she took the kids. Who the fuck cares? I'm home three hours a night, work seventeen hours some days; more'n sixty-five hours a week. I get off midnight, I gotta unwind; I get home at two, I'm up at five. Who can live with that?

LARRY: How can you?

PALE: I'm used to it.

LARRY: You'll burn yourself out, too. She should have taken a job as a waitress at the restaurant.

PALE: You got a real sense of humor there, that could be valuable to you. Her work? Not while I'm makin' nine hundred bucks a week. Six of it off the books, more like nineteen hundred.

LARRY: Jesus.

PALE: I bust my butt, don't worry.

LARRY: So you're divorced?

PALE: What's with questions, this hour the morning? I might want to experience the day here. Take inventory, somethin'. Her give me a divorce? She split, you should see how religious she got. The medals, the saints, the candles, never seen such crap. I coulda dragged her ass back. Who needs it? Sicka lookin' at her. Married a week outta school — what'd I know, I'm eighteen. It was good about six days. (*Pouring tea, adds milk.*)

LARRY: Milk?

PALE: Yeah, it — like — ties up the tannic acid, it don't burn your guts.

LARRY: There's lemon in the fridge.

PALE: Lemon'll kill ya.

LARRY: Citric acid's vitamin C — cure anything.

PALE: Acid's acid.

(*Phone rings; we hear Larry's voice*)

LARRY'S VOICE: Hello. Neither Anna nor I can come to the phone just now. Please leave a message when you hear the beep.

(*Pause — beep.*)

BURTON'S VOICE: Uh, Anna? It's Burton. Listen, I think I had too much blow last night, I —

PALE: He hang up? (*Pause.*) He hang up?

LARRY: She picked it up in the bedroom.

PALE (*to phone*): You got somethin' talk about, Bruce, come over, we'll talk. (*Laughs.*) He hung up.

LARRY (*lighting a cigarette*): You are hazardous to people's health, Pale.

ANNA (*enters, in jeans and T-shirt*): Goddamnit, Pale, what the hell do you think you're doing? That phone call happened to be — oh, real cute. Thanks. (*She slams down on the sofa. He goes to her. Sips his tea, offers her some.*) That looks strong.

PALE: You want a cup?

ANNA: I guess.

PALE: You want some eggs? (*He pours her a cup of tea.*)

LARRY: He cooks.

ANNA: No, I don't want to admit I'm still awake. Uh, Pale . . .

LARRY: I'm going to take a shower.

ANNA: In a minute, okay? Pale, would you do me a favor?

PALE: Sure.

ANNA: I don't want you to think that we've started something here.

PALE: . . . How come?

ANNA: I just don't. We're apples and oranges.

PALE: Yeah? Who's the apple and who's the orange?

ANNA: Pale.

PALE: You ever had that apple tart, glazed with marmalade?

ANNA: No, I haven't. I have to work; you have work to do.

PALE: Yeah? You get the job?

ANNA: What? Yes, I'm making a dance for a very important concert and it has me a little hysterical and it's occupying my time completely. This just isn't for me. I'm sorry if I led you on in any way. I don't feel well, and I'm not up for one of your scenes, but I'd like to not see you anymore.

PALE: How come?

ANNA: I don't know. I think you're dangerous.

PALE: Bullshit. You walk down the street, a brick falls on your head.

ANNA: But not in my apartment.

PALE: You gonna never leave your room, what?

ANNA: I might.

PALE: How come you don't feel good?

ANNA: I'm tired, my stomach's upset.

PALE: Who wouldn't be tired after what we did — ?

ANNA: Pale.

PALE: I'm tired, too; I'm fuckin' hung out to dry here. That tea's no good for a bad stomach. You want some milk?

ANNA: No. Please, Pale.

PALE: You're a real different person in the sack than you are standin' up.

ANNA: I know.

PALE: Which one's the lie? Were you fakin' it?

ANNA: I'm not lying now. And no, it isn't possible for me to fake it in bed.

PALE: You kiddin' me? Easiest thing in the world. Done it all my life. Half the time I'd fake it, too fuckin' tired to have interest. My o' lady'd run in and douche herself, come back feelin' fucked, cuddle up to me; I didn't know whether to hate the bitch for believin' me or for flushin' me out. Both of 'em lies. Lies happen like every ten seconds. Half the people you see on the street don't mean a thing they're doin'. Hug up some bitch, don't mean nothin' to them. Bitch smilin' up into his eyes, have more fun pushin' the bastard through a sausage grinder. My brother Sammy, older'n me, kissed his bride, said he wanted to bite the lips off her. People ain't easy.

ANNA: I know.

PALE: You said last night in the sack you ain't been with nobody since a month ago when you was with me. I ain't either. I figger one more time, we got us a hat trick. I got a vacation comin' up. I thought we'd go someplace.

ANNA: I'm working.

PALE: Hawaii, Brazil. See places.

ANNA: Really, Pale. Really.

LARRY (*after a long pause*): I think I should go straighten my room.

PALE: Naw, you stay here, like she wanted. I'll split. I don't hurt people. (*He goes into her room.*)

ANNA: No cracks, okay.

LARRY: Okay.

ANNA: No jokes.

LARRY: Even if it kills me.

ANNA: May I go to your room and lock the door? I don't want to see him.

LARRY: Of course you may.

PALE (*he has put his pants on, but nothing else; comes from her room*): No, I don't like it. You're gettin' me mad here. Lived with that bitch sixteen years, all we ever do is yell, never touched her once. Never felt nothin' for her.

ANNA: How would you be with someone you felt something for?

PALE: I never felt nothin' for nobody. How do I know? Whatta you want, a contract here? I'll write it out: I ever hit you, take my car or somethin'. What's causin' this crap?

ANNA: Pale, I don't even know how this nonsense started; it never should have.

PALE: It did.

ANNA: It didn't. Well, it did and it shouldn't have. I'm tired and sick, and I've got work to do.

PALE: Everybody's off today.

ANNA: Then I've got to sleep; you don't sleep, I sleep.

PALE: So we'll sleep.

ANNA: No . . . definitely not; I'm tired.

PALE: Me too. So what? My pants look like a pig's wearin' 'em, I got a hangover here, I'm puttin' on weight, I'm losin' my hair, and you're talkin' like that? I'm not dangerous. You don't think I'm dangerous; you think you're afraid of me is what you think.

ANNA: Okay, fine.

PALE: Why? (*Pause.*) You're afraid you might get interested. Have to feel somethin'.

ANNA: I feel, Pale, all the time. I'm a crackerjack feeler, thank you. (*Pause. To Larry.*) I'll go to your room.

LARRY: Sure. If he breaks the door in, somebody else pays for it.

PALE: I don't break in doors.

LARRY: I did once. Nearly killed myself. Cost three hundred dollars to replace.

PALE: Annie! Hey!

ANNA (*at Larry's door*): Pale, don't do this.

PALE: Do what? What am I doin'? You're the one doin' here.

ANNA: Oh, God. I'll try to say this so you can understand where . . . my point of view. I almost said "where I'm coming from." I have a friend that I'm seeing, Pale, and —

PALE: Who's that, Bruce?

ANNA: Burton. And we see —

PALE: You like him so much, why ain't you makin' it with him?

ANNA: . . . and we see things very similarly, and share a great deal, and I like being with him. I, at least, would like to give us the time to see if we're as compatible as we seem to be.

PALE: No, I can tell you.

ANNA: And I'm at a time in my life when — well, I just don't feel like fucking around. Sleeping around.

PALE: So don't.

ANNA: Pale, I have never had a personal life. I wasn't scared of it, I just had no place for it, it wasn't important. And all that is different now and I'm very vulnerable, I'm not going to be prey to something I don't want. I'm too easy. Go somewhere else.

PALE: I come to you.

ANNA: No. I said no. I don't want this. I'm not strong enough to kick you out physically. Why are you being so damned truculent? I said I don't like you. I don't want to know you. I don't want to see you again. There is no reason for you to come here. I have nothing for you. I don't like you and I'm frightened of you.

(*Pale looks at her, goes into the bedroom, comes out with his clothes. Goes to his cup of tea, finishing it. He doesn't look at her; they both stare at him.*)

PALE (*not looking up from tying his shoes*): What does that mean, "truculent"?

LARRY: Fierce, or actually, I think, uh, "like a truck."

PALE (*mumbles*): Like a truck. Great. (*He finishes and goes to her, kisses her, and leaves. Anna is on the brink of tears to the end of the scene.*)

LARRY: I didn't think you'd get rid of him by telling him to go. You say, "I'm desperately in love with you, never leave my side; I want to have your baby," and they'll leave.

ANNA: Could you go see if he actually is leaving?

LARRY: He actually is leaving.

ANNA: Go watch, I'm not kidding. Jesus, I reek of Jimmy.

LARRY: A little brandy-perspiraton and cologne. Not that bad, really. As he said, he's clean.

ANNA: The whole bedroom reeks of him. God. I'm going to have a shower, make the bed with clean sheets, and sleep the entire day. (*Leaving.*) Thanks for staying for that. (*She is gone.*)

LARRY (*half calling to her*): Think nothing of it. It was a completely new experience for me. And that is something I've never enjoyed. I'm not really that improvisational. I like having a rough copy to work from, at least. Something to go by.

(*She reenters with an enormous wad of sheets.*)

ANNA: What?

LARRY: Nothing.

ANNA: I'm sick of the age I'm living in. I don't like feeling ripped off and scared.

LARRY (*not campy*): You'd rather be pillaged and raped?

ANNA: I'm *being* pillaged and raped. I'm being pillaged and I'm being raped. And I don't like it. (*Stands in the middle of the pile of sheets. All the wind goes out of her.*)

LARRY: What? What is it, doll? Huh?

(*Anna almost cries; her shoulders shake.*)

ANNA: Ohhhhh! *I feel miserable!* Oh, damnit all. Did he leave?

LARRY: Yes.

ANNA: Aw, Jesus. Is he still out there, or did you see him drive off?

LARRY: I saw him drive off. If you didn't want him to go, you sure fooled me. It's okay, doll.

ANNA: It's not okay, doll; it fucking sucks.

LARRY: Okay, it sucks. You're absolutely right, it fucking sucks. Man, does it suck. It sucks so bad. God, does it suck.

ANNA: Don't. Come on.

LARRY: What?

ANNA: Goddamnit, I can't take it. (*She goes to the closet, gets her coat.*) I'm gonna have to see some more kids tomorrow — I'm working with four, I think I need six. Three couples. If I can't have a life at least I can work.

LARRY: Where you going?

ANNA: To Fred's studio. No one will be there today; I can get something done.

LARRY: Work here.

ANNA: No, no offense, but I want to be by myself.

LARRY: I'll leave.

ANNA: No.

LARRY: Eat something first.

ANNA: No, I'm not hungry. I'll pick up something later. Happy New Year. Get some rest.

LARRY: Well, don't just whip out of here, take a shower first.

(*She is at the door, coat on, bag in her hand, looking for her keys. She looks up at him steadily for a moment, studio keys in her hand. The music rises. She exits, closing the door behind her.*)

(*Blackout.*)

(*Burton stands center, still, rather in a daze. He holds a script. Larry comes from his room, putting on a sweatshirt. The door remains open; it's a gray day.*)

LARRY: Sorry — I had but nothing on. Foul day, huh? (*Beat.*) You want to get the door? (*Pause.*) Burt? You want to get the door? (*Pause. He goes to shut the door.*)

BURTON: Is Anna here?

LARRY: No. She's been busting her butt, you know, on the piece. It's glorious, of course.

BURTON: I'm, uh, I want to see it.

LARRY: It starts tonight, so she's probably there. It's only on for four nights — which is a long run for that kind of thing, if you can believe it. It's wonderful. I saw a tech run-through last night — It's miles and away the best piece on the program.

BURTON: She hasn't answered any of my messages. I wrote; I've been calling for a month.

LARRY: Maybe our machine isn't working; I don't think we're getting our messages . . .

BURTON: No, that's okay, you don't have to do that.

LARRY: . . . Good. You been working?

BURTON: Yeah, I did . . . the city thing. Most of it. I wanted to — I wanted her to read it.

LARRY: That's great. She'd love to. So would I.

BURTON: No, I don't think I'm ready for . . . well, okay. You're in it, sure. Don't pass it around.

LARRY: I'm in it?

BURTON: Nobody's safe around a writer. I thought you knew that.

LARRY: What do I do? Never mind, I'll find out. You want a drink?

BURTON: No, I haven't been drinking. Sure, what you got?

LARRY: Anything. Well, actually, vodka and Wild Turkey.

BURTON: Wild Turkey neat.

LARRY: Why not?

BURTON: Has she been seeing him?

LARRY: "Him"?

BURTON: Yeah.

LARRY (*making two drinks, vodka on the rocks*): I'm wondering what my procedure is here. We haven't talked about anything. She's not been out one night this month. But it kinda doesn't matter. I mean, except work. She comes home, I say, Hi, how was it, and she says, It's going well but it's difficult, and I say, You want something to eat, and she says, I stopped by some Chinese place on the way home, and she makes a drink and picks up a book and I go out to eat, and when I come home she's in her room with the light on and the door closed. Reading, I presume. She's working. But I *can* testify that the work she's doing is phenomenal. It's great.

BURTON: Then she's not seeing him?

LARRY: Burton, at least say, Good, she's working, or, Terrific, the work's good. Nothing else is important. She's already got a commission from it; no one's even seen it except a few bigwigs.

BURTON (*drinking, second sip*): What the hell is this?

LARRY: What?

BURTON: I asked for Turkey up; this is vodka rocks.

LARRY: I'm sorry.

BURTON: That's okay.

LARRY: No, that's just my mind. (*Pours Burton's drink into his, makes another.*)

BURTON: So, has she been seeing him?

LARRY: I thought I answered that.

BURTON: What'd you say?

LARRY: . . . What'd I say? You tell me.

BURTON (*thinking*): You said — I was listening; I was just listening too closely. You said, "I'm wondering about my procedure. We haven't talked at all; she's not been out one night in a month, but it kinda doesn't matter, she comes home, I say, Hi — "

LARRY: Stop. That's phenomenal.

BURTON: What? She's not been out one night this month?

LARRY: I said it kinda doesn't matter.

BURTON: What does that mean?

LARRY: It doesn't matter if she's seen him. It doesn't matter. The dance she's done is Pale and Anna. No, he hasn't been over. No, she hasn't seen him; it doesn't matter.

BURTON: Is that what it's called? Pale and Anna? Pale and me? What music are they using?

LARRY: You're not thinking. You've seen Fred's stuff; when have you ever heard music? It's a synthesized kind of city noise, with a foghorn and gulls and — it's here. This loft. Only more so. It's kind of epic. Well, for twelve minutes.

BURTON: How do you know it's supposed to be he?

LARRY: Well, for one thing, I've never seen a man on stage in a dance — it's a man and a — It's very startling. It just has to do with the center of gravity, I guess, but . . . or something. I mean it's a regular man — dancing like a man dances — in a bar or something, with his girl. You've never seen anything like it. I can't describe a dance; you might as well try to describe a piece of music.

BURTON: No, I know what you mean. I have this problem I'm trying to cope with here. I was a rich kid, you know.

LARRY: I know.

BURTON: And I've never really — I've always had pretty much my own — I've never lost anything before. Or, I've never lost. Before. (*Pause.*) See, what gets to me is, I keep feeling angry. You know, I could tear the shithead apart.

LARRY: I know.

BURTON: I could. But, you know, that doesn't mean anything. What's bothering me is, I keep feeling "Fuck *her*," you know? — and then I know that that's not really what I'm feeling — that's just a protective mechanism sort of thing that I've always used so I wouldn't lose. You know? 'Cause I've never lost. And I don't really feel "Fuck her" at all. That's just my immune system defending me.

LARRY: It's a handy thing to have.

BURTON (*setting his glass on the table*): Hit me.

LARRY: I beg your pardon? Oh, another, sure. (*Pours, leaves the bottle.*) It's perfectly natural you'd be pissed.

BURTON: Well, see . . . uh . . . I think you were supposed to say, "Hell, the race isn't over yet, kid, hang in there and fight."

LARRY: I'm sorry, Burton. "Win one for the Gipper" sticks in my craw.

BURTON: That's all right. So, I guess she really is in love with someone. We ought to celebrate. How's he feel about her?

LARRY: His entire mechanism is beyond my pale, doll. Anyway, we've not seen him. He hasn't come around. I would say he feels pretty much the same, but she threw him out so . . .

BURTON: She what? She threw him out? Boy, she is a piece of work, isn't she? And then goes off and makes a dance about him, great.

LARRY: She's had a very protected life. I mean, she's never had to even carry her own passport or plane tickets — she's not had to make her own way much.

BURTON: Yeah, I know. So what's she planning to do with her life? Live here with you?

LARRY (*pause*): I . . . uh . . . think I'll duck that one, if you don't mind.

BURTON: Sorry, I didn't intend that to sound like it did.

LARRY: No, actually that's very vivid. Put like that. (*Makes himself another drink.*) And by extension, what the fuck am I doing?

BURTON: Well, listen, it's none of my business. Tell her, you know, what we said, if you want to. Or not.

LARRY (*beat*): Huh? . . . Oh, uh . . . no, I definitely will.

BURTON: This isn't the way I was hoping . . .

LARRY: Tell me about it.

BURTON: Well . . . I got work. Read that, let me know what you think. I don't know. Give it to her. Tell her I'd like to hear — you know — what she thought about its — whatever.

LARRY: It's starting to snow, Burton, it's getting dark. Surely we could find a welcoming doorway somewhere on the block.

BURTON (*smiles*): Are you going to make me sorry I told you that?

LARRY: No. Thought I should mention it.

BURTON: I just haven't felt that open to the world since those days. Have a good life.

(*He leaves. Larry stands in the middle of the room. Music up, lights fade.*)

(*The apartment is dark; it is after midnight. Anna unlocks the door and comes in. She is in a party dress and a coat. She goes immediately toward the back without turning on the light, taking off her coat.*)

PALE: I'm here. Don't be scared.

ANNA: Oh, God!

PALE: Don't be scared. I'm stone-cold sober.

ANNA: I'm half drunk. How the hell'd you get in?

PALE: Your friend gave me a key.

ANNA: Larry? Why?

PALE: He come by the bar, he left me a note and the key and shit. The ticket.

ANNA: What ticket?

PALE: I saw your dance tonight. (*Pause.*) I looked for you, I didn't see you.

ANNA: I was hiding in the light booth.

PALE: You shoulda had Robbie for it. That guy didn't look right. He moved okay, he dances good, but he didn't look right.

ANNA: . . . I did it for Robbie, actually. In my mind Robbie did it.

PALE: I could tell. (*Pause.*) It wasn't what I thought it'd be.

ANNA: . . . Me either.

PALE: The other stuff — those first two things was shit. That's why I never went to no modern dance. I knew that's what it was gonna be. I almost had to leave. I didn't stay for that piece after yours.

ANNA: You would have hated it.

PALE: Your thing was good.

ANNA: Thank you.

PALE (*pause*): It was real good. Everybody stood up and yelled.

ANNA: Eight or ten people stood up.

PALE: How'd that feel when they did that?

ANNA: I was very surprised. I was afraid everyone would hate it. It was a relief.

PALE: Made me feel good, too. (*Pause.*) That was me and you up there. Only we ain't never danced. I could probably sue you for that.

ANNA: Probably.

PALE: I was kind — it's kinda embarrassing . . . to see somebody being you up there.

ANNA: Yes, it is.

PALE: He did okay. He moves good. She was good. She ain't as pretty as you.

ANNA: What are you doing going to a dance in the middle of the — Did you take off work?

PALE: Shit. Yeah, I quit. Bust my nuts twenty years, that guy. Been managing three years, not one day off. I'm tending bar at Danny's. You know . . . Ray? Fuckin' vacation. Work eight hours, like not workin'. (*Pause.*) You didn't go to the party? I thought there was a party for you.

ANNA: . . . I went; it was too noisy. Larry said he'd be here. I came home.

PALE: You been set up. Me too. He said he'd be here.

(*A long pause.*)

ANNA: Pale . . . I don't want this. (*She begins to cry softly.*)

PALE: I know. I don't want it, too.

ANNA: What'd he say? The bastard. In the note?

PALE: I read it ten times already. I wasn't gonna come. I almost know it by heart. (*Fishes it out of his pocket, hands it to her.*)

ANNA (*trying to read it, gives up*): That's okay. I can't . . .

PALE: . . . What?

ANNA: I can't read it.

PALE: . . . You cryin'? Somebody's always cryin' at your house.

ANNA: I know. I'm sorry. (*Hands it back to him.*) I can't read it.

PALE: It says: "Pale, doll. Here's a ticket for the program tonight and my keys.

We're going to the cast party and won't be home until three. I don't know how you're doing, but Anna is in pretty bad shape. This isn't opera, this is life, why should love always be tragic? Burn this." (*He hands it to her. She folds it into a tent, puts it in an ashtray.*) I been in pretty bad shape here, too. I'm thirty-six years old, I got a wife, I got two kids, I never felt nothin' like this.

ANNA: . . . I . . . uh . . . I haven't either.

PALE: I don't know what to do with myself here.

ANNA: I know. (*She lights a match, puts it under Larry's note; they watch it burn.*)

PALE: I thought you didn't like me, so I got lost. You know? 'Cause I didn't want you to do something you didn't like.

ANNA: I know. I was having a pretty difficult time not calling you.

PALE: I didn't know. (*Pause.*) I'm real scared here.

ANNA: I don't want this . . . Oh, Lord, I didn't want this . . .

PALE: I know. I don't want it, either. (*He stands beside one end of the sofa; she sits at the other. They look at each other.*) I didn't expect nothin' like this. (*He reaches his hand toward her; she reaches toward him. They touch. He moves over the back of the sofa and sits at the other end. She lies down, her back against his chest.*) I'm gonna cry all over your hair.

(*The music rises as the lights fade.*)   1987

INVESTIGATIONS

1. In what ways does Pale disprove Burton's notion that people in the past, especially "the wives waiting on their widow's walk" and "the men out there on the sea," "felt things in a much more profound way" than we do now? In what ways is Pale "totally foreign" to Anna's "urban microcosm" (p. 687)? In what ways can Anna be seen as "waiting on her widow's walk"? In what ways can Pale be seen as "out there on the sea"?

2. Note each time Anna tries to get rid of Pale during their initial conversation. Why doesn't she succeed? How do her motivations for not insisting he leave change as the encounter unfolds?

3. On page 722, Pale says, "You're afraid you might get interested. Have to feel somethin,' " to which Anna replies, "I feel, Pale, all the time. I'm a crackerjack feeler, thank you." After reviewing the play, write a 500–750-page essay in which you examine the ways in which each of them is correct.

4. Write a 500–750-word persuasive essay beginning with one of the following sentences:

   a. Anna should tell Burton and Pale to get lost and devote herself to her work till someone better comes along.

   b. Anna has a richer and more fulfilling relationship with Larry than she'd ever have with Burton or Pale.

c. Anna should ignore everything but what her instincts tell her to do about Pale.

d. Much of Anna's behavior, as well as her attraction for Pale, can be explained by her grief at Robbie's death.

e. Burton and Pale are both products of a macho ethic and can't be held entirely responsible for how they act toward Anna.

f. Pale reveals more complex and genuine emotion during the play than the rest of the characters put together.

ADRIENNE RICH

Love Poem

Tell me, bristler, where
do you get such hair
so quick a flare   so strong a tongue

Green eyes   fierce curls
there and here a mole   5
a girl's
dimples   a warrior's mind

dark blood under gold skin
testing, testing the world
the word   10

and so to write for you
a pretty sonnet
would be untrue

to your mud-river flashing
over rocks   your delicate   15
coffee-bushes

ADRIENNE RICH (b. 1929) is the winner of numerous honors, including a Fund for Human Dignity Award from the National Gay Task Force and two Guggenheim Fellowships. She grew up in Baltimore, Maryland, and graduated from Radcliffe College in 1951. Her two most recent poetry collections are *Your Native Land, Your Life* (1986) and *Time's Power: Poems 1985–88* (1989).

and more I cannot know
and some I labor with
and I mean to stay true

even in poems, to you   20
But there's something more

Beauty, when you were young
we both thought we were young
now that's all done

we're serious now   25
about death   we talk to her
daily, as to a neighbor

we're learning to be true
with her   she has the keys
to this house   if she must   30

she can sleep over   1986

INVESTIGATIONS

1. Describe the similarities between the speaker's feelings toward her beloved and those embodied in Berry's "Except," and Dobler's "Hospital Call," (p. 732). What do these poems suggest about the relationship between time and love?
2. What elements of friendship do you find in this poem? What details in it lie outside the realm of friendship?
3. Why does the speaker think writing "a pretty sonnet" for her lover "would be untrue" (lines 11–13)? In what ways have you found "pretty" expressions of love untrue? What does staying true to a lover have to do with "learning to be true" with death (line 28)?
4. Note each reference the poem makes to physical characteristics ("Green eyes," for example). Where do these references stop? How would your response to the poem change if it began at this point?

Hospital Call

The angel hunching on the TV set is bored.
I won't look at her, but can feel
the irritated whirr of wings
as I lean over my husband,
watching his thick chest fill and fall,   5
letting his breath wash my face.
The angel's not waiting for him.
She wants the black man in the next bed,
the one with cold fingers
and no wife to stand over him and pray   10
the sweat to break from his body.

The angel visits so many rooms like this one —
fluids pumping into bodies, pumping out,
nightsweat and vomit, dank hair spread on pillows —
she likes this taking to be easy.   15
She wants us to be beautiful and good,
cool as white nightgowns carved in stone.

I want a barroom brawl,
the TV blaring the Steelers score,
the black man banging his glass,   20
poking his finger in my husband's chest,
while I pull out
the angel's cotton candy hair
by its black roots.   1986

INVESTIGATIONS

1. Why is the angel bored? Why does she want "us to be beautiful and good, / cool as white nightgowns carved in stone" (lines 16–17)?
2. Discuss the speaker's attitude toward "the angel" as it compares to the attitude toward death expressed in Rich's "Love Poem." Where along the

For PATRICIA DOBLER (b. 1939), "following a poem is . . . the best way to understand." A native of Middletown, Ohio, Dobler is the author of three collections of poems: *Forget Your Life* (1982), *Talking to Strangers* (1986), and *UXB* (1991). She directs the Women's Creative Writing Center at Carlow College.

continuum you constructed in "Write Before Reading" would you place the love expressed by these speakers? Why?

3. Write a 500–750-word essay that begins, "The speaker of Patricia Dobler's 'Hospital Call' knows full well 'the angel' will get whatever it wants."

JANE SMILEY

Long Distance

Kirby Christianson is standing under the shower, fiddling with the hot-water spigot and thinking four apparently simultaneous thoughts: that there is never enough hot water in this apartment, that there was always plenty of hot water in Japan, that Mieko will be here in four days, and that he is unable to control Mieko's expectations of him in any way. The thoughts of Mieko are accompanied by a feeling of anxiety as strong as the sensation of the hot water, and he would like the water to flow through him and wash it away. He turns from the shower head and bends backward, so that the stream can pour over his face.

When he shuts off the shower, the phone is ringing. A sense that it has been ringing for a long time — can a mechanical noise have a quality of desperation? — propels him naked and dripping into the living room. He picks up the phone and his caller, as he has suspected, is Mieko. Perhaps he is psychic; perhaps this is only a coincidence, or perhaps no one else has called him in the past week or so.

The connection has a crystalline clarity that tricks him into not allowing for the satellite delay. He is already annoyed after the first hello. Mieko's voice is sharp, high, very Japanese, although she speaks superb English. He says, "Hello, Mieko," and he *sounds* annoyed, as if she called him too much, although she has only called once to give him her airline information and once to change it. Uncannily attuned to the nuances of his voice, she says, "Oh, Kirby," and falls silent.

Now there will be a flurry of tedious apologies, on both sides. He is tempted to hang up on her, call her back, and blame his telephone — faulty American technology. But he can't be certain that she is at home. So he says, "Hello, Mieko? Hello, Mieko? Hello, Mieko?" more and more loudly, as if her voice

JANE SMILEY (b. 1949), author most recently of *The Greenlanders* (1988), a novel, and the paired novellas, *Ordinary Love* and *Good Will* (1989), was raised in Los Angeles and now lives in Ames, Iowa. She is professor of English at Iowa State University.

were fading. His strategy works. She shouts, "Can you hear me, Kirby? I can hear you, Kirby."

He holds the phone away from his ear. He says, "That's better. Yes, I can hear you now."

"Kirby, I cannot come. I cannot go through with my plan. My father has lung cancer, we learned this morning."

He has never met the father, has seen the mother and the sister only from a distance, at a department store.

"Can you hear me, Kirby?"

"Yes, Mieko. I don't know what to say."

"You don't have to say anything. I have said to my mother that I am happy to stay with her. She is considerably relieved."

"Can you come later, in the spring?"

"My lie was that this Melville seminar I was supposed to attend would be offered just this one time, which was why I had to go now."

"I'm sorry."

"I know that I am only giving up pleasure. I know that my father might die."

As she says this, Kirby is looking out his front window at the snowy roof of the house across the street, and he understands at once from the hopeless tone of her voice that to give up the pleasure that Mieko has promised herself is harder than to die. He understands that in his whole life he has never given up a pleasure that he cherished as much as Mieko cherished this one. He understands that in a just universe the father would rather die alone than steal such a pleasure from his daughter. All these thoughts occur simultaneously, and are accompanied by a lifting of the anxiety he felt in the shower. She isn't coming. She is never coming. He is off the hook. He says, "But it's hard for you to give it up, Mieko. It is for me, too. I'm sorry."

The sympathetic tones in his voice wreck her self-control, and she begins to weep. In the five months that Kirby knew Mieko in Japan, and in the calls between them since, she has never shed a tear, hardly ever let herself be caught in a low moment, but now she weeps with absolute abandon, in long, heaving sobs, saying, "Oh, oh, oh," every so often. Once the sounds fade, as if she has put down the phone, but he does not dare hang up, does not even dare move the phone from one ear to the other. This attentive listening is what he owes to her grief, isn't it? If she had come, and he had disappointed her, as he would have, this is how she would have wept in solitude after swallowing her disappointment in front of him. But her father has done it, not him. He can give her a little company after all. He presses the phone so hard to his ear that it hurts. The weeping goes on for a long time and he is afraid to speak and interfere with what will certainly be her only opportunity to give way to her feelings. She gives one final wailing "Ohhh" and begins to cough and choke. Finally she quiets, and then sighs. After a moment of silence she says, "Kirby, you should not have listened."

"How could I hang up?"

"A Japanese man would have."

"You sound better, if you are back to comparing me with Japanese men."

"I am going to hang up now, Kirby. I am sorry not to come. Good-bye."   20

"Don't hang up."

"Good-bye."

"Mieko?"

"Good-bye, Kirby."

"Call me! Call me again!" He is not sure that she hears him. He looks at   25
the phone and then puts it on the cradle.

Two hours later he is on the highway. This is, after all, two days before
Christmas, and he is on his way to spend the holidays with his two brothers
and their wives and children, whom he hasn't seen in years. He has thought
little about this visit, beyond buying a few presents. Mieko's coming loomed,
imposing and problematic. They had planned to drive out west together — she
had paid extra so that she could land in Minneapolis and return from San
Francisco — and he had looked forward to seeing the mountains again. They
had made reservations on a bus that carries tourists into Yellowstone Park in
the winter, to look at the smoky geysers and the wildlife and the snow. The
trip would have seemed very American to her — buffalo and men in cowboy
boots and hats. But it seemed very Japanese to him — deep snow, dark pines,
sharp mountains.

The storm rolls in suddenly, the way it sometimes does on I-35 in Iowa,
startling him out of every thought except alertness. Snow swirls everywhere,
blotting out the road, the other cars, sometimes even his own front end. The
white of his headlights reflects back at him, so that he seems to be driving into
a wall. He can hardly force himself to maintain thirty-five miles an hour,
although he knows he must. To stop would be to invite a rear-end collision.
And the shoulder of the road is invisible. Only the white line, just beside the
left front corner of the car, reveals itself intermittently as the wind blows the
snow off the pavement. He ejects the tape he is playing and turns on the radio,
to the state weather station. He notices that his hand is shaking. He could be
killed. The utter blankness of the snowy whirl gives him a way of imagining
what it would be like to be dead. He doesn't like the feeling.

He remembers reading two winters ago about an elderly woman whose
son dropped her off at her apartment. She discovered that she had forgotten
her key, and with the wind-chill factor at eighty below zero, she froze before
she got to the manager's office. The winter before that a kid who broke his
legs in a snowmobile accident crawled three miles to the nearest farmhouse,
no gloves, only a feed cap on his head.

Twenty below, thirty below — the papers always make a big deal of the
temperature. Including wind chill, seventy, a hundred below. Kirby carries a
flashlight, a down sleeping bag, a sweatshirt that reads UNIVERSITY OF NE-
BRASKA, gloves and mittens. His car has new tires, front-wheel drive, and plenty
of antifreeze. He has a thermos of coffee. But the horror stories roll through

his mind anyway. A family without boots or mittens struggles two miles to a McDonald's through high winds, blowing snow, thirty below. *Why would they travel in that weather?* Kirby always thinks when he reads the papers, but of course they do. He does. Always has.

A gust takes the car, just for a second, and Kirby grips the wheel more tightly. The same gust twists the enveloping snow aloft and reveals the Clear Lake rest stop. Kirby is tempted to stop, tempted not to. He has, after all, never died before, and he has driven through worse than this. He passes the rest stop. Lots of cars are huddled there; but then, lots of cars are still on the highway. Maybe the storm is letting up.

As soon as he is past the rest stop, he thinks of Mieko, her weeping. She might never weep like that again, even if she heard of his death. The connection in her mind between the two of them, the connection that she allowed to stretch into the future despite all his admonitions and all her resolutions, is broken now. Her weeping was the sound of its breaking. And if he died here, in the next ten minutes, how would she learn of it? His brothers wouldn't call her, not even if she were still coming, because they didn't know she had planned to come. And if she were ever to call him back, she would get only a disconnect message and would assume that he had moved. He can think of no way that she could hear of his death, even though no one would care more than she would. These thoughts fill him with self-pity, but at least they drive out the catalogue of horror: station wagon skids into bridge abutment, two people are killed, two paralyzed from the neck down, mother survives unharmed, walks to nearby farmhouse. Kirby weighs the boredom and good fellowship he will encounter sitting out the storm at a truck stop against possible tragedy. Fewer cars are on the road; more are scattered on the median strip. Inertia carries him onward. He is almost to Minnesota, after all, where they really know how to take care of the roads. He will stop at the tourist center and ask about conditions.

But he drives past the tourist center by mistake, lost in thought. He decides to stop in Faribault. But by then the snow seems to be tapering off. Considering the distance he has traveled, Minneapolis isn't far now. He checks the odometer. Only fifty miles or so. An hour and a half away, at this speed. His mind eases over the numbers with customary superhighway confidence, but at once he imagines himself reduced to walking, walking in this storm, with only a flashlight, a thermos of coffee, a University of Nebraska sweatshirt — and the distance swells to infinity. Were he reduced to his own body, his own power, it might be too far to walk just to find a telephone.

For comfort he calls up images of Japan and southern China, something he often does. That he produces these images is the one tangible change that his travels have made in him. So many human eyes have looked upon every scene there for so many eons that every sight has an arranged quality: a flowering branch in the foreground, a precipitous mountainside in the background, a small bridge between. A path, with two women in red kimonos, that winds up a hillside. A white room with pearly rice-paper walls and a futon on the mat-covered floor, branches of cherry blossoms in a vase in the corner. They seem like pictures, but they are scenes he has actually looked upon: on a three-day trip out of Hong Kong into southern China, with some other teachers from his school on a trip to Kyoto, and at Akira's house. Akira was a fellow teacher at his school who befriended him. His house had four rooms, two Japanese style and two Western style.

He remembers, of course, other scenes of Japan — acres of buses, faces staring at his Westernness, the polite but bored rows of students in his class-room — when he is trying to decide whether to go back there. But these are not fixed, have no power; they are just memories, like memories of bars in Lincoln or the pig houses on his grandfather's farm.

And so, he survives the storm. He pulls into the driveway of Harold's new house, one he has not seen, though it is in a neighborhood he remembers from junior high school. The storm is over. Harold has his snowblower out and is making a path from the driveway to his front door. With the noise and because his back is turned, he is unaware of Kirby's arrival. Kirby stops the car, stretches, and looks at his watch. Seven hours for a four-hour trip. Kirby lifts his shoulders and rotates his head but does not beep his horn just yet. The fact is that he has frightened himself with the blinding snow, the miles of slick and featureless landscape, thoughts of Japan, and the thousands and thousands of miles between here and there. His car might be a marble that has rolled, only by luck, into a safe corner. He presses his fingers against his eyes and stills his breathing. 35

Harold turns around, grins, and shuts off the snowblower. It is a Harold identical to the Harold that Kirby has always known. Same bright snowflake ski hat, same bright ski clothing. Harold has spent his whole life skiing and ski-jumping. His bushy beard grows up to the hollows of his eyes, and when he leans into the car his moustache is, as always, crusted with ice.

"Hey!" he says. He backs away, and Kirby opens the car door.

"Made it!" Kirby says. That is all he will say about the trip. The last thing he wants to do is start a discussion about near misses. Compared with some of Harold's near misses, this is nothing. In fact, near misses on the highway aren't worth mentioning unless a lot of damage has been done to the car. Kirby knows of near misses that Harold has never dared to describe to anyone besides him, because they show a pure stupidity that even Harold has the sense to be ashamed of.

Over dinner, sweet and savory Nordic fare that Kirby is used to but doesn't much like, he begins to react to his day. The people around the table, his relatives, waver in the smoky candlelight, and Kirby imagines that he can feel the heat of the flames on his face. The other people at the table seem unfamiliar. Leanne, Harold's wife, he has seen only once, at their wedding. She is handsome and self-possessed-looking, but she sits at the corner of the table, like a guest in her own house. Eric sits at the head, and Mary Beth, his wife, jumps up and down to replenish the food. This assumption of primogeniture is a peculiarity of Eric's that has always annoyed Kirby, but even aside from that they have never gotten along. Eric does his best — earnest handshake and smile each time they meet, two newsy letters every year, pictures of the children (known between Harold and Kirby as "the little victims"). Eric has a Ph.D. from Columbia in American history, but he does not teach. He writes for a conservative think tank — articles that appear on the op-ed pages of newspapers and in the think tank's own publications. He specializes in "the family." Kirby and Harold have made countless jokes at Eric's expense. Kirby knows that more will be made this trip, if only in the form of conspiratorial looks, rolling eyes. Eric's hobby — Mary Beth's, too, for they share everything — is developing each nuance of his Norwegian heritage into a fully realized ostentation. Mary Beth is always busy, usually baking. That's all Kirby knows about her, and all he cares to know.

Across the table Anna, their older daughter, pale, blue-eyed, cool, seems   40
to be staring at him, but Kirby can hardly see her. He is thinking about Mieko. Kirby looks at his watch. It is very early morning in Osaka. She is probably about to wake up. Her disappointment will have receded hardly a particle, will suck her down as soon as she thuds into consciousness. "Oh, oh, oh": He can hear her cries as clearly as if they were vibrating in the air. He is amazed at having heard such a thing, and he looks carefully at the women around the table. Mieko would be too eager to please here, always looking after Mary Beth and Leanne, trying to divine how she might be helpful. Finally, Mary Beth would speak to her with just a hint of sharpness, and Mieko would be crushed. Her eyes would seek Kirby's for reassurance, and he would have none to give. She would be too little, smaller even than Anna, and her voice would be too high and quick. These thoughts give him such pain that he stares for relief at Kristin, Eric's youngest, age three, who is humming over her dinner. She is round-faced and paunchy, with dark hair cut straight across her forehead and straight around her collar. From time to time she and Leanne exchange merry glances.

Harold is beside him; that, at least, is familiar and good, and it touches Kirby with a pleasant sense of expectation, as if Harold, at any moment, might pass him a comic book or a stick of gum. In fact, Harold does pass him something — an icy cold beer, which cuts the sweetness of the food and seems to adjust all the figures around the table so that they stop wavering.

Of course his eyes open well before daylight, but he dares not move. He is sharing a room with Harold the younger, Eric's son, whose bed is between his and the door. He worries that if he gets up he will stumble around and crash into walls and wake Harold. The digits on the clock beside Harold's bed read 5:37, but when Kirby is quiet, he can hear movement elsewhere in the house. When he closes his eyes, the footsteps present themselves as a needle and thread, stitching a line through his thoughts. He has just been driving. His arms ache from gripping the wheel. The car slides diagonally across the road, toward the median. It slides and slides, through streams of cars, toward a familiar exit, the Marshalltown exit, off to the left, upward. His eyes open again. The door of the room is open, and Anna is looking in. After a moment she turns and goes away. It is 6:02. Sometime later Leanne passes with Isaac, the baby, in her arms.

Kirby cannot bear to get up and face his brothers and their families. As always, despair presents itself aesthetically. The image of Harold's and Leanne's living room, matching plaid wing chairs and couch, a triple row of wooden pegs by the maple front door, seems to Kirby the image of the interior of a coffin. The idea of spending five years, ten years, a lifetime, with such furniture makes him gasp. But his own apartment, armchair facing the television, which sits on a spindly coffee table, is worse. Mary Beth and Eric's place, where he has been twice, is the worst, because it's pretentious; they have antique wooden trunks and high-backed benches painted blue with stenciled flowers in red and white. Everything, everything, they own is blue and white, or white and blue, and Nordic primatif. Now even the Japanese images he calls up are painful. The pearly white Japanese-style room in Akira's house was bitterly cold in the winter, and he spent one night there only half-sleeping, his thighs drawn to his chest, the perimeters of the bed too cold even to touch. His head throbbing, Kirby lies pinned to the bed by impossibility. He literally can't summon up a room, a stick of furniture, that he can bear to think of. Harold the younger rolls over and groans, turning his twelve-year-old face toward Kirby's. His mouth opens and he breathes noisily. It is 6:27.

Not until breakfast, when Leanne sets a bowl of raisin bran before him on the table, does he recall the appearance of Anna in the door to his room, and then it seems odd, especially when, ten minutes later, she enters the kitchen in her bathrobe, yawning. Fifth grade. Only fifth grade. He can see that now, but the night before, and in the predawn darkness, she had seemed older, more threatening, the way girls get at fourteen and fifteen. "Cereal, sweetie?" Leanne says, and Anna nods, scratching. She sits down without a word and focuses on the back of the Cheerios box. Kirby decides that he was dreaming and puts the incident out of his mind.

Harold, of course, is at his store, managing the Christmas rush, and the house is less festive in his absence. Eric has sequestered himself in Leanne's sewing room, with his computer, and as soon as Anna stands up from breakfast, Mary Beth begins to arrange the day's kitchen schedule. Kirby rinses his cup and goes into the living room. It is nine in the morning, and the day stretches before him, empty. He walks through the plaid living room to the window, where he regards the outdoor thermometer. It reads four degrees below zero. Moments later it is five degrees below zero. Moments after that he is standing beside Harold's bar, pouring himself a glass of bourbon. He has already drunk it when Anna appears in the doorway, dressed now, and staring at him again. She makes him think of Mieko again — though the child is blonde and self-contained, she is Mieko's size. Last evening, when he was thinking of Mieko, he was looking at Anna. He says, attempting jovial warmth, "Good morning, Anna. Why do you keep staring at me?"

45

She is startled. "I don't. I was looking at the bookshelves."

"But you stared at me last night, at dinner. And you came to the door of my room early this morning. I know because I was awake."

"No, I didn't." But then she softens, and says with eager curiosity, "Are you a socialist?"

While Kirby is trying not to laugh, he hears Mary Beth sing from the kitchen. "Anna? Your brother is going sledding. You want to go?"

Anna turns away before Kirby can answer, and mounts the stairs. A "No!"   50
floats, glassy and definite, from the second floor.

Kirby sits down in one of the plaid armchairs and gazes at an arrangement of greenery and shiny red balls and candles that sits on a table behind the couch. He gazes and gazes, contemplating the notion of Eric and Mary Beth discussing his politics and his life. He is offended. He knows that if he were to get up and do something he would stop being offended, but he gets up only to pour himself another drink. It is nearly ten. Books are around everywhere, and Kirby picks one up.

People keep opening doors and coming in, having been elsewhere. Harold comes home for lunch; Leanne and Isaac return from the grocery store and the hardware store; Harold the younger stomps in, covered with snow from sledding, eats a sandwich, and stomps out again. Eric opens the sewing-room door, takes a turn through the house, goes back in again. He does this three times, each time failing to speak to Kirby, who is sitting quietly. Perhaps he does not see him. He is an old man, Kirby thinks, and his rear has spread considerably in the past four years; he is thirty-six going on fifty, round-shouldered, wearing slacks rather than jeans. What a jerk.

But then Kirby's bad mood twists into him, and he lets his head drop on the back of his chair. What is a man? Kirby thinks. What is a man, what is a man? It is someone, Eric would say, who votes, owns property, has a wife, worries. It is someone, Harold would say, who can chop wood all day and make love all night, who can lift his twenty-five-pound son above his head on the palm of his hand.

After lunch the men all vanish again, even Isaac, who is taking a nap. In various rooms the women do things. They make no noise. Harold's house is the house of a wealthy man, Kirby realizes. It is large enough to be silent and neat most of the time, the sort of house Kirby will never own. It is Harold and Eric who are alike now. Only Kirby's being does not extend past his fingertips and toes to family, real estate, reputation.

Sometime in the afternoon, when Kirby is still sitting quietly and his part   55
of the room is shadowed by the movement of the sun to the other side of the house, Kristin comes in from the kitchen, goes straight to the sofa, pulls off one of the cushions, and begins to jump repeatedly from the cushion to the floor. When he says, "Kristin, what are you doing?" she is not startled. She says, "Jumping."

"Do you like to jump?"

She says, "It's a beautiful thing to do," in her matter-of-fact, deep, three-year-old voice. Kirby can't believe she knows what she is saying. She jumps three or four more times and then runs out again.

At dinner she is tired and tiresome. When Eric tells her to eat a bite of her meat (ham cooked with apricots), she looks him right in the face and says, "No."

"One bite," he says. "I mean it."

"No. I mean it." She looks up at him. He puts his napkin on the table and pushes back his chair. In a moment he has swept her through the doorway and up the stairs. She is screaming. A door slams and the screaming is muffled. When he comes down and seats himself, carefully laying his napkin over his slacks, Anna says, "It's her body."

The table quiets. Eric says, "What?"

"It's her body."

"What does that mean?"

"She should have control over her own body. Food. Other stuff. I don't know." She has started strong but weakens in the face of her father's glare. Eric inhales sharply, and Kirby cannot restrain himself. He says, "How can you disagree with that? It sounds self-evident to me."

"Does it? The child is three years old. How can she have control over her own body when she doesn't know anything about it? Does she go out without a coat if it's twenty below zero? Does she eat only cookies for three days? Does she wear a diaper until she's five? This is one of those phrases they are using these days. They all mean the same thing."

"What do they mean?" As Kirby speaks, Leanne and Mary Beth look up, no doubt wishing that he had a wife or a girlfriend here to restrain him. Harold looks up too. He is grinning.

Eric shifts in his chair, uncomfortable, Kirby suddenly realizes, at being predictably stuffy once again. Eric says, "It's Christmas. Let's enjoy it."

Harold says, "Principles are principles, any day of the year."

Eric takes the bait and lets himself say, "The family is constituted for a purpose, which is the sometimes difficult socialization of children. For a certain period of their lives others control them. In early childhood others control their bodies. They are taught to control themselves. Even Freud says that the young barbarian has to be taught to relinquish his feces, sometimes by force."

"Good Lord, Eric," Leanne says.

Eric is red in the face. "Authority is a principle I believe in." He looks around the table and then at Anna, openly angry that she has gotten him into this. Across Anna's face flits a look that Kirby has seen before, has seen on Mieko's face, a combination of self-doubt and resentment molded into composure.

"Patriarchy is what you mean," Kirby says, realizing from the tone of his own voice that rage has replaced sympathy and, moreover, is about to get the better of him.

"Why not? It works."

"For some people, at a great cost. Why should daughters be sacrificed to the whims of the father?" He should stop now. He doesn't. "Just because he put his dick somewhere once or twice." The result of too many bourbons too early in the day.

"In my opinion — " Eric seems not to notice the vulgarity, but Harold, beside Kirby, snorts with pleasure. 75

"I don't want to talk about this," Leanne says. Kirby blushes and falls silent, knowing that he has offended her. It is one of those long holiday meals, and by the time they get up from the table, Kirby feels as if he has been sitting in a dim, candlelit corner most of his life.

There is another ritual — the Christmas Eve unwrapping of presents — and by that time Kirby realizes that he is actively intoxicated and had better watch his tone of voice and his movements. Anna hands out the gifts with a kind of rude bashfulness, and Kirby is surprised at the richness of the array: From Harold he has gotten a cotton turtleneck and a wool sweater, in bright, stylish colors; from Leanne a pair of very fancy gloves; from Isaac three pairs of ragg wool socks; from Eric's family, as a group, a blue terry-cloth robe and sheepskin slippers. When they open his gifts, he is curious to see what the wrappings reveal: He has bought it all so long before. Almost everything is some gadget available in Japan but not yet in the States. Everyone peers and oohs and aahs. It gives Kirby a headache and a sense of his eyeballs expanding and contracting. Tomorrow night he will be on his way home again, and though he cannot bear to stay here after all, he cannot bear to go, either.

He drifts toward the stairs, intending to go to bed, but Harold looms before him, grinning and commanding. "Your brain needs some oxygen, brother," he says. Then they are putting on their parkas, and then they are outside, in a cold so sharp that Kirby's nose, the only exposed part of him, stings. Harold strides down the driveway, slightly ahead of him, and Kirby expects him to speak, either for or against Eric, but he doesn't. He only walks. The deep snow is so solidly frozen that it squeaks beneath their boots. The only thing Harold says the whole time they are walking is, "Twenty-two below, not counting the wind chill. Feels good, doesn't it?"

"Feels dangerous," Kirby says.

"It is," Harold says. 80

The neighborhood is brightly decorated, and the colored lights have their effect on Kirby. For the first time in three Christmases he feels a touch of the mystery that he thinks of as the Christmas spirit. Or maybe it is love for Harold.

Back at the house, everyone has gone to bed except Leanne and Mary Beth, who are drying dishes and putting them away. They are also, Kirby realizes — after Harold strides through the kitchen and up the stairs — arguing, although with smiles and in polite tones. Kirby goes to a cabinet and lingers over getting himself a glass for milk. Mary Beth says, "Kristin will make the connection. She's old enough."

"I can't believe that."

"She saw all the presents being handed out and unwrapped. And Anna will certainly make the connection."

"Anna surely doesn't believe in Santa Claus anymore."   85

"Unofficially, probably not."

"It's Isaac's first Christmas," Leanne says. "He'll like all the wrappings."

"I wish you'd thought of that before you wrapped the family presents and his Santa presents in the same paper."

"That's a point too. They're his presents. I don't think Kristin will notice them."

"If they're the only wrapped presents, she will. She notices everything."   90

Now Leanne turns and gazes at Mary Beth, her hands on her hips. A long silence follows. Leanne flicks a glance at Kirby, who pretends not to notice. Finally she says, "All right, Mary Beth. I'll unwrap them."

"Thank you," Mary Beth says. "I'll finish this, if you want." Kirby goes out of the kitchen and up to his bedroom. The light is already off, and Harold the younger is on his back, snoring.

When he gets up an hour later, too drunk to sleep, Kirby sees Leanne arranging the last of Santa's gifts under the tree. She turns the flash of her glance upon him as he passes through the living room to the kitchen. "Mmm," he says, uncomfortable, "can't sleep."

"Want some cocoa? I always make some before I go to bed."

He stops. "Yeah. Why not? Am I mistaken, or have you been up since   95
about six A.M.?"

"About that. But I'm always wired at midnight, no matter what."

He follows her into the kitchen, remembering now that they have never conversed, and wishing that he had stayed in bed. He has drunk himself stupid. Whatever words he has in him have to be summoned from very far down. He sits at the table. After a minute he puts his chin in his hand. After a long, blank, rather pleasant time, the cocoa is before him, marshmallow and all. He looks at it. When Leanne speaks, Kirby is startled, as if he had forgotten that she was there.

"Tired?" she says.

"Too much to drink."

"I noticed."   100

"I don't have anything more to say about it."

"I'm not asking."

He takes a sip of his cocoa. He says, "Do you all see much of Eric and family?"

"They came last Christmas. He came by himself in the summer. To a conference on the future of the family."

"And so you have to put up with him, right?"   105

"Harold has a three-day limit. I don't care."

"I noticed you unwrapped all Isaac's presents."

She shrugs, picks at the sole of her boot. She yawns without covering her mouth, and then says, "Oh, I'm sorry." She smiles warmly, looking right at him. "I am crazy about Kristin. Crazy enough to not chance messing up Christmas for her."

"Today she told me that jumping off a cushion was a beautiful thing to do."

Leanne smiles. "Yesterday she said that it was wonderful of me to give her   110
a napkin. You know, I don't agree with Eric about that body stuff. I think they naturally do what is healthy for them. Somebody did an experiment with one-year-olds, gave them a range of foods to choose from, and they always chose a balanced diet. They also want to be toilet trained sooner or later. I think it's weird the way Eric thinks that every little thing is learned rather than realized."

"That's a nice phrase." He turns his cup handle so that it points away and then back in his direction. Finally he says, "Can I tell you about something?"

"Sure."

"Yesterday a friend of mine called me from Japan, a woman, to say that she couldn't come visit me. Her father has cancer. She had planned to arrive here the day after tomorrow, and we were going to take a trip out west. It isn't important, exactly. I don't know."

Leanne is silent but attentive, picking at the sole of her boot. Now that he has mentioned it, the memory of Mieko's anguish returns to him like a glaring light or a thundering noise, so enormous that he is nearly robbed of the power to speak. He pushes it out. "She can't come now, ever. She probably won't ever call or write me again. And really, this has saved her. She had all sorts of expectations that I couldn't have . . . well, wouldn't have fulfilled, and if she had come she would have been permanently compromised."

"Did you have some kind of affair when you were there?"   115

"For a few months. She's very pretty. I think she's the prettiest woman I've ever seen. She teaches mathematics at the school where I was teaching. After I had been with Mieko for a few weeks, I realized that no one, maybe in her whole adult life, had asked her how she was, or had put his arm around her shoulders, or had taken care of her in any way. The slightest affection was like a drug she couldn't get enough of."

"What did you feel?"

"I liked her. I really did. I was happy to see her when she came by. But she longed for me more than I have ever longed for anything."

"You were glad to leave."

"I was glad to leave."   120

"So what's the problem?"

"When she called yesterday, she broke down completely. I listened. I thought it was the least I could do, but now I think that she is compromised. Japanese people are very private. It scares me how much I must have embarrassed her. I look back on the spring and the summer and yesterday's call, and I see that, one by one, I broke down every single one of her strengths, everything she had equipped herself with to live in a Japanese way. I was so careful for a year and a half. I didn't date Japanese women, and I was very distant — but then I was so lonely, and she was so pretty, and I thought, well, she's twenty-seven, and she lives in this sophisticated city, Osaka. But mostly I was lonely."

Leanne gazes across the table in that way of hers, calm and considering. Finally she says, "Eric comes in for a lot of criticism around here. His style's all wrong, for one thing. And he drives Harold the younger and Anna crazy. But I've noticed something about him. He never tries to get something for nothing. I admire that."

Now Kirby looks around the room, at the plants on the windowsill, the hoarfrost on the windowpanes, the fluorescent light harsh on the stainless-steel sink, and it seems to him that all at once, now that he realizes it, his life and Mieko's have taken their final form. She is nearly too old to marry, and by the end of her father's cancer and his life she will be much too old. And himself. Himself. Leanne's cool remark has revealed his permanent smallness. He looks at his hands, first his knuckles, then his palms. He says, "It seems so dramatic to say that I will never get over this."

"Does it? To me it seems like saying that what people do is important."   125 And though he looks at her intently, seeking some sort of pardon, she says nothing more, only picks at her boot for a moment or two, and then gets up and puts their cups in the sink. He follows her out of the kitchen, through the living room. She turns out all the lights, so that the house is utterly dark. At the bottom of the stairs, unable to see anything, he stumbles against her and excuses himself. There, soft and fleeting, he feels a disembodied kiss on his cheek, and her voice, nearly a whisper, says, "Merry Christmas, Kirby. I'm glad you're here."   1987

INVESTIGATIONS

1. Early in the story, despite his relief that Mieko won't be visiting him, Kirby yells "Call me! Call me again!" as Mieko hangs up. Why? Why doesn't he offer to return to her?

2. Reread paragraphs 25–34 and 93–125. How might Kirby relieve the pain he experiences during his journey? If you were Leanne, what would you have said to Kirby?

3. How does Kirby feel about the fact that his "being does not extend past his fingertips and toes to family, real estate, reputation" (para. 54)? How are his feelings about his family connected to those he has for Mieko?

4. In paragraph 124, Kirby thinks "his life and Mieko's have taken their final form." What does he mean? Why does he think he'll " 'never get over this' "?

5. Write a 500–750-word essay that begins with one of these two sentences:

   a. The characters in "Long Distance" provide substantial evidence of how each of us has a different capacity to love.

b. If Kirby would quit feeling sorry for himself and realize that love doesn't cure anything, he'd probably find out he can be a lot happier than he thinks.

BOBBIE ANN MASON

Shiloh

Leroy Moffitt's wife, Norma Jean, is working on her pectorals. She lifts three-pound dumbbells to warm up, then progresses to a twenty-pound barbell. Standing with her legs apart, she reminds Leroy of Wonder Woman.

"I'd give anything if I could just get these muscles to where they're real hard," says Norma Jean. "Feel this arm. It's not as hard as the other one."

"That's 'cause you're right-handed," says Leroy, dodging as she swings the barbell in an arc.

"Do you think so?"

"Sure." 5

Leroy is a truckdriver. He injured his leg in a highway accident four months ago, and his physical therapy, which involves weights and a pulley, prompted Norma Jean to try building herself up. Now she is attending a body-uilding class. Leroy has been collecting temporary disability since his tractor-trailer jackknifed in Missouri, badly twisting his left leg in its socket. He has a steel pin in his hip. He will probably not be able to drive his rig again. It sits in the backyard, like a gigantic bird that has flown home to roost. Leroy has been home in Kentucky for three months, and his leg is almost healed, but the accident frightened him and he does not want to drive any more long hauls. He is not sure what to do next. In the meantime, he makes things from craft kits. He started by building a miniature log cabin from notched Popsicle sticks. He varnished it and placed it on the TV set, where it remains. It reminds him of a rustic Nativity scene. Then he tried string art (sailing ships on black velvet), a macramé owl kit, a snap-together B-17 Flying Fortress, and a lamp made out of a model truck, with a light fixture screwed in the top of the cab. At first the kits were diversions, something to kill time, but now he is thinking about building a full-scale log house from a kit. It would be considerably cheaper than building a regular house, and besides, Leroy has grown to appreciate how

For BOBBIE ANN MASON (b. 1940), "the style of the narrative, the cadence of it, is very important . . . It imitates that country speech that I hear in my ear." Born in Mayfield, Kentucky, Mason now lives near Mansfield, Pennsylvania. Her books include *Spence + Lila* (1988), a novel, and *Love Life: Stories* (1989).

things are put together. He has begun to realize that in all the years he was on the road he never took time to examine anything. He was always flying past scenery.

"They won't let you build a log cabin in any of the new subdivisions," Norma Jean tells him.

"They will if I tell them it's for you," he says, teasing her. Ever since they were married, he has promised Norma Jean he would build her a new home one day. They have always rented, and the house they live in is small and nondescript. It does not even feel like a home, Leroy realizes now.

Norma Jean works at the Rexall drugstore, and she has acquired an amazing amount of information about cosmetics. When she explains to Leroy the three stages of complexion care, involving creams, toners, and moisturizers, he thinks happily of other petroleum products — axle grease, diesel fuel. This is a connection between him and Norma Jean. Since he has been home, he has felt unusually tender about his wife and guilty over his long absences. But he can't tell what she feels about him. Norma Jean has never complained about his traveling, she has never made hurt remarks, like calling his truck a "widow-maker." He is reasonably certain she has been faithful to him, but he wishes she could celebrate his permanent homecoming more happily. Norma Jean is often startled to find Leroy at home, and he thinks she seems a little disappointed about it. Perhaps it reminds her too much of the early days of their marriage, before he went on the road. They had a child who died as an infant, years ago. They never speak about their memories of Randy, which have almost faded, but now that Leroy is home all the time, they sometimes feel awkward around each other, and Leroy wonders if one of them should mention the child. He has the feeling that they are waking up out of a dream together — that they must create a new marriage, start afresh. They are lucky they are still married. Leroy has read that for most people losing a child destroys the marriage — or else he heard this on "Donahue." He can't always remember where he learns things anymore.

At Christmas, Leroy bought an electric organ for Norma Jean. She used to play the piano when she was in high school. "It don't leave you," she told him once. "It's like riding a bicycle."

The new instrument had so many keys and buttons that she was bewildered by it at first. She touched the keys tentatively, pushed some buttons, then pecked out "Chopsticks." It came out in an amplified fox-trot rhythm, with marimba sounds.

"It's an orchestra!" she cried.

The organ had a pecan-look finish and eighteen preset chords, with optional flute, violin, trumpet, clarinet, and banjo accompaniments. Norma Jean mastered the organ almost immediately. At first she played Christmas songs. Then she bought *The Sixties Songbook* and learned every tune in it, adding variations to each with the rows of brightly colored buttons.

"I didn't like these old songs back then," she said. "But I have this crazy feeling I missed something."

"You didn't miss a thing," said Leroy.   15

Leroy likes to lie on the couch and smoke a joint and listen to Norma Jean play "Can't Take My Eyes Off You" and "I'll Be Back." He is back again. After fifteen years on the road, he is finally settling down with the woman he loves. She is still pretty. Her skin is flawless. Her frosted curls resemble pencil trimmings.

Now that Leroy has come home to stay, he notices how much the town has changed. Subdivisions are spreading across western Kentucky like an oil slick. The sign at the edge of town says "Pop: 11,500" — only seven hundred more than it said twenty years before. Leroy can't figure out who is living in all the new houses. The farmers who used to gather around the courthouse square on Saturday afternoons to play checkers and spit tobacco juice have gone. It has been years since Leroy has thought about the farmers, and they have disappeared without his noticing.

Leroy meets a kid named Stevie Hamilton in the parking lot at the new shopping center. While they pretend to be strangers meeting over a stalled car, Stevie tosses an ounce of marijuana under the front seat of Leroy's car. Stevie is wearing orange jogging shoes and a T-shirt that says CHATTAHOOCHEE SUPER-RAT. His father is a prominent doctor who lives in one of the expensive subdivisions in a new white-columned brick house that looks like a funeral parlor. In the phone book under his name there is a separate number, with the listing "Teenagers."

"Where do you get this stuff?" asks Leroy. "From your pappy?"

"That's for me to know and you to find out," Stevie says. He is slit-eyed   20
and skinny.

"What else you got?"

"What you interested in?"

"Nothing special. Just wondered."

Leroy used to take speed on the road. Now he has to go slowly. He needs to be mellow. He leans back against the car and says, "I'm aiming to build me a log house, soon as I get time. My wife, though, I don't think she likes the idea."

"Well, let me know when you want me again," Stevie says. He has a   25
cigarette in his cupped palm, as though sheltering it from the wind. He takes a long drag, then stomps it on the asphalt and slouches away.

Stevie's father was two years ahead of Leroy in high school. Leroy is thirty-four. He married Norma Jean when they were both eighteen, and their child Randy was born a few months later, but he died at the age of four months and three days. He would be about Stevie's age now. Norma Jean and Leroy were at the drive-in, watching a double feature (*Dr. Strangelove* and *Lover Come Back*), and the baby was sleeping in the back seat. When the first movie ended, the baby was dead. It was the sudden infant death syndrome. Leroy remembers handing Randy to a nurse at the emergency room, as though he were offering her a large doll as a present. A dead baby feels like a sack of flour. "It just happens sometimes," said the doctor, in what Leroy always recalls as a nonchalant tone. Leroy can hardly remember the child anymore, but he still sees vividly a scene from *Dr. Strangelove* in which the president of the United States was talking in a folksy voice on the hot line to the Soviet premier about the bomber accidentally headed toward Russia. He was in the War Room, and the world map was lit up. Leroy remembers Norma Jean standing catatonically beside him in the hospital and himself thinking: Who is this strange girl? He had forgotten who she was. Now scientists are saying that crib death is caused by a virus. Nobody knows anything. Leroy thinks. The answers are always changing.

When Leroy gets home from the shopping center, Norma Jean's mother, Mabel Beasley, is there. Until this year, Leroy has not realized how much time she spends with Norma Jean. When she visits, she inspects the closets and then the plants, informing Norma Jean when a plant is droopy or yellow. Mabel calls the plants "flowers," although there are never any blooms. She always notices if Norma Jean's laundry is piling up. Mabel is a short, overweight woman whose tight, brown-dyed curls look more like a wig than the actual wig she sometimes wears. Today she has brought Norma Jean an off-white dust ruffle she made for the bed; Mabel works in a custom-upholstery shop.

"This is the tenth one I made this year," Mabel says. "I got started and couldn't stop."

"It's real pretty," says Norma Jean.

"Now we can hide things under the bed," says Leroy, who gets along with   30
his mother-in-law primarily by joking with her. Mabel has never really forgiven him for disgracing her by getting Norma Jean pregnant. When the baby died, she said that fate was mocking her.

"What's that thing?" Mabel says to Leroy in a loud voice, pointing to a tangle of yarn on a piece of canvas.

Leroy holds it up for Mabel to see. "It's my needlepoint," he explains. "This is a 'Star Trek' pillow cover."

"That's what a woman would do," says Mabel. "Great day in the morning!"

"All the big football players on TV do it," he says.

"Why, Leroy, you're always trying to fool me. I don't believe you for one   35
minute. You don't know what to do with yourself — that's the whole trouble. Sewing!"

"I'm aiming to build us a log house," says Leroy. "Soon as my plans come."

"Like *heck* you are," says Norma Jean. She takes Leroy's needlepoint and shoves it into a drawer. "You have to find a job first. Nobody can afford to build now anyway."

Mabel straightens her girdle and says, "I still think before you get tied down y'all ought to take a little run to Shiloh."

"One of these days, Mama," Norma Jean says impatiently.

Mabel is talking about Shiloh, Tennessee. For the past few years, she has   40
been urging Leroy and Norma Jean to visit the Civil War battleground there.
Mabel went there on her honeymoon — the only real trip she ever took. Her
husband died of a perforated ulcer when Norma Jean was ten, but Mabel, who
was accepted into the United Daughters of the Confederacy in 1975, is still
preoccupied with going back to Shiloh.

"I've been to kingdom come and back in that truck out yonder," Leroy
says to Mabel, "but we never yet set foot in that battleground. Ain't that
something? How did I miss it?"

"It's not even that far," Mabel says.

After Mabel leaves, Norma Jean reads to Leroy from a list she has made.
"Things you could do," she announces. "You could get a job as a guard at
Union Carbide, where they'd let you set on a stool. You could get on at the
lumberyard. You could do a little carpenter work, if you want to build so bad.
You could — "

"I can't do something where I'd have to stand up all day."

"You ought to try standing up all day behind a cosmetics counter. It's   45
amazing that I have strong feet, coming from two parents that never had strong
feet at all." At the moment Norma Jean is holding on to the kitchen counter,
raising her knees one at a time as she talks. She is wearing two-pound ankle
weights.

"Don't worry," says Leroy. "I'll do something."

"You could truck calves to slaughter for somebody. You wouldn't have to
drive any big old truck for that."

"I'm going to build you this house," says Leroy. "I want to make you a
real home."

"I don't want to live in any log cabin."

"It's not a cabin. It's a house."   50

"I don't care. It looks like a cabin."

"You and me together could lift those logs. It's just like lifting weights."

Norma Jean doesn't answer. Under her breath, she is counting. Now she
is marching through the kitchen. She is doing goose steps.

Before his accident, when Leroy came home he used to stay in the house
with Norma Jean, watching TV in bed and playing cards. She would cook fried
chicken, picnic ham, chocolate pie — all his favorites. Now he is home alone
much of the time. In the mornings, Norma Jean disappears, leaving a cooling
place in the bed. She eats a cereal called Body Buddies, and she leaves the bowl
on the table, with the soggy tan balls floating in a milk puddle. He sees things
about Norma Jean that he never realized before. When she chops onions, she
stares off into a corner, as if she can't bear to look. She puts on her house
slippers almost precisely at nine o'clock every evening and nudges her jogging
shoes under the couch. She saves bread heels for the birds. Leroy watches the
birds at the feeder. He notices the peculiar way goldfinches fly past the window.
They close their wings, then fall, then spread their wings to catch and lift

themselves. He wonders if they close their eyes when they fall. Norma Jean closes her eyes when they are in bed. She wants the lights turned out. Even then, he is sure she closes her eyes.

He goes for long drives around town. He tends to drive a car rather 55 carelessly. Power steering and an automatic shift make a car feel so small and inconsequential that his body is hardly involved in the driving process. His injured leg stretches out comfortably. Once or twice he has almost hit something, but even the prospect of an accident seems minor in a car. He cruises the new subdivisions, feeling like a criminal rehearsing for a robbery. Norma Jean is probably right about a log house being inappropriate here in the new subdivisions. All the houses look grand and complicated. They depress him.

One day when Leroy comes home from a drive he finds Norma Jean in tears. She is in the kitchen making a potato and mushroom-soup casserole, with grated-cheese topping. She is crying because her mother caught her smoking.

"I didn't hear her coming. I was standing here puffing away pretty as you please," Norma Jean says, wiping her eyes.

"I knew it would happen sooner or later," says Leroy, putting his arm around her.

"She don't know the meaning of the word 'knock,' " says Norma Jean. "It's a wonder she hadn't caught me years ago."

"Think of it this way," Leroy says. "What if she caught me with a joint?" 60

"You better not let her!" Norma Jean shrieks. "I'm warning you, Leroy Moffitt!"

"I'm just kidding. Here, play me a tune. That'll help you relax."

Norma Jean puts the casserole in the oven and sets the timer. Then she plays a ragtime tune, with horns and banjo, as Leroy lights up a joint and lies on the couch, laughing to himself about Mabel's catching him at it. He thinks of Stevie Hamilton — a doctor's son pushing grass. Everything is funny. The whole town seems crazy and small. He is reminded of Virgil Mathis, a boastful policeman Leroy used to shoot pool with. Virgil recently led a drug bust in a back room at a bowling alley, where he seized ten thousand dollars' worth of marijuana. The newspaper had a picture of him holding up the bags of grass and grinning widely. Right now, Leroy can imagine Virgil breaking down the door and arresting him with a lungful of smoke. Virgil would probably have been alerted to the scene because of all the racket Norma Jean is making. Now she sounds like a hard-rock band. Norma Jean is terrific. When she switches to a Latin-rhythm version of "Sunshine Superman," Leroy hums along. Norma Jean's foot goes up and down, up and down.

"Well, what do you think?" Leroy says, when Norma Jean pauses to search through her music.

"What do I think about what?" 65

His mind has gone blank. Then he says, "I'll sell my rig and build us a house." That wasn't what he wanted to say. He wanted to know what she thought — what she *really* thought — about them.

"Don't start in on that again," says Norma Jean. She begins playing "Who'll Be the Next in Line?"

Leroy used to tell hitchhikers his whole life story — about his travels, his hometown, the baby. He would end with a question: "Well, what do you think?" It was just a rhetorical question. In time, he had the feeling that he'd been telling the same story over and over to the same hitchhikers. He quit talking to hitchhikers when he realized how his voice sounded — whining and self-pitying, like some teenage-tragedy song. Now Leroy has the sudden impulse to tell Norma Jean about himself, as if he had just met her. They have known each other so long they have forgotten a lot about each other. They could become reacquainted. But when the oven timer goes off and she runs to the kitchen, he forgets why he wants to do this.

The next day, Mabel drops by. It is Saturday and Norma Jean is cleaning. Leroy is studying the plans of his log house, which have finally come in the mail. He has them spread out on the table — big sheets of stiff blue paper, with diagrams and numbers printed in white. While Norma Jean runs the vacuum, Mabel drinks coffee. She sets her coffee cup on a blueprint.

"I'm just waiting for time to pass," she says to Leroy, drumming her fingers   70
on the table.

As soon as Norma Jean switches off the vacuum, Mabel says in a loud voice, "Did you hear about the datsun dog that killed the baby?"

Norma Jean says, "The word is 'dachshund.' "

"They put the dog on trial. It chewed the baby's legs off. The mother was in the next room all the time." She raises her voice. "They thought it was neglect."

Norma Jean is holding her ears. Leroy manages to open the refrigerator and get some Diet Pepsi to offer Mabel. Mabel still has some coffee and she waves away the Pepsi.

"Datsuns are like that," Mabel says. "They're jealous dogs. They'll tear a   75
place to pieces if you don't keep an eye on them."

"You better watch out what you're saying, Mabel," says Leroy.

"Well, facts is facts."

Leroy looks out the window at his rig. It is like a huge piece of furniture gathering dust in the backyard. Pretty soon it will be an antique. He hears the vacuum cleaner. Norma Jean seems to be cleaning the living room rug again.

Later, she says to Leroy, "She just said that about the baby because she caught me smoking. She's trying to pay me back."

"What are you talking about?" Leroy says, nervously shuffling blueprints.   80

"You know good and well," Norma Jean says. She is sitting in a kitchen chair with her feet up and her arms wrapped around her knees. She looks small and helpless. She says, "The very idea, her bringing up a subject like that! Saying it was neglect."

"She didn't mean that," Leroy says.

"She might not have *thought* she meant it. She always says things like that. You don't know how she goes on."

"But she didn't really mean it. She was just talking."

Leroy opens a king-sized bottle of beer and pours it into two glasses, dividing it carefully. He hands a glass to Norma Jean and she takes it from him mechanically. For a long time, they sit by the kitchen window watching the birds at the feeder.

Something is happening. Norma Jean is going to night school. She has graduated from her six-week body-building course and now she is taking an adult-education course in composition at Paducah Community College. She spends her evenings outlining paragraphs.

"First you have a topic sentence," she explains to Leroy. "Then you divide it up. Your secondary topic has to be connected to your primary topic."

To Leroy, this sounds intimidating. "I never was any good in English," he says.

"It makes a lot of sense."

"What are you doing this for, anyhow?"

She shrugs. "It's something to do." She stands up and lifts her dumbbells a few times.

"Driving a rig, nobody cared about my English."

"I'm not criticizing your English."

Norma Jean used to say, "If I lose ten minutes' sleep, I just drag all day." Now she stays up late, writing compositions. She got a B on her first paper — a how-to theme on soup-based casseroles. Recently Norma Jean has been cooking unusual foods — tacos, lasagna, Bombay chicken. She doesn't play the organ anymore, though her second paper was called "Why Music Is Important to Me." She sits at the kitchen table, concentrating on her outlines, while Leroy plays with his log house plans, practicing with a set of Lincoln Logs. The thought of getting a truckload of notched, numbered logs scares him, and he wants to be prepared. As he and Norma Jean work together at the kitchen table, Leroy has the hopeful thought that they are sharing something, but he knows he is a fool to think this. Norma Jean is miles away. He knows he is going to lose her. Like Mabel, he is just waiting for time to pass.

One day, Mabel is there before Norma Jean gets home from work, and Leroy finds himself confiding in her. Mabel, he realizes, must know Norma Jean better than he does.

"I don't know what's got into that girl," Mabel says. "She used to go to bed with the chickens. Now you say she's up all hours. Plus her a-smoking. I like to died."

"I want to make her this beautiful home," Leroy says, indicating the Lincoln Logs. "I don't think she even wants it. Maybe she was happier with me gone."

"She don't know what to make of you, coming home like this."

"Is that it?"

Mabel takes the roof off his Lincoln Log cabin. "You couldn't get *me* in   100
a log cabin," she says. "I was raised in one. It's no picnic, let me tell you."

"They're different now," says Leroy.

"I tell you what," Mabel says, smiling oddly at Leroy.

"What?"

"Take her on down to Shiloh. Y'all need to get out together, stir a little.
Her brain's all balled up over them books."

Leroy can see traces of Norma Jean's features in her mother's face. Mabel's   105
worn face has the texture of crinkled cotton, but suddenly she looks pretty. It
occurs to Leroy that Mabel has been hinting all along that she wants them to
take her with them to Shiloh.

"Let's all go to Shiloh," he says. "You and me and her. Come Sunday."

Mabel throws up her hands in protest. "Oh, no, not me. Young folks want
to be by theirselves."

When Norma Jean comes in with groceries, Leroy says excitedly, "Your
mama here's been dying to go to Shiloh for thirty-five years. It's about time
we went, don't you think?"

"I'm not going to butt in on anybody's second honeymoon," Mabel says.

"Who's going on a honeymoon, for Christ's sake?" Norma Jean says   110
loudly.

"I never raised no daughter of mine to talk that-a-way," Mabel says.

"You ain't seen nothing yet," says Norma Jean. She starts putting away
boxes and cans, slamming cabinet doors.

"There's a log cabin at Shiloh," Mabel says. "It was there during the battle.
There's bullet holes in it."

"When are you going to *shut up* about Shiloh, Mama?" asks Norma Jean.

"I always thought Shiloh was the prettiest place, so full of history," Mabel   115
goes on. "I just hoped y'all could see it once before I die, so you could tell me
about it." Later, she whispers to Leroy, "You do what I said. A little change
is what she needs."

"Your name means 'the king,' " Norma Jean says to Leroy that evening.
He is trying to get her to go to Shiloh, and she is reading a book about another
century.

"Well, I reckon I ought to be right proud."

"I guess so."

"Am I still king around here?"

Norma Jean flexes her biceps and feels them for hardness. "I'm not fooling   120
around with anybody, if that's what you mean," she says.

"Would you tell me if you were?"

"I don't know."

"What does *your* name mean?"

"It was Marilyn Monroe's real name."

"No kidding!"   125

"Norma comes from the Normans. They were invaders," she says. She closes her book and looks hard at Leroy. "I'll go to Shiloh with you if you'll stop staring at me."

On Sunday, Norma Jean packs a picnic and they go to Shiloh. To Leroy's relief, Mabel says she does not want to come with them. Norma Jean drives, and Leroy, sitting beside her, feels like some boring hitchhiker she has picked up. He tries some conversation, but she answers him in monosyllables. At Shiloh, she drives aimlessly through the park, past bluffs and trails and steep ravines. Shiloh is an immense place, and Leroy cannot see it as a battleground. It is not what he expected. He thought it would look like a golf course. Monuments are everywhere, showing through the thick clusters of trees. Norma Jean passes the log cabin Mabel mentioned. It is surrounded by tourists looking for bullet holes.

"That's not the kind of log house I've got in mind," says Leroy apologetically.

"I know *that*."

"This is a pretty place. Your mama was right."   130

"It's OK," says Norma Jean. "Well, we've seen it. I hope she's satisfied."

They burst out laughing together.

At the park museum, a movie on Shiloh is shown every half hour, but they decide that they don't want to see it. They buy a souvenir Confederate flag for Mabel, and then they find a picnic spot near the cemetery. Norma Jean has brought a picnic cooler, with pimiento sandwiches, soft drinks, and Yodels. Leroy eats a sandwich and then smokes a joint, hiding it behind the picnic cooler. Norma Jean has quit smoking altogether. She is picking cake crumbs from the cellophane wrapper, like a fussy bird.

Leroy says, "So the boys in gray ended up in Corinth. The Union soldiers zapped 'em finally. April 7, 1862."

They both know that he doesn't know any history. He is just talking about   135
some of the historical plaques they have read. He feels awkward, like a boy on a date with an older girl. They are still just making conversation.

"Corinth is where Mama eloped to," says Norma Jean.

They sit in silence and stare at the cemetery for the Union dead and, beyond, at a tall cluster of trees. Campers are parked nearby, bumper to bumper, and small children in bright clothing are cavorting and squealing. Norma Jean wads up the cake wrapper and squeezes it tightly in her hand. Without looking at Leroy, she says, "I want to leave you."

Leroy takes a bottle of Coke out of the cooler and flips off the cap. He holds the bottle poised near his mouth but cannot remember to take a drink. Finally he says, "No, you don't."

"Yes, I do."

"I won't let you."   140

"You can't stop me."

"Don't do me that way."

Leroy knows Norma Jean will have her own way. "Didn't I promise to be home from now on?" he says.

"In some ways, a woman prefers a man who wanders," says Norma Jean. "That sounds crazy, I know."

"You're not crazy."

Leroy remembers to drink from his Coke. Then he says, "Yes, you *are* crazy. You and me could start all over again. Right back at the beginning."

"We *have* started all over again," says Norma Jean. "And this is how it turned out."

"What did I do wrong?"

"Nothing."

"Is this one of those women's lib things?" Leroy asks.

"Don't be funny."

The cemetery, a green slope dotted with white markers, looks like a subdivision site. Leroy is trying to comprehend that his marriage is breaking up but for some reason he is wondering about white slabs in a graveyard.

"Everything was fine till Mama caught me smoking," says Norma Jean, standing up. "That set something off."

"What are you talking about?"

"She won't leave me alone — *you* won't leave me alone." Norma Jean seems to be crying, but she is looking away from him. "I feel eighteen again. I can't face that all over again." She starts walking away. "No, it *wasn't* fine. I don't know what I'm saying. Forget it."

Leroy takes a lungful of smoke and closes his eyes as Norma Jean's words sink in. He tries to focus on the fact that thirty-five hundred soldiers died on the grounds around him. He can only think of that war as a board game with plastic soldiers. Leroy almost smiles, as he compares the Confederates' daring attack on the Union camps and Virgil Mathis's raid on the bowling alley. General Grant, drunk and furious, shoved the Southerners back to Corinth, where Mabel and Jet Beasley were married years later, when Mabel was still thin and good-looking. The next day, Mabel and Jet visited the battleground and then Norma Jean was born, and then she married Leroy and they had a baby, which they lost, and now Leroy and Norma Jean are here at the same battleground. Leroy knows he is leaving out a lot. He is leaving out the insides of history. History was always just names and dates to him. It occurs to him that building a house out of logs is similarly empty — too simple. And the real inner workings of a marriage, like most of history, have escaped him. Now he sees that building a log house is the dumbest idea he could have had. It was clumsy of him to think Norma Jean would want a log house. It was a crazy idea. He'll have to think of something else, quickly. He will wad the blueprints into tight balls and fling them into the lake. Then he'll get moving again. He opens his eyes. Norma Jean has moved away and is walking through the cemetery, following a serpentine brick path.

Leroy gets up to follow his wife, but his good leg is asleep and his bad leg still hurts him. Norma Jean is far away, walking rapidly toward the bluff by

145

150

155

the river, and he tries to hobble toward her. Some children run past him, screaming noisily. Norma Jean has reached the bluff, and she is looking out over the Tennessee River. Now she turns toward Leroy and waves her arms. Is she beckoning to him? She seems to be doing an exercise for her chest muscles. The sky is unusually pale — the color of the dust ruffle Mabel made for their bed.   1982

INVESTIGATIONS

1. In paragraph 26, Leroy thinks, "Nobody knows anything. . . . The answers are always changing," yet at several points in the story he feels certain he knows he'll lose Norma Jean. How do you account for this?

2. How is it possible that Norma Jean and Leroy "have known each other so long they have forgotten a lot about each other" (para. 68)? If you could, what would you tell each about the other? Why might every possible reminder still be no help?

3. In what ways can this story be seen as a battle? How might both the Shiloh battlefield and Leroy's dream of building a log house be seen as illusory?

4. In paragraph 156, Leroy thinks that "the real inner workings of a marriage, like most of history, have escaped him." What evidence do you find that they've also escaped Norma Jean? What do you think are "the real inner workings of a marriage"? How does one find out what they are?

5. Compare Kirby's attempts to come to terms with his feelings for Mieko in "Long Distance" to Leroy's concern about losing Norma Jean. What similarities do you find between them that would help account for their inability to comprehend what's happening to them? Why can't they take more effective action?

The Widow

Her life was spent in deference to his comfort.
The rocking chair was his, the window seat,
the firm side of the mattress.

Hers were the midnights with sickly children,
pickups after guests left, the single   5
misery of childbirth. She had duties:

to feed him and to follow and to forgive his few
excesses. Sometimes he drank, he puffed cigars,
he belched, he brought the money in

and brought Belleek and Waterford for birthdays,   10
rings and rare scents for Christmas; twice he sent
a card with flowers: "All my love, always."

At night she spread herself like linen out
for him to take his feastly pleasures in
and liked it well enough, or said she did, day in,   15

day out. For thirty years they agreed on this
until one night, after dinner dancing,
he died a gassy death at fifty — turned

a quiet purple in his chair, quit breathing.
She grieved for him with a real grief for she missed him   20
sorely. After six months of this, she felt relieved.   1986

INVESTIGATIONS

1. To what extent is this marriage the product of outmoded attitudes toward
   the proper roles of men and women? What evidence does the poem provide
   that the partners saw each other as equals? To what extent do partners in

---

Descended from the Lynches of County Clare, Ireland, THOMAS LYNCH (b. 1948) grew up in Detroit and now lives in Milford, Michigan, where he works as an undertaker. He is the author of *Skating with Heather Grace* (1986), a collection of poems.

all long-term intimate relationships spend their lives "in deference" to one another's "comfort" (line 1)?

2. In what ways does the poem's final line describe a final stage in marriage? How did you account for this stage in "Write Before Reading" (p. 652)?

3. If the widow and her husband had talked to death "daily, as to a neighbor" (Rich's "Love Poem," line 27), how might the story this poem tells have been different?

4. After rereading Berry's "Except," Rich's "Love Poem," and Dobler's "Hospital Call," write a 250–500-word essay in which you classify the kinds of love displayed in these poems and provide a rationale for your classification.

LESLIE MARMON SILKO

Lullaby

The sun had gone down but the snow in the wind gave off its own light. It came in thick tufts like new wool — washed before the weaver spins it. Ayah reached out for it like her own babies had, and she smiled when she remembered how she had laughed at them. She was an old woman now, and her life had become memories. She sat down with her back against the wide cottonwood tree, feeling the rough bark on her back bones; she faced east and listened to the wind and snow sing a high-pitched Yeibechei song. Out of the wind she felt warmer, and she could watch the wide, fluffy snow fill in her tracks, steadily, until the direction she had come from was gone. By the light of the snow she could see the dark outline of the big arroyo a few feet away. She was sitting on the edge of Cebolleta Creek, where in the springtime the thin cows would graze on grass already chewed flat to the ground. In the wide, deep creek bed where only a trickle of water flowed in the summer, the skinny cows would wander, looking for new grass along winding paths splashed with manure.

Ayah pulled the old Army blanket over her head like a shawl. Jimmie's blanket — the one he had sent to her. That was a long time ago and the green wool was faded, and it was unraveling on the edges. She did not want to think about Jimmie. So she thought about the weaving and the way her mother had done it. On the tall wooden loom set into the sand under a tamarack tree for

---

Born in Albuquerque, New Mexico, in 1948, LESLIE MARMON SILKO grew up at Laguna Pueblo and now lives in Tucson, Arizona. Author of *Ceremony* (1977), one of the first novels published by an American Indian woman, Silko has also published *Laguna Woman: Poems* (1974) and *Storyteller* (1981), a collection of poems and short stories.

shade. She could see it clearly. She had been only a little girl when her grandma gave her the wooden combs to pull the twigs and burrs from the raw, freshly washed wool. And while she combed the wool, her grandma sat beside her, spinning a silvery strand of yarn around the smooth cedar spindle. Her mother worked at the loom with yarns dyed bright yellow and red and gold. She watched them dye the yarn in boiling black pots full of beeweed petals, juniper berries, and sage. The blankets her mother made were soft and woven so tight that rain rolled off them like birds' feathers. Ayah remembered sleeping warm on cold windy nights, wrapped in her mother's blankets on the hogan's sandy floor.

The snow drifted now, with the northwest wind hurling it in gusts. It drifted up around her black overshoes — old ones with little metal buckles. She smiled at the snow which was trying to cover her little by little. She could remember when they had no black rubber overshoes; only the high buckskin leggings that they wrapped over their elkhide moccasins. If the snow was dry or frozen, a person could walk all day and not get wet; and in the evenings the beams of the ceiling would hang with lengths of pale buckskin leggings, drying out slowly.

She felt peaceful remembering. She didn't feel cold any more. Jimmie's blanket seemed warmer than it had ever been. And she could remember the morning he was born. She could remember whispering to her mother, who was sleeping on the other side of the hogan, to tell her it was time now. She did not want to wake the others. The second time she called to her, her mother stood up and pulled on her shoes; she knew. They walked to the old stone hogan together, Ayah walking a step behind her mother. She waited alone, learning the rhythms of the pains while her mother went to call the old woman to help them. The morning was already warm even before dawn and Ayah smelled the bee flowers blooming and the young willow growing at the springs. She could remember that so clearly, but his birth merged into the births of the other children and to her it became all the same birth. They named him for the summer morning and in English they called him Jimmie.

It wasn't like Jimmie died. He just never came back, and one day a dark   5
blue sedan with white writing on its doors pulled up in front of the boxcar shack where the rancher let the Indians live. A man in a khaki uniform trimmed in gold gave them a yellow piece of paper and told them that Jimmie was dead. He said the Army would try to get the body back and then it would be shipped to them; but it wasn't likely because the helicopter had burned after it crashed. All of this was told to Chato because he could understand English. She stood inside the doorway holding the baby while Chato listened. Chato spoke English like a white man and he spoke Spanish too. He was taller than the white man and he stood straighter too. Chato didn't explain why; he just told the military man they could keep the body if they found it. The white man looked bewildered; he nodded his head and he left. Then Chato looked at her and shook his head, and then he told her, "Jimmie isn't coming home anymore," and

when he spoke, he used the words to speak of the dead. She didn't cry then, but she hurt inside with anger. And she mourned him as the years passed, when a horse fell with Chato and broke his leg, and the white rancher told them he wouldn't pay Chato until he could work again. She mourned Jimmie because he would have worked for his father then; he would have saddled the big bay horse and ridden the fence lines each day, with wire cutters and heavy gloves, fixing the breaks in the barbed wire and putting the stray cattle back inside again.

She mourned him after the white doctors came to take Danny and Ella away. She was at the shack alone that day they came. It was back in the days before they hired Navajo women to go with them as interpreters. She recognized one of the doctors. She had seen him at the children's clinic at Cañoncito about a month ago. They were wearing khaki uniforms and they waved papers at her and a black ball-point pen, trying to make her understand their English words. She was frightened by the way they looked at the children, like the lizard watches the fly. Danny was swinging on the tire swing on the elm tree behind the rancher's house, and Ella was toddling around the front door, dragging the broomstick horse Chato made for her. Ayah could see they wanted her to sign the papers, and Chato had taught her to sign her name. It was something she was proud of. She only wanted them to go, and to take their eyes away from her children.

She took the pen from the man without looking at his face and she signed the papers in three different places he pointed to. She stared at the ground by their feet and waited for them to leave. But they stood there and began to point and gesture at the children. Danny stopped swinging. Ayah could see his fear. She moved suddenly and grabbed Ella into her arms; the child squirmed, trying to get back to her toys. Ayah ran with the baby toward Danny; she screamed for him to run and then she grabbed him around his chest and carried him too. She ran south into the foothills of juniper trees and black lava rock. Behind her she heard the doctors running, but they had been taken by surprise, and as the hills became steeper and the cholla cactus were thicker, they stopped. When she reached the top of the hill, she stopped to listen in case they were circling around her. But in a few minutes she heard a car engine start and they drove away. The children had been too surprised to cry while she ran with them. Danny was shaking and Ella's little fingers were gripping Ayah's blouse.

She stayed up in the hills for the rest of the day, sitting on a black lava boulder in the sunshine where she could see for miles all around her. The sky was light blue and cloudless, and it was warm for late April. The sun warmth relaxed her and took the fear and anger away. She lay back on the rock and watched the sky. It seemed to her that she could walk into the sky, stepping through clouds endlessly. Danny played with little pebbles and stones, pretending they were birds eggs and then little rabbits. Ella sat at her feet and dropped fistfuls of dirt into the breeze, watching the dust and particles of sand intently. Ayah watched a hawk soar high above them, dark wings gliding; hunting or only watching, she did not know. The hawk was patient and he circled all afternoon before he disappeared around the high volcanic peak the Mexicans called Guadalupe.

Late in the afternoon, Ayah looked down at the gray boxcar shack with the paint all peeled from the wood: the stove pipe on the roof was rusted and crooked. The fire she had built that morning in the oil drum stove had burned out. Ella was asleep in her lap now and Danny sat close to her, complaining that he was hungry; he asked when they would go to the house. "We will stay up here until your father comes," she told him, "because those white men were chasing us." The boy remembered then and he nodded at her silently.

If Jimmie had been there he could have read those papers and explained   10 to her what they said. Ayah would have known then, never to sign them. The doctors came back the next day and they brought a BIA[1] policeman with them. They told Chato they had her signature and that was all they needed. Except for the kids. She listened to Chato sullenly; she hated him when he told her it was the old woman who died in the winter, spitting blood; it was her old grandma who had given the children this disease. "They don't spit blood," she said coldly. "The whites lie." She held Ella and Danny close to her, ready to run to the hills again. "I want a medicine man first," she said to Chato, not looking at him. He shook his head. "It's too late now. The policeman is with them. You signed the paper." His voice was gentle.

It was worse than if they had died: to lose the children and to know that somewhere, in a place called Colorado, in a place full of sick and dying strangers, her children were without her. There had been babies that died soon after they were born, and one that died before he could walk. She had carried them herself, up to the boulders and great pieces of the cliff that long ago crashed down from Long Mesa; she laid them in the crevices of sandstone and buried them in fine brown sand with round quartz pebbles that washed down the hills in the rain. She had endured it because they had been with her. But she could not bear this pain. She did not sleep for a long time after they took her children. She stayed on the hill where they had fled the first time, and she slept rolled up in the blanket Jimmie had sent her. She carried the pain in her belly and it was fed by everything she saw: the blue sky of their last day together and the dust and pebbles they played with; the swing in the elm tree and broomstick horse choked life from her. The pain filled her stomach and there was no room for food or for her lungs to fill with air. The air and the food would have been theirs.

She hated Chato, not because he let the policeman and doctors put the screaming children in the government car, but because he had taught her to sign her name. Because it was like the old ones always told her about learning their language or any of their ways: It endangers you. She slept alone on the hill until the middle of November when the first snows came. Then she made a bed for herself where the children had slept. She did not lie down beside

---

[1] Bureau of Indian Affairs. [Ed.]

Chato again until many years later, when he was sick and shivering and only her body could keep him warm. The illness came after the white rancher told Chato he was too old to work for him anymore, and Chato and his old woman should be out of the shack by the next afternoon because the rancher had hired new people to work there. That had satisfied her. To see how the white man repaid Chato's years of loyalty and work. All of Chato's fine-sounding English talk didn't change things.

It snowed steadily and the luminous light from the snow gradually diminished into the darkness. Somewhere in Cebolleta a dog barked and other village dogs joined with it. Ayah looked in the direction she had come, from the bar where Chato was buying the wine. Sometimes he told her to go on ahead and wait; and then he never came. And when she finally went back looking for him, she would find him passed out at the bottom of the wooden steps to Azzie's Bar. All the wine would be gone and most of the money too, from the pale blue check that came to them once a month in a government envelope. It was then that she would look at his face and his hands, scarred by ropes and the barbed wire of all those years, and she would think, this man is a stranger; for forty years she had smiled at him and cooked his food, but he remained a stranger. She stood up again, with the snow almost to her knees, and she walked back to find Chato.

It was hard to walk in the deep snow and she felt the air burn in her lungs. She stopped a short distance from the bar to rest and readjust the blanket. But this time he wasn't waiting for her on the bottom step with his old Stetson hat pulled down and his shoulders hunched up in his long wool overcoat.

She was careful not to slip on the wooden steps. When she pushed the   15
door open, warm air and cigarette smoke hit her face. She looked around slowly and deliberately, in every corner, in every dark place that the old man might find to sleep. The bar owner didn't like Indians in there, especially Navajos, but he let Chato come in because he could talk Spanish like he was one of them. The men at the bar stared at her, and the bartender saw that she left the door open wide. Snowflakes were flying inside like moths and melting into a puddle on the oiled wood floor. He motioned to her to close the door, but she did not see him. She held herself straight and walked across the room slowly, searching the room with every step. The snow in her hair melted and she could feel it on her forehead. At the far corner of the room, she saw red flames at the mica window of the old stove door; she looked behind the stove just to make sure. The bar got quiet except for the Spanish polka music playing on the jukebox. She stood by the stove and shook the snow from her blanket and held it near the stove to dry. The wet wool smell reminded her of newborn goats in early March, brought inside to warm near the fire. She felt calm.

In past years they would have told her to get out. But her hair was white now and her face was wrinkled. They looked at her like she was a spider crawling slowly across the room. They were afraid; she could feel the fear. She looked at their faces steadily. They reminded her of the first time the white people brought her children back to her that winter. Danny had been shy and hid behind the thin white woman who brought them. And the baby had not known her until Ayah took her into her arms, and then Ella had nuzzled close to her as she had when she was nursing. The blonde woman was nervous and kept looking at a dainty gold watch on her wrist. She sat on the bench near the small window and watched the dark snow clouds gather around the mountains; she was worrying about the unpaved road. She was frightened by what she saw inside too: the strips of venison drying on a rope across the ceiling and the children jabbering excitedly in a language she did not know. So they stayed for only a few hours. Ayah watched the government car disappear down the road and she knew they were already being weaned from these lava hills and from this sky. The last time they came was in early June, and Ella stared at her the way the men in the bar were now staring. Ayah did not try to pick her up; she smiled at her instead and spoke cheerfully to Danny. When he tried to answer her, he could not seem to remember and he spoke English words with the Navajo. But he gave her a scrap of paper that he had found somewhere and carried in his pocket; it was folded in half, and he shyly looked up at her and said it was a bird. She asked Chato if they were home for good this time. He spoke to the white woman and she shook her head. "How much longer?" he asked, and she said she didn't know; but Chato saw how she stared at the boxcar shack. Ayah turned away then. She did not say good-bye.

She felt satisfied that the men in the bar feared her. Maybe it was her face and the way she held her mouth with teeth clenched tight, like there was nothing anyone could do to her now. She walked north down the road, searching for the old man. She did this because she had the blanket, and there would be no place for him except with her and the blanket in the old adobe barn near the arroyo. They always slept there when they came to Cebolleta. If the money and the wine were gone, she would be relieved because then they could go home again; back to the old hogan with a dirt roof and rock walls where she herself had been born. And the next day the old man could go back to the few sheep they still had, to follow along behind them, guiding them, into dry sandy arroyos where sparse grass grew. She knew he did not like walking behind old ewes when for so many years he rode big quarter horses and worked with cattle. But she wasn't sorry for him; he should have known all along what would happen.

There had not been enough rain for their garden in five years; and that was when Chato finally hitched a ride into the town and brought back brown boxes of rice and sugar and big tin cans of welfare peaches. After that, at the first of the month they went to Cebolleta to ask the postmaster for the check; and then Chato would go to the bar and cash it. They did this as they planted the garden every May, not because anything would survive the summer dust, but because it was time to do this. The journey passed the days that smelled silent and dry like the caves above the canyon with yellow painted buffaloes on their walls.

He was walking along the pavement when she found him. He did not stop or turn around when he heard her behind him. She walked beside him and she noticed how slowly he moved now. He smelled strong of woodsmoke and urine. Lately he had been forgetting. Sometimes he called her by his sister's name and she had been gone for a long time. Once she had found him wandering on the road to the white man's ranch, and she asked him why he was going that way; he laughed at her and said, "You know they can't run that ranch without me," and he walked on determined, limping on the leg that had been crushed many years before. Now he looked at her curiously, as if for the first time, but he kept shuffling along, moving slowly along the side of the highway. His gray hair had grown long and spread out on the shoulders of the long overcoat. He wore the old felt hat pulled down over his ears. His boots were worn out at the toes and he had stuffed pieces of an old red shirt in the holes. The rags made his feet look like little animals up to their ears in snow. She laughed at his feet; the snow muffled the sound of her laugh. He stopped and looked at her again. The wind had quit blowing and the snow was falling straight down; the southeast sky was beginning to clear and Ayah could see a star.

"Let's rest awhile," she said to him. They walked away from the road and 20 up the slope to the giant boulders that had tumbled down from the red sandrock mesa throughout the centuries of rainstorms and earth tremors. In a place where the boulders shut out the wind, they sat down with their backs against the rock. She offered half of the blanket to him and they sat wrapped together.

The storm passed swiftly. The clouds moved east. They were massive and full, crowding together across the sky. She watched them with the feeling of horses — steely blue-gray horses startled across the sky. The powerful haunches pushed into the distances and the tail hairs streamed white mist behind them. The sky cleared. Ayah saw that there was nothing between her and the stars. The light was crystalline. There was no shimmer, no distortion through earth haze. She breathed the clarity of the night sky; she smelled the purity of the half moon and the stars. He was lying on his side with his knees pulled up near his belly for warmth. His eyes were closed now, and in the light from the stars and the moon, he looked young again.

She could see it descend out of the night sky: an icy stillness from the edge of the thin moon. She recognized the freezing. It came gradually, sinking snowflake by snowflake until the crust was heavy and deep. It had the strength of the stars in Orion, and its journey was endless. Ayah knew that with the wine he would sleep. He would not feel it. She tucked the blanket around him, remembering how it was when Ella had been with her; and she felt the rush so big inside her heart for the babies. And she sang the only song she knew to sing for babies. She could not remember if she had ever sung it to her children, but she knew that her grandmother had sung it and her mother had sung it:

> *The earth is your mother,*
> * she holds you.*
> *The sky is your father,*
> * he protects you.*
> *Sleep,*
> *sleep.*
> *Rainbow is your sister,*
> * she loves you.*
> *The winds are your brothers,*
> * they sing to you.*
> *Sleep,*
> *sleep.*
> *We are together always*
> *We are together always*
> *There never was a time*
> *when this*
> *was not so.*   1981

INVESTIGATIONS

1. Locate the places in the story where Ayah blames Chato or someone (or something) else for her and her children's suffering. How much responsibility do you think she bears for what happens to her? How could blaming Chato be seen as part of her love for him?
2. What circumstances shape the course of Ayah's life? What are the similarities between these circumstances and those that shape the life of Lynch's "The Widow"? What are the similarities between these circumstances and those you identified in your response to "Write Before Reading" (p. 652)?
3. In what ways might this story be considered an illustration of what the speaker of Rich's "Love Poem" means by "learning to be true" with death?
4. In what ways does this story illustrate how love frustrates rational explanation?

JOHN UPDIKE

Gesturing

She told him with a little gesture he had never seen her use before. Joan had called from the station, having lunched, Richard knew, with her lover. It was a Saturday, and his older son had taken his convertible; Joan's Volvo was new and for several minutes refused to go into first gear for him. By the time he had reached the center of town, she had walked down the main street and up the hill to the green. It was September, leafy and warm, yet with a crystal chill on things, an uncanny clarity. Even from a distance they smiled to see each other. She opened the door and seated herself, fastening the safety belt to silence its chastening buzz. Her face was rosy from her walk, her city clothes looked like a costume, she carried a small package or two, token of her "shopping." Richard tried to pull a U-turn on the narrow street, and in the long moment of his halting and groping for reverse gear, she told him. "Darley," she said and, oddly, tentatively, soundlessly, tapped the fingers of one hand into the palm of the other, a gesture between a child's clap of glee and an adult's signal for attention, "I've decided to kick you out. I'm going to ask you to leave town."

Abruptly full, his heart thumped; it was what he wanted. "OK," he said carefully. "If you think you can manage." He glanced at her rosy, alert face to see if she meant it; he could not believe she did. A red, white, and blue mail truck that had braked to a stop behind them tapped its horn, more reminder than rebuke; the Maples were known in the town. They had lived here most of their married life.

Richard found reverse, backed up, completed the turn, and they headed home, skimming. The car, so new and stiff, in motion felt high and light, as if it, too, had just been vaporized in her little playful clap. "Things are stagnant," she explained, "stuck; we're not going anywhere."

"I will not give her up," he interposed.

"Don't tell me, you've told me."   5

"Nor do I see you giving him up."

"I would if you asked. Are you asking?"

"No. Horrors. He's all I've got."

"Well, then. Go where you want, I think Boston would be most fun for the kids to visit. And the least boring for you."

JOHN UPDIKE (b. 1932) has published more than thirty books, including *Self-Consciousness: Memoirs* (1989), the novel *Rabbit at Rest* (1990), *Facing Nature: Poems* (1985), and *Trust Me: Short Stories* (1987). He once said, "Everything can be as interesting as every other thing. An old milk carton is worth a rose."

"I agree. When do you see this happening?" Her profile, in the side of his   10 vision, felt brittle, about to break if he said a wrong word, too rough a word. He was holding his breath, trying to stay up, high and light, like the car. They went over the bump this side of the bridge; cigarette smoke jarred loose from Joan's face.

"As soon as you can find a place," she said. "Next week. Is that too soon?"

"Probably."

"Is this too sad? Do I seem brutal to you?"

"No, you seem wonderful, very gentle and just, as always. It's right. It's just something I couldn't do myself. How can you possibly live without me?"

In the edge of his vision her face turned; he turned to see, and her expres-   15 sion was mischievous, brave, flushed. They must have had wine at lunch. "Easy," Joan said. He knew it was a bluff, a brave gesture; she was begging for reprieve. But he held silent, he refused to argue. This way, he had her pride on his side.

The curves of the road poured by, mailboxes, trees, some of which were already scorched by the turn of the year. He asked, "Is this your idea, or his?"

"Mine. It came to me on the train. All Andy said was, I seemed to be feeding you all the time."

Richard had been sleeping, most nights, in the weeks since their summer of separated vacations, in a borrowed seaside shack two miles from their home; he tried to sleep there, but each evening, as the nights grew longer, it seemed easier, and kinder to the children, to eat the dinner Joan had cooked. He was used to her cooking; indeed, his body, every cell, was composed of her cooking. Dinner would lead to a postdinner drink, while the children (two were off at school, two were still homebound) plodded through their homework or stared at television, and drinking would lead to talking, confidences, harsh words, maudlin tears, and an occasional uxorious collapse upward, into bed. She was right; it was not healthy, nor progressive. The twenty years were by when it would have been convenient to love each other.

He found the apartment in Boston on the second day of hunting. The real-estate agent had red hair, a round bottom, and a mask of make-up worn as if to conceal her youth. Richard felt happy and scared, going up and down stairs behind her. Wearier of him than he was of her, she fidgeted the key into the lock, bucked the door open with her shoulder, and made her little openhanded gesture of helpless display.

The floor was neither wall-to-wall shag nor splintered wood, but black-   20 and-white tile, like the floor in a Vermeer; he glanced to the window, saw the skyscraper, and knew this would do. The skyscraper, for years suspended in a famous state of incompletion, was a beautiful disaster, famous because it was a disaster (glass kept falling from it) and disastrous because it was beautiful: The architect had had a vision. He had dreamed of an invisible building, though immense; the glass was meant to reflect the sky and the old low brick skyline of Boston, and to melt into the sky. Instead, the windows of mirroring glass kept falling to the street and were replaced by ugly opacities of black plywood.

Yet enough reflecting surface remained to give an impression, through the wavery old window of this sudden apartment, of huge blueness, a vertical cousin to the horizontal huge blueness of the sea that Richard awoke to each morning, in the now bone-deep morning chill of his unheated shack. He said to the redhead, "Fine," and her charcoal eyebrows lifted. His hands trembled as he signed the lease, having written "Sep" in the space for marital status. From a drugstore he phoned the news, not to his wife, whom it would sadden, but to his mistress, equally far away. "Well," he told her in an accusing voice, "I found one. I signed the lease. Incredible. In the middle of all this fine print, there was the one simple sentence, 'There shall be no water beds.' "

"You sound so shaky."

"I feel I've given birth to a black hole."

"Don't do it, if you don't want to." From the way Ruth's voice paused and faded, he imagined she was reaching for a cigarette, or an ashtray, settling herself to a session of lover babying.

"I do want to. She wants me to. We all want me to. Even the children are turned on. Or pretend to be."

She ignored the "pretend." "Describe it to me."   25

All he could remember was the floor, and the view of the blue disaster with reflected clouds drifting across its face. And the redhead. She had told him where to shop for food, where to do his laundry. He would have laundry?

"It sounds nice," was Ruth's remote response, when he had finished saying what he could. Two people, one of them a sweating black mailman, were waiting to use the phone booth. He hated the city already, its crowding, its hunger.

"What sounds nice about it?" he snapped.

"Are you so upset? Don't do it if you don't want to."

"Stop *say*ing that." It was a tedious formality both observed, the pretense   30 that they were free, within each of their marriages, to do as they pleased; guilt avoidance was the game, and Ruth had grown expert at it. Her words often seemed not real words but blank counters, phrases of an etiquette, partitions in a maze. Whereas his wife's words always opened in, transparent with meaning.

"What else can I say," Ruth asked, "except that I love you?" And at its far end, the phone sharply sighed. He could picture the gesture: She had turned her face away from the mouthpiece and forcefully exhaled, in that way she had, expressive of exasperation even when she felt none, of exhaling and simultaneously stubbing out a cigarette smoked not halfway down its length, so it crumpled under her impatient fingers like an insect fighting to live. Her conspicuous unthriftiness pained him. All waste pained him. He wanted abruptly to hang up but saw that, too, as a wasteful, empty gesture, and hung on.

Alone in his apartment, he discovered himself a neat and thrifty house-keeper. When a woman left, he would promptly set about restoring his bachelor order, emptying the ashtrays that, if the visitor had been Ruth, brimmed with long pale bodies prematurely extinguished and, if Joan, with butts so short as to be scarcely more than filters. Neither woman, it somehow pleased him to observe, ever made more than a gesture toward cleaning up — the bed a wreck, the dishes dirty, each of his three ashtrays (one glass, one pottery, and one a tin cookie-jar lid) systematically touched, like the bases in baseball. Emptying them, he would smile, depending, at Ruth's messy morgue or at Joan's nest of filters, discreet as white pebbles in a bowl of narcissi. When he chastised Ruth for stubbing out cigarettes still so long, she pointed out, of course, with her beautiful unblinking assumption of her own primary worth, how much better it was for *her,* for her lungs, to kill the cigarette early; and, of course, she was right, better other-destructive than self-destructive. Ruth was love, she was life, that was why he loved her. Yet Joan's compulsive economy, her discreet death wish, was as dearly familiar to him as her tiny repressed handwriting and the tight curls of her pubic hair, so Richard smiled emptying her ashtrays also. His smile was a gesture without an audience. He, who had originated his act among parents and grandparents, siblings and pets, and who had developed it for a public of schoolmates and teachers, and who had carried it to new refinements before an initially rapt audience of his own children, could not in solitude stop performing. He had engendered a companion of sorts, a single grand spectator — the blue skyscraper. He felt it with him all the time.

Blue, it showed greener than the sky. For a time Richard was puzzled, why the clouds reflected in it drifted in the same direction as the clouds behind it. With an effort of spatial imagination he perceived that a mirror does not reverse our motion, though it does transpose our ears, and gives our mouths a tweak, so that the face even of a loved one looks unfamiliar and ugly when seen in a mirror, the way she — queer thought! — always sees it. He saw that a mirror posed in its midst would not affect the motion of an army; and often half a reflected cloud matched the half of another beyond the building's edge, moving as one, pierced by a jet trail as though by Cupid's arrow. The disaster sat light on the city's heart. At night, it showed as a dim row of little lights, as if a slender ship were sailing the sky, and during a rain or fog, it vanished entirely, while the brick chimney pots and ironstone steeples in Richard's foreground swarthily intensified their substance. He tried to analyze the logic of window replacement, as revealed in the patterns of gap and glass. He detected no logic, just the slow-motion labor of invisible workers, emptying and filling cells of glass with the brainlessness of bees. If he watched for many minutes, he might see, like the condensation of a dewdrop, a blank space go glassy, and reflective, and greenish blue. Days passed before he realized that, on the old glass near his nose, the wavery panes of his own window, ghostly previous tenants armed with diamonds had scratched initials, names, dates, and cut deepest and whitest of all, the touching, comical vow, incised in two trisyllabic lines:

> *With this ring*
> *I thee wed*

What a transparent wealth of previous lives overlay a city's present joy! As he walked the streets, how own happiness surprised him. He had expected to be sad, guilty, bored. Instead, his days were snugly filled with his lists, his quests for food and hardware, his encounters with such problematical wife substitutes as the laundromat, where students pored over Hesse and picked at their chins while their clothes tumbled in eternal circular fall, where young black housewives hummed as they folded white linen. What an unexpected pleasure, walking home in the dark hugging to himself clean clothes hot as fresh bread, past the bow windows of Back Bay glowing like display cases. He felt sober and exhilarated and justified at the hour when, in the suburbs, rumpled from the commute, he would be into his hurried second predinner drink. He liked the bringing home of food, the tautological satisfaction of cooking a meal and then eating it all, as the radio fed Bach or Bechet into his ears and a book gazed open-faced from the reading stand he had bought; he liked the odd orderly game of consuming before food spoiled and drinking before milk soured. He liked the way airplanes roamed the brown night sky, a second, thinner city laid upon this one, and the way police sirens sang, scooping up some disaster not his. It could not last, such happiness. It was an interim, a holiday. But an oddly clean and just one, rectilinear, dignified, though marred by gaps of sudden fear and disorientation. Each hour had to be scheduled, lest he fall through. He moved like a water bug, like a skipping stone, upon the glassy tense surface of his new life. He walked everywhere. Once he walked to the base of the blue skyscraper, his companion and witness. It was hideous. Heavily planked and chicken-wired tunnels, guarded by barking policemen, protected pedestrians from falling glass and the owners of the building, already millions in the hole, from more lawsuits. Trestles and trucks jammed the cacophonous area. The lower floors were solid plywood, of a Stygian black; the building, so lovely in air, had tangled mucky roots. Richard avoided walking that way again.

When Ruth visited, they played a game, of washing — scouring, with a ^{35} Brillo pad — one white square of the Vermeer floor, so eventually it would all appear clean. The black squares they ignored. Naked, scrubbing, Ruth seemed on her knees a plump little steed, long hair swinging, soft breasts swaying in rhythm to her energetic circular strokes. Behind, her pubic hair, uncurly, made a kind of nether mane. So lovably strange, she rarely was allowed to clean more than one square. Time, so careful and regular for him, sped for them, and vanished. There seemed time even to talk only at the end, her hand on the door. She asked, "Isn't that building amazing, with the sunset in it?"

"I love that building. And it loves me."

"No. It's me who loves you."

"Can't you share?"

"No."

She felt possessive about the apartment; when he told her Joan had been ^{40} there, too, and, just for "fun," had slept with him, her husband, Ruth wailed into the telephone, "In *our* bed?"

"In *my* bed," he said, with uncharacteristic firmness.

"In your bed," she conceded, her voice husky as a sleepy child's.

When the conversation finally ended, his mistress sufficiently soothed, he had to go lean his vision against his inanimate, giant friend, dimming to mauve on one side, still cerulean on the other, faintly streaked with reflections of high cirrus. It spoke to him, as the gaze of a dumb beast speaks, of beauty and suffering, of a simplicity that must perish, of loss. Evening would soften its shade to slate; night would envelop its sides. Richard's focus shortened and he read, with irritation, for the hundredth time, that impudent, pious marring, that bit of litany, etched bright by the sun's fading fire.

> *With this ring*
> *I thee wed*

Ruth, months ago, had removed her wedding ring. Coming here to embark with him upon an overnight trip, she wore on that naked finger, as a reluctant concession to imposture, an inherited diamond ring. In the hotel, Ruth had been distressed to lose her name in the false assumption of his, though he explained it to her as a mere convenience. "But I *like* who I am now," she protested. That was, indeed, her central jewel, infrangible and bright: She liked who she was. They had gone separate ways and, returning before him, she had asked at the hotel desk for the room key by number.

The clerk asked her her name. It was a policy. He would not give the key   45
to a number.

"And what did you tell him your name was?" Richard asked, in this pause of her story.

In her pause and dark-blue stare, he saw re-created her hesitation when challenged by the clerk. Also, she had been, before her marriage, a second-grade teacher, and Richard saw now the manner — prim, fearful, and commanding — with which she must have confronted those roomfuls of children. "I told him Maple."

Richard had smiled. "That sounds right."

Taking Joan out to dinner felt illicit. She suggested it, for "fun," at the end of one of the children's Sundays. He had been two months in Boston, new habits had replaced old, and it was tempting to leave their children, who were bored and found it easier to be bored by television than by their father, this bossy visitor. "Stop telling me you're bored," he had scolded John, the most docile of his children and the one he felt guiltiest about. "Fifteen is *supposed* to be a boring age. When I was fifteen, I lay around reading science fiction. You lie around looking at *Kung Fu*. At least I was learning to read."

"It's good," the child protested, his adolescent voice cracking in fear of   50
being distracted from an especially vivid piece of slow-motion *tai chi*. Richard, when living here, had watched the program with him often enough to know that it was, in a sense, good, that the hero's Oriental passivity, relieved by spurts of mystical violence, was insinuating into the child a system of ethics,

just as Richard had taken ideals of behavior from dime movies and comic books — coolness from Bogart, debonair recklessness from Errol Flynn, duality and deceit from Superman.

He dropped to one knee beside the sofa where John, his upper lip fuzzy and his eyebrows manly dark, stoically gazed into the transcendent flickering; Richard's own voice nearly cracked, asking, "Would it be less boring if Dad still lived here?"

"No-*oh*": The answer was instantaneous and impatient, as if the question had been anticipated. Did the boy mean it? His eyes did not for an instant glance sideways, perhaps out of fear of betraying himself, perhaps out of genuine boredom with grown-ups and their gestures. On television, satisfyingly, gestures killed. Richard rose from his supplicant position, relieved to hear Joan coming down the stairs. She was dressed to go out, in the timeless black dress with the scalloped neckline, and a collar of Mexican silver. At least — a mark, perhaps, of their fascinating maladjustment — he had never bored *her,* nor she, he dreaded to admit, him. He was wary. He must be wary. They had had it. They must have had it.

Yet the cocktails, and the seafood, and the wine, displaced his wariness; he heard himself saying, to the so familiar and so strange face across the table, "She's lovely, and loves me, you know" (he felt embarrassed, like a son suddenly aware that his mother, though politely attentive, is indifferent to the urgency of an athletic contest being described), "but she does spell everything out, and wants everything spelled out to her. It's like being back in the second grade. And the worst thing is, for all this explaining, for all this glorious fucking, she's still not real to me, the way — you are." His voice did break, he had gone too far.

Joan put her left hand, still bearing their wedding ring, flat on the tablecloth in a sensible, level gesture. "She will be," she said. "It's a matter of time."

The old pattern was still the one visible to the world. The waitress, who had taught their children in Sunday school, greeted them as if their marriage were unbroken; they ate in this restaurant three or four times a year, and were on schedule. They had known the contractor who had built it, this mock-antique wing, a dozen years ago, and then left town, bankrupt, disgraced, and oddly cheerful. His memory hovered between the beams. Another couple, older than the Maples — the husband had once worked with Richard on a town committee — came up to their booth beaming, jollying, loving, in that obligatory American way. Did they know? It didn't matter, in this country of temporary arrangements. The Maples jollied back as one, and tumbled loose only when the older couple moved away. Joan gazed after their backs. "I wonder what they have," she asked, "that we didn't?"

"Maybe they had less," Richard said, "so they didn't expect more."

"That's too easy." She was a shade resistant to his veiled compliments; he was grateful. Please resist.

He asked, "How do you think the kids are doing? John seemed withdrawn."

"That's how he is. Stop picking at him."

"I just don't want him to think he has to be your little husband. That 60
house feels huge now."

"You're telling me."

"I'm sorry." He was; he put his hands palms up on the table.

"Isn't it amazing," Joan said, "how a full bottle of wine isn't enough for
two people anymore?"

"Should I order another bottle?" He was dismayed, secretly: the waste.

She saw this and said, "No. Just give me half of what's in your glass." 65

"You can have it all." He poured.

She said, "So your fucking is really glorious?"

He was embarrassed by the remark now and feared it set a distasteful
trend. As with Ruth there was an etiquette of adultery, so with Joan some code
of separation must be maintained. "It usually is," he told her, "between people
who aren't married."

"Is dat right, white man?" A swallow of his wine inside her, Joan began
to swell with impending hilarity. She leaned as close as the table would permit.
"You must *promise*" — a gesture went with "promise," a protesting little
splaying of her hands — "never to tell this to anybody, not even Ruth."

"Maybe you shouldn't tell me. In fact, don't." He understood why she 70
had been laconic up to now; she had been wanting to talk about her lover,
holding him warm within her like a baby. She was going to betray him. "Please
don't," Richard said.

"Don't be such a prig. You're the only person I can talk to; it doesn't
mean a thing."

"That's what you said about our going to bed in my apartment."

"Did she mind?"

"Incredibly."

Joan laughed, and Richard was struck, for the thousandth time, by the 75
perfection of her teeth, even and rounded and white, bared by her lips as if in
proof of a perfect skull, an immaculate soul. Her glee whirled her to a kind of
heaven as she confided stories about herself and Andy — how he and a motel
manageress had quarreled over the lack of towels in a room taken for the
afternoon, how he fell asleep for exactly seven minutes each time after making
love. Richard had known Andy for years, a slender, swarthy specialist in
corporation law, himself divorced, though professionally engaged in the finick-
ing arrangement of giant mergers. A fussy dresser, a churchman, he brought to
many occasions an undue dignity and perhaps had been more attracted to
Joan's surface glaze, her smooth New England ice, than to the mischievous
demons underneath. "My psychiatrist thinks Andy was symbiotic with you,
and now that you're gone, I can see him as absurd."

"He's not absurd. He's good, loyal, handsome, prosperous. He tithes. He
has a twelve handicap. He loves you."

"He protects you from me, you mean. His buttons! — we have to allow a half hour afterward for him to do up all his buttons. If they made four-piece suits, he'd wear them. And he washes — he washes *everything,* every time."

"Stop," Richard begged. "Stop telling me all this."

But she was giddy amid the spinning mirrors of her betrayals, her face so flushed and tremulous the waitress sympathetically giggled, pouring the Maples their coffee. Joan's face was pink as a peony, her eyes a blue pale as ice, almost transparent. He saw through her words to what she was saying — that these lovers, however we love them, are not us, are not sacred as reality is sacred. We are reality. We have made children. We gave each other our young bodies. We promised to grow old together.

Joan described an incident in her house, once theirs, when the plumber   80 unexpectedly arrived. Richard had to laugh with her; that house's plumbing problems were an old joke, an ongoing saga. "The back-door bell rang, Mr. Kelly stomped right in, you know how the kitchen echoes in the bedroom, we had *had* it." She looked, to see if her meaning was clear. He nodded. Her eyes sparkled. She emphasized, of the knock, "Just at the *very* moment," and, with a gesture akin to the gentle clap in the car a world ago, drew with one fingertip a V in the air, as if beginning to write "very." The motion was eager, shy, exquisite, diffident, trusting: He saw all its meanings and knew that she would never stop gesturing within him, never; though a decree come between them, even death, her gestures would endure, cut into glass.   1978

INVESTIGATIONS

1. In Jen's "What Means Switch," Mona realizes she and her first boyfriend "don't see the same things at all," which deepens and complicates her experience of their relationship. How is this realization similar to the realizations the characters in "Gesturing" experience? What do these stories suggest about the power of love to transcend differences?

2. To what extent does Richard want to do what he does? To what extent is he a "victim of circumstance"? In what ways has love enhanced your freedom? In what ways has it imprisoned you?

3. Write a paragraph about each of the characters in which you discuss what their habitual gestures reveal about them. What do your habitual gestures reveal about you?

4. Why has Richard "engendered a companion of sorts, a single grand spectator" for whom he performs when he's alone (para. 32)? Why does he think "it could not last, such happiness" (para. 34)?

CAROLYN KIZER

Bitch

Now, when he and I meet, after all these years,
I say to the bitch inside me, don't start growling.
He isn't a trespasser anymore,
Just an old acquaintance tipping his hat.
My voice says, "Nice to see you,"   5
As the bitch starts to bark hysterically.
He isn't an enemy now,
Where are your manners, I say, as I say,
"How are the children? They must be growing up."
At a kind word from him, a look like the old days,   10
The bitch changes her tone: she begins to whimper.
She wants to snuggle up to him, to cringe.
Down, girl! Keep your distance
Or I'll give you a taste of the choke-chain.
"Fine, I'm just fine," I tell him.   15
She slobbers and grovels.
After all, I am her mistress. She is basically loyal.
It's just that she remembers how she came running
Each evening, when she heard his step;
How she lay at his feet and looked up adoringly   20
Though he was absorbed in his paper;
Or, bored with her devotion, ordered her to the kitchen
Until he was ready to play.
But the small careless kindnesses
When he'd had a good day, or a couple of drinks,   25
Come back to her now, seem more important
Than the casual cruelties, the ultimate dismissal.
"It's nice to know you are doing so well," I say.
He couldn't have taken you with him;
You were too demonstrative, too clumsy,   30
Not like the well-groomed pets of his new friends.
"Give my regards to your wife," I say. You gag

Born in Spokane, Washington, in 1925, CAROLYN KIZER was the first director of the Literature Program for the National Endowment for the Arts. Her recent books of poetry include *The Nearness of You* (1986), *Mermaids in the Basement: Poems for Women* (1984), and *Yin,* for which she won the Pulitzer Prize in 1985.

As I drag you off by the scruff,
Saying, "Good-bye! Good-bye! Nice to have seen you again."　　1984

INVESTIGATIONS

1. The narrator of the poem speaks to us in two voices. Describe the relationship between the voices. Do you find yourself getting confused as to which voice is which? If so, how does the confusion affect your understanding of the speaker? The situation? The poem?
2. In our culture, the term "bitch" is used to insult women. Look the word up in the dictionary. How does Kizer make use of the multiple meanings of the word throughout?
3. Reread lines 18–27. How has the speaker changed since the days of the relationship she describes? How has she "changed her tone"? Why isn't the "bitch" allowed to speak?
4. Write a short poem; make yourself the speaker and choose a situation in which the "bitch" in you wants to speak or act differently than you will allow yourself to do. You may use Kizer's poem as a model.

GALWAY KINNELL

After Making Love
We Hear Footsteps

For I can snore like a bullhorn
or play loud music
or sit up talking with any reasonably sober Irishman
and Fergus will only sink deeper
into his dreamless sleep, which goes by all in one flash,　　5
but let there be that heavy breathing
or a stifled come-cry anywhere in the house
and he will wrench himself awake

Vermont's state poet, GALWAY KINNELL was born in 1927 in Providence, Rhode Island, and educated at Princeton University and the University of Rochester. His many books of poetry include *When One Has Lived a Long Time Alone* (1990), *The Book of Nightmares* (1971), and *Selected Poems* (1982), which won the 1983 Pulitzer Prize.

and make for it on the run — as now, we lie together,
after making love, quiet, touching along the length of our bodies,   10
familiar touch of the long-married,
and he appears — in his baseball pajamas, it happens,
the neck opening so small
he has to screw them on, which one day may make him wonder
about the mental capacity of baseball payers —   15
and says, "Are you loving and snuggling? May I join?"
He flops down between us and hugs us and snuggles himself to sleep,
his face gleaming with satisfaction at being this very child.

In the half darkness we look at each other
and smile   20
and touch arms across his little, startlingly muscled body —
this one whom habit of memory propels to the ground of his making,
sleeper only the mortal sounds can sing awake,
this blessing love gives again into our arms.   1980

INVESTIGATIONS

1. In what ways does this couple's love make them "gleam with satisfaction" at being themselves? How has love deepened your satisfaction with who you are?
2. What are the differences between this poem's portrayal of sexuality and its portrayal in Wilson's *Burn This*? In Lynch's "The Widow"? How do you account for these differences?
3. Write a 500–750-word essay in which you use evidence from this poem and any other appropriate selections in Part Six to demonstrate the ways in which love can be defined as a blessing.

FENTON JOHNSON

The Limitless Heart

It is late March — the Saturday of Passover, to be exact — and I am driving an oversized rented car through west Los Angeles. This side of the city I have never seen except in the company of my lover, who died of AIDS-related complications in a Paris hospital in autumn of last year. He was an only child, and often asked that I promise to visit his parents after his death. Youngest son of a large family and a believer in brutal honesty, I refused. I have too much family already, I said. There are limits to how much love one can give.

Now I am driving along one of the lovelier streets of Santa Monica, San Vicente Boulevard west from Wilshire to the Pacific. The street is divided by a broad green median lined with coral trees, which the city has seen fit to register as landmarks. They spread airy, elegant crowns against a movie-set heaven, a Maxfield Parrish blue. Each branch bleeds at its end an impossibly scarlet blossom, as if the twigs themselves had pierced the thin-skinned sky.

My lover's parents — I'll call them Bill and Ruth — are too old to get about much. They are survivors of the Holocaust, German Jews who spent the war years hiding in a Dutch village a few miles from Germany itself. Beaten by Nazis before the war, Bill hid for four years with broken vertebrae, unable to see a doctor. When he was no longer able to move, his desperate wife descended to the street to find help, to see falling from the sky the parachutes of their liberators.

After the war they came to California, promised land of this promised land. Like Abraham and Sara, in their advanced years they had a single son; proof that it is possible, in the face of the worst, to pick up sticks and start again.

At their home Bill sits in chronic pain, uncomplaining. Unlike Ruth, he is reserved; he does not talk about his son with the women of his life — his wife or his surviving sister. No doubt he fears giving way before his grief, and his life has not allowed for much giving way. This much he and I share: A gay man who grew up in the rural South, I am no stranger to hiding.

Ruth always goes to bed early — partly by way of coping with grief — but tonight Bill all but asks her to retire. After she leaves he begins talking of his son, and I listen and respond with gratefulness. We are two men in control, who permit ourselves to speak to each other of these matters because we subscribe implicitly, jointly, unconditionally to this code of conduct.

Novelist FENTON JOHNSON (b. 1953), recipient of a National Endowment for the Arts Fellowship, the Wallace Stegner Fellowship, and the James Michener Fellowship, lives in San Francisco, where he occasionally teaches creative writing at San Francisco State University. Johnson is the author of *Crossing the River* (1989).

Bill tells of a day when his son, then eight years old, wanted to go fishing. The quintessential urban Jew, Bill nonetheless bought poles and hooks and drove fifty miles to Laguna Beach. There they dropped their lines from a pier to discover the hooks dangled some ten feet above the water. ("Thank God," Bill says. "Otherwise we might have caught something.") A passerby scoffed — "What the hell do you think you're trying to catch?" Bill shrugged, unperturbed. "Flying fish," he said.

I respond with my most vivid memory of Bill's son. A wiser man than I, he spoke many times across our years together of his great luck, his great good fortune. Denial pure and simple, or so I told myself at first. AZT, ddI, ACT-UP, CMV, DHPG, and what I came to think of as the big "A" itself — he endured this acronymed life, while I listened and learned and helped and participated when I could.

Until our third and last trip to Paris, the city of his dreams. On what would be his last night to walk about the city we sat in the courtyard of the Picasso Museum. There under a dusk-deep sapphire sky I turned to him and said, "I'm so lucky," and it was as if the time allotted to him to teach this lesson, the time allotted to me to learn it had been consumed, and there was nothing left but the facts of things to play out.

A long pause after this story — I have ventured beyond what I permit   10
myself, what I am permitted.

I change the subject, asking Bill to talk of the war years. He speaks not of his beating or of murdered family and friends but of moments of affection, loyalty, even humor; until he talks of winters spent confined to bed, huddled in Ruth's arms, their breaths freezing on the quilt as they sang together to pass time, to stay warm.

Another silence; now he has ventured too far. "I have tried to forget these stories," he says in his halting English.

In the presence of these extremes of love and horror I am reduced to cliché. "It's only by remembering them that we can hope to avoid repeating them."

"They are being repeated all the time," he says. "It is bad sometimes to watch too much television. You see these things and you know we have learned nothing."

Are we so dense that we can learn nothing from all this pain, all this   15
death? Is it impossible to learn from experience? The bitterness of these questions I can taste, as I drive east to spend the night at a relative's apartment.

Just south of the seedier section of Santa Monica Boulevard I stop at a bar recommended by a friend. I need a drink, I need the company of men like myself — survivors, for the moment anyway, albeit of a very different struggle.

The bar is filled with Latino drag queens wearing the most extraordinary clothes. Eighty years of B movies have left Hollywood the nation's most remarkable supply of secondhand dresses, most of which, judging from this evening, have made their ways to these guys' closets.

I am standing at the bar, very Anglo, very butch, very out of place, very much thinking of leaving, when I am given another lesson:

A tiny, wizened, gray-haired Latina approaches the stage, where under jerry-built lights (colored cellophane, Scotch tape) a man lip-syncs to Brazilian rock. His spike heels raise him to something more than six feet; he wears a floor-length sheath dress slit up the sides and so taut, so brilliantly silver, so lustrous that it catches and throws back the faces of his audience. The elderly Latina raises a dollar bill. On tottering heels he lowers himself, missing not a word of his song while half-crouching, half-bending so that she may tuck her dollar in his cleavage and kiss his cheek.

"*Su abuelita,*" the bartender says laconically. "His grandmother." 　　20

One A.M. in the City of Angels — the streets are clogged with cars. Stuck in traffic I am haunted by voices and visions: by the high thin songs of Bill and Ruth as they huddle under their frozen quilt, singing into their breath; by a small boy and his father sitting on a very long pier, their baitless fishhooks dangling above the vast Pacific; by the face of *su abuelita,* uplifted, reverent, peaceful, mirrored in her grandson's dress.

Somewhere a light changes; the traffic unglues itself. As cars begin moving I am visited by two last ghosts — the memory of myself and my lover in the courtyard of the Hôtel Salé, transfigured by the limitless heart.　　1991

INVESTIGATIONS

1. What kinds of love are illustrated in this memoir? What traits do these kinds of love share?

2. Write a 500–750-word essay that shows how this memoir demonstrates what Adrienne Rich ("Love Poem") means by "learning to be true" with death.

3. Johnson and Bill, his lover's father, "venture beyond" what they normally permit themselves when they exchange stories during their visit. To what extent can "venturing beyond" self-imposed restrictions be seen as an essential characteristic of love? What other evidence of this quality can be found in Johnson's memoir? In the other selections in Part Six?

4. In paragraph 15, Johnson asks, "Are we so dense that we can learn nothing from all this pain, all this death? Is it impossible to learn from experience?" After reviewing the specific pains and deaths to which he refers, write two or three paragraphs in which you use material in the essay to respond to Johnson's questions. Then write two or three paragraphs in which you use your own experience to answer him.

PART SIX
CONNECTIONS AND ELABORATIONS

1. Write an essay in which you first discuss how you would now respond to "Write Before Reading" (p. 652) and then demonstrate how the work you did with the selections changed your thinking about the stages of love and the outside influences that can affect the course of an intimate relationship.

2. After rereading Rich's "Love Poem" and reviewing all the work you've done in Part Six, identify the individuals who seem to be "serious . . . / about death" (p. 731, lines 25–26). Write an essay in which you show how this seriousness makes these people capable of the truest love.

3. Using as evidence material from Thompson's "Judgment," Wilson's *Burn This*, Rich's "Love Poem," Smiley's "Long Distance," Lynch's "The Widow," and Kizer's "Bitch,"

   a. write an essay in which you argue that living "in deference" to another person's "comfort" ("The Widow," line 1) is the very essence of love, *or*

   b. write an essay in which you argue that living "in deference" to another person's "comfort" is a destructive misunderstanding of what love is.

4. Using as evidence material from Jen's "What Means Switch," Thompson's "Judgment," Smiley's "Long Distance," Mason's "Shiloh," Silko's "Lullaby," and Updike's "Gesturing," write an essay in which you analyze the ways in which loving someone makes him or her no more familiar than a stranger.

5. After rereading Jen's "What Means Switch," Thompson's "Judgment," and Mason's "Shiloh,"

   a. select a scene from "What Means Switch" and rewrite it from Sherman's point of view, *or*

   b. select a scene from "Judgment" and rewrite it from Roxie's point of view, *or*

   c. select a scene from "Shiloh" and rewrite it from Norma Jean's point of view.

6. Using as evidence material from your response to "Write Before Reading" (p. 652), Berry's "Except," Mura's "Nantucket Honeymoon," Wilson's *Burn This*, Smiley's "Long Distance," and Johnson's "The Limitless Heart," write an essay that explores how love forces us to transcend our limitations.

7. Using as evidence your response to "Write Before Reading" and any other writing and thinking you've done in response to the selections in Part Six, write an essay in which you demonstrate that subjecting love to rational analysis is both absurd and absolutely necessary.

WITH ETERNAL
QUESTIONS
AND EVERYDAY
ABSURDITIES

Though one of the defining characteristics of American culture has been a preoccupation with the practical demands of life and making a living — and with the material rewards of that preoccupation — we are compelled to confront the nature of death, of blessings and curses, of belief and faith, of the nature of Nature itself.

In Part Seven delightful, terrifying, impossible things happen as the border between what we know and don't know gets crossed and re-crossed. A man joins "the plump lizards" gathering along an idyllic riverbank in James Wright's "Yes, But"; "Early Song," by Gogisgi/ Carroll Arnett, praises the "great circle" containing the human and the natural; in Maggie Anderson's "Heart Fire" a woman wrestles with suicide's unanswerable questions; in "Against Nature" Joyce Carol Oates urges us to foresake a romantic image of nature; in Charles Johnson's "Exchange Value" two young African-Americans suffer the curse of an old woman's inheritance; in Tobias Wolff's "The Other Miller" an odd young man is unsettled by his luck; Mary Oliver's "Some Questions You Might Ask" playfully considers the nature of the soul; *Roosters,* by Milcha Sanchez-Scott, dramatizes the ritual power of cockfighting and its effects on a Chicano family; in Charles Baxter's "Gryphon" a whimsical substitute teacher alters the world of her students; twin sisters bestow the blessing of sleep on their fellow villagers in Rosario Ferré's "Pico Rico, Mandorico"; a woman imagines her own death in "Staring at the Sea on the Day of the Death of Another," by May Swenson; David James's "Think Death" uses defiant humor to probe a serious subject; "The Moths," by Helena María Viramontes, confronts the nature of the soul and the power of gift-giving; Maxine Kumin's "In the Park" reflects on a nearly fatal encounter; and in Raymond Carver's "Cathedral," imagination builds a monument to our capacity for awe.

WRITE BEFORE READING

First, write a detailed account of the episode in your life that has most frustrated rational explanation. Next, describe the efforts you've made to explain the episode to yourself and to others. Finally, imagine the episode as a gift, a "lesson," and discuss what that gift might demand of you, what instruction that lesson might provide.

Yes, But

Even if it were true,
Even if I were dead and buried in Verona,
I believe I would come out and wash my face
In the chill spring.
I believe I would appear   5
Between noon and four, when nearly
Everybody else is asleep or making love,
And all the Germans turned down, the motorcycles
Muffled, chained, still.

Then the plump lizards along the Adige by San Giorgio   10
Come out and gaze,
Unpestered by temptation, across the water.
I would sit among them and join them in leaving
The golden mosquitoes alone.
Why should we sit by the Adige and destroy   15
Anything, even our enemies, even the prey
God caused to glitter for us
Defenseless in the sun?
We are not exhausted. We are not angry, or lonely,
Or sick at heart.   20
We are in love lightly, lightly. We know we are shining,
Though we cannot see one another.
The wind doesn't scatter us,
Because our very lungs have fallen and drifted
Away like leaves down the Adige,   25
Long ago.

We breathe light.   1977

INVESTIGATIONS

1. What is so powerful about what happens in this poem that the speaker
   "would come out and wash [his] face" even if he "were dead and buried
   in Verona" (lines 2–3)?

Born and raised in Martin's Ferry, Ohio, JAMES WRIGHT (1927–1980) once said, "My chief enemy in poetry is glibness. . . . My family background is partly Irish, and this means . . . that it is too easy for me to talk sometimes." Wright's collections of poetry include *To a Blossoming Pear Tree* (1977), *This Journey* (1982), and *Above the River: The Complete Poems* (1990).

2. Why doesn't the speaker say "I believe" after line 5? Why is line 13 the final time the speaker refers to himself as "I"?

3. How is it appropriate to the events in the poem that the lizards' "lungs" and not their eyes or legs or mouths "have fallen and drifted / Away like leaves down the Adige" (lines 24–25)? How does it affect your reading of the poem that this happened "long ago"?

4. Write a 250–500-word essay in which you argue against someone who says, "The natural world's a completely brutal place. The speaker of this poem is just trying to comfort himself by indulging in a romantic fantasy."

GOGISGI/CARROLL ARNETT

Early Song

As the sun rises
high enough to
warm the frost
off the pine needles,

I rise to make   5
four prayers of
thanksgiving for
this fine clear day,

for this good brown
earth, for all   10
brothers and sisters,
for the dark blood

that runs through me
in a great circle
back into this   15
good brown earth.
                                              1979

A Marine Corps veteran and author of ten collections of poetry, including *Tsalagi* (1976) and *Rounds* (1982), GOGISGI/CARROLL ARNETT (b. 1927) was born in Oklahoma City of Cherokee-French ancestry. (*Gogisgi*, his Cherokee name, means "smoke.") He is professor of English at Central Michigan University and lives in Mecosta, Michigan.

INVESTIGATIONS

1. Who are the "brothers and sisters" the speaker mentions in line 11?
2. Copy the poem as a prose sentence and compare this version with the original. How does the arrangement of lines add to the poem's impact?
3. Write a poem that embodies your sense of the natural world and how human beings fit or don't fit in.
4. What are the similarities between "Early Song" and Wright's "Yes, But"? To what extent do they deal with the same topics or themes? What are the differences in their treatments of these topics or themes?
5. What would the speaker of "Early Song" say about Joyce Carol Oates's "Against Nature" (p. 789)? What would Oates say about "Early Song"?

MAGGIE ANDERSON

Heart Fire

Three months since your young son shot himself
and, of course, no one knows why. It was October.
Maybe he was following the smell of dying leaves
or the warmth of the fire in the heart, so hard
to locate in a country always readying for war.   5

One afternoon we sat together on your floor, drinking
tea and listening to Brahms on the radio. He would
have liked this music, you told me. He would have liked
everything I like now and what he wouldn't like I don't
like either. He has made the whole world look like him.   10

Today, driving into Pittsburgh, I see you are right.
The sky is cold blue like a shirt I once saw him
wear and the bare trees are dark, like his hair.
I see how vulnerable the grasses are, pale and flimsy
by the roadsides, trying to stand straight in the wind.   15

For Maggie Anderson (b. 1948), "travel feeds the writing, as does translating, reading, walking, growing vegetables, making music — anything observed closely and lived intensely and fully." Author of three poetry collections, most recently *Cold Comfort* (1986), Anderson teaches writing at Kent State University.

At Canonsburg, all the pink and green and purple houses
have the same slant of roof toward the hill, like toys
because I'm thinking about children, how sometimes
we want to give them up if they seem odd and distant,
yet even if they die before us, we cannot let them go.   20

I see your son in landscapes as I drive, in a twist
of light behind a barn before the suburbs start,
or under a suburban street light where a tall boy
with a basketball has limbs like those he had just
outgrown. Because I want to think he's not alone,   25

I invent for him a heart fire even the unenlightened
living are sometimes allowed to see. It burns past
the white fluorescence of the city, past the steel mills
working off and on as they tell us we need, or don't
need, heavy industry for fuel, or war. Your son   30

keeps me company, driving down the last hill into Pittsburgh,
in the tunnel as I push for good position
in the lanes. He is with me as I spot the shiny cables
of the bridge and gear down, as all the lights beyond
the river come on now, across his safe, perfected face.   1986

INVESTIGATIONS

1. The speaker says, "of course, no one knows why" her friend's "young son
   shot himself" (lines 1–2). Look back at your response to the "Write Before
   Reading" exercise on page 784. Compare your efforts at explanation with
   the speaker's meditation on her friend's loss. To what extent does "the
   whole world look like" your "Write Before Reading" response whenever
   you think about it (line 10)? If both you and the speaker have realized
   that "no one knows why," what purposes are served by asking why?
2. What is the connection between lines 3–5 and lines 25–30? Why is "the
   warmth of the fire in the heart, so hard / to locate in a country always
   readying for war" (lines 4–5)? What use is it for the speaker to "invent
   . . . a heart fire" (line 26)?
3. To what extent does the speaker use illusion to comfort herself? In what
   sense is she relieving her own loneliness with her efforts "to think he's not
   alone" (line 25)?

Against Nature

> We soon get through with Nature. She excites an expectation which she cannot
> satisfy.   — Thoreau, *Journal,* 1854

> Sir, if a man has experienced the inexpressible, he is under no obligation to
> attempt to express it.   — Samuel Johnson

The writer's resistance to Nature.

It has no sense of humor: In its beauty, as in its ugliness, or its neutrality,
there is no laughter.

It lacks a moral purpose.

It lacks a satiric dimension, registers no irony.

Its pleasures lack resonance, being accidental; its horrors, even when pre-   5
meditated, are equally perfunctory, "red in tooth and claw" et cetera.

It lacks a symbolic subtext — excepting that provided by man.

It has no (verbal) language.

It has no interest in ours.

It inspires a painfully limited set of responses in "nature-writers" —
REVERENCE, AWE, PIETY, MYSTICAL ONENESS.

It eludes us even as it prepares to swallow us up, books and all.   10

I was lying on my back in the dirt-gravel of the towpath beside the
Delaware-Raritan Canal, Titusville, New Jersey, staring up at the sky and
trying, with no success, to overcome a sudden attack of tachycardia that had
come upon me out of nowhere — such attacks are always "out of nowhere,"
that's their charm — and all around me Nature thrummed with life, the air
smelling of moisture and sunlight, the canal reflecting the sky, red-winged
blackbirds testing their spring calls — the usual. I'd become the jar in Tennessee,
a fictitious center, or parenthesis, aware beyond my erratic heartbeat of the
numberless heartbeats of the earth, its pulsing pumping life, sheer life, incal-
culable. Struck down in the midst of motion — I'd been jogging a minute
before — I was "out of time" like a fallen, stunned boxer, privileged (in an
abstract manner of speaking) to be an involuntary witness to the random,
wayward, nameless motion on all sides of me.

Paroxysmal tachycardia is rarely fatal, but if the heartbeat accelerates to

---

Novelist, short-story writer, essayist, poet, and playwright, JOYCE CAROL OATES (b. 1938) is one of
the most prolific and admired contemporary American writers. She is also the Roger S. Berlind
Distinguished Professor of the Humanities at Princeton University and has recently published *The
Rise of Life on Earth* (1991) and *Because It Is Bitter, and Because It Is My Heart* (1991), both novels.

250–270 beats a minute you're in trouble. The average attack is about 100–150 beats and mine seemed so far to be about average; the trick now was to prevent it from getting worse. Brainy people try brainy strategies, such as thinking calming thoughts, pseudo-mystic thoughts, *If I die now it's a good death,* that sort of thing, *if I die this is a good place and a good time,* the idea is to deceive the frenzied heartbeat that, really, you don't care: You hadn't any other plans for the afternoon. The important thing with tachycardia is to prevent panic! you must prevent panic! otherwise you'll have to be taken by ambulance to the closest emergency room, which is not so very nice a way to spend the afternoon, really. So I contemplated the blue sky overhead. The earth beneath my head. Nature surrounding me on all sides, I couldn't quite see it but I could hear it, smell it, sense it — there is something *there,* no mistake about it. Completely oblivious to the predicament of the individual but that's only "natural" after all, one hardly expects otherwise.

When you discover yourself lying on the ground, limp and unresisting, head in the dirt, and helpless, the earth seems to shift forward as a presence; hard, emphatic, not mere surface but a genuine force — there is no other word for it but *presence.* To keep in motion is to keep in time and to be stopped, stilled, is to be abruptly out of time, in another time-dimension perhaps, an alien one, where human language has no resonance. Nothing to be said about it expresses it, nothing touches it, it's an absolute against which nothing human can be measured. . . . Moving through space and time by way of your own volition you inhabit an interior consciousness, a hallucinatory consciousness, it might be said, so long as breath, heartbeat, the body's autonomy hold; when motion is stopped you are jarred out of it. The interior is invaded by the exterior. The outside wants to come in, and only the self's fragile membrane prevents it.

The fly buzzing at Emily's death.

Still, the earth *is* your place. A tidy grave-site measured to your size. Or, from another angle of vision, one vast democratic grave.   15

Let's contemplate the sky. Forget the crazy hammering heartbeat, don't listen to it, don't start counting, remember that there is a clever way of breathing that conserves oxygen as if you're lying below the surface of a body of water breathing through a very thin straw but you *can* breathe through it if you're careful, if you don't panic, one breath and then another and then another, isn't that the story of all lives? careers? Just a matter of breathing. Of course it is. But contemplate the sky, it's there to be contemplated. A mild shock to see it so blank, blue, a thin airy ghostly blue, no clouds to disguise its emptiness. You are beginning to feel not only weightless but near-bodiless, lying on the earth like a scrap of paper about to be blown off. Two dimensions and you'd imagined you were there! And there's the sky rolling away forever, into infinity — if "infinity" can be "rolled into" — and the forlorn truth is, that's where you're going too. And the lovely blue isn't even blue, is it? isn't even there, is it? a mere optical illusion, isn't it? no matter what art has urged you to believe.

Early Nature memories. Which it's best not to suppress.

. . . Wading, as a small child, in Tonawanda Creek near our house, and afterward trying to tear off, in a frenzy of terror and revulsion, the sticky fat black bloodsuckers that had attached themselves to my feet, particularly between my toes.

. . . Coming upon a friend's dog in a drainage ditch, dead for several days, evidently the poor creature had been shot by a hunter and left to die, bleeding to death, and we're stupefied with grief and horror but can't resist sliding down to where he's lying on his belly, and we can't resist squatting over him, turning the body over . . .

. . . The raccoon, mad with rabies, frothing at the mouth and tearing at   20
his own belly with his teeth, so that his intestines spilled out onto the ground
. . . a sight I seem to remember though in fact I did not see. I've been told I did not see.

Consequently, my chronic uneasiness with Nature-mysticism; Nature-adoration; Nature-as-(moral)-instruction-for-mankind. My doubt that one can, with philosophical validity, address "Nature" as a single coherent noun, anything other than a Platonic, hence discredited, isness. My resistance to "Naturewriting" as a genre, except when it is brilliantly fictionalized in the service of a writer's individual vision — Thoreau's books and *Journal*, of course — but also, less known in this country, the miniaturist prose-poems of Colette (*Flowers and Fruit*) and Ponge (*Taking the Side of Things*) — in which case it becomes yet another, and ingenious, form of storytelling. The subject is *there* only by the grace of the author's language.

Nature has no instructions for mankind except that our poor beleaguered humanist-democratic way of life, our fantasies of the individual's high worth, our sense that the weak, no less than strong, have a right to survive, are absurd.

In any case, where *is* Nature? one might (skeptically) inquire. Who has looked upon her/its face and survived?

But isn't this all exaggeration, in the spirit of rhetorical contentiousness? Surely Nature is, for you, as for most reasonably intelligent people, a "perennial" source of beauty, comfort, peace, escape from the delirium of civilized life; a respite from the ego's ever-frantic strategies of self-promotion, as a way of insuring (at least in fantasy) some small measure of immortality? Surely Nature, as it is understood in the usual slapdash way, as human, if not dilettante, *experience* (hiking in a national park, jogging on the beach at dawn, even tending, with the usual comical frustrations, a suburban garden), is wonderfully consoling; a place where, when you go there, it has to take you in? — a palimpsest of sorts you choose to read, layer by layer, always with care, always cautiously, in proportion to your psychological strength?

Nature: as in Thoreau's upbeat Transcendentalist mode ("The indescrib-   25
ably innocence and beneficence of Nature, — such health, such cheer, they

afford forever! and such sympathy have they ever with our race, that all Nature would be affected . . . if any man should ever for a just cause grieve"), and not in Thoreau's grim mode ("Nature is hard to be overcome but she must be overcome").

Another way of saying, not *Nature-in-itself* but *Nature-as-experience*.

The former, Nature-in-itself, is, to allude slantwise to Melville, a blankness ten times blank; the latter is what we commonly, or perhaps always, mean when we speak of Nature as a noun, a single entity — something of ours. Most of the time it's just an activity, a sort of hobby, a weekend, a few days, perhaps a few hours, staring out of the window at the mind-dazzling autumn foliage of, say, Northern Michigan, being rendered speechless — temporarily — at the sight of Mt. Shasta, the Grand Canyon, Ansel Adams's West. Or Nature writ small, contained in the back yard. Nature filtered through our optical nerves, our "sense," our fiercely romantic expectations. Nature that pleases us because it mirrors our souls, or gives the comforting illusion of doing so. As in our first mother's awakening to the self's fatal beauty —

> I thither went
> With unexperienc't thought, and laid me down
> On the green bank, to look into the clear
> Smooth Lake, that to me seem'd another Sky.
> As I bent down to look, just opposite,
> A Shape within the watr'y gleam appear'd
> Bending to look on me, I started back,
> It started back, but pleas'd I soon return'd,
> Pleas'd it return'd as soon with answering looks
> Of sympathy and love; there I had fixt
> Mine eyes till now, and pin'd with vain desire.

— in these surpassingly beautiful lines from the Book IV of Milton's *Paradise Lost*.

Nature as the self's (flattering) mirror, but not ever, no never, Nature-in-itself.

Nature is mouths, or maybe a single mouth. Why glamorize it, romanticize it, well yes but we must, we're writers, poets, mystics (of a sort) aren't we, precisely what else are we to do but glamorize and romanticize and generally exaggerate the significance of anything we focus the white heat of our "creativity" upon . . . ? And why not Nature, since it's there, common property, mute, can't talk back, allows us the possibility of transcending the human condition for a while, writing prettily of mountain ranges, white-tailed deer, the purple crocuses outside this very window, the thrumming dazzling "life-force" we imagine we all support. Why not.

Nature *is* more than a mouth — it's a dazzling variety of mouths. And it pleases the senses, in any case, as the physicists' chill universe of numbers certainly does not.

30

Oscar Wilde, on our subject: "Nature is no great mother who has borne us. She is our creation. It is in our brain that she quickens to life. Things are because we see them, and what we see, and how we see it, depends on the Arts that have influenced us. To look at a thing is very different from seeing a thing. . . . At present, people see fogs, not because there are fogs, but because poets and painters have taught them the mysterious loveliness of such effects. There may have been fogs for centuries in London. I dare say there were. But no one saw them. They did not exist until Art had invented them. . . . Yesterday evening Mrs. Arundel insisted on my going to the window and looking at the glorious sky, as she called it. And so I had to look at it. . . . And what was it? It was simply a very second-rate Turner, a Turner of a bad period, with all the painter's worst faults exaggerated and over-emphasized.

(If we were to put it to Oscar Wilde that he exaggerates, his reply might well be: "Exaggeration? I don't know the meaning of the word.")

Walden, that most artfully composed of prose fictions, concludes, in the rhapsodic chapter "Spring," with Henry David Thoreau's contemplation of death, decay, and regeneration as it is suggested to him, or to his protagonist, by the spectacle of vultures feeding off carrion. There is a dead horse close by his cabin and the stench of its decomposition, in certain winds, is daunting. Yet: " . . . the assurance it gave me of the strong appetite and inviolable health of Nature was my compensation. I love to see that Nature is so rife with life that myriads can be afforded to be sacrificed and suffered to prey upon one another; that tender organizations can be so serenely squashed out of existence like pulp, — tadpoles which herons gobble up, and tortoises and toads run over in the road; and that sometimes it has rained flesh and blood! . . . The impression made on a wise man is that of universal innocence."

Come off it, Henry David. You've grieved these many years for your elder brother John, who dies a ghastly death of lockjaw, you've never wholly recovered from the experience of watching him die. And you know, or must know, that you're fated too to die young of consumption. . . . But this doctrinaire Transcendentalist passage ends *Walden* on just the right note. It's as impersonal, as coolly detached, as the Oversoul itself: A "wise man" filters his emotions through his brain.

Or through his prose.   35

Nietzsche: "We all pretend to ourselves that we are more simple-minded than we are: That is how we get a rest from our fellow men."

> Once out of nature I shall never take
> My bodily form from any natural thing,
> But such a form as Grecian goldsmiths make
> Of hammered gold and gold enamelling
> To keep a drowsy Emperor awake;
> Or set upon a golden bough to sing

To lords and ladies of Byzantium
Of what is past, or passing, or to come.
— William Butler Yeats, "Sailing to Byzantium"

Yet even the golden bird is a "bodily form taken from (a) natural thing." No, it's impossible to escape!

The writer's resistance to Nature.
Wallace Stevens: "In the presence of extraordinary actuality, consciousness takes the place of imagination."

Once, years ago, in 1972 to be precise, when I seemed to have been another person, related to the person I am now as one is related, tangentially, sometimes embarrassingly, to cousins not seen for decades, — once, when we were living in London, and I was very sick, I had a mystical vision. That is, I "had" a "mystical vision" — the heart sinks: such pretension — or something resembling one. A fever-dream, let's call it. It impressed me enormously and impresses me still, though I've long since lost the capacity to see it with my mind's eye, or even, I suppose, to believe in it. There is a statute of limitations on "mystical visions" as on romantic love.

I was very sick, and I imagined my life as a thread, a thread of breath, or   40
heartbeat, or pulse, or light, yes it was light, radiant light, I was burning with fever and I ascended to that plane of serenity that might be mistaken for (or *is,* in fact) Nirvana, where I had a waking dream of uncanny lucidity —

My body is a tall column of light and heat.
My body is not "I" but "it."
My body is not one but many.
My body, which "I" inhabit, is inhabited as well by other creatures, unknown to me, imperceptible — the smallest of them mere sparks of light.

My body, which I perceive as substance, is in fact an organization of   45
infinitely complex, overlapping, imbricated structures, radiant light their manifestation, the "body" a tall column of light and blood-heat, a temporary agreement among atoms, like a high-rise building with numberless rooms, corridors, corners, elevator shafts, windows. . . . In this fantastical structure the "I" is deluded as to its sovereignty, let alone its autonomy in the (outside) world; the most astonishing secret is that the "I" doesn't exist! — but it behaves as if it does, as if it were one and not many.

In any case, without the "I" the tall column of light and heat would die, and the microscopic life-particles would die with it . . . will die with it. The "I," which doesn't exist, is everything.

But Dr. Johnson is right, the inexpressible need not be expressed. And what resistance, finally? There is none.

This morning, an invasion of tiny black ants. One by one they appear, out of nowhere — that's their charm too! — moving single file across the white

Parsons table where I am sitting, trying without much success to write a poem. A poem of only three or four lines is what I want, something short, tight, mean. I want it to hurt like a white-hot wire up the nostrils, small and compact and turned in upon itself with the density of a hunk of rock from the planet Jupiter. . . .

But here come the black ants: harbingers, you might say, of spring. One by one they appear on the dazzling white table and one by one I kill them with a forefinger, my deft right forefinger, mashing each against the surface of the table and then dropping it into a wastebasket at my side. Idle labor, mesmerizing, effortless, and I'm curious as to how long I can do it, sit here in the brilliant March sunshine killing ants with my right forefinger, how long I, and the ants, can keep it up.

After a while I realize that I can do it a long time. And that I've written   50
my poem.   1986

INVESTIGATIONS

1. Write a "resistance to Joyce Carol Oates" in which you respond to her "resistance to Nature" in paragraphs 2–10.

2. In what ways might Oates see Wright's "Yes, But," Gogisgi/Arnett's "Early Song," Oliver's "Some Questions You Might Ask" (p. 813), and Swenson's "Staring at the Sea on the Day of the Death of Another" (p. 867) as nature writing that "is brilliantly fictionalized in the service of a writer's individual vision"? In what ways might she consider each of these poems "yet another, and ingenious, form of storytelling" (para. 21)? Do you agree that "the subject [Nature] is *there* only by the grace of the author's language"? Why or why not?

3. Write two or three paragraphs that describe a particularly compelling experience you've had "in Nature." Then write a 250–500-word essay in which you analyze that experience from Oates's point of view.

4. In what ways does this essay show how Oates is exaggerating "the significance of anything [she] focus[es] the white heat of [her] creativity upon" (para. 29)? In what ways does this essay demonstrate how writers must "glamorize and romanticize" what they write about? In what sense did you "glamorize and romanticize" what you wrote about in "Write Before Reading"? Think of two or three other essays you've written while using this book and comment on whether or not you glamorized and romanticized what you wrote about.

5. Write a 500–750-word essay in which you argue against Oates's assertion that "there is a statute of limitations on 'mystical visions' as on romantic love" (para. 39).

CHARLES JOHNSON

Exchange Value

Me and my brother Loftis came in by the old lady's window. There was some kinda boobytrap — boxes of broken glass — that shoulda warned us Miss Bailey wasn't the easy mark we made her to be. She had been living alone for twenty years in 4-B down the hall from Loftis and me, long before our folks died — a hincty, half-bald West Indian woman with a craglike face, who kept her door barricaded, shutters closed, and wore the same sorrylooking outfit — black wingtip shoes, cropfingered gloves in winter, and a man's floppy hat — like maybe she dressed half-asleep or in a dark attic. Loftis, he figured Miss Bailey had some grandtheft dough stashed inside, jim, or leastways a shoebox full of money, cause she never spent a nickel on herself, not even for food, and only left her place at night.

Anyway, we figured Miss Bailey was gone. Her mailbox be full, and Pookie White, who run the Thirty-ninth Street Creole restaurant, he say she ain't dropped by in days to collect the handouts he give her so she can get by. So here's me and Loftis, tipping around Miss Bailey's blackdark kitchen. The floor be littered with fruitrinds, roaches, old food furred with blue mold. Her dirty dishes be stacked in a sink spidered with cracks, and it looks like the old lady been living, lately, on Ritz crackers and Department of Agriculture (Welfare Office) peanut butter. Her toilet be stopped up, too, and, on the bathroom floor, there's five Maxwell House coffee cans full of shit. Me, I was closing her bathroom door when I whiffed this evil smell so bad, so thick, I could hardly breathe, and what breath I drew was horrible, like a solid thing in my throatpipes, like soup. "Cooter," Loftis whisper, low, across the room, "you smell that?" He went right on sniffing it, like people do for some reason when something be smelling stanky, then took out his headrag and held it over his mouth. "That's the awfulest stink I *ever* smelled!" Then, head low, he slipped his long self into the livingroom. Me, I stayed by the window, gulping air, and do you know why?

You oughta know, up front, that I ain't too good at this gangster stuff, and I had a real bad feeling about Miss Bailey from the get-go. Mama used to say it was Loftis, not me, who'd go places — I see her standing at the sideboard by the sink now, big as a Frigidaire, white with flour to her elbows, a washtowel

---

Charles Johnson (b. 1948) has devoted himself "to developing a genuinely philosophical black American fiction." Author of a collection of short fiction and three novels, including *Middle Passage* (1990), winner of the National Book Award for fiction, Johnson received a Guggenheim Fellowship in 1988 and teaches writing at the University of Washington.

over her shoulder, while we ate a breakfast of cornbread and syrup. He graduated fifth at DuSable High School, had two gigs, and, like Papa, he be always
wanting the things white people had out in Hyde Park, where Mama did
daywork. Loftis, he the kinda brother who buys *Esquire*, sews Hart, Schaffner
and Marx labels in Robert Hall suits, talks properlike, packs his hair with
Murrays, and took classes in politics and stuff at the Black People's Topograph-
ical Library in the late 1960s; who, at thirty, makes his bed military style, reads
Black Scholar on the bus he takes to the plant, and, come hell or high water,
plans to make a Big Score. Loftis, he say I'm bout as useful on a hustle — or
when it comes to getting ahead — as a headcold, and he say he has to count
my legs sometimes to be sure I ain't a mule, seeing how, for all my eighteen
years, I can't keep no job and sorta stay close to home, watching TV or reading
World's Finest comic books, or maybe just laying dead, listening to music,
imagining I see faces or foreign places in water stains on the wallpaper, cause
somedays when I remember Papa, then Mama killing theyselves for chump
change — a pitiful li'l bowl of porridge — I get to thinking that even if I ain't
had all I wanted, maybe I've had, you know, all I'm ever gonna get.

"Cooter," Loftis say from the livingroom. "You best get in here quick."

Loftis, he'd switched on Miss Bailey's sulfurcolored livingroom lights, so   5
for a second I couldn't see and started coughing — the smell be so powerful it
hit my nostrils like coke — and when my eyes cleared, shapes evolved from
the light, and I thought for an instant like I'd slipped in space. I seen why
Loftis called me, and went back two steps. See, 4-B is so small, if you ring
Miss Bailey's doorbell the toilet'd flush. But her livingroom, webbed in dust,
be filled to the max with dollars of all denominations, stacks of stock in General
Motors, Gulf Oil, and 3M Corporation in old White Owl cigar boxes, battered
purses, or bound in pink rubber bands. It be like the kind of cubbyhole kids
play in, but filled with . . . *things* — everything — like a world within the
world, you take it from me, so like picturebook scenes of plentifulness you
could seal yourself off in here and settle forever. Loftis and me both drew
breath suddenly. There be unopened cases of Jack Daniel's, three safes cemented
to the floor, hundreds of matchbooks, unworn clothes, a zinc laundry tub,
dozens of wedding rings, rubbish, World War II magazines, a carton of one
hundred canned sardines, mink stoles, old rags, a birdcage, a bucket of silver
dollars, thousands of books, paintings, quarters in tobacco cans, two pianos,
glass jars of pennies, a set of bagpipes, an almost complete Model A Ford
dappled with rust, and, I swear, three sections of a dead tree.

"Godamighty damn!" My head be light; I sat on an upended peachcrate
and picked me up a bottle of Jack Daniel's.

"Don't you touch *anything*!" Loftis, he panting a little; he slap both hands
on a table. "Not until we inventory this stuff."

"Inventory? Aw Lord, Loftis," I say, "something ain't *right* about this
stash. There could be a curse on it . . . "

"Boy, sometimes you act weakminded."

"For real, Loftis, I got a feeling . . . "   10

Loftis, he shucked off his shoes and sat down heavily on the lumpy arm of a stuffed chair. "Don't say *anything*." He chewed his knuckles, and for the first time Loftis looked like he didn't know his next move. "Let me think, okay?" He squeezed his nose in a way he has when thinking hard, sighed, then stood up, and say, "There's something you better see in that bedroom yonder. Cover up your mouth."

"Loftis, I ain't going in there."

He look at me right funny then. "She's a miser, that's all. She saves things."

"But a tree?" I say. "Loftis, a *tree* ain't normal!"

"Cooter, I ain't gonna tell you twice."   15

Like always, I followed Loftis, who swung his flashlight from the plant — he a nightwatchman — into Miss Bailey's bedroom, but me, I'm thinking how trippy this thing is getting, remember how, last year, when I had a paper route, the old lady, with her queer crablike walk, pulled my coat for some change in the hallway, and when I give her a handful of dimes, she say in her old Inner Sanctum voice, "Thank you, Co-o-oter," then gulped the coins down like aspirin, no lie, and scurried off like a hunchback. Me, I wanted no parts of this squirrelly old broad, but Loftis, he holding my wrist now, beaming his light onto a low bed. The room had a funny, museumlike smell. Real sour. It was full of dirty laundry. And I be sure the old lady's stuff had a terrible string attached when Loftis, looking away, lifted her bedsheets and a knot of black flies rose. I stepped back and held my breath. Miss Bailey be in her long-sleeved flannel nightgown, bloated, like she'd been inflated by a tire pump, her crazy putty face bald with rot, flyblown, her fingers big as bananas. Her wristwatch be ticking softly beside a stump of half-eaten bread. Above the bed, her wall had roaches squashed in little circles of bloodstain. Maggots clustered in her eyes, her ears, and one fistsized rat rattled in her flesh. My eyes snapped shut. My knees failed, then I did a Hollywood faint. When I surfaced, Loftis, he be sitting beside me in the livingroom, where he'd drug me, reading a wrinkled, yellow article from the Chicago *Daily Defender.*

"Listen to this," Loftis say. "'Elnora Bailey, forty-five, a Negro housemaid in the Highland Park home of Henry Conners, is the beneficiary of her employer's will. An old American family, the Connerses arrived in this country on the *Providence,* shortly after the voyage of the *Mayflower.* The family flourished in the early days of the 1900s'! . . . " He went on, getting breath. "'A distinguished and wealthy industrialist, without heirs or a wife, Conners willed his entire estate to Miss Bailey of 3347 N. Clark Street for her twenty years of service to his family' . . . " Loftis, he give that Geoffrey Holder laugh of his, low and deep, then it eased up his throat until it hit a high note and tipped his head back onto his shoulders. "Cooter, that was before we was born! Miss Bailey kept this in the Bible next to her bed."

Standing, I braced myself with one hand against the wall. "She didn't earn it?"

"Naw." Loftis, he folded the paper — "Not one penny" — and stuffed it in his shirt pocket. His jaw looked tight as a horseshoe. "Way *I* see it," he say, "this was her one shot in a lifetime to be rich, but, being country, she had backward ways and blew it." Rubbing his hands, he stood up to survey the livingroom. "Somebody's gonna find Miss Bailey soon, but if we stay on the case — Cooter, don't you square up on me now — we can tote everything to our place before daybreak. Best we start with the big stuff."

"But why didn't she *use* it, huh? Tell me that?"

Loftis, he don't pay me no mind. When he gets an idea in his head, you can't dig it out with a chisel. How long it took me and Loftis to inventory, then haul Miss Bailey's queer old stuff to our crib, I can't say, but that decrepit old ninnyhammer's hoard come to $879,543 in cash money, thirty-two bank books (some deposits be only $5), and me, I wasn't sure I was dreaming or what, but I suddenly flashed on this feeling, once we left her flat, that all the fears Loftis and me had about the future be gone, cause Miss Bailey's property was the past — the power of that fellah Henry Conners trapped like a bottle spirit, which we could live off, so it was the future, too, pure potential: can *do*. Loftis got to talking on about how that piano we pushed home be equal to a thousand bills, jim, which equals, say, a bad TEAC A-3340 tape deck, or a down payment on a deuce-and-a-quarter. Its value be (Loftis say) that of a universal standard of measure, relational, unreal as number, so that tape deck could turn, magically, into two gold lamé suits, a trip to Tijuana, or twenty-five rimjobs from a ho — we had $879,543 worth of wishes, if you can deal with that. Be like Miss Bailey's stuff is raw energy, and Loftis and me, like wizards, can transform her stuff into anything else at will. All we had to do, it seemed to me, was decide exactly what to exchange it for.

While Loftis studied this over (he looked funny, like a potato trying to say something, after the inventory, and sat, real quiet, in the kitchen), I filled my pockets with fifties, grabbed me a cab downtown to grease, yum, at one of them high-hat restaurants in the Loop . . . But then I thought better of it, you know, like I'd be out of place — just another jig putting on airs — and scarfed instead at a ribjoint till both my eyes bubbled. This fat lady making fishburgers in the back favored an old hardleg babysitter I once had, a Mrs. Paine who made me eat ochre, and I wanted so bad to say, "Loftis and me Got Ovuh," but I couldn't put that in the wind, could I, so I hatted up. Then I copped a boss silk necktie, cashmere socks, and a whistle-slick maxie leather jacket on State Street, took cabs *every*where, but when I got home that evening a funny, Pandoralike feeling hit me. I took off the jacket, boxed it — it looked so trifling in the hallway's weak light — and, tired, turned my key in the door. I couldn't get in. Loftis, he'd changed the lock and, when he finally let me in, looking vaguer, crabby, like something out of the Book of Revelations, I seen this elaborate boobytrapped tunnel of cardboard and razor blades behind him, with a two-foot space just big enough for him or me to crawl through. That wasn't all. Two bags of trash from the furnace room be sitting inside the door. Loftis, he give my leather jacket this evil look, hauled me inside, and hit me upside the head.

"How much this thing set us back?"

"Two fifty." My jaws be tight; I toss him my receipt. "You want me to take it back? Maybe I can get something else . . . "

Loftis, he say, not to me, but to the receipt, "Remember the time Mama give me that ring we had in the family for fifty years? And I took it to Merchandise Mart and sold it for a few pieces of candy?" He hitched his chair forward, and sat with his elbows on his knees. "That's what you did, Cooter. You crawled into a Clark bar." He commence to rip up my receipt, then picked up his flashlight and keys. "The instant you buy something you *lose* the power to buy something." He button up his coat with holes in the elbows, showing his blue shirt, then turned round at the tunnel to say: "Don't touch Miss Bailey's money, or drink her splo, or do *any*thing until I get back."

"Where you going?"

"To work. It's Wednesday, ain't it?"

"You going to work?"

"Yeah."

"You got to go *really*? Loftis," I say, "what you brang them bags of trash in here for?"

"It ain't trash!" He cut his eyes at me. "There's good clothes in there. Mr. Peterson tossed them out, he don't care, but I saw some use in them, that's all."

"Loftis . . . "

"Yeah?"

"What we gonna do with all this money?"

Loftis pressed his fingers to his eyelids, and for a second he looked caged, or like somebody'd kicked him in his stomach. Then he cut me some slack: "Let me think on it tonight — it don't pay to rush — then we can TCB, okay?"

Five hours after Loftis leave for work, that old blister Mr. Peterson, our landlord, he come collecting rent, find Miss Bailey's body in apartment 4-B, and phoned the Fire Department. Me, I be folding my new jacket in tissue paper to keep it fresh, adding the box to Miss Bailey's unsunned treasures, when two paramedics squeezed her on a long stretcher through a crowd in the hallway. See, I had to pin her from the stairhead, looking down one last time at this dizzy old lady, and I seen something in her face, like maybe she'd been poor as Job's turkey for thirty years, suffering that special Negro fear of using up what little we get in this life — Loftis, he call that entropy — believing in her belly, and for all her faith, jim, there just ain't no more coming tomorrow from grace, or the Lord, or from her own labor, like she can't kill nothing, and won't nothing die . . . so when Conners will her his wealth, it put her through changes, she be spellbound, possessed by the promise of life, panicky about depletion, and locked now in the past cause *every* purchase, you know, has to be a poor buy: a loss of life. Me, I wasn't worried none. Loftis, he got a brain trained by years of talking trash with people in Frog Hudson's Barber Shop on Thirty-fifth Street. By morning, I knew, he'd have some kinda wheeze worked out.

But Loftis, he don't come home. Me, I got plenty worried. I listen to the hi-fi all day Thursday, only pawing outside to peep down the stairs, like that'd make Loftis come sooner. So Thursday go by; and come Friday the head's out of kilter — first there's an ogrelike belch from the toiletbowl, then water bursts from the bathroom into the kitchen — and me, I can't call the super (How do I explain the tunnel?), so I gave up and quit bailing. But on Sat'day, I could smell greens cooking next door. Twice I almost opened Miss Bailey's sardines, even though starving be less an evil than eating up our stash, but I waited till it was dark and, lightheaded with hunger, I stepped outside to Pookie White's, lay a hardluck story on him, and Pookie, he give me some jambalaya and gumbo. Back home in the livingroom, fingerfeeding myself, barricaded in by all that hope made material, the Kid felt like a king in his countingroom, or God in February, the month before He made the world (Mama's saying), and I copped some z's in an armchair till I heard the door move on its hinges, then bumping in the tunnel, and a heavyfooted walk thumped into the bedroom.

"Loftis?" I rubbed my eyes. "You back?" It be Sunday morning. Six-thirty sharp. Darkness dissolved slowly into the strangeness of twilight, with the rays of sunlight flaring at exactly the same angle they fall each night, as if the hour be an island, a moment, outside time. Me, I'm afraid Loftis gonna fuss bout my not straightening up, letting things go. I went into the bathroom, poured water in the spigot washstand — brown rust come bursting out in flakes — and rinsed my face. "Loftis, you supposed to be home four days ago. Hey," I say, toweling my face, "you okay, brah?" How come he don't answer me? Wiping my hands on the seat of my trousers, I tipped into Loftis's room. He sleeping with his mouth open. His legs drawn up, both fists clenched between his knees. He'd kicked his blanket on the floor. In his sleep, Loftis laughed, or moaned, it be hard to tell. His eyelids, not quite shut, show slits of white. I decided to wait till Loftis wake up for his decision, but turning, I seen his watch, keys, and what looked in the first stain of sunlight to be a carefully wrapped piece of newspaper on his nightstand. The sun surged up in a bright shimmer, focusing the bedroom slowly like solution do a photographic image in the developer. And then something so freakish went down I ain't sure it took place. Fumblefingered, I unfolded the paper and inside be a blemished penny. It be like somebody hit me hard between the shoulderblades. Taped on the penny be a slip of paper, and on the paper be the note, "Found while walking down Devon Avenue." I hear Loftis mumble like he trapped in a nightmare. "Hold tight," I whisper, "it's all right." Me, I wanted to tell Loftis how Miss Bailey looked four days ago, that maybe it didn't have to be like that for us — did it? — because we could change. Couldn't we? Me, I pull his packed sheets over him, wrap up the penny, and, when I locate Miss Bailey's glass jar in the livingroom, put it away carefully, for now, with the rest of our things.   1986

INVESTIGATIONS

1. What gives Cooter the idea that "'something ain't *right* about this stash. There could be a curse on it . . . '" (para. 8). How would you have reacted in his place?
2. In paragraph 25 Loftis says, "The instant you buy something you *lose* the power to buy something." From what you know of him, how might this power be important to Loftis?
3. What is it about Miss Bailey's "hope made material" (para. 37) that's so destructive? To what extent is what Cooter says in paragraph 36 an adequate explanation?
4. In what ways might anything that's stolen exert power over the thief? In what ways do this story and your response to "Write Before Reading" (p. 784) show how gifts exert power over those who receive them?

TOBIAS WOLFF

The Other Miller

For two days now Miller has been standing in the rain with the rest of Bravo Company, waiting for some men from another company to blunder down the logging road where Bravo waits in ambush. When this happens, if this happens, Miller will stick his head out of the hole he is hiding in and shoot off all his blank ammunition in the direction of the road. So will everyone else in Bravo Company. Then they will climb out of their holes and get on some trucks and go home, back to the base.

This is the plan.

Miller has no faith in it. He has never yet seen a plan that worked, and this one won't either. He can tell. For one thing, the lieutenant who thought up the plan has been staying away a lot — "doing recon," he claims, but that's a lie. How can you do recon if you don't know where the enemy is? Miller's foxhole has about a foot of water in it. He has to stand on little shelves he's been digging out of the walls, but the soil is sandy and the shelves keep

---

TOBIAS WOLFF's books include the memoir *This Boy's Life* (1989), a novella called *The Barracks Thief* (1984), and a short-story collection called *Back in the World* (1985). Born in Alabama in 1945, Wolff grew up in the Pacific Northwest, served in Vietnam, worked as a reporter for the *Washington Post*, and now teaches creative writing at Syracuse University.

collapsing. That means his boots are wet. Plus his cigarettes are wet. Plus he broke the bridge on his molars the first night out while chewing up one of the lollipops he'd brought along for energy. It drives him crazy the way the broken bridge lifts and grates when he pushes it with his tongue, but last night he lost his willpower and now he can't keep his tongue away from it.

When he thinks of the other company, the one they're supposed to ambush, Miller sees a column of dry, well-fed men marching farther and farther away from the hole where he stands waiting for them. He sees them moving easily under light packs. He sees them stopping for a smoke break, stretching out on fragrant beds of pine needles under the trees, the murmur of their voices growing more and more faint as one by one they drift into sleep.

It's the truth, by God. Miller knows it like he knows he's going to catch   5
a cold, because that's his luck. If he were in the other company then they'd be the ones standing in holes.

Miller's tongue does something to the bridge, and a surge of pain shoots through him. He snaps up straight, eyes burning, teeth clenched against the yell in his throat. He fights it back and glares around him at the other men. The few he can see look stunned and ashen-faced. Of the rest he can make out only their poncho hoods. The poncho hoods stick out of the ground like bullet-shaped rocks.

At this moment, his mind swept clean by pain, Miller can hear the tapping of raindrops on his own poncho. Then he hears the pitchy whine of an engine. A jeep is splashing along the road, slipping from side to side and throwing up thick gouts of mud behind it. The jeep itself is caked with mud. It skids to a stop in front of Bravo Company's position, and the horn beeps twice.

Miller glances around to see what the others are doing. Nobody has moved. They're all just standing in their holes.

The horn beeps again.

A short figure in a poncho emerges from a clump of trees farther up the   10
road. Miller can tell it's the first sergeant by how little he is, so little that the poncho hangs almost to his ankles. The first sergeant walks slowly toward the jeep, big blobs of mud all around his boots. When he gets to the jeep, he leans his head inside; he pulls it out again a moment later. He looks down at the road. He kicks at one of the tires in a thoughtful way. Then he looks up and shouts Miller's name.

Miller keeps watching him. Not until the first sergeant shouts his name again does Miller begin the hard work of hoisting himself out of the foxhole. The other men turn their ashen faces up at him as he trudges past their heads.

"Come here, boy," the first sergeant says. He walks a little distance from the jeep and waves Miller over.

Miller follows him. Something is wrong. Miller can tell, because the first sergeant called him "boy," instead of "shitbird." Already he feels a burning in his left side, where his ulcer is.

The first sergeant stares down the road. "Here's the thing," he begins. He stops and turns to Miller. "Hell's bells, I don't know. Goddamn it. Listen. We got a priority here from the Red Cross. Did you know your mother was sick?"

Miller doesn't say anything. He pushes his lips tight together.   15

"She must have been sick, right?" When Miller remains silent the first sergeant says, "She passed away last night. I'm real sorry." The first sergeant looks sadly up at Miller, and Miller watches the sergeant's right arm beginning to rise under the poncho; then it falls to his side again. Miller can see that the first sergeant wants to give his shoulder a man-to-man kind of squeeze, but it just won't work. You can only do that if you're taller than the other fellow, or maybe the same size.

"These boys here will drive you back to base," the first sergeant says, nodding toward the jeep. "You give the Red Cross a call, and they'll take it from there. Get yourself some rest," he adds. He turns away and walks off toward the trees.

Miller retrieves his gear. One of the men he passes on his way back to the jeep says, "Hey, Miller, what's the story?"

Miller doesn't answer. He's afraid that if he opens his mouth he'll start laughing and ruin everything. He keeps his head down and his lips tight as he climbs into the back seat of the jeep, and he doesn't look up again until the company is a mile or so behind. The fat Pfc. sitting beside the driver is watching him. He says, "I'm sorry about your mother. That's a bummer."

"Maximum bummer," says the driver, another Pfc. He shoots a look over   20 his shoulder. Miller sees his own face reflected for an instant in the driver's sunglasses.

"Had to happen someday," he mumbles, and looks down again.

Miller's hands are shaking. He puts them between his knees and stares through the snapping plastic window at the trees going past. Raindrops rattle on the canvas overhead. He is inside, and everyone else is still outside. Miller can't stop thinking about the others standing around getting rained on, and the thought makes him want to laugh and slap his leg. This is the luckiest he has ever been.

"My grandmother died last year," the driver says. "But that's not the same thing as losing your mother. I feel for you, Miller."

"Don't worry about me," Miller tells him. "I'll get along."

The fat Pfc. beside the driver says, "Look, don't feel like you have to   25 repress just because we're here. If you want to cry or anything just go ahead. Right, Leb?"

The driver nods. "Just let it out."

"No problem," Miller says. He wishes he could set these fellows straight, so they won't feel like they have to act mournful all the way to Fort Ord. But if he tells them what happened they'll turn right around and drive him back to his foxhole.

This is what happened. Another Miller in the battalion has the same initials he's got, W. P., and this Miller is the one whose mother has died. His father passed away during the summer and Miller got that message by mistake too.

So he has the lay of the land now; as soon as the first sergeant started asking about his mother, he got the entire picture.

For once, everybody else is on the outside and Miller is on the inside. Inside, on his way to a hot shower, dry clothes, a pizza, and a warm bunk. He didn't even have to do anything wrong to get here; he just did as he was told. It was their own mistake. Tomorrow he'll rest up like the first sergeant ordered him to, go on sick call about his bridge, maybe go downtown to a movie after that. Then he'll call the Red Cross. By the time they get everything straightened out it will be too late to send him back to the field. And the best thing is, the other Miller won't know. The other Miller will have a whole other day of thinking his mother is still alive. You could even say that Miller is keeping her alive for him.

The man beside the driver turns around again and studies Miller. He has little dark eyes in a round, baby-white face covered with beads of sweat. His name tag reads KAISER. Showing little square teeth like a baby's, he says, "You're really coping, Miller. Most guys pretty much lose it when they get the word."

"I would too," the driver says. "Anybody would. Or maybe I should say almost anybody. It's *human*, Kaiser."

"For sure," Kaiser says. "I'm not saying any different. That's going to be my worst day, the day my mom dies." He blinks rapidly, but not before Miller sees his little eyes mist up.

"Everybody has to go sometime," Miller says. "Sooner or later. That's my philosophy."

"Heavy," the driver says. "Really deep."

Kaiser gives him a sharp look and says, "At ease, Lebowitz."

Miller leans forward. Lebowitz is a Jewish name. That means Lebowitz must be a Jew. Miller wants to ask him why he's in the army, but he's afraid Lebowitz might take it wrong. Instead, he says, conversationally, "You don't see too many Jewish people in the army nowadays."

Lebowitz looks into the rearview mirror. His thick eyebrows arch over his sunglasses, and then he shakes his head and says something Miller can't make out.

"At ease, Leb," Kaiser says again. He turns to Miller and asks him where the funeral is going to be held.

"What funeral?" Miller says.

Lebowitz laughs.

"Back off," Kaiser says. "Haven't you ever heard of shock?"

Lebowitz is quiet for a moment. Then he looks into the rearview mirror again and says, "Sorry, Miller. I was out of line."

Miller shrugs. His probing tongue pushes the bridge too hard and he stiffens suddenly.

"Where did your mom live?" Kaiser asks.

"Redding," Miller says.

Kaiser nods. "Redding," he repeats. He keeps watching Miller. So does

Lebowitz, glancing back and forth between the mirror and the road. Miller understands that they expected a different kind of performance from the one he's given them, more emotional and all. They have seen other personnel whose mothers died and now they have certain standards that he has failed to live up to. He looks out the window. They are driving along a ridgeline. Slices of blue flicker between the trees on the left-hand side of the road; then they hit a space without trees and Miller can see the ocean below them, clear to the horizon under a bright cloudless sky. Except for a few hazy wisps in the treetops they've left the clouds behind, back in the mountains, hanging over the soldiers there.

"Don't get me wrong," Miller says. "I'm sorry she's dead."

Kaiser says, "That's the way. Talk it out."

"It's just that I didn't know her all that well," Miller says, and after this monstrous lie a feeling of weightlessness comes over him. At first it makes him uncomfortable, but almost immediately he begins to enjoy it. From now on he can say anything.

He makes a sad face and says, "I guess I'd be more broken up and so on   50
if she hadn't taken off on us the way she did. Right in the middle of harvest season. Just leaving us like that."

"I'm hearing a lot of anger," Kaiser tells him. "Ventilate. Own it."

Miller got that stuff from a song, but he can't remember any more. He lowers his head and looks at his boots. "Killed my dad," he says, after a time. "Died of a broken heart. Left me with five kids to raise, not to mention the farm." Miller closes his eyes. He sees a field all plowed up with the sun setting behind it, a bunch of kids coming in from the field with rakes and hoes on their shoulders. As the jeep winds down through the switchbacks he describes his hardships as the oldest child in this family. He is at the end of his story when they reach the coast highway and turn north. All at once the jeep stops rattling and swaying. They pick up speed. The tires hum on the smooth road. The rushing air whistles a single note around the radio antenna. "Anyway," Miller says, "it's been two years since I even had a letter from her."

"You should make a movie," Lebowitz says.

Miller isn't sure how to take this. He waits to hear what else Lebowitz has to say, but Lebowitz is silent. So is Kaiser, who's had his back turned to Miller for several minutes now. Both men stare at the road ahead of them. Miller can see that they have lost interest in him. He is disappointed, because he was having a fine time pulling their leg.

One thing Miller told them was true: He hasn't had a letter from his   55
mother in two years. She wrote him a lot when he first joined the Army, at least once a week, sometimes twice, but Miller sent all her letters back unopened and after a year of this she finally gave up. She tried calling a few times but Miller wouldn't go to the telephone, so she gave that up too. Miller wants her to understand that her son is not a man to turn the other cheek. He is a serious man. Once you've crossed him, you've lost him.

Miller's mother crossed him by marrying a man she shouldn't have married: Phil Dove. Dove was a biology teacher in the high school. Miller was having trouble in the course, and his mother went to talk to Dove about it and ended up getting engaged to him. Miller tried to reason with her, but she wouldn't hear a word. You would think from the way she acted that she had landed herself a real catch instead of someone who talked with a stammer and spent his life taking crayfish apart.

Miller did everything he could to stop the marriage but his mother had blinded herself. She couldn't see what she already had, how good it was with just the two of them. How he was always there when she got home from work, with a pot of coffee already brewed. The two of them drinking their coffee together and talking about different things, or maybe not talking at all — maybe just sitting in the kitchen while the room got dark around them, until the telephone rang or the dog started whining to get out. Walking the dog around the reservoir. Coming back and eating whatever they wanted, sometimes nothing, sometimes the same dish three or four nights in a row, watching the programs they wanted to watch and going to bed when they wanted to and not because some other person wanted them to. Just being together in their own place.

Phil Dove got Miller's mother so mixed up that she forgot how good their life was. She refused to see what she was ruining. "You'll be leaving anyway," she told him. "You'll be moving on, next year or the year after" — which showed how wrong she was about Miller, because he would never have left her, not ever, not for anything. But when he said this she laughed as if she knew better, as if he wasn't serious. He was serious, though. He was serious when he promised he'd stay and he was serious when he promised he'd never speak to her again if she married Phil Dove.

She married him. Miller stayed at a motel that night and two more nights, until he ran out of money. Then he joined the Army. He knew that would get to her, because he was still a month shy of finishing high school, and because his father had been killed while serving in the Army. Not in Vietnam but in Georgia, killed in an accident. He and another man were dipping mess kits in a garbage can full of boiling water and somehow the can fell over on him. Miller was six at the time. Miller's mother hated the Army after that, not because her husband was dead — she knew about the war he was going to, she knew about snipers and booby traps and mines — but because of the way it happened. She said the Army couldn't even get a man killed in a decent fashion.

She was right, too. The Army was just as bad as she thought, and worse. You spent all your time waiting around. You lived a completely stupid existence. Miller hated every minute of it, but he found pleasure in his hatred, because he believed that his mother must know how unhappy he was. That knowledge would be a grief to her. It would not be as bad as the grief she had given him, which was spreading from his heart into his stomach and teeth and everywhere else, but it was the worst grief he had power to cause, and it would serve to keep her in mind of him.

Kaiser and Lebowitz are describing hamburgers to each other. Their idea of the perfect hamburger. Miller tries not to listen but their voices go on, and after a while he can't think of anything but beefsteak tomatoes and Gulden's mustard and steaming, onion-stuffed meat crisscrossed with black marks from the grill. He is on the point of asking them to change the subject when Kaiser turns and says, "Think you could handle some chow?"

"I don't know," Miller says. "I guess I could get something down."

"We were talking about a pit stop. But if you want to keep going, just say the word. It's your ball game. I mean, technically we're supposed to take you straight back to base."

"I could eat," Miller says.

"That's the spirit. At a time like this you've got to keep your strength up."   65

"I could eat," Miller says again.

Lebowitz looks up into the rearview mirror, shakes his head, and looks away again.

They take the next turnoff and drive inland to a crossroads where two gas stations face two restaurants. One of the restaurants is boarded up, so Lebowitz pulls into the parking lot of the Dairy Queen across the road. He turns the engine off and the three men sit motionless in the sudden silence that follows. It soon beings to fade. Miller hears the distant clang of metal on metal, the caw of a crow, the creak of Kaiser shifting in his seat. A dog barks in front of a rust-streaked trailer next door. A skinny white dog with yellow eyes. As it barks the dog rubs itself, one leg raised and twitching, against a sign that shows an outspread hand below the words KNOW YOUR FUTURE.

They get out of the jeep, and Miller follows Kaiser and Lebowitz across the parking lot. The air is warm and smells of oil. In the gas station across the road a pink-skinned man in a swimming suit is trying to put air in the tires of his bicycle, jerking at the hose and swearing loudly at his inability to make the pump work. Miller pushes his tongue against the broken bridge. He lifts it gently. He wonders if he should try eating a hamburger, and decides that it can't hurt as long as he is careful to chew on the other side of his mouth.

But it does hurt. After the first couple of bites Miller shoves his plate away.   70
He rests his chin on one hand and listens to Lebowitz and Kaiser argue about whether people can actually tell the future. Lebowitz is talking about a girl he used to know who had ESP. "We'd be driving along," he says, "and out of the blue she would tell me exactly what I was thinking about. It was unbelievable."

Kaiser finishes his hamburger and takes a drink of milk. "No big deal," he says. "I could do that." He pulls Miller's hamburger over to his side of the table and takes a bite.

"Go ahead," Lebowitz says. "Try it. I'm not thinking about what you think I'm thinking about," he adds.

"Yes, you are."

"All right, now I am," Lebowitz says. "but I wasn't before."

"I wouldn't let a fortune-teller near me," Miller says. "The way I see it,   75
the less you know the better off you are."

"More vintage philosophy from the private stock of W. P. Miller," Lebowitz says. He looks at Kaiser, who is eating the last of Miller's hamburger. "Well, how about it? I'm up for it if you are."

Kaiser chews ruminatively. He swallows and licks his lips. "Sure," he says. "Why not? As long as Miller here doesn't mind."

"Mind what?" Miller asks.

Lebowitz stands and puts his sunglasses back on. "Don't worry about Miller. Miller's cool. Miller keeps his head when men all around him are losing theirs."

Kaiser and Miller get up from the table and follow Lebowitz outside. Lebowitz is bending down in the shade of a dumpster, wiping off his boots with a paper towel. Shiny blue flies buzz around him. "Mind what?" Miller repeats.

"We thought we'd check out the prophet," Kaiser tells him.

Lebowitz straightens up, and the three of them start across the parking lot.

"I'd actually kind of like to get going," Miller says. When they reach the jeep he stops, but Lebowitz and Kaiser walk on. "Now, listen," Miller says, and skips a little to catch up. "I have a lot to do," he says to their backs. "I want to go home."

"We know how broken up you are," Lebowitz tells him. He keeps walking.

"This shouldn't take too long," Kaiser says.

The dog barks and then, when it sees that they really intend to come within range of its teeth, runs around the trailer. Lebowitz knocks on the door. It swings open, and there stands a round-faced woman with dark, sunken eyes and heavy lips. One of her eyes has a cast; it seems to be watching something beside her while the other looks down at the three soldiers at her door. Her hands are covered with flour. She is a gypsy, and actual gypsy. Miller has never seen a gypsy before, but he recognizes her just as he would recognize a wolf if he saw one. Her presence makes his blood pound in his veins. If he lived in this place he would come back at night with some other men, all of them yelling and waving torches, and drive her out.

"You on duty?" Lebowitz asks.

She nods, wiping her hands on her skirt. They leave chalky streaks on the bright patchwork. "All of you?" she asks.

"You bet," Kaiser says. His voice is unnaturally loud.

She nods again and turns her good eye from Lebowitz to Kaiser, and then to Miller. After she takes Miller in she smiles and rattles off a string of strange sounds, words from another language or maybe a spell, as if she expects him to understand. One of her front teeth is black.

"No," Miller says. "No, ma'am. Not me." He shakes his head.

"Come," she says, and stands aside.

Lebowitz and Kaiser mount the steps and disappear into the trailer. "Come," the woman repeats. She beckons with her white hands.

Miller backs away, still shaking his head. "Leave me alone," he tells her, and before she can answer he turns and walks away. He goes back to the jeep and sits in the driver's seat, leaving both doors open to catch the breeze. Miller feels the heat drawing the dampness out of his fatigues. He can smell the musty wet canvas overhead and the sourness of his own body. Through the windshield, covered with mud except for a pair of grimy half circles, he watches three boys solemnly urinating against the wall of the gas station across the road.

Miller bends down to loosen his boots. Blood rushes to his face as he fights   95 the wet laces, and his breath comes faster and faster. "Goddamn laces," he says. "Goddamn rain. Goddamn Army." He gets the laces untied and sits up, panting. He stares at the trailer. Goddamn gypsy.

He can't believe those two fools actually went inside there. Yukking it up. Playing around. That shows how stupid they are, because nobody knows that you don't play around with fortune-tellers. There is no predicting what a fortune-teller might say, and once it's said, no way to keep it from happening. Once you hear what's out there it isn't out there anymore, it's here. You might as well open your door to a murderer as to the future.

The future. Didn't everybody know enough about the future already, without digging up the details? There is only one thing you have to know about the future: Everything gets worse. Once you have that, you have it all. The specifics don't bear thinking about.

Miller certainly has no intention of thinking about the specifics. He peels off his damp socks and massages his white crinkled feet. Now and then he glances up toward the trailer, where the gypsy is pronouncing fate on Kaiser and Lebowitz. Miller makes humming noises. He will not think about the future.

Because it's true — everything gets worse. One day you are sitting in front of your house, poking sticks into an anthill, hearing the chink of silverware and the voices of your mother and father in the kitchen; then, at some moment you can't even remember, one of those voices is gone. And you never hear it again. When you go from today to tomorrow you're walking into an ambush.

A new boy, Nat Pranger, joins your Little League team. He lives in a   100 boardinghouse a couple of streets over from you. The first day you meet Nat you show him the place under the bleachers where you keep the change you steal from your mother. The next morning you remember doing this, and you push your half-eaten breakfast away and run to the ball park, blindly, your chest hurting. The change is still in its hiding place. You count it. Not a penny is missing. You kneel there in the shadows, catching your breath.

All summer you and Nat throw each other grounders and develop plans to acquire a large sailboat for use in the South Seas — that is Nat's term, "the South Seas." Then school starts, your first year of junior high, and Nat makes other friends but you don't, because something about you turns people cruel. Even the teachers. You want to have friends, you would change if you knew what it was that needed changing, but you don't know. You see Nat struggling to be loyal and you hate him for it. His kindness is worse than cruelty. By December you know exactly how things will be in June. All you can do is watch it happen.

What lies ahead doesn't bear thinking about. Already Miller has an ulcer, and his teeth are full of holes. His body is giving out on him. What will it be like when he's sixty? Or even five years from now? Miller was in a restaurant the other day and saw a fellow about his own age in a wheelchair, getting fed soup by a woman who was talking to some other people at the table. This boy's hands lay twisted in his lap like gloves dropped there; his pants had crawled halfway to his knees, showing pale, wasted legs no thicker than bones. He could barely move his head. The woman feeding him did a lousy job because she was too busy blabbing to her friends. Half the soup went over the boy's shirt. Yet his eyes were bright and watchful.

Miller thought, *That could happen to me.*

You could be going along just fine and then one day, through no fault of your own, something could get loose in your bloodstream and knock out part of your brain. Leave you like that. And if it didn't happen now, all at once, it was sure to happen slowly later on. That was the end you were bound for.

Someday Miller is going to die. He knows that, and he prides himself on knowing it when other people only pretend to know it, secretly believing that they will live forever. This is not the reason that the future is unthinkable to Miller. There is something worse than that, something not to be considered, and he will not consider it.

He will not consider it. Miller leans back against the seat and closes his eyes, but his effort to trick himself into somnolence fails. Behind his eyelids he is wide awake and fidgety with gloom, probing against his will for what he is afraid to find, until, with no surprise at all, he finds it. A simple truth. His mother is also going to die. Just like him. And there is no telling when. Miller cannot count on her to be there to come home to, and receive his pardon, when he finally decides that she has suffered enough.

Miller opens his eyes and looks at the raw shapes of the buildings across the road, their outlines lost in the grime on the windshield. He closes his eyes again. He listens to himself breathe and feels the familiar, almost muscular ache of knowing that he is beyond his mother's reach. He has put himself where she cannot see him or speak to him or touch him in that thoughtless way of her, resting her hand on his shoulder as she stops behind his chair to ask him a question or just stand for a moment, her mind somewhere else. This was supposed to be her punishment, but somehow it has become his own. He understands that it has to stop. It is killing him.

It has to stop now, and as if he has been planning for this day all along Miller knows exactly what he will do. Instead of reporting to the Red Cross when he gets back to base, he will pack his bag and catch the first bus home. No one will blame him for this. Even when they discover the mistake they've made they still won't blame him, because it would be the natural thing for a grieving son to do. Instead of punishing him they will probably apologize for giving him a scare.

He will take the first bus home, express or not. It will be full of Mexicans and soldiers. Miller will sit by a window and drowse. Now and then he will come up from his dreams to stare out at the passing green hills and loamy plowland and the stations where the bus puts in, stations cloudy with exhaust and loud with engine roar, where the people he sees through his window will

105

look groggily back at him as if they too have just come up from sleep. Salinas. Vacaville. Red Bluff. When he gets to Redding, Miller will hire a cab. He will ask the driver to stop at Schwartz's for a few minutes while he buys some flowers, and then he will ride on home, down Sutter and over to Serra, past the ball park, past the grade school, past the Mormon temple. Right on Belmont. Left on Park. Leaning over the seat, saying farther, farther, a little farther, that's it, that one, there.

The sound of voices behind the door as he rings the bell. Door swings open, voices hush. Who are these people? Men in suits, women wearing white gloves. Someone stammers his name, strange to him now, almost forgotten. "W-W-Wesley." A man's voice. He stands just inside the door, breathing perfume. Then the flowers are taken from his hand and laid with other flowers on the coffee table. He hears his name again. It is Phil Dove, moving toward him from across the room. He walks slowly, with his arms raised, like a blind man.   110

Wesley, he says. Thank God you're home.   1986

INVESTIGATIONS

1. Consider the initial encounter between Miller and the two men driving him back to the base (paras. 19–46). What does this encounter reveal about Miller? What does it reveal about his relationships with other people?

2. Miller refers to his "luck" throughout the story. What does his view of his luck suggest about his view of the way the world works? What does his view of the future suggest about his view of the world?

3. Discuss the relationship between the lie Miller tells about his mother (paras. 49–52) and the "real" story of his relationship with her? Tell the story of the mother's remarriage from her perspective.

4. The gypsy's presence makes Miller's blood pound in his veins: "If he lived in this place he would come back at night with some other men, all of them yelling and waving torches, and drive her out" (para. 86). How does this passage relate to other passages revealing Miller's feelings? What is it about Miller that "turns people cruel" (para. 101)?

5. Reread the last five paragraphs of the story (107–111). Notice each shift in verb tense from the present to the future to the present. What do these shifts signify?

MARY OLIVER

Some Questions
You Might Ask

Is the soul solid, like iron?
Or is it tender and breakable, like
the wings of a moth in the beak of the owl?
Who has it, and who doesn't?
I keep looking around me.   5
The face of the moose is as sad
as the face of Jesus.
The swan opens her white wings slowly.
In the fall, the black bear carries leaves into the darkness.
One question leads to another.   10
Does it have a shape? Like an iceberg?
Like the eye of a hummingbird?
Does it have one lung, like the snake and the scallop?
Why should I have it, and not the anteater
who loves her children?   15
Why should I have it, and not the camel?
Come to think of it, what about the maple trees?
What about the blue iris?
What about all the little stones, sitting alone in the moonlight?
What about roses, and lemons, and their shining leaves?   20
What about the grass?   1989

INVESTIGATIONS

1. In what ways does each thing Oliver names have a soul both "solid, like
   iron" and "tender and breakable, like / the wings of a moth in the beak
   of the owl" (lines 1–3)? In what ways are the things Oliver names not
   things at all?
2. Write a poem that answers, however fancifully, the speaker's questions.
3. How would Cooter, in Johnson's "Exchange Value," answer the speaker's
   questions? The speaker of Anderson's "Heart Fire"? The narrator of
   Carver's "Cathedral" (p. 876)?

Born in Cleveland, Ohio, in 1935, MARY OLIVER has published eight books of poetry, including
American Primitive (1983), winner of the Pulitzer Prize in poetry, and *House of Light* (1990). Oliver
has lived for many years in Provincetown, Massachusetts.

MILCHA SANCHEZ-SCOTT

Roosters

Characters

GALLO	CHATA
ZAPATA	ADAN
HECTOR	SHADOW #1
ANGELA	SHADOW #2
JUANA	SAN JUAN

Time and Place
The present. The Southwest.

ACT ONE

Scene I

(Stage and house are dark. Slowly a narrow pinspot of light comes up. We hear footsteps. Enter Gallo, a very, very handsome man in his forties. He is wearing a cheap dark suit, with a white open-neck shirt. He carries a suitcase. He puts the suitcase down. He faces the audience.)

GALLO: Lord Eagle, Lord Hawk, sainted ones, spirits and winds, Santa María Aurora of the Dawn. . . . I want no resentment, I want no rancor. . . . I had an old red Cuban hen. She was squirrel-tailed and sort of slab-sided and you wouldn't have given her a second look. But she was a queen. She could be thrown with any cock and you would get a hard-kicking stag every time.

I had a vision, of a hard-kicking flyer, the ultimate bird. The Filipinos were the ones with the pedigree Bolinas, the high flyers, but they had no real kick. To see those birds fighting in the air like dark avenging angels . . . well like my father use to say, "Son nobles . . . finos . . ."[1] I figured to mate that old red Cuban. This particular Filipino had the best. A dark burgundy flyer named MacArthur. He wouldn't sell. I began borrowing

---

[1] They are noble . . . fine . . . [Ed.]

MILCHA SANCHEZ-SCOTT was born in Bali in 1955 to an Indonesian, Chinese, and Dutch mother and a Colombian father. She immigrated with her family to La Jolla, California, when she was a teenager. A member of New Dramatists and the recipient of a First Level Award from the Rockefeller Foundation, Sanchez-Scott is the author of *Latina* (1980), *Dog Lady* (1984), *Evening Star* (1988), and *The Architect Piece* (1991).

MacArthur at night, bringing him back before dawn, no one the wiser, but one morning the Filipino's son caught me. He pulled out his blade. I pulled out mine. I was faster. I went up on manslaughter. . . . They never caught on . . . thought I was in the henhouse trying to steal their stags. . . . It took time — refining, inbreeding, cross-breeding, brother to sister, mother to son, adding power, rapid attack . . . but I think we got him.

(*Gallo stands still for a beat, checks his watch, takes off his jacket, and faces center stage. A slow, howling drumbeat begins. As it gradually goes higher in pitch and excitement mounts, we see narrow beams of light, the first light of dawn, filtering through chicken wire. The light reveals a heap of chicken feathers which turns out to be an actor/ dancer who represents the rooster Zapata. Zapata stretches his wings, then his neck, to greet the light. He stands and struts proudly, puffs his chest, and crows his salutation to the sun. Gallo stalks Zapata, as drums follow their movements.*)

Ya, ya, mi lindo . . . yeah, baby . . . you're a beauty, a real beauty. Now let's see whatcha got. (*He pulls out a switchblade stiletto. It gleams in the light as he tosses it from hand to hand.*) Come on, baby boy. Show Daddy whatcha got.

(*Gallo lunges at Zapata. The rooster parries with his beak and wings. This becomes a slow, rhythmic fight-dance, which continues until Gallo grabs Zapata by his comb, bending his head backwards until he is forced to sit. Gallo stands behind Zapata, straddling him, one hand still holding the comb, the other holding the knife against the rooster's neck.*)

Oh yeah, you like to fight? Huh? You gonna kill for me, baby boy? Huh?

(*Gallo sticks the tip of the knife into Zapata. The rooster squawks in pain.*)

Sssh! Baby boy, you gotta learn. Daddy's gotta teach you.

(*Gallo sticks it to Zapata again. This time the rooster snaps back in anger.*)

That's right, beauty. . . . Now you got it. . . . Come on, come.

(*Gallo waves his knife and hand close to Zapata's face. The rooster's head and eyes follow.*)

Oh yeah . . . that's it, baby, take it! Take it!

(*Suddenly Zapata attacks, drawing blood. Gallo's body contracts in orgasmic pleasure/pain.*)

Ay precioso! . . . Mi lindo. . . . You like that, eh? Taste good, huh? (*He waves the gleaming knife in a slow hypnotic movement which calms the rooster.*) Take my blood, honey. . . . I'm in you now. . . . Morales blood, the blood of kings . . . and you're my rooster . . . a Morales rooster. (*He slowly backs away from the rooster. He picks up his suitcase, still pointing the knife at Zapata.*) Kill. You're my son. Make me proud.

(*Gallo exits. Zapata puffs his chest and struts upstage. Lights go up a little on upstage left area as the rooster goes into the chicken-wire henhouse. He preens and scratches. Enter Hector, a young man of about twenty. He is very handsome. He wears gray sweatpants and no shirt. On his forehead is a sweatband. His hair and body are dripping wet. He has been running. Now he is panting as he leans on the henhouse looking at Zapata.*)

HECTOR: I saw what you did to those chicks. Don't look at me like you have a mind or a soul, or feelings. You kill your young . . . and we are so proud of your horrible animal vigor. . . . But you are my inheritance . . . Abuelo's gift to me . . . to get me out. Oh, Abuelo, Grandfather . . . you should have left me your courage, your sweet pacific strength.

(*A ray of light hits downstage right. In a semishadow, we see a miniature cemetery, with small white headstones and white crosses. We see the profile of a young angel/girl with wings and a pale dress. Angela is kneeling next to a bare desert tree with low scratchy branches. She has a Buster Brown haircut and a low tough voice. She is fifteen, but looks twelve.*)

ANGELA (*loudly*):
Angel of God
My Guardian Dear
To whom God's love
Commits me here
Ever this day be
At my side
To light and guard
To rule and guide
Amen.
(*Her paper wings get caught in a tree branch.*) Aw, shit! (*She exits.*)

Scene 2

(*As the light changes we hear the clapping of women making tortillas. Lights come up full. Center stage is a faded wood-frame house, with a porch that is bare except for a table and a few chairs. The house sits in the middle of a desert agricultural valley somewhere in the Southwest. Everything is sparse. There is a feeling of blue skies and space. One might see off on the horizon tall Nopales or Century cactus. Juana, a thin, worn-out-looking woman of thirty-five, comes out of*) *the house. She is wearing a faded housedress. She goes to midyard, faces front, and stares out.)*

JUANA: It's dry. Bone dry. There's a fire in the mountains . . . up near Jacinto Pass. (*The clapping stops for a beat, then continues. She starts to go back into the house, then stops. She sniffs the air, sniffs again, and again.*) Tres Rosas . . . I smell Tres Rosas. (*She hugs her body and rocks.*) Tres Rosas. . . . Ay, St. Anthony let him come home. . . . Let him be back.

(*The clapping stops. Chata enters from the house. She is a fleshy woman of forty, who gives new meaning to the word blowsy. She has the lumpy face of a hard boozer. She walks with a slight limp. She wears a black kimono, on the back of which is embroidered in red a dragon and the words "Korea, U.S.S. Perkins, 7th Fleet." A cigarette hangs from her lips. She carries a bowl containing balls of tortilla dough.*)

I smell Tres Rosas. . . . The brilliantine for his hair. . . . He musta been here. Why did he go?

CHATA: Men are shit.

JUANA: Where could he be?

CHATA: First day out of jail! My brother never comes home first day. You should know that. Gotta sniff around . . . gotta get use to things. See his friends.

JUANA: Sí, that's right. . . . He just gotta get used to things. I'll feel better when I see him . . . I gotta keep busy.

CHATA: You been busy all morning.

JUANA: I want him to feel good, be proud of us. . . . You hear anything when you come in yesterday?

CHATA: Who's gonna know anything at the Trailways bus station?

JUANA: You ain't heard anything?

CHATA: Juanita, he knows what he's doing. If there was gonna be any trouble he'd know. Ay, mujer, he's just an old warrior coming home.

JUANA: Ain't that old.

CHATA: For a fighting man, he's getting up there.

(*Juana slaps tortillas. Chata watches her.*)

Who taught you to make tortillas?

JUANA: I don't remember. I never make 'em. Kids don't ask.

CHATA: Look at this. You call this a tortilla? Have some pride. Show him you're a woman.

JUANA: Chata, you've been here one day, and you already —

CHATA: Ah, you people don't know what it is to eat fresh handmade tortillas. My grandmother Hortensia, the one they used to call "La India Condenada" . . . she would start making them at five o'clock in the morning. So the men would have something to eat when they went into the fields. Hijo!

She was tough. . . . Use to break her own horses . . . and her own men. Every day at five o'clock she would wake me up. "Buenos pinchi días,"[2] she would say. I was twelve or thirteen years old, still in braids. . . . "Press your hands into the dough," "Con fuerza,"[3] "Put your stamp on it." One day I woke up, tú sabes, con la sangre.[4] "Ah! So you're a woman now. Got your own cycle like the moon. Soon you'll want a man, well this is what you do. When you see the one you want, you roll the tortilla on the inside of your thigh and then you give it to him nice and warm. Be sure you give it to him and nobody else." Well, I been rolling tortillas on my thighs, on my nalgas,[5] and God only knows where else, but I've been giving my tortillas to the wrong men . . . and that's been the problem with my life. First there was Emilio. I gave him my first tortilla. Ay Mamacita, he use to say, these are delicious. Aye, he was handsome, a real lady-killer! After he did me the favor he didn't even have the cojones to stick around . . . took my TV set too. They're all shit . . . the Samoan bartender, what was his name . . .

JUANA: Nicky, Big Nicky.

CHATA: The guy from Pep Boys —

JUANA: Chata, you really think he'll be back?

CHATA: His son's first time in the pit? With "the" rooster? A real Morales rooster? Honey, he'll be back. Stop worrying.

JUANA: Let's put these on the griddle. Angela, Hector . . . breakfast.

Scene 3

(*Angela slides out from under the house, wearing her wings. She carries a white box which contains her cardboard tombstones, paper and crayons, a writing tablet, and a pen. She too sniffs the air. She runs to the little cemetery and looks up, as Hector appears at the window behind her.*)

ANGELA: Tres Rosas. . . . Did you hear? Sweet Jesus, Abuelo, Queen of Heaven, all the Saints, all the Angels. It is true. It is certain. He is coming, coming to stay forever and ever. Amen.

HECTOR: Don't count on it!

ANGELA (*to Heaven*): Protect me from those of little faith and substance.

HECTOR: I'm warning you. You're just going to be disappointed.

ANGELA: (*to Heaven*): Guard me against the enemies of my soul.

HECTOR: Your butt's getting bigger and bigger!

ANGELA: And keep me from falling in with low companions.

---

[2] Good morning. [Ed.]
[3] With force. [Ed.]
[4] You know, with the blood. [Ed.]
[5] Buttocks. [Ed.]

HECTOR: Listen, little hummingbird woman, you gotta be tough, and grown-up today.

(Angela digs up her collection can and two dolls. Both dolls are dressed in nuns' habits. One, the St. Lucy doll, has round sunglasses. She turns a box over to make a little tea table on which she places a doll's teapot and cups.)

ANGELA: As an act of faith and to celebrate her father's homecoming, Miss Angela Ester Morales will have a tea party.

HECTOR: No more tea parties.

ANGELA: Dancing in attendance will be that charming martyr St. Lucy.

HECTOR: He will not be impressed.

ANGELA: Due to the loss of her eyes and the sensitivity of her alabaster skin, St. Lucy will sit in the shade. *(She sits St. Lucy in the shade and picks up the other doll.)*

HECTOR: Who's that?

ANGELA: St. Teresa of Avignon, you will sit over here. *(She seats St. Teresa doll.)*

HECTOR: Just don't let him con you, Angela.

ANGELA *(pouring pretend tea)*: One lump or two, St. Lucy? St. Teresa has hyperglycemia, and only takes cream in her tea. Isn't that right, St. Teresa?

HECTOR: He's not like Abuelo.

(Angela animates the dolls like puppets and uses two different voices as St. Lucy and St. Teresa.)

ANGELA *(as St. Teresa)*: Shouldn't we wait for St. Luke?

HECTOR: Stop hiding. You can't be a little girl forever.

ANGELA *(as St. Lucy)*: St. Luke! St. Luke! Indeed! How that man got into Heaven I'll never know. That story about putting peas in his boots and offering the discomfort up to God is pure bunk. I happen to know he boiled the peas first.

HECTOR: I don't want you hurt. It's time to grow up.

ANGELA *(as St. Teresa)*: St. Lucy! I can only think that it is the loss of your eyes that makes you so disagreeable. Kindly remember that we have all suffered to be saints.

HECTOR: Are you listening to me, Angie?

ANGELA *(as St. Lucy)*: Easy for you to say! They took my eyes because I wouldn't put out! They put them on a plate. A dirty, chipped one, thank you very much indeed! To this day no true effort has been made to find them.

HECTOR: Excuse me! . . . Excuse me, St. Teresa, St. Lucy, I just thought I should tell you . . . a little secret . . . your hostess, Miss Angela Ester Morales, lies in her little, white, chaste, narrow bed, underneath the crucifix, and masturbates.

ANGELA: Heretic! Liar!

HECTOR: Poor Jesus, up there on the cross, right over her bed, his head tilted down. He sees everything.

ANGELA: Lies! Horrible lies!

HECTOR: Poor saint of the month, watching from the night table.

ANGELA: I hate you! I hate you! Horrible, horrible Hector.

JUANA (*from offstage*): Breakfast!

(*Hector leaves the window. Angela sits on the ground writing on a tombstone.*)

ANGELA (*lettering a tombstone*): Here lies Horrible Hector Morales. Died at age twenty, in great agony, for tormenting his little sister.

JUANA (*offstage*): You kids . . . breakfast!

HECTOR (*pops up at window*): Just be yourself. A normal sex-crazed fifteen-year-old girl with a big gigantic enormous butt. (*He exits.*)

ANGELA (*to Heaven*):
Send me to Alaska
Let me be frozen
Send me a contraction
A shrinking antidote
Make me little again
Please make my legs
Like tiny pink Vienna sausages
Give me back my little butt

(*Juana and Chata bring breakfast out on the porch and set it on the table.*)

JUANA: Angie! Hector! We ain't got all day.

(*Angela goes to the breakfast table with the St. Lucy doll and the collection can.*)

And take your wings off before you sit at the table. Ain't you kids got any manners?

(*Angela removes her wings, sits down, bows her head in prayer. Chata stares at St. Lucy. St. Lucy stares at Chata. Juana shoos flies and stares at the distant fire.*)

I hope he's on this side of the fire.

CHATA: That doll's staring at me.

ANGELA: She loves you.

(*Lights fade on the women, come up on the henhouse, Adan, a young man of twenty, is talking to Zapata — now a real rooster, not the actor/dancer — and preparing his feed.*)

ADAN: Hola Zapata . . . ya mi lindo . . . mi bonito. En Inglés. Tengo que hablar en English . . . pinchi English . . . verdad Zapata? En Español más romántico pero Hector say I must learned di English. (*Zapata starts squawking.*) Qué te pasa? Orita vas a comer.[6]

(*Hector enters.*)

HECTOR: English, Adan . . . English.

ADAN: No English . . . pinchi English.

HECTOR: Good morning, Adan.

ADAN: A que la fregada! . . . Okay this morning in the fields, I talk English pero this afternoon for a fight I talk puro Español.

HECTOR: Good morning, Adan.

ADAN: Sí, sí, good morning, muy fine. . . . Hector, el Filipino he say . . . (*He moves away from Zapata, so bird will not hear him.*) He say to tell you que Zapata no win. Porque Filipino bird fight more y your bird first fight y your first fight y you got no ex . . . ex . . .

HECTOR: Experience.

ADAN: Sí eso, he say you sell bird to him y no fight. . . . He say is not true Morales bird porque Gallo not here. El Filipino say if you fight bird . . . bird dead. If bird still alive after Filipino bird beat him. . . . Bird still dead porque nobody pay money for bird that lose.

HECTOR: But if he wins, everybody wants him.

ADAN: I say, ay di poor, poor Hector. His abuelo leave him bird. He can no sell. El Filipino say, "Good!" Inside, in my heart I am laughing so hard porque he not know Gallo gonna be here. We win, we make much money.

HECTOR: It's my bird, I have to do it myself.

ADAN: You tonto! You stupido! You mulo! Like donkey. . . . He help you, he the king . . . he you papa. For him all birds fight.

HECTOR: No!

ADAN: Why? Why for you do this? You no even like bird. Zapata he knows this, he feel this thing in his heart. You just want money to go from the fields, to go to the other side of the mountains . . . to go looking . . . to go looking for what? On the other side is only more stupid people like us.

HECTOR: How could you think I just wanted money? I want him to see me.

ADAN: Sorry. . . . I am sorry my friend. . . . I know. . . . I stay with you y we win vas a ver! Okay, Zapata! We win y est a noche estamos tomando Coors, Ripple, Lucky Lager, unas Buds, Johnnie Walkers, oh sí, y las beautiful señoritas. (*He gives Zapata his food.*) Eat, Zapata! Be strong.

HECTOR: I almost forgot, look what I have for you . . . fresh, warm homemade tortillas.

ADAN: Oh, now nice.

HECTOR: Yes, how nice. Aunt Chata made them.

ADAN: Oh, much nice.

HECTOR: Today she woke up at five o'clock, spit a green booger the size of a

---

[6] Now, my lovely . . . my pretty. In English. I have to speak in English, right Zapata? Spanish is more romantic, but Hector . . . what's the matter? Come and Eat. [Ed.]

small frog into a wad of Kleenex. She wrapped her soiled black "7th Fleet" kimono around her loose, flaccid, tortured, stretch-marked body and put her fat-toed, corned yellow hooves into a pair of pink satin slippers. She slap-padded over to the sink, where she opened her two hippo lips and looked into the mirror. She looked sad. I looked at those lips . . . those lips that had wrapped themselves warmly and lovingly around the cocks of a million campesinos, around thousands upon thousands of Mexicanos, Salvadoreños, Guatemaltecos. For the tide of brown men that flooded the fields of this country, she was there with her open hippo whore's lips, saying "Bienvenidos," "Welcome," "Hola," "Howdy." Those are legendary lips, Adan.

ADAN: Yes . . . muy yes.

HECTOR: What a woman, what a comfort. Up and down the state in her beat-up station wagon. A '56 Chevy with wood panels on the sides, in the back a sad, abused mattress. She followed the brown army of pickers through tomatoes, green beans, zucchinis, summer squash, winter squash, oranges, and finally Castroville, the artichoke capital of the world, where her career was stopped by the fists of a sun-crazed compañero. The ingratitude broke her heart.

ADAN: Oh my gooseness!

HECTOR: She was a river to her people, she should be rewarded, honored. No justice in the world.

ADAN: Pinchi world. (*He and Hector look to mountains.*) You look mountains. In my country I look mountains to come here. I am here and everybody still look mountains.

HECTOR: I want to fly right over them.

ADAN: No, my friend, we are here, we belong . . . la tierra.

JUANA (*from offstage*): Hector, I ain't calling you again.

(*Lights up on the porch. Juana and Chata are sitting at the table. Angela is sitting on the steps. She has her wings back on. St. Lucy and the collection can are by her side. She is writing on her tablet.*)

JUANA: Oh Gallo, what's keeping you?

CHATA: Men are shit! That's all. And it's Saturday. When do they get drunk? When do they lose their money? When do they shoot each other? Saturdays, that's when the shit hits the fan.

(*Enter Hector and Adan with Zapata in a traveling carrier.*)

JUANA: It's because I'm so plain.

HECTOR: We're better off without him.

CHATA: Buenos días, Adan. Un cafecito?

ADAN: Ah. Good morning, Mrs. Chata, no gracias, ah good morning, Mrs. Morales y Miss Angelita.

(*Angela sticks out her donation can. Adan automatically drops coins in.*)

JUANA: Angela!

ADAN: No, is good, is for the poor. Miss Angela, she good lady . . . eh, girl. (*He pats Angela on the head.*)

JUANA: Why don't you leave the bird, so your father can see him when he gets home.

HECTOR: He's my bird. He can see it later.

JUANA: I can't believe you would do this to your own father. Birds are his life . . . and he's so proud of you.

HECTOR: This is news. How would he know, he hasn't seen me in years.

JUANA: It isn't his fault.

HECTOR: It never is.

JUANA: Your father is with us all the time, he got his eye on us, he knows everything we're doing.

ANGELA: Everything!?

JUANA: I brag about you kids in my letters. . . . His friends they tell him what a smart boy you are . . . that you're good-looking like him. . . . He's proud. . . . "A real Morales," that's what he says.

HECTOR: And did he call me a winner? A champ? A prince? And did you tell him I was in the fields?

ANGELA: What did he say about me, Mama?

HECTOR: Nothing, you're a girl and a retard. What possible use could he have for you? Grow up!

CHATA: No, you grow up.

(*Angela buries herself in Chata's lap.*)

JUANA: Hector, please, Hector, for me.

HECTOR: No, Mother. Not even for you.

CHATA: You give him a chance.

HECTOR: What chance did he give us? Fighting his birds, in and out of trouble. He was never here for us, never a card, a little present for Angela. He forgot us.

JUANA: You don't understand him. He's different.

HECTOR: Just make it clear to him. Abuelo left the bird to me, not to him, to me.

JUANA: Me, me, me. You gonna choke on this me, me. Okay, okay, I'm not going to put my nose in the bird business. I just ask you for me, for Angie, be nice to him.

HECTOR: As long as we all understand the "bird business," I'll be nice to him even if it kills me, Mother.

JUANA: Now you're feeling sorry for yourself. Just eat. You can feel sorry for yourself later.

HECTOR: Why didn't I think of that. I'll eat now and feel sorry for myself later.

JUANA: Now, you kids gotta be nice and clean, your papa don't like dirty people.

CHATA: Me too, I hate dirty people.

JUANA: Angie, you take a bath.

HECTOR: Oh, Angela, how . . . how long has it been since you and water came together? (*Angela hits him.*) Oww!

JUANA: You put on a nice clean dress, and I don't wanna see you wearing no dirty wings.

HECTOR: Right, Angie, put on the clean ones.

JUANA: You say please and excuse me . . . and you watch your table manners. . . . I don't want to see any pigs at my table.

HECTOR (*making pig noises*): What a delicious breakfast! Cold eggs, sunny-side up. How cheery! How uplifting! Hmm, hmmm! (*He turns so Angela can see him. He picks up eggs with his hands and stuffs them in his mouth.*) Look, Angela, refried beans in a delicate pool of congealed fat. (*Still making pig noises, he picks up gobs of beans, stuffs them into his mouth.*)

CHATA: A que la fregada! Hector, stop playing with your food. You're making us sick.

JUANA (*looking at watch*): 7:20, you got ten minutes before work.

(*Hector drums his fingers on the table.*)

HECTOR: Nine minutes. . . . I will now put on the same old smelly, shit-encrusted boots, I will walk to the fields. The scent of cow dung and rotting vegetation will fill the air. I will wait with the same group of beaten-down, pathetic men . . . taking their last piss against a tree, dropping hard warm turds in the bushes. All adding to this fertile whore of a valley. At 7:30 that yellow mechanical grasshopper, the Deerfield tractor, will belch and move. At this exact moment, our foreman, John Knipe, will open his pig-sucking mouth, exposing his yellow, pointy, plaque-infested teeth. He yells, "Start picking boys." The daily war begins . . . the intimidation of violent growth . . . the expanding melons and squashes, the hardiness of potatoes, the waxy purple succulence of eggplant, the potency of ripening tomatoes. All so smug, so rich, so ready to burst with sheer generosity and exuberance. They mock me. . . . I hear them. . . . "Hey Hector," they say, "show us whatcha got," and "Yo Hector, we got bacteria out here more productive than you." . . . I look to the ground. Slugs, snails, worms slithering in the earth with such ferocious hunger they devour their own tails, flies oozing out larvae, aphids, bees, gnats, caterpillars their prolification only slightly dampened by our sprays. We will find eggsacks hiding, ready to burst forth. Their teeming life, their lust, is shameful . . . a mockery of me and my slender spirit. . . . Well it's time. . . . Bye, Ma. (*He exits.*)

JUANA (*yelling*): Hector! You gotta do something about your attitude. (*To herself.*) Try to see the bright side.

(*Juana and Chata exit into the house, leaving Angela on the porch steps. Adan runs up to her.*)

ADAN: Psst! Miss Angelita! . . . di . . . di cartas?

ANGELA: Oh, the letters . . . that will be one dollar.

ADAN: One dollar! Adan very poor man. . . .

(*Angela sticks the donation can out and shakes it. Adan reaches into his pockets and drops coins into the can.*)

Oh, sí, you are very good.

(*Angela puts on glasses and pulls out a letter.*)

ADAN (*reading letter*): Adored Señora Acosta: The impulses of my heart are such that they encourage even the most cautious man to commit indiscretion. My soul is carried to the extreme with the love that only you could inspire. Please know that I feel a true passion for your incomparable beauty and goodness. I tremulously send this declaration and anxiously await the result. Your devoted slave, Adan.

ADAN (*sighing*): Ay, que beautiful.

ANGELA: P.S. With due respect, Señora, if your husband should be home, do not turn on the porch light.

ADAN: Ah, thank you . . . thank you very much.

(*Adan hurriedly exits. Angela gathers her St. Lucy doll and her donation can, and exits quickly. Chata enters from the house wearing "colorful" street clothes. She looks around, then swiftly exits. Hector enters, picks up Zapata, hurries off. The stage darkens, as if smoke from the distant fire has covered the sun. Drum howls are heard. In the distance we hear a rooster crow and sounds of excited chickens as the henhouse comes to life. Gallo appears.*)

GALLO: Easy hens, shshsh! My beauties. (*He puts his suitcase down, cups his hands to his mouth, and yells to the house.*) Juana! Juana! Juana! (*Juana opens the door.*) How many times, in the fever of homesickness, have I written out that name on prison walls, on bits of paper, on the skin of my arms. . . . Let me look at you . . . my enduring rock, my anchor made from the hard parts of the earth — minerals, rocks, bits of glass, ground shells, the brittle bones of dead animals.

JUANA: I never seen you so pale, so thin. . . .

GALLO: I'm home to rest, to fatten up, to breathe, to mend, to you.

JUANA: How long? How long will you stay?

GALLO: Here. Here is where I'll put my chair. . . . I will sit here basking in the sun, like a fat old iguana catching flies, and watching my grandchildren replant the little cemetery with the bones of tiny sparrows. Here. Here I will build the walks for my champions. Morales roosters. The brave and gallant red Cubans, the hard and high-kicking Irish Warhorses, the spirited high-flying Bolinas.

JUANA: Don't say nothing you don't mean . . . you really gonna stay?

GALLO (*gently*): Here. Here is where I'll plant a garden of herbs. Blessed laurel to cure fright, wild marjoram for the agony of lovesickness, cempasuchie flowers for the grief of loneliness.

(*Gallo gently kisses Juana, picks her up, and carries her into the house. The door slams shut. Angela enters, her wings drooping behind her. She trips over Gallo's suitcase. She examines it. She smells it.*)

ANGELA: Tres Rosas!

(*Angela looks at the house. She sits on the suitcase, crosses her arms over her chest as if she were ready to wait an eternity. The shadows of two strangers fall on her.*)

ANGELA: What do you want?

SHADOW #1: Where's Gallo?

ANGELA: Nobody's home to you, rancor.

SHADOW #2: Just go in, tell him we got something for him.

ANGELA: Nobody's home to you, resentment.

SHADOW #1: Who are you supposed to be?

ANGELA (*holding St. Lucy doll*):
I am the angel of this yard
I am the angel of this door
I am the angel of light
I am the angel who shouts
I am the angel who thunders

SHADOW #1: She is pure crazy.

SHADOW #2: Don't play with it, it's serious.

ANGELA:
You are the shadow of resentment
You are the shadow of rancor
I am the angel of acid saliva
I will spit on you.

SHADOW #1: There's time.

SHADOW #2: Yeah, later.

(*Angela spits. The shadows leave. Angela crosses her hands over her chest and looks to Heaven.*)

ANGELA: Holy Father. . . . Listen, you don't want him, you want me. Please take me, claim me, launch me and I will be your shooting-star woman. I will be your comet woman. I will be your morning-star woman.

Scene 4

(*Lights become brighter. Angela exits under the house. The door opens. Gallo comes out in T-shirt and pants and goes to his suitcase. Juana comes to the door in slip and tight robe.*)

GALLO: I never sent him to the fields.

JUANA: I know.

GALLO: I never said for you to put him there.

JUANA: No, you never said. . . .

GALLO: Then why is my son in the fields? (*They look at each other. He looks away.*) Don't look at me. I see it in your eyes. You blame me. Just like the old man.

JUANA: Abuelo never said a word against you.

GALLO: I never let him down with the birds, nobody could match me. They were the best.

JUANA: He knew that. . . .

GALLO: So, he left the bird to Hector.

JUANA: He wanted him out of the fields. We didn't know when you would be out or maybe something would happen to you.

GALLO: He let the boy into the fields, that was his sin. He allowed a Morales into the fields.

JUANA: He was old, tired, heartbroken.

GALLO: Heartbroken, he wasn't a woman to be heartbroken.

JUANA: His only son was in jail.

GALLO: Yes, we know that, the whole valley knows that. You . . . what did you do? Didn't you lay out your hard, succulent, bitch's teat at the breakfast table? So he would have the strength to stand behind a hoe, with his back bent and his eyes on the mud for ten hours a day.

JUANA: Hard work never killed anybody.

GALLO: Ay, mujer! Can't you think what you've done, you bowed his head down.

JUANA: What was I suppose to do? There ain't no other work here. I can't see anything wrong with it for a little while.

GALLO: The difference between them and us, is we never put a foot into the fields. We stayed independent — we worked for nobody. They have to respect us, to respect our roosters.

(*Hector and Adan enter. They are both very dirty. Hector has Zapata, in his carrier. Adan has a carrier containing a second rooster. Gallo and Hector stare at each other.*)

Well . . . you are taller. This offshoot . . . this little bud has grown.

HECTOR: Yeah, well . . . that must be why you seem . . . smaller.

GALLO: Un abrazo![7]

---

[7] A hug. [Ed.]

HECTOR: I'm dirty. I'm sweaty.

GALLO: I see that.

HECTOR: I'm afraid I smell of the fields.

GALLO: Yes.

HECTOR: Of cheap abundant peon labor . . . the scent would gag you.

GALLO: It's going to kill you.

HECTOR: Mama says hard work never killed anyone . . . isn't that right, Mother?

JUANA: It's only for a little while. Your papa thinks that —

GALLO: I'll tell him what I think. Now what about those tamales you
     promised me?

JUANA: Ah sí, con permiso . . . I got some work in the kitchen.

ADAN: Oh sí, Mrs. Juana, los tamales . . . que rico.

JUANA (*smiling at Adan*): I hope they're the kind you like. (*She exits into
     house.*)

GALLO: Hijo, you always take the bird with you into the fields?

HECTOR: No, not always.

GALLO: This bird has to look like he's got secrets . . . no one but us should be
     familiar with him.

HECTOR: This is Adan.

ADAN: Es un honor, Mr. El Gallo.

(*Angela sticks her head out from under the house. Adan and Gallo
shake hands and greet each other.*)

GALLO: (*referring to Zapata*): Let him out . . . he needs a bigger carrier . . .
     he's a flyer.

ADAN: Como Filipino birds?

GALLO: Yes but this baby boy he's got a surprise. He's got a kick.

ADAN: Like Cuban bird?

GALLO: He'll fight in the air, he'll fight on the ground. You can put spurs or
     razors on that kick and he'll cut any bird to ribbons. You can put money
     on that.

ADAN: Hijo! Señor . . . how you know? He never fight. Maybe he only kick in
     cage.

GALLO: I know because I'm his papa. . . . (*Pointing to the other carrier.*) That
     your bird?

ADAN: Sí, pero no good . . . no fight. San Juan, he run away.

GALLO: I'll make him fight. Just let him out.

ADAN: Mr. El Gallo, you give this pendejo bird too much honor. Gracias Señor,
     pero this poor bird, he no can fight.

GALLO: Is it the bird, or you who will not fight?

HECTOR: The bird is too young. He doesn't want him to fight.

GALLO: I've never seen a bird that won't fight, but there are men who are
     cowards.

HECTOR: He is not a coward.

ADAN: This is true, pero I am not El Gallo. In my country all men who love di rooster know Mr. El Gallo. They tell of di famoso día de los muertos fight in Jacinto Park.

GALLO: Ah, you heard about that fight. You remember that fight, Hector?

HECTOR: No.

GALLO: First time you saw a real cockfight . . . Abuelo took you. . . . How could you forget your first cockfight? (*To Adan.*) Go on, take your bird out. I'll make him fight.

(*Gallo takes a drink from a bottle, then blows on San Juan. As he does this, lights go down almost to black. Pinspot comes up center stage, as other lights come up to a dark red. During this process, we hear Gallo's voice — "Ready," then a few beats later "Pit!" On this cue two dancer/roosters jump into the pinspot. This rooster dance is savage. The dancers wear razors on their feet. The Zapata dancer jumps very high. The poor San Juan dancer stays close to the ground. Throughout the dance, we hear drums and foot-stomping. At every hit, there is a big drum pound. During the fight, Hector appears on the porch.*)

HECTOR (*to himself*): It was in Jacinto Park . . . the crowd was a monster, made up of individual human beings stuck together by sweat and spittle. Their gaping mouths let out screams, curses, and foul gases, masticating, smacking, eager for the kill. You stood up. The monster roared. Quasimoto, your bird, in one hand. You lifted him high, "Pit!" went the call. "Pit!" roared the monster. And you threw him into the ring . . . soaring with the blades on his heels flashing I heard the mighty rage of his wings and my heart soared with him. He was a whirlwind flashing and slashing like a dark avenging angel then like some distant rainbow star exploding he was hit. The monster crowd inhaled, sucking back their hopes . . . in that vacuum he was pulled down. My heart went down the same dark shaft, my brains slammed against the earth's hard crust . . . my eyes clouded . . . my arteries gushed . . . my lungs collapsed. "Get up," said Abuelo, "up here with me, and you will see a miracle." You, Father, picked up Quasimoto, a lifeless pile of bloody feathers, holding his head oh so gently, you closed your eyes, and like a great wave receding, you drew a breath that came from deep within your ocean floor. I heard the stones rumble, the mountains shift, the topsoil move, and as your breath slammed on the beaches, Quasimoto sputtered back to life. Oh Papi, breathe on me.

(*Angela appears and stands behind her brother. Her wings are spread very far out. Drums and stomping crescendo as Zapata brutally kills San Juan. Blackout.*)

ACT TWO

Scene I

(*Early afternoon. The table is set up in the middle of the yard in a festive way, with tablecloth, flowers, a bowl of peaches, and bottles of whiskey and wine. Gallo is in the henhouse with Adan. Hector is in the bathroom, Juana and Chata are in the kitchen. Angela is by the little cemetery writing on a tombstone.*)

ANGELA: Here lies Angela Ester Morales died of acute neglect. Although she is mourned by many, she goes to a far, far better place, where they have better food.

(*Angela slides under the house as Juana comes out wearing a fresh housedress and carrying a steaming pot.*)

JUANA (*yelling*): Hector! Angela! You kids wash up, it's time to eat.

(*Juana hurries back into the house, almost knocking Chata down as she comes out with a tray of tortillas. She is heavily made up, wearing tight clothes, dangling earrings, high-heeled shoes. A cigarette dangles from her mouth.*)

CHATA: Why are you eating out here?
JUANA: He wants it. Says he don't wanta hide in the house.
CHATA: Begging for trouble.
JUANA: What can I do, he's the *man*. (*She goes into the house.*)
CHATA: Ah, they're all shit! Just want trouble. Soup's on!

(*Chata pours herself a quick shot of whiskey, shoots it down, and makes a face. Juana comes out with another pot.*)

JUANA: You better tell 'em that the food's ready. (*Chata goes to henhouse.*) Hector!
HECTOR (*coming out on porch*): What?
JUANA: It's time to eat . . . you look real nice, honey. Makes me proud to have your papa see you all dressed up.
HECTOR: Okay. Okay. Don't make a big deal about it. I just don't want him to think —
JUANA: I just feel so happy —
HECTOR: I just don't want him to think —
JUANA: Hijito! You love your papa . . . don't you?
HECTOR: Mother!
JUANA: I know you a little mad at him . . . pero when he comes home it's like the sun when it —
HECTOR: Shshshsh!

(*Chata, Gallo, and Adan come out of the henhouse.*)

GALLO: We have to sharpen and polish those spurs. I want them to flash.

JUANA (*to Gallo*): The food's ready . . . we fixed what you like . . . mole, rice, frijolitos . . . tamales.

GALLO: Tamales estilo Jalisco!

CHATA (*looking Hector over*): Ay Papi que rico estás! (*Hector quickly sits down.*) Honey! You gonna have to beat all them women off with a stick, when they see you and that rooster tonight.

ADAN: No worry, Hector, I be there . . . down, you mujeres, women leave de Mr. Hector and me alone. . . . Ay Mama! (*He has a giggling fit.*)

GALLO (*kissing Juana*): It's wonderful to be in love . . . to be touched by the noble fever.

CHATA: Ah, you're better off with a touch of typhoid.

JUANA: I . . . gracias al Señor que . . . my whole family is here. (*She looks around. She yells.*) Angela! Angie!

HECTOR: Mom!

JUANA: Where is she? Where is your sister?

HECTOR: Talking to the saints! I don't know.

(*Juana get up, goes to the spot where Angela slides under the house, gets down on her hands and knees, and yells.*)

JUANA: Angela! Angela! You leave them saints alone. You hear me!

(*As everybody looks at Juana, Angela comes from behind the house and tiptoes toward the henhouse. Hector is the only one to see her. Using hand signals, she pleads to him to be quiet. Juana peers under the house.*)

Angie! Honey . . . your mama worked for days to fix this food and now it's getting cold. (*To Gallo.*) You should see how sweet she looks when she's all dressed up. (*To under the house.*) You ain't got no manners . . . ain't even said hello to your father. (*To Gallo.*) She prays a lot . . . and she's got real pretty eyes.

CHATA (*to Gallo*): She's sorta . . . the bashful type . . . you know.

JUANA (*to Gallo*): And she ain't spoiled.

CHATA (*taking a drink*): Nah, all them kids smell like that.

JUANA (*to under the house*): Angie!

GALLO: Juana, leave her alone.

JUANA: Okay, Angie, I'm gonna ignore you, 'cause you spoiled my day, this day that I been looking forward to for years and years and now you making me look like a bad mama, what's your papa gonna think of us.

GALLO: Juana, she'll come out when she's ready.

(*Juana goes back to the table.*)

CHATA: Maybe was them roosters fighting got her scared.

ADAN: Poor San Juan.

GALLO: Adan, drink up and I'll see you get one of our famous Champion Morales birds.

HECTOR: What famous Champion Morales birds?

GALLO: The ones I paid for dearly, the ones I came home to raise . . . isn't that right mi amor?

JUANA: Yes . . . you see, honey, your papa's gonna stay home . . . raise birds . . . I think Abuelo would want that.

GALLO: And after they see our bird tonight . . . see first I want them to think it's just you and the bird up there. After the bets are down, I'll take over and they're gonna know we got roosters. A toast . . .

(*As Gallo stands up, everybody raises a glass, except Hector. Angela tiptoes from the henhouse carrying Zapata. She goes behind and under the house. Only Hector sees her.*)

To the finest fighting cocks ever to be seen. (*He slides bottle to Hector.*)

HECTOR (*sliding bottle back*): No.

(*Pause.*)

GALLO: Too good to drink with your old man.

HECTOR: I only drink with people I trust.

CHATA: Me . . . I drink with anybody. Maybe that's my problem.

GALLO: I am your father.

HECTOR: Yes. You are my father.

CHATA: I like it better when I drink alone. Ya meet a better class of people that way.

HECTOR: But it's my bird. Abuelo left it to me.

GALLO: Abuelo was my father, and you are my son. I see no problem. Now let's eat.

HECTOR: Mother!

JUANA: Let's eat, honey, and we can talk about it later.

ADAN: Ay the mole muy delicious . . . the mole muy rico . . . the mole muy beautiful y Mrs. Juana. Today, you look beautiful, like the mole.

GALLO: Hm, sabroso, exquisito.[8]

JUANA: I bet you been in plenty of fancy places got better food than this.

GALLO: This is home cooking, I know that your hands made it. . . . These . . . these are the hands of a beautiful woman. . . .

HECTOR: Ha! Bullshit.

GALLO: We say your mother is beautiful and you call it bullshit? I find that very disrespectful.

JUANA: Hijo, you're right . . . it's just the way people talk, I know I ain't beautiful.

GALLO: I say you are beautiful.

ADAN: Sí, muy beautiful.

---

[8] Tasty, exquisite. [Ed.]

833

GALLO: Ya ves! . . . If your son doesn't have the eyes, the soul, the imagination to see it . . . it's his loss.

HECTOR: That's right. I just can't seem to stretch my imagination that far.

GALLO: This is an insult to your mother.

HECTOR: It's the truth. That is a plain, tired, worn-out woman.

GALLO: Shut up.

HECTOR: The hands of a beautiful woman! Those aren't hands, they're claws because she has to scratch for her living.

JUANA: Please, Hector, let him say what he wants . . . I know I ain't beautiful. It don't go to my head.

HECTOR: But it goes to your heart which is worse. Did he every really take care of you? Did he ever go out and work to put food on the table, to buy you a dress? All he has is words, and he throws a few cheap words to you and you come to life. Don't you have any pride?

GALLO: Your mother has great courage to trust and believe in me.

HECTOR: Stupidity!

GALLO: You know nothing!

HECTOR: You don't seem to realize that it is my rooster. And that after the fight, depending on the outcome, I will sell him or eat him. I have made a deal with the Filipinos.

JUANA: Ay Hector! You've spoiled everything. All this food . . . I worked so hard . . . for this day.

GALLO: You're not selling anything to anybody. This is nothing to joke about.

HECTOR: I don't want to spend my life training chickens to be better killers. And I don't want to spend my whole life in this valley. Mother, Aunt Chata, excuse me.

CHATA: Ah? . . . O sí hijo pase[9] . . . sometimes Hector can be a real gentleman.

(*Hector starts to leave.*)

GALLO: Son! . . . You have no courage, no juice . . . you are a disgrace to me.

JUANA: Ay, Gallo, don't say that to him.

HECTOR: Do you think I care what you think . . . Father.

JUANA: Hijo no . . . for me just once for me. I don't wanna be alone no more.

HECTOR: What about me? You have me, you'll always have me, I'll work, I've always worked. I can take care of you. I won't leave you.

JUANA: It ain't the same, honey.

HECTOR: Yeah. . . . He comes first for you, he will always come first.

GALLO: If you sell that bird, it will be over your dead body.

HECTOR: You can't stop me.

(*Exit Hector. Chata takes a plate of food and bowl of peaches to the under-the-house area and tries to tempt Angela out.*)

GALLO: He doesn't seem to realize . . . coward . . . too bad.

---

[9] O yes, go ahead. [Ed.]

(*Gallo goes to the henhouse. Juana starts to follow him.*)

JUANA: Talk to him . . . he's a good boy . . . if you just talk . . . (*Seeing Adan still eating.*) Is it good? You really like it?

ADAN: Hm! Sabroso!

CHATA: Come on, Angie . . . it's real good.

(*Gallo returns running.*)

GALLO: He's gone . . . the bird is gone. . . .

ADAN: Yo no see nada, nada.

JUANA: He'll bring it back, he's a good boy. He's just a little upset . . . you know.

GALLO: Nobody fools with my roosters. Not even this over-petted, over-pampered viper you spawned. Go and pray to your Dark Virgin. You know what I'm capable of.

(*Exit Gallo. Adan stops eating and tries to comfort Juana as she puts her head down on the table and cries.*)

ADAN: No cry, no cry, Mrs. Juana. Di women cry y Adan, he not know what to do. (*Juana cries louder.*) Ay Mrs. Juana, for sure di flowers will die . . . di trees will be torn from di ground, freshness will leave di morning, softness will leave di night . . . (*Juana's cries increase.*) Ay Dios! (*From his pocket, he brings out the letter Angela wrote for him. He crosses himself.*) Mrs. di Juana . . . (*Reading with great difficulty.*) Di . . . impulses . . . of my . . . heart . . . are such . . . (*Throwing letter aside.*) A que la fregada! Mrs. Juana, Adan have mucho amor for you. My heart break to see you cry. I will not a breathe. When you no cry then I will breathe.

(*Adan takes a big breath and holds it. Slowly Juana stops crying and lifts her head. Adan, suffering some discomfort, continues to hold his breath.*)

JUANA: I been dreaming. Nothing's gonna change. I gotta face facts.

(*Adan lets his breath out in a great whoosh. Angela pops from under the house and takes a peach from Chata's hand. She stares at the peach with great intensity.*)

CHATA: Angie, ain't it nice to have the family all together again?

ANGELA: There is no pit in this peach. It is hollow. Instead of the pit, there is a whole little world, a little blue-green crystal-clear ocean, with little schools of tiny darting silver fish. On a tiny rock sits a mermaid with little teenie-weenie kinky yellow hair. A tiny sun is being pulled across a little china-blue sky by teenie-weenie white horses with itty-bitty wings. There is an island with tiny palm trees and tiny thatched hut. Next to the hut stand a tiny man and woman. She is wearing flowers and leaves. He is wearing one single leaf. On their heads are little bitty halos. In their arms is a little bitsy baby. He isn't wearing anything.

CHATA: Let me see . . . (*Looking at peach.*) I can't see dick!

(*Blackout.*)

Scene 2

(*Later in the afternoon. Chata sits on the porch steps, her legs spread out, fanning herself. Juana sits on a straight-back chair, her hands folded on her lap. She rocks herself gently. She watches Angela, who is sitting on the ground drawing circles in the dirt and humming softly. The circles get deeper and deeper.*)

CHATA: It's hot . . . I'm waiting for a cool breeze. . . .

ANGELA: Uh ha uh ha uh ha uh haa.

CHATA: Aire fresco . . . come on cool breeze, come right over here.

ANGELA: Uh ha uh ha uh haa.

CHATA: Women! We're always waiting.

(*Angela hums for a beat, then there is silence for a beat.*)

JUANA: It's because I'm so plain.

CHATA: Ah, you just work too much.

JUANA: Plainness runs in my family. My mother was plain, my grandmother was plain, my great-grandmother —

CHATA: It was the hard times . . . the hard work that did it.

JUANA: My Aunt Chona was the plainest.

CHATA: I don't remember her.

JUANA: The one with the crossed eyes and the little mustache.

CHATA: Ay, Juanita, that woman had a beautiful soul, sewing those little tiny outfits for the statues of the saints. That woman was a saint.

JUANA: She's the one told on you that time you was drinking beer with them sailors at the cockfight.

CHATA: Disgusting old bitch!

(*Angela hums for a beat as she continues drawing circles.*)

JUANA: I get up at six, I brush my teeth, no creams, no lotions, what they gonna do for me? I work that's all. I take care of people and I work. People look at me, they know that's all I do. I ain't got no secrets. No hidden gardens. I keep busy that's what I do. Don't stop, that's what I say to myself. Don't stop, 'cause you're not pretty enough, exciting enough, smart enough to just stand there.

ANGELA: Mama, I don't wanna be plain.

CHATA: Honey, you're too colorful to be plain.

ANGELA: Yeah, that's what I thought.

CHATA: Your mama forgets . . . those years when her heart was filled with wild dreams when she use to weave little white star jasmine vines in her hair and drive all the men crazy.

JUANA: It ain't true . . . she was the one always getting me in trouble.

CHATA: I wasn't the one they called Juanita la Morenita Sabrosita.

JUANA: Oh, Chata. We was young girls together . . . in the summer, at Jacinto Park . . . cockfights, fistfights, the music. At night we would jump out of our bedroom windows in our party dresses. With our good shoes in one hand, our hearts in the other, we ran barefoot through the wet grass, above us all the stars twinkling go, go, go.

CHATA: Nothing could stop us . . . we had such a short time being girls.

JUANA: Now, all I am is an old hag.

CHATA: It ain't true.

JUANA: Sí, it's true enough. I carry burdens, I hang sheets, I scrub, I gather, I pick up, "Here sit down," "I'll wash it," "Here's fifty cents," "Have my chair," "Take my coat," "Here's a piece of my own live flesh"!

CHATA: Es la menopause, that's what it is. You getting it early. I knew this woman once, use to pull out her hair.

JUANA: I don't care, I don't want any stories, I don't care what happens to Fulano Mangano . . . I just wanna stand still, I wanna be interesting, exciting enough to stand still.

CHATA: Ay, mujer!

JUANA: And I want to look like I got secrets.

CHATA: Juana!

JUANA: Don't call me Juana. Juana is a mule's name.

CHATA: Ah, you're crazy! That new gray hen, the kids named her Juana. See, they think of you.

JUANA: A gray hen! An old gray hen, that's all I am. An old gray hen in a family of roosters. No more! I want feathers, I wanna strut, too. I wanna crow.

ANGELA: Mama!

JUANA: Don't! Don't call me Mama. I am not Mama . . . I am . . . I am that movie star, that famous dancer and heartbreaker "Morenita Sabrosita" . . . and now if my fans will excuse me I'm gonna take a bath in champagne, eat cherry bonbons, and paint my toenails. (*She goes into the house.*)

CHATA (*to Juana*): We got champagne?

(*Chata goes into the house as Angela goes to the little cemetery and puts up a new tombstone.*)

ANGELA (*printing on tombstone*): Here lies Juana Morales. Beloved Wife of El Gallo, Blessed Mother to Angela and Horrible Hector. Died of acute identity crisis sustained during la menopause.

Scene 3

(*Lights go down, as Angela sits on her box/table at the little cemetery. The long shadows of men fall on Angela and the cemetery.*)

SHADOW #1: There's that spooky kid. You go, brother.

SHADOW #2: Ah, it's just a weird kid. Hey! You! Kid!

(*Angela does not acknowledge them.*)

SHADOW #1: Call her "Angel."

SHADOW #2: Hey, angel.

(*Angela looks up.*)

SHADOW #1: See what I mean.

SHADOW #2: Listen, kid, tell your old man, we got business to discuss.

SHADOW #1: Yeah, and you make sure he gets the message.

ANGELA: My old man, my Holy Father, my all powerful Father, sees no problems. If there are problems, I am the angel of this yard. I am the comet. I am the whirlwind. I am the shooting stars. Feel my vibrance.

SHADOW #1: I feel it, right behind my ears, like . . . like . . .

ANGELA: Locust wings.

SHADOW #1: Let's get outta here.

SHADOW #2: Tell Gallo some pals dropped by to settle an old score.

SHADOW #1: Come on!

SHADOW #2 (*voice trailing off*): Hey! That kid don't scare me, see.

SHADOW #1 (*voice trailing off*): I'm telling ya, my ears hurt.

(*Exit shadows. Lights go back up. Angela folds her hands in prayer.*)

ANGELA: Holy Father, please help me, I feel the illumination, the fever of grace slipping away. I need to know that you are with me, that you take an interest in my concerns. Send me a little demonstration, a sign. Any sign . . . I don't care. Stigmata, visions, voices, send an angel, burn a bush. . . . I am attracted to levitation . . . but you choose . . . I'll just lay here and wait.

(*Angela lies on the ground waiting. After a few beats Hector enters. He slowly walks up to Angela and looks down on her for a beat.*)

HECTOR: What are you doing?

ANGELA (*sitting up*): Ohhh . . . you're no sign.

HECTOR: What is going on?

ANGELA: Weird, shady men came here looking for Gallo. Two of them. They were not polite.

HECTOR: I see. . . . So your reaction is to lay stretched out on the dirt instead of going into the house.

ANGELA: Hector, please, I am scared. . . . I wanted a sign.

(*Hector sits down next to Angela.*)

HECTOR: Hey, you're the shooting-star woman, you can't be scared.

ANGELA: I am scared. Really scared. If I grow up will I still be scared? Are grown-ups scared?

HECTOR: Always scared, trembling . . . cowering . . . this . . . this second, now . . . this planet that we are sitting on is wobbling precariously on its lightning path around the sun and every second the sun is exploding . . . stars are shooting at us from deep distant space, comets zoom around us, meteor rocks are being hurled through distances we measure in light . . . this very earth which we call our home, our mother, has catastrophic moods, she keeps moving mountains, receding oceans, shifting poles, bucking and reeling like an overburdened beast trying to shake us off. . . . Life is violent.

ANGELA: You're scared about the fight . . . huh?

HECTOR: No. Whatever happens, Papi will still only care about the rooster. That's his son, that's who gets it all.

ANGELA: Maybe if we gave him the rooster he'd stay here and be happy.

HECTOR: He has to stay for us not the rooster . . . Angela . . . you . . . you were great taking the rooster.

ANGELA: He kept killing the little chicks. How could he do that, Hector? He's their papa.

HECTOR: Training. Look, Angela, you're the angel of this yard. You keep a close guard on that rooster. Don't let anyone near him . . . promise me.

ANGELA: Yes.

HECTOR: That's a real promise now. No crossed fingers behind your back.

ANGELA: I promise already. (*She spreads her hands out in front of her, then kisses the tip of her thumb.*) May God strike me dumb, make me a plain whiny person, and take away my gift of faith. Forever and ever, throughout my mortal years on earth, and throughout the everlasting fires of hell. Amen. Satisfied?

HECTOR: Yes.

ANGELA: Gee, maybe I should have given myself a little leeway, a little room for error.

(*Chata enters from the house with a bottle and glass.*)

HECTOR: Too late now. Can't take it back.

CHATA: Oh, oh, look who's here. Angie, your mama needs some cheering up, a nice hug, an angel's kiss, maybe a little song.

ANGELA: Litany to the Virgin. That's her favorite. (*She exits.*).

CHATA: Men are shit. Pure shit.

HECTOR: And you're still drinking.

CHATA: Stay outta my drinking. You hurt your mama, Hector.

HECTOR: Too bad.

CHATA: Ay Dios, what a man he is now.

HECTOR: Yeah, well what about you? Didn't you break Abuelo's heart when you became a whore?

CHATA: They called me the encyclopedia of love. You want to turn a few pages? Your Aunt Chata could show you a few things.

HECTOR: You're disgusting.

CHATA: Is that what fascinates you, honey? Is that why I always find you peeping at me, mirrors at the keyhole, your eyeballs in the cracks, spying when I'm sleeping, smelling my kimono.

HECTOR: You're drunk.

CHATA: I ain't drunk, honey.

HECTOR: You drink too much. It's not . . . good for you . . . it makes you ugly.

CHATA: Ain't none of your business. Don't tell me what to do, Hector.

HECTOR: I have to, it's for your own good.

CHATA: You got nothing to say about it, you ain't my man, and you ain't your mama's man. The sooner you learn that the better . . . take your bird, leave it, eat or sell it, but get out of here. (*Hector stands alone in the yard, as she goes to the door. She turns. They look at each other.*) What are you hanging around here for? Go on! Get out! It ain't your home anymore. (*She takes a broom and shoos Hector from the yard.*) Shoo! Shoo! You don't belong here, it ain't your place anymore.

HECTOR: Stop it, stop it, stop it.

(*Hector goes to the outside boundary of the yard, where he falls to his knees and buries his face in his hands, as Chata comes slowly up behind him.*)

CHATA: I feel like I'm tearing my own flesh from my bones. . . . He's back. Honey, we got too many roosters in this yard.

HECTOR: Did you sleep with my father? Did he yearn for you as you slept in your little white, chaste, narrow bed? Did he steal you when you were dreaming?

CHATA (*embracing him*): Shshsh . . .

HECTOR: I'm not like him.

CHATA: You're just like him, so handsome you make my teeth ache.

HECTOR: Whore, mother, sister, saint-woman, moon-woman, give me the shelter of your darkness, fold me like a fan and take me into your stillness, submerge me beneath the water, beneath the sea, beneath the mysteries, baptize me, bear me up, give me life, breathe on me.

(*Chata enfolds him as the lights fade. We hear Angela reciting the litany.*)

ANGELA (*offstage*): She is the Gate of Heaven, the Mystical Rose, the Flower of Consolation, the Fire of Transcendence, and the Queen of Love.

Scene 4

(*Lights come up to indicate that time has passed. Angela is alone in the yard. She sniffs the air.*)

ANGELA: Tres Rosas!

(*Angela slides under the house as Gallo enters. He sees a brief flash of Angela from the corner of his eye. He walks slowly into the yard. He stops by the little cemetery and reads the tombstones. Feeling the urge for a drink, he goes to the table and has a shot. He sits.*)

GALLO: Acute neglect? . . . uh-huh . . . I thought I felt a little spirit, slight, delicate . . . yes I feel it. A little tenderness . . . a little greenness . . . (*Examining the ground.*) What's this? Tracks . . . little tiny paws . . . there . . . (*Following tracks.*) and there . . .

(*Gallo pretends to be following tracks to the porch. Then with one great leap he jumps in the opposite direction, surprising the hell out of Angela, and pulls her from under the house by her heels.*)

Ah, ha!

ANGELA: Shit! Hey! You're ripping my wings! You shithead! Put me down! Don't touch me!

(*Gallo puts Angela down, throws his hands up to indicate he won't touch her. They stand and stare at each other. Angela goes to the little cemetery, never taking her eyes off Gallo. They continue to stare for a beat, then Angela looks up to Heaven, slapping her hands together in prayer.*)

There is a person here trying to con me, but I don't con that easy.

GALLO (*slapping his hands in prayer*): There is a person here who swallows saints but defecates devils.

ANGELA (*to Heaven*): He comes here smelling of rosas using sweet oily words . . . it's phony, it's obnoxious, it's obscene . . . I wanna throw up.

GALLO: I came here to see my baby, my little angel, my little woman of the shooting stars, my light delicate splendorous daughter. But she is as light, as delicate, as splendid as an angel's fart.

ANGELA: Angels do not fart. They do not have a digestive system. That's why they can all scrunch together on the head of a pin.

GALLO: Oh . . . I only come with my love —

ANGELA: You only came with words . . . well, where were these words on my birthday, Christmas, my saint's day? Where's my Easter outfit, my trip to Disneyland, the orthodontist. . . . You owe me.

GALLO: Sweet Jesus. . . . What a monster! I owe you . . . but Angela! Angela! Angela! How many times have I written that name on prison walls. On bits of paper, on the skin of my arms.

ANGELA (*to Heaven*): He's hopeless! You write everybody's name on your arms.

GALLO: Women like to know that they're on your flesh.

ANGELA: I am not a woman. I'm your baby daughter. You said so yourself.

GALLO: I'm afraid . . . fathers to daughters . . . that's so delicate. I don't know . . . what to do . . . help me, Angela. How do I know what to do?

ANGELA: Instinct! Ain't ya got no instinct? Don't you feel anything?

GALLO (*moving closer to Angela*): When you were a little baby, you were a miracle of tiny fingers and toes and dimples and you had a soft spot on the top of your head.

ANGELA: I still have it, see.

GALLO: I wanted to take you into my arms and crush you against my chest so that I could keep you forever and nobody, and nothing, could ever, ever hurt you because you would be safe . . . my little offshoot, my little bud, my little flower growing inside my chest.

ANGELA: Papi . . .

GALLO: Sí, sí, hijita. Your papi's here.

ANGELA: And, Papi, these men come all the —

GALLO (*holding Angela*): Shshsh . . . it's nothing, nothing and you thought I forgot about you . . . well it just hurt too much, do you understand?

ANGELA: You had to pull down some hard time and the only way to survive was to cut off all feelings and become an animal just like the rest of them.

GALLO: Well, something like that. Honey, you know what I wish —

ANGELA: Papa, did the lights really go down when the put the people in the electric chair?

GALLO: Angela, what a. . . . Honey, you know what I wish —

ANGELA: Did they force you to make license plates? Hector and I would look real close at the ones that started with a G. We thought you made them. "What craftsmanship!" Hector used to say.

GALLO: Don't you have any normal interests?

ANGELA: Like what?

GALLO: Like swimming . . . you know what I wish? That we could take a trip and see the ocean together.

ANGELA: I've never seen the ocean. When?

GALLO: Just you and me. Laying on our bellies, feeding the seagulls, riding the waves.

ANGELA: I can't swim.

GALLO: I will teach you, that's what fathers are for —

ANGELA (*to Heaven*): Angels and saints did you hear? My father's going to teach me to swim!

GALLO: Now, Angela, I didn't promise.

ANGELA: But you said —

GALLO: I want to but I have to hurry and fix things. I have to find Hector, talk to him and find that rooster fast before Hector sells him. Honey, you pray to St. Anthony, your prayers are powerful . . . unless . . . St. Anthony he listen to you?

ANGELA (*crossing her fingers*): Hey, we're like that.

GALLO: Ask St. Anthony, Angela . . . then we can go to the ocean.

ANGELA: Truly, Papi? Just you and me? And will you stay with us forever and ever?

GALLO: Wild horses couldn't drag me away.

ANGELA: Close your eyes. Tony! Tony! Look around, Zapata's lost and can't be found. (*She goes under the house, gets Zapata, and gives him to Gallo.*) I found him, Papi, he was —

GALLO: Ya lindo, ya. (*To bird*) Papa's got you now. Angela, you keep quiet now, honey, this is our secret.

HECTOR: What about Hector?

GALLO: I'm going to talk to Hector now. You go inside and get all dressed up. So I can be proud of my girl. I'll pick you up after the fight. (*He exits.*)

ANGELA: Your girl! (*Singing.*) We are going to the ocean, we are going to the sea, we are going to the ocean to see what we can see . . .

(*Angela goes into the house. We hear cha-cha music.*)

CHATA (*offstage*): One, two . . . not like that . . . I'm getting tired . . . what time's "Zorro" on?

JUANA (*offstage*): No, no. . . . Just one more. (*Singing.*) Cha, cha, cha, que rico, . . . cha, cha, cha. . . . Ay, I could do it all night.

(*Enter Gallo running, breathing hard. He has Zapata's carrier. He goes to the door and yells.*)

GALLO: Juana! Juana!

(*Juana and Chata come to the door.*)

I need money . . . and my stuff. I gotta leave . . . something's come up. . . . Do you hear me? I need money now.

JUANA: I hear ya . . . you ain't even been here a day and already you're gone . . . nothing's going to change with you . . . nothing. I was having fun, dancing, remembering old times, do you know how long —

GALLO: I don't have time for this, just give me the money.

JUANA: I ain't got any!

CHATA: I got some. (*She goes in the house.*)

GALLO: The Filipino, somebody told him about the bird. Oh, ya, ya my little hen, don't you ruffle those pretty feathers. I'll be back.

JUANA: No, you always gonna be running.

GALLO: If it was just me, I'd stay. You know that, Juana! You know I'd stay, but I got the bird to think of, gotta hide him, breed him good, soon as I get some good stags I'll come home . . . this is just a little setback.

(*Chata returns with suitcase and money.*)

JUANA: You know how long it's been since I went dancing?

CHATA: Here, you're gonna need this. (*Gives him the suitcase.*) And this is all the cash I got.

(*Angela enters as Gallo counts the money. She is dressed in a red strapless dress made tight by large visible safety pins, high heels, and a great deal of heavy makeup and jewelry. The effect is that of a young girl dressed like a tart for a costume party. She carries a suitcase, purse, and her donation can.*)

GALLO: Is this all you got?

ANGELA (*shaking the can*): Don't worry, Papa, I got my donation-can money.

(*They all stare at her for a beat.*)

JUANA AND CHATA: Angela?!!

JUANA: Angie, you got on your mama's old party dress.

CHATA: Yeah, and all my jewelry . . . where you going?

ANGELA: Papa, didn't you hear me? I have money. (*She shakes the can.*)

GALLO: Oh honey, don't you look pretty . . . now you got a little bit too much lipstick on, let your mama wipe some off.

ANGELA: Are we leaving now?

JUANA: Gallo!

GALLO: Shshsh Juana . . . Angela, I gotta talk to your mama for a few minutes. You go in the house and I'll come and get you.

ANGELA: Are you sure?

GALLO: Don't you trust me, Angie?

CHATA: Come on, Angie, I'll show you how to draw eyebrows. First you draw a straight line across your forehead and then spit on your finger and rub out the middle. Let's go in and try it.

ANGELA: Really, Aunt Chata, I'm not a child, you don't have to patronize me.

CHATA: Okay, I'll give you the low-down on blow-jobs.

(*Angela and Chata go into the house.*)

Now don't tell your mama . . .

GALLO: Juana, keep her in the house until I leave.

JUANA: You promised to take her with you?

GALLO: I had to get the bird. I said I would take her to the ocean.

JUANA: Ay bruto! How could you do it?

GALLO: How was I to know this would happen . . . and Juanita, it hurts me to say this but that kid is crazy . . .

JUANA: No, no Señor, she is not crazy and I ain't gonna let you call her crazy. She got the spirit they broke in me. I ain't gonna let it happen to her.

GALLO: Shshsh! Don't get so excited. It isn't important.

JUANA: It's important . . . it's her spirit, her soul, and you ain't gonna stomp on it . . . you hear me.

(*Adan enters running.*)

ADAN: Mr. El Gallo . . . bad men! Mucho bad, y mucho ugly. Looking for you y Zapata. All ober they look for you . . . Big Nicky's, Castro Fields, Don Pancho's. . . . You leave, Mr. El Gallo. You go far away. I take you. I go for my truck.

GALLO: You are a good friend, Adan, and my new partner.

ADAN: Oh, thank you, Mr. El Gallo. I am proud. But is better I come back here to Mrs. Juana y Hector.

JUANA: Thank you, Adan.

GALLO: We better hurry.

ADAN: Sí, sí, I come back with truck. (*He exits.*)

(*Juana goes into the house. Hector enters as Gallo starts to pack his suitcase.*)

HECTOR (*seeing Zapata*): You must have really sold her a bill of goods to get Zapata.

GALLO: Look, there's trouble . . . the Filipino send you?

HECTOR: No, how could you think I would work for him, but I came to get Zapata.

GALLO: You're the one told him about the bird.

HECTOR: Yes. I made a deal with the Filipino. He'll leave you alone if I give him the rooster.

GALLO: That's a lie and you fell for it.

HECTOR: No, he is an honorable man, we were here unprotected for seven years and he never bothered us. It's his bird, Papi.

GALLO: No, I paid seven years of my life for this baby.

HECTOR: And he lost his son. It's the right thing to do.

(*A truck horn is heard. Angela comes out of the house with her suitcase, Juana and Chata follow after her.*)

ANGELA: Papa? Are we leaving now, Papa?

JUANA: Angie! No!

HECTOR: So that's it . . . Angela, get back in the house.

ANGELA: I'm going with him, Hector.

HECTOR: Get back in the house, nobody's going anywhere.

ANGELA: No! I don't have to listen to you anymore. You're not my father.

JUANA: Angie . . . he's not going to the ocean . . . he can't take you.

(*We hear the sound of Adan's truck. The horn is heard as Gallo starts backing away, picking up Zapata's carrier.*)

ANGELA: Papi, wait for me! Papa, you promised.

GALLO: You're all grown up now, you don't need your old man.

CHATA: Hector!

(*Gallo turns, tries to run out. Angela grabs him, knocking Zapata's carrier out of his hand. Hector picks up the carrier.*)

ANGELA: No, Papa, we need you and Mama needs you, we've been waiting, and waiting, you can't leave, you promised me.

JUANA: They'll kill you, Gallo.

GALLO (*throwing Angela off*): Stop sucking off me. I got nothing for you.

ANGELA (*beating her fists on the ground*): No, no, Papa! You promised me! . . . Oh, Hector. . . . No, no, I promised Hector.

> (*Drums begin as punctuation of the pounding of Angela's fists on the ground. Lights change. A special on Angela and another on Gallo and Hector come up, as shadows appear. Angela sees them.*)

Ah. . . . Holy Father, Abuelo.

GALLO (*to Hector*): Give me that bird.

ANGELA: Saints, Angels, Mama.

JUANA (*trying to pick up Angela*): Come on, Angie, get up.

GALLO (*to Hector*): What do you want?

HECTOR: You, alive, Papi.

CHATA: Careful, Hector.

ANGELA: I've lost my faith. I am splintered.

GALLO (*imitating Hector*): You, Papi. . . . Give me life. . . . Make me a man. (*He whips out his stiletto.*) This is how you become a man. (*The drums get louder. We hear howling.*) Come on, baby boy, show Daddy whatcha got.

JUANA: Are you crazy! That's your son!

ANGELA: I am cast down! Exiled!

> (*Gallo stalks Hector as drums follow their movements.*)

JUANA: Oh, Gallo, you're killing your own children.

CHATA: Move, Hector, don't think, move!

GALLO: Oh yeah, mi lindo, you like to fight . . . eh?

JUANA: No, stop them! Please, please stop this.

ANGELA: Fallen from the light, condemned to the mud, to the shadows.

GALLO: You gotta learn, baby boy.

CHATA: Look at him, Hector. He's getting old, his hand is shaking . . . take the knife! Stay down, old warrior. Stay down.

ANGELA: Alone and diminished. This loneliness is unendurable.

JUANA: Hector!

HECTOR: Do I have it? Is this what you want me to be . . .

ANGELA (*looking to Heaven*):
My brains are slammed against the earth's hard crust.
My eyes are clouded
My arteries gush
My lungs collapsed.

HECTOR (*letting go of Gallo*): No! I am your son.

> (*Drums and cries stop.*)

ACT TWO
Scene 4

ANGELA: Holy Father, Abuelo, Hector, breathe on me.

(*Celestial sound as a white narrow shaft of light falls on Angela. She levitates, her wings spreading. Only Chata and Juana see this.*)

HECTOR (*taking a deep breath*): Oh sweet air! (*He gets the rooster and sees Angela.*) Angela!

ADAN (*rushing in*): I am here, I have truck . . . (*Seeing Angela, he crosses himself.*) Ay Dios. (*He kneels.*)

JUANA (*at Gallo's side*): Gallo, look!

GALLO: Did you see the hands on that kid, just like steel, never seen finer hands . . . (*Seeing Angela.*) Sweet Jesus, my beautiful monster. (*He crosses himself.*)

CHATA: No, it ain't true.

HECTOR (*standing before Angela holding the rooster*): Oh sweet hummingbird woman, shooting star, my comet, you are launched.

ANGELA: Abuelo, Queen of Heaven, All the Saints, All the Angels. It is true, I am back. I am restored. I am . . . Hector, take me with you.

HECTOR: Everywhere. . . . Over the mountains, up to the stars.

ANGELA: To the very edge.

ADAN: Hector! Angelita! You take Adan. (*He goes to Angela.*)

CHATA (*looking at Angela*): Shit happens . . . been happening all my life, that's all I know.

JUANA (*holding Gallo like the Pietà*): We seen it, Gallo, with our own eyes.

ANGELA (*to Hector and Adan*): And I want my doorstep heaped with floral offerings . . . and . . .

(*Hector, Adan, and Angela freeze. Chata removes the flower from her hair and holds it in her hand, trying to decide what to do. She freezes.*)

GALLO: Ay Juanita, I had a vision of a hard-kicking flyer . . . (*He yawns.*) the ultimate bird, noble, fino. (*He falls asleep.*)

(*Juana looks at Gallo, smiles, then looks out half-smiling.*)   1987

INVESTIGATIONS

1. In what ways might Gallo and Zapata's dance (Act One, Scene 1, p. 815) be seen as a dramatization of Joyce Carol Oates's ("Against Nature") claims about nature? To what extent could the dance be seen as a prayer?

2. Note each instance in the play of belief in the irrational or the nonhuman (Adan's belief in Act One, Scene 2, that "Zapata he knows" Hector doesn't like him is one example). How do these beliefs enrich the lives of the characters? How do they constrict them? What similar beliefs do you hold? How do they enrich your life? How do they constrict it?

3. Compare Hector's speech before going out to the field in Act One, Scene

3 (p. 824), to his speech at the end of Act One (p. 829). What similarities are there in his descriptions of people? To what extent do you think he includes himself in these descriptions? What, for Hector, sets him and Gallo apart from the other men in the community? What does Hector mean when he says, "Oh Papi, breathe on me" (p. 829)?

4. Write a 500–750-word essay in which you use evidence from the play to refute this assertion: "Cockfights are nothing but cruelty to animals practiced for profit."

5. In what ways does the humor in the play deepen the play's seriousness? In what ways do the characters use humor as a weapon, as a "rooster" in the "pit" of life?

CHARLES BAXTER

Gryphon

On Wednesday afternoon, between the geography lesson on ancient Egypt's hand-operated irrigation system and an art project that involved drawing a model city next to a mountain, our fourth-grade teacher, Mr. Hibler, developed a cough. This cough began with a series of muffled throat-clearings and progressed to propulsive noises contained within Mr. Hibler's closed mouth. "Listen to him," Carol Peterson whispered to me. "He's gonna blow up." Mr. Hibler's laughter — dazed and infrequent — sounded a bit like his cough, but as we worked on our model cities we would look up, thinking he was enjoying a joke, and see Mr. Hibler's face turning red, his cheeks puffed out. This was not laughter. Twice he bent over, and his loose tie, like a plumb line, hung down straight from his neck as he exploded himself into a Kleenex. He would excuse himself, then go on coughing. "I'll bet you a dime," Carol Peterson whispered, "we get a substitute tomorrow."

Carol sat at the desk in front of mine and was a bad person — when she thought no one was looking she would blow her nose on notebook paper, then crumple it up and throw it into the wastebasket — but at times of crisis she spoke the truth. I knew I'd lose the dime.

"No deal," I said.

When Mr. Hibler stood us in formation at the door just prior to the final

---

CHARLES BAXTER (b. 1947) once said, "The mind . . . is as remote and strange as South Dakota." Author most recently of a story collection called *A Relative Stranger* (1990), Baxter lives in Ann Arbor, Michigan, and teaches creative writing at the University of Michigan.

bell, he was almost incapable of speech. "I'm sorry, boys and girls," he said. "I seem to be coming down with something."

"I hope you feel better tomorrow, Mr. Hibler," Bobby Kryzanowicz, the   5 faultless brown-noser, said, and I heard Carol Peterson's evil giggle. Then Mr. Hibler opened the door and we walked out to the buses, a clique of us starting noisily to hawk and cough as soon as we thought we were a few feet beyond Mr. Hibler's earshot.

Since Five Oaks was a rural community, and in Michigan, the supply of substitute teachers was limited to the town's unemployed community college graduates, a pool of about four mothers. These ladies fluttered, provided easeful class days, and nervously covered material we had mastered weeks earlier. Therefore it was a surprise when a woman we had never seen came into the class the next day, carrying a purple purse, a checkerboard lunchbox, and a few books. She put the books on one side of Mr. Hibler's desk and the lunchbox on the other, next to the Voice of Music phonograph. Three of us in the back of the room were playing with Heever, the chameleon that lived in a terrarium and on one of the plastic drapes, when she walked in.

She clapped her hands at us. "Little boys," she said, "why are you bent over together like that?" She didn't wait for us to answer. "Are you tormenting an animal? Put it back. Please sit down at your desks. I want no cabals this time of the day." We just stared at her. "Boys," she repeated, "I asked you to sit down."

I put the chameleon in his terrarium and felt my way to my desk, never taking my eyes off the woman. With white and green chalk, she had started to draw a tree on the left side of the blackboard. She didn't look usual. Furthermore, her tree was outsized, disproportionate, for some reason.

"This room needs a tree," she said, with one line drawing the suggestion of a leaf. "A large, leafy, shady, deciduous . . . oak."

Her fine, light hair had been done up in what I would learn years later   10 was called a chignon, and she wore gold-rimmed glasses whose lenses seemed to have the faintest blue tint. Harold Knardahl, who sat across from me, whispered, "Mars," and I nodded slowly, savoring the imminent weirdness of the day. The substitute drew another branch with an extravagant arm gesture, then turned around and said, "Good morning. I don't believe I said good morning to all of you yet."

Facing us, she was no special age — an adult is an adult — but her face had two prominent lines, descending vertically from the sides of her mouth to her chin. I knew where I had seen those lines before: *Pinocchio*. They were marionette lines. "You may stare at me," she said to us, as a few more kids from the last bus came into the room, their eyes fixed on her, "for a few more seconds, until the bell rings. Then I will permit no more staring. Looking I will permit. Staring, no. It is impolite to stare, and a sign of bad breeding. You cannot make a social effort while staring."

Harold Knardahl did not glance at me, or nudge, but I heard him whisper

"Mars" again, trying to get more mileage out of his single joke with the kids who had just come in.

When everyone was seated, the substitute teacher finished her tree, put down her chalk fastidiously on the phonograph, brushed her hands, and faced us. "Good morning," she said. "I am Miss Ferenczi, your teacher for the day. I am fairly new to your community, and I don't believe any of you know me. I will therefore start by telling you a story about myself."

While we settled back, she launched into her tale. She said her grandfather had been a Hungarian prince; her mother had been born in some place called Flanders, had been a pianist, and had played concerts for people Miss Ferenczi referred to as "crowned heads." She gave us a knowing look. "Grieg," she said, "the Norwegian master, wrote a concerto for piano that was . . . " — she paused — "my mother's triumph at her debut concert in London." Her eyes searched the ceiling. Our eyes followed. Nothing up there but ceiling tile. "For reasons that I shall not go into, my family's fortunes took us to Detroit, then north to dreadful Saginaw, and now here I am in Five Oaks, as your substitute teacher, for today, Thursday, October the eleventh. I believe it will be a good day: All the forecasts coincide. We shall start with your reading lesson. Take out your reading book. I believe it is called *Broad Horizons,* or something along those lines."

Jeannie Vermeesch raised her hand. Miss Ferenczi nodded at her. "Mr. Hibler always starts the day with the Pledge of Allegiance," Jeannie whined.   15

"Oh, does he? In that case," Miss Ferenczi said, "you must know it *very* well by now, and we certainly need not spend our time on it. No, no allegiance pledging on the premises today, by my reckoning. Not with so much sunlight coming into the room. A pledge does not suit my mood." She glanced at her watch. "Time *is* flying. Take out *Broad Horizons.*"

She disappointed us by giving us an ordinary lesson, complete with vocabulary and drills, comprehension questions, and recitation. She didn't seem to care for the material, however. She sighed every few minutes and rubbed her glasses with a frilly handkerchief that she withdrew, magician-style, from her left sleeve.

After reading we moved on to arithmetic. It was my favorite time of the morning, when the lazy autumn sunlight dazzled its way through ribbons of clouds past the windows on the east side of the classroom and crept across the linoleum floor. On the playground the first group of children, the kindergartners, were running on the quack grass just beyond the monkey bars. We were doing multiplication tables. Miss Ferenczi had made John Wazny stand up at his desk in the front row. He was supposed to go through the tables of six. From where I was sitting, I could smell the Vitalis soaked into John's plastered hair. He was doing fine until he came to six times eleven and six times twelve. "Six times eleven," he said, "is sixty-eight. Six times twelve is . . . " He put his fingers to his head, quickly and secretly sniffed his fingertips, and said, ". . . seventy-two." Then he sat down.

"Fine," Miss Ferenczi said. "Well now. That was very good."

"Miss Ferenczi!" One of the Eddy twins was waving her hand desperately   20
in the air. "Miss Ferenczi! Miss Ferenczi!"

"Yes?"

"John said that six times eleven is sixty-eight and you said he was right!"

"*Did* I?" She gazed at the class with a jolly look breaking across her
marionette's face. "Did I say that? Well, what *is* six times eleven?"

"It's sixty-six!"

She nodded. "Yes. So it is. But, and I know some people will not entirely   25
agree with me, at some times it is sixty-eight."

"When? When is it sixty-eight?"

We were all waiting.

"In higher mathematics, which you children do not yet understand, six
times eleven can be considered to be sixty-eight." She laughed through her
nose. "In higher mathematics numbers are . . . more fluid. The only thing a
number does is contain a certain amount of something. Think of water. A cup
is not the only way to measure a certain amount of water, is it?" We were
staring, shaking our heads. "You could use saucepans or thimbles. In either
case, the water *would be the same*. Perhaps," she started again, "it would be
better for you to think that six times eleven is sixty-eight only when I am in
the room."

"Why is it sixty-eight," Mark Poole asked, "when you're in the room?"

"Because it's more interesting that way," she said, smiling very rapidly   30
behind her blue-tinted glasses. "Besides, I'm your substitute teacher, am I not?"
We all nodded. "Well, then, think of six times eleven equals sixty-eight as a
substitute fact."

"A substitute fact?"

"Yes." Then she looked at us carefully. "Do you think," she asked, "that
anyone is going to be hurt by a substitute fact?"

We looked back at her.

"Will the plants on the windowsill be hurt?" We glanced at them. There
were sensitive plants thriving in a green plastic tray, and several wilted ferns
in small clay pots. "Your dogs and cats, or your moms and dads?" She waited.
"So," she concluded, "what's the problem?"

"But it's wrong," Janice Weber said, "isn't it?"   35

"What's your name, young lady?"

"Janice Weber."

"And you think it's wrong, Janice?"

"I was just asking."

"Well, all right. You were just asking. I think we've spent enough time on   40
this matter by now, don't you, class? You are free to think what you like.
When your teacher, Mr. Hibler, returns, six times eleven will be sixty-six again,
you can rest assured. And it will be that for the rest of your lives in Five Oaks.
Too bad, eh?" She raised her eyebrows and glinted herself at us. "But for now,
it wasn't. So much for that. Let us go on to your assigned problems for today,

as painstakingly outlined, I see, in Mr. Hibler's lesson plan. Take out a sheet of paper and write your names on the upper left-hand corner."

For the next half hour we did the rest of our arithmetic problems. We handed them in and then went on to spelling, my worst subject. Spelling always came before lunch. We were taking spelling dictation and looking at the clock. "Thorough," Miss Ferenczi said. "Boundary." She walked in the aisles between the desks, holding the spelling book open and looking down at our papers. "Balcony." I clutched my pencil. Somehow, the way she said those words, they seemed foreign, misvoweled and mis-consonanted. I stared down at what I had spelled. *Balconie.* I turned the pencil upside down and erased my mistake. *Balconey.* That looked better, but still incorrect. I cursed the world of spelling and tried erasing it again and saw the paper beginning to wear away. *Balkony.* Suddenly I felt a hand on my shoulder.

"I don't like that word either," Miss Ferenczi whispered, bent over, her mouth near my ear. "It's ugly. My feeling is, if you don't like a word, you don't have to use it." She straightened up, leaving behind a slight odor of Clorets.

At lunchtime we went out to get our trays of sloppy joes, peaches in heavy syrup, coconut cookies, and milk, and brought them back to the classroom, where Miss Ferenczi was sitting at the desk, eating a brown sticky thing she had unwrapped from tightly rubber-banded waxed paper. "Miss Ferenczi," I said, raising my hand. "You don't have to eat with us. You can eat with the other teachers. There's a teacher's lounge," I ended up, "next to the principal's office."

"No, thank you," she said. "I prefer it here."

"We've got a room monitor," I said. "Mrs. Eddy." I pointed to where   45
Mrs. Eddy, Joyce and Judy's mother, sat silently at the back of the room, doing her knitting.

"That's fine," Miss Ferenczi said. "But I shall continue to eat here, with you children. I prefer it," she repeated.

"How come?" Wayne Razmer asked without raising his hand.

"I talked to the other teachers before class this morning," Miss Ferenczi said, biting into her brown food. "There was a great rattling of the words for the fewness of the ideas. I didn't care for their brand of hilarity. I don't like ditto-machine jokes."

"Oh," Wayne said.

"What's that you're eating?" Maxine Sylvester asked, twitching her nose.   50
"Is it food?"

"It most certainly *is* food. It's a stuffed fig. I had to drive almost down to Detroit to get it. I also brought some smoked sturgeon. And this," she said, lifting some green leaves out of her lunchbox, "is raw spinach, cleaned this morning."

"Why're you eating raw spinach?" Maxine asked.

"It's good for you," Miss Ferenczi said. "More stimulating than soda pop or smelling salts." I bit into my sloppy joe and stared blankly out the window.

An almost invisible moon was faintly silvered in the daytime autumn sky. "As far as food is concerned," Miss Ferenczi was saying, "you have to shuffle the pack. Mix it up. Too many people eat . . . well, never mind."

"Miss Ferenczi," Carol Peterson said, "what are we going to do this afternoon?"

"Well," she said, looking down at Mr. Hibler's lesson plan, "I see that 　55 your teacher, Mr. Hibler, has you scheduled for a unit on the Egyptians." Carol groaned. "Yessss," Miss Ferenczi continued, "that is what we will do: the Egyptians. A remarkable people. Almost as remarkable as the Americans. But not quite." She lowered her head, did her quick smile, and went back to eating her spinach.

After noon recess we came back into the classroom and saw that Miss Ferenczi had drawn a pyramid on the blackboard close to her oak tree. Some of us who had been playing baseball were messing around in the back of the room, dropping the bats and gloves into the playground box, and Ray Schontzeler had just slugged me when I heard Miss Ferenczi's high-pitched voice, quavering with emotions. "Boys," she said, "come to order right this minute and take your seats. I do not wish to waste a minute of class time. Take out your geography books." We trudged to our desks and, still sweating, pulled out *Distant Lands and Their People*. "Turn to page forty-two." She waited for thirty seconds, then looked over at Kelly Munger. "Young man," she said, "why are you still fossicking in your desk?"

Kelly looked as if his foot had been stepped on. "Why am I what?"

"Why are you . . . burrowing in your desk like that?"

"I'm lookin' for the book, Miss Ferenczi."

Bobby Kryzanowicz, the faultless brown-noser who sat in the first row by 　60 choice, softly said, "His name is Kelly Munger. He can't ever find his stuff. He always does that."

"I don't care what his name is, especially after lunch," Miss Ferenczi said. "*Where is your book?*"

"I just found it." Kelly was peering into his desk and with both hands pulled at the book, shoveling along in front of it several pencils and crayons, which fell into his lap and then to the floor.

"I hate a mess," Miss Ferenczi said. "I hate a mess in a desk or a mind. It's . . . unsanitary. You wouldn't want your house at home to look like your desk at school, now, would you?" She didn't wait for an answer. "I should think not. A house at home should be as neat as human hands can make it. What were we talking about? Egypt. Page forty-two. I note from Mr. Hibler's lesson plan that you have been discussing the modes of Egyptian irrigation. Interesting, in my view, but not so interesting as what we are about to cover. The pyramids, and Egyptian slave labor. A plus on one side, a minus on the other." We had our books open to page forty-two, where there was a picture of a pyramid, but Miss Ferenczi wasn't looking at the book. Instead, she was staring at some object just outside the window.

"Pyramids," Miss Ferenczi said, still looking past the window. "I want you to think about pyramids. And what was inside. The bodies of the pharaohs, of course, and their attendant treasures. Scrolls. Perhaps," Miss Ferenczi said, her face gleeful but unsmiling, "these scrolls were novels for the pharaohs, helping them to pass the time in their long voyage through the centuries. But then, I am joking." I was looking at the lines on Miss Ferenczi's skin. "Pyramids," Miss Ferenczi went on, "were the repositories of special cosmic powers. The nature of a pyramid is to guide cosmic energy forces into a concentrated point. The Egyptians knew that; we have generally forgotten it. Did you know," she asked, walking to the side of the room so that she was standing by the coat closet, "that George Washington had Egyptian blood, from his grandmother? Certain features of the Constitution of the United States are notable for their Egyptian ideas."

Without glancing down at the book, she began to talk about the movement of souls in Egyptian religion. She said that when people die, their souls return to Earth in the form of carpenter ants or walnut trees, depending on how they behaved — "well or ill" — in life. She said that the Egyptians believed that people act the way they do because of magnetism produced by tidal forces in the solar system, forces produced by the sun and by its "planetary ally," Jupiter. Jupiter, she said, was a planet, as we had been told, but had "certain properties of stars." She was speaking very fast. She said that the Egyptians were great explorers and conquerors. She said that the greatest of all the conquerors, Genghis Khan, had had forty horses and forty young women killed on the site of his grave. We listened. No one tried to stop her. "I myself have been in Egypt," she said, "and have witnessed much dust and many brutalities." She said that an old man in Egypt who worked for a circus had personally shown her an animal in a cage, a monster, half bird and half lion. She said that this monster was called a gryphon and that she had heard about them but never seen them until she traveled to the outskirts of Cairo. She wrote the word out on the blackboard in large capital letters: GRYPHON. She said that Egyptian astronomers had discovered the planet Saturn but had not seen its rings. She said that the Egyptians were the first to discover that dogs, when they are ill, will not drink from rivers, but wait for rain, and hold their jaws open to catch it.

"She lies."

We were on the school bus home. I was sitting next to Carl Whiteside, who had bad breath and a huge collection of marbles. We were arguing. Carl thought she was lying. I said she wasn't, probably.

"I didn't believe that stuff about the bird," Carl said, "and what she told us about the pyramids? I didn't believe that, either. She didn't know what she was talking about."

"Oh yeah?" I had liked her. She was strange. I thought I could nail him. "If she was lying," I said, "what'd she say that was a lie?"

"Six times eleven isn't sixty-eight. It isn't ever. It's sixty-six, I know for a fact."

"She said so. She admitted it. What else did she lie about?"

"I don't know," he said. "Stuff."

"What stuff?"

"Well." He swung his legs back and forth. "You ever see an animal that was half lion and half bird?" He crossed his arms. "It sounded real fakey to me."

"It could happen," I said. I had to improvise, to outrage him. "I read in this newspaper my mom bought in the IGA about this scientist, this mad scientist in the Swiss Alps, and he's been putting genes and chromosomes and stuff together in test tubes, and he combined a human being and a hamster." I waited, for effect. "It's called a humster." 75

"You never." Carl was staring at me, his mouth open, his terrible bad breath making its way toward me. "What newspaper was it?"

"*The National Enquirer*," I said, "that they sell next to the cash registers." When I saw his look of recognition, I knew I had him. "And this mad scientist," I said, "his name was, um, Dr. Frankenbush." I realized belatedly that this name was a mistake and waited for Carl to notice its resemblance to the name of the other famous mad master of permutations, but he only sat there.

"A man and a hamster?" He was staring at me, squinting, his mouth opening in distaste. "Jeez. What'd it look like?"

When the bus reached my stop, I took off down our dirt road and ran up through the backyard, kicking the tire swing for good luck. I dropped my books on the back steps so I could hug and kiss our dog, Mr. Selby. Then I hurried inside. I could smell brussels sprouts cooking, my unfavorite vegetable. My mother was washing other vegetables in the kitchen sink, and my baby brother was hollering in his yellow playpen on the kitchen floor.

"Hi, Mom," I said, hopping around the playpen to kiss her. "Guess what?" 80

"I have no idea."

"We had this substitute today, Miss Ferenczi, and I'd never seen her before, and she had all these stories and ideas and stuff."

"Well. That's good." My mother looked out the window in front of the sink, her eyes on the pine woods west of our house. That time of the afternoon her skin always looked so white to me. Strangers always said my mother looked like Betty Crocker, framed by the great spoon on the side of the Bisquick box. "Listen, Tommy," she said. "Would you please go upstairs and pick your clothes off the floor in the bathroom, and then go outside to the shed and put the shovel and ax away that your father left outside this morning?"

"She said that six times eleven was sometimes sixty-eight!" I said. "And she said she once saw a monster that was half lion and half bird." I waited. "In Egypt."

"Did you hear me?" my mother asked, raising her arm to wipe her forehead with the back of her hand. "You have chores to do." 85

"I know," I said. "I was just telling you about the substitute."

"It's very interesting," my mother said, quickly glancing down at me, "and we can talk about it later when your father gets home. But right now you have some work to do."

"Okay, Mom." I took a cookie out of the jar on the counter and was about to go outside when I had a thought. I ran into the living room, pulled out a dictionary next to the TV stand, and opened it to the Gs. After five minutes I found it. *Gryphon*: variant of griffin. *Griffin*: "a fabulous beast with the head and wings of an eagle and the body of a lion." Fabulous was right. I shouted with triumph and ran outside to put my father's tools in their proper places.

Miss Ferenczi was back the next day, slightly altered. She had pulled her hair down and twisted it into pigtails, with red rubber bands holding them tight one inch from the ends. She was wearing a green blouse and pink scarf, making her difficult to look at for a full class day. This time there was no pretense of doing a reading lesson or moving on to arithmetic. As soon as the bell rang, she simply began to talk.

She talked for forty minutes straight. There seemed to be less connection between her ideas, but the ideas themselves were, as the dictionary would say, fabulous. She said she had heard of a huge jewel, in what she called the antipodes, that was so brilliant that when light shone into it at a certain angle it would blind whoever was looking at its center. She said the biggest diamond in the world was cursed and had killed everyone who owned it, and that by a trick of fate it was called the Hope Diamond. Diamonds are magic, she said, and this is why women wear them on their fingers, as a sign of the magic of womanhood. Men have strength, Miss Ferenczi said, but no true magic. That is why men fall in love with women but women do not fall in love with men: They just love being loved. George Washington had died because of a mistake he made about a diamond. Washington was not the first *true* president, but she didn't say who was. In some places in the world, she said, men and women still live in the trees and eat monkeys for breakfast. Their doctors are magicians. At the bottom of the sea are creatures thin as pancakes who have never been studied by scientists because when you take them up to air, the fish explode.

There was not a sound in the classroom, except for Miss Ferenczi's voice, and Donna DeShano's coughing. No one even went to the bathroom.

Beethoven, she said, had not been deaf; it was a trick to make himself famous, and it worked. As she talked, Miss Ferenczi's pigtails swung back and forth. There are trees in the world, she said, that eat meat: Their leaves are sticky and close up on bugs like hands. She lifted her hands and brought them together, palm to palm. Venus, which most people think is the next closest planet to the sun, is not always closer, and, besides, it is the planet of greatest mystery because of its thick cloud cover. "I know what lies underneath those clouds," Miss Ferenczi said, and waited. After the silence, she said, "Angels. Angels live under those clouds." She said that angels were not invisible to everyone and were in fact smarter than most people. They did not dress in

90

robes as was often claimed but instead wore formal evening clothes, as if they were about to attend a concert. Often angels *do* attend concerts and sit in the aisles, where, she said, most people pay no attention to them. She said the most terrible angel had the shape of the Sphinx. "There is no running away from that one," she said. She said that unquenchable fires burn just under the surface of the earth in Ohio, and that the baby Mozart fainted dead away in his cradle when he first heard the sound of a trumpet. She said that someone named Narzim al Harrardim was the greatest writer who ever lived. She said that planets control behavior, and anyone conceived during a solar eclipse would be born with webbed feet.

"I know you children like to hear these things," she said, "these secrets, and that is why I am telling you all this." We nodded. It was better than doing comprehension questions for the readings in *Broad Horizons*.

"I will tell you one more story," she said, "and then we will have to do arithmetic." She leaned over, and her voice grew soft. "There is no death," she said. "You must never be afraid. Never. That which is, cannot die. It will change into different earthly and unearthly elements, but I know this as sure as I stand here in front of you, and I swear it: You must not be afraid. I have seen this truth with these eyes. I know it because in a dream God kissed me. Here." And she pointed with her right index finger to the side of her head, below the mouth where the vertical lines were carved into her skin.

Absentmindedly we all did our arithmetic problems. At recess the class   95
was out on the playground, but no one was playing. We were all standing in small groups, talking about Miss Ferenczi. We didn't know if she was crazy, or what. I looked out beyond the playground, at the rusted cars piled in a small heap behind a clump of sumac, and I wanted to see shapes there, approaching me.

On the way home, Carl sat next to me again. He didn't say much, and I didn't either. At last he turned to me. "You know what she said about the leaves that close up on bugs?"

"Huh?"

"The leaves," Carl insisted. "The meat-eating plants. I know it's true. I saw it on television. The leaves have this icky glue that the plants have got smeared all over them and the insects can't get off 'cause they're stuck. I saw it." He seemed demoralized. "She's tellin' the truth."

"Yeah."

"You think she's seen all those angels?"   100

I shrugged.

"I don't think she has," Carl informed me. "I think she made that part up."

"There's a tree," I suddenly said. I was looking out the window at the farms along County Road H. I knew every barn, every broken windmill, every fence, every anhydrous ammonia tank, by heart. "There's a tree that's . . . that I've seen . . . "

"Don't you try to do it," Carl said. "You'll just sound like a jerk."

I kissed my mother. She was standing in the front of the stove. "How was your day?" she asked.

"Fine."

"Did you have Miss Ferenczi again?"

"Yeah."

"Well?"

"She was fine. Mom," I asked, "can I go to my room?"

"No," she said, "not until you've gone out to the vegetable garden and picked me a few tomatoes." She glanced at the sky. "I think it's going to rain. Skedaddle and do it now. Then you come back inside and watch your brother for a few minutes while I go upstairs. I need to clean up before dinner." She looked down at me. "You're looking a little pale, Tommy." She touched the back of her hand to my forehead and I felt her diamond ring against my skin. "Do you feel all right?"

"I'm fine," I said, and went out to pick the tomatoes.

Coughing mutedly, Mr. Hibler was back the next day, slipping lozenges into his mouth when his back was turned at forty-five-minute intervals and asking us how much of his prepared lesson plan Miss Ferenczi had followed. Edith Atwater took the responsibility for the class of explaining to Mr. Hibler that the substitute hadn't always done exactly what he, Mr. Hibler, would have done, but we had worked hard even though she talked a lot. About what? he asked. All kinds of things, Edith said. I sort of forgot. To our relief, Mr. Hibler seemed not at all interested in what Miss Ferenczi had said to fill the day. He probably thought it was woman's talk: unserious and not suited for school. It was enough that he had a pile of arithmetic problems from us to correct.

For the next month, the sumac turned a distracting red in the field, and the sun traveled toward the southern sky, so that its rays reached Mr. Hibler's Halloween display on the bulletin board in the back of the room, fading the pumpkin-head scarecrow from orange to tan. Every three days I measured how much farther the sun had moved toward the southern horizon by making small marks with my black Crayola on the north wall, ant-sized marks only I knew were there.

And then in early December, four days after the first permanent snowfall, she appeared again in our classroom. The minute she came in the door, I felt my heart begin to pound. Once again, she was different: This time, her hair hung straight down and seemed hardly to have been combed. She hadn't brought her lunchbox with her, but she was carrying what seemed to be a

105

110

115

small box. She greeted all of us and talked about the weather. Donna DeShano had to remind her to take her overcoat off.

When the bell to start the day finally rang, Miss Ferenczi looked out at all of us and said, "Children, I have enjoyed your company in the past, and today I am going to reward you." She held up the small box. "Do you know what this is?" She waited. "Of course you don't. It is a Tarot pack."

Edith Atwater raised her hand. "What's a Tarot pack, Miss Ferenczi?"

"It is used to tell fortunes," she said. "And that is what I shall do this morning. I shall tell your fortunes, as I have been taught to do."

"What's fortune?" Bobby Kryzanowicz asked.

"The future, young man. I shall tell you what your future will be. I can't do your whole future, of course. I shall have to limit myself to the five-card system, the wands, cups, swords, pentacles, and the higher arcanes. Now who wants to be first?"   120

There was a long silence. Then Carol Peterson raised her hand.

"All right," Miss Ferenczi said. She divided the pack into five smaller packs and walked back to Carol's desk, in front of mine. "Pick one card from each one of these packs," she said. I saw that Carol had a four of cups and a six of swords, but I couldn't see the other cards. Miss Ferenczi studied the cards on Carol's desk for a minute. "Not bad," she said. "I do not see much higher education. Probably an early marriage. Many children. There's something bleak and dreary here, but I can't tell what. Perhaps just the tasks of a housewife life. I think you'll do very well, for the most part." She smiled at Carol, a smile with a certain lack of interest. "Who wants to be next?"

Carl Whiteside raised his hand slowly.

"Yes," Miss Ferenczi said, "let's do a boy." She walked over to where Carl sat. After he picked his five cards, she gazed at them for a long time. "Travel," she said. "Much distant travel. You might go into the army. Not too much romantic interest here. A late marriage, if at all. But the Sun in your major arcana, that's a very good card." She giggled. "You'll have a happy life."

Next I raised my hand. She told me my future. She did the same with Bobby Kryzanowicz, Kelly Munger, Edith Atwater, and Kim Foor. Then she came to Wayne Razmer. He picked his five cards, and I could see that the Death card was one of them.   125

"What's your name?" Miss Ferenczi asked.

"Wayne."

"Well, Wayne," she said, "you will undergo a great metamorphosis, a change, before you become an adult. Your earthly element will no doubt leap higher, because you seem to be a sweet boy. This card, this nine of swords, tells me of suffering and desolation. And this ten of wands, well, that's a heavy load."

"What about this one?" Wayne pointed at the Death card.

"It means, my sweet, that you will die soon." She gathered up the cards. We were all looking at Wayne. "But do not fear," she said. "It is not really   130 death. Just change. Out of your earthly shape." She put the cards on Mr. Hibler's desk. "And now, let's do some arithmetic."

At lunchtime Wayne went to Mr. Faegre, the principal, and informed him of what Miss Ferenczi had done. During the noon recess, we saw Miss Ferenczi drive out of the parking lot in her rusting green Rambler American. I stood under the slide, listening to the other kids coasting down and landing in the little depressive bowls at the bottom. I was kicking stones and tugging at my hair right up to the moment when I saw Wayne come out to the playground. He smiled, the dead fool, and with the fingers of his right hand he was showing everyone how he had told on Miss Ferenczi.

I made my way toward Wayne, pushing myself past two girls from another class. He was watching me with his little pinhead eyes.

"You told," I shouted at him. "She was just kidding."

"She shouldn't have," he shouted back. "We were supposed to be doing arithmetic."

"She just scared you," I said. "You're a chicken. You're a chicken, Wayne. You are. Scared of a little card," I singsonged.

Wayne fell at me, his two fists hammering down on my nose. I gave him a good one in the stomach and then I tried for his head. Aiming my fist, I saw that he was crying. I slugged him.

"She was right," I yelled. "She was always right! She told the truth!" Other kids were whooping. "You were just scared, that's all!"

And then large hands pulled at us, and it was my turn to speak to Mr. Faegre.

In the afternoon Miss Ferenczi was gone, and my nose was stuffed with cotton clotted with blood, and my lip had swelled, and our class had been combined with Mrs. Mantei's sixth-grade class for a crowded afternoon science unit on insect life in ditches and swamps. I knew where Mrs. Mantei lived: She had a new house trailer just down the road from us, at the Clearwater Park. She was no mystery. Somehow she and Mr. Bodine, the other fourth-grade teacher, had managed to fit forty-five desks into the room. Kelly Munger asked if Miss Ferenczi had been arrested, and Mrs. Mantei said no, of course not. All that afternoon, until the buses came to pick us up, we learned about field crickets and two-striped grasshoppers, water bugs, cicadas, mosquitoes, flies, and moths. We learned about insects' hard outer shell, the exoskeleton, and the usual parts of the mouth, including the labrum, mandible, maxilla, and glossa. We learned about compound eyes, and the four-stage metamorphosis from egg to larva to pupa to adult. We learned something, but not much, about mating. Mrs. Mantei drew, very skillfully, the internal anatomy of the grasshopper on the blackboard. We learned about the dance of the honeybee, directing other bees in the hive to pollen. We found out about which insects were pests to man, and which were not. On lined white pieces of paper we made lists of insects we might actually see, then a list of insects too small to be clearly visible, such as fleas; Mrs. Mantei said that our assignment would be to memorize these lists for the next day, when Mr. Hibler would certainly return and test us on our knowledge.   1985

INVESTIGATIONS

1. Answer Miss Ferenczi's question in paragraph 32: " 'Do you think . . . that anyone is going to be hurt by a substitute fact?' " How would you have answered this question when you were in the fourth grade? What is the point of Miss Ferenczi's math lesson?

2. After looking up "fabulous" in the dictionary, write two or three paragraphs describing how the word applies to the story and its characters.

3. Write a 250–300-word essay that begins with one of the following sentences:

   a. "Charles Baxter's 'Gryphon' provides numerous examples proving how easy it is for teachers to control the way their students see the world."

   b. "Charles Baxter's 'Gryphon' provides numerous examples of how our need for knowledge is second only to our need for wonder."

4. In what ways is Miss Ferenczi's "woman's talk" anything but "unserious and not suited for school" (para. 113)?

5. Compare your efforts at explanation in your response to "Write Before Reading" (p. 784) to Miss Ferenczi's students' explanations of what she says. Did you abandon these efforts as readily as the narrator does? Why or why not?

Pico Rico, Mandorico

There were once two girls who lived by themselves in a house on the edge of town. Their names were Alicia and Elisa and they were orphans, for their mother had died and their father had left town many years before. When she was on her deathbed, their kind mother called them to her side to give them her final blessing. Her parting words to them were:

"When the two of you were born, the midwife had to use great care when she untangled you from one another, for you were so tightly wrapped around each other that it was like prying open the two halves of a shell. Be sure to always work together as one and no evil shall ever befall you."

After their mother died, the two girls took charge of the house. They were twins and their faces were white sculptures made from the very same alabaster, so the townspeople had trouble telling them apart and soon came to call them simply "the Alisias." On hot summer days, whenever the two girls walked by them, the villagers would feel as if the icy notes of xylophones were playing gently on the surface of their skin or as if a breeze from the ocean had just whistled through the branches of the trees in the parched plaza square. At those moments, the townsfolk would find themselves irresistibly drawn to the arched doorways along the streets or to the shady carriage house eaves where they would sit and rest their heads against the cool and faded walls. Watching the patterns cut by the purple vines against the adobe, they would then close their eyes and go into their dreams once more.

But the twins rarely went beyond the wrought iron gates of their yard because they could no longer stand to see the sadness in the villagers' eyes. Most of them walked around with their heads bowed down and their eyes to the ground, never asking themselves why they were resigned to their unhappy fate, working from sunrise to sunset for the rich landowner who held most of the land in the province. At night, they would go to bed promptly, but since they had spent all day working their way around bubbling cauldrons of sticky molasses, digging their way along miles of trenches and irrigation ditches, planting their way along oceans of sugar cane that whipped across their backs in green welts, they could no longer coax the sandman and had lost all ability to sleep.

With every passing day the two sisters felt closer and closer, their affection for each other making them different somehow from other people around them. 5

Born in 1942 in Ponce, Puerto Rico, Rosario Ferré is a full-time writer of poetry, essays, and fiction whose most recent books include a novel entitled *Maldito Amor* (1986) and an essay collection called *El Coloquio de las Perras* (1990). "Pico Rico, Mandorico" was translated by Diana Velez.

Though they were already adolescents, they continued to wear white embroidered percale dresses, their long blonde hair woven up high into crowns of braids which they held together with large silver hairpins. They earned their living doing needlework — embroidery and weaving — so they each carried a pair of scissors, sharpened metal stars that hung from their waists.

The sisters shared every secret and told each other everything, so in time they became each like the shadow of the other, in the same way that dreams reflect the soul and the soul will mirror dreams. It was so much so that if one of them drank a glass of water too rapidly while in the midst of her housechores, the other, even if she were six miles away, would feel a sudden cold stabbing in her throat. If, while embroidering her lace some Sunday afternoon one of them would prick her finger, the other, even if she were visiting relatives in the next town, would suddenly see a drop of blood bubble up on her fingertip.

They taught themselves French at an early age, carefully doing their lessons together over breakfast. They would sit over their huge mugs of steaming milk into which they would slowly stir exactly two aromatic drops of coffee syrup kept in an emerald green jar on the table. They delighted in practicing the alphabet forwards and backwards, finding new and interesting combinations of words that they would then write down in their notebooks. They often told each other that they would someday send those words to the Language Academy as a way of marking its demise.

They knew many domestic secrets and arts as well: how to freshen up hands after their harsh contact with garlic and onion, soaking them for five minutes in an urn filled with goat's milk; how to keep fingers nimble for embroidery by soaking them in mineral water at least eight times a day and blowing on them gently afterwards. They didn't want to suffer the same fate as the other townspeople, who, because they had worked so hard, had forgotten how to coax their sleep. Instead, the sisters would always be sure to combine their labors with unusual fantasy games that would give free play to their imaginations. They spent hours trying to guess each other's thoughts and, by playing these innocent games, they came to acquire the difficult art of getting the soul to leave the body.

One time Elisa felt the sudden prickling pain of a migraine headache coming on, so she went to her bedroom to rest. Alicia said good-bye to her and went off to the marketplace to pick up some items for their evening meal. Elisa lay flat and still on her bed with the curtains drawn tightly but she could find no relief from the searing throb in her temples. Suddenly Alicia came swooping through the skylight, percale dress trailing behind her like sea foam, arms poised in a pensive way, like a Saint Ursula popping from a painting to make her midday rounds. She walked through the darkened chamber and made her way to the bed where her sister lay. She drew close to her and slowly stroked her forehead saying:

"Alicia, my sister, tell me how much you've missed me. Kiss me on the cheek and you'll see how much better you'll feel." 10

Blinded by the pain, Elisa opened her eyes slowly. She smiled, for she understood her sister's intent. She pulled herself up and leaned over to kiss her sister on the cheek, whispering:

"I'm feeling better, Elisa, much better, thanks to you."

Instantly her pain was gone, but they could never be sure after that if it had been Alicia or Elisa who had gone back out the skylight afterwards.

One afternoon they were sitting just inside their porch, embroidering, weaving, and sewing lace during the hottest part of the day, when they looked up to see a man on a horse approaching the house. He was dressed in black silk clothes, and he rode a pasofino horse with an English saddle. The slow clipclop of the horse's hooves left sharp, even marks on the road.

When the horseman drew close they could see he was wearing a finely woven wide-brimmed hat that hid half his face. On his shoulder sat a bronze-colored monkey making faces at the two sisters. Slung over the horse's back and strapped to the saddle was a wicker basket filled to the brim with mouth-watering fruit, harvested by the townspeople for the horseman. But his most attention-getting feature was his enormous nose, a nose that came clear to the brim of his hat.

The horseman came up to where the twins were and, letting the monkey's tail curl down onto his chest in a play of arabesques, he said to them in a deep voice:

> Soo, soo, roo, soo, soothing fruit
> ripe bananas, deep red cherries
> passion fruit and juicy pulp.
> All these goods I bring to you
> chew and swallow till you're full.
> Gifts are they for those girls who
> promise not to cry and brood
> when they see me passing through.

Alicia couldn't help but laugh at such an outlandish character, saying instead in a mocking tone:

> Pico Rico, what a nose!
> Who can know just where it goes?
> Hand me a mop, hand me a broom.
> We'll soon clean up this big old room.

But Elisa could not take her eyes off the fruit basket with its bananas, cherries, and passion fruit in their deep reds, yellows, and purples gleaming like jewels. She turned to her sister with tears in her eyes and begged her, please, to give her a little money, for she had suddenly gotten an irresistible urge to eat some of those fruits. When Alicia heard these words, they struck fear in her heart, for she suspected that the black-clad horseman was none other than the rich landowner, who by now owned almost all the land in the region. But she kept her silence, pretending she had not heard her sister's entreaties. In a loud voice, but more seriously this time, she repeated:

> *Pico Rico, what a nose!*
> *Heaven keep us from our foes.*
> *Wish number two*
> *and wish number one.*
> *Wish he'd soon be*
> *dead and gone.*

Annoyed at her sister, Elisa ran to the path where the horseman stood and, in exchange for the basket, she grabbed the scissors that hung from her waist, cut off one of her golden braids, and offered it to him with its two silver hairpins still attached.

That evening, Alicia begged her sister to please remember their mother's last words warning them to always act in unison, but Elisa ignored her and ate almost all the fruit in the basket until she was completely full. Late that night she began to complain to her sister that she couldn't sleep. Sitting by her sister's side, Alicia listened to her sing absently: 20

> *Pico Rico, far and wide*
> *leaves a mark where others hide.*
> *You who laugh while others perish*
> *please return the thing I cherish.*

After that night, Elisa became a workhorse, walking around with her head bowed down and her eyes to the ground, never asking herself why she was resigned to her unhappy fate, working from sunrise to sunset cleaning and waxing, polishing and shining until everything gleamed, sewing and weaving until her fingertips bled from the slightest contact with silk or linen. At bedtime she would collapse into bed, exhausted, and unbraid her hair, crying because she knew she would once again enter an endless battle with the dark forces of sleeplessness.

When she realized all her care and affection were to no avail, and that her sister was growing more distant, working her fingers to the bone, Alicia sat down to cry, just inside the porch. She knew her sister was dying and she didn't want to be there to see it. She had been sitting for some time wiping her tears on her percale dress, when she heard someone coming and a voice that sang:

> *Soo, soo, roo, soo, soothing fruit*
> *ripe bananas, deep red cherries*
> *passion fruit and juicy pulp.*
> *All these goods I bring to you*
> *chew and swallow till you're full.*
> *Gifts are they for those girls who*
> *promise not to cry and brood*
> *when they see me passing through.*

Alicia looked up and gazed at the funereal horseman. He, in turn, looked steadily at her from on high, his hat firmly placed on his head, his monkey on his left shoulder, and a new basket of fruit strapped to his horse. Alicia thought that if her sister were to eat of that fruit again she might recover her ability to sleep, so she ran to her sister's side to tell her the gentleman with the fruit was there and that she would buy her some fruit if she wanted it. But once having eaten of that fruit, it became impossible to hear the horseman's voice, so Elisa told her sister she must be imagining things, that there was no one there in front of the house. Realizing her hunch was right, Alicia ran to buy some fruit so as to make her sister eat of it once more. But the horseman, guessing what she was up to, spurred his horse on and galloped away, leaving behind a cloud of dust.

That very evening, Alicia hid her braids inside a kelly green silk bonnet and set out in search of the horseman. She was willing to traipse all around the region until she found him. She set about to observe all tracks carefully, for she knew his pasofino horse left such symmetrical marks that they would be impossible to miss. When she got to a town in the east, far from where she lived, she came upon a string of deep, even cuts in the road, and she knew right away she had found the horseman.

He was dozing under a shady elm and, when Alicia saw him there without his hat on, she was able to tell for sure that he was in fact the rich landowner. She approached him silently and when she was close up she realized that he was actually a handsome man: tall, olive-complected, with hair so dark it had a bluish cast. His slow, even breathing enveloped him in an aura of peaceful stillness. Alicia felt drawn to him. But suddenly she remembered her sister's tortured breathing and her nightly battles with sleeplessness and she was overcome with anger. She was convinced that what the dark horseman wanted was to be the only one left in the region able to sleep in peace. She decided to take her revenge. She came closer to him and, in a voice that was as sad as her sister's, she said:

> *Pico Rico, far and wide*
> *leaves a mark where others hide.*
> *You who laugh while others perish*
> *please return the thing I cherish.*

He thought Elisa had come back to join him at last so he let her come close. But as soon as she drew near the monkey jumped on her and pulled off her bonnet, making her two braids fall out onto her chest. When the horseman realized his mistake, he grabbed her by the arms and tried to force her to eat of the fruit, but she resisted, keeping her mouth tightly shut. Then he began to rub the fruit against her skin, covering her from head to toe with the poisonous juices. When Alicia looked down and saw that even to the folds of her voluminous skirts she was soaked in cherry juice, banana pulp, and the purple syrup of the passion fruit, she leaped out of his arms. In a flash, she grabbed the scissors that hung from her waist and snipped off the tip of his nose, leaving just a stump.

He grabbed his nose and howled in pain, forgetting all about Alicia, who ran home right away. Elisa was on the verge of dying when Alicia came flying through the skylight. She went over to her sister and, stroking her forehead, said gently:

"Alicia, my sister, tell me how much you've missed me. Kiss me on the cheek and you'll see how much better you'll feel."

Elisa opened her eyes slowly. Heavy with exhaustion, her limp hair splayed over the pillow, she was the picture of someone beaten by sleeplessness. When she saw her sister, she forced herself to smile and answer:

"Better, my sister, thanks to you."   30

Alicia leaned over to be kissed, but since her face was covered with juice, some drops inevitably fell onto her sister's lips. Elisa then avidly licked her sister's face, arms and back, which were covered with rivulets of fruit juice that looked like sparking drops of red perspiration. When she had quenched her thirst she saw that the folds of her sister's dress were smeared with banana and passion fruit pulp and she hungrily set about eating that, too. She felt better right away and, putting her arms around her sister, she promised never to act on her own again unless both were in complete agreement. And since from that day on the rich landowner was forced to walk around with a stump for a nose, the villagers were able to recognize him even from a distance and they refused to work for him from sunrise to sunset, thus regaining that wonderful ability to fall asleep once more.   1988

INVESTIGATIONS

1. What is the relationship between the twins and the townspeople? Why do the twins remain unaffected by the landowner for much of the story?

2. Why does Elisa's exchange of one of her "golden braids" (para. 19) for the horseman's fruit lead to her "walking around with her head bowed down and her eyes to the ground, never asking herself why she was resigned to her unhappy fate" (para. 21)? Why does the landowner lose his power when he loses his nose? Why does recognizing the landowner enable the villagers to sleep?

3. Locate each instance of thievery, exchange, or gift-giving in the story. What do the changes that accompany these instances suggest about the distinct powers of thievery, exchange, and gift-giving? What similarities exist among this story, Johnson's "Exchange Value," and your response to "Write Before Reading" (p. 784) in the portrayal of these powers?

4. To what extent would Miss Ferenczi ("Gryphon") consider the world of "Pico Rico, Mandorico" a world of "substitute facts"? Describe the "substitute logic" that operates in the story. In other words, describe how the events of the story fit into a pattern that makes consistent sense.

MAY SWENSON

Staring at the Sea
on the Day
of the Death of Another

The long body of the water fills its hollow,
slowly rolls upon its side,
and in the swaddlings of the waves,
their shadowed hollows falling forward with the tide,

like folds of Grecian garments molded to cling   5
around some classic immemorial marble thing,
I see the vanished bodies of friends who have died.

Each form is furled into its hollow,
white in the dark curl,
the sea a mausoleum, with countless shelves,   10
cradling the prone effigies of our unearthly selves,

some of the hollows empty, long niches in the tide.
One of them is mine
and gliding forward, gaping wide.   1990

INVESTIGATIONS

1. What effect does the repetition of "hollow" and "hollows" have on your reading of the poem? What distinct meanings of the word are suggested?
2. Locate instances of repeated sounds in the poem ("l" sounds are one example). How do these sound patterns enhance what the poem says? How, in other words, do these sounds help you *feel* what the poem means?
3. Compare the speaker's ideas about death to yours. In what ways are they similarly irrational?
4. Write a poem in which you address an "ultimate question" while devoting

The daughter of Swedish immigrants, MAY SWENSON (1919–1989) grew up in Logan, Utah, and graduated from Utah State University. Swenson's poetry brought her many honors, including the Shelley Poetry Award and a Guggenheim Fellowship, and was published most recently in *In Other Words: New Poems* (1987).

most of your effort to concretely describing a natural scene. In what ways does the resulting poem surprise you?

DAVID JAMES

Think Death

for Richard Shelton

I don't think Death
has much in store for us —
maybe a sale on silence,
a discount on all the darkness
we can carry.   5
Lowering ourselves into the ground,
blocking out any chance of sun or moonlight,
what do we expect?
Death is a hoarder by nature.
He keeps grabbing, pulling things   10
into him — dogs, insects, fish,
rhinos, trees, us.
A dark mass burrowing
under the surface,
his eyes are always open,   15
his hand forever clenched.

The idea that we live
a second life, or third,
makes for good science fiction
but no one really believes it.   20
We're born, we die.
In and out. Up and down.
Truth and truth.
In death,
the rich and poor,   25

A native of Detroit, Michigan, DAVID JAMES (b. 1955) writes, "The greatest gift we have is our imagination, our ability to generate possibilities in our lives." He is the author of the poetry collection *A Heart Out of This World* (1984).

the cursed and blessed,
all enter through the same door,
wide open from above,
locked tightly from below.

I don't think Death   30
has much to offer us
other than free cold storage,
a stillness close to infinity.
From birth, throughout our lives,
we create an enormous debt,   35
owing our parents, brothers, aunts,
neighbors, teachers, sisters,
husbands, wives, grandparents,
children, priests, strangers.
In death,   40
even someone who is a credit
to society gets tallied
in the loss column.

I don't think Death
wishes us any ill will.   45
He's got a job to do.
He adds up each life,
totaling each breath, each sin,
and when it's time,
he cashes in on us,   50
the ringing from his ancient register
like church bells
in the distance.   1990

INVESTIGATIONS

1. What comfort does the speaker find in his conviction that "the rich and poor, / the cursed and blessed, / all enter through the same door, / wide open from above, / locked tightly from below" (lines 25–29)? What comfort do you find in thinking of death this way?

2. Compare the speaker's attitude toward death with that of the speaker of Swenson's "Staring at the Sea on the Day of the Death of Another." To what extent could the differences in their attitudes be attributed to the fact that one of them has just lost someone close?

3. What would the speaker of Wright's "Yes, But" think of this poem's portrayal of death? The speaker of Gogisgi/Arnett's "Early Song"? The speaker of Anderson's "Heart Fire"?

HELENA MARÍA VIRAMONTES

The Moths

I was fourteen years old when Abuelita[1] requested my help. And it seemed only fair. Abuelita had pulled me through the rages of scarlet fever by placing, removing, and replacing potato slices on the temples of my forehead; she had seen me through several whippings, an arm broken by a dare jump off Tío[2] Enrique's toolshed, puberty, and my first lie. Really, I told Amá,[3] it was only fair.

Not that I was her favorite granddaughter or anything special. I wasn't even pretty or nice like my older sisters and I just couldn't do the girl things they could do. My hands were too big to handle the fineries of crocheting or embroidery and I always pricked my fingers or knotted my colored threads time and time again while my sisters laughed and called me bull hands with their cute waterlike voices. So I began keeping a piece of jagged brick in my sock to bash my sisters or anyone who called me bull hands. Once, while we all sat in the bedroom, I hit Teresa on the forehead, right above her eyebrow and she ran to Amá with her mouth open, her hand over her eye while blood seeped between her fingers. I was used to the whippings by then.

I wasn't respectful either. I even went so far as to doubt the power of Abuelita's slices, the slices she said absorbed my fever. "You're still alive, aren't you?" Abuelita snapped back, her pasty gray eye beaming at me and burning holes in my suspicions. Regretful that I had let secret questions drop out of my mouth, I couldn't look into her eyes. My hands began to fan out, grow like a liar's nose until they hung by my side like low weights. Abuelita made a balm out of dried moth wings and Vicks and rubbed my hands, shaped them back to size and it was the strangest feeling. Like bones melting. Like sun shining through the darkness of your eyelids. I didn't mind helping Abuelita after that, so Amá would always send me over to her.

In the early afternoon Amá would push her hair back, hand me my sweater and shoes, and tell me to go to Mama Luna's. This was to avoid another fight and another whipping, I knew. I would deliver one last direct shot on Marisela's arm and jump out of our house, the slam of the screen door burying her cries of anger, and I'd gladly go help Abuelita plant her wild lilies or jasmine or heliotrope or cilantro or hierbabuena in red Hills Brothers coffee cans. Abuelita

---

[1] Grandmother. [Ed.]   [2] Uncle. [Ed.]   [3] Mama. [Ed.]

HELENA MARÍA VIRAMONTES is the author of *The Moths and Other Stories* (1988) and coeditor of *Chicana Creativity and Criticism: Charting New Frontiers in American Literature* (1988). Born in East Los Angeles in 1954, Viramontes now lives and writes in Los Angeles.

would wait for me at the top step of her porch holding a hammer and nail and empty coffee cans. And although we hardly spoke, hardly looked at each other as we worked over root transplants, I always felt her gray eye on me. It made me feel, in a strange sort of way, safe and guarded and not alone. Like God was supposed to make you feel.

On Abuelita's porch, I would puncture holes in the bottom of the coffee   5
cans with a nail and a precise hit of a hammer. This completed, my job was to fill them with red clay mud from beneath her rose bushes, packing it softly, then making a perfect hole, four fingers round, to nest a sprouting avocado pit, or the spidery sweet potatoes that Abuelita rooted in mayonnaise jars with toothpicks and daily water, or prickly chayotes that produced vines that twisted and wound all over her porch pillars, crawling to the roof, up and over the roof, and down the other side, making her small brick house look like it was cradled within the vines that grew pear-shaped squashes ready for the pick, ready to be steamed with onions and cheese and butter. The roots would burst out of the rusted coffee cans and search for a place to connect. I would then feed the seedlings with water.

But this was a different kind of help, Amá said, because Abuelita was dying. Looking into her gray eye, then into her brown one, the doctor said it was just a matter of days. And so it seemed only fair that these hands she had melted and formed found use in rubbing her caving body with alcohol and marihuana, rubbing her arms and legs, turning her face to the window so that she could watch the Bird of Paradise blooming or smell the scent of clove in the air. I toweled her face frequently and held her hand for hours. Her gray wiry hair hung over the mattress. Since I could remember, she'd kept her long hair in braids. Her mouth was vacant and when she slept, her eyelids never closed all the way. Up close, you could see her gray eye beaming out the window, staring hard as if to remember everything. I never kissed her. I left the window open when I went to the market.

Across the street from Jay's Market there was a chapel. I never knew its denomination, but I went in just the same to search for candles. I sat down on one of the pews because there were none. After I cleaned my fingernails, I looked up at the high ceiling. I had forgotten the vastness of these places, the coolness of the marble pillars and the frozen statues with blank eyes. I was alone. I knew why I had never returned.

That was one of Apá's biggest complaints. He would pound his hands on the table, rocking the sugar dish or spilling a cup of coffee, and scream that if I didn't go to mass every Sunday to save my goddamn sinning soul, then I had no reason to go out of the house, period. Punto final. He would grab my arm and dig his nails into me to make sure I understood the importance of catechism. Did he make himself clear? Then he strategically directed his anger at Amá for her lousy ways of bringing up daughters, being disrespectful and unbelieving, and my older sisters would pull me aside and tell me if I didn't get to mass right this minute, they were all going to kick the holy shit out of me. Why am

I so selfish? Can't you see what it's doing to Amá, you idiot? So I would wash my feet and stuff them in my black Easter shoes that shone with Vaseline, grab a missal and veil, and wave good-bye to Amá.

I would walk slowly down Lorena to First to Evergreen, counting the cracks on the cement. On Evergreen I would turn left and walk to Abuelita's. I liked her porch because it was shielded by the vines of the chayotes and I could get a good look at the people and car traffic on Evergreen without them knowing. I would jump up the porch steps, knock on the screen door as I wiped my feet, and call Abuelita? mi Abuelita? As I opened the door and stuck my head in, I would catch the gagging scent of toasting chile on the placa. When I entered the sala, she would greet me from the kitchen, wringing her hands in her apron. I'd sit at the corner of the table to keep from being in her way. The chiles made my eyes water. Am I crying? No, Mama Luna, I'm sure not crying. I don't like going to mass, but my eyes watered anyway, the tears dropping on the tablecloth like candle wax. Abuelita lifted the burnt chiles from the fire and sprinkled water on them until the skins began to separate. Placing them in front of me, she turned to check the menudo. I peeled the skins off and put the flimsy, limp-looking green and yellow chiles in the molcajete and began to crush and crush and twist and crush the heart out of the tomato, the clove of garlic, the stupid chiles that made me cry, crushed them until they turned into liquid under my bull hand. With a wooden spoon, I scraped hard to destroy the guilt, and my tears were gone. I put the bowl of chile next to a vase filled with freshly cut roses. Abuelita touched my hand and pointed to the bowl of menudo that steamed in front of me. I spooned some chile into the menudo and rolled a corn tortilla thin with the palms of my hands. As I ate, a fine Sunday breeze entered the kitchen and a rose petal calmly feathered down to the table.

I left the chapel without blessing myself and walked to Jay's. Most of the time Jay didn't have much of anything. The tomatoes were always soft and the cans of Campbell soups had rusted spots on them. There was dust on the tops of cereal boxes. I picked up what I needed: rubbing alcohol, five cans of chicken broth, a big bottle of Pine Sol. At first Jay got mad because I thought I had forgotten the money. But it was there all the time, in my back pocket.

When I returned from the market, I heard Amá crying in Abuelita's kitchen. She looked up at me with puffy eyes. I placed the bags of groceries on the table and began putting the cans of soup away. Amá sobbed quietly. I never kissed her. After a while, I patted her on the back for comfort. Finally: "¿Y mi Amá?"[4] she asked in a whisper, then choked again and cried into her apron.

Abuelita fell off the bed twice yesterday, I said, knowing that I shouldn't have said it and wondering why I wanted to say it because it only made Amá cry harder. I guess I became angry and just so tired of the quarrels and beatings and unanswered prayers and my hands just there hanging helplessly by my side. Amá looked at me again, confused, angry, and her eyes were filled with

10

[4] "And my mother?" [Ed.]

sorrow. I went outside and sat on the porch swing and watched the people pass. I sat there until she left. I dozed off repeating the words to myself like rosary prayers: when do you stop giving when do you start giving when do you . . . and when my hands fell from my lap, I awoke to catch them. The sun was setting, an orange glow, and I knew Abuelita was hungry.

There comes a time when the sun is defiant. Just about the time when moods change, inevitable seasons of a day, transitions from one color to another, that hour or minute or second when the sun is finally defeated, finally sinks into the realization that it cannot with all its power to heal or burn, exist forever, there comes an illumination where the sun and earth meet, a final burst of burning red orange fury reminding us that although endings are inevitable, they are necessary for rebirths, and when that time came, just when I switched on the light in the kitchen to open Abuelita's can of soup, it was probably then that she died.

The room smelled of Pine Sol and vomit and Abuelita had defecated the remains of her cancerous stomach. She had turned to the window and tried to speak, but her mouth remained open and speechless. I heard you, Abuelita, I said, stroking her cheek, I heard you. I opened the windows of the house and let the soup simmer and overboil on the stove. I turned the stove off and poured the soup down the sink. From the cabinet I got a tin basin, filled it with lukewarm water and carried it carefully to the room. I went to the linen closet and took out some modest bleached white towels. With the sacredness of a priest preparing his vestments, I unfolded the towels one by one on my shoulders. I removed the sheets and blankets from her bed and peeled off her thick flannel nightgown. I toweled her puzzled face, stretching out the wrinkles, removing the coils of her neck, toweled her shoulders and breasts. Then I changed the water. I returned to towel the creases of her stretch-marked stomach, her sporadic vaginal hairs, and her sagging thighs. I removed the lint from between her toes and noticed a mapped birthmark on the fold of her buttock. The scars on her back which were as thin as the life lines on the palms of her hands made me realize how little I really knew of Abuelita. I covered her with a thin blanket and went into the bathroom. I washed my hands, and turned on the tub faucets and watched the water pour into the tub with vitality and steam. When it was full, I turned off the water and undressed. Then, I went to get Abuelita.

She was not as heavy as I thought and when I carried her in my arms, her body fell into a V, and yet my legs were tired, shaky, and I felt as if the distance between the bedroom and bathroom was miles and years away. Amá, where are you?

I stepped into the bathtub one leg first, then the other. I bent my knees slowly to descend into the water slowly so I wouldn't scald her skin. There, there, Abuelita, I said, cradling her, smoothing her as we descended, I heard you. Her hair fell back and spread across the water like eagle's wings. The water in the tub overflowed and poured onto the tile of the floor. Then the moths came. Small, gray ones that came from her soul and out through her mouth fluttering to light, circling the single dull light bulb of the bathroom. Dying is lonely and I wanted to go to where the moths were, stay with her and plant chayotes whose vines would crawl up her fingers and into the clouds; I wanted to rest my head on her chest with her stroking my hair, telling me about the moths that lay within the soul and slowly eat the spirit up; I wanted to return to the waters of the womb with her so that we would never be alone again. I wanted. I wanted my Amá. I removed a few strands of hair from Abuelita's face and held her small light head within the hollow of my neck. The bathroom was filled with moths, and for the first time in a long time I cried, rocking us, crying for her, for me, for Amá, the sobs emerging from the depths of anguish, the misery of feeling half born, sobbing until finally the sobs rippled into circles and circles of sadness and relief. There, there, I said to Abuelita, rocking us gently, there, there.   1985

INVESTIGATIONS

1. In the story's first three paragraphs, Mama Luna cures scarlet fever with potato slices and the narrator's enlarged hands with "a balm . . . of dried moth wings and Vicks" (para. 3). Do you think these cures unusual or surprising? Why or why not? Write two or three paragraphs describing an "unscientific" practice that has helped cure you of a problem. How do you explain this cure?

2. What does the narrator get in Mama Luna's house that she doesn't get in church? After looking up "catechism" in the dictionary, write a catechism that would apply to the "church of Mama Luna."

3. What do the moths at story's end have to do with the narrator's "feeling half born" (para. 16)? In what sense can Mama Luna's death be seen as her last gift to the narrator?

In the Park

You have forty-nine days between
death and rebirth if you're a Buddhist.
Even the smallest soul could swim
the English Channel in that time
or climb, like a ten-month-old child,   5
every step of the Washington Monument
to travel across, up, down, over or through
— you won't know till you get there which to do.

He laid on me for a few seconds
said Roscoe Black, who lived to tell   10
about his skirmish with a grizzly bear
in Glacier Park. *He laid on me*
not doing anything. I could feel
his heart beating against my heart.
Never mind *lie* and *lay,* the whole world   15
confuses them. For Roscoe Black you might say
all forty-nine days flew by.

I was raised on the Old Testament.
In it God talks to Moses, Noah,
Samuel, and they answer.   20
People confer with angels. Certain
animals converse with humans.
It's a simple world, full of crossovers.
Heaven's an airy Somewhere, and God
has a nasty temper when provoked,   25
but if there's a Hell, little is made of it.
No longtailed Devil, no eternal fire,
and no choosing what to come back as.
When the grizzly bear appears, he lies/lays down
on atheist and zealot. In the pitch-dark   30
each of us waits for him in Glacier Park.   1989

Winner of the 1973 Pulitzer Prize, MAXINE KUMIN has published eleven books of poetry, including *Nurture* (1989) and *Looking for Luck* (1991), as well as essays, four novels, and more than twenty children's books. Born in Philadelphia in 1925, Kumin has lived for many years on a horse farm in New Hampshire.

INVESTIGATIONS

1. Why do you think the speaker details particular beliefs of Buddhism and Judaism? What is the point of contrasting these two faiths?
2. The speaker quotes Roscoe Black's account of his "skirmish with a grizzly bear" (lines 9, 12–14). Why is this more effective than the speaker simply describing the encounter?
3. Consider the image of the grizzly bear in this poem. What about Roscoe's encounter with the bear prompts the speaker to associate it with religious imagery? What are the differences between Roscoe's encounter with the bear and the religious experiences described in the poem?

RAYMOND CARVER

Cathedral

This blind man, an old friend of my wife's, he was on his way to spend the night. His wife had died. So he was visiting the dead wife's relatives in Connecticut. He called my wife from his in-laws'. Arrangements were made. He would come by train, a five-hour trip, and my wife would meet him at the station. She hadn't seen him since she worked for him one summer in Seattle ten years ago. But she and the blind man had kept in touch. They made tapes and mailed them back and forth. I wasn't enthusiastic about his visit. He was no one I knew. And his being blind bothered me. My idea of blindness came from the movies. In the movies, the blind moved slowly and never laughed. Sometimes they were led by seeing-eye dogs. A blind man in my house was not something I looked forward to.

That summer in Seattle she had needed a job. She didn't have any money. The man she was going to marry at the end of the summer was in officers' training school. He didn't have any money, either. But she was in love with the guy, and he was in love with her, etc. She'd seen something in the paper: HELP WANTED — *Reading to Blind Man*, and a telephone number. She phoned and went over, was hired on the spot. She'd worked with this blind man all summer. She read stuff to him, case studies, reports, that sort of thing. She helped him

Born in Clatskanie, Oregon, RAYMOND CARVER (1938–1988) was a short-story writer and poet whose books include the poetry collection *A New Path to the Waterfall* (1989) and *Where I'm Calling From* (1988), a collection of stories. Surprised at the praise he'd received for vividly portraying working-class characters, Carver once said, "God, the country is filled with these people, They're good people. People doing the best they could."

organize his little office in the county social-service department. They'd become good friends, my wife and the blind man. How do I know these things? She told me. And she told me something else. On her last day in the office, the blind man asked if he could touch her face. She agreed to this. She told me he touched his fingers to every part of her face, her nose — even her neck! She never forgot it. She even tried to write a poem about it. She was always trying to write a poem. She wrote a poem or two every year, usually after something really important had happened to her.

When we first started going out together, she showed me the poem. In the poem, she recalled his fingers and the way they had moved around over her face. In the poem, she talked about what she had felt at the time, about what went through her mind when the blind man touched her nose and lips. I can remember I didn't think much of the poem. Of course, I didn't tell her that. Maybe I just don't understand poetry. I admit it's not the first thing I reach for when I pick up something to read.

Anyway, this man who'd first enjoyed her favors, the officer-to-be, he'd been her childhood sweetheart. So okay. I'm saying that at the end of the summer she let the blind man run his hands over her face, said good-bye to him, married her childhood etc., who was now a commissioned officer, and she moved away from Seattle. But they'd kept in touch, she and the blind man. She made the first contact after a year or so. She called him up one night from an Air Force base in Alabama. She wanted to talk. They talked. He asked her to send him a tape and tell him about her life. She did this. She sent the tape. On the tape, she told the blind man about her husband and about their life together in the military. She told the blind man she loved her husband but she didn't like it where they lived and she didn't like it that he was a part of the military-industrial thing. She told the blind man she'd written a poem and he was in it. She told him that she was writing a poem about what it was like to be an Air Force officer's wife. The poem wasn't finished yet. She was still writing it. The blind man made a tape. He sent her the tape. She made a tape. This went on for years. My wife's officer was posted to one base and then another. She sent tapes from Moody AFB, McGuire, McConnell, and finally Travis, near Sacramento, where one night she got to feeling lonely and cut off from people she kept losing in that moving-around life. She got to feeling she couldn't go it another step. She went in and swallowed all the pills and capsules in the medicine chest and washed them down with a bottle of gin. Then she got into a hot bath and passed out.

But instead of dying, she got sick. She threw up. Her officer — why should   5
he have a name? he was the childhood sweetheart, and what more does he want? — came home from somewhere, found her, and called the ambulance. In time, she put it all on a tape and sent the tape to the blind man. Over the years, she put all kinds of stuff on tapes and sent the tapes off lickety-split. Next to writing a poem every year, I think it was her chief means of recreation. On one tape, she told the blind man she'd decided to live away from her officer for a time. On another tape, she told him about her divorce. She and I began going out, and of course she told her blind man about it. She told him every-

thing, or so it seemed to me. Once she asked me if I'd like to hear the latest tape from the blind man. This was a year ago. I was on the tape, she said. So I said okay, I'd listen to it. I got us drinks and we settled down in the living room. We made ready to listen. First she inserted the tape into the player and adjusted a couple of dials. Then she pushed a lever. The tape squeaked and someone began to talk in this loud voice. She lowered the volume. After a few minutes of harmless chitchat, I heard my own name in the mouth of this stranger, this blind man I didn't even know! And then this: "From all you've said about him, I can only conclude — " But we were interrupted, a knock at the door, something, and we didn't ever get back to the tape. Maybe it was just as well. I'd heard all I wanted to.

Now this same blind man was coming to sleep in my house.

"Maybe I could take him bowling," I said to my wife. She was at the draining board doing scalloped potatoes. She put down the knife she was using and turned around.

"If you love me," she said, "you can do this for me. If you don't love me, okay. But if you had a friend, any friend, and the friend came to visit, I'd make him feel comfortable." She wiped her hands with the dish towel.

"I don't have any blind friends," I said.

"You don't have *any* friends," she said. "Period. Besides," she said, "god-   10 damn it, his wife's just died! Don't you understand that? The man's lost his wife!"

I didn't answer. She'd told me a little about the blind man's wife. Her name was Beulah. Beulah! That's a name for a colored woman.

"Was his wife a Negro?" I asked.

"Are you crazy?" my wife said. "Have you just flipped or something?" She picked up a potato. I saw it hit the floor, then roll under the stove. "What's wrong with you?" she said. "Are you drunk?"

"I'm just asking," I said.

Right then my wife filled me in with more detail than I cared to know. I   15 made a drink and sat at the kitchen table to listen. Pieces of the story began to fall into place.

Beulah had gone to work for the blind man the summer after my wife had stopped working for him. Pretty soon Beulah and the blind man had themselves a church wedding. It was a little wedding — who'd want to go to such a wedding in the first place? — just the two of them, plus the minister and the minister's wife. But it was a church wedding just the same. It was what Beulah had wanted, he'd said. But even then Beulah must have been carrying the cancer in her glands. After they had been inseparable for eight years — my wife's word, *inseparable* — Beulah's health went into a rapid decline. She died in a Seattle hospital room, the blind man sitting beside the bed and holding on to her hand. They'd married, lived and worked together, slept together — had sex, sure — and then the blind man had to bury her. All this without his having ever seen what the goddamned woman looked like. It was beyond my under-standing. Hearing this, I felt sorry for the blind man for a little bit. And then

I found myself thinking what a pitiful life this woman must have led. Imagine a woman who could never see herself as she was seen in the eyes of her loved one. A woman who could go on day after day and never receive the smallest compliment from her beloved. A woman whose husband could never read the expression on her face, be it misery or something better. Someone who could wear makeup or not — what difference to him? She could, if she wanted, wear green eye-shadow around one eye, a straight pin in her nostril, yellow slacks, and purple shoes, no matter. And then to slip off into death, the blind man's hand on her hand, his blind eyes streaming tears — I'm imagining now — her last thought maybe this: that he never even knew what she looked like, and she on an express to the grave. Robert was left with a small insurance policy and half of a twenty-peso Mexican coin. The other half of the coin went into the box with her. Pathetic.

So when the time rolled around, my wife went to the depot to pick him up. With nothing to do but wait — sure, I blamed him for that — I was having a drink and watching the TV when I heard the car pull into the drive. I got up from the sofa with my drink and went to the window to have a look.

I saw my wife laughing as she parked the car. I saw her get out of the car and shut the door. She was still wearing a smile. Just amazing. She went around to the other side of the car to where the blind man was already starting to get out. This blind man, feature this, he was wearing a full beard! A beard on a blind man! Too much, I say. The blind man reached into the back seat and dragged out a suitcase. My wife took his arm, shut the car door, and, talking all the way, moved him down the drive and then up the steps to the front porch. I turned off the TV. I finished my drink, rinsed the glass, dried my hands. Then I went to the door.

My wife said, "I want you to meet Robert. Robert, this is my husband. I've told you all about him." She was beaming. She had this blind man by his coat sleeve.

The blind man let go of his suitcase and up came his hand.   20

I took it. He squeezed hard, held my hand, and then he let it go.

"I feel like we've already met," he boomed.

"Likewise," I said. I didn't know what else to say. Then I said, "Welcome. I've heard a lot about you." We began to move then, a little group, from the porch into the living room, my wife guiding him by the arm. The blind man was carrying his suitcase in his other hand. My wife said things like, "To your left here, Robert. That's right. Now watch it, there's a chair. That's it. Sit down right here. This is the sofa. We just bought this sofa two weeks ago."

I started to say something about the old sofa. I'd liked that old sofa. But I didn't say anything. Then I wanted to say something else, small-talk, about the scenic ride along the Hudson. How going *to* New York, you should sit on the right-hand side of the train, and coming *from* New York, the left-hand side.

"Did you have a good train ride?" I said. "Which side of the train did you   25
sit on, by the way?"

"What a question, which side!" my wife said. "What's it matter which side?" she said.

"I just asked," I said.

"Right side," the blind man said. "I hadn't been on a train in nearly forty years. Not since I was a kid. With my folks. That's been a long time. I'd nearly forgotten the sensation. I have winter in my beard now," he said. "So I've been told, anyway. Do I look distinguished, my dear?" the blind man said to my wife.

"You look distinguished, Robert," she said. "Robert," she said. "Robert, it's just so good to see you."

My wife finally took her eyes off the blind man and looked at me. I had the feeling she didn't like what she saw. I shrugged.   30

I've never met, or personally known, anyone who was blind. This blind man was late forties, a heavyset, balding man with stooped shoulders, as if he carried a great weight there. He wore brown slacks, brown shoes, a light-brown shirt, a tie, a sports coat. Spiffy. He also had this full beard. But he didn't use a cane and he didn't wear dark glasses. I'd always thought dark glasses were a must for the blind. Fact was, I wished he had a pair. At first glance, his eyes looked like anyone else's eyes. But if you looked close, there was something different about them. Too much white in the iris, for one thing, and the pupils seemed to move around in the sockets without his knowing it or being able to stop it. Creepy. As I stared at his face, I saw the left pupil turn in toward his nose while the other made an effort to keep in one place. But it was only an effort, for that eye was on the roam without his knowing it or wanting it to be.

I said, "Let me get you a drink. What's your pleasure? We have a little of everything. It's one of our pastimes."

"Bub, I'm a scotch man myself," he said fast enough in this big voice.

"Right," I said. Bub! "Sure you are. I knew it."

He let his fingers touch his suitcase, which was sitting alongside the sofa.   35
He was taking his bearings. I didn't blame him for that.

"I'll move that up to your room," my wife said.

"No, that's fine," the blind man said loudly. "It can go up when I go up."

"A little water with the scotch?" I said.

"Very little," he said.

"I knew it," I said.   40

He said, "Just a tad. The Irish actor, Barry Fitzgerald? I'm like that fellow. When I drink water, Fitzgerald said, I drink water. When I drink whiskey, I drink whiskey." My wife laughed. The blind man brought his hand up under his beard. He lifted his beard slowly and let it drop.

I did the drinks, three big glasses of scotch with a splash of water in each. Then we made ourselves comfortable and talked about Robert's travels. First the long flight from the West Coast to Connecticut, we covered that. Then from Connecticut up here by train. We had another drink concerning that leg of the trip.

I remembered having read somewhere that the blind didn't smoke because, as speculation had it, they couldn't see the smoke they exhaled. I thought I knew that much and that much only about blind people. But this blind man smoked his cigarette down to the nubbin and then lit another one. This blind man filled his ashtray and my wife emptied it.

When we sat down at the table for dinner, we had another drink. My wife heaped Robert's plate with cube steak, scalloped potatoes, green beans. I buttered him two slices of bread. I said, "Here's bread and butter for you." I swallowed some of my drink. "Now let us pray," I said, and the blind man lowered his head. My wife looked at me, her mouth agape. "Pray the phone won't ring and the food doesn't get cold," I said.

We dug in. We ate everything there was to eat on the table. We ate like there was no tomorrow. We didn't talk. We ate. We scarfed. We grazed that table. We were into serious eating. The blind man had right away located his foods, he knew just where everything was on his plate. I watched with admiration as he used his knife and fork on the meat. He'd cut two pieces of meat, fork the meat into his mouth, and then go all out for the scalloped potatoes, the beans next, and then he'd tear off a hunk of buttered bread and eat that. He'd follow this up with a big drink of milk. It didn't seem to bother him to use his fingers once in a while, either. 45

We finished everything, including half a strawberry pie. For a few moments, we sat as if stunned. Sweat beaded on our faces. Finally, we got up from the table and left the dirty plates. We didn't look back. We took ourselves into the living room and sank into our places again. Robert and my wife sat on the sofa. I took the big chair. We had us two or three more drinks while they talked about the major things that had come to pass for them in the past ten years. For the most part, I just listened. Now and then I joined in. I didn't want him to think I'd left the room, and I didn't want her to think I was feeling left out. They talked of things that had happened to them — to them! — these past ten years. I waited in vain to hear my name on my wife's sweet lips: "And then my dear husband came into my life" — something like that. But I heard nothing of the sort. More talk of Robert. Robert had done a little of everything, it seemed, a regular blind jack-of-all-trades. But most recently he and his wife had had an Amway distributorship, from which, I gathered, they'd earned their living, such as it was. The blind man was also a ham radio operator. He talked in his loud voice about conversations he'd had with fellow operators in Guam, in the Philippines, in Alaska, and even in Tahiti. He said he'd have a lot of friends there if he ever wanted to go visit those places. From time to time, he'd turn his blind face toward me, put his hand under his beard, ask me something. How long had I been in my present position? (Three years.) Did I like my work? (I didn't.) Was I going to stay with it? (What were the options?) Finally, when I thought he was beginning to run down, I got up and turned on the TV.

My wife looked at me with irritation. She was heading toward a boil. Then she looked at the blind man and said, "Robert, do you have a TV?"

The blind man said, "My dear, I have two TVs. I have a color set and a black-and-white thing, an old relic. It's funny, but if I turn the TV on, and I'm always turning it on, I turn on the color set. It's funny, don't you think?"

I didn't know what to say to that. I had absolutely nothing to say to that. No opinion. So I watched the news program and tried to listen to what the announcer was saying.

"This is a color TV," the blind man said. "Don't ask me how, but I can tell."

"We traded up a while ago," I said.

The blind man had another taste of his drink. He lifted his beard, sniffed it, and let it fall. He leaned forward on the sofa. He positioned his ashtray on the coffee table, then put the lighter to his cigarette. He leaned back on the sofa and crossed his legs at the ankles.

My wife covered her mouth, and then she yawned. She stretched. She said, "I think I'll go upstairs and put on my robe. I think I'll change into something else. Robert, you make yourself comfortable," she said.

"I'm comfortable," the blind man said.

"I want you to feel comfortable in this house," she said.

"I am comfortable," the blind man said.

After she'd left the room, he and I listened to the weather report and then to the sports roundup. By that time, she'd been gone so long I didn't know if she was going to come back. I thought she might have gone to bed. I wished she'd come back downstairs. I didn't want to be left alone with a blind man. I asked him if he wanted another drink, and he said sure. Then I asked if he wanted to smoke some dope with me. I said I'd just rolled a number. I hadn't, but I planned to do so in about two shakes.

"I'll try some with you," he said.

"Damn right," I said. "That's the stuff."

I got our drinks and sat down on the sofa with him. Then I rolled us two fat numbers. I lit one and passed it. I brought it to his fingers. He took it and inhaled.

"Hold it as long as you can," I said. I could tell he didn't know the first thing.

My wife came back downstairs wearing her pink robe and her pink slippers.

"What do I smell?" she said.

"We thought we'd have us some cannabis," I said.

My wife gave me a savage look. Then she looked at the blind man and said, "Robert, I didn't know you smoked."

He said, "I do now, my dear. There's a first time for everything. But I don't feel anything yet."

"This stuff is pretty mellow," I said. "This stuff is mild. It's dope you can reason with," I said. "It doesn't mess you up."

"Not much it doesn't, bub," he said, and laughed.

My wife sat on the sofa between the blind man and me. I passed her the number. She took it and toked and then passed it back to me. "Which way is this going?" she said. Then she said, "I shouldn't be smoking this. I can hardly keep my eyes open as it is. That dinner did me in. I shouldn't have eaten so much."

"It was the strawberry pie," the blind man said. "That's what did it," he   70
said, and he laughed his big laugh. Then he shook his head.

"There's more strawberry pie," I said.

"Do you want some more, Robert?" my wife said.

"Maybe in a little while," he said.

We gave our attention to the TV. My wife yawned again. She said, "Your bed is made up when you feel like going to bed, Robert. I know you must have had a long day. When you're ready to go to bed, say so." She pulled his arm. "Robert?"

He came to and said, "I've had a real nice time. This beats tapes, doesn't   75
it?"

I said, "Coming at you," and I put the number between his fingers. He inhaled, held the smoke, and then let it go. It was like he'd been doing it since he was nine years old.

"Thanks, bub," he said. "But I think this is all for me. I think I'm beginning to feel it," he said. He held the burning roach out for my wife.

"Same here," she said. "Ditto. Me, too." She took the roach and passed it to me. "I may just sit here for a while between you two guys with my eyes closed. But don't let me bother you, okay? Either one of you. If it bothers you, say so. Otherwise, I may just sit here with my eyes closed until you're ready to go to bed," she said. "Your bed's made up, Robert, when you're ready. It's right next to our room at the top of the stairs. We'll show you up when you're ready. You wake me up now, you guys, if I fall asleep." She said that and then she closed her eyes and went to sleep.

The news program ended. I got up and changed the channel. I sat back down on the sofa. I wished my wife hadn't pooped out. Her head lay across the back of the sofa, her mouth open. She'd turned so that her robe had slipped away from her legs, exposing a juicy thigh. I reached to draw her robe back over her, and it was then that I glanced at the blind man. What the hell! I flipped the robe open again.

"You say when you want some strawberry pie," I said.   80

"I will," he said.

I said, "Are you tired? Do you want me to take you up to your bed? Are you ready to hit the hay?"

"Not yet," he said. "No, I'll stay up with you, bub. If that's all right. I'll stay up until you're ready to turn in. We haven't had a chance to talk. Know what I mean? I feel like me and her monopolized the evening." He lifted his beard and he let it fall. He picked up his cigarettes and his lighter.

"That's all right," I said. Then I said, "I'm glad for the company."

And I guess I was. Every night I smoked dope and stayed up as long as I   85
could before I fell asleep. My wife and I hardly ever went to bed at the same time. When I did go to sleep, I had these dreams. Sometimes I'd wake up from one of them, my heart going crazy.

Something about the church and the Middle Ages was on the TV. Not your run-of-the-mill TV fare. I wanted to watch something else. I turned to the other channels. But there was nothing on them, either. So I turned back to the first channel and apologized.

"Bub, it's all right," the blind man said. "It's fine with me. Whatever you want to watch is okay. I'm always learning something. Learning never ends. It won't hurt me to learn something tonight. I got ears," he said.

We didn't say anything for a time. He was leaning forward with his head turned at me, his right ear aimed in the direction of the set. Very disconcerting. Now and then his eyelids drooped and then they snapped open again. Now and then he put his fingers into his beard and tugged, like he was thinking about something he was hearing on the television.

On the screen, a group of men wearing cowls was being set upon and tormented by men dressed in skeleton costumes and men dressed as devils. The men dressed as devils wore devil masks, horns, and long tails. This pageant was part of a procession. The Englishman who was narrating the thing said it took place in Spain once a year. I tried to explain to the blind man what was happening.

"Skeletons," he said. "I know about skeletons," he said, and he nodded.   90

The TV showed this one cathedral. Then there was a long, slow look at another one. Finally, the picture switched to the famous one in Paris, with its flying buttresses and its spires reaching up to the clouds. The camera pulled away to show the whole of the cathedral rising above the skyline.

There were times when the Englishman who was telling the thing would shut up, would simply let the camera move around over the cathedrals. Or else the camera would tour the countryside, men in fields walking behind oxen. I waited as long as I could. Then I felt I had to say something. I said, "They're showing the outside of this cathedral now. Gargoyles. Little statues carved to look like monsters. Now I guess they're in Italy. Yeah, they're in Italy. There's paintings on the walls of this one church."

"Are those fresco paintings, bub?" he asked, and he sipped from his drink.

I reached for my glass. But it was empty. I tried to remember what I could remember. "You're asking me are those frescoes?" I said. "That's a good question. I don't know."

The camera moved to a cathedral outside Lisbon. The differences in the   95
Portuguese cathedral compared with the French and Italian were not that great. But they were there. Mostly the interior stuff. Then something occurred to me, and I said, "Something has occurred to me. Do you have any idea what a cathedral is? What they look like, that is? Do you follow me? If somebody says cathedral to you, do you have any notion what they're talking about? Do you know the difference between that and a Baptist church, say?"

He let the smoke dribble from his mouth. "I know they took hundreds of workers fifty or a hundred years to build," he said. "I just heard the man say that, of course. I know generations of the same families worked on a cathedral. I heard him say that, too. The men who began their life's work on them, they never lived to see the completion of their work. In that wise, bub, they're no different from the rest of us, right?" He laughed. Then his eyelids drooped again. His head nodded. He seemed to be snoozing. Maybe he was imagining himself in Portugal. The TV was showing another cathedral now. This one was in Germany. The Englishman's voice droned on. "Cathedrals," the blind man said. He sat up and rolled his head back and forth. "If you want the truth, bub, that's about all I know. What I just said. What I heard him say. But maybe you could describe one to me? I wish you'd do it. I'd like that. If you want to know. I really don't have a good idea."

I stared hard at the shot of the cathedral on the TV. How could I even begin to describe it? But say my life depended on it. Say my life was being threatened by an insane guy who said I had to do it or else.

I stared some more at the cathedral before the picture flipped off into the countryside. There was no use. I turned to the blind man and said, "To begin with, they're very tall." I was looking around the room for clues. "They reach way up. Up and up. Toward the sky. They're so big, some of them, they have to have these supports. To help hold them up, so to speak. These supports are called buttresses. They remind me of viaducts, for some reason. But maybe you don't know viaducts, either? Sometimes the cathedrals have devils and such carved into the front. Sometimes lords and ladies. Don't ask me why this is," I said.

He was nodding. The whole upper part of his body seemed to be moving back and forth.

"I'm not doing so good, am I?" I said.   100

He stopped nodding and leaned forward on the edge of the sofa. As he listened to me, he was running his fingers through his beard. I wasn't getting through to him, I could see that. But he waited for me to go on just the same. He nodded, like he was trying to encourage me. I tried to think what else to say. "They're really big," I said. "They're massive. They're built of stone. Marble, too, sometimes. In those olden days, when they built cathedrals, men wanted to be close to God. In those olden days, God was an important part of everyone's life. You could tell this from their cathedral-building. I'm sorry," I said, "but it looks like that's the best I can do for you. I'm just no good at it."

"That's all right, bub," the blind man said. "Hey, listen. I hope you don't mind my asking you. Can I ask you something? Let me ask you a simple question, yes or no. I'm just curious and there's no offense. You're my host. But let me ask if you are in any way religious? You don't mind my asking?"

I shook my head. He couldn't see that, though. A wink is the same as a nod to a blind man. "I guess I don't believe in it. In anything. Sometimes it's hard. You know what I'm saying?"

"Sure, I do," he said.

"Right," I said.

The Englishman was still holding forth. My wife sighed in her sleep. She drew a long breath and went on with her sleeping.

"You'll have to forgive me," I said. "But I can't tell you what a cathedral looks like. It just isn't in me to do it. I can't do any more than I've done."

The blind man sat very still, his head down, as he listened to me.

I said, "The truth is, cathedrals don't mean anything special to me. Nothing. Cathedrals. They're something to look at on late-night TV. That's all they are."

It was then that the blind man cleared his throat. He brought something up. He took a handkerchief from his back pocket. Then he said, "I get it, bub. It's okay. It happens. Don't worry about it," he said. "Hey, listen to me. Will you do me a favor? I got an idea. Why don't you find us some heavy paper? And a pen. We'll do something. We'll draw one together. Get us a pen and some heavy paper. Go on, bub, get the stuff," he said.

So I went upstairs. My legs felt like they didn't have any strength in them. They felt like they did after I'd done some running. In my wife's room, I looked around. I found some ballpoints in a little basket on her table. And then I tried to think where to look for the kind of paper he was talking about.

Downstairs, in the kitchen, I found a shopping bag with onion skins in the bottom of the bag. I emptied the bag and shook it. I brought it into the living room and sat down with it near his legs. I moved some things, smoothed the wrinkles from the bag, spread it out on the coffee table.

The blind man got down from the sofa and sat next to me on the carpet.

He ran his fingers over the paper. He went up and down the sides of the paper. The edges, even the edges. He fingered the corners.

"All right," he said. "All right, let's do her."

He found my hand, the hand with the pen. He closed his hand over my hand. "Go ahead, bub, draw," he said. "Draw. You'll see. I'll follow along with you. It'll be okay. Just begin now like I'm telling you. You'll see. Draw," the blind man said.

So I began. First I drew a box that looked like a house. It could have been the house I lived in. Then I put a roof on it. At either end of the roof, I drew spires. Crazy.

"Swell," he said. "Terrific. You're doing fine," he said. "Never thought anything like this could happen in your lifetime, did you, bub? Well, it's a strange life, we all know that. Go on now. Keep it up."

I put in windows with arches. I drew flying buttresses. I hung great doors. I couldn't stop. The TV station went off the air. I put down the pen and closed and opened my fingers. The blind man felt around over the paper. He moved the tips of his fingers over the paper, all over what I had drawn, and he nodded.

"Doing fine," the blind man said.

I took up the pen again, and he found my hand. I kept at it. I'm no artist. But I kept drawing just the same.

My wife opened up her eyes and gazed at us. She sat up on the sofa, her robe hanging open. She said, "What are you doing? Tell me, I want to know."

I didn't answer her.

The blind man said, "We're drawing a cathedral. Me and him are working on it. Press hard," he said to me. "That's right. That's good," he said. "Sure. You got it, bub. I can tell. You didn't think you could. But you can, can't you? You're cooking with gas now. You know what I'm saying? We're going to really have us something here in a minute. How's the old arm?" he said. "Put some people in there now. What's a cathedral without people?"

My wife said, "What's going on? Robert, what are you doing? What's going on?" 125

"It's all right," he said to her. "Close your eyes now," the blind man said to me.

I did it. I closed them just like he said.

"Are they closed?" he said. "Don't fudge."

"They're closed," I said.

"Keep them that way," he said. He said, "Don't stop now. Draw." 130

So we kept on with it. His fingers rode my fingers as my hand went over the paper. It was like nothing else in my life up to now.

Then he said, "I think that's it. I think you got it," he said. "Take a look. What do you think?"

But I had my eyes closed. I thought I'd keep them that way for a little longer. I thought it was something I ought to do.

"Well?" he said. "Are you looking?"

My eyes were still closed. I was in my house. I knew that. But I didn't feel like I was inside anything. 135

"It's really something," I said. 1981

INVESTIGATIONS

1. Why does the narrator's wife find Robert's touching her face such a powerful experience? In what sense might the tapes she and Robert exchange allow them to "see" more clearly than the narrator does?

2. Imagine that the narrator just walked in the room. Write two or three paragraphs describing him. To what extent can you trace your description to his tone of voice, to how he says what he says? To what extent does he protect himself with the way he talks?

3. In paragraph 16, the narrator imagines that Robert's married life was "pathetic." Do you agree? Why or why not? What's pathetic about the narrator's life? In what ways are both their lives full of pathos?

4. What does the narrator discover at the end of the story? Would he have made this discovery if he'd drawn a cathedral without Robert's participation? Why or why not? What answer would the narrator now give if Robert again asked if he was "in any way religious" (para. 102)? Why?

CONNECTIONS AND ELABORATIONS

1. Write a poem about the experience you explored in "Write Before Reading" (p. 784) using Mary Oliver's approach in "Some Questions You Might Ask."

2. Write a poem about the experience you explored in "Write Before Reading" using David James's approach in "Think Death."

3. Write a short story about the experience you explored in "Write Before Reading" using Rosario Ferré's approach in "Pico Rico, Mandorico."

4. Using as evidence material from the selections in Part Seven, your response to "Write Before Reading," and any other writing and thinking you've done during your work in Part Seven, write an essay in support of this assertion: "Though certain things that happen to us may always elude explanation, trying to explain them is crucial to living with them."

5. Using as evidence material from the selections in Part Seven, your response to "Write Before Reading," and any other writing and thinking you've done during your work in Part Seven, write an essay in support of this assertion: "Though belief ultimately lies outside logic, it's necessary to subject our beliefs to rational analysis."

6. Using as evidence material from Johnson's "Exchange Value," Sanchez-Scott's Roosters, Ferré's "Pico Rico, Mandorico," Viramontes's "The Moths," and Carver's "Cathedral," write an essay analyzing the obligations giving and receiving gifts place on us and how those obligations may be discharged.

7. Using as evidence material from Wright's "Yes, But," Gogisgi/Carroll Arnett's "Early Song," Oliver's "Some Questions You Might Ask," Baxter's "Gryphon," Ferré's "Pico Rico, Mandorico," Kumin's "In the Park," and your response to "Write Before Reading," write an essay analyzing the practical function of wonder.

8. Using as evidence material from appropriate selections in this book and from the writing you've done in conjunction with them, write an essay that demonstrates how writing, especially writing imaginative literature, is an act of faith.

(*Continued from page iv*)

Madison Smartt Bell, "Customs of the Country." Copyright © 1988 by *Harper's Magazine*. All rights reserved. Reprinted from the February 1988 issue by special permission.

Wendell Berry, "Except." Excerpted from *A Part* by Wendell Berry. Copyright © 1980 by Wendell Berry. Published by North Point Press and reprinted by permission.

Eric Bogosian, *Talk Radio*. Copyright © 1987 by Ararat Productions, Inc. Reprinted by permission of Vintage Books, a Division of Random House, Inc.

T. Coraghessan Boyle, "Sitting on Top of the World." Copyright © 1991 by T. Coraghessan Boyle. Reprinted by permission of Georges Borchardt, Inc.

Peter Cameron, "Jump or Dive." From *One Way or Another* by Peter Cameron. Copyright © 1986 by Peter Cameron. Reprinted by permission of HarperCollins Publishers, Inc.

Raymond Carver, "Cathedral." From *Cathedral* by Raymond Carver. Copyright © 1981 by Raymond Carver. Reprinted by permission of Alfred A. Knopf, Inc.

Lorna Dee Cervantes, "Refugee Ship." From *Revista Chicano Riquena*. Reprinted by permission of Arte Publico Press.

Sandra Cisneros, "My Lucy Friend Who Smells Like Corn." Copyright © 1991 by Sandra Cisneros. Published in *Woman Hollering Creek* by Sandra Cisneros (Random House, New York City, NY, 1990). First appeared in *Story*. Reprinted by permission of Susan Bergholtz Literary Services.

Lucille Clifton, "in white america." Copyright © 1987 by Lucille Clifton. Reprinted from *Next: New Poems* by Lucille Clifton with the permission of BOA Editions, Ltd., 92 Park Avenue, Brockport, NY 14420.

Judith Ortiz Cofer, "Silent Dancing." Reprinted by permission of the publisher from *Silent Dancing: A Partial Remembrance of a Puerto Rican Childhood* (Houston: Arte Publico Press–University of Houston, 1990).

Jim Daniels, "My Father Worked Late." From *Places/Everyone*, copyright © 1985 by The Board of Regents of the University of Wisconsin System. Reprinted by permission of The University of Wisconsin Press.

Ellen Darion, "Claudia." Reprinted by permission. Copyright 1991 *Special Report: Fiction*, Whittle Communications, 505 Market Street, Knoxville, TN 37902.

Rick DeMarinis, "The Flowers of Boredom." *The Coming Triumph of the Free World* by Rick DeMarinis. Copyright © 1988 by Rick DeMarinis. Used by permission of Viking Penguin, a division of Penguin Books USA Inc.

Patricia Dobler, "Hospital Call." From *Talking to Strangers*. Copyright © 1986 by The Board of Regents of the University of Wisconsin System. Reprinted by permission of The University of Wisconsin Press.

Michael Dorris, "Life Stories." From *Antaeus*, vol. 63, Fall 1989. Reprinted by permission of the author.

Rita Dove, "Grape Sherbet." From *Museum* by Rita Dove. Reprinted by permission of Carnegie Mellon University Press 1983.

Andre Dubus, "After the Game." From *The Last Worthless Evening* by Andre Dubus. Copyright © 1986 by Andre Dubus. Reprinted by permission of David R. Godine, Publisher.

Louise Erdrich, "The Leap." Copyright © 1990 by *Harper's Magazine*. Reprinted from the March 1990 issue by special permission.

Martín Espada, "Manuel Is Quiet Sometimes." From *Trumpets in the Island of Their Eviction* (1987) by Martín Espada. Reprinted by permission of the author and Bilingual Review/Press, Arizona State University, Tempe, AZ.

Trudy Pax Farr, "Steelworker." From *Hard-Hatted Women: Stories of Struggle and Success in the Trades*, edited by Molly Martin, (1988). Reprinted by permission of The Seal Press.

Rosario Ferré, "Pico Rico, Mandorico." Translated by Diana Velez. From *Reclaiming Medusa*. Reprinted by permission of the author and the translator.

Tess Gallagher, "The Lover of Horses," From *The Lover of Horses* by Tess Gallagher. Copyright © 1986 by Tess Gallagher. Reprinted by permission of the author.

Louise Glück, "Celestial Music." From *Ararat*, copyright © 1990 by Louise Glück. Published by The Ecco Press. Reprinted by permission.

Gogisgi/Carroll Arnett, "Early Song." from *An Ear to the Ground*, edited by Marie Harris and Kathleen Aguero (The University of Georgia Press). Reprinted by permission of the author.

Elizabeth Gordon, "On the Other Side of the War: A Story." From *Home to Stay*, edited by S. Watanabe and C. Bruchac (The Greenfield Review Press). Reprinted by permission of the author.

Vivian Gornick, "Twice an Outsider: On Being Jewish and a Woman." From *Tikkun*, vol. 4, no. 2. Reprinted by permission of the author.

Thom Gunn, "Memory Unsettled." From *AGNI*, no. 29/30, 1990. Reprinted by permission of the author.

John Haines, "Moments and Journeys." From *Living off the Country* by John Haines. Copyright © 1981 by the University of Michigan Press. First appeared in *Living Wilderness*, January–March 1978. Reprinted by permission of The University of Michigan Press, Ann Arbor, MI.

Donald Hall, "Ox Cart Man." From *Old and New Poems* (Ticknor & Fields). Copyright © 1977 The New Yorker Magazine, Inc. Reprinted by permission of *The New Yorker*.

Patricia Hampl, "Parish Streets." © 1986 by Patricia Hampl. First published in the *Graywolf Annual*. Permission granted by Rhoda Weyr Agency.

Joy Harjo, "Ordinary Spirit." Reprinted from *I Tell You Now: Autobiographical Essays by Native American Writers*, edited by Brian Swann and Arnold Krupat, by permission of University of Nebraska Press. Copyright © 1987 by the University of Nebraska Press.

Agnes G. Herman, "A Parent's Journey Out of the Closet." From *Reconstructionist*, vol. 51, no. 2, October 1985. Reprinted by permission of *Reconstructionist*.

Inés Hernandez, "Para Teresa." From *Con Razon Corazon: Poetry by Inés Hernandez Tovar*. Reprinted by permission of the author.

Richard Howard, "The Victor Vanquished." From *Antaeus*, vol. 64/65, Spring 1990. Reprinted by permission of the author.

David James, "Think Death." From *Passages North Anthology* (Milkweed Editions, 1990). Reprinted by permission of Milkweed Editions.

Gish Jen, "What Means Switch." Copyright © 1990 by Gish Jen. First published in *The Atlantic*, May 1990. Reprinted by permission of the author.

Charles Johnson, "Exchange Value." Reprinted with permission of Atheneum Publishers, an imprint of Macmillan Publishing Company, from *Sorcerer's Apprentice* by Charles Johnson. Copyright © 1986 by Charles Johnson.

Fenton Johnson, "The Limitless Heart." Original version, reprinted by permission of the author. This material appeared in slightly different form in *the New York Times Magazine*, June 23, 1991.

Rachel L. Jones, "The Price of Hate: Thoughts on Covering a Ku Klux Klan Rally." From the *St. Petersburg Times*, June 19, 1988. Reprinted by permission of the *St. Petersburg Times*.

Lawrence Joseph, "Driving Again." From *Shouting at No One* (Ontario Review Press, 1983). Reprinted by permission of the author.

Cynthia Kadohata, "Devils." Reprinted by permission. © 1989 Cynthia Kadohata. Originally in *The New Yorker*.

Jesse Lee Kercheval, "Willy." Reprinted from *The Dogeater: Stories* by Jesse Lee Kercheval, by permission of the University of Missouri Press. Copyright © 1987 by the author.

Galway Kinnell, "After Making Love We Hear Footsteps." From *Mortal Acts, Mortal Words* by Galway Kinnell. Copyright © 1980 by Galway Kinnell. Reprinted by permission of Houghton Mifflin Company. All rights reserved.

Walter Kirn, "The New Timothy." From *My Hard Bargain* by Walter Kirn. Copyright © 1990 by Walter Kirn. Reprinted by permission of Alfred A. Knopf, Inc.

Carolyn Kizer, "Bitch." From *The Mermaids in the Basement*. Copyright 1984 by Carolyn Kizer. Reprinted by permission of Copper Canyon Press.

Etheridge Knight, "Circling the Daughter." Reprinted from *The Essential Etheridge Knight* by Etheridge Knight, by permission of the University of Pittsburgh Press. Copyright © 1986 by Etheridge Knight.

Yusef Komunyakaa, "Facing It." Copyright © 1989 by Yusef Komunyakaa. Reprinted from *Dien Cai Dau* (Wesleyan University Press) by permission of University Press of New England.

Maxine Kumin, "In the Park." From *Nurture* by Maxine Kumin. Copyright © 1989 by Maxine Kumin. Used by permission of Viking Penguin, a division of Penguin Books USA Inc.

Philip Levine, "Buying and Selling." From *A Walk with Tom Jefferson* by Philip Levine. Copyright © 1988 by Philip Levine. Reprinted by permission of Alfred A. Knopf, Inc.

Ralph Lombreglia, "Late Early Man." © 1991 by Ralph Lombreglia. Reprinted with the permission of *The New Yorker*, where the story first appeared on July 15, 1991, and The Darhansoff & Verrill Literary Agency.

Thomas Lynch, "The Widow." From *Skating with Heather Grace* by Thomas Lynch. Copyright © 1986 by Thomas Lynch. Reprinted by permission of Alfred A. Knopf, Inc.

Richard McCann, "My Mother's Clothes: The School of Beauty and Shame." Appeared originally in *The Atlantic Monthly*. Copyright © 1986 by Richard McCann. Reprinted by permission of Brandt & Brandt Literary Agents, Inc.

Eduardo Machado, *Broken Eggs*. Copyright © 1984 by Eduardo Machado. All inquiries regarding rights should be addressed to William Craver, Writers & Artists Agency, 19 West 44th Street, New York, NY 10036.

Reginald McKnight, "The Kind of Light That Shines on Texas." From *The Kind of Light That Shines on Texas* (Little, Brown and Company, 1992). Reprinted by permission of the author.

Bobbie Ann Mason, "Shiloh." From *Shiloh and Other Stories* by Bobbie Ann Mason. Copyright © 1982 by Bobbie Ann Mason. Reprinted by permission of HarperCollins Publishers Inc.

James Masao Mitsui, "Allowance." Reprinted by permission of the author.

Rosario Morales, "I Am What I Am." From *This Bridge Called My Back*. Copyright © 1983 by Rosario Morales. Used by permission of Kitchen Table: Women of Color Press, P.O. Box 908, Latham, NY 12110.

Bharati Mukherjee, "Fathering." From *The Middleman and Other Stories*. Copyright © 1988 by Bharati Mukherjee. Used by permission of Grove Press, Inc.

David Mura, "Nantucket Honeymoon." From *After We Lost Our Way* (E. P. Dutton, 1989). Reprinted by permission of the author.

Lewis Nordan, "Sugar Among the Chickens." Reprinted by permission of Louisiana State University Press from *The All-Girl Football Team* by Lewis Nordan. Copyright © 1986 by Louisiana State University Press.

Marsha Norman, *'night, Mother*. Copyright © 1983 by Marsha Norman. Reprinted by permission of Hill and Wang, a division of Farrar, Straus and Giroux, Inc.

Joyce Carol Oates, "Against Nature." Copyright © 1988 by the Ontario Review, Inc. Reprinted by permission of the Ontario Review Press.

Tim O'Brien, "The Things They Carried." Published in *Esquire*, August 1986. Reprinted by permission of International Creative Management, Inc. Copyright © 1986 by Tim O'Brien.

Ed Ochester, "Changing the Name to Ochester." From *Changing the Name to Ochester* (Carnegie Mellon University Press, 1988). Reprinted by permission of the author.

Mary Oliver, "Some Questions You Might Ask." From *House of Light* by Mary Oliver. Copyright © 1990 by Mary Oliver. Reprinted by permission of Beacon Press.

Peter Oresick, "After the Deindustrialization of America, My Father Enters Television Repair." From *Definitions*. Reprinted by permission of West End Press.

Simon J. Ortiz, "The Language We Know." From *I Tell You Now: Autobiographical Essays by Native American Writers*, edited by Brian Swann and Arnold Krupat, by permission of University of Nebraska Press. Copyright © 1987 by the University of Nebraska Press.

Grace Paley, "Friends." From *Later the Same Day* by Grace Paley. Copyright © 1985 by Grace Paley. Reprinted by permission of Farrar, Straus and Giroux, Inc.

Jay Parini, "Working the Face." From *Anthracite Country* by Jay Parini. Copyright © 1982 by Jay Parini. Reprinted by permission of Random House, Inc.

Lucia Maria Perillo, "The Northside at Seven." From *Dangerous Life* by Lucia Maria Perillo. Copyright © 1989 by Lucia Maria Perillo. Reprinted with the permission of Northeastern University Press, Boston, MA.

David Rabe, *Hurlyburly*. Copyright © 1986 by Ralako Corp. Used by permission of Grove Press, Inc.

Adrienne Rich, "Love Poem." Reprinted from *Time's Power, Poems 1985–1988* by Adrienne Rich, by permission of W. W. Norton & Company, Inc. Copyright © 1989 by Adrienne Rich.

Richard Rodriguez, "Aria: A Bilingual Childhood" (editor's title). From *Hunger of Memory* by Richard Rodriguez. Copyright © 1982 by Richard Rodriguez. Reprinted by permission of David R. Godine, Publisher.

Wendy Rose, "For the White Poets Who Would Be Indian." From *Academic Squaw*. Reprinted by permission of the author.

Milcha Sanchez-Scott, *Roosters*. Copyright © 1987 by Milcha Sanchez-Scott. All inquiries regarding rights should be addressed to George Lane, William Morris Agency, 1350 Avenue of the Americas, New York, NY 10019.

Leslie Marmon Silko, "Lullaby." Copyright © 1981 by Leslie Marmon Silko. Reprinted from *Storyteller* by Leslie Marmon Silko, published by Seaver Books, New York, NY.

Jane Smiley, "Long Distance." From *The Age of Grief* by Jane Smiley. Copyright © 1987 by Jane Smiley. Reprinted by permission of Alfred A. Knopf, Inc.

Gary Snyder, "Building." From *Witness*. Reprinted by permission of the author.

Cathy Song, "Losing Track." Reprinted from *Frameless Windows, Squares of Light* by Cathy Song, by permission of W. W. Norton & Company, Inc. Copyright © 1988 by Cathy Song.

Jerry Sterner, *Other People's Money*. Copyright © 1989 by Jerry Sterner. All rights reserved. Reprinted by permission of Applause Theatre Books, 211 West 71st Street, New York, NY 10023. Richard Rodgers and Oscar Hammerstein II, "The Farmer and the Cowman" (p. 566). Copyright © 1943 by Williamson Music. Copyright renewed. International copyright secured. All rights reserved. Used by permission.

May Swenson, "Staring at the Sea on the Day of the Death of Another." Copyright © The Literary Estate of May Swenson. First appeared in *The New Yorker*.

Amy Tan, "Two Kinds." Reprinted from *The Joy Luck Club* by Amy Tan, by permission of The Putnam Publishing Group. Copyright © 1989 by Amy Tan.

Cliff Thompson, "Judgment." From *Breaking Ice: An Anthology of Contemporary African-American Fiction*, edited by Terry McMillan. Reprinted by permission of the author.

Kitty Tsui, "Don't Let Them Chip Away at Our Language." From *An Ear to the Ground: An Anthology of Contemporary American Poetry*, edited by Marie Harris and Kathleen Aguero (The University of Georgia Press).

John Updike, "Gesturing." From *Too Far to Go: The Maples Stories* by John Updike. Copyright © 1979 by John Updike. Reprinted by permission of Alfred A. Knopf, Inc.

Helena María Viramontes, "The Moths." From *The Moths and Other Stories*. Reprinted by permission of Arte Publico Press–University of Houston.

Anna Lee Walters, "The Warriors." From *The Sun Is Not Merciful* by Anna Lee Walters. Reprinted by permission of Firebrand Books, Ithaca, NY.

Theodore Weesner, "The Body Politic." Reprinted by permission of Sterling Lord Literistic, Inc.

John Edgar Wideman, "Valaida." From *Fever* by John Edgar Wideman. Copyright © 1989 by John Edgar Wideman. Reprinted by permission of Henry Holt and Company, Inc.

C. K. Williams, "Tar." From *Poems, 1963–1983* by C. K. Williams. Copyright © 1983, 1988 by C. K. Williams. Reprinted by permission of Farrar, Straus and Giroux, Inc.

Lanford Wilson, *Burn This.* Copyright © 1987 by Lanford Wilson. Reprinted by permission of Hill and Wang, a division of Farrar, Straus and Giroux, Inc.

Tobias Wolff, "The Other Miller." Copyright © 1986 by Tobias Wolff. First appeared in *The Atlantic Monthly.* Reprinted by permission of the author.

James Wright, "Yes, But." From *This Journey* by James Wright. Copyright © 1982 by Anne Wright, Executrix of the Estate of James Wright. Reprinted by permission of Random House, Inc.

Shay Youngblood, "Snuff Dippers." From *The Big Mama Stories* by Shay Youngblood. Reprinted by permission of Fireband Books, Ithaca, NY.

INDEX OF
AUTHORS AND TITLES

HOW WE LIVE NOW

JOHN REPP

CONTEMPORARY MULTICULTURAL LITERATURE

Prepared by Ellen Darion

6 5 4 3 2
f e d c b a

For information, write: St. Martin's Press, Inc.
175 Fifth Avenue, New York, NY 10010

Editorial Offices: Bedford Books *of* St. Martin's Press
29 Winchester Street, Boston, MA 02116

ISBN: 0–312–05256–1

PREFACE

This instructor's manual is designed to be a resource of observations and suggestions for teaching the selections in *How We Live Now*. In each of the book's seven thematic parts, an introductory overview discusses the theme and its various manifestations throughout the section. The overviews end with suggestions for condensing the parts if teaching time is limited.

The entries for individual selections begin by discussing the challenges instructors may encounter and by suggesting teaching strategies. Many of these introductory comments also include biographical information about the writer to supplement the biographical footnotes in the text.

Following these introductions, the manual offers discussions of the "Investigations," the numbered questions appearing after the selections in the text, and provides possible answers. The answers are intended to be neither definitive nor exhaustive; like all good writing, the selections in this book are rich enough to support many approaches.

Discussions of the "Write Before Reading" exercises and "Connections and Elaborations" assignments have been embedded within discussions of individual selections where appropriate. The "Write Before Reading" exercises, which appear at the end of each part introduction in the text, are intended to get students thinking about the part's themes in advance and to help them realize that, like the writers who appear in this book, they have something to say on this subject. As students work through a part, they encounter "Investigations" referring them back to their "Write Before Reading" exercise; at this point they can reconsider their own answers in light of what they have just read. The "Connections and Elaborations" assignments, which appear at the end of each part in the text, address connections between the selections within the unit and often refer students back to their "Write Before Reading" exercises as well.

CONTENTS

PART TWO

In Families

PART THREE

With Friends

Contents

PART FOUR

In and Out of Communities

PART FIVE

On and Off the Job

PART SIX

In and Out of Love

Contents

PART SEVEN

With Eternal Questions and Everyday Absurdities

PART ONE

WITH OURSELVES

OVERVIEW

The range of topics in this part is as broad as its title suggests: Students will read about everything from growing up and growing old to suicide and sexual orientation. The selections make it clear that, in order to live with ourselves, we must confront not only the question "Who am I?" but also the question "Who do I want to be?" Several pieces in this part present voices that confidently answer this question: Rosario Morales, John Haines, Joy Harjo, and Antler's speaker are all quite secure in their identities.

Other voices are much less sure of who they are or who they'd like to be. Clint Oates in "The Kind of Light That Shines on Texas" and the narrator of "My Mother's Clothes: The School of Beauty and Shame" both blatantly deny aspects of themselves that they find difficult or painful to face. And Evan in "Jump or Dive" hasn't quite figured out *what* he's about to deny or embrace.

The struggle isn't over once we think we know who we want to be, of course. The next step is figuring out how to get there. The speakers in the poems "Driving Again" and "The Northside at Seven" want to find a way to reconcile their pasts with their present lives. The narrators of "Customs of the Country" and "Valaida" and the speaker of "Facing It" are just now beginning to move out of their pasts, in which they experienced something so numbing they have been afraid to feel anything for quite some time. Finally, Jessie in *'night, Mother* knows that she doesn't want to be anything or anybody, and she's come to terms with what to do about it, too. For this reason some instructors (or students) might want to group Jessie with those characters and speakers who *are* secure in their identities. The main difference between them and Jessie, of course, is that they are all affirming life, while Jessie is denying it.

For instructors who don't have time to teach all the selections in Part One, the following groupings might be useful. Several of these selections would yield a revealing unit on prejudice: Consider assigning McKnight, Morales, Cameron, Wideman, and McCann to that end. Another interesting mini-unit might result from focusing on writers who come to know themselves through their families and ancestors: Joseph, Morales, Harjo, Haines, and Perillo.

1

REGINALD McKNIGHT

The Kind of Light
That Shines on Texas (p. 3)

Reginald McKnight won the Drue Heinz Prize for Literature in 1988 for his collection of short stories, *Moustapha's Eclipse*. "The Kind of Light That Shines on Texas" received an O. Henry Award. In Reginald McKnight's writing, "the development of a strong, independent sense of self is important" (*Essence*, March 1991). "The Kind of Light That Shines on Texas" beautifully depicts a twelve-year-old boy wrestling with just this challenge. One of three Black students in a recently integrated Texas elementary school, Clint Oates is also new to the class, having just moved to Connolly Air Force Base when his father was sent to Vietnam. Clint wants to be like his father: capable, manly, able to take charge and take care of things. When his father left for Vietnam, Clint "respected [himself], [his] manhood" (para. 59). During the course of the story, however, Clint betrays not only himself and one of his Black classmates, but also his father, who would — at least from Clint's description of him — never try to shunt his problems onto someone else. By the story's end, however, Clint begins to understand what he has done — and in this understanding is the beginning of the knowledge that he must change.

For further discussions of this story, see Investigation 2 in the entry for Rosario Morales's "I Am What I Am" (manual p. 6) and Investigation 3 in the entry for Madison Smartt Bell's "Customs of the Country" (manual p. 8).

INVESTIGATIONS (p. 12)

1. Clint Oates's "Tom-thing" involves hiding his pain at being the butt of racist jokes, hiding his true feelings about being Black — both from others and from himself — and doing whatever he has to do to get along with white people: "I sucked ass, too, I suppose" (7). Clint first does his "Tom-thing" in paragraph 7: "I, myself, would smile at Wickham's stupid jokes." He continues, here listing for us what activities constitute behaving like an Uncle Tom: "I kept my shoes shined, my desk neat, answered her questions as best I could, never brought gum to school, never cursed, never slept in class. I wanted to show her we [the Black students] were not all the same." (8). When Clint is permitted to be "eraser duster" (9), he says, "I didn't even care about the cracks my fellow students made about my finally having turned the right color." Then Clint tells his white classmates how much Marvin disgusts him (9–12). And when Clint and Oakley are the only two left at the end of a game of murderball, Clint naively believes he can buddy up to Oakley: "Good game, Oak Tree, I would say" (17). Finally, Clint's ultimate "Tom-thing" maneuver occurs (51), when he tries to get Oakley to fight Marvin instead of himself.

    If Marvin Pruitt did the "Tom-thing," Clint would certainly not despise him — especially if he no longer "smelled bad" and stopped sniffing his arm. But even if Marvin Pruitt ingratiated himself with their teacher and the white students in the class, Clint would probably still be somewhat put off by him, simply because he wasn't "smart," academically — and therefore, in Clint's eyes, would still make Black students like himself, who were smart, look bad.

2. This question would lend itself well to a creative assignment; students are essentially being asked to rewrite this story from Marvin's point of view.

    Marvin Pruitt might describe himself as having no use for school in general or white people in particular. (School, of course, is an institution run and almost entirely populated by white people.) Readers have no way of knowing how smart, academically, Marvin is, but since Texas schools "weren't afraid to flunk you" (5) and Marvin is at least two grades behind, it is apparent that he hasn't done well in school. His clothes, for which Clint pities him, suggest that he may be poor. On the other hand, since Clint is a "city boy," Marvin's clothes may simply not be sophisticated enough for Clint's taste. We don't have enough information about Marvin's background to know why he sleeps in class or behaves the way he does, though both lack of interest and an active refusal to participate in a world run by someone else's rules are reasonable guesses.

It's unclear whether Marvin is even awake to hear Mrs. Wickham's racist jokes, but they probably wouldn't surprise him or hurt him as much as they hurt Clint or even Ah-so, who stares down at her desk on these occasions. One gets the sense that Marvin is used to and even expects such things from white people.

Marvin probably sees Ah-so as at least a partially kindred spirit; though she'll read aloud — in a manner that demonstrates she could probably answer any question asked of her — she refuses to answer questions. Unlike Clint, but like Marvin, she too won't play the game, will not pretend this "integrated" classroom, where her teacher makes racist jokes, is a place she approves of or wants to be.

Since Oakley has never picked a fight with Marvin, Marvin probably has no more quarrel with Oakley than Oakley claims to have with him — at least until Clint arrives on the scene. (Of course, Oakley's tolerance of Marvin is not because he is tolerant of Blacks, but because he knows Marvin is the one person in class who could beat him in a fight. Still, he's never bothered Marvin.) Marvin might even feel some solidarity with Oakley because of their similar circumstances: They've both been left back and they share a similar disdain for school and authority.

Marvin might describe Clint as exactly the "suck-ass" Clint labels himself, and he would agree wholeheartedly with Clint's assessment of himself as an Uncle Tom. There's nothing to reveal this in the text, but like Oakley, Marvin *might* dislike Clint for being uppity, a "city boy," for saying "tennis shoes" instead of "sneakers" and "restroom" instead of "toilet." Marvin most likely despises Clint for doing his "Tom-thing," if in fact he has been awake to hear it prior to the incident in the locker room.

It is because of all this rather than in spite of it that Marvin fights Oakley. He does it to show Clint that in fact, he *is* the same as Marvin; to show Clint that, to much of the world, Black people *are* all the same: Oakley wants to fight one, and it doesn't matter which one, so long as that one is smaller than he is. Marvin wants Clint to see that all the Uncle Tom behavior in the world won't change the fact that he's as Black as Marvin is, and he might as well start to confront that fact *now*. If Marvin had let Oakley deck Clint, Clint would have just been another of Oakley's victims. But Clint is Black, and Marvin isn't going to let anyone Black get beaten up, on principle — but especially not a sniveling worm like Clint who (in Marvin's eyes) doesn't even know he's Black. Equally, if not more important, Marvin isn't going to pass up the chance to prove to Clint just how Black Clint is.

3. Clint Oates has a very strong sense of self — a little too strong, it turns out, for his own good. His desire to be seen as an individual is understandable, even commendable — he should no more be associated with Marvin's "negative" traits than Jack Preston should be associated with Oakley's, simply on the basis

of the colors of their skin. Clint is new in town and wants badly to be accepted; as a good student he also doesn't want to be "lumped" with the other Black students in the class, who are bad ones. His "Tom-thing" helps him ingratiate himself with the white students, and so, on the surface, he initially gets along better because of it. But the "Tom-thing" hurts him because it involves pretending racist attitudes don't bother him, when of course they do. He even recognizes these conflicting attitudes in himself: "I was ashamed. Ashamed for not defending Marvin and ashamed that Marvin even existed" (13). Clint's strong sense of self doesn't include a sense of pride in being who and what he is — Black— and his "Tom-thing" is a crutch that keeps him from having to deal with this internal conflict. When Marvin defends him, however — Marvin, the very person he tried to get Oakley to fight instead of himself, Marvin, who he was "ashamed even existed" — Clint is forced to face his "Tom-thing" head on.

4.   At the end of this story, when Clint and Ah-so exchange glances, Clint sees for the first time that she "had a very gentle-looking face, really. That surprised me" (71). Clint never noticed her gentle-looking face before because he never really looked. He is seeing her as an individual — rather than one of the three Black kids in class — for the first time. But he is also seeing her and himself as "the same" for the first time. The day's events have bonded Clint and Ah-so together, at least for this brief moment. Clint never saw Ah-so's smile before because she never offered one. It is only when she does that Clint begins to realize the importance of what Marvin Pruitt has done, that he begins to see the light that might reveal himself and Marvin (and Ah-so) as the same.

LAWRENCE JOSEPH

Driving Again (p. 13)

Among the awards Lawrence Joseph has received for his poetry are the Hopwood Award from the University of Michigan and, for his first collection of poems, *Shouting at No One* (1982), the Agnes Starret Poetry Prize from the University of Pittsburgh Press.

The speaker of this poem drifts from reality to memory to dream and back to reality again without always clearly indicating the transitions — much as these movements occur in real life. While this movement may seem natural to some students, it's liable to confuse others. It would be useful to begin by focusing on these transitions. Ask students to highlight transitional phrases to help them follow the movement of the poem. (See Investigation 1 for more on this.)

This poem compares usefully with both Lucia Maria Perillo's "The Northside at Seven" and John Haines's "Moments and Journeys." Note that the speakers in the two poems are in their cars, making both literal and metaphorical journeys. Both speakers are trying to reconcile their pasts with their presents. Ask students whether either succeeds. If so, to what extent? If not, what might be hindering that reconciliation?

John Haines believes that moving "without effort from waking into dreaming life" lends a "deep assurance that life has continuity and meaning" (Haines, para. 15). Ask students whether Joseph's poem seems to support that view. Certainly the speaker's dreams about his past and grandparents provide him with both a sense of continuity and with meaning, but what *is* that meaning? And is the speaker making this journey without effort? Indeed, can a journey such as Joseph's be made without effort?

INVESTIGATIONS (p. 14)

1. The first eight lines of the poem occur in the present; the speaker is literally driving his car down Van Dyke Avenue. Then the speaker, still in the present, records a memory from his past, his childhood (9–17). Point students to the key phrase in line 17: The smell of his grandmother's perfume and fur spun him "to sleep." Lines 18–32 are all a dream — or rather, the memory of a dream the speaker had as a boy, sitting next to his grandmother; and also a daydream the speaker is having now, as he drives. It is a dream, one can conjecture from the poem's title, the speaker has had before. Draw students' attention to the words "these" and "this" (29–32), the latter used repeatedly. The speaker uses these terms rather than less specific ones such as "a" or "the" because "this" street, smoke, and sky he sees now is the same street, smoke, and sky of his childhood, of his dream, and of his young adulthood, when he, too, worked on the loading dock.

   The speaker is realizing, here, the power of place in his life, the power "of this street, this smoke / from Eldon Axle foundry, these / motor blocks stacked against / this dull sky." (29–32). He is coming to terms with how this place has informed his life, how it has made him who he was and who he is today. Again this poem would make an interesting comparison with John Haines's essay: How does this speaker's sense of place differ from Haines's? Has this street, for the speaker, become what Haines describes as one of the "places that take on symbolic value to an individual" (18)? If so, what is that value, and how is it different from the value Haines attributes to the "'soul-resting places'" he cites in the same paragraph?

2. The speaker confronts his grief over his grandparents' death, which he has not, until now, been fully able to demonstrate. By crying now, he gives them the respect and mourning they deserved, but he was unable to proffer, in the past. The speaker may also be mourning how far he has come from his roots — the loading dock he used to work on is now part of his past, too.

   Answers to the second part of this question will vary. Many students have probably faced similar issues, such as the death of grandparents or parents.

3. The speaker cries for his dead grandparents, whose lives were hard, who died in pain, and who he has not, until now, properly mourned (see lines 39–48). The speaker cries specifically for his grandmother, who he misses not only for herself and for the comfort she provided, but also because she stood for his youth and innocence (13–16). Finally, the speaker cries for the woman whose face is "spotted purple" (19); the graffiti on the wall (24); the smoke, the foundry, and the dull sky (29–32); the bum on the loading dock (36) — all of which speak to the poverty and drudgery and misfortunes of the neighborhood. The speaker cries, as anyone might, because this is disturbing, but also because none of this has changed since he was a child.

ROSARIO MORALES

I Am What I Am (p. 15)

Rosario Morales was born in New York City and moved to Puerto Rico in 1950 where she lived with her family on a coffee farm. In 1967 she returned to the United States, publishing *Getting Home Alive* with her daughter, Aurora Levins Morales, in 1986. Morales is Puerto Rican, her husband, David Levins, is Jewish, so her daughter, Morales says, is "Puerto Rican–Jewish-American."

Morales's powerful and musical statement of personal identity may be difficult for some students because of its presentation: The stream-of-consciousness narration and prose-poem format may be unfamiliar and off-putting. A discussion of the relationship between form and content would provide a good entry to this selection. Ask students how the lack of punctuation affected their reading of "I Am What I Am." Have someone read the selection aloud and then ask students to provide the missing punctuation. (Make sure they know this isn't a quiz; there is certainly more than one acceptable way to punctuate these paragraphs.) Then have another student read the edited selection out loud. What differences do students hear? Has the intensity of the original been lessened? Or was the breathless quality of the original merely distracting to some students? Might that breathlessness have been intended as a reflection of the speaker's state of mind?

Another good initial approach might be to walk students through a close reading of the piece. Who is the "you" in the second and third line of the selection? What does the speaker mean when she says "I'm not hiding under no stoop"? If students find the opening of this selection confusing, it should come into focus toward the end of the first paragraph: "See! here's a real true honest-to-god Puerto Rican girl and she's in college . . . Ain't that something." Here students should recognize the irony in the speaker's voice. The "you" who would "take away the Puerto Rican" is anyone the speaker has encountered who has considered her somehow *not* American, or less capable or worthy than other Americans. She has been patronized and condescended to — and probably discriminated against, though this isn't explicitly illustrated in the text. Society has tried to make her feel she is not a *real* American, but she has refused to succumb to such prejudice.

INVESTIGATIONS (p. 16)

1. To Morales's speaker, a "U.S. American" is everything a U.S. citizen is made up of — all of the nationalities and ethnic groups that are in her blood, *plus* any external influences she absorbs, whether consciously or unconsciously. Given this definition, ask students what they make of all the Spanish and Yiddish words and references in the selection. You may have students who can provide translations; if so, invite them to do so. Ask students how much they think the ability to translate these words matters. While translations will certainly enhance a reader's understanding, can't the piece be understood without them?

2. Morales's speaker makes a point of saying how *like* other people — be they Puerto Rican American, Jewish American, Irish Catholic American, even British — she is. For her, it is not only *possible* to be both an assimilated citizen of the United States and maintain your individual cultural heritage or heritages, it is *essential* to do so for a healthy sense of self.

    Clint Oates, on the other hand, defines himself as someone who laughs at his teacher's and classmates' racist jokes, who wants his teacher to understand that he is "not like her other nigra children" (para. 7). Oates does what he calls his "Tom-thing" to get by — that is, he does whatever he can do to make white people like him, even at the expense of the other Black kids in his class. Clint would not only have to stop doing his "Tom-thing" for Morales to consider herself and Clint in any way the same; he would also have to admit that he was wrong to do it in the first place, and he would have to develop some pride, rather than shame, in being Black. (See Part One: Connections and Elaborations 2 for a related assignment.)

3. Responses will vary. Some students are likely to feel liberated by Morales's stream-of-consciousness approach. Others may feel stymied, especially if they are uncomfortable breaking rules. You might tell the latter group that they are free to use punctuation, but encourage them to try to replicate the rhythm of their thoughts and to pay attention to the rhythm of their spoken language or languages.

4. Morales's speaker might think that Jessie (*'night, Mother*) has spent much of her life (or at least the time since her husband left) "hiding under" a stoop. She would agree with Jessie that the world can be a pretty cruel place; note that the speaker in this prose poem is on the defensive from the beginning of this selection ("but I say go to hell"). People *have* tried to take things away from her, but her self-confidence is clearly too strong to be affected. Morales's speaker might tell Jessie that "she is who she is"; that her epilepsy and shyness and even the rosebuds on her mail-order bra are all part of who she is, and if these things bother other people, that's their problem, not Jessie's; that Jessie should tell them, "Take it or leave me alone." Unlike Morales's speaker, though, what bothers Jessie is not *other* people but herself: She doesn't *want* to be who she is. Nothing anyone says to Jessie is likely to make a difference.

MADISON SMARTT BELL
Customs of the Country (p. 16)

Madison Smartt Bell has taught at Goucher College in Baltimore, Maryland. "Customs of the Country," originally published in *Harper's* magazine, was reprinted in *Best American Stories 1989*. In addition to the books mentioned in the text footnote, Bell has published the novels *The Washington Square Ensemble* (1983), *Waiting for the End of the World* (1985), *Soldier's Joy* (1989), and the short-story collections *Zero db* (1987) and *Barking Man* (1990).

The narrator of this story has a strong sense of her identity in that she knows exactly what she wants: custody of her son and a decent life with him. She also has a strong sense of who she is, and, more importantly, who she has been: a very young mother, addicted to drugs, who, albeit unintentionally, broke her small son's leg by throwing him against the wall. She knows she has done the worst possible thing a mother can do to her child, and she'll suffer the consequences for the rest of her life.

In retrospect, she thinks she could have had more control over her life, but she knows there's nothing she can do to change that now. Nor is there anything she can do to change the wisdom of the state system in charge of the welfare of her son. She knows she would never hurt her child again, but the people in charge of foster care have no reason to give her that chance. Since they don't, the question becomes: How can she live with herself, and what kind of life can she lead? Knocking out her neighbor's abusive husband at the end of the story may be the beginning of an answer to that question, though the narrator herself doesn't realize this yet. (If you are teaching a literature class, this story presents an excellent opportunity to discuss point of view and unreliable narrators.)

The grim circumstances of this narrator's situation compare usefully with those of Jessie in Marsha Norman's *'night, Mother*. (See Part One: Connections and Elaborations 3a and 3c.) Some students may feel that Bell's narrator has had a *harder* life than Jessie, and yet suicide doesn't occur to her.

INVESTIGATIONS (p. 27)

1. The most disturbing custom in this story is the fact "that the man next door used to beat up his wife a couple of times a week" (para. 2). Equally disturbing is the narrator's custom of ignoring the beating. The custom of becoming inured to things that are very disturbing — be it a neighbor beating his wife or a woman losing her child — is at the heart of this story.

   Other customs include the narrator's figuring out what's expected of her and following those unwritten rules; she visits her son only so often that it won't look like she's "pressing too hard" (10); she plays with him only in ways she's sure his foster parents will approve of. She decorates her apartment in ways she "never cared a damn about" (3). Finally, she accepts the ruling that she'll lose her son without "any big tussle" (33), as her lawyer suggests.

   Davey's foster parents, the Bakers, also follow customs; they must pretend not to mind Davey's mother visiting. Since they want to adopt him, they can't possibly be pleased to see this woman — who broke his leg while she was under the influence of drugs — seeking custody, no matter how good they think their chances are of getting custody themselves.

2. The narrator ignores the fact that her neighbor abuses his wife: "I was that accustomed I barely noticed when they would start in" (7). Similarly, she shrugs off the fact that she can't make a friend of Susan (7); that her own whole apartment is "an act" (3). In her past, she ignored her husband' vices: his stealing drugs from the hospital and selling them, his being "unreliable, late, not showing up at all, gone out of the house for days sometime. Hindsight shows me he ran with other women, but I managed not to know anything about that at the time" (13). Finally, she ignored the fact that she was addicted to Dilaudid until, suffering from withdrawal symptoms she didn't even recognize at first, she did something so awful she was forced to face it.

   Students may be slow to admit to ignoring things they find disturbing. If discussion isn't forthcoming, ask them how they react when they see homeless people on the streets, or when they hear their parents fighting, or in the face of blatant prejudice against a group that they identify with or respect.

3. The narrator of "Customs of the Country" succeeds in understanding that she did a horrible thing to her son, that she did it because she was a drug addict, and that she lost her son forever because of it. Understanding this helps her trust herself and "believe it never would ever happen anymore" (23). During the course of this story she understands further that this mistake can never be "wiped out," that she can never "make it like it never had been" (32).

   When Clint Oates, the narrator of "The Kind of Light That Shines on Texas," tries to get Oakley to fight Marvin Pruitt (the only other Black boy in class besides Clint) instead of himself, he is implying that he (Clint) is better than Marvin, that Marvin is a more worthy punching bag; that Marvin's the one Oakley really wants; that Marvin's the one who's really Black. The truth is Clint is ashamed of being Black. He's also smart enough to be ashamed of that shame. Clint knows he shouldn't have said to Oakley "Why not him [Marvin]?" (51) — and believes now he'll have to fight Marvin as well as Oakley. Instead, Marvin steps in, takes over Clint's fight with Oakley, badly hurts his opponent, and is taken away. It's only after all this, when Clint exchanges a look with the only other Black student in the class, that he begins to understand why Marvin did what he did. With this understanding comes knowledge: knowledge that he must stop doing his "Tom-thing" and acknowledge who and what he is.

4.   Since Susan refuses the narrator's offer of a ride out of town and is taking care of her husband at the end of the story, apparently — the narrator's knocking him out hasn't made any difference in Susan's life — which is the difference the narrator had hoped to make. The act itself *might* make Susan realize in the future that she doesn't have to stay with her abusive husband, but neither the narrator, Susan, nor the reader has any way of knowing whether it will. The act does make a difference to the narrator, however, although the story's last line suggests she doesn't realize this yet. But the narrator *has* changed during the course of the story: She has broken the habit of ignoring things, she has broken the custom that has dictated her behavior until now.

> I kept on sitting there thinking about how used to everything I had got. . . . Some [people] were used to taking the pain and the rest were used to serving it up. About half of the world was screaming in misery, and it wasn't anything but a habit. (48)

She has realized she can break this cycle. She may not be able to get her son back, but she can do this one small good thing: "That's when it dawned on me that this was one thing I didn't really have to keep on being used to" (50). Though the narrator says she doesn't know what she's done at the end of this story, we have faith — just as she has faith in her act of knocking out her neighbor when she commits it — that someday she'll recognize what she has done as the redemptive act that it is.

Some readers might not accept the notion that the violence at the end is redemptive. The story presents a good opportunity to discuss violence and our different responses to it.

MARSHA NORMAN

'night, Mother (p. 28)

Marsha Norman's major in college was philosophy, which foreshadows her interest in the moral and ethical issues raised by the topic of suicide. Yet the characters in *'night, Mother* do not wax philosophical; instead, Norman brings a "dispassionate unflinching realism" to the subject, according to Alessandra Stanley in the *New York Times*.

Unlike any other selection in Part One, *'night, Mother* is about someone who chooses *not* to live with herself. If, as the introduction to Part One suggests, we are all brought up to believe that "each of us has a particular destiny to fulfill and the freedom to pursue it," Jessie Cates is exercising her freedom *not* to pursue her destiny. Jessie says she is tired, hurt, sad, and feels used, and she doesn't "have any reason to think it'll get anything but worse" (p. 38). Throughout the play she refers to being lonely, having hurt people, and being sick; this is not a destiny Jessie wants to pursue. She doesn't think she has the resources to do anything about it and has no interest in trying. Ironically, now that her "fits" have stopped and she could possibly lead a more normal life, she doesn't want that life. She says "I can't do anything, either, about my life, to change it, make it better . . . make it work. But I can stop it. . . . It's all I really have that belongs to me and I'm going to say what happens to it" (p. 41). Now that she finally has some control — because her medication has been adjusted properly — she's going to use it in the most compelling way she can: to make sure she never loses that control again. (See Part One: Connections and Elaborations 2; this play is likely to be cited by many students as challenging their ideas of how to maintain a healthy self.)

Students are liable to be unnerved by not only the outcome but also the very premise of the play; it is important that they see that Norman is not advocating suicide. Rather, her play documents two women actually facing this act, which allows her to explore this taboo subject in ways the playwright felt had not been done before. In an interview with Kathleen Betsko and Rachel Koenig in their book *Interviews with Contemporary Women Playwrights* (1987, Beach Tree Books), Norman acknowledges that she found other plays about suicide "unsatisfying": "I felt that if you were going to talk about suicide, there was really no way to talk about it without having someone argue back." Some students may think it would have been kinder of Jessie to leave a note than to announce her suicide plans to her mother, but it is precisely Jessie's feelings and reasons Norman wanted to explore. Ask students how the play would be different if Jessie *had* left a note. Almost all of the dramatic tension would be lost if we knew from the first scene that Jessie had already committed suicide. Other characters would also have to be introduced, unless the play were structured as a monologue — and it is hard to imagine this working as a full-length monologue. And Jessie's life would have to be revealed in flashbacks, which would be far less poignant than our hearing about it from her, firsthand.

Norman's use of humor in this play might also yield an interesting discussion or writing assignment. Have students cite any dialogue that made them laugh, and ask them to analyze its purpose in the play. Mama uses it as a defense mechanism to postpone addressing this issue seriously, and its presence in the play makes the subject more bearable for the readers and audience.

INVESTIGATIONS (p. 63)

1. *'night, Mother* won a Pulitzer prize and has been made into a movie, so students might be familiar with the plot and might know Jessie's intention before they read the play. Since the play is about the relationship between two women, their relationships to themselves, and their relationships to the larger world, however, this advance knowledge will in no way diminish a student's experience of reading the play. Students unfamiliar with the plot may not connect Jessie's requests for stacks of newspapers, towels, a rubber sheet, and pillows with suicide, but most will at least suspect her intention when she says of the gun: "It's not for him [Ricky], it's for me" (p. 31). Mama doesn't really register what Jessie's actions and requests add up to until her daughter announces "I'm going to kill myself, Mama" (p. 32). Even then, it's not clear that Mama begins to take Jessie seriously until Mama starts to dial the phone but then puts it down of her own accord (p. 35).

2. "Protection," to Mama, means protection from the outside world — from prowlers, for example (the reason Jessie told Dawson she needed bullets), or from the criminals she and Jessie see on television. To Jessie, "protection" means protection from herself: from the destiny she sees as hers, from a life in which she can't think of one thing she really likes, such as "rice pudding or cornflakes for breakfast or something" (p. 57).

3. Jessie really does want to make sure that Mama knows where things are and how to order groceries; part of her reason for returning to the list is her genuine concern for her mother. She's worried about Mama being alone and wants to help her with as many practical details as she can. But Jessie knows her mother can take care of herself; Mama says, "You don't have to take care of me, Jessie." Jessie replies, "I know that. You've just been letting me do it so I'll have something to do, haven't you?" (p. 39). In reality, Jessie keeps returning to her list to

avoid her mother's questions, all of which are aimed at changing Jessie's mind — which can't be changed. Jessie's list also provides a structure for this last evening of her life; it is a way to make this night easier for both herself and Mama. Together, they will enact some normal, relatively meaningless rituals as they talk, in an attempt to downplay the emotional impact of what is happening.

4. In response to Jessie's speech on page 41, Antler might tell Jessie she *could* change her life and make it better. He would probably agree with Jessie that the world is a pretty hard place, but he'd tell Jessie that she must create her own reasons to "raise her hand," to say yes instead of no, to continue living. He might tell her that *she* must create the "excitement and expectancy," that even "alone, in the wilds" (see "Raising My Hand," p. 101) — *especially* alone in the wild — there is a reason to live. Antler might say that we all have answers, we've had them all along, since we first tried to tell our teachers in grade school; we must believe in these answers, and call on ourselves when no one else will.

5. Students are most likely to single out the narrator of Madison Smartt Bell's "Customs of the Country," who, like Jessie, has had a very hard life. (Some may argue that the narrator of that story has had a *harder* life than Jessie. Part One: Connections and Elaborations 3a and 3c give students opportunities to explore this comparison further.) Both characters share a matter-of-fact tone and attitude about how bad things are and how they can't do anything to change them: "Sometimes you don't get but one mistake, if the one you pick is bad enough," says Bell's narrator (32). Unlike Jessie, though, Bell's narrator manages to keep going even after she loses custody of her son. Her final act of knocking out her wife-beating neighbor with a skillet can even be seen as life-affirming (though the narrator isn't convinced of this at the story's end).

YUSEF KOMUNYAKAA

Facing It (p. 64)

Komunyakaa's latest book is *Jazz Poetry Anthology* (1991); his other books are listed in the text's biographical footnote.

This powerful poem about a Vietnam veteran visiting the Vietnam Veterans Memorial in Washington, D.C. (also known as "the wall"), is quite accessible; its title should help students understand the speaker's mission. Some of your students may have visited the wall; if so, ask anyone willing to describe it, and their experience of seeing the wall, to the class. (This would also make an excellent additional writing assignment.) You might want to bring in some photographs of the wall to give students who haven't seen it a sense of how visually and emotionally striking it is.

You may want to spend some time defining "figurative language" and "metaphors" with your class to make sure they understand these terms; it will be difficult to discuss this poem *without* addressing the central metaphor of the wall. You might introduce the following statement Komunyakaa made about this poem and start discussion there: " 'Facing It' attempts to capture the pathos of the war through the reflective power of the Vietnam Veterans Memorial in Washington, D.C. The journey is from the external terrain to an internal one" (*Best American Poetry 1990*, p. 253).

INVESTIGATIONS (p. 65)

1. The speaker's face fades literally, since the reflection of a dark face in black granite would be difficult to see. The speaker's face also fades figuratively into the wall. Just as most of his reflection literally disappears, the speaker himself disappears metaphorically into the wall. The memorial does not merely commemorate the dead; it stands for the speaker's entire experience of the war, and encapsulates the horror of the experience. Looking at the wall, the speaker is drawn into that world again, pulled back into the war itself: "I touch the name Andrew Johnson; / I see the booby trap's white flash" (lines 17–18).

2. Literally, the speaker escapes the "bird of prey" of his reflection: "I turn / this way — the stone lets me go" (8–9). But then, in the next line, he's "inside" again. The poem suggests that the speaker is in some ways permanently caught, that his experiences in Vietnam were so harrowing they will be with him always. The transformations in the poem suggest that while he can temporarily escape, he can never fully leave the war behind — nor is trying to leave it behind his goal, as the poem's title suggests.

   Other images of transformation include the red bird turning into a plane (22–24); the speaker becoming a window (27); and the woman who appears to be erasing names on the wall but in fact is merely brushing a boy's hair (30–31).

3. The speaker has come to the wall for several reasons: He is there to remember both himself and Andrew Johnson; he is there to "face it," to try to confront his own emotions, which he has tried until now not to feel: "I said I wouldn't, / dammit: No tears" (3–4). He is there to come to terms with his own experiences in Vietnam as well as the experiences of everyone else who fought there or lost someone who fought there. And he is there to pay his respects to the 58,022 soldiers who knew the only real escape from this war that there is: death. He pays his respects; he seems to share some solidarity with the other visitors to the wall; and he remembers as much as he seems able or willing to bear, for the moment. It is clear that the speaker has much more to remember and "face," but it is also clear that these memories are extremely painful — so painful that the speaker must continue to keep his distance. Yet he has definitely made a start. Though there are repeated images of loss and violence in the poem (including the vet having "lost his right arm / inside the stone," (28–29), the poem ends on an affirmative image — a woman brushing a boy's hair, a gesture of caretaking and love.

4. The speakers in both "Facing It" and "Driving Again" are confronting death, and both speakers are afraid of — and have tried, until now, to distance themselves from — their emotions in response to these deaths. The poems share a dream-like quality, too; in each poem the speaker experiences events in such a way that he isn't always sure what is real and what's a dream.

PETER CAMERON

Jump or Dive (p. 65)

Some students may be initially uncomfortable with this short story in which a teenager, visiting his gay uncle and his uncle's lover, confronts his own sexual identity. (If you want to address the issue of homosexuality up front, you might assign Agnes Herman's memoir in Part Two, "A Parent's Journey Out of the Closet," which provides an excellent, nonjudgmental entry into this topic.) But Evan's relationship with his uncle is a healthy one, and there is nothing stereotypical about the author's presentation of Evan, either — this is, of course, part of the story's point.

Unlike some of the other characters and speakers students encounter in Part One, the protagonist of this story does not seem to have a very strong sense of self as the story opens. Evan is a keen observer of other people's characters, but prior to this vacation he doesn't seem to have thought much about his own. This is not to say that Evan is shallow, but merely that it is the events of this story that begin to make him take stock. Ask students to compare Evan to Reginald McKnight's or Richard McCann's twelve-year-old narrators, who have already given their identities quite a bit of thought, despite their youth. What might account for Evan's relative lack of self-examination to date, compared to these characters?

INVESTIGATIONS (p. 75)

1. Students' responses will vary. Evan certainly seems to be experiencing self-doubt, much as any teenager in his situation might. On vacation with his parents, he's the only person his age not only among his immediate party but also in the whole condominium complex, where children are allowed only as guests. "Everyone looked at me as if I was a freak," he observes (para. 7). He is self-conscious, though in a way that is typical of adolescents: He doesn't want to be the focus of the adults' attention (21); he's embarrassed to be seen shopping with his mother (41–51). Evan is at a transitional stage in life: He's used to a mother who "makes normal food" (107) and a father who reads the *Wall Street Journal*; he's also a boy used to doing as he's told and accepting what his parents tell him. For instance, he takes a practice golf swing "because [his] father . . . told [him] always to take a practice swing. Always" (113). But at the same time Evan is beginning to see the seams in his tidy, comfortable life. His mother is not invulnerable; she becomes hysterical in the Grand Canyon. His parents pretend not to be disturbed by the fact that Uncle Walter and Jason are homosexuals, but in fact Evan's mother says, "I can't face Villa Indigo without a drink" (52). When Evan asks what she means, she doesn't answer. And in the grocery store, where Jason pretends Evan and his mother are Jason's own son and wife, Evan's mother goes along with the lie. In the face of all this it is only natural that Evan would experience some self-doubt. He has not only witnessed his mother in a bold lie; but even Jason, who seems perfectly comfortable with his identity back at Villa Indigo, opts for a different identity in public.

2. Neither Evan nor his parents would be likely to describe Evan as a fatalist — at least not at the point in the story when Uncle Walter calls him one. Evan's comment about being a sophomore — "It's not something you like or dislike. . . . It's something you are" (90) — is not a statement intended to reveal Evan's beliefs; rather it is typical adolescent conversation from a kid who feels out of his element but is trying not to show it. It is simply Evan's attempt to remain cool and aloof, as is his earlier statement, "I don't talk on demand" (85). By the end of the story, though, Evan *is* feeling pretty fatalistic: If he goes to the Petrified Forest with his parents he knows he is running away from something — something he can be pretty sure will catch up with him later. If he stays at Villa Indigo instead he'll be forced to confront these unnerving feelings he has been experiencing.

The speaker in the poem "Facing It" is "a window" in part because of the physical play of light and dark in the poem. The white vet behind the speaker literally sees through him to his own reflection on the black wall. Similarly, it could be said that Uncle Walter sees through Evan: He seems to suspect even before Evan does that his nephew is approaching some kind of crisis or turning point in his life and identity.

3. Evan's decision about whether to go to the Petrified Forest is a big deal because either choice leaves him in a situation he won't control. The image of his mother crying hysterically in the Grand Canyon is still fresh in his mind; it would be disturbing for any child to see a parent helpless and out of control. The recognition of his mother's fallibility leads to another recognition: There are problems and decisions your parents can't help you with, decisions and situations you have to figure out on your own.

   For Evan, choosing to stay at Villa Indigo *is* one of those situations. Evan is both attracted to the idea and repelled by it; he doesn't want to see Jason "swimming in the dark water, slowly and nakedly" (172). Evan knows he will continue to feel uncomfortable around Jason, and staying at Villa Indigo would force him to confront why he feels this way, and why he felt the way he did when Jason coached him with his golf swing. Going with his parents to the Petrified Forest seems the safer option (by safe I am referring to *emotional* risk; there is no indication anywhere in the story that Evan is physically *afraid* of Jason, or that he has any reason to be.) By going to the Petrified Forest, Evan would be running from the important feelings he is just beginning to confront.

4. When Jason helps Evan with his golf swing, Evan seems to be "dropping dangerously, and much too fast" (115–118). Evan's response to Jason's physical attention is not what Evan (and probably many of your students) would have expected. He finds Jason's attention alone distracting enough almost to miss his first shot; when that attention turns physical, Evan is both unnerved and exhilarated: "He [Jason] leaned over me so that he was embracing me from behind, his large tan hands on top of mine, holding the club. . . . I tried to relax, but I couldn't. I suddenly felt very hot." Readers are privy, then, to Evan's thoughts — we know he couldn't relax and he felt very hot — but nowhere does he say anything along the lines of "I didn't want him touching me like that." Further, the scene ends on a satisfying note for Evan; he is hitting the ball well, as is everyone around him.

   Where Evan is "dropping" from and "dropping" into is not explicitly stated in the text, because the story is told from Evan's point of view and Evan himself isn't sure of the answer to this question. But he is on the road to figuring it out, and there are plenty of clues for the reader, too.

   Ask students how they interpret the story's last sentence. Why is it so important that Evan couldn't make his body turn? Simply because he didn't want to lose the game he was playing? Because he didn't want more "red welts from smacking the water at bad angles" (139)? Students should see that Evan is wrestling with something much more here, even though he's not able to articulate it. He's wrestling with his own sexual identity; the implication is that he's dropping, or jumping, from a familiar, comfortable, "acceptable" world in which he always assumed he was heterosexual into an unfamiliar, socially unacceptable, frightening new world in which he faces the possibility that he is *not* heterosexual.

JOHN EDGAR WIDEMAN

Valaida (p. 75)

In addition to the books mentioned in the text's footnote, Wideman is the author of *The Homewood Trilogy* (1985), consisting of *Damballah* (1981), *Hiding Place* (1981), and *Sent for You Yesterday* (1983); *Hurry Home* (1970); and *The Lynchers* (1973). Wideman, who was a Rhodes scholar at Oxford, is now a professor of English at the University of Massachusetts in Amherst. He has been hailed by Mel Watkins of the *New York Times* as "one of America's premier writers of fiction" (*New York Times Book Review*, April 11, 1982).

This profoundly moving story about the transformative powers of human emotion focuses on a white Holocaust survivor and his Black cleaning woman. The cleaning woman, who has worked for Mr. Cohen for decades, is much more than hired help: Mrs. Clara has kept his house, and him, decent and presentable all these years, and so helped him maintain his dignity. She has mended his shirts "so he is decent, safe within them" (para. 12). Mrs. Clara helps Mr. Cohen create this facade of neat, clean decency; it is the only thing between him and harrowing thoughts of his past like this: "All of it [this flesh], what's gray, what's pale, what's mottled with dark spots is meat that turns to lard and stinks a sweet sick stink to high heaven if you cook it" (13). Despite the horrors of the concentration camp, Mr. Cohen has found a way to live on. He does so in part thanks to Mrs. Clara's attentions and in part because he has been privy to the triumphant spirit of Valaida (the woman who saved his life in the camp) and knows that goodness does, in fact, exist somewhere in the universe. Mr. Cohen could not articulate all this, yet he carries on precisely because he recognizes, despite all he has been through, the intrinsic value of life: He speaks of leaving his apartment when it's spring and conquering

> the park again, shoes shined, the remnants of that glorious head of hair slicked back, freshly shaved cheeks raw as a baby's in the brisk sunshine of those first days welcoming life back and yes he's out there in it again, his splay-foot penguin walk and gentleman's attire, shirt like a pledge, a promise. (12)

(See Part One: Connections and Elaborations 3a; it is in this spirit that Mr. Cohen would argue with Jessie in *'night, Mother*, but Jessie simply lacks Mr. Cohen's fundamental interest in life, and Mr. Cohen would not succeed.)

Students may have difficulty with the shift in point of view after the story's second paragraph, especially given the stream-of-consciousness style of the opening narration. You may want to alert them to this before they read the story, lest they become frustrated when they tackle it on their own.

INVESTIGATIONS (p. 83)

1. The opening italicized passage is told from Valaida's perspective, *in heaven*. Her reminiscences are sparked by her bird's eye view of a reporter interviewing someone named Bobby, with whom she used to perform. Bobby never reappears in the story after it shifts to Mr. Cohen's point of view (he couldn't; Mr. Cohen didn't know him or even know he existed). Bobby's main purpose is to facilitate Valaida's reminiscences and establish her as the beautiful, but more important, humane, angel who saved Mr. Cohen's life. The focus on her musical career, the very musicality of her language, testify to a spirit that could not be broken. You might direct students' attention to Valaida's statement about her fancy clothes and cars and jewelry: "That's the foolishness the reporter's after" (2). Valaida knows the glamor is what people want to hear about; she also knows

that what *really* matters is the human spirit, the human soul, which is, in her case, exemplified by her music.

Once students meet Mr. Cohen and learn he is a Holocaust survivor, they may suspect that he is "the pitiful little stomped-down white boy in the camp" Valaida tried to keep alive; other students may not make this connection till paragraph 24.

2. Mr. Cohen observes of his relationship with Mrs. Clara that they had "developed an etiquette that spelled out precisely how close, how distant the two of them could be once a week while she cleaned his apartment" (4). And "seldom were they both in the same room at the same time more than a few minutes because clearly none was large enough to contain them and the distance they needed" (5). He observes: "They have grown old together, avoiding each other in these musty rooms" (21).

The intimacy of sharing an apartment as they do, with Mrs. Clara once a week taking care of Mr. Cohen's most personal needs (cleaning the bathroom, mending his shorts), *creates* a distance.

Mrs. Clara works *for* Mr. Cohen; she is Black and he is white; they are not, on the surface, equals, and this creates the distance between them. The distance is also there because they both want it there. We don't know the details of Mrs. Clara's past, but we do know that Mr. Cohen has been so badly degraded and debased, both spiritually and physically, that he is unable to risk an emotional bond with another person. He can't risk emotion because he can't risk loss; he has suffered more of that than anyone could be expected to bear. (Since he was in a camp at age thirteen, and the only mention of his mother and sister is when he is quite young, we can assume he lost his family in the camps, too.)

Two other simultaneously distant and intimate relationships revolve around Valaida. Her relationship with Bobby is distant because she's dead, in heaven, while he's alive, on earth; if she were alive, she'd speak to the reporter herself. But she's not alive. Her relationship with Bobby is intimate because they performed together, and she must speak to the reporter through him.

Valaida's relationship with Mr. Cohen is simultaneously as intimate and distant as a relationship between two people can be. She saved his life, yet Valaida and Mr. Cohen don't even know each other's names, much less their respective fates.

3. On the surface Mr. Cohen wants an audience for his story, but of course Mrs. Clara serves as much more than an audience. Mrs. Clara keeps Mr. Cohen and his apartment decent and presentable, but no emotional bond has ever been articulated between them. Now Mr. Cohen wants to bridge that distance. He wants to talk. And he wants her not to be suspicious when he asks her to sit down and talk, he wants her not to "refuse what's never been offered before" (20). Mr. Cohen wants not to be denied. But Mrs. Clara denies him (10), and his mother denies him, and then the night denies him (22). Mrs. Clara is the only person Mr. Cohen ever sees and the only one who would notice if he died; as his only human contact, she confirms his existence. And although Mrs. Clara initially says she'd rather work straight through and go home early, she does, in fact, listen to his story; she does not deny him.

It is unclear how much Mrs. Clara is changed by Mr. Cohen's story, but she is definitely affected. By listening at all, she has helped precipitate this change in their relationship, moving it one tiny step closer to a friendship.

And she has learned a fact she did not know: "Always thought it was just you people over there doing those terrible things to each other" (34). She has learned, too, that Mr. Cohen probably has more respect for Black people (hence herself) than she may have thought he did.

Mr. Cohen is profoundly changed by telling this story. In telling it he comes to realize what Mrs. Clara really means to him; she has helped to keep him alive in this world, as Valaida did in the camps. She has helped him maintain his dignity and is the closest thing to family he's got. The man who "sees the faces of her relatives become his" (35) no longer needs or wants to touch Mrs. Clara's hair (see 7). It has become the same as his.

4. If Mr. Cohen were talking to another Holocaust survivor he might not have dwelled so much on the physical horrors of the camps. Another survivor would probably have shared this experience, so words would be both unnecessary and insufficient.

To the speaker of "Facing It," Mr. Cohen would probably not place as much emphasis on the woman who saved him. Instead he might focus on the death of someone close to him. He might tell the speaker of "Facing It" that he must confront the horrors, that he *must* cry, for only then will he begin to heal.

To the speaker of "Driving Again," Mr. Cohen might well expand his story to relay the plight of his own family, in addition to emphasizing the heroism of Valaida, who sings much in the same way that the grandmother in Joseph's poem "smiled although cells / crushed her brain" (see "Driving Again," 47–48).

JOY HARJO

Ordinary Spirit (p. 83)

Joy Harjo is the poetry editor for *High Plains Literary Review*. In addition to the books mentioned in the text's footnote, she has published *In Mad Love and War* (1990).

In this memoir, Harjo tells us that through her writing, her "decision to live" (para. 1), and her belief that the many worlds she walks in and out of are all one, she has found her place in this world. It would be interesting to discuss the differences between this essay and John Haines's "Moments and Journeys": Both writers have a spiritual connection to the natural world and a very positive outlook on the world in general, but Haines emphasizes the physical world (his homesteading, and working with the land and animals), while Harjo emphasizes the intellectual (her writing). Ask your students whether they found one of these two essays more effective than the other, and have them explain why.

Note Harjo's statement, "When I first began writing, poetry was simply a way for me to speak" (11). Do any of your students share this experience with Harjo? For an additional writing assignment, ask them to write a poem or story in which they "speak" something about themselves they might otherwise be unable or unwilling to say.

INVESTIGATIONS (p. 87)

1. For the first part of this question, students' answers will vary. As for Evan in Peter Cameron's "Jump or Dive," any adolescent boy would be experiencing

some of his confusion. But Evan's confusion about his identity is certainly helped along by his mother's little lies and evasions, as well-intentioned as these might be. She makes every effort to "treat Uncle Walter normally" (23), but in fact, she "can't face Villa Indigo without a drink" (52). When Evan asks what she means by this, she won't tell him. She goes along with Jason's lie in the supermarket, pretending she's his wife not only to help him out, but also to help herself: She's more comfortable pretending they are a "regular" (hetero-sexual) family than acknowledging that the man she's shopping with is her gay brother-in-law's lover.

And then of course there is Evan's "forebear" Uncle Walter. Without suggesting that homosexuality is in some way inherited, it is reasonable to point out that one is certainly influenced by one's relatives. Whatever Evan's sexual orientation may eventually become, Uncle Walter's homosexuality is as much a part of his background as is the heterosexuality of his parents and other relatives. One's parents are usually one's most influential forebears; note that Evan's father is very supportive of Uncle Walter, and careful not to let anything negative be said about him or his homosexuality (23). At the same time, though, Evan's mother has revealed a glimpse of her true feelings on this subject to Evan. Evan, then, is not only unsure of what he feels, but also of what it's all right to feel, not only by society's larger standards, but by his own parents' standards.

As for Jessie in the play *'night, Mother,* her parents are the only forebears we know anything about, but what we do know is quite revealing. One key fact is that her parents apparently didn't love each other. Another is that her mother withheld vital information from both Jessie *and* her father (Jessie's father apparently had fits, though Mama never told him or Jessie; Jessie also had her fits long before she ever fell off a horse). Both the deception Jessie suffered and the knowledge she gains when her mother reveals this information confirm Jessie's feeling that there really is no point in living. More important, perhaps, is Mama's inherent ability to live in this world. Mama says about herself, "I don't know what I'm here for, but then, I don't think about it" (p. 46). She goes on to say "I don't like things to think about. I like things to go on" (p. 47). Jessie lacks the mindset or chemistry that allows her mother to operate in this way. Mama's having this ability, however, only highlights for Jessie the fact that she lacks it; she knows this is the kind of equipment she needs to live in the world, and she doesn't have it.

2. Students' responses to this question will vary. Many are liable to take issue with this statement, especially those who have experienced blatant prejudice or who feel they have been discriminated against for being in some way different from the majority of people around them. Ask whether such experiences in fact confirm that these many different worlds (for example, men vs. women; heterosexuals vs. homosexuals; white people vs. people of color) are separate. Couldn't it also be argued — as Harjo and Morales might claim — that these worlds are only separate insofar as people who want them separate *make* them so? Ask students to consider the behavior of Clint Oates ("The Kind of Light That Shines on Texas") in this light. Remind them of his statement: "I wanted to show her that we [the Black students in the class] were not all the same" (8).

3. Harjo's outlook is quite similar to Haines's. Haines praises the world "when men lived less complicated and distracted lives" and when this simplicity provided "a kind of radiance, a very old and deep assurance that life has continuity and meaning." Back then, he says, the dream journey and actual

18

life "were not separate at all, but continually one thing" (see "Moments and Journeys," 15). For Harjo, it is her work (her writing) rather than living in the natural world that provides this continuity and meaning: "And then, in the middle of working, the world gives way and I see the old, old Creek one who comes in here and watches over me" (5). Like Haines, Harjo celebrates nature.

On the other hand, neither Haines nor Harjo has much in common with Oates in Part Seven. Oates's essay title, "Against Nature," puts her immediately in conflict with anyone singing nature's praises. Oates tries to undo the romantic associations these writers, and many people, have with nature. Her feelings about nature have much to do with the ailment tachycardia — one that is, ironically, natural, in that it is a defect in her body she did not bring on herself. The nature Oates is surrounded by when she stops to control this "natural" malfunction of her body is no use to her; it can't save her, and in fact it is full of, to quote the passage of Thoreau that Oates quotes in her own essay, "tadpoles which herons gobble up, and tortoises and toads run over in the road; and . . . sometimes it [seems it] has rained flesh and blood!" (see "Against Nature," 33). These are not images Oates finds comforting or reassuring.

4. Mr. Cohen's soul might appear at least somewhat starved to Harjo, because of all the hatred and torment and loneliness he has experienced. But it should look better than the soul of the woman in paragraph 16 of Harjo's essay, since Mr. Cohen does not suffer from self-hatred, and is in fact allowing himself to care for another human being for the first time in a long time as "Valaida" ends.

RICHARD McCANN

My Mother's Clothes: The School of Beauty and Shame (p. 88)

Richard McCann codirects the M.F.A. Program in Creative Writing at the American University. His work has appeared in the *Atlantic* and *Esquire*, among other publications.

This complex and moving story is about a boy trying to come to terms with social definitions and expectations of the concepts "masculine" and "feminine," as well as with his own sexuality. The selection begins and ends as a conventional short story; ask students whether their expectations of a short story are fulfilled throughout. Direct their attention to paragraph 39. Whose voice is speaking here? Has the narrator changed? Why might the author have chosen to step outside of his narrator's voice and speak in his own at this point? What can McCann tell us that his narrator cannot? Would knowledge of the author's sexual orientation make a difference in understanding this story? If so, how? Finally, is the author in fact revealing his true self to his readers here? It is easy to misread the long sentence in the middle of this paragraph that ends "this costume having become the standard garb of the urban American gay man." The writer does not, in fact, explicitly state that he *is* a gay man, only that he is wearing the costume of one.

The costume metaphor is pervasive throughout this story, as is the closely related concept of labels. This story's narrator is preoccupied with the labels "masculine" and "feminine," along with the images that are associated with those labels. When the narrator calls his once–best friend Denny a "faggot" at the end of the story, he is rejecting, even spitting on, the very costumes and images he used to embrace.

INVESTIGATIONS (p. 100)

1. The story's narrator seems masculine when he and the other neighborhood kids listen to Bucky Trueblood's descriptions of his mother's naked body (para. 8). By social standards, there is nothing particularly abnormal about boys this age being preoccupied with the bodies of members of the opposite sex, but its presentation reveals exactly how grotesque this manner of learning about sex (by dropping a pencil on the floor to look under your mother's skirt, for instance) really is. It is clear that the narrator is not enjoying this as much as his peers; he feels uncomfortable and "moves outside the circle" (9).

   The narrator also seems masculine playing that favorite boyhood game of "War" (21), and when he's with his father on his annual tour of duty and the boy passes his afternoons "desultorily setting fires in ashtrays" (34).

   In two other scenes where the narrator is expected to be masculine (paragraph 28, when his father is reshingling the roof, separating power lines "with his bare hands," and paragraph 30, when the narrator is afraid of the slimy bottom of the reservoir), he depicts himself as grotesque: awkward, uncomfortable, unwilling or unable to do what's expected of him. A truly "masculine" boy wouldn't have been so scared when the hammer fell and would have been able to wade deep into the reservoir.

2. The narrator transcends being "split in two pieces" at the end of the story by denying the feminine side of himself. He not only denies, but also denigrates this part of his personality by joining Bucky's gang of hoods and cutting off his friendship with Denny. Prior to paragraph 52, when the narrator's mother discovers that he and Denny have been dressing up in her clothes, the narrator has not, in fact, transcended being "split in two pieces."

   > I saw myself as doubled — both an image and he who studied it. . . . Like Denny, I could neither dispense with images nor take their flexibility as pleasure, for the idea of self I had learned and was learning still was that one was constructed by one's images — " *When boys cross their legs, they cross one ankle atop the knee*" — so that one finally sought the protection of believing in one's own image and, in believing in it as reality, condemned oneself to its poverty. (37)

   The implication here is that if you cross your legs the other way, you're *not* a boy: You're either a girl, or you don't exist. The narrator is well aware of this bind at the story's end; he has chosen to exist.

   Bridging the gap between masculine and feminine might bring us into greater harmony with ourselves and each other in that males like Bucky and the narrator's father might see stereotypically feminine qualities (such as emotional vulnerability or physical beauty) as desirable rather than negative. The narrator's mother, on the other hand, might see her concepts of femininity as superficial: Isn't it possible that the other neighborhood mothers are good, intelligent people, despite the way they dress? Might there be something she herself could be interested in — perhaps even friendships with these women? — that would be more meaningful than her mysterious (and surely somewhat fabricated) moods?

3. Students' responses will vary, of course. Direct students back to paragraph 37 and ask them to consider whether they feel "condemned" to the poverty of any aspects of their own self-image. Ask students to consider not only social expectations regarding sex roles (the main image explored in this story) but also their expectations of themselves and their parents' expectations. Are there

male students who want to go into a profession in the arts, for example, whose parents want them to go into business? Are there female students who want to study physics or engineering whose parents deem these professions inappropriate?

ANTLER

Raising My Hand (p. 101)

In addition to the books mentioned in the text's footnote, Antler has written *Last Words* (1986). In 1987 he won the Witter Bynner Prize for Poetry from the American Academy and Institute of Arts and Letters.

This straightforward poem provides rich connections with other selections in Part One, and students should find it quite accessible. You might open discussion by asking students to link this poem with other selections in Part One and having them explain the connections they perceive. If the act of raising your hand can be seen as a metaphor for saying "yes" to life, Rosario Morales's "I Am What I Am" may be the first selection they mention. Ask students whether this metaphor can be applied to the character of Jessie in Marsha Norman's *'night, Mother* as well. (See Investigation 4, p. 11 in this manual for a further discussion of this connection.) Students might also compare what this poem's speaker learned in school to what Clint Oates learned there by the end of Reginald McKnight's "The Kind of Light That Shines on Texas." And what of the narrator in Madison Smartt Bell's "Customs of the Country"? She raises her hand to get her son back, but fails; she then literally raises her hand against her wife-beating neighbor — but the wife she tries to save does not want to be saved. On the surface, this narrator's actions fail — but is there a way these actions can be seen as life-affirming, too?

INVESTIGATIONS (p. 102)

1. Having to raise your hand before you speak curbs spontaneity, which in turn may curb enthusiasm; this in turn may curb a student's overall interest in school. Students are liable to feel rejected when someone else is called on — especially if the student called on has the wrong answer. But the custom of raising one's hand teaches many good things, too: patience, politeness, consideration, and respect for the rights of others. Students learn that everyone deserves a chance to speak, not just the loudest and most aggressive members of the class.

   If students never had to raise their hands, the result in most classrooms would probably be chaos. With everyone talking at once no one would be able to distinguish between correct or acceptable answers, unacceptable answers, irrelevant answers, and so forth. In short, especially in elementary school, when the focus is on basic skills, it is unlikely that much productive learning would go on.

2. The first thing school taught the speaker was how to get by in this world: Play by the rules, arbitrary as they may seem. In stanza 2 the speaker experiences a sort of bittersweet nostalgia for his early classroom days. It is clear he was a good student who liked school; it's also clear he was frustrated by *having* to raise his hand, by having to hold back, and especially by having to listen to incorrect answers when he knew the right ones (and he knew the teacher knew this as well). The speaker's sense of fair play was violated in school: A child who didn't know the correct answer didn't *deserve* the reward of being called on.

21

In stanza 3 the speaker moves into the present, some twenty-odd years later. His emotions are different now: he doesn't feel slighted, but appreciates the value of raising his hand. (See Investigation 3 below for more on this topic.)

3. School has taught the speaker that raising your hand is an affirmative gesture: It indicates not so much that you are willing to play by the rules but that you are willing to play at all. Students who raise their hands all think they have something valuable to say: The fact that some of them have the "wrong" answer is not as important as the fact that they have something to contribute and that they make that effort. *This* is the importance of the "excitement / and expectancy" the speaker feels in the poem's last stanza. The speaker knows now that the excitement and interest in life come from the *quest* for knowledge and understanding, rather than just knowing the right answer.

4. Students' responses will vary.

JOHN HAINES

Moments and Journeys (p. 103)

John Haines spends part of each year in Alaska. In addition to the books mentioned in the text's footnote, he has published *Living Off the Country: Essays on Poetry and Place* (1981).

John Haines devotes this memoir to celebrating the "reassuring vitality" he sees and feels in the earth's natural cycles. For Haines, the natural world is "symbolic of that hidden, original life we have done so much to destroy" (para. 18). Ask students to try to define this hidden original life. Can they identify with it? If not, why? Haines's visual imagery is quite effective, and he presents an enviably harmonic picture of his interdependence with nature. Ask students whether they feel a similar spiritual connection with nature. Clearly, Haines identifies very strongly with nature; it offers him not just beauty, but a sort of sustaining life force. It would be interesting to assign this with Joyce Carol Oates's "Against Nature" in Part Seven. Oates paints nature as sometimes indifferent, sometimes destructive, but never as prettily as Haines does. What might account for these differences in perspective?

If "our own life is a journey," as the embedded quotation from Edwin Muir in paragraph 1 states, ask students what kind of a journey Haines seems to have had so far. How does it compare to the journeys of other characters in this part? Haines writes:

> If such moments [the images of journeys and nature he provides throughout this memoir] are not as easily come by . . . it may be because they are not so clearly linked to the life that surrounds them and of which they are part. They are present nonetheless, available to imagination. (16)

Do your students feel these moments are equally "available" to the imagination of all the characters they have met in this part? You might want to start with Jessie, in Norman's '*night, Mother*. Students should see that apparently, at least from Jessie's point of view, these moments are quite unavailable to her. What about the narrator of Bell's "Customs of the Country"?

Haines may seem somewhat elitist to students who grew up in an urban environment — especially those who never had the call or the opportunity to leave that environment. But Haines is no weekend nature lover: Along with teaching and writing, he has supported himself through his hard work on the land as a hunter, trapper, and fisherman. Ask students whether they feel Haines sees lifestyles other than his own as equally valuable — or does he seem to believe that meaning is only found through connection with the natural world? In fact, Haines provides no instances of city dwellers experiencing anything close to a "kind of radiance, a very old and deep assurance that life has continuity and meaning" (15). Ask students to find key "meaningful" moments in some of the other selections in this part. You might suggest they look at Wideman's "Valaida"; certainly both Mr. Cohen and that story's title character have meaningful lives. And despite the horrors both have endured, they see much to celebrate: Even before the story's transforming ending, Mr. Cohen has his conquering of the park in the spring (12); Valaida has her music (1–2). Can these be considered the kinds of moments of radiance to which Haines later refers?

INVESTIGATIONS (p. 108)

1. Haines tells his story through a series of images that mark "moments and stages" in his existence (2). For example, in paragraph 4 he is on a trip with Fred Campbell, an old hunter and miner from whom he was "eager to learn" all he could. Later, he is no longer a novice so he no longer needs a guide to the Alaska wilds: "By then I had my own team" (6). Haines also speaks of "places that take on symbolic value to an individual or a tribe" (18).

   In McCann's story, the mother's clothes represent for the narrator both stages in his life and places (physical and spiritual) that are symbolic to him. Consider the period before the narrator knows Denny, when he adores his mother's belongings but does nothing about it. In the next stage, he and Denny start wearing his mother's clothes. Finally, he banishes Denny and stops wearing his mother's clothes. The clothes and certain behavior provide the images that construct the narrator. Note also that the narrator worships his mother (and *her* image) until he is caught wearing her clothes. After that, he adores neither his mother nor Denny; it is Bucky Trueblood's allegiance he seeks.

2. Responses will vary according to what students wrote in their original assignments. It may help to refer students to paragraph 12, where Haines defines a journey as consisting of "a place to start from, something to leave behind, . . . companions, . . . and . . . a destination."

3. Joseph's speaker might well embrace Haines's claim. In "Driving Again," the speaker's movement from waking into dreaming is hardly effortless — "Where was it? I stumbled / through the darkness to the door / before I realized / I was waking from a dream" (25–28) — but it *does* occur frequently in the poem. The reader also gets the sense that much of the hardship endured by both the speaker and his grandparents had to do with lives spent doing, or supervising, hard labor in a dirty city. Haines associates both cities and the kind of work done there with a movement *away* from things that bring us inner peace. One kind of work usually done in cities, of course, involves industries that in some ways destroy nature; another kind of work (white-collar desk jobs, for example) often provides the worker with absolutely no connection to the environment that sustains him or her. Whatever the work, to Haines cities are hardly the environments conducive to the Yuma Indians' ability to make these effortless, spiritually sustaining shifts from waking to dreaming.

LUCIA MARIA PERILLO

The Northside at Seven (p. 108)

This poem about a woman's past and present in an urban neighborhood contains imagery so vivid your students are likely to notice Perillo's language as much as her speaker's experience of coming to terms with where she came from and who she is. Perillo's language is not fancy, but its specificity and originality provide excellent models for students. For instances of fresh, innovative uses of language, direct students' attention to "the magazines flapping / from the gutters like broken skin" (lines 5–6) and "sometimes I feel history slipping from my body / like a guilty bone" (37–38).

This poem pairs especially well with Lawrence Joseph's "Driving Again." The two poems share the same framework: Both speakers remember their pasts and think about their forebears while they drive routes frequently traveled; during the course of these memories, both speakers are moved to tears. If you assign both these poems, ask students to focus on the differences between the two speakers: How does each answer the question "Who am I?" Is either speaker more at peace with him- or herself?

INVESTIGATIONS (p. 110)

1. The man at the bakery reminds the speaker of the men "who came to unload on" her father when she was a girl. The speaker is apparently repelled by or at least alienated from the world of her childhood. Her father was an important man in the Italian-American immigrant community in which the speaker grew up, and the speaker presents him as a somewhat stereotypical "godfather" type: He's the man family members and people in the neighborhood come to to have their problems solved. The speaker seems repelled by the ethos that ran the world of her childhood, the same world that the man at the bakery lives in: A man doesn't get paid, so he takes his client's car. The speaker can't absolve this man: She knows too little about the situation to know if there might have been other solutions, but she knows just enough to know that she doesn't approve of this manner of doing business.

    The speaker cries in part because she knows this ethos she hates is a part of her: It is who her father is; it is in her blood. She cries because she loves her father in spite of this, and to love her father is to accept her history — a history she is neither fond of nor comfortable with. She simultaneously wants to embrace and reject this history; it is a conflict she knows she cannot resolve: She is both different than her father and the same (see the poem's last line). She cries, too, for what she has forgotten — so much of her history that is *not* a part of her, that she has either rejected willfully or simply forgotten.

2. The most apparent thing the speaker shares with her father is food, which provides both nourishment and comfort (31–34, 39–40). The most important way in which the speaker and her father are the same is registered in the poem's last three lines: Both father and daughter recognize the "trap" of the working-class life the daughter was born into and want better for her. Both also realize — the father in lines 29–30, the speaker in the poem's last line — that no matter what their differences, their common histories will keep them in some ways always the same.

3. John Haines might say that the speaker's experience of memory confirms his own sense of one's personal journey; while "we would always hope to find

something" (Haines, 12), still each journey remains, for that person "the embodiment of an old story" (6). The speaker of this poem would be likely to agree that in many ways her life is the embodiment of an old story; lines 37–45 speak directly to how similar her life is to her father's. But she might not so readily embrace Haines's claim that all this engenders "a very old and deep assurance that life has continuity and meaning" (15). While her past has great meaning to the speaker in this poem, her present and future, and the ways in which she can make herself different and escape from the things about her past she does *not* like, are at least equally important.

PART TWO

IN FAMILIES

OVERVIEW

In this part students will read about families celebrated and denigrated, families that cohere and families that unravel, families as seen by children and those seen from a parent's point of view. Through all these selections, certain themes remain constant: loyalty and obligation, love and support, protection and nurturing. The narrator in "The Leap" honors her mother, the speaker in "Grape Sherbet" pays tribute to her father, and the speaker in "Circling the Daughter" celebrates his daughter — all with an intensity that would leave any parent or child proud and deeply moved. The speaker in "Words for My Daughter" looks to his innocent child to save not only him, but all of humanity, while the narrator of "Sugar Among the Chickens" learns he can earn his parents' pride and respect by saving himself. And the speakers in "Allowance" and "After the Deindustrialization of America, My Father Enters Television Repair" record the power of family legends to shape our lives.

The narrator of "The Lover of Horses," on the other hand, literally succumbs to the gypsies of her family legend, knowing that while this may lead to romance, it will also lead to no good. There is, of course, this darker side to family life: The most obvious illustration here is the play *Broken Eggs*, in which an already unstable Cuban American family disintegrates further during a daughter's wedding. In "Fathering," the narrator is so blinded by love for his daughter and by guilt (not only for leaving her behind but also for the Vietnam War in general) that he risks both their health and happiness by keeping outsiders at bay. And even the most devoted and well-intentioned family members can misinterpret situations: The narrator of "On the Other Side of the War: A Story" paints a cool portrait of a father who thinks he is providing his Vietnamese wife and Vietnamese American daughter with everything they need.

Most often, of course, our relationships with our families include both joy and pain, as we wrestle with issues of what we owe our families and what we need and want for ourselves. The speaker in "Changing the Name to Ochester" reconciles his love for his grandfather and father despite *their* lack of love for each other. Similarly, the narrator in "Devils" does something she knows is wrong (tells a lie) to correct a situation she *feels* is wrong (her mother marrying a man the narrator and her siblings don't like). And while Agnes Herman wants more than anything to love her son, she must overcome her prejudices against homosexuality before she can accept and embrace him.

Instructors who don't have time to teach all the selections in Part Two might focus on the following smaller grouping. Selections by Mukherjee, Gordon, Kadohata, Machado, and Herman all involve the conflict between family allegiance and allegiance to some other community as well — whether that community is Amerasian, Japanese American, Cuban American, or gay or lesbian. The tension caused by these different allegiances would provide an excellent focus.

TESS GALLAGHER

The Lover of Horses (p. 115)

Tess Gallagher lives in Port Angeles, Washington. Books not mentioned in the text's footnote include *Amplitude: New and Selected Poems* (1976), *Willingly* (1984), *Under Stars* (1978), *Instructions to the Double* (1976), *Stepping Outside* (1974), *A Concert of Tenses* (1986), and *The Lover of Horses* (1986), a collection of short stories. Gallagher has taught at many colleges and universities.

The father and great-grandfather in this mysterious story about a girl's relationship with her family are presented as simultaneously unpredictable and unreliable but lovable. They are drunks, but harmless drunks. Ask students to cite instances in the story where it is clear that the narrator is romanticizing her father and great-grandfather, and what life with them must have been like (at least for other members of the household). Note her reference to "the understandable wish to escape family obligations" (para. 7) and to "the harsh imaginings of his abandoned wife" (9). Meanwhile, the narrator's mother and grandmother refer repeatedly to her great-grandfather as a "good-for-nothing drunk" (10) and "a fool" (11). In most families, the wish to escape family obligations *might* be understandable, but acting on it would certainly be condemned. Similarly, an abandoned wife and mother would have good reason for "harsh imaginings."

Ask students what they make of the narrator's father cutting off his daughter's braids to pay off a card-playing debt (16). While the narrator claims to be happy to be free of her hair, she wasn't consulted beforehand and it's apparent that her father would have cut it regardless. How might the narrator's mother have related the same incident?

You may want to spend some time on the narrator's revealing theory that members of her family "have been stolen by things — by mad ambitions, by musical instruments . . . or, as was [her] father's case, by the more easily recognized and popular obsession with card playing" (12). In addition, the narrator's great-grandfather was stolen by a horse; her mother was stolen both *by* her father and "from a more fruitful and upright life which she was always imagining might have been hers" (14).

Ask students what they make of the word "stolen" as used in this context. It is clearly true, at least in the case of the narrator, that she did not *have* to be stolen. After all, she chose to leave this life for something more "ordinary" (21) once. Yet the word "stolen" implies a passivity on the part of the person who is stolen; such a person is acted *on*, rather than acting. Such a person is not really responsible for his or her actions, is at the mercy of powers stronger than her own. The narrator is clearly biased, then, in favor of the "disreputable" life led by her father and his forebears — a life that she claims as her own at the story's end. Ask students whether this bias makes a difference. That is, does it lessen the considerable magic of the story? Indeed, could *this* story be told by a narrator who did not share this bias? Probably not: It would be difficult, if not impossible, to perpetuate the existence of a legend (as the narrator does here) without believing in the legend in the first place. (Students may want to take this under consideration when revising their "Write Before Reading" assignments.)

INVESTIGATIONS (p. 124)

1. There are few concrete "facts" offered about the men in this family; note that the story begins with the words "They say," indicating hearsay rather than objective fact. You might ask your students what they think the role of "facts" is in this story. Is this narrator trying to determine verifiable truths? If not, what might her intentions be?

   The following facts are given about the narrator's great-grandfather: He drank; had eleven children, one of whom — the narrator's grandmother — was conceived in a horse's stall; he had some kind of special rapport with horses, of which he owned twenty-nine; at the age of fifty-two he abandoned his wife and family to join a circus; he returned seven years later with the trappings of one of the circus horses and asked to be taken back in; when drunk he would dance in the fields with this horse's blanket and plume. In most families, such a character would be described as eccentric at the very least. The same might be said of the narrator's father, who also drinks, but is obsessed with card playing rather than horses. Instead of gambling with money, he wrote IOU notes on everything from "fish he intended to catch next season to the sale of his daughter's hair" (15).

2. Students' responses to the first and last part of the question will vary.

   The narrator's mother "counseled her children severely against all manner of rash ambition and foolhardiness" (18), and the lesson apparently took, initially. It was her mother's influence and blood that made the narrator feel, as a teenager, that "the advantages of an ordinary existence among people of a less volatile nature had begun to appeal to [her]" (21). But it is her father's blood — that part of her which her mother tried to repress — that her mother now calls on when she needs help with the narrator's father. It is the very oddities that the narrator shares with her father and great-grandfather, her mother knows, that will allow her husband to die in peace.

3. The narrator takes on the "disreputable" characteristics of her forebears when she takes on her father's role in the family. He's on his deathbed but, she lets him know, "not forsaken" (66). She dons the mantle of the "crazy" or "gypsy" family line, lest it disappear forever. In taking on this role, partly out of love for her father but also because, like so many characters in this story, she has been "stolen" by a past she can no longer deny, she takes on the accompanying behavior: uttering sounds she doesn't understand and can't account for (26, 66); pulling the boughs from the trunk of the cedar tree her father loved (54), and sleeping outside on the ground "like a damned fool" (59).

4. The children's lives depend on playing in this frenzied manner because, simply, this is how children live: They don't repress anything; they don't yet have to moderate their behavior to meet social expectations; adults don't expect small children to "behave themselves." As soon as they start regulating or monitoring themselves, they lose some of the innocence, and wildness, of childhood.

The narrator's great-grandfather's life apparently depended hugely on "speed and darkness" and "laughter and cries brimming over" (62) — it was this need that drove him to join the circus, and that drove him out into the fields to dance with the horse's blanket and plume once he returned. He may have been stolen by a horse, but he also let it happen — just as the narrator's mother, "otherwise a deadly practical woman" (13), let herself fall in love with the narrator's father. She, too, had a need to be stolen away, a need for "speed and darkness," despite all the sentiments she expressed to the contrary.

As for the narrator, ever since she first spoke aloud at the age of eleven and subsequently sought out an "ordinary existence" (21), she had been denying the very part of her "that belonged exclusively to [her] father and his family's inexplicable manias" (23). At the story's end she realizes this and takes over, or takes on, her father's role in the family, embracing "the disreputable world of dancers and drunkards, gamblers and lovers of horses to which [she] most surely belonged." She says, "But from that night forward I vowed . . . to plunge myself into the heart of my life and be ruthlessly lost forever" (66).

RITA DOVE

Grape Sherbet (p. 124)

Rita Dove was born in Akron, Ohio. In addition to the books mentioned in the text's footnote, she has published the poetry collections *Grace Notes* (1989), *Museum* (1983), *The Yellow House on the Corner* (1980), and *Ten Poems* (1977); the short-story collection *Fifth Sunday* (1985). Her latest novel, *Through the Ivory Gate*, is forthcoming.

This wonderfully evocative poem is clearly about the kind of loving, happy family that members of "unhappy" families wish they were a part of. It is a moving testimony of the speaker's love for, and appreciation of, her father, and of the father's love for his children as well. The poem's power stems not from the fact that this event took place (it may or may not have; we have no way of knowing), but from the sentiments, which are universal: Children *do* feel this way about their fathers, and fathers *can* make their children this proud and happy.

INVESTIGATIONS (p. 125)

1. The speaker's father "bothered" to make the sherbet for pure pleasure — the pleasure of making his children happy, which in turn makes him happy. He does it for the simple but unsurpassable pleasure of hearing his children cheer, of creating something they think is wonderful, of making his small bit of magic for them, "a miracle" (line 14) of sweetness.

   In "The Lover of Horses," there is no indication that the narrator's father ever did anything routine with his family, much less anything special, as the father in this poem does. So while the narrator of that story does present a warm and loving portrait of her father, it is very different from the unqualified tribute that the speaker offers her father in "Grape Sherbet." Instead, Gallagher's narrator feels herself inexorably drawn, because of her father's unsavory blood, to enter the same "disreputable world" (para. 66) he inhabited. Perhaps if her father had spent more time fighting this bad blood himself, being more of a family man, like the father in "Grape Sherbet," the narrator wouldn't be following in his footsteps. In "Changing the Name to Ochester," the speaker's uncles and grandmother would certainly have benefited from that sort of "bothering," too.

2. Children are by nature not reflective in the same way as adults, and so don't usually appreciate the effort and love that goes into the "miracles," large and small, that their parents regularly perform. The poem's first three stanzas are devoted to recreating the miraculous sensation and taste of the grape sherbet. It is only in the poem's last stanza that the speaker addresses the memory from an adult perspective; it is only as an adult that she can appreciate the love and caring behind the gesture of making the sherbet.

3. The taste of the grape sherbet "doesn't exist" in part on a literal level — it was so wonderful, and so unlike anything the speaker and her siblings had ever tasted, that there *are* no words to describe it. More importantly, though, the taste was so much a part of those particular circumstances — that particular late spring day; a holiday; a family outing; the father's miraculous invention — that for the speaker it really does *not* exist, outside of those circumstances. Certainly there is grape sherbet in the world, but it will never again taste the way it did that day again.

ED OCHESTER

Changing the Name to Ochester (p. 126)

In addition to the collection mentioned in the text's footnote, Ed Ochester's books of poetry include *Weehawken Ferry* (1985), *Miracle Mile* (1984), and *Dancing on the Edges of Knives* (1973).

The speaker begins this moving poem about his father and grandfather with an anecdote about "other grandpas" rather than a story about his own grandfather. Ask students why they think he does so.

In fact, the speaker *has* no legends about his own grandfather: The speaker's father and uncles "never spoke of him" (line 37). The poem's first ten lines retell the legend common to many Poles and other Eastern European immigrants who came to this country in the early part of this century. But this is not the *speaker's* family legend: Note the word "other" modifying "grandpas" in the poem's first line, and then lines 11 and 12: "but my grandfather was born in this country / (no one living knows anything about *his* parents)." What little the speaker does know about his grandfather is hardly the stuff of celebrated legend. Rather, it seems the speaker's family managed to make good in this country, managed to take part in the American Dream, *in spite* of this grandfather, who deserted his wife and small children, leaving them "with nothing" (68).

Ask students how important they think family legends are to one's identity. What difference does it make whether we know stories about our forebears, or *which* stories we know? Does the speaker of this poem seem to have suffered for not knowing his grandfather? And would the speaker and his father be liable to answer that question the same way?

INVESTIGATIONS (p. 128)

1. Describing these details of his grandparents' lives allows the speaker to know his grandmother better and to know his grandfather at all. Putting these facts on paper is a way of putting flesh and blood on his grandfather's bones. The act of writing about his grandfather helps the speaker create this man he did not know and heard almost nothing about. So the speaker creates a narrative

for his grandfather: the story of his life. Thus the speaker has transformed a vague, shadowy presence into someone real, someone who can be forgiven. (One can't forgive someone who doesn't exist.)

The speaker is able to forgive his grandfather because his father and uncles have already punished him by refusing "to go to his funeral" (36) and never speaking of him. The speaker can afford to be generous, precisely because the sons who were abandoned were not generous. But the speaker's grandfather and all his sons are dead now, and the speaker, who never knew his grandfather and did not suffer directly from his desertion, can bring them all together again. More important, the speaker can make amends to his own father, whose bitterness toward *his* own father the speaker once condemned. So the speaker is forgiving both himself for deeming his father unfair, and his father, against whom the speaker had apparently held this unfairness for twenty years.

2. The speaker's father, uncles, and grandmother all draw on the financial and emotional support of the family when they are abandoned. Taking care of your own was obviously a given in this family, and the fact that the speaker's grandfather did not live up to this responsibility only made the ethos stronger for other family members (in addition to making their financial straits more dire, of course). You did what was required to take care of each other, even if it meant foregoing individual dreams. Once old enough, the uncles all "had to work to support the family like everybody else" (45). One uncle became a fireman; another worked in city government; the speaker's father sold insurance door to door. The "rags to riches" (or at least to the middle class) legend in this family belongs not to the grandfather, but to the next generation, the speaker's father and his brothers.

3. A traditional essay by nature relies heavily on narration to report on, explain, or describe its subject. Agnes G. Herman's "A Parent's Journey Out of the Closet" in Part Two is such an essay, as are John Haines's essay in Part One, Richard Rodriguez's in Part Four, and Trudy Pax Farr's in Part Five. A poem, on the other hand, typically depends more on imagery and figurative language, on pictures and associations that lead up to an emotional center. There are, of course, exceptions to the type of essay described above. Rosario Morales's stream-of-consciousness memoir in Part One and Joyce Carol Oates's fragmented essay in Part Seven are good examples of nonfiction that employ both poetic and fictional techniques.

BHARATI MUKHERJEE

Fathering (p. 129)

In addition to the book mentioned in the text footnote, Bharati Mukherjee is the author of three novels, *Wife* (1975), *The Tiger's Daughter* (1971), and *Jasmine* (1989); the short-story collection *Darkness* (1985); and several works of nonfiction. She has been awarded grants from the Guggenheim Foundation and the National Endowment for the Arts, and has taught at numerous schools, including McGill University, Columbia University, and the University of California at Berkeley.

"Fathering" is a powerful and disturbing story about a divorced Vietnam veteran who is trying to make his new family work. Like the family in Elizabeth Gordon's "On the Other Side of the War: A Story," this family includes an American GI who fathered a child in Vietnam and brought that child to the United States. The two stories yield an interesting comparison: Ask students to outline the differences between these two children and their fathers. What do they think accounts for those differences? This story also connects well with John Balaban's poem "Words for My Daughter." Both fathers share (or consider sharing) with their daughters certain knowledge of their experiences in Vietnam. What does each father hope each daughter will do with this knowledge?

The ending of this story bears some discussion. While Jason's rescuing his daughter may feel "right" to students — in part because his love for her is so strong, in part because of the value we place on family and taking responsibility for that family — what kind of a rescue is he really providing? Doesn't Eng really need some kind of help?

INVESTIGATIONS (p. 134)

1. Eng manipulates Jason by making him choose between herself and Sharon. She knows she can get away with being mean and irrational because she is a child, while Sharon will be expected to be understanding, patient, and forgiving because she is an adult. Eng manipulates Jason when she says, "Dad, let's go down to the kitchen. Just you and me" (para. 12). In paragraph 13 she thrusts the knife further, saying, "Not her, Dad. We don't want her with us." What Eng gains from this is Sharon's growing displeasure with Jason and Jason's undivided attention for herself. Of course, Eng cannot be held entirely responsible for her actions; she has been through experiences horrific enough to traumatize any adult, and the reader cannot legitimately judge how much of her behavior is calculated and how much is out of her control. Her delirium certainly seems genuine.

   In allowing himself to be manipulated by Eng, Jason, too, gains something more than the love and loyalty of his own child — a powerful enough motivation in its own right. He also uses Eng to avoid having to commit himself to Sharon. Eng is, after all, his helpless "sick, frightened, foreign" (14) child; it is easy to claim that she should take priority over a self-sustaining, healthy adult.

   Sharon, in turn, gets to be a martyr by putting up with this situation. As long as she labels Eng "manipulative," Sharon can perceive the situation as unfair to herself. If she were to admit, however, that Eng really is a deeply scarred and troubled child who *can't* control all her actions, Sharon would be obliged to be more understanding. She too would have to make a choice — either to stand by Jason and support him, which means she would also have to learn to accept and try to help Eng, or to give them both up.

2. Jason blames himself for leaving Eng in Vietnam in the first place, and for letting "a lot of people down already" (57). This line refers not only to Eng, whom he deserted, but also to his ex-wife, with whom his marriage did not work out; his twins, whose lives he is no longer a significant part of; and Sharon, whom he has caused to look "old, harrowed, depressed" (29).

   At the same time, however, Jason claims to have "brought the twins up without much help ten years ago" (3) — suggesting that he believes he was a good father to them. And he hates it when Sharon "treats Eng like a deaf-mute" (5) because she resents the girl. Instead of believing Sharon's accusation that he is manipulated by Eng, Jason thinks Sharon isn't sufficiently sympathetic. He clearly feels tremendous guilt about his participation in the Vietnam War and what his country did there (11). Yet his method of coping with this pain is also denial: "Vietnam didn't happen" (6).

Denial is the only answer Jason has come up with to deal with these internal struggles. Until he begins to recognize and accept his problems, there is no way he can begin to solve them.

3. Jason perceives himself as both Sharon's and Eng's protector: He is strong, his women are weak, and they couldn't get along without him. Jason thinks of Eng more possessively than he does of Sharon, for he perceives her as the more helpless of the two, both because she has suffered more and because she is a child. Throughout the story he refers to her through possessive pronouns: "my girl" (26), "my kid" (9), "my baby" (13), "my poor girl" (24), "my Rambo" (80). But Jason's "poor girl" survived postwar Saigon until he rescued her. Eng probably resents both having been deserted in the first place and having been thrust into an alien world inhabited by the very people who destroyed her country and everyone she loved.

    As for Sharon, although we don't know the specifics, she obviously had a life before she met Jason, and she no doubt resents his perception of her as helpless.

4. On the surface, Kearns and Sharon are the enemies because they want to "sedate" Eng; they want to Americanize her and turn her into a "normal" child. Jason is proud of her toughness; he sees it as a survival instinct — one she developed in Saigon but still needs now, since in both his mind and Eng's, the war continues. Jason believes he is rescuing Eng from anything that could hurt her, especially the "Yankee bastards" who killed her family. Though he claims "Vietnam didn't happen" and that he "put it behind" him (6), in fact, psychologically, in many ways he is still there. Eng serves as Jason's buffer between Vietnam and his current life in the United States. Taking care of her both expiates his guilt over the war and allows him to avoid confronting his own shortcomings here at home.

JOHN BALABAN

Words for My Daughter (p. 135)

In addition to the books listed in the text footnote, John Balaban's books include the poetry collection *After Our War* (1974), a children's book called *The Hawk's Tale* (1988), and the memoir *Remembering Heaven's Face: A Moral Witness in Vietnam* (1991). He translated and edited the books *Vietnamese Folk Poetry* (1974) and *Ca Dao Vietnam: A Bilingual Anthology of Vietnamese Folk Poetry* (1980). Among Balaban's many honors are the Lamont Award from the Academy of American Poets and fellowships from the National Endowment for the Arts and the National Endowment for the Humanities.

Students may be confused by Balaban's role in Vietnam, which is not clearly defined in the poem. (There is the suggestion, in stanza 6, that he is there to translate rather than to fight, but this is not explicitly stated.) Balaban declared himself a conscientious objector. In lieu of military service, he served as an instructor in a Vietnamese university and as a field representative for the Committee of Responsibility to Save War-Injured Children.

Ask students why they think Balaban devotes so much of the poem to describing the speaker's "playmates" and only one stanza to describing "the worst" that he has ever seen. The effect is clear: The anecdotes about Reds, the Connelly kids, and the girl and her brother (stanza 3), all set readers up for "the worst"; we are exposed to the horrors of the world in the same order the speaker witnessed them in his life. Until he was in Vietnam, the speaker thought he'd seen the worst there was to see. Until readers reach the fifth stanza, they think this chronicle of what human beings can do to each other is about as bad as it gets. And yet this is an essentially hopeful poem. The last stanza focuses not on "the worst" but on the best: an innocent child, one who will *not* be given guns and war toys, and who, her father hopes, will not only be a better person for it but will, in her goodness, help redeem us all.

INVESTIGATIONS (p. 137)

1. The worst, for John Balaban, was the horror of his experiences in Vietnam, especially the senseless maiming and death of helpless civilians and children, all of whom were simply in the wrong place at the wrong time. (Other characters mentioned in this poem are also in the wrong place at the wrong time: Reds and his mother in the first stanza; the Connelly kid, his mother, and the milkman in the second stanza; the girl with a dart in her back and her brother hung from an oak in the third stanza. Ask students whether they think the cruelties perpetrated in the poem's first three stanzas are less horrible than what Balaban considers "the worst." If so, why?)

   While being told "the worst" is unlikely to "free" anyone from a horror (whatever that specific horror might be), the very knowledge of that horror should ideally help keep someone from perpetrating similar evils, and also help him or her to do what can be done to help prevent such horrors from being perpetrated. Acting or speaking out against evil is one way of finding "good" — but one's ability to do this is, of course, finally a question of individual character.

2. The speaker in this poem is simultaneously exulting in and using his daughter's innocence — an innocence that helps him live in this far-from-innocent world. (In this way "Words for My Daughter" ties in very neatly with the story "Fathering"; the narrator of that story uses his daughter in similar ways, yet the father-daughter relationships described in this poem and story are very different.) The fact that the speaker helped create this perfect, unflawed creature, still too young to do anything anyone could construe as "wrong" or "bad," also helps him live in a world where he has seen terrible things. Unlike the speaker's daughter, Eng (the daughter in "Fathering") is far from passive, but she, too, is a victim of this horrible war; for her father, she is the one good thing that came out of it, the result of one positive, creative act in the midst of many negative and destructive ones.

3. Since horrible things *do* happen, protecting someone from the knowledge of life's pain can result in naivete, at best, or a very unrealistic perspective on life, at worst. A person who doesn't expect awful things to happen is likely to be ill-equipped to deal with them, both practically and emotionally.

ELIZABETH GORDON

On the Other Side of the War: A Story (p. 138)

In a note accompanying the original publication of this story in *Home to Stay* (1990), an anthology of Asian American women's fiction, Elizabeth Gordon said, "I've found there's a certain built-in tension in having a mixed heritage. All kinds of questions arise from it: questions of identity, of belonging, of home. Since I've moved out of the South, though, I've been learning to . . . explore those questions in my writing." You might open class discussion by asking students to discuss the nature of this exploration. Do they feel Gordon has resolved any of the tensions arising from having a mixed heritage? Do they think a simple "resolution" is her goal — and if so, is such a resolution likely, or even possible?

Students may need to be reminded that this short, apparently autobiographical tale about a girl whose father was an American soldier and whose mother is Vietnamese is fiction rather than fact. The voice is so straightforward that they may be tempted to think otherwise. Ask students if they think this distinction matters, and if so, why. (For more on this, see Investigation 1, below.)

This story pairs well with Bharati Mukherjee's "Fathering," another story about a child fathered in Vietnam. An interesting writing assignment might emerge from a comparison of the two stories: What are the differences between these two children, and what might account for some of them?

INVESTIGATIONS (p. 140)

1. The narrator is certainly sharp: She understands how out of place a very dark-haired mother and her child, both with heavy eyelids, look among symbols of white, suburban well-being such as "frame houses and a shiny Chevrolet" (para. 18). She is sharp enough to know that common sense often makes no sense, and she's sharp enough to label this selection "a story." If it were labeled "a memoir," the reader's expectation would be that she was telling the truth. Since she is telling "a story," just exactly what was understood by whom is in question. In those early years, how much did the narrator's mother really understand or misunderstand? How much did the narrator's father take for granted, and how could he have made her early years in this country easier for her?

    The narrator is also stubborn: She pretends not to know why her father is angry when he reads the question about her race. She knows that he wants her to be seen as the same as all the other "white" children, when of course she is not the same, since she is only half "white."

    With her mother, the narrator seems to share the quality of adaptability: Her mother learned to accept strange things, such as the cows being unprotected from inclement weather; the narrator has learned to accept strange things, such as prejudice against her because she has eyes that are "round at the center, narrow at the corners, and heavy-lidded" — in other words, because she's different.

2. The narrator thinks it's reasonable to wonder about being "different" because she wondered about it when she discovered it, too. In school and in her neighborhood, she hasn't seen anyone who looks like her mother or herself. Since everyone else wonders about it, and since she has been taught, like her mother, to accept that she is different, it seems perfectly reasonable to wonder along with them.

3. Skip reinforces racial distinctions by *not* letting his wife identify the ethnic background of their daughter. She *is* obviously different, and the answer "human" is intended to minimize that difference — that is, to erase the categories on the form. What it really does, of course, is make the girl stand out more. From the fact that "none of the answers seemed to fit" (21) we know that there was no answer for "Vietnamese" and probably not even one for "Asian American,"

either. Since Skip was already writing in an answer that wasn't on the form, there's no reason he couldn't have written in his daughter's true ethnic identity.

4. If students have trouble answering this question, ask them to think back to their "Write Before Reading" assignment in Part One (p. 2). If they related an experience that caused them self-doubt, they may well find that their notions of common sense were challenged at that time. You might also ask them to apply the notion of common sense being "rendered senseless" to other selections they've read in this text. For example, does it make sense to the narrator of Tess Gallagher's story to sleep on the ground in the garden the night of her father's death? In Part One does it make sense to the narrator of Richard McCann's story that boys have to behave in one way while girls have to behave in another? Ask students to come up with other examples.

ETHERIDGE KNIGHT

Circling the Daughter (p. 141)

This poem is sheer celebration: a father's beautiful homage to a daughter he obviously loves very much. The use of alliteration, internal rhyme, and a refrain make the poem seem almost a song, with the rhythm and language creating the music. Note that the second line of the refrain could be a song lyric: In fact, students can probably name several songs that include this line off the tops of their heads. And of course the poem's title, "Circling the Daughter," suggests a dance, which in turn suggests music.

Students unfamiliar with Knight's work may be confused by the reference to the "Month of Malcolm" in the first line. This most likely refers to Malcolm X, though whether the month in question is the month he was born or the month he was assassinated is unclear.

INVESTIGATIONS (p. 142)

1. The speaker means that life itself is beautiful — be it a flower or a child. Both are born innocent, not "in sin" (line 14). The speaker believes beauty is good, not sinful.

2. The speakers in Knight's and Balaban's poems both celebrate their daughters; indeed, they are both in awe of their daughters and the power their daughters have. But there are great differences between these speakers, too. While both see their daughters as innocent, Knight's poem has a simple message: Tandi is beautiful; her beauty and power are good; she should go out in the world and enjoy these things. Balaban's speaker, too, sees his daughter as good — but this speaker acknowledges the evil in the world, while Knight's speaker does not. Balaban's speaker thinks the evil should be confronted — that only in this way can any of us hope to make a difference.

   Knight's speaker might tell the narrator of "On the Other Side of the War: A Story" to celebrate the fact that she is different, to embrace her Vietnamese heritage. As the Gordon selection ends, the narrator says "it [the human race] sounded like a good race to me" (p. 140). On the surface this comment suggests that the narrator thinks race distinctions are unimportant and that she won't play this game of succumbing to labels. But in fact the narrator of this story never does embrace her heritage; she only observes that she is different. By dismissing the issue, she's not really avoiding the labeling game.

Balaban's speaker might tell Gordon to confront the "race" issue directly, rather than observing, as she does, from the sidelines. He would encourage her to tell everyone exactly what her ethnic background is: Only by confronting the truth can we learn to accept and deal with it.

CYNTHIA KADOHATA

Devils (p. 142)

Cynthia Kadohata is the author of the novel *The Floating World* (1989) and the recipient of a grant from the National Endowment for the Arts. Her work has appeared in *The New Yorker, The Mississippi Review,* and *Grand Street,* among other publications.

This deceptively simple story works well with other stories in this unit that are told from a child's perspective. In "The Leap," the narrator says of her mother, "I owe her my existence three times" (para. 3). Her portrait of her mother is at times almost reverential; here is a character with complete faith in her mother's ability to save her. In "The Lover of Horses," the narrator reveals her unqualified love of her father — a love so powerful that when he dies, she resolves to follow in his footsteps, "to be filled with the first unsavory desire that would have me. To plunge myself into the heart of my life and be ruthlessly lost forever" (66). And at the end of "Sugar Among the Chickens," the narrator basks in his parents' "love and pride," which arises from the belief that "a man and his wife with such a son could not be ruined either, not yet, not forever" (106). Ask students to compare these visions of children full of love, pride, faith, respect, and trust with the vision offered by the narrator of "Devils." Why might she seem comparatively clear-eyed, unemotional, and realistic? In what ways are the narrators of the stories mentioned above *unrealistic?* What might account for these differences?

INVESTIGATIONS (p. 148)

1. Depending on your perspective, it could be argued that almost every character in this story does something "evil" — except Sean, who is arguably too young to know the difference between right and wrong. The narrator thinks of herself as evil for making voodoo dolls of Mr. Mason and his children (15) and possibly for lying about being slapped by Mr. Mason (22). Kate could be considered evil for backing up her sister's lie. The people in town can also be seen as evil, because of their prejudices against the Ryan family. Students might consider the narrator's father evil for leaving his family, or the narrator's mother evil for planning to marry a man who could provide them with material wealth but would make them all (including herself) unhappy. Most of these characters, though, believe, albeit sometimes wrongheadedly, that their actions will in some way genuinely benefit the other characters involved. Mr. Mason is the easiest target: He seems evil because he's trying to usurp the role of the narrator's father, because he fights with the narrator's mother, and because he throws a rock at the little Ryan boy.

2. Since the story is told from the middle daughter's perspective, there is no way for readers to tell whether her mother is in love with Mr. Mason — but the narrator certainly never mentions anything to make us think this is the case. Apparently, the narrator's mother wants to marry Mr. Mason because he is a businessman and is financially well off. "[He] owned a dry cleaner's, and a home in a nicer neighborhood than ours" (19). The narrator's mother's motivation

should not be seen as entirely selfish, however. She undoubtedly believes Mr. Mason's wealth will help her make a better life for her children.

The narrator wants "to hear an adult voice" (20) but neither of her parents is available to her. Her mother is clearly not an objective participant in this situation, and so can't be seen as an ally; after all, she hasn't consulted her children about her plans to marry this man in the first place. And the divorce of the narrator's parents has made her father inaccessible to her; while she talks to him regularly on the phone, she doubts his ability to help in family situations. He couldn't solve his own marital problems with her mother, so why would he be able to help now? (Note the narrator's musings in paragraph 13: "Where was Samson *now*?")

3. If this family were white, it is possible that the narrator's father would have had access to some job other than "sexing chickens at a hatchery, like most of the other Japanese in town" (2). Note that the Ryans, who *are* white, are working class, like the narrator's family. The town in general and Mr. Mason in particular perceive the Ryans as white trash, or at least as people to be avoided. This story is as much about class prejudice as prejudice against any individual ethnic group. If the narrator's mother were a lawyer, of course, they would be well-off and class would not be an issue for them. If the narrator's father had vanished like the grandfather in the poem "Changing the Name to Ochester," the narrator and her siblings might have felt betrayed by their father, and therefore less — or perhaps not at all — loyal. They might, in fact, have *wanted* their mother to remarry, both for her happiness and also to hurt their father.

4. Students' answers will vary.

JAMES MASAO MITSUI

Allowance (p. 149)

James Masao Mitsui, a nisei (second-generation Japanese American), was born in Skykomish, Washington. When he was one year old, his family was moved to the Tule Lake Relocation Camp in California, where they lived for a year and a half.

This brief poem about a boy's relationship with his mother is much denser than it might appear. It's a fairly common practice for a child to receive his allowance in exchange for doing some mundane chore, but this child's task — pulling his mother's white hairs — is both unusual and symbolic. For the speaker's mother, each white hair removed makes her look younger, and so is a movement back in time. So, too, are the stories she tells, which allow her to recreate the past.

INVESTIGATIONS (p. 149)

1. Readers are witnessing both duty and intimacy in this poem: The passing on of family stories and the pulling of white hairs are both very intimate acts. Yet there is duty involved, too: Apparently it is the speaker's "job" to pull these white hairs, just as it is his duty, as it is the duty of all children, to listen to parents — whether they are being told to do their homework, to make their beds, or to listen to family stories to understand where they came from and who they are.

The speaker "allows" his mother to tell him her stories. He also allows her to require him to pull out her white hairs. No one could be forced to do either of these things, and while the former could be faked — a child could pretend to be listening — there is no indication that the speaker would rather *not* listen to these stories. Nor is there any indication that he minds pulling his mother's white hairs.

The speaker's mother, in turn, allows her son some compensation — "A penny / for each white hair I pull" (lines 9–10) — for this chore. In turn, she not only gets her white hairs pulled, but gets to pass her heritage on to her son.

2. If the poem included the details of the mother's stories, the country school and ricefields might seem more vivid to the reader. But the speaker's brief description indicates that he *knows* the details, knows them so well, in fact, that he has internalized them. It is clear that he's heard these stories again and again, and that for him, they have much more substance than he reveals here. Were he to reveal these details and retell his mother's stories in a more concrete fashion, the stories would seem fresh and new, as if he were hearing something for the first time and discovering something about himself he didn't know. The result would be a different poem: The sense here is that he has been hearing these stories since he was old enough to listen, and that when his mother decides to live with her white hair, she will think of some other forum for telling her stories.

EDUARDO MACHADO

Broken Eggs (p. 150)

Eduardo Machado's *Broken Eggs* is the part of his Floating Islands Trilogy, which also includes the plays *The Modern Ladies of Guanabacoa* (1982) and *Fabiola* (1985). Among his other plays are *Finding Your Way* (1986), *Rosario and the Gypsies* (1981), *Once Removed* (1986), *Burning Beach* (1988), *Stevie Wants to Play the Blues* (1989), and *Eye of the Hurricane* (1990). Machado has been awarded a Rockefeller Grant and fellowships from the National Endowment for the Arts. Of his background, Machado says one "important thing that happened to me was marrying somebody who is Jewish and not right-wing like my parents. Harriett has taught me a thought process that has nothing to do with being Catholic or Spanish. That's one of the reasons I can write plays about Cuba that question the society" (*On New Ground: Contemporary Hispanic-American Plays* [1987]). This biographical note may be of interest to students who detect an anti-Semitic thread in *Broken Eggs*. You might also start by asking students what they think Machado means by "a thought process that has nothing to do with being Catholic or Spanish." What cultural and ethnic traits might he be referring to? To what extent do your students think it is accurate to assign these traits to Jews, Catholics, or people of Hispanic descent?

Students may find some background on Cuban history helpful in understanding the circumstances of the characters in this play. At the least, they should know that starting in the eighteenth century, Cuba's economy was based on sugar plantations worked by slaves; that after the Spanish-American War in 1898, the United States' economic influence became dominant; and that Fidel Castro overthrew the ruling Batista regime in 1959. Establishing a communist dictatorship, Castro persecuted and executed many of his opponents, which led many Cubans (including the characters in this play) to immigrate to the United States.

On the other hand, most students won't need any additional background to recognize some typical family dynamics at work in this play: The scene is a wedding, yet everyone is too wrapped up in themselves to pay much notice to the bride — who, ironically, is supposed to be the center of attention on this occasion. The wedding, in fact, is of such minimal importance to these characters that it takes place, literally, between the acts. Ask your students whether any of them have witnessed similar scenes among their own families or friends. These need not be limited to weddings; graduations, bar mitzvahs, confirmations, birthday parties, and holiday gatherings are all likely to reveal a family's traits and personality. Remind students to think back to the subject of their "Write Before Reading" assignment as well.

While the characters in this play exude quite a bit of hatred, there is much humor here, too. Ask students what they found amusing in this play. In what ways is the institution of marriage being satirized? What other elements of social satire can they identify? Direct students' attention to the way Sonia's family talks about the groom's family, "the Jews" (p. 153). See especially Lizette's line on page 177: "The Jews, they're a quiet people" and Alfredo's "They were being polite, Jews don't like to appear greedy" (p. 184). For a very lively class discussion, ask students what stereotypes they usually hear associated with Jews. With Hispanics? Italians? In fact two of the most prevalent stereotypes about Jews are that they are loud and greedy. Yet the Cuban characters in this play admit to being both. How do students interpret Machado's use of these stereotypes? (They should understand, of course, that a writer's use of stereotypes does not indicate that he or she believes those stereotypes to be true.)

INVESTIGATIONS (p. 189)

1. Sonia is both a bitter and a forgiving woman: While her mother, sister-in-law, father-in-law, and children all condemn her ex-husband for divorcing her, she still loves him and would take him back if he asked. She considers him her only friend and a partner in everything that has mattered in her life: the destruction of their prosperous lifestyle in Cuba; the decline of their parents and siblings who remained in Cuba; their emigration, and of course their children and the life they built together in the United States. By the end of the play, Sonia realizes that Osvaldo is not coming back to her; their daughter's wedding has merely been a catalyst for some warm moments between them. Though Sonia realizes this, she can't accept it, which is why she turns to the Valium Miriam offers. She isn't yet ready, or perhaps able, to cope with the pain of losing Osvaldo. Indeed, it's not clear whether Sonia could resolve her problems more successfully at the end of this play: She is not yet strong enough to forget about Osvaldo and start fresh, which both her son Oscar (see p. 179) and her ex-husband Osvaldo (see p. 186) encourage her to do.

2. If the garden represents the upper-class life Manuela, Alfredo, Miriam, Osvaldo, and Sonia all knew in Cuba, Osvaldo could be suggesting that none of them has done a very good job with their lives since being stripped of that comfort. The garden also suggests a Biblical allusion to the garden of Eden, where everything was perfect and uncorrupted. Like Adam and Eve, these characters enjoyed a happy innocence in Cuba, in their garden. When they fled Castro's communist regime, they were fleeing their version of Paradise — a paradise predicated on a class system that exploited the poor, a fact that these characters ironically ignore.

3. The families in *Broken Eggs* seem more inclined toward chaos than order; the fact that almost every character in the play has a drinking or drug habit is

certainly a sign of chaos. In emigrating from Cuba both Sonia's and Osvaldo's families began to disintegrate as family members were left behind. Sonia's husband has left her family, but back in Cuba the men in the family had mistresses and humiliated their families, too. The men in the play might argue that in Cuba such behavior *was* evidence of order, not chaos; this was the expected way for men to behave. Similarly, Manuela's exhortations to poison Osvaldo could also be seen as manifestations of an "order" that is acceptable to the women in this society, or as "chaos" in that it is an uncivilized, destructive way to behave.

Students' answers to the rest of this question will vary.

4. The strongest trait tying this family together is precisely the fact that they *are* immigrants — note that even when Osvaldo leaves his wife for another woman, that woman is an immigrant too, rather than someone born in the United States. Members of the family who lived in Cuba all miss it, and most mourn the loss of the life they had there. Even Mimi, who was born in the United States, romanticizes the family's life in Cuba. In fact, their life would undoubtedly have been worse had they stayed in Cuba, which is precisely why they emigrated. In Cuba, they would have been stripped of all their wealth. At least in America Osvaldo had the freedom to pursue a career in business (or anything else he desired). Still, the question of identity is a difficult one. The parents and grandparents in this play define themselves as Cubans, though they want no part of the Cuba that exists today. At least one of the children, however, defines herself as a "white Hispanic American." Her grandmother, on the other hand, instructs her to think of herself as "a Cuban girl" (p. 158).

PETER ORESICK

After the Deindustrialization of America, My Father Enters Television Repair (p. 190)

Peter Oresick is promotion and marketing manager for the University of Pittsburgh Press. In addition to the book mentioned in the text's footnote, he is coeditor (with Nicholas Coles) of the anthology *Working Classics: Poems on Industrial Life* (1990).

This poem speaks eloquently about the decay of an American industrial city and the people who live there. Although the speaker's occupation is not clear, his allegiance to the pensioners — people disenfranchised by the rapidly changing technology and economy in this country — outside the factory is apparent.

INVESTIGATIONS (p. 192)

1. While family legends will vary widely among your students, certain parallels are liable to emerge. Most Americans, for example, can trace their families back to some "old" country. The particular customs and traditions of a culture certainly play a strong role in individual family legends, as does the amount of time a family has been in the United States. The experience of new immigrants, for instance, is quite different from that of their children — a point illustrated quite clearly both in this poem and in Ed Ochester's "Changing the Name to Ochester." For a variety of reasons, people — even members of the same family — assimilate into their new culture with varying degrees of difficulty

or ease: Ask students to compare the narrator of Elizabeth Gordon's story with Eng in Bharati Mukherjee's "Fathering," or consider the different members of the same family in Eduardo Machado's *Broken Eggs*.

2. The TV show about Edward I reveals something about the characters of both the speaker and his father. The speaker's working-class father is interested in broken televisions, not "the English / with their damp, historical programming" (lines 8–9). The speaker, however — who has presumably had more education than his father and more opportunity to rise out of the working class — *is* interested in the program. It is through him, after all, that we hear about it.

    The story of Edward I, the subject of the television show, also initially parallels the story of the rise and fall of Ford City, and so underscores the history of the speaker's home town. On the TV show, we learn that in order to subdue the Welsh masses, Edward I used them as forced labor to build castles. The masses don't get along with the nobility, just as, in Ford City, labor doesn't get along with capital. But the parallel ends in the poem's sixth stanza. Back on TV, in the fifteenth century, the middle class was thriving and castles had become "obsolescent" (35). In Ford City, most of the factories (which were the castles built by the wealthy industrialists) are closed, but most of the workers are unemployed, too.

3. This family has roots in Ford City: It is where the speaker's grandfather built a new life once he came to America. It is home to the speaker's children; it's where this family thrived; it's where the speaker's parents and his children's grandparents live. It *is* this family's history in this country; they have never been anywhere else.

    Yet while roots and connections are an important aspect of one's identity, the history of this town is not all good. Once it was a thriving factory town, a place where people like the speaker's grandfather recreated themselves, started anew. But "the factories today are mostly closed down" (52). There is no longer any promise here, no guarantee of work or a future. Since we don't know what the speaker does for a living, we don't know what economic price the decline of Ford City exacts from him. (The emotional price, of course, is one of the poem's subjects.) But the city's decline is certainly one reason for the family to leave.

AGNES G. HERMAN

A Parent's Journey
Out of the Closet (p. 193)

Agnes G. Herman was a social worker until her retirement in 1979. Now a public speaker and writer, she is coauthor, with her husband, Rabbi Erwin Herman, of *The Yanov Torah* (1985).

This frank account of a mother's coming to terms with her son's homosexuality is direct, simple, and honest. In these pages the writer publicly confronts issues she avoided, even in the privacy of her own home, for many years. Although Herman focuses on the Jewish community, in which she and her husband, a rabbi, are very active, the message in paragraph 40 is universal:

> For us, our Jewish dedication to family left no room for such behavior [rejecting a gay or lesbian child]. Disappointment hurts, but is curable. Alienation, on the other hand, can kill relationships, love, and family.

This memoir provides an excellent starting point for a discussion of homosexuality, in part because of the writer's honesty, but especially because of her clear-eyed look at the myths associated with homosexuality: the myths of the strong mother; the absent father; seduction into homosexuality *by* a homosexual; and the myth that homosexuals can be "cured" (see para. 24). You might open class discussion (or even try this exercise before students read the selection) by addressing the first two myths: Ask students how they would characterize their mothers' personalities. Then ask whether their fathers were home a lot when they were growing up. Chances are a significant number of students will say they have strong mothers and fathers who often worked late. If this is the case, ask your students whether they believe these facts about their parents have influenced their own sexual orientation and that of their siblings. Alternatively, in the event that most of the students in your class do not come from families with either "strong" mothers or "absent" fathers, ask them to think back a generation. As far as they know, did their grandparents fit these roles — and if so, do students think this influenced their own parents' sexual orientation?

INVESTIGATIONS (p. 198)

1. Herman's fear that Jeff was a sissy comes from his preference for holding a rolling pin rather than a baseball bat (2), his sensitivity (5), his preference for the company of the girl next door rather than boys his own age, and his being "too good" (2), in his grandmother's words. Early on, when Jeff is young, his mother fears as much for the potential humiliation of the family as she does for any difficulty Jeff might encounter due to the stigma attached to being a homosexual (see 3).

2. Herman writes, "Would we have done anything differently? Yes. . . . We would have helped our son as early as possible to like himself and to make peace with himself" (42). Had Jeff's parents paid attention to the signs they were unwilling to admit they saw, they might not have insisted he spend more time on the ball field and less in the kitchen. They would probably have addressed his reading problems earlier, too.

3. The extended comparison between Jeff and his sister puts the writer's children on equal footing; their mother emphasizes the fact that they are both, first, human beings, rather than "homosexual" and "straight," respectively. The comparison is there to document that she loves her children equally, regardless of their sexual orientation. Further, she wants her readers to realize, as she now does, that one's sexual orientation is irrelevant when it comes to basic "human needs" (29). Like everyone else, homosexuals need and deserve food and shelter, love and affection, financial and emotional support, advice on their careers, help if they're sick, and so forth.

4. McCann's narrator would be liable to sympathize with Herman's "inner turmoil" over her son's sexual orientation, since he experiences a similar turmoil himself — though he articulates it very differently. He also resolves it differently. Because the narrator of McCann's story cannot embrace the "feminine" part of himself, he rejects his friend Denny (who continues to appear "effeminate"), hurting both Denny and himself. McCann's narrator might well admire Herman for her ability to accept and adjust to her son's sexual orientation, the more so because it is an ability he apparently lacks. When he and his friend Denny dress in his mother's clothes, they are tapping into the "feminine" part of themselves. But it is a part, finally, that McCann's narrator cannot accept — at least not in the course of that story.

43

LOUISE ERDRICH

The Leap (p. 199)

Louise Erdrich's highly acclaimed first novel, *Love Medicine* (1984), won the National Book Critics Circle Award. It was the first book in a projected quartet; the second and third books in the quartet are *The Beet Queen* (1986) and *Tracks* (1988), respectively. The elements of myth and magic that pervade these books are evident in "The Leap" as well.

This story about a mother saving her daughter's life beautifully illustrates the shifting roles in relationships between parents and children: All children are initially dependent on their parents; much later in life, however, these roles often reverse. The narrator of this story says "I owe her [my mother] my existence three times" (para. 3). Ask students in what way the narrator's mother, now sightless, owes her daughter *her* existence. (This dynamic, of course, is not always so clear; ask students to cite other instances in Part Two where the parent-child relationship takes a surprising turn. They might want to look specifically at the last three lines of John Balaban's poem "Words for My Daughter." Mukherjee's and Nordan's stories would also yield interesting comparisons.)

INVESTIGATIONS (p. 204)

1. The narrator's fierce love for her mother is what brings her home; reading, the narrator knows, is her mother's lifeline, her *raison d'être*. It is the "form of flight" Anna of the Flying Avalons exchanged for her trapeze artistry. Without books — the world opened up to her by her second husband — the narrator's mother would not wish to "hang on [to life] so dearly" (17). The narrator's powerful love is breathtaking, as is the role reversal that inevitably takes place in so many families. Parents take care of their children until their children can function independently. In this case the mother takes care of her daughter in exemplary fashion: Most parents would not have been able to save their children from the fire this narrator survives. Later, when parents need help, their children take care of them.

2. The first "leap" is the narrator's move from her "failed life where the land is flat" (15) to the house in New Hampshire to take care of her mother. While we don't know the nature of the "extreme elements" of the narrator's failed life in the West, apparently she was *not* comfortable among those elements; hence the reference to her "failed life" and her subsequent return.

   The first physical leap in the story is the one in which Anna Avalon's husband and partner, Harry Avalon, is killed. The necessity of being able to live comfortably in extreme elements is clear for a trapeze artist.

   Next is the leap the narrator's mother makes from illiteracy to being literate. This leap takes place while she is confined to bed after the accident that killed her first husband and is a leap from an active, performing life to a stationary and contemplative one. Here, too, the narrator's mother must have had enormous resources to make this adjustment.

   The final leap is the one the narrator's mother makes to save her daughter's life. Although there is a fantastic quality to Anna's art, and her past life as a trapeze artist is the only thing that makes her effort possible and successful, it is also true — and part of the story's point — that any mother (arguably, any parent) would risk her own life (which certainly qualifies as braving extreme elements) to save her child.

The ability to live comfortably in extreme elements is notable in several other stories in this part. For Jason in "Fathering," living with Eng is certainly living in an extreme element; he will take care of his daughter against all odds, against all enemies, real and imagined. In "The Lover of Horses," the narrator abandons herself to the extreme elements that held sway over her father: the "dancers and drunkards, gamblers and lovers of horses," and unsavory desire[s]" (66). And in "Sugar Among the Chickens," Sugar learns to live with the weight of the world on his head, literally and figuratively, in the form of a rooster.

3. In teaching Anna to read and write, the narrator's father offers his patient a new, relatively risk-free life. After an accident that killed both her husband and her unborn child, it's unlikely Anna would have continued in this line of work (especially since she no longer had a partner). Still, her life with the Avalons was the only life she had ever known. The narrator's father offered her a new one, exchanging a kind of mental flight and excitement for the physical adventures she was used to. One fundamental aspect of family is that members support each other, psychologically as well as financially; here the narrator's father is doing just that.

In paragraph 18, another sort of exchange is hinted at: The narrator says, "My father, forgetful around the house and perpetually exhausted from night hours on call, often emptied what he thought were ashes from cold stoves into wooden or cardboard containers." The suggestion here is that the narrator's father exchanged his work for his family; that is, that he paid a little too much attention to the former and not quite enough to the latter. But this, too, is a dynamic typical of families — whether it's the mother, father, or both parents working, there is always the conflict between time spent supporting the family outside the home and time spent *with* the family.

The narrator's mother, of course, exchanges both propriety — by stripping down to her underwear (a small matter, given the circumstances) — and her safety (a large matter under any circumstances, but something most parents would risk to save their children).

Finally, the narrator exchanges her current failed life in the West for a life where she knows she'll be valued and valuable. While we don't know the details of this failed life, whatever it consisted of was less important to the narrator than helping her mother live out her life with dignity and love.

LEWIS NORDAN

Sugar Among the Chickens (p. 204)

Lewis Nordan is associate professor at the University of Pittsburgh, where he teaches creative writing. His third collection of stories, *Music of the Swamp*, was published in 1991.

Nordan's ear for the rhythms of speech and the musicality of his language should engage students immediately. Simultaneously deeply moving and howlingly funny, "Sugar Among the Chickens" is also one of the most original coming-of-age stories ever written. Draw students' attention to the narrator's statement in paragraph 86: "I have become old enough to believe that doom will always surprise you, that doom is domestic and purrs like a cat." Ask students whether they think Sugar would have made such a comment at this story's beginning. In fact, if the ten-year-old Sugar were to say anything about doom at all, it would more likely be that he wasn't studying doom right now.

Nordan, *Sugar Among the Chickens* (text pp. 204–215)

Students may benefit from a brief discussion of both symbolism and metaphor in connection with this story; some may have trouble with the idea of a thirteen-year-old boy literally spending the rest of his life with a chicken on his head.

INVESTIGATIONS (p. 214)

1. Mrs. Mecklin believes "it would ruin your life if you fished for chickens" (6). To Sugar's mother, who apparently feels her own life is ruined, or pretty close to it (note her observation that "she was such a big failure in life" [27]), fishing for chickens is a waste of time and indicates a complete lack of common sense. Worse, it signifies to Mrs. Mecklin the local sensibility: crude, vulgar, even stupid. It signifies to her that her son is destined to be "a fool to geography" (105), doomed to the "ruination" that resulted from "spending your life in the place of your birth, absorbing its small particulars into your blood" (104).

   What Mrs. Mecklin likes to do best, we learn in paragraph 30, is sew herself new dresses. Sugar notes the "pleased look on her face" (44). The pictures of women modeling the dresses on the pattern package allow her entry into other peoples' lives, lives she believes she would prefer to her own. The women on the package, she imagines, live in penthouse apartments in New York City; they meet downtown and say, "Why don't we go somewhere real nice today" (48); they go shopping and to the picture show and to the opera. These women live in a world where no one would *have* chickens, much less have a son who was fishing for them. In this world of penthouses and operas, no one says "ain't" — another habit Sugar's mother believes will ruin his life (56), because it ties him to the lowly customs of his place of birth, and weighs him down so he can't escape to something or some place better, whatever that might be.

2. When Sugar first starts fishing for chickens, it's mostly to amuse himself: He's trying to catch a chicken because he's been told not to and because "it wasn't possible to catch a chicken" (17). Doing what you're not supposed to do and wanting what you can't have are pretty typical motivations and sentiments for ten-year-old boys. Before long, however, the rooster begins to take on some genuine symbolic stature: "Then there was the part where the rooster attacks you. Every day I forgot it was going to happen, and then it would happen and I would think, Now why didn't I remember that?" (37). And "the rooster's eye. . . . seemed lidless and magical, like it could see into a person's heart and know all his secrets and read his future" (38). Gradually, as the not-entirely-idyllic circumstances of Sugar's life are revealed (an alcoholic father, a mother who wishes she were someone else), fishing for first chickens, and then the rooster, becomes more urgent. By paragraph 61, after Sugar has begun to try to work the jigsaw puzzle of his life, the rooster has assumed mythic proportions. Ask students what they think the rooster stands for. Direct their attention to the lines from paragraph 37, quoted above, and also to paragraph 65.

   Fishing for the rooster, finally, becomes an extended metaphor for life itself: how it makes no sense sometimes, how it can all go wrong on you, how you can't control it, and it sometimes seems hopeless, but you keep going anyway, learning to cope and trying to do the best you can. By fishing for chickens, Sugar is trying to gain some degree of control over his life, however irrelevantly.

   Sugar begins to understand all this when the rooster catches his bait (84) and, a few paragraphs later, catches Sugar. After the initial shock of the attack, Sugar realizes that he can and must learn to live with his burden: "I could bear this pain forever" (104). Not only can he bear the pain, he can embrace

46

it and even triumph over it; he can "wear this living crowing rooster like a crown." The rooster is Sugar's salvation: If he can bear this, he can bear anything. He can triumph not only over the rooster, but over geography, a bad marriage, alcohol, or anything else the world might throw his way.

3. The pieces in the jigsaw puzzle of Sugar's life have all been touched on in the discussions above. Sugar's father is an alcoholic, though it's not clear, early in the story, that Sugar realizes the significance of this. In paragraph 32 he simply notes his father's drinking in a casual description: "He would smell like paint and turpentine and maybe a little whiskey." But by paragraph 57, Sugar describes his father as "wobbly and ripe with whiskey"; it is at the end of this scene that Sugar feels he has "to do something" (60).

 Sugar's mother, too, is unhappy for reasons he is mostly too young to understand: She's a housewife living on a chicken farm, with a goat and a trailer full of midgets for neighbors; she's married to an alcoholic who smells of paint and turpentine when he doesn't smell of whiskey; and she has a son who, as far as she can tell, shows no sign of turning out any better than his father. She longs for a more refined existence, where people go to the opera, shop in nice stores, don't drink too much, and don't say "ain't."

4. Students' answers will vary. As a variation on this assignment, you might suggest students bring in some of the other selections in Part Two to support this assertion. Specifically, they might turn to Louise Erdrich's "The Leap," Bharati Mukherjee's "Fathering," and especially Tess Gallagher's "The Lover of Horses." Regarding the latter, direct students to paragraph 9, in which the narrator says: "It is known that my great-grandfather became one of these dancers. After that he was reputed, in my mother's words, to have gone 'completely to ruin.'" (See also Part Two: Connections and Elaborations 6, p. 216.)

PART THREE

WITH FRIENDS

OVERVIEW

The selections in Part Three illustrate all the contradictions of friendship: Students will read about friends who delight in, and would do anything for, one another; friends who serve as a community and friends who react against a community; friends who save each other and friends who can't save each other; friends who instruct each other; and friends who lose or reject one another. These same dynamics, of course, are at play in all human relationships (including those addressed in Parts Two and Six, "In Families" and "In Love"), so the task at hand is to explore what makes friendship unique among these relationships. You might remind students of the following statement made by Mama in *'night, Mother* (Part One, p. 36): "Family is just accident, Jessie. It's nothing personal, hon. They don't mean to get on your nerves. They don't even mean to be your family, they just are." If friendships are deliberate and rest on choice rather than blood ties, then why do some of the speakers and narrators in this unit allude to friends as members of their family? How do the responsibilities of a friend differ from those of a family member? And if choice is the key dynamic involved, then how does friendship differ from romantic love, which is also a matter of choice?

The narrator of Cisneros's "My Lucy Friend Who Smells Like Corn" is young enough to dwell on the sheer joy of childhood friendship, while the narrators of Paley's "Friends," Darion's "Claudia," and Kercheval's "Willy" know that joy tinged with varying degrees of sadness. Both Adams's "Stella" and Rabe's *Hurlyburly* focus not on individual friendships but on groups of friends who serve as a community, while in "Willy," the title character's friendship with Helen develops in reaction *against* a community. The narrator of "Willy" is saved, in part, by her friend's dying words, while the characters in *Hurlyburly* are so enthralled to drugs and alcohol that they seem beyond saving, especially by one another. And the narrator of "Claudia," the speaker of Espada's "Manuel Is Quiet Sometimes," and the subject of Gunn's "Memory Unsettled" realize that they can't, finally, save their friends, who are lost to disease, drugs, or mental anguish that can't be shared.

Friends with very different beliefs learn mutual respect and more in Hernandez's "Para Teresa" and Glück's "Celestial Music"; the speaker of "Para Teresa" discovers something about personal identity and social and racial politics, while the speaker of "Celestial Music" ponders mortality and spirituality.

48

Finally, the speakers in Song's "Losing Track" and Howard's "The Victor Vanquished" both experience rejection by friends. Many students will have shared the experience of the speaker in "Losing Track": A friendship dissolves for no apparent reason (except perhaps geographic distance). Yet the lack of a real cause makes the dissolution of the friendship no easier to accept. On the other hand, many fewer readers (instructors and students alike) are likely to have suffered what the speaker in the "The Victor Vanquished" has: banishment from the deathbed of a friend.

The following grouping may be useful for instructors who don't have time to teach the entire part. Paley, Howard, Gunn, Kercheval, and Adams all address the difficult subject of death. An interesting class discussion or assignment might arise from discussing the "appropriate" response to a friend's death. Is there such a thing? To what extent does it depend on the circumstances of the death? Should the wishes of the dying person be respected, regardless of the circumstances?

GRACE PALEY

Friends (p. 219)

In addition to the titles mentioned in the text footnote, Grace Paley's story collections include *Enormous Changes at the Last Minute* (1974) and *The Little Disturbances of Man* (1959). She teaches at Sarah Lawrence College.

Paley's narrative style may be a departure for some students, but it is unlikely to keep them from appreciating her work. Her language is the language everyday people really speak, and the rhythms of her prose and even her characters' associative leaps are liable to ring familiar and true to most students. The absence of quotation marks may confuse students in some instances, especially when the narrator seems to be speaking directly to the readers after a line of dialogue (see paras. 15 and 82 for examples). Ask students how they respond to the unconventional aspects of Paley's style. Do they find it disruptive, or does it enhance the story's sense of immediacy? Why might Paley choose to present her characters' thoughts and discussions in this fashion?

INVESTIGATIONS (p. 228)

1. Selena's most "useful" quality to her friends has apparently been her ability to see the bright side of things, both in her own life and in theirs. Selena has always been the most optimistic and nurturing of the four friends. Note Faith's wry comment in paragraph 42: "We had a long journey ahead of us and had expected a little more comforting before we set off."

    Selena's bravery is an extension of her usual "comforting" stance: She uses it to help her friends (as well as herself) deal with her impending death. If Selena doesn't dwell on her own suffering, her friends can't, either. This makes her dying easier for all of them to bear.

    Friendship involves constant variations on this theme: We only befriend people who are in some way useful to us — that is, who offer us something we need or enjoy, whether it is love, support, encouragement, hope, etc. Selena provides this for all her friends, even when she is dying. When her friends arrive, she immediately tries to focus the discussion on them and their children. She does this in part because she really cares, but also to deflect the conversation from herself, a topic on which she could be neither hopeful nor encouraging — except to say, as she does in the story's first paragraph, that life "has not been an unrelieved horror."

2. In paragraph 30, Faith says she doesn't know where her son Richard is, when in fact she "knew exactly where he was" (31). Faith lies, she believes, out of politeness, "not to pour [her] boy's light, noisy face into that dark afternoon" (33). She is trying to keep Selena, who has lost one of her own children and is now on her own deathbed, "happy and innocent" (33), as she has done, we learn at this paragraph's end, for many years.

   When Faith's friend Ann accuses her of being "lucky," Faith again holds her tongue (68–69). And in paragraph 79 she withholds the details of her own mother's death, which she could have related to make Ann more miserable. For Faith, friendship sometimes depends on not telling the whole truth, because that truth can sometimes be too painful for a friend to hear or admit — so painful that it damages the friendship, perhaps irreparably.

3. The sense of loyalty among friends in both stories is quite powerful. That the narrator of "Claudia" doesn't express or articulate the same depth of love toward Claudia that Faith does toward Selena (and her other friends) is primarily the result of age; the narrator and Claudia have not shared the years and experiences that the characters in "Friends" have. The narrator of "Claudia" does share a history with her friend, however, the time span of which parallels the histories shared by the characters in "Friends": In both stories, the friends have known each other most of their lives. The similarities between the friendships in the two stories have to do with the nature of friendship itself. Regardless of your age, you are capable of overlooking, and are sometimes forced to overlook, your friends' foibles, just as at other times you are obliged to make your friends aware of their foibles.

4. Friendship is an invention in that friends choose each other, and then choose to believe whatever they believe of each other. It is easy to tell yourself, or your friend, partial truths about your relationship; a friendship between two people depends in part on whether both people believe the same things about each other and their friendship. Family relationships, on the other hand, are based on something tangible: You may hate your brother, but the fact remains that he is your brother. Many people feel that family relationships are inviolable; most feel that it is at least much more difficult to dismiss a connection based on blood than one that is not based on blood.

SANDRA CISNEROS

My Lucy Friend
Who Smells Like Corn (p. 229)

In addition to the books mentioned in the text footnote, Cisneros has published the poetry collection *Bad Boys* (1980) and the short-story collection *The House on Mango Street* (1984), which won the Before Columbus Foundation American Book Award.

This brief monologue celebrates the joys of childhood friendship as well as the joys of childhood in general. Note all the colorful details the narrator provides: the different-colored window frames, the wringer washer, the amount and type of laundry hanging on the clothesline, the bed full of little sisters, the old pissy mattress in the yard. Ask students whether the narrator seems aware of the ramifications of these details, most of which imply that the Anguianos don't have much money.

This story compares interestingly to Rosario Morales's essay "I Am What I Am" in Part One. Both selections are first-person monologues told in a colloquial voice. Ask students what similarities and differences they perceive between the two selections. Do they share any themes or messages? And what of the relative ages of the narrators? Could Morales's essay have been narrated by a child or Cisneros's story have been told by an adult?

INVESTIGATIONS (p. 230)

1. These girls are drawn to each other for the same reasons most young girls are friends: They have fun together. The narrator also likes Lucy because she is different from herself, so exotic. "Different" is interesting, especially for children who have not yet developed the prejudices many adults harbor. Lucy smells different from the narrator, her skin is darker, her eyes differently shaped. She has "so many sisters there's no time to count them" (para. 5), while the narrator, who apparently lives with her grandmother, is an only child. Lucy has a dog, windows painted different colors on her house, and clothing of all shapes and sizes hanging from the clothesline; the narrator has none of these things. Compared to the narrator's life, life at Lucy's house is relatively noisy, unsupervised, and full of surprises — in short, it is more fun than life at the narrator's house.

2. Paragraphs will vary, but to imitate Cisneros, they should be written as first-person monologues told from a child's point of view. In a monologue, only the narrator's perspective is revealed. When the narrator is a small child speaking in the present tense, as in this story, reflection on the part of the narrator is unlikely. While the story "Friends" is written in the first person, it is not a monologue — which allows us access to dialogue spoken by the other characters — and the narrator is an adult, capable of more sophisticated introspection and reflection than a child would be. Cisneros's narrator offers an immediate and uninterrupted view of young friendship, reflecting beautifully the intensity of daily childhood experiences, since children tend to focus on the present, giving little consideration to the past or future. If "Friends" were written in this style, the reader might have a very detailed picture of an afternoon Faith once spent with Selena, for example, but Faith's wry reflections on her friendships and on life in general would most likely be lost.

3. The friends are sisters, in a metaphorical sense, because they do everything together and share everything from Popsicle sticks to candy to paper dolls. But the differences between them make it clear that they are not sisters. These differences (listed above in Investigation 1) include the fact that the two girls come from very different economic backgrounds: Lucy's family apparently has much less money than the narrator's. Note that the narrator's grandmother doesn't want her to get her dress dirty, while order and cleanliness are apparently no great concern in Lucy's family. Even the narrator's observation that Lucy smells like corn differentiates the two girls: If they lived in the same house, they would be likely to smell the same. Lucy probably smells like corn because her mother frequently cooks or bakes with it, while corn and cornmeal are probably not such staples of the narrator's diet.

ELLEN DARION

Claudia (p. 231)

This coming-of-age story provides another example of an unreliable first-person narrator; the protagonist here is simultaneously sophisticated and naive. Ask students to cite instances of both aspects of her character. How do they reconcile these two facets of her personality? Is the narrator changed at the end of the story, and if so, did these two traits in any way precipitate that change? You might also ask students to consider the last paragraph of Grace Paley's story "Friends" (p. 228). In what way has the narrator of "Claudia" *invented* her friendship with the title character?

This story also provides a good entry into the "Write Before Reading" assignment at the beginning of Part Three. The narrator is torn between "being there" for her friend and her own safety; by the story's end, she knows that "being there" was not the answer to Claudia's problems.

INVESTIGATIONS (p. 239)

1. Despite the stories the narrator tells Mark about her childhood friendship with Claudia, he sees no evidence of this friendship in Claudia's current behavior. Mark sees what the reader sees: two dirty, bedraggled, desperate teenagers, one of whom appears to be on drugs. The other may or may not be, but certainly doesn't appear to be in control of her life. Mark sees two people he would never let into his own house, people he knows the narrator wouldn't let into her house, either, if she were not blinded by her childhood loyalty to Claudia.

2. The "Jimmy and Susie" game reveals the pattern of the friendship between the two girls: Claudia made the rules for the game, and Claudia always chose to be Susie, the girl who needed to be saved. In the present time of this story, Claudia is still calling the shots and still needs to be saved, and the narrator is still willing to do it. The narrator, who came from the more stable family and was surrounded by love and attention, has always been willing to help Claudia, in part because she felt she had so much more than Claudia did. (Though the concept of "sisterhood" is never stated explicitly in this story, as it is in "My Lucy Friend Who Smells Like Corn," the narrator's description of childhood outings and photographs implies that she thinks, or thought, of Claudia this way. See Part Three: Connections and Elaborations 5 for a related question.) But her main reason for accommodating Claudia is as simple as the reason most children become friends in the first place: She enjoyed Claudia's company.

3. In her own mind, the narrator succeeds completely — or so she initially thinks. (By the story's end, however, she's not so sure.) The narrator has saved her friend from spending another night in the park, in the middle of a thunderstorm. If she hadn't allowed Claudia and Ray into her apartment, she would have failed Claudia. Not providing Claudia with shelter would have been, in the narrator's eyes, a betrayal — and betrayals destroy friendships. Bear in mind, though, that the narrator is an adolescent — someone who therefore lacks the perspective to realize that by letting Claudia into her apartment, she may in fact be encouraging Claudia's "wild" behavior. (See Part Three: Connections and Elaborations 4 for a related question.) By providing shelter when Claudia needs it, the narrator is making it easier for Claudia to spend a few more nights on the street, once she has to return there. Being clean, refreshed, rested, and well fed will strengthen Claudia's ability to endure the next few days *without*

shelter. In the jargon of popular psychology, then, the narrator could be said to be "enabling" Claudia, by helping her continue her self-destructive behavior. Perhaps the most helpful thing the narrator could do would be to *let* Claudia spend the night out in the storm. If Claudia's situation became sufficiently intolerable, and she became desperate enough, eventually she would have to return home and seek the help she needed.

4. The narrator feels empty and sad because she realizes she has been naive. She realizes she gave Claudia and Ray more than "a little kindness" (para. 70); she risked her own safety for them. And she realizes that being "decent" and "humane" is not as clear-cut as she thought it was. If the choice is between putting yourself at risk and being "kind" to someone else, sometimes the smarter choice is to put yourself first. And sometimes the best thing for the person who is asking for help is not to give it to them. When the narrator says she realizes she didn't do the right thing, she means, first, that she shouldn't have risked her own safety, and second, that she knows taking Claudia in for the night won't do Claudia any good in the long run, either.

INÉS HERNANDEZ

Para Teresa (p. 240)

This poem about the conflict between two Chicana schoolgirls and their assimilation (or refusal to assimilate) into the predominantly white world of "Alamo which-had-to-be-its-name / Elementary" should be immediately accessible to students, despite the fact that a good portion of the poem is in Spanish. Ask students why they think Hernandez might have chosen to write this poem in both English and Spanish. Would the poem's effect be changed if it were written entirely in English? How?

This poem works beautifully with Reginald McKnight's story "The Kind of Light That Shines on Texas" (Part One) and Richard Rodriquez's "Aria: A Bilingual Childhood" (Part Four). All three selections address issues of race, ethnicity, and education in provocative ways.

INVESTIGATIONS (p. 242)

1. At twenty-eight, the speaker is mature enough to see that, back in school, both she and Teresa were doing the same thing in very different ways. Both were Chicanas trying to determine or forge their places in an "Anglo" culture; the speaker respects Teresa for *her* attempts to cope with this situation. The speaker chose to claim her place by excelling in school; if she did as well as the white students, she was proving that people of *her* culture were just as good as white people. Teresa and her friends (like Marvin Pruitt in "The Kind of Light That Shines on Texas") chose instead to reject white culture: It neither welcomed nor accommodated them, so they would stick with their own kind. As children, the girls' mutual lack of acceptance *did* prevent mutual respect, but as an adult looking back on the relationship, the speaker is sophisticated enough to know that one can disagree with someone's tactics but still respect that person's goals. Possibly more important, in the years since she knew Teresa, the speaker may have encountered sufficient bias and prejudice in the world to believe that Teresa's strategy for coping with white culture may sometimes be appropriate. While the poem itself doesn't provide any anecdotes to support this conclusion, the poem's *language* — or rather, *languages* — does. The speaker could have

spoken entirely in English, thereby accommodating readers who don't know Spanish, but the poet chose not to have her do so.

2. The girls are bound by the fact that they are both playing this "game" of trying to live and flourish as minorities in a majority culture. The game is "deadly" for two reasons. First, the speaker is pitted against other members of her culture who object to her approach to this situation. If someone angered Teresa and her friends enough, she would no doubt get hurt. Second and more important, learning to live in or with the majority culture is a survival technique: To defy the majority culture is to risk expulsion from it, and hence from all the allegedly good things that go along with being part of the "majority," such as education, jobs, reasonable salaries, and so on. In the speaker's eyes, both girls were being true to their "people" and their ethnic heritage and both were honestly doing what they thought was right; hence, they can be seen as "good, honorable," and "genuine."

3. Neither set of friends is related to each other by law or family; the sisterhood is instead based on a sense of closeness and community. In Cisneros's story, the girls are simply inseparable best friends. In Hernandez's poem, the girls are linked by being part of the same larger (Chicana/Chicano) community.

4. Since the poem does not allow us entry into Teresa's point of view, we can't know for sure what she might think. It's possible she might still consider the speaker something of a sellout, but it's more likely that as an adult, Teresa would have sufficient maturity and distance from the poem's events to offer the speaker the same respect the speaker offers her. The speaker's use of Spanish language where she could have spoken in English might further convince Teresa that the speaker had not "sold out" to majority culture to get ahead.

LOUISE GLÜCK

Celestial Music (p. 243)

In addition to the books mentioned in the text footnote, Louise Glück has published the poetry collections *Firstborn* (1968), *The House on Marshland* (1975), and *Descending Figure* (1980).

This poem is at least as concerned with spiritual issues and the concept of mortality as it is with friendship; if students feel "distracted" by these ideas, encourage them to pursue them. Mortality, after all, is a key issue in all human relationships, so it is not as beside the point as it might initially seem to some students.

INVESTIGATIONS (p. 244)

1. The mother-child relationships students are most likely to recall include those in Norman's *'night, Mother* (in Part One) and in Gallagher's "The Lover of Horses," Kadohata's "Devils," Mitsui's "Allowance," Herman's "A Parent's Journey Out of the Closet," Erdrich's "The Leap," and Nordan's "Sugar Among the Chickens" (all in Part Two). Since these relationships vary significantly, so will responses to this question. The friend in "Celestial Music" is "brave," patient, realistic, and "always trying to make something whole, something beautiful, an image / capable of life apart from her" (lines 32–33). This can certainly be interpreted as a maternal impulse, yet some mothers in the selections above, at least initially, seem to want to prevent their children from being "whole" and "capable of life apart" from their family.

2. The speaker fears that her friend, who "talks to god," is wrong: that there is no heaven, no god, no "celestial music," and that her friend is the childish one for her faith in these things; the speaker fears her friend will only be hurt and let down in the end. But in fact, the speaker, too, believes in *something*, though she may not know it. In her dream, she describes the clouds and snow as "a white business in the trees / like brides leaping to a great height" (23–24) This beautiful image suggests that the speaker *does* have a spiritual dimension; that she does, like her friend, perceive things that aren't there ("brides leaping to a great height"). It is not clear whether the speaker herself realizes the significance of her leaping brides: These are her own "celestial music."

3. Though they come to this ease differently, these friends share the same "ease with death" (30), and sharing is a crucial part of friendship. While the friends disagree on the subject of belief, they can accept each other's perspectives in part because of the other things they share, most of which can be seen as quite spiritual: their "ease with death"; "this stillness that we both love" (37); "the love of form" and "endings" (38).

4. Responses will vary, but most students will say that all friendships eventually end, at least in a tangible sense — whether because of an argument, because friends lose touch, or because someone dies. Thus, to have a friend is to risk loss and pain — the loss and pain that accompany "endings."

ALICE ADAMS

Waiting for Stella (p. 245)

This unnerving story about a group of people gathering to commemorate a friend's death pairs beautifully with Grace Paley's story "Friends," a very different look at how a community of friends copes with someone's death. If your class has read "Friends," ask them to compare the two stories. Among the more obvious differences are the moods at the end of the stories and the amount of distance the narrators of the two stories seem to have from the events they are describing. Ask students what might account for these differences. Paley's story ends on an affirmative note, while Adams's ending is rather bleak. Paley's first-person narrator seems quite close to her friends, including Selena, but Adams's omniscient narrator seems distanced and removed from both past and present events. (If you are teaching a literature class, an interesting discussion might focus on this narrator, who seems intended to represent a group consciousness — that is, the minds of all the people gathered to remember Stella.)

INVESTIGATIONS (p. 254)

1. Stella's friends simultaneously feel her "lively absence" (para. 3) but feel that in life, she "always, somehow, went too far" (9). They disapproved of her flamboyance, which manifested itself in her drinking too much, talking too much, marrying too many times, and dyeing her hair too red. Yet she was also "believed to have helped get him [Jimmy] off the bottle" (35). And Rachel is thankful that Stella turned Baxter down, long ago, when he made advances. Baxter calls Stella "a bitch" (18), but clearly he does so because he was, and remained till she died, quite taken with Stella — so much so that he is still bitter, so many years later, that she refused him. And Day describes Stella as "perfectly all right" (14). If Stella were able to speak for herself, she might very well support these different impressions, which add up to a flesh-and-blood person

with strengths and weaknesses, which make her just like everyone else. She's a believable character because she's three-dimensional: No one remembers her as a saint, or as all bad, either. (Baxter, who comes closest to doing the latter, is perhaps the least sympathetic character in the story. But even he is fleshed out fully enough not to seem one-dimensional; for more on Baxter, see Investigation 6.)

2. Responses will vary.

3. Day serves as a foil for the older characters in the story: She represents beauty, youth, hope, and the future, while they are all preoccupied with Stella, the first of their circle of friends to die. Each of them knows his or her turn can't be far off, while thoughts of mortality could not be further from Day's mind. Despite her problems with her boyfriend Allen, Day retains the optimism of the young and believes things will work out: Allen does, after all, come find her at Rachel's house. And Day seems to interpret Jimmy's choice of a sweater with stripes the color of Stella's hair as a sign of undying love (see 100), while Rachel, Stella's peer, interprets it quite differently. Allen's arrival allows Day to achieve her full radiance in the eyes of the older characters, and to remind them even more strongly of the future these two beautiful young people might have together. Yet Allen's arrival and the unsettled quarrel allow the reader to see through any picture of unmitigated joy the older characters might perceive: Day and Allen might separate permanently tomorrow; they might marry and cheat on each other, or try to, as Baxter tried; they might divorce and remarry several times, as Stella did. In other words, they are simply two more people in love, who will probably follow the same patterns others in their situation do. They have no secrets, no magic formulas for youth and happiness, and in the end they'll be like the story's other characters, coping first with middle age, then old age, and finally death.

4. Both women, in different ways, are good friends to their friends. Selena is described by her friends as optimistic, even innocent — sometimes too innocent to really face the truth. At least one of her friends, Ann, feels Selena whitewashes issues (such as her daughter's death or the way her family treated her) to make herself feel better. But one senses that Ann — who, with a missing son, is in the parental situation closest to Selena's — wishes she could share some of Selena's innocence; it would probably help her cope. As is, Selena herself helps Ann cope, and her other friends who come to visit her before she dies. She helps them cope with her own impending death and the fact of her dead daughter by telling them, "Life, after all, has not been an unrelieved horror — you know, I *did* have many wonderful years with her" (1). And she insists on talking to Ann about her missing son. "She [Ann] wouldn't lean too far into Selena's softness, but listening to Selena speak Mickey's name, she could sit in her chair more easily. . . . She was able to rest her body a little bit (111).

Stella's traits, according to her friends, include flamboyance (talking too much, drinking too much, marrying too often, dyeing her hair too red), but also excitement: They all feel her "lively absence" at the the lunch table. Stella was definitely a good friend to at least two people: Rachel, whose husband she would not sleep with (though we don't actually know her motives for this), and Jimmy, who she helped stop drinking. Refusing Baxter could also be seen as a gesture of friendship toward him — perhaps she did not want to destroy his marriage — though again, we can't be sure. While some of Stella's mannerisms may have bothered her friends, she clearly served as the live wire amidst this crowd, and she is clearly missed — hence the story's title, "Waiting for Stella."

5. Rachel, who, as a doctor, has presumably encountered many dying patients, probably understood Stella's need for privacy and her need to maintain her dignity as she neared death. Like the dying friend in Howard's "The Victor Vanquished," Stella rejected her friends' comfort and support (albeit for a much shorter period of time — but presumably she died a much quicker and less awful death than the subject of Howard's poem). Stella probably knew she lacked the necessary strength and resources to comfort the friends who wanted to visit her. Most likely she also wanted to be remembered as she had been up until she lay dying — lively, loud, even flamboyant, and certainly attractive — all behaviors and qualities she was unable to muster now. To Stella, the woman in her bed that last month was not the woman either she herself or her friends had known. She wanted to be remembered for what she was most of her life, not as she was on her deathbed.

6. Men might have been irritated by Stella's "flamboyant" manner: A woman who talked and drank a lot and had many love affairs might seem, to many men born early in this century, either immoral or simply too aggressive — a trait traditionally associated with men, not women. Women, in such men's eyes, were supposed to be quiet and demure, and defer to men. But Stella knew what she wanted and went after it — an attitude that was probably threatening to many men (as it certainly is to the men in the play *Hurlyburly*). Jimmy was apparently not threatened by Stella — possibly because he had more liberal attitudes about sex roles and stereotypes (though the story provides no real evidence for this). But Jimmy faced a much bigger threat than Stella ever could have posed — alcohol — and Stella's help against that threat no doubt made him "like" her more.

RICHARD HOWARD

The Victor Vanquished (p. 255)

This moving poem about a friend's death is less elegiac than other selections in this part; the speaker's message is not limited to mourning his lost friend or testifying to the transformative powers of friendship, as is the case in the stories "Willy" and "Claudia" and the poem "Losing Track." Ask students what they make of the poem's title. If the dying man was a victor, over what did he triumph? And if he triumphed over human connection by spurning all his friends, what kind of a victory, finally, could he claim? Ask students to characterize the speaker of this poem. They should see that he is simultaneously scolding his dead friend for not accepting the love and comfort his friends offered and commemorating him with a begrudging admiration for how he handled his death.

Students may have some difficulty with the content of lines 28–37: The speaker is discussing his friend's sexual identity here. Richard Howard provided the following information about this poem in his biographical note in *The Best American Poetry 1990*:

> The last two years of his life before he died of AIDS, Tom Victor, the photographer. . . , withdrew from his friends and died in silence and solitude in Detroit. The poem is an attempt to come to terms with such a cancellation of the usual ties of human community.

INVESTIGATIONS (p. 257)

1. This poem documents several "endings" — not just the ending of the friend's life, but also the ending of the dead man's friendships with both the speaker and his other friends. Thus, the poem is a testament to the speaker's "love of endings" — if he felt otherwise, presumably he would not have been moved to write this poem. The poem itself can be seen as an ending, too: The act of writing it seems to have provided the speaker with a sense of closure, a way of coming to terms with his friend's death.

2. All friendships involve the risk of loss; to care about someone is to risk being hurt, either intentionally or by the person's departure, whether that departure is death or merely moving out of town. The closer one is to a friend, the more one risks. In this case, the risk for the speaker involved not only having to cope with his friend's death, but also with being rejected by that friend as he was dying. (This poem provides an interesting twist on Part Three's "Write Before Reading" assignment: Here is a friend who *wanted* to be there, but was not permitted that access.)

3. The speaker's friendship with his dying friend requires the speaker to be extremely vulnerable. He must not only suffer the impending loss of his friend, but he must also abide by the friend's decision to remain alone. The dying man will not afford the speaker, or any of his friends, the opportunity to grieve in his presence. The speaker sacrifices, in fact, what many of us consider a key aspect of friendship: the opportunity, even the right, to provide comfort and to help a friend in need. The speaker also sacrifices, albeit involuntarily, the right to say good-bye to his friend. His dying friend, in turn, sacrifices any solace and comfort the speaker and other friends might have provided — probably at least in part because he knows there is no real help or comfort anyone can provide. He may also be trying to spare his friends his pain and simultaneously maintain whatever dignity he has left.

The speaker in "The Victor Vanquished" never shared the thoughts in this poem with his friend — in part because he was banished from the dying man's presence. (Had be not been banished, his thoughts might not have been this harsh.)

In "Friends," the narrator, Faith, doesn't always say everything she thinks, either. (Refer students to para. 69 of that story, where Faith says, "I said a couple of things out loud and kept a few structured remarks for interior mulling and righteousness.").

In "Claudia," the narrator's sentiments echo line 17 of this poem: "We want playmates we can own." The narrator wants Claudia to be the same person (and thus the same friend) she was when both girls were small. By the end of the story, when the narrator acknowledges that this is not the case, she can no longer idolize Claudia as she once did. Similarly, the speaker of this poem has sacrificed part of his admiration and love for his friend in putting his sometimes bitter words on paper.

Finally, in *Hurlyburly*, the male characters are unwilling to make any real sacrifices for each other: Under the guise of honesty, they are tactless and mean to each other, rather than being caring and supportive. Their version of sharing is to share insults and drugs and to agree that anyone who wronged one of them is a worthless jerk or "bitch." This kind of sympathy and support is destructive rather than constructive; both parties delude themselves about the real problems at hand, which are never addressed. To address them would require exactly the kind of emotional investment and risk that real friends make to try to help friends through difficult situations.

THOM GUNN

Memory Unsettled (p. 257)

This poem pairs beautifully with Richard Howard's "The Victor Vanquished": the speaker of "Memory Unsettled" has witnessed precisely the kind of behavior and emotions the speaker in "The Victor Vanquished" *wishes* he could have experienced. Ask students what they think the now-dead subject of Howard's poem might have learned from either of the friends in Gunn's poem.

INVESTIGATIONS (p. 258)

1. The speaker of this poem feels that our power to alleviate the suffering of illness is quite limited: The lines "Your pain still hangs in air" and "The voice of your despair — / That also is not ended" (lines 1, 3–4) document this sensibility. The second stanza, too, can be read in this light: We cannot heal or save our friends; all we do is offer comfort now and remember them later, once they are gone. Yet the message of this stanza is ambiguous: It is also a very positive, affirmative statement. Remembering someone is no small thing; rather, it can be seen as the ultimate gesture of friendship. The poem itself — the fulfillment of a promise made by a friend — is eloquent testimony to the strength of that friendship. (See Part Three: Connections and Elaborations 3 for a related question.)

2. The poem's rhyme scheme is not consistent — it breaks down completely in the third stanza and returns, modified, in the final stanza. But iambic trimeter is used throughout the poem, and this, coupled with the rhyme scheme, suggests exactly the kind of restricted feeling that springs from our inability to help and comfort our friends. We can't stop the pain, we can't find a cure, we are limited in our choices and power in the same way that the poet is limited in his word choice by adhering to a set meter and rhyme scheme. This restriction of language reflects the speaker's experience of a restricted power to help or change things. It is significant that stanza 3, where the rhyme scheme breaks down, is the most emotional segment of the poem. Here, emotions have been set free; the speaker allows himself to risk pain in remembering his friend. Indeed, he insists on sharing his friend's pain, and through this gesture comes the true joy friendship can offer.

3. Among the chief joys of friendship is the joy of sharing, both physical, tangible things and emotional, spiritual states. "My Lucy Friend Who Smells Like Corn" offers multiple examples of sharing: These girls share everything from Popsicles to mosquito bites, while the most important thing they share is each other's company. Children, of course, delight in such joys spontaneously, while adults, like the subject of "Memory Unsettled," think and then act; note lines 15–16: "you perceived that he / Had to be comforted." Such deliberations make the friend's act of hugging *his* sick friend that much more heroic, and the joy the friends share at that moment that much more profound. This question connects with the "Write Before Reading" assignment at the beginning of Part Three: Hugging a dying friend can be seen as the ultimate manifestation of "being there" — while someone who did not offer such solace could be said to have failed to "be there." (See Part Three: Connections and Elaborations 3 for a related question.)

DAVID RABE

Hurlyburly (p. 258)

In addition to the plays mentioned in the text footnote, David Rabe is the author of *The Basic Training of Pavlo Hummel* (1971), *The Orphan* (1973), and *In the Boom Boom Room* (1973).

Students are likely to find this play disturbing because of its emphasis on drugs, meaningless and misogynistic sex, and both verbal and physical violence. The central characters, all male, behave unconscionably, not just to women but to one another and to themselves, destroying their bodies and minds with every mind-altering substance they can get their hands on. In his afterword to *Hurlyburly*, Rabe describes these characters and his own motivations in writing about them as follows:

> Whether they were right or wrong was not at all my concern, but the fact that they had been raised in a certain manner with certain obligations, duties and expectations . . . which . . . carried with them certain hidden but equally inevitable effects of personal and emotional self-distortion, a crippling. . . . Trained to control their feelings and think, they must now stop thinking and feel. Having been trained to be determined, hard, and dominant, they must now swoon into the ecstasies of submission.

You might share this quotation with students and ask whether they find it in any way objectionable. Can anything Rabe says here be construed as unsympathetic to women? Then ask students to consider the following quotation from the critic John Simon's review of this play:

> Rabe has been accused of misogyny in this play, and his men are indeed beastly to and about women. Yet if *Hurlyburly* has any Pyrrhic winners in it, it is the women who, as mothers and daughters, wrest a tiny victory from their defeat as lovers and wives. (*New York* Magazine, July 16, 1984, pp. 43–44)

Introducing these two quotations in class is sure to start a lively debate.

INVESTIGATIONS (p. 350)

1. Eddie and Phil are similar (rather than being "totally dissimilar") in many ways, chief among them their attitudes toward women and their addiction to alcohol and drugs. They share an apparent inability to sustain meaningful relationships with women: Eddie's marriage has failed and Phil's is failing. Both men speak of women as possessions, and not particularly valuable ones at that. In the opening scene (p. 263) the two men agree that Phil's wife, specifically — and women in general, we can infer — should not only tolerate but also support juvenile, inconsiderate, self-indulgent behavior. Susie should, for instance, wake up cheerfully in the middle of the night and patiently listen to her husband's drug-induced rantings; she should let him do and say whatever he wants to whenever he wants to simply because he is under the influence of some drug and is consequently not in control of his actions. This attitude toward women binds the two men together; neither could be friends with anyone who actually respected women. Their drug and alcohol abuse binds them together because recreational drug use can masquerade as a social activity. Two or more friends might (and indeed do, in this play) spend a great deal of time together drinking, smoking, or snorting coke and *thinking* that they are actually talking to one another. Perhaps most important, though, is the emptiness, misery, and desperation that binds these men together, for this is the condition that led them to take drugs in the first place. All the men in this play are unhappy about

their relationships with women, about the cutthroat business they're all in, and about the fate of the world in general; drugs are the only way they can escape from these things.

2. Eddie's definition of friendship changes according to his own moods and needs: on page 266 he implies that a real friend always agrees with his friends ("And you'd know it, too, if you were my goddamn friend like you think you are."). But he suggests, through his treatment of both Artie and Phil (p. 269), that a friend's job is to be brutally honest. His inconsistency on this point, among others, suggests he doesn't understand the true purpose of either agreeing with or being honest with one's friends. The rest of the men in the play have similarly confused or shallow concepts of friendship. Artie makes the "friendly" gesture of "giving" Donna to his friends, as a pet they can "keep and fuck," because they "can use her" more than he can (p. 275). Also allegedly for the sake of friendship, Mickey makes the sacrifice of "giving" Darlene back to Eddie, whose date she was in the first place. Similarly, Eddie sets up Phil with his friend Bonnie.

   Phil and Eddie dance around the one serious discussion of friendship between any of the men (see pp. 294–296). Phil wants to know if Eddie will still respect him if he makes a considered decision with which Eddie disagrees. Eddie claims he will, but it's not clear, finally, that Eddie is capable of such respect.

   What little we see of the female characters, on the other hand, suggests that for them, friendship is indeed based on respect. The most obvious illustration of this is Bonnie's willingness to "help" out a friend of Eddie's simply because he's Eddie's friend. Eddie has always treated her well, so she trusts him to continue to do the same. So when Phil treats Bonnie badly, pushing her out of the moving car, she holds Eddie responsible. Nor will she accept Eddie's explanation that "Phil has been driven to the brink" (p. 320) as an excuse for Phil's behavior. To Eddie and the other men in this play, desperation is apparently a justification for hurting or taking advantage of your friends. For Bonnie, in contrast, such desperation is precisely the reason people should try to be nice to each other; we're all in the same boat. Though some readers may disapprove of Bonnie's morals, they are likely to approve of her instincts to "put some sort of fucking humanity" (p. 319) into her date with Phil. Similarly, Eddie uses his childhood as an excuse for being mean to Darlene. Like Bonnie, Darlene ultimately calls Eddie on this, saying it doesn't "exonerate" their behavior toward one another.

3. Answers will vary. Students will probably advise Eddie to be less self-absorbed, more giving, and less envious of his friends' various successes. Eddie might also be advised to develop some tact. Few friendships could withstand the harshness to which he subjects his friends in the name of being "honest" and "realistic." Human beings in general and friends in particular expect to be treated with more consideration and courtesy than Eddie is wont to offer.

4. Phil is the character in this play least in control of his primal urges: Though none of the other men respect women, none of them sanction hitting them, either, and both Eddie and Mickey are at least mildly disturbed to learn that Phil has hit his wife. Apparently Phil makes the other characters feel good, or at least better about themselves than they otherwise would, since he is, as Mickey states, a "safe investment" — "no matter how far you manage to fall, Phil will be lower" (p. 314). On the other hand, Phil's friends live vicariously through him, since he'll act on many impulses they also have but manage to

restrain for fear of the consequences. Clearly, neither of these are good motivations for friendship.

5. Eddie claims to be desperate about the state of the world (p. 267), especially the neutron bomb, but we sense that his horror about these issues is a smokescreen for his horror about the state of his own life. All the men in this play *sound* like they are desperate for sex, when in fact what they are really desperate for, but have no idea how to conduct, are meaningful relationships and friendships. Similarly, the men all sound desperate about their careers. Phil is also desperate about his marriage; Susie is apparently desperate to have a child; Bonnie is desperately trying to support her child; Donna is desperate for a place to live; and Darlene was desperate when she had an abortion.

    All four men are unable to relate to women as peers: They were apparently raised by and among women who tolerated this sort of behavior, or at least had very different expectations for their lives than women like Susie and Darlene, who have ambitions, needs, and expectations of their own. While the men's self-pity and paranoia stems in part from their perception of women as hostile and alien creatures, their extensive drug use is at least equally responsible. Eddie, Mickey, Artie, and Phil apparently feel that they could mold Phil's baby daughter into the type of woman they consider ideal: submissive, passive, deferential to men, but sexy and gorgeous at the same time. What they fail to realize is that no woman would want to fit that bill for long, if at all. She would eventually, if not immediately, take a look at the world around her, claim her place, and try to adapt to it — something the men in this play are incapable of doing.

CATHY SONG

Losing Track (p. 351)

This poignant poem depicts an experience many students will have already shared: growing apart from a close friend. That this painful phenomenon is common makes it no less difficult. Each of our friends is unique, and the speaker here paints a vivid, concrete picture of the friend she has lost. Losing a friend in this fashion, of course, is very different than losing a friend to death, or even to drugs; you might ask students to discuss how this speaker's sensibility differs from that of the narrators of the stories "Willy" or "Claudia."

INVESTIGATIONS (p. 353)

1. The girl in the documentary bore a strong physical resemblance to the speaker's friend; both girls had long braids, "sturdy and earnest" (line 15) faces, and reluctant smiles. The speaker seems to miss her friend's earnestness and seriousness: She speaks of her friend's precise speech, her writing, studying with her in the library, and, most important, "the English language [they] both loved" (59).

2. Immediately before seeing the documentary, the speaker had not been thinking about her friend. When one has lost track of a friend, it is usually only in thinking of that person that one remembers what has been lost. Having been reminded of her friend, the speaker is now *more* alone than she was before seeing the documentary, when her friend was not in her immediate thoughts. It is also likely that, until seeing the documentary, the speaker had not entirely accepted the fact that she and her friend really had lost touch.

3. Responses will vary.

JESSE LEE KERCHEVAL

Willy (p. 354)

This moving story about how the death of an old friend helps a woman "with problems" (para. 1) restore her perspective on life compares usefully with Grace Paley's story "Friends." Ask students to describe how Helen and Faith react to the deaths of their old friends. For Helen, Willy's death serves as a cathartic experience, while for Faith and her friends the experience, though equally sad, is much less dramatic. What might account for these differences? Note that in Paley's story, the narrator has been continually in touch with her dying friend, while in Kercheval's story, the two characters have been long separated. Is there a sense in which Helen could be said to be inventing, or reinventing, her friendship with Willy in the same way that Faith talks about inventing "a report on these private deaths" in the last paragraph of "Friends" (p. 228)?

INVESTIGATIONS (p. 361)

1. The neighborhood women are a "group friendship" in that they are "interchangeable" (7) — any of them could have been the one to find Willy after her fall, any of them could have brought her food, and indeed several of them do. They are all part of "the chain [that] was always there" (7); this is the "protection" that group friendships offer. Group friendships offer the pleasure of knowing there is always someone there, whether in an emergency or in case of the mundane need for someone to talk to. Group friendships also offer the pleasure, for those afraid of real intimacy, of companionship without deep emotional investment. Intense emotional attachments are frightening, of course, precisely because the more you feel, the more you can lose (through separation or through death, for example).

2. Willy's death makes Helen want to be alive because seeing Willy awakens emotions in her "that hadn't worked in years" (29). Willy and Helen, once extremely close friends, lost touch long ago. Once Helen's marriage went bad, she apparently had no intimate friends, which only made her pain worse. So she began to dull that pain with Valium and alcohol. Willy's death and the memory of that friendship cut through Helen's numbness, reminding her of the pleasures of "particular" friendships: pleasures that are worth staying sober and Valium-free to remember, to commemorate, and even to seek again.

3. Mrs. Rosen's grief cannot be entirely for Willy, whom she did not even know. It is partly for Helen, whom she does know and whose loss she shares. More important, Mrs. Rosen's grief is for all of *her* dead — the members of her family who died in concentration camps, who were never formally mourned and buried as Willy is being mourned and buried now.

4. Helen characterizes Willy as tough and strong and herself as weak and indecisive. Indeed, even on the verge of death Willy tells Helen what to do: "You get well and stay well. You hear me, Helen?" (17). And Helen does what Willy tells her, just as she did when the two women first parted and Willy commanded: "No fade-out friendship — you hear me?" (9). And so Helen does begin to get well, throwing out her pills immediately after Willy's death. In Willy, Helen found someone stronger than herself, someone whose best qualities Helen wanted but felt she did not have. In reclaiming her friendship with Willy (and apotheosizing her old friend), Helen is able to find these qualities of strength and the will to live in herself.

MARTÍN ESPADA

Manuel Is Quiet Sometimes (p. 362)

Martín Espada is a supervising attorney at *Su Clínica*, Suffolk Law School's bilingual legal services program. In addition to the book mentioned in the text footnote, his collections of poetry include *The Immigrant Iceboy's Bolero* (1982) and *Trumpets from the Islands of Their Eviction* (1987).

Students should have no trouble following the narrative line of this poem. It is the poem's subject — secrets that cannot be spoken — that lends the mystery here. The speaker knows more about Manuel than both the reader and most of Manuel's acquaintances; note lines 22–28, where he mentions "the wound" and "the time / he went AWOL." The speaker deliberately withholds information he apparently has about these two events; ask students why they think he does so. Possibly this is done to establish the strong friendship between the speaker and Manuel; the speaker knows Manuel's secrets, so the two men must be very close. Establishing this closeness makes the poem's outcome that much more jarring: The reader is as surprised as the speaker when, in line 60, Manuel sees "a stranger."

INVESTIGATIONS (p. 364)

1. Vietnam was a horrific secret full of waking nightmares — nightmares with which Manuel, like so many other veterans, could not come to terms. There are no terms for accepting the "burst of mortar" (15); the blood "still drying / from bright to dark" (18–19); the fact that "some men there collected ears / some gold teeth" (12–13). The poem is secretive in that the speaker, not Manuel, is telling Manuel's story, or as much of it as he knows. That Manuel himself will not speak of these things is, in fact, the subject of this poem.

    As for the part secrets play in friendships, it is often secrets that bring us closest to our friends — that is, we share the most personal things with people we trust most, and vice versa; subsequently, we often feel those people know us better, and care about us more, than people who don't know these secrets.

2. Manuel is jailed by his experiences and knowledge of the war. His crime is that he can't forget, or at least come to terms with, those memories and "readjust" to civilian life. Though Vietnam may be a secret, it is a secret that is ruining Manuel's life.

3. Neither the speaker nor the reader has any idea to whom Manuel is speaking when he says "I never lied / to you, man." The identity of the stranger is in Manuel's mind, but there is no way for anyone else to know whom he is seeing. The speaker is deeply disturbed by Manuel's behavior: He realizes that even though he knows something about Manuel's experiences in Vietnam, he really doesn't know much about it at all. In fact, he apparently knows nothing about the scene Manuel is reliving at the end of the poem, and the effect this event had on Manuel. While the speaker knows Manuel's behavior is due to his being drunk, he also knows that the side of Manuel that has surfaced is key to Manuel's personality, a key the speaker will never understand. (See Part Three: Connections and Elaborations 4 for a related question.)

4. For the speakers of these poems and the narrator of O'Brien's story, Vietnam was an experience so horrifying and so impossible to understand or cope with

that it has wreaked havoc on all of their lives. (You may want to ask students to consider Bharati Mukherjee's story "Fathering" in this grouping as well.) Some of these characters or speakers chose denial or avoidance as a way of coping: Note the depiction of Manuel as "a polite amnesiac" (45) and Jason's statement, in paragraph 6 of the story "Fathering," that "Vietnam didn't happen." Some, like Komunyakaa's speaker, tried to go numb. Others, like Balaban's speaker, feel that the war must be confronted: Only by addressing such horrors can we even hope to avoid repeating them.

PART FOUR

IN AND OUT OF COMMUNITIES

OVERVIEW

It is a basic human desire to "belong" somewhere, to have a sense of being a part of some group that not only accepts but supports you, both emotionally and, if need be, physically. But this belonging is not always a matter of choice. Students will read about a number of people born into communities whose members were treated for many years in this country as second-class citizens, if they were lucky enough to be treated as citizens at all. For the narrator of Shay Youngblood's "Snuff Dippers," for the speakers of Lucille Clifton's "in white america," Wendy Rose's "For the White Poets Who Would Be Indian," and Kitty Tsui's "Don't Let Them Chip Away at Our Language," and for Simon J. Ortiz, the pleasures of belonging to a community have always been tempered by messages from outside of those communities. Racism, discrimination, and prejudice have made some of these people bitter, but in some cases have strengthened their communities as well. Judith Ortiz Cofer and the speaker of Lorna Dee Cervantes's "Refugee Ship," also minorities in a majority culture, struggle to hold onto their heritages as they see their communities unraveling as a result of assimilation into that majority culture. In contrast, Patricia Hampl and the narrator of Walter Kirn's "The New Timothy" were born *into* the majority culture. They lived in communities so insular it was difficult to believe there was an "outside" world — an atmosphere simultaneously safe and stultifying.

Richard Rodriguez, Vivian Gornick, and the narrator of Theodore Weesner's "The Body Politic" all perceive themselves as having choices and recognize the costs inherent in those choices: Declare allegiance to one group and your relationship with everyone outside that group will be radically altered. Amy Tan's narrator in "Two Kinds" and Gary Snyder's speaker in "Building" seem to have found peace in their communities, while the characters in Tim O'Brien's "The Things They Carried" and Eric Bogosian's protagonist in *Talk Radio* are, literally and figuratively, at war. O'Brien's characters, who have not chosen to be where they are, form a community of men literally trying to stay alive. Bogosian's Barry Champlain, on the other hand, is engaged in a psychological war, battling the world's stupidity with an apocalyptic fervor that alienates everyone with whom he might once have been able to form a community.

Many selections in the other parts of *How We Live Now* address issues of community and might pair well with individual selections here: You might refer students to McKnight, Morales, Cameron, Antler, and Perillo in Part One; Mukherjee, Gordon, Machado, Oresick, and Herman in Part Two; Paley, Hernandez, Adams, Rabe, and Kercheval in Part Three; and Johnson in Part Six.

For instructors who don't have time to teach all the selections in Part Four, a smaller grouping on language could include selections by Rodriguez, Cervantes, O'Brien, Tsui, and Ortiz. How does language help form communities, keeping insiders in and outsiders out? Does a private or separate language harm or help a community?

Another option would be to focus on apparent dissolution of communities and the ensuing confusion, distress, and alienation felt by the members of those communities: See selections by Kirn, Bogosian, O'Brien, and Cofer. Or you might concentrate on communities in which the narrator or speaker seems to have come to terms with conflicting demands and expectations, as exemplified in selections by Gornick, Weesner, Hampl, Tan, and Snyder.

SHAY YOUNGBLOOD

Snuff Dippers (p. 369)

The last line of this story provides a good opening for discussion: Ask students to focus on the phrase "the ways things used to be." What are the implications of this phrase? Does the narrator believe that racial incidents such as the one described here no longer occur? Ask students whether they think Big Mama believes this. If so, why is she telling this story? If not, what does she hope telling the story will accomplish?

INVESTIGATIONS (p. 374)

1. Big Mama dips snuff in part because she enjoys it, and also because it's a habit — an addictive one, like smoking cigarettes. But there is also the sense that dipping snuff is part of her heritage, both cultural and spiritual. While Big Mama doesn't actually articulate this, she also dips snuff because it is her right, just as it was Emma Lou's right on the #99 bus the day of the story's focal incident. The very fact that Big Mama answers the narrator's question by telling the story makes this point clear: Dipping snuff was one of the only rights and one of the few pleasures these women had.

   In paragraph 23, the narrator interrupts Big Mama, who has just finished what the narrator perceives to be a digression about the general state of race relations during the summer Big Mama is talking about. The narrator is too young to understand that the general weather and mood and background of a story are all integral parts of that story. Digressions such as the one Big Mama makes in paragraph 22 usually provide key information that helps a story make sense and helps it resonate as well. (If you are teaching literature or use creative writing as an option in your classes, this point is worth dwelling on.)

2. The women of the #99 bus share pride in who they are and in their ability to take care of themselves. They don't need someone to manage their households, and think there is something ridiculous about people who do need that kind of help. They share the experience of being discriminated against because of who they are: "They all carried shopping bags made of plastic, paper, or straw,

advertising the names of places they would never see or stores where they weren't welcome" (10). These women also share a religious faith that God is "on the case recording everything in his Book of Life" (39).

Ralph fits into this community because as a working-class "foreigner" (an Irish immigrant), he, too, is denigrated by the rich established white community. If Ralph agreed with whites who took a stand against Blacks, the white community in the story would probably at least tolerate him. But Ralph tries to protect and defend the women on the bus, hence crossing the line himself. To the white policeman, he *is* Black; note, in paragraph 35, when the policeman "looking hard at Ralph," says, "I want all you niggers to get off the bus. That mean everybody."

Ralph's character serves a strategic purpose in this story. He allows Big Mama to tell her tale without stereotyping white people: She and her friends know that there are white people capable of treating Black people as equals. The other characters are also varied enough to avoid fitting easy stereotypical molds. Big Mama is apparently the storyteller of the group. Emma Lou is the toughest of the lot, the one who calls herself a domestic engineer and wears her uniform with pride. She is also practical: The title "domestic engineer" allows her to get paid a little more. And she suggests Mary "charge for the privilege of knowing people's future" (15). Mary, on the other hand, is a bit more spiritual, unwilling to charge "money for a gift give to her by God" (16).

3. Dictionary definitions of *mores* will vary slightly, but the *American Heritage Dictionary of the English Language* (Houghton Mifflin, 1971) lists the following:

> **1.** The accepted traditional customs and usages of a particular social group that come to be regarded as essential to its survival and welfare, thence often becoming, through general observance, part of a formalized legal code. **2.** Moral attitudes. **3.** Manners; ways.

While the last two definitions may be the most familiar to students, the first is especially useful, with its emphasis on "survival" and reference to a "legal code." Many violent acts by whites were perpetrated against Blacks precisely because whites felt their survival threatened; ironically, to ensure their own survival, Blacks had to endure many of these acts (such as being spit on by the driver of the Cadillac). A legal code, of course, was one instrument whites tried to use to prevent Blacks from becoming their equals, while Blacks had little or no recourse to such codes.

4. In most codes of ethics or religion, it is not, of course, thoroughly praiseworthy to wish others dead, even if they have done something horrible to you. Still, there is a strong sense of right and wrong in this story; refer students to paragraph 22 for a litany of the evils perpetrated against Blacks that summer alone. And the fact is, Emma Lou's spitting on the white woman was not intentional. This is never questioned, of course, nor would the Black women be believed if they said it was an accident. The people in the Cadillac are just two more white people looking for any opportunity to treat Black people like dirt. So while it may be difficult to morally condone Mary's curses and the women's general satisfaction when the Cadillac is wrecked, it is easy to sympathize with these women, too. It may well be easier to understand these religious beliefs (that the wreck happened because "the Lord watching they [the white people in the Cadillac's] every move") than to understand the religious beliefs in "Parish Streets," where meatballs are a subject of theological discussion and nothing, even God, "could keep you steadfastly happy" (24, p. 386).

VIVIAN GORNICK

Twice an Outsider:
On Being Jewish and a Woman (p. 375)

In addition to the works mentioned in the text footnote, Gornick's books include *In Search of Ali Mahmoud: An American Woman in Egypt* (1973), *The Romance of American Communism* (1977), *Essays in Feminism* (1978), and the anthology *Women in Sexist Society* (1971), which she coedited with Barbara K. Moran.

This frank and revealing essay should provoke lively and possibly controversial discussion. Ask students whether they have ever felt compelled to make a choice between two allegiances similar to the one Gornick makes here. You might also ask whether they agree with Gornick's assessment of the relative plights of Jews, Blacks, and women. Draw their attention to paragraph 34, where Gornick says, "This invisibility once made Jews manic and Blacks murderous. It works on women in a variety of ways." First, the implication is that this invisibility is no longer a problem for either Blacks or Jews. For a discussion of the former, see Investigation 3, below. As for "the stigma of Jewishness" (33), if this has completely faded, what of the incident Gornick records where a colleague calls someone "a smart Jew"? Such labeling may initially sound harmless enough, but is in fact a subtle yet potent form of racism.

INVESTIGATIONS (p. 382)

1. Gornick thinks one stops being invisible by confronting people who treat you as visible: by asking the man in the hardware store if he would have told a Black person he didn't know how to use a particular lock; by telling the professor in the small Western town that "in New York we don't hear ourselves described as smart Jews any more" (28); by causing a scene at the dinner party. By forcing people to acknowledge attitudes they may not even be intentionally broadcasting, we can at least make them aware of those attitudes. Once aware of them, they'll have to examine them, and decide whether they're fair or unfair, right or wrong, or at least something to be reconsidered.

2. Gornick identifies the fact that she is a woman as "an immutable condition of birth." She acknowledges that if she had been of her father's generation instead of her own, she might have described her Judaism the same way. Given her knowledge of history, and despite her claim that she hasn't experienced anti-Semitism (a fact belied by the comment she reports from the professor in the Western state where she once taught), what Gornick is saying here is that she has made a choice: Being a woman is more important to her than being a Jew. It is not a choice she made easily — indeed, it is the subject of this entire essay — but she has chosen to define herself first as a woman, second as a Jew. (For two related assignments, see Connections and Elaborations 5 and 6 at the end of Part Four.)

3. The speaker in "in white america" and Big Mama in "Snuff Dippers" would be unlikely to share Gornick's approach to her divided identity; their experiences are so different from Gornick's that to do so would be impossible. For Gornick, white Jewish men have paved the path of assimilation and acceptance for all Jews, but at the expense of women, Jewish and otherwise. Hence sexism is her battleground now.

   Clifton's speaker and Big Mama, who are both women and both Black, do not address these two aspects of themselves separately. But while Gornick

69

does not hear the word "kike," for example, Big Mama heard the word "nigger," was spat upon, and saw much worse. And Clifton's speaker feels the same "stomach-churning rage and pain" Gornick experiences, but Clifton feels it because she is being talked down to as a Black, not as a woman. Why else would the white woman taking her on a tour of what was once a "female school" assure her the town has a "liberal" history? To Clifton's speaker, the fact that women (white women, of course), could attend this school is not nearly as important as the fact that *Black* women could not worship in the church, though they scrubbed its floors. The "outsiderness" of Clifton's speaker and Big Mama is defined first by being Black in white America. Both are more likely to experience rage, then, at hearing a racist remark than at hearing a sexist one. This does not invalidate Gornick's perspective; rather, it reflects two different points of view.

4. Answers will vary. Gornick might say these murders are self-inflicted so long as the women permit them to be — that is, so long as the women don't try to prevent them by refusing to be invisible, by pointing out the crime to the party who commits it.

THEODORE WEESNER

The Body Politic (p. 383)

In addition to the books mentioned in the text footnote, Weesner's novels include *The Car Thief* (1972), which won the Great Lakes Writers Prize, and *A German Affair* (1976).

This moving story about an adolescent boy discovering his self-worth through basketball should resonate with any students who have ever played an organized sport. You might open class discussion by asking students to share such experiences, extending the subject beyond sports to include any activity involving a combination of fierce desire and physical work.

This story will also resonate with anyone who has betrayed a friend to join a group into which that friend was not invited; for this reason it ties in beautifully with Part Three, "With Friends."

INVESTIGATIONS (p. 396)

1. By picturing what the gym floor will look like during home games (para. 17), Glen imagines himself out of the tense situation of tryouts. The home games are a certainty that will take place whether he makes the team or not. And in paragraph 81, Glen imagines himself back in the church driveway where he first played basketball; this allows him to relax enough to make his foul shot, which in turn brings him closer to his goal of being invaluable to the team, and hence, an integral part of the community.

Among the other powers Glen uses to gain acceptance is his apparent nonchalance. In paragraph 19 we learn that Glen "gives little thought to what it will mean if he does or does not make the team," yet it is clear how badly he wants it. This nonchalance is evident early in Glen's basketball career, when he joins the boys playing in the church driveway. Invited to play, he doesn't let on that "he had just a moment ago touched a basketball for the first time in his life" (30). Nor does he express the elation he feels sinking his first basket, though by the end of that day "he had grown so happy a glow was in his eyes, and for the first time in his life he was falling in love with something" (34).

2. For Glen, basketball is a means to discovering and establishing his self-worth. Even though his forays in the church driveway should have assured that him that he had some talent, he arrives at junior high school tryouts a nonentity in his own mind, "a complete unknown" (1). Basketball, for this boy who often feels like he comes "from the wrong side of something" (52), is a way not only of fitting in but excelling at something that will bring him over to the right side: the side where kids have two parents, one of whom can drive them to games, and a bedroom full of sports equipment.

Without basketball, Glen feels not "actual" in that there is nothing special about him; he is a loner, he doesn't know how to talk to people, and "he is shy or maybe he doesn't have much that he wishes to say" (48). Being good at something, especially something physical, is a steppingstone to his believing that he is a good person in general, capable of contributing something worthwhile to the world. (For a related assignment, see Part Four: Connections and Elaborations 5.)

3. Becoming a member of a group guarantees twinges of betrayal if one feels any allegiance to some other individual or group. In this story, Glen initially betrays Rat Nose. In Vivian Gornick's essay, she claims Jewish men betrayed women to further their own acceptance into non-Jewish America; some might also claim that Gornick betrays her Jewishness by dedicating herself foremost to combating sexism rather than anti-Semitism.

4. What Glen and his teammates know, in the rush of winning their game, is a success that can only be the result of a team effort and an excitement that is much more powerful than any one of them could feel individually. They know that together they can accomplish great things and that each one of them is an integral part of those great things. This sense of power, invincibility, and belonging is discovered in community: Each member of the team is crucial. Separately, each player might be very good, but without good players to pass to and receive from, no one alone would be good enough.

This knowledge creates a bond that in ideal cases inspires working together for the best of reasons, but such bonds can also be used to ill effect. Ask students whether they can think of any negative effect of this "community spirit." An obvious one is what Glen almost does to Rat Nose. In the euphoria of belonging, it is easy to betray those we have left behind. What about larger-scale unpleasant, dangerous, or even misanthropic uses of community spirit? Some have a desperate enough need to belong that they must turn to something more potent than basketball. Ask students whether they are familiar with any cults that seem to serve this purpose. You might mention the Ku Klux Klan or other white supremacist groups currently in the news around the country.

PATRICIA HAMPL

Parish Streets (p. 397)

In addition to the works mentioned in the text footnote, Hampl's books include the poetry collection *Woman Before an Aquarium* (1978).

This autobiographical essay beautifully captures the love-hate relationship many of us have with the communities in which we were raised. Ask students how they feel about the communities in which they grew up. Hampl focuses on her Catholic upbringing because her community — St. Luke's Parish — was defined by Catholicism, all non-Catholics representing "just so much extraneous spiritual matter orbiting the nethersphere" (para. 28). While some of Hampl's sensibilities are related to her faith, she herself says in paragraph 24 that "God is not the problem." The problem has to do with just how much power *any* commmunity wields, how much happiness any community, and finally life itself, can guarantee.

INVESTIGATIONS (p. 404)

1. In Hampl's memory, the fathers who appear thin and spent reflect the "blankness" she saw in her community — the blankness of belonging for life to St. Luke's, a place which, while it provided everything a community could, did not provide everything its members needed. It could not, finally, guarantee permanence or happiness, a fact these men must have realized, as Hampl did, at an early age.

2. In "The Body Politic," Glen feels disappointed not only with himself but "with the group of five who has decided to take him in. He had imagined something else. . . . One thing Glen does seem to see; he is a person. Each of them is a person, and each of them is different, and so is he, which is something he had never thought about before" (48). Hampl's "unshivered shiver" is very similar to Glen's having "imagined something else." To an outsider, insiders are surrounded by a mystique: They are admired, respected, have friends, and generally "know the score," as Glen says in paragraph 12 of "The Body Politic." But once the outsider becomes an insider, a community rarely fulfills all his or her expectations. In Glen's case, being inside the community helps him see that the only real link between him and the boys on the basketball team is how well they play. There is nothing special or magical or even otherwise admirable about them; this realization helps Glen see the values of his friendship with Rat Nose, who is a person, too. Hampl, who was born an insider, never experienced the excitement of becoming one. Being a part of her parish was a given for Hampl, and not a very satisfying one, she discovers early on. "Life itself was a problem," she writes in paragraph 17. "The physical world, full of detail and interest, was a parched topsoil that could be blown away." Hampl's physical world was the people and streets of St. Luke's parish, but even St. Luke's couldn't keep anyone "steadfastly happy" (24).

3. Gornick might attribute the lack of contact between Hampl and Jimmy Guiliani to the fact that interaction between girls and boys in Hampl's community was discouraged, as was any knowledge of sex: "You were supposed to know what you had been *taught*" (39), but nothing more. Girls, of course, were not taken seriously, except as potential mothers-to-be: "Breeding was a low-grade fever pulsing amongst us unmentioned, like a buzz or hum you get used to and cease to hear. The white noise of matrimonial sex" (6). In Gornick's terms, the girls in Hampl's community were invisible — until they did something they weren't supposed to do, like kick Jimmy Guiliani. This contact threatens Hampl's place in the community because it leads her to a knowledge of sex — a knowledge she did not know she had and that she knows she's not supposed to have. The knowledge threatens Hampl herself because she realizes that not only does she possess this knowledge, but she likes having it and wants more.

4. The man Hampl meets at a party sounds wistful because he is remembering what was, to him, a simpler time and place. Back in the days when his behavior was governed by such concepts as "mortal sin," life was less complicated, and

one had fewer options: Catholicism posited a set of rules you lived and died (or thought you would die) by. It provided an infallible safety net as well: " *We* [Catholics] were the homeland" (29). Family was all-important; divorce was not an option; nominally meatless spaghetti sauce on Friday night was not merely an option, it was required. And maybe, if you were very lucky, you could learn even the smallest part of the secret known by the parish lady who appears at the end of Hampl's essay, the woman whose "smile was a brief flood of light" (62).

WALTER KIRN
The New Timothy (p. 405)

This coming-of-age story about a Mormon boy who is suddenly forced to question most of what he has always believed is quite affecting; most of us hit this crossroad at some point, usually in adolescence, regardless of our faith. Students are likely to respond to Karl's confusion and skepticism as fewer and fewer of his expectations about the way the world works are met.

INVESTIGATIONS (p. 412)

1. Life in Karl's Mormon ward and in St. Luke's parish are similar in that both communities are insular. Members of each are expected to marry a nice boy or girl from within their ward or parish but to have no knowledge of sex beforehand; they are expected to follow the seemingly arbitrary rules of their churches; both communities consider women to be of minor importance, except in the role of homemaker and producer of more little Catholics or Mormons. Both communities also pulsed with "stories" of illicit activities. Hampl tells of "nuns who beat kids with rulers in the coat room" and the "priest in love with an altar boy" (para. 49), while Karl speaks of "boys who came home from the mission field . . . on drugs, or in love with a girl from wherever they'd taught, or even in love with the boy they'd taught with" (35).

    But overall, attitudes toward the outside world in St. Luke's parish seem more benign than those in Karl's Mormon ward. Or at least the Catholics are less willing to admit they think ill of non-Catholics, dismissing them as "so much extraneous spiritual matter orbiting the nethersphere" (Hampl, 28). The Mormons, on the other hand, view foreigners at best as exotic but more often in a manner either condescending or even degrading: Of Mexicans, Karl's father believes "there is just no helping those people" (39). And Timothy refers to the Mexican children in the yard as "the meek." Donna's description of Timothy's Korean mission is quite revealing, too: You have to cook your own meals and they have "riots and murders all day long" (16). Clearly, this could not be an accurate description of any culture. Note, too, Donna's tragically comic equation of cooking one's own meals with riots and murders. Finally, the Mormon's goal is not to dismiss any of these foreigners, as Hampl says the members of her parish did, but to convert them.

2. Donna thinks Timothy is confused because he isn't doing what the church, the community, and especially Donna expected of him. He's not dating Donna, a beautiful Mormon girl any boy just back from his mission would become engaged to if he had the chance. Nor is he teaching Mormon doctrine; rather, he's teaching the martial arts he learned in Korea to a bunch of Mexican kids in the yard outside his squalid apartment where he chain smokes and allegedly practices Buddhism.

Timothy might think Donna is confused in part because she's interested in sex, which nice Mormon girls aren't supposed to be. He might also think her confused because she's unenlightened: Apparently Timothy has seen Korean girls open bottles of Coke, "no hands" (90), so any pictures Donna sent must have seemed pretty tame to him. And, since Donna is only a girl, from Timothy's perspective she can't be expected to understand "how outnumbered we [Mormons] are" (95), hence how frivolous romance and sex might seem in the face of all this.

3. Everything in Karl's world has suddenly been turned upside down. Nothing is as it should be, which is why jokes seem serious and everything else seems funny. Karl's parents are off baptizing the dead, the absurdity of which is suddenly apparent to Karl. Timothy is breaking church rules left and right, yet encouraging Karl to go on a mission. And, inexplicable as it seems, Timothy doesn't *want* Donna, who has practically been throwing herself at him. Karl, on the other hand, has been all but going crazy restraining himself from demonstrating his own affections toward Donna. Now suddenly she's free of Timothy, and Karl doesn't have to hold back anymore — a knowledge which is as serious as it is exhilarating.

4. Karl and Donna remain inside the Mormon church in that they are both still Mormons, neither has seen anything of the outside world, and neither has imagined any future for him or herself outside of this community. Even in the Day Rates Motel, Donna is probably imagining herself at BYU, married to Karl, who may well be imagining the same thing. Both, however, show some signs of at least moving in a different direction. Donna is suddenly interested in knowledge, even if it is the seventh-grade variety. And Karl suddenly finds it sad that she doesn't have any knowledge, unlike his earlier sentiments in paragraph 23, when he felt sad that "a girl with her [Donna's] looks suddenly felt she had something to gain by reading classic foreign literature."

LUCILLE CLIFTON

in white america (p. 413)

In addition to the books mentioned in the text footnote, Clifton is the author of the poetry collections *Good Times* (1969), *Good News About the Earth* (1972), *An Ordinary Woman* (1974), *Two-Headed Woman* (1980), and *Next: New Poems* (1987). Her work has been nominated twice for the Pulitzer Prize.

This poem resonates as a stinging indictment of a society that tolerates well-intentioned but unwittingly prejudiced white people who call themselves liberal; it suggests that we all still have something to learn on this subject. It works beautifully with Vivian Gornick's essay. Ask students what Clifton's speaker might have to say about Gornick's choice. If Clifton were asked to choose between fighting racism or sexism, which might she choose?

INVESTIGATIONS (p. 415)

1. The speaker's singed hands are burning metaphorically, from the speed or perhaps heat with which she juggles her metaphorical balls of light. The word "singed" also implies "burnt," which suggests the colors brown and black, hence the colors of the speaker's skin. Her hands are singed, in fact, because she *is* Black; the world has been burning her people, both literally and figuratively, for a long time.

The obvious distinction between the speaker and her audience is that she is Black and they are white. But the speaker is also an outsider in that she "come[s] to read them poems" (line 1), emphasis on "them." She is there as a novelty, a performer, to entertain and do tricks — not as part of the audience. She is an insider not as a member of the audience, but as one who knows what the audience expects and wants.

2. The speaker's knowledge of history pervades her thinking; she is unable to see the present without filtering it through all that has happened to her people in the past. In section 6, the speaker says:

> and for a moment only
> i feel the reverberation
> of myself
> in white america
> a black cat
> in the belfry
> hanging
> and
> ringing.

This lynching image makes clear that the evil that was done to the speaker's people in this country will never be forgotten or forgiven. Even if America were devoid of racism — which the speaker certainly feels is not the case — wrongs once done would still resonate. The image of the cat "hanging and ringing" also suggests that America hears what the speaker has to say but doesn't do anything about it.

3. The "dark women" who cleaned the church were indeed not considered "persons," or at least not persons with brains and hearts and souls similar to white people's. It was all right for these women to scrub the floors, but it was not all right for them to pray there, the alleged "liberal history" (25) of the church notwithstanding.

4. By "none of my faces," the speaker means she is not looking into any Black faces; there are no Blacks in the audience. Despite the fact that the woman who shows the speaker around says that the church has a liberal history, it was only white women who were taught in this "female school," just as it was only white women who could pray in the church.

WENDY ROSE

For the White Poets
Who Would Be Indian (p. 416)

In addition to the books mentioned in the text footnote, Wendy Rose is the author of the poetry collections *Hopi Roadrunner Dancing* (1973), *Long Division: A Tribal History* (1976), and *Academic Squaw: Reports to the World from the Ivory Tower* (1977).

This poem works well with the Ortiz and Rodriguez selections; ask students how each of those writers might respond to the speaker here. Where do these three writers stand in relation to each other on the question of whether minority cultures can be understood by the mainstream white culture of this country? On whether minority cultures should *try* to be understood by this mainstream culture? Where do your students stand on these questions?

INVESTIGATIONS (p. 416)

1. The speaker thinks that, to "be Indian," one must share not only the values, philosophies, and entire cultural heritage of Indians, but also the experience of *being* Indian in a white culture. Sharing a mother, which may be meant here both literally and figuratively (we might all consider the earth our mother) is, or can be, merely an accident — whether or not we are *raised by* that mother determines how much of her knowledge, blood, values, and experience we really share. The statement "instant and primal knowledge" is a wonderfully caustic contradiction. The word "primal" implies a deep and powerful importance, one that could not be gained in an instant. Rather, a primal knowledge of what it takes to be an Indian would have to come from having lived as one, experiencing both the joys and hardships of that life, as the speaker presumably has.

2. Answers will vary, but some may well hearken back to Vivian Gornick's phrase "immutable condition of birth." The speaker might claim that she has always been defined in a way that no white person can ever really understand; to be seen as a white woman in a white society, for example, is in no way parallel to being seen as an Indian (or Black, or any other minority) in a white society. This is not to deny that women have their own problems of identity and place in this society, but to suggest that some nonwhite women, such as Rose or Lucille Clifton, might well say that they are entirely different problems.

   You may also have students who wish to take a different tack, and to try, as Simon J. Ortiz might try, to describe the speaker's experience "from the inside." Of course this belies the original premise of this assignment, but it should result in lively discussion, should any of your students choose this approach.

3. Presumably, the white poets go back to their white world. The very fact that they have this option and are not only welcome but are also established in this world explains why the speaker feels white poets can never really know the Indian experience. Unlike the whites, Indians have never been a part of this other, mainstream world; the speaker here feels that if you have never been excluded from the mainstream in this way, you really can't know what it's like "from the inside." The white poets may or may not feel they have gotten what they came for. The speaker, however, feels emphatically that the white poets have not succeeded in understanding or depicting the "Indian" experience.

RICHARD RODRIGUEZ

Aria: A Bilingual Childhood (p. 417)

In this excerpt from his highly acclaimed and highly controversial book, *Hunger of Memory* (1982), Rodriguez recounts his childhood struggle to learn English and argues *against* bilingual education, claiming that the costs of joining the English-speaking community are high, but well worth the price. If any of your students have firsthand experience with bilingual education or are bilingual but were not accommodated in school in any special way, ask them to share these experiences with the class. In retrospect, do they feel they were insufficiently immersed in the language of mass society to successfully compete? Or do they feel that they lost too much of their private language in the process of assimilation?

INVESTIGATIONS (p. 426)

1. The higher one's social class, the more likely the transition from a private, family language to the public language of school will go smoothly. This is in part because education is usually a privilege of class; the private family language of a wealthy child is likely already to be similar to the language spoken in school. If that child is from another culture, his or her parents will be more likely to go out of their way to make sure their child learns the language he or she needs to get on in the world as early as possible. In Rodriguez's case, his parents needed some encouragement (from the nuns who taught their children), but were eager to comply. Rodriguez's parents were well on their way to being assimilated before Richard ever went to school: What other motive could there be for moving to a white neighborhood? This willingness to strive for the "good life" made Richard's parents more open to change than some other parents might be — parents who did not always have jobs, for example, and so did not cope so well in America. (For more on this topic, see Investigation 2, below.)

2. Richard is the first to admit that his "parents coped very well in America." They lived far from the barrio, "the Mexican south side of town" (para. 7). So while Spanish may have been Richard's family language, it was not the language of his neighborhood, not the language he heard spoken in the streets. Nor was it the language his classmates spoke in school. "An accident of geography," he writes, "sent me to a school where all my classmates were white, many the children of doctors and lawyers and business executives" (3). A child of the barrio would have been surrounded by Spanish and only Spanish in his neighborhood and in his school. The parents of such a child might also be less receptive to any *gringos*, even nuns, who claimed they should stop speaking Spanish at home for the good of their children. (Of course it's also less likely that the nuns would try this strategy in the barrio in the first place.)

3. Answers will vary.

4. From Rodriguez's perspective, his private language had to be entirely forsaken to claim a public language. (You may want to refer students back to their "Write Before Reading" assignments here. Was it necessary for them to make such a dramatic sacrifice to move from being an "outsider" to being an "insider"?) In the essay's last paragraph, Rodriguez describes abandoning his private language as a necessary part of growing up. But as Rodriguez himself points out in this essay, many bilingual educators disagree. In fact, many of these educators strongly oppose Rodriguez's platform; they think it is entirely wrong-headed and culturally chauvinistic for non-English-speaking students to have to forsake their native language.

5. The color of Rodriguez's skin and his Hispanic-looking features are immutable in the same way that Vivian Gornick's gender is immutable. Even the best-intentioned observers tend to use labels to identify what they see: One looks at Gornick and sees a woman; one looks at Rodriguez and sees an Hispanic.

   But Rodriguez has made a point of changing the rest of his "condition of birth" — which is, for all of us, as changeable as we choose to make it, given certain opportunities and advantages. If, at a young age, Rodriguez was indistinguishable from other small boys in whose homes only Spanish was spoken, he spent the rest of his life working hard to *make* that distinction. Some educators who disagree with Rodriguez's approach to education might argue that he has, in fact, betrayed his "actual self" — but Rodriguez spends this essay, and indeed much of his book, explaining how and why he created the self he is today.

AMY TAN

Two Kinds (p. 427)

This excerpt from Tan's best-selling novel *The Joy Luck Club* (1989) depicts a parent-child conflict that will no doubt resonate with your students. All parents want their children to make good, but this Chinese immigrant wants her daughter to be an American success with a ferocity that sometimes seems frightening, at least to her daughter. Ask students whether their own experiences wrestling with their parents' aspirations for them were similar to Jing-mei's. If not, how did they differ? What does Jing-mei's mother being an immigrant have to do with the intensity of her hopes for her daughter? And does Jing-mei's being Chinese American seem to hold her back in any way?

INVESTIGATIONS (p. 436)

1. Jing-mei is determined "not to try" precisely because her mother so badly wants her to try. As a child, Jing-mei wants to be accepted for who and what she is. While part of this attitude simply manifests the normal self-absorption typical of young children, and later the rebellion typical of adolescents, Jing-mei's mother *is* pushy. At first, Jing-mei is just as excited as her mother,

    > maybe even more so. I pictured this prodigy part of me as many different images. . . . In all of my imaginings, I was filled with a sense that I would soon become *perfect*. My mother and father would adore me. I would be beyond reproach. (paras. 9–10)

    But both Jing-mei and her mother, with her belief that her daughter "can be best anything" (2), set themselves up for failure by expecting too much.

    Jing-mei's mother is bent on her daughter's achieving public success because "America was where all" her hopes lay (3). In China, she had suffered losses most of us — and certainly her daughter — could not possibly imagine. To assuage that pain, she staked everything on the American dream. Her daughter would have all the advantages; her daughter would have fortune and fame; her daughter's success would at least in part redress the unspeakable disaster and misery of her mother's life in China. To Jing-mei's mother, her daughter's success will make the whole family truly American, a part of the great American community where freedom is paramount and what happened to her in China can never happen again. There is a classic mother-daughter conflict taking place here, one in which both parties are to blame. Jing-mei's mother wants too much, and her daughter offers too little.

2. Neither Jing-mei nor her mother feels part of this "whole world" of aspiring young prodigies and their parents at the talent show. For Jing-mei, the experience and everything leading up to it has been a fantasy: While she knew she wasn't doing the work to earn acclaim, she loved to imagine the curtsy and applause. For Jing-mei's mother, too, there is a fantasy of the ultimate acceptance into American society, born of success. She, too, is not being realistic: She must have known her daughter wasn't good when she heard her practice. And (Beethoven notwithstanding) how could she have expected the child to excel with a deaf teacher — especially when she knew her daughter was rebellious in the first place?

3. Answers will vary, but should include the understanding that both Jing-mei and her mother are mistaken. Jing-mei says, "I could only be me," but the fact is she never tried even half-seriously to learn the piano, which she admits repeatedly in the course of this story. On the other hand, she *did* try seriously when first confronted with her mother's tests (12–16). Yet she wasn't good enough at any of them: "And after seeing my mother's disappointed face once again, something inside of me began to die" (18). Jing-mei's mother was mistaken in thinking her daughter, or anyone, "can be best anything." Waverly Jong, for instance, turned out to be a chess prodigy, but might well have had no aptitude for the piano. In time, Jing-mei might well have found something she excelled at. But the sad fact is that we *don't* always excel at something simply because we try hard.

4. Jing-mei was constantly being pushed into public life by her mother — by forces inside her home, the forces behind her private life. While Rodriguez's parents valued education, the push he received toward public life came from outside the home, initially from the nuns at his school. Rodriguez might agree with Jing-mei's observation about the "two halves of the same song." What the narrator of "Two Kinds" has come to realize, looking back, is that her mother was no monster, nor was her own childhood as tortured as she once believed it was. As an adult, Jing-mei has come to terms with her past; she can even play the piano with affection. And she realizes that, painful as the experience was at the time, her mother really did want what she thought was best for Jing-mei. Similarly, while Rodriguez found leaving his private life quite painful as a child, he, too, is "perfectly contented" with the outcome as an adult.

LORNA DEE CERVANTES

Refugee Ship (p. 436)

You might open discussion by asking students to characterize the speaker's feelings. Although she is with her grandmother, she seems locked in a powerful sense of isolation. What images in the poem suggest her sense of solitude? Ask students to think about why the speaker imagines herself as a refugee. Is language alone the key to resolving her questions of identity? If not, what other issues seem to be involved?

INVESTIGATIONS (p. 437)

1. First, cornstarch is white, while the speaker is not. She is Chicana, with "brown skin, black hair" (line 10). Second, wet cornstarch would be slippery, hard to hold on to, perhaps even considered a mess, which is how the speaker feels about her own identity. "The pudding" in line 5 refers literally to what the speaker's grandmother sees without her glasses; her vision is blurred. But it also refers to the speaker's image of herself: Her identity is elusive. She has a Spanish name and a Spanish appearance, but she does not speak the language; apparently she feels something of an imposter. At best, her sense of self is shapeless, amorphous, like pudding. The speaker not only feels this way about herself, but since it is her grandmother seeing "the pudding," the speaker believes her grandmother (who presumably speaks fluent Spanish) sees her this way, too.

2. Apparently, the speaker knows a few very common Spanish words, but knowing the Spanish words for "mother" and "grandmother" hardly constitutes speaking

the language. The speaker calls herself an "orphan to my Spanish name" (7) because she feels unconnected to her cultural heritage. Her knowledge of these few words is not sufficient to change that feeling; it is, in fact, the knowledge of an outsider looking in.

3. Rodriguez might think the speaker is being sentimental and impractical: As an American, she should proudly embrace her right to speak English. The connection and intimacy she craves with her family and culture is precisely the intimacy he lost when he learned to speak English well. For Rodriguez, the public gain was worth this private loss. Since the speaker of "Refugee Ship" does not even know clearly what she has lost (though this is exactly what she wants to find out), Rodriguez might even consider her self-indulgent.

4. Were the speaker to learn Spanish, perhaps from her mother or grandmother, she might well be better able to come to terms with who she is, and hence feel more at peace, better able to "dock."

TIM O'BRIEN

The Things They Carried (p. 437)

In addition to the books mentioned in the text footnote, O'Brien's books include *If I Die in the Combat Zone, Box Me Up and Ship Me Home* (1973); *Northern Lights* (1975); and *The Nuclear Age* (1985). O'Brien is widely considered to be one of the most important contributors to the literature of Vietnam. His motivation, he says, is

> to write stories that are good. To do that requires a sense of passion, and my passion as a human being and as a writer intersect in Vietnam, not in the physical stuff but in the issues of Vietnam — of courage, rectitude, enlightenment, holiness, trying to do the right thing in the world. (*Publishers Weekly*, February 16, 1990, p. 61)

Ask students how well they feel this story addresses the issues O'Brien outlines above. The issue of courage is perhaps obvious, but what of "trying to do the right thing in the world"? In what way is Lieutenant Cross's burning of Martha's letters "the right thing"? Is Cross right in blaming himself for Ted Lavender's death in the first place? You might also direct students to the cyclical way this story is told: for instance, we read about Ted Lavender's death many times before we read the actual scene in which he gets killed; O'Brien returns to the scene describing his peers' reactions several times, too. Ask students what the effect of this strategy is. How would the story differ if it were narrated chronologically?

INVESTIGATIONS (p. 451)

1. The soldiers call themselves "legs or grunts" (para. 3) — short, functional, even guttural names, names with no mystique about them. Of Ted Lavender's death, they said he was "greased," "offed, lit up, zapped while zipping" (68). "They used a hard vocabulary" to distance themselves from their fear and pain, referring to death "by other names, as if to encyst and destroy the reality of death itself" (68). Their language is a private one, and can be considered a family language, in the sense that no one outside of the war would understand it, nor would the soldiers here be likely to speak this language to anyone who hadn't been there, too. Students may argue that they *do* understand this language, as well they should. O'Brien *makes* us understand it by showing it to us from the inside, from the point of view of these men — but we have been shown. Point out

information is provided for readers, not for the men themselves, who know full well what they are called.

2. Among the weightless items the soldiers carry are Kiowa's "grandmother's distrust of the white man" (2); Jimmy Cross's "responsibility for the lives of his men" (7); Ted Lavender's "unweighed fear" (11); and Cross's knowledge that "he had loved Martha more than his men, and as a consequence Lavender was now dead, and this was something he would have to carry like a stone in his stomach for the rest of the war" (42). In addition, the men carry "all they could bear, and then some, including a silent awe for the terrible power of the things they carried" (12); "ghosts" (17); "imagination" (18); "the weight of memory," "infections," "diseases," "the sky," "the atmosphere," "their own lives" (all in para. 39), "all the emotional baggage of men who might die," "shameful memories," the instinct to run or freeze or hide," "their reputations," and "the fear of blushing" (all in 77).

Though readers are unlikely to have firsthand knowledge of most of the above, it is obvious that carrying "the emotional baggage of men who might die" is a much more oppressive burden and much harder to get used to (if it is possible to get used to) than any piece of equipment, no matter how much it weighs.

3. The soldiers' relationship to one another is closer than friendship because it concerns death in a way that civilian friendships do not: It's about death on a day-to-day basis. As the selections in Part Three (specifically those by Paley, Howard, Gunn, and Kercheval) make clear, to have a real friend is to risk losing that friend. But there is a difference between the general knowledge that we are all going to die *some*day and the specific knowledge shared by the soldiers that each one of them has an excellent chance of dying every single day. Hospices and hospital wards for the terminally ill are among the other kinds of communities where an intimacy similar to that shared by the soldiers might be possible.

4. Sanders' response is not satisfactory to Dobbins, who responds by saying, "I don't see no moral." But what satisfactory moral can there be in a world where "men killed, and died, because they were embarrassed not to" (77) and the man who is most scared, so carries the most ammunition, is the first one to die? The moral, then, is that there is none. There is no morality in such a world, except for staying alive and helping your buddies stay alive, if you can. To Sanders, the moral seems to be that he is alive, and the Viet Cong boy is not. In this world, it is moral simply to be alive. Kiowa's pleasure in being alive is consequently moral for the same reason: He isn't glad Lavender is dead, but he's glad that he *isn't*.

KITTY TSUI

Don't Let Them Chip Away
at Our Language (p. 451)

The first three stanzas of this poem offer us a slice of the speaker's grandmother's language, most of which we either recognize easily (see lines 1–2) or can decipher without much trouble. There are phrases, however, that most of us probably can't understand. Ask students how they react to these phrases. How might the poem's effect differ without them? (For more on this subject, see Investigation 3, below.) This poem works well with Rodriguez's and Ortiz's essays and Cervantes's poem.

How might any of those writers respond to the speaker here?

INVESTIGATIONS (p. 454)

1. Our language, to the speaker, is "many tongues" (88), including "street talk" and "the queen's English." The speaker and many of the people she lists in lines 84–88 clearly speak grammatical English, the kind required by the Republican assemblyman. But many other people the speaker lists, including her grandmother, did or do not know English this well. Yet they knew it well enough to help build this country, not only as merchants, traders, cooks, sharecroppers, and maids — jobs familiar to most immigrant populations — but also as laborers "hired to do what no man would" (56). (Students may not know that building the railroad in this country was a job so dangerous that only those absolutely desperate for work and money would do it. As the newest group of immigrants to this country at the time, the Chinese earned that privilege as other immigrants moved on to safer, less difficult work.) The speaker sees any and all languages spoken by her people as legitimate; any law regulating their speech, or punishing them for a limited understanding of English, is a threat not just to her language, but to her cultural heritage and to her people as a whole.

   The details of the assemblyman's proposed bill aren't spelled out in the poem, but he is no doubt concerned with the number of immigrants and their descendants who can't speak or understand English. Apparently he feels the state has been making exceptions for these people and that these exceptions are in some way damaging the English language or its use in this country.

2. Both Tsui's and Clifton's poems describe the division between minority cultures and the majority culture in the United States. Both poems make historical references because both speakers feel that in order to understand anything about their cultures today, it is necessary to understand the history of their people in this country. Hence, both speakers cite instances of discrimination and use images of oppression to help reveal who they are today and how they got there.

3. The speaker, who presumably knows some Chinese, logically feels that any manifestation of this language, even its Chinatown slang, is part of her cultural heritage. Hence she feels bound to those who speak, or spoke, Chinese — sufficiently so that she uses phrases in this poem readers unfamiliar with the language will not understand ("du pont guy" [12], for example, or "sic gee mah go" [15] or "tong yan" [76]). While the meaning of this poem is quite clear, the inability to translate certain phrases may alienate many readers. Presumably, this has helped alienate the Republican assemblyman as well.

ERIC BOGOSIAN

Talk Radio (p. 454)

In addition to the works mentioned in the text footnote, Bogosian's plays include *Men Inside* (1982) and *FunHouse* (1983). His play *Drinking in America* (1986) won an Obie Award for Best New Play.

Some students may have seen the film adaptation of this disturbing play; if you have access to a videocassette recorder, Bogosian's powerful performance of his lead character is well worth watching. The film's ending, however, differs from the play's. At the end of the film Barry Champlain is killed, apparently by a crazed, hate-filled listener. The film adaptation is based loosely on the true story of Alan hate-filled listener. The film adaptation is based loosely on the true story of Alan Berg, a Denver talk show host who was killed by one of his listeners. You might begin discussion by mentioning either the film or the actual Alan Berg case and asking students how they react to such an ending. Is a talk show host who baits his audience as Champlain does in this play "asking for it"? Is he providing a valuable service by trying to expose the people's prejudices, violence, and hypocrisy, or is he wasting his time on people who won't hear him? Does answering hate with more hate seem like an effective strategy?

INVESTIGATIONS (p. 498)

1. Barry sees his job as shaking up "this decadent country" (p. 459), and his listeners help him do this in two ways. The first is the simple fact that they are there. He has a large, loyal audience that grows enough to allow the show to be aired nationally. As long as his audience grows, the sponsors are happy; as long as the sponsors are satisfied, Barry has a job. Barry's listeners, of course, serve another purpose: They provide him with examples of all the "lying, whoring, and intoxication . . . that makes this country . . . rotten to the core" (p. 459).

   Barry speaks the same language as those who call in because he's as angry as his angry listeners (though usually he is angry that they are ignorant enough to hold the views they hold). But Barry has listeners who aren't angry; these are usually desperate or lonely or both, and Barry shares those experiences, too.

   Barry's insults bind this community together in that the people he baits *call* to be baited. They know how he'll respond to what they have to say, and they want to fight about it, the more publicly the better. And while there is no evidence for this in the play, it is easy to imagine Barry thinking that it's better for these people to vent their rage on his show and direct it at him than to let it loose elsewhere. At best, he might actually convince such a caller that there's something wrong with his or her thinking; at worst, it is Barry rather than someone else who serves as the caller's victim.

2. While it might be possible to trace some of Barry's anger to the "blankness akin to chronic disappointment" some people feel as a result of belonging to a particular community, there must also be other causes. Patricia Hampl, for instance, whose phrase is quoted above, gives us a moving and revealing yet finally evenhanded picture of the world. Clearly both she and most of the parish members she sketches for us are better able to cope with the world than Barry is. And Glen Whalen (of Weesner's "The Body Politic"), too, finds a blankness in his community — both the community he grows up in and the one he joins when he becomes part of the basketball team (see para. 48 of that story). But it is a blankness that he, too, can come to terms with. So part of Barry's anger must be traced to something other than this "blankness" — perhaps to a short circuit in his personality, some glitch that makes him more sensitive and less tolerant than most of the rest of us. Certainly it is not good to tolerate evil and hypocrisy, but tolerating it, or even ignoring it, is how many of us cope with the harsh world we live in. So while Barry's sensitivity to, or intolerance of, these issues is in some ways admirable, it makes it harder for him to live in the world, and harder for others to live with him as well. Hence Linda's statement that she "wouldn't want to live there." It is how each of us responds to this "blankness akin to chronic disappointment" as well as the blankness itself that determines how difficult we are to live with. And Barry's response to this "blankness" drives him every moment a little closer to the edge.

3. Answers will vary.

4. Barry — and some readers — might well argue that one of the causes of the lying and hypocrisy in this country is our attitude toward work. To many people, a job is something in which you do the minimum to get by: Put in the minimum amount of effort, get your paycheck, and whatever you do, don't think about it. Such people (both people at the bottom of the totem pole and executives at the top) don't care about quality, about whether a product is well made or a service properly performed, nor do they mind cutting corners to save money or time, even if someone's safety is at stake. Barry is definitely doing more than a mere job. He is on a mission to expose and eradicate such values. Barry is obsessed with his job: He simultaneously loves people and is alienated by them, and therein lies his tragic flaw. Any disc jockey could fill the airwaves during his time slot; any talk show host could let people ramble on about whatever they chose. Barry's job, as he sees it, is to slap this country in the face in the hopes of saving it. If Barry realized he *was* merely doing a job, his relationship with his listeners and coworkers would probably end; it is clear that he's not interested in being one of those other talk show hosts or disc jockeys.

5. Barry's public language is what his listeners want to hear. While his assessment that he is "providing a public service" (p. 496) is correct, his audience doesn't want to hear this, doesn't want to hear that their own lives have become their entertainment, that they are happiest when others are in pain. Because Barry's public language is what it is, in fact, he *has* no home. He says "I don't need your fear and your stupidity" (p. 496), but of course he does; it's the basis of his show. And he can't complain to his colleagues, either; as Stu says on page 495, "You don't like the heights, Barry, don't climb the mountains."

SIMON J. ORTIZ

The Language We Know (p. 499)

In addition to the books mentioned in the text footnote, Ortiz has published the poetry collections *Going for the Rain* (1976) and *A Good Journey* (1977) and the collection of short stories *The Howbah Indians* (1978). He is also the editor of *Earth Power Coming: Short Fiction in Native American Literature* (1983).

This essay about the difficulty of maintaining one's cultural heritage, values, philosophy, and language while becoming "truly American" (para. 10) pairs beautifully with Richard Rodriguez's essay "Aria: A Bilingual Childhood." Ask students what views these writers hold in common. Where do they differ? Like Rodriguez, Ortiz agrees about the importance of learning English. But Ortiz does not agree that losing one's ease and comfort with one's native language is either desirable or necessary. Rather, his stance is that "we were caught in a system inexorably, and we had to learn that system well in order to fight back" (11). Ortiz, then, believes it is necessary to work within the system both to preserve one's heritage and to change the system. What is Rodriguez's attitude toward preserving one's heritage? Does he perceive a need to change the system?

INVESTIGATIONS (p. 505)

1. Ortiz had little awareness of the non-Indian, non-Acoma world until his year in Skull Valley, Arizona, just as Hampl had little sense of a world outside St. Luke's parish: even the non-Catholics in St. Luke's were "claimed" (Hampl, 27)

by the parish. So despite the occasional Protestant, Jew, Lutheran, or Greek Orthodox neighbor, Hampl's community really was quite homogenous, as was Ortiz's. For both Ortiz and Hampl, the outside world posed threats to the nurturing safety of their childhood communities. For Hampl, though, the impulse was always *toward* the danger of the outside world, toward an investigation of that "unshivered shiver" (Hampl, 22), toward a knowledge of the unknown, of what went on beyond the boundaries (both literal and figurative) of St. Luke's. For Ortiz, the motivation was very different: Indians "had to leave home in order to become truly American by joining the mainstream" (10). Further, government policy "dictated that Indians . . . remove themselves from their lands and go to American cities for jobs and education" (10). For Hampl, the pressure to look beyond her Catholic community comes from within herself; for Ortiz, the pressure comes primarily from outside: it was "U.S. public policy that Indians were no longer to be Indians" (10).

2. Answers will vary.

3. "Staying home" can be perceived as un-American in that such behavior works against assimilation into the mainstream culture. This is precisely why Richard Rodriguez believes bilingual education is detrimental: It allows students, in effect, to stay home, where they will learn less of what they need to compete and succeed in the "outside" world they'll eventually have to enter. For Ortiz, happily, there was a less mechanistic motivation for and result of learning English: "Language opened up vistas of the world around me, and it allowed me to discover knowledge that would not be possible for me to know without the use of language" (3). And "acquiring knowledge about life was above all the most important item; it was a value that one had to have in order to be fulfilled personally and on behalf of his community" (5).

If each of us belonged in and to a particular place, misunderstandings and antagonism among communities would no doubt flourish, precisely as it did between the United States government and Native Americans in ways Ortiz outlines in this essay.

4. Answers will vary. Students might refer back to their answers to the "Write Before Reading" exercise on page 368; their heritage no doubt plays a part in at least one of the communities to which they feel they belong.

JUDITH ORTIZ COFER
Silent Dancing (p. 506)

In addition to the books mentioned in the text footnote, Cofer has published the poetry collections *The Native Dancer* (1981), *Peregrina* (1986), and *Reaching for the Mainland* (1986).

This haunting memoir provides fascinating insight into the life of a woman who, though she emigrated from Puerto Rico at the age of three, is still torn between two worlds. Cofer's use of detail is quite striking; students would no doubt benefit from studying the vivid, almost palpable pictures she creates of her childhood memories. You might draw students' attention to Cofer's use of concrete details — especially smells, sounds, and images — in paragraphs 3, 4, 10–12, 18, and 20–22. Then ask them to emulate Cofer's style and write a brief essay in which they attempt to recreate a community or scene they feel both close to and distant from.

INVESTIGATIONS (p. 512)

1.   The image of the "beehive" is a striking one. It conjures a vision of many separate, isolated compartments, and this indeed seems to be one of the main changes in Cofer's family life since they left Puerto Rico. There is the literal shift from living in a house, where there is open space around you yet still a space of your own, to living in an apartment, in which your pipes come out of one neighbor's apartment and lead into another neighbor's apartment. There is, too, Cofer's father's order to keep "ourselves to ourselves" (4) — that is, not to associate with the other Puerto Ricans in the building. Since Cofer's father could not yet meet his goal of getting his family out of the barrio, this avoidance of neighbors who would not be leaving so soon was his temporary version of upward mobility. But his whole attempt to keep his family from being stuck in what he saw as the mire of the barrio is part of the sensibility that helped the Puerto Rican community unravel from what it once was back on the island. This kind of isolationist attitude would only lead to the kind of "Americanization" Cofer's cousin had undergone. Here was a girl who was proud to "pass" as American, who never spoke Spanish, who considered the mores of "the island" old-fashioned and oppressive and couldn't wait to marry an American boy and have an American name. Cofer seems to see the move to America as at least partly responsible for the destruction of community values; in her dreams, the family is on a downward spiral, her dying great-uncle's face a mirror in which she can see the faces of everyone in her family, including her own.

2.   When Puerto Rican immigrants lose "la mancha," they have abandoned certain "traditional" Puerto Rican values and become thoroughly Americanized. Note that the *novia* (the girl just up from the island) is modest; she wears a full-skirted dress, which is pulled down over her knees. She has a "humble demeanor" and looks "insecure." In contrast, Cofer's cousin, born and raised in Paterson, wears a tight, gaudy dress, has dyed hair, smokes, and talks animatedly. The qualities of humility, modesty, and decency, we learn in paragraph 24, are associated with "Puerto Rican–style" women. American women, on the other hand, are considered to be somewhat corrupt: Cofer's cousin, who does as she pleases, doesn't even want to be identified as Puerto Rican.

3.   Both Cofer's father and Jing-mei's mother want what they think is best for their children. As immigrants who do not want their children to feel any limitations or run into any barriers, both Cofer's father and Jing-mei's mother encourage their children to be as "American" as they can. Jing-mei's mother wants her to be a success. If she's the "best" at something, this will be her (and consequently her whole family's) ticket to the American dream. The myth is that in America anyone can be or do anything, and both parents want to live that myth as fully as possible. In Cofer's case, her father feels that if the family does not act like other Puerto Ricans (by not living where others live, or, if they must, then by not associating with them, and by not shopping where they shop), they won't be treated like other Puerto Ricans — in other words, they won't be discriminated against. Both parents are keenly aware that they are not only immigrants to a new culture but also minorities in a majority culture, and their aims are to make these distinctions matter for their families as little as possible.

4.   Answers will vary. Clearly, it is difficult to retain old values while assimilating new ones. Cofer has recurring dreams many would consider nightmares over precisely this issue. Richard Rodriguez, on the other hand, seems to have assimilated without holding on to much of his old life. And then there is Glen Whalen, the narrator of "The Body Politic," who seems to have managed to both assimilate *and* hold onto old values by the end of that story. Students

may want to consider some of the other selections in this light, specifically those by Gornick, Cervantes, and Ortiz. They might also want to look back at earlier parts. Selections by McKnight, Morales, Perillo, Gordon, Machado, and Hernandez all speak to this issue.

GARY SNYDER

Building (p. 513)

This poem is about the importance of community in our lives in general but especially in our work. Students may be interested to learn that Snyder, along with Jack Kerouac and Allen Ginsberg, was part of the Beat movement in San Francisco in the 1950s, and that he studied Zen Buddhism in Japan for several years. The poem contains some topical references with which students may need help, specifically the "Cultural Revolution" in China, and the "Peoples Forests," which presumably hearkens back to the 1960s sense of communal property.

INVESTIGATIONS (p. 514)

1. "We" is the community of people who worked on each of those buildings with the speaker. The reader is not literally a part of this community, since he or she was not actually present in any instance, peeling trees, burying vajras, blowing the conch, or filling the building with flowers. But in the poem's third-to-last stanza, the reader is invited in: "Our buildings are solid, to live, to teach" (line 31). And, in the penultimate stanza, "This is outside of history" (33). The poem is not so much a testimonial to the people who actually worked on these buildings; rather, it is an ode to communal work itself — an activity which, by its very nature, unites builders and readers or observers.

2. Like a building, a metaphor needs a strong foundation; metaphors are built on something concrete, and then carefully developed. The walls and beams in a building must be painstakingly planned, positioned, and executed, just as a metaphor must be developed one step at a time. Images and word choice must be exact and build upon one another, or the metaphor will fall apart, just as an ill-planned building would.

3. The home, schoolhouse, and hall described by the speaker are all built communally. But at least one hundred people worked on the schoolhouse (or so the hundred wheelbarrows imply), while only forty worked on the hall, ten years later. The number of people interested in doing this kind of work dropped considerably from the sixties to the seventies, as did the number of people rebelling against the system: "Hair is short" (18) and "single mothers go back to college to become lawyers" (20). Another sign of the seventies and the growing women's movement is the "women carpenters" (23) working on the hall — presumably women were not working on the earlier building, or the speaker would not have singled them out here. A final sign of the changing times is the location of the buildings: The first two structures were built in the forest, while the last is built in a meadow, since "the industry calls the shots in the Peoples Forests" (19). Whatever forest land was once available to this community has apparently been claimed by private industry.

4. The speaker is suggesting that, in light of the world political climate, "the sound of a bell" may in fact be one of the only things we can "know for sure" in contemporary life. Between terrorism and wars and instances of clandestine government activities in a country that supposedly does not sanction such

activity, the simple acts of sitting, teaching, learning, and listening are among the few things we can be sure of. The bell suggests both school and, echoing the Liberty Bell, freedom.

5. Buildings are both "history," in that they represent the era during which they were built, and "not history" in that they are timeless. Barring some natural or unnatural disaster (such as, for example, either a fire or a bomb, respectively) buildings can last hundreds, even thousands, of years. Their presence is simultaneously a testimony to the work done to build them and to the spirit of renewal that keeps them in use, that allows people to adapt them, in each era, for their present needs.

ON AND OFF THE JOB

OVERVIEW

Part Five is peopled by lawn cutters, athletes, auto workers, steelworkers, people buying everything from obsolete machine parts to entire businesses, advertising writers, farmers, journalists, masons, miners, roofers, and employees of the Forest Service, private defense industry, and federal government. It is impossible to represent every profession here, but this range is quite broad — broad enough to confirm that "work" serves many functions in our society. While most people work first and foremost to support themselves and their families, the selections in Part Five reveal that work means, or can mean, much more than a paycheck.

Almost half the selections in this part feature workers who seem to want the jobs they have; they seem content or genuinely happy in their work. The pleasures of these jobs — which usually include both a sense of competence and some sense of power — seem to outweigh any drawbacks the workers may perceive, making the overall experience a positive one. Both Michael Dorris and Rachel L. Jones learn more about who they are and who they will become through their jobs. In Jones's case, coming face to face with potent racism for the first time was hardly a pleasant experience, but it taught her two important things: what hate truly means, and that she is incapable of it. In "After the Game," the exhaustion and anxiety pitcher Billy Wells sometimes feels is mitigated by the elation of winning a game. Both Garfinkle and Kate in *Other People's Money* feel similar elation when winning their legal and corporate games. All of the characters in "Late Early Man" enjoy their work a great deal; their jobs inherently involve creativity and a strong sense of play. Perfecto Flores *brings* that creativity and sense of play into his job as a mason and loves his work because of it. And both Elaine in "Sitting on Top of the World" and Lamar in "The Flowers of Boredom" experience a heady if bizarre sense of power from their work. (Certainly there are aspects of Lamar's job he dislikes, but the story's final paragraph makes it clear that whatever else he feels, he is in awe of the entire industry.)

In the poems by Donald Hall, Jay Parini, and C. K. Williams, students will meet characters who fall into a different category. The speakers in each case maintain some distance from the farmer, miner, and roofers they respectively describe, but each worker seems settled into his work. If these characters are anxious to change their lives, there's no evidence of this in the poems. (Note that in the poem "Tar," this statement refers only to the *roofers*; the speaker here, an entity clearly distinct from the roofers, most definitely wants a change in all of our lives.)

Finally, students will encounter characters who are, for a variety of reasons, dissatisfied with their work or what it has become. In "My Father Worked Late," Daniels's speaker feels that his father's job cost his family more than it could ultimately bear. And in Levine's "Buying and Selling," the speaker's job leaves him with a deep feeling of emptiness. In *Other People's Money*, Jorgenson, Bea, and Coles all *liked* their jobs, but fell victim, as did Trudy Pax Farr, to a changing economy in which their jobs simply disappeared. A similar fate can be described for Uncle Ralph in Anna Lee Walters's "The Warrior." In this rapidly changing world where traditional and decent values seem to have no place, the context in which Ralph could *do* the work of "living beautifully" has been pulled out from under his feet.

Instructors who don't have time to teach all the selections in Part Five might want to use the following grouping to focus on the role business plays in this country, and society's attitude toward that role: "My Father Worked Late," "Steelworker," "Ox Cart Man," *Other People's Money*, "Late Early Man," "The Flowers of Boredom," and "Tar." The steel, advertising, defense, and nuclear industries are represented here, along with corporate business and farming. Ask students whether these selections support Andrew Jorgenson's notion that a business is "the very fabric that binds our society together." (For a related assignment, see Part Five: Connections and Elaborations 4.)

MICHAEL DORRIS

Life Stories (p. 519)

In addition to the books mentioned in the text footnote, Dorris has written *Native Americans: Five Hundred Years After* (1975) and *A Guide to Research on Native American Studies* (1983).

The form of this autobiographical essay is familiar from paragraph 4 on, but ask students what they make of the first three paragraphs. They might be interested to know that Dorris is an anthropologist. Do they think he's suggesting that those of us in twentieth-century Western society have it soft, in comparison to other societies? Or that we're spiritually diminished? Does he think the experience of the Plains Indian male has any analogue in our culture? And does he suggest that he himself has experienced anything similar to those moments of "personal, enabling insight"?

INVESTIGATIONS (p. 524)

1. Answers will vary, but receiving their first paycheck may well be the closest many students will have come to this moment of "enabling insight"; at that moment they initially tasted "the satisfaction of remuneration that is earned, not merely doled" (para. 4). In the last paragraph, Dorris himself acknowledges that he "didn't wind up in an occupation with any obvious connection to the careers" he sampled during his summers, but together these jobs combined to help form his "adult persona."

2. School is neutral ground in that it is a holding zone: As long as you're a student, decisions about your vocation and avocation can be postponed. Even if you are following a specific educational track for an intended career, as a student you're still not officially a member of that profession. You haven't yet had to

hold your own as an adult member of the working world. Work is not neutral ground in that you are being judged and paid by the standard of the adult working world, though you are not yet really a part of it.

3. Dorris's jobs, and the circumstances surrounding them, taught him some of the most important things we can learn from our early work experiences: responsibility, humility, flexibility, resilience, and self-confidence — all skills and attitudes we need not only for future jobs, but for all aspects of our lives in this complicated world. As a lawn cutter, from the woman who called his "attention to each blade of missed grass" (7), Dorris learned patience. As a soon-to-be bank teller in France and the Coordinator of Tribal Youth Programs, Dorris learned that advertised jobs may not always be what they seem. In the Youth Programs job, he also learned to work with people who did not like him. In Paris he learned a great deal of resourcefulness. He also learned that if there are people like M. Dupont who will lie to you without a second thought, there are also people like M. Saint and Mademoiselle, who will be extraordinarily generous, too.

4. Answers will vary.

ANDRE DUBUS
After the Game (p. 525)

In addition to the books listed in the text footnote, Dubus has published the essay collection *Broken Vessels* (1991), the novel *The Lieutenant* (1967), the novella *Voices from the Moon* (1984), and the short-story collections *Separate Flights* (1975), *Adultery and Other Choices* (1977), *Finding a Girl in America* (1980), and *The Times Are Never So Bad* (1983).

In this short, tense story, Dubus beautifully depicts a man recognizing his own mortality, though this recognition is indirect. On the surface, he recognizes how little control he has over his success in his profession. Baseball, and sports in general, is a short-lived career: It's only a matter of time before even the best players slow down, betrayed by their aging bodies. Billy Wells knows this — it's why he's sending his father money to build a ranch — but until his teammate goes crazy, Billy imagines his own transition going very smoothly. His retirement from baseball will be a willed, logical, mature decision based on his own and his team's assessment of when his arm is giving out. Joaquin's seizure shows him that other pressures could get him, or any of his teammates, first. It makes Billy realize that he is more vulnerable than he thought he was and allows him simultaneously to appreciate the power of the magic he feels when he plays well and to realize how fleeting that magic is.

INVESTIGATIONS (p. 530)

1. Dialogues will vary. It's true that no job is really predictable, though some are more than others. If you work in a service industry (as a sales clerk or waiter or waitress, for example), an armed thief or lunatic could walk into your workplace at any time. If you work in business, a big financial deal you've just made could go sour; it happens all the time. If you work a farm or ranch, you're at the mercy of bad weather, which can ruin an entire year's crop, or disease, which could wipe out your livestock. From the outside looking in, other jobs may seem more predictable than playing ball, and may even be so on a day-to-day basis. But if the cook ruins everyone's food or you drop

a patron's meal you'll probably lose only your night's tips; if there's an early freeze on your ranch, you could lose a year's income.

2. Quintana is in the grip of something none of the players, including Joaquin himself, understands. He's staring at something that isn't there (except in his mind) and holding the shoe as if his life depends on it. There's nothing dangerous about the shoe, but it's the only tangible thing Quintana's teammates have to latch onto. It's as if Quintana is under some spell, and getting the shoe away from him will break it.

3. Any job with a physical component requires some form of this dancelike precision. The risk of depending on someone else, of course, is that everyone is fallible — the other guy *could* make a mistake, move too slowly, be in the wrong place at the wrong time. Worse, your partner could get sick, as Quintana does here; then you'd be forced to work with someone unfamiliar, who would have to learn all your moves afresh, just as you would have to learn his. The pressure on both parties is bad enough when you're used to each other; with a new partner, it would be tremendous.

Dancelike precision can be required in solitary efforts as well, but in those instances you only have to worry about one person's dependability and predictability: your own. This makes the pressure greater in some ways — everything is up to you — but your control of the situation is greater, too.

4. Depending on how well a player has played, he'll sleep "very well" or "very badly" (para. 2). The narrator says this is "one of the things that makes the game exciting" (2). The more predictable a job is, the less of this excitement it provides; but at the same time, the person with a less exciting job enjoys more security and stability. For some people, a job is merely a way to make a living; they seek excitement and satisfaction elsewhere, so their job needn't provide it. Others have jobs so demanding that they are left with no time or energy for any other pursuits; for them, without the kind of excitement Billy Wells enjoys, such work can be truly spiritually deadening.

JIM DANIELS

My Father Worked Late (p. 531)

Students should have little trouble with this moving poem about a father-son relationship thwarted in part by the demands of the father's job. Some may wish for a different resolution; the ending might seem depressing or even cruel, considering the father's recent stroke. Ask students whether any of them have had experiences similar to the speaker's. Do they share the speaker's attitude? How would they characterize the speaker's tone: Bitter? Matter of fact? Do students think the speaker's father was a *bad* father? Why or why not?

Ask students to point to other examples of children whose parents weren't there for them in selections they've read earlier in this book. The situations are all very different, but Jason in "Fathering" (Part Two) is not there for Eng until he brings her to the United States; Agnes G. Herman and her husband ("A Parent's Journey Out of the Closet," Part Two) are initially not there for their gay son; and neither Clint in "The Kind of Light That Shines on Texas" (Part One), Glen Whalen in "The Body Politic" (Part Four), nor Judith Ortiz Cofer ("Silent Dancing," Part Four) spend much time with their fathers. Ask students what these narrators and writers have in common with Daniels's speaker. What about their experiences is different?

INVESTIGATIONS (p. 532)

1. The speaker's father's weariness is similar to Billy Wells's in that both are exhausted after a hard day of physical work. In both cases, their loved ones suffer: Wells "lost a wife in [his] first year in professional ball"; she "felt like she was chasing the team bus all season long" (para. 24). The speaker and his brother in Daniels's poem had perhaps more to lose: The speaker remembers "the distance of those missing years" (line 34); he recalls his father looking "right through us" (23), "mechanically eating" (24), and "yelling at anything that moved" (25).

   But the satisfaction each man gets from his work is where the difference lies. In "My Father Worked Late," there is no indication that the speaker's father got any satisfaction from his work beyond a paycheck. Billy Wells, on the other hand, loves his work at least half the time. He gets rushes of adrenaline when he's pitching well, and the feeling he can dance like the beautiful, elegant couple he used to watch in the movies, the feeling that he knows how to move.

2. This poem is testimony to the fact that the speaker has "weighed, absorbed and incorporated" the lessons of his father's work. The main lesson the speaker seems to have taken from his father's work is that his father was rarely home to give his children the time or love they needed. Lines 41 and 42 indicate that the speaker's father seems to have realized this himself, long after the fact. But the speaker notes, in the poem's last two lines, that it is too late; the damage has already been done. One has no way of knowing whether the speaker will repeat his father's mistakes, but his very awareness of them certainly makes it less likely. (For a related assignment, see Part Five: Connections and Elaborations 4a.)

3. When the speaker and his brother use the phrase "Do you give?" initially, they use it specifically in the context of play wrestling: "Do you give up?" or "Do we win?" But by the poem's end it has taken on a broader and more powerful resonance: The phrase now means "do you give" emotionally. The speaker is asking, rhetorically, did you give me any of the love and support I need?

4. Answers will vary.

TRUDY PAX FARR

Steelworker (p. 533)

This poignant memoir by a steelworker is frank and unsentimental: Farr doesn't whitewash the dangers or drawbacks of her job, so her appreciation of its positive aspects is quite believable. A lively discussion might arise from asking students what they think about women holding "traditionally male jobs." Do they see any evidence of sexism in this workplace? Interestingly, it doesn't seem to come from Farr's male coworkers. But how do students explain the attitudes of the older women in the mill? And while the managers are not specifically mentioned, do we read of any women operating forklifts or cranes?

INVESTIGATIONS (p. 538)

1. The tools and language of any job are specific to that job. As several of the selections in Part Four demonstrate, language helps form community, and this is especially true in the workplace. (For a related assignment, see Part Five: Connections and Elaborations 4d.) The jargon of any job includes names of

tools, places, processes, and events that combine to compose a language insiders use fluently and unconsciously but outsiders don't understand at all. This language develops not primarily for the purpose of excluding outsiders, but for the purpose of recognizing the bond between the insiders: We are all in this together; we have common knowledge and abilities, we know things and have abilities other people don't. This knowledge is a form of power held by those who belong, by those with special skills, those who can say, with dignity and self-assurance, "There is something important I know how to do."

2. In paragraph 14 Farr feels immune to the danger posed by her work because up to that point none of the people who have died were doing the specific job she does. She has adopted an attitude that anyone with a dangerous job must: it can't happen to me. This is a self-preservation mechanism — she believes what she needs to believe in order to keep doing her job. But when someone with her job does get hurt, her defense mechanism is shattered.

These accidents aren't accidental in that they are inevitable: "Accidents happen everywhere in the mill" (para. 14). Equipment breaks or malfunctions, trucks tip over, molten steel spills or backfires. Things go wrong in all jobs, but when it happens here it's often fatal. It is the price these workers pay for a decent salary and the sense of self-worth they get from doing this job.

3. Stories form communities. Like language (of which stories are composed), they create and enforce bonds between storytellers and their listeners: I'm an insider, I remember that, I was there.

4. Few people like everything about their jobs, and this sentiment extends to pink- and white-collar employment. The problems in Farr's job — danger, extreme heat, noise, dirt, and scheduling — are factors in most construction or factory jobs as well. The nostalgia comes from having lost a strong sense of community, of no longer "being part of something BIG" (35). A sense of empowerment is also lost: Farr was part of something difficult; she "felt the satisfaction of overcoming trepidation" (35), which gave her confidence and strength.

PHILIP LEVINE
Buying and Selling (p. 538)

In addition to the books mentioned in the text footnote, Levine has published the poetry collections *On the Edge* (1963), *Silent in America: Vivas for Those Who Failed* (1965), *Not This Pig* (1968), *Five Detroits* (1970), *Pili's Wall* (1971), *Red Dust* (1971), *They Feed They Lion* (1972), *1933* (1974), *The Names of the Lost* (1976), *Ashes: Poems Old and New* (1979), *7 Years from Somewhere* (1979), *One for the Rose* (1981), *Selected Poems* (1984), and *Sweet Will* (1985).

Students may be unfamiliar with the particular job the speaker has (buying obsolete materials from warehouses for junk companies across the country), but once this is clear they should be able to work their way through this poem. And the sheer musicality of Levine's lines should be apparent to them and lure them through. You may need to define alliteration, assonance, and internal rhyme for some students; then pursue a discussion of these techniques. Note that the speaker even introduces the image of singing in the first line. You might focus on the *B*'s used in the poem's first three lines (Bay, Bridge, buffeting, buying); the repetition of the long *I* sound (I, my, I, my, life, buying); the internal rhyme of "way" and "Bay." Ask students to find further examples of the techniques, which are plentiful throughout the poem. What is their cumulative effect? Can they find other ways Levine controls the poem's rhythm?

INVESTIGATIONS (p. 540)

1. When a salesperson or steelworker describes his or her work, that person describes concrete things — the items being sold or made — and physical processes, the steps being taken to sell or make those things. When lawyers, doctors, teachers, or takeover artists describe their work, they usually talk about ideas or concepts rather than things. A lawyer traffics in laws, which exist on paper but are not tangible entities, just as for a doctor most disease is not tangible, though many treatments are. Takeover artists deal in imaginary numbers, in stocks that represent money but are not the thing itself. They work with predictions and manipulate numbers to do their jobs.

   Both Levine's speaker and Farr offer us lists that evoke their affection for the things with which they work. Both Levine's speaker and Garfinkle relish their work, but Levine's speaker nurses a sadness it is unlikely Garfinkle will ever know.

2. "The gospels" refers literally, of course, to the first four books of the New Testament, in which Matthew, Mark, Luke, and John relate the "good news" of Jesus's life and teachings. In secular parlance, "gospel" is usually used to mean something that is considered to be absolutely true. The speaker uses the term "the new gospels" ironically; he is referring to "the maker's name, letters, numbers / all of which translated into functions / and values known only to the old moguls / of the great international junk companies . . . / whose young emissary I was" (lines 22–27). Apparently the speaker's information tells the junkyard moguls the good news that he has found highly desirable merchandise. The "gospels" are connected to the "pittances" in that the sale gives the loaders and drivers work: "The bids were / awarded, so trucks were dispatched." The loaders and drivers must be "tipped" so they won't steal.

3. The speaker feels sadness at the end of the poem in part because he's experiencing an anticlimax: The work is done. Any excitement or satisfaction he got from buying important goods, from supervising its loading onto trucks, from securing the loaders' and drivers' honesty by paying them off, is gone. The work has been completed, and he's alone in a strange city recognizing that it's only work; it's not something that matters to him the way he wants his life to matter to him. The speaker wants to be the boy he used to be, who "wept publicly in the Dexter- / Davison branch of the public library / over the death of Keats in the Colvin / biography and had prayed like him / to be among the immortals" (28–32). The speaker feels he has abandoned that boy, as the children in the poem's last two lines have been abandoned.

JERRY STERNER

Other People's Money (p. 541)

In addition to *Other People's Money*, Sterner has written the play *Be Happy for Me* (1987).

This disturbing play presents a frightening picture of the world of business and finance in the United States. It tells the story of a small, once-successful business that simply cannot compete in today's cutthroat corporate world. While most of your students will not have firsthand knowledge of this world, many will know or know of someone who works in a small business or in an industry that is now becoming obsolete. Ask students whether they know anyone who has lost his or her job or company as a result of the current recession. Who do students think is to blame? Might they suggest any course of action, such as legislation, to resolve such problems?

Some students will no doubt be offended by Garfinkle's frequent and extremely crude sexual comments. Some may also be disturbed by Kate's response to him. On page 559, Kate says, "Garfinkle is a blatant sexist. I love blatant sexists. They're my meat." The implication is that she loves to tear sexists apart, but in fact she does nothing of the kind. Ask students whether they would call Kate a feminist. Does being a woman and having a high-powered corporate job make you a feminist? What might Vivian Gornick ("Twice an Outsider: On Being Jewish and a Woman," Part Four) say about the way Kate responds to Garfinkle's sexist comments?

Ask students whether they observe any stereotypes in this play. Examine the characters' last names and the personalities that go with those names. You may want to share the following author's note Sterner wrote addressing this subject:

> The character of Garfinkle can be played many ways. The one way he should not be played is overly, coarsely, "ethnic". Though he boasts of his Bronx upbringing he is an educated man and no doubt has an M.B.A. from some top university. His speech patterns are those of a third-generation New Yorker.

Ask students whether they think these instructions make Garfinkle any less a stereotype. Would the meaning of this play be changed for students if Garfinkle and Jorgenson exchanged names? Or if Garfinkle's name were Smith? Do they think these changes would alter the play's meaning from the playwright's perspective?

INVESTIGATIONS (p. 583)

1. Kate *claims* she doesn't consider her job a game, just as she claims to be repelled by Garfinkle. She protests that "for some people business means more than making money. They don't know how to play your game" (p. 565). But in fact the only reason she seems to feel anything at all for Jorgenson's company is that her mother is involved. Her motivation doesn't seem to have anything to do with Jorgenson's desire to save his company and his workers' jobs. Rather, Kate is excited by the challenge, by the opportunity to play hardball, to use all the tricks of the business she knows to manipulate the situation. So in fact it *is* the game that appeals to her.

   Neither Farr nor the speaker in Daniels's poem seems to consider the work they discuss a game. The nature of blue-collar work is repetitive and physically demanding; there is little opportunity for flexibility or creativity, and any mental or physical game workers devised to make the time pass more quickly would at least run the risk of being dangerous, since it would distract them from their work and so could encourage accidents. Though Michael Dorris reveals a lighthearted attitude toward his work, he himself points out that "summer jobs had the luxury of being temporary."

   Game playing can be rewarding in that it provides a challenge that can be exhilarating: Billy Wells gets his rush of adrenaline, his thrill at "knowing how to move." For Wells, of course, work is literally a game. It certainly has consequences that more casually played games do not, but the element of play remains a prominent part of the job in a way that play is not present in blue-collar work. Game playing encourages creative thinking and problem-solving, and those who win are rewarded. Taken too far, however, games can cross ethical boundaries, which some readers will feel is the case in this play.

2. Students may want to castigate Coles for dealing with Garfinkle, but Jorgenson didn't give him much of a choice. It's all right to take a noble stand if you have enough money to live on, as Jorgenson and Bea do. But Coles is the one whose future is unsettled: He's middle-aged, has twenty years to retirement, a family to support, and a business he *thought* he was going to take over. It was his security; if the company is sold, he has none. Coles has the real ethical dilemma in this play; he despises Garfinkle and everything he stands for, but Coles has to do something to save himself.

3. Needs and wants have a great deal to do with each other; as often as not, however, they are in conflict. In "Buying and Selling," the speaker *wants* some kind of meaning in his life greater than that provided by purchasing junk from navy shipyards, but he doesn't really know how to get it. In the meantime, like everyone else, he *needs* a job, so he has stuck with some version of buying and selling for the past ten years.

In "My Father Worked Late," needs and wants are directly opposed: The speaker's family *needs* the father's paycheck, but they *want* his presence, love, and attention. Ironically, it is his job, which provides the paycheck, that keeps the speaker's father from meeting his children's *wants*. Most of us would argue that parental love and attention are also needs, but from a strictly practical point of view, the family can get by without the father's presence; they can't get by without his income.

Rachel L. Jones *wants* to be unaffected by the Klan rally — in part because she believes this is the appropriate response for her profession — but her *need* to respond emotionally turns out to be uncontrollable.

RALPH LOMBREGLIA

Late Early Man (p. 584)

It is hard to know exactly what to take seriously in this tale of modern life and love, but the word "tale" is certainly appropriate. It cannot be intended as entirely realistic; a man with the powers of observation to describe the receptionist, a very minor character, as appearing "in our doorway in a state of excited wonder, her arms and eyelids fluttering like hovering birds" (para. 68), would certainly provide at least a few more graphic details about a close friend's giving birth in the car he is driving, if realism were the aim here. Nor does Anita's almost effortless birth seem plausible. There is a great deal of humor in this story, much of it ironic; ask students to locate some examples. They might point to Walter and Dwight's exchange of sandpaper jokes in paragraphs 32–35; Suzie's infelicities with the English language in paragraphs 70–75; the image of Tempesto "stir-frying hundreds of pounds of chicken in an old satellite dish over a bonfire" (121); *The Journal of Irreproducible Results*, or the lists of food served at both Tempesto's place and the belt-sander race. Ask students what makes these scenes funny. Can they find a common element among these funny moments?

INVESTIGATIONS (p. 603)

1. "Early man" is someone who was born before the technological revolution that brought us microwave ovens, cellular phones, personal computers, and all the

paraphernalia that accompanies them. The title "Late Early Man" seems to be a play on anthropological labels — as if Walter represents a particular stage of human development, and not the most advanced stage. He is *late* early man because he lives surrounded by these technological advances, but he doesn't seem to embrace them in the same way that others do, including Dwight, Anita, and even Benny. Walter has an air of beguilement about him, as if all this technical wizardry is almost too much for him.

2. Tempesto's perspective on life, let alone the events of this story, is radically different from Walter's. If the world in which Walter lives seems chaotic or at times hard to believe, there are aspects of his life and job that are familiar, too. Walter, Dwight, and Anita have recognizable jobs as actor-scriptwriter, producer, and editor at Paradise productions. Walter interacts with his colleagues, both professionally and socially. Walter is also romantically involved with Rebecca. While their relationship may have its problems, it is Walter's participation in and *openness* to human contact that makes what happens in this story matter. To Tempesto, who is often busy "simulating reality on a computer somewhere" (1), Anita's baby is probably an interesting digression from the evening's main story: the belt-sander races. Tempesto is a high-tech wizard whose primary interests seem to be inanimate; he is interested in entertaining people, but the most meaningful human contact he engages in is serving gourmet leftovers to Dwight and Walter. Tempesto's story might focus on precisely which items he bought but could not pay for at the computer store and what crucial adjustments he had to make to his belt sander in paragraph 22 so it would win the race. If Tempesto were telling this story, its last scene might well include his figuring out a way to outsmart the ambulance lights so his laser beams could still be seen.

3. Tempesto is the most "contemporary" character in this story simply because both his art and work revolve around the use of high technology, such as lasers, computers, holograms, and oscilloscopes. Tempesto is likable in part because he is so good at what he does but also because he has a child's sense of fun; the sheer pleasure he takes in zapping street lights, for instance, is contagious. On the other hand, it's also juvenile, and this is an unlikable aspect of his character. Everything seems to be a game to him, so he charges things he can't pay for on his Visa card, knowing he'll be bailed out.

Dwight shares Tempesto's happy-go-lucky attitude, but this seems less attractive in his character: A man with a very pregnant wife should behave a bit more responsibly. Most clients, especially those who are as happy as Benny is by paragraph 239, would not only understand but encourage a husband's leaving to take his wife to the hospital when she went into labor. Dwight's determination to *make* the deal, and his ability to execute it, of course, is admirable. He is clearly good at what he does.

Anita is likable both because she's good at what she does and because of her independence; most women would not insist on working when their baby was literally due any second, when they couldn't even sit up and the temperature was 98 degrees. Like Tempesto and Dwight she clearly enjoys her work, but her practical judgment is rather flawed; in fact, it is probably unhealthy for her to be out in that heat, and it's not the most intelligent idea for her to be gadding about without quick and easy access to a hospital. Luckily, since she is risking her own safety, her delivery is uneventful, but she had no way of knowing it would be.

4. Garfinkle and Tempesto are similar in that they are both self-absorbed and more interested in things than in people. (It's true that Garfinkle is interested in Kate, but her presence or absence wouldn't change his basic desire for money "because it's there.") But Garfinkle and Tempesto are different in that Tempesto's attitude toward his work usually doesn't hurt other people (the broken air conditioner notwithstanding), while Garfinkle seems to take pleasure in ruining people's lives.

5. In some ways the relationship between men and women in this story can be summarized by Anita's answer to Rebecca's question, "Do men ever grow up?"; the answer is "No" (197–198). Both Dwight and Anita are at least as preoccupied with their work as they are with each other; Anita seems so determined to keep working that perhaps Dwight really couldn't have gotten her to stay home. But he certainly should have gotten the air conditioner fixed. More important, he should have taken Anita to the hospital instead of staying at the belt-sander races to clinch his deal. Of course, Anita is a party to all this. She's the one who wants to keep working even though her baby's going to be born any second. And she doesn't seem perturbed by Dwight's not taking her to the hospital.

    We don't know as much about how work affects Rebecca and Walter's relationship, in part because Walter, who is narrating the story, doesn't understand it himself. "We fight all the time," he says in paragraph 9, "and later I can never remember what the fights were about." In paragraph 104, he says "I'm drama. She's documentary. It's a constant struggle," as if this explains something. In fact, it may: Rebecca does seem to be the most down-to-earth character in this story. Unlike Anita, she *is* the family-planning type. She knows she wants Walter's baby and she claims she has tried to tell him this, but he doesn't listen: In paragraph 100 she says, "A man who was somewhere besides on Mars would have taken the hint."

6. While many women do have relatively easy deliveries, Anita's is one for the record books: It takes about five minutes and includes no screams and only one passing reference to pain. Anita's labor is not unlike the other kinds of labor in the story because it doesn't really seem like work. Tempesto's work all seems like a game to him, and Walter and Anita certainly seem to be having fun when they're editing Benny's infomercial early in the story. And Dwight, as producer, is playing the game of trying to hook his client, Benny.

    One crucial difference between the delivery and the other labor in this story is that in spite of the mother's and especially the father's love of the latest technical gadgets, the baby is delivered without the aid of technology, in the way the babies of the earliest early women and men were delivered (not counting, of course, *The Wall Street Journal*). This irony is surely at the heart of Lombreglia's story.

DONALD HALL

Ox Cart Man (p. 604)

The ox cart man's work consists of hard, repetitive physical labor. Ask students to cite other workers in Part Five of whom this is true. How does the ox cart man's labor differ from theirs? The roofers in "Tar" and Perfecto Flores are affected by the seasons, though not to the same extent as the ox cart man. They can't work outdoors in inclement weather, just as the ox cart man must do each task in its proper season. Like Trudy Pax Farr, however, the roofers and Perfecto Flores do not work alone. (Perfecto may, sometimes, but he works with the speaker, his friend, in the poem printed here.) Only the miner in "Working the Face" and the ox cart man work consistently alone, yet even the miner has a grandeur the ox cart man seems to lack. Does the ox cart man's understanding of and respect for nature mitigate this lack?

INVESTIGATIONS (p. 605)

1. October is the month for harvesting (at least for harvesting potatoes) — a signal that the growing season is over. April, the month in which the wool was sheared, is the first full month of spring — when the growing cycle resumes. "Cold" November is the beginning of the waiting season — a time for indoor work, such as stitching the harness and "building the cart again" (line 25). Almost all the images in the poem reinforce our sense of nature's cycle, since the poem exclusively documents the ox cart man's preparations for his seasonal trip to market, the trip itself, and his return from that trip. Farming is dependent on nature's cycles, as are, for instance, counting and bagging potatoes, tapping maple sugar, plucking geese, going to market to sell your goods. Even paying taxes is seasonal, although it doesn't depend on natural cycles.

2. The ox cart man is clearly a very hard worker, diligent and dependable. One gets the sense, though, that his life consists only of work, only of the repetitious tasks described to us here. Of course this is the nature of farming, especially in the ox cart man's day. Today's farmers have the advantages of modern equipment, not the least of which is trucks to take their goods to market. Still, there is no indication that the ox cart man gets satisfaction from his work, or even his life; note that there is no mention of any family, or even helper, working with him.

   Among the most obvious examples of repetition are the words "counts" and "counting" in lines 2 and 3; "potatoes" in lines 12 and 13; "cart" in lines 16, 17, and 25; and "sells" in lines 12, 16, and 17. The repetition of these words, especially "counting" and "sells," reinforces the sameness of the work itself.

3. It might seem that the money for salt and taxes is not an even trade for all the goods the ox cart man has sold, but there's no sense that he himself is complaining about this, or expected anything "fair" in the first place. It is simply the trade he had to make. The walk to the market is full of life and promise; the ox cart man "walks by the ox's head" (11) and has a cart full of goods to sell. On the walk home, the goods are sold and he is alone, save "the year's coin" (20) in his pockets.

RACHEL L. JONES

The Price of Hate:
Thoughts on Covering
a Ku Klux Klan Rally (p. 606)

This moving essay in which a Black reporter recounts her experience covering a Ku Klux Klan rally provides a wonderful opportunity to discuss with your class the concept of emotional distance. Looking back on the rally, Jones successfully renders an extremely disturbing incident in a thoughtful and powerful essay, without losing any of the emotional power of the moment. (For more on this subject, see Investigation 2 below.)

INVESTIGATIONS (p. 609)

1. Had Jones asked her editor to excuse her from covering the Klan rally, she would have risked, in her own mind, both her professional standing and her security in the knowledge that she was not afraid of hate-mongers, that she would not allow fear of racism to prevent her from doing whatever she wanted to do. Regarding her professionalism, Jones felt that she *should* be able to cover this, or any event that was loathsome to her. As a journalist her training was to be objective, so she should be able to record and report on these events without emotional involvement. Covering the rally was simply doing her job. Regarding her own fears, Jones tells us that, in part because she had never personally experienced the worst kinds of racism, she was able to teach herself not to hate. By covering the rally she was deliberately exposing herself to "that kind of racism" (para. 32); had she declined to cover it, she would have avoided that challenge.

2. Jones is able to be "so clinical" for two reasons. The first is her training as a reporter. It is a journalist's job to be objective, to be able to be "clinical" in difficult emotional situations.

   The second is that Jones is looking back on this incident; she has had time to reflect on and articulate her feelings. When a writer is too close to her subject, her emotions can interfere with her writing. She may be unable to render a scene or argument in a way that makes it matter to readers as much as it matters to her. Note Jones's account of her attempt to tell her story to her editors immediately after the rally (20–29). In the heat of the moment, she simply can't do it; she is too emotionally involved. But the essay itself, written once she has come to terms with the disturbing event, is quite successful. When a writer has sufficient distance from her subject, she can choose the right details, scenes, tone, and moment to make her point. She can shift back and forth, as Jones deftly does, from narrating events to analyzing her own feelings. The result is hardly cold or clinical; rather, it is the powerful piece of writing we see here.

3. Jones will most likely perceive journalism as more difficult than she previously thought. She has learned that it is sometimes a tremendous challenge and effort to put yourself in someone else's shoes; in some cases it may be impossible. And she knows now that feeling this way once in a while *doesn't* make her a bad person or a bad reporter; it merely makes her "human" (43).

   You might ask students whether they can remember any instances when they've seen journalists become emotionally involved in their material. Two recent examples are the television news coverage of the first few days of the Persian Gulf War in January 1991 and the explosion of the space shuttle *Challenger* in 1986. In both cases, broadcasters were visibly shaken; in the former, some literally feared for their lives. Did students think any worse of these journalists for displaying their emotions? Might they have thought worse of them if they *didn't* display these emotions?

4. Answers will vary.

JIMMY SANTIAGO BACA

Perfecto Flores (p. 610)

In addition to the books mentioned in the text footnote, Baca has written *Martin and Meditations on the South Valley* (1987).

More than any other selection in Part Five, this poem unequivocally celebrates work. Both the speaker and his subject get tremendous satisfaction and enjoyment from their work, despite the fact that this work involves hard labor. Ask students what might account for the differences between Perfecto's attitude toward work and the attitude of the father in "My Father Worked Late" (p. 531). Of all the characters and speakers you've met in this part, who has an attitude closest to Perfecto's?

INVESTIGATIONS (p. 612)

1. The speaker means that Perfecto finds uses for things he himself would have thrown away: Perfecto instills these things with life. Perfecto's relationship with the speaker is clearly personal, while the exchange of money for goods or labor is impersonal. But the speaker and Perfecto are friends. This bartering, in fact, is part of the relationship. Were the speaker to pay Perfecto only in cash, he would be treating Perfecto as an anonymous worker rather than as a good friend.

2. Competition is an integral part of the relationship between the speaker and Perfecto because they both enjoy it. Both are storytellers, so they enjoy competing in that arena as well. In lines 5–16, Perfecto tells the speaker a story about why he should be paid more, and Perfecto wins. Though the speaker loses, he hasn't lost much: He's still paying Perfecto less than he'd have to pay anyone else. The negotiating that takes place here is part of a game Perfecto and the speaker play; they know they're going to do it and they know they're going to come up with a mutually agreeable price.

3. Some of the details in the poem students might mention are when Perfecto "poured cement / and troweled it smooth" (lines 28–29); when he "built three houses / for his daughters with construction site / scraps" (32–34); and when "he proudly hefts a wheelbarrow / brimmed with cement" (55–56).

   Perfecto himself can be seen as a work of art in that he is such a good worker — conscientious and skillful — and a worker who loves his work. And as we learn from the poem's last image, Perfecto's hands have no blisters, which are a sign of skin that is not used to the work it has just done. *His* hands are so rough and calloused "you could sharpen a file" (81) on them, a fact Perfecto is quite proud of.

   As to whether or not Garfinkle's work could be called an art, it is fair to say that people in the field of corporate takeovers probably consider it an "art" to orchestrate a particularly clever or difficult takeover. Donald Trump's very popular book *The Art of the Deal* employs the word "art" in precisely this fashion.

   You might also refer students back to "After the Game" (p. 525) and "Steelworker" (p. 533) to pursue this topic further. Billy Wells and his teammates certainly consider baseball an art; Wells's equating Joaquin and Tommy's turning a double play with elegant, formal dancing (Dubus, para. 20) makes this clear. And Farr's description of lining a ladle in paragraph 19 of "Steelworker" also depicts an art: "Like a mason, I tap the brick with my hammer to make it break just so, the exact place, the exact size I need to fit this space, to snug this row." (For a related question, see Part Five: Connections and Elaborations 6.)

JAY PARINI

Working the Face (p. 612)

In addition to the books mentioned in the text footnote, Parini has published the poetry collections *Singing in Time* (1972) and *Town Life* (1988) and the novels *The Love Run* (1980) and *The Patch Boys* (1986).

As is the case with many speakers and characters in Part Five, the miner's work gives him a sense of power. Ask students what other selections in this part depict similar situations. They might mention selections by Dubus, Farr, Levine, Lombreglia, Baca, Sterner, Boyle, or DeMarinis. How do each of these characters and speakers differ from the miner? Do any of them enjoy or experience anything he doesn't?

INVESTIGATIONS (p. 613)

1. A taproot is the main root of a plant, the root from which all other roots spring. It is therefore the strongest and most nourishing part of the plant; if something happened to it, the plant would die. Similarly, the miner "working the face" is the backbone of this operation, the most important part. No further work can take place until he has dug the initial tunnel. He is also "thick as a slug" (line 14): dependable, moving slowly and steadily toward his goal. He is a man of power, with "eyes like points of fire" (9) and the ability to turn the walls around him into "a million stars" (17).

   Finally, he is the "prince of darkness" (18), an ambiguous phrase. "Prince" itself suggests royalty, someone who, in an ideal scenario, would be honored and obeyed. "Prince of darkness," however, is another name for the devil — certainly a man of power, but a power that is destructive rather than benign. The benefits of a miner's job can be seen as ambiguous as well; it requires a tough and steady worker with a remarkable tolerance for working in a frighteningly enclosed and dark space; this tolerance and ability are rewarded both by high pay and a sense, on the worker's part, that he is able to do something others cannot. But there is a destructive side to this power as well: Though the poem itself does not allude to this, "working the face" must take a tremendous psychological toll. And of course many miners suffer from serious — sometimes fatal — respiratory ailments as well.

2. The speakers in both poems betray not a little awe in their descriptions of the roofers' and miner's work. They feel a certain reverence for those who work so hard at such dangerous, unpleasant jobs. The workers in Williams's poem would probably be less inclined to romanticize their work; the miner in Parini's poem would probably be less likely to describe himself in such figurative language. He might well describe himself as filthy, but probably not as "prince" of anything at all — except possibly the mining company's payroll.

3. The miner might feel a similar hatred since, like Farr, he would have lost a job that paid very well and that gave him a sense of power. Any nostalgia he felt would be quite different from Farr's. Farr misses the community that developed at the steel mill, but the miner works alone. In fact, he might have some difficulty adapting to working with a community; his nostalgia might be for the opportunity to work alone, undisturbed and unsupervised.

4. The miner is an artist in that he can thrive in an environment many would find themselves unable even to enter. He can tunnel under extraordinarily difficult physical conditions. He can even make magic: "Wherever he turned, the facets / showered a million stars" (16–17). To see him solely as an artist, however, is to ignore the hellish physical and psychological conditions of his job. (See Investigation 1 for more on this topic.)

T. CORAGHESSAN BOYLE
Sitting on Top of the World (p. 614)

This unnerving story lends new meaning to the concepts of both "empowerment" and "job stress." Elaine clearly finds her job both intoxicating and "beautiful" and "peaceful" (para. 1).

> Nine thousand feet up, she could see the distant hazy rim of the world . . . she could see stars that haven't been discovered yet. In the morning, she was the first to watch the sun emerge from the hills to the east, and in the evening . . . she was the last to see it set. (2)

Ask students whether similar feelings of empowerment or intoxication appear elsewhere in Part Five. They might mention sections by Dubus, Farr, Levine, Sterner, Lombreglia, or Baca. What do these jobs have in common? How do they differ? In each case, how much of this heady feeling derives from the worker rather than from the job itself? What, if anything, does this say about how much a person's mind set can influence his or her attitude toward a job?

INVESTIGATIONS (p. 626)

1. Some students will think Elaine should have made the emergency call — by not doing so she is clearly courting danger. Instead of putting out an emergency call she calls Zack; hearing his voice seems to be sufficiently reassuring for her, especially since the stranger can see and hear the conversation. Apparently letting him know that she can call for help if she needs to makes Elaine feel safe enough, for the moment. She stops short of making an emergency call in part because she is used to taking care of herself. Her ability to do so is clearly a source of pride to her, and she is reluctant to admit that something might interfere with this ability, with her feeling of "sitting on top of the world." She is also loathe to fall into the "helpless female syndrome" (38). Finally, though, there is another reason she doesn't make the call or tell Zack about the stranger — one we discover, along with Elaine, at the story's end. Elaine is *attracted* to danger. You'd have to be at least somewhat attracted to danger to take this job in the first place, and Elaine's willingness to wait out the storm is another indication of this side of her personality. The truth is, Elaine is attracted to the danger of this situation, and to the stranger himself. (See Investigation 5 for more on this topic.)

2. Answers will vary. Students will have to decide for themselves whether the stranger actually intends Elaine harm; the evidence in the story is deliberately ambiguous.

3. Elaine breaks away from stereotypical images of women in her attraction to power and danger — both of which are key elements of her job with the Forest Service. The job itself, of course, is one more often held by men. It requires a good deal of physical strength and a self-reliant nature; neither of these traits

thwarts convention: Apparently his father has custody, since he is only with her alternate weeks in the summer and she takes an apartment to be near Todd in the winters.

Elaine fulfills stereotypical images of women in that she's attracted to very "masculine" men — men of strength and size and power, who make her feel vulnerable.

4. The jobs Elaine refers to (waitressing or fast food) are menial, low-paying service jobs — positions in which one must be more than merely cordial to people, which is all her forestry job requires along those lines. Jobs like these offer none of the physical or spiritual beauty Elaine's current job offers, and they require you to answer to people constantly. A worker in these positions tends to feel demeaned rather than powerful, which is how Elaine's job looking for fires makes her feel.

5. Elaine's radio was her safety net, her connection to the outside world. Her knife was her only protection. When she disconnects the radio and puts the knife away, it's clear that she's no longer afraid of the stranger. In fact, she's welcoming him. In truth, she has been physically attracted to him from the first moment she saw him: "He was tall and powerful across the chest and shoulders" (24); "she saw the generosity in his shoulders and hands" (25); and "she felt something she hadn't felt in a long time, in an ice age, and she knew her cheeks were flushed" (28). Elaine, a powerful and vital woman, finds those characteristics attractive, even compelling. They are traits the stranger certainly has to offer, unlike her ex-husband, who was "sexless, pale . . . in love with death itself" (75).

ANNA LEE WALTERS

The Warriors (p. 626)

In addition to the books mentioned in the text footnote, Walters is the author of *The Otoe-Missouria Tribe Centennial Memoirs* (1980), *Ghost Singer* (1988), and, with Peggy V. Beck, *The Sacred: Ways of Knowledge, Sources of Life* (1977).

This moving story in which a Native American girl remembers her uncle is about a different kind of work than most of the other selections in this chapter. It is about the work of maintaining, or trying to maintain, a culture and set of values in a world that doesn't encourage those values. Ask students whether this description could be applied to any other selections in Part Five *Other People's Money* should come to mind.

INVESTIGATIONS (p. 636)

1. Like Uncle Ralph, the steelworkers and Jorgenson tell stories that foster a sense of community. The stories confirm a feeling of belonging for both the storyteller and for his or her audience. But both the steelworkers' and Jorgenson's stories are specifically about work; it is the labor done in the steel mill or building a business that ties these communities together. Uncle Ralph's stories have a spiritual quality that is missing in the work stories mentioned above. Ralph is concerned with beauty and retaining the ability to "see things different" — concepts that don't enter into the steelworkers' or Jorgenson's stories.

2. To Pumpkin Flower, the warrior life involves living for beauty (para. 4), dying with honor (5), and "what you see and feel when you look at this old world" (10). Specifically, it involves preserving the old customs and attitudes, living "beautifully with prayers and song" (109), with believing.

   The selection in Part Five that most obviously illustrates the loss of the warrior life is "My Father Worked Late." The speaker's father has apparently not managed to hold on to enough beauty or value in his life to share any of it with his children; in the speaker's eyes, his father has no dignity left at all.

3. The "more than just repeating words" part of Uncle Ralph's labor is described in Investigation 2. It consists not only of keeping the old values and attitudes alive but fully living by them, of believing in living "beautifully with prayers and song" (109).

   The story itself is the main evidence that Pumpkin Flower has learned well what her uncle taught her. The story is an elegy for him, and more: Pumpkin Flower wants to record Uncle Ralph's values for posterity because she knows they are important.

4. Uncle Ralph's alcoholism makes it difficult for him to "live beautifully." He knows that his drinking is wrong in that it doesn't represent "living beautifully," and it destroys his dignity and ability to be who he wants to be. Some would say the enemy is alcohol, or the changes in the world that have driven Uncle Ralph to alcohol. Others will say Uncle Ralph's enemy is himself, since he is the one who picked up the bottle. Since alcoholism is a disease, some will say it is his body that is his enemy.

RICK DeMARINIS

The Flowers of Boredom (p. 637)

In addition to the books mentioned in the text footnote, DeMarinis is the author of the collections *Jack and Jill: Two Novellas and a Short Story* (1979), *Under the Wheat* (1986), and *The Coming Triumph of the Free World* (1988) and the novels *A Lovely Monster: The Adventures of Claude Rains and Dr. Tellenbeck* (1976), *Scimitar* (1977), *Cinder* (1978), and *The Burning Woman of Far Cry* (1986).

In an interview with *Publisher's Weekly* (May 10, 1991), DeMarinis said, "Humor humanizes things that are so dreadful they threaten to dehumanize us. The ability to laugh is the ability to get a distance on things and think, 'Well, we're still in control to some degree.'" This story certainly focuses on work that dehumanizes; ask students whether they think Lamar looks at his job with a sense of humor. If so, does this seem to help him feel "in control"? Where else do they find humor in this story?

INVESTIGATIONS (p. 644)

1. Uncle Ralph would probably disapprove of the defense industry in and of itself, on the grounds that its products destroy the earth on which we are all trying, or should be trying, to live beautifully. Though Uncle Ralph calls himself a warrior, he is fighting to save the earth and its people and keep them humble. The goal of the defense industry, on the other hand, according to Lamar, is "to keep itself well nourished with cost-plus money, to increase steadily in

manpower and physical plant, and to reveal itself to the gullible citizenry as an economic savior as well as a vital necessity in a dangerous world" (para. 7).

Lamar tries to live beautifully in that he has "genuine sympathy for his men" and feels that "we are all in the same boat" (2). Lamar isn't interested in lording his power or authority over his men; in fact he wishes his men well. He knows the system is a difficult one and will eat some of them alive; he hopes some of them survive it, too — either by resigning in time to save their belief in "what they are doing" (8) or by adapting, as he has.

2. Students are likely to mention *Other People's Money*, "The Warriors," and "The Price of Hate: Thoughts on Covering a Ku Klux Klan Rally." Jorgenson's noble project is to keep his company alive; his old-fashioned values include rewarding hard work — which means not closing a business simply because it's there — and caring about his workers' jobs. But today's business climate has rendered these values obsolete. Uncle Ralph's values and beliefs seem similarly obsolete; it is his inability to carry them out that drives him to alcohol. And Rachel L. Jones's belief that the Ku Klux Klan rally should be covered and that she can handle the assignment ends up causing her a great deal of pain.

3. An innovative and energetic employee would threaten the extremely bureaucratic system that guides Advanced Proposals Engineering; such an employee would rock the boat. He or she might come up with cheaper or faster ways to produce or improve a product — neither of which would be in the company's best interest, from management's point of view. APE has "its own rules, rituals, and arcana" (7), with which it is quite comfortable. Since it manages to "produce weapons of ever-increasing sophistication" (7) within these rules, it sees no reason to change. Management would also suspect that anyone innovative was angling for a promotion — a hard-won distinction in this business.

Lamar might advise someone who wanted to get ahead in this field not to "frighten the man immediately above you on the ladder" (6), not to question the way things work, to strive to do exactly the job assigned to him or her, even if it seems insanely wasteful. This method of getting ahead would probably work well in many blue-collar fields, where creativity is not usually encouraged or rewarded. Ironically, Lamar's field is white-collar.

4. Both Uncle Ralph and Randy Voss believe in some sort of higher power that governs what *should* happen in the world (in Uncle Ralph's case) or what *does* happen in the industry (in Voss's case).

To some readers, Uncle Ralph may not seem crazy at all; he may be living in the past, but his concept of living beautifully is a spiritual one not easily dismissed. To Uncle Ralph, the world in which everyone wants to go to the moon seems crazy — and indeed, technological advancements usually do have some human cost. This is not in either story, but from a Native American's perspective, the white man's vision of progress was usually considered destructive — whether of land, animals, or cultures. This vision of progress, in turn, can be considered crazy.

Voss's contention that the "intelligence" that sweeps things along to their conclusion "is not human" certainly sounds crazy, but then the industry itself is crazy. It spends huge amounts of money on "redundant systems" (1) and routinely hires "a large, well-paid work force" (4) to sit around doing nothing.

C. K. WILLIAMS
Tar (p. 645)

In addition to the books mentioned in the text footnote, C. K. Williams has written the poetry collections *A Day for Anne Frank* (1968), *Lies* (1969), *I Am the Bitter Name* (1972), *With Ignorance* (1977), and *Tar* (1983).

This powerful poem juxtaposes a nuclear accident against the routine, if dangerous, task of roofing. The speaker says, "I never realized what brutal work it is, how matter-of-factly and harrowingly dangerous" (line 12). Ask students if they can cite similar epiphanal moments in other selections in this part; essays by Trudy Pax Farr and Rachel L. Jones should come to mind. What do these moments have in common? Students should note that fear is responsible in each instance; in Farr's and Williams's speaker's case, it is fear of death. In Jones's case, it is fear of hatred rather than death, but of course the hatred prejudice generates has been responsible for many deaths, a fact Jones knows all too well, though she may never have really confronted it before.

INVESTIGATIONS (p. 647)

1. The roofers can't be liars because their work is visible, concrete, matter-of-fact. All layers of the task are apparent: Their ladders shriek up the speaker's wall; "they hack away the leaden layers of asbestos paper and disassemble the disintegrating drains" (4); they set "winch-frames, sledging rounds of tar apart, and there I am, on the curb across, gawking" (11). It's all done out in the open, so each stage of the roofers' work can be seen not only by the speaker but by anyone else who cares to know what's going on.

   The federal spokesmen, in contrast, have told people "less than nothing" (8). It is their job to keep the country informed but calm; if the truth is not known, or if it's not calming, it can be withheld. We, the public, will have no way of knowing. In line 14 the speaker observes of his house: "the under-roofing crumbles." But if the under-roofing of a nuclear power plant, and consequently our safety and the safety of our planet, crumbles, the federal spokesmen deal with the event behind closed doors, if they deal with it at all. If the truth is too disturbing, it is their job to keep it from us.

2. Answers will vary. The question asks students to think metaphorically, and some may need encouragement to do so, but the results should be rewarding.

3. The roofers stay so clear because the work they do is visible and concrete, and therefore easy to describe. Terror, on the other hand, is intangible: Like the evasions of the federal spokesmen, it is huge, amorphous, and abstract. It is easier to forget the terror of that time in part because it is harder to remember something abstract, something that can't be touched or seen or described. It is also easier to forget the terror of that time because we *prefer* to forget knowledge so horrible. We would prefer not to know that we are all "going to perish of all of this . . . someday" (26), just as we would prefer not to imagine "some final generation, hysterically aswarm beneath an atmosphere as unrelenting as rock" (27), cursing "our surfeits and submissions" (28).

PART SIX

IN AND OUT OF LOVE

OVERVIEW

The book's introduction to Part Six encourages students to think systematically about love, to try to understand and define love by examining their assumptions, their own experiences, and the experiences they read about in these selections. Though a definition of love is liable to remain elusive even after students have read this part, they will no doubt learn something new about the forms love can take and the powers it can wield.

Students may identify most closely with the young characters in the stories by Gish Jen and Cliff Thompson. These characters experience love in its earliest stages, but the feeling is still strong enough to wreak significant psychological and emotional turmoil.

The poems by Adrienne Rich, Patricia Dobler, and Galway Kinnell all illustrate what most of us would label "good" relationships: relationships in which partners are equals; unions predicated on some combination of warmth, patience, wisdom, understanding, and passion; relationships in which the couple's love is, or seems to be, strong enough to last a lifetime.

In David Mura's "Nantucket Honeymoon," the speaker can only learn to love himself once he is loved by another. Similarly, in Lanford Wilson's *Burn This*, Anna's emotional life is on hold and Pale's is in complete upheaval until they decide to get serious about their mutual attraction.

Wendell Berry's "Except," Leslie Marmon Silko's "Lullaby," and John Updike's "Gesturing" depict some of the contradictions inherent in romantic relationships. Berry's speaker reveals how we can love someone but still want to be alone; Silko's story shows us a woman who can love someone and hate him at the same time; Updike's story illustrates not only how we can love more than one person at a time, but, stranger still, how we can love someone but leave them anyway. Updike's characters demonstrate a tenderness toward one another that would be a mystery to the speaker in Carolyn Kizer's poem "Bitch," who has no kind thoughts for the man with whom she once shared her life.

The stories by Jane Smiley and Bobbie Ann Mason also chronicle the ends of relationships, here narrated by men who don't understand what is happening to them but do understand that there is nothing they can do to stop it from happening.

Finally, Fenton Johnson and the speaker in Thomas Lynch's poem "The Widow" learn from the deaths of their beloveds. The widow learns that a whole new world has opened up before her, and Johnson learns that there is not, in fact, a limit to the amount of love he can give.

Instructors who don't have time to teach all the selections in Part Six might want to use selections by Jen, Thompson, Mura, and Smiley to focus on the role cultural differences can play in romantic relationships.

GISH JEN
What Means Switch (p. 653)

This story is as much about crossing cultures as it is about first love; note the narrator's introduction to and assimilation into the predominantly Jewish culture of her new neighborhood. Ask students to provide details that illustrate Mona's adoption of Jewish culture. They might mention her frequent use of the word "oy," the many bar and bas mitzvahs she attends, her knowledge of bagels, and her syntax in such sentences as "Also, I know what is schmaltz" (para. 11) and "I think maybe he doesn't get what means switch" (115). Note too Mona's learning the distinctions between Sherman's Japanese values and her own assimilated Chinese American values. What are these differences, and how do they both cause and affect the relationship between Mona and Sherman?

This story also provides an excellent opportunity to discuss narrative distance. Ask students to characterize the narrator's voice in this story. Is it consistent? Direct them to statements that could only be made by an adult looking back on a situation, not by a child presently experiencing the situation. In paragraph 11, for example, Mona says "In another ten years there'll be so many Orientals we'll turn into Asians. . . ." And in paragraph 34 Mona alludes to a statement a friend once made about having "something people value," inferring that in her own case, that "something" is being Chinese. Ask students what statements like this, statements thirteen-year-old Mona could not possibly have made, add to the story.

INVESTIGATIONS (p. 666)

1. Mona first bends the truth in paragraph 5, when she says she knows karate; later she lies about knowing how to get pregnant with tea. She says these things to appear special and interesting, which will make her popular. In paragraph 154, she lies about the extent of her relationship with Sherman, but it's worth noting that her initial responses to her friends on this subject are honest. In paragraph 97 she says, "I dunno," when asked whether she and Sherman are going out; later she says, "I think we're just friends" (144). Once she starts to lie about this relationship, a combination of peer pressure and natural adolescent curiosity do their work; in paragraph 153 she says, "The more I intimate that Sherman and I are hot and heavy, the more it seems we actually are."

2. The public Mona and Sherman don't talk much, while in private they joke and tell stories. Most thirteen-year-olds are as embarrassed about being interested in members of the opposite sex as they are interested in them, so Mona's and Sherman's youth is partly responsible for their inconsistent behavior. Age notwithstanding, a couple's public and private expressions of love can be very different and their love still genuine: Some differences between a couple's "public" and "private" personae *are* both inevitable and appropriate. People often behave differently in public than they do in private, whether as part of

a couple, members of a family, or even when they are alone. Certain differences, however, might well indicate something amiss in a romantic relationship: Couples who refuse to acknowledge that they are couples, or to express any affection, or who ignore or are mean to each other in public are probably having some problems in private, too.

3. Mona's uncertainty about the nature of her relationship with Sherman helps propel that relationship; in examining and reexamining her feelings, she realizes she must really like him. Why else would she keep thinking about him? After she realizes she's fallen for him, Mona's uncertainty about *his* interest keeps her from making first moves, like holding hands or kissing him, though she provides him with all the opportunities to do so.

4. Answers will vary.

5. It's true that Mona wants a boyfriend, as do all the girls in this story. So her being thrown together with Sherman is in that way fortuitous: She wants a boyfriend, and here's a boy who's a captive audience and cute in the bargain. But Sherman's attracted to her too, so the relationship can't be attributed entirely to wish fulfillment.

Mona and Sherman *don't* see eye to eye: Sherman doesn't want to kiss her the way she wants to be kissed and he doesn't want to unbutton her blouse, either. Nor does he want to be assimilated into American culture in the way Mona and her family are assimilated. To Sherman, Mona's idea of a relationship is thoroughly American and thoroughly unacceptable. Sherman thinks Mona should follow his traditions, in part because this is his upbringing and in part to prove that she likes him for himself, not just because she wanted a boyfriend. Mona, on the other hand, is almost thoroughly assimilated. Despite their youth, Mona knows she isn't like Sherman and couldn't ever be what he wanted.

CLIFF THOMPSON

Judgment (p. 667)

You might start discussion of this story by referring students back to the "Write Before Reading" assignment at the beginning of Part Six. Ask them to identify the stages of Wayne's and Roxie's relationship. Do Wayne and Roxie seem to be on the same wavelength when they say good-bye at the end of their freshman year? Why don't they discuss their feelings, beyond agreeing that they had some good times together? And what about their feelings for each other when Roxie visits Wayne at the beginning of sophomore year?

You might also ask students what this story has in common with Gish Jen's "What Means Switch." Both stories involve crossing racial barriers. How do the barriers between Mona and Sherman differ from those between Wayne and Joanne?

INVESTIGATIONS (p. 680)

1. Leaving home for college is Wayne's first big step toward adulthood. Having a girlfriend in this relatively independent situation is the next step: He's an adult now (or thinks he is) and is therefore deserving and capable of an unsupervised yet responsible romantic relationship. His relationship with Joanne takes him one step further. By crossing racial lines, he is breaking an unspoken rule that he (and many of the rest of us) grew up with: Stick to your own kind. (For more on this topic, see Investigation 3, below.)

But of course Wayne's relationship with Roxie is not really an adult relationship; he floats through it without ever seeming to reflect on why they like each other or what they have in common in the first place, and he never examines his feelings or tries to put himself in Roxie's place once things begin to go sour. While he is involved with Roxie, Wayne seems to think this reticent behavior is appropriate to being "a man." In his relationship with Joanne, he begins to open up a bit emotionally — though this seems to be at least partly a result of the racial issues he has to address.

2. When Roxie comes to visit Wayne at the beginning of their sophomore year, he says he's busy that night. Outside the movie theater, Roxie sees the girl he's busy with, and she knows she's been jilted. On the surface, then, Wayne feels accused of dropping her — which in fact he has done. But the phrase he imagines Roxie thinking — "I've got your number now" (para. 162) — could suggest more than that. It could suggest that Wayne thinks Roxie's accusing him of betraying his "race" by dumping her for a white girl. Roxie doesn't say anything on this subject, but Wayne reflects on it often enough that it's clear he's wrestling with this issue himself.

3. Friendships, especially among male college roommates, are relatively safe in that they lack, or at least don't *require*, the kind of intimacy that romantic relationships involve. It's easy enough to have a friend of a different race, especially in the very tolerant environment of a small liberal arts college. In fact, it isn't the white people on campus who make it hard for Wayne to cross the racial line with Joanne; they're apparently comfortable with and accepting of the situation. It's Wayne himself who is scared of making this leap, because it has ramifications for his life in the world outside of this isolated, tolerant environment. He knows this from his trip into town with Joanne and from having grown up in Washington, D.C., where he "hadn't spent much time around white people before" (18), although, in fact, there are plenty of white people in that city. But the ethos many of us grow up with is to "stick with our own"; this means it's okay to be civil to other people, but there's no point in getting really close to them; it will only cause trouble in the long run. Some people feel that the majority culture in this country will never really accept or approve of interracial relationships and families, so the person who enters a "mixed" relationship is only asking for heartache and controversy. Others feel that members of the majority culture can never share or understand what minorities have experienced, so trying to get close to members of the majority culture is not really possible — or, worse, it's selling out. These are just some of the prevalent attitudes toward interracial love a couple is likely to encounter.

If Joanne were Asian or Hispanic, Wayne's involvement with her would still require crossing the racial line. It might be easier in these cases since an Asian or Hispanic woman would come from a minority group, like Wayne. But most likely Wayne would still have to face accusations of being the "wrong color" in the outside world, along with having to resolve his *own* feelings about interracial relationships.

WENDELL BERRY

Except (p. 680)

In addition to the books mentioned in the text footnote, of Berry's other books include the essay collections *The Long-Legged House* (1969) and *The Unsettling of*

America: Culture and Agriculture (1977), the poetry collections *The Broken Ground* (1964) and *Openings* (1968), and the novel *Nathan Coulter* (1960).

This poem works well with other selections featuring speakers or narrators who recognize the complexities of love. Ask students whether they can imagine other characters they've read about in Part Six feeling similar to Berry's speaker. Anna in *Burn This* and Richard in "Gesturing" are likely candidates. For Anna, Pale is a whirlwind of noisy emotion; apparently she needs and wants this emotion, but she will certainly crave her solitude and time to work, too. In "Gesturing," Richard too is concerned with controlling his environment — he loves Ruth, but balks when Ruth calls the bed in this new apartment "*our* bed" (Updike, para. 40). The bed is his and his alone.

INVESTIGATIONS (p. 681)

1. The love addressed by Rich, Dobler, and Silko is in each instance an adult love: These speakers and narrators have all experienced both the pain and joy of love. Berry's poem doesn't provide us with enough context to know how long the speaker and Tanya have been together, but the speaker is sophisticated enough to recognize the irony of his feelings: He wants to be alone, but once he is alone he wants to be able to share the contentment he feels with Tanya — the very person he was so glad to see leave just moments before.

   Wayne, whose experience with love is quite limited, would probably not understand why Berry's contentment was not complete. Wayne is young and unsophisticated; the love relationships we see in "Judgment" reveal a good deal of selfishness and immaturity. He doesn't reflect at all on his relationship with Roxie; even with Joanne his introspection has to do primarily with the fact that she's white and he's Black rather than with their feelings for one another. Wayne seems to be at a stage in his emotional development where even if he did experience the conflicting emotions Berry's speaker feels, he probably wouldn't recognize them. And if he recognized them, he probably wouldn't articulate them. Wayne would most likely want to be with his girlfriend at designated times they had already arranged; the rest of the time he probably wouldn't think about her at all.

2. Berry's speaker is mature enough to know that love does not require us to be around our beloved twenty-four hours a day, and that solitude is invaluable as well. But he's also mature enough — and in love enough — to know that he doesn't feel complete without his beloved, that any pleasures he gets, even solitary ones, would be enhanced if he could share them, or at least share the knowledge of them, with his beloved.

3. Individual needs for solitude vary, so answers will vary accordingly. But most people need *some* privacy and solitude. To be inseparable from one's beloved is also to be dependent on that person; the danger here is that either party might be ignoring his or her individual goals or needs.

DAVID MURA

Nantucket Honeymoon (p. 681)

In an interview with *Transpacific* magazine (May/June 1991, p. 48), David Mura says, "I grew up thinking that White women were more attractive than Asian women which is a product of racial self-hatred." At twenty, Mura thought he could prove he was "as good as these White guys" by going out with a white woman — an attitude he now realizes was "fueled by buying into racist thinking." This poem describes the poet's experience of coming to this realization.

INVESTIGATIONS (p. 682)

1. We would all like to think we possess great inner strength and the ability to tell right from wrong, even if our actions don't always illustrate that ability and knowledge. It also makes a better story to be able to say, "Here is the dramatic moment when I realized something profound." But in fact there was no dramatic moment: "It wasn't like that" (line 11). The speaker is being honest about his experience. Most of what we learn we learn the hard way: A combination of things — not the least of which was time, or "growing up" (15) — taught the speaker to be comfortable with his heritage and thus with himself.

2. Line 1 depicts how bees live and reproduce; they operate in a realm of simplicity that does not include pondering the mysteries of love or thinking about racial difference. "It's easy" (1) for them to carry on. The poem's last line is where the speaker finally names his struggle. Prior to this, the only information we have about his conflict is the reference to his skin color in the second stanza and to "that Asian island [Japan]" in line 25. "They'll think I felt American" clarifies "the tirade" the speaker describes in lines 3–5: He tried to feel American by denying his Asian heritage, by thinking of himself as white.

3. Answers will vary, but the speaker is influenced by people "growing up" all around him. His friends were marrying and starting families, and his wife (or girlfriend; the poem doesn't indicate whether the speaker is married at that point) was starting medical school. It was her love as well as her entering the adult world of medical school and a career that helped the speaker learn to love himself.

4. The speaker wants his grandchildren to feel both American and proud of their Japanese heritage — a heritage he was not initially proud of or comfortable with. He doesn't want them to have to struggle with the sense of divided identity he had.

Mura's speaker is alone in a very different way than Berry's. Mura's speaker suffers a feeling of emptiness in the poem's first two stanzas, no matter how many lovers he tries to fill it with. Berry's speaker, on the other hand, is experiencing the wry pangs of love. He is temporarily alone in a place he and Tanya sometimes share; she means a great deal to the speaker, who feels her absence keenly.

LANFORD WILSON

Burn This (p. 683)

In addition to the plays mentioned in the text footnote, Lanford Wilson has written *Balm in Gilead* (1965), *Wandering* (1967), *Lemon Sky* (1970), and *The Rimers of Eldritch* (1967).

Newsweek reviewer Jack Kroll described *Burn This* as "a comedy that laughs at its own tragic roots, a love story in which the lovers are scared to death of one another, a play about art in which the strongest sensibility belongs to a character who looks upon artists as frauds." Ask students what all these contradictions add up to. Do students agree that this is a comedy? If so, what did they laugh at? What left them emotionally moved? Do these elements combine to create a believable, realistic drama? Would they describe the play's ending as happy? Satisfying?

INVESTIGATIONS (p. 729)

1. Pale certainly feels things profoundly; he's an emotional powerhouse. Pale is "foreign" to Anna's "urban microcosm" in that he's not interested in dance, music, or art; he works in a restaurant rather than as an artist or in a cerebral, white-collar trade like advertising (as Larry does); his demeanor is coarse and his personality wild. Compared to Pale, Anna and her friends seem polite and refined. Anna can be seen as "waiting on her widow's walk," though she has never been married, because she *is* waiting. She has "decided it might be interesting to have a personal life" (p. 697), but it hasn't yet happened, despite the fact that Burton is more than interested in helping her toward this goal. Pale is "out there on the sea" foundering, filled with some angry "humongous mega-passion" (p. 687) he doesn't understand. He's trying to cope simultaneously with his brother's death, his crazy family, his lousy job, and now his totally unexpected passion for Anna.

2. Anna first tries to get Pale to leave on page 695, saying "Actually, I've got to get back to — " and then again on p. 697: "Look, if you wanted to come back seven, seven-thirty. . . ." But Pale is a powder keg of exploding interruptions. Anna doesn't succeed in getting rid of him in part because she finds him interesting, so keeps responding to these interruptions. Initially she's only talking to him in an attempt to calm him down, and out of a sense of obligation because he's Robbie's brother. She wants him to leave so she can get some sleep; she's also annoyed by his presumptuousness, bursting in unannounced after she's been trying to contact him for weeks. But she's also curious about him, and responsive to him *because* he's Robbie's brother — he's the one Robbie "liked" (p. 696). Eventually she gets her second wind; not only is she unable to go back to sleep, but by this point she's so attracted to Pale she doesn't want him to leave.

3. Anna *does* feel all the time: She feels anger and grief over Robbie's death; she feels a great warmth and friendship for both Larry and Burton; she feels excited, enthusiastic, and supportive when Burton is working on a new idea. But apparently — given the play's conclusion — she feels something for Pale that she doesn't feel for Burton, something so powerful she can't control it. This makes Anna uncomfortable, for she likes to be in control. But Pale can tell she feels it anyway; if she didn't she wouldn't have let him stay and made Burton leave on New Year's Eve. (It's true her obvious motivation for getting Burton out of the house was to keep the two men from fighting, but she could have put Pale out on the street afterward as well.)

4. Students' answers will vary, but whichever option they choose, they should be encouraged to challenge the assumptions behind the statement.

   a. The answer to this question must first attempt a definition of "better" from Anna's perspective. It's easy enough to find negative traits in Pale, but what's wrong with Burton? Don't he and Anna seem well matched? In this question (and in c and d below), the key is that love is not, in fact, a rational, logical feeling or process that can be neatly analyzed or disposed of.

   b. Anna's relationship with Larry is a friendship, not a romantic or sexual relationship, which is what Anna is looking for (see p. 697, where Anna says,

"I decided it might be nice to have a personal life" and the reference to her "biological clock" on p. 707). Larry's friendship, important as it may be, is irrelevant here.

c. Anna *is* following her instincts through most of the play; instincts which tell her, at different times, to do different things. They tell her both to embrace Pale and to run from him, and sometimes they tell her to choose Burton instead.

d. Certainly Anna's first encounter with Pale can be explained in part by her grief at Robbie's death; Pale is Robbie's brother, and is grieving too, and this brings Anna and Pale together in a way she could not be brought together with Burton, who was not as close to Robbie as either Anna or Pale. But this doesn't make the attraction any less real; in time, it becomes independent of this grief and the connection Anna and Pale share.

e. Burton and Pale are both responsible adults (or should be, given their ages and positions in the world); they can and should be held entirely responsible for how they act not only toward Anna but toward each other as well.

f. Pale certainly displays more emotion that anyone else in the play. Burton is rather controlled, except in the scene when he and Pale fight. Larry is warm and supportive, but his character isn't really developed. And Anna only begins to open up emotionally at the play's end.

ADRIENNE RICH

Love Poem (p. 730)

In addition to the books mentioned in the text footnote, some of Rich's other works include the poetry collections *Diving into the Wreck* (1973) and *A Wild Patience Has Taken Me This Far* (1981) and the essay collections *On Lies, Secrets, and Silence* (1979) and *Blood, Bread, and Poetry* (1986).

Some students may be unnerved by the frank sexual references in the poem's first five stanzas. If so, you might remind them of some of the sexual banter and activity in *Burn This* and *Other People's Money* (Part Five). Ask students whose attitudes toward sex they are more comfortable with. Why? It's possible you'll encounter some homophobic responses to this poem, but if your class responded well to selections by Peter Cameron, Richard McCann, and Agnes Herman, this selection shouldn't prove too controversial.

INVESTIGATIONS (p. 731)

1. All three speakers express warmth and affection toward their partners. But Berry's speaker expresses a reticence that is absent from Rich's and Dobler's poems; his "contentment" was contingent (or so he thought) on being "alone and quiet." Dobler's speaker expresses a fierce passion not heard in Rich's or Berry's poems. And Rich's poem reveals a peaceful quality the other poems don't share.

    We don't have much to go on in Berry's poem, but its ironic tone suggests a mature relationship: The speaker knows the value of being alone, but also the feeling of missing his partner when he *is* alone. In a new relationship, couples are often inseparable.

    Rich's speaker is in the later stages of a long-term relationship: "We both thought we were young / now that's all done / we're serious now / about death" (lines 23–28). Partners who have been together this long ponder being "alone and quiet" in a very different way than Berry's speaker does; Rich's speaker knows either she or her beloved will soon be alone because one of them will die.

Dobler's speaker is married, but has probably been with her husband for a shorter time than Rich's speaker and her beloved have been together. Her ferocity suggests someone who has not been talking to death at all, much less as a neighbor; she has certainly not begun to accept death's inevitability.

2. In line 7, the speaker mentions her lover's "warrior mind"; in line 9 she refers to her "testing the world." These details refer to the beloved's mind and spirit, qualities that might be noted by a friend *or* a lover. And from line 21 on, the poem refers to "something more," a shared history the partners have, a shared past. The last three stanzas of the poem could be read as if the speaker and her subject were best friends, or even sisters. It is the poem's first five stanzas, in which the speaker evokes her subject primarily through physical — often sexual — details, that establish these women as lovers.

3. The speaker thinks writing a pretty sonnet for her lover would be untrue because a sonnet would not accurately reflect either her lover or her own feelings *for* her lover. Ask students to locate the phrases the speaker uses to describe her lover: "bristler," "quick," "strong," "fierce," "a warrior's mind," "testing," "mud-river flashing / over rocks." These are not "pretty" words in any traditional sense, neither soft nor gentle nor calming. To a certain extent "pretty" expressions of love are clichés — and so would not describe *anyone* particularly accurately.

Staying true to a lover means staying with that person, loving, caring, and supporting him or her forever. If a couple does stay true to each other, ultimately, eventually, they will have to face death together as well. Staying true, then, also means accepting the fact that one of the pair will inevitably lose the other to death.

4. The poem's physical references include "such hair," "so strong a tongue," "green eyes," "fierce curls," "a mole," "a girl's dimples," and "dark blood under gold skin." The last physical reference appears on line 16. If the poem began at this point, we would have no sense of who the speaker's subject was; in fact, we wouldn't know that she was anything more than a friend of the speaker. (See Investigation 2, above.) If the poem began after line 16, the speaker's subject would be little more than an abstraction, and it is difficult to picture, much less care about, an abstraction. Hence the poem's impact would be minimized. This is an excellent opportunity to discuss the importance of concrete description with your students. It is the tangible, specific details in the poem's first half that bring the speaker's beloved to life for us, so that we care about her, as the speaker does, throughout the poem.

PATRICIA DOBLER

Hospital Call (p. 732)

This poem pairs well with Adrienne Rich's "Love Poem"; you might also ask students to juxtapose it against Leslie Marmon Silko's "Lullaby." Each of these selections depicts a mature love relationship and each of the speakers or narrators has to confront the idea or possibility of the death of her beloved. What parallels can students draw from these selections? Is there such a thing as an appropriate response to the death of a lover or spouse?

INVESTIGATIONS (p. 732)

1. The angel is bored because she's tired of waiting, whether for the speaker's husband or the man in the next bed. Presumably she wants the speaker to leave so she can do her job quickly, neatly, without interference: "She likes this taking to be easy" (line 15). She wants "us to be beautiful and good" so her work doesn't have to be so hard, and so death doesn't get a bad reputation. If death occurs calmly, quietly, without a fuss, without a lot of sound and fury, it won't look so bad to others. They, and perhaps even their loved ones, will be less resistant to death, which will make the angel's job much easier.

   The line "cool as white nightgowns carved in stone" evokes both death and beauty. "Carved in stone" suggests a statue, a memorial or monument, perhaps; while the "cool white nightgown" conjures an image both beautiful and serene.

2. The speaker's attitude toward the angel is one of fierce resistance; the speaker does *not* accept the inevitability of her husband's death, and is nowhere near admitting that death "has the keys / to this house" (Rich, lines 29–30), as the speaker of Rich's poem does. Dobler's speaker isn't interested in talking to death at all, much less doing so daily; instead she wants a knock-down drag-out fight, "a barroom brawl" (18). Dobler's speaker perceives death as evil: "the angel's cotton candy hair" has "black roots" (23–24). Rich's speaker, on the other hand, recognizes death as natural and inevitable. This doesn't mean that the love expressed in Rich's "Love Poem" is any less strong than the love expressed in "Hospital Call." Rather, it means that the speakers are at different stages in their understanding of and attitudes toward death. Dobler's speaker is denying it, while Rich's is "learning to be true" with it.

3. Answers will vary, but students should recognize that the willingness to fight to keep death, or any opponent it seems impossible to beat, away from a lover can be seen as one more illustration of love.

JANE SMILEY

Long Distance (p. 733)

In addition to the books mentioned in the text footnote, Smiley's fiction includes the novels *Barn Blind* (1980), *At Paradise Gate* (1981), and *Duplicate Keys* (1984), and the collection *The Age of Grief* (1987).

This moving story about a young man's attempt to come to terms with a relationship's abrupt end raises more questions than it answers. Why *can't* Kirby offer Mieko what she wants from him? Why doesn't Kirby realize he's in love with Mieko? Or, if he's not in love, what *is* he feeling? Ask students whether these unresolved issues weaken the story for them. Or do they increase the story's poignancy because it so accurately reflects real life? Ask students whether any of them have been in (or have been privy to) romantic relationships in which one partner couldn't give the other what he or she needed emotionally. If so, can they articulate why?

INVESTIGATIONS (p. 745)

1. Kirby wants Mieko to call back because he cares about her, because this change of plans — and apparent end to their relationship — is quite sudden and unexpected; it has caught him by surprise. He also feels guilty, because "he

understands . . . that to give up the pleasure that Mieko has promised herself is harder than to die. He understands that in his whole life he has never given up a pleasure that he cherished as much as Mieko cherished this one" (para. 15). Kirby doesn't offer to return to Mieko because he can't give Mieko what she wants or needs from him: "She had all sorts of expectations that I couldn't have . . . well, wouldn't have fulfilled" (114).

2. Kirby might have relieved his pain first by not driving in weather that was likely to kill him: Clearly the danger the storm presents encourages his melodramatic fantasies. Beyond this there is nothing he can do to relieve his pain short of calling Mieko from the nearest phone and catching the next plane to Osaka, which he can't do because he doesn't realize that he wants to do this; even at the story's end, he hasn't fully realized that he is, in fact, in love with Mieko. He's so wrapped up in her pain and his guilt over causing it that he doesn't even register the significance of his calling up "images of Japan and southern China, something he often does" (33) for comfort.

   Students might encourage Leanne to be more direct with Kirby, though her statement that Eric "never tries to get something for nothing" (123) is pretty effective in revealing to Kirby his "permanent smallness" (124). Of course that smallness doesn't *have* to be permanent; it is Kirby's own paralysis, his own fear of risking love and all the potential joy and pain that goes with it, that keeps him small. Mieko might soon be too old to marry in *her* society, but Kirby need not be bound by those rules.

   Leanne might tell Kirby that he used Mieko — an admission he makes himself when he says, at the end of paragraph 122, "But mostly I was lonely" — and that he deserves what he gets. But what Kirby is feeling is way beyond remorse for hurting someone; Kirby is feeling the pain of lost love. So finally, Leanne might encourage Kirby to try to transcend his limitations, to call Mieko, to do something about this love. (For a related assignment, see Part Six: Connections and Elaborations 6.)

3. Kirby feels alone and estranged about the fact that his "being does not extend past his fingertips and toes to family, real estate, reputation." He used to think he and his brother Harold were alike, and Eric, with all his stuffiness, was the outsider. But now he realizes that *he* is the outsider. When he makes this observation Kirby is drunk, feeling sorry for himself and disdain for his family. He sneers at their values, their nice houses full of matching furniture, but in fact Kirby is aware of the sense of warmth and community and interdependence that fills the air, even as various arguments start and stop. In paragraph 81 he notes that "For the first time in three Christmases he feels a touch of the mystery that he thinks of as the Christmas spirit. Or maybe it is love for Harold." He's aware of what's good about all this, but won't admit it. Kirby is apparently afraid of the intimacy of marriage, of children, of family life. He's afraid of commitment, of settling down, which he knows is precisely what Mieko would have wanted from him.

4. Kirby thinks he'll never get over this because he feels incapable of changing this "final form" his life and Mieko's have taken. Despite everything he feels for Mieko, it is not enough to make him return to her, to save her from being "permanently compromised" (114) and "much too old" (124) to marry, and to save himself from never getting "over this" (124).

5. Answers will vary. For a related assignment, see Part Six: Connections and Elaborations 6.

BOBBIE ANN MASON

Shiloh (p. 746)

In addition to the books mentioned in the text footnote, Mason's fiction includes the collection *Shiloh and Other Stories* (1982) and the novel *In Country* (1985).

This story about a couple's unraveling marriage presents an excellent opportunity to talk about the significance of setting in short fiction. Only the story's last scene takes place at Shiloh, yet the name of this Civil War battlefield is the story's title. Ask students why they think the battlefield is so important. Then have them describe the setting for the rest of the story: Norma Jean and Leroy's home. What details are provided, and what do these reveal about Norma Jean and Leroy?

You might also ask students the significance of the story's final image, in which Leroy likens the sky to "the color of the dust ruffle Mabel made for their bed" (para. 157). You may need to refer students back to paragraph 30, in which Mabel gives the couple the dust ruffle and Leroy jokes, "Now we can hide things under the bed." Can this statement be read as something other than a joke? Indeed, in calling up Leroy's earlier statement, the final image confirms the statement's importance: Leroy and Norma Jean have swept their problems under the bed, specifically the problem of their long-dead child — a tragedy they were unable to cope with and so taught themselves to avoid, deny, and even ignore.

INVESTIGATIONS (p. 757)

1. Having lost his job and being unsure of what he'll do next, Leroy feels completely adrift. The only knowledge he is certain of is his love for Norma Jean and the love he and Norma Jean once shared. He is certain enough to trust his perceptions that things have changed between them, that she no longer loves him, at least not the way she once did.

2. It's not unusual for people who live together for a long time to begin to take one another for granted, to forget about everything but the daily routine of working and eating and sleeping. Part of the challenge of a marriage, in fact, is to work hard at preventing this from happening. (For more on this topic, see Investigation 4.) And in Leroy and Norma Jean's case, they *chose* to forget about the baby — who was both the reason they got married in the first place and a product of their love for each other. This choice was not a conscious one; it was a defense mechanism, the only way they knew how to cope with their loss. It could also be argued that Leroy and Norma Jean never knew each other very well to begin with. They were only eighteen when they got married, so were still kids themselves when their own baby died. Students might want to remind Norma Jean and Leroy how much they once loved each other, but it probably wouldn't help. The cost of not confronting the grief and pain of losing their baby for fourteen years is too high; the emotional damage has been done. Both parents have buried this wound so deep it's too late to try to address it now, and Norma Jean is ready to move ahead with her life.

3. Leroy and Norma Jean's marriage can be seen as a battle. The couple is constantly (albeit unconsciously) fighting the memory and pain of having lost their baby. They are fighting each other, too. Norma Jean is trying to rise from her past numbness into a new life; she is developing interests and learning to care about things, especially herself. Leroy wants to make a new start with Norma Jean, but for Norma Jean to leave the past behind she must leave Leroy as well.

Just as a log cabin must be physically constructed, the battle at Shiloh must be imaginatively constructed by visitors to the battlefield; the battle itself isn't there.

To perceive the Shiloh battlefield, a national military park, as a place that will cure what ails Norma Jean is extremely ironic. Because Mabel had her honeymoon there she romanticizes it, and Shiloh may well be very pretty. But in fact it is a somber place, commemorating a major military defeat and the death of thousands of soldiers. The very presence of families with children playing amidst this huge cemetery would be enough to send Norma Jean over the edge, if she hadn't already decided to leave Leroy by the time they got there.

Leroy's dream of building a log house is just as wrong-headed. Norma Jean doesn't need a new home, a new structure around her. What they both needed long ago was to dig down into the foundation of their marriage, to try to excavate their pain from deep down inside — not to try to fix things cosmetically by hiding behind a new and different set of walls.

4. The "real inner workings" of marriage have escaped Norma Jean in that she "is often startled to find Leroy at home, and . . . she seems a little disappointed about it" (9). It's a tremendous shock and adjustment for Leroy to be out of work and injured when he's used to the freedom of driving all over the country for weeks on end. The adjustment is made harder still by the knowledge that his injury will prevent him from returning to the only job he's had in the past fourteen years. Leroy literally doesn't know what he's going to do, and while it's certainly an adjustment for Norma Jean to have him around all the time, she could demonstrate a little more support and sympathy than she does. Leroy, on the other hand, discourages her from doing this by dwelling on all his "projects," which at best strike Norma Jean as impractical.

Most students won't have firsthand experience of the real inner workings of a marriage, but will probably see that the basic problem between Leroy and Norma Jean is that they don't talk to each other about their feelings. One finds out about the inner workings of a marriage by trial and error — that is, by "working" on the marriage, by communicating with one's spouse. Leroy and Norma Jean don't do this, though Leroy *considers* doing so several times in the course of the story. He tells his marital problems to hitchhikers and the boy who sells him marijuana, but apparently he has never talked this way with Norma Jean herself — nor has she talked this way with him. The fact is that Norma Jean and Leroy don't really know each other — a circumstance under which no relationship can succeed. (For a related assignment, see Part Six: Connections and Elaborations 4.)

5. Both Kirby and Leroy are self-absorbed; Kirby so much so that he doesn't realize he probably is in love with Mieko after all. Leroy is so wrapped up in his plans to "make" things that will fix his marriage that he doesn't realize that this is not the kind of change his marriage really needs. Neither man is comfortable with his emotions; if Kirby were, he would have realized sooner how strongly he felt about Mieko. He might have offered to return to Japan. Or he might have acted more responsibly in the first place, acknowledging that he was lonely but still resisting getting involved with Mieko, knowing how different her society's expectations of women are from ours. And Leroy is paralyzed by even the thought of feeling something: His response to any emotional tug is to squelch it with some practical project. Even in the story's

last paragraph when he realizes the log cabin was a "crazy" idea, his response is to "think of something else, quickly."

THOMAS LYNCH

The Widow (p. 758)

Students may glean from this poem knowledge of one of the less satisfying relationships they've encountered in Part Six. But ask them to recall other characters and speakers in this part who deferred to their partner's comfort in some way. Both Ayah in "Lullaby" and the speaker in "Bitch" share some of the widow's experiences, but is deference *always* a bad thing? In "Long Distance," Mieko deferred to Kirby's comfort by getting involved with him in the first place. If he had decided to join her in Japan, would it be possible to then see Mieko's initial deference as having had positive results? In "Gesturing," both Joan and Ruth have allowed Richard to carry on as he pleases, presumably for years. Do we have a clue as to why they put up with this? And in "The Limitless Heart," Fenton Johnson visits his dead lover's parents, deferring to a request made by his lover that Johnson thought he couldn't honor. In which of these cases can the deference be seen as a destructive act or force? Are there any cases in which it can be seen as constructive? (For more on this topic, see Investigation 1 below. For a related assignment, see Part Six: Connections and Elaborations 3.)

INVESTIGATIONS (p. 758)

1. The marriage in this poem definitely reflects old-fashioned attitudes about the proper roles of men and women; there is little evidence here that the husband sees his wife as an equal. The occasional gifts he bestowed upon her do not make up for "midnights with sickly children" (line 4), the "misery of childbirth" (6), the single-handed housekeeping, his always having the more comfortable chair or side of the bed.

   Living "in deference" to another's "comfort" is in some ways mature, necessary, and desirable; if your spouse sleeps late and you turn on the stereo full blast first thing in the morning, odds are your relationship is not going to last too long. In the course of a long-term intimate relationship, much more significant issues are likely to loom. Should you take the new job that requires you to move your entire family to a part of the country they hate? If you and your spouse have different religious backgrounds, in what tradition should the children be raised? These situations involve compromise on the part of both partners, and compromise is essential to any successful long-term relationship. But "deference" is something else again: It implies submitting to another's will and wishes, and no one can be happy doing this on a long-term basis. The widow in this poem apparently believed it was her place to live this way; in fact she only fully realizes she *was* living this way after her husband has been dead for six months.

2. Few students will be commenting on the basis of firsthand experience here, though they may have family or friends whose experiences they can draw on. Indeed, many may not have accounted for this stage of marriage at all. Their concept of marriage or long-term intimate relationships may well have included two people growing old together, but not the death of one of the partners.

3. There are many differences between the relationships depicted in these two poems. Rich's speaker focuses first on physical appearance and then on

emotions; Lynch's speaker focuses on domestic details, suggesting that the marriage described here is composed primarily *of* those details.

If the couple in "The Widow" ever *discussed* their feelings, they might be closer to being equals, like the lovers in Rich's "Love Poem." To talk to death "daily, as to a neighbor" (Rich, line 27), is to confront both your own mortality and your lover's. Confronting the inevitability of death requires a great deal of strength and support from those you love. To be capable of this you must be able to share your emotions in the first place, something the couple in "Love Poem" does, but the couple in "The Widow" does *not* do.

4. Berry's poem provides no context about the relationship at hand, but the speaker's simultaneous desire to be alone and his ironic acknowledgment that he wants Tanya around after all suggest a mature relationship. The speaker knows there is value in being alone, but he's also aware of his partner's absence when he *is* alone.

"Love Poem" focuses on the long-term love of a couple who see each other as equals, equals who have been together so long that they're beginning to confront the fact that death will leave one of them alone in the not-too-distant future.

Lynch's poem also depicts a long-term relationship, but these partners were not equals. The fact that the widow feels "relieved" six months after her husband's death suggests that prior to his death she was feeling (though apparently not consciously) the opposite: oppressed, stymied, unappreciated.

Dobler's poem, too, depicts a long-term relationship whose partners are confronting death — but the speaker here is far from accepting death's inevitability. The ferocity of her love does not suggest that the love felt by Rich's speaker is any less strong, but Dobler's speaker is clearly not at peace with herself and her relationship in the same way that Rich's speaker is.

LESLIE MARMON SILKO

Lullaby (p. 759)

In reviewing Silko's work for *The Southwest Review*, Edith Blicksilver made the following statement about Ayah:

> The Indian woman may not have been liberated according to the modern definition, but she knew her worth. Then life changed. A reservation environment and the white man's paternalism robbed the Native Americans of their self-esteem. The woman's role as wife and mother changed when her man no longer had freedom of movement, challenge, or self-determination in his life. (*The Southwest Review*, Spring 1979, pp. 149–160)

Both Ayah's and Chato's roles changed significantly even before Chato lost his job; the role of parents and providers was denied them when the government took their children. Ask students how Ayah's role changed further once Chato lost his job. What is the connection between "freedom of movement, challenge, or self-determination" and Chato's drinking?

INVESTIGATIONS (p. 766)

1. Ayah blames the whites and the government (which is, of course, white) in general for the impasse she and her family have come to. She blames the white doctors for taking her children, and they deserve this blame: They knew she

couldn't understand English and couldn't read the papers she was signing. It's true they believed their actions were in the children's best interests, but they took advantage of the Navajo woman's ignorance of English to get what they wanted. Surely they would be appalled and would fight back if someone decided *their* children were not being raised in an ideal environment and took them away.

She blames Chato for teaching her to sign her name, but this skill was "something she was proud of" (para. 6), so she shares some blame here. She *knew* that she didn't know what she was signing, that she didn't know what these papers said. She blames Chato for knowing English in the first place: "It was like the old ones always told her about learning their language or any of their ways: It endangers you" (12). If Chato hadn't known English, he wouldn't have been able to teach her to sign her name.

She blames Chato for all this, finally, because there is no one else to blame. She knows there's nothing Chato, or anyone else, can do about government policies, but she can't really accept this. Blaming him can be seen as a way of acknowledging that they're in this mess together.

2. Ayah's life is shaped in large part by the U.S. government policy which forced Native Americans to live on reservations, denied them free access to the land they had previously lived on and worked, forced them to work for white men because these were the only jobs they could get, and took away their control over their children's educations and lives.

    Her life is shaped, too, by a husband who has provided her with little if any company or emotional support, and who seems to take for granted whatever she does to keep the family and household going. Of course, once Danny and Ella are taken away, she and Chato *are* the family — a development that must have put a great strain on their relationship. Like the widow in Thomas Lynch's poem, Ayah's life was spent in deference to Chato's comfort.

3. In Rich's poem, "learning to be true" with death means accepting its inevitability. Ayah knows she and Chato are growing closer to that time, and that she'll have to watch Chato — who is sick already, moves slowly, is an alcoholic, and forgets things — die first.

4. Despite the hard life and all the disappointments Ayah and Chato have shared, despite her hatred for him for many years after the children had been taken away, Ayah still, finally, loves him. When he really needs her, when he is sick and shivering and "only her body could keep him warm" (12), when he has to be rescued, drunk, from snowstorms, she is there. If love were based on rational feelings, she would probably have left him long ago.

JOHN UPDIKE

Gesturing (p. 767)

In addition to the books mentioned in the text footnote, some of Updike's better known works are the novels *Rabbit Run* (1960), *Rabbit Redux* (1970), and *Rabbit Is Rich* (1981), which won the Pulitzer Prize.

Updike has said of his own work: "The idea of a hero is aristocratic. Now either nobody is a hero or everyone is. I vote for everyone. My subject is the American Protestant small-town middle class. I like middles. It is in middles that extremes clash, where ambiguity restlessly rules" (*Contemporary Authors*, Vol. 33). Ask students how this story bears out Updike's claims. Are Richard, Joan, and Ruth all heroic? How? Is any one of these characters more heroic than the others? What, if anything, is left ambiguous in this story?

Students may argue that Joan is most heroic in the end. She wins a small victory over Richard by dishing out a bit of his own medicine; she makes him uncomfortable by sharing stories about her lover, something he has done repeatedly to her. All the characters can be deemed heroic in their civility to one another; despite the charged circumstances, any animosity seems well controlled. The ambiguity in this story arises from a situation students have encountered repeatedly in Part Six: It is rarely clear exactly how or why a marriage or relationship falls apart. Richard's future with Ruth, too, seems ambiguous; although they love each other, it's not clear where their relationship is headed.

INVESTIGATIONS (p. 775)

1. "What Means Switch" and "Gesturing" suggest, finally, that love is *not* powerful enough to transcend all differences. From what we see of the Maples, their relationship does not seem irretrievably negative or destructive. (This is in part due to the scenes Richard chooses to share with us; no doubt there are ugly scenes he could have shown us that would make us feel differently about this marriage.) But what appears to us as a marriage that might be saved appears to Richard as unsalvageable, or at least not worth the work and sacrifices that would be involved. Richard and Joan actually do seem to "see the same things" about their marriage and their relationships with their lovers; they see that they are hurting one another by staying together, but also that their relationships with their respective lovers don't provide them with the same things their marital relationship did. They see, in other words, that they cannot make the present situation work.

   The characters in "What Means Switch," at thirteen, are a bit young to be concerned with the transcendent power of love, but still old enough to know that some differences — in this case, cultural mores — would be extremely difficult to overcome. At the story's end, Mona says, "If I could, I'd switch everything to be different. But since I can't, I might as well sit here at the table for a while, discussing what I know how to discuss" (Jen, 230).

2. It would be difficult to describe Richard as a "victim of circumstance": He wants to leave his wife; he states this in the story's second paragraph. Evenings with Joan dissolve into "harsh words, maudlin tears"; their marriage is neither "healthy, nor progressive" (18). And Richard wants to keep his lover — a condition unacceptable to his wife if they are to remain married. In paragraph 7, Joan makes it clear that she *would* give up her lover, if Richard wanted her to — but this is not what he wants. Joan's having a lover allows Richard to leave Joan without feeling *too* guilty for his transgressions. All of these details add up to Richard's doing *exactly* what he wants to do. It's true that he also still loves Joan — but not enough, clearly, to try to start over again.

3. The story opens with Joan's initial gesture, one Richard "had never seen her use before" (1). This gesture reveals that Joan is changing, has taken a step out of the circumscribed world of their marriage. Some of her gestures include "a compulsive economy" (32); smoking cigarettes down to their filters; "tiny repressed handwriting" (32); and a "protesting little splaying of her hands" (69). Those are all signs of a tense woman keeping things orderly and under control, holding back emotion and chaos.

Richard's habitual gestures include eating Joan's cooking; sleeping with Joan and Ruth and keeping both at a distance by telling each about the other; and, once he's moved to Boston, being a "neat and thrifty housekeeper" (32) and finding solace in the skyscraper he sees out his window. Although "all waste pained him" (31), Richard doesn't seem to recognize his own compulsive economy. Like Joan, he is a man of careful emotional habits, but he demonstrates a selfishness neither Joan nor Ruth share. Each of these women wants Richard to herself, but Richard wants to have them both on his own terms.

Ruth's gestures reveal her to be in many ways Joan's opposite: She is full of life and a "beautiful unblinking assumption of her own primary worth" (32). Her "conspicuous unthriftiness" (31) bothers Richard, but he appreciates her motivation: "better other-destructive than self-destructive." Ruth is also emotive, perhaps even theatrical: She expresses "exasperation even when she felt none" (31) and feels possessive of Richard's apartment.

All we know about Andy is a few gestures: He's a fussy dresser, worries about the towels in his hotel room, and has what Joan perceives to be an absurd number of buttons on his clothing. This general fussiness makes him perfect for Joan: He's predictable and won't disturb the emotional environment she tries so hard to control.

4. Richard finds that he "could not in solitude stop performing"; he isn't used to being alone, "without an audience" (32). The skyscraper provides that audience; it is his "inanimate, giant friend" (43). He sees in the skyscraper all the qualities and circumstances of his life: It is "a beautiful disaster" (20), a mass of seemingly unresolvable contradictions, "so lovely in air" but with "tangled mucky roots" (34). Richard knows that he has carefully constructed his current happiness; note that even now it is "marred by gaps of sudden fear and disorientation. Each hour had to be scheduled, lest he fall through" (34). He knows this happiness is just a "holiday" (34) from the sadness and pain he feels in the story's last paragraph, when he acknowledges that Joan "would never stop gesturing within him, never . . . her gestures would endure, cut into glass" — like the wedding vows etched into the window of his new apartment.

CAROLYN KIZER

Bitch (p. 776)

In addition to the books mentioned in the text footnote, Kizer has written *Poems* (1959), *The Ungrateful Garden* (1961), *Knock upon Silence* (1965–66), and *Midnight Was My Cry: New and Selected Poems* (1971).

This poem expresses more bitterness over a failed relationship than any other selection in Part Six. Roxie in "Judgment" and Burton in *Burn This* are also jilted, but these characters lack the sometimes vindictive attitude of this speaker. Ask students why they think this is the case. We don't see Roxie after the breakup with Wayne, so we don't really know what she's feeling, but that relationship was an odd one anyway; how hurt or surprised could Roxie be about its ending when she made no effort herself to call Wayne all summer? And in *Burn This*, apparently Anna and Burton had an on-again, off-again romantic relationship, though they remained friends throughout. In "Bitch," the speaker and the man she meets were once married (or at least lived together) for some time; this relationship appears to have been more significant and longer than the others mentioned above.

INVESTIGATIONS (p. 777)

1. One voice is the speaker's actual voice — the one that speaks aloud, saying the statements that appear in quotation marks. The other is the speaker's internal voice, which reports the speaker's thoughts rather than her actual words. These thoughts are presented to us as "the bitch's" thoughts, the bitch being one aspect of the speaker's personality. Students may be initially confused by the voices, but once they realize any words spoken aloud are in quotation marks, they should have no trouble following the poem. Students may remark that this initial confusion between the two voices reflects the speaker's initial emotional turmoil over running into her ex-husband or lover; talking to "the bitch inside" (line 2) her is her way of getting a grip on herself, of calming herself down.

2. Most students will know that, in addition to its use as a derogatory term for "woman," bitch also means "female dog." Kizer alludes to canine behavior throughout the poem. In line 2 she tells the bitch, "don't start growling"; "the bitch starts to bark hysterically" (6); "she begins to whimper" (11); "she slobbers and grovels" (16) and is dragged "off by the scruff" (33). In each instance that the female dog image is used, however, the image of a woman scorned, a woman who was ill-treated and finally "dismissed" by her lover, is equally appropriate.

    "Bitch" has one more important dictionary definition: "a complaint," or "to complain." In fact, the speaker is "bitching" or complaining about the man she used to be involved with, just as he, in turn, must have complained about her before they finally split.

3. When the speaker was involved with the man in question, she "came running / Each evening, when she heard his step" (18–19); she was submissive, adoring, and devoted and took whatever this man dished out. In speaking this poem, however, the speaker reveals a self-knowledge that suggests she would never allow herself to be treated this way — like a dog — again. The tone of her actual spoken voice is polite and detached but the tone of her other voice — the internal one — is at times vindictive, at times sarcastic. The bitch is not allowed to speak because the speaker doesn't want to give this man the satisfaction of knowing how much he affects her, even "after all these years" (1). She also wants the bitch to mind her "manners" (8), not to be "demonstrative" or "clumsy" (30) but rather "like the well-groomed pets of his new friends" (31).

GALWAY KINNELL

After Making Love
We Hear Footsteps (p. 777)

In addition to the books mentioned in the text footnote, Kinnell's collections of poetry include *What a Kingdom It Was* (1960), *Body Rags* (1968), *The Avenue Bearing the Initial of Christ into the New World: Poems 1946–1964* (1974); and *Mortal Acts, Mortal Words* (1980).

You might want to begin by reading this poem aloud, or having a student do so, so your class can hear the music of Kinnell's verse. Then have students read it again to themselves, noting instances of assonance, alliteration, and internal rhyme. (They might cite the repeated "or" sound in the first three lines, the repeated "l" in the first two lines; the "s" sounds and the long "e" sounds in lines 4 and 5.) Ask students how the sound of the poem enhances the speaker's tribute to his marriage and his child.

INVESTIGATIONS (p. 778)

1. This couple gleams "with satisfaction" *because* they love each other; to be in love is to be very lucky, and for at least part of the time, to be very happy as well. Not only are they in love, but through their love they have produced "this very child" (18), "this one whom habit of memory propels to the ground of his making," who is both an extension of themselves and a precious, independent entity all his own. In an ideal love relationship, each half of a couple brings out the best in the other half: There is a balance of discovery, sharing, giving, and taking that results in a harmonious sense of well-being for both parties.

2. In this poem, sexuality is portrayed as an entirely good thing: It both results from and is a manifestation of the love this couple shares. Sexuality here involves the "familiar touch of the long-married" (11) and "loving and snuggling" (16). Along with love, it involves warmth, humor, and spirituality: Sex is the act that resulted in their son, "this blessing love gives again into our arms" (24).

   In *Burn This*, sexuality is the subject of a great deal of crude joking; this talk and the act itself involve a kind of desperation and urgency absent from Kinnell's poem, where sex is associated with love throughout. This difference can be attributed primarily to the fact that none of the characters in *Burn This* have close, stable emotional relationships with the people with whom they are sexually involved. Sex in *Burn This* involves great emotional risk; participants can't entirely trust each other or relax with their partners, since they don't know what they really mean to one another or where their relationship is going.

   In Lynch's "The Widow," the couple's marriage lacks the joy shared by the couple in Kinnell's poem. The widow "spread herself like linen out / for him to take his feastly pleasures in / and liked it well enough, or said she did" (Lynch, 13–15). It is the phrase "said she did" that tips us off: If she was enjoying the experience at all, there is no indication of this. In this marriage sex seems more of a duty, or at best an expectation, rather than the celebration of love it is in Kinnell's poem.

3. The blessing in this poem is the couple's son Fergus, who is a result of their love. For the speaker in David Mura's poem, "Nantucket Honeymoon," love was a blessing that enabled the speaker to love his "own sweet skin" (Mura, 16). In *Burn This*, love *may* turn out to be a blessing for Anna and Pale, since Anna wants to settle down and start a family and Pale seems like he could benefit a great deal from some loving and nurturing. In Patricia Dobler's "Hospital Call," love is a blessing in that it is a weapon against death: The angel "wants the black man in the next bed, / the one with cold fingers / and no wife to stand over him and pray / the sweat to break from his body" (Dobler, 8–11). In Adrienne Rich's "Love Poem" and in Fenton Johnson's "The Limitless Heart," love is a blessing in that it helps lovers and survivors learn to accept the inevitability of death and cope with it once it occurs.

FENTON JOHNSON

The Limitless Heart (p. 779)

This moving essay recounts the writer's visit to the parents of his now-dead lover, who dies of complications related to AIDS. Ask students how Johnson's loss differs from other deaths they've read about in Part Six. How is it similar?

Johnson's loss differs from that of the widow of Lynch's poem in that although she loses her husband, after six months she is "relieved." Her deferential relationship to her husband was such that her pain is relatively short-lived; before long a whole new life has opened up to her.

The characters in *Burn This* lose their friend and brother, Robbie, as the play opens. Heartbreaking as this is, losing a friend or sibling does differ from losing a spouse or lover; one way Anna and Pale are able to carry on after Robbie's death is by finding solace in each other. Sex is an outlet not available to, or at least not usually desired by, someone who has just lost the person he or she was romantically involved with.

INVESTIGATIONS (p. 781)

1. This memoir illustrates both romantic love between the narrator and his lover and Bill and Ruth; it also illustrates parental love on Bill and Ruth's part, and on the part of the grandmother and her "drag queen" grandson. Both kinds of love require sacrifice and acceptance. Ruth risked her safety coming out of hiding to find medical help for her husband before she knew that the war was over. Bill and Ruth apparently accepted their son's homosexuality, just as the drag queen's grandmother loves and supports her grandson even as he sings in his spiked heels. Each of these people shares the knowledge that we can accept anything if we love someone enough.

2. "Learning to be true with death" means acknowledging that death "has the keys / to this house" (Rich, lines 29–30); it means acknowledging death's inevitability. It means learning to transcend those "limits to how much love one can give" (para. 1), since the opportunities to give that love turn out to be limited. And so Johnson can visit, even love, Bill and Ruth — who transcended any limitations they might have thought they had during their years of hiding during World War II.

3. Johnson initially ventures beyond self-imposed restrictions by visiting his lover's parents, something he had not only *not* promised but had told his lover he refused to do. Johnson had thought there were "limits to how much love" (1) he could give — but in fact visiting his lovers' parents turns out to be another manifestation of Johnson's love for his late lover.

   Venturing beyond self-imposed restrictions is an essential characteristic of love: In "Long Distance," Kirby can't venture beyond his own fears of intimacy and so can't actively love Mieko. In *Burn This*, Anna and Pale are terrified of what they feel toward one another, but ultimately decide the risk is worth taking to find out whether they can meet each other's needs and expectations.

4. Johnson refers to the pain of losing a lover or son at all, and especially to death caused by AIDS and AIDS-related complications; the pain of losing families in the Holocaust; being beaten by Nazis; hiding for years with broken bones; and the pain of having to hide being gay. Johnson and his lover's parents *have* learned from their experiences; they are able to share intimacies they might

not have thought possible prior to the death of Johnson's lover and Bill and Ruth's only son. And the drag queen's grandmother, who knows her grandson is at a high risk for AIDS, certainly loves and supports him unreservedly.

PART SEVEN

WITH ETERNAL QUESTIONS
AND EVERYDAY ABSURDITIES

OVERVIEW

In the last part of this text, students will encounter a variety of voices speaking about such profound issues as death, the soul, afterlife, and the power of the human imagination. They will also read about such apparently mundane incidents as a writer observing ants crawling across her writing table as she works and a fourth-grade class being appointed a strange substitute teacher. But who is to say what's really profound and what's mundane? Or what's strange, or normal, or fantastic? Part Seven should yield fascinating debates as your class attempts to define these concepts. Perhaps they will come to the conclusion that rigid definitions of these terms are impossible.

The events of Charles Baxter's and Raymond Carver's stories are realistic; it is the changes that take place in the characters' hearts and minds here that give us pause. Have Tommy and his classmates been permanently affected by their substitute teacher, Miss Ferenczi, and will they ever know the truth about her? Exactly what is the narrator of "Cathedral" feeling at the end of that story, and will it help him lead a better, happier life?

Unresolved questions abound in the selections in Part Seven. The events of "The Other Miller" *seem* realistic — but we can't be sure whether or not Miller is imagining his mother's death at the story's end. Maggie Anderson's speaker wonders why her son's friend committed suicide, and Mary Oliver's speaker wonders about the nature of the soul. The speaker of Maxine Kumin's "In the Park" suggests that all the religions in the world can't keep death from our doorstep, and that only someone who has faced death directly has even a clue about the power of this experience. But the speaker of David James's "Think Death," who shares Kumin's speaker's acceptance of death's inevitability, claims to be less in awe of the prospect: "We're born, we die," he says in line 21. And Joyce Carol Oates attempts to demystify death in particular and nature in general: Death is not romantic; rather, it is painful, it is messy, and it is the end.

The speakers in two other poems have different ways of coming to terms with death: May Swenson's speaker doesn't see death as romantic, but uses the natural setting of the sea to mentally organize her grief and pain. And Gogisgi/Carroll Arnett's speaker sees death as merely one stage in the great cycle of all life, human and otherwise.

Several selections in Part Seven contain fantastic or surreal elements, and in each of these selections, a profound transformation occurs. The effectiveness of Charles Johnson's "Exchange Value" rests upon the reader's willingness to accept the premise that Miss Bailey's inheritance is cursed, just as the reader must accept the moths and enlarging of the narrator's hands in Helena María Viramontes's story "The Moths" and Angela's levitation in Milcha Sanchez-Scott's *Roosters*. In other ways, these three selections are fairly realistic: The action unfolds in recognizable settings, and the characters, motivated by familiar human emotions, behave in understandable ways. Yet both Loftis and Cooter are transformed by Miss Bailey's intangible curse, the narrator of "The Moths" is transformed by her grandmother's death, and Angela's entire family is transformed by her levitation.

While James Wright's "Yes, But" and Rosario Ferré's "Pico Rico, Mandorico" are the least "realistic" selections in Part Seven, students will not find the two equally difficult. "Pico Rico, Mandorico" takes the familiar form of a fairy tale, and students will bring their knowledge and expectations of this genre to the story without even realizing it. Wright's poem, on the other hand, requires students to accept the speaker's merging with the lizards without providing any familiar narrative frame or realistic conventions to help them do so.

Instructors who don't have time to teach the entire part might focus on selections in which characters undergo a transformation that clearly does *not* involve fantastic or supernatural elements. What kind of transformation *has* taken place in each of the selections by Anderson, Wolff, Baxter, Kumin, and Carver? Or a unit could be constructed around the different views of nature presented in this part, using some or all of the following selections: Wright, Gogisgi/Arnett, Oates, Oliver, Swenson, James, and Kumin.

JAMES WRIGHT

Yes, But (p. 785)

In addition to the books mentioned in the text footnote, Wright is the author of the poetry collections *The Green Wall* (1957), *Saint Judas* (1959), *The Branch Will Not Break* (1963), *We Shall Gather at the River* (1968), *Two Citizens* (1973), *Moments of the Italian Summer* (1976), *Leave It to the Sunlight* (1981), *A Reply to Matthew Arnold* (1981), and *The Shape of Light* (1986).

Students may have difficulty with this mystical poem, which demands of its readers a very willing suspension of disbelief. Specifically, it demands that the reader accept that the speaker's becoming a lizard is not ridiculous. Even with that knowledge, some students may remain confused; you may want to walk them through the poem from line 5 on, when the speaker imagines that, even if he were dead, he would appear, during siesta time, and join the lizards gazing across the water. Ask students to observe the serenity and emotional warmth throughout the poem: Everything is peaceful and quiet "between noon and four" (line 6). Everyone "is asleep or making love" (7); the motorcycles are "still" (9); the lizards, "unpestered by temptation" (12), leave their prey alone. (The reference to the Germans in line 8 is vague; this could be a reference to noisy German tourists, but that interpretation is based on speculation, not on evidence in the poem.) The lizards leave their prey alone because they have no need for food (and note that, as of line 15, the speaker refers to the lizards as "we" rather than "they"; he has become one of them at this point in the poem). They don't need food because they have evolved or transcended to some mystical state where the body is irrelevant: "Our very lungs have fallen and drifted / Away like leaves down the Adige, / Long ago" (lines 24–26). In this state they experience neither hunger nor the human emotions of fatigue, anger, loneliness, or malaise; they are, simply, "in love" (21) with life, with existence.

INVESTIGATIONS (p. 785)

1. The speaker's existence and the existence of the physical world around him are so compelling and beautiful to him that he would "come out" even if he "were dead and buried." The speaker feels his love of life, and of this place he's in, so strongly that he would let nothing interfere with that feeling, even commonly held assumptions about death. To be dead and therefore not conscious of "the chill spring" (4) and the "golden mosquitoes" (14) glittering "defenseless in the sun" (18) would be a waste. So, the speaker is saying, he would defy the rules; dead or not, he would emerge to savor the world.

2. The speaker doesn't say "I believe" after line 5 because that which he "believed" in lines 1–5 — that he would join the lizards — has now happened: Note the shift from the conditional to the present tense in line 6. After line 13, the speaker doesn't refer to himself as "I" because he is no longer "I"; he has become part of the "we" first mentioned in line 15. After line 13, the speaker is among the lizards sitting by the Adige.

3. Lungs are the organs through which humans and reptiles breathe and breathing is the activity we consider most crucial to life. But these lizards can exist without lungs and oxygen, just as the speaker can defy the rules of death and join them. The leap to accepting lizards who "breathe light" should not be a problem for the reader who has already accepted the speaker's becoming a lizard. Once the speaker has joined the lizards, the poem's events exist in a magical realm. If a man can merge with lizards, those lizards are no more normal than that man. If they don't have to fulfill the reader's expectations of what's normal, then they don't need lungs, nor to necessarily "see one another" (22), nor to breathe anything other than light. Nor do they need to exist in linear time: hence the reference to this all happening "long ago." Along with conventional concepts of what the body can and cannot do, conventional concepts of time are also denied; the events of this poem took place both "long ago" and in the present, the tense of the poem's last line.

   Ask students whether the "logic" of this poem, detailed in the above paragraph, could be understood as a "substitute" logic based on "substitute facts" like those Miss Ferenczi mentions in Charles Baxter's story, "Gryphon."

4. Answers will vary.

GOGISGI/CARROLL ARNETT

Early Song (p. 786)

In addition to the books mentioned in the text footnote, Gogisgi/Arnett has published the poetry collections *Then* (1965), *The Intentions* (1966), *Not Only That* (1967), *Like a Wall* (1969), *Through the Woods* (1971), *Earlier* (1972), *Come* (1973), and *South Line* (1979).

This poem works well with Wright's, Oliver's, and Swenson's poems and contrasts usefully with Oates's "Against Nature." It also provides an excellent opportunity to discuss the connection between form and content. For more on this topic, see Investigation 2 below.

INVESTIGATIONS (p. 787)

1. Presumably, the "brothers and sisters" are all things that live on "this good brown / earth" (lines 9–10): Humans, animals, plants, and perhaps even the sun, stars, and sky are all part of the "great circle" mentioned in line 14.

2. Note that, as prose, the poem becomes one long sentence, punctuated by four commas. The sentence is prosaic: dull, flat, matter of fact. Ask your students what this suggests to them about the relationship between form and content. It is the poem's structure — its line breaks and division into stanzas — that provides it with its rhythm. And rhythm is crucial to this poem, reinforcing the sense of the natural cycle the poem describes.

3. Answers will vary.

4. Both poems depict a merging of man with nature and suggest that the soul or spirit does not remain forever in our own bodies but travels instead, whether into a lizard, the "good brown earth," or some other place. But Wright's speaker's vision is fanciful, even fantastic, and seems more connected to magical realism and sense of play than does Gogisgi/Arnett's speaker. Gogisgi/Arnett's speaker reveals a more traditional perspective on nature's primacy: All living things come from the earth and eventually return to the earth, from whence they will grow, in some form, again.

5. The speaker of "Early Song" engages some system of belief that Oates, at least from the evidence in "Against Nature," does not share. That system of belief includes a general sense of wonder at the beauty, efficiency, and cyclical nature of the physical world. The poem's speaker sees nature as an overarching power that creates a harmonic universe, and would take issue with Oates's depiction of nature as cruel and uncaring.

   Oates might say in turn that "Early Song" was full of false or misguided piety and mysticism. She might tell the speaker that the frost on his pine needles could kill all his plants or crops if it fell too early, or that it's merely a harbinger of a cold so severe that people will freeze to death in their sleep in the night. She might further tell the speaker that when his blood runs into the good brown earth, it will be because he is dead.

MAGGIE ANDERSON

Heart Fire (p. 787)

In addition to the books mentioned in the text footnote, Anderson is the author of the poetry collections *The Great Horned Owl* (1979) and *Years That Answer* (1980).

In this moving poem the speaker tries to come to terms with her friend's son's suicide. Ask students whether they think she succeeds. Do they think it's possible to come to terms with someone's suicide? Ask them to think back to Jessie in *'night, Mother* (Part One, p. 28). After all of Jessie's revelations, is her mother better equipped to deal with her daughter's suicide than the speaker's friend is equipped to deal with her son's?

INVESTIGATIONS (p. 788)

1. Answers will vary. There are many reasons we continue to pose questions we know to be unanswerable. In the case of this poem — and probably in the case of all suicides, and many other deaths as well — we ask these questions to create an opportunity to talk about, or remember, the deceased. We ask these questions for company, too; even if we don't know the answer, there is solace in the knowledge that no one else does, either. There is a whole community of us who can't answer these questions. Together, it is easier to keep faith and believe that if only the deceased could tell us what it is, there *is* a reason we could understand. Together we can also believe the deceased is happier where he or she is now. These are difficult thoughts, hard enough to face at all, much less alone. We ask these questions in part as a way of coping with our grief.

2. To one who feels he lives in a country always readying for war, the fire would be easy to locate *outside* the heart — figuratively in the minds and speeches of those who want to go to war and literally in the guns and bombs that would be used in that war. Amidst all this external heat and fire, it would be easy to forget about the importance of the individual spirit. Or it would be easy for that spirit to grow cold in the midst of such senseless goings-on. This is all conjecture on the part of the speaker; note the word "maybe" at the beginning of line 3. The speaker invents a heart fire because she wants to think her friend's son is not cold and alone. So she gives him this fire to keep him warm and give him company; it was, in the speaker's mind, a fire he was unable to keep lit while living. It is the speaker's way of trying to believe that he is happier where he is; he is able to keep his spirit burning, something he couldn't do while he was alive.

3. The speaker *does* use illusion to comfort herself: Illusion is one of the most remarkable defense mechanisms with which the human spirit is equipped. It is true that the speaker sees her friend's son everywhere, and that each sighting is an illusion: his shirt in the sky; his hair in the bare limbs of trees; his vulnerability in the wind-buffeted grass; his image in a boy under a suburban streetlight. The speaker is relieving her own loneliness in that she misses her friend's son, and, like her friend, has difficulty accepting that he is gone forever. Also, most of us feel anxiety about what, if anything, we'll experience after death; to many of us, loneliness — or at least the sense that we will be alone, away from our friends and loved ones — seems very likely. In this sense the speaker is projecting her own fears onto her friend's dead son: The speaker wants to think he's not alone because the thought of being alone, either for herself or for him, is frightening to her.

JOYCE CAROL OATES

Against Nature (p. 789)

This fascinating essay pairs well with David James's "Think Death"; both selections present unsentimental views of subjects that are not often approached with such candor. Both selections work well juxtaposed against the more romantic perspectives of Wright, Gogisgi/Arnett, Oliver, and Swenson. (For more on this comparison, see Investigation 2 below.)

The fragmented structure of this essay is a good place to start discussion. Ask students how the essay's structure influenced their reading. Was the essay coherent, or did they have difficulty making transitions from section to section? Why do they think Oates might have chosen this unconventional form? In what way does the form reflect what Oates is saying?

With the exception of some of the literary references — which may be lost on students unfamiliar, for example, with Melville or transcendentalism — students should have little trouble with Oates's central ideas, since they are all illustrated by graphic anecdotes such as her attack of paroxysmal tachycardia and her early memories of nature.

INVESTIGATIONS (p. 795)

1. Since one's attitude toward nature is subjective, responses will vary. One criticism of Oates's "resistance to nature" might be that she anthropomorphizes it: *People* have a sense of humor, a satiric dimension, and moral purpose; things do not, nor do we usually expect this of them.

   And what does being accidental have to do with lacking resonance? It is humans who bestow symbolic resonance upon something, and not the other way around, so in a sense all symbolism is accidental: We find the image that fits our needs.

   While it is true that nature lacks verbal language, that statement implies a powerful judgment: Is lacking language necessarily a negative quality? Certainly it makes nature (or anything else lacking verbal language) difficult for us to understand — but this mystery is precisely what so many writers and artists find so inspiring and compelling about nature.

2. Oates might well see all these writers, or at least their speakers, as guilty of varying degrees of "REVERENCE, AWE, PIETY, MYSTICAL ONENESS" (para. 9). In Wright's "Yes, But," the speaker merges with a lizard, basking in the sun on a river bank, "in love" and "shining" (Wright, 21), breathing light. Though Oates doesn't say so specifically, she is unlikely to believe in any sort of magical transference of souls; a writer who did would surely have mentioned it while thinking her "calming . . . pseudo-mystic thoughts" in paragraph 12. Anyone who sees the blue of the sky as "a mere optical illusion" (16) is unlikely to indulge in "comforting illusion[s]" (27) of any kind.

   Gogisgi/Arnett's speaker also believes in a continuous life cycle; he makes "prayers of / thanksgiving" (Gogisgi/Arnett, 6–7) "for the dark blood / that runs through me / in a great circle / back into this / good brown earth" (12–16).

   Oates might charge Oliver, too, with being guilty of a reverential mysticism. In her poem contemplating the nature of the soul, she personifies everything from swans to stones.

   In Swenson's case, the speaker is not glamorizing nature, but has certainly constructed a powerful "individual vision" to deal with her pain. The concept of the sea as a giant "mausoleum, with countless shelves" (Swenson, 10) helps the speaker organize and come to terms with her feelings, but it is just that: a concept. Were "the vanished bodies of friends who have died" (7) really in the sea, of course, they would be strewn wildly about, limbs askew, bodies everywhere, rather than tucked neatly into the hollows of the waves.

3. Answers will vary. When analyzing their own experience from Oates's point of view, students should be sure to single out any instances of glamorizing or romanticizing nature.

4. Oates has focused "the white heat of [her] 'creativity' upon" (29) her resistance to nature. She could be said to be exaggerating the importance of every episode she reports in this essay: her attack of paroxysmal tachycardia, which she acknowledges is "rarely fatal"; her "early nature memories" — all grim, when in fact she could surely remember some pretty scenes too, if she chose. Her point, of course, is that the pretty scenes are just that: pretty. Nothing special. They don't stay with us, haunt us, the way the violent scenes do. Still, in choosing to thrust her bloodsuckers and dead dog and rabid raccoon upon us, Oates can be seen as glorifying the crueler, uglier, destructive side of nature. The reason Oates's essay is so effective is precisely *because* she exaggerates the significance of her subject.

5. Answers will vary.

CHARLES JOHNSON

Exchange Value (p. 796)

In addition to the books mentioned in the text footnote, Johnson has written the novels *Faith and the Good Thing* (1974) and *Oxherding Tale* (1982) and the short-story collection *The Sorcerer's Apprentice* (1986).

In paragraph 36, Cooter describes "that special Negro fear of using up what little we get in this life," an attitude Loftis describes as "entropy." Ask students which of the two brothers seems more sensitive to Miss Bailey and what happened to her. Why? (You might need to steer students to paragraph 8, where Cooter suggests Miss Bailey's stash may be cursed, and to paragraph 36.) Loftis may be the better educated of the two, but Cooter seems to have a more instinctive understanding of their neighbor's goals, motivations, and fears.

Toward the story's end, when Loftis finally returns home, it is with a penny he found on the street. The fact that he picked up this penny despite his newfound wealth suggests that he, too, has fallen prey to the curse on Miss Bailey's inheritance. Cooter tells him it doesn't "have to be like that for us . . . because we could change" (38). Ask students whether they agree with Cooter: Can he or Loftis change? Refer them back to their "Write Before Reading" assignment. What lesson has Cooter learned, if any? Will he get a chance to put what he's learned into practice, or is it too late for that? Ask students what they make of Cooter's final gesture of placing the penny in Miss Bailey's jar "for now, with the rest of our things" (38). They should see that Cooter, too, has fallen prey to the curse.

INVESTIGATIONS (p. 802)

1. The sheer wealth of Miss Bailey's stash is incredible to Cooter, as it might be to anyone who stumbled upon it: it looked "so like picturebook scenes of plentifulness you could seal yourself off in here and settle forever" (5). But picture books are unreal: They are fantasy, products of the writer's and artist's imagination, and Cooter knows this. Since Cooter's imaginative tendencies run toward reading comic books and seeing "faces or foreign places in water stains on the wallpaper" (3), he probably associates picture books with fairy tales — a form he recognizes as fantasy. Cooter suspects something's wrong in part because such sudden wealth would simply be too good to be true. He's also made leery by the strange assortment of items, including items of no apparent value, like the "three sections of a dead tree" (5). Why would someone keep all this valuable stuff rather than spend it to improve the quality

of one's life? And what possible explanation could there be for keeping part of a dead tree? To Cooter at that moment there is no possible rational answer, so there must be something wrong with Miss Bailey's stash.

2. Loftis aspires to rise out of the squalid poverty from which he came; unlike his brother, he doesn't believe he's had all he's "ever gonna get" (3). Most of us would agree — if we received a huge sum of unexpected money — that it was important to take our time and plan wisely, and this seems to describe Loftis's behavior until he leaves for work on Wednesday. Loftis knows he has to be careful with his windfall; the very act of transforming it, of deciding "exactly what to exchange it for" (21) could make it disappear. In its untouched state, Miss Bailey's stash is worth all 879,453 dollars, but for every dollar spent, the psychological cost is much higher than a dollar: It's the knowledge that the *power* of the stash — that is, Loftis's future wealth and comfort — is diminished.

3. Miss Bailey's stash, her "hope made material," is destructive in that it has left her paralyzed, "panicky about depletion" (36), unable to make any use of her gift. Once she received Henry Conner's estate, she became "spellbound," considering "every purchase . . . a loss of life" (36). Some students will no doubt assert that Miss Bailey is crazy, and there is nothing in the story to refute that assumption. Cooter himself calls her "dizzy" (36). His explanation doesn't eliminate this as a possibility; rather, it suggests the circumstances that might have sent Miss Bailey over the edge.

4. Stolen property or goods exert their power over a thief the moment he or she takes them. Something must always be *done* with these goods — whether they are to be hidden, bartered or sold, or destroyed — and this activity must usually be performed in secret. Even if disposing of the stolen goods is not difficult, the thief may be subject to guilt and will certainly be subject to a certain amount of anxiety and fear.

Loftis and Cooter initially see Miss Bailey's stash as a gift, but its power turns out to be worse than the power of stolen goods; these goods are cursed. For Miss Bailey, of course, the stash was a gift, so not stolen. Yet it still, unfortunately, exerted the negative power over her described in Investigation 3 above — though presumably it was not intended to do so.

TOBIAS WOLFF

The Other Miller (p. 802)

This disturbing story reveals a man so motivated by spite that his main goal seems to be to inflict grief on his mother. Ask students if they can recall selections illustrating hatred elsewhere in the book. Students may cite Eng's hatred of Sharon in "Fathering" (Part Two, p. 129); the hatred of Blacks by whites as revealed in both "Snuff Dippers" (Part Four, p. 369) and "The Price of Hate: Thoughts on Covering a Ku Klux Klan Rally" (Part Five, p. 606); or Ayah's hatred of her husband Chato in "Lullaby" (Part Six, p. 759). How do these instances of hatred differ from Miller's feelings toward his mother? Are they in any way similar?

In paragraph 105, Miller acknowledges that he knows he's "going to die. He knows that, and he prides himself on knowing it when other people only pretend to know it, secretly believing that they will live forever." Ask students to compare Miller's understanding of death with Roscoe Brown's in "In the Park" (p. 875). Do Miller and Roscoe Brown know the same things about death?

INVESTIGATIONS (p. 812)

1. Miller's initial encounter with Kaiser and Lebowitz reveals Miller's inability to respond appropriately to a given situation, to respond, as Lebowitz implies in paragraph 31, the way a human would. While Miller's decision to grab this opportunity of mistaken identity to get out of the field may seem unethical to some students, it is understandable, since he hates being in the army. His decision to act out this charade is one thing; his ability to be convincing, however, is another. Until paragraph 47, Miller makes only the lamest attempts to act like a man whose mother has just died. It takes him all that time to realize that Kaiser and Lebowitz "expected a different kind of performance from the one he's given them, more emotional and all" (46).

   And Miller's observations about Lebowitz's religion indicate a further lack of tact, sensitivity, and general propriety: For some reason Miller thinks it will be less offensive to say "You don't see too many Jewish people in the army nowadays" (36) than to ask Lebowitz why he is in the army. Ask students whether they see any difference between the two statements. What is it that's offensive about either one?

   Overall, the scene depicted in paragraphs 19–46 reveals Miller's inability to communicate with other people, to establish any sort of real connection.

2. Miller is a fatalist who views luck as the controlling factor in his life: It killed his father; it made his mother marry his biology teacher; it made him the soldier who would always be the one "standing in holes" (5) in the rain. In the story's third paragraph, he says "he has never yet seen a plan that worked, and this one won't either." Until the story's end, he believes the events in his life are predetermined and that they are predetermined to be bad. His view of the future — that "everything gets worse" (97) — confirms that he thinks he's doomed to bad luck. This brief reprieve, when he is lucky enough to be mistaken (he thinks) for the guy whose mother died, is just that — a fluke. As long as Miller thinks everything is controlled by luck, he doesn't have to take responsibility for anything, nor does he have to make any effort to change things. As long as he believes his problem is bad luck, he doesn't have to take any emotional risks or give anything to anybody.

3. The lie Miller tells about his mother is basically an extremely exaggerated version of what Miller believes really happened: His mother deserted him. The other children and his father dying of a broken heart are all embellishment, but they serve to make Miller's tale a sadder story, and Miller believes that what actually happened — his mother marrying his biology teacher and disrupting the home, he, Miller, was so happy in — is very sad indeed, even tragic.

   From all the evidence we have, Miller's mother's remarriage was an entirely reasonable, "normal" event. She had been a widow for over ten years when she met Phil Dove; she fell in love; she got married. She had an almost-grown son who should have been mature enough to cope with her remarriage, and even if Wesley wasn't wild about the man, her son would soon be taking off to lead his own life anyway, so wouldn't have to put up with her new husband for long. Certainly she deserved to have a life, too, after all these years.

4. On the surface, Miller's reaction to the gypsy is a fear and consequent dislike of her powers: He doesn't want to know anything about his future. But his desire to drive her out of town is probably related to stereotypes about gypsies; they are supposed to be crude, wild, nomadic people. Miller is so obsessed with his mother and the concept of what a good mother should be that all

he can see when he looks at the gypsy is a "bad" woman, a woman who would be a bad mother: irresponsible, inviting strange men into her house to read their fortunes and do who knows what else, creating a generally unsavory environment for a child to grow up in.

From the time Miller's father died, he became extremely jealous of and possessive toward anyone he got close to. This is true of both his mother and Nat Pranger. There is no generosity in Miller's spirit, no ability to share either his love or the people he loves, no desire for them to be happy unless he is the sole cause of that happiness; this is what "turns people cruel."

5. In paragraphs 108–109, Miller is imagining the immediate future: He has realized, in paragraph 107, that he must reconcile with his mother, whom he really loves, before it's too late. In these two paragraphs, he imagines the journey home, step by step. But in paragraph 110 he is back in the present; the action has shifted out of his imagination and back into the real world. The change in tense suggests that the events in the story's last two paragraphs are really happening. He isn't the "wrong" Miller; his mother is really dead.

But the story's end is deliberately ambiguous. While the shift in tense *suggests* the scenario above, it's impossible to know whether this scene is actually taking place, or whether it too occurs in Miller's mind. There is, after all, no transition from paragraph 109 to paragraph 110, no indication that Miller has actually gotten out of the jeep, boarded a bus, and journeyed home. The shift in tense could merely be reflecting what is going on in Miller's mind, which, against his will, is dredging up his deepest fears.

MARY OLIVER

Some Questions You Might Ask (p. 813)

In addition to the books mentioned in the text footnote, Oliver has published the poetry collections *No Voyage and Other Poems* (1965), *The River Styx, Ohio and Other Poems* (1972), *The Night Traveler* (1978), *Sleeping in the Forest* (1979), *Twelve Moons* (1979), and *Dreamwork* (1986).

This whimsical poem pairs well with both "Early Song" and "Yes, But." Like these two poems, it also serves as a foil to Oates's essay "Against Nature."

INVESTIGATIONS (p. 813)

1. Answers will vary.

2. The things Oliver names are not things at all in that they are animate (with the exception of the iceberg and the little stones, but even these change form, appearance, and nature over time). The word "thing" usually refers to something *in*animate, something that is *not* alive in the way that organisms such as moths, owls, moose, swans, bears, hummingbirds, snakes, scallops, anteaters, camels, maple trees, irises, roses, lemons, leaves, and grass are. The "soul" of each of these things could be described as "solid, like iron" because it exists (*if* it exists; this is indeed the question at the heart of this poem); like the human soul (which the poem's speaker assumes exists), this soul has remarkable resilience. At the same time it is "tender and breakable," as are all living things and all spirits: If physical or emotional conditions are too harsh, they can be damaged or destroyed entirely.

3. Cooter might say all these things have souls, and we'd best not cross any of them. Cooter, after all, suspected there was something "not right" about Miss Bailey's stash to begin with. Cooter would be likely to think the soul was breakable, considering his brother's condition at the story's end.

The speaker of "Heart Fire" might want to believe that the soul is solid, because she would wish this for her friend's son; on the other hand, a broken soul might better account for his suicide. If it were broken, the speaker would like to believe that her "heart fire" could somehow make it solid again. And since she pictured her friend's son in shadows and in the sky, she would probably believe that the things Oliver's speaker names have souls as well.

The narrator of "Cathedral" claimed he was not religious during the course of the story; this suggests that he probably didn't believe in souls at all. Once he and the blind man drew their cathedral, however, he might well believe in spirituality of some kind. It's hard to know what he'd think of souls, specifically, and whether he'd attribute them to all living plants and creatures.

MILCHA SANCHEZ-SCOTT

Roosters (p. 814)

Students may need help interpreting this play's ambiguous ending. Hector apparently takes his father's knife away, so the son has clearly won the fight over who controls the rooster. Hector has promised the rooster to the Filipino if the Filipino will leave Gallo alone; yet the rooster remains, at the play's end, in Hector's possession. To protect his father, Hector will almost certainly keep his end of the bargain. But what is less clear is whether Hector is really through with cockfighting. There's no reason he and his father can't start over now with new roosters, nor is there any reason to assume his father won't regain his former status in this arena. Despite Hector's harsh words about his father throughout the play, he is clearly drawn both to Gallo and to the concept of being independent, of not having to work in the fields. But Hector doesn't just want to be independent: He wants to be his father's son, and he wants to be a Morales, a king, someone who is *best* at something.

INVESTIGATIONS (p. 846)

1. Oates claims that while most of us romanticize nature, there is in fact nothing romantic about bloodsuckers, rabid raccoons and the ants following one another across her writing table, one after one, only to die under her index finger. One might certainly say the same about a couple of birds with spurs and razor blades attached to their feet who slash each other to death. And Hector's speech in which he calls the field he works "this fertile whore of a valley" (p. 824) certainly echoes Oates's perspective on this subject.

In paragraph 22 of Oates's essay, she comments that "our sense that the weak . . . have a right to survive" is absurd. In *Roosters*, Gallo would seem to agree: By encouraging Zapata to respond aggressively to being attacked, Gallo is making the rooster stronger, thus giving him more of a right to survive.

The dance can be seen as a prayer in that Gallo is supplicating Zapata to fight well, to maintain the family honor — which, for Gallo, is integrally linked with winning cockfights. Gallo is praying for Zapata to help him regain his position as preeminent cockfighter — and thus a wealthy, independent man — now that he is out of jail.

2. All of the characters except Chata express religious or spiritual beliefs at some point in the play, even if it is only in the form of passing lip service to a saint. In his opening speech, Gallo supplicates Santa María Aurora of the Dawn; Juana addresses St. Anthony; and Angela prays throughout the play. Hector calls upon his dead grandfather on page 816, and Chata calls up her grandmother's instructions on catching the man you want by rolling a warm tortilla on your thigh.

   Genuine religious beliefs can provide people with great inner peace and solace; Angela's beliefs apparently serve this purpose in her life, but they also serve as a refuge from reality. Her levitation at the play's end, however, suggests that her religious faith is genuine.

   Irrational beliefs can serve as a crutch, which they do for other characters in this play. Gallo can make himself feel pious by supplicating a saint or two, but an honest man would admit that he should have looked out better for his family, Santa María Aurora of the Dawn notwithstanding. Both Chata and Hector also seem to adhere, to varying degrees, to the idea of fate: My luck is bad, or my father left me, therefore I'm not responsible.

3. In both speeches Hector refers to people en masse, rather than as individuals; in both cases he is part of the crowd but does not want to be. In the first speech on page 824, he describes the field workers as "beaten-down, pathetic men" at war with the valley's "violent growth." To Hector, that growth is "shameful," "a mockery of me and my slender spirit." While these ironic statements are partly intended as jabs at his absent father, it is also clear that Hector despises his job. In Hector's second speech, he is part of "the crowd [that] was a monster, made up of individual human beings stuck together by sweat and spittle" (p. 829). Yet he is an individual, separate from the crowd because he is the proud son of the best cockfighter in the region, a man who can even bring a dead bird back to life. Hector is special because he is a Morales, and carries "the blood of kings" (p. 816) in his veins.

   For Gallo, he and his family are different than other men in the community because "we never put a foot into the fields. We stayed independent — we worked for nobody" (p. 827). But for Hector this dream has yet to come true; since his father went to jail when he was young, Hector ended up in the fields after all. When Hector says "Oh Papi, breathe on me" (p. 829) he's asking his father to rejuvenate him just as he once rejuvenated the rooster Quasimoto in the cockfight described at the end of Act One.

4. Answers will vary, but essays should include references to the independence Gallo could claim when he had the best roosters, and the dignity and self-esteem that accompanied this independence. You may well have students who wish to support, rather than refute, this argument. Encourage them to examine the profit motive behind cockfighting. Is there something besides money the roosters' owners gain from this enterprise? If so, does this make the activity any less cruel to the roosters?

5. Humor is one of the human psyche's most powerful defense mechanisms, and defenses serve, or can serve, as weapons against the enemy. Humor allows us to take ourselves, and our problems, less seriously — not because those problems aren't serious, but because we need to go on living in spite of them. The characters in this play use humor to distance themselves from their pain: Chato, who has had a hard life in which she has had terrible luck with, or judgment about, men; Juana, whose husband comes home only to leave her again; Hector and Angela who were deserted by their father and treated badly by him once he came back.

Humor helps people distance themselves from difficult subjects and situations; David James uses it in his poem "Think Death," as does Lanford Wilson in *Burn This* (Part Six, p. 683) and Lewis Nordan in "Sugar Among the Chickens" (Part Two, p. 204). Ask students to provide other examples.

CHARLES BAXTER

Gryphon (p. 847)

In addition to telling strange and wonderful stories and suggesting the notion of "substitute facts," Miss Ferenczi uses words her students (and possibly yours) are unlikely to know. Words like "cabals" (para. 7) and "fossicking" (56) are unlikely to be a part of a fourth-grader's vocabulary. Ask the class what they think Miss Ferenczi gains by using such words. In the predictable and repetitive environment of an elementary school classroom, Miss Ferenczi's unusual "secrets" and vocabulary snare her students' attention. But these are generally well-behaved children, used to paying attention in class even when they have a substitute. Miss Ferenczi wants more than their attention; she wants wonder; she wants to stimulate their curiosity for knowledge beyond the classroom, for knowledge they can't get out of books. All of which sounds quite admirable, but many students may have a different fix on this story. It is also entirely reasonable to assume that Miss Ferenczi is not entirely sane. For a lively class session, you might open discussion of this story by posing the question: How many of you think Miss Ferenczi is simply crazy? Ask students for evidence to support their beliefs. On the one hand, her discussion of "substitute facts" is quite lucid — coherent enough that the nine-year-old narrator understands that Miss Ferenczi knows full well that six times eleven is sixty-six. On the other hand, her introduction of Tarot cards into the classroom can be seen as irresponsible at best. And few of us could condone her telling a nine-year-old boy that he is going to die.

INVESTIGATIONS (p. 860)

1. There is no simple answer to Miss Ferenczi's question. No one would be hurt by a substitute fact as long as he or she realized it *was* a substitute fact; that is, as long as he or she realized that the substitute fact should not be used as an answer on a math exam, for example, or in calculating the cost of a purchase at the grocery store. The danger of these substitute facts, of course, is that many fourth graders would not be sophisticated enough to understand Miss Ferenczi's lesson, and wouldn't be able to discern when the use of such a fact was appropriate and when it wasn't.

    The point of Miss Ferenczi's math lesson is to shake the students up, to make them question what they are told, to make things "more interesting" (30). She wants to show them that there is a world beyond Five Oaks, beyond multiplication tables, comprehension questions, and spelling drills, a world in which concrete facts are not only unimportant but possibly even irrelevant. By telling students that they are "free to think what" they like (40), she is forcing them to think for themselves; she is forcing them to question, analyze, and make judgments, activities that are not always required — and are often discouraged — in an elementary-school classroom.

    On the other hand, there is no evidence that Miss Ferenczi arrived with the intention of teaching this lesson; that is, she does not behave as if she had this material planned, and indeed she would have let the student's wrong answer go had another student not called her attention to it. Her behavior on

143

her second day, when "there seemed to be less connection between her ideas" (90), suggests that she does not plan her lessons, or the "points" of these lessons, at all.

2. Miss Ferenczi and her behavior are fabulous in several senses of the word. First, she *is* "legendary." This story exists because of her; the narrator tells this tale in an attempt to document and understand her affect on himself and his classmates. She is also "barely credible" and "astonishing." Her appearance, actions, and statements are all at least surprising and more often extremely difficult to believe. Finally, the narrator and most of his classmates find her "extremely pleasing" — she is different, mysterious, strange, and therefore interesting, and fun. (All the dictionary definitions in this response were taken from *The American Heritage Dictionary of the English Language*, Houghton Mifflin Company, 1969.)

3. Answers will vary. Miss Ferenczi's behavior can be used to support both sentences — one of the story's main points. Of course, Mr. Hibler's and Mrs. Mantei's behavior can also be used to support the former statement. Students who pick up on this would then need to address the questions: Which type of control is better? Which is more valuable and useful? Can these two types of control coexist?

4. Miss Ferenczi's talk is quite serious. Her aim is to introduce students to the kind of knowledge that can't be tested, graded, or perhaps even fully articulated or understood. It is a mysterious world full of philosophical and spiritual concerns about the nature of reality, the universe, our souls, and death — all of which would be seen, by some people, as much more serious than spelling drills or arithmetic lessons.

5. Answers will vary.

ROSARIO FERRÉ

Pico Rico, Mandorico (p. 861)

This story works well with "Exchange Value," "Gryphon," and "The Moths." Ask students to identify the fairy-tale elements and the importance of gifts in each story. The central characters in each of these stories receive gifts, though in all but "Exchange Value" the gifts received are not tangible. Is there a lesson to be learned in any of these stories? If so, what do these lessons have in common? How do they differ? (For a related assignment see Part Six: Connections and Elaborations 4).

INVESTIGATIONS (p. 866)

1. The twins are "different somehow from other people around them" (para. 5) because their affection for each other is so strong. Their unity gives them a power the townspeople lack. As long as they always worked "together as one" (2), their mother counseled them, no evil would befall them.

   The twins also seem to have a soothing, magical effect on the townspeople:

   On hot summer days, whenever the two girls walked by them, the villagers would feel as if the icy notes of xylophones were playing gently on the surface of their skin or as if a breeze from the ocean had just whistled through the branches of the trees in the parched plaza square. (3)

144

The twins remain unaffected by the landowner because they earn their living doing needlework instead of working his land.

2. The answers to each of these questions rests on a kind of fairy-tale logic, a logic we are all familiar with from our childhood, from picture books and make-believe. Elisa's braid bought her the horseman's fruit — fruit that was tainted because it belonged to the landowner, and because it had been harvested by the townspeople, who were all miserable, laboring under the landowner's curse. (Though the landowner's fruit doesn't come from the Tree of the Knowledge of Good and Evil, and though the horseman-landowner is not, literally, a serpent, students might detect a parallel to the biblical story of Eve's temptation in the Garden of Eden here.)

    The landowner's power resides in and is symbolized by "his most attention-getting feature": "his enormous nose" (15).

    Apparently, in the past, the landlord had tricked the villagers into working for him (just as he almost tricks Alicia into loving him in paragraph 25). Now that "the rich landowner was forced to walk around with a stump for a nose, the villagers were able to recognize him even from a distance and they refused to work for him from sunrise to sunset" (31), so they regained their ability to "coax the sandman" (4) and get to sleep.

3. Thievery, exchange, and gift-giving all have the power to transform. At the beginning of this story the girls gain each other — once their mother has revealed to them the secret of their birth — but lose their mother. The girls exchange their identities and souls to cure each other, and even, at the story's end, so that one can save the other's life. In "Exchange Value," the gift of Miss Bailey's inheritance has the power to transform as well. But it transforms in a negative way, paralyzing the recipient so that he or she not only can't spend the money but goes crazy because of it.

4. Miss Ferenczi would probably think the world of this story makes perfect sense, precisely because it is full of amazing and wonderful events that *can't*, in fact, be rationally explained. In Miss Ferenczi's world, there are circumstances under which things that are not true (such as six times eleven equaling 68) *are* true. So why shouldn't the townspeople be better able to recognize the landowner once he has a stump for a nose — even though logic suggests he should have been just as easy to recognize before, *because* of his enormous nose?

    The premise of "Pico Rico, Mandorico" is that the sisters are good and pure and have the power not only to save themselves but also to save the townspeople as well. All of the events in the story do work toward this: The sisters' power resides in their working "together as one"; when one feels pain and *lets* the other help her, the pain disappears. So when one sister breaks rank, she weakens and moves toward death. But Alicia saves her sister by figuring out that, just as partaking of the fruit made Elisa forlorn and rendered her unable to hear the horseman's voice, eating *more* of the fruit will break the spell altogether. (The theory seems related to the concept that two negatives make a positive.) In the end, Alicia is able to save not only her sister — first by switching souls and then by letting Elisa eat the fruit with which she, Alicia, is covered — but the whole town.

MAY SWENSON

Staring at the Sea on the Day
of the Death of Another (p. 867)

Although this poem has a formal feel to it, the rhyme scheme is in fact irregular. Ask students to track the rhymes throughout the poem, noting instances of both end and internal rhyme. Then have them look for instances of assonance and alliteration. (For more on this topic see Investigation 2 below.) How do these poetic techniques reinforce the meaning of the poem?

INVESTIGATIONS (p. 867)

1. The words "hollow" and "hollows" suggest emptiness, both literal and spiritual; they also suggest images of holes, graves, troughs, perhaps even the image of an empty hand grasping. The speaker's sadness and emptiness resonates with each use of these words.

2. The "l" sounds in the poem create, literally, a lulling feeling. The repetition of this sound is both calming and numbing, and numbness is a common early reaction to the death of a loved one. Note how the "water fi*ll*s its ho*ll*ow, / slow*l*y ro*ll*s . . . " (lines 1–2). This effect could be described as hypnotic or mesmerizing, as could the effect of watching the repetitive motion of the waves in the ocean.

   The repeated "w"s (see the quote above as well as the poem's next two lines) approximate a crying sound; the "wa" in "water" and "swaddling" and "waves" suggests sobbing or moaning. The repeated long "e" and long "i" sounds ("slowl*y*," "s*i*de," "t*i*de," "Gr*e*cian," and so on) also suggest the keening noises that often accompany grief.

3. Answers will vary, but students will probably observe that the speaker's friends are not literally "furled" into the waves' hollows, though she sees them there; nor does one of those hollows literally have her name on it. The idea of the sea as a mausoleum is, logically speaking, irrational; how can the waves be "shelves" when they are in constant motion? And since the motion of the sea is tempestuous, rather than gentle and controlled, how could these hollows "cradle" anyone? If the speaker's "prone effigies" really existed, they would be tossed every which way and strewn in all directions rather than "cradled" in one of these "countless shelves." This is a good opportunity to discuss the purpose of metaphor: Students should realize that the point of these comparisons is not to provide logical, exchangeable definitions but to suggest connections between the two things being compared.

4. Answers will vary.

DAVID JAMES

Think Death (p. 868)

This poem provides an excellent opportunity to discuss extended metaphors with the class. Have students identify the "money" metaphor here, beginning with the concept of death not having "much in store for us" (line 2) — emphasis on the word "store" — and then pursue it throughout the poem. They should note "a sale on silence" (3); "a discount on . . . darkness" (4); "Death is a hoarder"

(9); "his hand forever clenched" (16); "free cold storage" (32), and so on. How does this carefully wrought metaphor control the way they think about death as they read the poem? Why might the writer have chosen to organize his poem so tightly around this metaphor?

INVESTIGATIONS (p. 869)

1. The speaker seems to find some comfort in his belief that "all enter through the same door" (27) and that death doesn't wish "us any ill will" (45). The message is that we're all in this together, no one's exempt, we're all going to die, regardless of what privileges we may have had during our lifetime. Some readers may find the speaker's dry, evenhanded tone a bit hard to accept. But it's likely that the humor in this poem, along with the carefully wrought extended metaphor, serve as defense mechanisms for the speaker. Like most of us, he has his fears, but hides them under this veneer of clever talk.

2. The speaker of Swenson's poem is mourning her friend who has just died and friends who have died earlier; her tone is mournful, sad, and fearful, both for them and for herself. James's speaker, on the other hand, is musing abstractly on death, rather than thinking about a specific person or persons he's lost. Hence he is able to say things that sound harsh — death offers us "a stillness close to infinity" (33) — yet maintain his distance: This is what will happen, one day, to each of us. There's nothing immediate about his concern. In fact, compared to Swenson's and Anderson's speakers, some readers might consider James's speaker a bit flip or glib.

3. The speakers of both "Yes, But" and "Early Song" would take issue with this portrayal of death. Clearly, they both think something else happens once we're lowered "into the ground, / blocking out any chance of sun or moonlight" (6–7). They wouldn't agree that the door is "locked tightly from below" (29) and that we all get "tallied / in the loss column" (42–43) in the end. The speaker of "Yes, But" thinks there are amazing things waiting for us after death, things unimaginably wonderful. And the speaker of "Early Song" thinks we are all part of "a great circle" (Gogisgi/Arnett, 14), and will rise from the earth, in some form, again.

   The speaker of "Heart Fire" would be distressed by this poem's portrayal of death, at least regarding the fate of her friend's son, who she wants to think is "not alone" (Anderson, 25). Because of this, she invents "for him a heart fire" (26). But James's speaker suspects that there's only darkness after death, darkness and silence and "a stillness close to infinity" (33).

HELENA MARÍA VIRAMONTES

The Moths (p. 870)

Students accustomed to reading only realistic fiction may be uncomfortable with the fantastic elements of this story. Ask the class first to identify these elements. Are we to literally believe that the narrator's "hands began to fan out, grow like a liar's nose until they hung by my side like low weights" (para. 3)? The "liar's nose" should provide a clue: Students will recognize the reference is to Pinocchio, a fairy-tale character whose nose grew whenever he told a lie. What is important here is not so much whether the narrator's already large hands actually grew larger, but the fact that she *felt* they did, and that her grandmother not only believed her but made them feel (or appear) normal again. And what of the moths flying out of the grandmother's mouth at the story's end? There is no question whether the narrator really saw these, for she believed in them as firmly as her grandmother did. By convincingly rendering the characters and their feelings, the author has convinced us, at least for the period of time that we're reading the story, that these things are really happening.

INVESTIGATIONS (p. 874)

1. By today's medical standards, Mama Luna's cures are certainly "unscientific," but many students will know that herbs, plants, and other natural substances have been used to heal ailments and illnesses for centuries. We can't know whether the narrator's scarlet fever might have abated without the potato slices, but as Mama Luna points out in paragraph 3, the narrator is "still alive." As for the narrator's enlarged hands, we learn in paragraph 2 that her hands were "too big" to do the "girl things" her sisters did. Ask students whether they think they are really being asked to believe that the narrator's hands literally enlarged further. If they did actually swell, what caused this? If not, why did Mama Luna make and apply a special balm to the narrator's hands?

2. In Mama Luna's house the narrator feels "safe and guarded and not alone" (4). She gets love and the company of her grandmother there, while in the church she "was alone" (7). In her grandmother's house the narrator also gets warmth, both emotional and literal, from the cooking going on inside. The church, in contrast, is a cold place to the narrator; in the chapel she feels "the vastness" of the place, " the coolness of the marble pillars and the frozen statues with blank eyes" (7). The narrator also gets to feel useful at her grandmother's house, something she doesn't feel at home. She helps plant flowers, herbs, and vegetables, things that are literally full of life.

   Students' catechisms will vary, but the church of Mama Luna would instruct its students on familial love and respect, especially respecting one's parents and not fighting with one's siblings. It would instruct its students on the importance of *showing* that love, by word, gesture, and deed — of kissing someone when the thought "I never kissed her" enters your mind, as it does the narrator's in paragraphs 6 and 11. The church of Mama Luna would also instruct its students on the importance of self-love; apparently the narrator doesn't like herself very much, and this is why she is so bitter toward everyone in her family with the exception of her grandmother, whom she has mainly to herself.

3. The narrator feels half born because, by not allowing herself to love anyone until now, she has only felt half alive. And now the only person she really loves has died, so she feels even more bereft. It's as if "the moths that lay within the soul and slowly eat the spirit" (16) of her grandmother had also been at work on the narrator, despite her youth. Now that the moths are leaving both her grandmother and the narrator, the half of the narrator's spirit that is dead or missing can be replaced or rejuvenated.

   Mama Luna's death is a gift in that it forces the narrator to express her emotions; it breaks down her defenses so that she can love and express love, which she was unable to do in the past.

MAXINE KUMIN

In the Park (p. 875)

You might approach this poem by asking students what they make of the discussion of the words "lie" and "lay" in lines 15–16 and again in line 29. Why do they think the speaker pursues this apparent digression?

The discussion of "lie" and "lay" can be seen as analogous to the comparisons between Buddhism, Judaism, and Christianity in this poem. When you're facing death, whether or not your diction is correct doesn't matter, just as the particular religion you believe in doesn't matter. Whichever word you use, whichever religion you're a member of, you're still facing death. And, if you're lucky enough to escape it, you're still alive — and it isn't because the "correct" word, or the "correct" religion, saved you.

Ask students to focus on the poem's last three lines. Can they apply this concept to any other selections in Part Seven or in the rest of the book? Could Cooter in "Exchange Value" be said to have met the grizzly bear in the last paragraph of that story? What about the soldiers in "The Things They Carried" (Part Four, p. 437)?

INVESTIGATIONS (p. 876)

1. The speaker contrasts three faiths in this poem: Buddhism is discussed in the first two lines, Judaism in lines 18–25, and lines 26–27 contain references to Christianity.

   The details are used to document the fact that one of the functions of religion is to provide those who believe with a means of understanding and coping with death. The details are also necessary to contrast the faiths: Specific details are always needed to show how any two or more things — in this case religions — are different. The point of contrasting these faiths is to show that regardless of our faith (or lack of faith), we are all alike in our need for some way to understand death.

2. Roscoe Brown's words ring with the power of authenticity. Sometimes the simplest statements have the strongest effect. In the case of a man who has come face to face with something that almost killed him, it is unlikely anyone else's description can tell us more than his own. The speaker could only report what Roscoe *said* it was like, in which case the immediacy of Roscoe's words would be lost.

3. Roscoe's encounter with the bear was real, concrete, tangible: It happened. The religious experiences described here are generalized: Here is what Buddhists believe happens when you die; here is what Jews believe; here Christians. But these beliefs are just that: "beliefs." There is no way to officially document them (though some will claim the Bible or Bhagavad-Gita does this). Roscoe's near-death encounter, on the other hand, is a fact. He lived to tell it; he lived to bring back a report from the front. He knows how it feels to have a bear breathe in his face, to smell the bear's breath, to feel "*his heart beating against my heart*" (14). He knows how it feels to face certain death; he knows that when that moment comes, no system of belief can change what happens, and no religion can save you; it's up to the bear.

149

RAYMOND CARVER

Cathedral (p. 876)

In addition to the books mentioned in the text footnote, Carver published the short-story collections *Will You Please Be Quiet, Please?* (1976), *What We Talk About When We Talk About Love* (1981), and *Cathedral* (1984) and the poetry collections *Winter Insomnia* (1970), *Where Water Comes Together with Water* (1985), and *Ultramarine* (1986).

This story about a blind man's visit to an old friend and her husband is as mysterious as it is moving. Ask the class in what ways the phrase "the blind leading the blind" might be an appropriate description of the story's last scene.

Ask students to describe what they think happens at the story's end. Does the narrator understand what it's like to be blind, or does he learn something more? (For more on this topic, see Investigation 4 below.) What gifts are exchanged in this story? What do these gifts have in common with those exchanged in "Pico Rico, Mandorico" and "The Moths"?

INVESTIGATIONS (p. 887)

1. The narrator's wife finds Robert's touching her face so powerful because she understands the intimacy of the gesture; Robert will remember her by his map of her face as sighted people remember others by photographs. Touch, in other words, is one way that Robert "sees." The narrator's wife is also moved because during the brief time that Robert is touching her face, she has been let into another world, a world to which she would otherwise never have access.

   The tapes exchanged by the narrator's wife and Robert contain real dialogue; the two friends tell each other about their feelings, something the narrator and his wife apparently do not do. A man whose descriptions of his wife's first husband all end in the word "etc." and who describes her exchange of tapes with her blind friend as "her chief means of recreation" (para. 5) does not seem comfortable with his own emotions, much less his feelings toward his wife.

2. Any description of the narrator has to be based entirely on what he says and how he says it; the narrator provides us with neither a physical nor psychological description of himself, so everything we know about him must be inferred by his thoughts, speech, and action. Most of what the narrator thinks or says is delivered in the form of a blunt observation: Consider such statements as "I wasn't enthusiastic about his visit" (1) and "I'd heard all I wanted to" (5). Such observations reveal the narrator's immediate state of mind, but allow the narrator to remain safely on the surface of his own emotions. He protects himself by not examining these feelings, by not asking himself *why* he wasn't enthusiastic about the blind man's visit, or *why* he didn't want to hear the rest of the tape.

   What can be inferred from the narrator's tone and thoughts, however, is that he is unhappy and insecure: He doesn't like his job but doesn't see any other options (46); he doesn't have any friends (at least according to his wife); and he is threatened by the blind man — threatened by Robert's intimacy with his wife and by the fact that Robert and his wife have a shared history apart from him.

   The narrator is also prejudiced. In paragraph 11 we learn that in the narrator's mind, Beulah is "a name for a colored woman"; similarly, he has the preconceived notion that blind men shouldn't have beards, don't smoke, and wear dark glasses.

Until paragraph 86, he persists in mean-spirited thoughts. Of Robert's wedding he asks "who'd want to go to such a wedding in the first place?" (16). He also calls Robert "a regular blind jack-of-all-trades" (46).

The narrator is also self-absorbed. Except for the story's first and sixteenth paragraphs, he seems to completely forget that Robert's wife has just died. And when he does imagine that relationship, he assumes Robert's wife's last miserable thoughts were that her husband "never even knew what she looked like" (16). It's quite possible she did think this at some point, but the essential emotion behind this thought is self-pity, an emotion that is apparently easy for the narrator to conjure. On her deathbed, Robert's wife might have thought many other things, including how much she would miss Robert or that she wanted him to be happy once she was gone.

3. The narrator's perception of Robert and Beulah's marriage as pathetic is based entirely on the fact that Robert could never know what his wife looked like in the way that sighted people can know what someone looks like. Many students will argue that physical beauty is not the most important component in a relationship; in fact, relationships based on physical attraction are not liable to last if they don't include emotional and intellectual components too. In paragraph 16 the narrator imagines Beulah as "a woman who could go on day after day and never receive the smallest compliment from her beloved." But of course Beulah could have received thousands of compliments from her beloved, even physical ones ranging from how soft her skin was to how silky her hair or sweet her perfume. And then there are the infinite number of possible compliments that have nothing to do with sensuality.

The narrator is completely oblivious to the fact that happiness can be, and almost always is, based on something other than physical attraction alone. He is also unaware that he overrates the power of sight, or any one sense; when someone is deprived of one of their senses, he or she usually compensates by developing other senses more keenly. Hence Robert could probably read his wife's mood by sound or touch every bit as well as "sighted" people read facial expressions. The narrator's paucity of imagination and emotional resources, then, could be described as pathetic (along with some of the small-mindedness described in Investigation 2). His life is full of pathos for all the same reasons: He suffers limitations he's unaware of, at least until the story's end.

4. At the story's end the narrator discovers and participates in the kind of vision Robert has. He learns that there is more than one way to see, and experiences the exhilarating power of that knowledge. Drawing the cathedral without Robert's participation would not have led him to this discovery, because it is sharing Robert's experience of "seeing" — feeling Robert's hand moving with his, and realizing how this movement can be "read," as can the lines he draws if he presses hard enough — that leads to the discovery. The narrator is having some kind of spiritual experience at the story's end: "It was like nothing else in my life up to now," he says in paragraph 131. "I didn't feel like I was inside anything" (135). The narrator might not be able to articulate it beyond "It's really something" (136), but he would certainly no longer say, as he does in paragraph 109, that "Cathedrals don't mean anything special to me. . . . They're something to look at on late-night TV. That's all they are." This experience frees the narrator not only from his preconceptions about Robert and blind people, but also from the preconceptions that have ruled his life. He has learned something tremendous about both the power of the human imagination and the human spirit.